Great Lives from History

The 19th Century

1801-1900

Great Lives from History

The 19th Century

1801-1900

Volume 2
Charles Dickens - Ferdinand Lassalle

Editor
John Powell
Oklahoma Baptist University

Editor, First Edition
Frank N. Magill

SALEM PRESS
Pasadena, California   Hackensack, New Jersey

Editor in Chief: Dawn P. Dawson	*Indexer:* Rowena Wildin Dehanke
Editorial Director: Christina J. Moose	*Production Editor:* Andrea E. Miller
Acquisitions Editor: Mark Rehn	*Graphics and Design:* James Hutson
Research Supervisor: Jeffry Jensen	*Layout:* Eddie Murillo
Research Assistant: Rebecca Kuzins	*Photo Editor:* Cynthia Breslin Beres
Manuscript Editor: R. Kent Rasmussen	*Editorial Assistant:* Dana Garey

Cover photos: The Granger Collection, New York (Pictured left to right, top to bottom: Sitting Bull, Charles Darwin, Liliuokalani, Louisa May Alcott, Ludwig van Beethoven, Saʿīd ibn Sulṭān, Simón Bolívar, Cixi, Mark Twain)

Some of the essays in this work originally appeared in the following Salem Press sets: *Dictionary of World Biography* (© 1998-1999, edited by Frank N. Magill) and *Great Lives from History* (© 1987-1995, edited by Frank N. Magill). New material has been added.

Library of Congress Cataloging-in-Publication Data

Great lives from history. The 19th century, 1801-1900 / editor, John Powell.
    p. cm.
  "Editor, first edition, Frank N. Magill."
  Some of the essays in this work were originally published in Dictionary of world biography and the series of works collectively titled, Great lives from history, both edited by Frank N. Magill; with new material added.
  Includes bibliographical references and index.
  ISBN-13: 978-1-58765-292-9 (set : alk. paper)
  ISBN-10: 1-58765-292-7 (set : alk. paper)
  ISBN-13: 978-1-58765-294-3 (v. 2 : alk. paper)
  ISBN-10: 1-58765-294-3 (v. 2 : alk. paper)
  [etc.]

 1. Biography—19th century. I. Powell, John, 1954- II. Magill, Frank Northen, 1907-1997 III. Dictionary of world biography. IV. Great lives from history. V. Title: 19th century, 1801-1900. VI. Title: Nineteenth century, 1801-1900.
  CT119.G69 2006
  920.009′034—dc22

2006020187

First Printing

CONTENTS

CONTENTS

KEY TO PRONUNCIATION

Many of the names of personages covered in *Great Lives from History: The Nineteenth Century, 1801-1900* may be unfamiliar to students and general readers. For these unfamiliar names, guides to pronunciation have been provided upon first mention of the names in the text. These guidelines do not purport to achieve the subtleties of the languages in question but will offer readers a rough equivalent of how English speakers may approximate the proper pronunciation.

Vowel Sounds

Symbol	Spelled (Pronounced)
a	answer (AN-suhr), laugh (laf), sample (SAM-puhl), that (that)
ah	father (FAH-thur), hospital (HAHS-pih-tuhl)
aw	awful (AW-fuhl), caught (kawt)
ay	blaze (blayz), fade (fayd), waiter (WAYT-ur), weigh (way)
eh	bed (behd), head (hehd), said (sehd)
ee	believe (bee-LEEV), cedar (SEE-dur), leader (LEED-ur), liter (LEE-tur)
ew	boot (bewt), lose (lewz)
i	buy (bi), height (hit), lie (li), surprise (sur-PRIZ)
ih	bitter (BIH-tur), pill (pihl)
o	cotton (KO-tuhn), hot (hot)
oh	below (bee-LOH), coat (koht), note (noht), wholesome (HOHL-suhm)
oo	good (good), look (look)
ow	couch (kowch), how (how)
oy	boy (boy), coin (koyn)
uh	about (uh-BOWT), butter (BUH-tuhr), enough (ee-NUHF), other (UH-thur)

Consonant Sounds

Symbol	Spelled (Pronounced)
ch	beach (beech), chimp (chihmp)
g	beg (behg), disguise (dihs-GIZ), get (geht)
j	digit (DIH-juht), edge (ehj), jet (jeht)
k	cat (kat), kitten (KIH-tuhn), hex (hehks)
s	cellar (SEHL-ur), save (sayv), scent (sehnt)
sh	champagne (sham-PAYN), issue (IH-shew), shop (shop)
ur	birth (burth), disturb (dihs-TURB), earth (urth), letter (LEH-tur)
y	useful (YEWS-fuhl), young (yuhng)
z	business (BIHZ-nehs), zest (zehst)
zh	vision (VIH-zhuhn)

COMPLETE LIST OF CONTENTS

VOLUME I

VOLUME 2

Volume 3

VOLUME 4

LIST OF MAPS AND SIDEBARS

VOLUME I

VOLUME 2

Volume 3

VOLUME 4

THE WORLD IN 1801

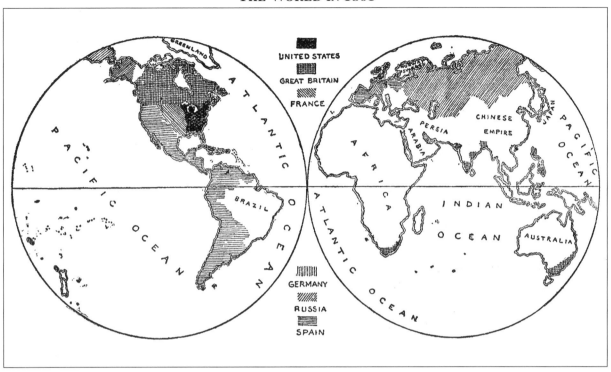

THE WORLD IN 1900

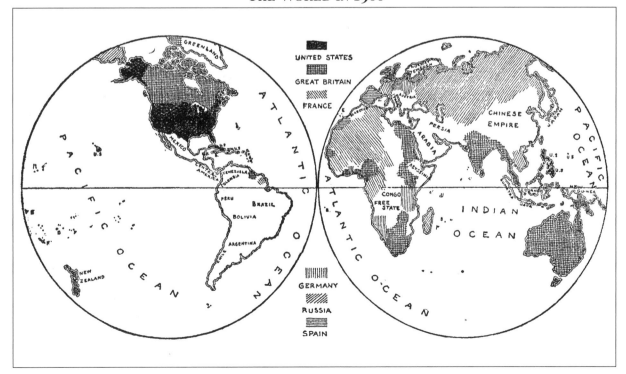

AFRICA AT THE END OF THE NINETEENTH CENTURY

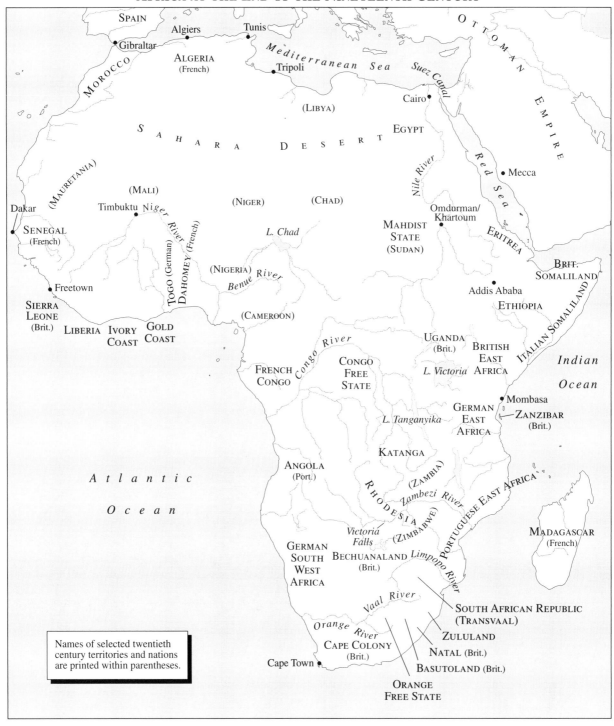

SPAIN

Gibraltar

Algiers

Tunis

MOROCCO

ALGERIA
(French)

Tripoli

Mediterranean Sea

Suez Canal

OTTOMAN EMPIRE

Cairo

(LIBYA)

EGYPT

SAHARA DESERT

Nile River

Red Sea

Mecca

(MAURETANIA)

(MALI)

Dakar

Timbuktu

Niger River

(NIGER)

(CHAD)

L. Chad

Omdurman/
Khartoum

MAHDIST
STATE
(SUDAN)

ERITREA

BRIT.
SOMALILAND

SENEGAL
(French)

TOGO (German)

DAHOMEY (French)

(NIGERIA)

Benue River

Addis Ababa

ETHIOPIA

ITALIAN SOMALILAND

Freetown

SIERRA
LEONE
(Brit.)

LIBERIA

IVORY
COAST

GOLD
COAST

(CAMEROON)

FRENCH
CONGO

Congo River

CONGO
FREE
STATE

UGANDA
(Brit.)

L. Victoria

BRITISH
EAST
AFRICA

Indian
Ocean

Mombasa

ZANZIBAR
(Brit.)

GERMAN
EAST
AFRICA

L. Tanganyika

Atlantic

Ocean

KATANGA

ANGOLA
(Port.)

RHODESIA

(ZAMBIA)

Zambezi River

PORTUGUESE EAST AFRICA

MADAGASCAR
(French)

Victoria
Falls

(ZIMBABWE)

GERMAN
SOUTH
WEST
AFRICA

BECHUANALAND
(Brit.)

Limpopo River

Vaal River

SOUTH AFRICAN REPUBLIC
(TRANSVAAL)

ZULULAND

NATAL (Brit.)

Orange River

CAPE COLONY
(Brit.)

BASUTOLAND (Brit.)

Cape Town

ORANGE
FREE STATE

Names of selected twentieth
century territories and nations
are printed within parentheses.

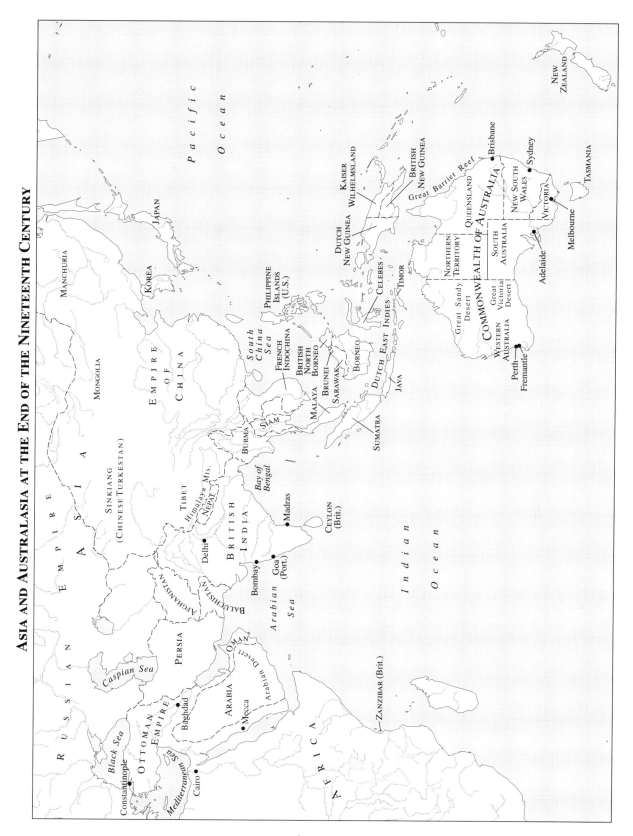

ASIA AND AUSTRALASIA AT THE END OF THE NINETEENTH CENTURY

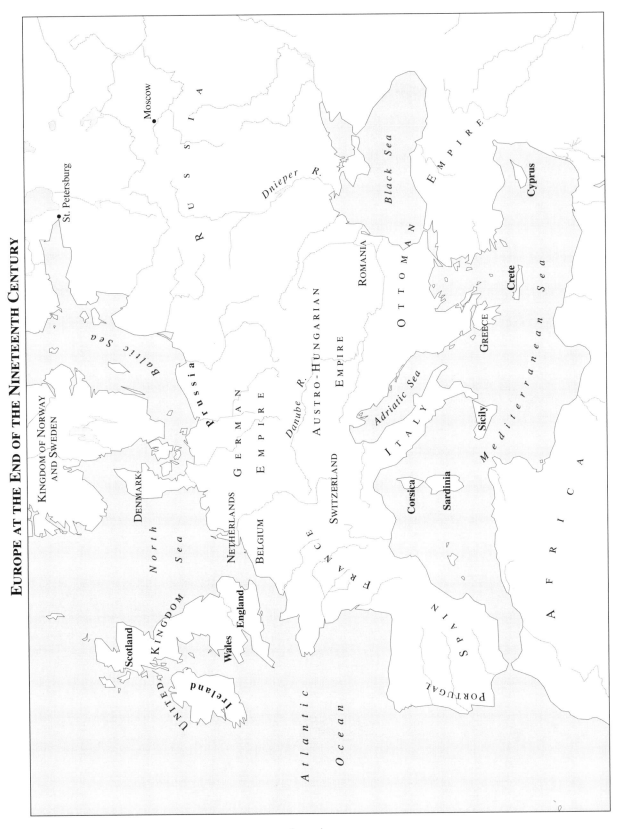

EUROPE AT THE END OF THE NINETEENTH CENTURY

Moscow

St. Petersburg

R U S S I A

Black Sea

Dnieper R.

OTTOMAN EMPIRE

Cyprus

Prussia

Baltic Sea

ROMANIA

Crete

Kingdom of Norway and Sweden

AUSTRO-HUNGARIAN EMPIRE

Danube R.

GERMAN EMPIRE

DENMARK

NETHERLANDS

BELGIUM

North Sea

SWITZERLAND

FRANCE

Adriatic Sea

I T A L Y

GREECE

Mediterranean Sea

Sicily

Corsica

Sardinia

AFRICA

Scotland

UNITED KINGDOM

Wales

England

Ireland

Atlantic Ocean

S P A I N

PORTUGAL

NORTH AMERICA AT THE END OF THE NINETEENTH CENTURY

Bering Sea

Bering Strait

Arctic Ocean

ALASKA

KLONDIKE

GREENLAND
(Denmark)

Baffin Bay

DOMINION OF CANADA

Hudson Bay

NEWFOUNDLAND

St. Lawrence River

Washington

Oregon

Montana

North Dakota

Minnesota

Great Lakes

Michigan

Wisconsin

Maine

Vermont

New Hampshire

Massachusetts

Rhode Island

Connecticut

New Jersey

Delaware

Maryland

Virginia

West Virginia

North Carolina

South Carolina

Idaho

South Dakota

New York

Wyoming

Nevada

Nebraska

Iowa

Indiana Ohio

Illinois

Penn-sylvania

Utah

Colorado River

Colorado

Kansas

Missouri River

Ohio River

Kentucky

California

Arizona (terr.)

Rio Grande

New Mexico (terr.)

Oklahoma (terr.)

Arkansas

Tennessee

Mississippi River

Mississippi

Alabama

Georgia

Florida

Texas

MEXICO

Louisiana

Pacific Ocean

Gulf of Mexico

CENTRAL AMERICA

CUBA

JAMAICA

HAITI

PUERTO RICO

DOMINICAN REPUBLIC

Atlantic Ocean

Caribbean Sea

SOUTH AMERICA

SOUTH AMERICA AT THE END OF THE NINETEENTH CENTURY

Galápagos Islands

North Atlantic Ocean

Caracas

BRITISH GUIANA

VENEZUELA

DUTCH GUIANA

FRENCH GUIANA

Bogotá

COLOMBIA

ECUADOR

Quito

Amazon River

Amazon Basin

BRAZIL

São Francisco River

PERU

Andes

Lima

La Paz

BOLIVIA

Sucre

South Pacific Ocean

Mountains

Paraná River

PARAGUAY

Rio de Janeiro

CHILE

Santiago

ARGENTINA

Buenos Aires

URUGUAY

Montevideo

South Atlantic Ocean

Negro River

Falkland Islands (British)

Stanley

South Georgia

Cape Horn

Great Lives from History

The 19th Century

1801-1900

CHARLES DICKENS
English novelist

The most popular novelist of his time, Dickens created a fictional world that reflected the social and technological changes of the Victorian era in which he lived. He created numerous immortal characters and is still one of the most widely read novelists in the world.

BORN: February 7, 1812; Portsmouth, Hampshire, England

DIED: June 9, 1870; Gad's Hill, near Rochester, Kent, England

ALSO KNOWN AS: Charles John Huffam Dickens (full name)

AREA OF ACHIEVEMENT: Literature

EARLY LIFE

Charles John Huffam Dickens was the second of eight children. His father, John Dickens, a clerk in the Naval Pay Office, was always hard-pressed to support his family. Because his father's work made it necessary for him to travel, Dickens spent his youth in several different places, including London and Chatham. When he was only twelve years old, his father's financial difficulty made it necessary for the young Dickens to work in a shoeblacking warehouse while his father was placed in a debtor's prison at Marshalsea—an event that was to have a powerful influence on Dickens throughout his life. Oliver Twist's experience in the workhouse is one of the best-known results of what Dickens considered to be an act of desertion by his parents.

After his father was released from prison, Dickens was sent to school at an academy in London, where he was a good student. When he was fifteen, he worked as a solicitor's clerk in law offices and two years later became a shorthand reporter of parliamentary proceedings and a freelance reporter in the courts. In 1829, he fell in love with Maria Beadnell, the daughter of a banker, but broke with her in 1833. At the age of twenty-one, he began publishing his *Sketches by Boz* and joined the *Morning Chronicle* as a reporter. His first collection of *Sketches by Boz* appeared in 1836, the same year he began a series of sketches titled *Pickwick Papers* (1836-1837). Also in 1836, he married Catherine Hogarth, the daughter of a journalist. As *Pickwick Papers* became a striking popular success in serial publication, the Dickens phenomenon began, and Dickens was on his way to becoming the most powerful and widely read author in nineteenth century England.

LIFE'S WORK

With Dickens's sudden fame came offers of more literary work. He began editing a new monthly magazine for which he contracted to write another serial story, which he called *Oliver Twist* (1837-1839) and that began to appear while *Pickwick Papers* was still running. Thus, Dickens started the breakneck speed of writing that was to characterize the energy of his work throughout his life. While *Oliver Twist* was still running in serial form, Dickens also began publishing *Nicholas Nickleby*, another great success, first in serial form (1838) and then as a book (1839). Immediately thereafter, he began the serialization of *The Old Curiosity Shop* (1840-1841) in a weekly publication, followed soon after by *Barnaby Rudge: A Tale of the Riots of '80* (1841).

Dickens paused from his writing between 1836 and 1841 to travel in the United States, the result of which was *American Notes* (1842) and, more important, the serialization of *Martin Chuzzlewit* (1843-1844), outraging many American readers with its caricature of life in the United States. During the Christmas season of 1843, Dickens achieved one of his most memorable successes with *A Christmas Carol*, which gave the world the character of Ebenezer Scrooge. The poor circulation of *Martin Chuzzlewit* was cause enough for Dickens to cease his writing once again for an extended visit to the Continent. However, the poor reception of *A Christmas Carol* was not enough to prevent Dickens from publishing two more Christmas stories—*The Chimes* (1844) and *The Cricket on the Hearth* (1845).

Returning from Italy in 1845, Dickens began editing a new daily newspaper, *The Daily News*, but resigned from that job after only three weeks. He began instead the serialization of *Dombey and Son* (1846-1848), only to begin the serialization of *David Copperfield* (1849-1850) the following year. During this time, Dickens began working with amateur theatricals as an actor and a director, mostly to benefit literature and the arts. He then began editing the periodical *Household Words* and writing what many call his most ambitious work, *Bleak House*, in 1852, which ran for a year and a half.

In 1854, *Hard Times* was published serially in order to boost the failing circulation of *Household Words*, and soon thereafter, Dickens began serialization of *Little Dorrit* (1855-1857). At this time, Dickens purchased a home at Gad's Hill, on the road between London and Dover, but his home life was not to be that of country tran-

DICKENS'S MAJOR WORKS

1836	*Sketches by Boz*
1836-1837	*Pickwick Papers*
1837-1839	*Oliver Twist*
1838-1839	*Nicholas Nickleby*
1840-1841	*The Old Curiosity Shop*
1841	*Barnaby Rudge: A Tale of the Riots of '80*
1842	*American Notes*
1843	*A Christmas Carol*
1843-1844	*Martin Chuzzlewit*
1844	*The Chimes*
1845	*The Cricket on the Hearth*
1846	*The Battle of Life*
1846-1848	*Dombey and Son*
1848	*The Haunted Man*
1849-1850	*David Copperfield*
1852-1853	*Bleak House*
1854	*Hard Times*
1855-1857	*Little Dorrit*
1858	*Reprinted Pieces*
1859	*A Tale of Two Cities*
1860	*The Uncommercial Traveller*
1860-1861	*Great Expectations*
1864-1865	*Our Mutual Friend*
1868	*George Silverman's Explanation*
1870	*The Mystery of Edwin Drood* (unfinished)
1871	*Christmas Stories*

quillity. In 1858, he separated from his wife amid much bad publicity.

Also in 1858, Dickens began another major aspect of his professional life—a series of public readings from his own work. Although he published *A Tale of Two Cities* in 1859, the public readings in London did not abate. In 1860, he began writing *Great Expectations* (1860-1861) to increase the circulation of a new weekly, *All the Year Round*. London readings continued through 1863, when he went to Paris for another series of readings there. Although he was experiencing poor health, Dickens wrote *Our Mutual Friend* (1864-1865) and performed public readings in London until 1868, when he made his last trip to the United States for a tour of readings that brought him much money but that taxed his already failing health.

When Dickens returned to England after several months in the United States, he took up readings again in London, Scotland, and Ireland, in addition to beginning his last work (which he did not live to finish), *The Mystery of Edwin Drood* (1870). In 1870, on June 8, after working all day, Dickens suffered a stroke while at his Gad's Hill home and died the next day. He was buried in Westminster Abbey.

SIGNIFICANCE

As any account of his life makes clear, what most characterizes Charles Dickens is the amount of work he produced and the fact that all of it was originally written for serial publication—a demanding way to publish. To keep up with the demand, Dickens was writing constantly. Although audiences followed Dickens's work as closely as they follow television soap operas today, identifying with his characters as if they were real people and eagerly awaiting each new installment, the fact that Dickens had to keep writing continuously to meet the demands of serialization has made many academic critics scorn his work as popular melodrama catering to the tastes of the masses.

The widespread popularity of Dickens, which continues unabated into the twenty-first century, cannot be accounted for so simply. In spite of the fact that Dickens cranked out novel after novel, as if he were a one-man literary factory, he impresses even skeptics as a masterful storyteller and a genius at characterization.

Many critics have tried to account for what might be called the mystery of Dickens: his amazing aptitude for visualizing scenes in concrete detail, his ability to control and develop highly elaborate plots, and most of all, his puzzling method of creating characters that, even as they are obviously caricatures, seem somehow more real in their fictionality than most realistic characters are. Simply to name such characters as Mr. Pickwick, Scrooge, Fagin, and Mr. Micawber is to conjure up images that are destined to remain memorable.

The fact that Dickens's novels have been so easily adapted to film has added to the almost hallucinatory way with which his works are imprinted on the mind of modern readers and viewers. Such scenes as Oliver in the workhouse asking for more gruel, Sydney Carton on the scaffold in *A Tale of Two Cities*, saying what a far, far better thing he does, and Miss Havisham in her decayed wedding dress in *Great Expectations* have become part of the mind and memory of millions of Dickens's admirers.

Dickens drew his inspiration primarily from three sources. First, much of his writing is autobiographical. One can see the deserted, poverty-stricken child in Oliver Twist, the aspiring young writer in David Copperfield, and the misguided young man in Pip. Second, Dickens wrote about the many social and technological elements of Victorian society. *Bleak House* is a compendium of Dickens's knowledge about the complexities of the law courts, just as *Martin Chuzzlewit* is a satiric overview of Victorian (and American) social absurdities.

In such works as *Hard Times*, Dickens focused on the deficiencies of utilitarian philosophy of the period, and in *Little Dorrit*, he turned his attention to the bureaucracy of the business world. Finally, Dickens's fiction developed out of the same source from which all fiction ultimately springs, that is, the many conventions of fiction itself. In spite of the fact that Dickens was not highly educated, he was well-read, especially in the wellspring works of storytelling and character-making such as *The Arabian Nights' Entertainments*, Murasaki Shikibu's *The Tale of Genji*, and Miguel de Cervantes' *Don Quixote de la Mancha* (1605, 1615), as well as the masterworks of the novel's beginning in the eighteenth century, such as Daniel Defoe's *Robinson Crusoe* (1719), Henry Fielding's *Tom Jones* (1749), and Tobias Smollett's *Roderick Random* (1748). Thus, in spite of the fact that Dickens's characters seem so very real when the reader remembers them, they seem real precisely because they are so artificial; that is, they are pure fictional creations who can exist only in Dickens's imaginative world.

The number of Dickens's admirers seems to grow each year. Such adaptations of Dickens's work as the highly popular musical version of *Oliver Twist*, the ambitious (day-long) and masterful Royal Shakespeare Company's stage presentation of *Nicholas Nickleby*, and the yearly tradition of countless presentations of *A Christmas Carol* introduce new readers to Dickens's works over and over again. There is little doubt that he will continue to be the most popular and influential spokesman of Victorian England, for, in the minds of the majority, Victorian England is Dickens's England.

—*Charles E. May*

FURTHER READING

Ackroyd, Peter. *The Life and Times of Charles Dickens*. Irvington, N.Y.: Hydra, 2003. Ackroyd describes the public and private lives of Dickens in this illustrated biography. Despite the novelist's public fame and wealth, the private man was anxious about money and ashamed of his extramarital relationship. The British Broadcasting Company published this book in 2002 under the title *Dickens: Public Life and Private Passion*.

Ayers, Brenda. *Dissenting Women in Dickens' Novels: The Subversion of Domestic Ideology*. Westport, Conn.: Greenwood Press, 1998. The author argues that Dickens's novels actually subvert Victorian ideology with respect to their portrayal of women.

Coolidge, Archibald C., Jr. *Charles Dickens as Serial Novelist*. Ames: Iowa State University Press, 1967. A helpful study of a very important aspect of Dickens's work: The fact that his writing first appeared in serialization had a great influence on the nature of his narrative.

Forster, John. *The Life of Charles Dickens*. London: Chapman and Hall, 1872-1874. Rev. ed. 1876. The first authoritative biography, in three volumes (two in the revised edition), written by a friend and literary adviser of Dickens, and valuable for the many factual details and anecdotes it includes.

House, Humphrey. *The Dickens World*. London: Oxford University Press, 1941. An important book that helped to initiate the revival of the study of Dickens as a serious novelist; focuses on Victorian social issues in Dickens's work.

Johnson, Edgar. *Charles Dickens: His Tragedy and Triumph*. 2 vols. New York: Simon & Schuster, 1952. Rev. ed. New York: Viking Press, 1977. The definitive biography; also contains very good criticism of Dickens's work.

Kaplan, Fred. *Dickens: A Biography*. New York: William Morrow, Hodder & Stoughton, 1988. Acclaimed biography of Dickens, whose life in many ways mirrored those of his characters. Kaplan uses unpublished and abandoned sources to create a three-dimensional portrait of Dickens's life, including his passions, unhappy marriage, and complicated family life.

Leavis, F. R., and Q. D. Leavis. *Dickens the Novelist*. London: Chatto & Windus, 1970. Focuses on the novels from *Dombey and Son* through *Great Expectations*; excellent criticism by two highly respected British critics.

Marcus, Steven. *Dickens: From Pickwick to Dombey*. New York: Basic Books, 1965. A study of Dickens's early work, focusing on Victorian cultural life; a stimulating account by a well-known critic of Victorian literature and life.

Nelson, Harland S. *Charles Dickens*. Boston: Twayne, 1981. Not the usual introductory survey, this study focuses on the way Dickens wrote and published and how the basic elements of his novels engage the reader.

Smiley, Jane. *Charles Dickens.* New York: Viking Press, 2002. Smiley, a Pulitzer Prize-winning novelist, describes Dickens as the "first true celebrity in the modern sense," and portrays him as he was known to his contemporaries. Smiley examines how Dickens used incidents from his life in his fiction and how he carefully crafted a public image.

Wilson, Angus. *The World of Charles Dickens.* New York: Viking Press, 1970. Perhaps the best single-volume study of Dickens's life as well as his work as a popular novelist.

SEE ALSO: Hans Christian Andersen; Maria Edgeworth; William Charles Macready; William Makepeace Thackeray.

RELATED ARTICLES in *Great Events from History: The Nineteenth Century, 1801-1900:* 1843: Carlyle Publishes *Past and Present;* March, 1852-September, 1853: Dickens Publishes *Bleak House;* 1884: New Guilds Promote the Arts and Crafts Movement.

EMILY DICKINSON
American poet

The greatest American woman poet of the nineteenth century, Dickinson lived an unusually reclusive life but led an inner life of intense, imaginative creativity that made her one of the greatest American poets.

BORN: December 10, 1830; Amherst, Massachusetts
DIED: May 15, 1886; Amherst, Massachusetts
ALSO KNOWN AS: Emily Elizabeth Dickinson (full name)
AREA OF ACHIEVEMENT: Literature

EARLY LIFE
The sparse facts of Emily Elizabeth Dickinson's external life after her birth can be summarized in a few sentences: She spent her entire life in her family home, and died in it at the age of fifty-five. She was graduated from Amherst Academy in 1847, then attended nearby Mount Holyoke Female Seminary for one year. She traveled occasionally to Springfield and twice to Boston. In 1854, she and her family visited Washington and Philadelphia. She never married and had no romantic relationships. However, her interior life was so intense that a distinguished twentieth century poet and critic, Allen Tate, could write, "All pity for Miss Dickinson's 'starved life' is misdirected. Her life was one of the richest and deepest ever lived on this continent." It is a life that has proved a perplexing puzzle to many critics and biographers.

What led to Dickinson's monastic seclusion from society? Was it forced on her by a possessive, despotic father? Was it self-willed by her timid temperament, by rejected love, or by her neurotic need for utmost privacy while she pursued the muse of poetry? Speculation abounds, certainty eludes; nothing is simple and direct about her behavior. Perhaps the opening lines of her poem number 1129 are self-revealing:

Tell all the Truth but tell it slant—
Success in Circuit lies
Too bright for our infirm Delight
The Truth's superb surprise

At the time when Dickinson was born, Amherst was a farming village of four to five hundred families, with a cultural tradition of Puritanism and a devotion to education as well as devoutness. The Dickinsons were prominent in public and collegiate activities. Samuel Fowler Dickinson, Emily's grandfather, founded Amherst College in 1821 to train preachers, teachers, and missionaries. Edward Dickinson (1813-1874), Emily's father, was the eldest of nine children. He became a successful attorney and, at the age of thirty-two, was named treasurer of Amherst College, a position he kept for thirty-eight years. He served three terms in the Massachusetts legislature and one term as a member of Congress. Even political opponents respected him as forthright, courageous, diligent, solemn, intelligent, and reliable; he was the incarnation of responsibility and rectitude. In a letter to her brother, Dickinson mocked him (and her mother): "Father and Mother sit in state in the sitting-room perusing such papers, only, as they are well assured, have nothing carnal in them."

Emily's mother, Emily Norcross (1804-1882), was born in Monson, Massachusetts, twenty miles south of Amherst. Her father was a well-to-do farmer who sent his daughter to a reputable boarding school, where she behaved conventionally, preparing herself for the respectable, rational marriage that ensued after Edward Dickinson had courted her politely and passionlessly. The mother has received adverse treatment from most of

Dickinson's biographers because of several statements the daughter wrote to her confidant, Colonel Thomas Wentworth Higginson (1823-1911):

My Mother does not care for thought.

I never had a mother. I suppose a mother is one to whom you hurry when you are troubled.

I always ran Home to Awe when a child, if anything befell me. He was an awful Mother, but I liked him better than none.

Richard Sewall indicates in his magisterial two-volume *The Life of Emily Dickinson* (1974) that Emily's acerbic remarks should not be taken at their surface meaning in the light of the poet's continued preference for remaining in the familial home. To be sure, Dickinson's mother read meagerly and had a mediocre mind, but she was a tenderhearted, loving person who committed herself wholly to her family and to the household's management. While she never understood her daughter's complex nature, she also never intruded on Dickinson's inner life.

Dickinson's brother Austin (1829-1895) was closest to her in disposition. Personable, sensitive, empathic, and sociable, he became an attorney, joined his father's practice, and succeeded him as Amherst's treasurer in 1873. He shared his sister's wit, taste in books, and love of nature; his vitality was a tonic for her. He married one of her schoolmates, Susan Gilbert, vivacious, worldly, and articulate.

Dickinson and her sister-in-law, living next door to each other, were in each other's homes frequently during the first years of this marriage. Dickinson had a near-obsessive concern for her immediate family and greatly desired to make of her sister-in-law a true sister in spirit. She sent Sue nearly three hundred of her poems over the years—more than to anyone else. However, a satisfyingly soulful friendship never quite materialized. To be sure, Sue's parties did keep Dickinson in at least limited circulation in her early twenties. The two women exchanged books and letters, with Dickinson occasionally seeking Sue's criticism of her poems. Dickinson, always fond of children, was particularly delighted with her nephew Gilbert; tragically, he died of typhoid fever at the age of eight; Dickinson's letter of condolence called him "Dawn and Meridian in one."

The two women's paths ineluctably diverged. Sue had a husband and, eventually, three children and was an extroverted social climber. For unknown reasons, Dickinson and Sue quarreled in 1854, and Dickinson wrote her the only dismissive letter in her correspondence: "You can go or stay." They resumed their friendship, but it proved turbulent, as did Sue's and Austin's marriage. In 1866, Sue betrayed Emily's confidence by sending her poem "A Narrow Fellow in the Grass" to the *Springfield Republican*, which mutilated it by changing its punctuation. "It was robbed of me," Dickinson bitterly complained.

With her natural sister Lavinia (1833-1899), Dickinson bonded intimately all her life. Like her older sister, Lavinia remained a spinster, remained at home, and outlived her family. Dickinson and Lavinia were devotedly protective of each other. The younger sister was relatively uncomplicated, steady in temperament, pretty, and outgoing. Their only quasi-serious difference centered on Vinnie's love of cats, contrasted to Dickinson's care for birds. It was Lavinia who organized the first large-scale publication of Dickinson's poems after her death.

Outside her family circle, Dickinson had only a few friends, but they mattered greatly to her—she called them her "estate" and cultivated them intensely. While still in her teens, she established a pattern that was to recur throughout her life: She sought to attach herself to an older man who would be her confidant and mentor or, to use her terms, "preceptor" or "master." These pilots would, she hoped, teach her something of the qualities that she knew she lacked: knowledge of the outer world, firm opinions and principles, sociability, and intellectual stability.

DICKINSON'S "LETTER TO THE WORLD"

This is my letter to the world,
That never wrote to me, —
The simple news that Nature told,
With tender majesty.

Her message is committed
To hands I cannot see;
For love of her, sweet countrymen,
Judge tenderly of me!

Source: Emily Dickinson, *Poems*, edited by Mabel Loomis Todd and T. W. Higginson (Boston, 1890).

Dickinson's first candidate was Benjamin Newton (1821-1853), only nine years her senior, who was a law student in her father's office from 1847 to 1849. He served her in the roles of intellectual companion, guide in aesthetic and spiritual spheres, and older brother. He introduced her to Ralph Waldo Emerson's poetry, encouraged her to write her own, but died of consumption in his thirty-third year, before she became a serious poet. Her letters to him are not extant, but in a letter she wrote Higginson in 1862, she probably refers to Newton when she mentions a "friend who taught me Immortality—but venturing too near, himself—he never returned—."

Dickinson's first mature friendship was with Samuel Bowles (1834-1878), who inherited his father's *Springfield Republican* and made it one of the most admired newspapers in the United States. Bowles had a penetrating mind, warmth, wit, dynamic energy, strongly liberal convictions, and an engaging, vibrant personality. Extensively seasoned by travel, he knew virtually every important public leader and was a marvelous guest and companion. He, and sometimes his wife with him, became regular visitors in both Edward and Austin Dickinson's homes from 1858 onward.

Thirty-five of Dickinson's letters to Bowles survive, and they show her deep attachment to—perhaps even love for—him, even though she knew that he was out of her reach in every way—just as her poetry was out of his, because his taste in literature was wholly conventional. In April, 1862, Bowles left for a long European stay. Shortly thereafter, Emily wrote him, "I have the errand from my heart—I might forget to tell it. Would you please come home?" Then, in a second letter, "[I]t is a suffering to have a sea . . . between your soul and you." That November, the returned Bowles called at Amherst. Dickinson chose to remain in her room, sending him a note instead of encountering him.

LIFE'S WORK

The turning point in Dickinson's career as a poet, and hence in her life, came in her late twenties. Before 1858, her writing consisted of letters and desultory, sentimental verses; thereafter, particularly from 1858 to 1863, poetry became her primary activity. As far as scholars can ascertain, she wrote one hundred in 1859, sixty-five in 1860, at least eighty in 1861, and in 1862—her annus mirabilis—perhaps as many as 366, of a prosodic skill far superior to her previous achievement. What caused such a flood of creativity? Most—but not all—biographers attribute it to her unfulfilled love for the Reverend Mr. Charles Wadsworth (1814-1882).

Dickinson and Lavinia visited their father in Washington, D.C., during April, 1854, when he was serving his congressional term. On their return trip, they stopped over in Philadelphia as guests of a friend from school days and heard Wadsworth preach in the Arch Street Presbyterian Church, whose pastor he was from 1850 to April, 1862. Married and middle-aged, of rocklike rectitude, shy and reserved, Wadsworth nevertheless made an indelible impression as a "Man of sorrow" on Dickinson. He was generally regarded as second only to Henry Ward Beecher among the pulpit orators of his time. A contemporary newspaper profile described him in these terms:

> His person is slender, and his dark eyes, hair and complexion have decidedly a Jewish cast. The elements of his popularity are somewhat like those of the gifted Summerfield—a sweet touching voice, warmth of manner, and lively imagination. But Wadsworth's style, it is said, is vastly bolder, his fancy more vivid, and his action more violent.

It is presumed that Dickinson must have talked with Wadsworth during her Philadelphia visit. Few other facts are known: He called on her in Amherst in the spring of 1860, and again in the summer of 1880. She requested his and his children's pictures from his closest friend. In April, 1862, Wadsworth moved to San Francisco, becoming minister to the Calvary Presbyterian Society. Dickinson found this departure traumatic: She used "Calvary" ten times in poems of 1862 and 1863; she spoke of herself as "Empress of Calvary," and began one 1863 poem with the words, "Where Thou art—that is Home/Cashmere or Calvary—the Same . . ./ So I may come." With probable reference to her inner "Calvary" drama of loss and renunciation, she began at this time to dress entirely in white. By 1870, and until his death, Wadsworth was back in Philadelphia in another pastorate, but the anguished crisis he had caused her had ended by then.

After Dickinson's death, three long love letters were found in draft form among her papers, in her handwriting of the late 1850's and early 1860's. They address a "Master," and have therefore come to be called the "Master Letters." Their tone is urgent, their style, nervous and staccato. In the second of them, "Daisy" tells her "Master": "I want to see you more—Sir—than all I wish for in this world—and the wish—altered a little—will be my only one—for the skies." She invites him to come to Amherst and pledges not to disappoint him. However, the final letter shows the agony of a rejected lover, amounting to an almost incoherent cry of despair. For whom were these letters intended? Thomas Johnson and most other biographers designate Wadsworth. Richard Sewall, however, argues for Bowles, on the internal evidence that some of the images in the unsent letters parallel images in poems that Dickinson did send Bowles.

In 1861, Dickinson composed the most openly erotic of her poems, number 249, with the sea the element in which the speaker moors herself:

> Wild Nights—Wild Nights!
> Were I with thee
> Wild Nights should be
> Our luxury!
> Futile—the Winds—
> To a Heart in port—
> Done with the Compass—
> Done with the Chart!
> Rowing in Eden—
> Ah, the Sea!
> Might I but moor—Tonight
> —In Thee!

Is this poem derived from autobiographical experience—or, at least, intense longing for such experience—or is the first-person perspective no more than that of the poem's persona or speaker? Again, Dickinsonians divide on this question.

On April 15, 1862, having liked an article by Thomas Wentworth Higginson, Dickinson sent him four of her poems and a diffident note, asking him if he thought her verses were "alive" and "breathed." Trained as a minister, Higginson had held a Unitarian pulpit in Newburyport, Massachusetts, then resigned it to devote himself to social reforms, chief of which was abolitionism. He had made a reputation as a representative, influential mid-century literary critic, with particular interest in the work of female writers. The four poems Dickinson mailed him were among her best to date; in his evaluative replies, however, he showed an obtuse misunderstanding of them, as well as of her subsequent submissions, which were to total one hundred.

Dickinson undoubtedly felt a strong need for another "preceptor"—Wadsworth had just departed for San Francisco—and especially for a literary rather than romantic confidant. Higginson was to prove her "safest friend" for the remainder of her life. A warm, courteous, sympathetic man, he regarded her with mystified admiration. After their correspondence had been under way for several months, he asked her to send him a photograph. Her response was, "I had no portrait, now, but am small, like the Wren, and my Hair is bold, like the Chestnut Bur, and my eyes, like the Sherry in the Glass, that the Guest leaves." After Higginson had met her eight years later, he confirmed this self-portrait and added to it that Dickinson was a "plain, shy little person, the face without a single good feature."

Dickinson's poetry, unfortunately for both of them, was simply beyond Higginson's grasp. He immediately and consistently advised her not to seek its publication because it was "not strong enough." His critical judgments were invariably fatuous, showing deaf ears and blind eyes to her original language, syntax, meter, and rhyme. She resigned herself to his recommendation against publication but gently yet firmly ignored his strictures concerning her poems' construction. Thomas Johnson summarizes the relationship as "one of the most eventful, and at the same time elusive and insubstantial friendships in the annals of American literature."

During the late 1870's, nearing her fiftieth year, Dickinson fell in love with Otis Phillips Lord (1812-1884). He was a distinguished lawyer who, from 1875 to 1882, served as an associate justice of the Massachusetts Supreme Court. He answered Dickinson's constant need for a settled, senior friend-tutor, intellectually gifted and personally impressive; he became her last "preceptor." She had first known Judge Lord when he had called on Edward Dickinson; like her father, he was vigorous, conscientious, commanding, and highly disciplined. Their affection developed after December, 1877, when Lord's wife died. Fifteen of her letters to him survive and indicate that, over the objection of his nieces, Lord apparently offered to marry her. With her father and Bowles now dead and her mother an invalid requiring many hours of her time each week, Dickinson found considerable solace in their correspondence. However, she also knew that her reclusive life was too rigidly established for her to adapt to the major changes that marriage would require of her.

On April 1, 1882, Wadsworth, the man she had called "my closest earthly friend," died. On May 1 of that year, Lord suffered a stroke; on May 14, Dickinson wrote him a fervent letter of joy at his (temporary) recovery, assuring him of her "rapture" at his reprieve from impending death; on October 5 came news of her beloved nephew Gilbert's death; on November 14, her mother finally died, after years of serious illness. It is not surprising that Dickinson then underwent a "nervous prostration" that impaired her faculties for many weeks.

After an 1864 visit to Boston for eye treatment, Dickinson did not leave Amherst for the remainder of her life.

Her withdrawal from society became gradually more marked. By 1870, she did not venture beyond her house and garden, preferring to socialize by sending brief letters, some of them accompanied by poems, flowers, or fruit. She retreated upstairs when most visitors came to call, sometimes lurking on an upper landing or around corners. While strangers regarded her eccentricities as unnatural, her friends and family accepted them as the price of her retreat into the intensity of her poetry. Perhaps her most self-revealing poem is number 303, whose first stanza declares

> The Soul selects her own Society—
> Then—shuts the Door—
> To her divine Majority—
> Present no more—

Emily Dickinson died of nephritis on May 15, 1886.

SIGNIFICANCE

Emily Dickinson's nearly eighteen hundred poems, only seven of which saw print during her lifetime, constitute her "Letter to the World" (number 441), her real life. They establish her, along with Walt Whitman, as one of this nation's two most seminal poets. Her sharp intellectual wit, her playfulness, and her love of ambiguity, paradox, and irony liken her poetry to the seventeenth century metaphysical achievements of England's John Donne and George Herbert and New England's Edward Taylor. However, her language and rhythm are often uniquely individual, with a tumultuous rhetoric that sharply probes homely details for universal essence. She is a writer who defies boundaries and labels, standing alone as a contemporary not only of Herman Melville and Nathaniel Hawthorne but also, in the poetic sense, of T. S. Eliot, W. H. Auden, Robert Frost, Robert Lowell, and Sylvia Plath. Her work ranks with the most original in poetic history.

—Gerhard Brand

FURTHER READING

Dickinson, Emily. *The Complete Poems of Emily Dickinson*. Edited by Thomas H. Johnson. Boston: Little, Brown, 1960. The text of the three-volume edition with the variant readings omitted.

_____. *The Letters of Emily Dickinson*. Edited by Thomas H. Johnson and Theodora Ward. 3 vols. Cambridge, Mass.: Harvard University Press, 1958. The definitive editions of Dickinson's poetry and letters. They have been arranged in the most accurate chronological order possible and numbered. In 1890, the first collection of Dickinson's poems was brought out by Mabel Loomis Todd and Higginson, with two more volumes in 1891 and 1896, all in disorderly, random selections, with gross editorial violations of the poet's spelling and syntax. Johnson has therefore done an invaluable service to American literary scholarship by taking Dickinson's jottings, scribbles, and semifinal drafts and sorting them out. Even so, his choices of alternative language have sometimes been questioned by other Dickinson specialists.

_____. *The Poems of Emily Dickinson*. Edited by Thomas H. Johnson. 3 vols. Cambridge, Mass.: Harvard University Press, 1955. "Including variant readings critically compared with all known manuscripts."

Habegger, Alfred. *My Wars Are Laid Away in Books: The Life of Emily Dickinson*. New York: Random House, 2001. Acclaimed literary biography. Habegger agrees with feminist critics who rejected the traditional portrayal of Dickinson as a quaint homebody; he depicts the poet as a powerful personality who transcended the strictures of her father and Victorian society. Includes analyses of Dickinson's poetry.

Johnson, Thomas H. *Emily Dickinson: An Interpretive Biography*. New York: Atheneum, 1976. A gracefully written, authoritative critical biography by the dean of contemporary Dickinson scholars. It is the first that discusses in detail Higginson's significance in Dickinson's life and career.

Kirk, Connie Ann. *Emily Dickinson: A Biography*. Westport, Conn.: Greenwood Press, 2004. Using her own primary research, Kirk paints a picture of Dickinson as a complex and busy woman who influenced American life and culture. Includes a bibliography and chronology.

Sewall, Richard B. *The Life of Emily Dickinson*. 2 vols. New York: Farrar, Straus and Giroux, 1974. By far the most comprehensive Dickinson interpretive biography. Sewall devotes his first volume to Dickinson's family, his second to her friends, and intertwines her life with both circles with great tact, sympathetic understanding, and impressive learning. The prose is clear and often eloquent. One of the most admirable modern literary biographies.

_____, ed. *Emily Dickinson: A Collection of Critical Essays*. Englewood Cliffs, N.J.: Prentice-Hall, 1963. A rich and diverse collection of critical essays, displaying an almost bewildering range of interpretive views. Such important critics and scholars as Charles Anderson, R. P. Blackmur, John Crowe Ransom, Allen Tate, and George Whicher are represented.

See also: Elizabeth Barrett Browning; Thomas Wentworth Higginson; Helen Hunt Jackson; Christina Rossetti.

Related article in *Great Events from History: The Nineteenth Century, 1801-1900:* November 8, 1837: Mount Holyoke Female Seminary Opens.

Rudolf Diesel
German engineer and inventor

Diesel's greatest invention was the diesel engine, which was named after him. Its high thermal efficiency and the low cost of its fuel have made it an exceptionally economical engine that has found many applications—in automobiles, trucks, ships, and submarines, and for generating electricity.

Born: March 18, 1858; Paris, France
Died: September 29, 1913; at sea, in the English Channel
Also known as: Rudolf Christian Karl Diesel (full name)
Area of achievement: Engineering

Early Life

Born to Bavarian parents residing in France, Rudolf Diesel was exposed at an early age to the mechanical arts, both in his father's leather-goods shop and at the nearby Conservatoire des Arts et Métiers. The Diesel family fled to London in September, 1870, in the face of growing anti-German sentiment during the Franco-Prussian War. After eight weeks there, his father, realizing there were too many mouths to feed, sent twelve-year-old Rudolf to Augsburg, Bavaria, to live with an uncle.

Diesel's uncle enrolled him in a county trade school, where Diesel decided, at the age of fourteen, to become an engineer. At the trade school, he studied mathematics, physics, mechanical drawing, and modern languages. It was there also that Diesel realized that his life's ambitions would come true only through hard work and a mastery of science. In the summer of 1875, Diesel advanced to the next level of education in the German system by enrolling, on a scholarship, in the new Technische Hochschule in Munich.

At the Technische Hochschule, Diesel heard the lectures of Professor Carl von Linde on the subject of heat engines. He was particularly struck by the low efficiency of the steam engine and began to think about ways to improve that efficiency. The firm grounding in thermodynamics that he received from Linde's lectures later formed his approach to the problem of designing a better engine. In December, 1879, Diesel passed his final exams at the Technische Hochschule with honors and began his career as an engineer.

Life's Work

Linde, who had so impressed Diesel in school, became his first employer. Diesel took a job as the Paris representative of the refrigeration machinery business Linde had founded. By working with heat engines and heat pumps, Diesel gained experience with the subject that most interested him: thermodynamics.

For ten years, Diesel worked in his spare time on various heat engines, including a solar-powered air engine. A heat engine produces work by heating a working fluid; the fluid then expands and exerts pressure on a moving part, usually a piston. Like many of his contemporaries, Diesel investigated the use of ammonia, ether, and carbon dioxide as substitutes for steam as the working medium in a heat engine. He tried to build an ammonia engine but found ammonia too difficult to handle (even small leaks proved hazardous to the health of nearby workers). He then turned to air as a working medium for two reasons: It was abundant and the oxygen in air could support combustion, thus eliminating the need for a separate firebox.

Having thoroughly studied thermodynamics, Diesel understood the Carnot cycle and attempted to apply it to his new heat engine, in the belief that it would improve the engine's thermal efficiency. First published in 1824 by the French engineer Sadi Carnot, the Carnot cycle describes the ideal heat engine of maximum thermal efficiency and consists of four phases: isothermal (constant temperature) combustion, adiabatic (no loss or gain of heat) expansion, isothermal compression, and adiabatic compression to the initial state. In order to realize the highest possible efficiency, Carnot noted, the heat to be converted into work must be added at the highest temperature of the cycle, and it must not raise the temperature of the cycle.

The difficulty of adding heat (through combustion) while maintaining a constant temperature did not daunt Diesel; he felt confident that he could design such an engine—an ideal Carnot engine. His solution was to heat the air by compressing it with a piston inside a cylinder. At the top of the stroke, the air temperature would be at a maximum. He would then add a small amount of fuel, which the high air temperature would ignite. The heat produced by combustion would then be offset by the tendency of the air temperature to drop as the piston moved down and the air expanded, thus producing isothermal combustion. While theoretically correct, this idea met with many practical difficulties, the most formidable being that the engine had to work at extremely high pressures in order to achieve maximum efficiency.

In Diesel's 1892 patent application for his engine, he listed isothermal combustion as the essence of his invention. A year later, Diesel published *Theorie und Konstruktion eines rationellen Wärmemotors zum Ersatz der Dampfmaschinen und der heute bekannten Verbrennungsmotoren* (1893; *Theory and Construction of a Rational Heat Motor*, 1894), in which he fully described his ideas and supported them with calculations and drawings. This book was important to Diesel as a way of promoting his ideas and thus gaining financial backing. With the endorsement of some of Europe's leading thinkers in thermodynamics, Diesel gained the support of two industrial giants: Krupp and Maschinenfabrik Augsburg. Under the agreement that he reached with these firms, Diesel received a good salary and the use of their facilities. Despite this boost, it would take him four years of hard work to begin to realize his dream of a more efficient engine.

In the process of writing his book, Diesel realized that the ideal engine he had envisioned would be almost impossible to build because of the high air pressures required by the theory, which were well beyond the practice of the day. Thus, he began, in 1893, to scale down his ideas and to settle for good, but less-than-ideal, efficiencies. Even with the changes in his theoretical goals, building a working engine proved to be a challenge. His first experimental engine, tested in late 1893, exploded upon ignition of the fuel. His second engine ran under its own power for a minute, but only at idling speed. Not until 1897 did a prototype run smoothly, but it had neither the reliability nor the economy to be a marketable engine. Furthermore, it operated at a thermal efficiency far below what Diesel had originally set out to achieve.

Despite the remaining problems, Diesel announced in June, 1897, at a meeting of the Society of German Engineers that his engine was ready to be sold. The resulting fiasco almost ruined Diesel financially, brought him to

Rudolf Diesel. (Library of Congress)

the brink of a nervous breakdown, and gave his engine a bad name. Continued refinement of the engine over the next five years, however, restored the diesel engine's reputation. It eventually gained a respectable share of the market, as the number of engines being sold every year increased steadily. By 1908, when Diesel's basic patent expired, the diesel engine was firmly established as an important type of power plant.

By 1912, doubts were being raised as to Diesel's role in the invention of the engine that bore his name. By some accounts, men other than Diesel—those who had taken his highly theoretical ideas and produced a working engine—deserved credit for the diesel engine. Those same critics saw Diesel as little more than a promoter. Diesel had always been high-strung (he was prone to migraines when under extreme stress) so it is not surprising that these criticisms stung him sharply. When he heard, in 1912, that a history of the diesel engine was being written, he countered with his own history, "Die Entstehung des Dieselmotors" (he published a book of the same title the following year).

In November, 1912, Diesel presented this paper at a professional meeting of engineers, at which two professors attacked him, pointing out that the diesel engine bore little resemblance to his original concept. At the same time Diesel was suffering these attacks upon his integrity, he was also suffering financial setbacks; bad investments had taken a heavy toll, despite good income from various sources. On the night of September 29, 1913, Diesel disappeared from a steamer while crossing the English Channel. His son later identified the effects taken from a body at the mouth of the Schelde River as those of his father. The death was ruled a suicide.

SIGNIFICANCE

The diesel engine of today bears little resemblance to Rudolf Diesel's original rational engine, but one is still quite justified in calling him the inventor. Few inventions spring from their creator's mind without the need to refine and improve them, and Diesel's brainchild was no exception. Significantly, Diesel kept a hand in his engine's development throughout the lengthy development period. Furthermore, today's engine retains three essential features of Diesel's original concept. First, all diesel engines are high-compression engines that use air as the working medium. Second, fuel is still injected into the cylinder at the end of the compression stroke. Third, it is still the heat of the compressed air that ignites the fuel.

Diesel engine production grew dramatically after Diesel's death. It is difficult to estimate the number of diesel engines in service, but the fact that millions are built each year throughout the world helps put their importance in perspective. The diesel engine's high thermal efficiency and the low cost of diesel fuel combine to make it an extremely economical engine. As a result, diesel engines have found a growing number of applications such as submarines, ships, locomotives, heavy road and off-road vehicles, passenger cars, and electric generating plants. These engines aptly carry the name of the man who worked so hard to make them a reality.

—Brian J. Nichelson

FURTHER READING

Auer, Georg. "Renaissance Man Set the Automobile Industry on Fire." *Automotive News* 75, no. 5908 (December 18, 2000): 20H. A tribute to Diesel, describing how his interest in thermodynamics led to his creation of a thermodynamic engine. Explains how the engine has been used to power ships, pumps, cars, and other machines and vehicles.

Bryant, Lynwood. "The Development of the Diesel Engine." *Technology and Culture* 17 (July, 1976): 432-446. A carefully documented case study of the nature of invention, development, and innovation. Contains a brief but useful discussion of the claims against Diesel in 1912. Highlights the many difficulties Diesel encountered in developing his engine and the many modifications to his original idea. Contains footnotes.

_____. "Rudolf Diesel and His Rational Engine." *Scientific American* 221 (August, 1969): 108-117. A careful examination of the intellectual evolution of the diesel engine. Well illustrated and written for the layman, the article explains each step in Diesel's progress toward the diesel engine of today. Contains an especially useful section, with graphs and illustrations, of the Carnot cycle, Diesel's starting point.

Cummins, C. Lyle, Jr. *Diesel's Engine.* Wilsonville, Oreg.: Carnot Press, 1993. A biography written by a mechanical engineer. In addition to providing an overview of Diesel's life, the book describes the work of licensees who transformed Diesel's engine into a reliable source of power for numerous products and vehicles.

Diesel, Eugen. "Rudolf Diesel." In *From Engines to Autos: Five Pioneers in Engine Development and Their Contributions to the Automotive Industry*, by Eugen Diesel, Gustav Goldbeck, and Friedrich Schilderberger. Chicago: Henry Regnery, 1960. Written by Diesel's son, this is, nevertheless, a reasonably objective account of Diesel's life and work. Details of engine development follow a concise, ten-page summary of his early life. Suffers from a lack of documentation, but is notable for the insights it provides into Diesel's personality.

Grosser, Morton. *Diesel: The Man and the Engine.* New York: Atheneum, 1978. A very readable account of the development of the diesel engine from Diesel's original idea through the date of the book's publication. Generally dependable in technical details. Contains a glossary and a list of books for further reading, as well as photographs and illustrations.

Nitske, W. Robert, and Charles Morrow Wilson. *Rudolf Diesel: Pioneer of the Age of Power.* Norman: University of Oklahoma Press, 1965. Biography with two chapters at the end on the diesel engine in the modern world. Not totally reliable. Written mostly from secondary sources and without footnotes; as such, it offers little new information about Rudolf Diesel or his engine.

Thomas, Donald E., Jr. *Diesel: Technology and Society in Industrial Germany*. Tuscaloosa: University of Alabama Press, 1987. Biography of Diesel, placing his invention within the context of technological, economic, and societal developments in nineteenth century Germany.

SEE ALSO: Carl Benz; Gottlieb Daimler; Étienne Lenoir; Nikolaus August Otto.

RELATED ARTICLE in *Great Events from History: The Nineteenth Century, 1801-1900:* February, 1892: Diesel Patents the Diesel Engine.

BENJAMIN DISRAELI
Prime minister of Great Britain (1868, 1874-1880)

Disraeli overcame social and political prejudice against his Jewish heritage to become leader of Great Britain's Conservative Party. He served twice as prime minister and formulated a "Tory Radicalism" distinctively free from the prevalent Whig-Liberal philosophy of utilitarianism. He also wrote novels that reflected his views on British society and politics.

BORN: December 21, 1804; London, England
DIED: April 19, 1881; London, England
ALSO KNOWN AS: Viscount Hughenden of Hughenden; Benjamin Disraeli, First Earl of Beaconsfield (full name)
AREAS OF ACHIEVEMENT: Government and politics, literature

EARLY LIFE

Benjamin Disraeli was the oldest son of Isaac D'Israeli, an antiquarian, literary scholar, and writer, and his wife, Maria Basevi. The child was the namesake and grandson of Benjamin D'Israeli, an Italian-Jewish immigrant and successful businessperson. Isaac's dispute with the synagogue of Bevis Marks led to the baptism of the four D'Israeli children as Christians in 1817, a step that later made it possible for Disraeli to have a career in the House of Commons, from which Jews were excluded until 1858.

Benjamin's family relations with his father and older sister Sarah were especially close. The younger generation simplified the family name by dropping the apostrophe. As a youngster, Benjamin attended school at Blackheath near London and Higham Hall at Epping Forest. In 1821, Benjamin—now a man of medium height, slender build, and pale, aquiline features, with a high forehead, black, wavy hair, and an intellectual countenance—began legal training in the office of a London solicitor.

Bored with the law and hoping to attain fame and fortune quickly, Disraeli in 1824 plunged into stock market speculation, lost money beyond his resources, and was forced to borrow at interest rates so ruinous that his debts became too great for him to pay until he was past middle age. In 1825, Disraeli organized a political and literary newspaper, *The Representative*, which quickly foundered amid more debts and the ill feeling of such influential associates as John Murray and John Gibson Lockhart. In an anonymous roman à clef, *Vivian Grey* (1826-1827), Disraeli caricatured these and other figures in the world of literature and politics, gaining notoriety, but at some cost to his reputation.

From 1827 to 1830, Disraeli retreated into minor writings and ill health, producing *The Young Duke* (1831), a hack novel "delightfully adapted to the most corrupt taste," to help finance a sixteen-month (1830-1831) trip to Europe, the Mediterranean, the Balkans, the Levant, Palestine, and Egypt. This experience of the atmosphere and reality of "the East" was an influence on his later novels and perhaps on his statecraft. The year 1832 found him frequently invited to London parties as both a foppishly dressed raconteur on exotic lands and an author of the amusing "society" novels that were his main, if insufficient, source of income. During Disraeli's travels the long dominance of the Tories had ended, and the new Whig government's proposals for extending voting rights to more of the middle class were nearing enactment as the Reform Bill of 1832. Disraeli decided to seek a seat in the House of Commons to participate in this new political era.

LIFE'S WORK

Disraeli made three unsuccessful attempts at parliamentary election as a Radical, a role that gave him maximum independence but no significant financial or political support. In 1835, he joined the Tory Party and, after contesting a hopeless seat, was in 1837 elected as the junior member for Maidstone. His first speech in the House of Commons was howled down by Irish and Whig mem-

Benjamin Disraeli. (Library of Congress)

bers, but he soon established himself as an effective speaker among the Tory-Conservative opposition led by Sir Robert Peel. In 1839, Disraeli abandoned his previous well-publicized love affairs and married Mrs. Mary Anne Wyndham Lewis, a widow possessed of a generous income for life from the estate of her first husband. She was twelve years older than Disraeli and noticeably tactless in her conversation, but affectionate and admiring in her nature. The union was largely one of mutual devotion until her death from cancer in 1872.

Disraeli was given no part in the Conservative administration which Peel formed after the election of 1841. He lacked influence and did not represent any large interest. Peel had his pick of older Tories, close political associates, important ex-Whigs such as Edward Stanley (later the fourteenth earl of Derby), and rising young men of promise such as William Ewart Gladstone. There was no compelling reason for him to include in the ministry an outsider of conspicuously independent views and noticeably restless ambition, and indeed there was no prospect that Peel would ever want Disraeli as a colleague in government.

Disraeli's rejection by Peel prolonged the former's leisure for developing further his own political ideas. In the pamphlet of 1833 "What Is He?" he had presented himself as both a Radical and a Tory, and in his "Vindication of the English Constitution" in 1835, he pointed out that the utilitarian maxim of "the greatest good for the greatest number" depended very much on who judged what was good. The history of political change in England had been termed "progress" by the bourgeoisie, which gained wealth and power through the changes, and by 1832, with the Reform Bill's redistribution of seats, the Whig merchants and manufacturers had begun to overbalance the parliamentary representation of Tory landlords. Peel's new "Conservatism" appeared to accept the proposition that the Whigs were entitled to determine who had the right to vote and that henceforth the Conservatives could promise only to preserve the status-quo interests of the "middle class." Disraeli argued that because the aristocratic principle had collapsed, the Tory Party should now appeal to the democratic principle of government.

The Young England movement of George Smythe, Lord John Manners, Alexander Baillie Cochrane, and Henry Hope provided for a time Disraeli's only House of Commons allies, and his best-known political novels reflected this connection in *Coningsby: Or, The New Generation* (1844) and *Sybil: Or, The Two Nations* (1845). These novels gave a realistic picture of the distress of the poor and criticized the indifference of Peel and his Conservatives to these victims of the Industrial Revolution and the Whigs' New Poor Law of 1834. Disraeli's argument, clearly, was for a Tory economic and social policy to meet the plight of the people, and for a radical departure from the laissez-faire doctrines of Manchester economics embraced by the Whigs.

Disraeli's opportunity to challenge Peel's leadership came with the latter's 1846 proposal to repeal the Corn Laws. This abolition of the protective tariff on grain and conversion to free trade would not afford any quick relief for the immediate Irish famine resulting from the 1845 potato blight, and the cabinet had already split over what the "backwoods" Tories saw as a betrayal of British farm interests mostly beneficial to British factory owners.

A party revolt of some magnitude was almost inevitable, but Disraeli acted on his own in leading off the debate for the protectionists, scathingly recounting the inconsistencies of Peel's political record and pouring scorn on his appeals for party loyalty. Having already charged that Peel "found the Whigs bathing and walked off with their clothes," Disraeli now termed him a "burglar" of other men's ideas and denounced "this huckstering tyranny of the Treasury bench . . . these political pedlars that bought their party in the cheapest market and sold us in the dearest." No other spokesperson for the landed Tories could equal Disraeli for the brilliant invective that now expressed the feelings of a majority of the Tory Party.

Repeal of the Corn Laws passed with Whig votes, but the Conservative Party, divided and defeated on an Irish "coercion bill," was split between the Peelites (including the first marquis of Aberdeen and Gladstone) and the more numerous protectionists, headed by Edward Stanley, soon fourteenth earl of Derby, with Disraeli gradually winning acceptance as protectionist leader in the House of Commons. When, in 1852, Lord Derby was asked to form a minority government, he and Disraeli revived the "Conservative" label for the party. Their efforts to reconcile Peel's followers (Peel died in 1850), however, were unsuccessful. Disraeli served as Leader

of the Commons and Chancellor of the Exchequer for the 1852 government. His budget and the administration were doomed by the opposing coalition even before Gladstone, in the budget debate, made the bitter personal attack on Disraeli that began the open hostility of these two political rivals.

The coalition of Whigs, Liberals, and Radicals split in 1858 over Lord Palmerston's foreign policy, and Derby and Disraeli again headed a minority government, from 1858 to 1859. This time they succeeded in passing the Removal of Jewish Disabilities (1858), hitherto blocked by the House of Lords. Disraeli proposed in 1859 an extension of the vote based on profession, government or bank savings, government pensions, or residential qualifications. This was defeated by the Whigs, Liberals, and Radicals as they reunited to restore Palmerston to office.

In 1866, Derby and Disraeli formed a third minority government after Lord John Russell and Gladstone were defeated on a franchise bill. The Tories introduced their

---

DISRAELI'S *CONINGSBY*

Coningsby is one of Benjamin Disraeli's most political novels. In this passage, a liberal-minded duke agonizes over the implications of poor relief on his own finances.

His Grace had been a great patron and a zealous administrator of the New Poor Law. He had been persuaded that it would elevate the condition of the labouring class. His son-in-law, Lord Everingham, who was a Whig, and a clearheaded, cold-blooded man, looked upon the New Poor Law as another Magna Charta. Lord Everingham was completely master of the subject. He was himself the Chairman of one of the most considerable Unions of the kingdom. The Duke, if he ever had a misgiving, had no chance in argument with his son-in-law. Lord Everingham overwhelmed him with quotations from Commissioners' rules and Sub-commissioners' reports, statistical tables, and references to dietaries. Sometimes with a strong case, the Duke struggled to make a fight; but Lord Everingham, when he was at fault for a reply, which was very rare, upbraided his father-in-law with the abuses of the old system, and frightened him with visions of rates [taxes] exceeding rentals.

Of late, however, a considerable change had taken place in the Duke's feelings on this great question. His son Henry entertained strong opinions upon it, and had combated his father with all the fervour of a young votary. A victory over his Grace, indeed, was not very difficult. His natural impulse would have enlisted him on the side, if not of opposition to the new system, at least of critical suspicion of its spirit and provisions. It was only the statistics and sharp acuteness of his son-in-law that had, indeed, ever kept him to his colours. Lord Henry would not listen to statistics, dietary tables, Commissioners' rides, Sub-commissioners' reports. He went far higher than his father; far deeper than his brother-in-law. He represented to the Duke that the order of the peasantry was as ancient, legal, and recognised an order as the order of the nobility; that it had distinct rights and privileges, though for centuries they had been invaded and violated, and permitted to fall into desuetude. He impressed upon the Duke that the parochial constitution of this country was more important than its political constitution; that it was more ancient, more universal in its influence; and that this parochial constitution had already been shaken to its centre by the New Poor Law. He assured his father that it would never be well for England until this order of the peasantry was restored to its pristine condition; not merely in physical comfort, for that must vary according to the economical circumstances of the time, like that of every class; but to its condition in all those moral attributes which make a recognised rank in a nation; and which, in a great degree, are independent of economics, manners, customs, ceremonies, rights, and privileges.

Source: Benjamin Disraeli, *Coningsby; Or, The New Generation* (London: H. Colburn, 1844), book 3, chapter 3.

---

own franchise reform bill in 1867. Disraeli made extension of voting rights in the boroughs according to residence qualifications the main thrust of the bill and accepted several Radical amendments, while persuading the House to reject Gladstone's attempt to control the terms of the bill, describing him as "a candidate for power" who "has had his innings." Despite the coalition majority, Disraeli's bill passed. Lord Derby retired in 1868, and Disraeli became prime minister, a fulfillment that he described in the sardonic expression, "at last I have climbed to the top of the greasy pole." During the 1868 election, however, Gladstone made disestablishing the Anglican Church in Ireland the issue on which he gained enough votes from the "Celtic fringe" in Ireland, Scotland, and Wales to give the Liberals a majority.

From 1868 to 1874, Disraeli fought off challenges to his leadership, rebuilt party organization and finance, sustained a personal loss in his wife's death on December 15, 1872, and also expanded his political creed to include more emphasis on pride in the British Empire. The popular notion, however, then and since, of Disraeli as an imperialist and Gladstone as a "Little Englander" more accurately described their speeches than their policies in office. The Gladstone ministry meanwhile outlived the early years of its reforms, had no remedy for the hard times following 1872, and justified Disraeli's description of the Treasury bench as "a row of exhausted volcanoes." The election of 1874 gave the Tories a majority in the Commons, and Disraeli finally became prime minister of a workable government.

In his administration of 1874 to 1880, Disraeli promoted "social reform" in terms of the working and living conditions of the laboring class. The Artisans' and Laborers' Dwelling Act of 1875 was a pioneering step in the field of slum clearance and public housing, while the 1875 Public Health Act began a systematic and codified approach to this problem. The Factory Acts of 1874 and 1878 applied the same systematic approach to work safety regulations and also gave trade unions organizing, bargaining, and picketing rights, the so-called Magna Carta of Labor. The Merchant Shipping Act of 1876 owed more to Samuel Plimsoll than to the political leaders, but Disraeli gave government support to this reform of marine safety and insurance. This broad social welfare approach to industrial problems was very different in form from the rural society ideas of *Coningsby* and *Sybil*, but the principle of Tory reforms to help the working poor was essentially the same.

In foreign and colonial affairs, Disraeli conducted a generally successful policy. His 1875 purchase from the khedive of Egypt of about 45 percent of the shares in the Suez Canal was a bargain investment for Great Britain financially, an important improvement of the British route to India and the Orient, and a significant expansion of British military, economic, and political presence in the Middle East for the next eighty years. The creation of a new title for the queen, "Empress of India," in 1876, was a more debatable accomplishment, and Disraeli's attempt in 1876 to conserve his failing health by becoming earl of Beaconsfield naturally weakened his influence in the Commons.

The 1878 Congress of Berlin on Balkan problems raised by the Bulgarian Revolt of 1876 and the Russo-Turkish War of 1877-1878 saw Disraeli successfully combining British, Turkish, Austrian, and Italian interests and policies to check the expansion of Russian influence in southeastern Europe. Upon his triumphant return to London, Disraeli described the Berlin settlement as "peace with honor." The last years of Disraeli's ministry were, however, clouded by military problems in Afghanistan and Zululand and by the depression of 1873, which still gripped Great Britain. In the general election of 1880, the disorganized Conservative Party was defeated. For almost a year, Disraeli continued as the active leader of the Tory opposition to Gladstone's second administration, but in March of 1881, his health began to fail rapidly. He died on April 19, 1881, at his London house, and was buried beside his wife at their Hughenden estate.

SIGNIFICANCE

The legacy of Benjamin Disraeli was in great part the courage and determined perseverance of his career from outsider to prime minister and in some part the romantic extravagance and wit with which he dramatized his own legend. His writings, however, and his later legislation established a rationale and a record of rejecting a status-quo conservatism limited to accepting only past changes, and the later leaders of his party have accepted Disraeli's teaching that only by continuing to propose basic changes to meet the needs of the whole nation can Toryism succeed as a political faith.

—K. Fred Gillum

FURTHER READING

Blake, Robert. *Disraeli*. New York: St. Martin's Press, 1966. Accepted as the most useful one-volume biography available, this work skillfully incorporates the scholarship of Monypenny and Buckle (below), adds several matters they omitted, and makes good use of letters that came to light between 1920 and 1967. In the area of politics, the book is comprehensive; Lord

Blake's account is readable and enjoyable as well as scholarly.

Bradford, Sarah. *Disraeli*. New York: Stein & Day, 1983. An important supplement to Monypenny and Buckle and to Blake. Easily the best account and analysis so far of Disraeli's personal life. The author draws on previously unpublished letters that show Disraeli and Mary Anne in several "storms" in the first decade of their generally happy marriage; on the whole, the book gives a good sense of the emotional side of Disraeli's character.

Disraeli, Benjamin. *Benjamin Disraeli: Letters*. Edited by J. A. Gunn et al. Toronto: University of Toronto Press, 1982-2004. A major and ongoing international enterprise, the Disraeli Project aims to compile a virtually complete edition of Disraeli's letters.

Eldridge, C. C. *England's Mission*. Chapel Hill: University of North Carolina Press, 1973. The author reviews several historians' arguments about nineteenth century British imperialism and offers his own analysis of "the Empire of Disraeli's Dreams." Well documented.

Endelman, Todd M., and Tony Kushner, eds. *Disraeli's Jewishness*. London: Vallentine Mitchell, 2002. Collection of essays that seek to explore the Jewish dimension in Disraeli's life. The essays include an explanation of why Disraeli was the target of anti-Semitic abuse, and a discussion of how his Jewishness was constructed and contested in the United States and United Kingdom in the twentieth century.

Jerman, B. R. *The Young Disraeli*. Princeton, N.J.: Princeton University Press, 1960. Brief, general, scholarly, and readable. Covers the period to 1837.

Levine, Richard A. *Benjamin Disraeli*. New York: Twayne, 1968. A useful and appreciative evaluation of Disraeli's place in literature.

Monypenny, William Flavelle, and George Earl Buckle. *The Life of Benjamin Disraeli, Earl of Beaconsfield*. 6 vols. London: Macmillan, 1910-1920. Rev. ed. 2 vols. London: Macmillan, 1929. Reprint. 4 vols. New York: Russell & Russell, 1968. Volumes 1 and 2 were written by Monypenny, and after his death the work was completed by Buckle. This work, although dated in some respects, remains the definitive and indispensable biography for scholars or serious readers, or for reference purposes. Much of the work consists of extensive quotations from Disraeli's writings, letters, and speeches. The authors let their subject speak for himself, and Disraeli's rhetoric has a personality that communicates the man to the reader with a force for which ordinary biography is no substitute.

Richmond, Charles, and Paul Smith, eds. *The Self-Fashioning of Disraeli: 1818-1851*. New York: Cambridge University Press, 1998. Collection of essays by historians, psychiatrists, and experts in literature that combine to profile the "self-made" Disraeli. Topics include his educational background and politics.

Smith, Paul. *Disraeli: A Brief Life*. New York: Cambridge University Press, 1996. A brief study of Disraeli, offering a significant reappraisal of his personality and career.

SEE ALSO: Fourteenth Earl of Derby; William Ewart Gladstone; Third Marquis of Salisbury; Queen Victoria.

RELATED ARTICLES in *Great Events from History: The Nineteenth Century, 1801-1900:* July 26, 1858: Rothschild Is First Jewish Member of British Parliament; August, 1867: British Parliament Passes the Reform Act of 1867; December 3, 1868-February 20, 1874: Gladstone Becomes Prime Minister of Britain; June 13-July 13, 1878: Congress of Berlin.

DOROTHEA DIX
American educator and social reformer

A crusader for the rights of the mentally ill, Dix devoted her life to establishing psychiatric hospitals to provide proper care for those with mental and emotional problems and set the stage for worldwide reforms in the care and treatment of people with mental disabilities.

BORN: April 4, 1802; Hampden, District of Maine, Massachusetts (now in Maine)
DIED: July 17, 1887; Trenton, New Jersey
ALSO KNOWN AS: Dorothea Lynde Dix (full name)
AREA OF ACHIEVEMENT: Social reform

EARLY LIFE

Dorothea Lynde Dix had a difficult childhood. By his family's standards, her father married below his station. Because married students were not accepted at Harvard, where he was studying at the time, he was sent to manage family holdings in Maine—nothing less than the frontier during the early nineteenth century. Never a financial success, he did win some notice as a traveling Methodist preacher and a writer of tracts. Thus, Dorothea was often without her father, and unfortunately, her mother was often too ill to give her the attention that young children require.

Dorothea's happiest memories of her solitary childhood revolved around visits to her paternal grandparents in Boston. Her grandfather, a successful if curmudgeonly physician, and grandmother provided a warm welcome. Dorothea's first exposure to public service came from watching her grandfather practice medicine. She had few playmates her own age and was four years older than her nearest sibling. At least one biographer believes that isolation from children and involvement with adults led to a high degree of self-interest and blocked the development of personal emotional commitment. In any case, she never married, and most, though not all, of her friendships were with people involved in her charitable endeavors.

When Dix was around the age of twelve and unhappy at home, she began to live permanently with her then-widowed grandmother. To her dismay, her grandmother insisted on both academic and social discipline, and Dorothea's sense of rejection was actually worsened. After two years, she was sent off to live with a great-aunt, where she finally found a congenial home. Although still a teenager, she was allowed to open a school for small children, which she ran successfully for three years be-fore returning to Boston. Two years later, in 1821, she opened a school for girls. Education for women was unusual—public schools accepted girls only for the few months when many boys were out for agricultural labor—and even more unusual was Dix's insistence on including natural science in the curriculum. Dorothea Dix proved to be a gifted teacher, and she seemed to have found her life's work. In a gesture that was a harbinger of her future, she added a program for poor girls who otherwise had no opportunity for schooling.

Ill health—apparently tuberculosis—and the collapse of a romance with her cousin resulted in a new direction for Dix. While recovering her strength during the mid-1820's, she became interested in Unitarianism and the ideas of William Ellery Channing. This Christian sect's emphasis on the goodness of humanity and the obligation to serve it would inspire her for the rest of her life. A new attempt to run a school, however, led to her complete collapse in 1836 and her doctor's orders never to teach again.

LIFE'S WORK

While recuperating, Dorothea Dix visited England. During her two-year stay with the William Rathbone family, she met a variety of intellectuals and reformers. When she returned to the United States, she found that the deaths of her mother and grandmother had left her financially independent. She spent several years seeking some focus for her life. Then, in 1841, she was asked to teach Sunday school for women at the East Cambridge Jail. She found the innocent and guilty, young and old, sane and insane crowded into the same miserable, unheated facility. Those regarded as insane were often chained or otherwise restrained. Her discussions with humanitarians such as George Emerson, who would become a long-time friend, led her to understand that conditions in East Cambridge Jail were, if anything, better than those in most jails. There was virtually no distinction made between mental illness and impairment, and in the entire country there were only about 2,500 beds specifically for those with emotional problems. Dix quickly had a sense that she had come upon something important that needed doing.

Dix's first move was to demand and get heat for the insane in the East Cambridge Jail. Then, after talking with other reformers, including Samuel Gridley Howe and Charles Sumner (later a radical Republican leader

Dorothea Dix. (Library of Congress)

during Reconstruction), she began a survey of facilities for the insane in Massachusetts. Although the McLean Psychiatric Hospital was relatively progressive, most of the mentally ill were kept in local poorhouses, workhouses, and jails. She visited every one. Conditions were horrendous. Patients were often locked in dirty stalls, sometimes for years, and many were chained to the floor. Many were virtually naked, and physical restraint was virtually universal. She also found time to discuss treatment with the best doctors, finding that much more humane treatment was being successfully used in leading hospitals in Europe and a few in the United States. More common in the United States were strong sedatives to induce quiescence and the application of shocks, such as surprise dousings with ice water, to bring individuals back to reality.

After eighteen months, Dix prepared a petition to the Massachusetts legislature. The petition stated psychiatric facilities should provide for physical health and comfort (she would later expand this to prisons) and seek, with kindness and support, to cure diseased minds. When it was published, this document at first produced embarrassment and denial and then attacks upon the author. Her friends—Howe, Sumner, and others—rushed to defend her. She had her first victory when a bill providing

for more and better accommodations for the mentally ill was passed. Her career was beginning to take shape.

Dix's initial investigations had occasionally taken her outside Massachusetts, where she found conditions to be generally worse than in her home state. From the mid-1840's to the mid-1850's, she traveled many thousands of miles around the United States and Canada, finding and exposing the suffering of the indigent insane. Although she did not travel to the far West (she did work in Texas), Dix visited almost every one of the thirty-one states of that era.

Dix developed an investigative technique in which, by means of simple persistence and will, she forced her way into every facility where the insane were kept. There followed dramatic revelations of suffering and abuse that shamed all but the most hardened and/or fiscally conservative. Finally, she launched a petition to the legislature for the necessary funds and regulations to ensure improved care. She found the inevitable compromises necessary in any political campaign frustrating, but she settled for whatever state legislatures would fund and began again.

Results varied. New Jersey and Pennsylvania established state psychiatric hospitals as a result of Dix's efforts. New York, however, rejected her call for six hospitals and only expanded the beds available in an existing facility. In 1845, with the help of Horace Mann and George Emerson, Dix expanded her efforts to prison reform and published a manual on that subject. Proper care for the mentally ill, however, remained her main focus.

From 1845 to 1846, Dix worked in Kentucky, Tennessee, Louisiana, Alabama, Georgia, and Arkansas, and she was working her way up the Mississippi when, in September, she collapsed in Columbus, Ohio. By December, she was sufficiently recovered to resume traveling, and in January, 1847, she presented a petition to the Illinois legislature, which resulted in the passage of a bill creating a psychiatric hospital. Later that year and in the following year, she had similar successes in Tennessee and North Carolina. Her fame was growing enormously, as were the respect and love with which Americans regarded her. One of the greatest marks of the latter came in 1863, when Confederate troops invading Pennsylvania stopped a train on which Dix was riding. A North Carolina officer recognized her, and the train was released to continue on its way. Not even the passions of Civil War could change people's feelings about Dorothea Dix.

Despite local successes—between 1844 and 1854 Dix persuaded eleven states to open hospitals—Dix recognized by the late 1840's that only a national effort would resolve the problems of the insane. No more than one-fourth of those needing care got it. She began to push for a federal effort, suggesting that five million acres of public land be committed to set up a fund to provide care for insane, epileptic, and mentally impaired Americans. A bill to this effect was introduced in Congress in 1848. Dix was provided with a small office in Washington from which to lobby. Questions about cost and constitutionality blocked the various versions of the bill until 1854, when, to her joy, it passed both houses. Her exultation was brief, however, for President Franklin Pierce vetoed the bill on the grounds that Congress had no authority to make such grants outside the District of Columbia. It was the final blow—the effort was abandoned.

Exhausted and ill, Dix planned to renew efforts in individual states, but friends and doctors persuaded her to rest. She visited friends in England, and within two weeks she was involved in efforts to reform psychiatric care there. She went so far as to go personally to the home secretary, Sir George Grey, to argue for improvements in Scotland. Before she left, a Royal Commission to investigate the problem was in the works. She also helped to sustain a reform effort in the Channel Islands before touring the Continent, where she visited hospitals, asylums, and jails, exposing problems and demanding change. The force of her personality seems to have made her irresistible; even Pope Pius IX was forced to initiate improvements in the Vatican's handling of the mentally ill.

Dix's return to the United States in 1856 brought a large number of requests for aid. She was soon traveling again, seeking various reforms and funding. In the winter of 1859 alone, she asked state legislatures for a third of a million dollars, and in 1860, she got large appropriations for hospitals in South Carolina and Tennessee. The outbreak of the Civil War brought reform work to a halt, and Dix promptly volunteered her services.

After being appointed superintendent of U.S. Army nurses, Dix spent four years of very hard work developing the Medical Bureau from a service set up for an army of ten thousand to one that could handle more than that many casualties from one battle. Unfortunately, she was too straitlaced at the age of sixty to cope with the rough-and-tumble style of the military. Her New England Puritanism showed in her tendency to think that an army doctor who had had a few drinks should be dishonorably discharged. Although her work in ensuring the provision of nurses and medical supplies at the beginning of the war was of great importance, in 1863 her authority was quietly reduced, to her bitter disappointment. After the war, Dix spent another fifteen years traveling as the ad-

vocate of the insane. Worn out in 1881, she retired to the hospital (the first created by her efforts) in Trenton, New Jersey, where she lived until her death in 1887.

SIGNIFICANCE

Dorothea Dix's importance can be seen from simple statistics. In 1843, the United States had thirteen institutions for the mentally ill; in 1880, it had 123. Of the latter, 75 were state-owned, and Dix had been a key factor in the founding of 32 of them. She had also been able to get a number of training schools for the mentally impaired established, and specialized training for psychiatric nurses had begun.

More important, the lives of many unfortunate people had been made easier thanks to Dix's efforts. The idea that the insane, even if poor, deserved humane care and treatment intended to help them recover had been established in the United States. Dix's efforts began a process that has continued since her death and has left the United States a world leader in the treatment of mental illness.

—*Fred R. van Hartesveldt*

FURTHER READING

Brown, Thomas J. *Dorothea Dix: New England Reformer*. Cambridge, Mass.: Harvard University Press, 1998. This study of Dix provides new insight into her passions and methods.

Dain, Norman. *Concepts of Insanity in the United States, 1789-1865*. New Brunswick, N.J.: Rutgers University Press, 1964. A useful description of attitudes and problems that Dix had to confront during her career.

Dix, Dorothea. *Asylum, Prison, and Poorhouse: The Writings and Reform Work of Dorothea Dix in Illinois*. Edited by David L. Lightner. Carbondale: Southern Illinois University Press, 1999. Dix traveled to Illinois in 1846 and 1847 to publicize the need for more humane treatment of prisoners, the insane, and the poor. This book is a collection of her writings during that trip, including a series of newspaper articles about conditions in jails and poorhouses. There also are two memorials she presented to the state legislature: one describes the treatment of inmates at a state penitentiary, and the other urges the establishment of a state insane asylum. Lightner has provided detailed notes and introductions to these documents, and in a concluding essay he assesses the immediate and continuing impact of Dix's work.

_____. *On Behalf of the Insane Poor: Selected Reports*. New York: Arno Press, 1971. A valuable source of Dix's ideas and opinions expressed in her own words. Her eloquence and passion shine through.

Gollaher, David. *A Voice for the Mad: A Life of Dorothea Dix*. New York: Free Press, 1995. A balanced biography highlighting Dix's strengths and weaknesses, her efforts in the area of legislative reform, and her second career as head of the Civil War nurses.

Marshall, Helen. *Dorothea Dix: Forgotten Samaritan*. Chapel Hill: University of North Carolina Press, 1937. Although it is sometimes overly sympathetic to its subject, this is a solid and well-written biography.

Snyder, Charles M., ed. *The Lady and the President: The Letters of Dorothea Dix and Millard Fillmore*. Lexington: University Press of Kentucky, 1975. Provides interesting insights into one period in Dix's life.

Tuke, Daniel. *The Insane in the United States and Canada*. London: M. K. Lewis, 1885. This contemporary description of the problems Dix tried to solve gives a valuable perspective of the situation. It is very useful for modern students trying to achieve an understanding of her work.

SEE ALSO: Elizabeth Fry; Samuel Gridley Howe; Charles Sumner.

RELATED ARTICLES in *Great Events from History: The Nineteenth Century, 1801-1900:* May, 1819: Unitarian Church Is Founded; 1820's-1850's: Social Reform Movement.

GAETANO DONIZETTI
Italian composer

Donizetti was the most prolific composer of Italian operas during the first half of the nineteenth century. Although his works are uneven in quality, he was, at his best, the greatest and most vital exponent of Italian Romanticism before Giuseppe Verdi.

BORN: November 29, 1797; Bergamo, Cisalpine Republic (now in Italy)
DIED: April 8, 1848; Bergamo, Austrian Empire (now in Italy)
ALSO KNOWN AS: Domenico Gaetano Maria Donizetti (full name)
AREA OF ACHIEVEMENT: Music

EARLY LIFE
Gaetano Donizetti (dahn-ih-ZEHT-ee) was the fifth of six children born to Andrea and Domenica Nava Donizetti. He was born in a basement apartment, where, according to his later recollection, "no glimmer of light ever penetrated." His father, who discouraged him from pursuing a career as a composer, followed no particular trade; after 1808, he earned a miserable existence as the janitor of the local pawnshop.

In 1806, a free music school was established in Bergamo under the direction of Johann Simon Mayr. The eight-year-old Donizetti was one of the first students to enroll in the institution which would later bear his name (Istituto Musicale Gaetano Donizetti), and he continued his studies there until 1814. Donizetti's extraordinary fluency in composition in later years was a result at least in part of the rigorous training of Mayr, himself a successful composer of Italian operas.

At Mayr's urging, Donizetti went to Bologna to study counterpoint and fugue at the Liceo Filarmonico, then perhaps the most distinguished music school in Italy. His master in Bologna was the highly erudite Padre Mattei, who had formerly taught Gioacchino Rossini. Though Mattei did not inspire affection, Donizetti applied himself vigorously to the study of the contrapuntal forms; sixty-one exercises in his hand survive in manuscript.

Donizetti returned to Bergamo in 1817. Working with that facility and ease that was to mark his entire career, Donizetti composed four operas during a period of four years and a large body of nonoperatic works. In the latter category, Donizetti composed eighteen string quartets; though modest, these works have a certain vernal charm. Donizetti was also forced at this time to devote considerable energy to the avoidance of military service. With the help of a woman who admired his talent, Donizetti was able to purchase an exemption in 1818.

Donizetti had by this time matured into a well-favored young man. His passport of 1821 describes him as tall and slender, with blue eyes and chestnut hair; associates found him to be handsome, generous, and charming. As a young man, Donizetti was high-spirited; later, personal tragedies caused a melancholia to descend upon him.

LIFE'S WORK
Donizetti's career as a composer of opera was firmly launched in 1822, with the success of a serious opera in Rome. Donizetti was next offered a commission by the Teatro Nuovo in Naples. Then the most robust operatic center in Italy, Naples had been dominated musically by

Rossini since 1815. Donizetti's first offering to the Neapolitan public, the semiserious opera *La zingara* (1822) was an immense success. For the next several years, Donizetti made Naples the base of his activities; like all successful opera composers of his day, however, he was forced to travel frequently.

Though none of the operas before *Anna Bolena* (1830) has maintained a place in the active repertory, Donizetti was stunningly productive during the fifteen-year span from 1822 to 1837. Donizetti completed forty-nine operas in this remarkably fertile period. All the subgenres of Italian opera are represented in the canon of Donizetti's works: opera buffa (comic opera), opera seria (serious opera), and opera semiseria.

Donizetti relied largely on the formal conventions of Italian opera as established by Rossini. Most of the scenes in Donizettian opera are reducible ultimately to an opening recitative (rapid declamation of text) and a section in a brisk tempo (*tempo d'attacco*), in which the dramatic situation is presented; a slow reflective aria; an interruption of mood in a faster tempo (*tempo di mezzo*); and a brisk concluding section replete with vocal fireworks (*cabaletta*). This formula could be applied to ensembles as well as to solo scenes; in the former case, the brilliant concluding passage was called the *stretto*.

Donizetti deployed the basic pattern in an infinite variety of ways; moreover, in his intuitive understanding of its dramatic potential, he surpassed Rossini. Donizetti was not an inventive harmonist, and his scoring sometimes consisted of the simplest accompaniment patterns repeated shamelessly; yet in dramatic pacing, in the creation of adrenaline-charged melodies, and in sheer élan, he had few peers.

Though earlier works had given ample indications of a strong talent, Donizetti did not reach artistic maturity until the composition of *Anna Bolena*. This work marks the ascendancy of the full-blooded Romantic melodrama in Italian opera. *Anna Bolena* is one of four Donizettian operas based on Tudor history. Donizetti created a score of great power and emotional sincerity. The work also marks the beginning of a preoccupation on the part of Italian composers with libretti that depict fallible women, in this case Anne Boleyn, in pitiable circumstances. In the moving final scene, in which Boleyn is alternately delirious and lucid before her execution, Donizetti offers a foretaste of the famous "mad scene" from his later opera *Lucia di Lammermoor* (1835).

Anna Bolena brought Donizetti international acclaim, and it probably marked the peak of his personal fortunes as well. Donizetti had been married, in 1828, to Virginia

DONIZETTI'S OPERAS	
1822	*La zingara*
1830	*Anna Bolena*
1832	*L'elisir d'amore* (*The Elixir of Love*)
1833	*Lucrezia Borgia*
1833	*Parisina*
1835	*Lucia di Lammermoor*
1835	*Marino Faliero*
1837	*Roberto Devereux*
1840	*Elisabeth*
1840	*La favorite*
1840	*La fille du régiment*
1842	*Linda di Chamounix*
1843	*Don Pasquale*
1843	*Maria di Rohan*

Vasselli. By all accounts, the union was a happy one. During the 1830's, however, three children born to them died in infancy, and in 1837, Virginia died of cholera. Donizetti never fully recovered from these losses, though he remained artistically productive for several years after Virginia's death.

The years between 1830 and 1837 constituted the zenith of Donizetti's career as a composer of Italian opera. In a series of striking works, including *Parisina* (1833), *Lucrezia Borgia* (1833), *Marino Faliero* (1835), *Lucia di Lammermoor*, and *Roberto Devereux* (1837), Donizetti solidified his achievement in the genre of the *melodramma* and also composed a comic opera of enduring charm in *L'elisir d'amore* (1832; the elixir of love). *Lucrezia Borgia*, an adaptation of Victor Hugo's play by Felice Romani, is a lurid drama steeped in violence and touching upon incest; in its sensationalism and explosiveness, Donizetti's setting adumbrates the *Verismo* opera school of the end of the century. Donizetti also happened upon a new musical texture for the setting of conversation in this work: The characters Rustighello and Astolfo chat in recitative in act 1, while a portentous motive sings in the orchestra (a device often credited to Verdi). *Marino Faliero*, with text supplied by Emanuele Bidera based indirectly on Lord Byron, prefigures Verdi's *I due Foscari* (1844) and *Simon Boccanegra* (1857) in its Venetian local color and its liberal political undercurrents. *Roberto Devereux* is the last of Donizetti's forays into Tudor history; his musical portrait of Elizabeth I in this work is one of his finest.

Lucia di Lammermoor has proved to be Donizetti's most durable work. It was his first collaboration with the distinguished librettist Salvatore Cammarano, and their joint effort is regarded by many as the touchstone of the entire bel canto repertory (as the works of Rossini, Vincenzo Bellini, Donizetti, and their contemporaries are collectively known).

In the final phase of his compositional career from 1838 to 1845, Donizetti was drawn into the orb of Parisian grand opera. He composed four operas to French texts for the stages of Paris; of these, the comic *La fille du régiment* (1840; the daughter of the regiment) and the serious *La favorite* (1840) became repertory staples. Donizetti's greatest achievement in the category of Italian opera buffa was also written for a foreign commission: His comic masterpiece *Don Pasquale* (1843) was written for the Théâtre Italien in Paris. Two serious operas with Italian texts, *Linda di Chamounix* (1842) and *Maria di Rohan* (1843), were commissioned by a Viennese theater.

Donizetti's life was rapidly approaching its own tragic denouement. In 1844, Donizetti began to show unmistakable symptoms of the last stages of syphilis. His condition deteriorated to the point where institutionalization was required in 1846. In 1848, Donizetti died in Bergamo.

SIGNIFICANCE

It was Gaetano Donizetti's misfortune to be the middle child in the family of nineteenth century Italian opera composers, preceded and followed by the more towering figures of Rossini and Verdi. Donizetti's primitive orchestrations and predictable melodic formulas were seen as tokens of his inferiority. A later generation of scholars has by contrast marveled at the professional standard Donizetti maintained given the conditions under which he worked. More detailed knowledge of his works has also bred increased respect; many effects associated with Verdi (or known through Sir Arthur Sullivan's parodies) have been found to be the products of Donizetti's imagination.

Appreciation of Donizetti's contribution has also been retarded by a lack of understanding of the subgenre in which he did his finest work, the *melodramma*. Modern critics have realized that the *melodramma* should not be judged according to the dramaturgical standards of a later generation. Texts that struck later generations as ludicrous were understood by Donizetti and his colleagues to be mere verbal semaphores reinforcing the profound emotional content of the music. Donizetti's role in the creation of the *melodramma* earns for him an honored place in the company of Victor Hugo, Hector Berlioz,

and the other innovators who dismantled the edifice of artistic classicism.

—*Steven W. Shrader*

FURTHER READING

Ashbrook, William. *Donizetti and His Operas.* Cambridge, England: Cambridge University Press, 1982. The definitive work in English on Donizetti. Part 1 offers biographical information; part 2 provides analytic comment on all of his operas. Appendixes supply synopses and information about Donizetti's librettists.

Ashbrook, William, and Julian Budden. "Gaetano Donizetti." In *The New Grove Masters of Italian Opera.* New York: W. W. Norton, 1983. Concise account of Donizetti's life and valuable analytic commentary by two first-rate scholars of Italian opera. Contains the most accurate catalog of Donizetti's works available.

Glascow, E. Thomas. "Quarter Notes." (Editorial) *The Opera Quarterly* 14, no. 3 (Spring, 1998). Discusses Donizetti's prolific career and the criticism he sustained for producing "superficial" works.

Gossett, Philip. *"Anna Bolena" and the Artistic Maturity of Gaetano Donizetti.* New York: Oxford University Press, 1985. Detailed discussion of *Anna Bolena*, the watershed work in Donizetti's career. Gossett offers a revisionist view of Donizetti's achievement.

Gossett, Philip, and E. Thomas Glasow. "Donizetti: European Composer." *The Opera Quarterly* 14, no. 3 (Spring, 1998). Profile of Donizetti focusing on his time in Paris.

Osborne, Charles. *The Bel Canto Operas of Rossini, Donizetti, and Bellini.* Portland, Oreg.: Amadeus Press, 1994. Osborne provides musical analyses of all of Donizetti's 69 operas; he also describes the circumstances of each opera's first performance and explains the opera's libretto and plot. Includes a bibliography and discography.

Weinstock, Herbert. *Donizetti and the World of Opera in Italy, Paris, and Vienna in the First Half of the Nineteenth Century.* New York: Pantheon Books, 1963. Full-length study of Donizetti's life aimed at a popular audience. Slightly out of date given the increase in scholarly interest in Donizetti, but highly readable.

SEE ALSO: Victor Hugo; Jenny Lind; Gioacchino Rossini; Giuseppe Verdi.

RELATED ARTICLE in *Great Events from History: The Nineteenth Century, 1801-1900:* January 14, 1900: Puccini's *Tosca* Premieres in Rome.

FYODOR DOSTOEVSKI
Russian novelist

Long recognized as one of the world's greatest novelists, Dostoevski summoned to imaginative life areas of psychological, political, and aesthetic experience that have significantly shaped the modern sensibility, and his books are still widely read.

BORN: November 11, 1821; Moscow, Russia
DIED: February 9, 1881; St. Petersburg, Russia
ALSO KNOWN AS: Fyodor Mihaylovich Dostoevski (full name); Feodor Dostoyevsky
AREA OF ACHIEVEMENT: Literature

EARLY LIFE

Fyodor Dostoevski (DAH-teh-yehf-skee) was one of only two great nineteenth century Russian writers—Anton Chekhov is the other—who failed, unlike Alexander Pushkin, Nikolai Gogol, Ivan Turgenev, Leo Tolstoy, and others, to be born into the landed gentry. Whereas aristocrats such as Turgenev and Tolstoy depicted settled traditions of culture and fixed moral-social norms, Dostoevski spent his early years in an atmosphere that prepared him to treat the moral consequences of flux and change, and dramatize the breakup of the traditional forms of Russian society.

Dostoevski's father, Mikhail Andreevich, derived from the lowly class of the nonmonastic clergy, succeeded in rising to the status of civil servant by becoming a military doctor, and then became a surgeon attached to a hospital for the poor on the outskirts of Moscow. His mother, Marya Feodorovna, née Nechaev, was a merchant's daughter, meek, kind, gentle, pious—obviously the inspiration for most of Dostoevski's fictive heroines. The elder Dostoevski was not the repulsively dissolute prototype of Feodor Karamazov that many early biographies describe. He was, however, while devoted to his family, extremely strict, mistrustful, irritable, and easily depressed. The son was to acknowledge in later life his inheritance, from his father, of oversensitive nerves and uncontrollable explosions of temper. In addition, Dostoevski suffered from epilepsy, a condition that also ran in his family.

Fyodor was the second child and second son in the family. In 1838, the elder Dostoevski sent his sons to St. Petersburg's Academy of Engineers, determined to push them into secure careers despite their preference for literary achievement. In February, 1839, the father suffered a partial stroke when Fyodor failed to be promoted during his freshman year; in early June, 1839, Dostoevski's father died. All biographers assumed until modern times that he had been murdered on his small country estate by peasants outraged by his severity toward them. Joseph Frank, however, in *Dostoevsky: The Seeds of Revolt, 1821-1849* (1976), the first volume of his monumental biography of Dostoevski, shows that important new evidence points to the probability of the elder Dostoevski's dying of an apoplectic stroke rather than at the hands of killers. Nevertheless, Dostoevski all of his life believed that his father had been murdered and therefore assumed a heavy burden of parricidal guilt, for the peasants who—so he imagined—had killed his father were merely enacting an impulse that he had surely felt.

In August, 1843, Dostoevski was graduated from the academy and placed on duty in the drafting department of the St. Petersburg Engineering Command. He neglected his work, preferring to read widely among French and German Romantic authors. By far the deepest influence, however, was that of Gogol. In 1844, Dostoevski resigned from the army, published a translation of Honoré de Balzac's *Eugénie Grandet* (1833; English translation, 1859), and began to work on his first novel, which was published in January, 1846, as *Bednye lyudi* (*Poor Folk*, 1887).

This is a poignant story of frustrated love, told in the form of letters passed between a poor government clerk and an equally poor girl who lives near him. Dostoevski's insight into the tortures of humiliated sensibility constitutes his major departure from what is otherwise a Gogol-like protest against the upper class's condescension to the lower. The most influential literary critic of the 1840's, Vissarion Belinsky, hailed the book as Russia's first important social novel.

Belinsky was less enthusiastic about Dostoevski's second novel, *Dvoynik* (*The Double*, 1917), which also appeared in 1846. Gogol's fiction again served as the model, particularly "Nos" ("The Nose") and "Zapiski sumasshedshego" ("Diary of a Madman"). Dostoevski's protagonist, Golyadkin, a middle-ranking bureaucrat, is driven by inner demons. His unquenchable thirst for self-worth and dignity causes him to distort reality and create for himself a world that will mirror his self-conflicts. Golyadkin's split personality disintegrates into two independent entities: A double appears who confronts him with his worst faults, both reflecting the suppressed wishes of his subconscious and objectifying his accompanying guilt feelings. While Dostoevski erred in failing

Fyodor Dostoevski. (Library of Congress)

to establish a moral perspective from which the reader could evaluate Golyadkin either straightforwardly or ironically, he did succeed in hauntingly portraying, for the first time, the kind of obsessive, divided self that was to dominate his later, greater fiction.

LIFE'S WORK

Dostoevski's darkest decade began the night of April 22-23, 1849, when he was taken into police custody in St. Petersburg as a member of a circle headed by Mikhail Butashevich-Petrashevsky. A czarist court of inquiry concluded that fifteen of the accused, including Dostoevski, had been guilty of subversion and conspiracy. On December 22, 1849, the prisoners were taken to a public square and lined up before a firing squad. By prearrangement, literally in the last seconds before their expected execution, an aide-de-camp to the czar commuted their punishment to four years of hard prison labor and four additional years of military service as privates—both in Siberia.

From that moment onward, the secular, progressive, idealistic influences from such writers as Friedrich Schiller, Victor Hugo, and George Sand, which had determined Dostoevski's previous philosophy, receded be-

fore the onrush of a spiritual vitality that overwhelmed Dostoevski as a revelation. Always a believing Christian, he strove for the rest of his life to emphasize an ethic of expiation, forgiveness, and all-embracing love, based on a conviction of the imminence of the Day of Judgment and the Final Reckoning.

Some scholars interpret Dostoevski's consequent right-wing conservatism and mistrust of human nature as a psychic-emotive transformation caused by his disillusioning prison camp experiences. Joseph Frank takes a more acute view: Dostoevski came to regard each downtrodden convict as potentially capable of love and compassion but focused on the Russian peasant, regarding persons outside the Slavic culture and Orthodox faith as historically and religiously outcast. He became a fervent Slavophile, insisting that religious and cultural isolation from Western materialism had enabled the Russian people to avoid what he regarded as Europe's demoralization and decadence.

The Dostoevski who returned to St. Petersburg in mid-December, 1859, had matured enormously as a result of having confronted mortality, discovered the egotistic drives dominating his fellow convicts, and undergone a conversion crisis. In 1864, he published a novelette, *Zapiski iz podpolya* (*Notes from the Underground*, 1918), written primarily as a satirical parody of the views expressed in Nikolay Chernyshevsky's didactic novel *Chto delat'?* (1863; *What Is to Be Done?*, c. 1863), which affirmed rational egotism as the panacea for all human problems. Not at all, says the Underground Man. He is a malicious, brilliantly paradoxical skeptic who challenges the validity of reason and of rational solutions. He insists that, above all, humans are determined to follow their often foolish, perverse, and even absurd wills. Against the Enlightenment premises of utilitarianism, order, and good sense, the Undergroundling opposes chaos, self-destruction, cruelty, and caprice. This work is now generally recognized as the central text in Dostoevski's canon, the prologue to his greatest novels. The problem he would now confront is how to preserve human freedom from nihilism, how to restrain its destructive implications.

Raskolnikov, the protagonist of *Prestupleniye i nakazaniye* (1866; *Crime and Punishment*, 1886), is another Underground Man, despising ordinary people and conventional morality. He commits murder to test his theory that an extraordinary person is beyond good and evil. He then suffers harrowing isolation and self-disgust. Only his growing love for the sacrificial Sonia will open him slowly to processes of compassion, remorse, and regeneration. However, Raskolnikov's self-will continues to battle his surrender to selfless Christian atonement until his Creator finally nudges him into God's camp.

In *Idiot* (1868; *The Idiot*, 1887), Dostoevski presents a Christlike man, Prince Myshkin, yet shows all of his saintly virtues mocked by the world. Myshkin is innocent and gentle, a good-natured sufferer of insults who becomes involved in the whirlpool of others' egotistic drives; is broken by their pride, lust, avarice, and vanity; and ends back in the world of idiocy from which he had emerged. The love and sympathy he brings to the world only fans more intensely its flames of hate, resentment, and self-will.

Besy (1871-1872; *The Possessed*, 1913) is Dostoevski's bitterest and most reactionary novel. He bases his plot on a notorious historic episode: A Moscow student was murdered in 1869 by a group of nihilists who followed Mikhail Bakunin's terrorist doctrines. Dostoevski fills this work with crimes, fires, debasements, and other forms of social and psychological chaos. The political drama centers on the nihilistic leader Peter Verkhovensky, a cynical, slippery, vicious, and monstrously criminal man. Dostoevski also pursues a metaphysical drama at whose center stands his most enigmatic character, Nikolai Stavrogin, who is attracted equally to good and evil and is full of mystery, power, pride, and boredom. He dominates all events while remaining passive and aloof. He liberates himself from any fixed image by confounding everyone's expectations. He is a fallen angel, a Satan, who succeeds, unlike Raskolnikov, in destroying others without scruple or passion. His suicide is his only logical act.

Dostoevski's last novel, *Bratya Karamazovy* (1879-1880; *The Brothers Karamazov*, 1912), sums up his leading themes and ideas. Here Dostoevski tries for no less than a dramatization of the nature of humanity, caught in the conflicting claims of humankind's desire for sainthood, symbolized by the youngest brother, Alyosha; for sensuality, embodied by the lust-driven middle brother, Dmitry; and for intellectual achievement, exemplified by the eldest brother, Ivan.

The last, a brilliant rationalist, organizes a revolt against a God-ordered universe in his powerful "Legend of the Grand Inquisitor," which denounces a world tormented with senseless, undeserved suffering. In the legend, Dostoevski, through Ivan, depicts humankind as weak, slavish, and self-deceptive, willing to renounce freedom and dreams of salvation in exchange for economic security and autocratic guidance. Like Raskolnikov and Stavrogin, Ivan believes that everything is permissible, including the murder of his depraved father. The counterarguments are mounted by the Elder Zossima and his disciple, Alyosha: "All are responsible for all." They preach and practice meekness, humility, com-

---

DOSTOEVSKI'S MAJOR WORKS

1846	*Bednye lyudi* (*Poor Folk*, 1887)
1846	*Dvoynik* (*The Double*, 1917)
1849	*Netochka Nezvanova* (English translation, 1920)
1861	*Unizhennye i oskorblyonnye* (*Injury and Insult*, 1886; also known as *The Insulted and Injured*)
1861-1862	*Zapiski iz myortvogo doma* (*Buried Alive: Or, Ten Years of Penal Servitude in Siberia*, 1881; better known as *The House of the Dead*)
1864	*Zapiski iz podpolya* (*Letters from the Underworld*, 1913; better known as *Notes from the Underground*)
1866	*Prestupleniye i nakazaniye* (*Crime and Punishment*, 1886)
1866	*Igrok* (*The Gambler*, 1887)
1868	*Idiot* (*The Idiot*, 1887)
1870	*Vechny muzh* (*The Permanent Husband*, 1888; also known as *The Eternal Husband*)
1871-1872	*Besy* (*The Possessed*, 1913; also known as *The Devils*)
1875	*Podrostok* (*A Raw Youth*, 1916)
1879-1880	*Bratya Karamazovy* (*The Brothers Karamazov*, 1912)
1914	*The Gambler, and Other Stories*
1917	*A Christmas Tree and a Wedding, and an Honest Thief*
1918	*White Nights, and Other Stories*
1919	*An Honest Thief, and Other Stories*
1945	*The Short Novels of Dostoevsky*

passion, and Christian commitment. Whether Dostoevski succeeds in refuting Ivan's skeptical secularism in this novel is questionable; most critics believe that he fails. He planned a sequel, with Alyosha as the dominant character, but died of a pulmonary hemorrhage in 1881, before he could write it.

SIGNIFICANCE

Perhaps Fyodor Dostoevski's greatest literary achievement was to marry the novel of ideas to the novel of mystery and crime, thereby creating a philosophical novel-drama, or metaphysical thriller. To be sure, he has glaring faults: His construction and style are often congested; his tone tends to be feverish; his language has sometimes unnerving changes of pace and rhythm; his pathos can become bathos; he crowds his fiction with more characters, incidents, and ideas than most readers can reasonably absorb; and he can burden his plots with irrelevant excursions and pronouncements. However, his vision, grasp, and skill in dramatizing the complexities and contradictions of humankind's nature exceed those of any other novelist.

Dostoevski's psychology is amazingly modern in its emphasis on the irrational nature of humankind, on the human psyche as far subtler and more paradoxical than previous writers realized. He anticipates many of the findings of contemporary depth psychology in his awareness of the personality's duality, of the roles played by unconscious drives, and of the symbolic function of dreams. His is a creative process that grasps intuitively not only the outline but also the philosophical implications of events. His characters are wholly absorbed by their thoughts and emotions: They live as they think and feel, translating their ideas and passions into entirely appropriate actions. Dostoevski's hypnotic art, filled with a fury that sometimes verges on hysteria, prepares readers for the ideological and moral struggles that have characterized the twentieth century.

—*Gerhard Brand*

FURTHER READING

Bloom, Harold, ed. *Fyodor Dostoevsky*. Philadelphia: Chelsea House, 2005. One in a series of Bloom Biocritiques, designed for literature students seeking an overview of prominent authors. This collection of essays includes an analysis of Dostoevski's work and a brief biography.

Dostoevsky, Fyodor. *The Brothers Karamazov*. Edited by Ralph Matlaw. Translated by Constance Garnett. New York: W. W. Norton, 1976. Includes relevant letters by Dostoevski and a dozen critical essays that suggest a diversity of approaches to the text: thematic, stylistic, mythological, structural, and religious.

_____. *Crime and Punishment*. Edited by George Gibian. Translated by Jessie Coulson. Rev. ed. New York: W. W. Norton, 1975. This valuable edition has extracts from Dostoevski's letters and notebooks and more than a score of outstanding critical essays representing distinguished Russian, Italian, and German as well as American scholarship; eight were not previously translated into English.

Frank, Joseph. *Dostoevsky: The Seeds of Revolt, 1821-1849*. Princeton, N.J.: Princeton University Press, 1976.

_____. *Dostoevsky: The Years of Ordeal, 1850-1859*. Princeton, N.J.: Princeton University Press, 1983.

_____. *Dostoevsky: The Stir of Liberation, 1860-1865*. Princeton, N.J.: Princeton University Press, 1986.

_____. *Dostoevsky: The Miraculous Years, 1865-1871*. Princeton, N.J.: Princeton University Press, 1995.

_____. *Dostoevsky: The Mantle of the Prophet, 1871-1881*. Princeton, N.J.: Princeton University Press, 2002. A five-volume study of Dostoevski's life and career. Because Frank specializes in intellectual history, his study subordinates the melodramatic personal struggles that have dominated most biographies. Instead, he stresses the social and cultural context in which his subject lived and wrote, taking particular care to analyze the great contemporaneous issues in which Dostoevski participated. Indispensable.

Freud, Sigmund. "Dostoevsky and Parricide." In *Dostoevsky: A Collection of Critical Essays*, edited by René Wellek. Englewood Cliffs, N.J.: Prentice-Hall, 1962. Freud's famous essay traces Dostoevski's epilepsy and gambling mania to what the great psychoanalyst regards as his Oedipus complex and links the parricidal theme of *The Brothers Karamazov* and Dostoevski's trauma suffered after his father's death to his masochistic need for self-punishment to atone for his unconscious drive to kill his father. Though based on flawed historical sources, it remains a striking application of depth psychology to literature.

Leatherbarrow, W. J., ed. *The Cambridge Companion to Dostoevskii*. New York: Cambridge University Press, 2002. Collection of essays interpreting various aspects of Dostoevski's work, including his relationship to the Russian folk heritage, literature, religion, the family, money, and psychology.

Mochulsky, K. V. *Dostoevsky: His Life and Work*. Translated with an introduction by Michael A. Minihan.

Princeton, N.J.: Princeton University Press, 1967. Commonly regarded as the best one-volume interpretation of Dostoevski. Mochulsky has a particularly brilliant analysis of *Crime and Punishment* as a five-act tragedy with a prologue and epilogue.

SEE ALSO: Nikolai Gogol; Mikhail Lermontov; Leo Tolstoy; Ivan Turgenev.
RELATED ARTICLE in *Great Events from History: The Nineteenth Century, 1801-1900:* December, 1849: Dostoevski Is Exiled to Siberia.

STEPHEN A. DOUGLAS
American politician

Best remembered for the political debates he waged with Abraham Lincoln, Douglas was endowed with a vision of nationalism and worked to develop the United States internally and to preserve the Union on the eve of the Civil War.

BORN: April 23, 1813; Brandon, Vermont
DIED: June 3, 1861; Chicago, Illinois
ALSO KNOWN AS: Stephen Arnold Douglas (full name)
AREA OF ACHIEVEMENT: Government and politics

EARLY LIFE
Stephen A. Douglas spent his early life in Vermont and western New York State. When he was only two months old, his father died, and he lived on a farm with his widowed mother until he was fifteen. At that point, he set off for Middlebury, Vermont, to see "what I could do for myself in the wide world among strangers." He apprenticed himself to a cabinetmaker, but a dispute developed and he returned home after eight months. His mother remarried in late 1830 and moved with her new husband to his home in western New York near Canandaigua, and Douglas accompanied them.

Douglas's early schooling in Vermont had been of the sketchy common-school variety, but in New York he entered the Canandaigua Academy, where he boarded and studied. There, he began to read law as well as study the classics, until he left school on January 1, 1833, to devote himself to full-time legal study. Early interested in politics, and particularly that of Andrew Jackson, Douglas associated himself for six months with the law office of Walter and Levi Hubbell, prominent local Jacksonians. New York State requirements for admission to the bar being very stringent—four years of classical studies and three of legal—Douglas decided to move. He was a young man in a hurry, and in June, 1833 (at twenty years of age), he moved west to seek his fortune.

Douglas went first to Cleveland, Ohio, before finally settling further west in Illinois. Douglas taught school briefly in Winchester, Illinois, and then decided to apply for his law certificate. Requirements for admission to the bar were far easier to satisfy on the frontier than they were in the settled East, and in March, 1834, Douglas was examined by Illinois Supreme Court justice Samuel D. Lockwood and received his license to practice. At the age of twenty-one, he had a vocation as a licensed attorney and could pursue his real love, which was politics. Douglas was not physically imposing, standing only five feet, four inches, with a head too large for his body, but he possessed tremendous energy. He would later receive such nicknames as the "Little Giant" and "a steam engine in britches."

Douglas's climb up the political ladder was meteoric. In 1835, he was elected state's attorney for the Morgan (Illinois) Circuit, and his political career was launched. He held a series of elective and appointive offices at the state level and was elected to the U.S. House of Representatives for the first time in 1843, at the age of thirty. He held that position until he resigned in 1847, having been elected to the U.S. Senate, a post he held until his death in 1861 at the age of forty-eight.

LIFE'S WORK
Douglas's life work was clearly political in nature. He had a vision of the United States as a great nation, and he wanted to use the political system to make his dream of "an ocean bound republic" a reality. He was willing to do whatever was necessary to develop and expand the United States and to preserve what was sacred to him, the Union. He expended enormous amounts of energy on his dream of developing the West by working to organize the Western territories and by urging the construction of a transcontinental railroad to bind the nation together.

Two of the highlights of Douglas's career in the Senate involved the Compromise of 1850 and the Kansas-Nebraska Act of 1854. There is a certain irony in the fact that the former was thought to have saved the Union while the latter destroyed it. Upon the acquisition of a vast amount of territory in the Mexican War, the nation was on the verge of disunion in 1849-1850 over the question of whether slavery should be allowed to expand into the area of the Mexican concession.

It was Douglas, taking over from an ailing Henry Clay, who put together the package that has come to be called the Compromise of 1850. That compromise, which required months of intense political maneuvering, included such items as California's entry into the Union as a free state, the organization of New Mexico and Utah as territories without restriction on slavery, a stronger fugitive slave law, the abolition of the slave trade in the District of Columbia, and the settlement of the Texas Bond issue. That this legislation was passed is a testimony to Douglas's ability to put together what appeared to be impossible voting coalitions.

With that compromise widely acclaimed as the "final settlement" of the nation's problems, Douglas sought but failed to get the Democratic nomination for the presidency in 1852. It went instead to Franklin Pierce, who defeated General Winfield Scott in the general election and who is regarded in retrospect as one of the weakest American presidents. Pierce, fearing Douglas's unconcealed political ambitions, excluded him from the inner circle of presidential power, and that exclusion compounded the great despair into which Douglas was plunged following the death of his first wife in January, 1853. His wife was the former Martha Martin of North Carolina, and her short life ended from the complications of childbirth. In an effort to overcome his grief, Douglas left the United States for a tour of Europe in the spring of 1853, and when he returned for the opening of the Thirty-third Congress that fall, he was out of touch with political developments in this country.

In the preceding session of Congress, Douglas's Senate Committee on Territories had reported a bill to organize Nebraska Territory with no mention of slavery. By the time he returned from Europe, the political dynamics had changed, and the pressure mounted to organize two territories and to include a section dealing directly with the slavery question. Kansas-Nebraska lay wholly within the area acquired by the Louisiana Purchase in 1803, where slavery had been forbidden by the Missouri Compromise of 1820.

Convinced that it was crucial to the national interest to get these territories organized as quickly as possible, and firmly believing that the slavery question was a phony issue, Douglas rewrote his organization bill. The new version called for two territories, Kansas and Nebraska, and included a sentence that stated that the 36 degrees,

30 minutes section of the Missouri Compromise was inoperative as it had been "superseded by the principles of the legislation" passed in 1850, which had made no reference to slavery. Such a statement was consistent with Douglas's long-standing belief in popular sovereignty, the idea that the people of a given territory should determine for themselves the institutions they would establish.

When the bill passed after months of the most hostile infighting in the U.S. Congress, and the president signed it into law in May, 1854, a storm of protest swept over the United States the likes of which had not been seen before and has not been seen since. The Kansas-Nebraska Bill split the Democratic Party and occasioned the rise of the Republican Party as the vehicle for antislavery sentiment. Douglas had misjudged the growing moral concern over slavery, and the nation was aflame; the flame would not be extinguished for more than a decade of controversy and bloody war. The situation was so critical as to make impossible an effective concentration by the government on other issues deserving of attention. The man who in 1850 and 1853 wanted to avoid the slavery issue and sought to consolidate and unify the United States became an instrument of its division.

Douglas's association with the Kansas-Nebraska Bill and his consistent failure to perceive the moral nature of the slavery question would haunt the rest of Douglas's abbreviated political career. It would frustrate his efforts to secure his party's nomination for the presidency in 1856 and would cost him dearly in the momentous election in 1860 that Abraham Lincoln won. In between, in 1858, Douglas defeated the Republican Lincoln for the U.S. Senate from Illinois, but that was a small victory in the overall scheme of national life.

SIGNIFICANCE

If ever a man represented the best and the worst of his times, it was Stephen A. Douglas. He was born in 1813 as the nation moved into an intensely nationalistic period; he lived through the Jacksonian period with its turbulent trends toward democracy; he died just as his beloved Union came apart in the Civil War. Douglas was devoted to the concept of democracy, but it was a democracy limited to white adult males. Given his view (widely held at the time) that black people were inferior beings, he saw no reason to be concerned about their civil rights—they simply had none. His political career was shaped by his love for the Union and by his desire to see the United States grow and expand, for he was truly a great nationalist. He thought in terms of the West and of the nation as a whole and did not constrict himself to a North-South view.

Douglas was, perhaps, the most talented politician of his generation, but his moral blindness, while understandable, was his tragic flaw. He alone among his contemporaries might have had the capacity and the vigor to deal with sectionalism and prevent the Civil War, but his fatal flaw kept him from the presidency. Once the war broke out, Douglas threw his support to his Republican rival Abraham Lincoln and in an attempt to rally northern Democrats to the cause of Union he said, "We must fight for our country and forget our differences."

Beset by a variety of infirmities at the age of forty-eight, Douglas hovered near death in early June, 1861. On June 3, 1861, with his beloved second wife Adele by his bed, he died. His last spoken words, passed through Adele as advice for his young sons, suggest Douglas's ultimate concern as a politician: "Tell them to obey the laws and support the Constitution of the United States."

—*Charles J. Bussey*

FURTHER READING

Capers, Gerald M. *Stephen A. Douglas: Defender of the Union*. Boston: Little, Brown, 1959. As the title suggests, this volume is generally pro-Douglas and forgives his moral blindness. It is fairly brief and is well written.

Hamilton, Holman. *Prologue to Conflict: The Crisis and Compromise of 1850*. New York: W. W. Norton, 1966. A valuable work and one that was a pioneering effort in quantitative history. Hamilton uses statistics to analyze voting patterns and to clarify the way Douglas put the compromise together. The writing is excellent, as one might expect from a former newspaper man. Hamilton was the first historian to give Douglas the credit he deserved.

Johannsen, Robert W. *The Frontier, the Union, and Stephen A. Douglas*. Urbana: University of Illinois Press, 1989. Johannsen's fifteen essays examine the issues of slavery, secession, and the nature of the Union during the 1850's, contrasting the views of Douglas and Abraham Lincoln on these questions. Johannsen describes Douglas's role as a spokesman for the Western frontier and an advocate for popular sovereignty, and explains his involvement in the election of 1860.

_____. *Stephen A. Douglas*. New York: Oxford University Press, 1973. This volume is the definitive work on Douglas. Johannsen is meticulous in his research, fair in his assessment, and thorough in his coverage.

Meyer, Daniel. *Stephen A. Douglas and the American Union*. Chicago: University of Chicago Library, 1994. Catalog of an exhibition held at the Library in 1994.

Nichols, Roy Frank. *The Democratic Machine: 1850-1854*. New York: Columbia University Press, 1923. While Nichols's book is dated, it is still worth reading. The author probably knew more about the politics of the 1850's than any single individual.

Potter, David M. *The Impending Crisis: 1848-1861*. New York: Harper & Row, 1976. This major interpretation puts Douglas's political activity in the context of his times and provides many insights into his character.

Waugh, John C. *On the Brink of Civil War: The Compromise of 1850 and How It Changed the Course of American History*. Wilmington, Del.: Scholarly Resources, 2003. An account of the congressional battling between Northern abolitionists, Southern secessionists, and moderates from both regions. Douglas is one of the lawmakers whose positions and actions on the compromise are examined.

SEE ALSO: James Buchanan; Henry Clay; Abraham Lincoln; Franklin Pierce.

RELATED ARTICLES in *Great Events from History: The Nineteenth Century, 1801-1900:* January 29-September 20, 1850: Compromise of 1850; May 30, 1854: Congress Passes Kansas-Nebraska Act; May, 1856-August, 1858: Bleeding Kansas; June 16-October 15, 1858: Lincoln-Douglas Debates; November 6, 1860: Lincoln Is Elected U.S. President.

FREDERICK DOUGLASS
American abolitionist, journalist, and social reformer

The best-known and most influential African American of his time, Douglass had a lifelong concern with freedom and human rights for all people. He articulated these concerns most specifically for black Americans and women.

BORN: February, 1817?; Tuckahoe, Talbot County, Maryland
DIED: February 20, 1895; Washington, D.C.
ALSO KNOWN AS: Frederick Augustus Washington Bailey (birth name)
AREAS OF ACHIEVEMENT: Journalism, social reform

EARLY LIFE

Born a slave, Frederick Douglass was originally named Frederick Augustus Washington Bailey. He was of mixed African, white, and Indian ancestry, but other than that, he knew little of his family background or even his exact date of birth. Douglass believed that he was born in February, 1817, yet subsequent research indicates that he may have been born a year later in February, 1818. Douglass never knew his father or anything about him except that he was a white man, possibly his master. Douglass's mother was Harriet Bailey, the daughter of Betsey and Isaac Bailey. Frederick, his mother, and his grandparents were the property of a Captain Aaron Anthony.

In his early years, Frederick experienced many aspects of the institution of slavery. Anthony engaged in the practice of hiring out slaves, and Douglass's mother and her four sisters were among the slaves Anthony hired out to work off the plantation. Consequently, Douglass seldom saw his mother and never really knew her. The first seven years of his life were spent with his grandmother, Betsey Bailey, not because she was his grandmother but because as an elderly woman too old for field work she had been assigned the duty of caring for young children on the plantation.

The boy loved his grandmother very much, and it was extremely painful for him when, at the age of seven, he was forced by his master to move to his main residence, a twelve-mile separation from Betsey. It was there, at Anthony's main residence, that Douglass received his initiation into the realities of slavery. The years with his grandmother had been relatively carefree and filled with love. Soon, he began to witness and to experience personally the brutalities of slavery. In 1825, however, Douglass's personal situation temporarily improved when Anthony sent him to Baltimore as a companion for young Tommy Auld, a family friend. Douglass spent seven years with the Aulds as a houseboy and later as a laborer in the Baltimore shipyards. The death of Anthony caused Douglass to be transferred to the country as a field hand and to the ownership of Anthony's son-in-law. Early in 1834, his new owner hired him out to Edward Covey, a farmer who also acted as a professional slave-breaker. This began the most brutal period of Douglass's life as a slave.

After months of being whipped weekly, Douglass fought a two-hour battle with Covey that ended in a standoff, and the beatings stopped. Douglass's owner next hired him out to a milder planter, but Douglass's victory over Covey had sealed his determination to be free. In 1836, Douglass and five other slaves planned an escape but were detected. Douglass was jailed and expected to be sold out of state, but the Aulds reprieved him and brought him back to Baltimore, where he first served as an apprentice and then worked as a ship caulker. However improved Douglass's situation might be in Baltimore, it was still slavery, and he was determined to be a free man. On September 3, 1838, Douglass borrowed the legal papers and a suit of clothes of a free black sailor and boarded a train for New York.

In New York, he was joined by Anna Murray, a free black woman with whom he had fallen in love in Baltimore. Douglass and Anna were married in New York on September 15, 1838, and almost immediately moved further north to New Bedford, Massachusetts, where there were fewer slave catchers hunting fugitives such as Douglass. It was also to elude slave catchers that Douglass changed his last name. He had long abandoned his middle names of Augustus Washington; he now dropped the surname Bailey and became Frederick Douglass. The move and the name change proved to be far more than symbolic; unknown to Douglass, he was about to launch on his life's work in a direction he had never anticipated.

LIFE'S WORK

New Bedford was a shipping town, and Douglass had expected to work as a ship caulker; however, race prejudice prevented his working in the shipyards and he had to earn a living doing any manual labor available: sawing wood, shoveling coal, sweeping chimneys, and so on. Anna worked as a domestic when she was not caring for their growing family. Anna bore Douglass five children: Rosetta, Lewis, Charles, Frederick, Jr., and Annie. Unexpectedly, the abolitionist movement of the 1830's, 1840's, and 1850's changed both Douglass's immediate situation and his whole future.

Within a few months of his escape to the North, Douglass chanced on a copy of William Lloyd Garrison's abolitionist newspaper, *The Liberator. The Liberator* so moved Douglass that, in spite of his poverty, he became a subscriber. Then, on August 9, 1841, less than three years after his escape, Douglass and Garrison met. This and subsequent meetings led to Garrison offering Douglass an annual salary of $450 to lecture for the abolitionist movement. Douglass was so convinced that he would not succeed as a lecturer that he accepted only a three-month appointment. In fact, he had begun his life's work.

Scholars have debated whether Douglass's greatest accomplishments were as an orator or a writer; both his speaking and his writing stemmed from his involvement with the abolition movement, and both were to be his primary activities for the remainder of his life.

From the beginning, Douglass was a powerful, effective orator. He had a deep, powerful voice that could hold his audiences transfixed. Moreover, Douglass was an impressive figure of a man. He had a handsome face, bronze skin, a leonine head, a muscular body, and was more than six feet in height. He stood with dignity and spoke eloquently and distinctly. Indeed, his bearing and speech caused critics to charge that Douglass had never been a slave; he did not conform to the stereotypic view of a slave's demeanor and address.

Even Douglass's allies in the abolition movement urged him to act more as the public expected. Douglass refused; instead, he wrote his autobiography to prove his identity and thus began his career as a writer. *Narrative of the Life of Frederick Douglass: An American Slave* (1845) remains his most famous and widely read book. It was an instant success. However, in the narrative, Douglass had revealed his identity as Frederick Bailey, as well as the identity of his owners, making himself more

vulnerable than ever to slave catchers. Anna was legally free, and because of her their children were free also, but Douglass was legally still a slave. To avoid capture, he went to England, where he remained for two years.

In England, Douglass was immensely successful as a lecturer and returned to the United States, in 1847, with enough money to purchase his freedom. By the end of the year, he was legally a free man. Also in 1847, Douglass moved to Rochester, New York, and began publication of his own newspaper, *The North Star*. While editing *The North Star*, Douglass continued to lecture and to write. In 1855, he published an expanded autobiography, *My Bondage and My Freedom*; he also published numerous lectures, articles, and even a short story, "The Heroic Slave," in 1853. Much later in life, he published his third, and most complete, autobiography, *Life and Times of Frederick Douglass* (1881).

In all of his writings and speeches, Douglass's major concerns were civil rights and human freedom. As a person born in slavery, and as a black man living in a racially prejudiced society, Douglass's most immediate and direct concerns were to end slavery, racial prejudice, and discrimination. However, he always insisted that there was little difference between one form of oppression and another. He proved the depth of his convictions in his

DOUGLASS'S UNCERTAINTY ABOUT HIS BIRTH

Like many African Americans born into slavery, Frederick Douglass knew little about the circumstances of his birth. He began his autobiography—which went through many editions—with this poignant commentary on his origins.

I was born in Tuckahoe, near Hillsborough, and about twelve miles from Easton, in Talbot county, Maryland. I have no accurate knowledge of my age, never having seen any authentic record containing it. By far the larger part of the slaves know as little of their ages as horses know of theirs, and it is the wish of most masters within my knowledge to keep their slaves thus ignorant. I do not remember to have ever met a slave who could tell of his birthday. They seldom come nearer to it than planting-time, harvest-time, cherry-time, springtime, or fall-time. A want of information concerning my own was a source of unhappiness to me even during childhood. The white children could tell their ages. I could not tell why I ought to be deprived of the same privilege. I was not allowed to make any inquiries of my master concerning it. He deemed all such inquiries on the part of a slave improper and impertinent, and evidence of a restless spirit. The nearest estimate I can give makes me now between twenty-seven and twenty-eight years of age. I come to this, from hearing my master say, some time during 1835, I was about seventeen years old.

Source: Frederick Douglass, *The Narrative of the Life of Frederick Douglass: An American Slave* (Boston: Anti-Slavery Office, 1845).

championing of the women's rights movement at the same time he was immersed in his abolitionist activities. In fact, Douglass was the only man to participate actively in the Seneca Falls Convention that launched the women's rights movement in the United States in 1848. Moreover, his commitment was lasting; on the day of his death, in 1895, Douglass had returned only a few hours earlier from addressing a women's rights meeting in Washington, D.C.

By the 1850's, Douglass was active in politics. He also knew and counseled with John Brown and was sufficiently implicated in Brown's Harpers Ferry raid to leave the country temporarily after Brown's capture and arrest. From the beginning of the Civil War, Douglass urged President Abraham Lincoln not only to save the Union but also to use the war as the means to end slavery. Douglass also urged black men to volunteer and the president to accept them as soldiers in the Union armies.

By the end of the Civil War, Douglass was the most prominent spokesperson for black Americans in the country. With the end of the war and the advent of Reconstruction, Douglass's work seemed to have reached fruition. By 1875, with the passage of the Civil Rights Act of that year, not only had slavery been ended and the Constitution amended but also the laws of the land had guaranteed black Americans their freedom, their citizenship, and the same rights as all other citizens. However, the victories were short-lived. The racism, both of North and of South, that had dominated the antebellum era triumphed again during the 1880's and 1890's. According to the Constitution, black Americans remained equal, but it was a paper equality. In fact, prejudice and discrimination became the order of the day across the whole United States.

For Douglass personally, the years following the Civil War contained a number of successes. He was financially solvent. He served in a number of governmental capacities: secretary of the Santo Domingo Commission, marshal and recorder of deeds in the District of Columbia, and United States minister to Haiti. For twenty-five years, he was a trustee on the board of Howard University. Nevertheless, these personal successes could not alleviate Douglass's bitter disappointment over the turn of public events, and he never ceased to fight. He continued to write, to lecture, and even began another newspaper, *New National Era*.

SIGNIFICANCE

Frederick Douglass's career and his personal life were all the more remarkable when one considers the times in which he lived. His life was an example of the human

will triumphing over adversity. Born into slavery, by law a piece of chattel, surrounded by poverty and illiteracy, he became one of the greatest American orators, an accomplished writer and editor, and for more than fifty years he was the most persistent and articulate voice in the United States speaking for civil rights, freedom, and human dignity regardless of race or sex. Douglass, more than any other individual, insisted that the ideals of the Declaration of Independence must be extended to all Americans.

Douglass's personal life reflected the principles for which he fought publicly. He always insisted that race should be irrelevant: Humanity was what mattered, not race, and not sex. In 1882, Anna Murray Douglass died after more than forty years of marriage to Frederick, and in 1884, Douglass married Helen Pitts, a white woman who had been his secretary. The marriage caused a storm of controversy and criticism from both black and white people and members of Douglass's own family. However, for Douglass there was no issue: It was the irrelevance of race again. His own comment on the criticism was that he had married from his mother's people the first time and his father's, the second.

Douglass is most frequently thought of as a spokesperson for black Americans and sometimes remembered as a champion of women's rights as well. Up to a point, this is accurate enough; Douglass was indeed a spokesman for black Americans and a champion of women's rights, because in his own lifetime these were among the most oppressed American people. Douglass's concern, however, was for all humanity, and his message, for all time.

—*D. Harland Hagler*

FURTHER READING

Chesebrough, David B. *Frederick Douglass: Oratory from Slavery*. Westport, Conn.: Greenwood Press, 1998. Analysis of Douglass's oratory skills and techniques. Beginning with a biographical sketch, the author moves to Douglass's techniques and finally presents three speeches from different periods in his career.

Douglass, Frederick. *Frederick Douglass: The Narrative and Selected Writings*. Edited by Michael Meyer. New York: Vintage Books, 1984. In addition to being a readily accessible, complete edition of *Narrative of the Life of Frederick Douglass*, this book includes excerpts from Douglass's two later autobiographies and twenty selected writings by Douglass on various topics that are not easily obtainable.

_____. *Narrative of the Life of Frederick Douglass: An American Slave*. Boston: Anti-Slavery Office, 1845. Reprint. Garden City, N.Y.: Doubleday, 1963. Originally published in 1845, the work covers Douglass's life up to that time; it was his first book and remains the most widely read of his three autobiographies.

_____. *My Bondage and My Freedom*. New York: Miller, Orton and Mulligan, 1855. Reprint. New York: Dover, 1969. Originally published in 1855, this is the least read of Douglass's autobiographies.

_____. *Life and Times of Frederick Douglass*. Hartford, Conn.: Park Publishing, 1881. Reprint. New York: Citadel Press, 1984. First published in 1881 and reissued in 1892. The 1892 edition is the most commonly reproduced and the most complete of the three autobiographies.

Factor, Robert L. *The Black Response to America: Men, Ideals, and Organization from Frederick Douglass to the NAACP*. Reading, Mass.: Addison-Wesley, 1970. Factor offers an interesting theoretical interpretation of Douglass as a black spokesman and informative comparison of Douglass with other black spokesmen and leaders.

Lawson, Bill E., and Frank M. Kirkland, eds. *Frederick Douglass: A Critical Reader*. Malden, Mass.: Blackwell, 1999. Essays by fifteen leading American philosophers who revisit Douglass and the place his work has in contemporary social and political thought.

Meier, August. *Negro Thought in America: 1880-1915*. Ann Arbor: University of Michigan Press, 1963. Meier offers a good account of the varieties of thought among black Americans for the period covered and suggests an intriguing, plausible thesis regarding shifts of opinion in the black community. Although the book covers only the last fifteen years of Douglass's life, it is still worth reading for insight into Douglass, especially for any comparison or contrast of Douglass with later black spokesmen such as Booker T. Washington and W. E. B. Du Bois.

Quarles, Benjamin. *Frederick Douglass*. Washington, D.C.: Associated Publishers, 1948. Reprint. New York: Atheneum, 1976. Originally published in 1948, this is an easily available, thorough biography.

Stauffer, John. *The Black Hearts of Men: Radical Abolitionists and the Transformation of Race*. Cambridge, Mass.: Harvard University Press, 2002. Describes the interracial alliance of Douglass, James McCune Smith, Gerrit Smith, and John Brown. The four men worked together on temperance and feminist issues as well as on abolition, seeking to achieve what Stauffer describes as a "vision of sacred, sin-free and pluralistic society."

Wu, Jin-Ping. *Frederick Douglass and the Black Liberation Movement: The North Star of American Blacks*. New York: Garland, 2000. Reassesses Douglass's place in the history of the black liberation movement, focusing on his impact on other black leaders and his Legitimate Reform Society.

SEE ALSO: John Brown; Mary Ann Shadd Cary; Paul Laurence Dunbar; William Lloyd Garrison; Harriet Tubman; Victoria Woodhull.

RELATED ARTICLES in *Great Events from History: The Nineteenth Century, 1801-1900:* December, 1833: American Anti-Slavery Society Is Founded; December 3, 1847: Douglass Launches *The North Star*; July 19-20, 1848: Seneca Falls Convention; July 6, 1853: National Council of Colored People Is Founded; December 6, 1865: Thirteenth Amendment Is Ratified.

SIR ARTHUR CONAN DOYLE
English physician and novelist

Doyle wrote on many subjects and was knighted for his contributions to the British cause during the South African War; however, his most enduring legacy was the creation of one of the first and most popular and long-lived of fictional detectives: Sherlock Holmes.

BORN: May 22, 1859; Edinburgh, Scotland
DIED: July 7, 1930; Crowborough, Sussex, England
ALSO KNOWN AS: Arthur Ignatius Conan Doyle (full name)
AREA OF ACHIEVEMENT: Literature

EARLY LIFE

Sir Arthur Conan Doyle was born into an artistic Roman Catholic family and grew up in Edinburgh, Scotland, a Protestant stronghold. His grandfather and his uncle were illustrators; Richard, his uncle, gained fame drawing for *Punch*. Doyle's father, Charles, became clerk of the Board of Works in Edinburgh, but he also drew. He illustrated the first edition of his son's *A Study in Scarlet* (1887), the first tale of Sherlock Holmes. Charles suffered from mental illness and alcoholism and was institutionalized from 1879 until his death in 1893. Doyle's mother, Mary Foley, was an Irish Catholic. She reared seven children, of whom Arthur was the fourth. Ever a practical woman, she oversaw Doyle's education, sending him to Jesuit schools at Stoneyhurst and at Feldkirch, Austria, despite the family's comparative poverty. She later encouraged him to study medicine at the University of Edinburgh. They remained close until her death in 1921.

Doyle grew into a large and sturdy man, over six feet tall. Photographs show him square-headed and mustached, with a direct, self-confident gaze. A fine athlete, he was welcomed on cricket and soccer teams well into his middle years.

After starting his medical studies in 1877, Doyle began his writing career soon after. He published his first story, "The Mystery of Sasassa Valley," in 1879. At the university, he met two professors who became models for his most famous literary creations: Dr. Joseph Bell, the inspiration for Sherlock Holmes, and William Rutherford, the prototype for Professor Challenger of *The Lost World* (1912). Before finishing his bachelor of medicine, Doyle sought adventure, signing on as surgeon for an arctic whaling cruise in 1880. After taking his degree in 1881, he tried a second cruise, this time to Africa.

Doyle practiced medicine in Plymouth, then in Southsea, a suburb of Portsmouth, and finally in London, but he was never notably successful. Upon completing his M.D. in 1885, he married Louise Hawkins. Within the first year of their marriage, Doyle wrote two novels but failed to publish them, though he continued to publish magazine pieces. A decisive moment in his career came in 1886, when he finished *A Study in Scarlet*, his first Sherlock Holmes adventure. The tale appeared in *Beeton's Christmas Annual*, where it attracted enough attention to warrant a separate edition in 1888.

As he entered fully into his writing career, Doyle seemed to be a man of balanced opposites: a lapsed Catholic who still respected the faith, a man of science turning to a profession in the arts, a man of reason already attracted to the Spiritualist movement, a man of physical strength and activity who also loved scholarship, a man who dreamed of producing great historical literature in the vein of Sir Walter Scott yet who was about to achieve greatness writing what he considered potboilers for a new popular magazine.

LIFE'S WORK

To an extent, Doyle captured this balance of opposites in Sherlock Holmes and Dr. Watson. In Holmes, the powers of reason are developed at the expense of the emotions. He solves crimes by keen observation, building hypotheses based on established facts, and testing those hypotheses. Watson, though quite competent, is a more ordinary man, a doctor who eventually marries and lives a prosaic life, except when with Holmes on a case. Then his life blossoms into adventure. Holmes is a creative genius, using a "scientific method" in an artistic manner to produce masterpieces of detection. Watson turns these masterpieces into what Holmes often describes as trivial romances, more entertaining than instructive.

Though Doyle proceeded to write what he considered great historical novels, some of which were quite well received, the public showed more interest in Holmes. At the request of *Lippincott's Magazine*, Doyle produced *The Sign of Four* (1890). Giving up his medical practice in 1891, he turned to writing for his living. He then wrote a series of Holmes stories for *The Strand*, beginning with "A Scandal in Bohemia." These were so popular that the editors asked for more. Before he had finished twelve— collected in *The Adventures of Sherlock Holmes* (1892)— he was tired of his characters and told his mother he intended to kill Holmes in the last one. She recommended against this course.

When *The Strand* asked for more Holmes stories in 1892, Doyle tried to put them off, as he had when they asked for the second six in 1891. Then he had asked the "ridiculous" price of fifty pounds, which *The Strand* gladly paid. This time he asked for one thousand pounds per story, and again, *The Strand* was eager. Eventually collected as *The Memoirs of Sherlock Holmes* (1894), this series ended with "The Final Problem," in which Holmes dies, falling down the Swiss Reichenbach Falls in the grip of Moriarty, "the Napoleon of crime."

Having taken Louise to Switzerland after discovering her tuberculosis, Doyle was away from London when *The Strand* readers learned of Holmes's death. Nevertheless, he heard in no uncertain terms the sorrow and anger of Holmes's fans. Still, he published no more Holmes stories until *The Hound of the Baskervilles* (1902).

Sir Arthur Conan Doyle. (Courtesy of The University of Texas at Austin)

Between 1892 and 1901, Doyle continued writing popular stories for *The Strand*, the best about Etienne Gerard, a comic soldier in Napoleon's army. He also made a successful reading tour of the United States, sailed up the Nile with Louise, and visited the Sudan as a war correspondent. Having been convinced that the climate of Surrey was good for tuberculosis patients, Doyle and Louise settled there in 1896. In 1897, Doyle met and fell in love with Jean Leckie, then twenty-four. With typical loyalty and honor, Doyle maintained a platonic relationship with her until after Louise's death. He married Jean in 1907. They had three children: Denis (1909), Adrian (1910), and Lena Jean (1912).

Before the outbreak of the South African (Boer) War in 1899, Doyle published story collections, novels, poetry, and drama. When the war began, he was turned down for combat because of his age, but he served under terrible conditions and without pay as a medical officer. His experiences in the war led to two books. In the second, *The War in South Africa: Its Causes and Conduct* (1902), he defended the British role in the war. For this service, he was knighted in 1902.

After running unsuccessfully for a seat in Parliament in 1900, Doyle visited Dartmoor. There, he heard legends that became the inspiration for *The Hound of the Baskervilles*. In this most famous Holmes story, Watson and Holmes solve the murder of a country gentleman and save the life of his heir, both of whom are beset by a "hell hound," supposedly the product of an ancestral curse.

While this novel was appearing in *The Strand*, William Gillette's play *Sherlock Holmes* (1899) opened successfully in London, and the demand for more Holmes stories increased. American and British publishers offered Doyle approximately seventy-five hundred dollars per story to write more. He began a new series with "The Adventure of the Empty House," in which Holmes returns after three years of hiding from surviving members of Moriarty's gang, for he had not really fallen with Moriarty over the falls. This series was collected in *The Return of Sherlock Holmes* (1905).

Doyle continued to produce Holmes stories sporadically for the rest of his life. *The Valley of Fear* (1915) recounts an encounter with agents of Moriarty. *His Last Bow* (1917) collects stories that had appeared in *The Strand* between 1893 and 1917. *The Case-Book of Sherlock Holmes* (1927) collects stories from 1921 to 1927. Doyle's last Holmes story was "The Adventure of Schoscombe Old Place."

Though his popularity and subsequent fame have rested mainly upon the Holmes tales, Doyle was reluctant to see these as his enduring achievements. Energetic, inquisitive, and ambitious, he sought to influence public opinion in many ways. In 1906, he ran for Parliament, again unsuccessfully. After Louise's death, he took humanitarian interest in English legal reform and in Belgian policy in the Congo. He spoke out on political issues such as Irish home rule, participated in an Anglo-German auto race, traveled widely in Europe and America, and was a war correspondent during World War I.

In 1916, Doyle became convinced that he had received a spirit message and proceeded to become a leader of the Spiritualist movement. He wrote several books on Spiritualism, including *The History of Spiritualism* (1926), a study that has been praised despite the prejudices of its author. He also came to believe in fairies and wrote about them. He gave generous financial support to research into the paranormal, especially communication with the dead. His friendship with Harry Houdini came to an end because Houdini exposed so many fraudulent claims.

The best-remembered creation from the last third of his life is another character, Professor Challenger, the hero of *The Lost World* (the novel that provided the basis for the classic film *King Kong*, 1933). Challenger is a passionate scientist, eager to explore unknown worlds. Like Holmes, Challenger eventually became a film hero as well as appearing in several successful novels and stories, but he never approached the popularity of Holmes.

Doyle fell ill with heart disease in 1929 and died in 1930 at his home, Windlesham, where he was buried.

SIGNIFICANCE

Sir Arthur Conan Doyle's biographers all characterize him as a late Victorian type. Throughout his life, he remained confident in the soundness of his own moral vision and in the basic goodness of British morality. As a public personage, he repeatedly took the lead, both in praising British principles and in criticizing particular policies. He is credited with helping to modernize British defense between the South African War and World War I, especially the defensive gear of common soldiers. He twice played detective himself, investigating cases of people unjustly condemned to prison. One of these, the Edalji case (1906), contributed to establishing a court of criminal appeal in 1907. Even

INTRODUCING SHERLOCK HOLMES

When Arthur Conan Doyle wrote his first Sherlock Holmes novel, A Study in Scarlet, *he had no idea that he would eventually write three more novels and numerous short stories about his brilliant consulting detective. As a consequence, some of his earliest descriptions of Holmes contradict the character's later descriptions. This passage in which Doyle's fictional narrator, Dr. Watson, describes his early impressions of Holmes is an example. The later Holmes was by no means as ignorant as this passage suggests.*

His ignorance was as remarkable as his knowledge. Of contemporary literature, philosophy and politics he appeared to know next to nothing. Upon my quoting Thomas Carlyle, he inquired in the naivest way who he might be and what he had done. My surprise reached a climax, however, when I found incidentally that he was ignorant of the Copernican Theory and of the composition of the Solar System. That any civilized human being in this nineteenth century should not be aware that the earth travelled round the sun appeared to be to me such an extraordinary fact that I could hardly realize it.

"You appear to be astonished," he said, smiling at my expression of surprise. "Now that I do know it I shall do my best to forget it."

"To forget it!"

"You see," he explained, "I consider that a man's brain originally is like a little empty attic, and you have to stock it with such furniture as you choose. A fool takes in all the lumber of every sort that he comes across, so that the knowledge which might be useful to him gets crowded out, or at best is jumbled up with a lot of other things so that he has a difficulty in laying his hands upon it. Now the skilful workman is very careful indeed as to what he takes into his brain-attic. He will have nothing but the tools which may help him in doing his work, but of these he has a large assortment, and all in the most perfect order. It is a mistake to think that that little room has elastic walls and can distend to any extent. Depend upon it there comes a time when for every addition of knowledge you forget something that you knew before. It is of the highest importance, therefore, not to have useless facts elbowing out the useful ones."

"But the Solar System!" I protested.

"What the deuce is it to me?" he interrupted impatiently; "you say that we go round the sun. If we went round the moon it would not make a pennyworth of difference to me or to my work."

Source: Arthur Conan Doyle, *A Study in Scarlet* (London, 1887), part 1, chapter 2.

his support of Spiritualism was a public crusade to effect the spiritual transformation of a nation he feared was in decline.

While his public services were many, including credit for introducing skiing to the Alps, Doyle will continue to be remembered mainly for the Sherlock Holmes stories. Holmes and Watson are indelible fixtures of Western culture, encountered in virtually every popular medium. These stories have influenced every important writer in the detective genre, from traditionalists such as Agatha Christie, Dorothy L. Sayers, and Ellery Queen to "hard-boiled" writers such as Raymond Chandler, Ross Macdonald, and P. D. James.

—Terry Heller

FURTHER READING

Barsham, Diana. *Arthur Conan Doyle and the Meaning of Masculinity*. Burlington, Vt.: Ashgate, 2000. Barsham explains how Doyle viewed himself and his work as models of British manhood, and describes his commitment to finding solutions to issues of nineteenth century masculinity.

Booth, Martin. *The Doctor, the Detective, and Arthur Conan Doyle: A Biography of Arthur Conan Doyle*. London: Hodder & Stoughton, 1997. A comprehensive, readable biography, describing the many activities and interests in Doyle's life. Booth recounts Doyle's experiences as a military doctor, war correspondent, spiritualist, cricket player, and politician, as well as the creator of Sherlock Holmes.

Carr, John Dickson. *The Life of Sir Arthur Conan Doyle*. New York: Harper & Row, 1949. Written with the help of Adrian Doyle, this biography draws on primary sources unavailable to subsequent biographers but avoids some problematic sides of his life.

Cox, Don Richard. *Arthur Conan Doyle*. New York: Frederick Ungar, 1985. Cox discusses virtually all of Doyle's writing, with chapters on historical fiction, Sherlock Holmes, other genres, and nonfiction. A portrait of Doyle as revealed in his writing.

Edwards, Owen Dudley. *The Quest for Sherlock Holmes*. Totawa, N.J.: Barnes & Noble Books, 1983. Concentrating on the years before *A Study in Scarlet*, Edwards uses records from Edinburgh and Doyle's schools to examine parental and educational influences.

Higham, Charles. *The Adventures of Conan Doyle*. New York: W. W. Norton, 1976. Combining biography and a critical review of Doyle's fiction, Higham consults uncollected materials such as Doyle's letters to the London *Times*. Gives special attention to the relationship between Doyle, Louise, and Jean Leckie.

Nordon, Pierre. *Conan Doyle: A Biography*. Translated by Frances Partridge. New York: Holt, Rinehart and Winston, 1966. This objective and scholarly biography focuses on relationships between Doyle's public life and his writing, with special attention to his interest in Spiritualism.

Shreffler, Philip A., ed. *The Baker Street Reader*. Westport, Conn.: Greenwood Press, 1984. A collection of critical material on Doyle's detective stories, this book helpfully places Doyle's work in the traditions of detective fiction and explores the reasons for its popularity.

Stashower, Daniel. *Teller of Tales: The Life of Arthur Conan Doyle*. New York: Henry Holt, 1999. Thorough, well-researched biography that attempts to separate Doyle from Sherlock Holmes and describe the entire range of Doyle's interests and activities. Places special emphasis on the psychic crusade upon which Doyle embarked in his final years.

SEE ALSO: Thomas Hardy; Edgar Allan Poe.

RELATED ARTICLES in *Great Events from History: The Nineteenth Century, 1801-1900:* 1878-1899: Irving Manages London's Lyceum Theatre; December, 1887: Conan Doyle Introduces Sherlock Holmes; October 11, 1899-May 31, 1902: South African War.

JAMES BUCHANAN DUKE
American industrialist

*From modest beginnings, Duke organized and built up
the largest conglomerate of tobacco companies in the
United States, founded power and textile companies,
and established an endowment in support of Duke
University—which was named after him—as well as
other educational and charitable institutions.*

BORN: December 23, 1856; Durham, North Carolina
DIED: October 10, 1925; New York, New York
AREA OF ACHIEVEMENT: Business

EARLY LIFE

Born in a six-room farmhouse in North Carolina, James
Buchanan Duke was the youngest in his family, which
had two half brothers from his father's first marriage, and
a brother and a sister had also preceded James. In 1858,
his mother, Artelia Roney Duke, died from typhoid fever, which also claimed his older half brother. His father,
Washington Duke, owned about three hundred acres of
land, on which he grew corn, wheat, oats, and some tobacco.

During the Civil War, Duke served for two years with
the Confederate artillery; in 1865, Union soldiers looted
his farm and left behind little but leaf tobacco. Immediately thereafter, however, demand for tobacco mounted,
and prices rose; between 1866 and 1872, the Duke family's production increased from 15,000 to 125,000
pounds. James took part in the planting and preparation
of their crop. His early education took place in local
schools. Evidently he learned quickly, but preferred
mathematics to the humanities. In 1872, he enrolled in
the New Garden Academy, near Greensboro, North Carolina; quite abruptly, he gave up his courses there and left
for the Eastman Business College in Poughkeepsie, New
York, where he studied bookkeeping and accounting.

By 1874, Washington Duke felt sufficiently confident
in the industry's future that he sold his farm and bought a
tobacco factory in downtown Durham. Although he originally intended to go into business on his own, James
Duke accepted with alacrity his father's offer that made
him, and his brother Benjamin Duke, one-third partners
in the new concern. Leaving correspondence and other
official functions to the others, James Buchanan Duke
kept their financial records and devised numerous means
by which to economize on the operations of their tobacco
firm.

Somewhat daunting in bearing if not precisely handsome, as he entered manhood Duke gave an impression
of strength and energy. He was six feet, two inches tall
and powerfully built; his features were distinguished by a
broad brow, a straight, thick nose, and piercing blue eyes.
His lank red hair, parted at the side, showed a tendency to
thinness in his later photographs. He spoke in a gentle
drawl; often among others he would remain silent for
protracted periods, and then hold forth at some length on
matters of concern to him.

LIFE'S WORK

Although the Dukes seemed overwhelmed by their competitors, notably the massive Durham Bull Company in
their native city, they began to advertise on local billboards. They also began to promote cigarettes, which
hitherto had not sold well but were peculiarly suited to
the bright tobacco leaf that was grown in abundance
across parts of North Carolina and Virginia. They
launched promotional campaigns in many states; they
obtained permission from a touring French actress to use
her picture in the company's cigarette advertisements.
The Dukes also readily adopted another innovation: In
1884, they had the newly invented Bonsack cigarette-
rolling machine installed in their plant. While it was
sometimes inclined to clog during use, this device could
produce more than two hundred cigarettes a minute, or
about fifty times as many as an expert artisan working by
hand.

Sensing that a national market might exist for the
company's cigarettes, in 1884 Duke moved to a small
apartment in New York City and opened an office there.
After two years, this branch was also turning a profit, in
part because of Duke's meticulous familiarity with all aspects of the tobacco trade, and in part as a result of his
flamboyant innovations in advertising. The company offered complimentary cigarette packs to immigrants coming into New York harbor; it sponsored sporting events;
it issued coupons, enclosed in its cigarette cartons, which
could be redeemed for cash. Billboards, posters, and advertisements in newspapers and magazines promoted the
various brands the company offered. By 1889, of some
2.1 billion cigarettes produced in the United States, about
940 million had come from the factories of W. Duke and
Sons. Its sales were well over $4 million, of which
$400,000 was profit.

After prolonged and tortuous negotiations, Duke persuaded the presidents of four other leading tobacco concerns to form the American Tobacco Company; to win

over his erstwhile rivals, Duke obtained a contract with the Bonsack company restricting sales of their rolling machines to the new trust. As president, Duke expanded upon his promotional methods: New coupon schemes were devised, and pictures of attractive women in tights were issued in packs of some of the company's brands. Moreover, the trust's vast resources allowed it to absorb smaller concerns, many of which were bought up outright or controlled through subsidiaries or holding companies. Duke also turned on the few powerful corporations that had remained independent.

The Durham Bull Company was taken over, and the trust acquired a controlling interest in the Liggett and Myers Company and the R. J. Reynolds Company. By 1900, the American Tobacco Company accounted for 92.7 percent of American cigarette production and 59.2 percent of the nation's output of pipe tobacco. By 1901, James B. Duke added the American Cigar Company to this business empire, and became its president; with this stroke, one-sixth of the country's cigar trade came under his control.

With annual sales of about $125 million, the American Tobacco Company was in a position to determine prices and wages as it saw fit. During the Spanish-American War of 1898, Congress had imposed a surtax on tobacco, and repealed it three years later; Duke's trust held their cigarette prices at the previous levels and kept the balance as profits. Competitive bidding for tobacco was curtailed; prices to farmers were held as low as three cents per pound, spawning organized violent outbreaks by "night riders" operating in Kentucky and Tennessee. Foreign markets were also exploited. The trust acquired subsidiaries in Australia and New Zealand; in 1895, it obtained several Canadian firms. In 1901, a two-thirds interest was obtained in one of the leading German cigarette dealers. It also opened offices in Japan and built factories in China to accommodate the demand for its products.

Seeking to reduce competition in international markets, in 1902 the American Tobacco Company reached agreement with representatives of the Imperial Tobacco Company, which delimited the areas where each company could do business. The British-American Tobacco Company was formed, with assets of about thirty million dollars and an established network in the British Empire; Duke became its president.

In the course of his work, Duke had occasionally seen Mrs. Lillian McCredy, a divorced woman with a dubious reputation. In 1904, after some years of intermittent and rather surreptitious courtship, they were married in a small private ceremony. It was a troubled and tempestuous union; after ten months, Duke claimed that his wife had been unfaithful and sued for divorce. In a sensational trial, he offered the evidence of company detectives and intercepted messages from his wife's paramour. In 1906, the court found in Duke's favor. He was later introduced to Mrs. Nanaline Holt Inman, the widow of a cotton merchant from Atlanta. Duke was captivated by her expressive, classical features. She responded to his attentions, and in 1907 they were married in a small church in Brooklyn. Their daughter and only child, Doris, was born in 1912; during his later years, Duke displayed a pronounced fondness for her.

Shortly before his second marriage, Duke was confronted with the most serious challenge of his business career. The American Tobacco Company, which was estimated to control 80 percent of all tobacco production in the United States, was brought to court in antitrust litigation by the Department of Justice. In 1908, Duke himself was required to testify. A federal court found that the American Tobacco Company had indeed operated in restraint of trade. The Supreme Court upheld this ruling, and in 1911 the defendants were ordered to dissolve the trust. Accordingly, snuff and cigar companies were cut loose. R. J. Reynolds and Liggett and Myers were severed from the American Tobacco Company, which after reorganization held perhaps two-fifths of its previous assets.

Already Duke had diversified his business interests, and after the antitrust suits he turned with redoubled attention to concerns in his native region. In 1905 he had provided support for hydroelectric works along the Catawba River, which flows through the western portions of North and South Carolina. Between 1907 and 1925, eleven plants were built for the Southern Power Company, which in 1924 was rechristened the Duke Power Company. In short order, Duke also came to own textile mills that used the electricity his plants supplied. Against the advice of others in the business, Duke also underwrote the construction of a hydroelectric complex along the Saguenay River in Upper Quebec, and in time this venture became profitable.

Over the years, the Duke family contributed in increasing amounts to Trinity College, a small Methodist institution in North Carolina; in 1892 a subvention from Washington Duke supported work on a campus in Durham. James Buchanan Duke, though possessing only a limited formal education, increasingly had come to believe that institutions of higher learning held out the best hopes for widespread social progress. In 1918, he became one of Trinity's trustees. In collaboration with the college's president, William P. Few, plans were devised for a series of gothic buildings, including a magnificent chapel and tower. Duke personally supervised the selection of the local stone that was used; he took great interest in plans for a new medical center. In all, Duke contributed nineteen million dollars to the college, of which eight million dollars were offered when Few agreed to change its name to Duke University. (There is no substance to stories that previously Duke had made similar, unsuccessful, offers to Princeton, Yale, or other universities.)

During the year before he died, Duke composed a will establishing the Duke endowment, which in all comprised about eighty million dollars in securities and at that time was the largest permanent foundation of its sort in the nation. In addition to providing continuing support for Duke University, it also left substantial sums for other colleges, hospitals, orphanages, and Methodist churches in North Carolina. Much of the remainder of his estate was left to Duke's wife Nanaline and their daughter Doris. Duke himself suffered from pernicious anemia; after his health declined for several months he died, rather suddenly, on October 10, 1925, at his home in New York. Ultimately, he was buried in the chapel of the university to which he had given his name.

SIGNIFICANCE

Duke was an accomplished businessperson; it was said that for years he would work twelve hours a day in his office, and then visit tobacco stores to learn more about the retail trade. He was able to capitalize upon three major developments: He realized early the potential popularity of cigarettes; he utilized advertising nearly to the limit of its effectiveness; in an age in which manifold business combinations became possible, he proved to be a shrewd, hard-bitten bargainer able to form and direct massive industrial organizations to his own advantage. Even when antitrust proceedings compelled its reorganization, Duke was able to retain control of more parts of his original company than his opponents had thought possible.

Duke's persistent exploitation of the opportunities that existed in his day, in the tobacco industry and in power and textiles, indicated the combination of business sense and ruthlessness that accompanied his rise. His philanthropic endeavors, which have left lasting monuments to the Duke family fortune in his native state, were inspired by his own notions of social betterment. Although he owned several magnificent houses, and in his later years enjoyed the pleasures his wealth could

buy, Duke seemed intent on achieving recognition that, as he expressed it to the university's president, would last for a thousand years. Driven by personal imperatives to achieve business supremacy, and then to provide philanthropic support for an institution and an endowment bearing his name, Duke left an enduring legacy that attests the curious and complementary duality of his ambitions.

—J. R. Broadus

FURTHER READING

Cunningham, Bill. *On Bended Knees: The Night Rider Story*. Nashville, Tenn.: McClanahan, 1983. Vivid though awkwardly written history of the armed bands that arose to resist farmers' collaboration with the American Tobacco Company. Despite its somewhat melodramatic tone, this work reflects extensive research.

Durden, Robert F. *Bold Entrepreneur: A Life of James B. Duke*. Durham, N.C.: Carolina Academic Press, 2003. Durden has written several books about the Duke family and its business activities. This book is a meticulously researched scholarly biography of James Buchanan Duke, describing the full range of his life and activities, including his tobacco business, electric company, philanthropy, and interest in horticulture.

_____. *The Dukes of Durham: 1865-1929*. Durham, N.C.: Duke University Press, 1975. Sound scholarly study that uses a number of manuscript collections at Duke University. Avoiding extremes of adulation or debunking, this work considers both the business activities and the philanthropic concerns of the family; particular attention is paid to their support for educational institutions.

_____. *Electrifying the Piedmont Carolinas: The Duke Power Company, 1904-1997*. Durham, N.C.: Carolina Academic Press, 2001. A history of the Duke Power Company from its inception until 1997. Durden describes how the Company's hydroelectric power transformed the Piedmont Carolinas from a rural to an industrialized region and changed the life of the area's residents.

Kluger, Richard. *Ashes to Ashes: America's Hundred-Year Cigarette War, the Public Health, and the Unabashed Triumph of Philip Morris*. New York: Vintage Books, 1997. Pulitzer Prize-winning, exhaustively researched examination of the American tobacco industry. Includes information about Duke's tobacco business, setting it within the context of the industry's history.

Kroll, Harry Harrison. *Rider in the Night.* Philadelphia: University of Pennsylvania Press, 1965. Although brisk and informal, this work on conflict in the tobacco-growing regions of Kentucky and Tennessee is well informed and steeped in local color. While evoking the plight of the farmers, the author does not explicitly take sides in the confrontations he discusses.

Massell, David. *Amassing Power: J. B. Duke and the Saguenay River, 1897-1927.* Montreal, Que.: McGill-Queen's University Press, 2000. Describes the Duke Power Company's operations on the river, and how these operations set off a battle between the Company and Quebec officials over the use of river water.

Porter, Earl W. *Trinity and Duke, 1892-1924: Foundations of Duke University.* Durham, N.C.: Duke University Press, 1964. Comprehensive work on the creation of Duke University. The book traces the university's formative years as Trinity College and considers the involvement of educators and administrators in securing support from the Duke family.

Tilley, Nannie May. *The Bright-Tobacco Industry: 1860-1929.* Chapel Hill: University of North Carolina Press, 1948. Massive treatment of the subject that is important for the general context of Duke's business activities. Both the technical and the economic aspects of tobacco marketing during this period are discussed in great detail.

Winkler, John K. *Tobacco Tycoon: The Story of James Buchanan Duke.* New York: Random House, 1942. Detailed biography that is somewhat derogatory in tone, and that relies heavily upon earlier works, such as that of Jenkins (see above). Provocative in its treatment of the more scandalous periods of Duke's life, such as his divorce and his reaction to antitrust litigation.

SEE ALSO: Andrew Carnegie.

RELATED ARTICLE in *Great Events from History: The Nineteenth Century, 1801-1900:* 1813: Founding of McGill University.

ALEXANDRE DUMAS, *PÈRE*
French playwright and novelist

A major playwright who helped to revolutionize French drama and theater, Dumas was also one of the best historical novelists of the nineteenth century and published more than two hundred novels, including such enduring classics as The Three Musketeers, The Count of Monte Cristo, *and* The Man in the Iron Mask.

BORN: July 24, 1802; Villers-Cotterêts, France
DIED: December 5, 1870; Puys, France
AREAS OF ACHIEVEMENT: Literature, theater

EARLY LIFE

Alexandre Dumas (dew-mah) is usually designated *père* to distinguish him from his father and son of the same name. The son, known as Alexandre Dumas, *fils*, was also an important writer of drama and of fiction. Dumas's father was an impoverished, disillusioned general in Napoleon's Egyptian campaign. His prowess and exploits were models for the character Porthos and for many incidents in Dumas's works.

Dumas spent his boyhood in the village of his birth and in neighboring villages. Early influences were his father, poachers with whom he lived and hunted in the nearby forest, and the sight of Napoleon I en route to and from Waterloo. An early visit to Paris brought him into contact with his father's friends, all field marshals under Napoleon. Dumas's early learning was limited to reading and penmanship, later enhanced only slightly by attendance at Abbé Grégoire's village day school. Literary influences were a production of William Shakespeare's *Hamlet* and reading the works of Friedrich Schiller, Johann Wolfgang von Goethe, Sir Walter Scott, and George Gordon, Lord Byron. At the age of fifteen, he was a clerk in a solicitor's office. At the age of eighteen, he met and collaborated on three vaudevilles with Adolphe de Leuven, a young Swedish aristocrat, who awakened him to drama. At this time he became a clerk to M. Lefèvre at Crépy.

In late 1822, following Leuven's return to Paris to attempt to stage the plays, Dumas and a fellow clerk went to Paris alternating walking and riding the clerk's horse, poaching game en route to barter for lodgings. At Paris, Dumas saw the Théâtre Française, met the famous actor François-Joseph Talma, attended a play, and received a touch on the forehead for luck; Leuven had been instrumental in arranging the meeting. Returning home, Dumas quit his job, pooled his assets, and re-embarked for Paris, this time in a coach.

LIFE'S WORK

After a series of successes and failures, Dumas became a major writer in several genres. His literary reputation rests primarily on his novels, his plays, his memoirs, and his many travel books, in which he recorded his experiences in as well as his impressions of Italy, Spain, Switzerland, Russia, Germany, the south of France, and Egypt.

Although Dumas published some fiction and other works between 1823 and 1844, he was primarily a playwright. His early success resulted partly from the acquaintances he made and partly from good luck. His first job at Paris was as a copyist for the duke of Orléans, the future King Louis-Philippe, in whose palace was housed an important theater, the Comédie-Française. On attending the Théâtre-Française, Dumas met the famous writer-theater critic Charles Nodier. Leading actresses often found Dumas attractive, and some were among his mistresses; Talma and other leading actors became his lifelong friends. Political figures, including the Marquis de Lafayette and Giuseppe Garibaldi, were his close associates and his commanders in two wars.

Dumas found his dramatic calling with *Christine* (1830). Seeing a bas-relief depicting an assassination or-

Alexandre Dumas, père. (Library of Congress)

dered by Queen Christina of Sweden, he studied the incident in a borrowed book. Collaborating with Leuven (the first of many collaborators for Dumas), he wrote the five-act verse drama in 1829. Through Nodier's influence, the play was accepted for staging, though such was delayed until the following year. Another historical drama, *Henri III et sa cour* (1829; *Catherine of Cleves*, 1831) was produced first. This work is historically significant because Dumas for the first time applied the methods of Sir Walter Scott to drama. A third important serious drama, *Antony*, was to appear in 1831 (English translation, 1904).

When the revolution of 1830 began, Dumas began his career as a soldier, following duty and his current mistress to Villers-Cotterêts and Soissons and leading insurgents to victory at his birthplace. At Soissons, he and two students stormed and took an arsenal, recovering powder kegs in the face of a garrison. Disillusioned that his commander and friend Lafayette allowed Louis-Philippe to be chosen king and spurning minor posts offered him, he resigned from the new king's employ. The next year, his first child was born by Belle Krebsamer, another mistress.

Events of interest during 1832 and 1833 included a dispute over billing for *La Tour de Nesle*, which was a rewriting by Dumas of an inferior play by Frédéric Gaillardet, the latter being given first billing, and M. Three Stars (Dumas) second; after the latter was given top billing, Gaillardet went to court and also challenged Dumas to a duel. About the same time, Dumas inadvertently discovered the cure for cholera when he mistakenly took undiluted ether. During Mardi Gras, Dumas gave an extended dinner party to which important artists, writers, actors, and actresses were invited. Drawing on his boyhood acquaintances, the poachers, and bartering the excess of game for other provisions, Dumas did the cooking and fed more than one hundred guests.

Dumas returned to the theater to stage *Antony* and his most popular serious drama, *La Tour de Nesle* (1832; English translation, 1906). In 1841, he turned to comedy, staging two of his three best that year, *Mademoiselle de Belle-Isle* (1839; *Gabrielle de Belle Isle*, 1842) and *Un Mariage sous Louis XV* (1841; *A Marriage of Convenience*, 1899). The third was staged in 1843; later, in 1855, it was selected as a command performance by Queen Victoria upon her and Prince Albert's visit to Paris.

Though Dumas had published fiction earlier and drama later, the real shift to fiction came in 1842, with the publication of his first great historical novel, *Le Chevalier d'Harmental* (1843; English translation, 1856). The following years saw the publication of his most pop-

DUMAS'S MAJOR WORKS

Novels

1843	*Le Chevalier d'Harmental* (with Auguste Maquet; *The Chevalier d'Harmental*, 1856)
1844	*Les Frères corses* (*The Corsican Brothers*, 1880)
1844	*Gabriel Lambert* (*The Galley Slave*, 1849; also as *Gabriel Lambert*, 1904)
1844	*Les Trois Mousquetaires* (*The Three Musketeers*, 1846)
1844-1845	*Le Comte de Monte-Cristo* (*The Count of Monte-Cristo*, 1846)
1845	*Vingt Ans après* (with Maquet; *Twenty Years After*, 1846)
1845-1846	*La Guerre des femmes* (*Nanon*, 1847; also as *The War of Women*, 1895)
1846	*Le Bâtard de Mauléon* (*The Bastard of Mauléon*, 1848)
1848	*Les Quarante-cinq* (with Maquet; *The Forty-five Guardsmen*, 1847)
1848-1850	*Le Vicomte de Bragelonne* (with Maquet; *The Vicomte de Bragelonne*, 1857; also as 3 volumes: *The Vicomte de Bragelonne*, 1893; *Louise de la Vallière*, 1893; and *The Man in the Iron Mask*, 1893)
1850	*La Tulipe noire* (with Maquet and Paul Lacroix; *The Black Tulip*, 1851)
1851	*Ange Pitou* (*Six Years Later*, 1851; also as *Ange Pitou*, 1859)
1852	*Conscience l'Innocent* (*Conscience*, 1905)
1852	*Mes Mémoires* (*My Memoirs*, 1907-1909)
1860	*Black* (*Black: The Story of a Dog*, 1895)

Drama

Years in left column are earliest dates of production or publication.

1829	*Henri III et sa cour* (*Catherine of Cleves*, 1831; also known as *Henry III and His Court*, 1904)
1830	*Christine: Ou, Stockholm, Fontainebleau, et Rome*
1831	*Antony* (English translation, 1904)
1832	*La Tour de Nesle* (English translation, 1906)
1839	*Mademoiselle de Belle-Isle* (English translation, 1855)
1841	*Un Mariage sous Louis XV* (*A Marriage of Convenience*, 1899)

ular, though not regarded as his best, novels, *Les Trois Mousquetaires* (1844; *The Three Musketeers*, 1846), *Le Comte de Monte-Cristo* (1844-1845; *The Count of Monte-Cristo*, 1846), and *La Tulipe Noire* (1850; *The Black Tulip*, 1851).

Dumas's recognized best novels are not always as well known. *Le Vicomte de Bragelonne* (1848-1850; English translation, 1857), perhaps the most popular of these, is the sequel to *Vingt Ans après* (1845; *Twenty Years After*, 1846) and *The Three Musketeers*, forming with them a trilogy. As noted in the publishing dates, Dumas, like Charles Dickens, often issued his novels in serial form in journals. The following are also among his best works in this genre of historical fiction, *Les Quarante-cinq* (1848; *The Forty-five Guardsmen*, 1847), *Ange Pitou* (1851; *Six Years Later*, 1851), *Black* (1860; *Black: The Story of a Dog*, 1895), and *Conscience l'Innocent* (1852; *Conscience*, 1905).

In January of 1860, Dumas met Garibaldi and traveled with a letter from him. Dumas purchased a schoo-

ner, *The Emma*, sailing the Mediterranean with friends. Eventually, he joined Garibaldi's campaign with the same spectacular success he and his father had previously enjoyed in Egypt and France. In freeing Naples from the Bourbons, he avenged his father of the imprisonment and torture he had suffered at their hands. In Palermo, Dumas was popular as a writer and a hero until the political climate changed: Garibaldi, like Napoleon and Lafayette before him, swerved from complete dedication to republicanism. After supporting and later criticizing Garibaldi publicly, Dumas returned to Paris.

Having been regarded as the most important playwright and now the most famous novelist in France, the aging Dumas found his luck failing him. Having made a fortune and having wasted it through his lavish lifestyle and his unbridled generosity, he worked furiously trying to save his palatial estate and his tarnished reputation. As his method had always been to work with collaborators who supplied ideas and minor works, or who provided details and basic plots, to which Dumas gave his touch of literary genius, he was now faced with accusations and even suits charging him with plagiarism.

Posterity has vindicated Dumas, because none of his collaborators has achieved anything of note unaided by him. His prolific productions came to be expanded by his need for money: He published novels in serials; he wrote accounts of his many travels (regarded as among the best travel literature); and he wrote and published *Mes Mémoires* (1852; *My Memoirs,* 1907-1909), sharing numerous details of his own experiences and observations as well as information about the people he had known, who numbered among them the most famous of his day. Eventually, after further travel, he lingered and died in bed at his son's estate in Puys.

SIGNIFICANCE

In writing about Alexandre Dumas, *père,* one is overwhelmed not only by the amount that he wrote (estimates run from seven hundred to more than one thousand volumes) but also by the great volume of information, often of much interest, about the man, his family, and his famous acquaintances. He, like his characters, was lavish, demonstrative, flamboyant, wealthy, and generous, as well as quarrelsome and forgiving.

A quadroon, Dumas was descended from paternal grandparents of the lower aristocracy and of West Indian black ancestry. His physical appearance changed from slender and military to portly with a large overhanging belly. He had fuzzy hair, thick lips, and blue eyes. His tastes in clothing were extravagant. After being rebuked for presenting his mistress Ida Ferrier to the king, he was boxed into an unwanted marriage, which, as was his wont, he graciously accepted. He would have publicly acknowledged all three of his illegitimate children, but the mother of his younger daughter refused to permit this. His friend Victor Hugo lacked his fame but surpassed him in poetic ability. The two share credit for revolutionizing the theater of France.

—*George W. Van Devender*

FURTHER READING

Bell, A. Craig. *Alexandre Dumas: A Biography and a Study.* London: Cassell, 1950. Attempts to vindicate the genius of Dumas in the light of hostile critics, flippant biographers, and neglectful literary historians. Lists authentic and spurious works and provides an index.

Castelar, Emilio. "Alexandre Dumas." In *The Life of Lord Byron, and Other Sketches.* Translated by Mrs. Arthur Arnold. New York: Harper & Row, 1876. A chapter of rhythmic prose on Dumas in a collection containing a lengthy life of Lord Byron and brief treatments of Dumas, Hugo, and three lesser-known writers.

Dumas, Alexandre. *An Autobiography-Anthology Including the Best of Dumas.* Edited by Guy Endore. Garden City, N.Y.: Doubleday, 1962. As the title suggests, included are excerpts from Dumas's own works, from *My Memoirs,* travel books, prose fiction, and others, interspersed with introductory comments by the editor, providing a running commentary on the life, writing career, and particular works.

_____. *The Road to Monte Cristo: A Condensation from the Memoirs of Alexandre Dumas.* Translated by Jules Eckert Goodman. New York: Charles Scribner's Sons, 1956. Goodman finds in the more than three thousand pages of the six volumes of the memoirs two types of material: much matter of lesser importance, because Dumas was paid by the line in his later years, and, interspersed among this matter, much that makes up an exciting and intriguing autobiography of Dumas for thirty years.

Foote-Greenwell, Victoria. "The Life and Resurrection of Alexandre Dumas." *Smithsonian* 27, no. 4 (July, 1996): 110. Discusses Dumas's life and the problems he experienced as the grandson of a Haitian slave.

Maurois, André. *Alexandre Dumas: A Great Life in Brief.* Translated by Jack Palmer White. New York: Alfred A. Knopf, 1964. Provides the basic facts in readable and limited fashion for readers seeking an introduction to Dumas's life and work. Maurois is one of the recognized authorities on Dumas.

_____. *The Titans: A Three-Generation Biography of the Dumas.* Translated by Gerard Hopkins. New York: Harper & Row, 1957. Emphasis in the first of ten parts is devoted to Dumas and his young son. Parts 2 through 6 focus on Dumas, *père,* 7 and 8 on *père* and *fils,* 9 and 10 on *fils.* The same work was published in England under the title *Three Musketeers.*

Schopp, Claude. *Alexandre Dumas: Genius of Life.* Translated by A. J. Koch. New York: Franklin Watts, 1988. Schopp provides a broad panoramic view of Dumas's life, which combined elements of farce and tragedy equal to any of the author's books.

SEE ALSO: Victor Hugo; Adah Isaacs Menken; Lola Montez; Jules Verne.

RELATED ARTICLE in *Great Events from History: The Nineteenth Century, 1801-1900:* March 3, 1830: Hugo's *Hernani* Incites Rioting.

JEAN-HENRI DUNANT
Swiss humanitarian

One of the most effective humanitarians of his time, Dunant won the Nobel Peace Prize for his work in founding the International Red Cross and was also a cofounder of the World's Young Men's Christian Association.

BORN: May 8, 1828; Geneva, Switzerland
DIED: October, 30, 1910; Heiden, Switzerland
AREA OF ACHIEVEMENT: Social reform

EARLY LIFE

The eldest of five children, Jean-Henri Dunant (dew-NAHN) was born in Geneva, Switzerland, at a time when there was great concern for a variety of humanitarian issues. His father, Jean-Jacques Dunant, was a prominent businessperson who held a position in the Office of Guardianships and Trusteeships, where he was charged with the welfare of prisoners and their families. His mother, Antoinette Colladon, nurtured his religious convictions and liberal humanitarian concerns. Dunant's interest in social issues was fostered early. At the age of six, an encounter with chained convicts so moved him that he vowed someday to help them. At thirteen, he was admitted to Geneva College.

At eighteen, Dunant became active in the League of Alms, a Christian organization whose members sought to aid Geneva's underprivileged, ill, and imprisoned, and he soon assumed a leadership role. In 1855, Dunant proposed international guidelines for a federation of Young Men's Christian Associations.

During that same period (1853-1859), Dunant was trying to earn his living in the banking profession. In the course of his work, he was sent to Algeria to manage the bank's interests, and there he succeeded in persuading many wealthy and influential Genevans and French to invest in the mills at Mons-Djémila. He sought additional land and water concessions from the French government but was unable to gain his ends. Undaunted, in the spring of 1859 Dunant set out to bring his ideas for Algeria to the French emperor Napoleon III, who was then on a campaign in Italy. Dunant followed the advancing French troops through northern Italy. Although he never met the emperor, his trip would set in motion a series of events that would forever change the way conflicts would be waged.

LIFE'S WORK

On June 24, 1859, in pursuit of the emperor, Dunant arrived in the town of Castiglione. All that day, only a few miles to the west, 150,000 French and Allied forces and 170,000 Austrian troops were waging one of the bloodiest conflicts of the nineteenth century, the Battle of Solferino.

Although it is not clear whether Dunant ever saw the fighting, he did see the casualties, estimated at forty thousand. He was so moved by the carnage and suffering that he spent the next eight days treating the wounded, seeking doctors, and procuring necessary medical supplies and food for the wounded of both sides. To the hundreds of wounded Dunant helped, the slender, handsome, dark-haired man in white became their symbol of hope. These eight days would serve as the focus for the remainder of Dunant's life.

After returning to Geneva, Dunant continued his business ventures but remained haunted by Solferino. In November, 1862, Dunant published *Un Souvenir de Solferino* (*A Memory of Solferino*, 1939), describing the plight of the wounded and proposing an organization of trained volunteers to aid them. Copies of the book were sent to influential people across Europe.

Response to Dunant's book was profound. Gustave Moynier, a Geneva lawyer, recommended that a special committee be organized to promote Dunant's plans on an international scale. That permanent international committee consisted of Dunant, Moynier, Guillaume-Henri Dufour, Louis Appia, and Theodore Maunoir. The committee proposed an international conference to be convened in Geneva on October 26. During the summer of 1863, Dunant traveled throughout Europe, artfully persuading government after government to send representatives to the Geneva meeting. This conference was followed in August, 1864, by a second, officially sponsored by the Swiss government. The product of this second conference was an international treaty, the first of the Geneva Conventions, which served as the foundation for the International Red Cross and set guidelines for the treatment and status of the wounded during wars.

Dunant's role in the conference was insignificant. His strengths were in his ideas and in dealing with people on an individual basis. Some sources suggest that Dunant did not even attend the meetings of the second conference, but such accounts appear unfounded. As the conference came to a close, Dunant had to turn his attention to his own financial problems. Since his visit to Solferino, he had not paid enough attention to his Algerian investments.

Dunant's only hope for his ailing Mons-Djémila ventures was to get concessions from the French government. However, even a meeting with the emperor in 1865 proved futile. In 1867, a rapid chain of events would lead Dunant to bankruptcy. During the early 1860's, Geneva had been hailing Dunant as one of its greatest sons, but after 1867, as the Calvinistic principles of the time dictated for the crime of bankruptcy, Genevans turned their backs on Dunant. Under these same rigid principles, he could never return to Geneva. In addition, under extreme pressure from Moynier, from whom he had become alienated, on August 25, 1867, Dunant was forced to resign from the international committee.

The period 1867-1887 was one of steady decline for Dunant, as he became an exile wandering about Europe. There were times when he was able to afford neither housing nor regular meals, and he slept on park benches or in train stations. However, he continued to work for a variety of causes, including a Jewish homeland in Palestine, a world library, and a broadening of the Geneva Conventions to include guidelines for conducting warfare at sea and for treatment of prisoners of war.

As his means for survival slowly ebbed and a variety of health problems sapped his vitality, his brother Pierre brought him home to Switzerland. For the last twenty-four years of his life, the small village of Heiden would be Dunant's home. Extreme bitterness and an intense paranoia made even the closest relationships difficult for Dunant.

In 1895, Dunant allowed a young Swiss journalist to interview him. Largely because of these published interviews, the world became aware that the founder of the Red Cross was still alive. Although virtually forgotten for nearly thirty years, he now received honors. The culmination of these occurred in 1901, when Dunant, along with Frédéric Passy, was awarded the first Nobel Peace Prize. Dunant died on October 30, 1910. In accordance with the conditions of his exile, Dunant's ashes were buried in an unmarked grave in Zurich.

SIGNIFICANCE

The life of Jean-Henri Dunant is one of profound irony. On one hand, he was an idealistic humanitarian, who changed the conduct of warfare forever and who must be credited with the saving of millions of lives. The International Red Cross, the Geneva Conventions, and the Young Men's Christian Association stand as monuments to his great vision. On the other, he was a tragic victim of his own weaknesses. He experienced the tributes of royalty and the pain of extreme poverty.

Nevertheless, Dunant was consistent in the belief that he could make a difference in the world. In 1906 and 1926, the Geneva Conventions were expanded to cover the victims of naval warfare and prisoners of war, respectively, causes that Dunant had championed since the late 1860's. For his many accomplishments, it is only fitting that each year the world celebrates May 8, his birthday, as World Red Cross Day.

—Ronald D. Tyler

FURTHER READING

Deming, Richard. *Heroes of the International Red Cross.* New York: E. P. Dutton, 1969. Chapter 1 provides a condensed biography of Dunant that emphasizes his role as the founder of the Red Cross.

Dunant, Jean-Henri. *A Memory of Solferino.* Washington, D.C.: American National Red Cross, 1959. A short, moving description of the Battle of Solferino, Dunant's role in the aftermath, and the genesis of the principles that would ultimately inspire formation of the International Red Cross.

Gagnebin, Bernard, and Marc Gazay. *Encounter with Henry Dunant.* Translated by Bernard C. Swift. Geneva, Switzerland: Georg Geneva, 1963. A short, readable account of Dunant's life, supplemented by photographs, paintings, maps, and photocopies of published and unpublished manuscripts.

Hutchinson, John F. *Champions of Charity: War and the Rise of the Red Cross.* Boulder, Colo.: Westview Press, 1996. Examines the organization's operations during the twentieth century, until the end of World War I. Hutchinson argues that the Red Cross initially tried to make war more humane, but eventually supported militarism. He describes how the organization launched campaigns to encourage women's involvement on the "home front" and to make war seem like a normal and desirable activity.

Libby, Violet Kelway. *Henry Dunant: Prophet of Peace.* New York: Pageant Press, 1964. A longer biography that focuses on how the evolution of the religious and business climate within Dunant's Geneva both provided an ideal atmosphere to foster his humanitarian concerns and severely punished him for his business failings. Includes a short list of other sources.

Moorehead, Caroline. *Dunant's Dream: War, Switzerland, and the History of the Red Cross.* New York: Carroll & Graf, 1999. Describes how Dunant founded the Red Cross and analyzes how the organization has responded to conflicts, issues, and moral dilemmas. Moorehead, who was given access to previously closed archival records, is critical of the International Committee that runs the organization, and charges that some of the committee's decisions have been ambiguous and politically motivated.

Peachment, Brian. *The Red Cross Story: The Life of Henry Dunant.* Elmsford, N.Y.: Pergamon Press, 1977. A brief account of Dunant's life, intended for younger readers.

Rich, Josephine. *Jean Henri Dunant: Founder of the International Red Cross.* New York: Julian Messner, 1956. A biography that focuses particularly on Dunant's relationships with his family. Also emphasizes

Henri's lifelong concern with social causes.

Rothkopf, Carol Z. *Jean Henri Dunant: Father of the Red Cross.* New York: Franklin Watts, 1969. Follows Dunant's life but focuses on how the principles behind the Red Cross are deeply rooted in history. Provides a modest secondary bibliography.

SEE ALSO: Clara Barton; Bertha von Suttner.

RELATED ARTICLE in *Great Events from History: The Nineteenth Century, 1801-1900:* August 22, 1864: International Red Cross Is Launched.

PAUL LAURENCE DUNBAR
American writer

Dunbar's writing is recognized as providing the most authentic representations of African American life in the United States during the late nineteenth and early twentieth centuries.

BORN: June 27, 1872; Dayton, Ohio
DIED: February 9, 1906; Dayton, Ohio
AREA OF ACHIEVEMENT: Literature

EARLY LIFE

Paul Laurence Dunbar's parents, Joshua and Matilda Murphy Dunbar, were slaves until the early or mid-1860's. Matilda had been married to another slave, Willis Murphy, with whom she had two sons, both born in slavery. Willis, who joined the Union army and was never heard from again, sent his wife and sons to Dayton, Ohio, where they remained, presuming Willis was dead. Matilda, ever eager to learn, attended night school. She soon became literate and mastered enough mathematics to keep her own accounts. In 1871, Matilda married Joshua Dunbar, who was twenty years her senior. In the following year, their first child, Paul Laurence Dunbar, was born.

Joshua never tired of telling his young son about his exploits, about how he clandestinely learned to read and write when slaves were punished, sometimes even killed, for trying to achieve literacy. Joshua recounted to his fascinated son details about his escape from slavery with the help of abolitionists via the Underground Railroad and his subsequent enlistment in the Fifty-fifth Division of the Union army, where he achieved the rank of sergeant. The tales Joshua wove eventually found their

way into Dunbar's writing, which his mother had encouraged from Dunbar's earliest days. When Joshua and Matilda's second child, Elizabeth, died before her first birthday, Matilda focused all her attention and centered all of her hopes upon Paul.

Meanwhile, Joshua, unable to find work despite being literate and having a spotless military record, began to drink, causing dissension in the household. To relieve tension, Matilda spun tales about plantation life, which helped create a basis for much of Dunbar's later writing. Matilda finally divorced Joshua, after which Joshua spent his remaining years in the Soldier's Retirement Home in Dayton, where Dunbar often visited him.

Dunbar, who was the only African American in his high school graduating class, was class president and class poet. While still in high school, Dunbar published poetry in the *Dayton Herald* and worked as an editor for the *Dayton Tattler.* One of his fellow students was Orville Wright, who, along with his brother Wilbur, constructed and flew the first airplane. Dunbar and Orville remained good friends throughout their lifetimes.

Too poor to attend college, Dunbar discovered that Dayton offered few desirable jobs to African Americans at that time. He finally took a job as an elevator operator, which gave him time to write. He produced a number of stories and poems during this period, some of them written in the black-dialect style that first drew national attention to his writing.

Dunbar was invited to address the Western Association of Writers at its 1892 convention in Dayton. This initial appearance was arranged by Helen Truesdell, one of Dunbar's high school English teachers. At this meeting,

Paul Laurence Dunbar. (Library of Congress)

Dunbar met James Newton Matthews, who wrote a letter praising Dunbar's writing. This letter was published in an Illinois newspaper and was subsequently reprinted in newspapers throughout the United States, bringing Dunbar considerable celebrity. James Whitcomb Riley read Matthews's letter and wrote an admiring letter to Dunbar. It was the encouragement the young poet received from Matthews and Riley that led him to collect his poems into the volume *Oak and Ivy* (1893). Printed at Dunbar's own expense, the poet quickly repaid the $125 printing costs by selling copies of the collection to people who rode his elevator.

LIFE'S WORK

The publication of *Oak and Ivy* changed the course of Dunbar's life. The collection contained many poems in standard English, which had been drilled into the young Dunbar by his mother. His "Ode to Ethiopia" remains among his most influential poems, recording as it does the accomplishments of African Americans and entreating them to have pride in their race. "Sympathy" focused on the dismal status of black people in American society. The poems that caught the attention of the white commu-

nity, however, were the collection's dialect poems that presented vivid portraits of plantation life and ruminated on the feelings of both free and enslaved black people. Many members of the black community resented Dunbar's dialect poems, arguing that they presented black people as uneducated, illiterate buffoons much like the exaggerated black characters presented by the minstrels of that day. On the other hand, white readers, some of them prominent in literary circles, applauded the dialect poems while dismissing Dunbar's poems in standard English as derivative and ordinary.

Oak and Ivy brought Dunbar to the attention of a prosperous Toledo attorney, Charles A. Thatcher, who was sufficiently impressed by Dunbar's writing that he offered to pay the poet's expenses if he wished to attend Harvard University. Bent on promoting his career as a writer, however, Dunbar rejected Thatcher's generous offer. Thatcher, nevertheless, did what he could to advance Dunbar's career, as did Thatcher's friend, Toledo psychiatrist Henry A. Tobey, who helped Dunbar through many difficult periods by lending him money and promoting his books.

Thatcher and Tobey encouraged Dunbar to publish a second volume of verse, *Majors and Minors* (1895). The book was divided into two sections: "Majors," or poems in standard English, and "Minors," or dialect poems. The publication of this volume drew considerable praise from William Dean Howells, probably the most prominent man of letters in the United States at that time. Although Howells's criticism of Dunbar's poems in standard English was somewhat dismissive, he heaped praise upon the dialect poems, calling Dunbar "the first man of his color to study his race objectively." The authenticity that Howells found in the dialect poems stemmed directly from Dunbar's early exposure to the tales his father and mother spun for him as he was growing up.

The publication of *Majors and Minors* marked the emergence of Dunbar as a nationally significant literary figure. Through Thatcher and Tobey, he was accepted as a client by Major James B. Pond, a New York City literary agent who represented such illustrious authors as Mark Twain, Henry Ward Beecher, and Frederick Douglass, whom Dunbar had met in 1893 and to whom he was close until Douglass's death in 1895. Pond persuaded Dunbar to leave Dayton and move to New York, which Paul did in the summer of 1896. Pond arranged numerous engagements for Dunbar to speak and to read his poetry. More important, however, he introduced him to publishers who were eager to offer him contracts.

Finally, Dodd, Mead offered Dunbar a four-hundred-dollar advance against royalties (an astronomical advance for a poet to receive at that time) and a generous royalty arrangement. The book for which Dodd, Mead contracted, *Lyrics of Lowly Life* (1896), which essentially drew poems from his two earlier volumes, was a resounding success among white readers and clearly established Dunbar as the leading black poet of his day. The success of this book led to a six-month reading tour of England.

Dunbar realized that the move to New York had been wise. Meanwhile, he began a correspondence with Alice Ruth Moore, a writer and teacher with whom he had fallen in love. Alice's parents discouraged her from marrying a writer whose income was uncertain at best. In 1897, however, Dunbar received a clerkship at the Library of Congress, affording him the means to marry Alice. The two moved to Washington, D.C., where Dunbar published his first collection of short stories, *Folks from Dixie* (1898), whose incisive insights into racial prejudice were well received by liberal white audiences.

Critics dismissed Dunbar's first novel, *The Uncalled* (1898), based on Nathaniel Hawthorne's *The Scarlet Letter* (1850), as trite and unconvincing. The book received little popular acceptance. The following year, however, a new collection of his poems, *Lyrics of the Hearthside* (1899), redeemed his literary reputation.

Long plagued by lung and respiratory problems made worse by Washington's climate and by the dust from the books he constantly handled at the Library of Congress, Dunbar was forced to quit his job in 1898. He immediately undertook another lecture tour, but within a few months his health had deteriorated so badly that he had to move first to New York's Catskill Mountains and then to Colorado for long periods of rest.

In *The Strength of Gideon, and Other Stories* (1900), which presented disturbing vignettes about black people during the days of slavery and emancipation that followed, Dunbar wrote passionately but without his usual humor about racial injustice. His next novel, *The Love of Landry* (1900), dealt with white characters and was generally unconvincing. His next novel, *The Fanatics* (1901), also focused on white characters and presented its minor black characters as

---

"REPRESENTATIVE AMERICAN NEGROES"

In 1903, Paul Laurence Dunbar was invited to contribute an article on "Representative American Negroes" to a collection of essays by such distinguished African Americans as Charles W. Chesnutt, W. E. B. Du Bois, and Booker T. Washington. This extract from the opening of his article reveals something of both his ideas on that subject and his writing style.

In considering who and what are representative Negroes there are circumstances which compel one to question what is a representative man of the colored race. Some men are born great, some achieve greatness and others lived during the reconstruction period. To have achieved something for the betterment of his race rather than for the aggrandizement of himself, seems to be a man's best title to be called representative. The street corner politician, who through questionable methods or even through skillful manipulation, succeeds in securing the janitorship of the Court House, may be written up in the local papers as "representative," but is he?

I have in mind a young man in Baltimore, Bernard Taylor by name, who to me is more truly representative of the race than half of the "Judges," "Colonels," "Doctors" and "Honorables" whose stock cuts burden the pages of our negro journals week after week. I have said that he is young. Beyond that he is quiet and unobtrusive; but quiet as he is, the worth of his work can be somewhat estimated when it is known that he has set the standard for young men in a city that has the largest colored population in the world.

It is not that as an individual he has ridden to success one enterprise after another. It is not that he has shown capabilities far beyond his years, nor yet that his personal energy will not let him stop at one triumph. The importance of him lies in the fact that his influence upon his fellows is all for good, and in a large community of young Negroes the worth of this cannot be over-estimated. He has taught them that striving is worth while, and by the very force of his example of industry and perseverance, he stands out from the mass. He does not tell how to do things, he does them. Nothing has contributed more to his success than his alertness, and nothing has been more closely followed by his observers, and yet I sometimes wonder when looking at him, how old he must be, how world weary, before the race turns from its worship of the political janitor and says of him, "this is one of our representative men."

This, however, is a matter of values and neither the negro himself, his friends, his enemies, his lauders, nor his critics has grown quite certain in appraising these. . . .

Source: Paul Laurence Dunbar, "Representative American Negroes," in *The Negro Problem: A Series of Articles by Representative American Negroes of Today* (New York, 1903).

caricatures. It was dismissed as an inconsequential work. Despite these setbacks, Dunbar was sufficiently esteemed to be an honored guest at the inauguration of President William McKinley in 1901.

Dunbar's last novel, *The Sport of Gods* (1902), was a strident protest novel focusing on a black servant falsely accused of theft who was vindicated only after serving time in prison and seeing his family disintegrate. It was followed by three more collections of poetry, bringing the total number of volumes of verse he produced in his lifetime to fourteen. Racked by illness, Dunbar controlled his pain by drinking. When Alice left him in 1902, Dunbar returned to Dayton, where he continued to write and from which he still made occasional speaking trips. His lungs destroyed by tuberculosis, he died in Dayton on February 9, 1906.

SIGNIFICANCE

Paul Laurence Dunbar brought views of plantation life, slavery, and racial inequality to a white reading public and became an influential voice in the struggle of black citizens to obtain their rightful place in American society. Dunbar also established black dialect as a reputable and legitimate literary vehicle, even though many black readers in his day, including his own wife, considered it demeaning and much preferred the work he produced in standard English.

—*R. Baird Shuman*

FURTHER READING

Alexander, Eleanor. *Lyrics of Sunshine and Shadow: The Tragic Courtship and Marriage of Paul Laurence Dunbar and Alice Ruth Moore: A History of Love and Violence Among the African American Elite.* New York: New York University Press, 2001. Describes the tempestuous romance of the celebrated African American literary couple. Alexander places the couple's courtship and marriage within the context of nineteenth century social conventions, both inside and outside the African American community.

Gentry, Tony. *Paul Laurence Dunbar: Poet.* Los Angeles: Melrose Square, 1993. Provides information about Dunbar's life and literary career, with excerpts from his works and many illustrations. Aimed at younger and student readers and people unfamiliar with Dunbar.

Hudson, Gossie Harold. *A Biography of Paul Laurence Dunbar.* Baltimore: Gateway Press, 1999. Comprehensive, detailed account of Dunbar's life. Contains biographical references.

McKissack, Patricia C. *Paul Laurence Dunbar: A Poet to Remember.* Chicago: Children's Press, 1984. Directed toward an adolescent audience, this book provides an accurate and engaging overview of Dunbar's life and writing.

Martin, Jay, ed. *Singers in the Dawn: Reinterpretations of Paul Laurence Dunbar.* New York: Dodd, Mead, 1972. Valuable contributions by scholars who participated in the Centenary Conference on Paul Laurence Dunbar at the University of California, Irvine, in 1972. Balanced and intellectually sound.

Redding, J. Saunders. *To Make a Poet Black.* Chapel Hill: University of North Carolina Press, 1939. This critical assessment by a major black author demonstrates the black bias against Dunbar's dialectal writing and the preference for his writing in standard English.

Revell, Peter. *Paul Laurence Dunbar.* Boston: Twayne, 1979. Following the usual format of Twayne's United States Authors Series, Revell presents a readable and accurate account of the author, his work, and his critical reception.

Wiggins, Lida Keck. *The Life and Works of Paul Laurence Dunbar.* Nashville, Tenn.: Winston-Derek Publishers, 1992. This profusely illustrated volume contains Dunbar's complete poetry and his best stories and anecdotes. It also includes William Dean Howells's introduction to *Lyrics of Lowly Life* and Wiggins's complete biography of Dunbar.

SEE ALSO: Frederick Douglass; Joel Chandler Harris; Nathaniel Hawthorne; Harriet Beecher Stowe.

RELATED ARTICLE in *Great Events from History: The Nineteenth Century, 1801-1900:* 1852: Stowe Publishes *Uncle Tom's Cabin.*

ELEUTHÈRE IRÉNÉE DU PONT
American industrialist

Combining sharp business acumen with innovative technical methods and tenacious moral principles, du Pont founded E. I. du Pont de Nemours and Company, which became a powerful commercial empire that endured into the twenty-first century.

BORN: June 24, 1771; Paris, France
DIED: October 31, 1834; Philadelphia, Pennsylvania
AREA OF ACHIEVEMENT: Business

EARLY LIFE

Eleuthère Irénée du Pont (ay-lew-tahr ee-ray-nay dew-pahn) was born on June 24, 1771, in Paris, France. He was named in honor of liberty and peace (after the Greek words for these ideals) at the insistence of his godfather, Turgot, who was also his father's benefactor. His father, Pierre Samuel du Pont, served the corrupt French throne for many years and was rewarded with nobility. His mother, Nicole Charlotte Marie Le Dée, died when Irénée was fourteen years old. He also had an older brother, Victor, to whom he was very close. Irénée grew up at the family estate at Bois-des-Fosses, about sixty miles south of Paris.

Irénée spent all of his young life in the harsh and oppressive political atmosphere of France during the epochs of Louis XVI, of the revolutionary mobs whose favorite instrument was the guillotine, and finally of Napoleon Bonaparte. After the death of his mother, Irénée's life became closely interwoven with that of his politically active father. In 1788, when Irénée was seventeen years old, the popular rebellion took place. As the nation's ideology was more and more identified with the political Left, Pierre remained on the Right.

Irénée and the Marquis de Lafayette, with whom he shared the title of commander of the National Guard, founded the Société de 1789, an organization constituting the most conservative wing of the bourgeoisie that favored a constitutional monarchy. Pierre and Irénée began to attack the Jacobins, the radical party of the petite bourgeoisie, from their newly acquired publishing house in Paris. On August 10, 1792, they led their sixty-man private guard to defend the king's palace from a Jacobinian assault that was demanding an end to the monarchy. During this period, at the age of twenty, Irénée married Sophie Madeleine Dalmas, with whom he had seven children during the course of their marriage.

After the uprising, Irénée served as apprentice to the chemist Antoine Lavoisier, the greatest scientist of his day and a close friend of his father. Lavoisier was the head of the French monarch's gunpowder mills, and it was there that Irénée learned the craft of gunpowder-making and acquired a precise sense of the scientific method. The revolution struck, however, and the king and Lavoisier were guillotined per the orders of Robespierre. Pierre was arrested shortly thereafter and would have also been guillotined had not the bourgeoisie, now convinced that their revolution was irreversible, asserted their control over the revolution by seizing power from the radicals. Robespierre was executed and Pierre was granted his freedom.

At this point, Irénée was making a precarious living operating the publishing house. The print shop, which was the main source of his income, had once been wrecked by the mob during a political uproar and there was no guarantee that the same thing might not happen again. His newspaper, *Le Républicain*, carried a revolutionary theme. Pierre's new newspaper, *L'Historien*, was a vehicle for reviving royalism and opposing Napoleon's appointment as commander-in-chief of the French forces in Italy. The bourgeoisie, however, struck and backed Napoleon's coup. Pierre and Irénée were imprisoned. With the help of a friend who was a member of the commission that prepared lists for deportation, Pierre regained their freedom under a plea of senility, but he had to pledge to leave France.

So it was that the du Pont family set sail aboard the *American Eagle* and arrived on the shores of Newport, Rhode Island, on December 31, 1800. It was in the United States that Irénée's individuality, creativity, innovative spirit, and strong character began to emerge. His physical appearance—he was small in size, with a cleft chin, a long sharp nose, and weak lips—belied the strength and courage he later displayed as he built his empire. His ability to restrain his emotions and his instinctive caution in befriending anyone who was not family also contributed to the building and solidifying of his dynasty in years to come.

LIFE'S WORK

Du Pont found in the United States a political climate that was very different from that of France. Insistence on freedom had led to the Declaration of Independence and the American Revolution. The American economy encouraged initiative, and the door of advancement was open to all.

Gunpowder was a much-needed commodity on the American frontier. It was needed for protection from Indians and wild animals, to shoot game for meat and skins, and to help clear land to build new homes and roads. American powder makers during the revolution had made some acceptable powder, although 90 percent had been bought from France. By 1800, explosions and British competition had put most of the domestic mills out of business.

Shortly after his arrival in the United States, du Pont went to purchase some gunpowder for hunting. His expert eye recognized its poor quality and its inability to meet the urgent needs of the American frontier. This discovery sparked his ingenuity and his dream was born. On July 19, 1802, at the age of thirty-one, he purchased land on the Brandywine Creek near Wilmington, Delaware, on the site of what had been the first cotton mill in America. He had originally planned to call his plant Lavoisier Mills out of respect for his mentor. He reconsidered, however, and decided to name it Eleutherian Mills, in honor of freedom, as a happy portent to political refugees. In the spring of 1804, the first du Pont gunpowder went on public sale.

Du Pont spent thirty-two years on the Brandywine Creek as president of E. I. du Pont de Nemours and Company. Throughout these years, the shortage of liquid capital was a constant problem for him. Although his original investors had pledged funds to build and run the mills, they did not give the amount promised, and he was forced to raise the difference through notes. When the mills began to show a profit, the stockholders demanded the earnings in dividends instead of reinvesting a portion to increase production and sales as he wanted to do. Du Pont had the business acumen of a modern-day entrepreneur, while his investors were stagnating in eighteenth century procedures. His way out of the impasse was to purchase their stock. They demanded exorbitant prices, so he signed more notes to meet them. In this way, he assured himself that only he and other family members would control the company, and by the time of his death, most of these notes had been paid off.

During his tenure with the company, du Pont established the technical, methodological, and ethical principles to which the company still adheres. With regard to the technical and methodological aspects, du Pont addressed the need to give careful attention to raw material preparation. Charcoal was made from willow trees because they always grew new branches and had an inexhaustible supply. Saltpeter was always thoroughly cleaned regardless of its state of cleanliness when it was received. Sulphur was always pure and clear in color.

Du Pont also had the foresight to install a labor-saving device for kerneling powder. In times of prosperity as well as in times of adversity, du Pont always sought out means to improve the quality of his product and improve his methods. This was the forerunner of the product and process improvement approach of modern industry. He even anticipated the modern principle of enlarging a company's income and usefulness through diversification. Du Pont provided one of the earliest examples of industrial integration by growing grain for the horses that transported the gunpowder in fields adjacent to the mills.

Du Pont was a man who abided by an exemplary code of ethics. The most salient example of this manifested itself during the tragedy that befell his mills in March, 1818. Explosions ruined much of the plant and killed forty men. At that time, there were no laws that committed the company to compensate the families of the victims, but du Pont pensioned the widows, gave them homes, and took responsibility for the education and medical care of the children. He paid these costs and those of rebuilding the plant by renewing his notes and signing more. Another example of du Pont's strong social and moral consciousness involved his principle that quality was a matter of pride, with which no compromise could be made. He constantly refused offers to manufacture inferior powder for shipping. He was once approached by the government of one of the states, which was irritated at a new federal tariff law and had threatened to resist its reinforcement by force of arms. Du Pont replied that he had no powder for such a purpose.

Du Pont's unyielding adherence to these principles brought him rewarding results. In 1804, during the first year of production, he made 44,907 pounds of gunpowder, which sold for $15,116.75. In 1805, both amounts had tripled. In 1808, an additional mill and new facilities accounted for the annual production of 300,000 pounds. In 1810, the profits exceeded thirty thousand dollars. In 1811, with a profit of forty-five thousand dollars, the du Pont mills were the largest in the Western Hemisphere.

The War of 1812 brought government orders totaling 750,000 pounds of gunpowder. Although this would appear to be a profitable assignment, the business realities proved to be the contrary. The company had to risk its cash and borrow heavily to extend the capacity of the mills. Du Pont purchased an adjoining property called the Hagley Estate, erected additional facilities, renamed it the Hagley Yards, and thereby completed the first major expansion in the company's history. By the time of his death on October 31, 1834, the output of corps of workmen, with constantly improving machinery and equipment, exceeded one million pounds. The Brandywine mills had become a major American enterprise.

SIGNIFICANCE

Du Pont created much more than a family business; he bred a tradition that has endured into the twenty-first century. This tradition espoused his code of business honor that was inseparable from his code of personal honor. His guiding principle was that privilege was inextricably bound to duty, and this principle ruled his entire life. He had a sense of obligation to his customers that was a rarity in the business world of his time. He staked personal fortunes on many occasions in order to fulfill a pledge. His commitment to technological innovations and increased productivity never undermined his commitment to top-quality products. His foresight and ingenuity antedated his century in technological and moral consciousness. These precepts, which originated from the Brandywine mills, still guide the Du Pont Company. The du Pont family empire is a global one that has expanded to include real estate, arms and defense industries, computers, communications, media, utilities, oil, food industries, banks, aviation, chemicals, rubber, insurance, and many other businesses.

When du Pont came to the United States in 1800, he was a strange man in a strange country. Nevertheless, he recognized that the United States was a land of opportunity, and the Du Pont Company grew because the fledgling nation's needs, and free traditions, encouraged progress. The United States grew because people such as du Pont contributed the seeds of growth that bloom in risk, courage, and innovation. He may have been forced to come to the United States, but he died as Delaware's most valuable citizen.

Generations of men and women contributed to the development of the Du Pont Company from a single gunpowder mill to a company that is international in scope and significance. The original Du Pont mills have been replaced by more modern and efficient buildings and procedures, but it is the spirit of du Pont that remains and reigns: His code of business honor and his code of personal integrity, of privilege and duty, still pervade his business empire.

—*Anne Laura Mattrella*

FURTHER READING

Dorian, Max. *The du Ponts: From Gunpowder to Nylon*. Boston: Little, Brown, 1961. Concentrates on the du Pont genealogy and the way in which each family member contributed to the building of the empire. Stresses the role of Pierre du Pont, his service to Louis XVI, his title of nobility, and the political connections that enabled him to migrate to America.

Du Pont de Nemours, E. I., et al. *Du Pont: The Autobiography of an American Enterprise*. Wilmington, Del.: E. I. du Pont de Nemours, 1952. The best book on du Pont's life and ingenuity. Also explores the century and a half that followed the first gunpowder mill on the Brandywine in terms of the parallel development of the Du Pont Company and the United States.

Du Pont de Nemours, Pierre Samuel. *Irénée Bonfils*. Wilmington, Del.: E. I. du Pont de Nemours, 1947. Discusses the religious beliefs of the du Pont family, which were somewhat redefined after the death of du Pont's mother, who was a Catholic. The tone is one of tolerance toward other religions and a strong appeal is made for a united church.

Kinnane, Adrian. *Du Pont: From the Banks of the Brandywine to Miracles of Science*. Wilmington, Del.: E. I du Pont de Nemours, 2002. An updated corporate history. Chapter 1, "A Vision and Product," describes how E. I. du Pont established his gunpowder business in 1802.

Winkler, John K. *The du Pont Dynasty*. New York: Reynal and Hitchcock, 1935. Explores the du Pont family history from their early days in France to their early days in Delaware. It also details the advancements and expansion of the company from its inception.

Zilg, Gerard Colby. *Du Pont: Behind the Nylon Curtain*. Englewood Cliffs, N.J.: Prentice-Hall, 1974. Chronicles the life of the du Pont family from France, their migration to America, the success of du Pont's first gunpowder mill, and the expansion of the du Pont dynasty.

SEE ALSO: Andrew Carnegie; Samuel Colt; Alfred Nobel.

RELATED ARTICLE in *Great Events from History: The Nineteenth Century, 1801-1900:* December 15, 1900: General Electric Opens Research Laboratory.

FIRST EARL OF DURHAM
British politician and colonial administrator

*Known as "Radical Jack" for his advanced ideas of
parliamentary reform and later appointed governor-
general of Canada, Lord Durham wrote a famous
report on British North America. Because the report
insisted upon British-style responsible government for
the colony, it has been regarded as the charter
document for the British Commonwealth of Nations.*

BORN: April 12, 1792; London, England
DIED: July 28, 1840; Cowes, Isle of Wight, England
ALSO KNOWN AS: John George Lambton (birth name);
   Viscount Lambton; Baron Durham; Radical Jack
AREA OF ACHIEVEMENT: Government and politics

EARLY LIFE

Although John George Lambton's father, William, died
when the child was but five years old, he bequeathed to
his son lively intelligence, fierce family pride, and dedication to liberal causes. At his guardian's insistence,
John was not sent away to school in his youth but received private tutoring in math and science and later
received his conventional education in Greek and Latin
at Eton. Lambton was not a distinguished scholar and
stubbornly resisted his guardian's plans for a university education, preferring instead a commission in the
Tenth Hussars, a prestigious cavalry regiment. Equally
headstrong in romance, Lambton eloped with Henrietta
Cholmondeley in 1812. Finally declared "of age," he settled with his wife at Lambton Hall in Durham County
and was elected to the House of Commons in 1813.

In the Commons, Lambton aligned himself with his
father's old faction, the liberal wing of the Whig Party.
As a new M.P., Lambton spoke occasionally for his
causes and against the conservative Tory government.
Just as he had begun to attract attention, he was struck by
a personal tragedy that would become a recurrent night-
mare. His young wife lay dead of tuberculosis—a disease that would later claim their three daughters and,
eventually, Lambton himself. His health had been and remained precarious following any intellectual or physical
exertion. His portraits reveal a handsome man, with dark
curls and fine features. His was not a robust beauty, but
he possessed enough aristocratic bearing to enforce his
presence anywhere.

Lambton considered quitting public life at his wife's
death, but his friend Henry Brougham (with whom he
would eventually quarrel) persuaded him to resume his
seat in the Commons. Marriage to Lady Louisa Grey on

December 9, 1816, brought him more than great personal
happiness; the marriage brought him into the inner councils of the Whig Party led by his father-in-law, Earl Grey.
Grey saw stern integrity behind the young man's petu-
lance and violent temper. As a result of his father-in-
law's patronage and forbearance, Lambton was included
in the Whig governments of the 1830's.

LIFE'S WORK

While his party was in opposition, Lambton's restless
energy flitted from the development of the Davy's safety
lantern for his coal miners to educational reform. He inspired acrimonious debate in Parliament and the press
when he espoused two highly controversial issues of the
decade: parliamentary and colonial reform. In 1821,
Lambton introduced legislation to reapportion the seats
in the House of Commons and extend the franchise. As a
bill without official support, it stood no real chance of
passing, but the Tories used political trickery to ensure
an especially humiliating defeat. His vindictive outburst
when he learned of his bill's fate earned for Lambton further opprobrium. The press referred to him deprecatingly
as "Radical Jack," "King Jog," "The Dictator," and
"Robert le Diable."

Outside the Commons, Lambton gave his name and
blessing to the New Zealand Company. Organized by
Edward Gibbon Wakefield, it advocated and sponsored
emigration. Colonies were not a popular cause during the
1820's; the loss of America was too fresh for men to appreciate new possibilities for the empire. Most ambitious
politicians would have shunned this as a dead issue and
Wakefield, a former convict, as an "improper gentleman." Lambton courageously, if eccentrically, publicly
approved of his ideas.

Though King William IV thoroughly despised Lambton and his causes, he created Lambton a Peer of the
Realm, Lord Durham, in 1827. His peerage recognized
generations of Lambton service to the state, but the Tory
press speculated that Baron Durham (as he was then
known) had been bribed away from his ideals. During the
1820's and 1830's, the press frequently suggested that
Lambton would head a third political party comprising
radicals, democrats, and popular demagogues. Those
who knew him well, however, never doubted his loyalty
to Earl Grey and to the Whig Party.

In 1830, the long Tory domination of government was
broken, and Earl Grey became prime minister. He ap-

pointed Durham Lord Privy Seal and asked his son-in-law to head a committee to draw up a bill for parliamentary reform. No minutes were kept by the committee, so it is impossible to determine each man's contribution, but the bill they created was much like Durham's 1821 failure.

The Whig bill proposed to abolish representation of "rotten" and "pocket" boroughs, shift their numbers to the new cities created by the Industrial Revolution, and extend the franchise to every male householder occupying premises worth ten pounds per annum. Though essentially moderate, the bill stirred passionate resistance by those who wished no change in the old, easily managed political system. It drew equally passionate support from those who wished to see the old oligarchical system dead. After a protracted struggle characterized by Tory intransigence, royal wavering, and Grey's resignation and return to power, the bill passed both houses and received the royal assent in 1832. Known as the Great Reform Bill, it did not bring mob rule to England as its critics feared but did allow the upper-middle classes the vote. Durham would not live to see the other reform bills of 1867 and 1884 that enfranchised most adult males, but his democratic spirit permeated them.

After a distinguished term as ambassador to the court at St. Petersburg (1835-1837), Durham returned home to honors and a great challenge. In 1838, Queen Victoria selected Durham to become a Knight of the Order of the Bath. He scarcely had time to savor his recognition before the new Whig prime minister, Lord Melbourne, requested his service. On March 31, 1838, Durham was commissioned governor-general of Canada and Lord High Commissioner, delegated to study the causes of recent rebellions there. When Durham and his staff, including Wakefield, Charles Buller, and Thomas Turton, arrived in Canada, they discovered the embers of rebellion still smoldering. Despite the fact that Canada was divided into Lower Canada (largely French) and Upper Canada (largely British), the causes of rebellion in both provinces were the same. Rebels in both provinces resented the fact that legislation passed by their elected assemblies could be ignored or defeated by appointed councils. Government, therefore, was by oligarchy, not by popular will.

Durham's first official act was the Ordinance of July 28, 1838, which freed all but several leaders of the rebels; these eight leaders were exiled to the British colony of Bermuda. The ordinance was welcomed as a generous solution that quickened Canadian hopes for a fair resolution of their grievances. Durham and his staff then set about the laborious process of interviewing disgruntled citizens and studying past policies. In the midst of these efforts, Durham learned that the home government had disallowed his ordinance on technical grounds. His former friend Henry Brougham and others had been undermining his mission since his departure, criticizing its expense, his inclusion of Wakefield and Turton, both of whom had scandalous pasts, and his failure to communicate properly with the Colonial Office. Durham resigned his post, announcing his betrayal to the Canadian press. For this, *The Times* of London titled him "Lord High Seditioner," and he returned to England in November under a cloud of suspicion and misunderstanding.

First Earl of Durham. (Library of Congress)

In January, 1839, Durham presented the Melbourne government with his *Report on the Affairs of British North America*. The "Durham Report," as it was popularly known, created a stir in Parliament and the press. Its most salient feature was an eloquent plea for the continuation of Great Britain's connection with Canada but within a new context. According to Durham, Great Britain could build this connection and avoid future rebellions only by granting responsible government to a single executive and legislature in a united Canada. Responsible government meant to Durham that in matters of domestic policy the executive would rule at the pleasure of a majority in the legislature that supported its program. In external or foreign affairs, the British Parliament would remain supreme.

By uniting the two Canadas, Durham believed that the French population would become Anglicized, thereby producing racial harmony. Responsible government was the heart of the Durham Report, though it contains numerous appendixes addressing other specific problems. The British government accepted the suggestion of union and passed a bill to that effect in the spring of 1840. Durham lived to see the bill passed but not long enough to see the evolution of responsible government. He died of tuberculosis on July 28, 1840.

SIGNIFICANCE

Lord Durham was a man whose vision of change continuously outdistanced his contemporaries. While he maintained a respect for tradition, he recognized that only those traditions that retained their integrity deserved to survive. He believed deeply that parliamentary government was stable enough to endure change and flexible enough to serve maturing nations. He was a statesman who hated oligarchical control of peoples even though he was born to oligarchic status.

Durham's greatest contribution to English history rested in his *Report on the Affairs of British North America*. Though some of his analyses were wrong (the French-Canadian identity would not be extinguished, and the line between internal and external affairs of a colony was vague), Durham's insistence upon responsible government meant that Canada would have self-government in the same form as it existed in England. It would be Durham's son-in-law, Lord Elgin, who would, as governor-general of Canada in 1848, first exercise the duties of a responsible executive. When Canada refined its constitution in the British North America Act of 1867, it would insist upon two principles—loyalty to the British Crown and responsible government. Canada led the

way for what became the journey of dozens of nations from colony to self-governing dominion. Though Durham's vision may not have stretched that far into the future, his ideas have been the charter for the British Commonwealth of Nations.

—*Kathryne S. McDorman*

FURTHER READING

Ajzenstat, Janet. *The Political Thought of Lord Durham*. Kingston, Ont.: McGill-Queen's University Press, 1987. Ajzenstat uses Durham's speeches, letters, and dispatches to analyze the political philosophy contained in his *Report on the Affairs of British North America*. She argues that the recommendations in the report demonstrate Durham's liberalism and toleration of minorities. Ajzenstat counters criticism that Durham was racist and prejudiced against French Canadians, maintaining his assimilation proposal actually aimed to widen political and economic opportunities for French Canadians.

Canadian Historical Review 20 (June, 1939). This entire issue is devoted to articles that commemorate the centenary of the report. The volume provides an excellent summary of the scholarship and interpretations of Durham's contribution to the idea of "dominion status."

Durham, John George Lambton. *The Durham Report*. Edited by Sir Reginald Coupland. Oxford, England: Clarendon Press, 1945. The first abridgment, aimed at acquainting post-World War II generations about to embark on a new phase of Commonwealth with Durham's ideas. Excellent brief introduction elucidating the report's main features.

_____. *Lord Durham's Report on the Affairs of British North America*. Edited by Sir Charles Lucas. 3 vols. Oxford, England: Clarendon Press, 1912. The finest, most complete edition of the report. Volume 1 contains some interpretive differences from the later standard biography by Chester New (see below). Volume 2 is a complete text of the report, while volume 3 provides a complete set of appendixes.

New, Chester. *Lord Durham*. Oxford, England: Clarendon Press, 1929. The standard scholarly biography, with an extensive bibliography of all pertinent works to date. New writes elegantly and presents a balanced look at Durham's career—neither tipped toward hero worship and overemphasis of his accomplishments, nor hesitant to insist upon a restored appreciation for Durham's work.

Reid, Stuart J., ed. *Life and Letters of the First Earl of Durham, 1792-1840*. 2 vols. London: Longmans,

Green, 1906. Reacting to other scholars' tendency to ignore Durham because his contemporaries underrated him, Reid makes the most extended case for his inclusion as a major figure in early nineteenth century affairs. Reid tends to be a bit breathlessly enthusiastic and slips into a moralizing tone on occasion, but his work succeeds in its purpose.

Rose, J. Holland, A. P. Newton, and E. A. Benians, eds. *The Cambridge History of the British Empire*. Cambridge, England: Cambridge University Press, 1940. This venerable series is useful for anyone who has

need of a survey that goes beyond the superficial. Durham and his report are well covered in volume 2.

SEE ALSO: Robert Baldwin; Second Viscount Melbourne; Queen Victoria; Edward Gibbon Wakefield.

RELATED ARTICLES in *Great Events from History: The Nineteenth Century, 1801-1900:* October 23-December 16, 1837: Rebellions Rock British Canada; February 10, 1841: Upper and Lower Canada Unite; August 9, 1842: Webster-Ashburton Treaty Settles Maine's Canadian Border.

ANTONÍN DVOŘÁK
Czech composer

One of the most notable European composers of the nineteenth century, Dvořák became one of the chief creators of the Czech national style of music and also had a profound influence on the development of American music.

BORN: September 8, 1841; Nelahozeves, Bohemia (now in Czech Republic)
DIED: May 1, 1904; Prague, Bohemia (now in Czech Republic)
ALSO KNOWN AS: Antonín Leopold Dvořák (full name)
AREA OF ACHIEVEMENT: Music

EARLY LIFE

Born into the family of a butcher-innkeeper in a small Bohemian village, Antonín Leopold Dvořák (DVOHR-zhahk) did not seem destined to a musical career. As was the case with other young men at that time, Antonín was expected to carry on the family business, which his father had inherited from his own father. In spite of these expectations, Antonín began to play the violin with his father, who performed with the village orchestra at various rustic festivals and ceremonies. The young Dvořák soon proved more capable than his father at the bow, and his musical promise attracted the notice of the local schoolmaster, a musician named Josef Spitz.

From Spitz, Dvořák learned the elements of the violin. In 1853, Dvořák was sent to his maternal uncle's house in Zlonice to continue his studies. There, under the tutelage of Antonín Liehmann, Dvořák gained familiarity with the viola, organ, and figured bass. Liehmann tutored the boy in modulation as well as extemporization, which he called "brambuliring." It was with Liehmann

that Dvořák first came into contact with the German language, which, as Bohemia was then part of the Austrian Empire, was an important prerequisite to further study. In order to perfect his German, he was sent to live with a German family in the nearby village of Ceske Kamenice.

In Ceske Kamenice, Dvořák continued his musical progress under the choirmaster at St. Jakub's Church, for whom he frequently substituted at the organ. Liehmann's suggestion that the boy continue his musical studies at Prague was received unfavorably by Dvořák's father, who asserted that there was no money to finance such an undertaking. At Liehmann's insistence, however, Dvořák's childless uncle agreed to pay for the boy's schooling at the Organ Conservatory in Prague, which Dvořák entered in 1857. Dvořák's musical talents rapidly developed at the conservatory under the guidance of such men as Josef Leopold Zvonař (voice), Josef Bohuslav Foerster (organ), and František Blazěk (theory). Many of these men laid the initial foundations for the national style of Czech music.

During his days as a student, Dvořák found an extracurricular outlet for his creativity in the orchestra of the musical society Cecilia, in which he played viola. He participated in the weekly rehearsals of the society, which was at that time under the direction of Antonín Apt, an ardent admirer of Robert Schumann and Richard Wagner.

LIFE'S WORK

Dvořák's musical career began at the end of the Romantic era in Bohemia. After the cultural renaissance of the Czech nation, the *národní obrození*, during which time poets such as Jan Kollár, František Celakovský, and, above all, Karel Hynek Mácha carved out a wide area of cultural autonomy for the Czech nation, it became common for poets, musicians, and artists to find inspiration for their work in national hagiography and legend. During the 1860's, however, the vivid élan of Romanticism was slowing into the less revolutionary, nostalgic era of the Biedermeier. It is helpful to keep this literary distinction between Romantic and Biedermeier in mind when one speaks of the music of Dvořák. For, like the poet Karel Jaromir Erben, Dvořák, in this early period of his career, composed works suffused with languor and a certain *fin d'époque* melancholy. In addition to two symphonies that date from this period—the *Bells of Zlonice* in C minor and the Second Symphony in B flat major—Dvořák set Moravian poet Gustav Pfleger's "Cypress Trees" to music as a song cycle.

When the Czech National Opera opened in 1862, the members of the Cecilia society's orchestra formed its backbone. The contemporary atmosphere inspired Dvořák to compose his first venture for the musical stage: *Alfred* (1938), based on the lyric epic poem by Vítězslav Hálek. This work, however, was never produced on-stage. Its overture was published in 1912—eight years after Dvořák's death—and is noted for its technical finesse.

Much of Dvořák's work predating 1870 was destroyed by Dvořák himself. In 1872, he took a curious journey back to the period of literary Romanticism in Bohemia. It was in this year that he set to music a few songs from the Ossian-like "Old Czech" forgeries of Václav Hanka—the *Rukopis královédvorský* and *Rukopis zelenohorský*. Like the literary works themselves, Dvořák's adaptations of the *Rukopisy* achieved some measure of fame beyond the borders of Bohemia. In 1879, they were published in German and English translation.

In 1873, Dvořák turned to a mode of composition that was to reward him with much musical success—the composition of quartets. One of the most beautiful of these works—written in this year of Dvořák's marriage to his former student Anna Cermáková—is the String Quartet in F Minor, Op. 9. A growing sense of self-confidence, spawned perhaps by conjugal satisfaction, inspired Dvořák to resign from the National Opera and take a post in St. Vojtěch's Church. Then came the Symphony in D Minor, Op. 13, which, however, was to lie dormant for a full twenty years.

The lure of the opera continued to be strong, and the year 1874 brought Dvořák's return to the operatic stage with the adapted puppet show *King and Collier*. The work was an immediate success, and Dvořák was hailed as a promising representative of a revivified Slavic mu-

Antonín Dvořák. (Library of Congress)

sic. Dvořák followed this event with another quartet, this time in A minor. Dvořák's career began to take off in earnest after these successes. In 1875, he was awarded a generous stipend from the Austrian government for his musical achievements; on the award's selection committee was Johannes Brahms, later to become Dvořák's lifelong friend. More chamber pieces and another collection of folk songs (the *Moravian Duets*) followed, as did the Symphony in F, Op. 24, which was to add greatly to Dvořák's renown abroad.

Personal tragedy struck Dvořák at the zenith of this fecund period. In 1876, while Dvořák was at work on another opera (*Wanda*, based on an ancient Polish legend), his daughter became sick and died. This painful occurrence inspired Dvořák to create one of his greatest musical works, the *Stabat mater*. This work made Dvořák's name famous in Great Britain, where he conducted the work himself to rave reviews in 1884.

Dvořák's steady, conquering march on the musical world was continued with his *Slavonic Dances*. Curiously enough, critics initially looked upon these works with coolness, as they were commissioned by the German music publishing firm of Simrock. However, time has proven the great value of these sterling compositions, and the critics were soon silenced by voices such as Hans Richter's, who praised Dvořák's "God-given talent" after hearing the earlier *Symphonic Variations for Orchestra* (1877).

Dvořák consolidated his leading position among composers of the Czech national school during these years with the composition of various pieces of music deeply imbued with patriotic feeling. Such works are the *Hussite Overture* (1883), which contains as a theme the famous Hussite hymn "Ktoz jste Bozí bojovníci" ("You Who Art the Warriors of God"), and the tone poem suite *Ze Šumavy* (*From the Bohemian Forest*). Of special interest to the adept of comparative arts is Dvořák's chorale adaptation of Erben's Bürgeresque ballad *Svatební košile* (*The Spectre's Bride*).

About this time, Dvořák's fame began to burgeon in the Anglo-Saxon countries. In England, for example, his *Stabat mater* was hailed as "one of the finest works of our times" by a musical critic when it was performed for the eight hundredth anniversary of Worcester Cathedral under the baton of Dvořák himself. For the next few years, Dvořák was to divide his time between the British Isles and his native Bohemia, where he had just acquired a peaceful, rustic cottage as a quiet retreat for composition.

Dvořák's Symphony in G, Op. 88, although dedicated to the Imperial Bohemian Academy for the Fine Arts, has become known as the "English Symphony," as it was published uncharacteristically in London. His popularity in England is attested by the Birmingham Festival's invitation to set John Henry Newman's *Dream of Gerontius* to music for the year 1891. Dvořák opted instead for something less literary: the *Requiem Mass*, Op. 89. This work was again received favorably when performed at the festival yet did not win for Dvořák the same high accolades as the seemingly unsurpassable *Stabat mater*.

Dvořák soon put the pen aside for conservatory instruction. In 1891, he accepted the chair of composition at the Prague Conservatory and embarked on a teaching career that was to last for five years and carry him across the ocean. Only one year after his appointment to the Prague professorship, he was granted a leave of absence by the institution to undertake similar duties at the New York Conservatory for what was at that time a generous salary.

Dvořák was to remain in the United States until 1896. From this stay in New York came what is perhaps his most recognizable work to the American ear, the Symphony in E Minor, Op. 95, known popularly as the *New World* Symphony. As George Gershwin was to do in the next century, Dvořák infused new blood into the musical scene by incorporating heretofore exotic musical elements—of Indian, African, and American flavor—into his strong European musical heritage. This last great work of his had enormous consequences for American symphonic music. Karel Hoffmeister goes so far as to suggest—with some justification—that Dvořák's impact on American music can be compared to that of George Frideric Handel on the music of England.

Dvořák returned from the United States to the hero's welcome that had greeted him constantly in these last few years of artistic grandeur. As his stay on American soil seemed to have affected his composition by introducing new motifs and styles in his European background, so his return to Bohemia reawakened his Slavic muse. Among his greatest successes from this last period of his life are the symphonic poems he composed, based on Erben's highly popular collection of folk-styled ballads titled *Kytice* (*The Wreath*) and his final great opera *Rusalka* (*The Water-Nymph*).

Dvořák's last effort in this field, the opera *Armida*, built around Jaroslav Vrchlický's libretto, ended in fiasco. It seems strange that the brilliant career of such an artist should end in failure, yet this is indeed what happened. Falling ill toward the end of March, 1904, Dvořák died on May 1. As a sign of the great esteem in which the Czech people held him, Dvořák was laid to rest on the grounds of the royal castle of Vyšehrad in Prague on May 5, 1904.

SIGNIFICANCE

Antonín Dvořák is lauded as one of the greatest composers of the modern era. A technical genius whose absolute devotion to music gave birth to unforgettable symphonies, operas, and chamber works, Dvořák influenced and was highly regarded in his own day by colleagues such as Brahms and Richter. As pedagogue, he left his unique mark upon musicians such as Oskar Nedbal, who came under his tutelage at conservatories in Prague and New York. Nevertheless, Dvořák is most widely known as the one composer who, more than anyone else during the late nineteenth century, popularized Slavic themes and musical styles to European and American audiences unaccustomed to the fertile region of East and Central Europe. In this, Dvořák can be compared to Frédéric Chopin, who preceded him during the early part of the century.

Dvořák is also remembered as a musical innovator who introduced American rhythms to the older traditions of Europe. He is unique in modern musical history as a composer who has had a profound effect on at least two, if not three (counting Germany), musical cultures—that of Bohemia and the United States—and deserves to be held in honor by the American, as well as the Czech, public as an illustrious founder of a musical culture that might have developed in a radically different fashion had he not participated in its nurturing.

—*Charles Kraszewski*

FURTHER READING

Beckerman, Michael. *Dvořák and His World*. Princeton, N.J.: Princeton University Press, 1993. The first part of this book contains essays about various aspects of Dvořák's life and music, including the reception for his work, his relationship with Brahms, his operas, and his visit to the United States. The second part includes Dvořák's correspondence, unpublished reviews and criticism from Czech newspapers, and other documents that have been translated into English.

Clapham, John. *Dvořák*. New York: W. W. Norton, 1979. Clapham's biography contains a wealth of information concerning Dvořák's life and compositions; the book is particularly valuable for students interested in Dvořák's American years and British successes. Some illustrative musical annotation, a "Catalogue of Compositions," a generous bibliography, and a helpful "Chronicle of Events" make this biography an excellent and easy-to-use reference tool. Black-and-white photographs.

Fischl, Viktor, ed. *Antonín Dvořák: His Achievement*. London: L. Drummond, 1943. Reprint. Westport, Conn.: Greenwood Press, 1970. A helpful and enlightening collection of essays written by critics such as Edwin Evans, Thomas Dunhill, and Harriet Cohen. Topics discussed in the eleven papers cover every aspect of Dvořák's creative work, from his orchestral works and opera to his chamber music and sacral creations. An excellent text for both initiates and musically refined students because it presents Dvořák's life and compositional heritage in well-written, logically arranged sections.

Hoffmeister, Karel. *Antonín Dvořák*. Edited and translated by Rosa Newmarch. Westport, Conn.: Greenwood Press, 1970. This is a well-constructed biography, divided into two main sections. The first introduces Dvořák as a person and the second proceeds to a detailed discussion of his works, with generous snippets of musical notation which exemplify and reinforce the critical commentary. The reader, however, should be aware of a few minor miscues that detract from an otherwise excellent work. Hoffmeister at one point refers to a period in Dvořák's life as being quite "stormy and stressful," thus creating a misleading reference to the German literary period *Sturm und Drang* (late eighteenth century). Also, the author suggests that the Czech national revival began during the mid-nineteenth century, when it actually began as early as 1785.

Honolka, Kurt. *Dvořák*. Translated by Anne Wyburd. London: Haus, 2004. English translation of a book originally published in 1974. A brief introduction to Dvořák's life and work, setting his life against the backdrop of the political and social tensions in the final years of the Austro-Hungarian Empire.

Moore, Douglas. *A Guide to Musical Styles: From Madrigal to Modern Music*. New York: W. W. Norton, 1942, rev. ed. 1962. Although not totally devoted to Dvořák, Moore's book is a concise, excellent introduction to the European musical heritage, with generous commentary on composers and musical styles that had a profound influence on Dvořák. Aids greatly in understanding the composer and his place in, and significance for, music. The book's generous use of musical annotations, easy style, and helpful definitions make it an indispensable tool for both beginning and advanced students of musical history.

Schonzeler, Hans-Hubert. *Dvořák*. New York: Marion Boyars, 1984. A more illuminating biography of the composer than Hoffmeister's work (see above), featuring many excerpts from Dvořák's letters and writings. A good book for readers who wish to know Dvořák as a person rather than a composer. Contains sixty-seven well-chosen black-and-white photographs.

SEE ALSO: Frédéric Chopin.

RELATED ARTICLES in *Great Events from History: The Nineteenth Century, 1801-1900:* March 3, 1875: Bizet's *Carmen* Premieres in Paris; August 13-17, 1876: First Performance of Wagner's Ring Cycle; October 22, 1883: Metropolitan Opera House Opens in New York; January 14, 1900: Puccini's *Tosca* Premieres in Rome.

JAMES BUCHANAN EADS
American engineer and inventor

Eads so revolutionized long-span bridge construction that the Eads Bridge, which spans the Mississippi River at St. Louis, is the only such structure bearing an engineer's name. He was also a highly successful capitalist and an inventor of note, with more than fifty patents credited to him.

BORN: May 23, 1820; Lawrenceberg, Indiana
DIED: March 8, 1887; Nassau, New Providence Island, Bahamas
AREAS OF ACHIEVEMENT: Engineering, business

EARLY LIFE

James Buchanan Eads (eeds) was born in an Ohio River town. His family was of moderate means, moving in search of better fortune to Cincinnati, Ohio, then to Louisville, Kentucky. As a result of economic difficulties, between the ages of nine and thirteen Eads had only minimal formal education. Nevertheless, by the time he was eleven years old, Eads, working from observations made during family moves on steamers, had already constructed a small steam engine and models of sawmills, fire engines, steamboats, and electrotype machines.

In Louisville, Eads's father experienced serious business reverses, so at only thirteen Eads traveled to St. Louis, working passage on a river steamer and seeking employment. After suffering hardships, Eads found well-paying work in a St. Louis mercantile establishment. Recognizing Eads's abilities, an employer opened his library (reportedly one of the Mississippi Valley's finest) to him, and Eads used it intensively to study civil engineering, mechanics, and machinery. When he was nineteen, his family moved to Dubuque, Iowa, where young Eads signed as second clerk aboard the river steamer *Knickerbocker*, which operated between Dubuque and Cincinnati. In the next few years, having risen to purser, he served aboard several Mississippi steamers and became intimately acquainted with the navigational characteristics of the river with which his life became intimately linked.

LIFE'S WORK

In 1842, now an attractive, industrious, tactful, ingenious, and personable man, Eads placed his savings into copartnership with Case and Nelson, a firm of St. Louis boat builders, in order to help the company to expand into the salvage of river wrecks. Hundreds of steamers were lost annually during the mid-nineteenth century because

of boiler explosions, contact with bars or snags, and other accidents, and millions of dollars were lost to river pirates and to the unpredictabilities of the river itself. As a consequence, Eads and his partners extended their salvage operations the length of the Mississippi and to the Gulf countries of Central America, profiting greatly. Nevertheless, Eads sold his shares and established the first glass manufactory west of the Mississippi, an equally profitable enterprise.

Drawing upon his vast experience with the Mississippi and its tributaries, Eads founded his own salvage company in 1847. His success lay in his design and construction of a series of "submarines," diving bells raised and lowered by derricks and supplied with compressed air, which revolutionized salvage work. Not only were sunken cargoes recovered, but also vessels themselves could be refloated. His final salvage boat, bought from the American government and redesigned, was the largest, most powerful of its type ever built.

Eads was so successful with his diving bells and snag boats that in 1856-1857 he proposed a federal contract to clear obstructions and maintain free navigation of the Mississippi and other western rivers over subsequent years. His proposal was defeated, however, chiefly by the opposition of Senators Judah P. Benjamin of Louisiana and Jefferson Davis of Mississippi, the former to serve in several capacities Davis's Confederate cabinet. Thwarted, but already wealthy, at the age of thirty-seven Eads retired with his second wife to the comfort of a St. Louis suburb, ostensibly to recover from his latest bout with tuberculosis.

The most significant phases of Eads's career lay ahead. Edward Bates, a friend of the Eads family who had entered Abraham Lincoln's cabinet as attorney general, alerted Eads to the possible need for his services as secession of the South threatened in 1860; the administration was anxious to preserve free navigation of the Mississippi. Shortly after war erupted in 1861, Eads won federal contracts for construction of seven six-hundred-ton armored steamers to be ready for action in sixty-five days.

Greatly handicapped by his illness, Eads still assembled men and materials from ten states and from the mills of half a dozen cities, successfully completing his first delivery in forty-five days. Within one hundred days he designed and constructed an aggregate of five thousand tons of military shipping. These vessels contributed to Union victories at Forts Henry and Donelson and at Island No. 10, thereby opening the northern Mississippi. Indeed, at the time of these victories, Eads actually owned the vessels, having paid for them with his own funds (he had not yet been reimbursed by Washington).

Before 1865, Eads built fourteen heavily armored gunboats, four mortar boats, and seven armored transports, all delivered on time and to specifications. Furthermore, his revolving gun turrets later became standard. For this and other inventions, Eads was elected a Fellow of the American Academy for the Advancement of Science. Devoid of engineering training, Eads had amply demonstrated not only a mastery of novel shipbuilding but also a profound knowledge of iron and steel potentials. Combined with his grasp of the Mississippi's peculiarities, his ingenuity, tenacity, high civic esteem, and organizational abilities, he was brilliantly equipped for his next enterprise: bridging the Mississippi at St. Louis.

With canal building and the era of the river steamer waning, railway expansion dominated the postwar period. From 1865 until Eads's death in 1887, railway mileage increased from about 40,000 to more than 200,000 miles. Concurrently, need for bridges (hitherto of wooden or iron truss constructions) of long spans and heavy bearing capacities became imperative. Proposals for a St. Louis span had been made earlier than 1867 by Charles Ellet, Jr., as well as by John Augustus Roebling, engineers of distinction, but Eads's plan won the vital approval of the St. Louis business community and of the city's officials.

For his unprecedented scheme, Eads employed unprecedented means. Aware of his own weaknesses, he created a superb staff: Charles Shaler Smith joined him as chief engineering consultant, two other able men were chosen as assistant engineers, and the chancellor of Washington University served as mathematical consultant. With Bessemer steel then available, Eads selected steel as his basic construction material. This ran against the advice of many engineers; indeed, the British Board of Trade banned the use of steel for bridges until years later. Moreover, Eads helped transform Bessemer steel into chrome steel, that choice alone altering subsequent major bridge construction, in which special steels came to supersede iron.

Foundations created special problems. Eads knew the Mississippi, and by treading its bottom in his diving bell he confirmed that three or more feet of sand and silt moved along the river bed at speed of flow. Winter ice jams and the necessity of keeping navigational channels open further complicated planning. The pneumatic caissons devised for foundation work were not new in principle but they had seldom been tested and never on the scale or at the depths required to reach bedrock: 123 feet below the mean water level on the Illinois side and 86 feet at St. Louis. Moreover, these iron-shod timber caissons were seventy-five feet in diameter and designed to sink under their own weight as work progressed. Consequently, several lives were lost and others frequently endangered, and cases of "bends" from depths and pressures were numerous.

Double-decked for trains and for normal traffic, the bridge featured unique arches that had been cantilevered into position, the central sections coming last. Moreover, the three arched spans were of unprecedented length: 1,560 feet overall. Notwithstanding distinguished assistance, Eads designed and oversaw, as his engineers testified, every one-eighth of an inch of the structure, and his aesthetic sense produced a masterwork of great beauty, one still in service. It was completed in 1874, just as the nation's first and longest industrial depression struck. Bondholders foreclosed on the bridge's mortgage. Eads's own bank proved to be one of the great financial disasters of the day. By 1877, the financier and speculator Jay Gould assumed control of the bridge.

Eads, however, swiftly recovered from this crash. By 1875 he had begun overriding congressional opposition to a $5,250,000 contract for permanently clearing major bars at the mouth of the Mississippi and extending its South Pass jetties into deep Gulf waters. Again through ingenuity developed after study of European river jetties, Eads designed an inexpensive "mattress" construction, successfully completing the job and recouping his fortune. Indeed, he offered seventy-five million dollars of his own money if Congress would charter his company for construction of a ship-railway across the Mexican isthmus at Tehuantepec, thereby bringing the Pacific twelve hundred miles nearer to the Mississippi than Ferdinand de Lesseps's ongoing Panama project. Even as Congress moved to accept his proposal, however, Eads's health failed. He died on March 8, 1887, in Nassau, the Bahamas.

SIGNIFICANCE

Either as a great capitalist or as a great engineer, Eads would have enjoyed distinction. Essentially filling the ideal of the American self-made man, he combined both roles, distinguishing himself in both. He revolutionized the salvage business with his inventions, notably with his design of steam-driven centrifugal pumps and his diving bells. He revolutionized bridge construction with his arch designs and, above all, with his introduction of steel for such structures. He resolved through financial, political, and engineering inventiveness and skill the freeing of the river around which so much of his life revolved. In 1884, he became the first American recipient of the Albert Medal from the British Royal Society of Arts. Further, of the eighty-nine persons elected to the Hall of Fame for Great Americans, Eads (elected in 1920) was the sole engineer or architect chosen during the institution's first sixty years of existence.

—Clifton K. Yearley and Kerrie L. MacPherson

FURTHER READING

Barry, John M. *Rising Tide: The Great Mississippi Flood of 1927 and How It Changed America*. New York: Simon & Schuster, 1997. The title is deceptive; although the book is about the 1927 flood, Barry begins his tale during the 1870's, describing the first serious attempt to control the Mississippi River. The effort pitted Eads against Andrew Humphreys, chief of the Army Corps of Engineers. The two hated each other and bitterly fought over river control plans. A compromise policy eventually was adopted, and Barry explains how the failure of that policy resulted in the disastrous 1927 flood.

Condit, Carl W. *American Building: Materials and Techniques from the Beginning of the Colonial Settlements to the Present*. 2d ed. Chicago: University of Chicago Press, 1982. Sweeping and expert analysis. Chapter 12, "Long-Span Bridges in Iron and Steel," treats Eads in proper technical context.

Kouwenhoven, John A. "The Designing of the Eads Bridge." *Technology and Culture* 23 (1982): 535-568. Scholarly work in a widely available, learned journal.

_____. "James Buchanan Eads: The Engineer as Entrepreneur." In *Technology in America: A History of Individuals and Ideas*, edited by Carroll W. Pursell, Jr. Cambridge, Mass.: MIT Press, 1981. Chapter 8 on Eads is excellent; scholarly and well written.

Scott, Quinta, and Howard S. Miller. *The Eads Bridge: Photographic Essay*. New York: Columbia University Press, 1979. The fullest description of the bridge; less useful for the general context of Eads's other activities.

Weisberger, Bernard A. "He Mastered Old Man River." *American Heritage* 44, no. 8 (December, 1993): 22. Describes Eads's attempts to control the Mississippi River, including his invention of the diving bell.

Woodward, Calvin M. *A History of the St. Louis Bridge: Containing a Full Account of Every Step in Its Construction and Erection*. St. Louis: Janes, 1881. This account of the building of the Eads Bridge is old but is the most exhaustive.

Yager, Rosemary. *James Buchanan Eads: Master of the Great River*. New York: Van Nostrand Reinhold, 1968. Interesting overview of Eads's life and activities, but not the final word on Eads's work.

SEE ALSO: Sir Henry Bessemer; Andrew Carnegie; John Augustus Roebling; Thomas Telford.

RELATED ARTICLE in *Great Events from History: The Nineteenth Century, 1801-1900:* May 24, 1883: Brooklyn Bridge Opens.

THOMAS EAKINS
American painter

Eakins produced a small body of major paintings that were to add to the reputation of the United States as a center of art independent of Europe. He was also an important influence on art education in the United States.

BORN: July 25, 1844; Philadelphia, Pennsylvania
DIED: June 25, 1916; Philadelphia, Pennsylvania
AREA OF ACHIEVEMENT: Art

EARLY LIFE

Thomas Eakins (EE-kihns) was the son of Benjamin Eakins, a writing master of Scottish-Irish parentage in the Philadelphia school system. Eakins had early ambitions to follow his father into that work. His mother was of English and Dutch descent. It was a close, middle-class family with a modest private income that was to help support Eakins throughout his life, because his teaching and painting did not always do so. He was particularly close to his three sisters, and they often appear in his paintings.

Eakins evidenced early talents in draftsmanship and drawing and was to study them formally from high school onward, but he also had strengths in science, mathematics, and languages. Eakins was to use his knowledge of science and mathematics extensively in the preparation of his more complicated paintings.

Eakins studied at the Pennsylvania Academy of Fine Arts in Philadelphia, from 1861 to 1866. Drawing from casts of fine antique sculpture was the center of the technical studies at the school, and to Eakins's dissatisfaction, little drawing was done from live models. He supplemented his work by enrolling in anatomy classes at Jefferson Medical College, where he was allowed to watch surgeons operating, and where he began a practice that he admitted he disliked, but that he considered essential to the student artist—the study of anatomy—by taking part in dissection classes. By the end of his time at the academy, he had done very little painting. In September, 1866, he left for France in order to study in Paris.

Eakins entered the conservative École des Beaux-Arts, choosing to study under the painter Jean-Leon Gerome, who was himself somewhat conservative and old-fashioned, but who gave Eakins a thorough grounding in drawing, with emphasis on the use of live models. Eakins again added anatomy classes to his studies, and when he started to paint seriously in his second year, he took a studio where he could work alone while continuing his instruction under Gerome.

Eakins's correspondence evidences little interest in what was going on about him in Paris, although it was a time of considerable ferment in the art world, and the early work of the painters who were to become the Impressionists was being shown and discussed. At the end of his three years in Paris, he toured the galleries of Spain, showing particular enthusiasm for the technique and realistic subject matter of José Ribera and Diego Velázquez. On July 4, 1870, he returned to Philadelphia, where he was to live and work for the remainder of his life.

LIFE'S WORK

There had been indications of a fully formed skill in a few of Eakins's paintings during the late 1860's, and that maturity was soon confirmed in his work during the 1870's. A solid and stocky young man (he can be seen hovering in the middle-background of some of his paintings) with an active interest in rowing and hunting, he brought the world of his athletic pleasures into his paintings, and he is best known for a group of stunningly forceful studies of rowers that exemplify the American love of high athletic skill and outdoor life. *John Biglin in a Single Scull* (1873) and *Max Schmitt in a Single Scull* (1871) are the most popular examples of these intense, imploded moments of athletic focus, in which the subjects, patently modest, convey an aesthetic rightness, a kind of metaphysical truth about life that connects them with the earlier tradition of American paintings celebrating the rugged men working the rivers of America.

This paean to personal skill is explored again in Eakins's pictures of surgeons at work, musicians at play,

and prize-fighters in action. Eakins was, however, to run into trouble with the public, who found his paintings of surgeons at work in the operating theaters too gruesome and bloody, and his paintings of male and female nudes were often considered too crudely unblinkered. He could, on the other hand, be quietly tender in his paintings of musicians, particularly in his studies of his sisters.

As a result, Eakins established a reputation as one of the foremost realists of the latter half of the nineteenth century, but he did not sell many pictures. In his later years, he turned more and more to portraits, generally using friends and acquaintances as subjects, and he rarely was commissioned to do so. He showed little inclination to idealize his portraits. Rather, he tended to catch his sitters in the introspective moment, and he was often successful in getting something of their character on the canvas. His later portraits often went further and revealed physical and emotional vulnerabilities that did not always please his subjects.

It is possible to think of Eakins as a portraitist from beginning to end, with the athletes and men of action showing the best of prime human endeavor, and some of the latter sitters revealing the cruel, inexorable nature of time passing. However, it is those early pictures of sportsmen that are, quite rightly, best remembered.

This mixed reputation that Eakins developed as a painter, of being enormously talented but a bit crude, carried over into his parallel career as an art teacher and administrator. In 1876, he joined the Pennsylvania Academy of Fine Arts as its instructor in the life classes; gradually he became so important to the school's work that in 1882 he became the director. As he did in his own painting, he put heavy emphasis upon drawing from life, not because he did not appreciate the greatness of ancient sculpture but because he saw the naked human form as the best subject for the young artist. He also urged his students to take anatomy classes with medical students.

Over the years, opposition built up, inside the school and outside, over Eakins's insistence that students, male and female, should draw from life. In 1886, his exposure of a male model, completely nude, before a class of female students caused such an avalanche of protest that he was asked to resign. He took a large group of male students with him, and they formed the Art Students League of Philadelphia with Eakins as the sole, unpaid instructor. The school lasted for six years but foundered eventually for financial reasons. Eakins continued to teach in art schools as a guest lecturer, but his insistence on using nude models often got him into trouble, and by mid-life, he ceased to teach.

Eakins had a continuing interest in sculpture and left a few pieces that show considerable skill, but the later years were in the main confined to doing portraits, with occasional returns to his studies of athletes and nudes.

SIGNIFICANCE

Eakins made a double contribution to American culture. As an educator, he championed, to his own detriment, the need to repudiate the sometimes prurient sexual morality of the late nineteenth century in favor of an intelligent acceptance of the human body as the basis for study in art colleges. His fight, often played out in public, made it easier for such artistic and educational freedoms to become a common aspect of American art instruction.

Eakins was also the first prominent art teacher to bring science into the classroom and studio. His personal use of, and instruction in the preparation of, mathematically precise preliminary studies, his use of scale models, and particularly his pioneering use of photography were to become commonly applied tools.

Despite his training in France and his admiration for Spanish painters, Eakins was peculiarly American. His choice of subjects and his refusal to idealize them are examples of his solid, down-to-earth approach to art. Other painters romanticized the portrait; Eakins used it to record reality, however uncomplimentary. He has been called antiartistic, but he proved that art could be made out of life as it was seen. His refusal to compromise for profit and popularity is an example of his American forthrightness, and his affection for science, for mathematics, for photography, for sport, and for high professional endeavor may also be seen as marks of his American character.

Possessed of abundant painterly skills, Eakins often seems too skeptically stolid to make use of them, but at his best, particularly in his sporting pictures, he can make the simple moment accumulate a splendor that links him with painters such as Paul Cézanne and Jean-Baptiste-Siméon Chardin. At those moments of pastoral innocence, the paintings achieve a poetic density that transcends and glorifies the simplicity of the mundane act of living. Then, he is at his best—and his most American.

—*Charles H. Pullen*

FURTHER READING

Adams, Henry. *Eakins Revealed: The Secret Life of an American Artist.* New York: Oxford University Press, 2005. Adams offers a radically different view of Eakins than has been presented in past biographes. His Eakins was an exhibitionist who preyed on young women, was confused about his sexual identity, and was a possible victim of childhood abuse.

Berger, Martin A. *Man Made: Thomas Eakins and the Construction of Gilded Age Manhood.* Berkeley: University of California Press, 2000. In this account of Eakins's life and art, Berger describes how he used his paintings to portray white, middle-class manhood, reflecting American society's changing ideas about masculinity in the final years of the nineteenth century.

Foster, Kathleen A. *Thomas Eakins Rediscovered: Charles Bregler's Thomas Eakins Collection at the Pennsylvania Academy of the Fine Arts.* New Haven, Conn.: Yale University Press, 1997. Catalog of the artworks contained in the collection and an essay by Foster reassessing Eakins's work. Foster analyzes the techniques Eakins used when working in various media and describes the development of his imagery.

Goodrich, Lloyd. *Thomas Eakins.* Cambridge, Mass.: Harvard University Press, 1982. An updated look at Eakins, including interviews with Eakins's widow, students, and sitters. Good bibliography of articles about the artist.

_____. *Thomas Eakins: His Life and Work.* New York: Whitney Museum of American Art, 1933. A major study combining critical biography and catalog in which the reviving reputation of the artist is assessed in conjunction with the neglect that followed his death.

_____. *Thomas Eakins: Retrospective Exhibition.* New York: Whitney Museum of American Art, 1970. A paperback monograph, prepared for the major retrospective show at the Whitney Museum of American Art by the scholar most involved with putting Eakins into the mainstream of American art. Good, with numerous reproductions and an excellent short essay.

Hendricks, Gordon. *The Life and Work of Thomas Eakins.* New York: Grossman Publishers, 1974. An obsessively detailed study, provocative in its assumptions.

Homer, William Innes. *Thomas Eakins: His Life and Art.* 2d ed. New York: Abbeville Press, 2002. Presents an unflattering portrait of Eakins, depicting him as a self-righteous, domineering egotist, with unconscious hostility toward women. Homer describes how this failed individual produced complex and humane art.

Johns, Elizabeth. *Thomas Eakins: The Heroism of Modern Life.* Princeton, N.J.: Princeton University Press, 1983. An interesting study of specific subjects painted by Eakins, putting them into the context of how other artists have used the same subjects.

Siegl, Theodor. *The Thomas Eakins Collection*. Philadelphia: Philadelphia Museum of Art, 1978. A careful assessment of Eakins's individuality as a painter and a sympathetic consideration of his personality.

SEE ALSO: Paul Cézanne; James McNeill Whistler.
RELATED ARTICLE in *Great Events from History: The Nineteenth Century, 1801-1900:* 1878: Muybridge Photographs a Galloping Horse.

WYATT EARP
American frontier law officer

As a lawman in the early cow towns of the Old West, Earp established a reputation that made him an American legend. To some, he epitomized revenge; to others, he was an authentic American hero.

BORN: March 19, 1848; Monmouth, Illinois
DIED: January 13, 1929; Los Angeles, California
ALSO KNOWN AS: Wyatt Berry Stapp Earp (full name)
AREA OF ACHIEVEMENT: Law

EARLY LIFE
Wyatt Berry Stapp Earp (ehrp) was named after his father's company commander during the Mexican War. He was the third son to Nicholas and Virginia Earp. As an early settler of Monmouth, Illinois (1843), Nicholas provided law and order in the community. His father's principles would impact Earp throughout the rest of his life. Nicholas, a restless farmer, saw the opportunity of abundant farmland in Pella, Iowa. In 1850, he moved his wife, his daughter Martha, and his four sons, Newton (Nicholas's son from a previous marriage), James, Virgil, and Wyatt (age two). Newton, James, and Virgil fought for the Union during the Civil War. In 1863, during the middle of the Civil War, the Earp family, which now included three more children (Morgan, Warren, and Adelia), moved again, this time to San Bernardino, California, where lush fields and prospering cities promised wealth.

On the wagon train traveling westward to California, Earp learned to handle a gun, shoot, hunt, scout, and, most important, stay cool in pressure situations. All of these skills would aid Earp in his brief but famous career as a frontier marshal. However, at the young age of sixteen, Earp was still very uncertain as to what he wanted to do. It was not until he reached California that he determined that farming was not for him. Instead, he began driving stagecoaches across the deserts of California and Arizona. Though short-lived, the experience enhanced Earp's frontier skills.

In 1868, Earp's family returned to Iowa, then quickly moved to the small town of Lamar, Missouri. It was there that Earp married Urilla Sutherland in January, 1870.

Just two months later, he was appointed as the constable of Lamar, a job that he found much more enjoyable than farming for his father. Earp seemed to have everything in order. Suddenly, however, his world came crashing down around him. Before their first wedding anniversary, Urilla suddenly died. The cause of her death remains a mystery. Speculation has ranged from complications while giving birth to a stillborn baby to typhoid. It has been suggested that the Sutherlands blamed Earp for Urilla's death and engaged him and his brothers in a fight. Some biographers believe that Earp left his job and the town of Lamar because of the bitterness and the grief he felt over the death of his wife, but not before allegedly embezzling twenty dollars from the town. Charges were filed, but nothing ever came of it.

After leaving town, Earp headed to the Indian Territory, where the federal government charged him with stealing horses. However, he jumped bail and headed to Kansas. He was able to evade the law by blending into the West as a Kansas buffalo hunter. His reputation as a lawman eventually began in the rough-and-tumble cow towns of Kansas.

LIFE'S WORK
After he spent a few years buffalo hunting, Earp sought his livelihood in the cow towns of Kansas. As legend has it, he was forced into law enforcement in Ellsworth, Kansas, and found it to his liking. From there, he moved to Wichita, Kansas, where he spent three years breaking up fights, dealing with drunken cowboys, and defending the city.

In 1876, during an election for the town marshal, Earp physically attacked the opposing marshal for remarks made against his family. He was immediately fired. However, having heard of Earp's success with some of the ruffians of Wichita, the mayor of Dodge City immediately called upon him to come to what had become one of the wildest and wickedest cow towns in the West. Even though Earp thought he would be the marshal of Dodge, he was given the deputy marshal's job and became chief enforcer. He only stayed in Dodge for one season before, according to legend, he went to Deadwood, South Dakota, for the fall and winter. There he cut and sold firewood while learning to gamble. Thereafter, gambling became an added source of income for Earp.

During the next cattle season, Earp returned to Dodge City but not to his job. Instead, he spent the next year bounty hunting fugitives from Dodge throughout Kansas, the Indian Territory, and Texas. It was during an excursion to Fort Griffin, Texas, in 1877 that he met his lifelong friend Doc Holliday, a noted gambler, gunman, and killer. This friendship would always cast a dark shadow on Earp's reputation.

In 1878, Earp returned to Dodge and was hired back as a deputy and began his career with noted lawman Bat Masterson. Earp and Masterson were credited with taming Dodge. Earp was effective at keeping order without resorting to gunplay, which was precisely what the saloon keepers, merchants, and bankers who ran Western boomtowns wanted. By the time he left Dodge in 1879, he had established himself as the top lawman in the West. Some would argue that he attained this reputation through intimidation and excessive force, while others would say that he epitomized law enforcement with a cool temper and nerves of steel. Earp had tamed the Wild West of Kansas, no doubt with help from a progressive railroad that essentially killed the cattle trade and a temperance movement that restricted alcohol.

Meanwhile, Virgil, Earp's brother, had heard of a silver strike in the small mining camp of Tombstone, Arizona. He wrote to Earp to come and make his fortune. In December of 1879, Earp arrived in Arizona with Celia Ann "Mattie" Blaylock, his common-law wife whom he had met while in Dodge but had never married. Along with Earp and Mattie came Earp's brother James and James's family. Virgil and Morgan arrived shortly after.

Earp was soon back into law enforcement when he was named deputy sheriff of Pima County. Virgil had been named U.S. deputy marshal of the same region. The Earp brothers conflicted with some of the surrounding ranchers, cowboys, and suspected villains. The term "cowboy" had taken on a negative connotation by this time and referred to thieves, robbers, cutthroats, and lawless citizens. The Clantons and McLaurys, two families that have been perceived as lawless cowboys in history books, clashed with the Earps, who tried to reestablish the laws that had grown lax.

The cowboys claimed that the Earps were simply taking advantage of their position. These confrontations eventually blew up in a shootout near the O.K. Corral on

Wyatt Earp.

October 26, 1881. By that time, Earp and Morgan had been made special deputies under Virgil. According to most accounts, the Earps sought a peaceful resolution to threats that Ike Clanton had made. The incident placed Billy and Ike Clanton, Frank and Billy McLaury, and Billy Claiborne near the O.K. Corral.

Speculation still circulates as to whether these men were waiting to ambush the Earps or were just riding out of town. Whatever their intentions, their plans were severely changed when Virgil, Earp, Morgan, and Holliday, who had been deputized for the occasion, met them on Fremont Street. Again, legend varies as to who fired first, but after the shootout, Billy Clanton and both McLaurys lay dead. Virgil, Morgan, and Holliday were wounded. To this day it is debated whether the shootout was a cold-blooded murder by men who hid behind their badges or justified law enforcement for violence against innocent citizens of Tombstone.

Earp and Holliday stood trial for the shootout. They eventually were acquitted, but the Earps suffered much criticism from the local papers and citizenry. Attention to the trial added to the incident's infamy. In retaliation for the shootout, an assassination attempt was made on Virgil. He survived, but at the cost of losing the use of his right arm. Next, Earp's favorite brother, Morgan, was assassinated. It was not until Earp tried to move the rest of his family west and another assassination attempt was made that Earp responded with lethal vengeance by killing one of the assailants. This controversial act was seen by some as murder and by others as justified vengeance. Earp's lethal crusade continued until he felt that he had accounted for all of the men who had killed his brother. After killing two more men, Earp and his posse fled to Colorado to escape indictment.

Earp stayed in Colorado expecting a pardon that never came. It was not until late 1882 that he joined Virgil in San Francisco, California. Meanwhile, Mattie, who had returned to California with Earp's family, returned to Tombstone after realizing that Earp was not coming for her. She committed suicide in 1887. During that time, Earp rekindled a romance with Sadie Marcus that had begun in Tombstone. For forty-seven years, Sadie and Earp remained with each other, gambling, mining, working in saloons, and moving from boomtown to boomtown in the American West. Earp died in 1929 in Los Angeles, California, a few months before his eighty-first birthday.

SIGNIFICANCE

Wyatt Earp's career as frontier marshal, only a small portion of his eighty years, was the reason for his notoriety. The saga of a brave frontier lawman fighting for justice has captured the hearts of Americans. His initial biography was released in the dreary days of depression, prohibition, and gangster activity. Because of public perceptions of police who are less than effective or consumed by corruption and a court system that fails to adequately punish criminals, Americans continue to seek someone who will supersede the law to preserve order. Wyatt Earp stands as a powerful symbol of just such a lawman.

—*Tonya Huber*

FURTHER READING

Banks, Leo. "Wyatt Earp." *Arizona Highways* 70 (July, 1994): 4-13. This short but detailed article covers the chronology of Earp's life and his appeal to American society.

Barra, Allen. *Inventing Wyatt Earp: His Life and Many Legends*. New York: Carroll & Graf, 1998. Barra, a reporter for the *Wall Street Journal*, meticulously sifts through the events of Earp's life to distinguish fact from fiction.

Bartholomew, Ed. *Wyatt Earp: The Man and the Myth*. Toyahvale, Tex.: Frontier Book Company, 1964. This is one of the earliest books that attempted to account for errors in the Earp story by substantiating events with factual information.

Brooks, David. "Wyatt Usurped." *The National Interest* 37 (Fall, 1994): 66-70. Brooks's brief historic overview of Earp argues that motion pictures have perpetuated a Western myth that has become representative of America.

Lake, Stuart. *Wyatt Earp: Frontier Marshall*. Boston: Houghton Mifflin, 1931. Lake's biography was supposedly written with the help of Earp himself. This interesting but fantastic book is important because it has become one of the major sources of the Earp myth.

Lubet, Steven. *Murder in Tombstone: The Forgotten Trial of Wyatt Earp*. New Haven, Conn.: Yale University Press, 2004. Lubet, a law professor, provides a detailed description of the trial resulting from the gunfight near the O.K. Corral. In Lubet's account, the bitter, contested trial was almost as contentious as the gunfight, with prosecutors determined to send the Earps and Doc Holliday to the gallows, and defense lawyers insisting upon their clients' heroism.

Peterson, Roger. "Wyatt Earp: Man Versus Myth." *American History* 29 (August, 1994): 54-61. This magazine article provides a brief history of Earp, discussing how his legend began and how it may have been corrupted.

Tefertiller, Casey. *Wyatt Earp: The Life Behind the Legend*. New York: John Wiley & Sons, 1997. Tefertiller's book is an excellent source for explaining the myth of Earp and why it has been misunderstood.

SEE ALSO: Wild Bill Hickok; Jesse and Frank James.
RELATED ARTICLE in *Great Events from History: The Nineteenth Century, 1801-1900:* August 17, 1896: Klondike Gold Rush Begins.

MARY BAKER EDDY
American religious leader

A deeply religious thinker, Mary Baker Eddy established the Church of Christ, Scientist—the first church movement to be founded in the United States by a woman.

BORN: July 16, 1821; Bow, New Hampshire
DIED: December 3, 1910; Chestnut Hill, Massachusetts
ALSO KNOWN AS: Mary Morse Baker (birth name)
AREA OF ACHIEVEMENT: Religion and theology

EARLY LIFE

The youngest of six children, Mary Morse Baker was born on her parents' New Hampshire farm. Her father, Mark Baker, was a respected farmer whose deep interest in theology prompted him to engage in serious religious debates with his neighbors. Mary's mother, Abigail Ambrose Baker, had grown up as the daughter of a prominent deacon of the Congregational church in nearby Pembroke and was known for her tender solicitude toward her family and neighbors. Both parents were devout members of the Congregational church; Mary was nurtured in their Calvinist faith and joined the church herself at the age of twelve.

As a young girl, Mary began her formal education in 1826. An intelligent, highly sensitive child, Mary suffered from ill health that frequently kept her at home. She became a diligent reader and an avid writer of poetry. Mary received individual instruction from her second brother, Albert, who served as a schoolmaster at Mary's school when he was twenty. Her brother's instruction provided Mary with an education well in advance of that commonly available to young women of the period, and she was introduced to the rudiments of Greek, Latin, and Hebrew as well as contemporary works of literature and philosophy.

In December of 1843, Mary Baker was married to Major George Washington Glover, a successful builder with business interests in the Carolinas. The newlyweds eventually settled in Wilmington, North Carolina. By June of 1844, George Glover's investments in building supplies for a project in Haiti were lost, and he was stricken with yellow fever. He died on June 27, forcing his pregnant and impoverished widow to return to her parents' home. Despite her dangerously poor health, Mary gave birth in September to a healthy son, whom she named George in honor of his late father.

When Abigail Baker died in 1849, her daughter's grief and precarious health made further care for the boisterous young George Glover even more difficult. Mark Baker's second marriage less than one year later forced Mary and her son to leave the Baker house. Mary went to stay with her sister Abigail Tilton, but George Glover was placed in the care of Mary's former nurse. Mary was devastated by her separation from her son, but her family insisted that reuniting the two would further strain Mary's tenuous health.

In 1853, Mary was married to Daniel Patterson, a dentist who promised to provide a home for her and her son. That promise was never fulfilled, however, and Patterson's failings as a husband became increasingly evident. Mary's son moved with his foster parents to the West; they later told him that his mother had died. Mary's new husband was often absent in the course of his itinerant practice, and the couple found lodgings in various communities in New Hampshire. In the spring of 1862, while on commission to deliver state funds to Union sympathizers in the South, Patterson was taken prisoner by Confederate forces.

Barely able to care for herself, Mary sought relief from her persistent ill health at an institute in New Hampshire that promoted hydropathy, or the water cure. Finding little improvement during her visit, she traveled to Portland, Maine, to visit Phineas P. Quimby, a clockmaker who had developed a reputation as a magnetic healer and hypnotist. After her first treatment at his office, Mary experienced a marked improvement in her health. In her enthusiasm to learn more about the methods Quimby used, she sought to reconcile Quimby's ideas with the spiritually based biblical healings with which she was so familiar.

Reunited with her husband in December of 1862 after his escape from prison, Mary returned to New Hampshire, where she experienced relapses of ill health. She sought relief by visiting Quimby at various times but could not discover a permanent cure for her illnesses. After Quimby's death in early January of 1866, Mary was seriously injured when she fell on icy pavement in Lynn, Massachusetts, on February 1.

After being taken to a nearby house, Mary eventually regained consciousness sufficiently to persuade her doctor and friends to move her to her lodgings in nearby Swampscott, where she was given little hope of recovery from the injuries to her head and spine. Visited by a clergyman on the Sunday after her accident, she asked to be left alone with her Bible. Turning to the ninth chapter of

Matthew, she read the account of Jesus' healing of the man sick of the palsy (paralysis). Upon reading the story, she felt a profound change come over her and found that she was fully recovered from her injuries. Rising from her bed to dress and then greet the friends who waited outside her door, Mary astonished them with the rapidity and completeness of her healing, one that she credited to the power of God alone.

LIFE'S WORK

During the decade from 1866 to 1876, Mary Patterson's outward life seemed little improved, yet her conviction that she could discover the source of her healing experience inspired her to continue her study of the Bible. Her husband deserted her soon after her healing; they were divorced in 1873, and she resumed using the surname Glover.

Although her financial situation was precarious and she was still separated from her son, Mary realized that, at the age of forty-five, she was healthier than she had ever been in her entire life. For three years after her recovery, she dedicated herself solely to searching the Bible for answers to her questions regarding spiritual healing, withdrawing from social pursuits and her temperance movement activities in order to record the revelations she was gaining through her studies. She lived frugally in a series of boardinghouses, began sharing her notes and interpretations of Bible passages with individuals who seemed receptive to her new ideas, and occasionally offered instruction in her healing methods in exchange for the cost of her room and board. A group of committed students eventually began to gather around her. In October of 1875, she managed to publish the first edition of her work, entitled *Science and Health*, with the financial assistance of some of her students.

It was in March of 1876 that Asa Gilbert Eddy, a native of Vermont who was ten years her junior and worked in Massachusetts as a salesperson for the Singer Sewing Machine Company, became one of Mary's students. Asa Eddy, better known as Gilbert, became a successful healer. At a time when many of her most talented students were challenging her authority and attempting to undermine her teachings, Mary came to rely on Gilbert Eddy's sound judgment and his steady support of her leadership. The two were married on January 1, 1877.

Around this time, Mary Baker Eddy began revising *Science and Health*, adding five new chapters. This two-volume second edition was so rife with typographical errors that only the second volume was circulated. During this time, Eddy began to lecture weekly at the Baptist Ta-

Mary Baker Eddy. (Library of Congress)

bernacle in Boston. The success of her public sermons led her to make a motion at a meeting of her students in 1879 that they organize a church; it was called the Church of Christ, Scientist. In Eddy's own words, the purpose of this church was "to commemorate the word and works of our Master, which should reinstate primitive Christianity and its lost element of healing."

The new church was incorporated under a state charter, and Eddy was designated its president and appointed its first pastor. By the winter of 1879, Eddy and her husband had moved to rooms in Boston to be nearer to the growing church. She continued to teach new adult students about Christian Science, and the church established a Sunday school for the instruction of children in 1880. That same year, Eddy published the first of her many pamphlets: a sermon entitled *Christian Healing*. In an effort to give a more solid legal foundation to her classes, Eddy applied for a state charter in order to incorporate the Massachusetts Metaphysical College, a school dedicated to furthering the spread of her healing method by ensuring that students received unadulterated instruction directly from her.

Earlier, Mary Baker Eddy had begun revising and expanding *Science and Health* once again. The third edition of *Science and Health*, which appeared in 1881, was the first accurate edition of her writings to incorporate part of the treatise she used to instruct students in her classes. This publishing enterprise brought Eddy into contact with one of the leading printers of her day: John Wilson of the University Press in Cambridge, Massachusetts. Prospects for selling all one thousand copies of the third edition were not promising, but Wilson was convinced that Eddy would be able to finance the printing of her book through its sales. By 1882, the book had gone back to print for two additional editions of one thousand copies each.

Other publishing activities began. In April of 1883, Eddy published the first issue of *The Journal of Christian Science*. Originally a bimonthly periodical with articles designed to explore issues of interest to both newcomers and longtime students of Eddy's religion, the *Journal* was expanded to become a monthly publication and was one of the first authorized organs of the Christian Science church. A sixth edition of *Science and Health* appeared in 1883; it was the first to contain Eddy's "Key to the Scriptures," a section initially consisting of a glossary with her metaphysical interpretations of biblical terms and concepts. By 1885, nine additional printings were made, bringing the total number of copies in circulation during the book's first ten years to 15,000.

The years following the publication of the sixth edition of *Science and Health* were prosperous ones, with many new students working to spread Christian Science and its healing practice throughout the United States. Nevertheless, several events occurred in the period from 1889 to 1892 that radically altered the structure and direction of the Christian Science church. Schisms among her students and the burdens resulting from those who increasingly relied on her personal leadership in all matters led Eddy to close her college at the height of its popularity and resign her post as pastor of

EDDY'S ADVICE TO HER FOLLOWERS

This extract is from Mary Baker Eddy's introduction to her frequently reprinted pamphlet No and Yes, *in which she offers advice and encouragement to her followers on how to practice Christian Science beliefs properly. This passage is broadly representative of Eddy's writing style.*

To kindle in all minds a common sentiment of regard for the spiritual idea emanating from the infinite, is a most needful work; but this must be done gradually, for Truth is as "the still, small voice," which comes to our recognition only as our natures are changed by its silent influence.

Small streams are noisy and rush precipitately; and babbling brooks fill the rivers till they rise in floods, demolishing bridges and overwhelming cities. So men, when thrilled by a new idea, are sometimes impatient; and, when public sentiment is aroused, are liable to be borne on by the current of feeling. They should then turn temporarily from the tumult, for the silent cultivation of the true idea and the quiet practice of its virtues. When the noise and stir of contending sentiments cease, and the flames die away on the mount of revelation, we can read more clearly the tablets of Truth.

The theology and medicine of Jesus were one,—in the divine oneness of the trinity, Life, Truth, and Love, which healed the sick and cleansed the sinful. This trinity in unity, correcting the individual thought, is the only Mind-healing I vindicate; and on its standard have emblazoned that crystallized expression, CHRISTIAN SCIENCE.

A spurious and hydra-headed mind-healing is naturally glared at by the pulpit, ostracized by the medical faculty, and scorned by people of common sense. To aver that disease is normal, a God-bestowed and stubborn reality, but that you can heal it, leaves you to work against that which is natural and a law of being. It is scientific to rob disease of all reality; and to accomplish this, you cannot begin by admitting its reality. Our Master taught his students to deny self, sense, and take up the cross. Mental healers who admit that disease is real should be made to test the feasibility of what they say by healing one case audibly, through such an admission,—if this is possible. I have healed more disease by the spoken than the unspoken word.

The honest student of Christian Science is modest in his claims and conscientious in duty, waiting and working to mature what he has been taught. Institutes furnished with such teachers are becoming beacon-lights along the shores of erudition; and many who are not teachers have large practices and some marked success in healing the most defiant forms of disease.

Dishonesty destroys one's ability to heal mentally. Conceit cannot avert the effects of deceit. Taking advantage of the present ignorance in relation to Christian Science Mind-healing, many are flooding our land with conflicting theories and practice. We should not spread abroad patchwork ideas that in some vital points lack Science. . . .

Source: Mary Baker Eddy, *No and Yes* (Boston, 1919).

the Boston church. Services continued to be conducted in Christian Science churches, but students voted to adjourn the activities of the National Christian Scientist Association for three years beginning in 1890. Withdrawing to a new home in Concord, New Hampshire, Eddy commenced work on a major revision of *Science and Health* to be published as the fiftieth edition in 1891.

September 23, 1892, marked the establishment of Eddy's newly reorganized church: the First Church of Christ, Scientist, in Boston, Massachusetts, also known as The Mother Church. She consulted with attorneys familiar with Massachusetts statutes in order to find a legal means to incorporate her church that would place its corporate government on a solid basis without encouraging undue attachment to her personal authority. The new charter provided a powerful centralized structure in the form of a five-member board of directors responsible for management of the church's affairs; it also fostered the practice of democratic self-government already established in the branch churches outside of Boston that were affiliated with the growing church movement. All members of these branches were invited to apply for concurrent membership in The Mother Church.

Eddy was henceforth designated as the Discoverer and Founder of Christian Science. To her mind, this title expressed the scientific aspect of her work—emphasizing her role in formulating and articulating its religious teachings in much the same way that scientific laws and principles are formulated and articulated, but not created, by those who discover them.

In October of 1893, the building of the new church edifice was begun in Boston's Back Bay area, with the cornerstone of the church laid in May of 1894 and the first service held on December 30, 1894. Eddy took the unusual step of ordaining the Bible and *Science and Health*, rather than human ministers, as pastors of the church. When she published the *Manual of The Mother Church* in 1895, setting forth the rules by which the church was to be governed, she made provisions in its bylaws for the election of lay readers who would read texts from the Bible and from *Science and Health* relating to twenty-six topics she set forth.

The texts were selected by a special committee; the resulting lesson sermons were studied daily by individual members and were read Sundays at Christian Science church services throughout the world. These changes were instituted by Eddy in order to avoid the adulteration of her teachings through personal preaching. In this way, she believed that the healing message contained in the Bible and in her book would speak directly to all who at-

tended her church without the injection of personal opinion or conflicting interpretations.

In 1898, Eddy established a board of education to provide for the formal instruction of students in Christian Science by those who were approved to serve as teachers. She also established a Board of Lectureship to which practitioners (ordained healers within the church) and teachers of Christian Science were appointed. These lecturers were responsible for preparing and delivering public lectures on Christian Science in order to introduce and clarify its teachings to those unfamiliar with the religion. The Christian Science Publishing Society was created through a deed of trust and was charged with the responsibility for publishing and distributing *Science and Health* and Eddy's other books as well as *The Christian Science Journal* and the newly founded periodical, *The Christian Science Weekly* (renamed *The Christian Science Sentinel* in 1899). In 1902, Eddy completed work on her final major revision of *Science and Health*; it was the 226th edition of the book known as the Christian Science textbook.

Although she enjoyed the relative peace and seclusion of her New Hampshire estate, known as Pleasant View, Eddy faced bitter personal attacks in the popular press during the early twentieth century that threatened to undermine her church. These articles reflected the sensational "yellow journalism" of the period. Few pieces were more damaging than those published by Joseph Pulitzer, whose *New York World* newspaper claimed that Eddy was near death from cancer and that her alleged fortune of $15 million was being wrested from her control. Refusing to meet with Pulitzer's reporters, Eddy granted audience to representatives of several other leading newspapers and press associations. After answering three brief questions concerning her health, Eddy gave evidence of her well-being by departing to take her daily carriage ride.

Despite Eddy's efforts to disprove the rumors concerning her health, her son George was approached by the publishers of the *New York World* and was encouraged, on the basis of the paper's erroneous accounts of his mother's welfare, to begin legal proceedings to determine Eddy's mental competence and ability to conduct business affairs connected with her church. Although funded by Pulitzer's newspaper fortune, this lawsuit ultimately collapsed after a panel appointed to determine Eddy's competence held a one-hour interview and established that she was in full possession of her mental faculties.

Refusing to back down in the face of these personal attacks, Eddy was prompted to establish a trust for her property in order to preserve its orderly transfer to the church after her death. More important, Eddy was impelled to launch an enormous new undertaking: She directed the Trustees of the Publishing Society to establish a daily newspaper to be known as *The Christian Science Monitor*, which began publication in 1908. By bringing national and international events into clearer focus for its readers, *The Christian Science Monitor* would fulfill Eddy's vision of its purpose: to combat the apathy, indifference, and despair that were common responses to world affairs through its spiritually enlightened, problem-solving journalism. After witnessing the fruition of her long-cherished hopes, Eddy died quietly in her sleep near the end of 1910.

SIGNIFICANCE

Regardless of one's perspective on the validity of her religious beliefs, Mary Baker Eddy clearly led a remarkable life—one full of extraordinary success despite the prejudices that confronted her as a woman attempting to establish a spiritually minded religious movement during an age of rampant materialism. Novelist and humorist Mark Twain, who was one of Eddy's most outspoken critics, once remarked that she was "probably the most daring and masterful woman who has appeared on earth for centuries."

A pragmatic and capable administrator who inspired her followers by her example of single-minded dedication, Eddy was equally comfortable in her role as a religious thinker—one who refused to compromise her conscience "to suit the general drift of thought" and was convinced of the importance of maintaining the intellectual and spiritual purity of her writings. Her church remains an active presence in the United States and throughout the world, and her book *Science and Health* was recognized by the Women's National Book Association in 1992 as one of seventy-five important works by "women whose words have changed the world."

—*Wendy Sacket*

FURTHER READING

Eddy, Mary Baker. *Mary Baker Eddy: Speaking for Herself.* Boston: Writings of Mary Baker Eddy, 2002. Includes two of Eddy's books: her memoir, *Retrospection and Introspection*, first published in 1891, and *Footprints Fadeless*, a defense of one of her critics, written in 1901-1902, and published here for the first time. Jana K. Reiss, religion editor for *Publishers Weekly*, provides an introduction, analyzing Eddy's writings and placing Eddy's life and work in the context of late nineteenth century American religion and society.

Gill, Gillian. *Mary Baker Eddy.* Reading, Mass.: Perseus Books, 1998. Feminist biography. Gill portrays Eddy as a powerful woman who broke free from conventional gender roles to introduce radical new ideas. While acknowledging Eddy's faults, Gill is generally sympathetic, emphasizing her subject's gifts as a religious leader, administrator, and promoter of Christian Science.

Gottschalk, Stephen. *The Emergence of Christian Science in American Religious Life.* Berkeley: University of California Press, 1973. Although its examination of Christian Science from the perspective of intellectual history may make it less easily accessible to general readers, this work sets forth the distinctive contributions Christian Science has made to American theology and culture.

Orcutt, William Dana. *Mary Baker Eddy and Her Books.* Boston: Christian Science Publishing Society, 1950. Written by a distinguished bookmaker who worked closely with Eddy from 1897 to 1910 and helped design the oversize subscription edition of *Science and Health* that was released in 1941, this memoir provides an intriguing window on Eddy's career as an author.

Peel, Robert. *Mary Baker Eddy: The Years of Discovery.* New York: Holt, Rinehart and Winston, 1966.

_____. *Mary Baker Eddy: The Years of Trial.* New York: Holt, Rinehart and Winston, 1971.

_____. *Mary Baker Eddy: The Years of Authority.* New York: Holt, Rinehart and Winston, 1977. Written by a Harvard-educated scholar who had unprecedented access to church archival materials, this monumental three-volume biography remains the definitive work on Eddy's life. Although Peel was himself a Christian Scientist, his work gives evidence of his conscientious effort to provide "a straightforward, factual account free from either apologetics or polemics."

Satter, Beryl. *Each Mind a Kingdom: American Women, Sexual Purity, and the New Thought Movement, 1875-1920.* Berkeley: University of California Press, 1999. Focusing on the New Thought Movement in general, and Eddy's Christian Science in particular, Satter describes American women's intellectual and psychological relationships to progressive social movements and self-improvement cults during the late nineteenth and early twentieth centuries. She concludes that participation in these movements gave disenfranchised middle-class white women a way to escape their homes and refashion society and gender roles.

Thomas, Robert David. *"With Bleeding Footsteps":* *Mary Baker Eddy's Path to Religious Leadership.* New York: Alfred A. Knopf, 1994. Trained in the theories of psychoanalysis, Thomas brings this psychological perspective to bear on his study of Eddy's character and behavior. Despite his serious, scholarly approach, Thomas fails to provide a complete assessment of Eddy's significance as a religious leader and seems to fall short of bringing his subject fully alive.

Nevertheless, this biography is useful as one of the few fair-minded studies of Eddy to have appeared since Peel's three-volume work, cited above.

SEE ALSO: Dorothea Dix; Joseph Smith; Mark Twain.
RELATED ARTICLE in *Great Events from History: The Nineteenth Century, 1801-1900:* October 30, 1875: Eddy Establishes the Christian Science Movement.

MARIA EDGEWORTH
English novelist

Edgeworth achieved fame in her own time as a novelist and author of children's stories, but her lasting impact has been as a regional novelist who captured the lives of landlords and tenants living in Ireland during the late eighteenth and early nineteenth centuries.

BORN: January 1, 1768; Black Bourton, Oxfordshire, England
DIED: May 22, 1849; Edgeworthstown, Ireland
AREA OF ACHIEVEMENT: Literature

EARLY LIFE

Maria Edgeworth was the third child and first daughter of Richard Lovell Edgeworth and his wife, Anna Maria. The Edgeworths were descendants of an English family who had been given land in Ireland during the seventeenth century. The family lived in England until 1782, when Maria's father moved them to their Irish estate, Edgeworthtown in County Longford.

During Maria's childhood, her mother died, as did two stepmothers in later decades. Each time that her father lost a wife, he dutifully remarried. His fourth wife, Frances, whom he married in 1798, was a year younger than Maria herself. Edgeworth eventually had a total of twenty-two children by his four wives. As one of the oldest, Maria frequently found herself assisting in rearing younger siblings, an experience that would later influence her writing.

As a child, Maria attended private schools briefly, but her father directed her real education. An eclectic and somewhat eccentric thinker, Richard Lovell Edgeworth had a keen interest in science, engineering, and education. He exploited his eldest daughter's proclivity for writing by making her his assistant on a number of projects that resulted in publications on educational theory, and he later directed the work of many of her novels.

When she was a teenager, Maria began writing down stories she told to the family as evening entertainments. At the same time, her father began assigning projects to her, among them a translation of Madame Stephanie de Genlis's *Adèle et Théodore* (1782), an educational tract presented in the form of letters. Her father's friend Thomas Day, another educational theorist and author of the pioneering children's novel *The History of Sandford and Merton* (1783), prompted her to write philosophical tracts on subjects such as happiness. By the time Maria came of age, her future had been charted: She was to spend her life as an author, collaborating with her father on books about education and writing novels and stories illustrating principles of Richard Lovell Edgeworth's educational and social philosophy.

LIFE'S WORK

The first fruit of the collaboration between Maria Edgeworth and her father was a slim volume titled *Letters for Literary Ladies* (1795), her own version of *Adèle et Théodore* in which women exchange ideas about education. A year later she issued *The Parent's Assistant: Or, Stories for Children* (1796), a three-volume collection of children's stories based on her father's ideas about rearing children. Her father had a hand in both works, editing them carefully and advising his daughter about the virtues and vices her writing should depict. Maria published both books anonymously; when they were reissued in later years, their title pages bore her name alone.

Such was not the case with *Practical Education* (1798), a collection of essays that Maria wrote with her father outlining his theories. Its three volumes were influenced heavily by the work of John Locke and Jean-Jacques Rousseau, and the book's publication gave the

EDGEWORTH'S MAJOR FICTIONAL WORKS

Novels

1800	*Castle Rackrent*
1801	*Belinda*
1806	*Leonora*
1809	*Ennui*
1812	*The Absentee*
1812	*Vivian*
1814	*Patronage*
1817	*Harrington*
1817	*Ormond*
1834	*Helen*

Short Fiction

1805	*The Modern Griselda*
1809-1812	*Tales of Fashionable Life*
1825	*Tales and Miscellaneous Pieces*
1832	*Garry Owen: Or, The Snow-Woman, and Poor Bob, the Chimney-Sweeper*
1848	*Orlandino*
1883	*Classic Tales*

Children's Books

1796	*The Parent's Assistant: Or, Stories for Children*
1801	*Harry and Lucy* (with Richard Lovell Edgeworth)
1801	*Rosamond* (with Richard Lovell Edgeworth)
1801	*Frank* (with Richard Lovell Edgeworth)
1801	*Moral Tales for Young People*
1801	*The Mental Thermometer*
1804	*Popular Tales*
1814	*Continuation of Early Lessons*
1821	*Rosamond: A Sequel to Early Lessons*
1822	*Frank: A Sequel to Frank in Early Lessons*
1825	*Harry and Lucy Concluded*
1931	*The Purple Jar, and Other Stories*

Over the next seventeen years Maria wrote prolifically in the three genres for which she had prepared herself. She continued to write and publish children's stories while pursuing her career as a writer of tales for adults as well. Often, rather than writing what would have been considered novels by her contemporaries—multivolume stories such as those by Henry Fielding and her contemporary Mrs. Elizabeth Inchbald—she concentrated on works that normally occupied a single volume or less.

In 1809, Maria published the first series of *Tales of Fashionable Life*, a collection of four long tales that included one of her most memorable stories, *Ennui* (1809). Three years later she brought out the second series of the tales, one volume of which was *The Absentee*. This tale about an English landlord who returns to his Irish estates to find mismanagement and despair among his tenants is typical of the kind of social criticism that Edgeworth offered in many of her stories to give form to situations she had experienced or learned about as the daughter of an English landlord in Ireland.

In 1802, Maria accompanied her father to the Continent, where she was exposed at first hand to high society. While in Paris in November of 1802, she met Abraham N. C. Edelcrantz, the private secretary to the king of Sweden. A month after they met, Edelcrantz proposed marriage. Although her father thought well of her marrying Edelcrantz, Maria turned down his offer. She indicated in letters to family and friends that she preferred not to live in Sweden—or away from her father, to whom she was attached in a way that would raise speculation among scholars and biographers in later years.

By 1813, when the Edgeworths made an extended trip to England, Maria was lionized by high society not only for works such as *Belinda* (1801), *Tales of Fashionable Life*, and especially *Castle Rackrent*, but also for being her father's collaborator on works such as *Practical Education* and its sequel, *Essays on Professional Education*

Edgeworths a minor reputation as progressives in the field of educational theory. At the same time Maria was writing these volumes, she began a story based loosely on her reminiscences of John Langan, a former caretaker at Edgeworthtown. That Irishman had impressed the youthful Maria with his amusing stories and his lilting brogue, which Maria attempted to capture by making him the narrator of a tale about four generations of a dissolute English family who had ruined their Irish estate and its native tenant farmers. Published anonymously in 1800, *Castle Rackrent* became instantly popular in literary circles in both Ireland and England. Maria Edgeworth's career as a writer of adult novels was launched propitiously.

(1809). Among those who met her and expressed their admiration was the poet George Gordon—better known as Lord Byron—who said that he wished his future wife to be like a character from Edgeworth's novels. Maria's reputation as the premier English novelist of the first decades of the nineteenth century was solidified with the publication of *Patronage* (1814) and two shorter tales published in 1817, *Harrington* and *Ormond*.

After the death of her father in 1817, however, Maria's creativity seemed to diminish. She continued to work on revisions of earlier stories, but her principal work during the years after her father's death were spent in completing *Memoirs of Richard Lovell Edgeworth, Esq.* (1820), a two-volume biography of the man who had so dominated her life and for whom she had expressed abiding affection.

During the 1820's, Edgeworth produced a dozen volumes of stories and plays for children, but her next novel for adults, *Helen*, did not appear until 1834. It was to be the last work of serious fiction she would write. She spent the last three decades of her life at Edgeworthtown and paid occasional visits to England and Scotland. During her 1823 visit to Edinburgh, she met with Sir Walter Scott, who invited her to his home for an extended stay. She also received the poet William Wordsworth at her own home in Ireland in 1829. During her later years she oversaw the publication of two collected editions of her work. By the late 1830's, the popularity of her novels had given way the books of other writers, most notably Charles Dickens. She died in Ireland on May 22, 1849.

SIGNIFICANCE

From 1800 until the arrival of Dickens on the literary scene, Maria Edgeworth was considered one of the greatest living novelists. Only Sir Walter Scott rivaled her in reputation or popularity. She is considered the originator of the regional novel, having created in *Castle Rackrent* the formula for using local color and dialect as techniques for commenting on morality and society. Equally important, Edgeworth was the first notable writer of literature specifically aimed at children; her work provides simple stories with discernible morals woven into exciting tales that capture children's attention and help them learn while being entertained. The best of her novels of social commentary, *Ennui* and *The Absentee*, provide insights into the plight of the English and Irish during the turbulent period when Ireland was firmly under English rule.

—*Laurence W. Mazzeno*

FURTHER READING

Butler, Marilyn. *Maria Edgeworth: A Biography*. Oxford, England: Clarendon Press, 1972. This detailed account of Edgeworth's writing career is the standard twentieth century biography. Butler weaves throughout her story of Edgeworth's life and relationship with her eccentric father critical commentary that demonstrates how events shaped both her fiction and nonfiction. Her bibliography contains an extensive list of primary sources, including letters and other unpublished writings.

Gonda, Caroline. *Reading Daughters' Fictions, 1709-1834*. New York: Cambridge University Press, 1996. Gonda includes a chapter on Edgeworth's relationship with her father and the resultant influence the latter had in shaping his daughter's fiction. In the course of her critique, Gonda challenges earlier readings of Edgeworth's career offered by Butler and Kowaleski-Wallace.

Harden, O. E. *Maria Edgeworth*. Boston: Twayne, 1984. Harden provides a chronology and brief biographical sketch, examines a number of novels and nonfiction works Edgeworth completed with her father, and assesses Edgeworth's achievements. The volume also includes an annotated bibliography.

Hollingworth, Brian. *Maria Edgeworth's Irish Writings*. New York: St. Martin's Press, 1997. Hollingworth's principal interest is in Edgeworth's regional novels, a genre of which Edgeworth is frequently considered the first practitioner. He explains how Edgeworth's upbringing as the daughter of an English landlord in Ireland influenced her novels about that country.

Kowaleski-Wallace, Elizabeth. *Their Father's Daughters*. New York: Oxford University Press, 1991. Edgeworth's career is examined in detail in this study of several eighteenth and nineteenth century women authors whose fathers dominated their lives. Kowaleski-Wallace examines strategies these women used to react against patriarchal expectations of their appropriate role as writers.

SEE ALSO: Mary Elizabeth Braddon; The Brontë Sisters; Lord Byron; Charles Dickens; George Eliot; Sir Walter Scott; Mary Wollstonecraft Shelley; William Wordsworth; Charlotte Mary Yonge.

RELATED ARTICLES in *Great Events from History: The Nineteenth Century, 1801-1900:* 1814: Scott Publishes *Waverley*; May 9, 1828-April 13, 1829: Roman Catholic Emancipation; 1845-1854: Great Irish Famine.

THOMAS ALVA EDISON
American inventor

Edison was perhaps the greatest inventor in world history. His incandescent electric lights transformed electrical technology; his myriad other inventions included a stock ticker, duplex and quadraplex telegraphs, the phonograph, a telephone transmitter, the motion-picture camera, and the storage battery. He symbolized the ingenious, prolific, heroic, and professional American inventor in an age of invention, innovation, and industrialization.

BORN: February 11, 1847; Milan, Ohio
DIED: October 18, 1931; West Orange, New Jersey
AREA OF ACHIEVEMENT: Science and technology

EARLY LIFE

Thomas Alva Edison grew up in the midwestern industrial heartland of the United States during his country's transformation from an agrarian to an industrial nation. The seventh and last child of Samuel and Nancy (née Elliot) Edison, he was reared in Port Huron, Michigan, near Detroit. He found formal schooling disagreeable, so his mother, a former teacher, tutored young Tom at home. Gifted with a natural inquisitiveness, a love of science and experimentation, and access to the Detroit Free Library, he largely educated himself.

As a teenager, Edison worked, first selling newspapers and candy on the train between Port Huron and Detroit, and later as a telegraph operator in the Midwest. In both jobs he managed to find time to perform various chemical and electrical experiments and to continue his lifetime reading habit. By 1868, he had moved to Boston, where he came under the intellectual influence so strong in that city at the time. There his reading of Michael Faraday's work on electricity, with its heavy emphasis on experimentation and conceptualization of physical models, strengthened his own strong preference for applied science with its testing of hypotheses, its pragmatic approach to problems, and its interest in practical application. Inventing for profit became a goal for Edison as he directed his genius toward the industrial and economic climate of post-Civil War America.

Seeking fame and fortune, Edison moved to New York City in 1869, having neither a job nor money. A combination of luck and acumen at the Law's Gold Indicator Company resulted in his appointment as plant superintendent. Edison's working in Wall Street during an age of enterprise provided him with the basis for his first commercially successful invention, an improved stock ticker. His additional improvements of stock ticker technology brought Edison forty thousand dollars for his patent rights, a princely sum in 1870. With a small fortune and some fame, Edison turned to electrical technology, an arena that consumed much of his life's work.

LIFE'S WORK

Like so many of his fellow pioneers in the world of electrical invention, Edison was well versed in telegraphy. His many years as a first-rate telegraph operator, his familiarity with electrical devices and experiments, and his vision of an industrial, urban America directed his various endeavors. In the period from 1872 to 1874, he turned his attention to duplex and quadruplex telegraphy, the process of sending two or four simultaneous signals, respectively, over a single wire. His commercial success with these two processes led him to improvements with the telephone, itself a special type of telegraph.

In 1876, Edison sought and found a more efficient transmitter for the telephone. His carbon button device in the mouthpiece provided a stronger signal that would travel farther on transmission lines. With this success, he demonstrated his legendary ability to improve existing inventions. In this same year, he moved to Menlo Park, New Jersey, and established a research and development laboratory complete with support personnel and several workshops. Edison realized the central role of systematic inquiry for new enterprises, and Menlo Park became the prototype for the industrial research laboratories that have been so important for innovation in a technological society.

The phonograph was another Edison invention with its origins in telegraphy. The embossed paper tape that recorded the dots and dashes of telegraph messages gave off a musical sound when Edison moved the tape quickly through a repeater mechanism. From this stimulus he devised a tin-foil-covered cylinder that would record vibrations of sound entered through a recording diaphragm. A quickly conceived idea became a patented reality in 1877, although the phonograph required substantial modification before it became a commercial success. Edison's ability to invent a "talking machine" enhanced his reputation as a genius. His most prolific years of work on the phonograph came in the period 1887-1890, when he developed the wax-coated flat record and separate recording and playback components.

Thomas Alva Edison. (Library of Congress)

Success with the early phonograph led Edison to another challenge in the world of electricity: an incandescent electric lighting system. From 1878 to 1882, he and his Menlo Park staff devoted much of their time to the invention and innovation of a system that would subdivide the electric arc light. In this task, Edison was an entrepreneur as well as a pioneer developer of a new technology. He used the full resources of the Menlo Park laboratory and workshops to attack the problems of incandescent lighting and to seek commercially successful solutions to those problems, which required many painstaking hours of research and development; he relied on the best talent in Menlo Park, the scientific method of inquiry, and the systematic empirical approach to problem solving.

When Edison began his quest to provide a workable lighting system, he built on an awareness of arc lighting developments and on the achievements of other inventors seeking an incandescent system. He realized that he needed a high resistance lamp filament that would burn for several hours; an efficient generator; a distribution network with wires, switches, meters, and fuses; and a

central power station. A heavy reliance on a skilled and knowledgeable staff provided the successful lighting elements: a carbonized cotton filament, the "long legged Mary Ann" generator, and the prototype Pearl Street central station. He set his sights on the marketplace, used the familiar terminology and methods of gas illumination in his system, and displayed his entrepreneurial talents by promoting his own system, a promotion helped greatly by his reputation as an inventive genius (a reputation which Edison made no attempt to dispel). So successful was he in this enterprise that to generations of Americans, Thomas Edison was *the* inventor of the electric light.

Although Edison's business acumen was greater than most people believed, his chief interest was not the ledger book, and he soon tired of the business of electric lighting and turned to other areas of invention. By 1892, the Edison General Electric companies became part of a larger conglomerate known simply as the General Electric Company. With his name no longer associated with the operation, Edison lost interest in electric lighting developments and sold his stock in General Electric. He now had millions of dollars to use for new inventive challenges.

By 1887, Edison had moved his laboratories to West Orange, New Jersey, in a more extensive physical plant. With this move, he could engage in large-scale invention and innovation, as he did during the 1880's and 1890's with two major projects: the motion-picture camera and a magnetic ore separation process. The former was a commercial success; the latter was an economic disaster.

Although he began his work on the motion-picture camera in 1887, Edison performed most of the developmental work on it in the years from 1889 to 1891. His invention of a camera that took a series of still photographs in rapid succession resulted from mechanical insight rather than any electrical or chemical knowledge that was so important in almost all of his other inventions. That he could successfully devise a practical motion-picture camera through the strength of his mechanical ability attests his inventive talent.

From 1894 to 1899, Thomas Edison devoted his attention to another chiefly nonelectrical project: magnetic ore separation. Sensing that a market for low-grade Eastern iron ore existed if it could be extracted cheaply, he invested several years and millions of dollars in creating huge ore-crushing machines. These machines would pulverize the ore deposits, and the resulting powder would pass by electromagnets that separated the ore from the dross. Although a technical success, the process never could compete with the low-cost ores of the

Mesabi range; Edison found himself deeply in debt by 1900 and finally abandoned the scheme.

At the turn of the century, Edison returned to electrical technology with his invention of a durable storage battery. From 1899 to 1909, he and his West Orange technical staff developed an alkaline-iron-nickel storage battery as an improvement over the widely used lead-acid battery. Edison envisioned this lighter, more durable battery for use in the growing automobile industry, especially in electric cars. By the time Edison had a commercially successful battery available in 1909, however, electric cars had lost favor with the public, which preferred the vehicles powered by internal combustion engines that were being promoted by men such as Henry Ford. The Edison battery proved unreliable for intermittent automobile uses, was ineffective in cold temperatures, and never replaced the lead-acid storage battery in motor car applications. Edison's battery did find successful use in marine and railroad applications that required a durable, long-lived battery.

The storage battery was Edison's last major invention. In 1914, a fire destroyed most of the West Orange laboratories; World War I diverted his attention as he served as chairman of the Naval Consulting Board to direct the nation's inventive talent into the war effort. As he grew older, Edison spent the winter months at his home in Fort Myers, Florida, and established a modest laboratory there. In 1927, he began work trying to create artificial rubber but did not complete that endeavor. His fertile mind was active until his death at West Orange, New Jersey, on October 18, 1931.

SIGNIFICANCE

With the death of Thomas Alva Edison, the United States lost a legendary and heroic inventor. The example of his life and personality—simplicity, pragmatism, hard work, and self-education, linked to inventive genius—appealed to the egalitarian spirit of Americans in an age of enterprise. Edison was a self-made man whose mental capacity, ambition, and dedication brought him success in the tradition of the American spirit of private enterprise. In an age of invention and industrialism, he stood as a symbol of the modern spirit in the United States with his contributions of electrical inventions and innovations: duplex and quadraplex telegraphy, incandescent lighting, telephone transmitter, phonograph, motion-picture camera, and storage battery. These contributions alone guarantee his place among great Americans.

Thomas Edison the heroic inventor is as much myth as reality. His strong determination to conquer a problem

or task and his ability to work long hours in his laboratory are characteristic of the lone inventor, but Edison was much more complex than might be suggested by the familiar image of the simple genius at work alone. He was among the foremost professional American inventors. His success was a result in large measure of his prescience about changes in an urban, industrial America and the need for new technological systems to serve that new society.

Edison's technique matched his vision; he excelled at improving on existing designs, assessing the commercial potential of a device. He also relied heavily on a systematic and rational approach to invention and innovation and on a highly trained staff, as his Menlo Park and West Orange laboratory complexes attest. Edison's early use of the industrial research laboratory provided a model for American industry in the twentieth century. Further, Edison's talent for understanding complex processes, for seeing the need for technological systems, and for focusing on practical application mark him as a highly organized professional who was a pioneer inventor-innovator and entrepreneur. Just as his image as a heroic inventor appealed to the average American of his time, so his success as a professional inventor who held nearly eleven hundred patents should appeal to students of American technological, social, and economic history.

—Harry J. Eisenman

FURTHER READING

Baldwin, Neil. *Edison: Inventing the Century.* New York: Hyperion, 1995. Reprint. Chicago: University of Chicago Press, 2001. Critically acclaimed comprehensive biography, providing information on Edison's personal life and career. Baldwin argues that Edison embodied the American potential for technological change; his book describes the cultural context of Edison's inventions.

Conot, Robert. *A Streak of Luck.* New York: Seaview Books, 1979. A full-scale biography of Edison. Conot examines Edison's personal life and technological achievements, and treats Edison's successes and failures in a thorough and objective manner.

Dyer, Frank Lewis, and Thomas Commerford Martin. *Edison: His Life and Inventions.* 2 vols. New York: Harper & Brothers, 1910. The first authorized biography of Edison. Limited because it was published during Edison's lifetime. Praises Edison and lacks objectivity.

Israel, Paul. *Edison: A Life of Invention.* New York: John Wiley & Sons, 1998. Israel draws on Edison's notebooks to describe Edison's working methods, portraying him as a tireless experimenter who labored to create his many inventions.

Jehl, Francis. *Menlo Park Reminiscences.* 3 vols. Detroit: Edison Institute, 1936. Although written by an Edison associate and very subjective, this is an excellent source of material on the workings of the Edison laboratories and of Edison himself. Many useful illustrations.

Jenkins, Reese V. "Elements of Style: Continuities in Edison's Thinking." In *Bridge to the Future: A Centennial Celebration of the Brooklyn Bridge*, edited by Margaret Latimer, Brooke Hindle, and Melvin Kranzberg. New York: New York Academy of Sciences, 1984. Jenkins explores the fascinating subject of style as a factor in Edison's inventions; well worth considering.

Jonnes, Jill. *Empires of Light: Edison, Tesla, Westinghouse, and the Race to Electrify the World.* New York: Random House, 2003. Explains how the three inventors sought to create businesses that would provide safe, reliable electricity. Jonnes describes the inventions and careers of Edison, Tesla, and Westinghouse, and relates how they worked with bankers, lawyers, and financiers to create electrical "empires."

Josephson, Matthew. *Edison: A Biography.* New York: McGraw-Hill, 1959. An excellent full-scale biography of Edison which treats his professional and personal life in detail. Contains cogent discussions of Edison's inventions, innovations, and relationships with financial figures such as Jay Gould and J. P. Morgan.

SEE ALSO: Alexander Graham Bell; Joseph Wilson Swan; Nikola Tesla; George Westinghouse.

RELATED ARTICLES in *Great Events from History: The Nineteenth Century, 1801-1900:* December 24, 1877: Edison Patents the Cylinder Phonograph; October 21, 1879: Edison Demonstrates the Incandescent Lamp.

GUSTAVE EIFFEL
French engineer

A leading engineer of Europe's "second" industrial age, Eiffel specialized in the manufacture and design of iron structures—from bridges, exposition halls, and water locks to public buildings and monuments. He supplied the armature required to support New York's Statue of Liberty and erected one of France's best-known icons, the Eiffel Tower. His later research on wind resistance and airflow contributed to the early development of aviation.

BORN: December 15, 1832; Dijon, France
DIED: December 27, 1923; Paris, France
ALSO KNOWN AS: Gustave-Alexandre Eiffel (full name); Alexandre-Gustave Eiffel; Gustave Bönickhausen
AREAS OF ACHIEVEMENT: Engineering, architecture

EARLY LIFE
Gustave Alexandre Eiffel (goo-stahv ah-lehks-ahn-druh eh-fehl) grew up in a provincial middle-class family in Dijon, France. One of his ancestors, Wilhelm Heinrich Johann Bönickhausen, had migrated there from Eifeldorf, a small village near Marmagen, Germany, during the early eighteenth century and became known to the French as Jean-René Bönickhausen-Eiffel. Because of later Franco-Germanic tensions, the name Bönickhausen was later conveniently omitted from family documents.

Gustave's early life in Dijon was tranquil, happy, and secure. His parents, François Alexandre Eiffel (1795-1878) and Catherine Mélanie Moneuse (1799-1878), prospered as merchants in the nation's flourishing coal industry before investing their savings in a local brewery. As a student at the neighborhood Lycée Royal of Dijon, Gustave found most of his classes boring but later admitted having acquired some useful knowledge there during his final two years. In 1850, he went to Paris and enrolled in preparatory courses at the Saint-Barbe College, hoping to gain admission to the highly competitive Polytechnic Institute. At the end of his second year, however, his performance on the qualifying examination fell short of the mark; as a result, he was steered into a more purely vocational track at the Central School of Arts and Manufacturing, where he graduated in 1855 with a diploma in engineering.

After a few months of in-work training at a foundry in Châtillon-sur-Seine, Eiffel found employment in Paris as a personal assistant to Charles Nepveu, a railway engineer with important connections in the industry. In December, 1856, Nepveu formed a limited partnership with a Belgian company specializing in railroad materials and secured a position for Eiffel as the director of research in its Paris factories.

LIFE'S WORK

Eiffel's first major project for the Belgian company was the construction in 1858-1860 of a five-hundred-meter bridge over the Garonne River at Bordeaux, a crucial link between the northern and southern railway networks. Upon its successful completion, he became chief engineer for the company's railway division and received not only a substantial raise in salary but also a share in future projects. Between 1860 and 1861, he completed other railway bridges, notably at Bayonne on the river Nive, at Capdenac on the Lot, and at Floirac on the Dordogne, gaining financial stability and a solid reputation in the industry. Confident in his success, he married Marie Gaudelet (1845-1877) on July 8, 1862. His wife was the granddaughter of an established Dijon brewer. They later moved into a large house in northern Paris.

When an unstable market forced the Belgian company into bankruptcy, Eiffel took the initiative of securing contracts for the construction of railway stations in Toulouse and Agen (1864-1866), for the delivery of locomotives to Egypt (1864-1865), for miscellaneous bridges (1867 and later), and for exposition galleries at the Universal Exhibition of 1867. To meet the demands of these and future contracts, he established workshops at Levallois-Perret, a largely industrial zone in northern Paris, and, in 1868, founded G. Eiffel and Company in a limited partnership with a recent graduate of the École Centrale, Théophile Seyrig.

In addition to its many domestic ventures, G. Eiffel and Company obtained contracts for a number of international projects: bridges in Romania (1872), Bolivia (1873), Peru (1874), and Colombia (1874); floodgates for a dam in Russia (1874); and churches in Peru, Chile, and the Philippines (1875). A substantial portion of Eiffel's financial success after the late 1870's derived from the design and manufacture of modular bridges. They were cheap, versatile, and easy to erect; hundreds of such structures were employed not only in France and Western Europe, but throughout the world as well. Following Seyrig's departure in 1879, the company was renamed several times but survived in one form or another for more than one hundred years.

Eiffel undertook many of his most dramatic and resourceful construction projects between 1875 and 1890. Innovative in their use of exposed metal structure and glass, the Nyugati railway station in Budapest, Hungary (1874-1877), and the central office of the Crédit

Gustave Eiffel.

Lyonnais in Paris, France (1881), stand out as models of architectural integrity. The Maria Pia Bridge over the Douro at Porto, Portugal (1877), with its 160-meter central span, was advertised during its construction as the world's largest nonsuspension bridge; it later served as a model for the elegant Garabit Viaduct (1884) in the rugged Truyère Valley of France's Massif Central. The Cubzac Bridge at Lilbourne, France (1884), although similar in manufacture to other linear, steel-lattice bridges, benefited from improved construction techniques such as the use of hydraulic jacks to ensure proper height and tension.

Eiffel also designed the internal support structure for Frédéric Auguste Bartholdi's Statue of Liberty, which was shipped to the United States for assembly in 1885, and an ingenious revolving dome for the Observatory at Nice (1885-1886). The most remarkable engineering project of his career, however, was the three-hundred-meter-high Eiffel Tower (1886-1889), which was erected as a central attraction for the Universal Exposition of 1889. The exposition had been organized in Paris to commemorate the first centenary of the French Revolution, and the tower, the tallest in the world, was to symbolize France's industrial success and the triumph of republican ideals. Despite public protests during its construction and calls for its dismantlement in 1903, Eiffel prevailed over his critics and the tower that bore his name became a permanent landmark in the French capital.

In 1893, following his indictment in connection with France's Panama Canal project, Eiffel retired from the administration of his company and devoted himself increasingly to the study of aerodynamics. The research he presented in his book *La Résistance de l'air et l'aviation, expériences effectuées au laboratoire du Champs-de-Mars* (1910; *The Resistance of Air and Aviation Experiments Conducted at the Champs-de-Mars Laboratory*, 1913) drew international attention to his research and helped establish the science of aviation. He spent the final years of his life completing a *Biographie industrielle et scientifique* (industrial and scientific biography) that survives in original typescript (1922) at the Orsay Museum in Paris. Eiffel died in 1923 at the age of ninety-one.

SIGNIFICANCE

Perhaps the single greatest icon of modern French culture, the Eiffel Tower has virtually overshadowed the engineer's other noteworthy contributions to the history of nineteenth century engineering. By the time he began work on the tower, he had already acquired an international reputation for designing and building some of the world's largest and most elegant bridges and viaducts. His designs and wrought iron found their way into a wide variety of projects: a synagogue at Rue des Tournelles, Paris (1867), the Bon Marché department store (1872), churches, railway stations, exposition halls, pavilions, gasworks, water locks, lighthouses, and observatories.

In contrast to the armature that Eiffel designed for the Statue of Liberty, the Eiffel Tower stands out as a work of pure form, free from constraints other than those imposed by nature and physics. As the twentieth century French critic Roland Barthes argued, the tower has for more than a century symbolized many things to many people—from modern hubris and bad taste to the victory of France's republican ideals and the triumph of science and industry. Artists, poets, filmmakers, historians and philosophers have found inspiration in the tower's bold design and its secret harmony.

—*Jan Pendergrass*

FURTHER READING

Bermond, Daniel. *Gustave Eiffel*. Paris: Perrin, 2002. A comprehensive look at the architect's career, including his successes and failures, in the French language.

Carmona, Michel. *Eiffel*. Paris: Fayard, 2002. Examines every major aspect of Eiffel's life and work in historical context; written in French.

Grigsby, Darcy Grimaldo. "Geometry/Labor = Volume/Mass?" *October* 106 (2003): 3-34. Journal article examining the importance of geometric design and empty space in Eiffel's work on the Statue of Liberty, the Eiffel Tower, and the French plans for a Panama canal; appropriate for both specialists and nonspecialists.

Harvie, David I. *Eiffel: The Genius Who Reinvented Himself*. Stroud, England: Sutton, 2004. A comprehensive survey of Eiffel's life and his major contributions to engineering, architecture, and aeronautics; includes a discussion of the world's tallest buildings following the September 11, 2001, destruction of the World Trade Center's twin towers. The bibliography identifies major Web sites devoted to Eiffel.

Lemoine, Bertrand. *Architecture in France, 1800-1900*. New York: Harry N. Abrams, 1998. This illustrated survey of nineteenth century French architecture helps to situate Gustave Eiffel within a larger context; includes chapters on industrial architecture and civil engineering.

Loyrette, Henri. *Gustave Eiffel*. New York: Rizzoli, 1985. Illustrated, comprehensive survey of the man's life and work; includes discussion of the Eiffel Tower's representation in modern art; a standard reference for English-language readers.

Marrey, Bernard. *The Extraordinary Life and Work of Monsieur Gustave Eiffel: The Engineer Who Built the Statue of Liberty, the Porto Bridge, the Nice Observatory, the Garabit Viaduct, the Panama Locks, the Eiffel Tower, etc.* Paris: Graphite, 1984. An accurate survey for the general reader; includes illustrations but no bibliography.

Thompson, William. "'The Symbol of Paris': Writing the Eiffel Tower." *French Review* 73 (2000): 1130-1140. Examines symbolic interpretations of the Eiffel Tower, from Charles Garnier and Guy de Maupassant to Jean Cocteau and Roland Barthes.

SEE ALSO: Isambard Kingdom Brunel; Marc Isambard Brunel; James Buchanan Eads; Sophie Germain; John Augustus Roebling; Thomas Telford.

RELATED ARTICLES in *Great Events from History: The Nineteenth Century, 1801-1900:* May 24, 1883: Brooklyn Bridge Opens; October 28, 1886: Statue of Liberty Is Dedicated; March 31, 1889: Eiffel Tower Is Dedicated.

CHARLES WILLIAM ELIOT
American educator

Combining administrative skill with a readiness to undertake novel and irregular ventures, Eliot transformed the structure and function of higher education in the United States. During his long and productive career, universities became a prominent force in American culture and progress.

BORN: March 20, 1834; Boston, Massachusetts
DIED: August 22, 1926; Northeast Harbor, Mount Desert, Maine
AREA OF ACHIEVEMENT: Education

EARLY LIFE

Charles William Eliot was the only son of Mary Lyman and Samuel Atkins Eliot, who were both from prominent New England families. After graduating from Boston Latin Grammar School, he entered his father's alma mater, Harvard College, in 1849. There, he became especially interested in mathematics and science and profited greatly from his study with a number of notable professors, among whom were Louis Agassiz, Asa Gray, and Josiah Parsons Cooke. It was under Cooke, in fact, that the young Eliot was given the then unique opportunity for an undergraduate student to conduct laboratory and field work in science.

Eliot graduated in 1853, among the top three students in his class of eighty-eight, and the following year became a tutor in mathematics at Harvard. In 1858 he married his first wife, Ellen Derby Peabody, and in that same year he received a five-year appointment as assistant professor of mathematics and chemistry. While in this position, he introduced a number of curricular innovations at Harvard, including the first written examination and placing a greater emphasis on laboratory exercises as a learning tool.

Failing to secure promotion at the end of his five-year appointment as assistant professor, Eliot left Harvard in 1863 and even considered abandoning the teaching profession. The governor of Massachusetts offered him an appointment as lieutenant colonel of cavalry in the state's militia, but poor eyesight and family financial reverses forced Eliot to decline the offer. Instead, he embarked upon the first of two voyages to Europe for the purpose of further study. During his first trip abroad, Eliot was appointed to the faculty of the newly founded Massachusetts Institute of Technology, where he began teaching upon his return from Europe in September, 1865. Eliot gave four years of distinguished service to

that institution. He not only organized the chemistry department in collaboration with Francis Storer but also collaborated with him in writing the Eliot and Storer manuals of chemical analysis, the first textbooks to feature laboratory and experimental work along with theoretical principles.

Eliot's study of European education while abroad and his experiences as a teacher at Harvard and MIT convinced him that American colleges and high schools were inadequate for the needs of individual students and American society. His thoughts about secondary and higher education were presented in two notable articles on "the new education," which appeared in the *Atlantic Monthly* early in 1869 and were widely read and quoted. These articles brought him to the attention of Harvard's Board of Overseers, which was seeking a new president for the school. Despite initial opposition to his election by some board members, Eliot was inaugurated as the twenty-second president of Harvard on October 19, 1869.

LIFE'S WORK

Photographs of the beardless, bespectacled middle-aged Eliot show a profile befitting that of a late nineteenth century college president: a receding hairline, firmly set chin, and muttonchop whiskers. His presidency marked a new era at Harvard. Under Eliot's leadership, Harvard's faculty grew from sixty to six hundred and its endowment increased from a mere two and one-half million dollars to more than twenty million. He restructured Harvard into a university, concentrating all undergraduate studies in the college and building around it semiautonomous professional schools and research facilities. In 1872, he developed graduate master's and doctoral programs, followed in 1890 by the establishment of a Graduate School of Arts and Sciences. In the schools of medicine, law, and divinity, he formalized entrance requirements, courses of study, and written examinations. He assisted reformers who were interested in providing higher education for women, which led to the founding in 1894 of Radcliffe College.

Among Eliot's policies affecting Harvard, none was more fundamental than the improvement of faculty working conditions. He raised faculty salaries and introduced a liberal system of retirement pensions that Harvard maintained independently until 1906, when the Carnegie Foundation made provisions for this purpose. His introduction of the sabbatical year as well as French and

German exchange professorships provided faculty with greater opportunities for contact with European scholars and greater leisure for research.

The most radical and far-reaching innovation introduced during Eliot's administration was the elective principle. This reform grew out of Eliot's conviction that college students needed more freedom in selecting courses so that they might acquire self-reliance, discover their own hidden talents, rise to a higher level of attainment in their chosen fields, and demonstrate a greater interest in their studies. Eliot also believed that modern subjects such as English, French, German, history, economics, and especially the natural and physical sciences should have equal rank with Latin, Greek, and mathematics in the college curriculum.

Gradually under Eliot's leadership, Harvard adopted the elective principle. In 1872, all course restrictions for seniors were abolished. Seven years later, all junior course restrictions were abolished. In 1884 sophomore course restrictions came to an end, and the following year those for freshmen were greatly reduced. By 1897, the required course of study at Harvard had been reduced to a year of freshman rhetoric.

Eliot's influence was felt in other areas of college life. The long-standing rule requiring student attendance at

Charles William Eliot. (Library of Congress)

chapel was abolished, and participation in all religious activities was made voluntary. Eliot demonstrated a keen interest in athletic policy, too. He established a general athletic committee, comprising alumni, undergraduates, faculty, and administrators. In addition, Eliot played an important role in the introduction of stricter eligibility requirements for college athletes at Harvard and other American colleges.

Although higher educational reform occupied most of his energies, Eliot used his position to influence primary and secondary schools as well. His numerous published articles and addresses covered a wide range of subjects. He argued for better training and greater security of teachers and for improved sanitary conditions in schools; he supported Progressive Era educators' efforts to improve schooling; and he emphasized the need for teachers and schools to train the senses, the body, and the imagination of the student. At the same time, he raised and diversified admissions requirements at Harvard to exert pressure upon schools to improve the quality of their instruction.

After Eliot resigned from the presidency of Harvard in 1909, he continued to participate in a wide range of activities. As a member of Harvard's Board of Overseers, Eliot maintained an interest in campus affairs. He was influential in shaping the policies of the General Education Board, the Rockefeller Foundation, and the Carnegie Foundation for the Advancement of Teaching. Eliot devoted the remainder of his time to writing, speechmaking, and correspondence. Fully active until the last year of his life, he died at Northeast Harbor, Mount Desert, Maine, on August 22, 1926.

SIGNIFICANCE

In countless ways, Eliot exerted a powerful influence upon the development of higher education in the United States. During his long and productive career, the university emerged as a preeminent force in Americans' lives. It became the primary service organization which made possible the function of many other institutions in society. The university not only brought coherence and uniformity to the training of individuals for professional careers but also provided a formal structure for the techniques Americans employed in thinking about every level of human existence.

Eliot was able to accomplish so much because, to an extraordinary degree, his own outlook mirrored the hopes and fears of many other late nineteenth century Americans. Eliot's contribution to change in higher education made a difference in American history at a crucial moment, when aspiring middle-class individuals were struggling to define new career patterns, establish new institutions, pursue new occupations, and forge a new self-identity. The university was basic to this struggle; it became a central institution in a competitive, status-conscious society. Eliot played a key role in this process by giving vitality to the American college at a time when its remoteness from society imperiled the whole structure of higher education in the United States.

—Monroe H. Little, Jr.

FURTHER READING

Bledstein, Burton J. *The Culture of Professionalism: The Middle Class and the Development of Higher Education in America.* New York: W. W. Norton, 1976. The best single book about the activities and ideology of Eliot and other leaders of late nineteenth century American higher education. Although somewhat over-critical, offers a needed corrective to other accounts.

Eliot, Charles W. *Charles W. Eliot and Popular Education.* Edited by Edward A. Krug. New York: Teachers College Press, 1961. This short anthology includes nine of Eliot's articles, addresses, and reports on education in the United States during the late nineteenth and early twentieth centuries. It also contains a lengthy introduction which discusses and analyzes his contribution to the educational reform movement.

_____. *Educational Reform: Essays and Addresses.* New York: Century, 1898. Reprint. New York: Arno Press, 1969. Contains some of Eliot's early essays and addresses. Provides readers with a sample of his thinking on American education's problems and their solutions.

_____. *A Late Harvest: Miscellaneous Papers Written Between Eighty and Ninety.* Boston: Atlantic Monthly Press, 1924. This volume contains typical products of Eliot's thought during the last years of his life. In addition to a brief autobiographical piece, it includes papers on a wide range of subjects. Of particular note is a partial bibliography of Eliot's publications from 1914 to 1924.

Hawkins, Hugh. *Between Harvard and America: The Educational Leadership of Charles W. Eliot.* New York: Oxford University Press, 1972. The best single book on Eliot's tenure as president of Harvard. It analyzes his efforts to make the university ideal a reality in the changing, sometimes hostile social environment of late nineteenth century and early twentieth century America.

James, Henry. *Charles W. Eliot: President of Harvard University, 1869-1909.* 2 vols. Boston: Houghton Mifflin, 1930. Marred by its uncritical perspective, this nevertheless well-written, highly detailed biography of Eliot remains indispensable; all subsequent studies of Eliot's life have drawn on it.

Mahoney, Kathleen A. *Catholic Higher Education in Protestant America: The Jesuits and Harvard in the Age of the University.* Baltimore: Johns Hopkins University Press, 2003. In 1893, Eliot helped implement an admissions policy barring graduates of Jesuit colleges from regular admission to Harvard University. Mahoney explains how his decision set off a controversy about the terms of Catholic participation in higher education. Her book describes how Eliot and other liberal Protestant educators sought to link the modern university with the cause of Protestantism, and how Catholic educators and students responded to this development.

Rudolph, Frederick. *The American College and University: A History.* New York: Alfred A. Knopf, 1968. Provides a rich analysis of Eliot's early years as president and reformer at Harvard. Generally balanced and well researched, it provides a clear, objective account of the elective system's revolutionary impact on higher education in the United States.

Tyack, David B. *The One Best System: A History of American Urban Education.* Cambridge, Mass.: Harvard University Press, 1974. This highly readable, well-documented study only briefly discusses Eliot's activities on behalf of public schooling, but it provides a detailed account of the social milieu in which he worked and shaped his ideas about education.

Veysey, Laurence R. *The Emergence of the American University.* Chicago: University of Chicago Press, 1965. A massive study that includes more references to Eliot than to any other person. Valuable chiefly for its background information and incisive analysis of the social and intellectual context within which late nineteenth century American higher educational reform proceeded.

SEE ALSO: Elizabeth Cabot Agassiz; Louis Agassiz; Asa Gray; William Rainey Harper; Alice Freeman Palmer.

RELATED ARTICLE in *Great Events from History: The Nineteenth Century, 1801-1900:* September 26, 1865: Vassar College Opens.

GEORGE ELIOT
English novelist

Eliot's philosophical profundity and mastery of fictional technique earned her a reputation as one of the world's great novelists, and her writings helped to establish the novel as a powerful vehicle for the serious exploration of ideas. She expanded both the range and the technical resources of the novel by exploring the thoughts and feelings of her characters.

BORN: November 22, 1819; Chilvers Coton, Warwickshire, England

DIED: December 22, 1880; London, England

ALSO KNOWN AS: Marian Lewes; Marian Evans; Mary Ann Evans (birth name)

AREA OF ACHIEVEMENT: Literature

EARLY LIFE

The woman who wrote her novels under the male pseudonym George Eliot was born Mary Ann Evans on a farm near Coventry in the rich farming district of central England. Her father, a man with an almost legendary reputation for integrity and competence, worked as an estate agent, or general overseer, on the extensive lands of the aristocratic Newdigate family. Her upbringing in the evangelical traditions of the Church of England gave her strong moral convictions that remained with her all of her life and formed the basic moral imperatives of her fiction.

When Evans was twenty-two, she and her father, who had retired from active work, moved to a house just outside Coventry. Evans's closest friends in Coventry were Charles and Cara Bray and Cara's sister Sara Hennell. Like many others who took part in the intellectual and religious ferment of early Victorian England, the Brays questioned the validity of Christian theology, although they had no serious reservations about the value of Christian moral teachings. Contact with them reinforced the doubts about her evangelical religion that Evans had already begun to entertain. In 1844, she began translating *Das Leben Jesu* by the German theologian David Friedrich Strauss, which she published two years later under the title *The Life of Jesus, Critically Examined.* Her work on Strauss further undermined her Christian orthodoxy.

Shortly after her father's death in 1849, Mary Ann Evans, who was now spelling her name Marian, became associated with John Chapman, editor of the *Westminster Review*, a prestigious intellectual quarterly whose first editor had been John Stuart Mill. Although the social customs of Victorian England made it impossible for a woman to bear the title of editor of an important journal of opinion addressed largely to a male audience, Evans exercised primary editorial responsibility for the *Westminster Review*. She not only solicited and selected articles and planned the content of the issues, but she also wrote many reviews. ("Reviews" in Victorian intellectual journals were really independent essays that might run to fifteen or twenty pages in length.) Although shy and retiring by nature (her shyness may have been reinforced by her lack of physical beauty—she had a prominent nose and rather heavy features), Evans was at the center of intellectual life in Victorian England.

Among the many people with whom Evans became acquainted at this time was George Henry Lewes. One of the most versatile of the Victorian intellectuals, Lewes was a biologist, novelist, drama critic, biographer of Goethe, and author of a history of philosophy. Lewes's wife, Agnes, was openly adulterous, but Lewes had accepted her extramarital affairs and registered her illegitimate children as his own. When Lewes and Evans fell in love, there seemed to be no way that Lewes could divorce Agnes. Not only was divorce in Victorian England expensive and legally complex, but the usual grounds of divorce, adultery, had been eliminated by Lewes's generous acceptance of Agnes's illegitimate children. After deciding that they could hurt only themselves by a common-law marriage, Marian Evans and George Henry Lewes agreed to live together as husband and wife. In July, 1854, they began a honeymoon trip to Germany; Marian wrote to tell her friends of this relationship and to ask that they henceforth address her as Marian Lewes.

LIFE'S WORK

Her common-law marriage with Lewes initiated the most productive period in Evans's life. Lewes provided her with the emotional support she needed and encouraged her when she decided to try her hand at writing fiction. Because of the scandal that was associated with her relationship with Lewes and because she did not want to compromise her reputation as a translator and a reviewer, Evans wrote under a pen name; she selected "George Eliot." Lewes protected her anonymity and carried on all negotiations with publishers.

George Eliot's first published fiction was "The Sad Fortunes of the Reverend Amos Barton," which appeared in the issue of *Blackwood's Magazine* that came out on New Year's Day, 1857. With two other short works of fiction that also appeared in *Blackwood's Magazine*—"Mr. Gilfil's Love-Story" and "Janet's Repentance"—it was reprinted in book form in *Scenes of Clerical Life* in 1858. Her first major work of fiction was *Adam Bede*, published by Blackwood's in 1859. *Adam Bede* was a popular and critical success, and "George Eliot" was hailed as an important new talent. Among the principal writers of the time, Charles Dickens was one of the few who suspected that *Adam Bede* had been written by a woman.

In chapter 17 of *Adam Bede*, Eliot makes one of the most important statements of the creed of the realistic novelist. Art, she says, should always remind us of the world's "common coarse people, who have no picturesque sentimental wretchedness"; the artist should be "ready to give the loving pains of a life to the faithful representing of commonplace things." Moreover, the novelist's purpose is not only to achieve the kind of accuracy of representation one finds in Dutch painting but also to ensure that a "fibre of sympathy" ties the author—and, by implication, the reader—to the "vulgar citizen" with whom one is in contact in everyday life so that, as she says, "my heart should swell with loving admiration of some trait of gentle goodness in the faulty people who sit at the same hearth with me." The aim of the novelist, then, is not only to depict life accurately, but also to enlarge the reader's human sympathies.

George Eliot's second novel, *The Mill on the Floss* (1860), is her most autobiographical work, nostalgically recalling her own childhood with her brother Isaac Evans in her depiction of Maggie and Tom Tulliver. The novel also embodies, in the adult character of Maggie, the moral issues that Eliot was to explore again and again in her fiction: the dangers of self-indulgence and self-deception, often associated with some inappropriate sexual relationship, and the need for self-sacrifice and the renunciation of egotistical desires.

In 1861, *The Mill on the Floss* was followed by *Silas Marner*, which is perhaps the most familiar of Eliot's novels. Also her shortest major work, it suggests more directly than her other novels the way in which human relationships based on Christian morality provide the support that in previous ages might have been afforded by the institutional church. *Romola* (1863), a historical novel set in Renaissance Florence, is Eliot's only novel that does not have an English setting. The historical novel was a genre that enjoyed considerable prestige at the time, and Eliot's research into the historical background

of the novel was both exhaustive and exhausting. However, the novel, which was published in the *Cornhill Magazine*, then edited by William Makepeace Thackeray, was not a popular success. In order to compensate Thackeray for the comparative failure of *Romola*, Eliot gave him, without charge, a short story for publication in the *Cornhill Magazine*.

In her next fiction, *Felix Holt, Radical* (1866), Eliot returned to an English setting and to her previous publisher, Blackwood's. *Felix Holt, Radical*, perhaps Eliot's least-read novel, has a plot marred by excessive reliance on obscure coincidences but also contains some of her most profound psychological analysis. Her next work, *The Spanish Gypsy* (1868), is a blank verse tragedy, another genre that enjoyed considerable prestige in Victorian England. Eliot's literary gifts did not, however, include the ability to write good poetry, and *The Spanish Gypsy*, in spite of some commercial success, must be rated as her least effective major work.

Eliot's first three novels have a warmth and humor that has charmed her readers. Her works of the mid-1860's show an advance in psychological complexity and philosophical depth, but they often lack the seeming spontaneity of her early novels. All of her talents as a novelist, however, have their greatest expression in her next novel, *Middlemarch* (1871-1872), which is one of the supreme achievements of English fiction. A novel with dozens of deeply studied characters, *Middlemarch* examines the limitations and opportunities of life in a provincial English town during the early 1830's. Eliot's final novel, *Daniel Deronda* (1876), combines some of her most profound psychological analysis with a plot that anticipates the Zionist movement to establish a national homeland for the Jews in Palestine.

When *Daniel Deronda* was published, Eliot was widely regarded as the greatest living English novelist. Her literary achievement, the more liberal moral code of the late Victorian period, and the obvious respectability of her life with Lewes had largely dissipated the scandal once associated with their common-law marriage, and she and Lewes were received in the highest literary and social circles. Both, however, were afflicted with ill health, and on November 30, 1878, Lewes died at the age of sixty-one. Devastated by the loss of the man who had given her so much companionship and encouragement for more than twenty years, Eliot turned for support to John Cross, a young man who had been their close friend for several years. On May 6, 1880, she and Cross were married, but their marriage was to be a short one, for on December 22, 1880, Eliot died.

SIGNIFICANCE

George Eliot was approaching forty when she embarked on the career as a novelist for which she is known today. Her previous work as a translator of theological and philosophical treatises, her experience as the virtual editor of one of the leading intellectual quarterlies of the day, her authorship of many extensive essay reviews, and her friendship with leading Victorian thinkers had given her a depth of knowledge unmatched by any previous novelist. As her standing as an intellectual was widely recognized in her own day, Eliot probably did more than anyone else to change the view that the novel could be regarded only as popular entertainment and to win recognition for this genre as a vehicle for the serious examination of ideas.

Like other great novelists, Eliot expanded both the range and the technical resources of the novel. Whereas previous novelists had, in general, emphasized the external events in the lives of their characters, Eliot emphasized their thoughts and feelings. In her novels, her characters' psychological response to an event is almost always more significant than the event itself. The expansion of the subject matter of fiction often requires new techniques of novel writing; Eliot's examination of her characters' minds and emotions is frequently presented through elaborate patterns of imagery that allow her to express the subtleties and complexities of their emotional and ethical dilemmas.

Eliot is not generally considered a feminist, but what she accomplished in her career unquestionably did much to enhance the status of women. Other women—for example, Jane Austen and Charlotte Brontë—had achieved critical or popular success as novelists, but Eliot's recognition as the greatest living English novelist was an unprecedented achievement for a woman.

Although Eliot wrote primarily of English subjects, she was highly regarded in the United States as well. Her defense of realism in chapter 17 of *Adam Bede* was echoed on both sides of the Atlantic, and she was a major influence on some of the most important American novelists, among them William Dean Howells and Henry James.

—Erwin Hester

FURTHER READING

Ashton, Rosemary. *George Eliot: A Life*. New York: The Penguin Press, 1996. Ashton analyzes *Middlemarch*, *Adam Bede*, *Silas Marner*, and other Eliot novels to demonstrate how they explore tensions between the urge to conform and the desires of the mind and heart. Ashton describes how these tensions reflected the dilemma of Eliot's own life.

Haight, Gordon S. *George Eliot: A Biography*. New York: Oxford University Press, 1968. A careful and thorough biography by one of the leading Eliot scholars, this book avoids interpreting Eliot's personality beyond elaborating on a statement by Charles Bray that "she was not fitted to stand alone." It is the most reliable source for detailed factual information about Eliot.

_____. *George Eliot and John Chapman, with Chapman's Diaries*. New Haven, Conn.: Yale University Press, 1940. A detailed study of Eliot's work on the *Westminster Review* and of her personal relationship with John Chapman. Includes transcripts of Chapman's diaries.

Henry, Nancy. *George Eliot and the British Empire*. New York: Cambridge University Press, 2002. Examines Eliot's life and fiction within the context of nineteenth century British imperialism. Henry focuses on Eliot's investment in colonial stocks, her reading of colonial literature, and her role as a parent to emigrant sons.

Kitchel, Anna. *George Lewes and George Eliot*. New York: John Day, 1933. A standard work on Lewes as well as a useful study of the most important relationship in Eliot's life, this biography gives a good picture of Eliot's emotional and intellectual development.

Laski, Marghanita. *George Eliot and Her World*. New York: Charles Scribner's Sons, 1973. A richly illustrated short biography. Less sympathetic to Lewes than most biographers, Laski tends to support the conjecture, mentioned in other biographies as well, that Eliot's marriage to Cross soon after Lewes's death may have been prompted by her discovery of evidence that her common-law husband had been guilty of infidelity.

Menon, Patricia. *Austen, Eliot, Charlotte Brontë, and the Mentor-Lover*. New York: Palgrave Macmillan, 2003. An examination of how Eliot, Austen, and Brontë handled matters of gender, sexuality, family, behavior, and freedom in their work.

Redinger, Ruby. *George Eliot: The Emergent Self*. New York: Alfred A. Knopf, 1975. An interesting and often persuasive attempt to explore the interplay of events and personality traits that contributed to the development of Eliot as a writer. Redinger emphasizes the psychological damage caused by Eliot's father's insistence on evangelical orthodoxy and by her brother's cruel rejection of her when she associated herself with Lewes.

Sprague, Rosemary. *George Eliot: A Biography*. Philadelphia: Chilton Books, 1968. A well-written biography with a considerable appeal for the general reader. It includes critical comments on Eliot's novels.

Willey, Basil. *Nineteenth Century Studies*. New York: Columbia University Press, 1949. A classic study of the impact of German theology and "higher criticism" on Eliot's early evangelicalism. Of special interest are the chapters "George Eliot: Hennell, Strauss and Feuerbach" and "George Eliot, Conclusion."

SEE ALSO: Mary Elizabeth Braddon; William Makepeace Thackeray; Anthony Trollope.

RELATED ARTICLES in *Great Events from History: The Nineteenth Century, 1801-1900:* September 2, 1843: Wilson Launches *The Economist*; March, 1852-September, 1853: Dickens Publishes *Bleak House*.

FANNY ELSSLER
Austrian ballerina

Elssler's name has become synonymous with the Romantic Age. Elssler was one of the central figures responsible for inspiring the renaissance in ballet that occurred during the early nineteenth century. She was known for her remarkably individual style, which she often showcased in her various signature pieces.

BORN: June 23, 1810; Vienna, Austria
DIED: November 27, 1884; Vienna, Austria
ALSO KNOWN AS: Franziska Elssler (birth name)
AREA OF ACHIEVEMENT: Music

EARLY LIFE

Fanny Elssler (EHLS-lehr) was the youngest of five children, all of whom except her older brother, Johann, were to pursue careers in the arts. Her other brother, Joseph, became a professional tenor; her sisters, Therese and Anna, were instructed in ballet from a young age. Fanny's mother was a seamstress, but both her grandfather and father worked for the Austrian composer Josef Haydn as copyists and attendants. With such a background in the arts, Fanny was well placed to commence her ballet training with the Theater an der Wien.

In 1818, at the age of eight, Fanny joined the Vienna Court Opera and made her first billed appearance in the Kärntnertortheater production of Jean Aumer's *Die Hochzeit der Thetis und des Peleus* on April 20 of that year. During this first phase of her dancing career, the three dancing masters most influential in her ballet training were Filippo Taglioni, Louis Henry, and Armand Vestris. Fanny's sister Therese appeared with her and even collaborated with her almost exclusively throughout her own career, but it is Fanny's technical and dramatic brilliance that history most often recalls.

LIFE'S WORK

Considering Fanny's potential as a gifted ballerina, the decision to have her study in Italy was a natural one. The experience would prove to be influential because Fanny acquired the dramatic skills needed for many of the new ballets being written in Naples during the period. Presentations such as Gaetano Gioja's *Cesare in Egitto* (July, 1825) and Taglioni's *Alcibiade* (July, 1826) demanded more from choreography and dance than ever before. Similarly, Fanny also received many opportunities to develop her technical mastery, particularly her *pointe* work—on the tips of her toes—for which she later became famous.

Although Fanny made the most of her two years in Italy, her career was put on hold briefly when she returned to Vienna in 1827 to give birth to her illegitimate son, Franz Robert, on June 4. The boy's father, Prince Leopold of Salerno, had reportedly "purchased" Fanny from her mother. In fact, Fanny's career was put on hold again five years later when she gave birth to another illegitimate child, this time a daughter, Theresa Anne (born on October 26, 1833), whose father was the dancer Anton Stuhlmüller.

Fanny distinguished herself as technically skilled early in her career. From the occasion of her first appearance in a lead role as Mathilde in Luigi Astolfi's *Mathilde, Herzogin von Spoleto* in January, 1826, to that of Amalie in Amalia Brugnoli's *Ottavio Pinelli*, it was clear that Fanny was special. Such ballets were entirely new, and Fanny's execution was made all the more thrilling because she successfully emulated the *pointe* work that so distinguished Brugnoli's own style.

Fanny's successes soon took her across continental Europe. In Berlin, she debuted in *La Somnambule* in Oc-

Fanny Elssler.

tober, 1830; in London she debuted in *Faust* in March, 1833; and in Paris she debuted in *La Tempête* in September, 1834. She then undertook a two-year tour of the United States. In May, 1840, she debuted in *La Tarentule* in New York City. She also appeared in Havana, Cuba, in January, 1841, in *La Sylphide*; in Milan, Italy, in January, 1844, in *Armida*; and in Moscow, Russia's Bolshoi Theater in October, 1848, in *Giselle*.

Fanny's sensational performances not only attracted celebrity status and popularity but also inspired the opinions of many of the era's most noted contemporary critics. The German political theorist Friedrich von Gentz attended a number of her performances at the Vienna Opera in 1830 and became her lover shortly afterward. Later, Dr. Louis Véron, director of the Paris Opera, helped fuel a rumor that Fanny's lover was the duke of Reichstadt—a son of Napoleon I—ostensibly to publicize her Parisian debut in 1834. Similarly, the French critic Théophile Gautier's reviews of Fanny's performances in 1837 were so profound that they influenced the very genre of criticism itself.

Other artists were also influenced by Fanny's work. In 1836, Jean-Baptiste Barre's sculpture of Fanny, which he called *Cachucha* after her Spanish dance, was rivaled

only by the lithographs produced by Achille Deveria and Franz Seitz and the miniatures of Ferdinand Waldmüller and Madame de Mirbel. In fact, the *Cachucha* so inspired the senior Johann Strauss that he composed his *Cachucha Galop* in Vienna in 1837.

Many composers wrote premier pieces specifically for Fanny. These included Paulo Samengo's *Theodosia*, which debuted in Vienna in June, 1831, and the Marquis de Saint-Georges's *La Gipsy*, which premiered in Paris in January, 1839. *La Gipsy* was spectacularly successful as a vehicle showcasing Fanny's technical and dramatic merits. Later, Jean Coralli's ballet *La Tarentule* debuted in Paris in June, 1839, and became one of Fanny's most recognized signature performances.

Fanny Elssler retired from the stage on June 21, 1851, at the age of forty, shortly after she returned to Vienna from Russia. She outlived her two children and all her siblings. By the early 1880's her steadfast companion was her friend of sixty years, Katti Prinster. Prinster was by Fanny's side when she died in Vienna on November 27, 1884.

SIGNIFICANCE

Dualism has dominated the scholarship of Elssler's significance. Her technical merit is usually examined as the antithesis of Filippo Taglioni, and her cultural significance has been discussed in the light of the aesthetic imperatives of the Romantic movement. The so-called "pagan" quality of Elssler as a ballerina noted by Théophile Gautier contrasted with the so-called "Christian" dancer that was Taglioni. Similarly, while Taglioni embodied the "weightlessness" of a *danse ballonnée*, Elssler's performances as a *danse tacquetée* revitalized ballet with an "earthy" gritty flare.

The task of contrasting prima ballerinas such as Elssler and Taglioni and Grisi has been made simpler by the fact that these dancers exhibited different preferences in their repertoires. Taglioni's signature role of *Sylphide*—which demanded an ethereal quality of movement emphasized by a costume of white muslin—unavoidably contrasted greatly with Elssler's colorful costume and fleshy performances of the cachucha.

Similarly, when Elssler's other rival, Carlotta Grisi, created and performed the role of *Giselle*, her performances emphasized the melancholy of the narrative, thereby accentuating the romance of the piece. Elssler's presentation, however, focused much more on the sorrowful aspects of the material work, therefore creating a more compelling and dramatic spectacle. Hence, not only was Elssler's artistic skill distinctive, of equal significance was her interpretation of roles. That too was revolutionary.

Both Fanny and her sister Therese staged ballets themselves, such as *Die Maskerade* (Berlin, 1834), or wrote them, such as Therese's ballet *Armide* (London, May, 1834). In fact, Therese's arrangement of Fanny's *pas de deux* in the Paris debut of *Cachucha* (in 1836) was a focal point of the performance. Therese's other piece, *La Volière* (1838), although not entirely successful, was nonetheless important as a counterpoint to those written and staged by predominantly male choreographers.

As the first principal prima ballerina to visit the United States, Fanny Elssler was also significant in contributing to the popularization of ballet beyond continental Europe. In this she was spectacularly successful. In fact, her American tour inspired "Elsslermania." Her costumes set trends in contemporary fashion and, as in Europe, a whole industry of mass-marketed trinkets was based on her popularity.

During the early 1840's, there was a well-publicized division among American theater critics, some of whom questioned Fanny's technical skills as a dancer, while others were troubled by the sheer level of her public popularity. She also inspired shifts in performance review writing in continental Europe, and her name everywhere became synonymous with radically polarized public opinion. However, such narratives were not possible without the freshness of Elssler's technical skill and the unique contributions to dramatic recitation that she made throughout her career as a performance artist.

—*Nicole Anae*

FURTHER READING

Aloff, Mindy. *Dance Anecdotes: Stories from the Worlds of Ballet, Broadway, the Ballroom, and Modern Dance.* New York: Oxford University Press, 2006. A collection of interesting stories about dancers, including Elssler.

Delarue, Allison. *Fanny Elssler in America: Comprising Seven Facsimiles of Rare Americana—Never Before Offered the Public—Depicting her Astounding Conquest of America in 1840-42.* Brooklyn: Dance Horizons, 1976. Historical account of Fanny's American tour.

"Fanny Elssler." *The Modern Language Journal* 22, no. 7 (April, 1938): 556. Review of the film *Fanny Elssler*, in which Lilian Harvey played Elssler. Provides insights into how how Elssler's life translated to the screen.

Guest, Ivor. *Fanny Elssler.* London: Black, 1970. Noted and meticulously researched biography of Elssler's life by a leading ballet historian.

Hutchinson, Ann. *Fanny Elssler's Cachucha.* London: Dance Books, 1981. Study of the cachucha by the wife of Ivor Guest, complete with references to Elssler's interpretation of the dance.

SEE ALSO: Léo Delibes; Lola Montez; Napoleon I; Johann Strauss.

RELATED ARTICLE in *Great Events from History: The Nineteenth Century, 1801-1900:* March 12, 1832: *La Sylphide* Inaugurates Romantic Ballet's Golden Age.

RALPH WALDO EMERSON
American writer and philosopher

A leading spokesperson for New England Transcendentalism, Emerson articulated a peculiarly American culture in his writings, which contributed to that culture and encouraged others to add still further to it.

BORN: May 25, 1803; Boston, Massachusetts
DIED: April 27, 1882; Concord, Massachusetts
AREA OF ACHIEVEMENT: Literature

EARLY LIFE

Ralph Waldo Emerson was the fourth child of Unitarian minister William Emerson and Ruth Haskins Emerson, His father's death in 1811 left the family poor, and his mother had to maintain a boardinghouse to support the family of six young children. Despite this poverty, Emerson's education was not neglected. He attended the prestigious Boston Latin School (1812-1817) and in 1821 was graduated from Harvard. Even when he was an undergraduate, his interest in philosophy and writing was evident. In 1820, he won second prize in the Bowdoin competition for his essay "The Character of Socrates," and the following year, he won the prize again with "The Present State of Ethical Philosophy." In these pieces he demonstrated his preference for the present over the past, praising the modern Scottish common-sense philosophers more highly than Aristotle and Socrates.

This preference derived largely from Emerson's belief that the modern philosophers offered more guidance in how to live. Despite the mysticism that informs much of Emerson's writing, he remained concerned with daily life. Thus, his purpose in *Representative Men* (1850) was to draw from the lives of great men some lessons for everyday behavior, and during the 1850's he gave a series of lectures collected under the title *The Conduct of Life* (1860).

After graduation from Harvard, Emerson taught school for his brother William before entering Harvard Divinity School in 1825. In 1826, he delivered his first sermon in Waltham, Massachusetts; typically, it dealt with the conduct of life. Emerson warned that because prayers are always answered, people must be careful to pray for the right things. One sees here another strain that runs through Emerson's writings, the optimistic view that one gets what one seeks.

Three years later, in 1829, Emerson was ordained as minister of Boston's Second Church, once the Puritan bastion of Increase and Cotton Mather. In the course of his maiden sermon there, he spoke of the spiritual value of the commonplace. He reminded his audience that parables explain divine truths through homey allusions and noted that if Jesus were to address a nineteenth century congregation, he "would appeal to those arts and objects by which we are surrounded; to the printing-press and the loom, to the phenomena of steam and of gas." Again one finds this love of the commonplace as a persistent theme throughout his work. As he states in *Nature* (1836), "The meal in the firkin; the milk in the pan; the ballad in the street; the news of the boat" all embody universal truths.

In the same year that Emerson became minister of the Second Church, he married Ellen Louisa Tucker. Her death from tuberculosis in 1831 triggered an emotional and psychological crisis in Emerson, already troubled by elements of Unitarianism. In October, 1832, he resigned his ministry, claiming that he could not accept the church's view of communion, and in December he embarked for a year in Europe. Here he met a number of his literary heroes, including Samuel Taylor Coleridge, William Wordsworth, and Thomas Carlyle. He was less impressed with these men—Carlyle excepted—than he was with the Jardin des Plantes in Paris. At the French botanical garden he felt "moved by strange sympathies. I say I will listen to this invitation. I will be a naturalist."

Returning to Boston in 1833, Emerson soon began the first of numerous lecture series that would take him across the country many times during his life. From the lectern he would peer at his audience with his intense blue eyes. Tall and thin, habitually wearing an enigmatic smile, he possessed an angelic quality that contributed to his popularity as a speaker. The subject of his first lectures was science, a topic to which he often returned. His literary debut came, however, not from a scientific but from a philosophical examination of the physical world.

LIFE'S WORK

In 1835, Emerson married Lydia Jackson (rechristened Lidian by Emerson), and the couple moved to Concord, where Emerson lived the rest of his life. The next year Waldo, the first of their four children, was born. In 1836, too, Emerson published a small pamphlet called *Nature*. Condemning the age for looking to the past instead of the present, he reminded his readers that "the sun shines today also." To create a contemporary poetry and philosophy, all that was necessary was to place oneself in harmony with nature. Then "swine, spiders, snakes, pests, madhouses, prisons, enemies" will yield to "beautiful faces, warm hearts, wise discourse, and heroic acts . . . until evil is no more seen. . . . Build therefore your own world."

The volume was not popular: It sold only fifteen hundred copies in the United States in the eight years following its publication, and a second edition was not published until 1849. It served, though, as the rallying cry for the Transcendentalist movement. In literature this group looked to Carlyle and Johann Wolfgang von Goethe; indeed, Emerson arranged for the publication of Carlyle's first book, *Sartor Resartus* (1836), in the United States some years before it found a publisher in England. In philosophy the Transcendentalists followed Immanuel Kant in believing that humans can transcend sensory experience (hence the movement's name); they thus rejected the view of John Locke, who maintained that all knowledge comes from and is rooted in the senses. In religion it rejected miracles and emphasized instead the Bible's ethical teachings.

Addressing the Phi Beta Kappa Society at Harvard on August 31, 1837, Emerson returned to his theme in "The American Scholar." He warned against the tyranny of received opinion, particularly as it appeared in books: "Meek young men grow up in libraries, believing it their duty to accept the views, which Cicero, which Locke, which Bacon have given," but "Cicero, Locke, and Bacon were only young men in libraries, when they wrote these books." The American scholar should, therefore, read the book of nature. He should do so confidently, believing that in him "is the law of all nature, . . . the whole of Reason."

EMERSON'S MAJOR WORKS

1836	*Nature*
1837	*An Oration Delivered Before the Phi Beta Kappa Society, Cambridge* (better known as *The American Scholar*)
1838	*An Address Delivered Before the Senior Class in Divinity College, Cambridge . . .* (better known as *Divinity School Address*)
1841	*Essays: First Series*
1844	*Orations, Lectures and Addresses*
1844	*Essays: Second Series*
1847	*Poems*
1849	*Addresses and Lectures*
1850	*Representative Men: Seven Lectures*
1856	*English Traits*
1860	*The Conduct of Life*
1860	*Representative of Life*
1867	*May-Day and Other Pieces*
1870	*Society and Solitude*
1870	*Works and Days*
1875	*Letters and Social Aims*
1876	*Selected Poems*
1884	*Lectures and Biographical Sketches*
1884	*Miscellanies*
1893	*Natural History of Intellect*

Guided by his own insight and revelation rather than by outdated cultures, Emerson would lead others to a union with the spiritual source of life. This enlightened individual was to be American as well as scholarly, for the nature he was to take as his mentor was that of the New World rather than the Old.

In 1838, Emerson presented the controversial *Divinity School Address*. To his audience of intellectual, rational Unitarians he preached the doctrine of constant revelation and called each of his listeners "a newborn bard of the Holy Ghost." Once more he was urging the rejection of the past—in this case historical Christianity—in favor of the present and trust in personal feelings rather than doctrine and dogma. His criticism of what he saw as the cold lifelessness of Unitarianism so shocked his listeners that he was barred from Harvard for almost three decades.

Such a reaction, though, was what Emerson was seeking; he wanted to shock what he saw as a complacent nation into regeneration through an appreciation of the present. "What is man for but to be a Reformer," he wrote. First a person was to reform, that is remake, himself; hence, Emerson took little interest in political parties or the many utopian experiments—some started by members of the Transcendental Club—of the 1840's.

When enough individuals reformed themselves, society would necessarily be improved.

Among those who shared Emerson's vision were a number of neighbors: Bronson Alcott, William Ellery Channing, Margaret Fuller, Elizabeth Peabody, Jones Very, and Henry David Thoreau. From 1840 to 1844, this group published *The Dial*, a quarterly magazine rich in literature that expressed the Emersonian vision. Emerson frequently contributed to the journal, and for the magazine's last two years he was also its editor. Emerson's new philosophy spread well beyond Concord. In his journal in 1839, Emerson recorded that "a number of young and adult persons are at this moment the subject of a revolution [and] have silently given in their several adherence to a new hope."

In 1841, Emerson published *Essays*, which includes what is probably Emerson's most famous piece, "Self-Reliance." The themes of the essays were by now familiar, but the expression was forcefully aphoristic. Attacking contemporary religion, education, politics, art, and literature for their adherence to tradition, he declared, "Whoso would be a man must be a nonconformist." In 1844 appeared *Essays: Second Series*, with its call for an American poet who would sing of "our logrolling, our stumps, . . . our fisheries, our Negroes, and Indians, . . . the northern trade, the southern planting, the western clearing, Oregon, and Texas." The American poet would not care for "meters, but metermaking argument."

Emerson attempted to fill this role himself. His aunt Mary Moody had encouraged his youthful efforts in this area, and at the age of ten he had begun a poetic romance, "The History of Fortus." His early efforts had earned for him the role of class poet when he was graduated from Harvard in 1821. *Poems* (1847) suggests, however, that he lacked the ability or inclination to follow his own advice. The poems often remain tied to meter and rhyme rather than the rhythms of natural speech.

In "Days," one of Emerson's more successful pieces, Emerson described himself as sitting in his "pleached garden" and forgetting his "morning wishes." In "The Poet" he lamented, "I miss the grand design." Shortly before his second marriage, he had written to Lidian that though he saw himself as a poet, he knew he was one "of a low class, whose singing . . . is very husky." Some poems, though, like "The Snow Storm," reveal the power and beauty of nature through language that is fresh and immediate. Others, such as "Brahma" and "The Sphinx" (Emerson's favorite), use symbols well to convey spiritual messages and suggest the correspondence among humanity, nature, and the spiritual world that is one of the tenets of Transcendentalism.

In the next decade, Emerson published three important works based on his lectures: *Representative Men* (1850), *English Traits* (1856), and *The Conduct of Life* (1860). His lectures were not always well attended, even though he was in great demand. One course of lectures in Chicago brought only thirty-seven dollars; another audience in Illinois quickly left when it found a lecture lacking in humor.

The books that emerged from these lectures are more sober than Emerson's earlier writings. Emerson's youthful idealism is tempered by a darker sense of reality. In "Fate," the first chapter of *The Conduct of Life*, he recognizes the tyrannies of life and notes that humans are subject to limitations. In the concluding essay of the book, he reaffirms liberty and urges again, "Speak as you think, be what you are," but he concedes, too, the power of illusion to deceive and mislead.

After the Civil War, Emerson published two more collections of his essays, *Society and Solitude* (1870) and *Letters and Social Aims* (1875), this second with the help of James Elliot Cabot. Much of the contents of these books is drawn from lectures and journal entries written decades earlier.

Although Emerson was reusing old ideas, his popularity continued to grow. In 1867, he was invited to deliver the Phi Beta Kappa address again at Harvard; the previous year the school had indicated its forgiveness for the *Divinity School Address* by awarding Emerson an honorary doctorate. When he returned from a trip to Europe and the Middle East in 1873, the church bells of Concord rang to welcome him back, and the townspeople turned out in force to greet him.

Emerson recognized, however, that his powers were declining. As he wrote in "Terminus," "It is time to be old/ To take in sail/ . . . Fancy departs." John Muir saw him in California in 1871 and was amazed at the physical transformation, one mirrored by his fading mental abilities as his aphasia worsened. After John Burroughs attended a lecture by Emerson in 1872, he described the address as "pitiful." When Emerson attended the funeral of his neighbor Henry Wadsworth Longfellow in March, 1882, he could not remember the famous poet's name. A few weeks later, on April 27, 1882, Emerson died of pneumonia and was buried near his leading disciple, Thoreau.

SIGNIFICANCE

Emerson said that Goethe was the cow from which the rest drew their milk. The same may be said of Emerson himself. Walt Whitman derived his poetic inspiration from "The Poet," as Whitman acknowledged by sending a copy of the first edition of *Leaves of Grass* (1855) to Concord. Emerson was among the few contemporary readers of the book to recognize its genius. Thoreau, though an independent thinker, also took much from Emerson. In "Self-Reliance," Emerson had written,

> In the pleasing contrite wood-life which God allows me, let me record day by day my honest thoughts without prospect or retrospect. . . . My book should smell of pines and resound with the hum of insects.

Here is a summary of *Walden* (1854). Emerson's emphasis on the miraculous within the quotidian may even have influenced William Dean Howells and other American realists later in the century.

As an advocate of literary nationalism, of a truly American culture, Emerson urged his countrymen to look about them and celebrate their own surroundings. His was not the only voice calling for an intellectual and cultural independence to mirror the country's political autonomy, but it was an important and influential one. Oliver Wendell Holmes, Sr., referred to *The American Scholar* as "our intellectual Declaration of Independence."

In calling for a Renaissance rooted in the present of the New World rather than the past of the Old, Emerson was paradoxically joining the mainstream of the American spirit. Like John Winthrop in his sermon aboard the *Arbella* in 1630, he was advocating a new spirit for a new land.

Like his Puritan forerunners, too, Emerson stressed spiritual rather than material salvation. Having grown up poor, he harbored no illusions about poverty. He knew that "to be rich is to have a ticket of admission to the masterworks and chief men of every race." Because of such statements, H. L. Mencken said that Emerson would have made a fine Rotarian. This misreading of Emerson ignores the view that he expressed near the end of his life: "Our real estate is that amount of thought which we have." For Benjamin Franklin, the American Dream meant the opportunity to earn money. For Emerson, as for the Puritans, it meant the opportunity to live in harmony with oneself, to save not one's pennies but one's soul. Emerson's lectures and essays forcefully articulate a vision of the United States that has continued to inform American thought and writing.

—Joseph Rosenblum

FURTHER READING

Allen, Gay Wilson. *Waldo Emerson: A Biography*. New York: Viking Press, 1981. The definitive biography of Emerson, at once scholarly and readable. Allen is concerned with the personal as well as the public side of his subject. He also shows the evolution of Emerson's ideas by citing the stages of their development in journal entries, letters, lectures, essays, and poems.

Bode, Carl, ed. *Ralph Waldo Emerson: A Profile*. New York: Hill & Wang, 1969. How did Emerson's contemporaries view him? How has that view changed since his death? Bode offers a selection of biographical sketches by friends and scholars. Some of the earlier pieces are not readily available elsewhere.

Leary, Lewis Gaston. *Ralph Waldo Emerson: An Interpretive Essay*. Boston: Twayne, 1980. Offers an intellectual biography with a thematic arrangement. The focus is on understanding Emerson's ideas and their relationship to his life.

McAleer, John J. *Ralph Waldo Emerson: Days of Encounter*. Boston: Little, Brown, 1984. Each of the eighty short chapters treats a stage in Emerson's growth as a person, thinker, or writer. Much of the book deals with actual encounters between Emerson and his contemporaries to illustrate their mutual influence.

Matthiessen, Francis Otto. *American Renaissance: Art and Expression in the Age of Emerson and Whitman*. London: Oxford University Press, 1941. Investigates the intellectual climate that produced so much significant American literature between 1850 and 1855. Focus is on literary criticism of the works themselves. Appropriately, Matthiessen begins with Emerson and explores all of his major works, not simply his publications during the early 1850's.

Miller, Perry. "From Edwards to Emerson." In *Errand into the Wilderness*. Cambridge, Mass.: Belknap Press of Harvard University Press, 1956. An insightful essay exploring Emerson's intellectual debt to the Puritans at the same time that it shows the radical newness of Emerson's ideas.

Myerson, Joel, ed. *A Historical Guide to Ralph Waldo Emerson*. New York: Oxford University Press, 2000. Collection of essays, including a brief biography, and examinations of Emerson and individualism, nature, religion, antislavery, and the women's rights movement.

Rusk, Ralph Leslie. *The Life of Ralph Waldo Emerson*. New York: Charles Scribner's Sons, 1949. Rusk's was a pioneering study, the most detailed biography of Emerson up to that time and still useful for its meticulous detail. Rusk carefully examined unpublished material to present an authoritative picture of Emerson's life. Concentrates more on the man than on his ideas.

Sacks, Kenneth S. *Understanding Emerson: "The American Scholar" and His Struggle for Self-Reliance*. Princeton, N.J.: Princeton University Press, 2003. Recounts the circumstances under which Emerson wrote and delivered his address to the Phi Beta Kappa Society. Sacks portrays Emerson as a young intellectual, struggling to define his own principles and become self-reliant, while seeking the approval of others.

SEE ALSO: Bronson Alcott; William Ellery Channing; Margaret Fuller; Theodore Parker; Elizabeth Palmer Peabody; Henry David Thoreau.

RELATED ARTICLES in *Great Events from History: The Nineteenth Century, 1801-1900:* 1820's-1850's: Social Reform Movement; 1836: Transcendental Movement Arises in New England; March 9, 1875: *Minor v. Happersett.*

FRIEDRICH ENGELS
German socialist philosopher

In partnership with Karl Marx—with whom he wrote
The Communist Manifesto—*Engels analyzed the origins and nature of industrial capitalist society and worked to bring about the overthrow of that society by a working-class revolution.*

BORN: November 28, 1820; Barmen, Prussia (now in Germany)

DIED: August 5, 1895; London, England

AREAS OF ACHIEVEMENT: Social reform, government and politics

EARLY LIFE

Friedrich Engels (EHNG-ehls) was born into the social class whose domination he later strove to overturn. His father, Friedrich, owned one of the principal cotton mills in the Wupper Valley, in the Rhineland territory that Prussia had taken over in 1815 after the Napoleonic Wars. It was assumed that young Friedrich, the first of nine children, would enter the family business, and university education was considered unnecessary for a business career; Friedrich left grammar school in 1837 without taking the final examinations, having shown strong academic skills, particularly in languages. His literary inclinations, he believed, could be pursued without academic credentials; indeed, he became impressively self-educated.

By 1838, when he began a sort of businessperson's apprenticeship in the export business of a family friend in Bremen, Engels had already broken away from the strong Pietist fundamentalist Protestantism of his family and of Barmen. His letters also included sarcastic attacks on the Prussian king, Friedrich Wilhelm IV, calling him oppressive and stupid. His taste in philosophy favored D. F. Strauss and the Young Hegelians, in literature, Heinrich Heine and the Young German movement. Engels had defined himself as an alienated young man, but the newspaper articles that he wrote from Bremen were generally amusing, mocking rather than vehement in tone, though Engels did attack both capitalists and Pietists.

Engels returned to Barmen in 1841, and later that year went to Berlin to do his military service as a one-year volunteer in the Prussian artillery. His military duties, which he often avoided, were so undemanding that he was able to attend lectures at the university, associate with enthusiastic young radicals, and write copiously on political and philosophical issues. In October, 1842, his military service completed, he visited Cologne and the offices of the *Rheinische Zeitung*, whose editor, Moses Hess, claimed credit for converting Engels from generic revolutionary to communist.

From November, 1842, to August, 1844, Engels was in England, working in the Manchester branch of his father's firm and preparing his vivid attack on industrial capitalism, *Die Lage der arbeitenden Klasse in England* (1845; *The Condition of the Working Class in England in 1844*, 1887). In Paris, on the way home from England, Engels met Karl Marx, beginning a partnership that lasted till Marx's death. The two had met, coolly, in November, 1842. Now Engels's firsthand acquaintance with industrial society impressed Marx, who was beginning to interest himself in economic issues. The university-educated Marx, two years older than Engels, was profound, while Engels was quick; Marx mapped out huge projects that remained unfinished, and Engels responded to the needs of the moment. Together they attempted to change the world.

LIFE'S WORK

Marx and Engels defined their differences from other socialists of the day in their first collaborative writings and joined in organizing various revolutionary groups in Brussels, Paris, and London. One of these, the Communist League, aspired to be an international organization of the revolutionary working class, under the slogan "Workers of the World, unite!" Engels drafted this group's program and Marx revised it into *Manifest der Kommunistischen Partei* (1848; *The Communist Manifesto*, 1850). Although this program of a weak organization had little effect in 1848, it combined philosophy and economic history into a powerful prophecy that the course of history would soon make it possible to eliminate class rule and inaugurate true human freedom. The successes of the Industrial Revolution, carried out by the middle classes, were creating the conditions for a workers' revolution. Despite its dated denunciations of ephemeral leftist rivals, *The Communist Manifesto* remains the central expression of Marxism's ideas and style.

Revolution broke out in Paris in February, 1848, followed by upheavals elsewhere. Liberalism and nationalism were the issues of the day, not communism. Engels and Marx devoted their efforts to the *Neue Rheinische Zeitung*, published in Cologne, which advocated the unification of Germany as a democratic republic, ignoring for the moment the eventual goal of abolishing capitalism. Engels wrote caustically on the deliberations of the Frankfurt Assembly as that body failed to unite Germany, and he discussed revolution-related military campaigns in Hungary, Italy, and elsewhere. The authorities suspended the paper's publication in September and October, and Engels fled, taking an extended walking tour in France and returning to Cologne in January, 1849. He replaced Marx as editor in chief in April and May. In early May, uprisings occurred in several German areas, including Engels's hometown. He left Cologne to take part, but order was soon restored; he went back to Cologne, but the government, recovering its sense of initiative, shut down the *Neue Rheinische Zeitung* for good.

As revolutionary hopes faded everywhere in Europe, the Prussian king declined the invitation of the Frankfurt Assembly to serve as ruler of a new united Germany; only two small states supported the defiant, obviously doomed call to unite the country as a republic. Engels joined the volunteer corps, led by August Willich, as the revolutionary diehards held out for more than a month against overwhelming Prussian and other forces; he was among the last to cross into Switzerland. His sole experience of revolutionary combat showed the limitations of slogans and zeal against military organization.

Engels sailed from Genoa to London, already the refuge of Marx and many other revolutionary refugees. Debates on tactics and organization soon led to a split between the "party of the *Neue Rheinische Zeitung*," who argued that a real revolution would depend on years of preparation, education, and economic development, and those (including Engels's former commander Willich and other officers) who wished to revive the revolution by immediate conspiratorial and military action. As on several other occasions, Marx and Engels opposed more impatient revolutionaries. One consequence of this émigré discord (1850-1851) was that Engels took up the study of military science, to contest the opposing faction's monopoly on military expertise.

Bowing to economic necessity, Engels went to work at his father's company in Manchester. After his father's death in 1860, he became a partner in the firm, selling out his interest in 1869. His income from the textile mill, and later from successful investments, supported an official address where he met his business contacts, and a home where he lived with Mary Burns, a factory worker whom he had met during his visit to England in 1842-1844. It also furnished the chief, and often the only, source of support for the Marx family in London.

Until he was able to move to London in 1869, Engels corresponded daily with Marx. He wrote articles, often under Marx's name, for sale. When Eugen Dühring came forward with a rival socialist philosophy, Engels replied with *Herrn Eugen Dührings Umwälzung der Wissenschaft* (1877-1878; *Herr Eugen Dühring's Revolution in Science*, 1894), following Dühring into natural philosophy as well as politics. The work and an excerpt from it, *Die Entwicklung des Sozialismus von der Utopie zur Wissenschaft* (1882; *Socialism: Utopian and Scientific*, 1892), are Engels's best-known works, standing alongside *The Communist Manifesto* as summaries of Marxist thought, and sometimes accused of leading subsequent Marxists into simplistic materialist determinism.

Engels's foray into anthropology, *Der Ursprung der Familie, des Privateigentums und des Staats* (1884; *The Origin of the Family, Private*

ENGELS'S MAJOR WORKS	
1845	*Die Lage der arbeitenden Klasse in England* (*The Condition of the Working Class in England in 1844*, 1887)
1845	*Die deutsche Ideologie* (with Karl Marx; *The German Ideology*, 1938)
1847	*Grundsätze des Kommunismus* (*Principles of Communism*, 1925)
1848	*Manifest der Kommunistischen Partei* (with Marx; *The Communist Manifesto*, 1850)
1850	*Der deutsche Bauernkrieg* (serial; book: *The Peasant War in Germany*, 1926)
1877-1878	*Herrn Eugen Dührings Umwälzung der Wissenschaft* (*Herr Eugen Dühring's Revolution in Science*, 1894)
1882	*Die Entwicklung des Sozialismus von der Utopie zur Wissenschaft* (*Socialism: Utopian and Scientific*, 1892)
1884	*Der Ursprung der Familie, des Privateigenthums und des Staats* (*The Origin of the Family, Private Property, and the State*, 1902)
1887	*Zur Wohnunsfrage* (*The Housing Question*, 1935)
1888	*Ludwig Feuerbach und der Ausgang der klassischen deutschen Philosophie* (*Ludwig Feuerbach and the Outcome of Classical German Philosophy*, 1934)
1896	*Revolution and Counter-Revolution in Germany in 1848*

Property, and the State, 1902), has attracted some attention from feminist scholars. At great cost to his eyesight, Engels worked through vast quantities of overlapping, ill-organized drafts in Marx's wretched handwriting to produce volumes 2 and 3 of Marx's *Das Kapital* (1885, 1894; *Capital: A Critique of Political Economy*, 1907, 1908, best known as *Das Kapital*).

Described as military in bearing and nicknamed "General" by Marx's daughters after writing his brilliant articles on the Franco-Prussian War, Engels made a specialty of military science. In addition to writing about wars and crises as bread-and-butter journalism, he studied war as a phenomenon that might improve or diminish the prospects of revolution. Some capitalist states were more regressive and obnoxious than others, and Engels and Marx were never indifferent to the wars of their lifetimes. The most important fruit of Engels's military studies was his conclusion, after the Austro-Prussian War of 1866, that all the great powers would have to adopt the Prussian-style universal-service army. That meant that there was hope for the revolution, despite the folly of insurrection against an intact army; a socialist electoral majority would be reflected by a majority in the ranks, and the army would vanish as a counterrevolutionary instrument.

After Marx's death in 1883, Engels found himself in the role of interpreter of Marx's theories and as leader of the movement. He dispensed encouragement and advice to the younger socialists and presided over splendid parties in celebration of holidays and socialist election victories. His companion Mary Burns had died in 1863, succeeded in Engels's household by her sister Lizzie, whom Engels married on her deathbed in 1878. Engels presided at the Zurich Conference of the Second International in 1893, the grand old man of a growing, confident, worldwide movement. When Engels died of throat cancer in 1895, his ashes were scattered in the sea off Beachy Head.

SIGNIFICANCE

Friedrich Engels's name usually appears preceded by "Marx and." He was indeed important, not apart from Marx, but as a full partner in the creation of Marxism. In addition to providing Marx's material needs, protecting Marx's scholarly labors from interruption, and furnishing his friend vital psychological support for forty years, Engels brought to Marxism a quick intelligence and an acquaintance with the real world of capitalism. Involved in conceiving and elaborating all the varied aspects of Marxism and predominant in the crucial area of revolu-

tionary tactics, Engels played an indispensable part in creating Marxism as an intellectual system and as a political and social movement.

—Martin Berger

FURTHER READING

Berger, Martin. *Engels, Armies, and Revolution: The Revolutionary Tactics of Classical Marxism.* Hamden, Conn.: Archon Books, 1977. Emphasizes Engels's thought on war and military institutions as a key to Marxist views on international relations and the timing and tactics of revolution.

Carver, Terrell. *Engels: A Very Short Introduction.* New York: Oxford University Press, 2003. A concise (105-page) overview of Engels's life and thought. Carver traces the source of Engels's materialistic interpretation of history and explains how this interpretation affected the development of Marxist theory and practice. Includes an index and bibliography.

Henderson, W. O. *The Life of Friedrich Engels.* 2 vols. London: Frank Cass, 1976. A detailed study, strongest on Engels's business life in England.

Hunt, Richard N. *The Political Ideas of Marx and Engels.* 2 vols. Pittsburgh: University of Pittsburgh Press, 1974-1984. A standard account. Differentiates Marx and Engels from both Leninist and Social Democratic varieties of Marxism.

Lichtheim, George. *Marxism: An Historical and Critical Study.* 2d rev. ed. New York: Praeger, 1965. An unusually coherent account of Marxism, placing Engels in context.

McLellan, David. *Friedrich Engels.* New York: Viking Press, 1978. A concise (120-page) introduction in the Modern Masters series, a by-product of the author's major Marx biography.

Marcus, Steven. *Engels, Manchester, and the Working Class.* New York: Random House, 1974. A perceptive study of Engels's *The Condition of the Working Class in England in 1844* as a literary work.

Mayer, Gustav. *Friedrich Engels: A Biography.* Translated by Gilbert Highet and Helen Highet. New York: Alfred A. Knopf, 1936. A condensation of the great two-volume German original (1934). Still a sound treatment.

Steger, Manfred B., and Terrell Carver, eds. *Engels After Marx.* University Park: Pennsylvania State University Press, 1999. The title has a dual meaning: The essays in the book critically appraise Engels's relevance after the death of Marx and after the decline of Marxism. Essayists define the significance of Engels's contributions to philosophy, science, political economy, history, and socialist politics.

Wilson, Edmund. *To the Finland Station: A Study in the Writing and Acting of History*. Garden City, N.Y.: Doubleday, 1940. A classic popular account of the development of Marxism. Contains a good sketch of the Marx-Engels relationship.

SEE ALSO: Ferdinand Lassalle; Wilhelm Liebknecht; Karl Marx.

RELATED ARTICLES in *Great Events from History: The Nineteenth Century, 1801-1900:* February, 1848: Marx and Engels Publish *The Communist Manifesto*; September 28, 1864: First International Is Founded; 1867: Marx Publishes *Das Kapital*; March, 1898: Russian Social-Democratic Labor Party Is Formed.

SIR ARTHUR EVANS
British archaeologist

Evans is best known for his excavation of the Bronze Age site of Knossos on the island of Crete, where he discovered the remains of an advanced culture that he called "Minoan" after the legendary King Minos.

BORN: July 8, 1851; Nash Mills, Hertfordshire, England

DIED: July 11, 1941; Youlbury, near Oxford, England

ALSO KNOWN AS: Arthur John Evans (full name)

AREA OF ACHIEVEMENT: Scholarship

EARLY LIFE

Arthur Evans was the oldest of five children. His mother, Harriet Dickinson Evans, died when he was six, leaving a vacuum in his early life. His father, Sir John Evans, ran a prosperous paper manufacturing business but was more distinguished as an archaeologist, numismatist, antiquarian, and collector. Young Arthur shared his father's interests and accompanied him on archaeological quests. He was educated at Harrow School and from 1870 to 1874 attended Brasenose College in Oxford, where he received a degree in history.

Throughout his youth, Evans traveled widely, visiting sites in Europe, Finland, and Russian Lapland. Upon completion of his schooling, he toured the Balkans, the mountainous area north of Greece. There he pursued his interests in archaeology by locating and identifying ancient Roman roads and architectural sites. His studies led to a series of early scholarly works.

LIFE'S WORK

In 1878, Evans settled in the Dalmatian port city of Ragusa (now Dubrovnik, Croatia) and married Margaret Freeman. He came to be regarded as an expert on the Balkan region, which was then part of the Ottoman Empire. He openly sympathized with local Slavs who were rising against Turkish oppression and served as correspondent for the *Manchester Guardian*. In 1882, he was charged with complicity in a local insurrection and was arrested and imprisoned. When he was released seven weeks later, he was expelled from the region. He then returned to England with his wife and made Oxford his home. In 1884, he accepted the position of keeper of Oxford's Ashmolean Museum of art and archaeology, beginning an association that would continue for almost sixty years.

Continuing their travels, Evans and his wife visited Greece. There they met archaeologist Heinrich Schliemann, who had located and excavated Troy in Asia Minor and the palace at Mycenae in southern Greece. During the nineteenth century, little was known about the origins of the classical world. Although most scholars believed that early Greek narratives were purely mythological, Schliemann successfully pursued clues from ancient literature to locate early historical sites.

Schliemann's discoveries opened to Evans new perspectives on the distant past. Evans believed that the origins of the Mycenaean culture of the Greek mainland could be traced to the island of Crete, where ancient sealstones engraved with unknown symbols had been found. He thought the markings were an early form of Mycenaean writing. He first visited Crete in 1894, the year after his wife died, and repeatedly returned to the island to search for evidence of ancient writing.

Evans was familiar with the tradition that Knossos, the palace of the kings of Crete, stood on Kephala, the low hill near Candia (now Heraklion). He studied visible ruins at the site and met the Greek businessperson Minos Kalokairinos, who had uncovered ancient storage jars (*pithoi*) in that area. Evans began negotiations with local officials who had halted archaeological excavations, fearing that the island's Turkish rulers would confiscate valuable finds. In 1900, after Crete was freed from Turkish domination, Evans completed the purchase of Kephala Hill and obtained permission to excavate.

With the help of hired workers and the Scottish archaeologist Duncan Mackenzie, Evans began excavating on March 23, 1900. Financing the project with his own inherited family wealth, he began digging where Kalokairinos had worked. As the site had not been built over in later times, ancient remains were generally undisturbed and close to the surface. The dig produced results that were both immediate and astonishing. The very first day of digging revealed artifacts and remains of buildings. By the end of the first week, Evans had found inscribed clay tablets, fulfilling his goal of discovering early writing.

The site that Evans excavated at Knossos had been occupied in Neolithic times and had been built over with a series of Bronze Age palaces during the second millennium B.C.E. After an earthquake around the year 1700 B.C.E. damaged existing structures, rebuilding began. The new palace was a flat-roofed, multistory structure supported by wooden columns that tapered toward the bottom. It was organized around a stone-paved central court from which radiated a maze of passageways, including a three-story staircase. These led to additional courtyards, chambers, ritual areas, administrative areas, and storerooms. Sunlight and fresh air entered through transoms, shafts, staggered levels, and open stairways. A subterranean network of terra-cotta pipes provided an advanced plumbing system. Many of the plastered walls were painted with richly colored murals revealing major artistic motifs: double-bladed axes, horned bulls, bull leapers, women with snakes, and plant and animal life. The site encompassed six acres and fourteen hundred rooms. After Mycenaeans took over around the year 1450 B.C.E., Knossos remained in use for two more centuries.

Although Evans originally believed that Knossos represented an early Cretan counterpart of the Mycenaean civilization, it became apparent that he had discovered a culture that was both older and distinct from that which Schliemann had uncovered on the Greek mainland. The mazelike pattern of rooms, corridors, and courtyards at Knossos reminded Evans of the labyrinth of Greek mythology: according to ancient narratives, Crete was the stronghold of King Minos, who, according to legend, kept the half-man/half-bull Minotaur in a labyrinth in his palace. This prompted Evans to describe his excavation as the "Palace of Minos" and to give the name "Minoan" to its civilization.

As a result of Evans's spectacular find, his honors were numerous. In 1901 he was elected a fellow of Great

Sir Arthur Evans.

Britain's prestigious Royal Society. After receiving a large inheritance in 1908, he resigned his position at the Ashmolean Museum and was appointed the museum's honorary keeper with a seat on its Board of Visitors. He was also appointed professor of prehistoric archaeology at Oxford the following year. In 1911 he was knighted. From 1914 to 1919, he served as president of both the Society of Antiquaries and the Royal Numismatic Society. In addition, he was president of the British Association for the Advancement of Science from 1916 to 1919.

Meanwhile, Evans continued to devote himself to Minoan research. Pursuing his interest in ancient writing, he published the first volume of *Scripta Minoa* in 1909. (The second volume, edited by Sir John Myres, was published in 1952.) In 1921 the first volume of his monumental *The Palace of Minos* was published. It provided an encyclopedic account of everything then known about Minoan Crete. Additional volumes, in 1928, 1930, and 1935, recorded new material and updated earlier interpretations.

Evans also reconstructed parts of ancient Knossos that had fallen into ruin. Foundations and partial walls marked dimensions of chambers. Selected rooms, passageways, and frescoes were restored and repainted. Some reconstruction was necessary to protect uncovered remains from weathering and collapse; some was undertaken to offer visitors glimpses of the later palace as it may have appeared in ancient times. In 1927, Evans donated the site to the British School at Athens in 1927.

In 1938 failing health forced Evans into retirement at his estate at Youlbury, near Oxford. He died on July 11, 1941, three days after his ninetieth birthday.

SIGNIFICANCE

Sir Arthur Evans's accomplishments were numerous. His early explorations in the Balkans provided the basis for later archaeological studies of Roman roads and sites, many of which had been built over or destroyed. He also revitalized Oxford's Ashmolean Museum, vastly expanding the institution's holdings. His major accomplishment, however, was his discovery at Knossos.

Some of Evans's work has been controversial. Rather than serving as a dispassionate chronicler, it has been suggested that he projected his own vision onto his finds. For example, he identified his discovery as the Palace of Minos even though he found no evidence of King Minos or his legendary labyrinth at the site. He also referred to rooms as royal apartments without real evidence of their use. Although evidence of weaponry and stone fortifications has been uncovered, Evans created the widespread perception that Minoans were pleasure-loving people who lived peacefully on their unfortified island. Some of Evans's reconstructions at Knossos were necessary for preservation, but he and his restorers worked from fragmentary remains and created reconstructions that introduced new inaccuracies.

Nevertheless, Evans showed Knossos to be one of the most important sites of the Aegean region's Bronze Age. Using stratigraphy—identifying age of materials by the layers of earth in which they appear—he developed a broad chronology of Minoan history. His publications identified unique Minoan architectural features. He recovered frescoes and artifacts that revealed Minoan artistic and cultural characteristics. His careful excavation and documentation laid the foundation for study of this newly discovered civilization.

Evans also discovered previously unknown forms of ancient writing. In addition to pictorial writing, he uncovered two varieties of symbols arranged in rows, which he called Linear A and Linear B script. Linear B, which was later found to be an early form of ancient Greek that was used for administrative records, was deciphered in 1952. Linear A, which is thought to be the written form of Minoan language, remains undeciphered. Because of the failure to decipher Linear B, much about Minoan daily life and culture remains unknown.

Evans went to Crete in pursuit of ancient writing, but he looked far beyond. His discovery of Minoan Crete as a sea empire with contacts throughout the Mediterranean world revealed a unique chapter in ancient history. He recovered a lost civilization of unexpected size and richness.

—Cassandra Lee Tellier

FURTHER READING

Evans, Arthur. *The Palace of Minos: A Comparative Account of the Successive Stages of the Early Cretan Civilization as Illustrated by the Discoveries at Knossos*. 4 vols. New York: Biblo and Tannen, 1964. Complete edition of Evans's writings about Knossos.

Fitton, J. Lesley. *The Discovery of the Greek Bronze Age*. Cambridge, Mass.: Harvard University Press, 1996. Well-illustrated book that traces archaeological discoveries relating to Bronze Age Greece.

Harden, D. B. *Sir Arthur Evans, 1851-1941*. Oxford, England: Ashmolean Museum, University of Oxford, 1983. Biography of Evans that includes a useful chronology of his life.

Macgillivray, Joseph Alexander. *Minotaur: Sir Arthur Evans and the Archaeology of the Minoan Myth*. London: Random House, 2001. Biography that suggests that Evans anticipated his discoveries in Crete.

Sherratt, Susan. *Arthur Evans, Knossos, and the Priest-King*. Oxford, England: Ashmolean Museum, University of Oxford, 2000. History of the excavation at Knossos and examination of the famous "priest-king" fresco image. Notes and photographs.

SEE ALSO: Alexander von Humboldt; Heinrich Schliemann.

RELATED ARTICLES in *Great Events from History: The Nineteenth Century, 1801-1900:* 1803-1812: Elgin Ships Parthenon Marbles to England; 1839-1847: Layard Explores and Excavates Assyrian Ruins; November, 1839: Stephens Begins Uncovering Mayan Antiquities; April, 1870-1873: Schliemann Excavates Ancient Troy; March 23, 1900: Evans Discovers Crete's Minoan Civilization.

LOUIS FAIDHERBE
French imperialist

Through warfare and diplomacy, Faidherbe laid the foundation of France's West African empire. He stemmed the Muslim military advance in West Africa but respected Islam. He improved Senegal economically, socially, and culturally. His generalship also helped to retrieve France's honor during the Franco-German War.

BORN: June 3, 1818; Lille, France
DIED: September 29, 1889; Paris, France
ALSO KNOWN AS: Louis Léon César Faidherbe (full name)
AREAS OF ACHIEVEMENT: Military, government and politics

EARLY LIFE

Louis Léon César Faidherbe (feh-dehrb) was the son of a moderately successful merchant who had suffered imprisonment under the rule of Napoleon I. Louis studied at the Universities of Lille and Douai, the École Polytechnique, and the École d'Application. In 1842, he became a lieutenant in the French army's engineering corps. In Algeria, where he was stationed from 1843 to 1846 and again from 1849 to 1852, Faidherbe embraced French imperialism and became adept in warfare. He showed ingenuity in designing and supervising a fort's construction in newly occupied Bou-Saada, where he commanded for two years. While in Algeria, Faidherbe experienced an intellectual awakening. He learned Arabic and read Ibn-Khaldūn's history of the Berbers. He developed respect for Arabo-Berber culture and for Islam. Nevertheless, he supported French conquest, whatever the tactics, because it benefited the so-called barbaric peoples.

In the West Indian island of Guadeloupe, where he was stationed in 1848 and 1849, Faidherbe turned to republicanism and negrophilism, yet he did not allow these views to interfere with promoting French interests and his own career. The engineering detachment's reduction in Guadeloupe led to his recall and another stint in Algeria. In 1852, Faidherbe became subdirector of engineers in Senegal. He participated in seizing Podor and constructing its fort, attacking Diman's capital, and reinforcing Bakel's defenses in 1854. He wrote "Les Berbères" and began learning Wolof, Pular, and Sarakolé from his Sarakolé wife. He became interested in exploring the Niger River. Admiring Faidherbe's activities, major Bordeaux firms doing business with Senegal recommended him for Senegal's governorship.

LIFE'S WORK

Faidherbe served two terms as governor of Senegal, 1854-1861 and 1863-1865. Determined to erect a stable *Pax Francia*, he instituted an aggressive policy of conquest and expansion of trade. He took decisive steps to advance eastward from St. Louis through the Senegal River Valley and the vast Sudan region to Lake Chad. He even dreamed of a French African empire stretching from the Atlantic Ocean to the Red Sea. He sought to create a firm basis for its future development culturally as well as politically and economically.

Militarily, Faidherbe first sought to protect the gum trade along the Senegal River and to quell the Moorish Trarzas, who were raiding and opposing the Wolof peasants living along the river's south bank. In February, 1855, Faidherbe ordered his forces to expel Trarza clans from Walo. War ensued with Walo, whose leadership rebuffed Faidherbe's plan to "liberate" them; in April, Faidherbe had to fight the principal Trarza warrior clans. By the end of 1855, he had overcome Walo, which became the first sub-Saharan state dismembered and annexed by France. In 1858, having employed divide-and-conquer tactics, Faidherbe made treaties with the Trarzas of southern Mauretania. The Trarzas agreed to respect French traders and to commute the controversial "customs" charges into a fixed export duty of 3 percent.

Faidherbe's endeavor to end all African control over French navigation along the Senegal River, particularly the toll at Saldé-Tébékout in central Futa-Toro, brought greater hostilities. Conflict erupted with the traditional leaders of Futa-Toro and with the Tukolor Muslim reformer and state builder al-Hājj Umar Tal. In 1858-1859, Faidherbe forced the confederation of Futa-Toro to make peace with France on French terms. Faidherbe divided the confederation into four client states of France.

Faidherbe's greatest adversary, Umar, was the charismatic leader of the Tijaniyya fraternity in West Africa. Before Faidherbe's governorship, Umar had attacked the French because of their prohibiting the firearms trade in the Senegal Valley. Faidherbe resisted Umar's thrust along the Senegal. In July, 1857, Faidherbe gallantly led a small force with fixed bayonets in relieving Médine from Umar's three-month siege. In 1860, Faidherbe negotiated a demarcation line along the Bafing River with Umar's emissary and provisionally agreed to send his own envoy to discuss future relations with Umar. Faidherbe hoped that, in return for political support and supplies of firearms, Umar would permit France to enact a line of fortified trading posts from Senegal to a base for navigation on the Niger.

With Umar's cooperation, Faidherbe envisioned pushing French trade and influence downstream and averting the monopoly that Great Britain, through traders in the delta, threatened to establish over the Niger. Returning as governor in 1863, Faidherbe sent Lieutenant Eugène Mage to contact Umar. Eventually Mage negotiated a treaty with Umar's successor, Ahmadu Tal, wherein Ahmadu renounced holy war against France and permitted French trade and exploration in his territories, while France allowed him to buy goods in St. Louis. While fighting Umar, Faidherbe's forces gutted the principal villages of Buoye, Kaméra, and Guidimakha, after which Faidherbe made treaties with new client rulers in each state.

As early as 1859, Faidherbe had also turned his attention to the kingdom of Cayor. His aim was to prevent its warriors' interference in the collection of peanuts by peasants and to open a trail with three small forts placed along it and a telegraph line to link St. Louis to Dakar and Gorée via the coastal route. Faidherbe first tried peaceful

means but, rebuffed by Damel Biraima, he used force. When Biraima died, Faidherbe claimed that Biraima had agreed on his deathbed to France's demands. Biraima's successor, Macodu, would not recognize the treaty. Faidherbe declared war and sought to replace Macodu with Madiodio. Thereupon Lat Dior progressed in seizing power. Faidherbe's replacement, Governor Jean Jauréguiberry, allowed Lat Dior to expel Madiodio and become ruler. In his second governorship, Faidherbe moved to restore Madiodio, who ceded more territory to France. As disorder still prevailed in Cayor, Faidherbe retired Madiodio and annexed the remainder of Cayor in 1865.

Faidherbe's military successes owed much to his personal touch. In 1857, he organized the Senegalese Riflemen. He created two battalions of volunteers recruited as much as possible from the free population of Senegambia. The first recruits were paid relatively well; they served short, two-year terms; wore special, colorful uniforms; were allowed a looser discipline than that of European troops; and received traditional food. Faidherbe labored in numerous ways in Senegal. He founded a school for the sons of chiefs, and lay schools for Muslims. He established scholarships for primary education in St. Louis and secondary education in France. He built small technical schools at Dakar. He opened a museum and a newspaper at St. Louis. Faidherbe founded the Bank of Senegal, laid out St. Louis afresh as befitted a capital city, promoted the export of groundnuts, made valuable and detailed studies of the indigenous people, and founded Dakar.

After the conclusion of his second term as governor of Senegal, Faidherbe returned to Algeria, where he spent the years from 1865 to 1870. In addition to his military duties, he gave considerable time to writing during this period. In December, 1870, Faidherbe became Commander in Chief of the Army of the North in the Franco-Prussian War. Despite fever and exhaustion, he commanded superbly in the Battles of Pont Noyelles, Bapaume, and St. Quentin. A confirmed republican, Faidherbe in 1871 declined election to the National Assembly because of its reactionary character. In 1879, he accepted election to the Senate. In 1880, he became grand chancellor of the Legion of Honor. He continued his writing until his death, in 1889. After a public funeral in Paris, he was buried in Lille.

Louis Faidherbe. (Library of Congress)

SIGNIFICANCE

Louis Faidherbe stood center stage in modern French imperialism. He initiated firm French control of the Senegal valley, which became the springboard for further expansion in West Africa. By opening the trade of Senegal, he provided the means for reaching the Niger Basin. His plan for railroad construction eventually materialized. His proposal, rejected by his superiors, for France and Great Britain, and France and Portugal mutually to arrange exchange of territories in West Africa would have created the French Gambia valley. Faidherbe grappled firmly but humanely with Islam in West Africa. He used war and diplomacy to stop the westward push of the great al-Hājj Umar Tal. Faidherbe's policy of opposing Christian proselytism of Muslims caused a lasting prestigious francophile Muslim community and tradition in Senegal.

Faidherbe further affected West Africa. In Senegal, his governorship distinguished priorities and allocated limited resources. Faidherbe started new public works and aided the peasants. His policies of non-French settlement and restricted assimilation into French citizenship became models for French West Africa. Faidherbe accomplished still more. He reorganized the Legion of Honor and reformed its educational work. He wrote extensively on ancient Egypt, Carthage, Numidia, the Franco-Prussian War, West Africa, and army reorganization. His scholarship gained for him election to the Academy of Inscriptions and Belles-Lettres.

—*Erving E. Beauregard*

FURTHER READING

Abun-Nasr, Jamil M. *The Tijaniyya: A Sufi Order in the Modern World.* London: Oxford University Press, 1965. An excellent, impartial treatment of the movement led by Faidherbe's major foe, Umar. Clear analysis of the reasons for the clash between Faidherbe and Umar, the warfare between the French and Umarians, and the negotiations bringing peace.

Barrows, Leland C. "Faidherbe and Senegal: A Critical Discussion." *African Studies Review* 19 (April, 1976). A scholarly and detailed study of Faidherbe's governorship of Senegal. Critical of Faidherbe's so-called radicalism, especially his stand on slavery and his ambiguity in defining the positions of blacks and mulattoes. Stresses Faidherbe's militarism as his chief contribution to the creation of French West Africa.

Barry, Boubacar. *Senegambia and the Atlantic Slave Trade.* Translated from the French by Ayi Kwei Armah. New York: Cambridge University Press, 1998. Originally published in French in 1988, this book provides a meticulously detailed examination of four centuries of the West African slave trade, including trading practices during the nineteenth century co-

lonial era. Information about Faidherbe is included in numerous pages that are listed in the index.

Cohen, William B. *Rulers of Empire: The French Colonial Service in Africa.* Stanford, Calif.: Hoover Institution Press, 1971. Cohen emphasizes Faidherbe's founding of a workable administrative organization in West Africa, which remained unchanged and lasted with few modifications until the end of the French occupation.

Hargreaves, John D. *Prelude to the Partition of West Africa.* New York: St. Martin's Press, 1963. Pinpoints Faidherbe's faith in the possibilities of penetrating the Sudan by the upper Senegal route and his freedom from strong anti-Muslim prejudice achieved during service in Algeria. Good on Anglo-French relations in West Africa.

Howard, Michael. *The Franco-Prussian War: The German Invasion of France, 1870-1871.* New York: Macmillan, 1961. Shows that Faidherbe's objective was not to defeat the enemy but to pin down the greatest possible number of Germans and, by attacks, to facilitate Paris's relief.

Kanya-Forstner, A. S. *The Conquest of the Western Sudan: A Study in French Military Imperialism.* Cambridge, England: Cambridge University Press, 1969. Underlines Faidherbe's vigor and his vision for a future French African empire. Notes the declining fortunes of Senegal following his departure in 1865 but the revival of his Niger plan after 1876. Contains valuable footnotes, a bibliography, an index, and two maps.

Klein, Martin A. *Islam and Imperialism in Senegal: Sine-Saloum, 1847-1914.* Stanford, Calif.: Stanford University Press, 1968. Stresses how Faidherbe laid the foundation for France's West African empire in spite of the skepticism of the French government. A first-rate consideration of Faidherbe's relations with the Senegambian rulers. Notes Faidherbe's compromise with slavery but his enlightened outlook toward Islam.

Robinson, David. *The Holy War of Umar Tal: The Western Sudan in the Mid-Nineteenth Century.* Oxford, England: Clarendon Press, 1985. A reliable account of Faidherbe's encounter with Umar. Shows Faidherbe's ingenuity: use of intelligence reports and manufacturing his own propaganda to counter the appeal of Umar's holy war.

Singer, Barnett, and John Langdon. *Cultured Force: Makers and Defenders of the French Colonial Empire.* Madison: University of Wisconsin Press, 2004.

The authors reassess the nature of French imperialism by focusing on the lives and careers of French leaders in African and Asian colonies. One of those leaders is Faidherbe, whose experiences are discussed in the chapter "Faidherbe of Senegal and West Africa."

SEE ALSO: Abdelkader.

RELATED ARTICLES in *Great Events from History: The Nineteenth Century, 1801-1900:* May 4, 1805-1830: Exploration of West Africa; June 14-July 5, 1830: France Conquers Algeria.

MICHAEL FARADAY
British physicist

Considered by many to have been the greatest British physicist of the nineteenth century, Faraday made discoveries in electromagnetism that were fundamental to the development of field physics. His inventions of the dynamo and electric motor provided the basis for modern electrical industry.

BORN: September 22, 1791; Newington, Surrey, England
DIED: August 25, 1867; Hampton Court, Surrey, England
AREAS OF ACHIEVEMENT: Physics, chemistry

EARLY LIFE

Michael Faraday (FAHR-ah-day) was the third of four children born to James Faraday, a Yorkshire blacksmith, and Margaret Hastwell, the daughter of Yorkshire farmers. Both were of Irish descent. Shortly before his birth, the family moved to Newington, near London, in search of better opportunities. James Faraday's health deteriorated, limiting his ability to work, and the family had only the bare necessities for survival. Young Faraday's education consisted of the rudiments of reading, writing, and arithmetic. The family belonged to the small religious sect of Sandemanians, which emphasized the Bible as the sole and sufficient guide for each individual, and Faraday was a devoted, lifelong member.

In 1804, Faraday was an errand boy for George Riebau, a London bookseller and bookbinder. His seven-year apprenticeship produced an extraordinary manual dexterity, a skill characteristic of his experimental researches. He also read omnivorously, from *The Arabian Nights' Entertainments* to the *Encyclopaedia Britannica*. The latter's article on electricity awakened him to a new world, as did Jane Marcet's *Conversations on Chemistry* (1806), a book that converted him in his teenage years into a passionate student of science. With his apprenticeship nearing an end in 1812, it was not likely that Faraday would be anything but a bookbinder. A customer's gift of tickets to a series of lectures by Humphry Davy at the Royal Institution changed his life. Davy was a scientist of international stature and a brilliant lecturer, largely responsible for the success of the Royal Institution, a center both for research and for the dissemination of science to a general audience.

Faraday, enthralled by the lectures, desperately wanted to become a scientist. When Davy became temporarily blinded in a laboratory explosion, a customer at Riebau's bookshop recommended Faraday to him as secretary for a few days because of Faraday's fine penmanship. Faraday subsequently bound in the bookshop his neatly written lecture notes with his own illustrations and sent the volume to Davy asking for a job. Davy had nothing for him at the time. Suddenly, in 1813, however, Davy fired his laboratory assistant for brawling, and the twenty-one-year-old Faraday became his assistant.

In that same year, Davy married a rich widow and set out on a grand tour of Europe, including visits to the major scientific centers to meet the most distinguished Continental scientists. Faraday went along to assist Davy in his research. The tour was a remarkable experience; the young man had never been more than a few miles from London. His letters home were full of amazement over meeting renowned scientists during the eighteen-month tour. On his return to England, the Royal Institution appointed Faraday superintendent of apparatus. Now in his early twenties, he possessed a robust intelligence, considerable scientific knowledge, and the good fortune to be at the Royal Institution.

All Faraday's contemporaries described him as kind, gentle, and simple in manner. Serenity and calm marked his life and countenance; no scientist has been referred to more as humble or saintly. These attributes stemmed from his Sandemanian faith, with its stress on love and community. He had an unquestioning belief in God as creator and sustainer of the universe and saw himself as merely the instrument by which the divine truths of nature were exposed. His faith and his science meshed completely.

Otherworldly, Faraday had a contempt for money-making and trade, and he rejected all honors that raised him above others. He refused both knighthood and the presidency of the Royal Society. In 1821, he married a fellow Sandemanian, Sarah Barnard. The marriage was childless but most happy. She lavished her maternal feelings on the nieces who lived with them and on her husband. United by a deep, enduring love, secure in their faith, the tone of the household (they lived in rooms provided in the Royal Institution) was one of gaiety, and domestic life was completely satisfactory.

LIFE'S WORK

Faraday was a late bloomer with no important discovery until he was more than thirty. He lacked familiarity with mathematics, the language of physics, and remained outside the mathematical tradition of universities and of Continental physics. From 1815 to 1820, he earned a modest reputation as an analytical chemist, publishing several papers on subjects suggested by Davy. These were the years of his scientific apprenticeship.

In 1820, the Danish physicist Hans Christian Oersted discovered the magnetic effect of the electric current. This discovery of electromagnetism caused a sensation and provoked both an explosion of research and much confusion. In 1821, the editor of a journal asked Faraday to review the experiments and interpretations and present a coherent account of electromagnetism. Faraday's genius now became evident, for he demonstrated that there were no attractions or repulsions involved in the phenomenon; instead, a force in the conductor made a magnetic needle move around it in a circle. He also devised an instrument to illustrate the process, producing the first conversion of electrical into mechanical energy. He had discovered electromagnetic rotation, and as a by-product, he had invented the electric motor.

Faraday did not follow up this major discovery with anything comparable until 1831, although his chemical researches continued to be fruitful, notably the 1825 discovery of benzene, which he isolated from an oil that separated from illuminating gas. He also conducted a lengthy project for the Royal Society on the improvement of optical glass used in lenses. It ended with no apparent useful results, but he did prepare a heavy lead borosilicate glass that later proved indispensable to his electromagnetic work.

In 1825, the Royal Institution promoted Faraday to director of the laboratory. Faraday instituted the Friday Evening Discourses, which soon became one of the most famous series of lectures on the progress of science, serving to educate the English upper class in science and to influence those in government and education. In 1826, he began the Christmas Courses of Lectures for Juvenile Audiences, which further extended the appeal of the institution. His lectures, based on a careful study of oratory, were full of grace and earnestness, and exercised a magic on hearers. He was at his best with children: a sense of drama and wonder unfolded, and they reacted with enthusiasm to the marvels of his experiments. Two of his courses for juveniles were published as *The Chemical History of a Candle* (1861) and *The Various Forces of Nature* (1860). They have remained in print as classics of scientific literature.

In 1831, Faraday made his most famous discovery, reversing Oersted's experiment by converting magnetism into electricity. He used the Royal Institution's thick iron ring as an electromagnet, winding insulated wire on one side with a secondary winding on the other side. With a battery linked to one winding and a galvanometer to the other, he closed the battery circuit and the galvanometer needle moved. He had induced another electric current through the medium of the iron ring's expanding magnetic force. He called his discovery electromagnetic induction and elaborated a conception of curved magnetic lines of force to account for the phenomenon.

Over the next several weeks, Faraday devised variations and extensions of the phenomenon, the most famous one being the invention of the dynamo. He converted mechanical motion into electricity by turning a copper disc between the poles of a horseshoe magnet, thereby producing continuous flowing electricity. From this discovery came the whole of the electric-power industry. Faraday realized that he had a possible source of cheap electricity, but he was too immersed in discovery to pursue the practical application.

In 1833, Faraday made his most monumental contribution to chemistry. A study of the relationship between electricity and chemical action disclosed the two laws of electrochemistry. He then devised a beautiful, elegant theory of electrochemical decomposition that involved no poles, no action at a distance, no central forces. Faraday's theory, totally at odds with the thinking of his contemporaries, demanded a new language for electrochemistry. In 1834, in collaboration with the classical scholar William Whewell, he invented the vocabulary of electrode, anode, cathode, anion, cation, electrolysis, and electrolyte, the word *electrode* meaning not a pole or terminal but only the path taken by electricity. Faraday's stupendous labors of the 1830's were too much for him, however, and in 1838, he suffered a serious mental breakdown. So bad was his condition that he could not work for five years.

In 1845, William Thomson (Lord Kelvin) suggested to Faraday some experiments with polarized light that might reveal a relation between light and electricity. This stimulated Faraday into intense experimentation. He had no success until he tried a stronger force, an electromagnet, and passed a polarized light beam through the magnetic field. At first unsuccessful, he remembered his heavy borosilicate glass from the 1820's. Placing it between the poles of the magnet, he sent the light beam through the glass and the plane of polarization rotated; he had discovered the effect of magnetic force on light (magneto-optical rotation).

The fact that the magnetic force acted through the medium of glass suggested to Faraday a study of how substances react in a magnetic field. This study revealed the class of diamagnetics. Faraday listed more than fifty substances that reacted to magnets not by aligning themselves along the lines of magnetic force (paramagnetics) but by setting themselves across the lines of force, a finding that attracted more attention from scientists than any of his other discoveries.

During the 1850's, Faraday's theorizing led to the idea that a conductor or magnet causes stresses in its surroundings, a force field. The energy of action lay in the medium, not in the conductor or magnet. He came to envision the universe as crisscrossed by a network of lines of force, and he suggested that they could vibrate and thereby transmit the transverse waves of which light consists. (The notion of the electromagnetic theory of light first appeared in an 1846 Royal Institution lecture.) His speculations had no place for Newtonian central forces acting in straight lines between bodies, or for any kind of polarity. All were banished for a field theory in which magnets and conductors were habitations of bundles of lines of force that were continuous curves in, through, and around bodies.

Faraday's mental faculties gradually deteriorated after 1855. Concern for his health reached Prince Albert; at his request, Queen Victoria in 1858 placed a home near Hampton Court at Faraday's disposal for the rest of his life. There, he sank into senility until his death in 1867. Like his life, his funeral was simple and private.

SIGNIFICANCE

Michael Faraday was an unusual scientist. He never knew the language of mathematics. To compensate, he had an intuitive sense of how things must be, and he organized his thoughts in visual, pictorial terms. He imagined lines of force stretching and curving through the space near magnets and conductors. In this way, he mastered the phenomena. His vision of reality was incomprehensible to a scientific world preoccupied with the Newtonian model. Only when James Clerk Maxwell showed how Faraday's ideas could be treated rigorously and mathematically did the lines-of-force conception in the guise of field equations become an integral part of modern physics.

Faraday coupled his inventive thinking with an unmatched experimental ability. His ingenuity disclosed a host of fundamental physical phenomena. One of those phenomena, his seemingly humble discovery of the dynamo, became the symbol of the new age of electricity, with its incalculable effects on society and daily life.

—*Albert B. Costa*

FURTHER READING

Agassi, Joseph. *Faraday as a Natural Philosopher*. Chicago: University of Chicago Press, 1971. Faraday's biographers stressed his experimental contributions, downplaying his speculations until historians of science rediscovered him as a daring natural philosopher. This work is a product of that rediscovery.

Cantor, Geoffrey. *Michael Faraday: Sandemanian and Scientist—A Study of Science and Religion in the Nineteenth Century*. New York: St. Martin's Press, 1991. The first detailed account of Faraday's public and private life that shows how all facets of his life were closely linked to his Sandemanism, the doctrine of a small, strict sect of fundamentalist Christians.

Hamilton, James. *A Life of Discovery: Michael Faraday, Giant of the Scientific Revolution*. New York: Random House, 2002. Biography focusing on Faraday's life, including his relationships with friends and colleagues, and less on his scientific discoveries.

Ihde, Aaron. "Michael Faraday." In *Great Chemists*, edited by Eduard Farber. New York: Interscience, 1961. An excellent discussion of Faraday's contributions to chemistry.

Jones, Henry Bence. *Life and Letters of Faraday*. 2 vols. London: Longmans, Green, 1870. A collection of letters to and from Faraday and excerpts from diaries with a biography written by a close friend and colleague at the Royal Institution.

Kendall, James. *Michael Faraday: Man of Simplicity*. London: Faber & Faber, 1955. A popular biography with simple handling of difficult subject matter in a way understandable to the general reader.

Thomas, John Meurig. *Michael Faraday and the Royal Institution: The Genius of Man and Place*. Bristol, England: Institute for Physics, 1997. Thomas, the director of the Royal Institution of Great Britain, describes Faraday's life, work, and legacy in a style accessible to general readers as well as scientists. Includes numerous illustrations.

Tyndall, John. *Faraday as a Discoverer*. New York: D. Appleton, 1868. Reprint. New York: Thomas Y. Crowell, 1961. The first biography of Faraday, written by his successor at the Royal Institution. Essential reading, for it reveals what friends of Faraday thought of him and his physical theories. A lucid discussion of his vast basic contributions to science.

Williams, L. Pearce. *Michael Faraday: A Biography*. New York: Basic Books, 1965. Indispensable. The first major appraisal by a historian of science. Lively, readable, comprehensive, and based on painstaking scholarship, Williams's work traces the full context of Faraday's contributions and his genius as both a daring theorist and experimentalist.

SEE ALSO: William Fothergill Cooke and Charles Wheatstone; Sir Humphry Davy; Sir William Robert Grove; Joseph Henry; Baron Kelvin; James Clerk Maxwell.
RELATED ARTICLES in *Great Events from History: The Nineteenth Century, 1801-1900:* October, 1831: Faraday Converts Magnetic Force into Electricity; October 21, 1879: Edison Demonstrates the Incandescent Lamp.

DAVID G. FARRAGUT
American admiral

The first officer given the rank of admiral in the United States Navy, Farragut is most noted for his victory over Confederate forces in the Battle of Mobile Bay during the Civil War. He had served in the Navy for an exceptionally long period and is regarded as a model of a career military career officer.

BORN: July 5, 1801; Campbell's Station, Tennessee
DIED: August 14, 1870; Portsmouth, New Hampshire
ALSO KNOWN AS: James Glasgow; David Glasgow Farragut (full name)
AREA OF ACHIEVEMENT: Military

EARLY LIFE
David Glasgow Farragut (FARH-ah-geht) was the son of George Farragut and the former Elizabeth Shine. His mother was a native of Dobbs County, North Carolina, while his father was an immigrant of Spanish ancestry from the British (later French) island of Minorca. George Farragut served as both an army and then a naval officer during the American Revolution, then moved his family to Tennessee and again westward.

In Louisiana after 1807, George Farragut was a sailing master in the Navy who, the following year, suffered the loss of his wife to yellow fever at their home on the shore of Lake Pontchartrain. Because he did not expect to remarry and thought that he could no longer give proper care and attention to his children, the elder Farragut arranged for his son's adoption by his friend, Commander David Porter. Porter was the commandant of the naval station at New Orleans.

Porter took his adopted son with him to Washington in 1809, and there and at his later home in Chester, Pennsylvania, he gave him better schooling than he had hitherto known. He also introduced him to Paul Hamilton, secretary of the Navy, who promised him a commission as a midshipman. This was issued December 17, 1810, although Farragut was only nine years of age. From 1811 through 1815, Farragut served under Porter aboard the frigate *Essex*, saw action in the Atlantic and the Pacific in the War of 1812, and even had the brief opportunity at the age of twelve to command a captured prize ship, the *Barclay*. Although finally made a prisoner of war after an unsuccessful battle with the British ship *Phoebe*, the thrill of this early service and the pride he took in his adoptive father's growing reputation caused Farragut, upon release in 1814, to change his name legally to David. This was also the name of his foster brother, David Dixon Porter; the two maintained a healthy rivalry and friendship down through the years.

At home, in Chester, Farragut added to his education. He then served briefly apart from Porter following a paroled prisoner of war exchange, and concluded the war aboard the brig *Spark*. With never a thought toward a civilian occupation, Farragut immediately took service aboard a ship-of-the-line, the *Independence*, which sailed to the Mediterranean Sea to back up Commodore Stephen Decatur's squadron against the Barbary pirates in what was called the Algerine War.

After this Farragut served aboard a similar ship, the *Washington*, until he was afforded the opportunity to study under the American consul at Tunis, Charles Folsom. In addition to diplomacy, polite manners, and foreign languages, he was able to develop an understanding of English literature and mathematics. He was a bright young man, though impressive only in demeanor as he was five feet, six and a half inches tall and of average build. With his formal education complete late in 1818, Farragut embarked upon his naval career in earnest.

LIFE'S WORK

Duty was undertaken aboard the *Franklin* and the *Shark*, and while aboard the latter brig, Farragut was recommended for promotion to the rank of lieutenant at the unusually young age of eighteen. Recalled to Norfolk, Virginia, he was ordered to sea again in the sloop-of-war *John Adams*; in 1823 he volunteered for duty aboard the *Greyhound* when he heard that this ship was to be placed under the command of Captain Porter's brother, Lieutenant John Porter, and that the captain himself was to command the squadron of which it was a part. The squadron was prepared to fight pirates in the Caribbean Sea, and this was especially welcome duty to Farragut, who had come to detest piracy.

Confiscating the booty of numerous pirates and burning their ships, the "Mosquito Fleet," as the squadron was known, did effective service over the next two years. British forces then arrived to finish the job, and piracy was virtually eliminated as a common practice in Caribbean waters. An incident that occurred in the town of Foxardo, Puerto Rico, however, while he was in command of the squadron led to Commodore Porter's courtmartial and resignation from the Navy. In later years he would serve his country as a diplomat.

After six months' service in the Caribbean in 1823, Farragut returned to Norfolk to marry a young woman he had met there. On September 24, 1823, Susan C. Marchant became his wife. With his formal promotion to lieutenant in 1825, Farragut was ordered once again to active duty aboard the frigate *Brandywine*, which carried the celebrated old hero of that Revolutionary War battle, the Marquis de Lafayette, back to France. When he returned to the United States, Farragut found his wife suf-

David G. Farragut. (Library of Congress)

fering greatly from neuralgia. Despite a convalescence at New Haven, Connecticut, she continued to decline from the disease until her death on December 27, 1840.

While in New Haven, Farragut had come to attend lectures at Yale and reflect on the lack of educational opportunities available to young boys aboard ships. Upon returning to Norfolk, he organized a school for "ship's boys," said to be the first of its kind.

From 1828 to 1829, from 1833 to 1834, and again from 1841 to 1843, Farragut served in the South Atlantic waters off South America. He rose from first lieutenant (executive officer) of the sloop-of-war *Vandalia* to captain of the schooner *Boxer*. Several years of shore duty were then followed by orders to Pensacola, Florida, in 1838, where he was placed in command of the sloop-of-war *Erie* and given duty off Veracruz, Mexico. He was then advanced to the rank of commander in 1841.

Returning to Norfolk early in 1843, Farragut met and married Virginia Loyall, a native of that community, on December 26, 1843. They would have one child, a son, Loyall, born in 1844. As war with Mexico approached, Farragut anxiously requested duty off Veracruz and pressed his ideas for an attack on its fort, Castle San Juan de Ulloa, upon George Bancroft, secretary of the Navy. His overzealousness in doing so, however, delayed his being given a proper command. Finally, in February, 1847, almost a year after the war got under way, he was given the sloop-of-war *Saratoga* and sent to the port. By that time, however, Veracruz had already been captured by army forces under General Winfield Scott. Nothing came of his service in this war except frustration, a bout with yellow fever, bitterness, and ill feelings.

Assignment to the Norfolk Navy Yard followed the Mexican War in 1848. Posted in California in 1854, Farragut was responsible for the establishment of the soon-to-be-important navy yard at Mare Island. In 1855, he was promoted to the rank of captain. Returning to the east three years later, he was named to command a new steamship, the wooden sloop-of-war *Brooklyn*. From 1858 to 1860, he remained her captain, assigned primarily to the Gulf of Mexico.

With the election of Abraham Lincoln, the secession of Southern states began in late 1860. As his native state of Tennessee and adopted state of Virginia threatened to follow others and join the Confederacy, Farragut had the same mixed feelings that struck Scott and other Southern unionists; like them, however, he professed his loyalty and stood by the same colors he had served so long.

The war's beginning, on April 12, 1861, with the firing upon Fort Sumter, was formalized by Lincoln's call for seventy-five thousand volunteers and establishment of a naval blockade of the Confederate coast. Farragut took his family out of Norfolk and established a home for them at Hastings, New York. On December 21, 1861, Farragut met the Assistant Secretary of the Navy, Gustavus Vasa Fox, and received from him orders to take command of the Western Gulf Blockading Squadron, gather all available vessels, and proceed to capture New Orleans.

Farragut designated the steam sloop-of-war *Hartford* his flagship and departed Hampton Roads in February, 1862, for Ship Island in the Gulf. Seventeen vessels, mostly gunboats, were brought in and sailed up the Mississippi; on April 18, 1862, Farragut, as his orders directed, set his mortar boats to work bombarding Fort Jackson. The fort, however, was too strong to be reduced in this manner, and so Farragut took it upon himself to run past this fort, and Fort St. Philip upstream, at night. After 2:00 A.M. on August 24, the run was successfully completed, Confederate vessels sent against them were destroyed, and New Orleans was taken through the instrument of Benjamin Butler's army. Farragut then

passed Vicksburg on June 28. Instantly he became a national hero and was promoted to rear admiral on July 16, 1862. He added little to his fame with further actions on the Mississippi, which was soon in the capable hands of David Dixon Porter.

In August, Farragut made his headquarters in the evacuated harbor of Pensacola. His blockade of the Gulf coast was now complete save for the fortified Confederate port of Mobile. This was a hornets' nest of blockade runners and Farragut's last objective. Receiving added ships and support from Secretary of the Navy Gideon Welles, he took a fleet of nineteen ships into Mobile Bay on August 5, 1864, past the Confederate batteries of Fort Morgan and through a minefield.

When Farragut's lead ship, the *Brooklyn*, hesitated upon spotting the mines, and the monitor *Tecumseh* was sunk by one (then called a "torpedo"), Farragut ordered his flagship to take the lead and not to slow down. "Damn the torpedoes!" he said, and ordered the *Hartford* ahead at full speed. Successful at moving by the fort and through the mine field, Farragut's fleet defeated all Confederate vessels easily except for the *Tennessee*, a ram that held out through a desperate battle until it had suffered so badly that it surrendered at last. Soon Fort Morgan was in Union hands and the Confederate coast was closed.

As Farragut's health, ravaged by many tropical diseases, was declining, he was recalled to New York in November, 1864. There he became a communicant of the Episcopal Church. A month later, as of Christmas, he was promoted as the first to hold the rank of vice admiral of the U.S. Navy. The people of New York claimed him as a citizen of their city and bestowed a gift of fifty thousand dollars upon him as the war drew to a close.

On July 25, 1866, Congress created the new rank of admiral for Farragut. He served aboard the flagship *Franklin* in command of the European Squadron, returning to New York in 1868. He then traveled to California the following year but suffered a heart attack on the return via Chicago. Taken by steamship to be the guest of an admiral at the Portsmouth, New Hampshire, naval yard, Farragut died there on August 14, 1870.

SIGNIFICANCE

David Farragut is regarded by many twentieth century historians as an ideal example of the nineteenth century career naval officer. Despite numerous disappointments while in uniform, his adoptive father's court-martial, and his roots in the South, Farragut remained constant in his allegiance to the United States Navy and the government it represents. His patriotism, coolness and courage under fire, thorough preparation, and belief in education are part of the heritage he and others like him left for later generations of naval officers.

Farragut's career of fifty-nine years in the service of his country has been equaled by few. What is more, it was a career featuring promotion as the first American to hold the rank of admiral, and it was crowned with the glory of the preeminent naval victory of the Civil War— the Battle of Mobile Bay. Had his health been better at the war's close, and had he been so inclined, virtually no appointive or elective office would have been beyond his reach.

As it was, Farragut died, like Lincoln, near the peak of his fame and at the high tide of his fortunes. His passing was not so dramatic, but neither was much of his life. It was simply a life of dedicated service.

—Joseph E. Suppiger

FURTHER READING

Duffy, James P. *Lincoln's Admiral: The Civil War Campaigns of David Farragut*. New York: Wiley, 1997. Duffy offers new insight into the life of the American first full admiral. Based on source materials made available in the last twenty years.

Farragut, Loyall. *The Life of David Glasgow Farragut: First Admiral of the United States Navy, Embodying His Journal and Letters*. New York: D. Appleton, 1879. Reprint. New York: D. Appleton, 1907. The author, Farragut's only child, has written a hagiography greatly improved by his use of Farragut's letters and journal.

Hearn, Chester G. *Admiral David Glasgow Farragut: The Civil War Years*. Annapolis, Md.: Naval Institute Press, 1998. An account of Farragut's life and naval exploits, based in part on previously unused family and archival records. Focuses on Farragut's participation in the Civil War, describing his command of the Western Gulf Blockading Squadron and his victory at the Battle of Mobile Bay.

Lewis, Charles Lee. *David Glasgow Farragut*. 2 vols. Annapolis, Md.: United States Naval Institute, 1941-1943. Reprint. Salem, N.H.: Ayer, 1980. The author of several excellent books on naval officers has here produced a scholarly biography enriched by original research.

Mahon, A. T. *Admiral Farragut*. New York: D. Appleton, 1892. A classic work on the subject written by another famous admiral, this biography nevertheless is dated and deemed unnecessarily laudatory.

Nash, Howard P., Jr. *A Naval History of the Civil War*. Cranbury, N.J.: A. S. Barnes, 1972. Concise and to the point, this is an outstanding one-volume history of the naval struggle between the North and the South. Many references are made to Farragut.

Schneller, Robert J., Jr. *Farragut*. Washington, D.C.: Brassey's, 2002. One in a series of concise biographies of military leaders. Schneller analyzes Farragut's personality and military leadership style, and concludes that Farragut's intelligence, confidence, and courage were some of the character traits that made him the most outstanding naval officer of the nineteenth century.

SEE ALSO: Stephen Decatur; George Dewey; Matthew C. Perry; Augustus Saint-Gaudens.

RELATED ARTICLE in *Great Events from History: The Nineteenth Century, 1801-1900:* March 9, 1862: Battle of the *Monitor* and the *Virginia*.

DAME MILLICENT GARRETT FAWCETT
English social reformer

A leader in advancing the causes of woman suffrage, education, and social reform. Fawcett also worked to end the double standard in the grounds for divorce, to improve women's rights of guardianship over their children, and to open the legal profession to women.

BORN: June 11, 1847; Aldeburgh, Suffolk, England
DIED: August 5, 1929; London, England
ALSO KNOWN AS: Millicent Garrett (birth name)
AREAS OF ACHIEVEMENT: Women's rights, social reform

EARLY LIFE

Millicent Garrett Fawcett (FAH-set) was the fifth daughter among the ten children of Newson Garrett, a self-made wealthy corn and coal merchant and shipowner, and Louisa Dunnell. Her mother was deeply religious and had less influence on her than her father. Millicent attended a school run by the aunt of the poet Robert Browning at Blackheath until she was fifteen. An apocryphal story recounted by Ray Strachey in her history of woman suffrage, *The Cause* (1928), tells how one night, after Millicent, her sister Elizabeth, and their friend Emily Davis had discussed what each might accomplish, Emily responded,

> I must devote myself to securing higher education, while you open the medical profession to women. After these things are done, we must see about getting the vote.... You are younger than we are Milli, so you must attend to that.

They all succeeded.

In 1864, Elizabeth met Henry Fawcett, a blind professor of political economy at Cambridge. He proposed to her but was spurned. In the meantime, Millicent frequently visited Louise, the oldest of the Garrett sisters, in London. Louise, like Elizabeth, was a feminist. In 1865 she took Millicent to hear a speech on women's rights by John Stuart Mill. There Millicent, who was eighteen, also met Fawcett, a disciple of John Stuart Mill. Eighteen months later, in April, 1867, over the objections of Elizabeth, who saw his modest income and his blindness as obstacles, they were married. A year later, Philippa, their only child, was born.

LIFE'S WORK

In 1865, Henry Fawcett entered Parliament as the member from Brighton. A Liberal free-trader, his feminism was derived from his opposition to government regulation. Mrs. Fawcett acted as his secretary and soon added to her education. He encouraged her to submit articles to journals such as *Macmillan's Magazine* in 1868 and to write *Political Economy for Beginners* in 1870. It provided, in simplified form, the economic gospel of Mill, heavily salted with self-help and individualism. It was an immediate success and went to ten editions. Together, the Fawcetts wrote *Essays and Lectures in Political Subjects* in 1872. At that time, Mrs. Fawcett's views on self-help were extreme. She even opposed free education because, as a result, a father otherwise prone to alcoholism might instead strive to provide an education for his children.

Henry Fawcett supported Mill's effort to give women the vote in 1867, favoring a bill that included not only widows and spinsters (who had become heads of households) but also married women. In 1884, as postmaster general in Gladstone's cabinet, he clashed with the prime minister's opposition to including women in the 1884 Franchise Reform Act. He also opposed legislation in 1874 regulating the labor of women in the textile industry. Unfortunately, Henry Fawcett died in 1884 from pleurisy.

Before his death, Mrs. Fawcett published a successful novel, *Janet Doncaster* (1875). It was slow-moving, with little action, and was mainly a temperance tract. Her second novel, published under a pseudonym so that she could see if it could stand on its own merits, was not as successful.

A widow at the age of thirty-seven, Mrs. Fawcett intensified her interest in the cause of women's rights. Even while she had written about economic topics during the 1870's, she had continued her interest in the cause of woman suffrage. In July, 1867, she had become a member of the first regular Women's Suffrage Committee in London and had made her first speech in Manchester in 1868. Now, during the 1880's and 1890's, she became active in two related causes of interest to women: the Contagious Diseases Acts controversy and the Henry Cust case.

When the Contagious Diseases Acts controversy had first emerged as an issue during the 1860's, Mrs. Fawcett had refused to become involved for fear that it might split the suffrage movement. The acts aimed to protect members of the armed forces from venereal diseases by requiring the compulsory examination of suspected prostitutes. Both feminists and moralists opposed the acts for seeming to accept prostitution while discriminating against women by forcing them to submit to involuntary medical examination. The appearance of William Thomas Stead's articles on white slavery in the *Pall Mall Gazette* came in 1885, shortly after Mrs. Fawcett's husband's death. It provided her with a cause she could support in her husband's memory and on behalf of women's rights. She became a leader in the Vigilance Society, which was formed to repeal the acts and protect the virtue of young women. Later, in 1927, she wrote a biography of Josephine Butler, its leader.

Mrs. Fawcett waged another moral crusade in 1894, over Henry Cust, a Conservative M.P. from Manchester. Cust had seduced and made pregnant a young girl whom he subsequently abandoned; he then proposed marriage to another woman. When the girl wrote Cust a letter begging him to marry her, he flaunted its contents to some friends. As a Vigilance Society member, Mrs. Fawcett launched a campaign that finally succeeded in forcing Cust to abandon his candidacy and marry the girl whom he had seduced. Unfortunately, Mrs. Fawcett continued attacks on Cust until her friends had to restrain her zeal because of the damage it was doing to the cause of woman suffrage.

As a women's rights advocate, Mrs. Fawcett argued for equal grounds for divorce and improvement in the rights of women as guardians of children. She was a staunch defender of the family; her championing of the rights of women did not extend to supporting sexual freedom. Even her daughter Philippa contributed to the cause of women's equality when, in 1890, she proved superior to the senior wrangler (the Cambridge honors graduate in mathematics) on the mathematical tripos list.

Throughout the 1880's, Mrs. Fawcett tried to remain aloof from party commitment. The 1867 Reform Act had given the right to vote to all male borough householders who personally paid rates or rented lodgings at more than ten pounds a year. The 1884 Reform Act extended these provisions to the rural areas of Great Britain. The strenuous efforts by Liberal Party managers to exclude women householders from the Reform Bill of 1884 made Mrs. Fawcett reject an invitation to join the Council of the Women's Liberal Federation, and finally in 1887, as a nationalist, she abandoned her husband's party to join the Liberal Unionists over the issue of home rule. She broke with it in 1903 because of her commitment to free trade. Throughout her life, she remained committed to liberal principles and evolutionary politics but not economic reform. She championed the right of women to work in the mining industry. In 1898, she opposed attempts to prohibit women working with phosphorus. Her opposition was based on feminist and libertarian grounds.

The 1890's witnessed some gains and some reversals in the woman suffrage movement. In order to understand the irregular progress of the woman suffrage movement in Great Britain and the obstacles facing Mrs. Fawcett, it must be realized that even opponents of woman suffrage believed that all rate payers ought to vote in local municipal elections, if not for members of Parliament. In 1869, the Municipal Franchise Act had enfranchised women taxpayers, although the courts later ruled that this included only single women. Married women who were taxpayers, however, could vote for school boards in 1870, poor law boards in 1875, county councils in 1888, and parish and district councils in 1894. Moderate women suffragists could look to the past with some satisfaction as a precedent for a gradual strategy.

In 1887, Lydia Becker, the leader of the Manchester Women's Suffrage Society and editor of the *Women's Suffrage Journal*, died. In April, 1892, Sir Arthur

Dame Millicent Garrett Fawcett. (Library of Congress)

Rollitt's private member's bill to enfranchise widows and spinsters who already had the right to vote failed by a mere twenty-three votes. Between 1890 and 1897, the number of woman suffrage societies dwindled from one thousand to fewer than two hundred. Finally, in 1897, a committee met in Westminster Town Hall and elected Mrs. Fawcett president of a new umbrella organization, the National Union of Women's Suffrage Societies (NUWSS).

The union was made up of independent societies in all parts of the nation and proposed to gain the same terms for suffrage as were currently or might eventually be granted to men. A petition drive netted more than a quarter million signatures, and more than 140 meetings were held. Mrs. Fawcett was busy speaking, lobbying individual members of Parliament, and organizing parades in all parts of the country. By 1906, the majority of NUWSS members were supporters of the Liberal Party, and the majority of Liberal M.P.'s elected in the 1906 landslide had individually pledged themselves to the women's cause.

Before 1906, however, the center stage of political concern was occupied by the South African (Boer) War, which had begun in 1899, and Mrs. Fawcett was sent in July, 1901, to South Africa as a leader of an all-woman commission to investigate the conditions in British concentration camps exposed by Emily Hobhouse.

Throughout her life, Mrs. Fawcett was a nationalist and imperialist, and while her report was on the whole sympathetic to government goals, her criticisms entitle her to be considered the "Florence Nightingale" of the South African War. Her recommendations were implemented by Viscount Milner, and within a year the camp mortality rate fell below that of Glasgow, although not

---

REMEMBERING JOHN STUART MILL

In 1873, Millicent Garrett Fawcett contributed to a collection of essays honoring John Stuart Mill on the occasion of his death. She wrote on the subject of Mill's influence as a politician and naturally emphasized Mill's efforts on behalf of women's rights.

Every one must be familiar with the often expressed opinion, that, as a practical politician, Mr. Mill's career was essentially a failure. It has been said a thousand times that the principal result of his brief representation of Westminster was to furnish an additional proof, if one were wanted, that a philosopher is totally incapable of exercising any useful influence in the direction of practical politics. . . .

When, it is said that Mr. Mill failed as a practical politician, there are two questions to be asked: "Who says he has failed?" And "What is it said that he failed in?" Now, it seems that the persons who are loudest in the assertion of his failure are precisely those to whom the reforms advocated by Mr. Mill in his writings are distasteful. They are those who pronounce all schemes of electoral reform embodying the principle of proportional representation to be the result of a conspiracy of fools and rogues; they are those who sneer at the "fanciful rights of women;" they are those who think our present land tenure eminently calculated to make the rich contented, and keep the poor in their proper places; they are those who believe that republicans and atheists ought to be treated like vermin, and exterminated accordingly; they are those who think that all must be well with England if her imports and exports are increasing, and that we are justified in repudiating our foreign engagements, if to maintain them would have an injurious effect upon trade. The assertion of failure coming from such persons does not mean that Mr. Mill failed to promote the practical success of those objects the advocacy of which forms the chief feature of his political writings. It is rather a measure of his success in promoting these objects, and of the disgust with which his success is regarded by those who are opposed to his political ideas. It was known, or ought to have been known, by every one who supported Mr. Mill's candidature in 1865, that he was a powerful advocate of proportional representation, and that he attributed the very greatest importance to the political, industrial, and social emancipation of women; he advocated years ago, in his "Political Economy," the scheme of land tenure reform with which his name is now practically associated. . . . Just as radical heirs apparent are said to lay aside all inconvenient revolutionary opinions when they come to the throne, it was believed that Mr. Mill in Parliament would be an entirely different person from Mr. Mill in his study. It was one thing to write an essay in favor of proportional representation; it was another thing to assist in the insertion of the principle of proportional representation in the Reform Bill, and to form a school of practical politicians who took care to insure the adoption of this principle in the school board elections. It was one thing to advocate theoretically the claims of women to representation; it was another to introduce the subject into the House of Commons, to promote an active political organization in its favor, and thus to convert it, from a philosophical dream, into a question of pressing and practical importance. . . .

Source: Millicent Garrett Fawcett, "His Influence as a Practical Politician," in *John Stuart Mill: His Life and Works* (Boston: J. R. Osgood, 1873).

before more than twenty-five thousand had died from measles and typhoid epidemics.

The suffrage cause therefore languished between 1899 and 1905, when the Women's Social and Political Union (WSPU) was founded. At first its militancy was welcomed by Mrs. Fawcett for the discussion it drew to the issue, but as eccentricity turned to violence she strongly condemned the use of physical violence in propaganda in 1908. She had earlier supported Ann Cobden Sanderson, who had been imprisoned, and her sister Elizabeth, who was a WSPU member for three years. In 1910, a temporary truce between the WSPU and NUWSS was reached and a joint parade and demonstration were staged.

The NUWSS during this period received heavy financial support from Mrs. Fawcett. She donated more than one hundred pounds to it, and by 1900 organizers received salaries totaling one thousand pounds and included six workingwomen. Until May, 1912, Mrs. Fawcett supported a policy that endorsed individual M.P.'s rather than parties to secure suffrage, but at that time she accepted the decision of the NUWSS to support Labour Party candidates because it had become the only party to support woman suffrage. It was in essence a declaration of war on the Liberal Party, given her opposition to socialism and support of self-help.

When the outbreak of World War I was imminent, the NUWSS held a large peace meeting in London, on August 4, but after the declaration of war, Mrs. Fawcett and most of the membership of the NUWSS called upon women to sustain the vital forces of the nation. In 1915, she defeated an attempt by pacifists to alter NUWSS policy. When the problem of adjusting the franchise to accommodate servicemen arose near the end of 1915 and the question of woman suffrage was raised, she reinitiated private lobbying efforts.

Later, as compulsory service legislation in February, 1917, rekindled interest in change of suffrage, Mrs. Fawcett supported a limited measure of woman suffrage and was encouraged when David Lloyd George replaced H. H. Asquith, whom she no longer trusted. In June, 1917, the measure passed the House of Commons, and in January, the House of Lords. In gratitude, Mrs. Fawcett broke her former attitude of nonpartisanship and became an outspoken supporter of Lloyd George and the coalition government. It was at the celebration of the suffrage victory in 1918 that the suffrage hymn utilizing William Blake's poem *Jerusalem* was set to music by Sir Hubert Parry.

After World War I, the granting of family allowances, which was supported by Eleanor Rathbone, caused a split in the NUWSS. Mrs. Fawcett was convinced that al-

lowances would destroy family life and were still another example of creeping socialism. As a consequence, she resigned from the National Union of Societies for Equal Citizenship (the new name for the NUWSS). Even so, she continued to support efforts to open the legal profession to women and to grant equal franchise to women under thirty years of age. The latter was achieved in 1928 while she was in Palestine. In 1929, she died of pneumonia.

SIGNIFICANCE

Dame Millicent Garrett Fawcett was not flashy or charismatic. She epitomized the type of woman voter who supporters of woman suffrage believed would exercise the privilege responsibly: She was dignified and reliable, conciliatory yet determined. Though she disliked making speeches, her efforts were well prepared and logical; her delivery was clear and spiced with her keen sense of humor. Though lacking the beauty of the Pankhurst family, Mrs. Fawcett was an attractive woman, with a serene face, radiant complexion, and shiny brown hair. She was a hard worker and never employed a secretary. Her hobby was listening to music. While she championed women's rights, she never believed in war between the sexes. As the *Daily Telegraph*'s obituary read,

> The name of militants . . . are sometimes quoted as the leaders to victory, but in reality it was the woman of sweet reasonableness, womanly manner, quiet dress and cultured style who did more than any other in the cause of emancipation.
>
> —*Norbert C. Soldon*

FURTHER READING

Banks, Olive. *Faces of Feminism: A Study of a Social Movement*. New York: St. Martin's Press, 1981. Best balanced, overall treatment of the subject. It covers more than suffrage, treating family, legal, and economic subjects.

Fawcett, Henry, and Millicent Garrett Fawcett. *Essays and Lectures on Social and Political Subjects*. London: Macmillan, 1872. Contains four essays by Henry Fawcett and eight by Millicent Garrett Fawcett that show the influence of John Stuart Mill and opposition to overprotective legislation that might retard women's independence and their ability to compete in society.

Fawcett, Millicent Garrett. *What I Remember*. London: T. Fisher Unwin, 1924. Typically understates Mrs. Fawcett's role but demonstrates the methodical planning and organization that characterized her leadership.

_____. *The Women's Victory and After: Personal Reminiscences*. London: Sidgwick and Jackson, 1920. Interesting on the war years and the role of Lloyd George in achieving the partial attainment of woman suffrage.

Fawcett, Millicent Garrett, T. C. Jack, and E. C. Jack. *Women's Suffrage: A Short History of a Great Movement*. London: People's Books, 1912. Written during the period of WSPU militancy, this book shows Mrs. Fawcett's faith in democracy within the ranks of the movement.

Goldman, Lawrence, ed. *The Blind Victorian: Henry Fawcett and British Liberalism*. New York: Cambridge University Press, 1989. Collection of essays analyzing Fawcett's personal life, her friendship with John Stuart Mill, and his views on economics and politics. Includes an essay by David Rubinstein (see below), "Victorian Feminism: Henry and Millicent Garrett Fawcett."

Oakley, Ann. "Millicent Garrett Fawcett: Duty and Determination." In *Feminist Theorists*, edited by Dale Spender. New York: Random House, 1983. At times this book fails to allow for historical perspective and to understand the ideological stance of mid-Victorian liberalism. Interestingly, Oakley is one of few modern feminists to have studied Mrs. Fawcett.

Pugh, Martin. *Women's Suffrage in Britain, 1867-1929*. London: Historical Association, 1980. A good historiographic survey that analyzes succinctly the rela-

tionship between the Edwardian period and wartime suffrage for franchise reform.

Rover, Constance. *Women's Suffrage and Party Politics in Britain, 1866-1914*. London: Routledge & Kegan Paul, 1967. A lively account of the political aspects of woman suffrage and narratives of the cabinet-WSPU battle.

Rubinstein, David. *A Different World for Women: The Life of Millicent Garrett Fawcett*. Columbus: Ohio State University Press, 1991. Comprehensive biography, describing Fawcett's life, career, and personality.

Stephen, Leslie. *The Life of Henry Fawcett*. London: Smith, Elder, 1886. Details Fawcett's views on woman suffrage and feminism and is valuable for understanding why his wife did not become an antimale crusader.

Strachey, Ray. *Millicent Garrett Fawcett*. London: John Murray, 1931. Written by her close friend of many years, this work is bland and uncontroversial. It views Mrs. Fawcett and NUWSS as part of a development broader even than the women's movement.

SEE ALSO: Susan B. Anthony; Helene Lange; Anna Howard Shaw; Elizabeth Cady Stanton; Lucy Stone.

RELATED ARTICLES in *Great Events from History: The Nineteenth Century, 1801-1900:* May, 1869: Woman Suffrage Associations Begin Forming; December, 1869: Wyoming Gives Women the Vote.

GUSTAV THEODOR FECHNER
German psychologist

Fechner is widely regarded as both the founder of psychophysics—the science of the mind-body relation—and a pioneer in experimental psychology. His most important contributions are a number of quantitative methods for measuring absolute and differential thresholds that are still employed by psychologists to study sensitivity to stimulation.

BORN: April 19, 1801; Gross-Särchen, Lusatia (now in Germany)
DIED: November 18, 1887; Leipzig, Germany
AREAS OF ACHIEVEMENT: Philosophy, physics

EARLY LIFE

Gustav Theodor Fechner (FEHK-nehr) was the second of five children of Samuel Traugott Fechner and Johanna

Dorothea Fischer Fechner. His father was a progressive Lutheran preacher who is said to have astounded the local villagers by mounting a lightning rod on the church tower and by adopting the unorthodox practice of preaching without a wig. Although he died when Gustav was only five years old, already the young Fechner was infused with his father's fierce intellectual independence and his passion for the human spirit.

Fechner attended the gymnasium at Soran, near Dresden, and was matriculated in medicine at the University of Leipzig in 1817. He was not a model student, opting to read on his own rather than attend lectures. During this period, Fechner became disenchanted with establishment views: He professed atheism and was never able to complete the doctorate that would have entitled him to practice medicine. His studies were not a waste of time, however, because he began composing satires on medicine and the materialism that flourished in Germany during this period. Some fourteen satirical works were published by Fechner under the pseudonym "Dr. Mises" between 1821 and 1876.

In 1824, Fechner began to lecture on physics and mathematics at the University of Leipzig without any remuneration. Translating scientific treatises from French into German (about a dozen volumes in six years), although onerous work, helped him to make a living. He managed to publish numerous scientific papers during this period, and a particularly important paper on quantitative measurements of direct currents finally secured for him an appointment with a substantial salary as professor of physics in 1834.

This period marked the happiest time in Fechner's life. The year before his appointment, he had married Clara Volkmann, the sister of a colleague at the university. The security of a permanent position and marital bliss did nothing to dampen his enthusiasm for hard work; an enviable social life was simply incorporated into his already cramped schedule. Evenings at the local symphony conducted by Felix Mendelssohn were regular events to which, on occasion, the Fechners were accompanied by Robert and Clara Schumann, his niece by marriage.

Fechner's idyllic life was shattered in 1839 by an illness that forced him to resign his position at the university. At first, he experienced partial blindness caused by gazing at the sun through colored glasses as part of a series of experiments on colors and afterimages; depression, severe headaches, and loss of appetite soon followed. For three years, Fechner sheltered himself in a darkened room, and his promising career seemed to be over. One day, however, he wandered into his garden and removed the bandages that had adorned his eyes since the onset of his illness. He reported that his vision not only was restored but also was more powerful than before because he could now experience the souls of flowers. After the initial trauma of restored eyesight faded, Fechner recovered with a revitalized religious consciousness. It was this newfound awareness of the importance of the human spirit that marked the beginning of Fechner's mature period.

LIFE'S WORK

The focal point of Fechner's work was a deep-seated antipathy toward materialism, or the view that nothing exists except for matter and its modifications. His first volley against materialism was the enigmatic *Nanna: Oder,*

Über das Seelenleben der Pflanzen (1848; Nanna, or the soul life of plants), which advanced the notion that even plants have a mental life. Three years later, his *Zend-Avesta: Oder, Über die Dinge des Himmels und des Jenseits* (1851; *Zend-Avesta: On the Things of Heaven and the Hereafter*, 1882) proclaimed a new gospel based on the notion that the entire material universe is consciously animated and alive in every particular. The phenomenal world explored by physics, Fechner asserted, is merely the form in which inner experiences appear to one another. Because consciousness and the physical world are coeternal aspects of the same reality, materialism (or what Fechner referred to as the "night view") must be repudiated because it examines the universe in only one of its aspects.

More pertinent, Fechner submitted that his alternative "day view" dissolves the traditional problem of the mind-body relation. There is no need to worry about how the physical is converted into the mental, because mind and body are not distinct kinds of things. All that one needs is to display the functional relationship between consciousness and its physical manifestations. Because it was uncontested that physical qualities could be measured, Fechner discerned that he would have to specify a means for measuring mental properties if the scientific establishment was to be convinced that his alternative program represented a legitimate contender to materialism.

The German physiologist Ernst Heinrich Weber had submitted in 1846 that a difference between two stimuli (or an addition to or subtraction from one or the other stimulus) is always perceived as equal if its ratio to the stimulus remains the same, regardless of how the absolute size changes. If a change of one unit from five can be detected, Weber's result specifies that so can a change of ten from fifty, of one hundred from five hundred, and the like. On the morning of October 22, 1850, Fechner discovered what he regarded as the fundamental relation between the mental and the physical world. Where Weber's result was restricted to external stimulation, Fechner posited a general mathematical relationship between stimulus and sensation, such that for every increase in stimulation there is a corresponding increase in sensation. This functional relationship is now known as the Weber-Fechner law. It asserts that the psychological sensation produced by a stimulus is proportional to the logarithm of the external stimulation.

Although Fechner's law represents a development of Weber's work, he did not rely on Weber's substantive result. Indeed, it was Fechner who realized that his psychophysical principle corresponded to Weber's result and gave it the name Weber's law. Perhaps he was overly generous. Weber's result conflicts with low-stimulus intensities. By incorporating the activity of the subject's sensory system into the equation, Fechner was able to overcome this difficulty.

Fechner's law is a genuine psychophysical law in the sense that it relates mental phenomena to external stimulation. Comparing it with Sir Isaac Newton's law of gravitation, Fechner laid out his ambitious program for a science of the functional relations of mind and body in his classic work, *Elemente der Psychophysik* (1860; *Elements of Psychophysics*, 1966). Along with his method for measuring the relationship between psychological and physical phenomena, Fechner refined three methods—the method of barely noticeable differences, the method of right and wrong cases, and the method of average error—for measuring thresholds, or the point at which a stimulus (or a stimulus difference) becomes noticeable or disappears. These techniques for measuring sense discrimination are still prominent in psychological research. Fechner also established the mathematical expressions of these methods and contributed to the literature a series of classical experiments on human sensitivity to external stimulation.

Fechner's program for a psychophysics attracted few converts. Vocal opponents, such as William James, the eminent American philosopher and psychologist, objected that mental properties are not quantifiable. Fechner sought to measure sensations by measuring their stimuli, but he furnished no independent evidence for the presupposition that it is sensations that are measured. This objection was significant granted that there was good reason to suppose that sensations cannot be measured. Sensations are not additive; a larger sensation is not simply a sum of smaller sensations. Anything that is not additive, Fechner's opponents declared, cannot be measured. What he had measured, rather, was observer response to stimulation; Fechner had produced an account of sensitivity and so had confused the sensation with the excitation of the subject.

These and related objections led to the downfall of psychophysics. Although Fechner's ideas were examined by Hermann von Helmholtz, Ernst Mach, and other scientists who were interested in related subjects, Fechner's attempt to place the mental on a par with the physical was dismissed as pure whimsy. The failure of Fechner's program, however, does not diminish his importance as a philosopher. Fechner's methods for measuring sensitivity were assimilated into the basis of empirical psychology. Because Fechner's methods presume that chance is a characteristic of physical systems, Fechner achieved a measure of victory over materialism. If he was right, mental phenomena could not be straightforwardly reduced to matter and its modifications.

Although Fechner continued to contribute to the literature on psychophysics, he turned to other matters late in his life. An interest in aesthetics proved to be a rather natural development of his interest in stimulation and his long-standing affection for the arts. The culmination of his work on the study of beauty was *Vorschule der Aesthetik* (1876; introduction to aesthetics), which argued that aesthetics is the study of the objects that produce aesthetic experiences. This work proved to be seminal in the history of experimental aesthetics.

SIGNIFICANCE

Gustav Theodor Fechner was a man of great erudition—not only was he a physicist and a philosopher but he also was the author of a detailed theological theory, a poet, and a satirist. What united his diverse pursuits was a struggle to reconcile the empirical rigor of the exact sciences with a spiritual conception of the universe. Although Fechner's attempt to place consciousness on a par with the physical was rejected by the scientific community, his vision helped to lay the foundations for the emerging science of empirical psychology.

Fechner's greatest contributions, the functional proportion between sensation and stimulus and his numerous techniques for measuring psychological response to stimulation, do not compare favorably with the concept of universal gravitation. Fechner's philosophy of nature as consciously animated and alive in every particular was rejected by the scientific community, and so his contributions did not revolutionize science. However, without his techniques for measuring psychological variables, the science of empirical psychology would not have reached maturity.

—Brian S. Baigrie

FURTHER READING

Boring, Edwin G. *A History of Experimental Psychology.* 2d ed. New York: Appleton-Century-Crofts, 1950. A comprehensive account of the emergence of experimental psychology. Although Boring credits Fechner with laying the foundations for empirical psychology, he contends that it was merely an unexpected by-product of Fechner's philosophical interests.

Fechner, Gustav Theodor. *Elements of Psychophysics.* Translated with a foreword by Helmut E. Adler. New

York: Holt, Rinehart and Winston, 1966. The author's introduction provides an overview of the problem concerning the mind-body relation and an outline of his program for a science of psychophysics. The translator's foreword places Fechner's contributions in their nineteenth century historical context.

Heidelberger, Michael. *Nature from Within: Gustav Theodor Fechner and His Psychophysical Worldview*. Translated by Cynthia Klohr. Pittsburgh: University of Pittsburgh Press, 2004. A biography that includes a detailed examination of Fechner's writings. Heidelberger views Fechner's work from three perspectives: history, philosophy, and what Fechner called his "day view" approach of studying across fields.

James, William. *The Principles of Psychology*. New York: Henry Holt, 1890. Reprint. New York: Dover, 1950. Contains a faithful presentation of Fechner's contributions and a searching critique of his philosophical outlook. Perhaps the best indicator of why psychophysics fell into disfavor.

Savage, C. Wade. *The Measurement of Sensation: A Critique of Perceptual Psychophysics*. Berkeley: University of California Press, 1970. A thorough discussion of the central philosophical issues in the measurement of sensation. The excellent bibliography is a useful guide to the wealth of literature on this topic.

Snodgrass, Joan Gay. "Psychophysics." In *Experimental Sensory Psychology*, edited by Bertram Scharf. Glenview, Ill.: Scott, Foresman, 1975. A concise introduction to the history of psychophysical theory and its methods. For the technically minded reader, the analysis of the relationship between Weber's result and Fechner's psychophysical law helps to illustrate Fechner's contributions to the measurement of sensation.

SEE ALSO: Francis Galton; William James.

RELATED ARTICLE in *Great Events from History: The Nineteenth Century, 1801-1900:* 1900: Freud Publishes *The Interpretation of Dreams*.

MARSHALL FIELD
American merchant

The founder of Marshall Field and Company, which became the largest wholesale and retail dry-goods store in the world, Field introduced many retailing concepts that set standards for modern merchandising that have endured into the twenty-first century.

BORN: August 18, 1834; near Conway, Massachusetts
DIED: January 16, 1906; New York, New York
AREA OF ACHIEVEMENT: Business

EARLY LIFE
Marshall Field was the son of John and Fidelia (née Nash) Field. His family had lived in Massachusetts since 1629, when his ancestor Zechariah Field had come over from England. Although his father was a farmer, the agrarian life did not appeal to young Marshall. Instead, he left home at the age of seventeen and took a job in a dry-goods store owned by Deacon Davis in Pittsfield, Massachusetts. He worked there for five years, but even though Davis offered him a partnership in the business, Field had other plans. He saw the West as the site of his future, as the place where huge fortunes could be made by those ambitious and talented enough to take advantage of the tremendous opportunities caused by its rapid

development and population growth. Accordingly, he left New England in 1856 and moved to the rude and dirty, but potentially thriving, city of Chicago, Illinois.

Field arrived in Chicago with little money and secured a job as a clerk with Cooley, Wadsworth and Company, the largest wholesale dry-goods firm in the city at the time. His starting salary was four hundred dollars a year and, as an indication of his future business sense, he managed to save half of this amount by living and sleeping in the store. A small, handsome young man with a serious and polite demeanor and a large handlebar mustache, Field also displayed a true flair for the dry-goods business and a unique appeal to and concern for the customer. As a result, he rapidly advanced through the hierarchy of the firm.

Within a year of Field's arrival in Chicago, he was made a traveling salesperson for the company, and in 1861 he became general manager of the Chicago store. His rapid rise culminated in 1862, when he was invited to be a full partner in the company, which changed its name to Cooley, Farwell and Company. In 1864, when the financial wizard Levi Z. Leiter joined as a new partner, Field finally had his name added to the company's title, Farwell, Field and Company. Impressed by the entrepre-

Marshall Field. (Library of Congress)

neurial and financial skill of Field and Leiter, the millionaire Potter S. Palmer offered to sell them his retail and wholesale dry-goods business in 1865. The two men jumped at the chance and, with money borrowed from Palmer himself, they formed the new firm of Field, Palmer, and Leiter. Palmer dropped completely out of the business two years later in order to concentrate exclusively on his hotel interests, leaving Field and Leiter in sole control of the growing firm. In only eight years, and by the age of thirty, Marshall Field had risen from a lowly clerk to the co-owner of one of the largest dry-goods operations in Chicago.

LIFE'S WORK

After Palmer retired from the firm in 1867, Field invited his two younger brothers, Henry and Joseph Field, to join as partners, thus consolidating his control of the business at Leiter's expense. Nevertheless, Leiter remained a partner until he sold his interest to Field in 1881. Wholesale and retail sales, which had stood at approximately ten million dollars annually at the time of Palmer's with-

drawal, climbed to nearly thirty-five million dollars by the early 1890's and had surpassed sixty-eight million dollars by the time of Field's death in 1906. Not even such catastrophes as the Chicago fire of 1871 (which completely destroyed his retail store and wholesale warehouse), the financial panic of 1873 (which ruined many Chicago merchants), or another fire in 1877 in his main retail outlet at the corner of State and Washington streets significantly slowed this pattern of expansion. As an example of this powerful drive to succeed, Field led Chicago in its recovery from the 1871 fire by establishing a temporary store in a horse barn at State and Twentieth streets only two weeks after the flames had died out.

At first, the wholesale aspect of the business interested Field more than the retail side. As time went on, however, and Field realized the immense profit potential of quality retailing, he devoted more and more of his energy to it, to the exclusion of the wholesale part of the firm. In 1873, the retail branch was physically separated from the wholesale branch with the opening of a new store at State and Washington streets. A program of continual expansion followed, culminating in the creation of the magnificent, city block-square entrepôt in 1912, six years after Field's death. This massive structure still stands and serves as the flagship store of the Field Company as well as a familiar landmark in the heart of downtown Chicago.

Field was not a merchandising innovator but was adept at adopting new methods in retailing pioneered by others. His store plainly marked prices on all goods, so that customers knew exactly what the costs of items were when they examined them. He established resident buyers in England, France, and Germany in order to ensure his store a steady supply of quality foreign-made goods and frequently made it a practice to become the exclusive agent of popular products in Chicago—thus making sure that if customers wanted a certain product, they had to come to Fields to buy it.

Field's reputation for honesty and courtesy was legendary, and he is credited with coining the motto The Customer Is Always Right. He also was among the first to adopt what is now the accepted practice in retailing marketing: purchasing products at wholesale for cash before there was any real customer demand for them and then, through advertising and attractive window displays, creating that demand. This practice allowed Field to undersell his numerous competitors, who waited for demand to materialize before placing an order with a manufacturer, thus paying a higher wholesale price for the time. Marshall Field and Company was also the first retail outlet in the Midwest to employ window displays, to offer such personal services as gift wrapping to customers, to establish a "bargain basement," and to open a restaurant within the store.

Field recognized ability when he saw it and often promoted talented managers to partners in his firm as a reward for their dedicated service. Former employees such as Harlow N. Higinbotham, Harry Gordon Selfridge, and John Shedd all became millionaires as a result of this practice. Once they had earned their fortunes as Field's partners, however, he then frequently proceeded to buy out their interest in the company in order to provide room for younger up-and-comers. The achievement of the American Dream was a real possibility for those who worked for Marshall Field, as long as they demonstrated the ambition, imagination, and ability he admired.

The American Dream was certainly good to Marshall Field as well. By the time of his death, he had amassed a fortune of $120 million. He did not waste this wealth on ostentatious display, as did so many other self-made millionaires of his era. Although he did build himself a grand mansion on Chicago's prestigious Prairie Avenue (constructed in 1873, at a cost of $100,000, by Richard Morris Hunt, the famous architect who had designed the fabulous palaces of William Vanderbilt and John Jacob Astor in New York), he otherwise lived a rather simple life dominated by his devotion to his work. He preferred to walk to his office and frequently ridiculed the pretensions of the wealthy. For example, when he was informed that a clerk was dating his daughter, he responded, "Thank God, there is no disgrace in being a clerk."

Field was not a prolific philanthropist, but when he did give, he made his gifts count. After he first arrived in Chicago, he became active in such diverse organizations as the Chicago Relief and Aid Society, the Young Men's Christian Association, the Chicago Historical Association, the Art Institute, and the Civic Federation. However, as the years went by, business concerns monopolized an increasing portion of his time, and he let his membership in most of these organizations lapse. The year 1889 saw the rejuvenation of his charitable generosity. In that year he donated a ten-acre parcel of land, valued at $125,000, to serve as the site of the new University of Chicago. He later supplemented that gift with a $100,000 endowment to the school.

In 1891, Field gave $50,000 worth of land to the Chicago Home for Incurables, and, in 1893, he gave $1 million to create the Columbian Museum at the Chicago World's Fair. A provision in his will for a further $8 million allowed this museum to construct a permanent

building on Chicago's Lake Shore Drive and to enlarge its collection. In appreciation of his support, the institution took the name the Field Museum of Natural History; it remains one of the best museums of its type in the United States.

Field's personal life contained a large share of tragedy. His first wife, Nannie Scott (they were married in January, 1863), left him during the late 1880's and took up permanent residence in France. After she died in 1896, he secretly courted Mrs. Delia Spencer Caton and married her shortly after her husband's death in 1905. Then, in November, 1905, his only son, Marshall Field, Jr., accidentally shot and killed himself while preparing for a hunting trip. This last blow proved to be too much for the elderly multimillionaire. He came down with pneumonia in late December, 1905, and died on January 16, 1906. The bulk of his huge estate was left in trust to his two grandsons, Henry Field and Marshall Field III. The latter would become the founder and first publisher of the *Chicago Sun-Times*.

SIGNIFICANCE

Marshall Field embodied those characteristics of ambition, business sense, hard work, and simplicity that Americans of his era valued so highly. The fact that a New England dry-goods clerk could become one of the wealthiest men in the United States suggested that success was within the grasp of anyone willing to work hard enough. Although there were thousands of failed clerks for every Marshall Field, Field nevertheless served as a shining example for every ambitious young man who entered the business world.

Field's impact on the American retail trade was equally striking. Although not an innovator himself, Field was willing to gamble on the innovations of others. He thus introduced many ideas first pioneered on the East Coast to Chicago and made his store the most progressive in the city throughout the nineteenth and early twentieth centuries. His emphasis on fairness and "the customer is always right" also won for him millions of loyal customers. As a result, in Chicago the name Marshall Field is still associated with honesty, courtesy, and high-quality merchandise at a fair price.

Finally, Field also had a profound influence on the history and institutions of the city of Chicago. Without his generosity, it is doubtful that the University of Chicago and the Field Museum of Natural History would exist. The prosperous State Street business district grew up around his State and Washington store and thus owes its life to Field's initial decision to locate there in 1873.

His descendants, notably Marshall Field III, would play prominent roles in local politics and the press. Finally, several generations of Chicagoans have grown up with fond memories of Christmas trips to Field's to talk to Santa Claus, to gaze at the gigantic Christmas tree towering from the center of the Walnut Room, and to be dazzled by those magical Christmas window displays. Christmas and Field's go hand in hand in the hearts of Chicagoans and in the memories of ex-Chicagoans. Perhaps it is this feeling that represents Marshall Field's most profound gift to his beloved adopted city.

—Christopher E. Guthrie

FURTHER READING

Cromie, Robert. *The Great Chicago Fire*. New York: McGraw-Hill, 1958. A detailed account of the holocaust that destroyed a good portion of the city in 1871. Also provides an informative description of Field's efforts to get both his business and the city back on their feet after the fire.

Drury, John. *Old Chicago Houses*. Skokie, Ill.: Rand McNally, 1941. Includes drawings, photographs, and an accurate description of Field's mansion on Prairie Avenue.

Madsen, Axel. *The Marshall Fields: The Evolution of an American Business Dynasty*. New York: John Wiley & Sons, 2002. A history of six generations of the Fields family, beginning with Marshall Field. Madsen provides an account of Marshall Field's career, detailing his business methods and creation of his department store empire. The author also describes Field's failed personal life and focuses on the controversial and most important members of the succeeding five generations of this family.

Pierce, Bessie Louise. *The Rise of a Modern City, 1871-1893*. Vol. 3 in *A History of Chicago*. New York: Alfred A. Knopf, 1957. An excruciatingly minute history of the city during the late nineteenth century that includes numerous, and often colorful, anecdotes on the life, business, and contributions of Field.

Pridmore, Jay. *Marshall Field's: A Building from the Chicago Architecture Foundation*. San Francisco: Pomegranate, 2002. At the time of its construction, Field's flagship building was the largest department store in the world. Today, the building is a Chicago architectural landmark. This book's text and photographs provide architectural details of the building and its annexes, and describe earlier buildings in which the store was housed.

Twyman, Robert W. *Marshall Field and Company, 1852-1906*. Philadelphia: University of Pennsylvania Press, 1906. Based on the author's doctoral dissertation, the book provides an excellent, although occasionally dry, analysis of the rise of Field's retailing empire.

Wagenknecht, Edward C. *Chicago*. Norman: University of Oklahoma Press, 1964. A brief, rather impressionistic, portrait of the history of the city that also presents a spotty but productive investigation of Field's influence during the late nineteenth century.

Wendt, Lloyd, and Herman Kogan. *Chicago: A Pictorial History*. New York: Bonanza Books, 1958. Although brief on text, this visual history contains photographs of Field, his stores, and his mansion.

_____. *Give the Lady What She Wants*. Skokie, Ill.: Rand McNally, 1952. An exciting and well-written history of Marshall Field and Company until 1950.

SEE ALSO: Henry Hobson Richardson; Montgomery Ward.

RELATED ARTICLES in *Great Events from History: The Nineteenth Century, 1801-1900:* 1869: First Modern Department Store Opens in Paris; May 1-October 30, 1893: Chicago World's Fair.

STEPHEN J. FIELD
American Supreme Court justice

During the last quarter of the nineteenth century, Justice Field's brilliant and often ingenious legal opinions protected American entrepreneurs from what they perceived to be the destructive power of popular government.

BORN: November 4, 1816; Haddam, Connecticut
DIED: April 9, 1899; Washington, D.C.
ALSO KNOWN AS: Stephen Johnson Field (full name)
AREA OF ACHIEVEMENT: Law

EARLY LIFE

Stephen Johnson Field was the sixth child of seven boys and two girls born to David and Submit Field. His father was an austere Congregational minister. His mother, whose Puritan father had given her the name "Submit" as an expression of Christian virtue, imbued her son with an independence of mind and motives that graphically demonstrated that she had been misnamed. Field's earliest education was the product of his parents' unchangeable convictions. "Our whole domestic life," wrote his brother, "received its tone from this unaffected piety of our parents, who taught their children to lie down and rise up in that fear of the Lord, which is the beginning of wisdom." At thirteen, Field's hearthside education ended when he accompanied his older sister and her husband to Greece, where they were to establish a school for young women. Two and a half years later, Field returned to Massachusetts with a less provincial view of the world and a determination to enroll at Williams College. In 1833, he entered Williams and was graduated valedictorian four years later.

Faced with the problem of choosing a vocation at the age of twenty-one, Field joined his brother's law firm in New York City. In 1841, he passed the New York bar. After ten years of service in the family law firm, however, he was eager to set off on his own; with his brother's encouragement, he moved to San Francisco to try his luck at gold mining and lawyering. In California, it soon became apparent that he was a better lawyer than a miner. San Francisco was much too expensive for his meager purse, however, so he made his way up the Sacramento River to the frontier town of Marysville.

In Marysville, Field had the good fortune of rendering legal services to General John Augustus Sutter, on whose land gold had been discovered in 1849. With Sutter's help, he was elected the *alcalde* (the Mexican equivalent to the justice of the peace) of the Marysville township. A

year later, with the installation of the newly drafted California constitution, he exchanged his position of *alcalde* for a seat in the legislature. In 1853, he ran for the California senate but was defeated by two votes and, with the defeat, never again sought a political position in the state.

Field devoted the next six years to establishing a successful law practice and becoming financially independent. Indeed, by 1857 he had acquired enough influence with the rich and powerful people in California to be nominated and appointed to the state supreme court. A few years later, as a result of his brilliantly reasoned and orderly laissez-faire legal opinions, he became the chief justice of the court. In 1863, although a Democrat, Field was appointed by the Republican president Abraham Lincoln to the U.S. Supreme Court.

LIFE'S WORK

Field's judicial activities covered more than forty years, thirty-four of which were on the federal bench, and during which time he wrote more than one thousand opinions. It was not the number of opinions but rather their quality that was to become his national legacy, a legacy in defense of the entrepreneurial class that was to last for more than half a century. Often he was the minority voice in his own court, yet long after majority decisions had lost their influence and had grown silent, his opinions directed the course of law in the United States.

Field's appearance, when he sat on the Supreme Court bench, was reported by some to be reminiscent of that of a Hebrew prophet. He was, in fact, short and stout, with a rounded body and an oval face covered with a white flowing beard that curled around the back of his neck and ears; yet this profusion of hair was wholly missing from the top of his head.

It is not difficult to find the foundations for Field's arguments in his religious training as a child. It was the inexorable propositions of the Bible that solidified his moral convictions and were later to mold his notions of natural and inalienable rights. As a mature judge, he found easy the transition from the God of the Bible to the Creator of inalienable rights. These autonomous, God-given rights became the bedrock conviction of nineteenth century American judicial conservatism. In his earliest opinions, Field was hard put to find precedent for his inalienable rights arguments. While the Declaration of Independence mentioned inalienable rights, the Constitution itself, which was the primary document for legal decisions, had nothing to say about such rights. With the drafting of the Fourteenth Amendment, however, Field finally had a federal document wholly adequate to his legal mission.

The critical passage in the Fourteenth Amendment read:

> No state shall make or enforce any law which shall abridge the privileges or immunities of citizens of the United States; nor shall any state deprive any person of life, liberty, or property without due process of law; nor deny to any person within its jurisdiction the equal protection of the laws.

In later years, the "due process" and "equal protection of the laws" clauses were to become the most quoted words in the amendment, but for Field the "shall [not] abridge the privileges or immunities" clause was exactly the terminology he was looking for to secure his doctrine of inalienable rights.

In his earliest opinions, Field consistently applied the "privileges or immunities" clause to those cases in which individuals were seeking redress from the intrusion of government into their private lives. Eventually, however, as his influence and leadership in the Court grew, so also did his more collective definition of inalienable rights grow.

Soon he transposed and expanded his doctrine so as to accommodate the concept of citizen to include "citizens in the aggregate." Ostensibly, he argued that natural or inalienable constitutional rights applied to groups *qua* groups, and specifically to corporations. Business institutions and corporations had the same rights of protection from the invidious usurpation of privileges as did the individual citizen. This transposition from private to public rights was dramatically exhibited in a series of landmark opinions he wrote between 1865 and 1885. The earliest of these opinions was concerned with the abridgment of rights that individuals suffer at the hands of majoritarian legislation, but by 1875 he was applying the rationale he had employed in private rights cases to corporate business and industry.

For example, in 1865 there was a series of cases commonly described as "test-oath" cases that came before the Court. *Cummings v. Missouri* was one such case. In this case, the state of Missouri had required those seeking public office to declare under oath that they had not been disloyal to the United States or to the state of Missouri. This was divisive legislation since, in this border state, roughly half the population's sympathies lay with the

South during the Civil War. It was legislation clearly intended to punish those who had backed the wrong side. As a consequence, anyone refusing to take this oath was to be prohibited access to various public stations and privileges. For example, they could not vote, hold public office, teach, preach, practice law, or administer public trusts.

Field was unequivocally opposed to test-oath restrictions. He argued that the requirement was punitive and in no manner tested the fitness or unfitness of citizens. Such a law, he continued, was *ex post facto*, intended to punish people without trial for past allegiances—punishment, in fact, for behavior that at the time committed was not a prosecutorial offense. Field joined a majority of the Court in striking down this legislation on the grounds that it was an abrogation of a citizen's inalienable right not to be subjected to sanctions for an act performed before the institution of a statute.

A second set of so-called due process cases was known as the "Chinese immigration" laws. Soon after the gold rush of 1849, enterprising shipping merchants began importing Chinese workers into California to do the menial labor brought on by the rapid industrial

Stephen J. Field. (Library of Congress)

growth. In order to complete the transcontinental railroad, greater and greater numbers of Chinese were brought into California, and by 1869 government authorities were devising ways to limit the influx of these immigrants into the state. They enacted a series of laws that were unabashedly discriminatory.

The Supreme Court had the task of determining the constitutionality of these laws. One law, for example, declared in the most general terms that "undesirable" Chinese were forbidden entry into the port of San Francisco, leaving the definition of undesirable up to city officials. Undesirables might mean prostitutes, or the poor, or unbonded workers. Another particularly pernicious law required that imprisoned Chinese men have their hair shorn, even though the cutting off of their plaited hair (*queue*) was for them an act of religious degradation. Again, there was a law requiring those Chinese wishing to establish a laundry business to obtain in writing the support of at least twelve taxpayers in the same city block. This was obviously a law intended to restrain the trade of the Chinese. In almost all these cases, Field argued that these laws accomplished nothing worthwhile and were merely acts of "hostility and spitefulness," clearly intended to deprive the Chinese of their natural and inalienable rights.

By 1870, Field was ready to transfer his inalienable rights doctrine from individuals to corporations and to expand his definition of persons to include "bodies of persons with a common interest." One of the earliest constitutional cases in which he argued in this fashion was *Hepburn v. Griswold. Hepburn v. Griswold* was a "legal-tender" or "greenback" case. Greenbacks referred to paper money, and many people had no confidence in paper money, particularly in its inflated state immediately after the Civil War.

Despite private protests, the government insisted on paying its postwar debts with paper currency; creditors of the government regarded this practice as unstable because the government could print currency as it was needed, thus making it less and less valuable. For this reason, creditors began demanding payment in gold and silver.

In most of these legal-tender cases the Court majority supported the right of the government to pay its debts in greenbacks. Field, however, at times single-handedly, supported the creditors' right not to be required to accept these highly fluctuating, unstable paper notes. These creditors, he argued, had the right to payment special basis: They had the right to assess the worth of the payment, once it could be shown that the debtor had agreed to the

value of the original contract. Legal-tender cases were clear evidence of Field's defense of his inalienable rights doctrine applied not only to aggrieved individuals but also to aggrieved groups of individuals, specifically, to corporations and industry.

Some of Field's most noteworthy "corporate citizen" arguments revolve around a series of cases pertaining to the country's railroads, and particularly to the railroad interests of some of Field's most influential California friends, men with controlling interests in midwestern and far-western railroads (Leland Stanford, Collis P. Huntington, Charles Crocker, and Mark Hopkins). During the 1840's and 1850's, in order to stimulate the growth of railroad building across the continent, Congress had provided railroad companies with enormous financial subsidies, tax exemptions, and outright land donations. As a result, these companies grew at an unbounded pace with an apparently unfair economic advantage over other commercial institutions. This advantage grew even larger during the next two decades because the railroads were able to escape the country's rising tax burden.

The railroads also demonstrated an arrogance indicative of their power. They charged exorbitant and discriminatory rates, undercut their competitors, and refused to service the communities that they judged antirailroad. In due course, legislators, with popular support, began to introduce initiatives whose express purpose was to reduce the power and influence of these companies. In an effort to regain years of lost tax revenue, for example, the California constitutional convention of 1878 introduced a provision that would levy a tax against these companies' vast housing and equipment holdings. It was clear to everyone that this legislative maneuver was discriminatory because most of the inventory held by railroads was mortgaged inventory, and mortgage holdings were tax-exempt for private citizens in California.

The railroads refused to pay what they perceived as an inequitable tax and brought the disputed provision before the Supreme Court in 1882 (*San Mateo v. Southern Pacific*). This case gave Field an unambiguous opportunity to defend his "corporate citizen" argument once again. The Fourteenth Amendment, he declared, is intended to protect corporations in the same manner that individual citizens are protected. "Due process" requires that railroads, despite their vast wealth and holdings, are entitled to the same provisions of justice afforded the humblest citizen. Congress, he argued, fully intended that corporate interests receive "equal protection of the laws," and those lawyers who argued that this amendment was intended solely for black Americans were interpreting the amendment much too narrowly.

Field had considerable personal charm and was known as an enjoyable party guest. However, he was also intensely disliked by many—with good reason, for he had some very unlikable character traits. He was a constant public moralizer, insatiably ambitious, at times vindictive, and not above making ethical compromises. Two of his brothers, David Dudley Field and Cyrus Field, became powerful, influential industrialists, and Stephen Field was accused, and not without some provocation, of tailoring his legal judgments to fit his brothers' financial interests. Off the bench, Stephen Field was intimate with Stanford, Huntington, J. P. Morgan, Jay Gould, and other wealthy industrialists, and on one occasion he even attended a private dinner party with them the night before he was to hear legal arguments in his court against their business holdings.

Stephen Field's tenure on the Supreme Court was longer than that of any justice who had gone before. He finally stepped down as a result of failing health at the age of eighty-two. While his devotion to individual rights was not always steadfast (he later ruled against private citizens such as women, laborers, and Chinese immigrants), his commitment to the interests of corporations and business never faltered. He died in Washington, D.C., on a cold, gray day in April, 1899, with the wealthy and powerful in government and business close at hand. There was also his wife, Sue Virginia, to whom he had been devoted for more than forty years.

SIGNIFICANCE

Stephen Field's significant contribution to American society was unquestionably his brilliant legal opinions in defense of private rights. This defense was consistently sustained in support of private over public jurisdictions, opposition to loyalty oaths, opinions against the government's "legal tender" arguments, and his antislavery sympathies manifested in the "Chinese immigration" decisions. This fearless independence of mind set the direction of the Court for many years.

—*Donald Burrill*

FURTHER READING

Black, Chauncey F. *Some Account of the Work of Stephen J. Field.* New York: Samuel B. Smith, 1881. A systematic collection of Field's legal opinions. Includes his work as a member of the California Supreme Court as well as his decisions on the U.S. Supreme Court. The introduction by John Norton Pomeroy, who was a law professor at the University

of California during Field's lifetime, is of high scholarly quality but overly favorable to Field. One must, however, expect this from a volume put together by Field's political and legal friends during his lifetime.

Field, Stephen J. *California Alcalde.* Oakland, Calif.: Biobooks, 1950. Field's personal record of his reasons for coming to California, and how he became the administrative judge of Marysville and eventually ran for the newly formed California legislature. There is also a description of his stormy struggle to obtain various political and judicial appointments, culminating in his appointment to the California Supreme Court.

_____. *Personal Reminiscences of Early Days in California.* Washington, D.C.: Privately printed, 1893. Reprint. New York: Da Capo Press, 1968. Field produces, in lively fashion, personal sketches of his early days in California, his first few days in San Francisco, his success and good luck in Marysville, his legislative years, and his membership on the California Supreme Court. Also included is his version of what he describes as an attempt to assassinate him by former chief justice of the California Supreme Court, David S. Terry, in 1889.

Kens, Paul. *Justice Stephen Field: Shaping Liberty from the Gold Rush to the Gilded Age.* Lawrence: University Press of Kansas, 1997. Comprehensive biography chronicling Field's life and career. Kens describes the influences that shaped Field's legal thought and judicial opinions, and explains why his opinions remain relevant today.

McCloskey, Robert Green. *American Conservatism in the Age of Enterprise.* Cambridge, Mass.: Harvard University Press, 1951. A provocative, albeit unsympathetic analysis of Field's legal influences in the post-Civil War era. McCloskey attempts to show a conceptual line of influence, from the social Darwinism of William Graham Sumner through the legal conservatism of Field to the entrepreneurial, laissez-faire ideology of the capitalist Andrew Carnegie. McCloskey argues that Sumner and Field produced the moral and legal foundation for American capitalism.

Swisher, Carl Brent. *Stephen J. Field: Craftsman of Law.* Washington, D.C.: Brookings Institution, 1930. This is the best account of Field's career. It offers a rich record of his early years, his appointment as a Democrat from California to the U.S. Supreme Court by the Republican president Abraham Lincoln, and his political aspirations to be the Democratic nominee for president in 1880. Field had a dramatic and strenuous career, and Swisher's book covers it with literary skill.

Warren, Charles. *The Supreme Court in United States History*. 2 vols. Boston: Little, Brown, 1926. This two-volume work is one of the greatest treatments of American constitutional history available. In volume 2, chapters 30-34, Warren offers a concise record of the constitutional period between 1863-1888, the period in which Field's legal decisions so indelibly influenced the bench. Readers may find Warren's style excessively juridical, but the work is an invaluable account of Field's and other justices' supporting and dissenting opinions.

SEE ALSO: Salmon P. Chase; John Marshall; Roger Brooke Taney.

RELATED ARTICLE in *Great Events from History: The Nineteenth Century, 1801-1900:* October 24, 1861: Transcontinental Telegraph Is Completed.

MILLARD FILLMORE
President of the United States (1850-1853)

Fillmore's record as the thirteenth president of the United States is generally regarded as undistinguished; however, his push for legislation to resolve a deadlock between northern and southern states over the admission of California to the Union and the extension of slavery into new territories may have postponed the Civil War for a decade.

BORN: January 7, 1800; Summerhill, New York
DIED: March 8, 1874; Buffalo, New York
AREA OF ACHIEVEMENT: Government and politics

EARLY LIFE

Millard Fillmore was born in a log cabin on the farm that his father, Nathaniel, and his uncle Calvin had purchased in 1799. Nathaniel and his wife, Phoebe Millard Fillmore, had come to the western frontier from Vermont, prompted by the prospect of more fertile land in the Military Tract set aside by New York State after the American Revolution in order to pay bonuses to veterans. In time, there were nine children in the Fillmore family; Millard was the second child and first son.

In 1815, Millard Fillmore was apprenticed to a wool carder and cloth-dresser at New Hope, near the farm in Niles, New York, that Nathaniel Fillmore had leased after title to the property in Locke proved invalid. He attended the district school in New Hope, teaching there and in Buffalo schools after 1818, and there he met his future wife Abigail Powers. Fillmore spent the years between this first acquaintance and their marriage, on February 5, 1826, establishing himself as a lawyer. He studied law from 1820 under Judge Walter Wood in Montville, New York, and in 1822 began work as a clerk in the Buffalo, New York, law firm of Asa Rice and Joseph Clary. Even though he had not completed the usual seven-year period of study, Fillmore was admitted to practice before the Court of Common Pleas and opened his own law practice in East Aurora, New York, in 1823. He moved to Buffalo in 1830 and in time went into law partnership with Nathan K. Hall and Solomon G. Haven.

Fillmore's appearance and public manner marked him for a career in politics. Just under six feet tall, he had broad shoulders, an erect carriage, and bright blue eyes. His hair was thick and yellow, but by middle age it had turned snowy white. His voice was deep and masculine. Never an orator like Daniel Webster or Edward Everett, both of whom served him as secretary of state, Fillmore struck juries and audiences as carefully prepared, sincere, and unaffected. An associate of Thurlow Weed in formation of the Anti-Masonic Party, he was elected three times to the New York State Assembly (1829-1831). Fillmore's chief accomplishment in the legislature was authorship of a law eliminating the imprisonment of debtors and providing for a bankruptcy law. Characteristic of his mature political style was the careful balancing of individual and business interests that this legislation achieved.

LIFE'S WORK

Because the chief impetus behind the formation of the Anti-Masonic Party was reelection of John Quincy Adams and defeat of Andrew Jackson in the election of 1828, the party lost strength when Jackson was elected, although it retained local influence chiefly in New York, Pennsylvania, and New England. Fillmore was elected to the House of Representatives as an Anti-Mason (1833-1835), but he followed Thurlow Weed into the newly formed Whig Party in 1834. Subsequently, he was sent to Congress as a Whig (1837-1843) after William Henry Harrison was elected president in 1840. Fillmore served as chairman of the House Ways and Means Committee, and in that position he engineered congressional approval of protective tariff legislation in 1842.

Mentioned as a senatorial or vice presidential candidate prior to the 1844 election, Fillmore accepted Weed's advice—perhaps intended to keep the vice presidential prospects of William H. Seward alive—that he run for governor of New York. He was defeated by the popular Democrat Silas Wright but came back in 1847 to win election as New York's comptroller. Fillmore and Seward were both favorite son prospects for the Whig vice presidential nomination in 1848. The presidential candidates were Henry Clay, General Winfield Scott, and General Zachary Taylor.

When the convention chose Taylor, and some delegates objected to Abbott Lawrence of Massachusetts as his running mate, the antislavery Clay delegates put their votes behind Fillmore and assured him the vice presidential slot. He was not assured of influence within the Taylor administration itself when, having won the election, the new president took office in 1849. William H. Seward, Weed's ally and the newly elected senator for New York, worked to minimize Fillmore's influence on the new president. Unable to control party patronage in

Millard Fillmore. (Library of Congress)

his home state, Fillmore was limited chiefly to his constitutional duty of presiding over the debates of the U.S. Senate.

California had petitioned for admission to the Union. There were thirty states at the time, fifteen slave and fifteen free, and California would tip the balance in the debate over slavery. The same issue complicated discussion of territorial governments for Utah and New Mexico, acquired at the end of the Mexican War, and an outstanding Texas-New Mexico border dispute. Abolitionists and Free-Soilers campaigned to limit the expansion of slavery into new states and territories, even trying to prohibit the slave trade in the District of Columbia, while southern political leaders argued for the extension of slavery and for more vigorous enforcement of laws requiring the capture and return of fugitive slaves.

Senator Henry Clay, the support of whose delegates at the Whig convention of 1848 had assured Fillmore the vice presidential nomination, proposed an omnibus package of compromise legislation to deal with these issues. President Taylor, though a slaveholder from Louisiana, indicated that he would veto the bill if it extended slavery into the territories gained from Mexico. He also claimed he would use federal troops to resolve the Texas-New Mexico boundary dispute. Initially, Fillmore supported Taylor's position on Clay's omnibus bill, but in 1850, he advised the president that he would vote to accept the package if required to cast a tiebreaking vote in the Senate. Fillmore never had to cast that vote. Taylor became ill after attending ceremonies at the Washington Monument on July 4, and died on July 9, 1850, making Millard Fillmore the thirteenth president of the United States.

After taking the oath of office and accepting the resignations of Taylor's entire cabinet, Fillmore moved to occupy a pro-Union political position. He appointed Daniel Webster as secretary of state and John Crittenden as attorney general, and he filled the rest of the cabinet with equally moderate men. Fillmore repeatedly insisted that slavery was morally repugnant to him, but he also said that he intended to be the president of the entire United States. He was prepared to make compromises in the interest of national unity.

When Senator Stephen A. Douglas, a Democrat, took over Senate management of Clay's stalled "omnibus bill," Fillmore indicated his willingness to sign the provisions of the omnibus as separate pieces of legislation. Between September 9 and September 20, 1850, he signed five measures designed to hammer out a compro-

FILLMORE'S FIRST STATE OF THE UNION ADDRESS

Unexpectedly cast into the presidency by Zachary Taylor's sudden death on July 9, 1850, Millard Fillmore delivered his first state the union address only five months later. He naturally opened his speech with a tribute to his predecessor.

Being suddenly called in the midst of the last session of Congress by a painful dispensation of Divine Providence to the responsible station which I now hold, I contented myself with such communications to the Legislature as the exigency of the moment seemed to require. The country was shrouded in mourning for the loss of its venerable Chief Magistrate and all hearts were penetrated with grief. Neither the time nor the occasion appeared to require or to justify on my part any general expression of political opinions or any announcement of the principles which would govern me in the discharge of the duties to the performance of which I had been so unexpectedly called. I trust, therefore, that it may not be deemed inappropriate if I avail myself of this opportunity of the reassembling of Congress to make known my sentiments in a general manner in regard to the policy which ought to be pursued by the Government both in its intercourse with foreign nations and its management and administration of internal affairs. . . .

Source: Millard Fillmore, "State of the Union Address," December 2, 1850.

Party in 1856. He attempted to distance himself from the proslavery, anti-Catholic, nativist principles of the party and to run his campaign on the Unionist basis he had advocated while president. The strategy did not work. In a three-way race against Democrat James Buchanan and Republican John C. Frémont, Fillmore came in a poor third.

With the election of Buchanan in 1856, Fillmore's national political career came to an end. Abigail Powers Fillmore died in Washington, D.C., on March 30, 1853, only a few weeks after her husband had left the White House. On February 10, 1858, Fillmore married Caroline Carmichael McIntosh, a widow, in Albany, New York. He died in Buffalo, New York on March 8, 1874; Caroline McIntosh Fillmore died there on August 11, 1881.

mise between northern and southern interests. California was admitted as a free state; Utah and New Mexico were given territorial status, with the citizens eventually to determine the status of slavery there; and Texas was compensated for the loss of territory in the adjustment of its border with New Mexico. Fillmore also signed a tougher law dealing with fugitive slaves and another prohibiting the slave trade, but not slavery itself, in the District of Columbia.

This reversal of Taylor's position achieved a political solution to a conflict threatening to erupt into military action. Fillmore had to send troops into South Carolina to deal with threats of secession and threatened to use them in the North to enforce the Fugitive Slave Act before there was general acceptance of these measures. While moderate men of all political parties supported Fillmore's position, both the southern and New England factions of his own Whig Party blamed him for those parts of the compromise package of which they disapproved. Therefore, Fillmore did not get the Whig presidential nomination in 1852 and retired to Buffalo in 1853, turning over the powers of the office to the Democrat Franklin Pierce.

In the face of the virtual dissolution of the Whigs as a national political party, Fillmore accepted the presidential nomination of the American, or Know-Nothing,

SIGNIFICANCE

During the Civil War and in the years following, the popular press depicted Millard Fillmore as a southern sympathizer. He supported the candidacy of General George B. McClellan in 1864, and he also expressed approval of Andrew Johnson's efforts to achieve reconciliation with the South at the war's end. Properly speaking, Fillmore's positions were not so much pro-southern as conservative, exactly as they had been when he accepted the compromise legislation of 1850 in the name of preserving the Union. His role in passage of that legislation was the central achievement of his term as president.

Fillmore's initiatives in foreign policy were modest, but they too reflected his unwillingness to adopt extreme positions. Fillmore resisted moves to annex Cuba and Nicaragua; he expressed disapproval of Austria's handling of the Hungarian uprising led by Lajos Kossuth, and he blocked French attempts to make the Hawaiian Islands a protectorate. Fillmore's administration moved to normalize relations with Mexico and opened negotiations to build a canal connecting the Atlantic and Pacific oceans through Nicaragua. He sent Commodore Matthew Perry on his mission to open the ports of Japan to merchant ships of the United States.

Like Taylor, Pierce, and Buchanan, Fillmore's reputation has been diminished by the failure of nineteenth century American politics to avert the Civil War. The administration of each of these presidents struggled to control the forces that led to military conflict. The legislation passed in 1850 was the most significant attempt to defuse the sectional conflict, and Millard Fillmore's role in its passage is his chief claim to historical importance.

—*Robert C. Petersen*

FURTHER READING

Barre, W. L. *The Life and Public Services of Millard Fillmore*. New York: Burt Franklin, 1971. Reprint of a campaign biography originally published in 1856. Barre's book provides an undocumented contemporary account of Fillmore's life and tenure as president.

Fillmore, Millard. *Millard Fillmore Papers*. Edited by Frank H. Severance. 2 vols. Buffalo, N.Y.: Buffalo Historical Society, 1907. Reprint. New York: Kraus Reprint, 1970. These volumes contain the only printed collection of Fillmore's public papers.

Goodman, Mark. *High Hopes: The Rise and Decline of Buffalo, New York*. Albany: State University of New York Press, 1983. While Goodman's book deals with Fillmore only in passing, it contains a fascinating account of local reactions to his 1856 campaign as the presidential nominee of the American, or Know-Nothing, Party.

Holt, Michael F. *The Political Crisis of the 1850's*. New York: John Wiley & Sons, 1978. Reprint. New York: W. W. Norton, 1983. Holt argues that disintegration of the Whig-Democrat two-party structure was a cause and not an effect of the political crisis of the 1850's.

Potter, David M. *The Impending Crisis, 1848-1861*. Edited by Don E. Fehrenbacher. New York: Harper & Row, 1976. This excellent history of the period places the various conflicts Fillmore dealt with squarely within the ideological framework of Manifest Destiny.

Rayback, Robert J. *Millard Fillmore: Biography of a President*. Buffalo, N.Y.: Henry Stewart, 1959. The book explains the complex factors that drew Fillmore into the Anti-Masonic, Whig, and American parties and the effects of these associations on his political career.

Scarry, Robert J. *Millard Fillmore*. Jefferson, N.C.: McFarland, 2001. Extensively researched review of Fillmore's life and career, based partly upon previously unavailable correspondence and personal papers. Scarry refutes the image of Fillmore as stodgy and ineffectual, maintaining he was a complex, energetic, and successful president.

Smith, Elbert B. *The Presidencies of Zachary Taylor and Millard Fillmore*. Lawrence: University Press of Kansas, 1988. A concise reinterpretation of the two men's presidencies. Smith concludes that, contrary to conventional wisdom, Taylor and Fillmore were misrepresented and underrated presidents.

Snyder, Charles M., ed. *The Lady and the President: The Letters of Dorothea Dix and Millard Fillmore*. Lexington: University Press of Kentucky, 1975. The correspondence of Fillmore and Dix, the chief nineteenth century American advocate for reform in the treatment of the mentally ill, gives insight into Fillmore's personality and actions as a public official and political candidate.

SEE ALSO: Henry Clay; Stephen A. Douglas; Matthew C. Perry; William H. Seward; Zachary Taylor.

RELATED ARTICLES in *Great Events from History: The Nineteenth Century, 1801-1900:* January 29-September 20, 1850: Compromise of 1850; March 31, 1854: Perry Opens Japan to Western Trade; May 29, 1867: Austrian Ausgleich.

GUSTAVE FLAUBERT
French novelist

The most influential European novelist of the nineteenth century, Flaubert is regarded as the leader of the realist school of French literature. He is especially well known for his masterpiece, Madame Bovary.

BORN: December 12, 1821; Rouen, France
DIED: May 8, 1880; Croisset, France
AREA OF ACHIEVEMENT: Literature

EARLY LIFE

Gustave Flaubert (floh-behr) was the son of Achille Cléophas Flaubert, a noted surgeon and professor of medicine, and Caroline (Fleuriot) Flaubert, a woman from a distinguished provincial family. As a child Flaubert was high-strung, delicate, and precocious. He developed a love of literature early.

In his adolescence, Flaubert became attracted to the Romantic movement. Consequently he declared a hatred for bourgeois values and a passionate devotion to art; he maintained these attitudes throughout his life. They were strengthened through his youthful friendship with Alfred Le Poittevin, a young philosopher, whose pessimistic outlook affected Flaubert deeply. Another formative influence was his father's practice and teaching of medicine, which led him to value the discipline, intelligence, and clinical eye of the surgeon and helped shape his own approach to his literary materials.

In 1836, at the age of about fifteen, Flaubert met Élisa Schlésinger, a married woman eleven years his senior, and succumbed to a devastating romantic passion for her that was destined to remain unrequited and to serve in his mind as an ideal that was never to be reached in his subsequent relationships with women.

Flaubert was sent to Paris in the autumn of 1842 to study law, a profession that did not attract him. He was committed to literature but reluctant to publish his work and susceptible to episodes of serious depression. In January, 1844, he gave up the study of the law upon suffering a nervous breakdown that was then diagnosed, probably erroneously, as epilepsy. Following a yearlong recuperation, he began to devote his time and energy to literary creation and to turn away from his earlier romantic subjectivism.

Flaubert's father died in January, 1846, leaving him an inheritance that enabled him to pursue his literary career full time. His sister Caroline died the following March, leaving an infant daughter. Flaubert and his mother adopted the child and began living at their estate at Croisset, near Rouen, where he spent most of the remainder of his life. In July, 1846, Flaubert met the poet Louise Colet in Paris and began a tempestuous, intermittent affair with her that ended ten years later, in 1856.

In 1847, Flaubert went on a walking tour through Brittany with his writer friend Maxime Du Camp and wrote about the tour in *Par les champs et par les grèves* (with Du Camp; *Over Strand and Field*, 1904), which was published posthumously (1885). At this time, he was also engaged in writing the first version of *La Tentation de Saint Antoine* (1874; *The Temptation of Saint Anthony*, 1895), begun in 1846. Although he expended much energy and care on the manuscript, his friends found it florid and rhetorical and advised him to burn it. Disheartened, he set it aside and set out with Du Camp in November, 1849, on travels through Egypt, Palestine, Syria, Turkey, Greece, and Italy. Upon his return to Croisset in the summer of 1851, he was preparing to begin a very different kind of novel.

LIFE'S WORK

Flaubert spent the next five years of his life hard at work on *Madame Bovary* (1857; English translation, 1886). In the first two months of 1857, the French government brought Flaubert to trial, charging him with writing an immoral work, but he was acquitted and *Madame Bovary* won widespread success.

In the writing of *Madame Bovary*, Flaubert found himself, both as a man and as an artist. The novel relates dispassionately the story of a young provincial girl whose incurably romantic notions about life and passion lead her to adultery, financial ruin, and suicide. Her yearnings are of a kind with which Flaubert himself had been all too familiar, as is evidenced in his famous remark, "Madame Bovary, c'est moi" (Madame Bovary is myself). In projecting his own temperament upon this fictional character and subjecting it to relentlessly objective scrutiny, Flaubert was working to exorcise inner weaknesses that had bedeviled him all of his life.

Flaubert's painstaking care with the observation of concrete facts and psychological details in *Madame Bovary* and his constant concern to present his materials impersonally constituted a revolution in the art of the novel and earned for him recognition as the leader of a

FLAUBERT'S MAJOR WORKS

1857	*Madame Bovary* (English translation, 1886)
1862	*Salammbô* (English translation, 1886)
1869	*L'Éducation sentimentale* (*A Sentimental Education*, 1898)
1874	*La Tentation de Saint Antoine* (*The Temptation of Saint Anthony*, 1895)
1874	*Le Candidat* (*The Candidate*, 1904)
1874	*Le Château des cœurs* (with Louis Bouilhet; *The Castle of Hearts*, 1904)
1877	*Trois Contes* (*Three Tales*, 1903)
1881	*Bouvard et Pécuchet* (*Bouvard and Pécuchet*, 1896)
1885	*Novembre* (*November*, 1932)
1885	*Par les champs et par les grèves* (with Maxime Du Camp; *Over Strand and Field*, 1904)

new realist school of literature. This designation is misleading, however, and, in fact, somewhat ironic. Flaubert himself detested it, commenting, "People think I am in love with reality, though I hate it; for it is out of hatred of realism that I undertook the writing of this novel."

It is important to note the prevailing idealism in Flaubert's temperament and art. He saw art as an escape from life's ugliness; the paradox of *Madame Bovary* is that it takes a story that is essentially sordid and commonplace and transforms it into a vessel of beauty. The medium of this transformation is Flaubert's language: Through his ideas about and use of this medium, he has come to epitomize the dedicated literary artist. He refused to rush his art, and would spend hours in anguish searching for the right word or phrase to express his vision.

From *Madame Bovary* Flaubert turned to the subject of ancient Carthage; in 1862, he published *Salammbô* (English translation, 1886), a minutely researched novel whose fictitious narrative is set against the actual historical background of the 240-237 B.C.E. uprising of the mercenaries against Carthage. *Salammbô* was a popular success, but, to Flaubert's disappointment, it failed to win approval from the critics.

After writing three unsuccessful plays, Flaubert took up for extensive revision the manuscript of *L'Éducation sentimentale* (1869; *A Sentimental Education*, 1898). The novel, which Flaubert called a "moral history of the men of my generation," is set in Paris during the 1840's, and it fictionalizes Flaubert's personal experiences within the panoramic and solidly realized historical context of France under the July Monarchy. Flaubert considered this novel his masterpiece, but the reviews

were very unfavorable and the reading public unsympathetic.

Other troubles also plagued Flaubert in his last years. He was beset by financial problems after sacrificing his own fortune in 1875 to save his niece's husband from bankruptcy. He was, nevertheless, highly respected by other writers and generous in his advice to young authors, including Guy de Maupassant—who became his disciple—as well as Émile Zola and Alphonse Daudet. He formed friendships with the novelists Ivan Turgenev and George Sand.

Flaubert's last novel, which he left unfinished, was *Bouvard et Pécuchet* (1881; English translation, 1896). He interrupted his work on this long novel in 1875-1877 to write *Trois Contes* (1877; *Three Tales*, 1903), three stories that display the range and diversity of Flaubert's art and received immediate recognition. *Bouvard et Pécuchet* is a portrayal of human folly and frailty, specifically in its modern manifestation as an uncritical confusion of science and truth.

Flaubert died at home in Croisset after suffering a stroke on May 8, 1880. He was buried in Rouen.

SIGNIFICANCE

Gustave Flaubert greatly influenced the development of the modern novel. In the historical context of French literature, his work forms a bridge between romanticism and realism, and his art arises out of the conflict within his mind and temperament between these two tendencies. *Madame Bovary* has been called the first modern novel and is widely hailed as one of the greatest works of fiction ever written.

Although he was a kindhearted man and a loyal friend, Flaubert's vision of life in his fiction was tragic and pessimistic. It epitomizes for many a quintessentially modern outlook. His ironic stance; his understanding of solitude, ennui, suffering, and loss; his dissatisfaction with materialistic and empty bourgeois values and the pursuit of ideal beauty; and his fascination with the destructive force of time and the preserving power of memory are attitudes that are found in the works of many writers of the late nineteenth and twentieth centuries. His understanding of human psychology was precise and deep. Flaubert's painstaking devotion to style and form raised the status of the novel to a form of high art and made him a model of the literary artist for subsequent generations of writers and readers.

—*Eileen Tess Tyler*

FURTHER READING

Bart, Benjamin F. *Flaubert*. Syracuse, N.Y.: Syracuse University Press, 1967. This lengthy and comprehensive critical biography makes copious use of Flaubert's letters, private papers, and drafts for his novels to present a detailed account of his life, aesthetic, and ideas about prose fiction.

Brombert, Victor. *The Novels of Flaubert: A Study of Themes and Techniques*. Princeton, N.J.: Princeton University Press, 1966. A thorough study of the texture, structure, patterns, and themes in Flaubert's fiction, stressing the nonrealistic and autobiographical aspects of his art. Brombert argues that Flaubert is essentially a tragic novelist.

Buck, Stratton. *Gustave Flaubert*. Boston: Twayne, 1966. A comprehensive and authoritative introduction, for students and general readers, to Flaubert's novels and correspondence. Buck traces the evolution and composition of each of Flaubert's novels, describes their nature and contents, and assesses their artistic importance.

Culler, Jonathan. *Flaubert: The Uses of Uncertainty*. Ithaca, N.Y.: Cornell University Press, 1974. A sophisticated study, with a critical approach influenced by structuralism. Culler addresses Flaubert's early writings in sequence, identifying predominant themes, especially human stupidity and irony, in the later novels, which he then treats at length together. Culler concludes by discussing Flaubert's writings in terms of their value and sources of interest for modern readers.

Flaubert, Gustave. *The Letters of Gustave Flaubert*. Selected, edited, and translated by Francis Steegmuller. 2 vols. Cambridge, Mass.: Harvard University Press, 1980-1982. Flaubert's letters are crucial to an understanding of his personality, life, and works. This edition, which includes authoritative notes, appendixes, indexes, and illustrations, presents Flaubert's letters from 1830 through 1880.

Gay, Peter. *Savage Reprisals: "Bleak House," "Madame Bovary," "Buddenbooks."* New York: W. W. Norton, 2002. Gay refutes the view that "realistic novels" are a documentary account of their times. He maintains that all novels are subjective reflections of their authors' prejudices and obsessions. Gay advances his theory by closely analyzing three novels, including *Madame Bovary*, which he argues is less a true depiction of provincial French life than a "weapon of harassment," reflecting Flaubert's cynical view of society.

Nadeau, Maurice. *The Greatness of Flaubert*. Translated by Barbara Bray. New York: Library Press, 1972. A general introduction to Flaubert's life and career by the editor of the author's complete works. Nadeau stresses Flaubert's lifelong and never fully realized quest, as he became an artist, for a coherent sense of his own identity. Nadeau characterizes Flaubert's work as a body of "social, philosophical, and moral criticism."

Spencer, Philip H. *Flaubert: A Biography*. New York: Grove Press, 1952. A sensible and highly readable narrative that provides a vivid introduction to Flaubert's life. Spencer views Flaubert in terms of an interrelated set of conflicts between self and society, idealism and disillusionment, beauty and ugliness, and escapism and commitment, and explores these conflicts as they manifest themselves in his life and motivate him as an artist.

Starkie, Enid. *Flaubert: The Making of the Master*. New York: Atheneum, 1967. Starkie draws upon previously unused materials from manuscripts, notes, and letters in this comprehensive and well-documented critical biography of Flaubert through 1857, concluding with a study of *Madame Bovary*, its antecedents, its publication and censorship trial, and Flaubert's aesthetic doctrine. Includes illustrations, bibliography, notes, and index.

_____. *Flaubert: The Master—A Critical and Biographical Study, 1856-1880*. New York: Atheneum, 1971. In this, the sequel volume to her *Flaubert: The Making of the Master* (1967), Starkie presents a sympathetic and thorough analysis of Flaubert's life and art after the publication of *Madame Bovary*. She argues that Flaubert's later works represent the fundamental aspects of his genius. Includes illustrations, bibliography, notes, and index.

Vargas Llosa, Mario. *The Perpetual Orgy: Flaubert and Madame Bovary*. Translated by Helen Lane. New York: Farrar, Straus and Giroux, 1986. A thoroughgoing study of Flaubert's art in *Madame Bovary* by the celebrated Peruvian novelist. Vargas Llosa begins by charting vividly his particular experiences with this novel. He then addresses in depth the biographical, historical, and geographical origins of *Madame Bovary*, and analyzes important recurring themes and innovative techniques.

Wall, Geoffrey. *Flaubert: A Life*. London: Faber & Faber, 2001. Well-reviewed biography, showing the contradictions of Flaubert's settled life in provincial France and his more dramatic experiences in Paris and the foreign countries he visited. Wall demonstrates how these contradictory experiences influenced Flaubert's fiction, including the creation of his characters.

SEE ALSO: Anatole France; Guy de Maupassant; George Sand; Anaïs Ségalas; Émile Zola.
RELATED ARTICLES in *Great Events from History: The Nineteenth Century, 1801-1900:* October 1-December 15, 1856: Flaubert Publishes *Madame Bovary;* c. 1865: Naturalist Movement Begins; c. 1884-1924: Decadent Movement Flourishes.

WILLIAMINA PATON STEVENS FLEMING
Scottish-born American astronomer

Fleming pioneered the analysis of stellar spectra and discovered more than three hundred variable stars and ten exploding stars (novas). Her work made her the leading woman astronomer of her time.

BORN: May 15, 1857; Dundee, Scotland
DIED: May 21, 1911; Boston, Massachusetts
ALSO KNOWN AS: Williamina Paton Stevens (birth name); Williamina Fleming; Mina Fleming
AREA OF ACHIEVEMENT: Astronomy

EARLY LIFE

Williamina Paton Stevens Fleming was born in Scotland to Robert Stevens and Mary Walker Stevens. Her father was a craftsperson in the carving and gilding trade and was among the first in Dundee, Scotland, to experiment with the new daguerreotype photographic process. He died when Williamina was seven.

Williamina became a pupil-teacher at the age of fourteen. In 1877, after five years of teaching, she married James Orr Fleming; the following year they emigrated to the United States and settled in Boston. After her husband abandoned her two years later, she took a job as a maid in the home of Edward C. Pickering, who was director of the Harvard College Observatory from 1877 to 1919. A few months later she took a short leave to return to Scotland for the birth of her son, Edward Pickering Fleming, who would later graduate from the Massachusetts Institute of Technology and become a mining engineer and metallurgist.

At the Harvard College Observatory, Pickering pioneered in employing women as "computers"—people who measured and analyzed the vast number of stellar-spectrum photographs he was producing. At that time, women were not allowed to work in the observatory at night, when observations of the skies were made, but they could be employed during the daytime to analyze photographs at salaries that were lower than those of male astronomers. When Pickering became impatient with the inefficiency of a male assistant, he claimed that his Scottish maid could do a better job. In 1881, he invited Fleming to work as a computer at Harvard, even though she had neither a college education nor training in astronomy. However, her work was so good that Pickering decided to hire other young women to work with her. Over the next thirty years, Fleming worked closely with Pickering, first in clerical and computing work, but advancing rapidly to become one of the leading astronomers of her day and to supervise many other women computers at Harvard.

LIFE'S WORK

During the nineteenth century astronomy underwent a major revolution. New techniques for lens making, more advanced telescope designs, and the use of photography led to measurements of fainter stars with greater precision than ever before. In 1872, the American physician Henry Draper made the first successful photograph of the spectrum of a star. After Draper died in 1882, his widow established the Henry Draper Memorial to assist the program of stellar spectroscopy at the Harvard College Observatory. When a thin prism was placed in front of the objective lens of a refracting telescope, each star formed its own spectrum on a photographic plate at the focus, making it possible to record long exposures of spectra of as many as two hundred stars on a single photographic plate. In 1886, Fleming was placed in charge of the Draper project to measure, analyze, and classify stellar spectra.

Fleming's chief assignment was classifying stars on the basis of the various patterns of lines and bands that appeared in their spectral photographs. Because photographs were more sensitive than the human eye, they revealed new features that required a more complex classification scheme than earlier systems based solely on visual observations. In the "Pickering-Fleming system" light spectra were organized into fifteen categories, using most of the letters from A to Q according to the complexity of their lines and bands, but about 99 percent of the stars were in the six classes designated A, B, F, G, K, and M.

In 1890, the *Draper Catalogue of Stellar Spectra* was published as volume 27 of the *Annals of Harvard College Observatory*. Fleming's earlier work had been published in the customary way under the name of the director of the observatory. However, by the year 1890, the signature "M. Fleming" began to appear along with Pickering's on reports in astronomy journals. In the *Draper Catalogue*, Pickering acknowledged that "Mrs. M. Fleming" did most of the work in measuring and classifying spectra and preparing the catalog for publication. In the preparation of the catalog, Fleming used 633 photographic plates taken with the eight-inch Bache telescope. She measured 28,266 spectra and classified 10,351 stars brighter than seventh magnitude.

In the course of her work on the *Draper Catalogue*, Fleming found that the spectra of many variable red stars contained bright emission lines in addition to the usual dark absorption lines. Her further investigation showed that all stars with such unusual spectral features are variable in their luminosity. Her finding provided a new tool for discovering long-period variables. Using this technique, she discovered 222 variable stars. In her 1907 paper "A Photographic Study of Variable Stars," which was published as volume 47 of the *Annals of Harvard College Observatory*, she gave the variation in brightness of each star based on a selected list of companion stars.

In addition to Fleming's work on variable stars, she made a special study of other stars with peculiar spectra. This led her to the discovery of ten novas—or exploding stars—more than a third of the twenty-eight novas known at the time of her death. She also discovered 94 of the 107 known Wolf-Rayet stars, which are massive stars characterized by broad emission lines. Shortly after she died, her list of "Stars Having Peculiar Spectra" was published as volume 56 of the *Annals of Harvard College Observatory* in 1912.

Fleming combined her diligence and research ability with effective administrative skill in her supervision of several dozen young women. She also served as editor of all the publications issued by the Harvard College Observatory. In 1898, the Harvard Corporation named her curator of astronomical photographs. Under her supervision, nearly 200,000 photographic plates taken at Cambridge and in Peru between 1882 and 1910 were examined and cataloged. In 1906, she became the first American woman elected to the British Royal Astronomical Society, and she was also a charter member of the American Astronomical and Astrophysical Society. In 1911 she became ill with pneumonia and died in Boston at the age of fifty-four.

SIGNIFICANCE

Williamina Fleming's discovery and analysis of 222 variable stars and ten novas was unprecedented. The unusual nature of this achievement can be better appreciated when it is understood that most astronomers were proud to discover even one variable star and that they then typically left the further study of its properties to others. Fleming's influence on the many assistants who worked under her was even more significant. Her pioneering classification scheme led to major contributions by other women who followed her example at Harvard. Two of the most important of these were Annie Jump Cannon and Henrietta Leavitt, both of whom began as her assistants.

Annie Cannon joined the Harvard staff in 1896 and developed the definitive Harvard system of spectral classification based on the work of Fleming. She organized Fleming's alphabetical system according to increasing spectral complexity, and her system led to a later correlation with decreasing temperatures and an understanding of the evolution of stars. Henrietta Leavitt continued Fleming's study of variable stars and became a full staff member in 1902. Ten years later, she announced her discovery of the relation between the pulsation period and luminosity of a type of variable star called Cepheids that later led to measurements of the distances of galaxies and the discovery of the expansion of the universe.

—*Joseph L. Spradley*

FURTHER READING

Belkora, Leila. *Minding the Heavens: The Story of Our Discovery of the Milky Way*. Bristol, England: Institute of Physics, 2003. Fleming is briefly discussed in a chapter on William Huggins and astronomical spectroscopy.

Cannon, Annie J. "Williamina Paton Fleming." *Astrophysical Journal* 34 (July, 1911): 314-317. Obituary of Fleming written by one of her colleagues at the Harvard College Observatory.

Dobson, Andrea K., and Katherine Bracher. "Urania's Heritage: A Historical Introduction to Women in Astronomy." *Mercury: The Journal of the Astronomical Society of the Pacific* 21 (January/February, 1992): 4-15. This well-illustrated article includes a discussion of the work of Fleming and Cannon.

Jones, Bessie, and Lyle Boyd. *The Harvard College Observatory, 1839-1919.* Cambridge, Mass.: Harvard University Press, 1971. Several sections of this history discuss Fleming's work and contributions.

Kass-Simons, G., and Patricia Farnes, eds. *Women of Science: Righting the Record.* Bloomington: Indiana University Press, 1990. A chapter on "Women in Astronomy in America" has a good discussion of the Harvard College Observatory women.

Spradley, Joseph L. "The Industrious Mrs. Fleming." *Astronomy 18* (July, 1990): 48-51. A short account of Fleming's life and work with several photographs of her and others of the Harvard College Observatory women.

SEE ALSO: Margaret Lindsay Huggins; Samuel Pierpont Langley; Sir Joseph Norman Lockyer; Albert A. Michelson; Maria Mitchell.

RELATED ARTICLES in *Great Events from History: The Nineteenth Century, 1801-1900:* January 1, 1801: First Asteroid Is Discovered; 1814: Fraunhofer Invents the Spectroscope.

EDWIN FORREST
American actor

Despite early obstacles in his career, Forrest became the first great American actor and the first to gain international acclaim.

BORN: March 9, 1806; Philadelphia, Pennsylvania
DIED: December 12, 1872; Philadelphia, Pennsylvania
AREA OF ACHIEVEMENT: Theater

EARLY LIFE

By temperament and circumstance, Edwin Forrest typified the rough, self-reliant individualism of the early nineteenth century pioneer. Though he was born into a comfortable middle-class environment, his choice of an acting career compelled him to leave the security of his home and to learn his craft in some of the wildest places amid some of the wildest men in the country.

Forrest's father, a bank clerk, died when Forrest was thirteen, but he had already made plans for him to enter the safe, prestigious career of the ministry. The boy's remarkable memory, gift for mimicry, and already distinctive voice, however, were better suited to the playhouse than the pulpit. At ten, he was a member of an amateur theatrical troupe, playing female roles. Tradition suggests that he was shrieked and laughed at on the stage, but this early failure only cemented his determination to act.

By his early teens, Forrest had held a number of jobs, including one as an apprentice printer. In the meantime, he was studying, reading, running his own juvenile acting company, and performing his first recitations in a neighbor's old barn.

Forrest's early commitment to the stage was abetted by the fortuitousness of geography, for Philadelphia, his native city, was a vital cultural hub, a theatrical center whose playhouses were among the oldest, liveliest, and most important in the country. It seems likely that the young actor enjoyed easy access to the many plays both produced and published in Philadelphia, as well as ample opportunity to study the styles and techniques of many actors in a variety of roles.

What is certain is that one of his youthful recitations so impressed several well-to-do citizens that they supported him in his studies for the next few years. Incredibly, Forrest made his professional debut at the Walnut Street Theatre in Philadelphia on November 27, 1820, playing Young Norval, a popular juvenile lead in John Home's *Douglas* (1756). The part was perfect for him, requiring an amount of physical action that allowed him to show his grace and agility, and declamatory speech that showed to advantage his already impressive timbral voice. His success was unqualified; Forrest was only fourteen.

LIFE'S WORK

Though he performed in several plays over the next few months, Forrest was convinced that he had to break the image of a juvenile actor and gain broader experience. To do this, he decided to travel west, across the Allegheny Mountains, where he would have more freedom to learn the profession, to experiment, to grow. Thus, in 1821, having been engaged by the theatrical company of Collins and Jones, Forrest embarked on a career as a strolling player for eight dollars a week.

By October, 1822, he was in Pittsburgh, once again playing Young Norval, developing the rugged physique and booming voice that were to become the crucial ingredients in his acting style. A few months later, he and his fellow strollers sailed a flatboat down the Ohio, stopping at Lexington, Kentucky, for several performances, and then traveling overland by covered wagon to Cincinnati, opening there in February, 1823.

The experience gained in these Western cities was decisive in shaping Forrest's career. He learned the importance of holding an audience under exacting and restrictive conditions—theaters with poor lighting, a paucity of props and scenery, and a change of bill nightly. Each member of the small troupe was expected to play a variety of parts: the dramatic lead in one play, the clown in the other, the dancer in the encore or afterpiece.

In 1823, the troupe went bankrupt and Forrest was out of a job. Broke, he stayed on in Cincinnati, living with a theatrical family who admired his work. He spent the next few months in poverty, reading the works of William Shakespeare.

Finally, he accepted an offer to play in New Orleans, a key city in the southern and western circuit. By the winter of 1824, just short of his eighteenth birthday, Forrest opened there in a Restoration tragedy, but his leisure time in that city was spent carousing with James Bowie (who gave the young man one of his famous knives), with a roustabout steamboat captain, and with "domesticated" Indian chiefs and other frontier types. Such figures comported with his robust, hot-tempered, and impulsive spirit, complementing his basically unrefined education.

Throughout the spring of 1825, Forrest played a variety of roles in New Orleans, including Iago in Shakespeare's *Othello, the Moor of Venice* (1604) and the title role in John Howard Payne's *Brutus: Or, The Fall of Tarquin* (1818), one of his most popular portrayals. His persistence was finally rewarded. The following year, he obtained an engagement in Albany, New York, playing with Edmund Kean, the famous British actor. Shortly thereafter, he arrived in New York City, still poor but rich in experience and in a deepened understanding of his craft.

The turning point of his career was this New York debut. Opening at the Bowery Theater in November, 1826, playing Othello, he brought to the role all the experience his life on the road and in the Western playhouses had given him. He was a brilliant success. At the age of twenty, Edwin Forrest had conquered the American stage. His New York triumph was the beginning of a reputation that was to last for the next thirty years. In less than a year, he became the most famous and highest paid American actor of the period, advancing from a salary of

Edwin Forrest. (Library of Congress)

twenty-eight dollars a week in 1826 to two hundred dollars per night in 1827-1828 to five hundred dollars per night during the late 1830's.

At this point in his career, Forrest dedicated himself to the production of American plays. To encourage the development of a national drama and, shrewdly, to find just those plays in which he could use his tall, powerfully built body to advantage, Forrest sponsored a yearly competition to attract the best work. Among the many plays submitted, two in particular became important contributions to American dramatic literature of the nineteenth century. *The Gladiator* (1831), by Robert Montgomery

Bird, and *Metamora: Or, The Last of the Wampanoags* (1829), by John A. Stone, were significant examples of the history play and the play on Indian themes, respectively. Both were well suited to Forrest's gifts, containing sonorous, orotund poetry that displayed his powerful voice and quick, physical action that demonstrated his athletic prowess. Both supplied him with his most famous and popular roles to the end of his career.

Twice during the 1830's he went to England, becoming the first great American actor appearing on the London stage. With nationalistic zeal, he opened his London engagement with *The Gladiator*, playing the role of Spartacus. In England, he met Catherine Sinclair, an actor, marrying her in 1837, at the peak of his fame. It was eventually an unhappy relationship. Often rash, jealous, and increasingly petulant, Forrest sued her for divorce in 1850. The trial was nasty and scandalous, becoming more notorious by Forrest's frequent exercises in public self-justification. Though the episode did little damage to his career as an actor, it did reveal the weaker side of his character as a man.

Even before this public squabbling about his domestic life, however, Forrest's role in one of the most infamous events in the history of the American theater gave further proof of a truculence that characterized much of his professional life. For years, Forrest was the chief American rival of William Macready, the noted British actor; the two were barely civil to each other. When Forrest was hissed on opening night in his second London tour of 1845, he bluntly attributed the heckling to a Macready faction, and when, in turn, Macready played in the United States and Forrest bitterly denounced him in the press, the feud took on a nationalistic, patriotic hue. On the night of May 7, 1848, supporters of Forrest stormed the Astor Place Opera House in New York City, where Macready was playing. Before the police broke up the riot, some thirty people had been killed. This so-called Astor Place Riot was the beginning of Forrest's decline.

Forrest's decline was assured, as well, by his body. Riddled with gout and arthritis, he was by the 1850's in great pain; his imposing, muscular frame, which had been in large measure responsible for his success, now became an impediment to his active, robust acting style. His retirement was imminent. Trying to recapture his past glories, Forrest accepted an invitation to visit California. He played Cardinal Richelieu, a favorite role, but the audience saw only a gouty, ill-tempered old actor, and a month later, the play closed.

Because California had been a failure for him, Forrest returned to Philadelphia, now taking any engagement,

anywhere, that would keep him going. At this point in his career, just before the Civil War, he was living on his reputation, but it was steadily eroding as younger actors such as Edwin Booth began to eclipse him.

By the late 1860's, Forrest was in virtual, enforced retirement, living alone in his gloomy Philadelphia mansion. Few engagements were left him. His last performance was as Richelieu in Boston, during April, 1872. A few public readings closed his career, though he never stopped exercising, trying to keep his failing body in shape. On the morning of December 12, while pursuing rigorous exercise, Edwin Forrest sustained a massive stroke and was found dead later that day. In his will, he had made a provision for the establishment of a home for aged actors, but his estranged wife and an army of lawyers dismembered the will, and the provision died with Forrest.

SIGNIFICANCE

Edwin Forrest's rise to fame and fortune was a phenomenon characteristic of the period in American history when the country was just beginning to recognize its nationalistic aspirations and to realize its political identity. The country was ready to take a native cultural hero to its heart, especially one who could compete favorably with the British and with the rest of Europe. For the American theater, Forrest came along at the right time. He had a physical dynamism that projected an image of strength, agility, and forthrightness, those traits that Americans most cherished. Critical opinion of his ability has varied, ranging from William Winter's famous remark about Forrest being "a vast animal bewildered by a grain of genius" to more recent studies that appraise Forrest's contributions from the vantage point of history and his influence on generations of later actors.

Forrest was intensely patriotic, and his efforts to promote the American drama at a time when English drama and English actors held preference on the stage constituted a pioneering achievement from a man who had the strengths—and the moral weaknesses—of the pioneer spirit.

—*Edward Fiorelli*

FURTHER READING

Barrett, Lawrence. *Edwin Forrest*. Boston: J. R. Osgood, 1881. A fine early biography. Written less than a decade after Forrest's death, the book is valuable as an accurate and brief account by a contemporary fellow actor. The style is often laden with Victorian circumlocutions and overripe delicacies, but the assessment of Forrest that emerges is largely sympathetic and well balanced.

Boardman, Gerald. *American Theatre: A Chronicle of Comedy and Drama, 1869-1914.* New York: Oxford University Press, 1994. A year-by-year description of plays produced primarily in first-class New York theaters. An index lists Edwin Forrest and other actors that have six or more pages of information. Provides an idea of the type of theater that was produced in Forrest's day.

Csida, Joseph, and June Bundy. *American Entertainment: A Unique History of Popular Show Business.* New York: Billboard Books, 1978. A largely pictorial panorama of American theatrical history, with reproductions of playbills, posters, and advertisements, as well as portraits of famous actors. The book contains a lively assessment of Forrest's character and acting ability by fellow actor John W. Blaisdell. Also treats the theatrical milieu of the Forrest era.

Hughes, Glenn Arthur. *A History of the American Theatre: 1700-1950.* New York: Samuel French, 1951. Discusses, sometimes too sketchily, the theatrical times, customs, and personalities during Forrest's rise. A good overview rather than a specific treatment.

Moses, Montrose J., and John Mason Brown, eds. *The American Theatre as Seen by Its Critics: 1752-1934.* New York: W. W. Norton, 1934. Contains William Winter's famous critique of what he called Forrest's "ranting" style. Winter dismissed Forrest as an actor who lacked intellectual depth but possessed a "puissant animal splendour." An important anti-Forrest assessment.

Schanke, Robert A., and Kim Marra, eds. *Passing Performances: Queer Readings of Leading Players in American Theater History.* Ann Arbor: University of Michigan Press, 1998. Information about Edwin Forrest is included in this collection of critical and biographical essays about actors with unconventional sexual inclinations, on- and offstage.

Wilson, C. B. *A History of American Acting.* Bloomington: Indiana University Press, 1966. Provides an incisive account of Forrest's acting style, emphasizing the influence of Edmund Kean; rich in detail and quite readable. Most of the more important critics are cited.

SEE ALSO: Edwin Booth; Edmund Kean; William Charles Macready.

RELATED ARTICLE in *Great Events from History: The Nineteenth Century, 1801-1900:* c. 1801-1850: Professional Theaters Spread Throughout America.

WILLIAM EDWARD FORSTER
English educator

Forster was most famous for his reform in British education. An "advanced" Liberal, he was responsible for the Education Act of 1870, the Ballot Act of 1872, and advancement of other Radical causes. He was less revered for his policy of coercion in Ireland, where he served as Great Britain's chief secretary.

BORN: July 11, 1818; Bradpole, Dorsetshire, England
DIED: April 5, 1886; London, England
AREAS OF ACHIEVEMENT: Education, government and politics

EARLY LIFE

William Edward Forster grew up in a prominent Quaker family but was expelled from the Society of Friends in 1850 when he married Jane Martha, the eldest daughter of Dr. Thomas Arnold of Rugby School. His parents, William and Anna Buxton Forster, were Quaker missionaries. His father died on an antislavery mission in Tennessee in the United States in 1854. All William's formal education was in Quaker schools of Bristol and Tottenham. He traveled in Ireland as a representative of the Friends' Relief Fund during the famine.

After his marriage, Forster joined the Church of England and became a successful woolens manufacturer. A model employer, Forster was known as the "workingman's friend." He was in sympathy with the goals of Chartism and was acquainted with Robert Owen, Thomas Cooper, the Reverend Frederick Denison Maurice, Thomas and Jane Carlyle, Richard Cobden, and John Bright. Between 1861 and 1886, Forster represented Bradford in the House of Commons. Forster remained childless, but he adopted four orphans of his wife's brother, one of whom, H. O. Arnold-Forster, became a cabinet minister.

LIFE'S WORK

Other nicknames given to Forster were "Education Forster," "Buckshot Forster," and the "English Robespierre"—not all were terms of endearment. These names reflect phases of his career: Early in his parliamentary career, on the occasion of the death of Lord Palmerston, he was made undersecretary for the colonies, launching his national political career and representing a continuing interest for the rest of his life. He became a privy councillor in 1868.

During William Ewart Gladstone's government of the late 1860's and early 1870's, Forster became the equivalent of minister of education. His title was Vice President of the Committee of Council on Education. He formulated and guided through Parliament the Education Act of 1870, which provided for the first national system of elementary education for England and Wales. There were later provisions for Ireland and Scotland, as well as universally obligatory and free education provisions. The Forster Education Act did lay the foundation for a comprehensive centralized system of education, and it introduced changes in the concept of the child and the child's place in society and the community.

Like most other legislation, the bill underwent a process of political compromise. Most controversy centered on the "religious difficulty," concerns of Roman Catholics, Anglicans, and Nonconformists, the latter being especially determined to prevent monopolistic domination by the Church of England, the established religion. The "conscience clause," the denominational system, and "the Cowper-Temple amendment" excluding the teaching of catechisms all entered into the conflicts. The resulting act pleased no one and especially displeased the Nonconformists and some powerful Radicals, notably Joseph Chamberlain. (Indeed, Gladstone later blamed his defeat of 1874 on the Education Act.) The act provided for a "dual system" of elementary education: side-by-side and separate voluntary schools and local authority schools. Local school boards, elected by secret ballot and under national oversight, were established. They were empowered to provide education for all.

Forster is credited for this unprecedented achievement, but it came at a price. His constituents at Bradford were among those disappointed with the act and censured him. Perhaps more significant, Forster, in effect, was passed over for party leadership. In 1875 Gladstone "retired" for the first time. (He would return to the prime ministership twice.) In the political manipulating within the Liberal Party, Joseph Chamberlain and the powerful Nonconformists made sure that the choice for his replacement was Lord Hartington and not Forster.

Forster's obituary in *The Times* included an observation by a contemporary: "The invective of both [extremes] of irreconcilables was mercilessly poured out upon Mr. Forster." A modern analysis of educational provisions in England during the nineteenth century by Philip Gardner laments the demise of many good working-class private schools, "the people's schools," displaced by the state system.

With great tactical ability during the parliamentary sessions of 1871 and 1872, Forster guided the famous secret Ballot Act of 1872 through both houses. Debates were especially lengthy. Moving on to other reforms, he participated in such causes as antislavery, arbitration, and working men's interests; he was pro-North during the American Civil War and anti-Russian in international affairs. It was Forster's persistent questioning, in 1876, that elicited Prime Minister Benjamin Disraeli's disastrous attempt to explain the Bulgarian atrocities, the murdering of Christians by Turkish authorities. Forster, a former Quaker who obviously was moving toward the political and religious center, was an enthusiastic "volunteer," a kind of national guard or militia leader.

Gladstone resumed his leadership of the Liberal Party and was returned to office as prime minister in 1880. Forster wanted the Colonial Office but received instead the chief secretaryship for Ireland, a most challenging position at a time when the Irish leader, Charles Stewart Parnell, and his Land League were establishing positions of enormous power within and outside Ireland. Forster determined to suppress crime and violence in Ireland. He formulated and had passed, again despite extraordinary parliamentary obstruction, the Irish Coercion Bill of 1881, which provided for suspension of habeas corpus and arrest of suspects without trial.

The Irish bill was ruthlessly enforced, gaining for Forster the sobriquets "Buckshot Forster" and the "English Robespierre." In fact, the bill was counterproductive: Violence increased. It was later determined that several assassination plots were aimed at Forster. In the meantime, Gladstone and the cabinet sought alternative policies. Parnell, in a Dublin prison himself, was secretly approached. Negotiation and promises of conciliation led to an agreement, the Kilmainham (prison) Treaty of May, 1882. Forster mistrusted Parnell, objected, and announced his resignation. Four days later, his successor, Lord Frederick Cavendish, and another Irish official were brutally murdered in Phoenix Park, Dublin.

Forster continued to maintain special interest in colonial matters. He went to great lengths, including personal tours of the area, to become an expert on the Eastern Question (concerning British affairs in Egypt). He increasingly opposed Gladstone, voting for censure of the government in the sensational case of Charles "Chinese" Gordon and the Khartoum disaster (1885). Forster opposed home rule for Ireland. Shortly before his death, he became the first head of the Imperial Federation League, an imperialist pressure group.

While still a Quaker, Forster wrote his first work, an apology for the leader of the Society of Friends, William Penn, in response to a critique by the historian Thomas Babington Macaulay. Subsequently, he contributed to the *Leader, Westminster Review*, and *Edinburgh Review* on issues associated with his causes such as right to work, distress in colonial areas, and opposition to slavery. In 1875 he was elected Lord Rector of the University of Aberdeen. There is a revealing exchange between Gladstone and Forster's biographer, Thomas Wemyss Reid, editor of the *Leeds Mercury*, in the periodical *Nineteenth Century*, in 1888. Gladstone summarized the career and contributions of Forster, pointing out that Forster had often stood up for his convictions even when it brought conflict with close friends: "By political creed a Radical, he dissented from the first article of Radicalism . . . the maintenance of the Church Establishment in England."

Forster's funeral was held in Westminster Abbey, and he was buried at Burley-in-Wharfedale. His portrait, by H. T. Wells, hangs in the National Portrait Gallery in London, and a statue stands on the banks of the Thames near the location of the London School Board building. His widow died in 1890.

SIGNIFICANCE

The nicknames given to this Quaker turned Anglican statesman illustrate trends of his career and his political development: "Lond" was an affectionate appellation for a sensitive employer, "Education" signifies his most important contribution, and "Buckshot" indicates his unfortunate and coercive policies as Irish minister toward the end of his life.

William Edward Forster was a brilliant and successful politician and parliamentarian. He was particularly persuasive in debate and particularly effective in manipulating votes. Repeatedly he sacrificed personal political advancement and special interests in colonial-imperial matters to lead controversial and essential reforms. He was the quintessential Victorian reformer.

—*Eugene L. Rasor*

FURTHER READING

Armytage, W. H. "The 1870 Education Act." *British Journal of Educational Studies* 18 (June, 1970): 121-133. A detailed account of the formative education legislation, describing the areas of dispute and compromise, such as election of boards, the conscience clause, and permissive compulsion. There is a chro-nology of the legislative process; more than two hundred members spoke in the debates.

Gardner, Philip. *The Lost Elementary Schools of Victorian England*. London: Croom Helm, 1984. A modern revisionist critique of Forster's Education Act. There existed in nineteenth century England a working system of traditional, working-class, private schools, an "alternative educational culture." Some schools were linked to Chartism and Owenism. They were practical and purposeful, and they had contributed to a relatively high literacy rate. Gardner laments their demise, as they were bureaucratically replaced after 1870.

Jackson, Patrick. *Education Act Forster: A Political Biography of W. E. Forster (1818-1886)*. Madison, N.J.: Fairleigh Dickinson University Press, 1997. Biography examining Forster's life and career. Explains how Forster was one of the era's "new men"—a person from a manufacturing background, without public school or university education or connections to the political establishment, who held a significant position in British politics.

Middleton, Nigel. "The Education Act of 1870 as the Start of the Modern Concept of the Child." *British Journal of Educational Studies* 18 (June, 1970): 166-179. Forster's act brought neither free nor compulsory education, but it was quite significant because it introduced fundamental changes: a new type of society that radically altered the place and the concept of the child.

Murphy, James. *Church, State, and Schools in Britain, 1800-1970*. London: Routledge & Kegan Paul, 1971. A chapter is devoted to the impact of the Education Act of 1870 on the church-state and interdenominational controversies in Great Britain during the past two centuries. Good at sorting out the complexities associated with the denominations, radicals, Nonconformists, Anglicans, pressure groups, and other activists.

O'Callaghan, Margaret. *British High Politics and a Nationalist Ireland: Criminality, Land, and the Law Under Forster and Balfour*. New York: St. Martin's Press, 1994. Scholarly examination of the "land question" in Ireland, describing the role of Forster and others who devised and upheld British policy on this issue, and the Irish response to that policy.

Reid, Thomas Wemyss. *Life of the Right Honourable William Edward Forster*. 1888. New York: A. M. Kelley, 1970. The standard biography by a close friend, editor of the *Leeds Mercury* and a political supporter—Forster's apologist.

Roper, Henry. "W. E. Forster's Memorandum of 21 October 1869: A Re-Examination." *British Journal of Educational Studies* 21 (February, 1973): 64-75. An intriguing and speculative thesis based on new research. Roper claims there were two drafts by Forster outlining the education bill. Gladstone insisted on alterations. The omitted sections related to the two most controversial issues: religion and attendance. Contends that the original version would have forestalled basic objections by critics.

SEE ALSO: Thomas Arnold; John Bright; Joseph Chamberlain; Richard Cobden; Benjamin Disraeli; William Ewart Gladstone; Thomas Babington Macaulay; Frederick Denison Maurice; Robert Owen; Lord Palmerston; Charles Stewart Parnell.

RELATED ARTICLES in *Great Events from History: The Nineteenth Century, 1801-1900:* 19th century: Development of Working-Class Libraries; August, 1867: British Parliament Passes the Reform Act of 1867.

CHARLOTTE FORTEN
American educator and abolitionist leader

An educator, author, and abolitionist, Forten spent her life in the service of others, particularly in working for bettering the condition of her fellow African Americans.

BORN: August 17, 1837; Philadelphia, Pennsylvania
DIED: July 22, 1914; Washington, D.C.
ALSO KNOWN AS: Charlotte Forten Grimké; Charlotte Lottie Forten (full name)
AREAS OF ACHIEVEMENT: Education, social reform

EARLY LIFE

An African American, Charlotte Lottie Forten represented the fourth generation of the Forten family who were born free in the United States. She was the only child of Robert Bridges Forten and his first wife, Mary Virginia Woods Forten. Acknowledged as the most prominent and wealthy free black family in America, the Fortens avidly pursued reform, equality, and the abolition of slavery. Mary Virginia Woods Forten died when Charlotte was three. After her mother's death, Charlotte grew up under the tutelage of her aunts and other relatives.

The ideals and influences of Charlotte's family shaped the rest of her life. Her grandfather, James Forten, Sr., petitioned the U.S. Congress in 1800 to end the African American slave trade, establish guidelines to abolish slavery, and provide legislation that would weaken the Fugitive Slave Act of 1793. Congress denied the petition with a vote of eighty-five to one. Forten and his friends were not easily discouraged as they continued their pursuit for equality. Forten actively criticized legislation that would ban free blacks from Pennsylvania and the colonizationists' efforts to move free blacks to Africa. James Forten, Sr., believed that black people in the

United States were entitled to the country's resources and equal protection under the law. Similarly, Charlotte Forten's father, her aunts, and her uncles played vital roles in the abolitionist movement. The family also supported women's rights.

Surrounded by the most prominent intellectuals of the era, Charlotte knew the importance of scholarly achievement. Robert Forten arranged for his daughter to have private tutors until she could have an excellent public education in Salem, Massachusetts. At the age of sixteen in 1854, she moved to Salem, where she prepared herself for a teaching career. Determined to please her father, Charlotte applied herself to her studies. Residing with prominent black abolitionist Charles Lenox Remond and his wife in Salem, Charlotte acquainted herself with William Lloyd Garrison, Wendell Phillips, John Whittier, Abigail and Stephen Foster, and many other notable figures of the time. She thrived in her intellectual duties at the Higginson Grammar School. In 1855, she entered Salem Normal School and was graduated in 1856. Gaining a reputation as a local poet, she often submitted poems for publication. One of her poems, written in praise of William Lloyd Garrison, was published in *The Liberator* magazine in March, 1855.

LIFE'S WORK

After graduation, Charlotte Forten began teaching and continued studying in her free time. She practiced French, German, and Latin and studied European and classical history. She also enjoyed literature, including the works of her contemporaries.

The pursuit of knowledge became Forten's primary interest. As a deeply religious person, she believed that God intended her to uplift and educate the people of her race. Her self-sacrificing nature made it difficult for Forten to appreciate herself and the contributions she made. She was aware of the racial hostility around her and sometimes allowed it to influence her self-image, in spite of compliments on her appearance, her manners, and her intelligence. Furthermore, her father's move to Canada in 1853 left her somewhat estranged from her immediate family.

During her stay in Salem, Forten began the first of her series of five journals in which she discussed all aspects of her life including family, politics, education, and important leaders of the time. In 1856, she accepted a teaching position at Epes Grammar School in Salem. Soon, however, she had to return to Philadelphia after suffering from a respiratory illness and severe headaches. By July of 1857, she was back at Epes, only to resign in March, 1858, because of her recurrent health problems.

Again Charlotte returned home, where she rested and taught privately. The extra time allowed her to write poetry and essays for publication. In May of 1858, her poem entitled "Flowers" was published in *Christian Recorder* magazine. In June of that year, her essay "Glimpses of New England" appeared in the *National*

Anti-Slavery Standard. "The Two Voices" and "The Wind Among the Poplars" were printed in 1859. In January of 1860, "The Slave Girl's Prayer" was published in the *National Anti-Slavery Standard*.

Forten regained her health sufficiently to return to Salem in September of 1859, to accept a teaching post at the Higginson Grammar School. During the next spring, however, she again fell ill. While battling to regain her health, she taught briefly in a school for black children. She visited John Whittier upon her return to Salem in the summer of 1862. During this visit Whittier proposed that Forten could further the cause of her people if she went to teach the contraband slaves in the South.

On October 22, 1862, Charlotte Forten sailed to Port Royal, South Carolina. Stationed on St. Helena Island, she secured a position as a teacher among the slaves. With a fond regard for her students, she sought to prepare them for life as freed men and women. Her primary task included teaching the fundamentals of a formal education to contraband children of all ages. Forten taught reading, writing, spelling, history, and math. She emphasized the importance of proper moral and social behavior to the older black people. She leaned toward assimilation, believing that black people would find it difficult to interact with society if they remained culturally different.

Charlotte also met with prominent whites during her stay on St. Helena. As the first black teacher among the slaves, she had to face the reactions of white teachers and Union soldiers. Usually she was politely received, and people associated with her even more when abolitionist friends and acquaintances arrived. Among some of her close friends were Colonel Thomas Wentworth Higginson, who commanded the First South Carolina Volunteers, and Colonel Robert Gould Shaw, commander of the all-black Fifty-fourth Massachusetts regiment. Forten also had a close friendship with Dr. Seth Rogers, a white surgeon in Higginson's First South Carolina Volunteers.

Forten's friendships and the teaching she accomplished made her stay on St. Helena a rewarding one; eventually, however, her health failed her once again. Her declining health and news of her father's death from typhoid fever on April 25, 1864, persuaded her to move back to the North permanently. Although she still suffered from poor health, she accepted a position as secretary of the Teachers Committee of the New England Branch of the Freedmen's Union Commission in October of 1865.

Forten continued to further her own education by studying and translating French literature. Her transla-

Charlotte Forten. (Courtesy of Salem State College)

tion of *Madame Thérèse: Or, The Volunteers of '92*, a novel by Emile Erckmann and Alexandre Chatrain, was published by Scribner in 1869. Charlotte's role as secretary of the Teachers Committee required her to act as a liaison between teachers in the South who taught former slaves, and the people in the North who sent financial and material support. In October of 1871, she resigned from that position to teach at the Shaw Memorial School in Charleston, South Carolina. Forten then moved to Washington, D.C., where she taught in a black preparatory high school from 1872 to 1873. She left that position and accepted a job in the Fourth Auditor's Office of the United States Treasury Department as a first-class clerk. Although poor health continued to frustrate her, she continued to work in Washington, D.C.

Charlotte Forten married Francis Grimké on December 19, 1878. The Princeton-trained minister was twelve years her junior; he was described as intelligent, noble, and morally upright. The couple had one daughter who died in infancy. Charlotte and Francis Grimké worked hard to dispel discrimination in society. They attacked racial oppression in numerous essays and sermons. In 1885, they moved to Florida, where Francis Grimké accepted the pastorate at Laura Street Presbyterian Church. After four years they returned to Washington, D.C., and continued missionary work.

Although Charlotte Forten Grimké combined her efforts with those of her husband, she did not abandon her interest in writing poetry and essays. Several poems from that period include "A June Song" (1885), "Charlotte Corday" (1885), "At Newport" (1888); some essays that survive are "On Mr. Savage's Sermon: 'The Problem of the Hour'" (1885) and "One Phase of the Race Question" (1885). Evidently essays and poetry remained an important facet of her life. Throughout her life she continued writing her journals, of which there are five, titled by number, date, and the locations of her residence.

Forten spent her last years surrounded by family and friends. Her home was enlivened socially and intellectually with well-known political activists. She also enjoyed a close relationship with her niece Angelina Grimké, who lived in Washington, D.C., with the Grimkés. In spite of her illnesses, Charlotte lived a full, happy life. She died on July 22, 1914, in her home at the age of seventy-six.

SIGNIFICANCE

Charlotte Forten did not complete any single monumental task for which she is well known. Instead, she worked diligently to help others. In spite of frequent illnesses and insecurities, she willingly dedicated her time and energies to further the cause of her oppressed race. As a woman, Charlotte Forten far exceeded the intellectual expectations of the time. She tirelessly pursued knowledge and shared it with others. As a poet and writer, she voiced her opinions and interests to the American public. It was her philanthropic deeds, however, that she performed in the name of her race. As a free black woman, she tirelessly sought liberation, equality, and education for her people.

In an era when the white society oppressed the black, Charlotte stood out as a person who tried to correct injustices. Her quiet demeanor belied the active mind and spirit that were revealed by her pen. Her unassuming personality and eagerness to please led her in a life of service to others. The quiet dignity of Charlotte Forten and her lifelong efforts made her one of the most notable American women and an inspiration to all Americans.

—Dover C. Watkins and Elisabeth A. Cawthon

FURTHER READING

Andrews, William L., ed. *Classic African American Women's Narratives*. New York: Oxford University Press, 2003. Anthology of prose written by African American women before 1865. Includes Forten's article "Life on the Sea Islands," a description of her experiences in South Carolina, published in *Atlantic Monthly* in 1865, the first contribution by an African American woman to a major American literary magazine.

Barker-Benfield, G. J., and Catherine Clinton. *Portraits of American Women: From Settlement to the Present*. New York: St. Martin's Press, 1991. This publication is a combined volume presenting biographies of American women, arranged according to historical eras. Each biography discusses the impact each woman made on her contemporaries. The book is amply illustrated.

Braxton, Joanne M. "Charlotte Forten Grimké and the Search for a Public Voice." In *The Private Self: Theory and Practice of Women's Autobiographical Writings*, edited by Shari Benstock. Chapel Hill: University of North Carolina Press, 1988. An analysis of Forten's complete journals, based on archival research and a personal appreciation of the journals. The author maintains that, as a young woman, Forten used her journal as a means to try out different poetic voices.

Eldred, Janet Carey, and Peter Mortensen. *Imaging Rhetoric: Composing Women of the Early United States*.

Pittsburgh: University of Pittsburgh Press, 2002. Analyzes work by Forten and others to determine how women's writing developed between the American Revolution and the Civil War. Examines how women writers perceived education as a means of furthering civic goals.

Forten, Charlotte L. *The Journals of Charlotte Forten Grimké*. Edited by Brenda Stevenson. New York: Oxford University Press, 1988. This volume comprises the five journals written by Charlotte Forten. They provide insight into the politics and people of the abolitionist era. The editor provides an introduction and notes for each journal, as well as a chronology and brief biographies of people mentioned.

McPherson, James M. *The Struggle for Equality: Abolitionists and the Negro in the Civil War and Reconstruction*. Princeton, N.J.: Princeton University Press, 1964. A complete and thorough analysis of the abolitionists, including Forten, and the roles they played during and after the Civil War. Includes a biblio-graphic essay describing the manuscripts, correspondence, publications, and archives used.

Quarles, Benjamin. *Black Abolitionists*. New York: Oxford University Press, 1969. Reprint. New York: Da Capo Press, 1991. Providing the reader with a thorough background of the African American abolitionists, the author covers the early efforts of black preachers and writers to the antislavery underground; the book also describes the organizational efforts of later abolitionists. This volume includes detailed bibliographic notes separated by chapter.

SEE ALSO: Frederick Douglass; William Lloyd Garrison; Sarah and Angelina Grimké; Thomas Wentworth Higginson; Wendell Phillips.

RELATED ARTICLES in *Great Events from History: The Nineteenth Century, 1801-1900:* January 1, 1831: Garrison Begins Publishing *The Liberator*; December 3, 1847: Douglass Launches *The North Star*; December 6, 1865: Thirteenth Amendment Is Ratified.

ABBY KELLEY FOSTER
American abolitionist

A tireless opponent of slavery, Foster traveled and lectured widely to promote the establishment of antislavery societies. Her election to the business committee of the American Anti-Slavery Society in 1840 prompted a schism in the abolitionist movement over the issue of women's equality, but she recruited many women to the abolitionist cause who went on to prominence in the suffrage movement.

BORN: January 15, 1810; Pelham, Massachusetts
DIED: January 14, 1887; Worcester, Massachusetts
ALSO KNOWN AS: Abigail Kelley (birth name); Abigail Kelley Foster
AREAS OF ACHIEVEMENT: Social reform, women's rights

EARLY LIFE

Abby Kelley Foster was born Abigail Kelley, the fifth of seven children of Wing Kelley, a New England farmer descended from recent Irish immigrants, and Diana Daniels, whose family came to Massachusetts from England during the early eighteenth century. Both her parents were Quakers, and Abigail was steeped in Quaker morality and asceticism as a child. A few months after she was born, her family moved to a one-hundred-acre farm in Worcester, Massachusetts, where she spent her childhood assisting her parents in running the farm. The family periodically attended Quaker meetings at Uxbridge, but because this was some distance from their home, Abby's mother undertook most of the religious education of her children.

In 1822, Abby's father sold the Worcester farm and moved his family to a 167-acre farm near the town of Tatnuck on the outskirts of Worcester. Abby attended the one-room school in Tatnuck and a private girls' school in Worcester. With dreams of becoming a teacher, she required additional education. Her parents could not afford to send her away to school, but an older sister lent her the tuition money to attend the New England Friends Boarding School in Providence, Rhode Island.

Abby enrolled in the boarding school in 1826 and again in 1829, spending the interim at home earning more money for her tuition. Meanwhile, she received an unconventionally thorough education that included writing and rhetoric as well as mathematics, botany, astronomy, and bookkeeping. In 1830, she returned to the Worcester area and began teaching, using some of her earning to pay for two younger siblings to attend the boarding school. She continued teaching in 1835 after she moved with her parents to a new farm in the town of Millbury, six miles from Tatnuck. By the spring of 1836, her father's finances were stable, and her youngest sister's last year of schooling was paid for. Abby moved to Lynn, Massachusetts, about an hour's travel north of Boston, to begin teaching in a Quaker school there.

LIFE'S WORK

Abby was introduced to the abolitionist movement by members of Lynn's Quaker community. She joined Lynn's Female Anti-Slavery Society shortly after her arrival there and helped to sew and sell pincushions, aprons, and other articles to raise money for state and national antislavery societies. In the summer of 1836, she gathered signatures for a petition to the U.S. Congress to abolish slavery in the national capital, Washington, D.C.

Inspired by Angelina and Sarah Grimké, the first women to lecture before mixed-gender audiences, Abby began to participate more vocally in the public debate over slavery. Despite an angry mob that pelted the windows of the meeting hall with stones, she made her first speaking appearance before women affiliates of the American Anti-Slavery Society in May, 1838. A few months later, she was among the first women admitted to membership and appointed to committees in the New England Anti-Slavery Society.

Abby's activities reflected growing agitation among antislavery women, as well as some men, that women should be accorded equal status in abolitionist organizations. Resistance to this idea also intensified, however, with opponents contending that extending equality to women would alienate potential supporters and damage the cause of abolition. The matter finally boiled over at the society's May, 1840, meeting when Abby was nominated to serve on the business committee. After a majority of delegates approved her nomination, Lewis Tappan led an exodus of nearly three hundred men from the meeting in protest. The result of the walkout was the formation of the American and Foreign Anti-Slavery Society and a schism within abolitionism over the question of women's equality. In the decades that followed, many abolitionists would blame Abby for causing the schism.

After the 1840 meeting, Abby continued the efforts she had begun in the previous year to establish an antislavery society in Connecticut. She traveled and lectured throughout the state, even when hostile townspeople heckled her for being a woman who spoke publicly. Despite these challenges, her commitment to abolitionism strengthened. Dismayed by the organization's aban-

donment of its earlier antislavery leadership, Abby left the Society of Friends in 1841. She joined other abolitionists, including Frederick Douglass, in Dorr's Rebellion—a successful effort to remove the word "white" from voting provisions in the Rhode Island constitution in 1842.

Meanwhile, Abby's renown as a lecturer spread, and she was invited to appear before other antislavery audiences. Throughout the 1840's and early 1850's, she lectured, helped build abolition societies, and solicited subscriptions for abolitionist newspapers in New York, Pennsylvania, and western frontier states, including Ohio, Michigan, and Illinois. She shared many of these tours with fellow abolitionists, free blacks, and former slaves, including Sojourner Truth, Sarah Parker Remond, Charles Lenox Remond, and Stephen Symonds Foster. Foster was a former ministry student and fiery lecturer for the New Hampshire Anti-Slavery Society whom Abby married on December 21, 1845.

In April, 1847, the Fosters purchased a farm in Tatnuck. Abby gave birth to their daughter, Paulina Wright Foster—whom they nicknamed Alla—during the following month. Their farm served as a station on the Underground Railroad during the 1850's. During Abby's travels on behalf of the abolitionist movement, her husband often remained at home to care for Alla.

Abby recruited several future suffragists to the abolitionist movement. In 1848, Lucy Stone became an antislavery lecturer after graduating from Oberlin College. Susan B. Anthony met Abby in upstate New York and also became a lecturer during the 1850's. Abby herself participated in the first two National Woman's Rights Conventions in Worcester in 1850 and 1851. She also helped establish the New England Woman Suffrage Association, the first regional organization of its kind in the United States, in 1868. However, Abby diverged from these other women's rights activists by continuing to emphasize abolitionism over woman suffrage until the 1870's.

Problems with the health of both Abby and her daughter limited Abby's travels during the late 1850's. During the Civil War, Abby formed the Women's Loyal National League with Elizabeth Cady Stanton and Susan B. Anthony to collect signatures for a petition to Congress for a constitutional amendment abolishing slavery. She returned to the American Anti-Slavery Society in 1865, serving on its executive committee and urging its members that despite the end of the Civil War, their work was not complete without a constitutional amendment guaranteeing African Americans the right to vote.

After the Fifteenth Amendment, guaranteeing African American men the right to vote, was ratified in early 1870, Abby directed her energies toward the temperance and woman suffrage causes. Between 1872 and 1880, she and her husband refused to pay taxes on their Tatnuck farm as protest against Abby's inability to vote. However, they abandoned the protest when Stephen's health began to fail. He died at the farm on September 8, 1881. Abby sold the farm in 1883 and moved into a Worcester boardinghouse, where she spent her last years writing her memoirs of the abolitionist movement. On January 14, 1887—one day short of her seventy-seventh birthday—she died of asthenia in Worcester. The home that she had shared with her husband and daughter, now called Liberty Farm, became a National Historic Landmark on May 30, 1974.

SIGNIFICANCE

All too often forgotten in histories of abolitionism, Abby Kelley Foster was one of its most dedicated voices—one that helped carry the antislavery message to western frontier states far removed from the abolitionist hotbeds of the Northeast. Despite the fact that gender issues prompted the 1840 schism in the movement, Abby's persistence then and after indicates that the causes of racial integration and sexual equality could reinforce each other. However, Abby also had conflicts with woman suffrage activists, as well as abolitionists, by seeking to ensure the right of African American men to vote before women got that right.

Foster made a place of her own within the public sphere of the nineteenth century. She pursued a social and political vision that, despite her respective disagreements with each movement, nonetheless moved both African Americans and women toward greater equality.

—*Francesca Gamber*

FURTHER READING

Greene, Richard E. "Abby Kelley Foster: A Feminist Voice Reconsidered, 1810-1887." In *Multiculturalism: Roots and Realities*, edited by C. James Trotman. Bloomington: Indiana University Press, 2002. Concise overview of Foster's life that seeks to transcend the conflicts between the abolitionist and women's rights movements by describing Foster as a universal reformer.

Jeffrey, Julie Roy. *The Great Silent Army of Abolitionism: Ordinary Women in the Antislavery Movement.* Chapel Hill: University of North Carolina Press, 1998. Emphasizes the community of women abolitionists of which Foster was a part and their importance to the daily maintenance of antislavery societies.

Sterling, Dorothy. *Ahead of Her Time: Abby Kelley and the Politics of Antislavery.* New York: W. W. Norton, 1991. Detailed study of Foster, the abolitionist world in which lived, and those who populated it.

SEE ALSO: Susan B. Anthony; Frederick Douglass; Sarah and Angelina Grimké; Elizabeth Cady Stanton; Lucy Stone; Sojourner Truth; Harriet Tubman.

RELATED ARTICLES in *Great Events from History: The Nineteenth Century, 1801-1900:* July 19-20, 1848: Seneca Falls Convention; May 28-29, 1851: Akron Woman's Rights Convention; May, 1869: Woman Suffrage Associations Begin Forming; July 4, 1876: Declaration of the Rights of Women.

STEPHEN COLLINS FOSTER
American composer

Working within the most popular, sometimes vulgar, musical style of the day, Foster wrote works of unaffected simplicity and melodic beauty that became among the finest representatives of the American folk song.

BORN: July 4, 1826; Lawrenceville, Pennsylvania
DIED: January 13, 1864; New York, New York
ALSO KNOWN AS: America's Troubadour
AREA OF ACHIEVEMENT: Music

EARLY LIFE

In one of history's notable small coincidences, Stephen Collins Foster—who would become known as "America's Troubadour"—was born precisely fifty years after the day on which the Declaration of Independence was signed and on the same day that the Founders Thomas Jefferson and John Adams died. The ninth child of William and Eliza Collins, "Stephy," as he was sometimes called, was the baby of the family, nurtured in a warm and loving environment. His father, one of the pioneers in the establishment of Pittsburgh as a thriving "Western" city, was a middle-class businessperson, would-be entrepreneur, and minor public official whose fortunes were always tottering between solvency and indigence, a condition that would carry over into Stephen's own later life.

Tutored first by his older sisters, Foster was educated at a number of private academies in and around Pittsburgh and in Towanda in northern Pennsylvania. Gentle, sensitive, and often pensive, he was never the scholar, and he chafed under the discipline of academic life. His only real interest was in music, a subject that he studied on his own and for which he early showed a rare ability. Even his father, who wished a business career for his youngest son, could not help but observe the boy's "strange talent." Family anecdotes describe the seven-year-old boy as picking up a flute for the first time and in a few minutes playing "Hail Columbia" and of his teaching himself to play the piano. Sent to Jefferson College in Canonsburg, Pennsylvania, Foster dropped out after a week, homesick, and returned to his family in the summer of 1841.

Over the next few years, Foster lived at home, visiting relatives with his mother and occasionally attending theatrical events and concerts with his favorite brother, Morrison, his first official biographer. During this tranquil period, Foster became increasingly absorbed in his music. In December, 1844, he published his first composition, the music to a poem, "Open Thy Lattice, Love." Derivative and harmonically awkward, the song was a creditable piece of work for a boy of sixteen and already bore the naturalness that was to be its composer's trademark.

LIFE'S WORK

Home life was thus somehow a catalyst to Foster's inspiration. Even after the publication of his first song, Foster continued living with his family despite efforts on their part to find him some employment. "Stephy" was always the dreamer, though the only photograph of him, taken years later when he had become famous, shows a strong face, with prominent brow, large, dark eyes, and full, almost pouting lips.

In 1845, Foster joined the Knights of S.T., a club of young men who met twice weekly at the Foster home. The members wrote verses and sang popular songs of the day. Membership in this club was probably crucial in determining Foster's career, for it provided the young composer with both a ready audience for his work and a further source of inspiration. Through the club, he came into contact with examples of the minstrel song, or, as it was then called, the "Ethiopian" melody.

Additionally, the minstrel show was just coming into its prime as a popular American form of entertainment. Pittsburgh, in fact, had, in the fall of 1830, been the scene of one of the earliest minstrel shows when a twenty-two-year-old Thomas "Daddy" Rice, the "father" of American minstrelsy, first put on blackface and cavorted on the stage as Jim Crow, a good-humored, illiterate black man. Whether Foster had seen this first performance is uncertain, but it is clear that by the 1840's he had become friends with Daddy Rice and had submitted to him a number of pieces in the minstrel style, which Rice politely refused.

Foster kept composing, however, and the Knights kept singing his songs "in almost every parlor in Pittsburgh," so that by 1847 Foster's songs were being circulated largely from singer to singer, a fact that explains their success as authentic creations of a basically oral folk culture rather than as products of a formal musical tradition. Emerging from this oral culture was the first of his great songs. "Oh! Susanna," a nonsense song in the American minstrel manner, was first sung in Andrews's Eagle Ice Cream Saloon in Pittsburgh in September,

1847, though it was not published until the following year.

"Oh! Susanna" made Foster famous, not only because minstrel companies all over the country appropriated it and publishers and other songwriters altered and rearranged it, but also because thousands of pioneers carried the song along with their hopes to the goldfields of California.

Curiously, Foster was at first somewhat blasé about payment for his early work. In a letter dated 1849, for example, he mentions that he gave manuscript copies of "Oh! Susanna" to "several persons" before submitting a copy to W. C. Peters for publication. Scores of pirated editions of this and later songs point out the laxity in those days with regard to copyrights, but it is clear also that Foster at first regarded songwriting as a questionable occupation for a gentleman. The fact that he was at least partially embarrassed by or indifferent to fame as a songwriter is evident in the fact that he gave permission to the famous minstrel impresario Edwin P. Christy to perform and publish his "Old Folks at Home"—popularly known as "Swanee River"—as Christy's own. In return, Foster was paid fifteen dollars and was encouraged to submit further work.

Foster's association with Christy, in fact, was crucial to his career. The Christy Minstrels were among the most popular theatrical troupes before the Civil War, and Foster's connection with Christy assured him of both a steady income and a ready market. Christy's Minstrels performed all over the country, transmitting Foster's songs orally months before they were ever published.

The early 1850's were Foster's most prolific period and the happiest of his life. In July, 1850, he had married Jane McDowell, daughter of an eminent Pittsburgh physician who had treated Charles Dickens on his stopover in Pittsburgh during his famous American tour during the 1840's.

Always close to his family, Foster took his young wife to live with his parents, and once again the surroundings of familial love and contentment fueled his creative powers. Often locking himself in his study for hours—a labor that belied the spontaneity of the finished compositions—he produced dozens of his best songs during the next two or three years, securing Firth and Pond of New York as his principal publisher. During this period, Foster composed "Camptown Races" (1850), "Ring de Banjo" (1851), "Old Folks at Home" (1851), "Massa's in de Cold, Cold Ground" (1852), "My Old Kentucky Home" (1853), "Jeanie with the Light Brown Hair" (1854)—inspired by his wife—and "Come Where My

Love Lies Dreaming" (1855), all masterpieces that have never lost popular appeal and that have secured for their composer a preeminent place in nineteenth century American music.

The year 1855 marked a turning point in Foster's life and career. At the peak of his fame and at the height of his creative powers, Foster could now command unusual prerogatives from his publishers, one of which was to prove disastrous. He was temperamentally unfit for the plodding routine of the businessperson, but songwriting was a joy, and he soon convinced himself that he could live comfortably on his *potential* as a composer. In effect, Foster pawned his future for a secure present. He developed the practice of drawing advances from his publishers, selling outright all future royalties from his published songs. As soon as a song was printed, he would calculate its future value and sell its royalties.

Living thus beyond his means, and having to write songs to live, Foster composed over the next few years scores of works, most of which were markedly inferior to his early material. "Come Where My Love Lies Dreaming" was written in 1855, but not until 1860, with

Stephen Collins Foster. (Library of Congress)

"Old Black Joe," did he write a song with the powerful simplicity of his best work. In between were temperance songs and sentimental ballads, the spontaneous gaiety of his minstrel style all but gone. Not unexpectedly, Foster was experiencing domestic problems as well. His relationship with Jane became strained, and on several occasions the couple separated because of Foster's inability to support her.

By the advent of the Civil War in 1860, Foster had moved to New York City to be nearer his publishers. From this time on, he became a sort of song factory, churning out to order virtual potboilers for a public eager to hear anything new from him. Deeper in debt, he produced work that was facile, commercial, and dull: saccharine hymns, topical comic pieces, patriotic war songs, and the usual sentimental ballads of mother, home, and sloe-eyed love. Little of this work is of any importance in the canon of Foster's songs. It represents, rather, a pitiful decline in his art and fortunes.

Eventually, Foster received less and less for his work—work that he must have sensed was inferior to his earlier compositions. He began drinking heavily, getting steadily weaker and falling into states of depression. Poor and in ill health, Foster was taken to Bellevue Hospital in January, 1864, where he died three days later. Found in his pockets were a few scraps of paper and a few coins totaling thirty-eight cents. In March of that year, a last great song was published from among his final papers. Called "Beautiful Dreamer," it was a final return to the gentle lyricism and honesty of his greatest work.

SIGNIFICANCE

It is ironic that the man whose music is richly evocative of the Old South never traveled below the Mason-Dixon line. Such irony suggests the most telling characteristic of Foster as a composer—his instinctive, unschooled, spontaneous lyricism. Foster was a self-taught composer whose lack of formal, technical knowledge of the rules of composition hampered the success of his instrumental pieces, his dozen or so attempts to write "serious" music. For simple, unaffected melody, however—for "parlor" songs sung by respectable, middle-class folks—Foster's songs are unsurpassed among the works of nineteenth century composers.

Though at first reluctant, Foster steadfastly held to his commitment to become the best of the "Ethiopian" melodists. He produced songs that in effect reformed the American minstrel style. His best work bore none of the vulgarity common to the minstrel show; there was no coarseness, no crudity even in his nonsense and comic songs. His work reveals the honest, homespun simplicity that was the strength of the oral folk tradition.

—*Edward Fiorelli*

FURTHER READING

Emerson, Ken. *Doo-dah!: Stephen Foster and the Rise of American Popular Culture.* New York: Simon & Schuster, 1997. Well-researched and documented biography, examining Foster's life and music within the context of events and personalities of his era. Emerson describes the combination of racism and genuine compassion for African Americans that are reflected in Foster's songs.

Foster, Morrison. *My Brother Stephen.* Indianapolis: Hollenbeck Press, 1932. A brief account of Foster's life, particularly his relationship with his family. Not totally objective, it ignores much of the less flattering aspects of Foster's life and character but does provide, as the earliest biography, some important information about his music.

Howard, John Tasker. *Stephen Foster: America's Troubadour.* New York: Thomas Y. Crowell, 1962. The definitive biography, well researched and unbiased. Drawing almost too minutely on private collections of Foster material, including family papers, Howard recounts Foster's schooling, travel, relationships, and financial habits. A thorough appendix includes a complete list of Foster's compositions.

Lott, Eric. *Love and Theft: Blackface Minstrelsy and the American Working Class.* New York: Oxford University Press, 1993. Lott analyzes the complex racial meaning of minstrelsy, arguing that to white working-class audiences, blackface entertainment expressed their paradoxical admiration and contempt, envy and fear, of African Americans. He focuses on Foster's music in chapter 7, "California Gold and European Revolution: Stephen Foster and the American, 1848."

Milligan, Harold Vincent. *Stephen Collins Foster: A Biography of America's Folk-Song Composer.* New York: G. Schirmir, 1920. The first objective biography. Pays particular attention to Foster's early life and to what its author perceives as a major drawback to Foster's cultivation of serious musical taste. Also treats Foster's final days and his undramatic death.

Walters, Raymond. *Stephen Foster, Youth's Golden Gleam: A Sketch of His Life and Background in Cincinnati, 1846-1850.* Princeton, N.J.: Princeton University Press, 1936. Treats a period of Foster's life while the composer was a bookkeeper for his brother,

Dunning. Suggests that the Cincinnati waterfront, with its wharves and its black music, was a profound influence on Foster's creative achievements. Both Howard and Milligan (see above) also discuss this period, though both regard it as somewhat "sketchy."

Wittke, Carl. *Tambo and Bones.* Durham, N.C.: Duke University Press, 1930. An accurate and entertaining history of the American minstrel show, the book provides a clear perspective through which to appreciate

Foster's success and his contribution to American music.

SEE ALSO: Joel Chandler Harris; Scott Joplin.

RELATED ARTICLES in *Great Events from History: The Nineteenth Century, 1801-1900:* February 6, 1843: First Minstrel Shows; 1850's-1880's: Rise of Burlesque and Vaudeville; 1890's: Rise of Tin Pan Alley Music.

CHARLES FOURIER
French social reformer

Fourier was one of the founders of nineteenth century utopian socialism. Although the few experiments in building a model community based upon his theories proved short-lived, his writings have continued to attract interest.

BORN: April 7, 1772; Besançon, France
DIED: October 10, 1837; Paris, France
ALSO KNOWN AS: François-Marie-Charles Fourrier (full name)
AREA OF ACHIEVEMENT: Social reform

EARLY LIFE

Charles Fourier (few-ree-ay) was born François-Marie-Charles Fourrier; he dropped the second *r* in his surname around the time he turned eighteen. He was the fifth child and only son of a prosperous cloth merchant. In 1781, his father died, leaving him a substantial inheritance. He attended the local Collège de Besançon, where he received a solid if uninspiring classical education. His ambition appears to have been to study military engineering at the École de Génie Militaire, but he lacked the noble status requisite for admission. He was apprenticed to a cloth merchant around 1790, first at Rouen, then at Lyons. He was ill-suited for, and unhappy in, the world of business.

Fourier was involved in the savagely suppressed 1793 counterrevolutionary uprising in Lyons against the Convention (central government). As a result, he was imprisoned and narrowly escaped execution. In 1794, he was called for military service; he was discharged two years later. Although the details remain unclear, he lost the bulk of his inheritance. He thereafter worked as a traveling salesperson and then as an unlicensed broker.

Fourier also began writing short articles and poems, which appeared in the Lyons newspapers starting in

1801. He set forth an outline of his developing ideas in two papers written in late 1803, "Harmonie universelle" and "Lettre au Grand-Juge." In 1808, he published—anonymously and with a false place of publication to protect himself against prosecution by the authorities—his first major work, *Théorie des quatre mouvements and des destinées générales* (*The Social Destiny of Man: Or, Theory of the Four Movements*, 1857).

In 1812, Fourier's mother died, leaving him a modest lifetime annuity. The money allowed him to devote himself full time to elaborating his ideas in a projected *Grand Traité* (great treatise). Although he never finished this great treatise, he did publish in 1822 his two-volume *Traité de l'association domestique-agricole* (later retitled *Théorie de l'unité universelle*; *Social Science: The Theory of Universal Unity*, 185?). A briefer and more accessible statement of his position would appear in his *Le Nouveau Monde industriel et sociétaire: Ou, Invention du procédé d'industrie attrayante et naturelle distribuée en series passionées* (1829).

Fourier never married, appears to have had no lasting romantic attachment, and lived most of his life in cheap lodging houses and hotels. He was a deeply neurotic personality—what the French call a *maniaque* (crank). There is even evidence that he seriously thought himself to be the son of God. As he grew older, he became increasingly paranoid about his supposed persecution by his enemies. His jealousy of rival would-be saviors of humanity resulted in an 1831 pamphlet, *Pièges et charlatanisme des deux sectes Saint-Simon et Owen, qui promettent l'association et le progrès* (traps and charlatanism of the Saint-Simonian and Owen sects, who promise association and progress). The last of his major writings to be published during his lifetime was the two-volume *La Fausse Industrie morcelée, répugnante, men-*

songère, et l'antidote, l'industrie naturelle, combinée, attrayante, veridique, donnant quadruple produit et perfection extrème en tous qualités (1835-1836). A manuscript entitled *Le Nouveau Monde amoureux*—written around 1817-1818 and demonstrating the central place in his thinking of his vision of a sexual revolution—was not published until 1967.

LIFE'S WORK

Fourier's starting point was his repudiation of the eighteenth century philosophes, who had enthroned reason as humankind's guide. He dismissed reason as a weak force compared with the passions, or instinctual drives. He postulated the existence of twelve fundamental human passions. These in turn fell into three major categories. There were the so-called luxurious passions (the desires of the five senses of sight, hearing, taste, smell, and touch); the four group, or affective, passions (ambition, friendship, love, and family feeling or parenthood); and the serial, or distributive, passions (the "cabalist" desire for intrigue, the "butterfly" yearning for variety, and the "composite," or desire for the simultaneous satisfaction

Charles Fourier. (Library of Congress)

of more than a single passion). Fourier held that because all the passions were created by God, they were naturally good and harmonious. Thus, they should be allowed the freest and fullest expression. He preached that humankind had achieved sufficient mastery over the forces of the natural world to make possible the satisfaction of all human wants.

The trouble was that in capitalist society—which Fourier in his sixteen-stage scheme of human history termed Civilization—most people found their passions repressed or, even worse, so distorted as to become vices. What was required was a new social order that would channel the passions in salutary directions. His ideal world—which he called Harmony—was a paradise of sensuous enjoyments: a continuous round of eating, drinking, and lovemaking. The prerequisite for its attainment was a properly designed community, or phalanx, that would constitute the basic social unit. Each phalanx would consist of sixteen hundred to two thousand persons. This number would allow inclusion within the phalanx of the full range of different individual personality types and thus of potential combinations of passions. There were, he calculated, no more than 810 fundamentally different varieties of men and the same number for women. The perfect society required that each type interact with all other types.

All the members of the phalanx would live in one large building, known as the phalanstery. He even specified the architectural design: a building about six stories high, consisting of a long main body and two wings with inner courtyards and a parade ground immediately in front. Almost always, individuals would not engage in their occupations or pastimes alone or as part of a haphazard gathering, but rather as members of scientifically arranged groupings. Individuals with the same interests would voluntarily form a small group, and groups with like occupations would similarly combine naturally into what he termed a series. This organizational scheme would give full scope simultaneously to the cooperative and competitive impulses, because each group would consist of volunteers passionately devoted to the purpose of the group and the different groups would vie with one another to win the praise of the other members of the phalanx.

Boredom would be eliminated because of frequent changes in jobs and sex partners. Phalanx members would work at any given task typically only one hour per day, with two hours as the maximum. Leadership would be similarly rotated depending upon the activity. Most important, phalanx members would join only those groups and series that attracted them. Within each group, they would perform only that part of the work that appealed to them. Thus, for example, the would-be Nero would find an outlet for his bloodthirsty tastes by working as a butcher. This matching of job with personality was the fundamental difference between Civilization and Harmony. "In the former," Fourier explained,

> a man or a woman performs twenty different functions belonging to a single kind of work. In the latter a man performs a single function in twenty kinds of work, and he chooses the function which he likes while rejecting the other nineteen.

Fourier did not propose to abolish private property. He allowed differential rewards for those with superior creative abilities and, accordingly, differences in the degree of pleasures according to resources. Even the poorest in the phalanx would lead much richer and more pleasurable lives than was attainable by even the richest in the existing society. As for who would do society's so-called dirty jobs, he had a simple answer: children. "God," he explained,

> gave children these strange tastes to provide for the execution of various repulsive tasks. If manure has to be spread over a field, youths will find it a repugnant job but groups of children will devote themselves to it with greater zeal than to clean work.

A revolutionary educational policy was at the heart of Fourier's system. Whereas civilized education repressed the faculties of the child, the new education that he envisaged would be aimed at developing all the child's physical and intellectual faculties, especially the capacities for pleasure and enjoyment. He most antagonized contemporary opinion—and dismayed even many of his disciples—by his advocacy of free love. He was convinced that the amorous desires of most people were polygamous. He thus attacked the family as the number one example of an unnatural institution, stifling both men and women. Marriage in contemporary society, he charged, was "pure brutality, a casual pairing off provoked by the domestic bond without any illusion of mind or heart."

From 1822 on—except for a brief return to Lyons in 1825—Fourier lived in Paris. He was constantly appealing to would-be patrons to finance the establishment of an experimental phalanx to provide scientific proof of the correctness of his theories. Every day on the stroke of twelve noon, he would return to his lodgings to await the arrival of the hoped-for benefactor. He was the target of frequent newspaper ridicule, but he attracted a small but loyal band of disciples. In 1832, the first Fourierist journal, *Le Phalanstère*, was launched; the same year witnessed the first attempt to establish a model phalanx at Condé-sur-Vesgre. From 1833 on, Fourier suffered from worsening intestinal problems that sapped his health. For the last year of his life, he was an invalid confined to his apartment. On the morning of October 10, 1837, the building concierge found him dead, kneeling by his bed dressed in his frock coat.

SIGNIFICANCE

Charles Fourier himself constitutes a fascinating psychological problem, given the contrast between his free-ranging, sensual imagination and the crabbed drabness of his personal life. Much of his writing is simply incoherent—rambling, repetitive, and filled with invented pseudoscientific jargon. He goes into flights of fantasy—such as his portrayal of the planets copulating, his prophecy of the oceans turning into lemonade, and his vision of the pests of man, such as fleas, rats, crocodiles, and lions, becoming transformed into more pleasant species, antifleas, antirats, anticrocodiles, and antilions—that raise questions about his sanity. However, his vision of a freer, happier, and more harmonious social order to replace the poverty, misery, and conflict of early industrial society exerted a strong attraction upon his sensitive-minded contemporaries, ranging from the young Fyodor Dostoevski to the New England Transcendentalists assembled at Brook Farm.

Although all the attempts to establish a model phalanx proved failures, Fourier has received renewed attention as the prophet of what have become the animating values for much of Western society—liberation of the senses from the repressions of middle-class life, exaltation of the instincts, and an all-pervading impulse toward self-gratification. He has attracted perhaps most interest as the precursor of the sexual revolution because of his calls for freedom from sexual taboos, his attacks on the barrenness of the marriage relationship, and his implicit assumption that there was no such thing as a sexual norm. He anticipated Sigmund Freud in key respects, particularly in his recognition of the importance of the sexual drive and the mechanisms for its repression and sublimation. Fourier's direct contribution to these later developments was minor, if not nil. However, he was a more astute reader of human nature—and thus of the future—than the eighteenth century philosophes whom he so strongly attacked.

—John Braeman

FURTHER READING

Altman, Elizabeth C. "The Philosophical Bases of Feminism: The Feminist Doctrines of the Saint-Simonians and Charles Fourier." *Philosophical Forum* 7 (Spring/Summer, 1974): 277-293. A laudatory examination of Fourier's advanced (at least from a present-day feminist perspective) ideas concerning the stifling effects of middle-class marriage upon women and his egalitarian views about the role of women in the phalanx.

Beecher, Jonathan. *Charles Fourier: The Visionary and His World.* Berkeley: University of California Press, 1986. An impressive piece of research into the extant published and manuscript materials on Fourier, this work should remain for the foreseeable future the definitive biography. The book is divided into three major parts: Part 1 details Fourier's life up to 1822, part 2 is a penetrating explication of his ideas, and part 3 traces his efforts to publicize and implement his program.

Blaug, Mark, ed. *Dissenters: Charles Fourier (1772-1837), Henri de St. Simon (1760-1825), Pierre-Joseph Proudhon (1809-1865), John A. Hobson (1858-1940).* Brookfield, Vt.: E. Elgar, 1992. Examines the economic theories of Fourier and three other philosophers with alternative social visions.

Fourier, Charles. *The Theory of the Four Movements.* Edited by Gareth Stedman Jones and Ian Patterson. New York: Cambridge University Press, 1996. An English translation of Fourier's first book, in which he describes some of his utopian ideas.

_____. *The Utopian Vision of Charles Fourier: Selected Texts on Work, Love, and Passionate Attraction.* Edited and translated by Jonathan Beecher and Richard Bienvenu. Boston: Beacon Press, 1971. As the subtitle indicates, the book contains English translations of selections from Fourier's writings. The editor-translators have avoided the temptation of pruning the nonsense and even gibberish with which Fourier filled so many of his pages; students without a knowledge of French thus can get at least a taste of Fourier's style. The seventy-five-page introduction provides an excellent, relatively brief introduction to Fourier's thinking.

Guarneri, Carl J. *The Utopian Alternative: Fourierism in Nineteenth-Century America.* Ithaca, N.Y.: Cornell University Press, 1991. Explores Fourier's influence in the United States, where the religious, social, and economic turmoil of the 1830's led some Americans to create communal living arrangements and other utopian experiments in the years before the Civil War.

Manuel, Frank E. *The Prophets of Paris.* Cambridge, Mass.: Harvard University Press, 1962. The author has written a perceptive account of five late eighteenth/early nineteenth century French prophets of a transformed social order—Anne-Robert-Jacques Turgot, Marquis de Condorcet, and Comte de Saint-Simon, and Auguste Comte, along with Fourier. Manuel explains the similarities and differences in their ideas. He gives a sympathetic appraisal of Fourier as Freud's precursor in his psychological insights.

Poster, Mark, ed. *Harmonian Man: Selected Writings of Charles Fourier.* Garden City, N.Y.: Doubleday, 1971. Although Poster's introduction is short, the volume offers a handy selection of translated excerpts from Fourier's writings. Approximately half of the selections are nineteenth century translations, mostly by Arthur Brisbane. The rest—including excerpts from *Le Nouveau Monde amoureux*—were translated for this volume by Susan Ann Hanson.

Riasanovsky, Nicholas V. *The Teaching of Charles Fourier.* Berkeley: University of California Press, 1969. A lucidly written, comprehensive, and systematic analysis of the major themes in Fourier's thinking that should be the starting point for any serious examination of his ideas. An admirer of Fourier, Riasanovsky makes him appear too sensible and perhaps too modern by downplaying the fantastic and bizarre elements in his writings.

Spencer, M. C. *Charles Fourier.* Boston: Twayne, 1981. The volume includes a brief biographical sketch along with a summary of the major points in Fourier's thinking. Spencer's interest lies on the aesthetic side, and he has suggestive comments about Fourier's influence on French literature from Charles Baudelaire to the Surrealists.

SEE ALSO: Charles Baudelaire; Auguste Comte; Fyodor Dostoevski; Aleksandr Herzen; Karl Marx; Pierre-Joseph Proudhon.

RELATED ARTICLES in *Great Events from History: The Nineteenth Century, 1801-1900:* 1819: Schopenhauer Publishes *The World as Will and Idea*; 1820's-1850's: Social Reform Movement; 1839: Blanc Publishes *The Organization of Labour.*

JOSEPH FOURIER
French mathematician and physicist

In deriving and solving equations representing the flow of heat in bodies, Fourier developed analytical methods that proved to be useful in the fields of pure mathematics, applied mathematics, and theoretical physics.

BORN: March 21, 1768; Auxerre, France
DIED: May 16, 1830; Paris, France
ALSO KNOWN AS: Baron Fourier; Jean-Baptiste-Joseph Fourier (full name)
AREAS OF ACHIEVEMENT: Mathematics, physics

EARLY LIFE

The twelfth child of master tailor Joseph Fourier and the ninth child of Édmie Fourier, Jean-Baptiste-Joseph Fourier (few-ree-ay) became an orphan at the age of nine. He was placed in the local Royal Military School run by the Benedictine Order and soon demonstrated his passion for mathematics. Fourier and many biographers after him attribute the onset of his lifelong poor health to his habit of staying up late, reading mathematical texts in the empty classrooms of the school. He completed his studies in Paris. He was denied entry into the military and decided to enter the Church and teach mathematics.

Fourier remained at the Benedictine Abbey of St. Benoit-sur-Loire from 1787 to 1789, occupied with teaching and frustrated that he had little time for mathematical research. Whether he left Paris because of the impending revolution or because he did not want to take his vows is uncertain. He returned to Auxerre and from 1789 to 1794 served as professor and taught a variety of subjects at the Royal Military School. The school was run by the Congregation of St. Maur, the only religious order excluded from the postrevolutionary decree confiscating the property of religious orders.

Fourier became involved in local politics in 1793 and was drawn deep into the whirlpool as internal unrest and external military threats turned the committees on which he served into agents of the Terror. Fourier made the mistake of defending a group of men who turned out to be enemies of Robespierre. He was arrested and nearly guillotined, spared only by the death of Robespierre. He became a student at the short-lived École Normale, mainly to have the opportunity to go to Paris and meet Pierre-Simon Laplace, Joseph-Louis Lagrange, and Gaspard Monge, the foremost mathematicians in France. In 1795, the École Polytechnique was opened, and Fourier was invited to join the faculty, but he was arrested once again,

this time by the extreme reactionaries who hated him for his role in the Terror, even though he did much to moderate the excesses of the Terror in Auxerre. As with many other aspects of Fourier's life during the Revolution, the exact reason for his release is unknown. In any case, he was released and occupied himself with teaching and administrative duties at the École Polytechnique.

In 1798, Fourier was chosen to be part of Napoleon I's expedition to Egypt. Fourier was elected permanent secretary of the newly formed Institute of Egypt, held a succession of administrative and diplomatic posts in the French expedition, and conducted some mathematical research. Upon his return to France in 1801, Fourier was named by Napoleon to be the prefect of Isère, one of the eighty-four newly formed divisions of France. It is during his prefecture that Fourier began his life's work.

LIFE'S WORK

Fourier's work in the development of an analytical theory of heat diffusion dates from the early nineteenth century, when he was in his early thirties, and after he had distinguished himself in administration of scientific and political institutions in Egypt. He had demonstrated a talent and passion for mathematics early, but he had not yet made significant contributions to the field. It was during whatever time he could spare from his administrative duties as prefect that he made his lasting contribution to physics and mathematics.

Fourier remained at Grenoble until Napoleon's downfall in 1814. He turned a poorly managed department into a well-managed one in a short time. It is not clear why Fourier began to study the diffusion of heat, but in 1804 he began with a rather mathematically abstract derivation of heat flow in a metal plate. He conducted numerous experiments in an attempt to establish the laws regulating the flow of heat. He expanded the scope of problems addressed, polished the mathematical formalism, and infused physical concepts into the derivation of the equations that expressed heat flow. In 1807, he presented a long paper to the French Academy of Sciences, but opposition from Laplace and others prevented its publication. At issue was a fundamental disagreement over mathematical rigor and the underlying physical concepts.

Laplace's first objection was that Fourier's methods were not mathematically rigorous. Fourier claimed that any function could be represented by an infinite trigonometric series—a sum of an infinite number of sine and cosine functions each with a determinable coefficient. Such series were instrumental in Fourier's formulation and solution of the problems of the diffusion of heat. Only later were Fourier's methods shown to be strictly rigorous mathematically. The second objection concerned the method of derivation. Laplace preferred to explain phenomena by the action of central forces acting between particles of matter. Fourier, while not denying the correctness or the usefulness of that approach, took a different approach. Heat, for Fourier, was the flow of a substance and not some relation between atoms and their motions. He attempted, successfully, to account for the phenomenon of heat diffusion through mathematical analysis. His paper of 1807 languished in the archives of the Academy of Sciences, unpublished.

As a result of his work in Egypt and his position as permanent secretary of the Institute of Egypt, Fourier edited and wrote the historical introduction to the *Description de l'Égypte* (1809-1828; description of Egypt). He worked on this project from around 1802 until 1810.

A prize was offered in 1810 by the Academy of Sciences on the subject of heat diffusion, and Fourier slightly revised and expanded his 1807 paper to include discussion of diffusion in infinite bodies and terrestrial and radiant heat. Fourier won the prize, but he had faced no serious competition. The jury criticized the paper in much the same way as the 1807 paper had been criticized, and again Fourier's work was not published. Eventually, after years of prodding, the work was published in 1815.

Fourier was probably not happy being virtually exiled from Paris, the scientific capital of France. He seemed destined to live out his days in Grenoble. With Napoleon's abdication in April, 1814, Fourier provisionally retained his job as prefect during the transfer of power to Louis XVIII. He also managed to alter the route Napoleon took from Paris to exile in Elba, bypassing Grenoble, in order to avoid a confrontation between himself and Napoleon. Upon Napoleon's return in March, 1815, Fourier prepared the defenses of the town and made a diplomatic retreat to Lyons. Fourier returned before completing the journey upon learning that Napoleon had made him prefect of the Rhône department. He was dismissed before Napoleon fell once again.

Fourier's scientific work began again after 1815. One of his former pupils was now a prefect and appointed Fourier director of the Bureau of Statistics for the Seine department, which included Paris. He now had a modest income and few demands on his time. Fourier was named to the Academy of Sciences in 1817. During the next five years, he actively participated in the affairs of the Academy, sitting on commissions, writing reports, and conducting his own research. His administrative duties increased in 1822, when he was elected to the powerful position of permanent secretary of the mathematical section of the Academy. His *Théorie analytique de la chaleur* (1822; *The Analytical Theory of Heat*, 1878) differs only slightly from his 1810 essay. The papers he wrote in his later years contained little that was new. He led a satisfying academic life in his last years, but his health began to deteriorate. His rheumatism had returned, he had trouble breathing, and he was sensitive to cold. Fourier died from a heart attack in May, 1830.

SIGNIFICANCE

The core of Joseph Fourier's scientific work is *The Analytical Theory of Heat*. This work is basically a textbook describing the application of theorems from pure mathematics applied to the problem of the diffusion of heat in bodies. Fourier was able to express the distribution of heat inside and on the surface of a variety of bodies, both at equilibrium and when the distribution was changing because of heat loss or gain.

Fourier significantly influenced three different fields: pure mathematics, applied mathematics, and theoretical physics. In pure mathematics, Fourier's most lasting influence has been the definition of a mathematical function. He realized that any mathematical function can be represented by a trigonometric series, no matter how difficult to manipulate the function may appear. Some scholars single out this concept as the stepping-stone to the work of pure mathematicians later in the century, which resulted in the modern definition of a function. Additional influences are that of a clarification of a notational issue involving integral calculus and properties of infinite trigonometric series.

Applied mathematics has been influenced to a great extent by Fourier's use of trigonometric series and techniques of integration. The class of problems that Fourier series and Fourier integrals can solve extends far beyond diffusion of heat. His methods form the foundation of applied mathematics techniques taught to undergraduates. Some mathematicians before him had used trigonometric series in the solutions of problems, but the clarity, scope, and rigor that he brought to the field were significant.

Fourier's influence in theoretical physics is more subdued, perhaps because of the completeness of his results. There was little room for others to extend the physical aspects of Fourier's work—his results did not need extending. Other branches of physics appear to have been influenced by his approach, and a direct influence on the issue of determining the age of the earth by calculating its heat loss has been documented.

—*Roger Sensenbaugh*

FURTHER READING

Bell, Eric T. *The Development of Mathematics*. 2d ed. New York: McGraw-Hill, 1945. Presents a narrative history of the decisive epochs in the development of mathematics without becoming overly technical. The majority of references to Fourier appear in chapter 13.

_____. *Men of Mathematics*. New York: Simon & Schuster, 1986. First published in 1937, this book remains one of the best accounts of the history of mathematics. The contributions of Fourier are discussed in chapter 12, "Friends of an Emperor."

Fourier, Joseph. *The Analytical Theory of Heat*. Translated by Alexander Freeman. 1878. Reprint. Mineola, N.Y.: Dover, 2003. Fourier's preliminary discourse to his most famous work explains in clear terms what he is attempting in the work. Devoid of technical matters, this book offers the reader a glimpse of why Fourier has achieved the status he has.

Fox, Robert. "The Rise and Fall of Laplacian Physics." *Historical Studies in the Physical Sciences* 4 (1974): 89-136. This paper presents a description of the research program of Laplace, which dominated French science at one of its most successful periods, from 1805 to 1815. Fourier led the revolt against this program.

Friedman, Robert Marc. "The Creation of a New Science: Joseph Fourier's Analytical Theory of Heat." *Historical Studies in the Physical Sciences* 8 (1977): 73-100. This paper concentrates on conceptual and physical issues rather than the mathematical aspects stressed in most older works. Also discusses how Fourier's philosophy of science compared to that of his contemporaries.

Grattan-Guinness, Ivor, with J. R. Ravetz. *Joseph Fourier, 1768-1830: A Survey of His Life and Work, Based on a Critical Edition of His Monograph on the Propagation of Heat, Presented to the Institute de France in 1807*. Cambridge, Mass.: MIT Press, 1972. Intertwines a close study of Fourier's life and work with a critical edition of his 1807 monograph. The 1807 monograph is in French, but everything else is in English. Contains a bibliography of Fourier's writings, a list of translations of his works, and a secondary bibliography.

Herivel, John. *Joseph Fourier: The Man and the Physicist*. Oxford, England: Clarendon Press, 1975. Although this work does not claim to be the definitive biography of Fourier, it goes much further than any other work written in English. Although the book is almost devoid of technical detail, the prospective reader would benefit from a knowledge of the history of France from 1789 to 1830.

James, Ioan. *Remarkable Physicists: From Galileo to Yukawa*. New York: Cambridge University Press, 2004. This collection of brief biographies of famous physicists contains a five-page biography of Fourier. Written in a nontechnical style for readers with limited knowledge of science.

Purrington, Robert D. *Physics in the Nineteenth Century*. New Brunswick, N.J.: Rutgers University Press, 1997. Fourier is mentioned in several places, and his work is placed in a historical context, in this survey of nineteenth century physics; references to Fourier are listed in the index. Chapter 4, "Heat and Thermodynamics," contains information about the Fourier series.

SEE ALSO: Évariste Galois; Sophie Germain; Pierre-Simon Laplace; Napoleon I.

RELATED ARTICLE in *Great Events from History: The Nineteenth Century, 1801-1900:* 1900: Lebesgue Develops New Integration Theory.

LYDIA FOLGER FOWLER
American physiologist

The first woman to become a professor at an American medical school, Fowler became well known as a lecturer on physiology, temperance, and women's rights during the years in which the medical field gradually opened to the entry of women.

BORN: May 5, 1822; Nantucket, Massachusetts
DIED: January 26, 1879; London, England
ALSO KNOWN AS: Lydia Folger (birth name)
AREAS OF ACHIEVEMENT: Medicine, women's rights

EARLY LIFE

The daughter of Gideon and Eunice Macy Folger, Lydia Folger was born on the small island of Nantucket off the coast of Massachusetts. Her father, who had spent various periods in his life as a mechanic, a farmer, a candle-maker, a shipowner, and even a sometime politician, was a direct descendant of Peter Folger, who had arrived on Nantucket in 1663 as one of the earliest settlers of the island. The Folger clan, which also includes Benjamin Franklin, can be traced back to English nobility in the person of the earl of Shrewsbury.

Another well-known relative of Lydia Folger Fowler was her distant cousin Maria Mitchell, who grew up in Nantucket as a contemporary of Fowler and who would one day become a professor of astronomy at Vassar College. In fact, it was through Maria Mitchell's father, a popular teacher in the community, that Fowler gained a consuming interest in her studies, particularly in math and science. Additionally supported by an uncle who fancied himself an amateur astronomer, Lydia Folger Fowler felt a special devotion to the field in which her cousin Maria would find such distinction. All in all, Fowler's early education, with its inclusion of subjects generally thought of as unsuitable for women students, appears to have been quite extensive when compared with that of other women of the era.

One possible explanation for this circumstance is the distinctive character of the community in Nantucket. For the most part, the men of Nantucket worked in sea-faring trades—trades that demanded that they leave the island for weeks and months at a time. Such necessities helped to form an atmosphere of independence and self-reliance among the women of the island, who were often forced to run the affairs of the community while the men were away. Lucretia Mott, one of the early leaders of the women's rights movement and a native of Nantucket, is a good example of the kind of attitudes fostered

there. Add to this the fact that the island at this time was inhabited primarily by Quakers, who were defined by an openness to social reform and a devotion to the ideal of equality, and one can begin to imagine more clearly the environment from which Lydia Folger Fowler emerged.

LIFE'S WORK

Lydia Folger left Nantucket in 1838 to study for a year in Norton, Massachusetts, at the Wheaton Seminary, where she would later spend two years (1842-1844) as a teacher. This stint ended with her marriage, on September 19, 1844, to Lorenzo Niles Fowler. They would have but one child together, a daughter named Jessie Allen, born in 1856.

Lorenzo Fowler was at this time one of the best-known and most vocal proponents of the budding science of phrenology. He and his brother Orson had been exposed to phrenological theories during the 1830's while they were both studying at Amherst College in preparation for a life in the ministry. Convinced of the tenets of this new science, the brothers became two of its most famous adherents by embarking on numerous lecture tours and even establishing the publishing house of Fowlers and Wells in 1842 in order to become the publishers of the *American Phrenological Journal.*

Beginning in 1845, Lydia Folger Fowler accompanied her husband during the journeys to his speaking engagements, and later, in 1847, she began to give lectures of her own at the opening of each congregation. These lectures covered such topics as anatomy, physiology, and hygiene, and formed the basis for the two books Fowler would publish in 1847 through the auspices of her husband's publishing operation. *Familiar Lessons on Physiology* and *Familiar Lessons on Phrenology* (to be followed in 1848 by a third volume, *Familiar Lessons in Astronomy*) appeared as books intended for young readers and enjoyed some sales success.

Heartened by her successes as a lecturer and author, Lydia Folger Fowler decided to pursue a medical degree and enrolled at Central Medical College in November, 1849. Located first in Syracuse, New York, and later moving to Rochester in 1850, Central was the first medical school to make a regular policy of admitting women. The school even included a so-called "Female Department," of which Fowler served as principal during her second term of study. Although there was this emphasis on Central's campus and though there were several other women who joined her entering class, Lydia Folger Fowler was the lone female graduate in June of 1850, making her only the second woman ever, after Elizabeth Blackwell, to receive a medical degree in the United States.

Fowler was soon to achieve a first of her own. After she had worked briefly as a "demonstrator of anatomy" to students at Central, Fowler was promoted in 1851 to the position of professor of midwifery and diseases of women and children, thereby becoming the first woman professor at an American medical college. The professorship was not long-lived, however, because Central Medical College merged with a rival institution in 1852 and Fowler left to practice privately in New York City. While in New York, Fowler resumed teaching, and in 1854, she began a series of private medical lectures for women at Metropolitan Medical College, a physiopathic school that existed between 1852 and 1862. Fowler also succeeded in publishing three articles in the pages of Metropolitan College's alternative medical journal. These articles were entitled "Medical Progression," "Female Medical Education," and "Suggestions to Female Medical Students." These articles argued the necessity of women physicians, noting that women needing medical care were often precluded by their modesty from seeking help from the heretofore exclusively male profession.

The early 1850's also witnessed Fowler's increased politicization, as she became involved in several causes for reform. Twice she served as secretary to national women's rights conventions (1852 and 1853), and once she was a delegate to a meeting of the state Daughters of Temperance (1852). In February of 1853, Fowler presided over a women's temperance meeting in New York City, during which she utilized her well-honed skills at public speaking. In addition to supporting these reform movements, Fowler continued to give public lectures on the topics of physiology and hygiene. She remained in New York City until 1860, when she left with her husband as he embarked on a speaking tour of Europe. After spending the year studying and working in Paris and London, Fowler returned to New York in 1861. In 1862, she became an instructor in midwifery at the New York Hygeio-Therapeutic College. The next year, Lorenzo Fowler left the publishing house, and he and Lydia Fowler moved to London, where they would spend the rest of their days.

While in London, Lydia Folger Fowler chose not to practice medicine but continued to remain extremely ac-

tive within the temperance movement, becoming an honorary secretary of the Woman's British Temperance Society. This period also allowed Folger the leisure to focus on her writing. *Nora: The Lost and the Redeemed*, a temperance novel that earlier had been serialized in America, appeared in book form in 1863. A series of Folger's lectures on child care was published in 1865 as *The Pet of the Household and How to Save It*. Finally, in 1870, a book of poems entitled *Heart Melodies* became Folger's last published work. Lydia Folger Fowler died in London of pleuropneumonia on January 26, 1879.

SIGNIFICANCE

Lydia Folger Fowler's list of accomplishments easily leads one to see her as an inspiring symbol of women's determination to break down the social and institutional barriers that excluded them from the study and practice of medicine. The fact that she made such great strides and enjoyed so much success at Central Medical College, becoming the second American woman to receive a medical degree and the first to become a professor in an American medical school, secures forever Fowler's place among the early pioneers of women's rights within the medical field.

To stress Fowler's symbolic importance, however, is to misrepresent the true nature of her influence upon the other women of her era. Fowler's efforts were of a much more practical kind. During her many extended tours of public lectures, Fowler addressed wide and varied audiences, meeting and speaking with countless admirers and skeptics. It was during these moments, when she brought her message and personal example so immediately to those in attendance, that Lydia Folger Fowler had her greatest impact. No other woman physician of the moment could claim to have influenced so many people in so direct and intimate a manner. Although it is true that much of Fowler's lecturing was done in connection with the thoroughly debunked science of phrenology and that she continually found herself working in alternative or marginal situations, this does not seem so surprising if one considers the hostility she must have felt emanating from a medical institution that sensed that its days as a closed fraternity were numbered.

—*Bonnie L. Ford*

FURTHER READING

Abrams, Ruth J., ed. *"Send Us a Lady Physician": Women Doctors in America, 1835-1920*. New York: W. W. Norton, 1986. Collection of essays compiled to accompany a museum exhibit. The essays describe the experience of women in the health professions during the nineteenth and early twentieth centuries. A good book for placing Fowler's experiences into historical context.

Hume, Ruth Fox. *Great Women of Medicine*. New York: Random House, 1964. Fowler is mentioned as an able practitioner though a graduate of an eclectic college. The portrayals of the six women in the book—Elizabeth Blackwell, Florence Nightingale, Elizabeth Garrett Anderson, Sophia Jex-Blake, Mary Putnam Jacobi, and Marie Curie—provide the reader with a good introduction to the medical profession during in the nineteenth century.

Lopate, Carol. *Women in Medicine*. Baltimore: Johns Hopkins University Press, 1968. In the first chapter, Lopate provides good background concerning the entrance of American women into the medical profession. She explains the importance of eclectic schools such as the one Lydia Folger Fowler attended in offering women entrance.

Morantz-Sanchez, Regina Markell. *Sympathy and Science: Women Physicians in American Medicine*. New York: Oxford University Press, 1985. Reprint. Chapel Hill: University of North Carolina, 2000. The best discussion of Lydia Folger Fowler appears in this comprehensive history of women in American medicine. Morantz-Sanchez explores the role of feminism in this history as well as the unique contributions women made to the field of medicine.

More, Ellen S. *Restoring the Balance: Women Physicians and the Profession of Medicine, 1850-1995*. Cambridge, Mass.: Harvard University Press, 1999. Fowler is mentioned twice in this history examining how women physicians work to balance the demands of their profession with society's expectations for women.

Stille, Darlene R. *Extraordinary Women of Medicine*. New York: Children's Press, 1997. A four-page biography of Fowler is included in this collection of brief biographies aimed at young adult readers.

Walsh, Mary Roth. *"Doctors Wanted: No Women Need Apply": Sexual Barriers in the Medical Profession, 1835-1975*. New Haven, Conn.: Yale University Press, 1977. Lydia Folger Fowler is mentioned on the first page of this book as the first American woman to be graduated from an American medical college. This book is an excellent study of the barriers women faced in entering the medical profession in the United States as well as a good overview of the progress of medicine in the nineteenth century, helping to put Fowler in perspective.

Wilson, Dorothy Clarke. *Lone Woman: The Story of Elizabeth Blackwell, the First Woman Doctor*. Boston: Little, Brown, 1970. Wilson shows how Elizabeth Blackwell's achievement led to the adoption of a coeducational policy by the Rochester Eclectic College of Medicine. Fowler was the first woman graduate of Rochester and thereby benefited from Blackwell's endeavor.

SEE ALSO: Elizabeth Blackwell; Mary Putnam Jacobi; Maria Mitchell; Lucretia Mott; Florence Nightingale; Emma Willard.

RELATED ARTICLE in *Great Events from History: The Nineteenth Century, 1801-1900:* May 12, 1857: New York Infirmary for Indigent Women and Children Opens.

ANATOLE FRANCE
French novelist

France's reclusive devotion to books turned to militancy in the wake of the late nineteenth century Dreyfus affair, and he used his satirical skills thereafter to campaign against intolerance and social injustice. He was awarded the Nobel Prize in Literature in 1921.

BORN: April 16, 1844; Paris, France
DIED: October 12, 1924; La Béchellerie, near Tours, Saint-Cyr-sur-Loire, France
ALSO KNOWN AS: Jacques-Anatole-François Thibault (birth name)
AREA OF ACHIEVEMENT: Literature

EARLY LIFE

Born Jacques-Anatole-François Thibault, Anatole France was the son of François Noël Thibault, a devoutly Roman Catholic and politically conservative bookseller. Anatole grew to adolescence surrounded by the cultural heritage of France and quickly acquired a keen appreciation of its worth. To begin with, he took aboard his father's religious and political beliefs in a meekly obedient fashion, with the result that his childhood was untroubled by conflict.

France remembered his childhood as a comfortable and happy time that he revisited nostalgically throughout his writing life, evoking aspects of it in *Le Livre de mon ami* (1885; *My Friend's Book*, 1913), *Pierre Nozière* (1899; English translation, 1916), *Le Petit Pierre* (1919; *Little Pierre*, 1920), and his final novel, *Le Vie en fleur* (1922; *The Bloom of Life*, 1923). A portrait painted when he was six shows him with a serious expression, a Cupid's-bow mouth and a narrow chin (which he was to conceal throughout adult life with a luxuriant beard and mustache).

The young Anatole became a devoted scholar, although he left the Collège Stanislas in 1862 without qualifications for reasons that his biographers have been unable to clarify. He refused to take over his father's business—which the elder Thibault then liquidated—and set out to make a living from his pen using the pseudonym Anatole France. He began to frequent the salon of the Parnassian poet Charles Leconte de Lisle in 1867 but supported himself in the field of academic journalism, which was unusually lucrative in nineteenth century France by virtue of the rapid postrevolutionary establishment of universal literacy and an attendant hunger for education.

France's subjects ranged from such writers of ancient Greece and Rome as Lucius Apuleius and Terence to such contemporaries as Paul Bourget and Émile Zola. The classical philosophy of Epicurus and the social upheavals of revolutionary France became particularly fascinating for Anatole. The Catholic faith and monarchist sympathies that Anatole had inherited from his father were ameliorated by polite Epicurean skepticism and an idealistic commitment to liberty, equality, and fraternity.

Early manhood proved to be a more troubling period of his life. A passionate infatuation with Élise Devoyod in 1865-1866 was unreciprocated. He married Marie-Valérie Guérin de Sauville in 1877, but the marriage was disrupted by a hectic love affair with a married woman, Léontine Arman de Caillavet, that turned his gradual retreat from moral orthodoxy into a headlong rush during the late 1880's. His marriage was dissolved in 1893, shortly before his involvement with the celebrated case of Alfred Dreyfus—a Jewish army officer wrongly convicted of selling military secrets—presented his newfound radicalism a cause that he could pursue in the public arena.

LIFE'S WORK

France's first full-length work, issued in 1868, was a study of the poet Alfred de Vigny. He published a poetry collection of his own in 1873 and a poetic drama, *Les Noces corinthiennes*, in 1876, but the latter was not performed until he had become famous; it was first produced at the Odéon in 1902. His first book of prose, *Jocasta et le chat maigre* (1879; *Jocasta and the Famished Cat*, 1912), consisted of two novellas, but his breakthrough to popular success was *Le Crime de Sylvestre Bonnard* (1881; *The Crime of Sylvestre Bonnard*, 1890), a novel about an unworldly book lover's struggle to cope with the vicissitudes of everyday life. This was followed in 1883 by the long, moralistic fairy tale "L'Abeille," variously known in English as "Honey-Bee," "Bee," and "The Kingdom of the Dwarfs," which became the longest item in the story collection *Balthasar* (1889; English translation, 1909).

France wrote two novels dramatizing his feelings for Léontine Arman de Caillavet. The first, written while he was still married, was *Thaïs* (1890; English translation, 1891), based on a legend that he had already recapitulated in a poem written in 1867. Paphnuce, a hermit liv-

Anatole France. (Library of Congress)

ing in the same locale as Saint Anthony (whose oft-illustrated temptations had been vividly described in an extravagant novel by Gustave Flaubert), persuades a famous Alexandrian courtesan to repent her wicked ways and become a nun but is then driven mad by the erotic feelings she has awakened in him. The second novel, set in the city of Florence, which he and Madame Arman de Caillavet visited while touring Italy in the wake of his divorce, was the infinitely more relaxed and sentimental love story *Le Lys rouge* (1894; *The Red Lily*, 1898).

The resentment against Christian asceticism embodied in *Thaïs* was further extended in the stories in *L'Étui de nacre* (1892; *Tales from a Mother of Pearl Casket*, 1896), which opens with the notorious "Le procurateur de Judea" ("The Procurator of Judea"), in which an aged Pontius Pilate, reminiscing about old times, reveals that he has no memory whatsoever of his brief encounter with Christ, although he remembers Mary Magdalene well. The collection also includes further ironic pastiches of the legends of the saints in the same vein as *Thaïs*. The trend continued in *Le Puits de Sainte-Claire* (1895; *The Well of Santa Clara*, 1909), which included a fine tale of a satyr saint that summarized France's arguments about the tragedy of the Church's rejection of the pagan heritage and the novella "L'humaine tragédie" ("The Human

Tragedy"), in which a medieval holy man discovers that the Church has become the enemy of true Christian ideals and that the rebellious spirit of its traditional enemy— Satan—better embraces the traditional ideals of hope and charity.

Other works elaborating France's new spirit of dissent included the Rabelaisian satire *La Rôtisserie de la Reine Pédauque* (1893; *At the Sign of the Reine Pédauque*, 1912) and *Les Opinions de M. Jérome Coignard* (1893; *The Opinions of Jerome Coignard*, 1913), but his work changed direction markedly in 1897 when he began a four-volume series of novels set in contemporary France. This consisted of *L'Orme du mail* (1897; *The Elm Tree on the Mall*, 1910), *Le Mannequin d'osier* (1897; *The Wicker Work Woman*, 1910), *L'Anneau d'améthyste* (1899; *The Amethyst Ring*, 1919), and the semiautobiographical *Monsieur Bergeret à Paris* (1901; *Monsieur Bergeret in Paris*, 1922).

The last book features a hero whose decision to remain aloof from politics is overturned by outrage at the refusal of the French military authorities to admit that Captain Dreyfus had been wrongly convicted and at the consequent continuation of Dreyfus's imprisonment on Devil's Island. France's own sense of outrage broadened to include other social injustices, some of which were scathingly chronicled in the sarcastic tales collected in *Crainquebille, Putois, Riquet et plusieurs autres récits profitables* (1904; *Crainquebille, Putois, Riquet and Other Profitable Tales*, 1915). The Dreyfus affair formed the basis for the final sequence of his hugely successful satire *L'Île des pingouins* (1908; *Penguin Island*, 1914), in which a population of accidentally baptized penguins reproduces all the errors and follies of human social evolution.

France offered more earnest accounts of his philosophical development in his reconstruction of debates in *Le Jardin d'Épicure* (1894; *The Garden of Epicurus*, 1908) and a novel examining the difficulties of predicting the future, *Sur le pierre blanche* (1905; *The White Stone*, 1909), whose attempted description of a future Marxist utopia reflected France's increasing attachment to socialism. He eventually joined the Communist Party, but only briefly; he found its narrow faith as stultifying as the one he had deserted in adolescence.

France always preferred to develop his ideas satirically and relatively lightheartedly, as in *Contes de Jacques Tournebroche* (1908; *The Merrie Tales of Jacques Tournebroche*, 1910), which contained stories in the same slightly bawdy mock-medieval vein as Honoré de Balzac's *Droll Tales*, and *Les Sept Femmes de la Barbe-*

Bleue et autres contes merveilleux (1909; *The Seven Wives of Bluebeard and Other Marvellous Tales*, 1920), a collection of ironic fairy tales that concludes with a long exercise in moral symbolism in which emissaries of an unhappy king search in vain for the shirt of a happy man with which to redeem the king's melancholy spirit. France had been much troubled himself by the contro-

versial remarriage of his divorced daughter Suzanne in 1908; he refused to speak to her thereafter, and the estrangement continued until her death during the 1918 Spanish flu epidemic.

The ultimate satirical product of France's conversion to radicalism was his literary masterpiece, *La Révolte des anges* (1914; *The Revolt of the Angels*, 1914), written on the eve of World War I. The story tells how a guardian angel is converted to free thought by *De rerum natura* (Lucretius's summary of Epicurean philosophy) and sends out a new call to arms to the fallen angels, most of whom have become teachers and artists. He offers the commanding role to Satan, who is working as a humble gardener and who politely declines on the grounds that liberation from divine tyranny must be won within the hearts and minds of men, not on the field of battle.

The carefully considered rejection of violent means was carried forward from *Les Dieux ont soif* (1912; *The Gods Are Athirst*, 1913), his heartfelt historical novel analyzing the French Revolution of 1789 and the consequent Reign of Terror. He had turned to that subject in the wake of the death, in 1910, of his longtime companion Madame Arman de Caillavet. He did marry again in 1920, and in 1921 he received the Nobel Prize in Literature at the age of seventy-six. He was still working despite his age, and his last few published works, although slight, showed that he had lost none of his clarity of mind.

ST. MAEL CONVERTS THE PENGUINS TO CHRISTIANITY

The Anatole France novel best known to modern readers is probably Penguin Island. *Set in the distant past, it is about a Breton monk named Mael who is diligent in gathering converts to the Church. One day the devil causes Mael to be transported to an island near the North Pole that is inhabited by penguins. Partly blinded by the snow, he mistakes the birds for people and preaches to them. Then, taking their silence as assent, he baptizes them into the Christian faith. Here, France describes Mael's first encounter with the penguins.*

Now what he had taken for men of small stature but of grave bearing were penguins whom the spring had gathered together, and who were ranged in couples on the natural steps of the rock, erect in the majesty of their large white bellies. From moment to moment they moved their winglets like arms, and uttered peaceful cries. They did not fear men, for they did not know them, and had never received any harm from them; and there was in the monk a certain gentleness that reassured the most timid animals and that pleased these penguins extremely. With a friendly curiosity they turned towards him their little round eyes lengthened in front by a white oval spot that gave something odd and human to their appearance.

Touched by their attention, the holy man taught them the Gospel.

Inhabitants of this island, the earthly day that has just risen over your rocks is the image of the heavenly day that rises in your souls. For I bring you the inner light; I bring you the light and heat of the soul. Just as the sun melts the ice of your mountains so Jesus Christ will melt the ice of your hearts.

Thus the old man spoke. As everywhere throughout nature voice calls to voice, as all which breathes in the light of day loves alternate strains, these penguins answered the old man by the sounds of their throats. And their voices were soft, for it was the season of their loves.

The holy man, persuaded that they belonged to some idolatrous people and that in their own language they gave adherence to the Christian faith, invited them to receive baptism.

"I think," said he to them, "that you bathe often, for all the hollows of the rocks are full of pure water, and as I came to your assembly I saw several of you plunging into these natural baths. Now purity of body is the image of spiritual purity."

And he taught them the origin, the nature, and the effects of baptism. . . .

And thus for three days and three nights he baptized the birds.

Source: Anatole France, *Penguin Island* (1908).

SIGNIFICANCE

Despite the fact that Anatole France won a Nobel Prize, his international reputation has always suffered somewhat from the fact that he does not fit into either of the literary categories currently regarded as the most prestigious. His early adventures in poetry were undistinguished, and the bare handful of realistic novels that he produced are obviously novels of ideas rather than novels of character.

France's best work is in the tradition of Voltairean *contes philosophiques*, which never won much acclaim outside France and petered out even within their native land. He remains, however, one of the finest contributors to the later days of that tradition (and a significant influence on James Branch Cabell, the one writer who tried hard to import it into the United States). France's greatest virtues—his painstaking erudition and the dispassionate coolness of his intelligence and wit—are sometimes held against him by critics who prefer more intimate narratives and more intricate plots, but they are rare virtues that ought to be accounted more precious than they often are. *The Revolt of the Angels* remains the classic work of the tradition of "literary Satanism" that sprang from William Blake's observation that the author of *Paradise Lost*, John Milton, had been "of the devil's party without knowing it." Such literature raises the important question of whether the commandments of a jealous God are really the best basis for human morality.

—*Brian Stableford*

FURTHER READING

George, W. L. *Anatole France*. London: Nisbet, 1915. This was the first study of France in English. Written shortly after publication of *The Revolt of the Angels*, it deftly summarizes his career from that viewpoint.

Jefferson, A. C. *Anatole France: The Politics of Skepticism*. New Brunswick, N.J.: Rutgers University Press, 1965. A careful analysis of France's philosophical progress, his involvement in contemporary issues, and the position he eventually adopted.

Levy, D. W. *Techniques of Irony in Anatole France: Essay on "Les Sept Femmes de la Barbe-Bleue."* Chapel Hill: University of North Carolina Press, 1978. A minute dissection of a key exemplar of France's satirical method.

Sachs, M. *France: The Short Stories*. London: Arnold, 1974. A comprehensive survey of France's short fiction, offering a useful account of work that is sometimes neglected in more conventional studies that tend to place the novels in the foreground.

Virtanen, R. *Anatole France*. New York: Twayne, 1968. A useful general survey of the author's life and work.

SEE ALSO: Honoré de Balzac; Gustave Flaubert; Joaquim Maria Machado de Assis; Émile Zola.

RELATED ARTICLE in *Great Events from History: The Nineteenth Century, 1801-1900:* October 1-December 15, 1856: Flaubert Publishes *Madame Bovary*.

FRANCIS JOSEPH I
Emperor of Austria (r. 1848-1916) and king of Hungary (r. 1867-1916)

The reign of Emperor Francis Joseph I was one of the longest in European history. Ascending the throne at the age of eighteen, he eventually became the living symbol of an imperial ideal of government that was doomed to vanish at his death, which occurred during the middle of World War I.

BORN: August 18, 1830; Schönbrunn Palace, near Vienna, Austria
DIED: November 21, 1916; Schönbrunn Palace, near Vienna, Austria
ALSO KNOWN AS: Francis (birth name)
AREA OF ACHIEVEMENT: Government and politics

EARLY LIFE

The person who had the most profound effect upon the character of Francis Joseph was his mother, Princess Sophie of Bavaria. This younger daughter of Maximilian I married Charles Francis, the second son of Emperor Francis I, in 1824, and, until the birth of her first son, she devoted her time to mastering the bewildering etiquette of the Austrian court as well as the maze of imperial politics.

The heir to the throne, Archduke Ferdinand, had a mental disability and suffered from epilepsy. It was expected that the crown would pass to Sophie's retiring and irresolute husband. Because she was already regarded as the best political mind in the family, few had any doubts about who would govern the empire. Metternich, the man who had redrawn the map of Europe in 1815, dashed Sophie's hopes by arranging a marriage for the hapless Ferdinand and persuading the emperor that his heir was capable of ruling Austria. In 1835, Francis died and Ferdinand ascended the throne.

Archduke Charles Francis was a loving and devoted father to his children, but their mother was in charge. Although young Francis had been given a household of his own at birth, his mother totally controlled his upbringing. Slowly, the charming prince began to evolve into a devout and gallant young gentleman. Although he was not a scholar, Francis was a conscientious student, but his real love was military science. At the age of thirteen, he was appointed a colonel of dragoons and began to train seriously for a career as a soldier. The handsome, graceful youth proved an instant favorite who fit easily into the carefree world of Vienna in the last years before the revolutions of 1848.

The events that shook the foundations of the empire between March and December of 1848 provided the opportunity for which the Archduchess Sophie had long waited. With Metternich a fugitive in England, she easily persuaded her husband to renounce his claim to the throne in favor of their eldest son. On December 2, 1848, Emperor Ferdinand gladly abdicated in favor of his nephew, who assumed the name Francis Joseph in memory of Joseph II, the great reforming emperor of the late eighteenth century. As the imperial family journeyed from Vienna, however, it was the new empress-mother who was busily charting the course of the new reign, not the young emperor.

LIFE'S WORK

During the first three years of his reign Francis Joseph demonstrated his hostility to liberalism and constitutional government by methodically revoking most of the changes that had been made by the revolutionaries. Even freedom of the press was denied lest criticism of the regime become too widespread. With the confidence of youth, the emperor sought to fashion a centralized absolutism in which all power and responsibility would reside in him. Although a number of worthy administrative reforms were made to implement this policy, he totally ignored the potent force of nationalism. When the Hungarians under Lajos Kossuth resisted, their fledgling republic was crushed by troops sent from Russia by Czar Nicholas I, who was delighted to further the cause of reaction.

When a Hungarian patriot tried unsuccessfully to assassinate Francis Joseph in February, 1853, the young sovereign's sense of mission only deepened. He believed that he had been sent to revive the defunct Holy Roman Empire in partnership with a revitalized Roman Catholic Church. Apart from this rather grand scheme, his foreign policy was rather erratic and unimpressive.

Against his mother's wishes, Francis Joseph married his sixteen-year-old cousin, Elizabeth of Bavaria, on

April 24, 1854. Unfortunately for the young couple, Sophie decided to mold her niece into her image of an empress. Elizabeth was equally determined to resist, and the struggle of these two strong-willed women eventually led to an estrangement between Francis Joseph and his wife. Sophie then assumed the responsibility for rearing her three grandchildren while their mother frequented fashionable spas, seeking to restore her health.

At the moment his personal happiness began to vanish, the emperor was forced to face the loss of all of his Italian possessions except Venetia. The combined armies of France and Piedmont-Savoy defeated the Austrians at Solferino on June 24, 1859. This bloody battle and the peace terms arranged at Villafranca the next month forced Francis Joseph to make some drastic changes in the way in which the empire was governed.

The liberals, whom the emperor had rejected at the beginning of his reign, were now wooed with the creation of an imperial parliament, whose membership was effectively restricted to the moneyed classes. The Hungarians, Poles, and Czechs refused to cooperate, but Francis Joseph proceeded with his plan for a largely German legislature. Having lost most of his Italian possessions, the emperor turned his attention to regional affairs. His dream of an Austrian-led central Europe brought Francis Joseph unwittingly into conflict with Otto von Bismarck.

In 1864, Bismarck lured the Austrians into a war against Denmark to prevent the incorporation of the largely German duchies of Schleswig and Holstein into that kingdom. The war lasted barely six months, and with its end, the control of Schleswig passed to Prussia and the control of Holstein to Austria. Although he diplomatically isolated Austria, Bismarck began a war of nerves over the administration of Holstein. Goaded beyond endurance, Austria went to war against Prussia in June, 1866. On July 2, 1866, the Prussians and their allies won a decisive victory at Königgrätz. Francis Joseph was forced to acquiesce to the absorption of most of northern and central Germany into the Prussian-dominated North German Confederation. There were repeated calls for the emperor's abdication in favor of his younger brother Maximilian. The final humiliation was the seizure by Italy of Venetia with the blessing of Prussia.

To prevent the complete disintegration of the empire, Francis Joseph agreed to the Compromise of 1867, which created an independent Hungary within a dual monarchy. As emperor of Austria and king of Hungary, he presided over a government that shared control of foreign affairs, armed forces, and finances between Vienna and Budapest. Shortly after his coronation in Hungary in June, 1867, Francis Joseph learned of the death of Maximilian before a firing squad in Mexico. For three years Maximilian had been emperor of that turbulent country with the support of the French, but the desertion of his allies left him at the mercy of his rebellious subjects.

The death of his brother was the first of a series of personal tragedies that haunted the remaining years of Francis Joseph's life. When Sophie died in 1873, the possible reconciliation between her son and daughter-in-law did not take place; instead, the gulf that separated them grew wider. Although intelligent and liberal in his political outlook, Crown Prince Rudolf did not display the same dedication to duty that his father prized, nor was his personal life exemplary. When Rudolf and his mistress committed suicide in January, 1889, the foundations of the empire were shaken. The empress never recovered from her son's death, and her wanderings became more aimless until she died at the hands of an assassin in Geneva in September, 1898.

Francis Joseph's last years were marred by the murder of his nephew and heir, Franz Ferdinand, at Sarajevo in June, 1914, and by World War I. A man of peace, he would have preferred to spend his last days with his grandchildren. Instead, he died like a good soldier, immersed in war-related work, on November 21, 1916.

SIGNIFICANCE

The rapid disintegration of the Austro-Hungarian Empire in the last months of the war surprised a number of experts. It had survived so many crises since the end of the Napoleonic era, including revolution and the constantly disruptive force of nationalism, that it seemed eternal. Francis Joseph I was the force that held together the diverse elements that made up his empire. The ideas that he brought to the throne were those of his mother, Metternich, and Felix Schwarzenberg, his first prime minister. As he matured, these youthful ideas were modified or discarded. Personal tragedy tempered his nature and endeared him to his people.

It may well be that he perceived the incurable weaknesses in his empire long before they became apparent to others, but with a tenacity born of adversity he devoted his life to preserving the rather antiquated structure. With age and infirmity, he was forced to curtail his public duties and leave the cares of state to lesser men. By then he was already a legend, almost a national icon. He was the

one element that held the Austro-Hungarian Empire together, and when he died, it died with him.

— *Clifton W. Potter, Jr.*

FURTHER READING

Bagger, Eugene S. *Francis Joseph, Emperor of Austria—King of Hungary*. New York: G. P. Putnam's Sons, 1927. This standard biography, while almost contemporary with its subject, remains a work of solid and reliable scholarship. The author tends to avoid a penetrating analysis of private and personal matters in favor of a strict historical narrative. It should be read as background to other, later works.

Beller, Steven. *Francis Joseph*. London: Longman, 1996. One of the volumes in the Profiles in Power series, this book chronicles the events of Francis Joseph's long reign and analyzes the importance of his reign on his times.

Crankshaw, Edward. *The Fall of the House of Habsburg*. New York: Viking Press, 1963. The bulk of this work is devoted to the reign of Francis Joseph and the collapse of the Austro-Hungarian Empire after his death. Well written and well documented. Contains a useful bibliography.

Gerö, András. *Emperor Francis Joseph, King of the Hungarians*. Translated from the Hungarian by James Patterson and Enikö Koncz. Boulder, Colo.: Social Science Monographs, 2001. Examines the relationship between Francis Joseph, king of Hungary, and his subjects from the crushing of the Hungarian Revolution of 1849 until World War I. Describes the evolution of Francis Joseph's attitudes toward the Hungarians, whose public adulation masked historical enmity.

McGuigan, Dorothy Gies. *The Habsburgs*. Garden City, N.Y.: Doubleday, 1966. Although a general history of the Habsburg Dynasty, one-quarter of this work is devoted to Francis Joseph. The notes and bibliography are extremely valuable. Useful for its sensitivity to the forces that destroyed the empire and to the destiny that trapped the last Habsburgs.

Marek, George R. *The Eagles Die: Franz Joseph, Elisabeth, and Their Austria*. New York: Harper & Row, 1974. The rather complicated, yet tragic relationship between Francis Joseph and his wife is the theme of this work. The men and women who influenced their lives are carefully profiled. The portrait of the emperor is particularly sensitive and complete.

May, Arthur J. *The Habsburg Monarchy, 1867-1914*. Cambridge, Mass.: Harvard University Press, 1951.

The primary focus of this work is the period from the Compromise of 1867 to the outbreak of World War I. A work of depth and scholarship. The chapter notes are particularly valuable.

Palmer, Alan. *Twilight of the Habsburgs: The Life and Times of Emperor Francis Joseph.* New York: Grove Press, 1995. Comprehensive biography. Palmer seeks to provide a three-dimensional portrait of Francis Joseph, and he chronicles the emperor's personal tragedies and public concern for his empire's survival.

Wandruszka, Adam. *The House of Habsburg: Six Hundred Years of a European Dynasty.* Translated by Cathleen Epstein and Hans Epstein. Garden City, N.Y.: Doubleday, 1964. Gives a valuable overview of the entire dynasty with a brief but incisive treatment of Francis Joseph. The genealogical charts are particularly useful.

SEE ALSO: Otto von Bismarck; Ferenc Deák; Maximilian; Metternich; Nicholas I; Johann Strauss.

RELATED ARTICLES in *Great Events from History: The Nineteenth Century, 1801-1900:* July 11, 1859: Napoleon III and Francis Joseph I Meet at Villafranca; June 15-August 23, 1866: Austria and Prussia's Seven Weeks' War; May 29, 1867: Austrian Ausgleich; January 18, 1871: German States Unite Within German Empire; May 6-October 22, 1873: Three Emperors' League Is Formed.

CÉSAR FRANCK
French composer

Franck's mastery of the principles of orchestration and the harmonic theories of the nineteenth century made him the acknowledged leader of French music of his era and one of the world's great composers.

BORN: December 10, 1822; Liège, the Netherlands (now in Belgium)
DIED: November 8, 1890; Paris, France
ALSO KNOWN AS: César Auguste Franck (full name)
AREA OF ACHIEVEMENT: Music

EARLY LIFE

César Auguste Franck was the firstborn son of a minor bank official who had come from Aix to settle in Liège in 1817 and had married a German woman in 1820. His father, Nicholas-Joseph, was an ambitious, frustrated man; a lover of music and amateur musician, he curried the favor of the writers and artists of Liège and transferred his thwarted ambition for fame and fortune onto César, who early displayed musical ability. Nicholas-Joseph arranged a strict schedule for the boy, forcing him to rigorous study of the piano and composition. By the time César was eight years old, the elder Franck enrolled him at the local conservatory, where his musical aptitude gained for him the notice of his teachers.

In 1835, when Franck was thirteen, his father sent him to Paris to study counterpoint and harmony under the most notable music masters of the day. Eager to succeed through the merits of his son, Nicholas-Joseph arranged a number of public concerts at which his young son performed as a prodigy, along with such established musicians as Franz Liszt. At these concerts, Franck played some of his own compositions. Though competent, they were undistinguished.

Realizing that a foreigner had little chance to make his way into the musical establishment of Paris, Nicholas-Joseph became a naturalized French citizen and won for Franck the right to enroll in the prestigious Paris Conservatory in 1837. Franck's talents were so extraordinary that by the end of the first year he had taken a special first prize for playing a difficult piano piece, astonishing his examiners by transposing the work into another key while sight reading.

For four years the young Franck pursued his studies, especially of the organ, an instrument that was to be a crucial factor in his career. Then—probably at his father's perverse insistence—Franck resigned from the conservatory in 1842. His father had arranged a series of weekly concerts to be held in his own home, and Franck obligingly performed, playing some of his own pieces—fantasias, adaptations of tunes from popular light operas, and other theatrical music. He also composed a set of four piano trios (1843), works that brought him some serious attention, but by and large the music of this concert period was more attuned to public taste and personal profit than to serious artistic concerns.

Gradually, Franck grew restive under the despotism of his father. Though he had made a number of artistic friendships through his father's contrivances—people such as Franz Liszt and Hector Berlioz—Franck bridled under his father's overbearing control, which forced him to produce the kind of music that the old man thought would advance his son's, and his own, career.

One such composition was *Ruth* (1846), an oratorio composed from earlier musical jottings. Based on the Old Testament story of Ruth and Boaz, the work comprised fifteen numbers, and when first performed it drew a number of serious reviews. Critics noted its simplicity, its almost childlike directness, and though the work was a failure, it remains Franck's first major achievement, one that he would come back to and revise some thirty years later.

Meanwhile, Franck had met and fallen in love with one of his piano pupils, Félicité Saillot-Desmousseaux, whose parents were actors in the Comédie Française. Franck married Saillot in February, 1848. The marriage signaled a formal break with his father; Franck was now on his own.

Retiring from public music, Franck began making his living primarily as a teacher, as accompanist at a conservatory in Orléans, and, significantly, as organist at the Church of Saint-Jean-Saint-François-au-Marais and, more important, at the Church of Sainte-Clotilde. These were key stages in his artistic career. The modern organ of Franck's time, especially the wonderful instrument at Sainte-Clotilde, was capable of producing a wide range of tones and orchestral coloring, and it presented Franck with the opportunity of developing a musical technique based on this symphonic capability. For the rest of his life, Franck was to dedicate himself to the mastery of the organ, though his duties as church organist kept him, for almost two decades, from creating any music more significant than improvisational pieces and routine liturgical works. Thus, from the late 1840's to the beginning of the Franco-Prussian War in 1870, Franck lived and worked in virtual obscurity.

LIFE'S WORK

In retrospect, this obscurity was a period of creative gestation during which Franck worked out his musical ideas. *Six Pièces* (1862) were short, improvisational experiments filled with a majestic tonality and a melodiousness

César Franck.

that were to characterize his later masterpieces. Liszt, who was one of Franck's earliest and most important friends, regarded these pieces as worthy of comparison to those of Johann Sebastian Bach.

Meanwhile, the contacts he had made during a thirty-year career as musician, teacher, and minor composer began to bear fruit. Liszt had been playing Franck's 1843 trios in Germany and had gained for the composer some small measure of fame. Additionally, Franck's mastery of the organ now brought him into contact with French musicians who specialized in that instrument. The Franco-Prussian War raised French nationalistic sentiment, so that by late 1871 a group of French composers and musicians organized the National Society of Music. Its purpose was to promote, through concerts, the music of French composers. At fifty, Franck was the oldest in the group, but he was to become one of its most important artists.

The years immediately after Franck's fiftieth birthday were central in his career as a composer. He was appointed professor of the organ at the conservatory in

1872, and though the position did little for him financially, it did establish his preeminence and brought his music more serious attention. Parts of his oratorio *Ruth*, which had laid in comparative neglect since the late 1840's, were given fresh performances. Amid such renewed interest in his music, Franck determined to compose an ambitious work.

The work was *Rédemption* (1873), which Franck conceived as a symphonic poem for orchestra and voice. The text is in three parts. Part 1 tells of humankind's paganism and its expectations of the coming of Christ. Part 2 records humanity's Christian joy through the centuries, and part 3 laments the Fall of Man and contemplates a second redemption through prayer.

Though the obvious religiosity of the subject deeply appealed to Franck, the work was a resounding failure, not only because of poor copies of the orchestration and bad conducting but also because the piece lacked dramatic tension. Nevertheless, *Rédemption* is important in the Franck canon as a transitional work, particularly the section of symphonic interlude, bearing characteristics of harmony and tonality that distinguish the best of Franck's music.

Despite this setback, however, Franck continued his duties as teacher, establishing a profound influence on the younger generation of French composers and musicians who embraced his ideas of harmony and the relationship of chords and keys. One of his pupils, Vincent d'Indy, a composer in his own right and one of Franck's first biographers, records his famous impression of Franck at the organ, his flowing white hair and whiskers setting off his dark, piercing eyes.

In 1874, Franck first heard the prelude to Richard Wagner's *Tristan und Isolde* and was reassured about his own harmonic techniques. The following year, Franck composed *Les Éolides*, first performed in Paris in 1876. A major orchestral work, this symphonic poem is the first composition that fully integrates structure and tonality, combining lyrical delicacy with structural grace. *Les Éolides* introduced the last phase of Franck's achievement. The work ushered in a period of creative efflorescence that continued unabated until Franck's death some fifteen years later. At the age of fifty-three, when most composers had already completed most of their best work, Franck was just beginning to produce his masterpieces.

Les Béatitudes was completed in 1879 and published the following year. A large-scale oratorio based on Christ's Sermon on the Mount, the work is impressive in its structural integrity and its use of certain keys to denote psychological states. Also in 1879, Franck astonished

the musical world with one of his greatest works, Quintet in F Minor for Piano and Strings. Filled with dramatic energy and passion, it still retains a formal structure that provides a balance and cohesiveness, making the quintet among Franck's most popular works. Still another oratorio, *Rebecca*, appeared the following year, but it was the two symphonic poems, *Le Chasseur maudit* (1882) and *Les Djinns* (1884), and the *Variations symphoniques* (1885) that finally established Franck as one of France's greatest composers. These works are characterized by a lush harmony within a tightly structured cyclical form, a technique of restating themes and chords as a principle of musical organization.

The awarding of the Legion of Honor to Franck in 1885 was a tribute no less to his achievement as a composer as to his standing as a professor and his character as a man. Such official recognition was thus the culmination of the public's belated acknowledgment. With the Sonata in A Major for Violin and Piano (1886), he produced a masterpiece of chamber music—concise, eloquent, and finely structured. It is one of his most popular compositions.

At the height of his creative powers, Franck climaxed his career as a composer in the production of his only symphony, the magnificent Symphony in D Minor. For sheer expressiveness, controlled by classical form, and as an example of chromatic richness and harmonic beauty, the symphony ranks as Franck's crowning work. Though it earned for him a mixed reception at its first performance—some of the criticism leveled particularly at the use of the English horn in the first movement—the symphony has never lost its appeal. It is regarded by many as one of the great symphonies of the world.

The String Quartet in D Major (1889), his last major composition, is also one of his best. Typical of his greatest work, the quartet is masterfully structured and melodically rich, a superb example of the cyclical form at its most subtle and concise.

In October, 1890, still involved in several projects, Franck caught cold. By November, his condition worsened. Pleurisy developed, and he died on November 8.

SIGNIFICANCE

Of the great composers, César Franck was among the least prolific. He contributed only one symphony to the orchestral repertory and only three major works in chamber music. However, the quality of these compositions assures for Franck a place as the foremost composer of absolute—that is, nonprogrammatic—music in France during the nineteenth century.

Though Franck wrote numerous choral works throughout his career, his genius was not as a composer for the voice. His oratorios, while creditable, lack the texture of harmonic fullness, even the drama, of his orchestral scores. His opera *Hulda*, written hastily between 1884 and 1886, was never produced during Franck's lifetime; another, "Ghiselle," was never completed. Neither is of any consequence.

In his symphonic poems, his chamber music, and his symphony, Franck led the way among all French composers of the nineteenth century. In a period when French music was dominated by theatrical forms, especially the opera and operetta, Franck looked back to the classical forms of Bach and Ludwig van Beethoven and created works of forceful and melodic character. As a teacher, Franck influenced a generation of French composers who carried their master's dedication to well-designed harmonic structure into the twentieth century.

—*Edward Fiorelli*

FURTHER READING

Abraham, Gerald, ed. *Romanticism (1830-1890)*. Vol. 9 in *New Oxford History of Music*. New York: Oxford University Press, 1990. This standard reference work on music includes an essay analyzing Franck's life and music.

Archbold, Lawrence, and William J. Peterson, eds. *French Organ Music: From the Revolution to Franck and Widor*. Rochester, N.Y.: University of Rochester Press, 1995. Collection of essays analyzing organ compositions by Franck and other French composers. The essays place the music within its political and cultural context, describe how some compositions were created, and provide new information about organ technique.

Davies, Laurence. *César Franck and His Circle*. Boston: Houghton Mifflin, 1970. A classic study not only of Franck but also of his influence on the lives and works of his pupils and musical descendants. Such composers as Ernest Chausson, Henri Duparc, and Vincent d'Indy brought to their music the principles of their master, who must thus be considered a precursor of modern music.

Demuth, Norman. *César Franck*. London: Dennis Dobson, 1949. A musical study of the composer with copious examples of notation and scoring. Suggests that Franck was a pioneer in the creation of the symphonic poem. A good biography, though rather technical for the lay reader.

Douglass, Fenner. *Cavaille-Coll and the French Romantic Tradition*. New Haven, Conn.: Yale University Press, 1999. A biography of Aristide Cavaille-Coll, the greatest French organ builder of the nineteenth century. Examines his relations with Franck and other composers and performers; describes how he built an organ for Franck at the Church of Sainte-Clotilde in Paris.

Indy, Vincent d'. *César Franck*. Translated by Rosa Newmarch. London: John Lane, 1910. An important early biography, representing the biased view of one of Franck's pupils. Himself a composer, d'Indy writes reverently of Franck and his music, glorifying the composer in tones amounting almost to deification. Assessments aside, historical details are accurate.

Smith, Rollin. *Toward an Authentic Interpretation of the Organ Works of César Franck*. 2d ed., rev. and enlarged. Hillsdale, N.Y.: Pendragon Press, 2002. An updated version of the doctoral thesis Smith wrote in 1983 when he was a student at the Juilliard School of Music. Smith discusses Franck, his music, and the organs on which he performed, and offers suggestions for organists wishing to perform Franck's compositions.

Ulrich, Homer. *Chamber Music*. 2d ed. New York: Columbia University Press, 1966. A good, brief examination of Franck's chamber works, noting particularly their cyclical form. A basic knowledge of musical composition would help the lay reader to fully appreciate Franck's structural methods.

_____. *Symphonic Music: Its Evolution Since the Renaissance*. New York: Columbia University Press, 1952. Views Franck as a late Romanticist and notes his mastery of the cyclical form, with several examples of notation. Interesting reference to Franck's skill as master organist and the effect of such on his orchestral writing.

Vallas, Léon. *César Franck*. Translated by Hubert Foss. Reprint. Westport, Conn.: Greenwood Press, 1973. The avowed purpose of this study is to demythologize the life and work of Franck as established by d'Indy and others. Though accurate, it devotes as much space to Franck's choral music as to his more important orchestral works and is thus somewhat too detailed.

SEE ALSO: Ludwig van Beethoven; Hector Berlioz; Georges Bizet; Léo Delibes; Franz Liszt; Richard Wagner.

RELATED ARTICLE in *Great Events from History: The Nineteenth Century, 1801-1900:* August 13-17, 1876: First Performance of Wagner's Ring Cycle.

SIR JOHN FRANKLIN
British Arctic explorer

Franklin commanded three exploratory expeditions to the northern parts of Canada and the Arctic and died proving the existence of the long-sought Northwest Passage. He is remembered for his upright character and the disasters that accompanied his adventures.

BORN: April 16, 1786; Spilsby, Lincolnshire, England

DIED: June 11, 1847; near King William Island, British Arctic Islands (now in Nunavut Territory, Canada)

AREA OF ACHIEVEMENT: Exploration

EARLY LIFE

The ninth of twelve children of Willingham Franklin and Hannah Weekes, John Franklin attended prep school in St. Ives, Huntingdonshire, England, and grammar school in Spilsby. While living in Spilsby, which is only ten miles from the North Sea, Franklin grew fascinated with the sea from a young age. Although his parents hoped his education would lead him into the church, he preferred to imagine a life at sea. In an effort to cure him of this fantasy, his parents sent him aboard a merchant ship to Lisbon, Portugal, and back. However, the experience merely convinced Franklin that a life in the navy was for him. In 1800, at the age of fourteen, he joined the Royal Navy, in which he rose quickly through the ranks because of his enthusiasm and skill.

Franklin joined the navy at the time of Great Britain's long war with Napoleonic France. During his first six months in the service, he saw action in the Battle of Copenhagen. In 1801, his uncle Captain Matthew Flinders made him a midshipman on HMS *Investigator*, which became the first ship to circumnavigate Australia. During the voyage, Franklin was noted for his skill in astronomical observations; when the ship reached Sydney, he acted as an assistant in an observatory.

After returning to England, Franklin was appointed to HMS *Bellerophon*, on which he served during the epic Battle of Trafalgar in 1805. On February 11, 1808, he was promoted to lieutenant while serving aboard HMS *Bedford*, on which he was slightly wounded at New Orleans. After the Napoleonic Wars ended in 1815, Franklin went on half pay until 1817, when John Barrow, the second secretary of the British admiralty, reopened the question of finding the Northwest Passage and began organizing naval expeditions to the far north. Franklin was chosen to be part of the first exploratory foray into Arctic waters in 1818, and his career of northern exploration began.

LIFE'S WORK

Franklin's Arctic career began inauspiciously, as his first two expeditions were complete failures. In 1818, he was appointed to command the *Trent*, the second ship of a two-ship expedition under Commander David Buchan of the *Dorothea*. Franklin was instructed to penetrate an ice pack in the eastern Arctic and explore westward. However, the two ships encountered a terrible storm off the coast of Greenland and were forced to return home without even reaching North America.

Despite that setback, Franklin was appointed to another northern adventure shortly after his return home. He was given command of a small overland expedition of navy men and Canadian voyagers to survey the mouth of the Coppermine River and the Arctic coastline adjacent to it. This expedition, too, was fraught with troubles. The birchbark canoes used to navigate the treacherous Coppermine River and the choppy Arctic Ocean waters constantly needed repairs. The Canadians did not know or follow naval protocol, and food was continually in short supply. By the late summer of 1821, the explorers found themselves critically short of provisions on their trek back to winter quarters at Fort Enterprise, and the party was overcome with hunger, fatigue, and dissension. Eleven of the twenty men perished—nine from hunger, and a naval officer and another man from violence. The survivors existed by eating rotted carcasses of animals they found, their own clothing, and tea that they made from a semipoisonous lichen. They were eventually rescued by hunters of the Yellowknife people, who nursed them back to health.

When Franklin returned to England in 1822, he was surprised to learned that he had been promoted to the rank of commander during the previous year. He was also elected a member of the Royal Society and was feted in London's fashionable drawing rooms as "the man who ate his boots." Publication of his journal of the expedition, *Narrative of a Journey to the Shores of the Polar Sea in the Years 1819, 20, 21, and 22* (1824), laid the basis for his long-term popularity. The book was a best seller of its time and fueled the growing British enthusiasm for Arctic exploration.

In the years between his first and second overland expeditions Franklin enjoyed personal success as well as

HUNGER IN THE ARCTIC

John Franklin's journal of his first Arctic expedition is filled with stories about the privations that he and his men endured. This passage from October, 1821, recounts a typical experience near Canada's Great Slave Lake.

The Indians expected to have found here a bear in its den and to have made a hearty meal of its flesh, indeed it had been the subject of conversation all day and they had even gone so far as to divide it, frequently asking me what part I preferred, but when we came to the spot—oh! lamentable! it had already fallen a prey to the devouring appetites of some more fortunate hunters who had only left sufficient evidence that such a thing had once existed, and we had merely the consolation of realising an old proverb. One of our men however caught a fish which, with the assistance of some weed scraped from the rocks (*tripe de roche*) which forms a glutinous substance, made us a tolerable supper; it was not of the most choice kind yet good enough for hungry men. While we were eating it I perceived one of the women busily employed scraping an old skin, the contents of which her husband presented us with. They consisted of pounded meat, fat, and a greater proportion of Indians' and deers' hair than either; and though such a mixture may not appear very alluring to an English stomach it was thought a great luxury after three days' privation in these cheerless regions of America. Indeed had it not been for the precaution and generosity of the Indians we must have gone without sustenance until we reached the fort.

Source: John Franklin, *The Journey to the Polar Sea* (London: Everyman's Library, 1910), chapter 8.

tragedy. On August 19, 1823, he married Eleanor Anne Porden, a poet and socialite. Franklin was often away from London laying plans for his second overland expedition, however, and was absent for the birth of his only child, Eleanor Isabella, on June 3, 1824. He left England for his second command on February 16, 1825. His wife died six days later. While traveling with the surviving officers of his 1819-1822 expedition—Captain George Back and Dr. John Richardson—Franklin explored the coastlines around the lower Mackenzie River in northwestern Canada and returned to England in 1827.

After returning home, Franklin found civilian life again good to him. In 1828, he married Jane Griffin, and on April 29, 1829, he was knighted. Between 1830 and 1833, he served in the Mediterranean Sea, where he was the senior British naval officer in Greece during that country's war of independence against the Ottoman Empire. In 1836, he was appointed lieutenant governor of Van Diemen's Land, as Australia's island of Tasmania was then known. During his tenure there, he and his wife attempted many social and institutional improvements. Though he was popular among the colonists of

Van Diemen's Land, his tenure as a colonial administrator was ultimately unsuccessful, mostly because of his guilelessness in the face of hidden political agendas in the British Colonial Office. He was not invited to renew his post after 1844.

Fresh from his unremarkable governorship, Franklin was determined to restore his professional reputation. With the encouragement of his wife, the fifty-nine-year-old Franklin accepted the captaincy of the most ambitious Arctic expedition yet outfitted. Its ships, *Erebus* and *Terror*, carried 129 officers and men and were supplied for three years. On May 19, 1845, the ships began what many believed would be the expedition to complete the puzzle of the Northwest Passage, and England eagerly awaited news of the expedition's success.

When nothing had been heard from Franklin's expedition by 1847, the Admiralty began to entertain the possibility that it had met with disaster. From 1848 until 1859, more than thirty American and British ships—both public and private—were sent to search for the missing sailors. News of the expedition's fate first appeared in an 1854 report by Dr. John Rae, a Hudson's Bay Company surveyor who had interviewed a band of Inuit hunters along the north mainland coast. Their news was tragic: A group of white travelers had been discovered starved to death on an island, after resorting to cannibalism in an attempt to survive.

Though the British Admiralty considered the mystery of Franklin's fate closed, his widow, Lady Franklin, disagreed. Convinced that her husband had died with honor, she personally outfitted a final search for her husband and his crews in the area delineated by Rae's report in 1857. In 1859, the question was finally settled on the west shore of King William Island. Lieutenant William Hobson discovered a paper recording Sir John Franklin's death on June 11, 1847.

The evidence of Franklin's death in 1847 absolved him from the charge of cannibalism leveled at other members of the expedition, as he had died before the men were forced to abandon their ships. The document found by Hobson also contained a record of the remaining crews' plans to cross to the mainland and follow the Back River, east of the Coppermine, in hopes of reaching a Hudson's Bay Company outpost. Although no crew member survived, the record of their intentions was considered conclusive evidence that Franklin's men had been the first discoverers of a Northwest Passage, which they died crossing in 1847-1848.

SIGNIFICANCE

Though Franklin was lauded as a hero in Victorian England, his reputation has suffered under the scrutiny of late twentieth century scholarship. Franklin's sense of naval propriety has often been identified as the sole cause for the disasters of which he was a part, but this assessment ignores his equally recognizable kindness and sense of right, and makes no mention of the pressure Franklin must have been under to succeed: With the alternative of half pay and no prospects for naval officers after the Napoleonic Wars, Franklin no doubt felt compelled to continue his dangerous explorations despite the risks.

Franklin still remains the most recognizable icon of Arctic exploration, whose romantic and quixotic nature his name and history have come to encapsulate. His published journals as well as his disappearance fueled an intense curiosity about the Arctic that continues today. His two published journals were enormously popular in the nineteenth century and established the image of the Arctic explorer as a living hero, while his last expedition still haunts discussions of imperialism, scientific ambition, and exploration.

—*Erika Behrisch*

FURTHER READING

Atwood, Margaret. *Strange Things: The Malevolent North in Canadian Literature*. Oxford, England: Clarendon Press, 1995. Offers a twentieth century perspective on Franklin, acknowledging the continued fascination with his disappearance.

Fleming, Fergus. *Barrow's Boys*. London: Granta Books, 1998. Provides an excellent overview of the development of Arctic exploration as a navy activity in post-Napoleonic Britain, and Franklin's involvement in it.

Franklin, John. *Narrative of a Journey to the Shores of the Polar Sea in the Years 1819-20-21-22*. Vancouver: Douglas & McIntyre, 2000. Reprint of Franklin's account of his first major Arctic expedition, with a new introduction by James P. Delgado.

Traill, Henry Duff. *The Life of Sir John Franklin, R.N.* London: John Murray, 1896. Published by the Admiralty's own publisher, this biography offers an official perspective on Franklin's life and work.

Woodman, David C. *Unravelling the Franklin Mystery: Inuit Testimony*. Kingston: McGill-Queen's University Press, 1991. A comprehensive transcription and analysis of Inuit accounts of Franklin's last expedition.

Woodward, Frances. *Portrait of Jane: A Life of Lady Franklin*. London: Hodder and Stoughton, 1951. A detailed account of Franklin's second marriage and later career, including his military service in Greece, his administrative post in Van Diemen's Land, and his final Arctic expedition.

SEE ALSO: Zebulon Pike; Sir James Clark Ross; David Thompson.

GOTTLOB FREGE
German mathematician

Frege's writings were never widely read or appreciated during his own time, and his complex system of symbols and functions was forbidding even to the best minds in mathematics. Nevertheless, he is recognized as the founder of modern symbolic logic and the creator of the first system of notations and quantifiers of modern logic.

BORN: November 8, 1848; Wismar, Mecklenburg-Schwerin (now in Germany)
DIED: July 26, 1925; Bad Kleinen, Germany
ALSO KNOWN AS: Friedrich Ludwig Gottlob Frege (full name)
AREA OF ACHIEVEMENT: Mathematics

EARLY LIFE

Friedrich Ludwig Gottlob Frege (FREH-gah) was the son of the principal of a private girls' high school. While Frege was in high school in Wismar, his father died. Frege was devoted to his mother, who was a teacher and later principal of the girls' school. He may have had a brother, Arnold Frege, who was born in Wismar in 1852. Nothing further is known about Frege until he entered the university at the age of twenty-one. From 1869 to 1871, he attended the University of Jena and proceeded to the University of Göttingen, where he took courses in mathematics, physics, chemistry, and philosophy. By 1873, Frege had completed his thesis and had received his doctorate from the university. Frege returned to the University of Jena and applied for an unsalaried position. His mother wrote to the university that she would support him until he acquired regular employment. In 1874, as a result of publication of his dissertation on mathematical functions, he was placed on the staff of the university. He spent the rest of his life at Jena, where he investigated the foundations of mathematics and produced seminal works in logic.

Frege's early years at Jena were probably the happiest period in his life. He was highly regarded by the faculty and attracted some of the best students in mathematics. During these years, he taught an extra load as he assumed the courses of a professor who had become ill. He also worked on a volume on logic and mathematics. Frege's lectures were thoughtful and clearly organized, and were greatly appreciated by his students. Much of Frege's personal life, however, was beset by tragedies. Not only did his father die while he was a young man but his children also died young, as did his wife. He dedicated twenty-

five years to developing a formal system, in which all of mathematics could be derived from logic, only to learn that a fatal paradox destroyed the system. During his life, he received little formal recognition of his monumental work and, with his death in 1925, passed virtually unnoticed by the academic world.

LIFE'S WORK

Frege's first major work in logic was published in 1879. Although this was a short book of only eighty-eight pages, it has remained one of the most important single works ever written in the field. *Begriffsschrift: Eine der Arithmetischen Nachgebildete Formelsprache des reinen Denkens* (conceptual treatise: a formal language, modeled upon that of arithmetic, for pure thought) presented for the first time a formal system of modern logic. He created a system of formal symbols that could be used more regularly than ordinary language for the purposes of deductive logic. Frege was by no means the first person to use symbols as representations of words, because Aristotle had used this device and was followed by others throughout the history of deductive logic.

Earlier logicians, however, had thought that in order to make a judgment on the validity of sentences, a distinction was necessary between subject and predicate. For the purposes of rhetoric, there is a difference between the statements "The North defeated the South in the Civil War" and "The South was defeated by the North in the Civil War." For Frege, however, the content of both sentences conveyed the same concept and hence must be given the same judgment. In this work, Frege achieved the ideal of nineteenth century mathematics: that if proofs were completely formal and no intuition was required to judge the correctness of the proofs, then there could be complete certainty that these proofs were the result of explicitly stated assumptions. During this period, Frege began to use universal quantifiers in his logic, which cover statements that contain "some" or "every." Consequently, it was now possible to cover a range of objects rather than a single object in a statement.

In 1884, Frege published *Die Grundlagen der Arithmetik* (*The Foundations of Arithmetic*, 1950), which followed his attempt to apply similar principles to arithmetic as his earlier application to logic. In this work, he first reviewed the works of his predecessors and then raised a number of fundamental questions on the nature of numbers and arithmetic truth. This work was more philosophical than mathematical.

Throughout the work, Frege enunciated three basic positions concerning the world of philosophical logic. Mental images of a word as perceived by the speaker are irrelevant to the meaning of a word in a sentence in terms of its truth or falsity. The word "grass" in the sentence "the grass is green" does not depend on the mental image of "grass" but on the way in which the word is used in the sentence. Thus the meaning of a word was found in its usage. A second idea was that words have meaning only in the context of a sentence. Rather than depending on the precise definition of a word, the sentence determined the truth-value of the word. If "all grubs are green," then it is possible to understand this sentence without necessarily knowing anything about "grubs." Also, it is possible to make a judgment about a sentence that contains "blue grubs" as false, because "all grubs are green."

Frege's third idea deals with the distinction between concepts and objects. This distinction raises serious questions concerning the nature of proper names, identity, universals, and predicates, all of which were historically troublesome philosophical and linguistic problems.

After the publication of *The Foundations of Arithmetic*, Frege became known not only as a logician and a mathematician but also as a linguistic philosopher. Although the notion of proper name is important for his system of logic, it also extends far beyond those concerns. There had existed an extended debate as to whether numbers such as "1,2,3, . . ." or directions such as "north" were proper names. Frege argued that it was not appropriate to determine what can be known about these words and then see if they can be classified as objects. Rather, like his theory of meaning, in which the meaning of a word is determined by its use in a sentence, if numbers are used as objects they are proper names.

Frege's insistence on the usage of words extended to the problem of universals. According to tradition, something that can be named is a particular, while a universal is predicated on a particular. For example, "red rose" comprises a universal "red" and a particular "rose." Question arose as to whether universals existed in the sense that the "red" of the "red rose" existed independently of the "rose." Frege had suggested that universals are used as proper names in such sentences as "The rose is red."

Between 1893 and 1903, Frege published two volumes of his unfinished work *Grundgesetze der Arithmetik* (the basic laws of arithmetic). These volumes contained both his greatest contribution to philosophy and logic and the greatest weaknesses of his logical system.

Frege made a distinction between sense and reference, in that words frequently had the same reference, but may imply a different sense. Words such as "lad," "boy," and "youth" all have the same reference or meaning, but not in the same sense. As a result, two statements may be logically identical, yet have a different sense. Hence, 2 + 2 = 4 involves two proper names of a number, namely "2 + 2" and "4," but are used in different senses. Extending this idea to a logical system, the meaning or reference of the proper names and the truth-value of the sentence depend only on the reference of the object and not its sense. Thus, a sentence such as "The boy wore a hat" is identical to the sentence "The lad wore a hat." Because the logical truth-value of a sentence depends on the meaning of the sentence, the inclusion of a sentence without any meaning within a complex statement means that the entire statement lacks any truth-value. This proved to be a problem that Frege could not resolve and became a roadblock to his later work.

A further problem that existed in *Grundgesetze der Arithmetik*, which was written as a formal system of logic including the use of terms, symbols, and derived proofs, was the theory of classes. Frege wanted to use logic to derive the entire structure of mathematics to include all real numbers. To achieve this, Frege included, as part of his axioms, a primitive theory of sets or classes.

While the second volume of *Grundgesetze der Arithmetik* was being prepared for publication, Frege received a letter from Bertrand Russell describing a contradiction that became known as the Russell Paradox. This paradox, sometimes known as the Stranger Loop, asks, is "the class of all classes that are not members of itself" a member of itself or not? For example, the "class of all dogs" is not a dog; the "class of all animals" is not an animal. If the class of all classes is a member of itself, then it is one of those classes that are not members of themselves. However, if it is not a member of itself, then it must be a member of all classes that are members of themselves, and the loop goes on forever. Frege replaced the class axiom with a modified and weaker axiom, but his formal system was weakened, and he never completed the third volume of the work.

Between 1904 and 1917, Frege added few contributions to his earlier works. During these years, he attempted to work through those contradictions that arose in his attempt to derive all of mathematics from logic. By 1918, he had begun to write a new book on logic, but he completed only three chapters. In 1923, he seemed to have broken through his intellectual dilemma and no longer believed that it was possible to create a foundation of mathematics based on logic. He began work in a new direction, beginning with geometry, but completed little of this work before his death.

SIGNIFICANCE

In *Begriffsschrift*, Gottlob Frege created the first comprehensive system of formal logic since the ancient Greeks. He provided some of the foundations of modern logic with the formulation of the principles of noncontradiction and excluded middle. Equally important, Frege introduced the use of quantifiers to bind variables, which distinguished modern symbolic logic from earlier systems.

Frege's works were never widely read or appreciated. His system of symbols and functions was forbidding even to the best minds in mathematics. Russell, however, made a careful study of Frege and was clearly influenced by his system of logic. Also, Ludwig Wittgenstein incorporated a number of Frege's linguistic ideas, such as the use of ordinary language, into his works. Frege's distinction between sense and reference later generated a renewed interest in his work, and a number of important philosophical and linguistic studies are based on his original research.

—Victor W. Chen

FURTHER READING

Bynum, Terrell W. Introduction to *Conceptual Notations*, by Gottlob Frege. Oxford, England: Clarendon Press, 1972. An eighty-page introduction to the logic of Frege. Although sections of the text on the logic are not suited for the general reader, the introductory text is clear, concise, and highly accessible. The significant works by Frege are outlined in simple terms, and the commentary is useful.

Currie, Gregory. *Frege: An Introduction to His Philosophy*. Brighton, England: Harvester Press, 1982. Discusses all the major developments in Frege's thought from a background chapter to the *Begriffsschrift*, theory of numbers, philosophical logic and methods, basic law, and the fatal paradox. Some parts of this text are accessible to the general reader; other parts require a deeper understanding of philosophical issues.

Dummett, Michael A. E. *Frege: Philosophy of Language*. London: Duckworth, 1973. One of the leading authorities on the philosophy of Frege. The advantage of this text over others is that Dummett is in part responsible for the idea that Frege is a linguistic philosopher. Somewhat difficult but good introduction to Frege.

Grossmann, Reinhardt. *Reflections on Frege's Philosophy*. Evanston, Ill.: Northwestern University Press, 1969. Delineates three major areas of Frege's thoughts as found in *Begriffsschrift* and *The Foundations of Arithmetic*, and describes the distinction between meaning, sense, and reference. Within these areas the author writes an exposition on a few selected problems that are of current interest.

Hill, Claire O. *Rethinking Identity and Metaphysics: The Foundations of Analytic Philosophy*. New Haven, Conn.: Yale University Press, 1997. The author provides a reassessment of twentieth century analytic philosophy by examining the writings of Frege, Bertrand Russell, and Willard Quine. Hill concludes that the lack of clarity inherent in the abstract issue of identity has implications for solid subjects, such as medical ethics.

Kneale, William, and Martha Kneale. *The Development of Logic*. Oxford, England: Clarendon Press, 1962. Three chapters in this work are useful. Chapter 7 covers Frege and his contemporaries, Frege's criticism of his predecessors, and Frege's definition of natural numbers. Chapter 8 covers Frege's three major works and outlines his contributions to the world of logic. Chapter 9 covers formal developments in logic after Frege and reveals his pivotal position in the development of modern symbolic logic.

Noonan, Harold W. *Frege: A Critical Introduction*. Malden, Mass.: Blackwell, 2001. An overview of Frege's ideas, emphasizing his logic, theory of meaning, distinctions between sense and reference, and ideas about object, concept, and function.

Reck, Erich H., ed. *From Frege to Wittgenstein: Perspectives on Early Analytic Philosophy*. New York: Oxford University Press, 2002. Considers how the two men developed an analytic philosophy, including a discussion of Wittgenstein's debt to Frege, an explanation of the roots of analytic philosophy, and interpretations of some of Frege's writings.

Salerno, Joseph. *On Frege*. Belmont, Calif.: Wadsworth/Thomson Learning, 2001. Brief, nontechnical overview of Frege's ideas aimed at students seeking a better understanding of his philosophy.

Weiner, Joan. *Frege Explained: From Arithmetic to Analytic Philosophy.* Chicago: Open Court, 2004. A summary of Frege's philosophy, tracing the development of his ideas about logic, sense, meaning, and other subjects. Includes a chapter about his life and character.

SEE ALSO: Lewis Carroll; John Stuart Mill.

RELATED ARTICLES in *Great Events from History: The Nineteenth Century, 1801-1900:* 1847: Boole Publishes *The Mathematical Analysis of Logic*; 1859: Mill Publishes *On Liberty*; 1899: Hilbert Publishes *The Foundations of Geometry.*

JOHN C. FRÉMONT
American explorer and military commander

Frémont's exploits as an explorer helped to propel the American nation westward toward Oregon and California. When the continental nation he helped to create was faced with civil war, he fought to maintain the Union and end slavery.

BORN: January 21, 1813; Savannah, Georgia
DIED: July 13, 1890; New York, New York
ALSO KNOWN AS: John Charles Frémont (full name)
AREAS OF ACHIEVEMENT: Exploration, government and politics

EARLY LIFE

When John Charles Frémont (free-mahnt) was born, his parents were not married. In 1811, Ann Beverly Whiting had left her elderly husband John Pryor to run away with Charles Frémon, a young French emigrant who taught dancing and French. For several years the struggling Frémon family traveled the South, but after the father died they settled in Charleston, South Carolina, where John Charles grew to maturity.

At the age of fourteen, Frémont clerked in the law office of John W. Mitchell, who soon sent the young man to Dr. John Roberton's academy. In 1829, Frémont entered the junior class of the College of Charleston. Showing promise, he nevertheless fell behind in his studies from a lack of diligence as well as the distraction of a young love. In 1831, the faculty reluctantly dismissed him for "incorrigible negligence," three months short of his graduation.

In 1833, saved from obscurity by Joel Poinsett, former minister to Mexico, Frémont taught mathematics on the USS *Natchez* on a South American cruise and then earned an appointment in 1835 as professor of mathematics in the navy. He nevertheless declined this position to join Captain William G. Williams in surveying part of a proposed railroad route from Charleston to Cincinnati. This first assignment earned for him a second as Williams's assistant in 1836-1837, surveying the lands of the Cherokee Indians in Georgia. Frémont showed little con-cern for the forced removal of the Cherokees across the Mississippi, but he did discover a longing to pursue a life in unexplored lands.

With the help of Secretary of War Poinsett, Frémont was assigned in 1838 to assist Joseph Nicolas Nicollet, a respected French scientist mapping the region between the Mississippi and Missouri Rivers. He was commissioned a second lieutenant in the United States Topographical Corps and from Nicollet received valuable experience in frontier survival, as well as rigorous training in mapmaking and scientific observation. As Nicollet's protégé, Frémont stood ready to replace the gravely ill scientist on future missions.

Bright and inquisitive, Frémont already possessed the knowledge of surveying, mathematics, and natural sciences, as well as the impulsiveness, that would shape his later career. Bearded and slightly but sturdily built, he was able to endure great physical and personal hardships. His dark hair, olive skin, and piercing blue eyes attracted the friendship and affection of men and women alike. In 1841, he won the lifelong admiration and love of the young and talented Jessie Benton, acquiring not only a bride but also another powerful benefactor in her father, Senator Thomas Hart Benton of Missouri.

LIFE'S WORK

Frémont received his first independent assignment in 1841 to survey the Des Moines River region. On his return, he secretly married Jessie, soon benefiting from his family connection with Senator Benton: Advocates of American expansion, led by Benton, were eager to encourage emigration to the Oregon country, and Frémont was thus given command of his first western expedition, assigned to examine part of the trail to Oregon while gathering information useful to emigrants and the government.

In Missouri, Frémont enlisted Kit Carson as his guide and set off from the Kansas River in June, 1842. Following the Platte to the Sweetwater River, he went on to cross the Rocky Mountains at South Pass in Wyoming, later describing the route as no more difficult than the ascent up Capitol Hill. He then explored the headwaters of the Green River in the Wind River Range, unfurling an American flag atop one of its loftiest peaks. Returning, Frémont led six men in a collapsible boat down the Platte. When the current became swift and dangerous, he rashly decided to run the rapids, resulting in an accident that destroyed much of his equipment and part of the expedition's records.

Frémont's second expedition of 1843-1844 was more ambitious. With a large, well-equipped party (including an unauthorized howitzer cannon), he was to complete his survey of the overland trail all the way to Oregon. Setting off in May, the explorer first sought a new pass through the Colorado mountains but soon rejoined the Oregon Trail. Crossing at South Pass, he pushed on to the British forts in the Oregon country, finally reaching Fort Vancouver on the Columbia. On this expedition, Frémont made the first scientific investigation of the Great Salt Lake; his reports inspired Brigham Young to lead his Mormon followers to settle there and make the region bloom, as Frémont had predicted.

John C. Frémont. (Library of Congress)

From Oregon, Frémont embarked on a perilous journey southward, exploring and naming the Great Basin and then attempting a risky winter crossing of the Sierra Nevada into California, successfully leading his men to Sutter's Fort in the Sacramento Valley. Inspired in part by American interest in the Mexican province of California, Frémont's adventures intensified American passions to possess this valuable Pacific prize. Returning via the old Spanish Trail, Utah Lake, and Bent's Fort on the Arkansas River, Frémont emerged in August, 1844, a national celebrity.

With Jessie's valuable help, Frémont prepared reports of his first and second expeditions that captured the excitement and promise of the new land. Congress ordered the reports published for public distribution, providing emigrants a guide for western travel. The popular reports helped to dispel the notion that the Plains region was an arid wasteland, showed the Oregon Trail passable, and praised the fertile valleys of Oregon and California.

With a well-armed party of sixty men, the brevet captain's third expedition would place him in California just as relations with Mexico worsened. Starting in June, 1845, the party followed the Arkansas and then crossed the central Colorado Rockies. Frémont paused to examine further the Great Salt Lake, then led his party across the desert to the west. While the main party followed a safer route, Frémont led a smaller group directly across the Great Basin and then attempted another winter crossing of the Sierras. Encountering less difficulty than on the previous trip, he arrived once again at Sutter's Fort, eager to play a role in California's future.

Frémont's formidable force earned the suspicion of Mexican officials, who ordered the party to leave the province. Although war with Mexico was months away, Frémont defied the order, raised the American flag, and prepared for a confrontation. When none developed, he slowly moved toward Oregon but retraced his steps after the arrival of a messenger from Washington. Marine Lieutenant Archibald Gillespie had carried important dispatches to Consul Thomas O. Larkin at Monterey, directing him to conciliate the native Californians to accept American rule. Gillespie repeated these instructions to Frémont and relayed news of trouble with Mexico. Frémont misinterpreted the government's instructions to mean that he should return to California and act to protect American interests there. After a bloody clash with Indians, he returned to the Sacramento Valley, assuming command of the "Bear Flag" revolt of American settlers in June, 1846.

Frémont's actions secured northern California for the United States but were contrary to the government's wishes to win the province peacefully with the aid of its citizens. Once hostilities with Mexico began, American naval forces seized the ports of Monterey and San Francisco in July, 1846. Frémont's frontiersmen and settlers then formed the "California Battalion" to assist Commodore Robert F. Stockton in securing southern California. San Diego and Los Angeles were quickly occupied, but a revolt by Californians forced the Americans to retake the south. Assembling a large force in the north, Frémont arrived too late to join in the battle for Los Angeles, but he did accept (without authority) the Californians' surrender at Cahuenga.

In January, 1847, Stockton appointed Frémont governor of California. This position embroiled the current lieutenant colonel in a bitter dispute over proper authority between the commodore and General Stephen Watts Kearny, who had arrived from Santa Fe only to be bloodied by Californians at San Pasqual. As governor in Los Angeles, Frémont recognized Commodore Stockton's authority while unwisely resisting General Kearny's commands, resulting in his arrest and return east virtually a prisoner. In a celebrated court-martial defense, he won public sympathy, but in January, 1848, was found guilty of mutiny, disobedience, and conduct prejudicial to military order. He was sentenced to dismissal from the service. President James K. Polk disallowed the mutiny conviction but upheld the lesser charges while suspending the punishment. Frémont spurned Polk's gesture and resigned his commission instead, ending his career as an explorer for the United States Army.

To regain his injured honor, Frémont organized a privately funded fourth expedition in late 1848. Intended to locate suitable passes for a central railroad route to the Pacific, the expedition attempted a midwinter passage of the severe San Juan Mountains in southern Colorado. Disregarding the advice of mountain men and perhaps misled by his guide "Old Bill" Williams, Frémont plunged into the snowy mountains, only to find disaster. Cold and starvation eventually took the lives of ten of his thirty-three men, while a few survivors may have resorted to cannibalism. Frémont withdrew to Taos, New Mexico, sending a relief party to his surviving men. With a smaller party, he pushed on to California by the Gila River route, arriving in early 1849.

Frémont's fortunes revived once more as gold had just been discovered in California. In 1847, he had directed Consul Larkin to buy a tract of land near San Francisco; instead Larkin had secured a large grant in the inte-

rior. At first apparently worthless, the Mariposa grant yielded immense wealth in gold and became the Frémonts' California home. Then in December, 1849, Frémont was selected one of California's first United States senators, serving a short term from 1850 to 1851 as an antislavery Democrat.

Not chosen to lead one of the five government parties surveying the best route for a Pacific railroad, Frémont in late 1853 undertook his fifth and final expedition to prove the superiority of a central route. On this venture, Frémont found less hardship in attempting another winter crossing of the Colorado mountains. Crossing into Utah, however, his men were again on the brink of starvation, whereupon he swore them not to resort to cannibalism. The party was finally saved in February, 1854, when it arrived at a Mormon settlement in Parowan. The route was not adopted for the Pacific railroad.

As tension grew between North and South, Frémont emerged as a candidate for president in 1856, first for the Democratic Party and then for the newly organized Republican Party. Hostile to slavery, he favored the Republican position, opposing slavery's westward expansion, and in June, 1856, accepted the first presidential nomination of the young party. In the general election, he faced both Democrat James Buchanan and the candidate of the Know-Nothing Party, Millard Fillmore. The "Pathfinder" made few campaign utterances, but his illegitimate origins and false campaign charges that he was a Catholic virtually overshadowed his opposition to the spread of slavery to Kansas. While he carried eleven free states, lack of campaign organization and money in politically critical states such as Pennsylvania and Indiana probably cost him the election. Perhaps Frémont was not the best man to lead his nation in time of crisis, but his popularity helped to establish the Republican Party and thus contributed to the election of Abraham Lincoln four years later.

After his disappointing defeat, Frémont temporarily retired to private life, absorbed in developing the Mariposa, by now encumbered with debt. When the Civil War erupted in April, 1861, he was in Europe on business. Born a southerner, he did not hesitate to support the Union in its greatest crisis. On his own authority he purchased arms and ammunition for the Union in England and France, then returned home to accept an appointment as a major general commanding the Western Department based in St. Louis.

Beginning in July, 1861, Frémont's challenging task was to pacify the divided state of Missouri while raising an army to undertake an offensive down the Mississippi.

He received little support from Washington, and his duties were overwhelming. Although he reinforced the strategic Illinois town of Cairo, he did not act quickly enough to aid Nathaniel Lyon, who was defeated and killed at Wilson's Creek on August 10. Charges of favoritism and corruption in government contracts haunted Frémont's command, but most controversial was his sudden order of August 30 declaring martial law in Missouri, threatening to shoot captured guerrillas, and freeing the slaves of rebel masters.

While antislavery advocates praised Frémont's emancipation edict, Lincoln feared its effect on the border states and directed him to modify the order. The general stubbornly refused to heed Lincoln, forcing the president to reverse the measure publicly. With Frémont's command assaulted by powerful political enemies, his wife went east to present his case, but her stormy interview with Lincoln did more harm than good. As Frémont sought to lead his troops to victory in southwestern Missouri, Lincoln removed him from command of the Western Department in November, 1861.

Outcry over Frémont's removal induced Lincoln to appoint him in March, 1862, to command the newly formed Mountain Department, designed to capture an important railroad at Knoxville, Tennessee. Abandoning this effort, Frémont was also outmarched by Stonewall Jackson in the Virginia Valley Campaign of 1862. At the Battle of Cross Keys on June 8, Frémont proved ineffective against Confederate troops, and when Lincoln added Frémont's force to the command of John Pope, Frémont asked to be relieved. In 1864, Frémont was nominated to the presidency by some Democrats and radical Republicans dissatisfied with Lincoln. At first accepting the nomination, he soon feared a Democratic victory and withdrew from the race, helping to ensure Lincoln's reelection.

As the war came to an end, Frémont lost much of his wealth as well as control of his beloved Mariposa. His ambitions turned to railroad finance, as he still hoped to realize his dream of a Pacific railroad. He became involved with unscrupulous business associates, however, squandering the remainder of his fortune and a good portion of his reputation when the Southwest Pacific failed in 1867 and the Memphis & El Paso did so in 1870.

From 1878 to 1883, Frémont served as governor of Arizona Territory. With Jessie's help he wrote his memoirs, published in 1887. Belated gratitude from his nation came in April, 1890, when he was restored to his rank as major general and placed on the retired list with pay. Death came in New York in July, 1890, from a sudden attack of peritonitis.

SIGNIFICANCE

Frémont's exploits as an explorer exemplified the restless energy and unbounded ambition of mid-nineteenth century America. Proud and self-reliant, Americans resented restraints and the rulings of authority. Frémont's career also reflected the lack of discipline and wisdom born of experience that led the young and sometimes careless American people into such tragedies as the brutal treatment of American Indians, the war on Mexico, and the spilling of brothers' blood in the Civil War. Like his nation, Frémont climbed heights of adventure and opportunity, but also found failure, conflict, and injustice.

Frémont never claimed to be a "Pathfinder"; his mapping expeditions usually followed paths already worn by fur traders and early emigrants. Nevertheless, his romantic journeys spurred American expansion to the Pacific, his reports encouraging western emigration while providing travelers with useful information. Frémont's mapping and scientific work rivaled that of earlier explorers, improving knowledge of the vast interior region from the Rockies to the Sierra Nevada, while helping to clarify the true natures of the Continental Divide and the Great Basin.

As politician, soldier, and financier, Frémont found less glory. His unauthorized actions in the California revolt remain controversial, while his service during the Civil War provoked charges of political opportunism and military ineffectiveness. His mining and railroad schemes typified the boom period of American industrial expansion but left him almost destitute. His death in 1890 coincided with the end of the romantic age of the American West, where he left his name and his mark.

—Vernon L. Volpe

FURTHER READING

Chaffin, Tom. *Pathfinder: John Charles Frémont and the Course of American Empire*. New York: Hill & Wang, 2002. Well-written, comprehensive, and balanced biography, describing Frémont's varied life and career. Includes information on his expeditions, relationships with allies and adversaries, and marriage to Jessie Benton Frémont.

Egan, Ferol. *Frémont: Explorer for a Restless Nation*. Garden City, N.Y.: Doubleday, 1977. By focusing on Frémont's career to 1854, this work praises his accomplishments more than most.

Frémont, Jessie Benton. *The Letters of Jessie Benton Frémont*. Edited by Pamela Herr and Mary Lee Spence. Urbana: University of Illinois Press, 1993. Collection of 271 of Jessie Frémont's letters, fully annotated by the editors. The letters reveal her relationship with her difficult husband and her outspokenness on abolition and other issues.

Frémont, John Charles. *Memoirs of My Life*. Chicago: Belford, Clarke, 1887. Frémont's memoirs are the only source for much of the available information on his personal life as well as his career. An intended second volume was not published.

Goodwin, Cardinal L. *John Charles Frémont: An Explanation of His Career*. Stanford, Calif.: Stanford University Press, 1930. This is perhaps the most critical account of Frémont's life. It views the explorer as a "drifter" who entered into corrupt financial dealings.

Harlow, Neal. *California Conquered: War and Peace on the Pacific, 1846-1850*. Berkeley: University of California Press, 1982. Much of this work examines Frémont's controversial role in the California conquest. It also discusses his dispute with Kearny and subsequent arrest.

Jackson, Donald, and Mary Lee Spence, eds. *The Expeditions of John Charles Frémont*. 3 vols. Champaign: University of Illinois Press, 1970-1984. This multivolume collection of documents is an invaluable source of information for Frémont's expeditions. It includes his reports, important correspondence, and the record of his court-martial.

Nevins, Allan. *Frémont: Pathmarker of the West*. 2 vols. New York: Frederick Ungar, 1961. Perhaps the best study of Frémont, this work by a famous American historian portrays the explorer as a flawed hero of American expansion.

Roberts, David. *A Newer World: Kit Carson, John C. Frémont, and the Claiming of the American West*. New York: Simon & Schuster, 2000. An account of Frémont's expeditions in the western United States from the early 1840's until the beginning of the Civil War. Describes Carson's role in the expeditions and the relationship of the two men.

Rolle, Andrew. *John Charles Frémont: Character as Destiny*. Norman: University of Oklahoma Press, 1991. A psychological examination of Frémont's character, resulting in a generally unflattering biography.

SEE ALSO: Thomas Hart Benton; James Buchanan; Kit Carson; Millard Fillmore; Stonewall Jackson; Abraham Lincoln; James K. Polk; Brigham Young.

RELATED ARTICLES in *Great Events from History: The Nineteenth Century, 1801-1900:* May, 1842-1854: Frémont Explores the American West; June 30, 1846-January 13, 1847: United States Occupies California and the Southwest; January 29-September 20, 1850: Compromise of 1850; March 2, 1853-1857: Pacific Railroad Surveys; July 6, 1854: Birth of the Republican Party.

FRIEDRICH FROEBEL
German educator

Froebel is best remembered for founding the first kindergarten. He believed in the underlying unity in nature, for him God, and emphasized that schools should provide pleasant surroundings, encourage self-activity, and offer physical training for children.

BORN: April 21, 1782; Oberweissbach, Thuringia (now in Germany)
DIED: June 21, 1852; Marienthal, Thuringia (now in Germany)
ALSO KNOWN AS: Friedrich Fröbel; Friedrich Wilhelm August Froebel (full name)
AREA OF ACHIEVEMENT: Education

EARLY LIFE
Friedrich Wilhelm August Froebel (FREW-bel) had an unhappy childhood that affected his entire life. The son of Johann Jakob and Eleonore Friderica Froebel, he was left motherless when he was nine months old. His father, a Lutheran pastor, was aloof and pompous. After he remarried, he lost interest in Friedrich, who was still too young for school. After Johann's wife bore their child, Friedrich was treated like an interloper. His stepmother addressed him in the formal third person rather than in the familiar second person normally used with children.

The father considered his son stupid and rebellious. He conveyed these feelings to Friedrich, who developed a sense of personal unworthiness. When Friedrich began school, his father insisted that he attend the girls' school, making Friedrich feel more unusual than he already considered himself.

When he was ten, Friedrich was sent to live with a kindly uncle in Stadt Ilm, remaining there for five years.

On his return home, however, the antagonisms that plagued his earlier days resurfaced, so his father apprenticed him to a woodcutter at Neuhof, the former home of educational reformer Johann Heinrich Pestalozzi, where he stayed for two years.

At the age of seventeen, Friedrich visited his brother, a medical student at the University of Jena. Although he was ill prepared for the university, Froebel attended elementary lectures in philosophy, the sciences, and mathematics until he was jailed by the university for indebtedness. After his father reluctantly posted his bail, Froebel drifted for five years. After a flirtation with architecture, he turned to tutoring and found that he loved teaching.

In 1805, Froebel made his first short visit to Yverdon, where Pestalozzi had just established his experimental school. After a brief stay in Frankfurt, he returned to Yverdon to spend four years as an assistant to Pestalozzi. He perceived that Pestalozzi's approach failed both to interconnect the subjects being taught and to give much attention to the students' spiritual connection with the universe. These reservations spurred Froebel into formulating his own philosophy of education.

Friedrich Froebel. (Library of Congress)

LIFE'S WORK

When Froebel completed his four-year stay at Yverdon in 1810, he returned to Frankfurt as a tutor. He soon decided, however, that he had a dual destiny. On one hand, he saw himself as a potential educational reformer. On the other, he was trying to find a unity in nature, an explanation of the mysteries of existence. Accordingly, he was enrolled in the University of Göttingen in 1811, first studying ancient languages in his search for the underlying unity in existence. He then turned his attention to mathematics, the sciences, and philosophy, subjects to which he had been exposed at Jena.

In 1812, Froebel moved to the University of Berlin to study crystallography; his interest in this subject was awakened by an essay he had written on the symbolism of spheres the preceding year at Göttingen. By 1813, he was assistant curator at the university's museum of mineralogy. He continued his research in crystals, viewing them always as symbols of an underlying unity.

Although Froebel was offered a teaching position at the University of Berlin in 1816, he believed that his greatest contribution could be made by opening a school. In that year, in a humble cottage not far from Pestalozzi's Neuhof, he founded the Allegemeine Deutsche Erziehungsanstalt (universal German institute of education). The student body consisted of five of Froebel's nephews.

His declared purpose was to teach people how to be free, something that he himself was still in the process of learning.

By 1817, the school had grown. Froebel moved it to more imposing quarters in nearby Keilhau. He was soon joined by Wilhelm Middendorff and Heinrich Langethal, friends he had made in 1813 during his brief service in the military. The school almost foundered in 1818 after Froebel's marriage to Wilhelmine Hoffmeister aroused contention in the closely knit school community. The origins of the discord are perhaps attributable to homosexual overtones, overt or covert, in Froebel's relationship with Middendorff and Langethal. One of Froebel's brothers rescued the school with both funds and a new approach to running its business. The school's enrollment rose to sixty.

As the enterprise succeeded, Froebel became increasingly absolutist, autocratic, and tyrannical. Students began to rebel against him, and word reached public officials that all was not well at the institution. An official investigation cleared the school of the charges against it, but the damage had been done. By 1820, Froebel's influence was minimal, although he was associated with the school until 1831. From the Keilhau experience Froebel wrote *Die Menschenerziehung* (1826; *The Education of*

Man, 1885), which details his philosophy of teaching children to age ten.

Essentially, the book is guided more by intuition than reason. It is based on nothing resembling scientific method. Froebel's stated aim is to help his students unlock what is inside them and to find a harmony between their inner selves and the external world, which to Froebel is the entire universe. The approach is mystical and shows Froebel as a deeply religious man who, presuming a divine origin for the universe, proceeds to suggest ways to bring human beings into a balance with that divine, creating force. As Froebel searched for absolutes, his search made him increasingly absolutist.

Froebel believed that everything, no matter how small, has a purpose. His scheme of education was to lead people to discover that purpose. He agreed with Pestalozzi's belief that, because the universe is constantly changing, nothing in life is static. This reasoning led him quite naturally to a dynamic *Weltanschauung* (worldview). For Froebel, people are themselves an inherent part of all activity. They can be guided by skillful teachers, but real teaching proceeds only from self-activity. Froebel's conception of human development is one in which infancy, childhood, youth, and maturity are separate entities, but one in which these stages are entities evolving into subsequent stages of which they are forever parts. Such speculation suggests the taxonomies of such educational theorists as Benjamin S. Bloom and Lawrence Kohlberg and also presages Sigmund Freud.

Froebel, like Jean-Jacques Rousseau, presumed that children are inherently good. He thought that evil resulted from bad education. He considered the ideal educational institution to be the earliest one—the family—at whose heart, he believed, is the mother as chief teacher of the young. Froebel's own education lacked the fundamental ingredient of effective learning—a mother who both loved and taught. Froebel virtually deified mothers, and in so doing, moved in the direction of what was to be his greatest educational contribution, the kindergarten—literally a garden whose blossoms are children. Froebel was rationalizing guilt feelings about what he perceived as his own evil when he wrote that wickedness proceeds from a mother's neglect of her young child.

Froebel left Keilhau in 1831 and went to Switzerland, where he opened a school; he opened a second at Lucerne. Soon, however, he was forced to disband these schools, partly because Lucerne's Catholic populace was suspicious of him and partly because his nephews, his former students at Keilhau, bore him great animosity and did everything they could to discredit him. By 1833, Froebel had developed a plan for the education of Bern's poor, but he had yet to find his real vocation.

In 1835, Froebel was appointed director of the orphanage at Burgdorf, the site of some of Pestalozzi's pre-Yverdon teaching, and he operated the orphanage according to Pestalozzi's methods, training teachers at the orphanage and teaching the children. At Burgdorf, Froebel began to concentrate on the education of young children and especially of those normally considered too young for school. He left Burgdorf in 1836 to go to Berlin, where he studied nursery schools.

In 1837, at the age of fifty-five, Froebel established a school in Blankenburg, not far from Keilhau, for the training of very young children. He called it a *Kleinkinderbeschäftigungsanstalt* (an institution for the occupation of small children), but in 1840 he changed the name to the less cumbersome, more familiar kindergarten. In this school, he instituted his method of teaching through gifts and occupations. Children received, over a period of time, ten boxes of gifts, objects from which they could learn, and they also were assigned ten

---

COINING THE NAME "KINDERGARTEN"

Around 1862, Johann Arnold Barop, Friedrich Froebel's nephew by marriage, remembered the moment that Froebel had come up with the name "kindergarten."

When Friedrich Froebel came back from Berlin, the idea of an institution for the education of little children had fully taken shape in his mind. I took rooms for him in the neighbouring Blankenburg. Long did he rack his brains for a suitable name for his new scheme. Middendorff and I were one day walking to Blankenburg with him over the Steiger Pass. He kept on repeating, "Oh, if I could only think of a suitable name for my youngest born!" Blankenburg lay at our feet, and he walked moodily towards it. Suddenly he stood still as if fettered fast to the spot, and his eyes assumed a wonderful, almost refulgent, brilliancy. Then he shouted to the mountains so that it echoed to the four winds of heaven, "*Eurêka!* I have it! KINDERGARTEN shall be the name of the new Institution!"

Source: Friedrich Froebel, *Autobiography of Friedrich Froebel*, translated and annotated by Emilie Michaelis (Syracuse, N.Y.: C. W. Bardeen, 1889).

occupations, activities that would result in their creating gifts.

Part of Froebel's technique was to devise games to interest and actively involve children both physically and mentally. He recorded these techniques in *Die Päda-gogik des Kindergartens* (1862; *Friedrich Froebel's Pedagogics of the Kindergarten: Or, His Ideas Concerning the Play and Playthings of the Child*, 1895), published posthumously. His most successful book of that period was *Mutter- und Kose-lieder* (1844; *Mother-Play and Nursery Songs*, 1878), a book containing fifty original songs and finger plays that would help mothers interact with their infants. This book attracted an enthusiastic following.

Successful though Froebel's first kindergarten was in many respects, it fell into debt by 1844, and he had to disband it. People expressed great fears about kindergartens, worrying about the political and religious philosophies to which very young, impressionable children were exposed in Froebel's institution, which enrolled students from ages one through seven. By 1851, the Prussian government had banned kindergartens as threats to society. Meanwhile, Froebel's influential nephews worked hard to discredit him.

On June 21, 1852, a year after he married Luisa Leven, his second wife, who was thirty years his junior, Froebel died at Marienthal, his kindergartens banned in Prussia until 1860.

SIGNIFICANCE

Friedrich Froebel's experimental school, the kindergarten, has affected education and society significantly. Froebel had vigorous supporters, among them his widow and the Baroness Berthe von Marenholtz-Bülow, both of whom traveled widely to disseminate his ideas. Indeed, Charles Dickens wrote a favorable account of a kindergarten he had seen.

Mrs. Carl Schurz and her sister, both trained by Froebel, imported the kindergarten to the United States in 1855, establishing a German-language kindergarten in Watertown, Wisconsin. Elizabeth Peabody established the first English-language kindergarten in the United States in Boston in 1860.

The term *kindergarten* has survived in the United States, although it now frequently designates that single year before a child enters the primary grades. The kindergarten as Froebel perceived it now exists in the United States as the preschool, attended by infants of several weeks to children of four or five.

—*R. Baird Shuman*

FURTHER READING

Brehony, Kevin J., ed. *The Origins of Nursery Education: Friedrich Froebel and the English System.* 6 vols. New York: Routledge, 2001. The first five volumes of this set are translations of Froebel's books, including *The Education of Man* and *Lessons on the Kindergarten*. The last volume reprints journal articles discussing the evolution of English nursery education.

Brosterman, Norman. *Inventing Kindergarten.* With original photography by Kiyoshi Togashi. New York: H. N. Abrams, 1997. Brosterman is a staunch proponent of Froebel's conception of kindergarten. His book provides biographical information on Froebel and an explanation of Froebel's theories to advance his argument that the Froebelian conception of kindergarten is the best form of schooling for very young children.

Bruce, Tina, Anne Findlay, Jane Read, and Mary Scarborough. *Recurring Themes in Education.* London: P. Chapman, 1995. Examines six recurring themes in Froebel's philosophy and explains the relationship of these ideas to the current British educational system.

Downs, Robert B. *Friedrich Froebel.* Boston: Twayne, 1978. An accurate, brief overview of Froebel. Solid presentation of facts, although generally short on analysis. The book serves the basic purpose for which it is intended, that of informing the reading public and college undergraduates.

Froebel, Friedrich. *Autobiography of Friedrich Froebel.* Translated and annotated by Emilie Michaelis and H. Keatley Moore. Syracuse, N.Y.: Bardeen, 1889. Froebel's only autobiographical record exists in two long letters, one written to the duke of Meiningen in 1827, the other to Karl Krause in 1828. These letters, well translated and accurate, along with Johann Barop's notes on the Froebel community, make up this useful volume. Helpful for biographical details.

Kilpatrick, William H. *Froebel's Kindergarten Principles Critically Examined.* New York: Macmillan, 1916. Despite its age, an indispensable book for Froebel scholarship because it describes how the intractability of the International Kindergartners Association, founded in 1892, eventually clashed with Granville Stanley Hall's more scientifically devised psychological approach to early childhood education. An accurate, objective assessment of an important topic.

Lawrence, Evelyn, ed. *Friedrich Froebel and English Education.* New York: Philosophical Library, 1953.

Six British educators discuss Froebel's influence on the schools of Great Britain and on education in general. A balanced view of Froebel's contributions outside Germany.

Liebschner, Joachim. *Child's Work: Freedom and Play in Froebel's Educational Theory and Practice*. Parkwest, N.Y.: Lutterworth Press, 2002. The title of this book comes from Froebel's famous remark: "A child's work is his play." The book describes Froebel's educational philosophy, his motivations, and his efforts to establish programs for early childhood education. Includes translations of some of Froebel's German texts.

Marenholtz-Bülow, Berthe von. *Reminiscences of Friedrich Froebel*. Translated by Mary Mann. Boston: Lee and Shepard, 1895. This book by one of Froebel's former students and staunchest supporters provides important details about his later years, during which he was implementing his concept of the kindergarten.

SEE ALSO: Felix Adler; Dorothea Beale; Charles Dickens; Elizabeth Palmer Peabody; Johann Heinrich Pestalozzi; Carl Schurz.

RELATED ARTICLE in *Great Events from History: The Nineteenth Century, 1801-1900:* 1820's-1830's: Free Public School Movement.

ELIZABETH FRY
English social reformer

Living during a time when prison convicts were generally assumed incorrigible, Fry believed that prisoners could and should be rehabilitated and treated humanely. Her work led to substantial prison reforms—especially for women, throughout Great Britain and abroad. She also worked to improve hospitals, nursing, and the treatment of the insane.

BORN: May 21, 1780; Norwich, Norfolk, England
DIED: October 12, 1845; Ramsgate, Kent, England
ALSO KNOWN AS: Elizabeth Gurney (birth name)
AREAS OF ACHIEVEMENT: Social reform, women's rights

EARLY LIFE

Elizabeth Fry was born Elizabeth Gurney, the fourth of twelve children of John Gurney and Catherine Bell, who both came from old Quaker families. She spent her first years in Norwich, England, until her family moved to nearby Earlham Hall in 1786. One of her great-grandfathers was the well-known Quaker apologist Robert Barclay. She herself became a devout believer, but the wealthy banker John Gurney raised his children to be skeptical of the strict teachings of the Quakers' Society of Friends. When she was twelve, her mother died.

Many members of Elizabeth's family became Anglicans, but in 1789, Elizabeth was so influenced by a speech delivered by the American William Savery that she chose to embrace traditional Quaker beliefs. Following a meeting with her cousin, the devout Quaker Priscilla Gurney, Elizabeth began to wear the black hood associated with strict Quakers and started to use "thou"

and "thee" in place of "you" in ordinary speech. Her conversion was both complete and permanent. Inspired by her faith, she distributed clothing to the poor and opened a Sunday school in her home for local children. She remained actively involved in the service of the Society of Friends for the rest of her life.

LIFE'S WORK

On August 19, 1800, at the age of twenty, Elizabeth married Joseph Fry, a merchant who came from a Quaker family much more orthodox than her own. Her personal diary entries suggest that despite the fact that she wore traditional Quaker garb and earnestly professed her faith, her husband and his family saw her polished social manners unbefitting a sincere Quaker. Her refinement also caused some of her detractors to question her sincerity after she became a public figure. However, whatever disagreements Elizabeth and Joseph may have had about their religion, they raised a large family in London and in East Ham after 1809. By 1816 they had ten children, and by 1828 they had eleven.

Even as a mother of a large family, Elizabeth Fry remained active in her church and worked to improve her community. In 1811, she was declared a Quaker minister. Besides providing education for the poor, she ran a soup kitchen out of a barn at Plashet House in East Ham. Prompted by family friend Stephen Grellet, she visited the women's section of London's Newgate Prison in 1813.

At Newgate, Fry saw hardened female criminals crammed together with women awaiting trial; some of the women had children with them. They all slept packed together on hard cell floors, and many were nearly naked.

In 1816, Fry began to make regular visits to Newgate. After establishing a school for the prison children, she introduced a system of supervision and classification of prisoners, in which only women supervised other women. She believed that society should strive both to save prisoners' souls and to reform their behavior by providing them with religious and secular education, clothing, and gainful employment so that those who were released or transported to Australia could enter society with a sense of self-worth and some skills. Also, prisoners destined for the gallows could at least be saved spiritually.

Reading the Bible to prison inmates and providing other religious instruction was as integral a part of Fry's plan as the more materially apparent improvements. To ensure the continuance of these reforms, she created the Ladies' Association for the Improvement of the Female Prisoners at Newgate in 1817. By 1821, this body had become the British Ladies' Society for Promoting the Reformation of Female Prisoners. It was the first national organization for women in England.

Even before her brother-in-law Thomas Fowell Buxton championed her cause in a speech to the House of Commons in 1818, Fry had begun to garner some fame. She herself addressed Parliament soon afterward. However, her methods and her strong stance against capital punishment conflicted with the views of many members of Parliament, including the home secretary, Lord Sidmouth, who publicly declared that Fry's actions were helping to keep criminals from fearing the law.

Sidmouth's successor as home secretary, Sir Robert Peel, was more amenable to Elizabeth Fry's petitions. His reforms included the Gaols Act of 1823, and under his tenure, prison guards received regular salaries so they would no longer have to rely on bribes from prisoners for their income. Regular visits from caregivers of various kinds were also instituted. Although many legislators and prison professionals saw Fry as an amateur, her correspondence with dignitaries and officials at home and abroad helped confirm her status as an expert. In 1827, she published *Observations on the Visiting, Superintendence, and Government, of Female Prisoners.*

In 1818, Fry began making journeys through northern England, Ireland, and Scotland to organize women's service groups and visit local jails. Her records of her journeys reveal the beginnings of her concern for the insane and her opposition to solitary confinement. For example, on the first of these travels she was appalled by the conditions under which a deranged man was kept in Haddington Prison. He had been locked up alone for eighteen

months merely for petty vandalism. Her own jottings and those of her younger brother, Joseph Gurney, served as evidence for the need to reform town prisons outside London that were not covered by the national Gaols Act. In 1819, Gurney published *Notes on a Visit to Some of the Prisons in Scotland and the North of England in Company with Elizabeth Fry.*

Gurney helped Elizabeth's family financially after his brother-in-law's bank went bankrupt in 1828—an event that temporarily hurt Elizabeth's reputation. Her brother's help allowed her to persevere in championing prison reform and other concerns, which eventually included the improvement of mental asylums, hospitals, nursing, and the abolition of slavery.

Prejudice against Fry's religion, philosophical differences about how to deal with criminals, and objections to the idea of women with families exercising professional expertise on public matters all brought Fry many enemies throughout her career. Whitworth Russell and William Crawford were assigned to inspect Newgate, and in their 1836 report, they concluded that her religious instruction was a threat to the prison's state-sanctioned Anglican services, and they strongly objected to her lenient methods.

Although Russell and Crawford's report seriously weakened Fry's influence, it did not stop her work at Newgate. Some of her most virulent detractors saw her many meetings with the young Queen Victoria and her 1842 tour of Newgate with the king of Prussia as snobbish self-aggrandizement at the expense of the prisoners. It did not help that she never shed the refined manners to which her husband and in-laws had originally objected. Nevertheless, she remained popular with the public until she died at Ramsgate in Kent on October 12, 1845, at the age of sixty-five. Quakers do not have formal funeral services, but about one thousand people came to witness her silent burial at Barking in Essex.

SIGNIFICANCE

Elizabeth Fry's work dramatically improved the quality of prison conditions in Europe and abroad. Although her opposition to solitary confinement never won out, her insistence that women be in charge of female prisoners is now broadly accepted. In addition to prison reform, she also founded a Servants' Society, district societies to assist the poor, and London's Institution for Nursing Sisters in 1840. The latter was a groundbreaking effort to improve nursing in Britain.

Fry's pioneering enterprise inspired both Florence Nightingale and Queen Victoria, and her example, in which officials from the Americas, Russia, and Australia solicited her advice, paved the way for women to take on leadership roles as professional experts and advocates of justice. What began as one woman's promotion of maternal compassion for women in England occasioned the development of women's associations of varying concerns and philosophies worldwide, including the Elizabeth Fry Society in Canada, established in Vancouver in 1939, which was the first of twenty-five member societies.

— *William Gahan*

FURTHER READING

Corder, Suzanna. *Life of Elizabeth Fry: Compiled from Her Journal as Edited by Her Daughters, and from Various Other Sources*. Philadelphia: H. Longstreth, 1853. This voluminous compilation is an excellent source for a firsthand familiarity with Fry's journal entries. It is available electronically through some academic institutions.

Kent, John. *Elizabeth Fry*. London: B. Batsford, 1962. In addition to briefly tracing Fry's life and work, Kent's well-indexed book historicizes her religious motivations in context with other religious and ideological currents of her day.

Rose, June. *Elizabeth Fry*. New York: St. Martin's Press, 1981. This biography chronicles the accomplishments of Fry's life and portrays a complex personality through a close analysis of her journal entries. Rose closely examines Fry's struggle between family obligations and public service.

Van Drenth, Annemieke, and Francisca de Haan. *The Rise of Caring Power: Elizabeth Fry and Josephine Butler in Britain and the Netherlands*. Amsterdam: Amsterdam University Press, 2000. This scholarly work traces the rise of the idea of "caring power" as it worked to formulate a political identity for women in society, focusing on both Fry and Butler.

Whitney, Janet. *Elizabeth Fry: Quaker Heroine*. Boston: Little, Brown, 1936. Whitney's clear prose pieces together information from various journals to construct an interesting, if somewhat lengthy, biography.

SEE ALSO: Josephine Butler; Sir Thomas Fowell Buxton; Dorothea Dix; Florence Nightingale; Sir Robert Peel; Queen Victoria.

RELATED ARTICLE in *Great Events from History: The Nineteenth Century, 1801-1900:* July, 1865: Booth Establishes the Salvation Army.

MARGARET FULLER
American journalist

A pioneering feminist far ahead of her time, Fuller was a perceptive literary and social critic, and the first American woman to work as a foreign journalist.

BORN: May 23, 1810; Cambridgeport, Massachusetts
DIED: July 19, 1850; off the coast of Fire Island, New York
ALSO KNOWN AS: Marchesa Ossoli; Sarah Margaret Fuller (full name)
AREAS OF ACHIEVEMENT: Journalism, social reform

EARLY LIFE

Sarah Margaret Fuller was the first of the nine children of Timothy Fuller and Margaret Crane Fuller. Her father, a prominent figure in Massachusetts politics, was a graduate of Harvard College and the absolute authority in his household. Keenly disappointed that his first child was a girl, Timothy Fuller nevertheless determined to educate her according to the classical curriculum of the day—an experience usually afforded only to boys.

Even as a small child, Margaret was directed by her father in a rigorous schedule of study. She learned both English and Latin grammar and, before she was ten years old, read Vergil, Ovid, and Horace as well as William Shakespeare. At the age of fourteen, Margaret went briefly to Miss Prescott's School in Groton but soon returned home to immerse herself again in study. Although Margaret was intellectually developed far beyond her years, the girl's intensity caused trouble in friendships, a pattern that continued throughout her life. Margaret was also uncomfortable with her physical appearance. Therefore, she decided to cultivate her intellect, spending fifteen-hour days reading literature and philosophy in four languages, breaking only for a few hours of music and walking each day.

By the late 1820's, Margaret was forming strong friendships with Harvard students such as James Freeman Clarke and Frederic Henry Hedge, many of whom would later become involved, as she did, with the Transcendentalist movement. She was becoming known in intellectual society in Cambridge and at Harvard as a for-midable conversationalist. The same determination that brought her such success, however, also brought criticism. Margaret tended toward sarcasm, offending even close friends in intellectual discussions, and the great demands that she placed upon herself she also placed upon others.

In 1833, Timothy Fuller moved his family to a farm in Groton. Margaret taught her younger siblings and, when her mother's health declined, took over the household. She continued to read, particularly German literature and philosophy, but her life at that time was a strain. Early in 1835, Margaret fell seriously ill, then recovered; in October of that year, her father died.

At this turning point, Margaret's future seemed uncertain and difficult. She had planned a European trip to expand her horizons but had to cancel it in order to support the family. After a three-week visit at the home of Ralph Waldo Emerson (a Transcendentalist and a literary figure) in Concord, she decided to take a teaching position at Bronson Alcott's experimental Temple School in Boston. In 1837, Margaret accepted a teaching position in Hiram Fuller's (no relation) Greene Street School in Providence, Rhode Island.

Margaret Fuller. (Library of Congress)

During her two years in Providence, Fuller also continued her scholarly work—often at the expense of her health—translating Johann P. Eckermann's *Conversation with Goethe*, for example, and publishing poems and international literature reviews in a liberal, Unitarian journal edited by James Freeman Clarke. In addition, she wrote her first piece of important criticism, which was published a year later in the first issue of the Transcendentalist publication the *Dial*. Although Margaret was a successful teacher, she missed the intellectual stimulation of Boston, so in 1839 she moved back to Jamaica Plain, a Boston suburb, where she was joined by her mother and younger siblings.

LIFE'S WORK

When Margaret Fuller moved back to Boston, her involvement with Transcendentalism (which began when she met Emerson in 1836) increased. As a movement, Transcendentalism focused around a common perspective on religion and philosophy rather than any particular doctrine, and intellectuals met regularly for discussion about the nature of freedom and spirit. In 1840, Fuller became the first editor of the Transcendentalist literary quarterly the *Dial*. She also wrote much of the copy and kept the periodical alive—almost single-handedly—until she resigned her editorship two years later.

Fuller supported herself during this time by conducting "Conversations," highly successful weekly discussions attended by the society women of Boston. Fuller believed that women were not taught how to think, and she determined to remedy this with discussions of topics from Greek mythology to ethics to women's rights. Through these "Conversations," which continued until she moved to New York in 1844, Fuller became known as a powerful speaker and intellectual critic. During this time, she was also involved with Brook Farm, a Transcendentalist experiment in the nature of ideal community that began in 1841 (she did not actually live there).

Fuller was frequently Emerson's houseguest in Concord. She said of Emerson, "From him I first learned what is meant by the inward life." They had a strong friendship, and through their discussions, both were able to develop their knowledge and appreciation of literature. The friendship was complex, however, and Fuller and Emerson were not always comfortable in each other's presence, much less with each other's ideas.

During this period, Fuller traveled outside the boundaries of New England. Her journey to the Midwest is recorded in her first book, *Summer on the Lake* (1843), in which she investigated the relationship between nature and society, focusing on people and social manners. While conducting research for this book, Fuller became the first woman to receive permission to enter the library at Harvard University. The book also brought Fuller to the attention of Horace Greeley, editor of the *New York Tribune*. He invited her to become the newspaper's literary critic, and—against the advice of friends such as Emerson—Fuller accepted. In December, 1844, she moved to New York, leaving the constraints of family and friends behind, to become the first female member of the working press in the United States.

Horace Greeley said that Fuller was, in some respects, the greatest woman America had yet known, and he gave her almost a free hand with her writing. Fuller's style became more solid, and her thinking deepened even further as she wrote regularly on major authors and ideas of her time. While at the *Tribune*, Fuller also became concerned about public education and social conditions. She visited prisons, poorhouses, and asylums, and her front-page articles about them moved people's feelings and laid the foundation for reforms.

In 1845, Greeley published Fuller's *Women in the Nineteenth Century*, the first American book-length discussion of equal rights for men and women. The book became a public sensation and made Fuller's name known throughout the English-speaking world. A classic in American feminist literature, it combined the spiritual focus of a transcendental vision with the need for practical action and was influential in the Seneca Falls conference on women's rights in 1848. In 1846, Fuller published *Papers on Literature and Art*, a compilation of her critical reviews that set a high standard for American literary criticism.

The strain of writing on deadline made Fuller's chronic headaches worse, however, and she was also trying to recover from a broken romance. In August, 1846, Greeley commissioned her as the first American foreign correspondent, and she visited first England, then France, and finally Rome, in April, 1847. Everywhere she went, Fuller met with major figures of the time and sent dispatches back to the *Tribune*. Fuller was disturbed by the misery that she saw around her, particularly that of working-class women. More and more, life—not art—became her preoccupation, and Fuller's articles on the common worker appeared prominently in the *Tribune*.

In the summer of 1847, Fuller made an extended tour of Italy. She was drawn into the Italian struggle for independence, and in the course of her travels she met Giovanni Angelo Ossoli, a young Italian count who was committed to the liberal cause. Ossoli and Fuller became lovers and, it seems, planned for a life together. Because Ossoli would have been disowned by his aristocratic family for marrying a non-Italian and a non-Catholic, however, the marriage was delayed for more than a year.

Ossoli and Fuller spent the winter of 1848 involved in the Republican struggle in Rome. Fuller continued to send detailed articles about the revolution to the *Tribune*, but she kept her relationship with Ossoli a secret for a long time, even from family and friends in America. Fuller was expecting a child, so she moved to Rieti, outside Rome, where she gave birth to a son, Angelo, on September 5, 1848. Fuller stayed with the child until April, then left him with a nurse and returned to Ossoli and the fighting in Rome, where she directed an emergency hospital and ran supplies to her husband's fighting unit. When the Italian liberals were finally defeated in July, 1849, Ossoli and Fuller were forced to leave Rome. They took Angelo and fled to Florence, where Fuller wrote what she thought was the most important work she had done to date: a history of the Italian revolution.

Fuller wanted to publish the manuscript in the United States, so the family set sail for New York City on May 17, 1850, despite Fuller's deep foreboding about the journey. Difficulties started soon after they set sail: The ship's captain died of smallpox; then Angelo became sick with the disease, and he almost died. On July 17, just after land was sighted, a storm came up and the inexperienced captain ran the ship aground near Fire Island, New York. Whenever the storm abated, people tried to swim to shore, only a few hundred feet away, but Fuller resigned herself to death and refused to leave the ship. She eventually allowed a sailor to try to save the baby, but Fuller and her husband stayed on board as the ship was pulled apart by the sea. Angelo's body finally washed ashore, but Fuller, Ossoli, and Fuller's manuscript were never found.

SIGNIFICANCE

Those who remember Margaret Fuller most often do so within the context of her association with New England Transcendentalism, but her most significant contributions were in the areas of literary criticism and social reform. Despite the fact that her own writing style was inconsistent, Fuller is nevertheless considered to be one of the two real literary critics of the nineteenth century, along with Edgar Allan Poe. She developed a theory of criticism that combined perspectives of realism and romanticism, and she held to high standards that did not fluctuate with the prevailing winds of the times.

Fuller was also a pioneering journalist and perceptive social critic on both the national and the international levels. In *Tribune* columns, her commentary on public education and social conditions looked deeply into American values. She visited and wrote about Sing-Sing and Blackwell's Island prisons, for example, and her visits led to the establishment of the first halfway house for newly released female convicts. Her dispatches from Europe—especially her account of the Italian revolution—helped Americans grow in their understanding of the world around them.

Although Fuller did find fulfillment as a wife and mother, her powerful character was not circumscribed by these traditional female roles. In her behavior, Fuller questioned economic, social, and political assumptions about women; in her writing, she propagated her belief in equality through. Her major work, *Women in the Nineteenth Century* (1845), is generally considered to be the first important feminist work by an American woman. Fuller fascinated the readers of her day and challenged their ideas about what a woman could and should be. More than a century later, her argument that people should be able to express themselves as individuals, not simply as representatives of their gender, continues to offer insights into the unlimited potential of human nature.

—*Jean C. Fulton*

FURTHER READING

Allen, Margaret Vanderhaar. *The Achievement of Margaret Fuller*. University Park: Pennsylvania State University Press, 1979. This biography presents a strikingly feminist perspective on Fuller's life and work. Allen concludes that Fuller was easily the equal of Ralph Waldo Emerson and Henry David Thoreau.

Blanchard, Paula. *Margaret Fuller: From Transcendentalism to Revolution*. New York: Delacorte Press, 1978. This biography is written from a clearly feminist perspective, but with a more subtle voice than Margaret Allen's (see above). It has helped to make Fuller more accessible to the general reading public.

Capper, Charles. *Margaret Fuller: An American Romantic Life*. 2 vols. New York: Oxford University Press, 1992, 2006. This stunning narrative deals comprehensively with Fuller's identity as a female intellectual, the primary issue in her life. Based on sources, many of which have never before been used, this volume covers her early years and her beginnings as an American prophet and critic.

Chevigny, Bell Gale, comp. *The Woman and the Myth: Margaret Fuller's Life and Writings*. Old Westbury, N.Y.: Feminist Press, 1976. This major study changed Fuller scholarship during the mid-1970's and is essential reading for anyone who is seriously interested in Fuller.

Edwards, Julia. *Women of the World: The Great Foreign Correspondents*. Boston: Houghton Mifflin, 1991. Presents a lively and vivid account of Fuller's activities in Europe and quotes liberally from her communiques to the *Tribune*. The book gives a real sense of Fuller within the context of her times.

James, Laurie. *Why Margaret Fuller Ossoli Is Forgotten*. New York: Golden Heritage Press, 1988. An actor, James has done extensive research in preparing her original one-person drama about Fuller, which has toured internationally. In this sixty-five-page book, James presents her thesis that Fuller has been buried in history because the authors of her "definitive" biography *Memoirs of Margaret Fuller Ossoli* (1852) intentionally misrepresented her life and works. James builds quite a case against Ralph Waldo Emerson, William Henry Channing, and James Freeman Clarke. She elaborates further in her *Men, Women, and Margaret Fuller* (1990).

_____, ed. *The Wit and Wisdom of Margaret Fuller Ossoli*. New York: Golden Heritage Press, 1988. This selection of quotations is organized around topics such as "love," "equality," "revolution," "toys," and "faith and soul." Fuller's astute, often wry observations have not gone out of date, and the reader can get a real taste of Fuller from this small book. It also includes a list of Fuller's major achievements and a bibliography.

Myerson, Joel, comp. *Critical Essays on Margaret Fuller*. Boston: G. K. Hall, 1980. These articles represent Fuller criticism from 1840 to the date of this publication. As Myerson observes, it is obvious that from the start, critics were more interested in Fuller's personality than in her work. The fifty-three mostly short selections make interesting reading.

Steele, Jeffrey. *Transfiguring America: Myth, Ideology, and Mourning in Margaret Fuller's Writing*. Columbia: University of Missouri Press, 2001. Traces the development of Fuller's feminist consciousness and social theories, showing how she combined her personal experiences and cultural criticism to create a new vision for American society. Includes detailed analyses of her major texts, including her *Dial* essays and her correspondence with Ralph Waldo Emerson.

Von Mehren, Joan. *Minerva and the Muse: A Life of Margaret Fuller*. Amherst: University of Massachusetts Press, 1994. A biography, tracing Fuller's evolution from child prodigy to New England intellectual. Focuses on her character, including the relationship of her private life to her ideas about personal development and democratic culture.

Watson, David. *Margaret Fuller: An American Romantic*. New York: Berg, 1988. This is a useful account of Fuller's life, work, and reputation. Watson examines Fuller's roles as romantic, feminist, and socialist, suggesting that she deserves to be taken seriously as a contributor to historically important bodies of thought. Of particular interest is Watson's examina-

tion of modern feminist Fuller scholarship. He concludes that modern attempts to "rescue" Fuller do not always escape the myopic traps to which they are opposed.

SEE ALSO: Bronson Alcott; Amelia Bloomer; Ralph Waldo Emerson; Horace Greeley; Sarah Josepha Hale; Thomas Wentworth Higginson; Elizabeth Palmer Peabody; Edgar Allan Poe; Henry David Thoreau.

RELATED ARTICLES in *Great Events from History: The Nineteenth Century, 1801-1900:* 1836: Transcendental Movement Arises in New England; May 28-29, 1851: Akron Woman's Rights Convention.

ROBERT FULTON
American inventor

Fulton did not invent the steam engine; however, he built the first profitable steamboat, established the traditions that distinguished American steamboats for the remainder of the century, and laid the groundwork for future submarine and torpedo warfare.

BORN: November 14, 1765; Little Britain Township, Pennsylvania
DIED: February 24, 1815; New York, New York
ALSO KNOWN AS: Robert Fulton, Jr. (full name)
AREA OF ACHIEVEMENT: Engineering

EARLY LIFE

At the beginning of 1765, Robert Fulton, Sr., a successful tailor and leading citizen of Lancaster, Pennsylvania, sold most of his possessions and borrowed money in order to purchase a large farm, thirty miles to the south in Little Britain Township. There, his first son, Robert Fulton, Jr., was born toward the end of that year. Nothing else went well for the inexperienced farmer. Six years later, the elder Fulton returned to Lancaster, a bankrupt and dispirited man. He died in 1774, leaving his wife and six children without means of support other than the charity of relatives. Thus, at the age of nine, Robert Fulton learned the meaning of failure and poverty. For the remainder of his life, he struggled to achieve financial success and social status.

With the outbreak of the American Revolution, Lancaster changed from a small, isolated agricultural community to a bustling military and economic center. The

population swelled with refugees, soldiers on the march, military prisoners, and gunsmiths. As young Fulton's curiosity attracted him to the new inhabitants, his quick intelligence and enthusiasm induced strangers to give time to the dark, handsome boy. Fulton spent an increasing amount of time with the gunsmiths, for whom he made mechanical drawings and painted signs. Perhaps he was having too good a time: His mother apprenticed him to a Philadelphia jeweler.

Little is known about Fulton's Philadelphia years. His master was a former London jeweler named Jeremiah Andrews. Fulton's talent at drawing and painting prepared him to produce miniature portraits on ivory lockets. By 1785, Fulton was listed in a city directory as a "miniature painter." The following year saw Fulton struck with two burdens that characterized the remainder of his life. He borrowed money to help his mother and sisters purchase another farm. At the same time, he was ill with respiratory ailments.

Despite his debts, Fulton borrowed money and took the waters at Bath, a spa in northern Virginia favored by the upper class. There, Fulton recovered his health and doubtlessly heard about the steamboat experiments of a local man named James Rumsey. Upon his return to Philadelphia, Fulton found another steamboat pioneer, John Fitch, running his strange vessel across the Delaware River. At this time, however, Fulton displayed no interest in steam engines. He was a painter who desired to improve his skills and status. That meant that he, like other American painters before and since, had to work in Great

Britain. Thus, in the summer of 1787, Fulton sailed for England. He would be absent from the United States for the next thirteen years.

Thanks to a letter of introduction, Fulton settled in London as a student of Benjamin West, an American painter popular with Britain's upper class. Fulton was not a gifted painter; he was, however, successful at cultivating wealthy friends and patrons. Thus, Fulton managed to survive for several years as a painter. By the early 1790's, Fulton turned toward machines and canals. He devoted considerable time to studying canals and, in 1796, wrote *Treatise on the Improvement of Canal Navigation*. Many of his ideas were quite dated, but the volume was distinguished by its format. Fulton demonstrated details with excellent drawings, attempted to base designs upon mathematical calculations, and focused all canal features toward the concept of an inexpensive and national transportation system. The book established Fulton as a canal engineer.

LIFE'S WORK

With France and Great Britain at war during the mid-1790's, the patents of citizens of one nation were freely copied by the citizens of the other nation. Fulton believed that his canal ideas were valuable and ought to be patented in France. He arrived in France in 1797 and soon abandoned canals. After all, that nation had been building canals for more than a century and had little use for experts who lacked experience. Anyway, Fulton already had a new patron and a new mechanical passion.

Benjamin West had given Fulton an introduction to Joel Barlow, a Yale graduate who was making much money by running American ships through the British blockade and into French ports. Barlow and his wife, Ruth, welcomed Fulton into their Paris residence. The three lived together for the next seven years. The educated Barlow tutored Fulton in science and mathematics, and it was probably Barlow who introduced Fulton to the subject of submarine warfare. Barlow had been at Yale when another student, Robert Bushnell, designed *Turtle*, a submarine that had engaged in unsuccessful attacks upon British warships during the American Revolution. Bushnell, living in seclusion in Georgia, had sent Thomas Jefferson a detailed description of his submarine efforts, and the latter made the material available to Barlow. By the end of 1797, Fulton was working on submarines.

Within three years, Fulton completed a submarine, and in late 1800, he launched several unsuccessful attacks against British warships off French ports. His submarine *Nautilus* was an enlarged and refined version of the craft that Bushnell had built more than twenty years earlier. The method of attack was similar: The submarine carried a mine (which Fulton called a "torpedo") to the enemy vessel. If the intended victim moved, it was safe from the slow, awkward submarine. Moreover, the hand-cranked *Nautilus* could not overcome contrary tides or currents. In one attempt, however, Fulton and his crew of two remained submerged for more than six hours. That record was unequaled until the late nineteenth century. Fulton reached the obvious conclusion that *Nautilus* was inadequate as a weapon; he dismantled the submarine—perhaps to protect its secrets from imitators and its weaknesses from critics.

While still trying to collect funds from the French government for past submarine activities and future proposals, Fulton opened negotiations with British agents. In exchange for a substantial monthly payment, Fulton agreed to develop plans for small rowboats to tow torpedoes against French ships. In the midst of this scheme, Robert Fulton found a new patron.

Robert R. Livingston was one of the wealthiest men in America. Since helping to draft the Declaration of Independence, he had been active in public service. In 1801, Livingston became the American minister to the French government. For the past three years, the wealthy New Yorker had tried to promote steam navigation. While his brother-in-law, John Stevens, had set up a machine shop in New Jersey to conduct steamboat experiments, Livingston had secured a monopoly to steam navigation on New York waters. The two men, however, were not suited as partners. Hence Robert Fulton, the engineer eager to win fame and fortune, and Livingston satisfied each other's needs. They became partners.

Fulton first studied the design of earlier steamboats and their engines. Next, he built models to test his own designs. Finally, in 1803, he placed a British engine aboard a craft of his own design, but the vessel moved too slowly. Fulton then left France, telling Livingston that he would return within two weeks. Fulton remained in England for two years working on his favorite project, undersea warfare. Fulton finally left England and sailed for New York.

The tall, handsome man who landed in the United States after nearly twenty years abroad was often mistaken for a foreign aristocrat. The boy from Lancaster had come a long way. Robert Fulton wasted no time: In the remarkably brief space of eight months, Fulton assembled the first steamboat to earn money for its owners. Fulton hired one of the best builders, Charles Brown, to

Robert Fulton. (Library of Congress)

construct the hull. The boat was supposed to have been designed in accordance with Fulton's study of water and wind resistance. Nevertheless, the vessel looked like an enlarged British canal boat. The engine was the best that could be bought, a Boulton and Watt from England. After a brief trial run, Fulton informed Livingston that the vessel was ready.

On August 17, 1807, *The North River Steamboat* left New York City with forty passengers, mostly apprehensive relatives of Livingston. On its way up the Hudson River to Albany, the vessel stopped at Livingston's river estate, Clermont, the origin of the steamboat's unofficial but popular name, *Clermont*. Only a few passengers ventured aboard the steamboat for its first commercial run several weeks later. Public acceptance of the vessel increased, however, as it maintained a regular schedule. By the time river transportation closed for the winter, Livingston was earning a small but steady return on his investment.

During the winter of 1807-1808, Fulton rebuilt the steamboat with more comfortable accommodations. Because the vessel lacked sails to roll her about and voyaged on the relatively smooth waters of the Hudson River

(locally called the North River), Fulton could install furniture that a sailing vessel could not accommodate. In the remaining seven years of his life, Fulton completed twenty more steamboats, each with fancier fittings than its predecessor. Thus, Fulton established the tradition of steamboat luxury. This tradition distinguished steam vessels from sailing vessels and attracted passengers.

In January, 1808, Fulton married Harriet Livingston, the beautiful niece of Robert Livingston. Once again, Fulton was working on torpedoes. In 1810, he published *Torpedo War and Submarine Explosions*, the first "do-it-yourself" book on that subject. Besides an expanding transportation system, a growing family, and torpedo work, Fulton was spending much time defending the steamboat monopoly that Livingston had pushed through the legislature years earlier. Other builders saw no more reason for a steamboat monopoly than one for sailing ships. Further, New Jersey citizens resented the Livingston-Fulton claim that New York's waters extended to the Jersey shore. The lawsuits dragged on for years.

When the War of 1812 began, Fulton concentrated on naval weapons. In marked contrast with his numerous letters and public demonstrations that characterized his earlier work in France and England, Fulton now worked in secret. He built a semisubmersible vessel to tow torpedoes against British warships off New London, Connecticut. A storm washed the vessel ashore, and the British later blew it up. Fulton's major work during the war was *Demologes*, a steam-driven battery. With its heavy cannon and thick sides, people (including British officers) expected the warship to destroy British blockaders near New York.

On February 24, 1815, shortly before the vessel was finished and just as news of peace reached the United States, Robert Fulton died. Exhausted by rushing the steam battery toward completion, by court actions over the steamboat monopoly, and by overexposure to a cold winter, he was too weak to resist another bout with respiratory problems.

SIGNIFICANCE

The achievement of Robert Fulton was in developing a commercially successful steamboat. Other men may vie for the honor of inventing the steamboat, but their work failed to alter marine transportation. Robert Fulton and *The North River Steamboat* ended the dependence of ships upon the wind. Moreover, whereas travel had always involved varying degrees of hardship, Fulton developed the concept of voyaging in comfort. Finally, in an age suspicious of change, Fulton introduced the modern practice of continual product development.

It is ironic that Fulton's fame in steamboats came so easily when compared with the brief time involved. The fact that he succeeded in steam navigation was because of his willingness to build upon the work of others, to cooperate with financial backers, and to follow a logical pattern. Research, conceptualization, scale models, and mathematical calculations distinguished his work method. As a result of Fulton's efforts, the vision of steamboat pioneers became a reality.

In turn, Fulton's pioneering work in submarines and torpedoes had to wait upon further advances in technology. However, his vision of undersea warfare fascinated contemporaries and inspired people throughout the nineteenth century. Fulton's ideas were employed with some success by the Confederacy during the Civil War, and Jules Verne named his imaginary submarine after Fulton's *Nautilus*. The United States Navy completed Fulton's *Demologos*, the world's first steam warship, renamed it *Fulton*, and then left the vessel to rot.

Robert Fulton belonged to a select group of Americans. Along with Francis Cabot Lowell and Eli Whitney, Fulton introduced technology to American society and laid the foundation for the nation to become the industrial leader of the world.

—*Joseph A. Goldenberg*

FURTHER READING

Chapelle, Howard I. *Fulton's Steam Battery: Blockship and Catamaran*. Washington, D.C.: Smithsonian Institution Press, 1964. Most detailed account of the steam battery based upon plans located in Denmark in 1960. Although the author is best known for his many books on American sailing vessels, he devoted the same care and expertise to collecting and analyzing the plans of steamships. Using copies of the steam battery's plans that were located in Danish archives, the author has produced the lost detailed account of Robert Fulton's last work.

Flexner, James T. *Steamboats Come True: American Inventors in Action*. Boston: Little, Brown, 1978. An excellent account of steamboat pioneers before Fulton.

Fulton, Robert. *Torpedo War and Submarine Explosions*. New York: W. Elliot, 1810. Fulton's descriptions of underwater warfare not only guided the efforts of Americans who attempted to attack British warships during the War of 1812 but also became re-

quired reading for British officers aboard those same ships.

Hutcheon, Wallace, Jr. *Robert Fulton: Pioneer of Undersea Warfare*. Annapolis, Md.: Naval Institute Press, 1981. The best account of Fulton's underwater work. Draws on many different sources for its information.

Morgan, John S. *Robert Fulton*. New York: Mason/Charter, 1977. Provides a clear and well-written summary of Fulton's life and work. This book meets the needs of the general reader.

Philip, Cynthia O. *Robert Fulton*. New York: Franklin Watts, 1985. This well-researched biography is particularly good for its thoughtful analysis of Fulton's character and behavior. The author's conclusions about the relationship between Fulton and the Barlows are not accepted by all scholars.

Sale, Kirkpatrick. *The Fire of His Genius: Robert Fulton and the American Dream*. New York: Free Press, 2001. Well-written, balanced biography, describing how Fulton's steamboat transformed nineteenth century America, for good and ill. While the steamboat boosted the American economy and opened up the western United States to settlement, this settlement facilitated the destruction of Native American civilizations.

Shagena, Jack L. *Who Really Invented the Steamboat? Fulton's Clermont Coup: A History of the Steamboat Contributions of William Henry, James Rumsey, John Fitch, Oliver Evans, Nathan Read, Samuel Morey, Robert Fulton, John Stevens, and Others*. Amherst, N.Y.: Humanity Books, 2004. Shagena, a retired aerospace engineer, traces the technological contributions of the many inventors, including Fulton, who helped create the steamboat.

Taylor, George R. *The Transportation Revolution: 1815-1850*. New York: Harper & Row, 1951. This standard history examines the role of the steamboat in the expansion of the American economy and society during the first half of the nineteenth century.

SEE ALSO: Benjamin Henry Latrobe; Cornelius Vanderbilt; Jules Verne.

RELATED ARTICLES in *Great Events from History: The Nineteenth Century, 1801-1900:* August 17, 1807: Maiden Voyage of the *Clermont*; May 22-June 20, 1819: *Savannah* Is the First Steamship to Cross the Atlantic; March 2, 1824: *Gibbons v. Ogden*.

JAMES GADSDEN
American diplomat

Although Gadsden was an accomplished soldier, engineer, and railroad executive, his lasting fame came as the U.S. minister to Mexico during the mid-1850's. While in Mexico City, he negotiated what became known as the Gadsden Purchase, by which the United States acquired a strip of Mexican territory that now forms the southern portions of Arizona and New Mexico.

BORN: May 15, 1788; Charleston, South Carolina
DIED: December 26, 1858; Charleston, South Carolina
AREAS OF ACHIEVEMENT: Diplomacy, military

EARLY LIFE

James Gadsden was born into one of South Carolina's most reputable families. The family's prominence came from Gadsden's paternal grandfather, Christopher Gadsden, who owned several stores, a commercial wharf, and a plantation. He also served in the South Carolina Assembly and organized Charleston's resistance to the Stamp Act in 1765. Ten years later, Christopher acted as a delegate to the Continental Congress and eventually served as a Revolutionary War general.

Christopher's son, Philip, lived in the shadow of his famous father. Philip entered his family's mercantile business and stayed in Charleston his entire life. He married Catherine Edwards, whose father was also a local businessperson and Revolutionary War patriot. Desirous of a large family, the couple managed sixteen offspring. Philip, a devout member of the Protestant Episcopal Church, taught his children, through mild discipline, about Christian moral principles. He also gave his sons the best formal education. They were sent to a well-known preparatory school, the Associated Academy of Charleston, and then shipped to Connecticut for a classical education at Yale.

In 1803, when Philip's third son, James, reached Connecticut, he was welcomed by his two older brothers, C. E. and John. Away from home for the first time, young Gadsden found comfort in the companionship of his siblings. There were also new friendships, including one with John C. Calhoun, a fellow South Carolinian. Within a few decades, Calhoun would become a national political figure exerting great influence on James. It is possible that in later years the pious Philip was most proud of his eldest son C. E., who pursued the ministry and became a Protestant bishop. His son John emerged as a U.S. attorney but died at a relatively young age. The path of the younger James often appeared uncertain, and in the end, more closely resembled the diverse pursuits of his grandfather, General Christopher Gadsden.

LIFE'S WORK

James Gadsden graduated from Yale in 1806 and returned to Charleston. The recent death of his grandfather led him to enter the family's mercantile business. After several years, he grew restless and prayed for new opportunities. His prayers were answered in 1812 with the outbreak of war between the United States and Great Britain. With the help of his congressman, he was commissioned a second lieutenant in the U.S. Army and trained in the Army Corps of Engineers. Military service changed his life forever.

Gadsden's military career lasted ten years. Early in the war he helped prepare for the invasion of Canada and saw action in several major battles. He was later dispatched to New York to build defenses in Brooklyn and Harlem Heights. In 1815 Gadsden transferred to New Orleans, Louisiana, to assist General Andrew Jackson in the construction of fortifications along the Gulf of Mexico and the southwestern frontier. The flamboyant Jackson took the young lieutenant under his wing, making him his personal aide-de-camp. President James Madison asked Gadsden, who was already the chief engineer of the New Orleans district by 1816, to evaluate all regional defense posts. The next year, Gadsden accompanied Jackson in a campaign against the Seminole Indians of Spanish Florida. Jackson, on his own initiative, captured several Spanish garrisons—actions that soon led to the acquisition of Florida by the United States.

Gadsden had distinguished himself in the Seminole War; as a result, he was promoted to captain and placed in charge of all construction works in the Gulf of Mexico frontier. Several years later he received two of the army's most senior administrative positions. In October, 1820, he was appointed inspector general of Jackson's Southern Division with the rank of colonel. In 1822, at the request of Secretary of War John Calhoun, President James Monroe appointed Gadsden adjutant general of the entire army. His appointment was opposed, however, by many politicians who disliked Monroe and Calhoun; ultimately, the Senate forced Gadsden out of office.

In late 1822 Gadsden returned to Charleston to resume his business career. However, Calhoun once again intervened by asking his friend to negotiate a treaty with the Seminoles. Gadsden consented, moved to Florida, and did not return to South Carolina for sixteen years. In September, 1823, he signed the Treaty of Fort Moultrie, which effectively relocated the Seminole Indians from central to southern Florida. Afterward, he agreed to survey the boundaries of the new reservation. In 1824, he received appointment to Florida's first legislative council, accepted a federal contract to survey a major roadway in the territory, and married Suzanna Gibbes Horte.

After his marriage, Gadsden tried to establish roots as a planter near Tallahassee, Florida, but, bored with the slow pace of plantation life, he set his sights on politics. He attempted to associate himself with the legend of war hero Jackson and relied on the general's friends for political support. Between 1825 and 1837, he campaigned five times, all unsuccessfully, to become the territory's delegate to the U.S. Congress. During this time he declined several federal job offers and finally settled for a position as Florida's assistant engineer. His primary activities focused on improving the territory's transportation network with new roadways, canals, and railroads. This brought him into frequent contact with local Seminole Indians. In 1832 he became involved in new treaty negotiations to move the Seminoles west. When President Andrew Jackson dispatched the army to remove the American Indians, the Indians resisted, starting the seven-year Seminole War. Gadsden served in various administrative capacities during the war, but by 1839 he had grown disillusioned and moved to the safety and stability of South Carolina.

Gadsden quickly immersed himself in Charleston's business community. He had brought from Florida new ideas for increasing commercial activity in the port city and the entire South. Several years earlier he had recognized the potential of coordinated railroad networks for Florida's economic development. For that purpose he had advocated a southern rail line from New Orleans to the Atlantic coast. He promoted this vision in Charleston but on an increasingly large scale. In 1840 Gadsden was elected president of the new Louisville, Cincinnati, and Charleston Railroad and remained in that position for ten years while the company was reorganized as the South Carolina Railroad Company. Throughout the 1840's, he actively promoted the idea of a southern transcontinental railroad stretching from Charleston to San Diego, California.

Plans for a transcontinental railroad had political ramifications. Northerners also wanted the economic benefits of a national railroad and had proposed a northern line running through Chicago, Illinois, to San Francisco,

California. Moreover, they feared that a southern route would expand slavery to the southwestern territories. Such fears were well founded. Gadsden, for example, owned more than one hundred slaves and supported the practice of slavery in the West. In fact, he wanted to use slave labor to build the new railroad. As slavery became an increasingly controversial issue during the 1850's, he joined his friend Calhoun in the secessionist movement that ultimately led to the Civil War. However, it was diplomacy, not rebellion, that brought him lasting fame.

Through the influence of Secretary of War Jefferson Davis, a fellow Southerner, Gadsden was appointed U.S. minister to Mexico in May, 1853. He hoped to resolve various disputes between the United States and Mexico that had arisen since the 1848 Treaty of Guadalupe Hidalgo. Most important was the demarcation of a border separating the two nations that allowed adequate land for a southern transcontinental railroad. In December, 1853, after months of negotiation, Mexican dictator Antonio López de Santa Anna signed a treaty to sell land (45,535 square miles) in northern Mexico to the United States for fifteen million dollars. The U.S. diplomat proceeded to Washington, D.C., and presented the treaty for ratification.

Congressional approval of the Gadsden Purchase did not come easily. The Senate, like much of the country, was divided over the issue of slavery in the Western territories. Many northerners were not inclined to buy Mexican land likely to benefit southern slave owners. When some senators revised the treaty by radically decreasing the size and price of the land purchase, it failed to attract enough votes for passage. Finally, a new compromise was reached and ratified on April 25, 1854. In its final version, the treaty stated that the United States would buy 29,640 square miles of land for ten million dollars and that certain protections would be given to U.S. railroad investments in Mexico. Gadsden returned to Mexico City and received de Santa Anna's approval of the revisions. He remained the U.S. minister to Mexico until October, 1856. After retiring to South Carolina, his health declined rapidly. He died the day after Christmas, 1858, at the age of seventy-one.

SIGNIFICANCE

Like his paternal grandfather, James Gadsden lived a remarkable life and participated in many important currents in antebellum U.S. history. As a soldier, engineer, and negotiator, he played a central role in the development of Florida and the Old Southwest. Consequently, several military installations, towns, and counties in the southeastern United States have been named in his honor. The significance of Gadsden's life, however, transcends regional importance.

From a national perspective, Gadsden's activities often signaled the progress and problems associated with U.S. territorial expansion. At the time of his birth, the nation consisted of only the original thirteen states, but the country expanded rapidly south and west. A dozen years after the Louisiana Purchase, he joined Andrew Jackson's conquest of Florida at the expense of native people and a European power. In the spirit of manifest destiny, Gadsden also welcomed the annexation of Texas and other territories farther west, especially after the United States defeated Mexico in war.

During this time Gadsden became one of the nation's leading proponents of a transcontinental railroad. An ardent southern Democrat who favored free trade and the expansion of slavery, his motivations for a southern rail line were economic and political. As the U.S. envoy to Mexico, Gadsden enthusiastically acquired land crucial to the construction of a southern railroad extending from the Atlantic to the Pacific. Although this railroad was not realized in his lifetime, the ratification of the Gadsden Purchase represented one of the last major sectional compromises before the Civil War and signaled the end of contiguous U.S. expansion on the continent.

—Jeffrey J. Matthews

FURTHER READING

Blassingame, Wyatt. *The First Book of American Expansion.* New York: Franklin Watts, 1965. This elementary book describes the Gadsden Purchase within the context of the territorial expansion of the United States from the Louisiana Purchase to the annexation of Hawaii.

Clary, David A., and Joseph W. A. Whitehorne. *The Inspector General of the U.S. Army, 1777-1903.* Washington, D.C.: Center of Military History, 1987. Contains brief discussions of Gadsden's career as inspector general of the Southern Division and as adjutant general. It is a detailed source for understanding the U.S. Army's early development and administration.

Devine, David. *Slavery, Scandal and Steel Rails: The 1854 Gadsden Purchase and the Building of the Second Transcontinental Railroad Across Arizona and New Mexico Twenty-Five Years Later.* Lincoln, Nebr.: iUniverse, 2004. Describes how Gadsden advocated the need for a southern cross-country railroad, and explains his role in acquiring land from Mexico to eventually construct this route. Also examines how the Southern Pacific Railroad Company began constructing lines east of California in 1875, more than twenty years after the Gadsden Purchase.

Garber, Paul N. *The Gadsden Treaty.* Philadelphia: University of Pennsylvania Press, 1923. For many decades this book has served as the standard account of the Gadsden Treaty. It remains the most descriptive book and provides considerable background on James Gadsden.

Godbold, E. Stanly. *Christopher Gadsden and the American Revolution.* Knoxville: University of Tennessee Press, 1982. This is a full-length biography of Gadsden's influential grandfather. Aside from analyzing Christopher's role in the American Revolution, the book is an excellent source that describes the Gadsden family and antebellum life in South Carolina.

SEE ALSO: John C. Calhoun; Jefferson Davis; Andrew Jackson; James Monroe; Franklin Pierce; Antonio López de Santa Anna.

RELATED ARTICLES in *Great Events from History: The Nineteenth Century, 1801-1900:* November 21, 1817-March 27, 1858: Seminole Wars; February 2, 1848: Treaty of Guadalupe Hidalgo Ends Mexican War; December 31, 1853: Gadsden Purchase Completes the U.S.-Mexican Border; May 20, 1862: Lincoln Signs the Homestead Act.

MATILDA JOSLYN GAGE
American feminist

Along with Elizabeth Cady Stanton and Susan B. Anthony, Gage was one of the three best-known American feminists of her time, but her radical views and opposition to organized religion have caused her to be underappreciated in histories of the woman suffrage movement. She saw woman suffrage not as an end in itself but rather as a tool by which to lift one-half of humanity from degradation caused by what she believed to be the fourfold bondage of women to the state, the church, the capitalist economy, and social pressures to remain at home, away from the professional world.

BORN: March 24, 1826; Cicero, New York
DIED: March 18, 1898; Chicago, Illinois
ALSO KNOWN AS: Matilda Joslyn (birth name)
AREA OF ACHIEVEMENT: Women's rights

EARLY LIFE

Born Matilda Joslyn in a town located a few miles east of Syracuse, New York, Matilda Gage spent most of her life within a thirty-mile radius of Syracuse. She was raised in an abolitionist home that served as a station on the Underground Railroad, and as a child, she circulated antislavery petitions.

When Matilda was an adult, her home, like that of her parents, became a station on the Underground Railroad during the years immediately before the Civil War. As a young wife and mother in 1850, Gage signed a petition stating that she would face the penalty of a six-month prison term and a two-thousand-dollar fine rather than obey a newly enacted fugitive-slave law, which made a criminal of anyone who assisted slaves toward freedom anywhere in the United States. She said,

> Until liberty is attained—the broadest, the deepest, the highest liberty for all—not one set alone, one clique alone, but for men and women, black and white, Irish, Germans, Americans, and Negroes, there can be no permanent peace.

Gage entered the women's rights movement with Susan B. Anthony during 1852, four years after the first women's rights convention in Seneca Falls. She made her first public speech at the third national woman's rights convention in Syracuse during that same year and rapidly became a leader in the expanding women's rights movement.

LIFE'S WORK

Along with Elizabeth Cady Stanton, Gage and Anthony formed the "triumvirate" of the radical wing of the women's rights movement, the largely separatist National Woman Suffrage Association (NWSA), which chose civil disobedience as a major tactic during the early 1870's. Gage was one of many women who broke existing laws by attempting to vote in 1871. In 1880, she also became the first woman to vote in Fayetteville under a state law permitting women to vote in school board elections. However, she lost a suit challenging the legality of her vote, so the limited right to school suffrage was taken away from New York women.

Although busy with her state and national work, Gage always found time for door-to-door petitioning and local organizing work that was the backbone of the women's movement. During 1880, when the New York Women's Suffrage Association gained women the right to vote and run for office in school elections, Gage helped organize the women of her village, Fayetteville, and they elected an all-woman slate of officers.

With Stanton, Gage coauthored the major documents of the NWSA The group's yearly "Plan of Action," the addresses to the presidential conventions every four years, and the day-to-day formulations of theory and strategy came primarily from their pens. When the United States prepared to celebrate its centennial in 1876, the NWSA used Gage's words to counter that "Liberty today is . . . but the heritage of one-half the people, the men who alone could vote." The women "determined to place on record for the daughters of 1976, the fact that their mothers of 1876 had thus asserted their equality of rights, and thus impeached the government of today for its injustice towards women."

Gage and Stanton drew up the "Declaration of Rights of Women" that Anthony and Gage presented at the official July 4 ceremony in Philadelphia, even though they were denied permission to do so and knew that they faced possible arrest for their action. Gage, who was fifty years of age at the time, was unmoved by the danger and declared: "We of this Centennial year must not forget that this country owes its birth to disobedience to law."

During the 1870's, Gage also wrote a series of controversial articles decrying the brutal and unjust treatment of American Indians. She was adopted into the wolf clan of the Mohawk nation and given the name *Ka-ron-ien-ha-wi* (Sky Carrier) after describing the equality of women with men in the Iroquois system of government.

In 1879, Gage's newspaper, *The National Citizen and Ballot Box* published portions of *History of Woman Suffrage*, which she coedited with Stanton and Anthony. This publication also included Stanton's account of the 1848 Seneca Falls Convention. The newspaper was used as a prepublication forum for commentary before publication of the books in final form. Gage also worked with Stanton on *The Woman's Bible*; in 1893 she published *Woman, Church and State*, the most widely known publication that she wrote entirely on her own.

In "Who Planned the Tennessee Campaign of 1862?" Gage argued that this important Union military campaign that altered the course of the Civil War and was generally credited to General Ulysses S. Grant was actually the idea of Anna Ella Carroll. President Abraham Lincoln asked that the matter be kept quiet, Gage asserted, because he feared that Union troops would be demoralized if they had known that this brilliant strategy was the product not only of a civilian but also a woman.

Sometimes described as one of the most logical, fearless, and scientific writers of her day, Gage made important contributions to feminist thought in her pioneering work on the origins of the oppression of women. At a time when women's rights advocates almost universally believed that steady progress characterized the history of the condition of women, Gage asserted that the opposite was true. She believed in the existence of prehistoric matriarchies—what she called the "Matriarchate"—in which women carried strong political influence.

According to feminist scholar Sally Roesch Wagner, the director of the Gage Foundation, Gage was fascinated by the Haudenosaunee branch of the Iroquois people because of their matrilineal society that was so unlike the male-dominated culture of nineteenth century America. Gage encountered stiff resistance to her suggestion that the downfall of womankind in the West corresponded with the rise of Christianity. She believed that ancient matriarchies were replaced, violently in some cases, by Roman Catholicism's Patriarchate. Wagner says that, steeped in the triple doctrines of obedience to authority, woman's subordination to man, and woman's responsibility for original sin, Gage believed that organized religion was the primary enemy of women's rights.

Gage died in Chicago on March 18, 1898, at the age of seventy-two years. A few years after her death, her son-in-law L. Frank Baum won enduring literary fame with his publication of *The Wonderful Wizard of Oz* (1900).

SIGNIFICANCE

Many of Gage's contributions to the women's rights movement were literary and theoretical. Stanton said of Gage that she had a knack for rummaging through old libraries, bringing more interesting facts to light than any woman she had known. For example, in her pamphlet "Woman as Inventor," Gage maintained that the cotton gin was not invented by Eli Whitney, but by Catherine Littlefield Greene, who had the idea for the gin and engaged Whitney to construct it.

As the suffrage campaign failed to win women the right to vote, Gage grew increasingly weary of pursuing that one issue on its own. A person who always saw common interests among disparate groups, she argued that reform measures such as suffrage were only partial solutions that left intact the underlying causes of social injustice. Increasingly, the ballot seemed to her to be an ineffective tool.

Gage's home in Fayetteville, New York, is now utilized by a nonprofit foundation in her name. The inscription on her gravestone in the Fayetteville Cemetery was a lifelong motto with which she frequently signed autographs, including the 1876 Centennial memorial: "There

Matilda Joslyn Gage. (The Granger Collection, New York)

is a word sweeter than Mother, Home or Heaven, that word is Liberty."

—*Bruce E. Johansen*

FURTHER READING

Anthony, Susan B., Elizabeth Cady Stanton, and Matilda Joslyn Gage, eds. *History of Woman Suffrage*. Salem, N.H.: Ayer Company, 1985. Reprint edition of a major work that provided the intellectual basis for nineteenth century feminism.

Buhle, Mary Jo, and Paul Bulhe. *A Concise History of Woman Suffrage: Selections from the Classic Works of Stanton, Anthony, Gage, and Harper*. Urbana: University of Illinois Press, 1978. Abridged edition of the most basic sources on the woman suffrage movement. Provides useful selections from the writings of Gage and other eminent suffrage leaders.

Flexner, Eleanor. *Century of Struggle: The Woman's Rights Movement in the United States*. Cambridge, Mass.: Harvard University Press, 1959. An overview of the women's rights movement that offers insights into the intellectual origins of American feminism that remains the standard history of the movement.

Gage, Matilda Joslyn. *Woman, Church, and State*. 1893. Watertown, Mass.: Peresphone Press, 1980. Gage's views on women's oppression by the state and religious organizations, updated to the present in a new edition.

SEE ALSO: Susan B. Anthony; L. Frank Baum; Amelia Bloomer; Ulysses S. Grant; Abraham Lincoln; Elizabeth Cady Stanton; Lucy Stone; Victoria Woodhull.

RELATED ARTICLES in *Great Events from History: The Nineteenth Century, 1801-1900:* July 19-20, 1848: Seneca Falls Convention; May 28-29, 1851: Akron Woman's Rights Convention; May, 1869: Woman Suffrage Associations Begin Forming; June 27, 1874-June 2, 1875: Red River War; February 17-18, 1890: Women's Rights Associations Unite.

ALBERT GALLATIN
American anthropologist and government administrator

While serving as secretary of the treasury in the presidential administrations of Thomas Jefferson and James Madison, Gallatin drew upon the social philosophy of the French Enlightenment to improve the fiscal stability of the new nation. As the first president of the American Ethnological Society, he made significant contributions to the development of American anthropology.

BORN: January 29, 1761; Geneva, Switzerland
DIED: August 12, 1849; Astoria, New York
ALSO KNOWN AS: Abraham Alfonse Albert Gallatin (full name)
AREAS OF ACHIEVEMENT: Government and politics, scholarship

EARLY LIFE

The parents of Abraham Alfonse Albert Gallatin (gahl-ah-tihn), Jean Gallatin and Sophie Albertine (née Rolaz) Gallatin, both died when he was an infant, and his care was entrusted to a distant relative of his mother, Mlle Catherine Pictet. Part of the Geneva aristocracy and supplier of lords and councillors to the city-state, the Gallatin family saw to it that young Gallatin was provided an excellent education. Despite access to the rich cultural heritage of his family, who counted Voltaire as a close friend, and a fine education at the academy, from which he was graduated in 1779, Gallatin resisted the aristocratic trappings of his family and identified with a growing number of students who supported Jean-Jacques Rousseau's Romantic call of "back to nature."

Gallatin's grandmother secured him an appointment as lieutenant colonel in the army of her friend Frederich, the Langrave of Hesse, who was then preparing to fight as a mercenary for England against the American colonies. In response, Gallatin rebelled and with a friend fled Geneva at the age of eighteen for America. He arrived in Massachusetts in 1780 and, without much money, set off for the frontier of Maine. After spending a year there, he returned to Boston, where he eked out a living as a tutor teaching French to students at Harvard College.

Finding the atmosphere in Boston too cold for his tastes, Gallatin moved to the backcountry of Pennsylvania in 1782. Through business dealings, he acquired land in the region and, as a good Romantic, settled down to devote his life to farming. At one point, Gallatin hoped to establish a Swiss colony on the American frontier, but these plans came to nothing. Gallatin was successful as

Albert Gallatin. (Library of Congress)

neither farmer nor land speculator. Personal tragedy also touched him when his wife of a few months, Sophia Allegre, whom he had met in Richmond, Virginia, died at his farm, Friendship Hill. Despondent, Gallatin contemplated returning to Geneva, but an inability to sell his farm and the fighting in Geneva triggered by the French Revolution caused him to remain in America.

Gallatin's intelligence and gregariousness led him to politics, first in Pennsylvania as a member of the Harrisburg conference of 1788, which met to consider ways in which the U.S. Constitution could be strengthened, and then as a member of the convention that met in 1789-1790 to revise the Pennsylvania constitution. In 1790, he was elected representative of Fayette County to the Pennsylvania state legislature.

LIFE'S WORK

Gallatin had three careers: politics, business, and science. Although he believed that his investigations in science, rather than his work in government, would cause his name to be remembered in history, the reverse, ironically, proved to be the case. Western Pennsylvania elected Gallatin twice to the state legislature, and then he was elected by the legislature to the Senate of the United

States. There, his eligibility was challenged because he had not been a citizen for nine years. Removed from the Senate, Gallatin returned to Pennsylvania, taking his new bride Hannah, daughter of Commodore James Nicholson of New York. His stay in Pennsylvania proved short, for in 1794 the voters of western Pennsylvania sent him to the House of Representatives, in which he served three terms. A Republican, Gallatin defended the farming interests of western Pennsylvania; at the same time, his grasp of international law and public finance and his reasoning ability and cogent arguments made him a valuable legislator at a critical time in early American history.

In May of 1801, Thomas Jefferson appointed Gallatin secretary of the treasury. Gallatin held this post through Jefferson's two administrations and through part of James Madison's first administration. Accusations that his financial policies hindered American efforts to fight the British in the War of 1812 prompted Gallatin to leave the treasury in 1813 and accept an appointment as a special envoy to Russia, which had offered to mediate the conflict between Great Britain and the United States. Great Britain, however, refused to accept mediation and, thus, frustrated Gallatin's mission. Rather than returning to the treasury, as Madison expected, Gallatin chose to remain in Europe in diplomatic service. So began Gallatin's career as diplomat.

Along with John Quincy Adams and Henry Clay, Gallatin drew up the Treaty of Ghent, which ended the War of 1812. With the work on the treaty concluded, Gallatin, Adams, and Clay traveled to England and negotiated a commercial treaty with the British. On his return to the United States, Gallatin accepted the post of minister to France, which he held from 1816 to 1832. Upon his return from France, he intended to retire from government service and to devote the rest of life to being a gentleman farmer at Friendship Hill, but, although Gallatin was increasingly upset with the emphasis on gain in American politics, he allowed his name to be put forward for vice president. Henry Clay's ultimate acceptance of the nomination allowed Gallatin happily to withdraw his name. Life at Friendship Hill proved boring for the Gallatins after seven years in Paris, and so Gallatin once again accepted diplomatic assignment, his last, in 1826, as minister to England.

The United States to which Gallatin returned in 1827 seemed foreign to him. The robust activity of Jacksonian America seemed to make a shambles of the Jeffersonian idealism to which Gallatin subscribed. So disorienting did the new United States seem to him that he seriously considered leaving the country and returning with his family to Geneva. Although he did not return to Europe, he did retire from government service, beginning a new career in business.

Gallatin moved to New York City, where John Jacob Astor urged him to accept the presidency of Astor's new National Bank. In this position, which Gallatin held from 1831 to 1839, he not only wrote on fiscal reform in articles such as *Considerations on the Currency and Banking System of the United States* (1831) but also protested slavery, the annexation of Texas by the United States, and the war with Mexico. In addition, he found time to indulge his interests in ethnology and, especially, linguistics.

While Gallatin had been living in Paris, he had made the acquaintance of the famous German scientist Alexander von Humboldt. Gallatin's knowledge of several European languages and his interest in linguistics complemented Humboldt's study of linguistics and American Indian languages. Humboldt prevailed upon Gallatin to write on Indian languages, and thus, even before Gallatin left public service, he had begun his scientific career. His first major publication in this field was *A Synopsis of the Indian Tribes Within the United States East of the Rocky Mountains and in the British and Russian Possessions in North America* (1836), followed by *Notes on the Semi-Civilized Nations of Mexico, Yucatan, and Central America* (1845) and *Indians of North-west America* (1848). Besides writing in the field of ethnology, Gallatin served as president of the American Ethnological Society, an organization he helped to found in 1842.

SIGNIFICANCE

Although sometimes indulging in Romantic notions, Gallatin was first and foremost a gentleman of the Enlightenment. With his superb forensic skills and his ability to remain calm under personal attack, Gallatin proved a consummate politician, negotiator, and diplomat. His brilliance of mind led Jefferson to rely on Gallatin not only to oversee national finance but also to proofread his speeches and act as personal confidant. As secretary of the treasury and disbursing agent, Gallatin assumed a major role in promoting the exploration of the West and settlement of the Western frontier.

Governed by an Enlightenment philosophy that emphasized idealism and humanism in politics, learning, and society, Gallatin became uncomfortable with the raw commercialism of Jacksonian America, which seemed to him to promote only the base side of human potential.

By the time of his death, Gallatin was out of step with his time: an Enlightenment figure in Jacksonian America. Nevertheless, for many he remained the Enlightenment conscience of America's idealistic beginnings.

—*Robert E. Bieder*

FURTHER READING

Adams, Henry. *The Life of Albert Gallatin*. Philadelphia: J. B. Lippincott, 1880. Still a classic account of Gallatin's life. Henry Adams, the grandson of John Adams, provides an intimate glimpse into Gallatin's life and values and places both in the context of Gallatin's European experience and a rapidly developing American society.

Allen, John Logan. *Passage Through the Garden: Lewis and Clark and the Image of the American Northwest*. Urbana: University of Illinois Press, 1975. Allen's work discusses Gallatin's economic contribution as secretary of the treasury and his intellectual contribution to the exploration of the West.

Balinky, Alexander. *Albert Gallatin: Fiscal Theories and Policies*. New Brunswick, N.J.: Rutgers University Press, 1958. An extensive study of Gallatin's theories and policies on public finance.

Bieder, Robert E. *Science Encounters the Indian, 1820-1880: The Early Years of American Ethnology*. Norman: University of Oklahoma Press, 1986. Contains a chapter on Gallatin, his study of American Indians, and his place in the early development of American ethnology.

Elazar, Daniel Judah, and Ellis Katz, eds. *American Models of Revolutionary Leadership: George Washington and Other Founders*. Lanham, Md.: University Press of America, 1992. Collection of essays assessing how America's earliest leaders enabled the country to make the transition from revolutionary upheaval to stable democratic government. Includes an essay by Rozann Rothman entitled "Albert Gallatin: Political Method in Leadership."

Gallatin, James. *The Diary of James Gallatin, Secretary to Albert Gallatin, a Great Peace Maker, 1813-1827*. Edited by Count Gallatin. New York: Charles Scribner's Sons, 1931. A highly intimate and entertaining account of Gallatin's years in Paris and London, written by his son, who served as Gallatin's secretary.

Kuppenheimer, L. B. *Albert Gallatin's Vision of Democratic Stability: An Interpretive Profile*. Westport, Conn.: Praeger, 1996. The author builds a profile of Gallatin based on analysis of the intellectual climate in Europe that influenced his philosophical and political perspectives.

Smelser, Marshall. *The Democratic Republic: 1801-1815.* Edited by Henry S. Commager and Richard B. Morris. New York: Harper & Row, 1968. Mentions Gallatin in the larger context of the growth of the American republic.

Walters, Raymond, Jr. *Albert Gallatin: Jeffersonian Financier and Diplomat.* New York: Macmillan, 1957. Walters differs from Balinky in emphasizing Gallatin's Jeffersonian ties and diplomatic career.

White, Leonard D. *The Jeffersonians: A Study in Administrative History, 1801-1829.* New York: Macmillan,

1951. Now dated but still useful in its consideration of Gallatin's administration of the treasury.

SEE ALSO: Henry Adams; John Quincy Adams; Henry Clay; Alexander von Humboldt; Lewis Henry Morgan.

RELATED ARTICLES in *Great Events from History: The Nineteenth Century, 1801-1900:* 1811-1840: Construction of the National Road; February 17, 1815: Treaty of Ghent Takes Effect; April 24, 1820: Congress Passes Land Act of 1820; October 26, 1825: Erie Canal Opens; May, 1831-February, 1832: Tocqueville Visits America.

ÉVARISTE GALOIS
French mathematician

With the aid of group theory, Galois produced a definitive answer to the problem of the solvability of algebraic equations, a problem that had preoccupied mathematicians since the eighteenth century. Consequently, he laid one of the foundations of modern algebra.

BORN: October 25, 1811; Bourg-la-Reine, near Paris, France
DIED: May 31, 1832; Paris, France
AREA OF ACHIEVEMENT: Mathematics

EARLY LIFE
Évariste Galois (gah-lwah) was the son of Nicolas-Gabriel Galois, a friendly and witty liberal thinker who headed a school that accommodated about sixty boarders. Elected mayor of Bourg-la-Reine during the Hundred Days after Napoleon's escape from Elba, the elder Galois retained office under the second Restoration. Galois's mother, Adelaïde-Marie Demante, was from a long line of jurists and had received a more traditional education. She had a headstrong and eccentric personality. Having taken control of her son's early education, she attempted to implant in him, along with the elements of classical culture, strict religious principles as well as respect for a stoic morality. Influenced by his father's imagination and liberalism, the eccentricity of his mother, and the affection of his elder sister Nathalie-Théodore, Galois seems to have had a childhood that was both happy and studious.

Galois continued his studies at the Collège Louis-le-Grand in Paris, entering in October, 1823. He found it

difficult to adjust to the harsh discipline imposed by the school during the Restoration at the orders of the political authorities and the Church, and, although a brilliant student, he was rebellious. During the early months of 1827, he attended the first-year preparatory mathematics courses taught by H. J. Vernier; this first exposure to mathematics was a revelation for him. He rapidly became bored with the elementary nature of this instruction and with the inadequacies of some of his textbooks and began reading the original works themselves.

After appreciating the difficulty of Adrien-Marie Legendre's geometry, Galois acquired a solid background from the major works of Joseph-Louis Lagrange. During the next two years, he attended Vernier's second-year preparatory mathematics courses, then the more advanced ones of L. P. E. Richard, who was the first to recognize Galois's superiority in mathematics. With this perceptive teacher, Galois excelled in his studies, even though he was already devoting much more of his time to his personal work than to his classwork. In 1828, he began to study some then-recent works on the theory of equations, on number theory, and on the theory of elliptic functions.

This was the time period in which Galois's first memoir appeared. Published in March, 1829, in the *Annales de mathématiques pures et appliquées* (annals of pure and applied mathematics), it demonstrated and clarified a result of Lagrange concerning continuous fractions. Although it revealed a certain astuteness, it did not demonstrate exceptional talent.

LIFE'S WORK

In 1828, by his own admission Galois falsely believed—as Niels Henrik Abel had eight years earlier—that he had solved the general fifth-degree equation. Quickly enlightened, he resumed with a new approach the study of the theory of equations, a subject that he pursued until he elucidated the general problem with the aid of group theory. The results he obtained in May, 1829, were sent to the Academy of Sciences by a particularly competent judge, Augustin-Louis Cauchy. Fate was to frustrate these brilliant beginnings, however, and to leave a lasting impression on the personality of the young mathematician.

First, at the beginning of July, his father, a man who had been persecuted for his liberal beliefs, committed suicide. A month later, Galois failed the entrance examination for the École Polytechnique, because he refused to use the expository method suggested by the examiner. Barred from entering the school that attracted him because of its scientific prestige and liberal tradition, he took the entrance examination for the École Normale Supérieure (then called the École Préparatoire), which trained future secondary school teachers. He entered the institution in November, 1829.

At this time he learned of Abel's death and, at the same time, that Abel's last published memoir contained several original results that Galois himself had presented as original in his memoir to the Academy. Cauchy, assigned to supervise Galois's work, advised his student to revise his memoir, taking into account Abel's research and new results. Galois wrote a new text that he submitted to the Academy in February, 1830, that he hoped would win for him the grand prix in mathematics. However, this memoir was lost upon the death of Joseph Fourier, who had been appointed to study it. Eliminated from the competition, Galois believed himself to be the object of a new persecution by both the representatives of institutional science and society in general. His manuscripts preserve a partial record of the revision of this memoir of February, 1830.

In June, 1830, Galois published in *Bulletin des sciences mathématiques* (bulletin of mathematical sciences) a short note on the resolution of numerical equations, as well as a much more significant article, "Sur la théorie des nombres" (on number theory). The fact that this same issue contained original works by Cauchy and Siméon-Denis Poisson sufficiently confirms the reputation that Galois had already acquired. The July Revolution of 1830, however, was to initiate a drastic change in his career.

Galois became politicized. Before returning for a second year to the École Normale Supérieure in November, 1830, he had already developed friendships with several republican leaders. Even less able to tolerate his school's strict discipline than before, he published a violent article against its director in an opposition journal. For this action he was expelled on December 8, 1830.

Left alone, Galois devoted most of his time to political propaganda. He participated in the riots and demonstrations then agitating Paris and was even arrested (but was eventually acquitted). Meanwhile, to a limited degree, he continued his mathematical research. His last two publications were a short note on analysis in the *Bulletin des sciences mathématiques* of December, 1830, and "Lettre sur l'enseignement des sciences" (letter on the teaching of the sciences), which appeared on January 2, 1831, in the *Gazette des écoles*. On January 13, he began to teach a public course on advanced algebra in which he planned to present his own discoveries; this project appears not to have been successful.

On January 17, 1831, Galois presented the Academy a new version of his memoir, hastily written at Poisson's request. However, in Poisson's report of July 4, 1831, on this, Galois's most important piece of work, Poisson suggested that a portion of the results could be found in several posthumous writings of Abel and that the rest was incomprehensible. Such a judgment, the profound injustice of which would become apparent in the future, only encouraged Galois's rebellion.

Arrested again during a republican demonstration on July 14, 1831, and imprisoned, Galois nevertheless continued his mathematical research, revised his memoir on equations, and worked on the applications of his theory and on elliptic functions. After the announcement of a cholera epidemic on March 16, 1832, he was transferred to a nursing home, where he resumed his investigations, wrote several essays on the philosophy of science, and became immersed in a love affair that ended unhappily. Galois sank into a deep depression.

Provoked into a duel under unclear circumstances following this breakup, Galois sensed that he was near death. On May 29, he wrote desperate letters to his republican friends, hastily sorted his papers, and addressed to his friend Auguste Chevalier—but intended for Carl Friedrich Gauss and Carl Gustav Jacob Jacobi—a testamentary letter, a tragic document in which he attempted to outline the principal results that he had attained. On May 30, fatally wounded by an unknown opponent, he was hospitalized; he died the following day, not even twenty-one years of age.

SIGNIFICANCE

Èvariste Galois's work seems not to have been fully appreciated by anyone during his lifetime. Cauchy, who would have been able to understand its significance, left France in September, 1830, having seen only its initial outlines. In addition, the few fragments published during his lifetime did not give an overall view of his achievement and, in particular, did not provide a means of judging the exceptional interest of the results regarding the theory of equations rejected by Poisson. Also, the publication of the famous testamentary letter does not appear to have attracted the attention it deserved.

It was not until September, 1843, that Joseph Liouville, who prepared Galois's manuscripts for publication, announced officially that the young mathematician had effectively solved the problem, already investigated by Abel, of deciding whether an irreducible first-degree equation is solvable with the use of radicals. Although announced and prepared for the end of 1843, the memoir of 1831 did not appear until the October/November, 1846, issue of the *Journal de mathématiques pures et appliquées*, when it was published with a fragment on the primitive equations solvable by radicals.

Beginning with Liouville's edition, which appeared in book form in 1897, Galois's work became progressively known to mathematicians and subsequently exerted a profound influence on the development of modern mathematics. Also important, although they came too late to contribute to the advancement of mathematics, are the previously unpublished texts that appeared later.

Although he formulated more precisely essential ideas that were already being investigated, Galois also introduced others that, once stated, played an important role in the genesis of modern algebra. Furthermore, he boldly generalized certain classic methods in other fields and succeeded in providing a complete solution and a generalization of problems by systematically drawing upon group theory—one of the most important structural concepts that unified the multiplicity of algebras in the nineteenth century.

—Genevieve Slomski

FURTHER READING

Bell, Eric T. *Men of Mathematics*. New York: Simon & Schuster, 1937. Historical account of the major figures in mathematics from the Greeks to Georg Cantor, written in an interesting if at times exaggerated style. In a relatively brief chapter, "Genius and Stupidity," Bell describes the life and work of Galois in a tone that both worships and scorns the young mathematician and mixes fact with legend in his discussion.

Boyer, Carl B. *A History of Mathematics*. New York: John Wiley & Sons, 1968. In this standard and reputable history of mathematics, Boyer devotes a brief section to Galois. Galois is described as the individual who most contributed to the vital discovery of the group concept. The author also assesses Galois's impact on future generations of mathematicians.

Infeld, Leopold. *Whom the Gods Love: The Story of Èvariste Galois*. New York: Whittlesey House, 1948. This biography takes great license with the facts (many of which are unknown) of Galois's life and creates an interesting, if fictional, account. The author, maintaining that biography always mixes truth and fiction, puts Galois's life in the historical context of nineteenth century France by creating scenes and dialogues that might have occurred.

Kline, Morris. *Mathematical Thought from Ancient Times to Modern Times*. New York: Oxford University Press, 1972. In this voluminous work, the author surveys the major mathematical creators and developments through the first few decades of the twentieth century. The emphasis is on the leading mathematical themes rather than on the men. The brief section on Galois gives some biographical information and discusses the mathematician's work in finite fields, group theory, and the theory of equations.

Struik, Dirk J. *A Concise History of Mathematics*. Vol. 2 in *The Seventeenth Century-Nineteenth Century*. New York: Dover, 1948. In this book devoted to a concise overview of the major figures and trends in mathematics during the time period covered, a brief section is devoted to Galois. The author spends approximately equal time discussing Galois's life and major achievements, and views the mathematician both as a product of his times and as a unique genius.

Tota Rigatelli, Laura. *Evariste Galois, 1811-1832*. Translated from the Italian by John Denton. Boston: Birkhäuser Verlag, 1996. Brief biography based on new research offering a more accurate account of Galois's life than previous biographies. Includes a chapter describing Galois's mathematical work and a comprehensive bibliography.

SEE ALSO: Richard Dedekind; Joseph Fourier; Carl Friedrich Gauss; Henri Poincaré; Charlotte Angas Scott.

RELATED ARTICLE in *Great Events from History: The Nineteenth Century, 1801-1900:* 1899: Hilbert Publishes *The Foundations of Geometry*.

FRANCIS GALTON
English eugenicist

Galton is credited with the development of modern statistical methods that have made immense contributions in all areas of science, and he also laid the foundation for modern psychology and for the eugenics movement.

BORN: February 16, 1822; Birmingham, near Sparkbrook, England
DIED: January 17, 1911; Haslemere, Surrey, England
ALSO KNOWN AS: Sir Francis Galton
AREAS OF ACHIEVEMENT: Mathematics, science and technology

EARLY LIFE

Francis Galton was the son of Samuel Tertius Galton and Violetta Darwin Galton, the daughter of Erasmus Darwin. Thus, Francis Galton and the great naturalist Charles Darwin were cousins. Galton's early education was provided by his sister Adele—his elder by twelve years—who took a special interest in his education. Before Francis enrolled in school for formal education, Adele taught him to read English, Greek, and Latin and taught him simple arithmetic. In 1836, at the age of fourteen, Galton was enrolled in King Edward's School in Birmingham, where the curriculum was primarily Latin and Greek. In *Memories of My Life* (1908), Galton wrote that while at the school he craved "an abundance of good English reading, well-taught mathematics, and solid science."

After attending King Edward's School for two years, Galton became a pupil at the Birmingham General Hospital to prepare for a career in medicine. For a young boy of sixteen, he was immediately given a position of much responsibility in the dispensary. He prepared infusions, decoctions, tinctures, and extracts. In *Memories of My Life*, his early medical experiences are emotionally described. Galton's inquisitiveness led him to sample the various medicines in the dispensary, stopping when croton oil, with its emetic effects, temporarily cured his investigative tendencies. In 1839, he continued his formal theoretical medical training at King's College, London.

In 1840, Galton left medical study at King's College and enrolled at Cambridge (Trinity College) to study mathematics. A nervous breakdown forced him to miss a term and abandon his plans to receive honors in mathematics. Instead, he finished studies for a medical degree. Galton's stay at Trinity College proved to be influential

as he met, socialized with, and was stimulated by many prominent educators.

Undoubtedly inspired by Charles Darwin's *The Voyage of the Beagle* (1839), Galton had a propensity for travel, of which his first taste came during the summer of 1840. In *Memories of My Life*, Galton said, "in the Spring of 1840 a passion for travel seized me as if I had been a migratory bird." The "passion" took him to various countries on the Continent.

In 1844, after the death of his father, who left him independently wealthy, Galton "abandoned all thought of becoming a physician." With no apparent sense of vocation, he traveled for several years.

LIFE'S WORK

Having abandoned his medical studies and being independently wealthy, Galton resumed his interest in traveling, climbing, and mountaineering. He traveled to Egypt and Spain in 1845 and under the aegis of the Royal Geographical Society visited Southeast Africa from 1850 to 1852. His travels won for him the gold medal of the Royal Geographical Society and established his position in the scientific world. His account of his travels to Southeast Africa was published in 1853 as *Tropical South Africa*. He published in 1855 *Art of Travel*, which became the most popular of all publications of the Royal Geographical Society. Galton eventually became editor of the *Proceedings of the Royal Geographical Society*. His work for the Royal Geographical Society secured his election as a fellow of the Royal Society in 1856.

Through his association with the Royal Geographical Society, Galton became a member of the Managing Committee of the Kew Observatory in 1858. His work at the observatory included the establishment of a means for standardizing sextants and other angular instruments and verifying the accuracy of thermometers. He also developed a photographic method used to record readings from a barometer, discovered anticyclones, took part in the construction of weather charts for publication in daily newspapers, and made several minor inventions. He became chairman of the observatory in 1889 and held that post until 1901.

During the 1860's, while still at Cambridge, Galton noticed that academic talent ran in families, and he became interested in heredity, especially of human characteristics. This interest was sparked by Darwin's *On the Origin of Species by Means of Natural Selection* (1859).

Galton stated in *Memories of My Life* that *On the Origin of Species* "made a marked epoch in my own mental development."

Galton first outlined his ideas on human heredity in the June and August, 1865, issues of *Macmillan* magazine in an article titled "Hereditary Talent and Character" but elaborated on them and developed them more fully in a book, published in 1869 and titled *Hereditary Genius: An Inquiry into Its Laws and Consequences*. Galton's purpose as stated in the introduction of the book was to show "that a man's natural abilities are derived from inheritance, under exactly the same limitations as are the forms and physical features of the whole organic world."

In his book, Galton describes his method based on the normal distribution of classifying people by ability. He outlines the kinships of judges, statesmen, scientists, poets, and so on. His conclusions about the power of heredity are clear: "I object to pretensions of natural equality. The experiences of the nursery, the school, the community, and of the professional careers, are a chain of proofs to the contrary." Galton believed that human intelligence and behavior were under the same influences as any physical trait.

Galton concluded that if one can breed horses with "peculiar powers of running . . . so it would be quite practicable to produce a highly gifted race of men by judicious marriages during several consecutive generations." Galton, believing that "heredity was a far more powerful agent in human development than nurture," decided to explore "the range of human faculty . . . in order to ascertain the degree to which heredity might . . . modify the human race."

Galton realized that the development and spread of his ideas on heredity were hampered by a lack of knowledge of a hereditary mechanism. In 1871, he succeeded in establishing cross-circulation between two breeds of rabbits in an effort to study Darwin's gemmule theory of inheritance. Neither breed was altered by the experiment, casting doubt on a gemmulelike theory. In later studies, Galton came close to discovering the principles of the continuity of the germ plasm and corroborating Gregor Mendel's principle of segregation.

Galton's own theory of inheritance was a biometrical one:

> The laws of heredity are concerned only with deviations from the median. . . . It supposes all variability are a result of different and equally probable combinations of a multitude of small independent causes.

This work led to his development of the correlation coefficient.

In 1872, Alphonse de Candolle published a response to *Hereditary Genius: An Inquiry into Its Laws and Consequences*, in which de Candolle concluded that environment and not heredity was more important in determining mental character. In an effort to determine the relative importance of nature and nurture, Galton sent questionnaires to 180 selected fellows of the Royal Society. The questionnaires inquired about parents, physique, comparable success of relatives, energy, memory, mechanical aptitude, religious beliefs, and origin of the interest in science. The results of the questionnaires formed the foundation for *English Men of Science* (1874). Although one could interpret Galton's results in favor of an environmental influence, he said that "the results of the inquiry showed how largely the aptitude for science was an inborn and not an acquired gift, and therefore apt to be hereditary."

Realizing the wealth of information on the nature/nurture debate to be gained from the study of twins, Galton located and questioned several pairs of twins. The results, which supported Galton's suspicions about the power of

Francis Galton. (Library of Congress)

heredity, were published in the *Journal of the Anthropological Institute* in 1875 and 1876. Galton concluded:

> The impression that all this evidence leaves on the mind is one of some wonder whether nurture can do anything at all. There is no escape from the conclusion that nature prevails enormously over nurture when the differences of nurture do not exceed what is commonly to be found among persons of the same rank of society and in the same country.

In his continuing quest to obtain hereditary data on humans, Galton published the *Record of Family Faculties* in 1884. The *Record of Family Faculties* was a list of questions about topics ranging from mental powers to temperament. Prizes were awarded to those who provided the most complete answers. The information from the questionnaires was used for *Natural Inheritance*, published in 1889.

Galton's interest in human characteristics provided the stimulus for the opening in 1885 of an anthropometric laboratory at the South Kensington Museum, where data on height, weight, sight, hearing, and so on, were collected. The laboratory remained open for eight years. His studies at the laboratory on children's ability to remember number and letter spans were noticed by Alfred Binet and incorporated into Binet's intelligence test. One emphasis of the laboratory was in the use of fingerprints as a means of identification, a technique pioneered by Galton. *Finger-Prints* was published in 1893.

In Galton's attempts to discover the mechanisms involved with hereditary phenomena, he studied, as suggested by Darwin, inheritance in sweet peas. The results of the sweet-pea experiments and subsequent studies on humans showed a direct correlation between parent and offspring for the various characteristics he studied. The studies directly led to the discovery of the correlation coefficient and the concept of regression. Many of his results were published in *Natural Inheritance*, the publication of which led to the formation of the biometric school of heredity, a direct rival of the Mendelian school. Galton's work on the inheritance of human characteristics secured his election as president of the Anthropological Society in 1885. Six years later, Galton helped launch *Biometrika*, of which he became a consulting editor. The journal was intended as a forum for the publication of biological studies of a statistical nature.

Galton is best known for his work in eugenics, an interest that directly evolved from his work on the inheritance of human characteristics. In *Inquiries into the Human Faculty and Its Development* (1883), he defined eugenics as

> the science of improving stock which is by no means confined to questions of judicious mating but which, especially in the case of man, takes cognizance of all influences that tend in however remote a degree to give the more suitable races or strains of blood a better chance of prevailing speedily over the less suitable than they otherwise would have had.

Galton's conviction that intelligence and virtually all other behavioral characteristics were inherited led him to believe that social ills could be cured by controlling the reproduction of undesirables (negative eugenics) and encouraging the breeding of superior individuals (positive eugenics) to the end of breeding a better race. It was clear to Galton that the breeding of criminals, the insane, the feebleminded, and paupers should be limited, by compulsory means if necessary. In the Huxley Lecture delivered in 1900, Galton stated that doing so "would abolish a source of suffering and misery for a future generation." Again, his ideas attracted little attention.

In May, 1904, Galton lectured before the Sociological Society. In that lecture, he defined eugenics as

> the science which deals with all influences that improve the inborn qualities of a race; also with those that develop them to the utmost advantage. . . . What Nature does blindly, slowly, and ruthlessly man may do providently, quickly and kindly.

Late in 1904, Galton gave the University of London five hundred pounds per year for three years to set up a eugenics laboratory. Galton acted as superintendent. Monies were also given for a research fellow and a research assistant. The laboratory was called the Eugenics Record Office; the lab's official definition of eugenics was "the study of the agencies under social control that may improve or impair the social qualities of future generations either physically or mentally." The Eugenics Education Society was founded three years later, and Galton was appointed honorary president.

Galton was knighted in 1909. He died on January 17, 1911, in Haslemere, Surrey, England. On his death, he bequeathed forty-five thousand pounds to the University of London to endow a Chair of Eugenics.

SIGNIFICANCE

Francis Galton's work had a profound impact on scientific research. His development of the correlation coefficient and the concept of regression marked the dawn of the statistical era of scientific inquiry and revolutionized the way scientists analyze their experimental results.

Work on the inheritance of psychological characteristics, the use of twin studies, and the use and development of statistical methods made Galton the founder of modern psychology. Galton is best known for his work in eugenics. He was convinced that heredity was the most important factor in determining psychological characteristics. There is little doubt that he was influenced by Darwin's theory of natural selection. Galton saw that Darwin's theory easily applied to humankind and that the process of natural selection could be accelerated by human intervention. At first, his eugenic proposals attracted little attention and few followers.

After the rediscovery of Mendel's law in 1900, Galton's eugenic ideas began to take hold. His ideas spread throughout Europe and to the Americas and quickly found influence in the United States. The eugenics movement was seen as a large-scale social-hygiene program aimed at curing social ills. In the United States, the movement culminated with the passing in 1924 of an immigration restriction law. The rise of Nazism clearly demonstrated how eugenics could be misused by those in authority. Adolf Hitler delivered the final death knell to eugenics as an organized movement.

—*Charles L. Vigue*

FURTHER READING

Brookes, Martin. *Extreme Measures: The Dark Visions and Bright Ideas of Francis Galton*. New York: Bloomsbury, 2004. Comprehensive biography written by a former evolutionary biologist who worked at the University College of London's Galton Laboratory. Brookes is impressed by the breadth of Galton's achievements, but condemns Galton's racist ideas, Victorian prejudices, and failure to understand the statistical ideas he devised.

Bulmer, Michael. *Francis Galton: Pioneer of Heredity and Biometry*. Baltimore: Johns Hopkins University Press, 2003. Bulmer, a biometrician, describes Galton's life and ideas about the use of biometrical methods in genetics.

Forrest, D. W. *Francis Galton: The Life and Work of a Victorian Genius*. New York: Taplinger, 1974. Biog-raphy containing many letters written to family members and colleagues.

Galton, Francis. *Memories of My Life*. London: Methuen, 1908. An account of Galton's personal and scientific life from his own perspective. There are some errors that have probably resulted from Galton's failing memory.

Gillham, Nicholas Wright. *A Life of Sir Francis Galton: From African Exploration to the Birth of Eugenics*. New York: Oxford University Press, 2001. Biography describing the full range of Galton's accomplishments, placing his achievements in relation to Victorian social ideas and Darwinism.

Haller, Mark. *Eugenics: Hereditary Attitudes in American Thought*. New Brunswick, N.J.: Rutgers University Press, 1963. An excellent account of the origin and development of the eugenics movement in both Great Britain and the United States.

Porter, Theodore M. *The Rise of Statistical Thinking, 1820-1900*. Princeton, N.J.: Princeton University Press, 1986. An excellent study of the development of statistical thinking among nineteenth century social scientists, biologists, and physicists; includes extensive discussion of Galton. The author is a historian, and his account demands little mathematical background.

Stigler, Stephen M. *The History of Statistics: The Measurement of Uncertainty Before 1900*. Cambridge, Mass.: Harvard University Press, 1986. A magisterial history of statistics, from its origins in the seventeenth century to the full-fledged development of statistical methods at the beginning of the twentieth century. In contrast to Porter (see above), Stigler writes for the mathematically knowledgeable reader, and his engagingly written book is dense with equations, formulas, and statistical tables. Includes a biographical sketch of Galton and thorough discussion of his probability machine. Illustrated.

SEE ALSO: Charles Darwin; Gregor Mendel.
RELATED ARTICLES in *Great Events from History: The Nineteenth Century, 1801-1900:* 1883: Galton Defines "Eugenics"; 1899-1900: Rediscovery of Mendel's Hereditary Theory.

LÉON GAMBETTA
French politician

One of the most vocal critics of the Second Empire of Napoleon III during the 1860's, Gambetta became the virtual dictator of France in 1870 during the resistance to the Prussian invasion. He was one of the most prominent and the most popular republican politicians of the period.

BORN: April 2, 1838; Cahors, near Toulouse, France
DIED: December 31, 1882; Ville-d'Avray, near Paris, France
AREA OF ACHIEVEMENT: Government and politics

EARLY LIFE

Léon Gambetta (gahm-BEHT-ah) was born in southern France, where his Italian grandfather had settled his family in 1818. There the Gambettas became shopkeepers. In 1837, Gambetta's father, Joseph, married Marie Magdeleine Massabie, the daughter of a local chemist; Gambetta's family, on both sides, might best be described as lower middle class. Gambetta's father wished him to follow in the family business, but in 1857 Gambetta went to Paris to study law. He had long been an opponent of the Second Empire of Napoleon III, and during the 1860's he began to write and speak against the regime. He made his mark during that decade in his defense of various individuals accused of political crimes against the empire. In 1869, he was elected to the French Legislative Assembly, representing the southern city of Marseilles though he had also been victorious in the working-class Parisian district of Belleville. Though young, he was already a recognized leader of the opposition.

Throughout his life, Gambetta suffered from various medical problems, including the loss of an eye as a child. He was of less than average height and put on substantial weight as a young man, but his long hair and his pronounced nose gave him a dramatic appearance, especially in profile. This imposing physical presence was complemented by a charismatic rhetorical style.

LIFE'S WORK

In 1870, France and Prussia went to war as a result of Otto von Bismarck's Machiavellian diplomatic machinations. The French public demanded war, and although Napoleon III's own inclinations were toward peace, he led France against its enemy from across the Rhine. This action proved disastrous. Napoleon was captured and soon abdicated, French armies were defeated, and in Paris on September 4, 1870, the former regime was re-

placed by a republic and a government of national defense was established. The new government was composed primarily of those elected to represent the various Parisian districts in the previous year's election. Gambetta, who had been elected from Belleville, became minister of the interior. As Prussian troops approached Paris, it was decided to establish another governmental presence in Tours, and soon the decision was made to reinforce the Tours government with Gambetta, the youngest member of the cabinet. In Tours, he became minister of war as well as minister of the interior and became the most powerful individual in France.

Earlier, Gambetta had joined with a number of his fellow republicans to warn against the war with Prussia, but, unlike some of his republican allies, Gambetta was no pacifist. He fervently believed in France and was willing to resort to arms to save France and the republic. In Tours, Gambetta faced what he considered internal treason as well as foreign invasion; the result was that by the end of the year Gambetta had become in effect dictator of France. Some of his critics had their doubts.

Although impressively assembled, the French troops were no match for the Prussians. Gambetta wished to continue the war, but as the winter elapsed the opinion of the French public turned toward peace. Eventually, Gambetta was forced to give way, and he resigned on February 6, 1871. He had both saved France's honor and left a residue of considerable controversy.

In the elections to the National Assembly that followed, Gambetta was victorious in ten different constituencies but chose to represent a department in Alsace, fated to be lost, along with Lorraine, to Germany as a result of the peace. When the treaty was accepted, Gambetta resigned in protest, the cause of the lost provinces remaining of paramount concern to Gambetta and to France. In the following months, Gambetta attempted to recover his damaged health, and in July he was again elected to the assembly, choosing to represent working-class Belleville.

In the years that followed, Gambetta's prestige and influence remained widespread. Fully committed to the ideals of the republic, he initially demanded that the assembly be quickly dissolved and a new one elected with the clear objective of producing a republican constitution. He feared, along with many other republicans, that the existing assembly was too monarchist in sentiment, intent on restoring either the house of Bourbon or that of

Orléans. He particularly feared a Napoleonic revival. Gambetta was also concerned about the power of the Church. Sympathetic to the positivism of Auguste Comte, he had few orthodox religious feelings. His animosity toward the Church was based less on its claims to spiritual truth than on its institutional influences on French society, particularly in education.

In time, Gambetta began to believe that the assembly could in itself become safely republican and that there might be no need to call a new constituent assembly. That attitude required compromise on his part, particularly in his acceptance of a senate, that many conservatives demanded as a curb on the democratically elected Chamber of Deputies. Accepting a senate not chosen directly by the voters, he argued that democratic reforms could be made in the future, but his willingness to compromise gained for him a reputation as an opportunist.

The future of the republic remained problematical during the early 1870's. In 1875, the assembly adopted, by a narrow vote, a method to choose the eventual successor to the president of France, the conservative Marshal MacMahon, thus transforming the provisional republic into a more permanent one. There was no formal constitution, merely the acceptance of a series of laws that established the powers of the president, a senate, and a Chamber of Deputies.

Gambetta, as he had done earlier, pushed for Republican Union, the name of his bloc in the Chamber of Deputies, but there were more radical republicans to the left and more conservative republicans to the right. Although no socialist, Gambetta did believe in the right of labor to organize and the necessity for some government regulation of business. Unlike many of his fellow republicans on both the right and the left, Gambetta, the nationalist, believed in the need for a strong government, both internally and externally.

In 1876, Gambetta was chosen head of the important Budget Committee of the Chamber of Deputies. In early 1879, he became president of the chamber, a position of considerable prestige but one that compromised Gambetta's political leadership. Many argued that the president of the chamber should remain above the party fray, but it was difficult for Gambetta to distance himself. Soon some claimed that Gambetta was wielding hidden power. Many predicted that Gambetta would soon become premier and form his own government, but MacMahon's successor, the conservative republican Jules Grevy, refused to summon Gambetta, a longtime rival, until November, 1881.

Only then did Gambetta form his long-awaited Grand Ministry. There were great expectations, but, for both personal and political reasons, Gambetta was unable to fulfill his ideal of republican unity. Many of the most prominent of his republican colleagues refused to join his government, and he was forced to rely upon his own often young and untried supporters. He himself often acted too imperiously when several years earlier he might have been more accommodating. In attempting to strengthen the central government, he alienated various local interests; in advocating railroad regulation, he caused consternation among some conservative republican businesspeople. He took the Foreign Affairs ministry himself and was particularly concerned to ally France with England in Egypt.

The issue that caused his downfall was an issue with which he was long associated. Gambetta, in order to create a stronger unity among republicans, had long urged that deputies should be selected not from individual districts but collectively representing larger areas. For once, Gambetta's opportunism failed him, and the legislature, elected by individual districts, was unwilling to adopt a different system, especially so early in its term of

Léon Gambetta.

office. Also, many were suspicious of Gambetta's possible dictatorial bent, and when he lost a key vote in the chamber, his government resigned after only seventy-four days.

SIGNIFICANCE

Léon Gambetta was only forty-three years old when he resigned. His health had long been poor, and after resigning he took time away from politics to recover his strength. When he returned, he took up the cause of military reform. Gambetta's reputation ever since 1870 had been connected to the fortunes of the military, and many accused him of being too adventurous, particularly in his desire to regain Alsace and Lorraine. Gambetta was conscious of those accusations, and while he never forgot the lost provinces he remained hopeful that someday Germany might be willing to exchange them for overseas territory. Unlike many of his countrymen, Gambetta was interested in colonial development, both in Africa and in Southeast Asia. A colonial empire would add to France's strength; in addition, colonies might someday be traded for Alsace and Lorraine.

On November 27, 1882, while handling a revolver, Gambetta accidentally shot himself in the hand. The wound, itself minor, became infected. Gambetta gradually weakened, dying on the last day of the year. He was given a state funeral, and his body, at his father's demand, was buried in Nice. In 1920, with the return of Alsace and Lorraine after World War I, Gambetta's heart was placed in the Pantheon in Paris, coinciding with the golden jubilee of the Third French Republic, the republic to which he had been so committed.

An oft-expressed criticism of Gambetta was that he was too closely tied to the working classes of Belleville and that they would ensure that his words and actions would remain too radical for the moderate inclinations of most French voters. However, he did not see himself as representing only the working classes. He did speak of the "new social strata" that would come to power under the republic, but for Gambetta that controversial phrase referred not to the working classes exclusively but rather to the majority of the French population, including the middle classes, who, he argued, had been excluded from power under the kings and emperors of France's past. Gambetta was always more a political than an economic radical, committed to majority political rule instead of advancing the claims of particular economic classes. In that he was a nineteenth century liberal, not a Marxist. Nevertheless, his opponents accused him of revolutionary radicalism.

Léon Gambetta's career had been full of paradoxes: a half-Italian who personified French patriotism; a moderate republican who in the eyes of many epitomized revolutionary radicalism; a pragmatic politician accused of being both an ideologue and an opportunist; a representative of the proletariat, or the middle classes, who wished to become dictator. When he died, some argued that he was still posed between Left and Right, and it is impossible to say in which direction he might have turned. What can be said is that he dominated French politics from 1870 until his death in 1882 as did no one else of that time.

—*Eugene S. Larson*

FURTHER READING

Brogan, D. W. *France Under the Republic: The Development of Modern France, 1870-1939*. New York: Harper & Brothers, 1940. Brogan's elegantly written study of the Third Republic is considered one of the classic historical accounts of the subject. Gambetta plays a significant role in the first part of the work, sometimes published separately under the title *From the Fall of the Empire to the Dreyfus Affair*.

Bury, J. P. T. *Gambetta and the Making of the Third Republic*. London: Longman, 1973. The author is the major English biographer of Gambetta. In *Gambetta and the National Defense* (1970), he analyzed Gambetta's role during the Prussian invasion of France in 1870-1871. Here he carries the story of Gambetta and the Third Republic through 1877.

_____. *Gambetta's Final Years: "The Era of Difficulties," 1877-1882*. New York: Longman, 1982. Bury concludes his exhaustive study of Gambetta. The author is sympathetic toward his subject, finding Gambetta to be perhaps the crucial figure in the founding of the Third Republic. Bury is not uncritical, however, suggesting that in his later years Gambetta's judgment was corrupted by his power and popularity.

Deschanel, Paul. *Gambetta*. New York: Dodd, Mead, 1920. Written by a later president of the Third Republic. Well written and sympathetic to the subject. Less a scholarly work than an interpretation of Gambetta's contributions to later French history.

Horne, Alistair. *The Fall of Paris: The Siege of the Commune, 1870-71*. New York: St. Martin's Press, 1965. The author is a specialist in modern French history. Horne presents a readable story of the aftermath of the Franco-Prussian War, in which Gambetta plays a central role.

Lehning, James R. _To Be a Citizen: The Political Culture of the Early French Third Republic_. Ithaca, N.Y.: Cornell University Press, 2001. A history of the early years of the republic, in which the French government worked to implement political reforms, including universal male suffrage.

Mayeur, Jean-Marie, and Madeleine Reberioux. _The Third Republic from Its Origins to the Great War, 1871-1914_. Cambridge, England: Cambridge University Press, 1984. This valuable work is more analytical and more structured than Brogan's work, which was published a generation earlier. Gambetta plays a major role in the early chapters.

Stannard, Harold. _Gambetta and the Foundation of the Third Republic_. London: Methuen, 1921. Like Deschanel's, this study of Gambetta was also written soon after Germany's defeat in World War I. In contrast to Deschanel, however, Stannard is not French, and although he admires Gambetta, Stannard is more critical. Suggests that regardless of Gambetta's own motives, some of his statements and actions did seem to imply, to others, the turn toward dictatorship.

Taithe, Bertrand. _Citizenship and Wars: France in Turmoil, 1870-1871_. London: Routledge, 2001. Information about Gambetta, including his role in assembly during the Third Republic, is included in this examination of the concept of citizenship during this period of social and political upheaval in France.

SEE ALSO: Otto von Bismarck; Auguste Comte; Napoleon III; Henry Morton Stanley; Adolphe Thiers.

RELATED ARTICLES in _Great Events from History: The Nineteenth Century, 1801-1900:_ July 19, 1870-January 28, 1871: Franco-Prussian War; February 13, 1871-1875: Third French Republic Is Established.

JAMES A. GARFIELD
President of the United States (1881)

During his nearly two-decade-long political career as a congressman and as president of the United States, Garfield played a key role in every issue of national importance. As party leader, he helped resolve the factionalism within the Republican Party and enabled the Republicans to lead the United States into the twentieth century.

BORN: November 19, 1831; Orange Township, Ohio
DIED: September 19, 1881; Elberon, New Jersey
ALSO KNOWN AS: James Abram Garfield (full name)
AREA OF ACHIEVEMENT: Government and politics

EARLY LIFE

Born in a log cabin, James Abram Garfield was the son of Abram and Eliza Garfield, members of the Disciples of Christ Church, which had been founded by Alexander Campbell. Abram died in 1833, thus leaving Eliza a widow, the sole provider for her family. Next to hunting, reading was young Garfield's greatest interest. He liked history and fiction, especially stories of the American Revolution and stories of the sea.

At the age of sixteen, Garfield went to Cleveland, where he was shocked and disappointed by a drunken captain to whom he had applied for work. On that same day, August 16, 1848, Garfield secured a job as driver with his cousin on a canal boat that carried goods between Cleveland and Pittsburgh. After six weeks of working on the canal, Garfield became quite ill and returned home. During his recuperation, his mother and Samuel Bates, a schoolteacher, convinced Garfield of the importance of education. Garfield enrolled and studied at Geauga Academy in Chester, where he became the academy's prize Latin student. He originally planned to spend the winter months at the academy and the spring and summer months on the canal, but after he absorbed himself in his studies, he decided to forget the canal life.

In the fall of 1851, Garfield enrolled in the newly established Western Reserve Eclectic Institute at Hiram, Ohio, where he plunged into his studies with a fierce determination to excel. His popularity and prominence at the Western Reserve Eclectic Institute were based on his scholastic ability as well as his physical prowess. His commanding physical appearance—he stood almost six feet tall, with broad shoulders and a massive head topped by a shock of unruly tawny hair—and his ability to outrun and outwrestle his schoolmates instilled automatic respect. This, combined with his serious demeanor, which gave an impression of quiet dignity, and his unaffected friendliness contributed to Garfield's popularity. Enjoying success as a debater, Garfield discovered that he possessed the ability to sway an audience, and the oratorical techniques that he learned during this period prepared him to become one of the most effective political speakers of his time.

In 1853, Garfield began preaching at neighboring churches. The following year, having completed his studies at the Eclectic Institute, he enrolled in Williams College. There, he was elected president of two major campus organizations—the Philogian Society, a literary society, and the Equitable Fraternity, an organization designed to combat the influence of the Greek fraternities. In addition, in spite of his Campbellite beliefs, Garfield was elected president of the Mills Theological Society, a Calvinist organization. He was also elected editor of the *Williams Quarterly*, a pioneer college journal of exceptional quality, to which he contributed extensively. Garfield never lost an election at Williams College or any election in which he was a candidate through the rest of his life. On August 7, 1856, he was graduated from Wil-

liams College with honors in a ceremony that included his delivering an oration on the conflict between matter and spirit.

LIFE'S WORK

As an inspiring and electrifying evangelist, Garfield preached continually during the last of the series of so-called Great Awakenings—periodic religious revivals that had begun in the colonial era. In 1857, at the age of twenty-six, Garfield was elected president of Western Reserve Eclectic Institute, defeating his former teacher, the institute's oldest and most distinguished faculty member. As president, Garfield made the Eclectic Institute the educational center of the region, changing a sectarian academy into an institution that welcomed students of all denominations.

Garfield believed educational curricula should reflect the trends of the time and serve as a medium through which students could prepare for successful living. He sponsored teacher-training workshops and seminars on teaching methods and school administration, and he prepared a series of lectures on American history, a subject that had not been included in the curricula of American colleges.

Garfield did not confine himself to administrative duties; he taught a full load of classes in a style designed to encourage students to think independently. Garfield's kindness and immense vitality, his readiness to praise, his deep concern for the overall welfare of his students, his enthusiasm, his ability to introduce his students to the meaning of education and the high ideals of life, and his participation with them in the extracurricular activities, especially athletic events, inspired great loyalty. The Eclectic Institute prospered under Garfield's leadership. On November 11, 1858, Garfield married Lucretia Rudolph, daughter of Zeb Rudolph, a pioneer Hiram Disciple and one of the school's most prominent trustees.

Moved by Garfield's prominent background and popularity, the Republican Party of the Twenty-sixth Ohio Senatorial District nominated him for the state senate on August 23, 1859. He won the seat handily on October 11. This feat ultimately led

James A. Garfield. (Library of Congress)

him to the center stage of the national political arena. Garfield distinguished himself on a number of key issues, especially those pertaining to slavery and the impending crisis—the Civil War. He stood strong against slavery and, shedding his pacifism, believed that war was the best solution to the problem of slavery. When the war began, he took an active role in raising troops and persuaded the governor of his state to appoint him lieutenant colonel in the Twenty-fourth Ohio Infantry; later, he was put in charge of the Forty-second Ohio Volunteer Infantry as a full colonel. Learning about Garfield's commission, the young men of Hiram, who held Garfield in the highest esteem, enthusiastically joined the Forty-second Ohio Volunteer Infantry to follow and fight with their hero.

At the outset of Garfield's military service, General Don Carlos Buell assigned him command of the Eighteenth Brigade and gave him the responsibility of planning the campaign to drive the Confederate army out of eastern Kentucky. In spite of the fact that Garfield had no military education or military experience, he accepted the task, presenting a plan that Buell accepted. Under Garfield's leadership, the Confederate forces were driven out of Kentucky.

Assuming control of the administration of eastern Kentucky after the conclusion of the campaign, Garfield pursued a policy of reconciliation. Promoted to brigadier general, he served outstandingly as chief of staff under General William S. Rosecrans, commander of the Army of the Cumberland. Garfield reached the peak of his military career in the Chattanooga campaign, fighting in one of the epic battles of military history, the Battle of Chickamauga. Garfield's outstanding achievements in the Kentucky campaign led his friends and the Republican Party of the Nineteenth Congressional District to nominate him as their representative to Congress on September 2, 1862. While still in the army carrying out his military duties and without participating in the campaign, he won the right to represent the Nineteenth District by an impressive victory, in the congressional election of October, 1862.

Beginning with the election of 1862, Garfield easily won nine consecutive terms, splendidly serving the people of the Nineteenth District for the next eighteen years as chairman of the Military Affairs Committee (in which capacity he was the first to introduce a bill that proposed a reserve officer training corps, or ROTC program for the colleges), chairman of the Banking and Currency Committee, and chairman of the powerful and prestigious Appropriations Committee.

When the Democratic Party won a majority of the seats in the House of Representatives in the congressional election of 1874, Garfield assumed the leadership of the Republican minority in the House. Having lost his chairmanships, he skillfully and relentlessly spoke out against the policies of the Democratic Party. As a member of a bipartisan committee selected to investigate the 1876 presidential election in the state of Louisiana, Garfield submitted a thorough report based on data presented to him by the election board and interviews he held with those who participated in the election and those denied participation, especially voters who were terrorized by white secret societies such as the Ku Klux Klan, the Knights of the White Camellia, and the Rifle Clubs. His report helped influence the election board to nullify Samuel Tilden's majority, and Rutherford B. Hayes was granted the electoral votes of Louisiana.

The 1876 election ended in an intense controversy involving the returns of Florida, Louisiana, and South Carolina. This situation produced a political stalemate that set the stage for a potential crisis that might have led the opposing parties back to the battlefields in a new civil war. Garfield served as a member of a special Electoral Commission to elect the president and participated in the historic conference that led to the compromise between the leaders of the Republican Party and the southern Democrats. These actions resolved the impending crisis, and Hayes became the nineteenth president of the United States.

On March 29, 1879, Garfield established himself as the outstanding leader of the Republican Party when he delivered one of the most dynamic speeches in the history of Congress. The Democrats' dogged advocacy of the principle of states' rights motivated Garfield to present his greatest speech—a speech that upheld the principle of federalism and inspired the Republicans to quit squabbling and act together as a strong united party. This speech influenced his state's legislature to elect him to serve in the U.S. Senate, and ultimately led to his nomination and election as president of the United States.

In 1880, Garfield was elected to serve as a delegate to the Seventh National Nominating Convention of the Republican Party, which met in Chicago. He came to the convention without any intention of seeking the nomination, but because of his great popularity, he was considered a dark-horse candidate. On the thirty-sixth ballot, the deadlocked delegates chose Garfield, hoping that he could unify the party. In a move that displeased a large number of Republicans, but as a means of placating the highly disappointed Stalwarts, who had supported Ulysses S. Grant for a third term, the imperious political boss of the New York Republican Party, Chester Alan Arthur, was selected as the party's candidate for vice president.

In November, Garfield's ability to control the various factions of his party and brilliantly manage his campaign resulted in his winning the presidency in the closest presidential election of the century. In view of the fact that he did nothing either before or during the convention to obtain his party's nomination (he strongly opposed the effort that culminated in his nomination) and the fact that his party had all but self-destructed since the assassination of President Abraham Lincoln, Garfield achieved a magnificent victory.

On July 2, 1881, only a few months after his inauguration, Garfield was shot by a crazed office-seeker, Charles Guiteau. He died on September 19, 1881. It is widely believed that Garfield's death was partly due to the incompetence of his physicians, who probed his bullet wound with their unwashed fingers.

SIGNIFICANCE

Garfield's election to the presidency was the crowning achievement of a spectacular and glorious career that began as the driver of a towboat on the Ohio Erie Canal. His was a classic American success story, brought to a tragically premature end.

The legacy of Garfield's brief term suggests what he might have accomplished had he lived to complete it. He laid the foundation for the development of a more independent and vigorous presidency that proved vital for a nation destined to become one of the most powerful nations in the world. The Pendleton Act of 1883, which led to the end of the spoils system in the federal government, was the logical conclusion of his efforts.

—*James D. Lockett*

FURTHER READING

Ackerman, Kenneth D. *Dark Horse: The Surprise Election and Political Murder of President James A. Garfield*. New York: Carroll & Graf, 2003. Describes Garfield's unanticipated presidential nomination, the presidential campaign of 1880, Garfield's few months in office, and his assassination. Focuses on the battling among Republicans for patronage and spoils, describing how this fighting resulted in Garfield's assassination by Charles Guiteau, a disappointed patronage seeker.

Brisbin, James S. *From the Tow-Path to the White House: The Early Life and Public Career of James A. Garfield*. Philadelphia: J. C. McCurdy, 1880. A flattering campaign biography, written in a romantic style shortly after Garfield's nomination. Although hurriedly written, Brisbin's work vividly recounts the story of a leader who exemplified fundamental American values. Includes illustrations.

Caldwell, Robert G. *James A. Garfield, Party Chieftain*. New York: Dodd, Mead, 1934. An exhaustive scholarly chronicle of the life of Garfield that, in effect, summarizes American political history from 1861 to 1881. Includes an excellent bibliography.

Clark, James C. *The Murder of James A. Garfield: The President's Last Days and the Trial and Execution of His Assassin*. Jefferson, N.C.: McFarland, 1993. An objective treatment of the subject in an enjoyable narrative style. Clark profiles Garfield's killer, Charles Guiteau, and covers the assassination plot, the medical care given to Garfield afterward, the president's funeral, and the trial and execution of Guiteau.

Doenecke, Justus D. *The Presidencies of James A. Garfield and Chester A. Arthur*. Lawrence: University Press of Kansas, 1981. This is one of the volumes of the American Presidency series, intended to present historians and the general public with interesting, scholarly assessments of the various presidential administrations. Includes excellent notes and bibliographical essays.

Hinsdale, Mary L., ed. *Garfield-Hinsdale Letters: Correspondence Between James Abram Garfield and Burke Aaron Hinsdale*. Ann Arbor: University of Michigan Press, 1949. The correspondence between James A. Garfield and his lifelong friend, Burke A. Hinsdale, a former pupil of Garfield, superintendent of Cleveland's Public School System, outstanding teacher at the University of Michigan, and president of Hiram College. The letters between Garfield and Hinsdale discuss the various issues that confronted the United States between 1857 and 1881, as well as the most popular books of the period; they also reveal the writers in their lighter moods. Their correspondence, which began when Hinsdale was nineteen and continued until Garfield's death, provides graphic self-portraits of Garfield and Hinsdale, and is a significant resource for scholars of Garfield.

Leech, Margaret, and Harry J. Brown. *The Garfield Orbit*. New York: Harper & Row, 1978. An absorbing story of the life of Garfield, showing him as a man of complex and contradictory character, in whom ambition and desire warred with firm principle. The book reveals more of the man and less of the vital issues that he confronted. Includes a Garfield genealogy; a selection of Garfield's letters; notes and references; sixty-three illustrations, mainly photographs and sketches; and maps of the Western Reserve and the military campaigns of Garfield during the Civil War.

Riddle, Albert G. *The Life, Character and Public Services of James A. Garfield.* Chicago: Tyler, 1880. This is a classic biography of Garfield that covers the period from his birth to his nomination as the standard-bearer of the Republican Party.

Smith, Theodore Clark. *The Life and Letters of James Abram Garfield.* 2 vols. New Haven, Conn.: Yale University Press, 1925. Smith's biographical study is principally based on Garfield's own words contained in his letters, journals, school and college notes,

speeches, and memorabilia. The author's masterful selection and arrangement of the materials produces the effect of Garfield himself interpreting his life.

SEE ALSO: Chester A. Arthur; James G. Blaine; Alexander Campbell; Ulysses S. Grant; Marcus A. Hanna; Rutherford B. Hayes.

RELATED ARTICLES in *Great Events from History: The Nineteenth Century, 1801-1900:* 1835: Finney Lectures on "Revivals of Religion"; March 2, 1867: U.S. Department of Education Is Created; November 4, 1884: U.S. Election of 1884.

GIUSEPPE GARIBALDI
Italian military leader

The hero of the Risorgimento, Garibaldi inspired Italy to unite under the leadership of Victor Emanuel of Piedmont and Sardinia. His victory over Naples was the key achievement in bringing about a unified Italy and capped a life devoted to wars of liberation.

BORN: July 4, 1807; Nice, France
DIED: June 2, 1882; Island of Caprera, Italy
AREAS OF ACHIEVEMENT: Military, government and politics

EARLY LIFE

Giuseppe Garibaldi (gahr-ih-BAHL-dee) was the son and grandson of sailors. At the time he was born, his birthplace, Nice, was a French town, but it was ceded to the Kingdom of Sardinia and Piedmont in 1815. Garibaldi is said to have learned to speak and read Italian from a priest, who also taught him the history of Italy and filled him with an enthusiasm for his country. His youth was marked by numerous events, some difficult to distinguish from the legends that naturally arise around a charismatic figure. One such story describes an escape with friends from school at the age of fourteen, including the seizure of a sailboat and embarkation in it for Constantinople. Garibaldi's disinclination toward disciplined intellectual activity induced him to leave school at an early age and to embark upon a career as a seaman, and he first pursued a sailor's life working on cargo ships in trade with the eastern Mediterranean and Black Sea.

On one of his voyages, a shipmate informed him of an organization inspired by the Italian nationalist leader

Giuseppe Mazzini, Young Italy, pledged to the cause of liberating Italy from foreigners. By 1834 an ardent member of the society, Garibaldi participated in a plot to seize a ship in the port of Genoa; the plot was discovered and Garibaldi fled to Marseilles, where he learned from an Italian newspaper that he had been condemned to death.

From Marseilles, Garibaldi sailed for South America, reaching Rio de Janeiro. Brazil and the republic Rio Grande do Sul were at war. After talking to some prisoners, Garibaldi quickly resolved to help the small state in its war, and the rest of his twelve years on the continent were spent fighting for Rio Grande in its war with Brazil and for Uruguay in its war with Argentina. He fought primarily at sea as a pirate, attacking Brazilian shipping until 1843, when he formed an Italian legion, whose "uniform" consisted of red shirts (from a happy opportunity to buy at a good price shirts otherwise destined for workers in slaughterhouses). During this time, he carried off (1839) and later married Anna Maria Ribeiro da Silva, who shared his exploits and glory until her death in 1849.

In South America, Garibaldi practiced and mastered the techniques of guerrilla fighting that were to serve him in Italy. He also learned how to command and inspire men. In later life, he was criticized for being a rather lax disciplinarian, but it may be said in his defense that comradeship is perhaps better than strict discipline at inspiring a volunteer guerrilla army. Surely he gained more experience in military matters than any other Italian of his generation.

Garibaldi's greatest battles were perhaps fought toward the end of his South American exile, in behalf of

Uruguay. His victory at Sant'Antonio in 1846 won for him fame in Italy, where a sword of honor was inscribed for him. In 1847, commanding the defense of the capital, Montevideo, he met Alexandre Dumas, *père*, whose life of Garibaldi added adventures to an already adventuresome life.

LIFE'S WORK

Early in 1848, news reached Garibaldi of the revolutions taking place in Europe, and, together with his wife and children and many members of his Italian legion, he set sail for Italy, intending to participate in the war for independence against Austria. In Italy, his offers to fight were rebuffed first by Pope Pius IX, then by King Charles of Piedmont-Sardinia. Garibaldi and his men fought for Charles anyway and engaged in several bloody fights at Como, Varese, and Laveno. His troops were finally scattered, and Garibaldi retired into Switzerland. Soon afterward, he made his way to his childhood home of Nice, where he and his wife enjoyed a few months of domestic life.

The intense fervor to unify Italy, still seen as a visionary and quixotic dream by all but the most ardent followers of Mazzini, stirred Garibaldi to go to Rome when, with the pope in flight, an opportunity presented itself in late 1848. There he tried to organize Rome's independence, but, when the French planned to reinstate the pope as head of the government, Garibaldi fought against the French siege of the city. Although victory was highly unlikely, Garibaldi, his men, and indeed the people of Rome fought gallantly for nearly three months, ringing the bells of the city at the approach of the French and erecting barricades in the streets to prevent or delay their entrance. Eager not to fall into the hands of French and papal supporters, Garibaldi and about four thousand of his men began a retreat across Campagna to the Adriatic. The enemy pursued him hotly, and Garibaldi was compelled to hasten his retreat. He managed to escape, but at the cost of his dear wife, who died from the exertions.

A fugitive again, unwelcomed by the king of Piedmont-Sardinia, hunted by the Austrians, Garibaldi left his children with his parents in Nice and went to live and work on Staten Island, New York. He soon returned to sea and became the commander of a Peruvian sailing vessel. Learning in 1853 of the death of his mother and the repeal of the order banishing him from Italy, he returned to Nice. In 1856, he bought a parcel of land on the island of Caprera, between Sardinia and Corsica, and planned to retire. In 1859, when the war of France and

Giuseppe Garibaldi. (Library of Congress)

Sardinia against Austria broke out, King Victor Emmanuel of Piedmont-Sardinia and his minister Count Cavour invited Garibaldi to form an army and fight with them. He formed the Cacciatori delle Alpi and achieved notable success by guerrilla maneuvers in the Tirol region of the Alps.

In May, 1860, Garibaldi set sail for Sicily with about one thousand volunteers, who were later to be celebrated in Italian history as the mythical *Mille*, who made the Italian peninsula into a modern nation. His aim was ostensibly to aid an insurgent revolt against Sicily's master, Naples. Garibaldi landed at Marsala amid artillery fire from several Neapolitan frigates and at once met with success. With additional volunteers constantly joining his ranks, he defeated the Neapolitan army at Calatafimi and marched toward Palermo, the largest and most important city in Sicily.

Palermo was well fortified with Neapolitan soldiers, but, after several feints, Garibaldi entered the city in the dawn of May 26 and had the city in his control by midmorning. Additional volunteers kept coming from all Sicily to join him, and the Neapolitan troops withdrew. He declared himself dictator and established provisional governments throughout the island. Taking advantage of his victories, he hastened across the Strait of Messina and charged through Calabria to Naples, which he entered on September 7, 1860. As "Dictator of the Two Sicilies" he fought a battle against a Neapolitan army in October. By then, his army had increased to thirty thousand, the largest number of men Garibaldi had ever commanded, and it held the line victoriously at the Volturno River.

Plebiscites conducted throughout the southern peninsula and in Sicily gave Garibaldi the authority to present these lands to Victor Emmanuel. When the king arrived in November, Garibaldi met him ceremoniously, but when the king and his court—perhaps anxious about some of Garibaldi's radical and revolutionary ideas, perhaps envious of Garibaldi's enormous popularity— would not grant him powers over these newly added lands, Garibaldi retired to his home in Caprera. His retirement was short-lived. In April, 1861, he was elected to the Chamber of Deputies, where he opposed Cavour and the king.

Garibaldi also caused embarrassment when in July, 1862, he appealed to Hungary to revolt against Austria. When some of his officers were arrested, Garibaldi threatened to attack Rome. Slipping through a blockade of Napoleon III, he landed in Italy and, with more than two thousand of his followers, fought a battle near Aspromonte. Garibaldi was badly wounded and imprisoned but was soon released and returned to Caprera. Though he had seemed to be independent, it became clear that he was working with the king to effect Rome's accession to the kingdom. Between 1867 and 1871, Garibaldi participated in two more campaigns, another unsuccessful expedition to the Papal States and an attempt to help France in its war with Prussia. He then retired to his home in Caprera, wrote his memoirs, and tried to overcome the infirmities of age and of a body scarred with thirty battle wounds. He died in 1882.

SIGNIFICANCE

Few in their own lifetimes enjoyed as much repute as did Giuseppe Garibaldi. Abraham Lincoln invited him to take a command at the beginning of the Civil War; unhappy with Lincoln's refusal to take a stronger stand against slavery, however, Garibaldi refused. When in 1864 Garibaldi went to England, he was received by thousands of well-wishers. The peoples of the world recognized in Garibaldi a man sincere in his love of freedom, a man selfless in his devotion to his cause, a man absolutely incorruptible. Because he was uncompromisingly idealistic, he was an inspiration to his people; indeed, more than Mazzini, Cavour, or even Victor Emmanuel himself, Garibaldi represented the spirit of Italian unification.

Garibaldi's military successes were perhaps also a manifestation of his character and most particularly of his courage. What academy-trained military man would have ventured the risks he did and against such overwhelming odds? Indeed, the very riskiness of his adventures often secured their success, for surprise was easier to achieve when the hazards seemed overwhelming. Garibaldi stands as one of the great patriots of all time, a "hero of two worlds" and for all times. If he was at times overcredulous and naïve, such may be attributed to his good heart, the same good heart that was the source of his heroic splendor.

—James A. Arieti

FURTHER READING

Davis, John A., ed. *Italy in the Nineteenth Century: 1796-1900.* New York: Oxford University Press, 2000. Collection of essays, including "Garibaldi and the South" by Lucy Riall.

DiScala, Spencer M. *Italy from Revolution to Republic: 1700 to the Present.* 3d ed. Boulder, Colo.: Westview Press, 2004. Part 3 of this history of Italy focuses on the Risorgimento, including Garibaldi and the Thousand. There are other references to Garibaldi throughout the book that are listed in the index.

Garibaldi, Giuseppe. *Autobiography of Giuseppe Garibaldi.* Translated by A. Werner, with a supplement by Jessie White Mario. London: W. Smith and Innes, 1889. A two-volume translation of Garibaldi's memoirs, certainly the starting place for serious study of Garibaldi. The supplement provides insights by one of the subject's friends.

Hibbert, Christopher. *Garibaldi and His Enemies: The Clash of Arms and Personalities in the Making of Italy.* Boston: Little, Brown, 1966. Deliberately not a social history. The subtitle suggests its focus: the personalities and events out of which came the Risorgimento. A less flattering biography than older accounts.

Mack Smith, Denis. *Garibaldi: A Great Life in Brief.* New York: Alfred A. Knopf, 1956. A readable biography, providing a portrait of Garibaldi as more a passionate than an intellectual figure.

_____, ed. *Garibaldi.* Englewood Cliffs, N.J.: Prentice-Hall, 1969. A biography put together from original documents, here all conveniently translated into English.

Ridley, Jasper. *Garibaldi*. New York: Viking Press, 1976. A highly detailed and massive biography, perhaps relying too much on secondary sources for Italian history, but vivid in its portrayal of Garibaldi as a personality.

Trevelyan, G. M. *Garibaldi's Defence of the Roman Republic, 1848-9*. 1907. London: Longmans, Green, 1949.

_____. *Garibaldi and the Thousand, May, 1860*. Reprint. London: Longmans, Green, 1948.

_____. *Garibaldi and the Making of Italy, June-November, 1860*. Reprint. London: Longmans, Green, 1948. For many years the most widely read books about Garibaldi in the English-speaking world. Notable for their romantic portrait of Garibaldi as hero.

Valerio, Anthony. *Anita Garibaldi: A Biography*. Westport, Conn.: Praeger, 2001. A biography of Garibaldi's wife, the illiterate daughter of a poor Brazilian herdsman. Describes the couple's life in South America and Italy.

SEE ALSO: Count Cavour; Alexandre Dumas, *père*; Abraham Lincoln; Giuseppe Mazzini; Napoleon III; Pius IX.

RELATED ARTICLES in *Great Events from History: The Nineteenth Century, 1801-1900:* 1831: Mazzini Founds Young Italy; January 12, 1848-August 28, 1849: Italian Revolution of 1848; May-July, 1860: Garibaldi's Redshirts Land in Sicily; March 17, 1861: Italy Is Proclaimed a Kingdom.

WILLIAM LLOYD GARRISON
American journalist and abolitionist

A crucial figure in the abolition of American slavery and the coming of the Civil War, Garrison combined Protestant evangelicalism, Jeffersonian liberalism, and Quaker humanism into a radical antislavery doctrine that called for the immediate end of the institution of slavery.

BORN: December 10, 1805; Newburyport, Massachusetts
DIED: May 24, 1879; New York, New York
AREAS OF ACHIEVEMENT: Social reform, journalism

EARLY LIFE

In his 1913 biography of William Lloyd Garrison, John Jay Chapman described his subject's emergence as a radical abolitionist in 1830 as a streaking, white-hot meteorite crashing into the middle of Boston Common. However, little in Garrison's background would have foretold of his career as a professional reformer and founder of a radical antislavery movement. His parents, Abijah and Frances (Fanny) Maria Lloyd Garrison, had once lived simply and obscurely in wealthy Newburyport, Massachusetts. By the summer of 1808, however, President Thomas Jefferson's embargo had nearly destroyed New England's merchant marine, inflicting immense suffering upon lower middle-class sailing masters such as Abijah.

During that same summer, the Garrisons' five-year-old daughter died from an accidental poisoning. Abijah

Garrison could not withstand the pressure and grief of this period. He took to heavy drinking and then deserted his struggling family of three. The childhood of young William Lloyd was then an even greater ordeal, and he often had to beg for food from the homes of Newburyport's wealthy residents.

In 1815, Lloyd, as he was called, was apprenticed to a Maryland shoemaker, but the young boy simply lacked the physical strength to do the work. In 1817, Lloyd found himself back in Newburyport, alone and apprenticed to a cabinetmaker. That work also proved unsuitable. When he was thirteen, his luck began to change when he secured an apprenticeship with the editor of the Newburyport *Herald*. Lloyd feared another failure, but within weeks he displayed remarkable skill and speed. The editor quickly made him shop foreman. Garrison had found his life's work.

After mastering the mechanics of the trade, Lloyd was eager to print his own writing. Like Benjamin Franklin a century before, he submitted editorials under a pseudonym (Garrison used "An Old Bachelor") that his boss liked and published. "An Old Bachelor" gained much attention, even from conservative political leaders. In 1826, with a loan from his former employer, Garrison purchased his own newspaper, which he immediately named the *Free Press*. Seeking respectability and entrance into the ruling elite of Massachusetts, Garrison advocated the conservative politics and social ideas of the Federalist Party. The *Free Press* became bellicose in its political stands, denouncing everything that smacked of Jeffersonian democracy. During his brief tenure at the paper, Garrison discovered the poet John Greenleaf Whittier, published his first poetry, and also made some oblique criticisms of the institution of slavery, but he revealed nothing that gave the slightest indication of what lay only four years in the future.

Following this relatively conservative initiation into his journalistic career, Garrison became more and more strident in his style and radical in the opinions he voiced in editorials, to the extent that he lost subscribers, defaulted on his loan, and lost his paper. In 1828, he drifted to the *National Philanthropist*, a temperance paper, and attacked dancing, theatergoing, dueling, and gambling. The fiery editor denounced war and began to display a more thoroughgoing disdain for the institution of slavery by decrying a South Carolina law outlawing black education. Garrison soon repeated his familiar pattern and within six months found himself without a job. He managed to secure a position at the *Journal of the Times* in Bennington, Vermont, and there railed at intemperance and advanced his ideas concerning peace and gradual emancipation.

In 1829, Garrison had become radicalized on the issue of slavery, about one year after reading Benjamin Lundy's newspaper, the *Genius of Universal Emancipation*. Garrison had met Lundy, a Quaker abolitionist, in 1828 and had adopted his views on the gradual emancipation of American slaves. On July 4, 1829, again unemployed, Garrison delivered his first antislavery speech, indicting the North for its racism and declaring that gradual emancipation was the only possible way to end slavery. Then, after reading the works of black Americans such as David Walker and English abolitionists such as James Cropper, Garrison decided to dedicate his life to ending what he viewed as the greatest abomination in American history. He went to work for Lundy and moved back to Baltimore, Maryland, where he coedited the *Genius of Universal Emancipation*.

Before the end of 1829, Garrison had abandoned gradual emancipation—Lundy had not—and called for the immediate end of slavery. He lashed out against

William Lloyd Garrison. (Library of Congress)

slaveholders and even against New Englanders who countenanced the institution. On April 17, 1830, he was confined to a Baltimore jail for criminal libel against a New England merchant. Word of Garrison's imprisonment circulated throughout the North and eventually reached the ears of the wealthy New York merchants and reformers, Arthur and Lewis Tappan. They bailed Garrison out of jail and paid his fines. He wandered back to Boston and decided to set up a new paper there.

On October 16, 1830, Garrison advertised a series of public lectures on the subject of slavery and the American Colonization Society. The ACS, established in 1817, claimed to oppose slavery and favored black uplift and the evangelization of Africa, but Garrison sought to expose it as a tool of the slaveocrats who actually perpetuated slavery. At the October lectures, Garrison denounced the ACS as a racist organization that intended to expel free black Americans if they refused to leave voluntarily. Boston's liberal and conservative clergy alike reacted to the lectures with disgust. Other thinkers, such as Samuel Joseph May, a renegade Unitarian minister and reformer, Bronson Alcott, a Transcendentalist educator and May's brother-in-law, and Samuel E. Sewall, May's cousin, became captivated by Garrison's moral vigor and earnestness. They instantly converted to radical abolitionism and pledged to aid the young editor. Emergence of *The Liberator* the following year established Garrison as the leader of the radical antislavery movement.

LIFE'S WORK

William Lloyd Garrison stood about five feet, six inches tall. His slender, almost fragile frame supported a massive bald head, and his powerful blue eyes were framed by tiny, steel, oval-shaped spectacles. Although relentless on the lecture platform, in private Garrison comported himself with great dignity and grace. Like many reformers, he married late. While lecturing in Providence, Rhode Island, in 1829, he met Helen Benson, the daughter of the Quaker philanthropist George Benson. Timid in the presence of women and lacking a stable career, Garrison initiated a long courtship, finally marrying Helen on September 4, 1834.

On January 1, 1831, Garrison published the first issue of *The Liberator*. It angered northerners as irrational and incendiary and struck fear in slaveholders as an uncompromising condemnation. Garrison, as a pacifist, eschewed violent rebellion, but his strident language—something entirely new in the long history of American antislavery thought—inaugurated a new era in American history. He denounced slavery as sin, called upon all true Christians immediately to abandon it no matter what the cost to the Union, and blasted those who thought slavery might be gradually abandoned. What, gradually stop sin? Tell a man to rescue his wife from a rapist gradually? Garrison thundered. Why complain of the severity of my language, he cried, when so unutterable an evil abounded. Ignoring his critics, Garrison lashed out: "I *will be* as harsh as truth, and as uncompromising as justice. . . . I will not excuse—I will not retreat a single inch—AND I WILL BE HEARD."

Garrison's antislavery appeal fused the evangelical fervor of the Second Great Awakening, which had begun during the 1790's, with the long-standing Quaker opposition to slavery. He had tapped an essential root of American thought, and if he could convince Americans that slavery was, in fact, sin, then they would have to accept his second proposition that it be immediately abandoned. Southerners understandably recoiled from his rhetoric, but they were horrified when, eight months after appearance of *The Liberator*, Nat Turner turned Virginia inside out by fomenting a slave rebellion and killing dozens of whites, including women and children. Southerners connected the two events, blamed Garrison for the killings, put a price on his head, and demanded that Massachusetts suppress the newspaper and its editor.

In January, 1832, Garrison and twelve men—antislavery apostles—founded the New England Anti-Slavery Society. In June, he published his influential *Thoughts on African Colonization* (1832), and, for the next three years, Garrison and his associates dedicated themselves to destroying the credibility of the American Colonization Society. He helped found the American Anti-Slavery Society on December 4, 1833. Between 1833 and 1840, two hundred Auxiliaries of the American Anti-Slavery Society were organized from Massachusetts to Michigan with about 200,000 members. They sent antislavery agents throughout the North to whip up controversy and support for the cause.

The growth of radical antislavery thought caused great consternation. Between 1830 and 1840, abolitionists suffered from personal and physical abuse. Rocks, bricks, and the contents of outhouses were thrown at them. They were denounced as anarchists who would destroy the Union if it suited their whim. In 1836, southern states requested Governor Edward Everett of Massachusetts to suppress Garrison and his friends. On November 7, 1837, Illinois abolitionist editor Elijah P. Lovejoy was assassinated by a rampaging mob determined to destroy his newspaper, the *Alton Observer*. The attacks on abolitionists and the murder of Lovejoy sparked unprecedented sympathy for the antislavery advocates, who could now justifiably claim that abolitionism and a defense of a free press and free speech were inseparable.

To Garrison, abolitionism was only the most important of a collection of reforms, from women's rights to temperance, connected by a liberal Christian faith in a benevolent God and the rejection of all forms of force and violence. In 1836, Garrison learned of two extraordinary women from Charleston, South Carolina. Sarah and Angelina Grimké, born into a slaveholding family, had rejected their home and human bondage, converted to Quakerism, and moved north. In 1837, Garrison arranged a speaking tour for them in New England. Huge crowds turned out for the sisters, who risked their reputations to ignore the social restrictions against women speaking in public. Indeed, during the course of their tour, the Grimkés became ardent exponents of women's rights, having seen how prominent clergymen denounced their violation of women's restricted sphere. Garrison supported the sisters and opened up the Massachusetts Anti-Slavery Society to women, urging his conservative colleagues to do the same.

Garrison's support for women's rights brought howls of protest from other abolitionists, who urged him to avoid "extraneous" issues and stick to antislavery work. He refused to compromise and answered his critics by becoming even more radical. At the September, 1838, meeting of the American Peace Society, Garrison, May, and Henry C. Wright, a radical Garrisonian, attempted to gain the society's acceptance of nonresistance thought. They wanted to outlaw as utterly unchristian all forms of war, force, and violence, even denying one's right to defend oneself. When faced with an attacker, according to nonresistance thought, one could only respond with Christian meekness and manifestations of love. Garrison, May, and Wright all claimed that they had personally disarmed robbers or criminals with love. Conservatives refused to accept the new doctrine or to permit women to participate in their society, and they left the meeting. In response, Garrison and his friends formed the New England Nonresistance Society to spread what they saw as true Christian principles.

Garrison's extreme ideas fractured his own Massachusetts Anti-Slavery Society in 1839 and the American Anti-Slavery Society in 1840. Although the antislavery movement seemed to be crumbling, Garrison responded in typical fashion. While many of the best young male abolitionists avoided Garrison's organizations and went into politics, Garrison damned the political system. In 1842, he advocated the dissolution of the Union. The nation had become so corrupt, so dominated by slave power that no hope existed for slavery's end so long as the South remained in the Union.

Although Garrison's critics argued that no hope for the end of slavery existed if the South left the Union, Garrison ignored them. In 1843, *The Liberator* adopted its most radical stand yet. The "compact which exists between the North and the South is 'a covenant with death, and an agreement with hell'—involving both parties in atrocious criminality; and should be immediately annulled." On March 17, 1843, Garrison began placing the slogan "NO UNION WITH SLAVE-HOLDERS!" on the masthead of his newspaper, where it remained until the Civil War.

Split over women's rights and nonresistance ideas, the antislavery movement nearly ended by the mid-1840's. Little money flowed in and few Americans could accept disunionism, no matter how much they hated slavery. Passage of the Fugitive Slave Act in 1850 boosted the American Anti-Slavery Society's prospects, because most northerners came to hate the law as an infringement of constitutionally protected rights. As the nation moved toward civil war during the 1850's, Garrison increased his attacks on slavery, the Constitution, and the Union.

With the firing on Fort Sumter in April, 1861, Garrison supported Abraham Lincoln and the Union cause. Although many of his associates thought the South ought to leave the Union peacefully, Garrison saw the war as perhaps the only opportunity to end slavery, even if it did violate his peace principles. He thus supported the Lincoln administration's war policy, all the while urging the president to abolish slavery. When Lincoln signed the Emancipation Proclamation in 1863, Garrison was ecstatic, and when the nation adopted the Thirteenth Amendment, abolishing slavery, in 1865, he felt vindicated. Believing his life's purpose fulfilled, Garrison retired from activism, though he continued to support the Republican Party and causes such as temperance and women's rights. He died in New York City on May 24, 1879.

SIGNIFICANCE

Although Garrison harbored some racial prejudice, he was a pioneer of racial justice. He argued that racism and slavery worked hand-in-hand and that northern prejudice and southern intransigence shared equally in the responsibility for perpetuating slavery. Garrison's message of racial justice and abolitionism threatened the nation's class system, which exploited northern free blacks as well as southern slaves and endangered the tenuous bonds that had kept the Union together since the formation of the Constitution. Public reaction to Garrison did not change until passage of the Emancipation Proclamation in 1863. Before the war's end, he became a prophetic figure to Americans. The Boston mobs that tried to lynch him in 1834 raised statues to him in 1865. Modern historians have recognized Garrison's indispensable role in the ending of American slavery and have hailed him for his simple claim that the Declaration of Independence ought to speak for everyone, black and white, male and female.

—*Donald Yacovone*

FURTHER READING

Chapman, John Jay. *William Lloyd Garrison*. New York: Moffat, Yard, 1913. A sympathetic early biography by the son of one of Garrison's associates.

Friedman, Lawrence J. *Gregarious Saints: Self and Community in American Abolitionism, 1830-1870*. New York: Cambridge University Press, 1982. Representative of the best modern studies of the abolitionist movement. Gives an inside look at the subtle distinctions the reformers made on a variety of topics related to voting, the Constitution, and how distinct groups of reformers sprang up around charismatic figures such as Garrison, Gerrit Smith, or the Tappan brothers.

Garrison, William Lloyd. *The Letters of William Lloyd Garrison*. Edited by Walter M. Merrill and Louis Ruchames. 6 vols. Cambridge, Mass.: Harvard University Press, 1971-1981. The best way for the student to become acquainted with Garrison is to read the activist's own work. These are copiously annotated personal and public letters that fully display the thinking and the sometimes idiosyncratic personality of *The Liberator*'s chief editor.

_____. *William Lloyd Garrison and the Fight Against Slavery: Selections from "The Liberator."* Edited with an introduction by William E. Cain. Boston: Bedford Books of St. Martin's Press, 1995. Includes forty-one selections from the newspaper dealing with issues related to slavery. The introduction provides historical background on slavery and the abolition movement in the United States and the events in Garrison's career.

Kraditor, Alieen S. *Means and Ends in American Abolitionism: Garrison and His Critics on Strategy and Tactics, 1834-1850*. New York: Pantheon Books, 1969. Far and away the best book on Garrison's movement and thought. Kraditor fully explores the controversy of the "woman question" and argues convincingly that, in order for Garrison to gain acceptance of a minimum of antislavery thought, he had to remain more radical than the nation and many of his antislavery brethren.

Merrill, Walter M. *Against Wind and Tide: A Biography of William Lloyd Garrison*. Cambridge, Mass.: Harvard University Press, 1963. A thorough and often critical examination of the abolitionist's career. The text emphasizes Garrison's personality, which could be extremely abrasive and unforgiving. The author recognizes, however, that it took an abrasive personality to challenge the foundations of American society.

Perry, Lewis. *Radical Abolitionism: Anarchy and the Government of God in Antislavery Thought*. Ithaca, N.Y.: Cornell University Press, 1973. The most sophisticated treatment of antislavery thought, concentrating on Garrison and his nonresistance colleagues. Perry examines the origins of Garrison's thinking and connects it to wider trends in Western Christian thought.

Rogers, William B. *"We Are All Together Now": Frederick Douglass, William Lloyd Garrison, and the Prophetic Tradition*. New York: Garland, 1995. Describes how Douglass and Garrison drew on the tradition of Biblical prophecy in their struggle against slavery, intemperance, and the oppression of women and minorities.

Stewart, James B. *Holy Warriors: The Abolitionists and American Slavery*. New York: Hill & Wang, 1976. A good, readable survey of the antislavery movement, emphasizing Garrison's role and the religious nature of the movement that stemmed from the influence of the Second Great Awakening.

Thomas, John L. *"The Liberator": William Lloyd Garrison—A Biography*. Boston: Little, Brown, 1963. The best study of Garrison; it appreciates his central role in the movement but remains critical of his tactics and personality. Thoroughly researched, and more detailed than Merrill's biography.

SEE ALSO: Bronson Alcott; Frederick Douglass; Sarah and Angelina Grimké; Lucretia Mott; Wendell Phillips; Nat Turner; John Greenleaf Whittier.

RELATED ARTICLES in *Great Events from History: The Nineteenth Century, 1801-1900:* 1820's-1850's: Social Reform Movement; c. 1830-1865: Southerners Advance Proslavery Arguments; January 1, 1831: Garrison Begins Publishing *The Liberator*; December, 1833: American Anti-Slavery Society Is Founded; December 3, 1847: Douglass Launches *The North Star*; 1852: Stowe Publishes *Uncle Tom's Cabin*; December 6, 1865: Thirteenth Amendment Is Ratified.

PAUL GAUGUIN
French painter

Gauguin epitomized a rejection of nineteenth century realism and its final phase, Impressionism, in favor of a new approach to painting based on primitive art; a simplification of lines, colors, and forms; and a suppression of detail, all intended to enhance the intellectual-emotional impact of a work of art. His program amounted in fact to a deliberate overthrow of the primacy of the optical sensation that had dictated all art since the Renaissance and is therefore the single most revolutionary thought introduced by a nineteenth century artist.

BORN: June 7, 1848; Paris, France
DIED: May 8, 1903; Atuana, Marquesas Islands,
  French Polynesia
ALSO KNOWN AS: Eugene-Henri-Paul Gauguin (full
  name)
AREA OF ACHIEVEMENT: Art

EARLY LIFE

An extraordinary childhood and youth preceded the entry of Paul Gauguin (goh-gahn) into the bourgeois world of business and finance. His parents, Clovis and Aline, active in liberal circles, felt forced to flee Paris (after the coup d'état of Napoleon III in 1851) and to seek refuge in Peru, where Aline's uncle, Don Piot Tristán y Moscoso, who would soon adopt her as his daughter, lived a life of leisure and luxury. Clovis died during the ocean voyage, but Aline, with children Marie and Paul, arrived in Lima to remain there for four years. Although only a small child during his stay in Lima, Gauguin was never to forget that country. Indeed, his persistent longing for the faraway and exotic no doubt had its roots in his rich, unencumbered childhood years in Peru.

Mother and children returned to France in 1855, and Paul spent the next seven years as a solitary, morose, and withdrawn schoolboy who learned "to hate hypocrisy, false virtues, tale-bearing, and to beware of everything that was contrary to my instincts, my heart, and my reason." In his seventeenth year, he hired on as a seaman on a ship sailing to South America, beginning a career that would keep him at sea for six years, part of that time as an enlisted man in the French navy.

Aline, who died at the age of forty-two in 1865, had appointed a business friend as guardian to her children, and it was through him that Gauguin in 1871 became a stockbroker, sufficiently successful to offer marriage to a Danish woman, Mette Sophie Gad, in 1873. In his finan-cial career, he met Émile Schuffenecker, a Sunday painter who persuaded Gauguin to take up the same hobby; his interest in art, together with a reasonable affluence that enabled him to become an art patron, brought him into contact with Camille Pissarro, the paterfamilias of the Impressionist group, whose influence is readily detected in Gauguin's early, still-hesitant paintings. In 1883, by now the father of five children, he resigned as a stockbroker to devote all of his energy to the arts.

LIFE'S WORK

Gauguin's first official entry into the art world took place in 1876, when he exhibited a canvas in the Impressionist style at the annual Parisian Salon. From 1879 until 1886, he showed in the last five exhibits of the Impressionists. Shortly thereafter, with his family settled in Copenhagen, he set out for Central America, working for a time on the construction site of the Panama Canal, then stopping in Martinique, where he produced his first canvas depicting a tropical paradise, a view of the Bay of Saint-Pierre, still in the Impressionist spirit, yet with a color vibrancy that reflects his emotional reaction to the subject.

Back in France in 1888, Gauguin took up residence in Pont-Aven, Brittany. "I love Brittany," he said in a letter to Schuffenecker. "I find here the wild and the primitive. When my clogs ring out on its granite soil, I hear the low, flat, powerful note I seek in painting." Joining him in Pont-Aven were Émile Bernard and Louis Anquetin, young experimental painters whose ideas were close to Gauguin's. All three felt moved by the rich colors of medieval enamelwork and cloisonné, and favored reducing visual phenomena to abstract lines and flat colors, a pictorial method clearly employed by Japanese printmakers, whose works were then much in vogue.

Gauguin's Brittany paintings, such as *The Vision After the Sermon* (1888), must be seen as an affirmation of these ideas, with its use of receding planes of flat primary colors enclosed by angular, dark lines and dramatized by a drastic perspective. The result is an overall effect far removed from any visual reality. This intense concentration on the visual and emotional totality of the subject rather than on its separate components, the synthetic view, would characterize the majority of Gauguin's paintings. The landscape and people of French Polynesia, where he spent most of his creative life, tended to mellow his temperament and turn his pictures into vibrantly colorful, sinewy linear, often mysteriously muted paeans to primitive nature.

On his return to Paris from Pont-Aven in the summer of 1888, Gauguin met Vincent van Gogh. During the autumn, he joined van Gogh in Arles in the Midi of France. In spite of turbulent conflicts during the three months they spent together, the Arles experience left its positive impact on both artists, as seen in canvases of closely related subjects produced during their joint outings in the fertile Provençal countryside.

In 1889, during the World's Fair in Paris, Gauguin and his friends from the artist colony in Pont-Aven arranged a private exhibit of one hundred of their works in an Italian bistro within the fairground, Café Volpini. Hardly taken seriously by the public at that time, the Volpini Exhibit is today considered one of the milestones in nineteenth century art. Although the exhibitors called themselves "Impressionists" and "Synthetists" they had clearly abandoned the gracefully textured, retinally oriented approach of Claude Monet, Pierre-Auguste Renoir, and Pissarro. Instead, they presented pictures with large patches of contrasting colors separated by dark lines, minimal emphasis on depth and perspective, and, in Gauguin's case, a steady procession of peasants at their melancholy tasks or in worshipful contemplation.

During his stay in Brittany, and more so after his return to Paris in 1890, Gauguin continually toyed with the idea of settling in a more exotic part of the world, preferably with fellow painters in a new "Barbizon" of primitive nature, but if necessary he would go alone. Prior to his departure for Tahiti in the spring of 1891, his Paris friends—and by now there were many of them, artists, writers, government officials—eased his transition, helping him with an auction of his works, which brought a substantial amount of money, and arranging a farewell banquet presided over by Stéphane Mallarmé, the avant-garde poet.

During the two years of his first stay in Tahiti, Gauguin produced some of his most stunning canvases depicting the landscape, the people, and a civilization of beauty and innocence in the process of vanishing. A Tahitian landscape with a village surrounded by wildly exotic, swirling trees, backed up by mountains in sharp, receding planes and surmounted by white clouds against a cerulean sky, is reminiscent of his landscapes in Brittany, except that the dark, angular lines separating the color surfaces in the Brittany scenes have yielded to softer, more undulant patterns in this new, exotic setting. Similarly, his depiction of people of Tahiti, though in form and color resembling his efforts in Brittany, has some-

thing new and mysterious in it, close-up views mostly of women, singly or in clusters, with guarded, secretive mien and in hushed poses of ritual solemnity. "Always this haunting silence," Gauguin wrote in a letter to his wife. "I understand why these individuals can rest seated for hours and days without saying a word and look at the sky with melancholy."

Despite Gauguin's enchantment with the Polynesian ambience, he felt confined and out of touch with the art world. Besides, he was financially destitute, incapable of providing for his daily bread. He decided to return to France and succeeded in finding a lender to advance his travel expenses. During the early fall of 1893, he was back in Paris with his Tahitian paintings, preparing for an exhibit and hoping for wide acceptance. His display of more than forty canvases generated few sales, and even his presentation to the French state of the magnificent *Ia Orana Maria* (1891; we hail thee, Mary) was rejected. A few close supporters, Edgar Degas and Mallarmé among them, helped Gauguin—Degas by making a purchase and Mallarmé by praising the Tahitian works.

Paul Gauguin.

Such signs of approval, however, were scarce, and Gauguin soon regretted his return to the insensitive, overcivilized world he had once abandoned. An unfortunate altercation during a visit to Brittany left him hospitalized and maimed, and an encounter with a Parisian prostitute resulted in syphilis. All of this resulted in a life of creative stagnation and physical agony, and as soon as he was able to move about he began to prepare for his second and final journey to Tahiti.

A major sale of Gauguin's paintings and belongings was arranged to finance the venture, and, planning to issue a catalog of the items on view, he asked a new acquaintance, the dramatist August Strindberg, to write a preface. In a long and detailed letter, Strindberg enumerated the reasons for his refusal to do so.

It appears that Strindberg understood Gauguin's creative impulse, sensed its depth. Gauguin, detecting a positive note in Strindberg's rejection, printed the letter as the preface. The sale, however, was a failure. In fact, in a letter to his wife, he records a detailed account showing a net loss of 464 francs. Nevertheless, with the assistance of several picture dealers and a guarantee that they would market his subsequent works, he was able to raise a sum sufficient for the voyage and his immediate subsequent needs; he left France in June of 1895, never to return.

In his second Tahitian period, Gauguin produced one hundred paintings, more than four hundred prints, and numerous pieces of sculpted wood. In addition, he wrote hundreds of letters, an intriguing journal, and reworked text and illustrations in his *Noa Noa* (English translation, 1919), published in France in 1900.

During Gauguin's first stay, his works, like his visual reactions to life in Brittany, had reflected the primal quality of the Tahitian landscape, the natural innocence of a people still close to the beginnings of time, and the legendary quality of Tahitian spirituality. Thus, desiring to share his experiences with the art audience at home, he had attempted to serve as a messenger from a remote world and a civilization still unspoiled yet inevitably doomed.

In Gauguin's second stay, he found these subtle links with the past already severely eroded through Western colonization. His works from this final period are therefore more introspective and deliberately ponderous. Typical of this approach is his monumental masterpiece *Where Do We Come From? What Are We? Where Are We Going?* (1897-1898), "designed to embody a total philosophy of life, civilization, and sexuality." As in early Renaissance altar panels, it is a work whose imagery transcends time and place, a composite of ritual epi-sodes moving from the outer perimeter toward a central, all-embracing Godhead. A significant and influential aspect of his last Tahitian stay is found in a series of tropical woodblocks carved and hand printed in 1898-1899. Viewed in sequence as in a frieze, they seem to constitute a summary of his visual and spiritual experiences in the land and society he had adopted.

Gauguin never denied his admiration for certain other artists of the nineteenth century, and among his last works are paintings reminiscent of Eugène Delacroix's epochal depictions of women of Morocco, nudes and horses clearly indebted to Degas, and still-lifes of fruits and flowers echoing those of van Gogh painted in Arles.

Still on his easel at the time of his death was his final work, *Breton Village Covered by Snow*. Painted in feverish, death-conscious agony, it is a profoundly melancholy dream evoking the beginnings of a career devoted to a futile search for an earthly paradise.

SIGNIFICANCE

Paul Gauguin was the first nineteenth century artist to move away from naturalism to a world of visual dreams inspired by the primitive magic of the medieval past and intensified by a direct exposure to societies less marred by Western civilization. From childhood experiences in Latin America and a turbulent youth at sea and in the Caribbean, he was irresistibly drawn to the untamed and the exotic, finding part of it in a Brittany still steeped in its past and more in the faraway islands of the South Seas. With their purity of line and surface, vibrancy of color, and subtle evocation of the human condition in a tenuous state of innocence, his paintings opened up entirely new vistas in the world of the arts, through the depiction of rare and exotic subject matter. They also paved the way for equally bold strivings among artists of future generations.

> I wanted to establish the right to dare everything. My capacity was not capable of great results, but the machine is none the less launched. The public owes me nothing . . . but the painters who today profit from this liberty owe me something.

—*Reidar Dittmann*

FURTHER READING

Andersen, Wayne. *Gauguin's Paradise Lost*. New York: Viking Press, 1979. An American scholar's attempt at reaching an understanding of the artist's psychological development through a parallel probing of his works and writings.

Brettell, Richard, et al. *The Art of Paul Gauguin*. Boston: New York Graphic Society Books, 1988. This catalog, accompanying an exhibit jointly sponsored by the National Gallery and the Art Institute of Chicago, is so comprehensive, so authoritative, and so richly illustrated that it supersedes all previous efforts in that direction. Drawn from collections in North and South America, Europe, and Asia, the exhibit included 280 separate items, nearly all described in terse but excellent articles.

Druick, Douglas W., et al. *Van Gogh and Gauguin: The Studio of the South*. Chicago: Thames and Hudson and Art Institute of Chicago, 2001. Catalog accompanying an exhibit of the two artists' work that was displayed at the Art Institute of Chicago and the Van Gogh Museum in 2001-2002. Contains 510 reproductions of the artists' works, 300 of which are in a sensuously beautiful color. Also contains essays examining the artwork, character analysis of the two men, some of their correspondence to each other, and a description of their inspiring yet antagonistic relationship.

Eisenman, Stephen. *Gauguin's Skirt*. New York: Thames and Hudson, 1997. Gauguin traveled to Tahiti in search of a tropical paradise, but instead found a French colony divided by race, sex, and class. Eisenman analyzes the artworks Gauguin created in Tahiti, describing how they represented the complexities of the island's social conditions.

Gauguin, Paul. *The Intimate Journals of Paul Gauguin*. Translated by Van Wyck Brooks, with a preface by Émile Gauguin. London: Heinemann, 1923. The original manuscript, finished in 1903, has the title *Avant et après* and was published in facsimile editions in 1913 and 1953. The English edition was endorsed by Gauguin's son, who in his preface says, "These journals are the spontaneous expression of the same free, fearless, sensitive spirit that speaks in the canvases of Paul Gauguin."

_____. *Paul Gauguin: Letters to His Wife and Friends*. Edited by Maurice Mallinge. Translated by Henry F. Stenning. Cleveland: World, 1949. This collection sheds much light on the strained relationship between Gauguin and his estranged wife, Mette Gad, who at the time of Gauguin's first stay in Brittany returned with their five children to her childhood home in Copenhagen. Characterized by Gauguin's continual quest for understanding and her pervasive bitterness, the letters also contain much information on his creative activities.

Gauguin, Pola. *My Father, Paul Gauguin*. Translated by Arthur G. Chater. New York: Alfred A. Knopf, 1937. Written by Gauguin's youngest son, an artist and art historian who lived in Norway, this biography draws much of its information from family letters and documents whose content up to that time had been unavailable to the public. Remarkably dispassionate in its narration, it tends to counterbalance the relentless bitterness of Gauguin's wife.

Gray, Christopher. *Sculpture and Ceramics of Paul Gauguin*. Baltimore: Johns Hopkins University Press, 1963. Gray's volume spans Gauguin's entire career and shows how his early efforts in ceramics foreshadowed the three-dimensional works produced in Tahiti. An appendix twice the size of the principal text contains a detailed catalog of the artist's known works in these media.

Rewald, John. *Post-Impressionism: From Van Gogh to Gauguin*. 3d rev. ed. New York: Museum of Modern Art, 1979. This magnificently illustrated work by a principal authority in late nineteenth century European painting presents the total fabric of the post-Impressionist movement in which van Gogh and Gauguin occupied center stage, with many others playing supporting roles.

Sweetman, David. *Paul Gauguin: A Complete Life*. New York: Simon & Schuster, 1995. In the best Gauguin biography yet published, Sweetman unearths facts and presents them in an original way. Attention is paid to the importance of Gauguin's early life in Peru and its effect on his self-image, his relationships with unconventional women, and more.

SEE ALSO: Edgar Degas; Eugène Delacroix; Vincent van Gogh; Napoleon III; Camille Pissarro; Pierre-Auguste Renoir; Henri Rousseau; Henri de Toulouse-Lautrec.

RELATED ARTICLES in *Great Events from History: The Nineteenth Century, 1801-1900:* April 15, 1874: First Impressionist Exhibition; Late 1870's: Post-Impressionist Movement Begins.

CARL FRIEDRICH GAUSS
German scientist

A great scientific thinker who is often ranked with Archimedes and Isaac Newton, Gauss made significant contributions in many branches of science. His most notable achievement was the articulation of the two most revolutionary mathematical ideas of the nineteenth century: non-Euclidean geometry and noncommutative algebra.

BORN: April 30, 1777; Brunswick, Duchy of Brunswick (now in Germany)
DIED: February 23, 1855; Göttingen, Hanover (now in Germany)
ALSO KNOWN AS: Johann Friedrich Carl Gauss (full name)
AREAS OF ACHIEVEMENT: Mathematics, science and technology

EARLY LIFE

Carl Friedrich Gauss (gowz) was born into a family of town workers who were struggling to achieve lower-middle-class status. Without assistance, Gauss learned to calculate before he could talk; he also taught himself to read. At the age of three, he corrected an error in his father's wage calculations. In his first arithmetic class, at the age of eight, he astonished his teacher by instantly solving a word problem that involved finding the sum of the first hundred integers. However, his teacher had the insight to furnish the child with books and encourage his intellectual development.

When he was eleven, Gauss studied with Martin Bartels, then an assistant in the school and later a teacher of Nikolay Ivanovich Lobachevsky at Kazan. Gauss's father was persuaded to allow his son to enter the gymnasium in 1788. At the gymnasium, Gauss made rapid progress in all subjects, especially in classics and mathematics, largely on his own. E. A. W. Zimmermann, then professor at the local Collegium Carolinum and later privy councillor to the duke of Brunswick, encouraged Gauss; in 1792, Duke Carl Wilhelm Ferdinand began the stipend that would assure Gauss's independence.

When Gauss entered the Brunswick Collegium Carolinum in 1792, he possessed a scientific and classical education far beyond his years. He was acquainted with elementary geometry, algebra, and analysis (often having discovered important theorems before reaching them in his books), but he also possessed much arithmetical information and number-theoretic insights. His lifelong pattern of research had become established: Exten-

sive empirical investigation led to conjectures, and new insights guided further experiment and observation. By such methods, he had already discovered Johann Elert Bode's law of planetary distances, the binomial theorem for rational exponents, and the arithmetic-geometric mean.

During his three years at the Collegium, among other things, Gauss formulated the principle of least squares. Before entering the University of Göttingen in 1795, he had rediscovered the law of quadratic reciprocity, related the arithmetic-geometric mean to infinite series expansions, and conjectured the prime number theorem (first proved by Jacques-Salomon Hadamard in 1896).

While Gauss was in Brunswick, most mathematical classics had been unavailable to him. At Göttingen, however, he devoured masterworks and back issues of journals and often found that his discoveries were not new. Attracted more by the brilliant classicist Christian Gottlob Heyne than by the mediocre mathematician A. G. Kästner, Gauss planned to be a philologist, but in 1796 he made a dramatic discovery that marked him as a mathematician. As a result of a systematic investigation of the cyclotomic equation (whose solution has the geometric counterpart of dividing a circle into equal arcs), Gauss declared that the regular seventeen-sided polygon was constructible by ruler and compasses, the first advance on this subject in two thousand years.

The logical aspect of Gauss's method matured at Göttingen. Although he adopted the spirit of Greek rigor, it was without the classical geometric form; Gauss, rather, thought numerically and algebraically, in the manner of Leonhard Euler. By the age of twenty, Gauss was conducting large-scale empirical investigations and rigorous theoretical constructions, and during the years from 1796 to 1800 mathematical ideas came so quickly that Gauss could hardly write them down.

LIFE'S WORK

In 1798, Gauss returned to Brunswick, and the next year, with the first of his four proofs of the fundamental theorem of algebra, earned a doctorate from the University of Helmstedt. In 1801, the creativity of the previous years was reflected in two extraordinary achievements, the *Disquisitiones arithmeticae* (1801; *Arithmetical Inquisitions*, 1966) and the calculation of the orbit of the newly discovered planet Ceres.

Although number theory was developed from the ear-

Carl Friedrich Gauss.

liest times, during the late eighteenth century it consisted of a large collection of isolated results. In *Arithmetical Inquisitions*, Gauss systematically summarized previous work, solved some of the most difficult outstanding questions, and formulated concepts and questions that established the pattern of research for a century. The work almost instantly won for Gauss recognition by mathematicians, although readership was small.

In January, 1801, Giuseppi Piazzi had briefly discovered but lost track of a new planet he had observed, and during the rest of that year astronomers unsuccessfully attempted to relocate it. Gauss decided to pursue the matter. Applying both a more accurate orbit theory and improved numerical methods, he accomplished the task by December. Ceres was soon found in the predicted position. This feat of locating a distant, tiny planet from apparently insufficient information was astonishing, especially because Gauss did not reveal his methods. Along with *Arithmetical Inquisitions*, it established his reputation as a first-rate mathematical and scientific genius.

The decade of these achievements (1801-1810) was decisive for Gauss. Scientifically it was a period of exploiting ideas accumulated from the previous decade, and it ended with a work in which Gauss systematically

developed his methods of orbit calculation, including a theory of and use of least squares. Professionally this decade was one of transition from mathematician to astronomer and physical scientist. Gauss accepted the post of director of the Göttingen Observatory in 1807.

This decade also provided Gauss with his one period of personal happiness. In 1805, he married Johanna Osthoff, with whom he had a son and a daughter. She created a happy family life around him. When she died in 1809, Gauss was plunged into a loneliness from which he never fully recovered. Less than a year later, he married Minna Waldeck, his deceased wife's best friend. Although she bore him two sons and a daughter, she was unhealthy and often unhappy. Gauss did not achieve a peaceful home life until his youngest daughter, Therese, assumed management of the household after her mother's death in 1831 and became his companion for the last twenty-four years of his life.

In his first years as director of the Göttingen Observatory, Gauss experienced a second burst of ideas and publications in various fields of mathematics and matured his conception of non-Euclidean geometry. However, astronomical tasks soon dominated Gauss's life.

By 1817, Gauss moved toward geodesy, which was to be his preoccupation for the next eight years. The invention of the heliotrope, an instrument for reflecting the sun's rays in a measured direction, was an early by-product of fieldwork. The invention was motivated by dissatisfaction with the existing methods of observing distant points by using lamps or powder flares at night. In spite of failures and dissatisfactions, the period of geodesic investigation was one of the most scientifically creative of Gauss's long career. The difficulties of mapping the terrestrial ellipsoid on a sphere and plane led him, in 1816, to formulate and solve in outline the general problem of mapping one surface on another so that the two were "similar in their smallest parts." In 1822, the chance of winning a prize offered by the Copenhagen Academy motivated him to write these ideas in a paper that won for him first place and was published in 1825.

Surveying problems also inspired Gauss to develop his ideas on least squares and more general problems of what is now called mathematical statistics. His most significant contribution during this period, and his last breakthrough in a major new direction of mathematical research, was *Disquisitiones generales circa superficies curvas* (1828; *General Investigations of Curved Surfaces*, 1902), which was the result of three decades of geodesic investigations and that drew upon more than a century of work on differential geometry.

After the mid-1820's, Gauss, feeling harassed and overworked and suffering from asthma and heart disease, turned to investigations in physics. Gauss accepted an offer from Alexander von Humboldt to come to Berlin to work. An incentive was his meeting in Berlin with Wilhelm Eduard Weber, a young and brilliant experimental physicist with whom Gauss would eventually collaborate on many significant discoveries. They were also to organize a worldwide network of magnetic observatories and to publish extensively on magnetic force. From the early 1840's, the intensity of Gauss's activity gradually decreased. Increasingly bedridden as a result of heart disease, he died in his sleep in late February, 1855.

SIGNIFICANCE

Carl Friedrich Gauss's impact as a scientist falls far short of his reputation. His inventions were usually minor improvements of temporary importance. In theoretical astronomy, he perfected classical methods in orbit calculation but otherwise made only fairly routine observations. His personal involvement in calculating orbits saved others work but was of little long-lasting scientific importance. His work in geodesy was influential only in its mathematical by-products. Furthermore, his collaboration with Weber led to only two achievements of significant impact: The use of absolute units set a pattern that became standard, and the worldwide network of magnetic observatories established a precedent for international scientific cooperation. Also, his work in physics may have been of the highest quality, but it seems to have had little influence.

In the area of mathematics, however, his influence was powerful. Carl Gustav Jacobi and Niels Henrik Abel testified that their work on elliptic functions was triggered by a hint in the *Arithmetical Inquisitions*. Évariste Galois, on the eve of his death, asked that his rough notes be sent to Gauss. Thus, in mathematics, in spite of delays, Gauss reached and inspired countless mathematicians. Although he was more of a systematizer and solver of old problems than a creator of new paths, the completeness of his results laid the basis for new departures—especially in number theory, differential geometry, and statistics.

—*Genevieve Slomski*

FURTHER READING

Bell, Eric T. *Men of Mathematics*. Reprint. New York: Simon & Schuster, 1961. Historical account of the major figures in mathematics from the Greeks to Georg Cantor, written in an interesting, if at times exaggerated, style. In a lengthy chapter devoted to Gauss titled "The Prince of Mathematicians," Bell describes the life and work of Gauss, focusing almost exclusively on the mathematical contributions. No bibliography.

Boyer, Carl B. *A History of Mathematics*. New York: John Wiley & Sons, 1968. In "The Time of Gauss and Cauchy," chapter 23 of this standard history of mathematics, Boyer briefly discusses biographical details of Gauss's life before summarizing the proofs of Gauss's major theorems. Boyer also discusses Gauss's work in the context of the leading contemporary figures in mathematics of the day. Includes charts, an extensive bibliography, and student exercises.

Buhler, W. K. *Gauss: A Biographical Study*. New York: Springer-Verlag, 1981. The author's purpose is not to write a definitive life history but to select from Gauss's life and work those aspects that are interesting and comprehensible to a lay reader. Contains quotations from Gauss's writings, illustrations, a bibliography, lengthy footnotes, appendixes on his collected works, a useful survey of the secondary literature, and an index to Gauss's works.

Dunnington, Guy Waldo. *Carl Friedrich Gauss, Titan of Science*. With additional material by Jeremy Gray and Fritz-Egbert Dohse. Washington, D.C.: Mathematical Association of America, 2004. Originally published in 1955, this is an expanded version of a biography describing Gauss's life and times to reveal the man as well as the scientist. The new edition includes introductory remarks, an updated bibliography, and a commentary on Gauss's mathematical diary. It also reprints the features contained in the original edition, including appendixes on honors and diplomas, children, genealogy, a chronology, books borrowed from the college library, courses taught, and views and opinions.

Goldman, Jay. *The Queen of Mathematics: An Historically Motivated Guide to Number Theory*. Wellesley, Mass.: A. K. Peters, 1998. A history of number theory, described by Gauss as the "queen of mathematics," describing how number theory developed from the seventeenth through the nineteenth centuries. Includes a chapter on Gauss and his work, and another chapter on the ideas contained in *Disquisitiones arithmeticae*. Aimed at readers with a knowledge of mathematics.

Turnbull, H. W. *The Great Mathematicians*. New York: New York University Press, 1962. Useful as a quick reference guide to the lives and works of the major figures in mathematics from the Greeks to the twentieth century.

SEE ALSO: Niels Henrik Abel; Richard Dedekind; Évariste Galois; Sophie Germain; Alexander von Humboldt; Nikolay Ivanovich Lobachevsky; Maria Mitchell; Charlotte Angas Scott.

RELATED ARTICLES in *Great Events from History: The Nineteenth Century, 1801-1900:* January 1, 1801: First Asteroid Is Discovered; 1899: Hilbert Publishes *The Foundations of Geometry.*

JOSEPH-LOUIS GAY-LUSSAC
French physical scientist

A preeminent scientist of his generation, Gay-Lussac helped prepare the way, through his discoveries in chemistry and physics, for the modern atomic-molecular theory of matter. His investigations of gases led to the law describing how they react with each other in simple proportions by volume, and his chemical investigations led to the discovery of a new element, boron, and to the development of new techniques in qualitative and quantitative analysis.

BORN: December 6, 1778; Saint-Léonard-de-Noblat, France
DIED: May 9, 1850; Paris, France
ALSO KNOWN AS: Joseph-Louis Gay (birth name)
AREAS OF ACHIEVEMENT: Chemistry, physics

EARLY LIFE

Born in a small market town in west central France, Joseph-Louis Gay was the eldest son of five children of Antoine Gay, a lawyer and public prosecutor, who, to distinguish himself from others called Gay, later changed his surname to Gay-Lussac (gay-lew-sahk), after the family property in the nearby hamlet of Lussac. Joseph-Louis used this expanded name throughout his life. His early education from a priest and his comfortable social and economic position were ended by the French Revolution of 1789, and in the turbulent years that followed, his teacher fled the country, and his father was arrested.

With the fall of Robespierre in 1794, the Revolution took a more moderate direction, and Gay-Lussac's father was freed. Antoine Gay-Lussac was then able to send Joseph-Louis to Paris to continue his education at religious boarding schools. His father expected him to study law, but Gay-Lussac became increasingly interested in mathematics and science. His excellent record in mathematics gave him the opportunity to enter the École Polytechnique, then a young but already prestigious revolutionary institution for the training of civil and military engineers. Gay-Lussac completed his studies there with distinction, and he was graduated in November, 1800. He then entered the École des Ponts et Chaussées. He saw engineering not as a career but as a position to fall back on if he did not succeed in pure science.

During these years of study, Gay-Lussac came under the wing of Claude Louis Berthollet, a distinguished chemist and former companion to Napoleon I in Egypt. In his triple role as teacher, father-substitute, and patron, Berthollet became the most important influence on Gay-Lussac's life. Some of Gay-Lussac's greatest early work was done at Berthollet's country house at Arcueil, where important scientists would gather and where the Society of Arcueil was later formed. Gay-Lussac continued his studies at the École des Ponts et Chaussées, but his relationship with the school grew more nominal as he spent more and more time on scientific research at Arcueil.

LIFE'S WORK

Gay-Lussac's initial research was of considerable importance both because of its permanent scientific value and because it marked his successful initiation into a career of pure science. In 1802, after painstaking measurements, he showed that many different gases expand equally over the temperature range from 0 to +100 degrees Celsius. Despite the thoroughness of his studies and the significance of his results, Gay-Lussac is not generally credited with the discovery of the quantitative law of the thermal expansion of gases. Some chemists recalled that Jacques Charles, a French physicist, had found in 1787 that certain gases expanded equally, but Charles had also found that other gases, those that dissolved in water, had different rates of expansion. Because Charles never published his work and because he did not completely understand the phenomenon of thermal expansion, many scholars believe that justice demands that this discovery should be known as Gay-Lussac's law.

Gases were central to another of Gay-Lussac's early research projects. During the early nineteenth century, scientists debated whether the percentage of nitrogen, oxygen, and other gases was different in the upper and lower atmosphere. A similar diversity of opinion existed about the behavior of a magnet at low and high altitudes.

To resolve these differences, Gay-Lussac and Jean-Baptiste Biot, a young colleague, made a daring ascent from Paris in a hydrogen-filled balloon on August 24, 1804. By observing oscillations of a magnetic needle, they concluded that the intensity of the earth's magnetism was constant up to four thousand meters, but they did not have time to collect samples of air. Therefore, to answer the question about the atmosphere's composition, Gay-Lussac made a solo balloon ascent over Paris on September 16, 1804. He reached a height of more than seven thousand meters, an altitude record that would remain unmatched for a half century. He discovered that the temperature of the atmosphere decreased by one degree Celsius for every 174-meter increase in elevation. When he analyzed the air samples that he had collected, he found that the composition of air was the same at seven thousand meters as it was at sea level (his technique was not sensitive enough to detect the differences that were later found).

Shortly after the balloon flights, Gay-Lussac began to collaborate with Alexander von Humboldt, a Prussian nobleman, world traveler, and scientist. Gay-Lussac had just received an appointment to a junior post at the École Polytechnique when he met Humboldt, who was interested in his analysis of the atmosphere. Humboldt and Gay-Lussac agreed to collaborate in a series of experiments on atmospheric gases. Their research led to a precise determination of the relative proportions with which hydrogen and oxygen combine to form water: almost exactly two hundred parts to one hundred parts by volume. Though they were not the first to discover this 2:1 ratio (Henry Cavendish had noted it in 1784), the experiment convinced Gay-Lussac that scientists should study the reactions of gases by volume instead of by weight.

Because of the fruitfulness of their collaboration, Gay-Lussac wanted to accompany Humboldt on a European tour he was planning, to make a systematic survey of magnetic intensities. Gay-Lussac was granted a leave of absence from the École Polytechnique, and in March, 1805, he and Humboldt embarked on a year of travel through Italy, Switzerland, and Germany. Through their tour, Gay-Lussac made many contacts with important physicists and chemists such as Alessandro Volta, the inventor of the electric battery. A tangible result of his European travels was a paper on terrestrial magnetism. Because of this and other studies, he was elected in 1806 to the National Institute (the revolutionary replacement for

the Royal Academy of Sciences). Although this was a major step in Gay-Lussac's career, his base of operations remained the École Polytechnique and Arcueil.

In 1807, Gay-Lussac completed a series of experiments to see if there was a general relationship between the specific heat of a gas and its density. Specific heat is a measure of a substance's capacity to attract its own particular quantity of heat. For example, mercury has less capacity for heat than water; that is, mercury requires a smaller quantity of heat than does water to raise its temperature by the same number of degrees. Gay-Lussac knew that the compression of gases was accompanied by the evolution of heat and their expansion by the absorption of heat, but he wanted to find the relationship between the absorbed and evolved heat. Through an ingenious series of experiments, he discovered that the heat lost by expansion was equal to the heat gained by compression, a result significant in the history of physics, particularly for the law of the conservation of energy.

Although Gay-Lussac had studied the 2:1 chemical combination of hydrogen and oxygen in 1805, he did not generalize his results until 1808, when he again became interested in gas reactions. At that time, he began his long collaboration with Louis Jacques Thenard, a peasant's son who had risen from laboratory boy to Polytechnique professor. In one of their early experiments, they heated a mixture of calcium fluoride and boric acid in an iron tube. Instead of getting the expected fluorine, they obtained fluoric acid (now called boron trifluoride), a gas that, on coming into contact with air, produced dense white fumes that reminded them of those produced by muriatic acid (now called hydrogen chloride) and ammonia. In fact, they found that boron trifluoride and ammonia reacted in a 1:1 ratio by volume, just as hydrogen chloride and ammonia did.

With these and other examples from his own experiments, along with results reported by others in various papers, Gay-Lussac felt secure enough to state that all gases combine in simple volumetric proportions. He announced this law, now known as Gay-Lussac's law of combining volumes, at a meeting of the Société Philomatique in Paris on December 31, 1808. This law would later be used to teach students about the evidence for the atomic theory, but at the time of its proposal Gay-Lussac rejected John Dalton's atomic theory.

Despite Gay-Lussac's important research at the École Polytechnique and Arcueil, his career was stalled. During the years 1808 and 1809, his friends tried to lobby on his behalf for a position commensurate with his accomplishments. The death of Antoine Fourcroy in 1809 provided the opportunity for which Gay-Lussac's friends had been waiting, and on February 17, 1810, Gay-Lussac became Fourcroy's successor to the chemistry chair at the École Polytechnique. Another reason for this activity on Gay-Lussac's behalf was his impending marriage to Geneviève-Marie-Joseph Riot, to whom he was married in May, 1809. The marriage was a happy one, eventually producing five children.

During the time that Gay-Lussac's friends were trying to find him a position, Gay-Lussac and Thenard were doing important work on the alkali metals. These soft metals with great chemical reactivity had recently been isolated by Humphry Davy, the great English chemist who would become Gay-Lussac's competitor in many discoveries. Davy had used the giant voltaic batteries at the Royal Institution to discover sodium and potassium. Because of the rivalry between Great Britain and France, Napoleon ordered the construction of an even larger collection of batteries at the École Polytechnique, and he urged Gay-Lussac and Thenard to do experiments with this voltaic pile. Ironically, they actually found that they could ignore electrolysis and use chemical means to produce large quantities of sodium and potassium. Davy's electrical method had liberated only tiny amounts of the new metals, whereas Gay-Lussac and Thenard's method of fusing potassium and sodium salts with iron filings at high temperatures produced great amounts of sodium and potassium more cheaply.

Gay-Lussac and Davy were both interested in isolating the element contained in boric acid. On June 21, 1808, Gay-Lussac and Thenard heated boric acid with potassium in a copper tube, producing a mixture of products, one of which was the new element. Their first published claim to the discovery of boron was in November, a month before Davy submitted a similar claim to the Royal Society. They delayed publishing their discovery because they wanted not only to decompose boric acid but also to recompose it.

After their work on boron, Gay-Lussac and Thenard examined oxymuriatic acid. At the beginning of the nineteenth century, chlorine was called oxymuriatic acid because chemists thought that it was a compound of oxygen and muriatic acid. This belief was based on its preparation by heating muriatic (now called hydrochloric) acid with a substance such as manganese dioxide with its abundance of oxygen. Gay-Lussac and Thenard were therefore astonished when they passed oxymuriatic acid gas over red-hot charcoal and the oxygen that was supposedly in the acid refused to combine with the charcoal. This led them to doubt that the gas contained oxygen and

to suggest that it might be an element. Historians of chemistry usually report that Davy first recognized the elementary nature of chlorine, because in Gay-Lussac and Thenard's report in the 1809 volume of the Arcueil Memoires, which was known to Davy, they conservatively stated that their experiments caused them to doubt the existence of oxygen in oxymuriatic acid, whereas Davy in 1810 unambiguously stated that it was an element, for which he proposed the name chlorine.

In addition to the misconception about chlorine, chemists of the time were also grappling with a faulty theory of acids since Antoine Lavoisier had earlier proposed that all acids contained oxygen. Until Gay-Lussac's research on iodine in 1814 and on prussic acid in 1815, he had accepted Lavoisier's theory of acidity. Gay-Lussac's discovery and investigation of hydriodic acid reopened the question for him, and he concluded that hydrogen, not oxygen, was necessary to convert iodine to an acid. He clearly stated that hydrogen played the same role for one class of substances that oxygen did for another. He introduced the concept and name "hydracid" for the first class, and his studies of hydrogen chloride, hydrogen iodide, and hydrogen fluoride prepared the way for a new theory of acids.

Gay-Lussac's early work was based on the recognition, common among chemists since the eighteenth century, that each substance possessed a unique chemical composition that could be represented by a unique formula. During the 1820's, Gay-Lussac and other chemists discovered pairs of compounds, each member of which had the same number of the same atoms but with quite distinct properties. Gay-Lussac straightforwardly interpreted this phenomenon, called isomerism, as a result of the different atomic arrangements in the two substances. This idea, that different structures result in different chemical properties, would become an extremely important theme in the history of modern chemistry.

During the final decades of Gay-Lussac's career, he turned his attention more and more to applied science. The economic needs created by his growing family caused him to do more industrial research, where the financial rewards were greater than in theoretical work. Particularly noteworthy was his development of a superior method of assaying silver using a standard solution of common salt. This precise method, which he developed after he became chief assayer to the mint in 1829, is still used.

In 1832, Gay-Lussac accepted a distinguished position at the Museum of Natural History. In his last years, he worked so hard to provide for his family that he produced little theoretical work, but he continued to reap honors for his brilliant early discoveries. In 1839, he became a Peer of France, even though his election was accepted reluctantly by those who thought that he worked too much with his hands to be a gentleman. He had a brief political career during the 1830's, after which he held a number of advisory positions, where he used his technical knowledge to suggest improvements in such industrial chemical processes as the production of gunpowder and oxalic acid. He died in Paris on May 9, 1850, lamenting his departure from the world just when science was becoming interesting.

SIGNIFICANCE

The quest for laws dominated Joseph-Louis Gay-Lussac's scientific life. He believed that if a scientist lacked this desire, then the laws of nature would escape his attention. His most important discovery was the law of combining volumes, which helped pave the way for the modern atomic-molecular theory of matter.

Gay-Lussac managed to pass relatively unscathed through three political revolutions. Nevertheless, his life reflected the social and political changes taking place around him. His education occurred largely in schools founded or modified by the Revolution. Berthollet and the Society of Arcueil, the shapers of Gay-Lussac as a scientist, owed much to the patronage of Napoleon. During the 1830's and 1840's, under Louis-Philippe, Gay-Lussac became a conservative member of the professional class or upper bourgeoisie. Through all these changes he continued to be a French patriot. This chauvinism surfaced in his scientific controversies with the British chemists Humphry Davy and John Dalton.

Just as Gay-Lussac's political life was a curious blend of liberalism and conservatism, so too was his scientific life. In his early career, devoted to pure science, he made so many important discoveries in so many areas that no one in post-Napoleonic France could teach chemistry without frequent references to his work. During the Restoration, however, he made few contributions to pure science, and he seemed to many young scientists to represent an enervating conservatism. For example, he adhered to the caloric theory of heat (heat as a substance) rather than embracing what most scientists saw as the superior kinetic theory (heat as motion).

Despite these weaknesses in his later career, Gay-Lussac's place in the history of science is secure. His achievements in chemistry, physics, meteorology, and geology led him to become a central figure in the French scientific establishment, and he was influential in shaping such institutions as the École Polytechnique and the Museum of Natural History. His facility in applying chemistry to practical problems set an example that had wide repercussions later in the century. He also had great influence internationally—he emerges as a key figure of European science in the first third of the nineteenth century.

—Robert J. Paradowski

FURTHER READING

Crosland, Maurice. *Gay-Lussac, Scientist and Bourgeois.* New York: Cambridge University Press, 1978. Crosland takes a thematic rather than a strictly chronological approach to the life and work of Gay-Lussac. He relates Gay-Lussac both to the history of science and to contemporary social and political history. His account, which is refreshingly frank in dealing with issues of scientific rivalry and academic politics, is intended for historians of science as well as for social and economic historians, but because Crosland explains the science of the times so well, his work should be accessible to a wider audience.

_____. *The Society of Arcueil: A View of French Science at the Time of Napoleon I.* Cambridge, Mass.: Harvard University Press, 1967. This book contains an important account of the social context of Gay-Lussac's early work. Crosland also uses Arcueil to make some good general points about the nature of patronage and about French science.

Ihde, Aaron J. *The Development of Modern Chemistry.* New York: Harper & Row, 1964. Ihde, who taught the history of chemistry for many years at the University of Wisconsin, emphasizes the period from the eighteenth to the twentieth centuries. His approach is more encyclopedic than analytic, but descriptive enough so that it is readable by high school and college chemistry students. Contains an extensive annotated bibliography.

Nye, Mary Jo. *Before Big Science: The Pursuit of Modern Chemistry and Physics, 1800-1940.* New York: Twayne, and London: Prentice Hall, 1996. A social and intellectual history of the physical sciences from the early nineteenth century until the beginning of World War II. Chapter 2, "Dalton's Atom and Two Paths for the Study of Matter," includes information on Gay-Lussac.

Purrington, Robert D. *Physics in the Nineteenth Century.* New Brunswick, N.J.: Rutgers University Press, 1997. An historical overview of nineteenth century physics, placing the science within the context of the

Industrial Revolution and the rise of European nation states. Includes information about Gay-Lussac's caloric theory of heat and his ideas about atoms.

Scott, Wilson L. *The Conflict Between Atomism and Conservation Theory, 1644-1860.* New York: Elsevier, 1970. Scott focuses on the conflict between groups of scientists over the issue of whether force (later called energy) is conserved when one hard body strikes another. This debate had important implications for the atomic theory, and Gay-Lussac's ideas and experiments were integral to it. The book is based on extensive research, but because the author can tell a story and explain scientific concepts clearly, his account is accessible to readers without any special scientific knowledge.

Szabadvary, Ferenc. *History of Analytical Chemistry.* Elmsford, N.Y.: Pergamon Press, 1966. This book, first published in Hungarian in 1960, is a detailed account of the historical development of analytical chemistry. Gay-Lussac's contributions to qualitative and quantitative, gravimetric and volumetric analyses are extensively discussed. The book is based largely on original sources and is intended for the reader with some knowledge of chemistry.

SEE ALSO: Amedeo Avogadro; John Dalton; Sir Humphry Davy; Alexander von Humboldt; Justus von Liebig; Napoleon I; Friedrich Wöhler.

RELATED ARTICLES in *Great Events from History: The Nineteenth Century, 1801-1900:* 1803-1808: Dalton Formulates the Atomic Theory of Matter; April, 1898-1903: Stratosphere and Troposphere Are Discovered.

GEORGE IV
King of Great Britain (r. 1820-1830)

Through his incompetence and disreputable personal behavior, King George IV eroded traditional British respect for and reliance upon the monarchy as a functioning governing institution, thereby inadvertently strengthening the powers of Parliament and weakening those of the British monarchy.

BORN: August 12, 1762; St. James's Palace, London, England

DIED: June 26, 1830; Windsor Castle, Windsor, England

ALSO KNOWN AS: George Augustus Frederick (birth name); Georg August Friedrich

AREA OF ACHIEVEMENT: Government and politics

EARLY LIFE

George Augustus Frederick—the eventual George IV, king of Great Britain—was the first child of George III (who reigned from 1760 to 1820) and Queen Charlotte Sophia, the former princess of Mecklenburg-Strelitz. As heir to the throne of one of the world's great powers, George received the finest education possible, in accordance with the standards of the eighteenth century. Beginning at the age of five, he was privately tutored under a disciplined regimen, learning the classics, English, and the rudiments of French, German, and Italian. He would eventually achieve fluency in French. At the age of thir-teen, the rigor of George's education was intensified by order of his father, the king. His tutors added history, religion, ethics, law, government, mathematics, and the natural sciences to his studies, while in his spare time he learned to play the cello, fence, box, sing, and appreciate the fine arts. Music, sculpture, and painting would remain lifelong interests.

As a child, George was universally popular with his teachers, family, the court, and friends. He was variously described as amiable, affectionate, cheerful, and intelligent, while he achieved a reputation as an enthusiastic and responsive pupil. He already possessed that wit and charm for which he would later become both famous and notorious. Altogether, George's early years were as promising as any enjoyed by a Prince of Wales (the traditional title bestowed by the English upon the heir to the throne).

The future king's difficulties began in his late teens, when he developed an obsessive desire for heavy drinking and womanizing. In these endeavors, he was assisted by numerous roguish companions, an excellent physique, and irresistible handsomeness. Soon, his drunken escapades, numerous love affairs, and casual sexual liaisons became well known to the British public. His heavy spending, supported by the taxpayers, and his constant philandering cost him the esteem and affection of the nation. He never fully recovered from the playboy image he earned as the Prince of Wales.

George's behavior also cost him the respect and trust of his father. King George III regularly excluded the prince from consultation on the affairs of state, while begging him to mend his ways. Relations between father and son became especially strained when, during the 1780's, the prince gradually began to align himself with the opposition Whig Party. The Whigs generally favored liberal causes, such as Catholic emancipation, political reform, and the curtailment of the king's prerogatives. Carlton House, the prince's residence in London, became the meeting place for Whig politicians and intriguers. The Whigs' opponents, the Tory Party, could remain in power, however, as long as George III reigned. The king nevertheless deeply resented the prince's collusion in attacks upon his political favorites, the Tories.

Public disapproval of George III swelled during the so-called Regency Crisis of 1788-1789. The king suffered from a rare, hereditary metabolic disorder known as porphyria, whose effects upon the central nervous system caused extreme pain and sometimes insanity. When George III endured a particularly acute attack of the disease in late 1788, the prince and the Whigs scrambled to establish George IV as Prince Regent with unrestricted powers. George III's sudden recovery in early 1789 caused much embarrassment for the prince and disappointment for the Whigs. The British people, who dearly loved George III, long remembered and resented the eagerness with which the prince hastened to supplant his father.

A new source of friction between the king and his son emerged after 1792, when Great Britain became involved in war with revolutionary France. The prince desired an important, active military command similar to those possessed by his younger brothers. George III refused to comply with his son's request, citing the need for the prince to prepare himself for the kingship, as well as the foolishness of exposing to combat the heir to the throne. The young George's vanity was wounded by this denial of the opportunity to participate in the military glory that others garnered. The quarrel between father and son lasted for almost two decades, as the war with France continued almost without respite until 1815.

George's romantic life assumed some stability after 1785, when he married Mrs. Maria Anne Weld Fitzherbert (née Smythe), a wealthy widow who had been married twice before. The wedding ceremony and the prince's relationship to his new wife were loosely guarded secrets, however, because the marriage was contracted without the king's permission and Mrs. Fitzherbert was a Roman Catholic, both violations of British law. Despite

George IV.

bitter quarrels and prolonged separations, the couple remained devoted to each other until 1809, when they mutually agreed to end their relationship. The prince's love for Mrs. Fitzherbert had not stopped his philandering entirely, merely slowing him down—the most important factor in the deterioration of their relations.

Although the king was much distressed by persistent rumors of George's wedding, the illegality of the union with Mrs. Fitzherbert permitted a royal marriage. Burdened by stupendous debts and faced with the need to produce an heir to the throne, George married Princess Caroline Amelia Elizabeth of Brunswick in 1795, casting a covetous eye upon her dowry and income. This union was to become a marriage in name only, as George conceived an instant distaste for his bride. Sexual relations between the couple ceased after the birth of their only child, Princess Charlotte, in 1796. An informal separation was also arranged in that year, George claiming to be revolted by his wife's vulgar behavior and conversation.

In late 1810, George III, slowed by blindness and old age, was struck once again by an acute attack of porphyria and lapsed into an insanity from which he never recovered. For a few months, the nation awaited the possibility of the king's restoration to health. Discouraged by the doctors' poor prognoses, Parliament voted to establish Prince George as regent with full royal powers, a position he assumed on February 5, 1811.

LIFE'S WORK

The Whigs greeted George's regency with high expectations. With the pro-Tory George III out of the way, they anticipated an invitation from his son to form a new government. Unfortunately for them, the prince's political attitudes had gradually changed markedly over the preceding decade. Like many Europeans, he had been appalled by the violence, the excesses, and the aggressiveness of revolutionary France. He was no longer the enthusiastic supporter of liberal causes that he had once been. Moreover, George admired the doggedness with which the Tories were pursuing the war against Napoleon. By the end of 1812, it was clear to the Whigs that the prince would retain the Tories in power.

By then it was equally clear that George was not a well man. The illness that afflicted him bore symptoms similar to those exhibited by his father. It is probable that the prince also suffered from porphyria, although not in the acute form that caused George III's insanity. The prince's health problems would contribute to his indecisiveness and ineffectiveness as a political leader in the years ahead.

In 1815, following the Battle of Waterloo, Great Britain emerged victorious from the long war with France. The nation that the prince regent viewed in its hour of triumph was considerably different from that of his youth. Rapid commercial and economic growth, coupled with advancing industrialization, was causing much social dislocation and distress. The influence of the French Revolution aroused many Englishmen to favor further democratization of British politics. Discontent was expressed through riots (the Peterloo Massacre), assassination plots (the Cato Street Conspiracy), and vociferous demands for political reform. During the next fifteen years, George aligned himself with conservative Tories in defense of the status quo. The death in 1817 of Princess Charlotte, whose liberal views were well known, caused the Whigs to despair of ever achieving their political program.

On January 29, 1820, George III died, and his son became king in his own right. The first crisis of George IV's reign occurred when he attempted to exclude Princess Caroline from enjoying the prerogatives and benefits of being queen. George's legal maneuverings caused Caro-

line to return to England from the Continent, where she had been residing since 1814. The populace greeted her arrival with great acclaim, perceiving her as the hapless, innocent victim of George's infidelities and cruelties. Caroline's popularity was an accurate gauge of the dislike of ordinary Englishmen for George and the Tory government. The king was outraged by Caroline's courting of the populace and caused a divorce bill to be introduced in the House of Lords in August of 1820.

Caroline's extramarital affairs had been known to George and his advisers since the early nineteenth century. In 1806, a special Commission of Enquiry had established that she had probably engaged in several illicit affairs since her marriage to George. To the information gathered by this committee—known as the "Delicate Investigation"—there had been added massive, new evidence of Caroline's riotous living and immoral life on the Continent after 1814. This new investigating body, the Milan Commission, depicted Caroline as romantically involved with an Italian nobleman, appearing seminude in public on several occasions, and openly boasting of her numerous sexual liaisons. Confronted by overwhelming evidence, the Lords voted in favor of the divorce bill, but only marginally.

The public response, moreover, was intimidating. Mobs, some of them egged on by the Whig opposition, protested against the queen's conviction. The ministers, prominent Tory politicians, and even George himself were booed and heckled when they appeared in public. The Whigs seemed determined to use this opportunity to bring the ministry down. In the face of potentially violent disturbances, George's advisers suggested that he quietly withdraw the divorce bill from further consideration by the House of Commons. This he did, but only with great reluctance. George was relieved from further mortifying embarrassment by the queen's behavior when she died suddenly in 1821. The incident had graphically demonstrated to the Tories the extent of their unpopularity, and, consequently, slow progress toward Tory liberalization began.

Nevertheless, despite the urgent need for change, reform proceeded at a snail's pace under the Tory administrations of the 1820's. George proved to be even more conservative than his ministers, opposing reformist ideas and initiatives and espousing a strong royal prerogative. Initially, he resisted the liberalization of British foreign policy under Foreign Secretary George Canning (who served from 1822 to 1827), whereby Great Britain withdrew unqualified support for the suppression of revolutionary movements and subsequently recognized the independence of Latin America from Spain. As George's esteem and affection for Canning replaced an earlier hatred, the foreign secretary's ideas became more attractive to him. George's later acceptance of Canning's policy demonstrated a serious defect in the king's use of the royal prerogatives: To a great extent, he was easily swayed by his personal feelings toward individual ministers and politicians.

The king's resistance to the Tories' one substantial piece of reformist legislation, the Roman Catholic Relief Act of 1829, was more typical of his stubbornness and reactionary political attitudes. Only after months of obstructive behavior—including threats to abdicate or veto the bill—did he finally relent in the face of a tactful lobbying effort by his most esteemed friends and advisers, led by the duke of Wellington. George's strong opposition to Catholic emancipation was all the more incredible in the light of the potentially revolutionary situation in Ireland.

In spite of occasional fits of assertiveness, George's royal style was characterized more often by indecisiveness and deliberate inattention to his duties. Ministers frequently had to hound him for weeks to secure his signature on important documents. As he had been wont to do in his youth, he dissipated his time in heavy drinking and social events. The greater part of his positive energies was devoted to the refurbishing of Windsor Castle and Buckingham Palace in unsurpassed opulence at great expense to the British public. In his final years, George's social activities were curtailed by obesity, gout, and arteriosclerosis. These debilitating conditions made him an invalid during the waning months of his life. He died on June 26, 1830, from a ruptured blood vessel in the stomach region.

SIGNIFICANCE

George IV was one of the more incompetent and ineffective monarchs of Great Britain. His alcoholism, sexual promiscuity, financial extravagance, and general irresponsibility made him extremely unpopular with most segments of British society, and hampered his abilities to govern the nation in the aggressive style forged by his father, George III. During his regency and reign, the royal prerogatives were further eroded through lack of intelligent and consistent use. In this way, George inadvertently contributed to the strengthening of parliamentary institutions and the concomitant deterioration of royal power in Great Britain.

—*Michael S. Fitzgerald*

FURTHER READING

Cowie, Leonard W. *Hanoverian England, 1714-1837.* London: G. Bell and Sons, 1967. A brief but comprehensive account of Great Britain under the Hanoverian dynasty.

David, Saul. *The Prince of Pleasure: The Prince of Wales and the Making of the Regency.* London: Little, Brown, 1998. Comprehensive, balanced biography. David recounts anecdotes about George's scandalous lifestyle, but also credits George for his patronage of the arts and his crucial role in the multinational campaign against Napoleon.

Gash, Norman. *Lord Liverpool: The Life and Political Career of Robert Banks Jenkinson, Second Earl of Liverpool, 1770-1828.* Cambridge, Mass.: Harvard University Press, 1984. Much more than a simple biography, Gash's work provides a brief introduction to English politics in the era of George IV. Liverpool was prime minister from 1812 to 1827 and was much detested, but he was indispensable to George IV.

Hibbert, Christopher. *George IV: Prince of Wales, 1762-1811.* New York: Harper & Row, 1972. A fine biography of George. Comprehensive in its scope and based upon extensive research in archival sources. Fairminded and judicious in its evaluations.

_____. *George IV: Regent and King, 1811-1830.* New York: Harper & Row, 1973. Continues the story begun in the author's above-cited work.

Leslie, Doris. *The Great Corinthian: A Portrait of the Prince Regent.* London: Eyre & Spottiswoode, 1952. A well-written, colorful narrative of George's life before 1821. Describes the pageantry and beauty of aristocratic life in Regency England. Distressingly short on that political and character analysis necessary to an understanding of George IV.

Machin, G. I. T. *The Catholic Question in English Politics, 1820 to 1830.* Oxford, England: Clarendon Press, 1964. Scholarly background to the Roman Catholic Relief Act of 1829. Places the question of Ireland and Catholic emancipation clearly in the context of politics during the reign of George IV.

Parissien, Steven. *George IV: Inspiration of the Regency.* New York: St. Martin's Press, 2002. Parissien's biography is generally critical of George IV, describing his inconstancy, selfishness, and ill-conceived emulation of the French monarchy. Parissien concludes that George was one of the most hated monarchs who "sundered the contract between monarch and nation."

Richardson, Joanna. *George IV: A Portrait.* London: Sidgwick and Jackson, 1966. A short biography of

George, attempting to rehabilitate his character by neglecting the political and private sides of his life. Places great stress on George's role as a patron of scholars, writers, architects, and artists.

Smith, E. A. *George IV*. New Haven, Conn.: Yale University Press, 1999. This biography, one in the Yale English Monarchs series, provides a less critical view of George than many other books. Smith reconsiders George's accomplishments, crediting the king with significant achievements in politics and for his patronage of the arts.

SEE ALSO: Henry Brougham; George Canning; Charles Grey; Second Earl of Liverpool; Second Viscount Melbourne; Queen Victoria; Duke of Wellington.

RELATED ARTICLES in *Great Events from History: The Nineteenth Century, 1801-1900:* January, 1802: Cobbett Founds the *Political Register*; May 9, 1828-April 13, 1829: Roman Catholic Emancipation; June 4, 1832: British Parliament Passes the Reform Act of 1832; June 28, 1838: Queen Victoria's Coronation.

HENRY GEORGE
American economist and social reformer

George's writings and lectures on land, labor, and economic policies expressed a popular radicalism that challenged established economic doctrines and dominant political practices, exercising a profound influence for reform both in the United States and abroad.

BORN: September 2, 1839; Philadelphia, Pennsylvania
DIED: October 29, 1897; New York, New York
AREA OF ACHIEVEMENT: Social reform

EARLY LIFE

An oldest son, Henry George was born into a large, devoutly Episcopalian family. His birthplace was close to Philadelphia's Independence Hall, which would become a source of lifelong inspiration to him. His father, Richard Samuel Henry George, was a sea captain's son whose once prosperous resources were depleted prior to his death. Accordingly, throughout his life Richard earned a steady, but modest, income working variously as a schoolteacher, a dealer in religious books, and for a longer period as a clerk in Philadelphia's United States Customs House—a Democratic Party political appointment. Catharine Vallance, Henry's mother, was as devout as her husband; also a former schoolteacher, she bore nine children and was proud of her descent from a close friend of Benjamin Franklin. Overall, the George household was warmly Christian and modestly comfortable. Henry George remained attached to his family all of his life.

Apart from receiving some primary instruction at home, the young George's formal education was brief. What there was of it failed to impress him. At the age of six, he entered a small private school, and at the age of nine moved on to Philadelphia's famed Episcopal Academy but performed poorly and withdrew. He was subsequently coached for admission to the city's esteemed public high school—this tutoring, he later believed, providing his best educational experience. Once enrolled, however, he quit almost immediately, thus ending his formal education at the age of thirteen. When fully mature, he was to praise only vocational or practical learning, but in his early years there were other cultural advantages that derived from his regular use of the libraries of the Franklin Institute, the American Philosophical Society, and a small, convivial literary society.

Regardless of George's formal deficiencies, they were never a handicap. Largely self-taught, reflective, ambitious, and combative, with a romantic sense of individuality and a slowly acquired ability to concentrate his energies, George would eventually meet many of the Western world's best-educated, most learned, and most politically important figures, either directly or by debating them; at such times, George was equal to his discussion partners or debating adversaries in maintaining his own faith—and, almost without exception, he gained the respect of these men.

Two sets of events brought Henry George to youthful independence and helped pave a path toward his life's work. In 1855, through family connections, he sailed as foremast boy on a sixteen-month voyage from New York to Melbourne and Calcutta. After returning to Philadelphia, he secured a job from which he rose to journeyman typesetter, a skill that carried a number of his famous contemporaries into journalism or writing. In the depressed economy of 1857, however, his friends and relatives were already living on the Pacific coast, and he determined to join them. With an offer for a job in his pocket, he thus started his journey west. Again, thanks to parental persuasions, he sailed as an ordinary seaman on a government lighthouse vessel, which, upon arrival in San Francisco, he deserted. He would remain in the new and bustling state of California from 1858 to 1880.

LIFE'S WORK

Initially there was an unsteady quality to George's California days, especially during the Civil War. Like many, he caught "gold fever" and explored northward as far as British Columbia. He weighed rice, served as a foreman, dabbled in journalism, joined in the operation of a San Francisco newspaper, and even abandoned the Democratic Party for California's liberal brand of Republicanism, at least through the Grant administrations. Such ventures or allegiances, however, were either short-lived or failures. Consequently, along with many young eastern emigrants during the 1860's, he suffered economic hardships, at one point verging on desperation. Nevertheless, he was establishing mature foundations.

In 1861, George married Annie Fox, a Catholic orphaned by a broken British colonial marriage, and they started a family of their own. Moreover, in March, 1865, by his own account, he determined to devote his life to writing, exploring social issues through the economic contrasts and conflicts that appeared so stark in California. Between 1866 and 1879, he pursued this course as editor variously of eight San Francisco, Oakland, and Sacramento newspapers. Editorially he advocated (and sometimes joined) movements toward free trade and public ownership and regulation of railroads, the telegraph, and municipal utilities. He sought revisions in the state's land policies, as well as revisions in national land policy under the Morrill Act, thus encouraging more equitable land distribution both in California and in the nation.

Generally George favored trade unionism, the eight-hour day, and strikes as a last resort. He believed that high wages, leading to a greater respect for labor, would help lead to an economy of abundance. Favoring competition, he staunchly opposed its excesses or monopolies in any form. Similarly, on the then hotly debated "currency question," he proposed an end to credit manipulations by bankers and by government and a gradual restoration of wartime greenbacks (inflated currency) to equivalency in gold: a gradual return to a hard-money policy. Distressed by the cornering of California lands by a handful of speculators and wealthy individuals and anxious to see the state continue as a utopia for the com-

mon man, he urged restrictions on immigration, particularly Chinese immigration. The issues with which he dealt were current ones, engaging wide popular attention and commentary by American and British political economists of whom George was aware and whom he acknowledged, but his faith, common sense, keen personal observations, and experienced reflections lent special force to his writings.

George's editorials and lectures brought him notoriety. It was two books specifically, however, that won for him national and even international recognition. In 1871, he published *Our Land and Land Policy, National and State* (really a 130-page pamphlet) in San Francisco. In it he argued that public lands should be made more available to ordinary homesteaders (80-acre or 40-acre allotments rather than 160-acre allotments); that existing enormous landholdings should be divested and their future restricted chiefly through the fairest and most collectible of all taxes: a tax on land. Barring the rapid drift toward land monopolies and a reopening of accessibility, he predicted revolutions in Europe and America that would begin among the dispossessed peoples of their growing and spreading urban areas. Thus spoke the frail,

Henry George. (Library of Congress)

bald, but bearded, mustachioed, flashing-eyed "Prophet of San Francisco," a man by then inspiring pragmatic land reform movements.

In 1879, George published *Progress and Poverty: An Inquiry into the Causes of Industrial Depressions, and of Increase of Want with Increase of Wealth—The Remedy*. Injustices were explicit in the subtitle. The remedy was nationalization of land and imposition of one single tax (later known as the "Single Tax"). Land values, George argued, as personal knowledge of stark contrasts between extraordinary wealth and dire need in San Francisco and New York convinced him, were communal, societal creations inherent in the scarcity of land. Pressures of population, production necessities, or monopolistic urges thus raised land and rental values and depressed wages. The mere possession of land often made millionaires of nonproducers or noncontributors to human welfare. A tax, therefore, on such socially created rents would allow government to redistribute such gains to alleviate want and enhance community life. George was no socialist. Indeed, because the basis of local revenues was a general property tax and because George abhorred centralization over local responsibilities, he expected local governments to fulfill these necessary functions.

Progress and Poverty earned for George international fame even greater than the fame he was enjoying at home. In 1880, he moved to New York City, there to write, lecture, and carry his message abroad. He was active among reformers, land restoration leaguers, and labor and economic circles in England and Ireland in 1882 and again in England and Scotland (with particular success in the latter) in 1884. By the end of the 1880's, he had been active on the Continent as well as in Australia. In fact, he had, with some justice, come to believe that *Progress and Poverty* was the most influential work of its kind since Adam Smith's *The Wealth of Nations* (1776). Even Karl Marx, while critical, regarded George's work as a significant assault upon economic orthodoxy.

Inevitably George's prominence brought him into the political forum. After the Civil War and Reconstruction era, he had returned to the Democratic Party, though not uncritically. Although many reformers championed him for the nation's and for New York State's highest political offices, he either avoided selection or lost the votes. In fact, it was the politics of New York City that claimed him. His prolabor positions were well known. So too were his urban progressive reforms: an end to bossism, municipal ownership of utilities, and the secret ballot, among others. His idea for a single tax and his other eco-

nomic proposals, such as free trade and antipoverty activities, also had wide currency.

Attuned to rural dissents, George was recognized also for his awareness that the future of the United States lay with the consciences of its growing urban citizenry. Nominated by New York's Central Labor Union for the mayoralty in 1886, he lost in a hotly disputed three-way race. Afterward, he continued with his mission, writing and lecturing, until he tried once more to become New York's mayor in 1897 as the candidate of the democracy of Thomas Jefferson. Indefatigable to the end, but exhausted from campaigning, he died on October 29, 1897.

SIGNIFICANCE

No American reformer loomed larger in his generation nationally and internationally than Henry George. *Progress and Poverty* was widely translated and received a degree of attention that few other books ever have; it was in its time far more influential than the first volume of Karl Marx's *Das Kapital* (1867). George's idealism and devotion to democracy, though professional economists found his single-tax idea flawed, did more to shake economic thinking by directing it to profound social and related political problems than anyone else's.

In a narrow economic sense, George came close to developing the idea of marginal productivity. More practically, his ideas linked land questions with taxation and helped spawn tax reforms that were placed in effect not only in parts of the United States but also in Canada and Australia. If George represented popular radicalism, his roots were natively American, drawing from the best of the Jeffersonian and Jacksonian traditions. He was firmly procapitalist and a believer in fair competition. Despite flirtations with socialism, he had little regard for any type of governmental centralization. Rather, the somewhat utopian visions of democracy in which he placed his faith emphasized local government and local responsibilities. Finally, as he carried his ideas into the heart of the world's greatest city, his forceful Christianity influenced most major reformers of the Progressive era that followed his death.

—Clifton K. Yearley and Kerrie L. MacPherson

FURTHER READING

Barker, Charles Albro. *Henry George*. New York: Oxford University Press, 1955. The richest, most exhaustively researched, perhaps definitive biography. Coverage is meticulously chronological, but Barker makes his own careful evaluations of George's development and ideas, both in the context of his time and in historical perspective.

DeMille, Anna George. *Henry George: Citizen of the World*. Edited by Don C. Shoemaker. Chapel Hill: University of North Carolina Press, 1950. George's daughter concentrates upon her father as a family man and devotes more attention to her mother's role than is to be found in any other work.

Dorfman, Joseph. *The Economic Mind in American Civilization*. Vol. 3. New York: Viking Press, 1959. Chapter 6 places George, with depth and excellence, in a context of the economic history of Popular Radicalism between 1865 and 1918.

Geiger, George Raymond. *The Philosophy of Henry George*. New York: Macmillan, 1933. A close, if pedantic and somewhat ahistorical analysis. Stresses George's pragmatism.

George, Henry. *Henry George: Collected Journalistic Writings*. 4 vols. Edited by Kenneth C. Wenzer. Armonk, N.Y.: M. E. Sharpe, 2003. This four-volume collection brings together all of George's journalistic writings, with annotations for each writing and introductions to each volume. Vol. 1 contains his earliest writings plus a never-before published biography written in 1884; vols. 2 and 3 contain writings from the 1880's and 1890's, respectively; vol. 4 contains writings he produced while visiting Australia in 1890.

George, Henry, Jr. *The Life of Henry George by His Son*. 2 vols. Garden City, N.Y.: Doubleday, Page, 1911. Reprint. New York: AMS Press, 1973. Much material later incorporated in George, Jr.'s *The Complete Works of Henry George*. 10 vols. Garden City, N.Y.: Fels Fund Library Edition, 1906-1911. An associate of his father from his adolescence onward, George, Jr., later a congressman, faithfully reflects paternal decisions and ideas in this memoir.

Hill, Malcolm. *The Man Who Said No! The Life of Henry George*. London: Othila Press, 1997. Brief (147-page) biography covering George's ideas and the major events in his life. Although it does not contain any new information or insights, the book provides a good introduction to George.

Nock, Albert Jay. *Henry George, an Essay*. New York: William Morrow, 1939. A brilliant analysis of George's character and mind.

Seligman, Edwin R. A. *Essays in Taxation*. 9th rev. ed. New York: Macmillan, 1921. Still readily available, this work by the foremost American authority on taxation concludes that on political, social, economic, and moral grounds, the single tax was a mistake. However, Seligman freely acknowledges its great usefulness in drawing attention to abuses of medieval land systems abroad, to inequities in the general property tax in the United States, and to unjust privilege.

Thomas, John L. "Utopia for an Urban Age: Henry George, Henry Demarest Lloyd, Edward Bellamy." *Perspectives in American History* 6 (1974): 135-166. A lucid comparison of George's utopian strains with those of two famous contemporaries.

SEE ALSO: Samuel Gompers; Karl Marx.

RELATED ARTICLES in *Great Events from History: The Nineteenth Century, 1801-1900:* January 24, 1848: California Gold Rush Begins; 1867: Marx Publishes *Das Kapital*; December 8, 1886: American Federation of Labor Is Founded.

THÉODORE GÉRICAULT
French painter

Géricault helped to move French art away from neoclassicism, which was the dominant form between the revolutionary and Napoleonic eras, into new, more modern directions. Nineteenth century Romantic and realistic painters alike claimed to have been inspired by his work.

BORN: September 26, 1791; Rouen, France
DIED: January 26, 1824; Paris, France
ALSO KNOWN AS: Jean-Louis-André-Théodore
Géricault (full name)
AREA OF ACHIEVEMENT: Art

EARLY LIFE

Jean-Louis-André-Théodore Géricault (zhay-ree-koh) was a descendant of a respectable Norman line. His father, Georges-Nicolas Géricault, a prosperous lawyer and later businessperson, was forty-eight at the birth of his only child. His mother, Louise-Jeanne-Marie (née Caruel), had turned thirty-nine.

The Géricaults moved to Paris around 1796. Théodore soon entered boarding school and in 1806 commenced study at the Lycée Impérial, an academy known for its fine, classical education. Only an average student, he nevertheless showed artistic talent. Théodore also was fortunate to have been taught by Pierre Bouillon, winner of the 1797 Grand Prix de Rome. Géricault later competed for this government-sponsored award, which carried with it art study in Italy.

The death of his mother in 1808 caused Théodore to reconsider his circumstances. It also brought him closer to home: Théodore decided that he had had enough of academic training and decided to live with Georges-Nicolas. Furthermore, his mother's large estate and his father's business interests allowed the young man to devote himself wholly to art, without concern for finances. One obstacle remained: Georges-Nicolas objected to Théodore's career pursuit. With moral support from his maternal uncle, Jean-Baptiste Caruel, the younger Géricault allegedly went to work but actually entered the studio of Carle Vernet. Thus, Géricault eased his way into art.

LIFE'S WORK

According to the professional codes of the day, enrollment in a master's studio was the first of many steps toward status as a painter. Géricault's affinity for Vernet, primarily an equestrian artist, appears logical: One of

Géricault's first actions after the death of his mother had been to buy a horse.

As a teacher, Vernet ran a loose studio, providing his own atmosphere and personal warmth but little artistic direction. Géricault nevertheless maintained a lifelong enthusiasm for both riding and equestrian art. The early twentieth century Parisian critic Louis Dimier ventured, "Only when it came to horses did he paint to perfection." This verdict is open to much scrutiny. It may be more accurate to say that Géricault took equestrian painting from a rather stodgy, still form and gave it life, placing the animals in motion and illustrating their diverse work and sporting roles. To do that, he frequently employed gouache or watercolor washes with brown ink or pencil on beige paper. However, Géricault used oils for his larger, more ambitious works.

After spending roughly two years in Vernet's studio, Géricault may have felt the need for a more rigorous, professional approach. He then became affiliated with Pierre-Narcisse Guérin, a painter who had attained considerable renown in his day and owed inspiration to the revered Jacques-Louis David. A method instructor, Guérin required his students—Eugène Delacroix also was one of them—to paint antiquarian and heavenly subjects. Géricault, however, asserted his individuality. During a particular session, he first began to copy, then radically alter, the composition of his master's work. When queried by a perturbed Guérin, the younger artist allegedly responded, "I had taken it into my head to inject some energy into it, and you can imagine how that turned out." Géricault stayed with the classical painter for only eleven months, into 1811. He then studied independently, frequenting the Louvre. Most authorities admit that the young artist was influenced by the warm colors, brush techniques, and lifelike images of Peter-Paul Rubens, Titian, and the Italian masters.

If scholars disagree on Géricault's style, perhaps this stems from the fact that contemporary French society underwent many changes quickly—from the turbulent Revolution to the Napoleonic conquests to the restoration of the Bourbon monarchy. Some of the democratic ideals advocated during the Revolution, for example, harked back to classical Greece and Rome; hence, the philosophical commitment and tremendous popularity of the neoclassicist David. Napoleon I, on the other hand, sought to ennoble his own image and contributions. In 1810, the emperor identified two thematic classifications—

historic and current—by which the government-sponsored Salon was to judge its art competition. Napoleon also brought to Paris cultural riches from his far-flung conquered lands, rendering the Louvre a truly eclectic treasure chest. Thus, Géricault benefited from a much broader exposure than did, for example, David.

If influences were widening, the attainment of status followed an established track. Géricault therefore enrolled in the École des Beaux Arts and, because of his affiliation, began to enter competitions. Certainly the largest and best known of these, the Salon, accepted his *Charging Chasseur* for its 1812 exhibition. Géricault's work depicted a mounted officer of the Imperial Guard, poised for action. Although executed quickly, it won critical acclaim, more so, in fact, than any of Géricault's subsequent Salon showings. The *Charging Chasseur*—with its warm colors and effective sense of light and motion—also emphasized the artist's interest in military subjects.

Two years later, the Salon displayed both the *Charging Chasseur* and a new creation, the *Wounded Cuirassier* (1814). Reception this time proved to be rather poor. The less buoyant tone of the *Wounded Cuirassier* followed Napoleon's military losses, but the critical ambivalence also may be attributed to stylistic

Théodore Géricault. (Library of Congress)

factors and disappointment over the painting's failure to fulfill expectations.

In 1816, Géricault vied for the top award: the Prix de Rome. When he did not capture the honors, he decided to finance his own studies in Italy. Personal as well as art-related reasons motivated him: Géricault had become involved with Alexandrine-Modeste de Saint-Martin Caruel, his uncle's young wife. Perhaps the painter was depressed over this relationship, or maybe he sought foreign refuge before the family became embroiled in a full-fledged scandal. His affair with Alexandrine, continuing after his return from Italy, never proved to be happy, although it produced one son, Georges-Hippolyte, in 1818.

Géricault's Italian odyssey lasted for a year, during which time he became entranced with the work of Michelangelo and other masters. The youthful painter also witnessed a uniquely Roman event, the riderless horse race of Barberi, which meshed his artistic and equestrian interests. Although Géricault rendered many sketches of this intended life-size project, it remained unfinished. Most authorities agree that the tall, slender, handsome painter—with his curly reddish-blond hair and deep-set eyes—was suffering from a lack of confidence. The artistic grandeur of Rome possibly aggravated his perceived inadequacies.

Returning to France in September, 1817, Géricault resumed his friendship with Horace Vernet, the son of his former teacher and an artist in his own right. It was under Vernet's influence that Géricault first produced lithographs, again using military subjects as a theme. However, the works hardly sold. Knowing of Géricault's financial independence, his art publisher even advised him to seek another career.

Disappointed over the lithographs and with his child on the way, Géricault spent eighteen intensive months preparing the most important work of his life, *The Raft of the Medusa* (1818-1819), which was based on a controversial contemporary event. A government frigate, the *Medusa*, sank off the coast of Africa, largely because of the incompetence of its captain, who owed his commission to political patronage. The errant officer also retained the most serviceable lifeboats for himself and his friends, forcing the rest of the passengers to construct a raft from the sinking ship's parts. Of the 149 people stranded aboard the improvised vessel, only fifteen survived. Cannibalism, among other horrors, had occurred.

Géricault tackled his project in the manner of a chronicler: He interviewed the survivors and went to local hospitals and morgues to observe the dead and dying. Intensely committed to a realistic portrayal, he prepared numerous sketches. A model, possibly commenting on this frenetic process, said, "Monsieur Géricault had to have complete silence, nobody dared speak or move near him; the least thing disturbed him."

The dramatic, monumental masterpiece—measuring sixteen by twenty-four feet—appeared in the Salon of 1819 but bore the brunt of debate. Disparate factions blamed one another for the circumstances that ultimately determined the *Medusa*'s fate, and many argued about Géricault's political interpretations. Writing in typically partisan journals, art critics also viewed the painting harshly. Its dark tones and frank depiction of human torment also worked against it. Nevertheless, the Salon awarded Géricault a medal for his labor of love. One judge even commissioned him to do another painting. Fatigued from the intensive preparation and controversial aftermath of *The Raft of the Medusa*, however, Géricault transferred the proposed assignment to his friend Delacroix. French art circles may have been divided in their assessment of *The Raft of the Medusa*, but in 1820 an English gallery owner invited Géricault to show his work in London, where it was praised. The painting subsequently traveled to Dublin.

Géricault returned to Paris in December, 1821. The following year, a friend who specialized in mental disorders commissioned the artist to paint portraits of ten psychiatric patients; five of these portraits survive. Notwithstanding the radical changes in psychiatry, the series deserves respect for its realistic approach: a study of men and women with problems rather than the subhumans popularly perceived during the early nineteenth century.

A normal existence, and therefore painting, would become increasingly difficult for Géricault toward the end of his life. In 1822, he suffered two falls while horseback riding. Undaunted, he continued to pursue his favorite sport and also to sketch more advanced versions of *African Slave Trade* (1823) and *Liberation of the Prisoners of the Spanish Inquisition* (1823). Both of these paintings took an enlightened view; the second was critical of the restored Bourbon monarchy.

Géricault never allowed his wounds to heal properly. By 1823, the riding injuries caused his spine to deteriorate. Doctors operated several times but ultimately failed to save him. Géricault died on January 26, 1824, at the age of thirty-two.

SIGNIFICANCE

The three paintings that Théodore Géricault exhibited during his lifetime currently hang in the Louvre, testimony to his endurance as an artist. When his studio was cleared for sale ten months after his death, many works surfaced, far more than had been known to exist.

Géricault likely doubted his compositional and drawing skills and, therefore, sketched numerous life studies before proceeding with a master painting. Once confident of his ability to portray people and events realistically, he added the motion, lighting effects, and drama that often characterize him as a Romantic. If experts disagree on Géricault's style, they also ponder his social consciousness. The artist, in his later years, expanded his repertoire from military and equestrian themes to controversial political subjects and studies of the downtrodden. During his British tenure, for example, he sketched a public hanging, a paralytic woman, and an impoverished man. Géricault nevertheless became increasingly enamored of the relatively highbrow, distinctly English, equestrian crowd.

The artist's premature death left his life open to speculation and, occasionally, legend. Yet, from 1824 through much of the twentieth century, various patrons of the arts—collectors, gallery owners, scholars, and museum directors—have shown consistent interest in what now appear to be his prodigious efforts.

—*Lynn C. Kronzek*

FURTHER READING

Alhadeff, Albert. *The Raft of the Medusa: Géricault, Art, and Race*. Munich, Germany: Prestel, 2002. Alhadeff analyzes this artwork, describing how it reflects early abolitionist sentiment and was one of the first times a work of European art used a black figure to symbolize the hopes of all humanity.

Canaday, John. *The Lives of the Painters*. Vol. 3 in *Neoclassic to Post-Impressionist*. New York: W. W. Norton, 1969. A chapter describing the classic-Romantic schism in France contains a short synopsis of Géricault's life and creative output. The painter appears as a prominent force, whose work embodied a number of nineteenth century trends.

Eitner, Lorenz. *Géricault*. Los Angeles: Los Angeles County Museum of Art, 1971. Text accompanies this catalog of 125 paintings (plates) displayed during a 1971 exhibition. The introductory chapter mostly discusses the posthumous fame and changing perceptions of Géricault's art. Also includes a ten-page timeline and a table of exhibitions and literature.

_____. *Géricault: His Life and Work*. Ithaca, N.Y.: Cornell University Press, 1982. Fusing biography and art history, nearly four hundred pages yield a comprehensive study of Géricault. Extremely useful for assessing the creative process: how his original ideas and subject matter changed during the course of a painting. Contains many color and black-and-white plates.

Grigsby, Darcy Grimaldo. *Extremities: Painting Empire in Post-Revolutionary France*. New Haven, Conn.: Yale University Press, 2002. Analyzes six paintings by four artists, including Géricault's *The Raft of the Medusa*. Grigsby argues these paintings depict the history and politics of the French colonial empire, an empire that forced painters who previously advocated freedom to depict slavery and cultural and racial differences.

Grunchec, Philippe. *Géricault's Horses: Drawings and Watercolors*. New York: Vendome Press, 1985. Although more than an equestrian artist, Géricault elevated the genre to new heights and broadened its dimensions. This book examines horse painting as the primary nexus between the master's career and outside life. Contains a bibliography, a chronology of exhibitions, and numerous plates, most of which are in color.

_____. *Master Drawings by Géricault*. Washington, D.C.: International Exhibitions Foundation, 1985. Heavily illustrated with reproductions of Géricault's sketches, this work seeks to demonstrate his stylistic

and thematic tendencies. Text also discusses friends and other artists who influenced him, as well as the posthumous dispersal of his art. Contains a timeline and a well-annotated list of paintings.

Lethève, Jacques. *Daily Life of French Artists in the Nineteenth Century*. Translated by Hilary E. Paddon. New York: Praeger, 1972. The book offers insights into how artists lived, executed and marketed their work, and gained recognition. Students of Géricault will find several interesting details and quotations, but the most important contribution is an understanding of the institutions (such as the Salon) that made an impact upon his professional career. Contains notes, a bibliography, and illustrations.

Whitney, Wheelock. *Géricault in Italy*. New Haven, Conn.: Yale University Press, 1997. Whitney creates a detailed account of Géricault's year in Italy (1817) with emphasis on the works produced during this time and the influence the trip had on his later career.

SEE ALSO: Jacques-Louis David; Eugène Delacroix; Jean-Auguste-Dominique Ingres; Napoleon I.

RELATED ARTICLE in *Great Events from History: The Nineteenth Century, 1801-1900:* October-December, 1830: Delacroix Paints *Liberty Leading the People*.

SOPHIE GERMAIN
French mathematician

Germain overcame the limits of a haphazard education and a variety of social and institutional impediments to make fundamental advances in the proof of Fermat's last theorem and in the physics of elasticity. Those achievements represent the most original and significant contribution to mathematics by any woman before the end of the nineteenth century.

BORN: April 1, 1776; Paris, France
DIED: June 27, 1831; Paris, France
ALSO KNOWN AS: Marie-Sophie Germain (full name); Sophia Germain
AREA OF ACHIEVEMENT: Mathematics

EARLY LIFE
Sophie Germain (zhayr-mehn) was born Marie-Sophie Germain, the daughter of Ambroise-François Germain, a prosperous French silk merchant. All that is known of her

mother is the latter's name: Marie-Madeleine Gruguelin. Sophie also had two sisters—Marie-Madeleine, who was six years older, and Angélique-Ambroise, who was three years younger. That she shared the given name "Marie" with her mother and older sister probably explains her lifelong use of "Sophie" by itself. Destined to lead conventional lives of Parisian upper-middle-class women, both of Sophie's sisters married prominent professional men. In contrast to her sisters, Sophie never married, and her life was anything but conventional.

In 1789, the year of the French Revolution, Sophie's father was elected to the Estates General that King Louis XVI had been forced to convene. Over the next two years, the family shop and home was a center of political discussion. The earliest account of Sophie's life by her friend and fellow mathematician Guglielmo Libri-Carucci suggests that she disliked these discussions. Retreating to her father's study, she became absorbed in Jean-Etienne Montucla's *Histoire des mathématiques* (1799). In that book she discovered the story of the famous ancient Greek mathematician Archimedes, who, lost in the beauty of a geometrical demonstration and oblivious to the turmoil of the Roman conquest of Syracuse, was killed when he failed to respond to a soldier's order.

Ignoring the political drama of the revolution and the social expectations of her family, Sophie was similarly captivated by the study of mathematics. Libri-Carucci's account of her life depicts concerned parents depriving their daughter of candles and even heat, all in an effort to discourage her new interest, but all to no avail. Sophie soon taught herself Latin so she could read the works of Isaac Newton and Leonhard Euler. Eventually, her parents relented. As her father's foray into politics ended, the Germain house on the rue St. Denis increasingly played host to a company of scholars.

LIFE'S WORK

The years of the French Revolution constituted one of the most formative periods in the history of mathematics. The center of this ferment was the École Polytechnique, which opened in 1794. Its faculty included a true pantheon of late Enlightenment scientists. However, its

Sophie Germain. (The Granger Collection, New York)

classrooms excluded women. Nonetheless, an innovative pedagogy that made professors' lecture notes public and that invited student observations offered Sophie Germain an opportunity. She obtained the lecture notes from the college and, borrowing the name of a male student, Monsieur Le Blanc, she offered observations on Joseph-Louis Lagrange's mathematics lectures. It was not long before Lagrange uncovered Germain's deception, but he was so impressed with her ability he encouraged her to continue her work.

Pursuing an interest in number theory in 1798, Germain initiated a correspondence with Adrien-Marie Legendre, the author of an important recent treatise on the subject, and began to study the *Disquisitions arithmetical* that Carl Friedrich Gauss published in 1801. Again under the name M. Le Blanc, she began a correspondence with Gauss in 1804. Her identity was revealed only in the aftermath of the French-Prussian battle at Jena in October, 1806. Fearing that Gauss might suffer the same fate as Archimedes, Germain used her family connections in the French military to ensure the safety of the German mathematician.

Germain's correspondences with Legendre and Gauss are the source of the first of her two major contributions to mathematics. Around the year 1638, the French mathematician Pierre Fermat articulated a theorem while annotating a copy of the third century Greek mathematician Diophantus of Alexandria's *Arithmetica*. Fermat observed that, in contrast to the Pythagorean theorem, which holds that the square of the hypotenuse of a right triangle is equal to the sum of the squares of its other two legs, there were no solutions for the equation $x^n + y^n = z^n$ when the factor n is greater than 2. When Fermat published his notes on Diophantus's *Arithmetica* in 1670, his observation stimulated important advances in number theory. However, proof of the tantalizing intuition that it was impossible to find a cube that was the sum of two other cubes or indeed to find any number raised to a power greater than 2 that was the sum of two other numbers raised to the same power—Fermat's so-called "last theorem"—turned out to be one of the most intractable problems in the history of mathematics.

Fermat himself had offered a proof of the case $n = 4$. In 1738, Euler proved the case $n = 3$. Germain demonstrated that the conditions for the case in which n is an odd prime number, such that $2p + 1$ was also prime, were so stringent as to be virtually impossible. In short, she moved beyond proofs of singular cases to a general strategy for many cases. Modern mathematics honors her achievement by referring to those prime numbers p

in which $2p + 1$ is also prime as "Sophie Germain primes."

During 1807-1808, Germain's interests turned to applied mathematics. In 1809, the Institute of France announced a two-year prize competition for a mathematical theory of elasticity. Two years later, Germain submitted the only entry in the competition. The institute acknowledged that her "experiments presented ingenious results" but judged the rigor of her analysis inadequate and renewed the competition. Working with Lagrange, Germain again submitted the only entry in 1813. This time the institute awarded her an honorable mention but questioned the derivation of her equations from established principles of physics. Only after a second extension did the institute finally award Germain the prize, making her the first women ever to achieve such a public recognition in mathematics.

Germain did not attend the award ceremony on January 8, 1816. Some historians speculate that she wished to avoid the attendant notoriety that the event would bring to her. Other historians suggest that she was angry that the institute had made its award to her with reservations and that one of her judges, Siméon-Denis Poisson, was using her work without attribution for his own alternative theory of elasticity.

During the 1820's, Germain's friendship with the mathematician Joseph Fourier, another rival of Poisson, played a role in allowing Germain to be the first woman who was not a wife of a member to attend sessions of the French Academy of Sciences. By this time, she was increasingly writing on the philosophy of science. In her essay, "General Considerations on the Condition of the Arts and Sciences at Different Stages of their Cultivation," she—much as her younger contemporary Auguste Comte—argued that just as the natural sciences proceeded from observation and classification of phenomena through generalization and mathematical systemization, so similar progress was possible in the human sciences. Germain herself, however, was unable to contribute to this progress. On June 27, 1831, she died in Paris after a two-year battle with breast cancer.

SIGNIFICANCE

Shortly before Sophie Germain died, Gauss recommended her to the University of Göttingen for an honorary degree, but his request was refused. Germain never received a university degree, she never attended university classes, and, indeed, never seems to have had much formal education at all. Nevertheless, in number theory, she took what at that time was the single most significant

step forward in the proof of Fermat's last theorem—a theorem that was finally proved only in 1994. Likewise, in applied mathematics, it was not the model of the impeccably rigorous scientific insider Poisson that provided the foundation for the physics of elasticity but the model of the self-taught scientific outsider Sophie Germain.

The life of Sophie Germain is eloquent testimony to the difficulties women have historically faced in pursuing scientific careers. Through sheer determination, Germain was able to transcend social expectations. In the end, her parents' generosity provided her enough income to live independently. She was also able to challenge some of the institutional barriers to women in science. Through what Libri-Carucci aptly called her courage, Germain secured the support of many of the most eminent professional mathematicians of her time. However, subtle pressures always weighed on her while she worked. For example, when she was preparing her theory of elasticity and had to visit the École Polytechnique or Institute of France, she needed formal invitations and escorts. When she submitted a paper to the Academy of Sciences extending her theory in 1825, her submission was simply ignored.

Posthumous recognition has come to Germain almost as reluctantly. In 1889, when the opening of Paris's Eiffel Tower commemorated seventy-two people whose contributions to the mathematics of elasticity made possible the tower's construction, there was no mention of Sophie Germain. Thanks to the increase in interest in women's history in late twentieth century Europe, Germain's name now appears on Parisian schools and streets. However, in many standard histories of mathematics and science, the achievements of Sophie Germain are still overlooked.

—Charles R. Sullivan

FURTHER READING

Bucciarelli, Louis L., and Nancy Dworsky. *Sophie Germain: An Essay in the History of the Theory of Elasticity*. Dordrecht, Netherlands: D. Reidel, 1980. This is the only extended study in English of Germain's achievements, but Bucciarelli and Dworsky present a lifeless Germain, and their presentation of the theory of elasticity is too technical for average readers.

Dahan Dalmédico Amy. "Sophie Germain." *Scientific American* 265, no. 6 (December, 1991): 116-122. A clear, if brief, summary of Germain's career by a leading historian of mathematics.

Petrovich, Vesna Crnjanski. "Women and the Paris Academy of Sciences." *Eighteenth-Century Studies*

22, no. 3 (1999): 383-390. Places Germain in the context of the strategies that eighteenth and early nineteenth century women used to achieve recognition for their scientific work.

Singh, Simon. *Fermat's Enigma*. New York: Doubleday-Anchor, 1997. This lucid introduction to the history of Fermat's last theorem includes an appreciative discussion of Germain's contribution.

SEE ALSO: Auguste Comte; Gustave Eiffel; Joseph Fourier; Évariste Galois; Carl Friedrich Gauss; Sofya Kovalevskaya; Pierre-Simon Laplace; Countess of Lovelace; Henri Poincaré; Charlotte Angas Scott.
RELATED ARTICLES in *Great Events from History: The Nineteenth Century, 1801-1900:* 1899: Hilbert Publishes *The Foundations of Geometry*; 1900: Lebesgue Develops New Integration Theory.

GERONIMO
Native American leader

Through two decades, Geronimo was the most feared and vilified person in the Southwest, but in his old age, he became a freak attraction at fairs and expositions. His maligned and misunderstood career epitomized the troubles of a withering Apache culture struggling to survive in a hostile modern world.

BORN: June, 1829; near present-day Clifton, Arizona
DIED: February 17, 1909; Fort Sill, Oklahoma
ALSO KNOWN AS: Goyathlay (birth name)
AREA OF ACHIEVEMENT: Warfare and conquest

EARLY LIFE
Although the precise date and location of Geronimo's (jeh-RAHN-ih-moh) birth are not known, he was most likely born around June, 1929, near the head of the Gila River in a part of the Southwest then controlled by Mexico. Named Goyathlay (One Who Yawns) by his Behonkohe parents, the legendary Apache warrior later came to be called Geronimo—a name taken from the sound that terrified Mexican soldiers allegedly cried when calling on Saint Jerome to protect them from his relentless charge.

Geronimo's early life, like that of other Apache youth, was filled with complex religious ritual and ceremony. From the placing of amulets on his cradle to guard him against early death to the ceremonial putting on of the first moccasins, Geronimo's relatives prepared their infant for Apache life, teaching him the origin myths of his people and the legends of supernatural beings and benevolent mountain spirits that hid in the caverns of their homeland.

Through ritual observances and instruction, Geronimo learned about Usen, a remote and nebulous god who, though unconcerned with petty quarrels among men, was the Life Giver and provider for his people. "When Usen created the Apaches," Geronimo later asserted, "he also created their homes in the West. He gave to them such

grain, fruits, and game as they needed to eat. . . . He gave to them a climate and all they needed for clothing and shelter was at hand." Geronimo's religious heritage taught him to be self-sufficient, to love and revere his mountain homeland, and never to betray a promise made with oath and ceremony.

Geronimo grew into adulthood during a brief period of peace, a rare interlude that interrupted the chronic wars between the Apache and Mexican peoples. Even in times of peace, however, Apache culture placed a priority on the skills of warfare. Through parental instruction and childhood games, Geronimo learned how to hunt, hide, track, and shoot—necessary survival skills in an economy based upon game, wild fruits, and booty taken from neighboring peoples.

Geronimo also heard the often repeated stories of conquests of his heroic grandfather Mahko, an Apache chief renowned for his great size, strength, and valor in battle. Like his grandfather, Geronimo had unusual physical prowess and courage. Tall and slender, strong and quick, Geronimo proved at an early age to be a good provider for his mother, whom he supported following his father's premature death, and later for his bride, Alope, whom he acquired from her father for "a herd of ponies" stolen most likely from unsuspecting Mexican victims. By his early twenties, Geronimo (still called Goyathlay) was a member of the council of warriors, a proven booty taker, a husband, and a father of three.

LIFE'S WORK
In 1850, a band of Mexican scalp hunters raided an Apache camp while the warriors were away. During the ensuing massacre, Geronimo's mother, wife, and three children were slain. Shortly after this tragedy, Geronimo had a religious experience that figured prominently in his subsequent life. As he later reported the incident, while

in a trancelike state, a voice called his name four times (the magic number among the Apache) and then informed him, "No gun can ever kill you. I will take the bullets from the guns of the Mexicans, so they will have nothing but powder. And I will guide your arrows." After receiving this gift of power, Geronimo's vengeance against Mexicans was equaled by his confidence that harm would not come his way.

While still unknown to most Americans, during the 1850's, Geronimo rose among the ranks of the Apache warriors. A participant in numerous raids into Mexico, Geronimo fought bravely under the Apache chief Cochise. Although wounded on several occasions, Geronimo remained convinced that no bullet could kill him. It was during this period that he changed his name from Goyathlay to Geronimo.

War between the U.S. government and the Apache first erupted in 1861 following a kidnapping-charge incident involving Cochise. The war lingered for nearly a dozen years until Cochise and General Oliver Otis Howard signed a truce. According to the terms of the agreement, the mountain homeland of the Chiricahua (one of the tribes that made up the Apache and Geronimo's tribe) was set aside as a reservation, on which the Chiricahua promised to remain.

Following Cochise's death in 1874, the United States attempted to relocate the Chiricahua to the San Carlos Agency in the parched bottomlands of the Gila River. Although some Apache accepted relocation, Geronimo led a small band off the reservation into the Sierra Madre range in Mexico. From this base, Geronimo's warriors conducted raids into the United States, hitting wagon trains and ranches for the supplies needed for survival.

In 1877, for the first and only time in his life, Geronimo was captured by John Clum of the United States Army. After spending some time in a guardhouse in San Carlos, Geronimo was released, being told not to leave the reservation. Within a year, however, he was again in Mexico. Although a fugitive, he was blamed in the American press for virtually all crimes committed by Apache "renegades" of the reservation.

Upon the promise of protection, Geronimo voluntarily returned to the San Carlos Agency in 1879. This time, he remained two years until an unfortunate incident involving the death of Noch-ay-del-klinne, a popular Apache religious prophet, triggered another escape into the Sierra Madre. In 1882, Geronimo daringly attempted a raid into Arizona to rescue the remainder of his people on the reservation and to secure for himself reinforcements for his forces hiding in Mexico. This campaign,

Geronimo. (Library of Congress)

which resulted in the forced abduction of many unwilling Apache women and children, brought heavy losses to his band and nearly cost Geronimo his life. The newspaper coverage of the campaign also made Geronimo the most despised and feared villain in the United States.

In May, 1883, General George Crook of the United States Army crossed into Mexico in search of Geronimo. Not wanting war, Geronimo sent word to Crook of his willingness to return to the reservation if his people were guaranteed just treatment. Crook consented, and Geronimo persuaded his band to retire to San Carlos.

Geronimo, however, never adjusted to life on the reservation. Troubled by newspaper headlines demanding his execution and resentful of reservation rules (in particular, the prohibition against alcoholic drink), Geronimo in the spring of 1885 planned a final breakaway from the San Carlos Agency. With his typical ingenuity, Geronimo led his 144 followers off the reservation. Cutting telegraph lines behind him, he eluded the cavalry and crossed into Mexico, finding sanctuary in his old Sierra Madre refuge. Although pursued by an army of five thousand regulars and five hundred Apache scouts, Geronimo avoided capture until September, 1886, when he voluntarily surrendered to General Nelson Miles. (He had agreed to a surrender to General George Crook in March but had escaped his troops.)

Rejoicing that the Apache wars were over, the army loaded Geronimo and his tribesmen on railroad cars and shipped them first to Fort Pickens in Florida and then to the Mount Vernon Barracks in Alabama. Unaccustomed to the warm, humid climate, so unlike the high, dry country of their birth, thousands of the Apache captives died of tuberculosis and other diseases. In 1894, after the government rejected another appeal to allow their return to Arizona, the Kiowa and Comanche offered their former Apache foes a part of their reservation near Fort Sill, Oklahoma.

Geronimo spent the remainder of his life on the Oklahoma reservation. Adapting quickly to the white man's economic system, the aged Apache warrior survived by growing watermelons and selling his now infamous signature to curious autograph seekers. Although the government technically still viewed him as a prisoner of war, the army permitted Geronimo to attend, under guard, the international fairs and expositions at Buffalo, Omaha, and St. Louis. In 1905, Theodore Roosevelt even invited him to Washington, D.C., to attend the inaugural presidential parade. Wherever Geronimo went, he attracted great crowds and made handsome profits by selling autographs, buttons, hats, and photographs of himself.

In February, 1909, while returning home from selling bows and arrows in nearby Lawton, Oklahoma, an inebriated Geronimo fell from his horse into a creek bed. For several hours, Geronimo's body lay exposed. Three days later, the Apache octogenarian died of pneumonia. As promised, no bullet ever killed him.

SIGNIFICANCE

The Industrial Age of the late nineteenth century altered the life patterns of American farmers and entrepreneurs, women and laborers. No groups, however, were more affected by the forces of modernization than were the Native American Indians. Geronimo's tragic career as warrior and prisoner epitomized the inevitable demise of an ancient Apache culture trapped in a web of white man's history.

Although a stubbornly independent and uncompromising warrior, Geronimo symbolized to countless Americans the treacherous savagery of a vicious race that could not be trusted. Highly conscious of his wrath and unrelenting hatred, the American public never knew the deeply religious family man who yearned to abide in his mountain homeland.

During his last twenty-three years of captivity, the legend of Geronimo grew, even as the public's hatred of the once-powerful Apache mellowed into admiration. Always a good provider, Geronimo established for himself a profitable business by peddling souvenirs and performing stunts at Wild West shows. A living artifact of a world that no longer existed, Geronimo became the comic image of the tamed American Indian finally brought into white man's civilization.

—*Terry D. Bilhartz*

FURTHER READING

Adams, Alexander B. *Geronimo: A Biography.* New York: G. P. Putnam's Sons, 1971. A well-researched history of the Apache wars that contains much material on Mangas Coloradas, Cochise, and other warriors as well as Geronimo. Replete with documentation of the connivance, blunders, and savagery that characterized the removal of the Apache from their homelands, this biography exposes the limitations of General Nelson Miles and the inexperience of the white leadership in Indian affairs.

Betzinez, Jason, with Wilbur Sturtevant Nye. *I Fought with Geronimo.* Harrisburg, Pa.: Stackpole Books, 1960. Another first-hand narrative account of the Apache wars written by the son of Geronimo's first cousin. Includes stories told more than half a century after the event. An entertaining primary source, but it must be used with caution.

Brown, Dee. "Geronimo." *American History Illustrated* 15 (May, 1980): 12-21; 15 (July, 1980): 31-45. The best article-length introduction to the life of Geronimo. A lively and sympathetic overview of the career of this clever Apache warrior.

Clum, Woodworth. *Apache Agent: The Story of John P. Clum.* Boston: Houghton Mifflin, 1936. Reprint. Lincoln: University of Nebraska Press, 1978. A story of the only man who ever captured Geronimo. Written from the notes of John Clum, a man who hated Geronimo with a passion. Biased yet entertaining account.

Cozzens, Peter, ed. *Eyewitnesses to the Indian Wars, 1865-1890: The Struggle for Apacheria.* Harrisburg, Pa.: Stackpole Books, 2001-   . This book is the first in a five-volume series containing army reports, diaries, news articles, and other contemporaneous accounts of Indian wars. This volume focuses on military campaigns against the Apaches, with part five, "Chasing Geronimo, 1885-1886," containing accounts of Geronimo's escape and eventual surrender.

Davis, Britton. *The Truth About Geronimo.* New Haven, Conn.: Yale University Press, 1929, 1963. An entertaining narrative filled with humorous and thrilling incidents written by an author who spent three years in the United States Army attempting to locate and capture this Apache warrior.

Debo, Angie. *Geronimo: The Man, His Time, His Place.* Norman: University of Oklahoma Press, 1976. The best of the many Geronimo biographies. Carefully researched and documented, this balanced account portrays Geronimo neither as villain nor as hero, but as a maligned and misunderstood individual trapped in an increasingly hostile environment. Highly recommended.

Faulk, Odie B. *The Geronimo Campaign.* New York: Oxford University Press, 1969. A reassessment of the military campaign that ended with the surrender of Geronimo in 1886. Includes much information collected by the son of Lieutenant Charles B. Gatewood, who arranged the surrender and was one of the few white men Geronimo trusted.

Geronimo. *Geronimo: His Own Story.* Edited by S. M. Barrett and Frederick Turner. New York: Duffield, 1906. The personal autobiography dictated by Geronimo to Barrett in 1905. A chronicle of Geronimo's grievances, in particular against the Mexican nationals. Includes informative sections on Apache religion, methods in dealing with crimes, ceremonies, festivals, and appreciation of nature.

Kraft, Louis. *Gatewood and Geronimo.* Albuquerque: University of New Mexico Press, 2000. A biography of Geronimo and Lieutenant Charles B. Gatewood, a cavalryman posted in Arizona who was criticized by the military and civilians for his equitable treatment of Apaches.

SEE ALSO: Black Hawk; Crazy Horse; Chief Joseph; Sitting Bull.

RELATED ARTICLES in *Great Events from History: The Nineteenth Century, 1801-1900:* February 6, 1861-September 4, 1886: Apache Wars; 1890: U.S. Census Bureau Announces Closing of the Frontier.

GIA LONG
Emperor of Vietnam (r. 1802-1820)

The only Nguyen prince who survived his family's massacre by Tay Son rebels, Gia Long fought the Tay Son for twenty-five years until achieving a victory that reunified Vietnam and allowed him to found Vietnam's last imperial dynasty. While reorganizing his domain on a conservative Confucian and Chinese model, he increased its power in Southeast Asia and kept at bay Western imperialist nations. However, he was unable to spur economic growth and earned a reputation for cruelty.

BORN: February 8, 1762; Phu Xuan (now Hue), Vietnam
DIED: January 25 or February 3, 1820; Hue, Vietnam
ALSO KNOWN AS: Nguyen Phuc Anh (birth name); Nguyen Anh; Nguyen Vuong
AREAS OF ACHIEVEMENT: Government and politics, warfare and conquest

EARLY LIFE

Emperor Gia Long (zih-ah long, northern Vietnamese pronunciation; yih-ah long, southern pronunciation) was born Nguyen Phuc Anh in Phu Xuan, the capital of the Nguyen lords who ruled southern Vietnam. His father, Chuong Vo, was the legitimate heir of his grandfather Nguyen Phuc Khoat, the first Nguyen lord to become king in the south. However, when Ahn was three years old, his royal grandfather decided to disinherit his father. The grandfather then appointed his twelve-year-old son by a favorite new concubine, Nguyen Phuc Thuen, who was to rule as Denh Vuong, or King Denh.

When Anh's grandfather died in 1765, the teenage King Denh's maternal grandfather, Truong Phuc Loan, became regent. Anh's father was thrown in jail, where he died two years later, but Ahn was left alive. In 1771, while Anh was receiving the classical education that befitted a young Vietnamese noble, the Tay Son Rebellion broke out. Rebel success led to an invasion of the south by the Nguyen's northern rival, the Trenh king. Breaking a century-old peace, a Trenh army besieged Phu Xuan, where Anh lived. Even surrendering the regent did not lead the Trenh to withdraw from the south. In early 1775, the Trenh occupied Phu Xuan. Anh fled with his uncle south to Gia Denh (close to modern Saigon), only to have to flee once more, as the Tay Son looted that city before being driven out in early 1776.

LIFE'S WORK

In 1777, Nguyen Anh became the sole surviving Nguyen heir, when the Tay Son conquered Gia Denh, killing King Denh and most of Anh's Nguyen relatives. Anh escaped into the swamps near Cambodia, where in October, 1777, he was saved by Pierre Joseph Georges Pigneau de Béhaine, the Roman Catholic bishop of Adran. After the Tay Son leaders withdrew, Anh led a force that recaptured Gia Denh late in 1777. During the following year, he concluded a peace treaty with Thailand. He married, and in 1779 his first son, Nguyen Phuc Cenh, was born.

In 1780, while he was only eighteen years old, Nguyen Anh proclaimed himself king of southern Vietnam. His claim was contested by the Tay Son, whom he would fight over the next twenty-two years. At the beginning of this struggle, the Tay Son repeatedly drove Anh out of Gia Denh. By 1783, he was in Thailand with his wife, mother, sister and son. Late in 1784, he sent Cenh with Bishop Pigneau to get French military aid, and accepted the help of a Thai army to fight the Tay Son. In Vietnam, Tay Son leader Nguyen Hue defeated Anh's army on February 19, 1785. Nguyen Anh fled to Thailand but returned in August, 1787. Three months later, on November 28, 1787, Bishop Pigneau signed a treaty in Paris that would give France military bases and commercial privileges in Vietnam in exchange for giving Anh military aid.

After Nguyen Anh captured Gia Denh in September, 1788, France decided not to honor its treaty with him. Bishop Pigneau gathered a private army and landed with two warships in Vietnam on July 24, 1789. With his southern base secure, Nguyen Anh fought a seasonal war from 1790 to 1799, sailing north in spring and returning in autumn. He also welcomed Laotian aid. In July, 1799, Ahn's son Cenh took Qui Nhon, and on October 9, Bishop Pigneau died there of dysentery. The Tay Son besieged the city in April, 1800. In February, 1801, Anh defeated the Tay Son fleet, while Cenh died of a fever. On June 15, 1801, Anh suddenly captured Phu Xuan. As Qui Nhon fell to the Tay Son army, in September, 1801, the Tay Son forces were encircled. A desperate counterattack in March, 1802, failed, and they fled north.

On June 1, 1802, Nguyen Anh celebrated his victory and opened the Gia Long era, which combined the names of the southern capital city, Gia Denh (Saigon), and the northern capital Thang Long (Hanoi). Western historians generally call Anh "Emperor Gia Long" from that moment, but he was actually ruling as king.

On July 22, 1802, Anh captured Thang Long. The captured Tay Son emperor had to witness Anh's soldiers digging up the bones of Nguyen Hue and his brother and

urinating on them before he himself was torn to pieces. The wife and daughter of the Tay Son general who had retaken Qui Nhon were stripped naked and publicly crushed to death. Afterward, Nguyen Anh made Phu Xuan his capital, naming it Hue. In 1803, the Chinese government recognized his government. He opened a mint and the National College at Hue and began issuing a new coinage. In 1804, he officially changed the name of his country from Dai Viet to Viet Nam. In his relations with Westerners, he remained cautious and did not give a trading post to the British in 1804.

In June, 1802, Anh assumed the name of Gia Long and proclaimed himself emperor of Vietnam. He then set about reorganizing his government along centralized lines. From the earlier Le emperors he adopted a system of six ministries. He created twenty-seven provinces, and updated land and population records. He kept a standing army of 113,000 men, 42,000 of whom were French trained, and 200 war elephants. His navy had 18,800 men. In 1812, he instituted a conservative law code that replaced the more progressive Heng Dec code, which had been in effect since 1483. The 398 articles of the Gia Long code were based on a Confucian Chinese model that was harsh on women's rights and adequately adjusted to the needs of Vietnamese society.

In 1813, Gia Long intervened in Cambodia, leaving 1,000 Vietnamese soldiers in Phnom Penh. Meanwhile, he was growing weary of the increasing French presence in Vietnam. When the French warship *Cybele* arrived at Da Neng on December 30, 1817, to inquire about France's treaty with him, Gia Long refused to meet its commander and indicated that he considered the treaty invalidated.

Gia Long decided to appoint his son by a favorite concubine as heir. He chose Nguyen Phuc Dem because of his strong Confucian beliefs, distrust of Europeans and rejection of Christianity. His son reigned as Emperor Minh Mang.

Gia Long died in Hue on either January 25 or February 3 of 1820. With his wife and concubines, among them Ngec Bich, the youngest daughter of the last Le emperor and former wife of the Tay Son emperor whom Gia Long had had executed, Gia Long had thirteen sons and eighteen daughters.

SIGNIFICANCE

During a struggle of twenty-five years, Gia Long defeated the Tay Son and reunified Vietnam. He also founded a dynasty that would last until the abdication of Vietnam's last emperor in 1955. Nevertheless, his national legacy is disputed. His deep conservatism and favoring of Confucian philosophy that legitimizes imperial and patriarchal rule led to the promulgation of a law code, which was used until 1880, that took away women's rights and tried to impose a Chinese system on Vietnamese society. His alliance with foreigners is seen as problematical by modern Vietnamese historians. Using Thai soldiers to fight his Vietnamese enemies nearly ruined Vietnam.

Gia Long's friendship with the French bishop Pigneau gave him access to Western military science and medicine. However, had his treaty with France become effective, the French would have gained Vietnamese land. The conservative economic policies of Gia Long did not promote modernization. Instead, they established state monopolies and based tax and labor burdens solely on the backs of peasants and commoners. Gia Long's military was strong in Southeast Asia, and he manufactured modern guns for his navy. However, his military strategies remained conservative and static, and Vietnam eventually fell behind European and American advances.

After Gia Long died, his chosen successor, Minh Mang, quickly killed the wife and children of his dead stepbrother, Cenh. Throughout his own reign, which lasted until 1840, he lived up to his father's trust to keep out Westerners and reject Christianity. However, his rule increasingly clashed with his people. Although Gia Long's reign saw seventy-three recorded instances of uprisings and riots, that number more than tripled to 234 during his son's reign.

—*R. C. Lutz*

FURTHER READING

Chapuis, Oscar. *A History of Vietnam*. Westport, Conn.: Greenwood Press, 1995. Discusses Gia Long's life in detail, beginning in the context of the Tay Son rebellion when he was still Nguyen Anh, and devotes a substantial part of one chapter to his reign. Contains useful maps.

Hall, Daniel George. *A History of Southeast Asia*. 4th ed. London: Macmillan Press, 1981. Still a standard work on the period, this general history's chapter 24 thoroughly covers Gia Long's life, arguing that he was no innovator as emperor.

Karnow, Stanley. *Vietnam: A History*. 2d ed. New York: Viking Press, 1997. Still the most widely available source in English, this story places Gia Long's fight and reign in the context of rising European influence in Vietnam, focusing also on his French advisers. Includes a useful chronology.

Lamb, Helen. *Vietnam's Will to Live*. New York: Monthly Review Press, 1972. Chapters 3 and 4 deal with Nguyen Anh's use of French help to fight the Tay Son; his later disenchantment with the French is seen in the context of Vietnamese resistance to European colonialization.

Li, Tana. *Nguyen Cochinchina*. Ithaca, N.Y.: Cornell University Press, 1998. Thorough discussion of the heterogeneous society of southern Vietnam where Gia Long was born and which served as his base while fighting the Tay Son rebellion, which is described as a local uprising against deteriorating Nguyen rule.

SEE ALSO: Ho Xuan Huong; Tu Duc.

RELATED ARTICLES in *Great Events from History: The Nineteenth Century, 1801-1900:* August, 1858: France and Spain Invade Vietnam; April, 1882-1885: French Indochina War.

JAMES GIBBONS
American Roman Catholic cleric

The most influential American archbishop of the late nineteenth century Roman Catholic Church, Gibbons helped establish Catholicism as an important and vital religion in modern American society.

BORN: July 23, 1834; Baltimore, Maryland
DIED: March 24, 1921; Baltimore, Maryland
AREA OF ACHIEVEMENT: Religion and theology

EARLY LIFE

James Gibbons was the eldest son in a family of five children. His parents, Thomas Gibbons and Bridget (Walsh) Gibbons, were Irish immigrants. When James was three, his family returned to Ireland because of his father's poor health. They resettled in New Orleans in 1853, six years after his father's death. Upon his return to the United States, Gibbons worked as a clerk in a grocery store for two years. In 1855, he entered Saint Charles College, Ellicott City, Maryland. He moved on to Saint Mary's Seminary in his native Baltimore in 1857 and was ordained a priest of the Roman Catholic Church on June 30, 1861.

Throughout the Civil War, Gibbons pastored various congregations in the Chesapeake Bay area. In addition, he served as a volunteer chaplain at Forts McHenry and Marshall. His dedicated service earned for him much public admiration, and he was one of only three Catholic priests invited to pay their respects when the body of the assassinated President Abraham Lincoln passed through Baltimore.

Following the war, Gibbons's influence in the Roman Catholic Church rapidly increased. In 1865, he was appointed secretary to the archbishop of Baltimore. A year later, he became assistant chancellor for that archdiocese. Gibbons was consecrated as bishop of North Carolina in 1868 and in the following year attended the Vatican I Council in Rome as the youngest bishop among the more than seven hundred in attendance. In 1872, Gibbons assumed the duties of the vacant Richmond see in addition to retaining his responsibilities in North Carolina. Despite the extraordinary demands on his time, he wrote his best-known work, *The Faith of Our Fathers* (1877), in 1876. This extremely popular book, written for the general public, presented an explanation and defense of Catholicism.

Photographs of Gibbons reveal an individual of slight but well-defined physical features, with a calm and peaceful demeanor. His unassuming appearance did not indicate the acumen and depth of the spiritual resources that enabled him to provide decisive leadership to the Catholic Church in the United States during the most volatile period in its history.

LIFE'S WORK

In 1877, at the age of forty-three, Gibbons became the ninth archbishop of Baltimore—a position he would hold until his death in 1921. The oldest archdiocese in the United States, it was also the most prestigious. Such a position made Gibbons the unofficial leader of American Catholics.

Gibbons was a highly effective administrator and spiritual leader, although he did not gain national attention until he presided over the Third Plenary Council in Baltimore in 1884. The council brought together American bishops and archbishops to enact legislation on doctrine, ecclesiastical governance, and parochial education. A major accomplishment of the council was the establishment of Catholic University in Washington, D.C. There, Gibbons provided distinguished leadership as both its first chancellor and its principal advocate.

Gibbons's work at the Third Plenary Council was highly acclaimed. He had diplomatically avoided many controversial social issues that would bitterly divide conservative and liberal Catholics throughout the remainder of the nineteenth century. His efforts prompted Pope Leo XIII to make Gibbons a cardinal in 1886. With this rapid rise to national prominence, Gibbons was thrust into the role of resolving a number of social issues. With the aid of his principal allies, Archbishop John Ireland and Bishop John J. Keane, Gibbons faced the pressing problems of organized labor and immigration.

Because of the deplorable working conditions of late nineteenth century America—for example, twelve-hour workdays and inadequate wages—the Knights of Labor was formed in 1869 to establish various labor unions. Its goals were primarily to limit working hours, improve working conditions, and increase wages. Because labor organizers were routinely fired by their employers, however, the membership and activities of the Knights of Labor became secretive. The pope had declared that membership in an organization requiring secret oaths and activities was incompatible with the Catholic faith. For this reason, as well as fear of socialist tendencies, conservative Catholic leaders opposed the Knights of Labor. In 1884, Cardinal Elzéar Taschereau of Quebec obtained a ruling from the Vatican forbidding Catholics to belong to the labor organization. Conservatives argued that the ruling included the United States as well.

Gibbons fought for the laborers. He maintained that the prohibition applied only to Quebec and that it would be wrong for the Catholic Church to oppose the American labor movement. Although Gibbons and his liberal allies admired the achievements of capitalism, they believed that adequate wages, improved working conditions, and shorter working hours were demanded by the principles of Christian charity and justice. Furthermore, Gibbons warned that condemnation of the Knights of Labor would create an unnecessary conflict of conscience for Catholic laborers. A Catholic would be forced to choose between a union and the Church. Because the goals of the labor movement were just, Gibbons argued, opposition was uncalled for.

Gibbons backed a series of strikes in 1886 and a year later presented the pope with a lengthy document defending the Knights of Labor. In 1888, the Vatican removed

its ban on the organization. This reversal represented a major victory for Gibbons and set a precedent for strong Catholic support of labor reform in the following years.

The great wave of immigration in the nineteenth century created a second pressing issue for Gibbons. During this time, the Catholic population in the United States increased from three million in 1860 to more than twelve million by 1895. This rapid growth inspired strong anti-Catholic sentiments within American society, as seen in the formation of such organizations as the Know-Nothing Party (1854) and the American Protective Association (1887). These groups claimed that Catholic teachings opposed democracy and the separation of church and state, and they feared that priests would instruct their parishioners on how to vote based on orders from the Vatican. American society, they declared, was being attacked from an outside religious force.

Although such claims bore minimal influence on public opinion, they did create problems concerning how Catholics viewed their participation in American life. These attacks emphasized the ethnic differences that already existed among Catholics. For example, German Catholics tended to be rural, midwestern, and conservative, whereas Irish Catholics tended to be urban, eastern, and liberal. In response to these tensions, conservative Catholics began viewing American society as largely Protestant and hostile. They maintained that Catholics should not accommodate themselves to the larger culture but should preserve their religious and ethnic identity through traditional beliefs and customs.

Gibbons fought both the anti-Catholic claims and the conservative position. He countered that Catholicism was not opposed to democracy and could flourish in a nation where church and state were legally separated. He believed that Catholics could, and must, simultaneously be good citizens and faithful members of the Church. As a liberal, he argued that Catholics must adapt to the American situation rather than preserve their traditional beliefs and ethnic customs. Catholics should be assimilated into American society by actively participating in its social, political, and educational institutions.

The liberal position that Gibbons advocated was popularly titled "Americanism."

James Gibbons. (Library of Congress)

It was loudly condemned as heretical by its opponents and acclaimed as progressive by its supporters. The debate, however, was not decisive, because in 1895 Pope Leo XIII both praised the liberty of the Catholic Church in the United States and questioned whether the separation of church and state was the most desirable situation. Although Gibbons had not won a clear victory, he clearly set the pattern for full Catholic participation in an increasingly pluralistic American society.

SIGNIFICANCE

The lengthy career of this distinguished religious leader reflected the changing, often turbulent, character of American society at the close of the nineteenth century and beginning of the twentieth century. Gibbons's concern over labor and immigration reflected the problems of a nation that was simultaneously becoming prosperous and ethnically diverse. He brought a strong religious and moral commitment to the pressing political, economic, and social issues of his day.

Gibbons's range of interests was quite broad. He was routinely consulted on church-state issues and provided advice to a variety of political leaders. Often invited to preach in Protestant churches, he worked toward improving relations between different religions and participated in the World Parliament of Religions in Chicago in 1893. The patriotism of Gibbons was unparalleled as he helped establish the National Catholic War Council at U.S. entry into World War I in 1917. His tireless will helped not only Catholics but all Americans as well to define the national character at a crucial time in history.

—*Brent Waters*

FURTHER READING

Browne, Henry J. *The Catholic Church and the Knights of Labor*. Washington, D.C.: Catholic University of America Press, 1949. Reprint. New York: Arno Press, 1976. Close examination of the Knights of Labor controversy within the Roman Catholic Church. Particular attention is directed toward the role Gibbons played in changing his church's position on the labor organization.

Cross, Robert D. *The Emergence of Liberal Catholicism in America*. Cambridge, Mass.: Harvard University Press, 1958. A comprehensive overview of the various controversies between conservative and liberal Catholics in late nineteenth and early twentieth century America.

Dolan, Jay P. *The Immigrant Church*. Baltimore: Johns Hopkins University Press, 1977. Reprint. Notre Dame, Ind.: University of Notre Dame Press, 1983. Although this book concentrates on issues that divided German and Irish Catholics living in New York City during the mid-nineteenth century, it provides a good framework for understanding the various ethnic and immigrant issues that Gibbons and the Church faced.

Ellis, John Tracy. *American Catholicism*. Chicago: University of Chicago Press, 1956. An excellent concise introduction to the history of Catholicism in the United States.

Gibbons, James Cardinal. *A Retrospect of Fifty Years*. Baltimore: John Murphy, 1916. Reprint. New York: Arno Press, 1972. An autobiographical recounting of the major events that shaped the author's career.

McAvoy, Thomas T. *The Great Crisis in American Catholic History, 1895-1900*. Chicago: Henry Regnery, 1957. An extensive and excellent inquiry into the Americanism controversy.

_____, ed. *Roman Catholicism and the American Way of Life*. Notre Dame, Ind.: University of Notre Dame Press, 1960. A series of essays written by both Catholics and Protestants that review and evaluate the role of Catholicism in early twentieth century American society.

Marty, Martin E. *Pilgrims in Their Own Land*. Boston: Little, Brown, 1984. Reviews the history of various religions in the United States. The chapter "Adapting to America" provides a concise and helpful framework for understanding the immigration and labor issues of the late nineteenth century.

Spalding, Thomas W. *The Premier See: A History of the Archdiocese of Baltimore, 1789-1989*. Baltimore: Johns Hopkins University Press, 1989. A history of the archdiocese, covering its growth, tensions, politics, and how it influenced American Catholicism. Part 3, "The Gibbons Church, 1877-1921," offers an extensive description of Gibbons's activities as archbishop.

SEE ALSO: Frances Xavier Cabrini; Leo XIII; Daniel Mannix.

RELATED ARTICLE in *Great Events from History: The Nineteenth Century, 1801-1900:* December 8, 1869-October 20, 1870: Vatican I Decrees Papal Infallibility Dogma.

JOSIAH WILLARD GIBBS
American physical scientist

Gibbs established the theoretical basis for modern physical chemistry by quantifying the second law of thermodynamics and developing heterogeneous thermodynamics. This and other work earned for him recognition as the greatest American scientist of the nineteenth century.

BORN: February 11, 1839; New Haven, Connecticut
DIED: April 28, 1903; New Haven, Connecticut
ALSO KNOWN AS: J. Willard Gibbs
AREAS OF ACHIEVEMENT: Chemistry, physics

EARLY LIFE

Josiah Willard Gibbs, later known usually as J. Willard Gibbs—to distinguish him from his father, who bore the same name—was the fourth child and son among five children of J. W. Gibbs, a professor of sacred literature at Yale College Theological Seminary, and Mary Anna Van Cleve Gibbs. Born in New Haven, Connecticut, Gibbs would live all of his life in that city, leaving only to take one trip abroad, and dying in the same house in which he grew up.

Well educated in private schools, Gibbs was graduated from Yale College in 1858, receiving prizes in Latin and mathematics. In 1863, he took his doctoral degree in engineering at Yale—one of the first such degrees in the United States; his dissertation was entitled *On the Form of the Teeth of Wheels in Spur Gearing.* For the next three years he tutored at Yale in Latin and natural philosophy, working on several practical inventions and obtaining a patent for one of them, an improved railway brake. The foregoing points to a not inconsiderable practical element in the chiefly theoretical scientist that Gibbs would become.

In 1866, Gibbs embarked on a journey to Europe, where he attended lectures by the best-known mathematicians and physicists of that era, spending a year each at the Universities of Paris, Berlin, and Heidelberg. What he learned at these schools would form the basis for his later theoretical work. His parents having died, and two of his sisters as well, he traveled with his remaining sisters, Anna and Julia, the latter returning home early to marry Addison Van Name, later librarian of Connecticut Academy, in 1867.

Upon his return to New Haven in 1869, Gibbs began work at once on his great theoretical undertaking, which he would not complete until 1878. He lived in the Van Name household, as did his sister Anna; neither he nor

she was ever married. In 1871, he was appointed professor of mathematical physics at Yale—the first such chair in the United States—but without salary. He was obliged to live for nine years on his not very considerable inherited income. When The Johns Hopkins University, aware of the significance of his work, offered him a position at a good salary, Yale decided to offer Gibbs two-thirds of what Johns Hopkins would pay; it was enough for Gibbs.

In 1873, he published his first paper, "Graphical Methods in the Thermodynamics of Fluids," which clarified the concept of entropy, introduced in 1850 by Rudolf Clausius. The genius of this insight was immediately recognized by James Clerk Maxwell in England, to whom Gibbs had sent a copy of the paper. The work was published, however, in a relatively obscure journal, *The Transactions of the Connecticut Academy of Arts and Sciences,* where almost all of Gibbs's subsequent writings would appear. In addition, his style was so terse, austere, and condensed as to be unreadable to all but a few readers who were already well acquainted with his underlying assumptions. Consequently, for most of his life Gibbs would remain largely unknown, especially in the United States, except among a small circle of his scientific colleagues.

This undeserved obscurity never seemed to trouble Gibbs. By all accounts, he was a genuinely unassuming and unpretentious man, tolerant, kind, approachable, and seemingly unconscious of his intellectual eminence. He was by no means gregarious and probably more than a little aloof; he had few really close friends, though he kept up a large correspondence. He attended church regularly. Physically, he was of slight build and owed a certain frailty in health to a severe case of scarlet fever in childhood. However, he was strong enough to ride and was known as a good horseman. Photographs of him reveal a handsome but somewhat stern man with a well-trimmed, short beard. The photographic image leaves an apt impression of what he was in life: a gentleman, a professor, and a scientist of unimpeachable integrity.

LIFE'S WORK

Gibbs published yet another paper in 1873, "A Method of Geometrical Representation of the Thermodynamic Properties of Substances by Means of Surfaces." In 1876, the first 140 pages of his major work appeared (again in *Transactions*), the final 180 pages finally being published by that journal in 1878; both parts bore the title "On the Equilibrium of Heterogeneous Substances." This work, of the utmost importance to science, never appeared in book form in English in Gibbs's lifetime. Its significance was appreciated by Maxwell, who incorporated some of its findings into his own books, but he died in 1879.

Continental Europeans perceived the general importance of Gibbs's discoveries, but had real difficulty reading Gibbs's text. (Gibbs himself rejected all suggestions that he rewrite his treatise as a readable book.) Hermann Helmholtz and Max Planck both duplicated some of Gibbs's work, simply because they did not know of it. A German translation of it, by the great scientist Wilhelm Ostwald, appeared only in 1892. French translations of various sections of the treatise were published in 1899 and 1903. Meanwhile, scientists came to perceive—in the words of physics professor Paul Epstein—that a

> young investigator, having discovered an entirely new branch of science, gave in a single contribution an exhaustive treatment of it which foreshadowed the development of theoretical chemistry for a quarter of a century.

Gibbs's was thus an achievement almost unparalleled in the history of science. Ostwald predicted that the result of Gibbs's work would determine the form and content of chemistry for a century to come—and he was right. A French scientist compared Gibbs, in his importance to chemistry, with Antoine Lavoisier. It should be mentioned that the editors of *The Transactions of the Connecticut Academy of Arts and Sciences* published Gibbs's work on faith alone as they were not able to understand it completely; they obtained the money for publishing the long treatise through private subscription.

Of special importance in Gibbs's work is its sophisticated mathematics. It is therefore not possible to summarize his discoveries in a brief article. There are two features, however, that must be noted. First, Gibbs succeeded in precisely formulating the second law of thermodynamics, which states that the spontaneous flow of heat from hot to cold bodies is reversible only with the expenditure of mechanical or other nonthermal energy. Consequently, entropy (S), equal to heat (Q) divided by temperature change (T), must continually be increasing. Prior to Gibbs, thermodynamics simply did not exist as a science.

Second, Gibbs derived from his more complex heterogeneous thermodynamics the "phase rule," which shows the relationship between the degrees of freedom (F) of a thermodynamic system and the number of components (C) and the number of phases (P), so that $F = C + 2 - P$. He showed how these relationships could be expressed graphically, in three dimensions. Often phase-rule diagrams proved to be the only practical key to the solution of hitherto insoluble problems concerning the mixing of components so that they would remain in equilibrium and not separate out and destroy the mixture. The phase rule helped make it possible to calculate in advance the temperature, pressure, and concentration required for stability—thus eliminating months and possibly years of tedious trial-and-error experiments. This would have important application in industry as well as in the laboratory.

Interestingly, after Gibbs's one major treatise on thermodynamics, he never wrote another important paper on the subject. He had said the last word, and he knew it. He did not, however, remain idle. Between 1883 and 1889, he published five papers on the electromagnetic theory of light. This work, too, was well received.

Meanwhile, he had begun to receive a certain amount of more or less perfunctory recognition at home: He was elected to the National Academy of Sciences in 1879 and to the American Academy of Arts and Sciences in 1880; in 1880 he received the Rumford Medal from the latter; in 1885 he was elected a vice president of the American Association for the Advancement of Science.

In the period between 1889 and 1902, Gibbs lectured on the subject of statistical mechanics but published almost nothing on the topic except for a brief abstract. This would be his major work during the final portion of his life; it would require about the same gestation period as did his investigation of thermodynamics. Simultaneously, however, he was lecturing and publishing papers on vector analysis and multiple algebra; the theory of dyadics that appeared in these works is regarded as his most important published contribution to pure mathematics. A book based on his lectures, *Gibbs' Vector Analysis*, was edited and published by a student, E. B. Wilson, in 1901.

During that same year, Gibbs was awarded the Copley Medal by the Royal Society of London for being the first to apply the second law of thermodynamics to the exhaustive discussion of the relation between chemical, electrical, and thermal energy and the capacity for external work. This was the highest honor for scientists prior to the founding of the Nobel Prize.

In 1902, Gibbs's final important work was published under the title *Elementary Principles in Statistical Me-*

chanics Developed with Special Reference to the Rational Foundation of Thermodynamics. In this brilliant study, Gibbs was as far ahead of his time as he had been with his first major treatise. The later work has been called "a monument in the history of physics which marks the separation between the nineteenth and twentieth centuries." Gibbs's perception of the role played by probability in physical events made his last work a true precursor to quantum mechanics, which did not develop fully until the 1920's.

During the year following the publication of his final gift to the world, Gibbs suffered from several minor ailments. One of these resulted in a sudden and acute attack from an intestinal obstruction, which led to Gibbs's untimely death on April 28, 1903.

SIGNIFICANCE

Gibbs's contribution to American society occurred chiefly after his death. It is regrettable that few Americans had the capacity to recognize his achievements while he was alive, but it seems pointless to try to fix the blame for this. On the one hand, he himself declined to make his papers more accessible by revising them for a wider readership. On the other, physical chemistry was only beginning to develop in the United States. Few professors of either chemistry or physics had the background that would have enabled them to understand Gibbs's work; there were no grand figures such as Rudolf Clausius, James Clerk Maxwell, William Thomson (Baron Kelvin), or Wilhelm Ostwald in the United States to welcome the new young genius personally.

In addition, the chemical industry in the United States was conservative in the matter of adopting new methods derived chiefly from theory, while at the same time it was caught up in the chaos of a greatly expanding industrialism. There was virtually no one available to examine the implications for the chemical industry of Gibbs's new phase rule. Gradually, however, as the industry turned more and more to synthesizing new compounds and developing metal alloys, there came a demand for precisely the sort of tool that Gibbs long before had provided. The phase rule had an early application in alloys of iron and carbon to produce different types of steel. Another application involved the industrial synthesis of ammonia from nitrogen and hydrogen, and of nitric acid from ammonia. Although most of these applications were first worked out in Europe, American industry finally learned how to reap the benefits of bringing theory to bear on practical processes. It finally came to recognize what it owed to Gibbs.

The United States thus reaped the practical benefits of Gibbs's work; it also had the honor of claiming as its own one of the world's greatest theoretical scientists.

—*Donald M. Fiene*

FURTHER READING

Bumstead, H. A. "Josiah Willard Gibbs." In *The Collected Works of J. Willard Gibbs*, edited by H. A. Bumstead. 2 vols. New Haven, Conn.: Yale University Press, 1948. Reprinted, with some additions, from the *American Journal of Science* 4 (September, 1903). Also in a previous edition of *The Collected Works*, edited by W. R. Longley and R. G. Van Name. New York: Longmans, Green, 1928. Written by a former student who knew Gibbs well, this basic source for all other biographies includes a useful list of Gibbs's publications in chronological order.

Caldi, D. G., and G. D. Mostow, eds. *Proceedings of the Gibbs Symposium: Yale University, May 15-17, 1989*. Providence, R.I.: American Mathematical Society, 1990. Collection of papers delivered at a professional conference commemorating Gibbs. Includes three articles providing a perspective of Gibbs, the man, and his place in the history of science.

Crowther, J. G. "Josiah Willard Gibbs." In *Famous American Men of Science*, edited by J. G. Crowther. Freeport, N.Y.: Books for Libraries Press, 1969. Reprinted with minor changes from first edition. New York: W. W. Norton, 1937. Excellent psychological speculation about Gibbs's family and his social and academic life. Two portraits, brief bibliography.

Jaffe, Bernard. "J. Willard Gibbs (1839-1903): America in the New World of Chemistry." In *Men of Science in America: The Role of Science in the Growth of Our Country*. New York: Simon & Schuster, 1944. Excellent discussion of American reception (or lack of it) of Gibbs, and the consequences for American society. Good explanation of phase rule and its application in industry.

James, Ioan. *Remarkable Physicists: From Galileo to Yukawa*. New York: Cambridge University Press, 2004. This collection of brief biographies of prominent physicists includes a five-page overview of Gibbs's life and scientific contributions.

Kraus, Charles A. "Josiah Willard Gibbs." In *Great Chemists*, edited by Eduard Farber. New York: Interscience, 1961. Good discussion of experimental work and of phase rule.

Rukeyser, Muriel. *Willard Gibbs*. Garden City, N.Y.: Doubleday, Doran, 1942. Long text, reads almost like a novel, but offers good background detail that places Gibbs squarely within the context of the American culture of his time.

Seeger, Raymond John. *J. Willard Gibbs: American Mathematical Physicist Par Excellence*. Elmsford, N.Y.: Pergamon Press, 1974. Places greatest emphasis on details of mathematics and science. Includes useful chronology of life and work with a short bibliography.

Wheeler, Lynde Phelps. *Josiah Willard Gibbs: The History of a Great Mind*. Reprint. Woodbridge, Conn.:

Oxbow Press, 1998. The authorized biography. Wheeler was a student of Gibbs during the 1890's, and his account is comprehensive but rather genteel.

SEE ALSO: Baron Kelvin; James Clerk Maxwell.
RELATED ARTICLES in *Great Events from History: The Nineteenth Century, 1801-1900:* 1850-1865: Clausius Formulates the Second Law of Thermodynamics; December 14, 1900: Articulation of Quantum Theory.

W. S. GILBERT AND ARTHUR SULLIVAN
English composers

In their musical collaborations, Gilbert and Sullivan forged a truly British character for light opera, in the process establishing operetta as a major dramatic subgenre and extending its boundaries to include melodrama, satire, and serious drama. Sullivan was one of the foremost British composers of the nineteenth century; he displayed an amazing range, from overtures and oratorios to operettas and hymns, but is primarily remembered for his collaborations with Gilbert.

W. S. GILBERT

BORN: November 18, 1836; London, England
DIED: May 29, 1911; Grim's Dyke, Harrow Weald, Middlesex, England
ALSO KNOWN AS: F. Tomline (pseudonym); William Schwenck Gilbert (full name)

ARTHUR SULLIVAN

BORN: May 13, 1842; London, England
DIED: November 22, 1900; London, England
ALSO KNOWN AS: Arthur Seymour Sullivan (full name)
AREAS OF ACHIEVEMENT: Music, theater

EARLY LIVES

William Schwenck Gilbert was the eldest of five children and the only son of William Gilbert, a sometime naval surgeon who became a prolific if not a talented novelist and playwright, and Anne Morris Gilbert, a doctor's daughter who is remarkable only for the apparent lack of effect she had on her son's life. When he was a toddler, he

was kidnapped at Naples and held for ransom. His abductors demanded and received the princely sum of twenty-five pounds for their trouble, and it is possible that this experience provided part of the impetus behind the plot of *The Pirates of Penzance: Or, The Slave of Duty* (1879), in which a dim-witted nurse mistakes pirate for pilot, thus beginning the complications that dog young Frederick's life.

More important than the kidnapping, though, was the influence the elder William Gilbert exerted over his son. The two were entirely alike in temperament: combative, active, confident to a fault. The father instilled in the son an almost unhealthy need to win and an overweening sense of his own worth. This arrogance was Gilbert's early undoing, for at the Western Grammar School and later at Ealing he was a lazy student, until he realized, with a shock, that he was falling behind other boys whose intellectual capabilities he scorned. He began to apply himself, and at the age of sixteen he became head boy at Ealing, going on to enter King's College, London, in 1853, and taking his degree in 1857.

The next period in Gilbert's life looms large in its impact on his career as a dramatist. In 1855, he entered the Inner Temple to study law, and in 1857, the year he took his degree, he joined the militia, beginning twenty years of service there. Both his experiences at the bar and his military service provided grist for Gilbert's satirical mill, not only in his operettas, but in *The Bab Ballads* (1869) as well. At any rate, his desire for military service in the Crimea was thwarted when that war inconveniently ended, and his service at the bar, beginning in 1863, was only slightly more successful; he earned only seventy-five pounds in two years.

W. S. Gilbert. (The Granger Collection, New York)

In the meantime, Gilbert passed the long quiet time in his law office by becoming involved in literary affairs. His first lyric, a translation of the laughing song from Daniel-François-Esprit Auber's *Manon Lescaut*, debuted in 1858, and in 1861 Gilbert began contributing to a new satiric magazine, *Fun*, which would become the principal rival of *Punch*, to which Gilbert also contributed in 1865. More important, he began his stage-writing career with *Dulcamara: Or, The Little Duck and the Great Quack* (1866), an operatic burlesque, the first of five that he would produce during the 1860's. That same year also saw the publication of "The Yarn of the Nancy Bell" and in 1867 *The Bab Ballads* began to appear in *Fun*.

In August of 1867, Gilbert married Lucy Blois Turner, a military officer's daughter. A tall man with a military bearing, Gilbert cut a handsome figure. His short brown hair swept back from his broad forehead and, together with his long muttonchop whiskers, framed a narrow face. A square chin combined with these other attributes to give him a stolid, formidable appearance that seemed to heighten his personal characteristics of stubbornness and feistiness. These characteristics served him

well in his literary life, for he was so confident of his talent that he often went over editors' heads and persuaded the owners of journals to publish his material. For this reason, and because he displayed a genuine talent for satire and parody, his literary career began to flourish, and by 1869, when he first met Arthur Sullivan, he had already achieved considerable success.

Six years younger than Gilbert, Arthur Seymour Sullivan was the second child of Thomas and Mary Coghlan Sullivan. Thomas Sullivan was a poor military musician and band director who provided his sons with a very early introduction to music, to which Arthur immediately took. Before he was twelve, young Arthur had mastered practically every instrument in the band. Singing and composing were Arthur's fortes, and they gained for him entry to the Chapel Royal, even though, at the age of twelve, he was three years beyond the maximum age for admission. There he won, at the age of fourteen, the first Mendelssohn scholarship, an award that allowed him, two years later, to pursue his studies in Leipzig, at the conservatorium founded there by Felix Mendelssohn himself.

Thus began almost three years of incredible success for such a young musician. If Sullivan had been a prodigy before, he was now a marvel whose compositions gained public performance along with those of far more renowned artists. Indeed, his String Quartet in D Minor was played twice in rapid succession, a rare honor at that time, and both times the piece was received well. In addition, he was accorded the privilege of conducting the orchestra in its performance of his overture to a poem by Thomas Moore, an unheard-of honor for a mere student. The one-year scholarship had been extended for a second year, and at the end of that time, Sullivan was invited to stay on for further study, tuition-free. His masters were reluctant to see him go. Finally he was forced by financial exigency to return to London, where he faced his future with some trepidation. After the triumph in Leipzig, Sullivan feared that the know-it-all London critics would be waiting to ambush him.

Sullivan's worries were needless. His return to London in the spring of 1861 passed largely unnoticed. Like any young artist, he settled in for a period of struggle that, for him, would not last long. This short, olive-skinned, dark-eyed and curly-haired youth with an open and appealing manner was too talented to go unnoticed for long. An engaging young man, Sullivan soon attracted influential acquaintances, and by 1862 his *The Tempest* music debuted with the Crystal Palace orchestra, and public and critical acclaim followed. From that time

Sullivan's reputation grew, and by 1866, his *anno mirabilis*, it soared. He was appointed professor of composition at the Royal Academy of Music. Later that year, his *In Memoriam*, a musical response to the death of his father, firmly established him as the great hope of English music. He was twenty-four years old.

LIVES' WORK

As the 1860's progressed, Arthur Sullivan's reputation grew. He took on the specter of Georg Frideric Handel with *The Prodigal Son*, an oratorio, and in that year he was accorded an honor unprecedented in one so young: The queen requested a copy of his complete works. Sullivan, however, always eager to extend his range of accomplishment, began what would become his greatest achievement, the resurrection of light opera in Great Britain. His early collaborator was F. C. Burnand, with whom he wrote, among other productions, *The Contrabandistas* (1867) and *Cox and Box* (1867), works that bore a strongly Continental flavor reminiscent of Gioacchino Rossini and Charles-François Gounod. These two operettas achieved growing popularity, and the form was on its way.

"I AM THE VERY MODEL OF A MODERN MAJOR GENERAL"

One of the most memorable pieces in William Gilbert and Arthur S. Sullivan's operetta The Pirates of Penzance *is this song about a "modern major general."*

I am the very model of a modern Major-General,
I've information vegetable, animal, and mineral,
I know the kings of England, and I quote the fights historical
From Marathon to Waterloo, in order categorical;
I'm very well acquainted, too, with matters mathematical,
I understand equations, both the simple and quadratical,
About binomial theorem I'm teeming with a lot o' news
With many cheerful facts about the square of the hypotenuse.

With many cheerful facts about the square of the hypotenuse,
With many cheerful facts about the square of the hypotenuse,
With many cheerful facts about the square of the hypoten-potenuse.

I'm very good at integral and differential calculus;
I know the scientific names of beings animalculous;
In short, in matters vegetable, animal, and mineral,
I am the very model of a modern Major-General.

In short, in matters vegetable, animal, and mineral,
He is the very model of a modern Major-General.

I know our mythic history, King Arthur's and Sir Caradoc's;
I answer hard acrostics, I've a pretty taste for paradox,
I quote in elegiacs all the crimes of Heliogabalus,
In conics I can floor peculiarities parabolous;
I can tell undoubted Raphaels from Gerard Dows and Zoffanies,
I know the croaking chorus from the Frogs of Aristophanes!
Then I can hum a fugue of which I've heard the music's din afore,
And whistle all the airs from that infernal nonsense Pinafore.

Meanwhile, William Gilbert was achieving a measure of prominence as a drama critic who wrote parodic reviews for *Fun* and as a librettist in his own right, providing plays and librettos for German Reed's Royal Gallery of Illustration. At a rehearsal for one of these productions, the two men who would transform light opera into English operetta met, in 1869, but the meeting produced no immediate reaction. Sullivan was involved in a successful collaboration with Burnand, and Gilbert, at the time, was happy producing librettos for Frederic Clay and German Reed. Not until 1871 did Gilbert and Sullivan first collaborate, and then the product, *Thespis: Or, The Gods Grown Old*, was less than a triumph, for it closed within a month. That first stumbling effort was marked, nevertheless, by the kind of sensitive relationship between music and lyrics that would come to characterize

Gilbert and Sullivan's work and, as a result of their leadership, the English operetta.

Four years passed, during which Sullivan displayed his versatility, attempting oratorios, hymns (among which is "Onward Christian Soldiers," 1874), and further involvements with both the serious and the comic stages. The awards and commissions rolled in, and he became universally recognized as the premier composer in Great Britain. Meanwhile, Gilbert was also achieving a large measure of success. His *Pygmalion and Galatea* (1871) earned for him forty thousand pounds, he continued to write serious dramas, and *The Bab Ballads* had also won for him separate recognition as a poet. Both men were rich and famous before they experienced success together, but in 1875 events started to unfold that would firmly establish them as a team.

> *And whistle all the airs from that infernal nonsense Pinafore,*
> *And whistle all the airs from that infernal nonsense Pinafore,*
> *And whistle all the airs from that infernal nonsense Pina-Pinafore.*
>
> Then I can write a washing bill in Babylonic cuneiform,
> And tell you ev'ry detail of Caractacus's uniform:
> In short, in matters vegetable, animal, and mineral,
> I am the very model of a modern Major-General.
>
> *In short, in matters vegetable, animal, and mineral,*
> *He is the very model of a modern Major-General.*
>
> In fact, when I know what is meant by "mamelon" and "ravelin,"
> When I can tell at sight a Mauser rifle from a javelin,
> When such affairs as sorties and surprises I'm more wary at,
> And when I know precisely what is meant by "commissariat,"
> When I have learnt what progress has been made in modern gunnery,
> When I know more of tactics than a novice in a nunnery;
> In short, when I've a smattering of elemental strategy,
> You'll say a better Major-General had never sat a gee.
>
> *You'll say a better Major-General had never sat a gee,*
> *You'll say a better Major-General had never sat a gee,*
> *You'll say a better Major-General had never sat a, sat a gee.*
>
> For my military knowledge, though I'm plucky and adventury,
> Has only been brought down to the beginning of the century;
> But still, in matters vegetable, animal, and mineral,
> I am the very model of a modern Major-General.
>
> *But still, in matters vegetable, animal, and mineral,*
> *He is the very model of a modern Major-General.*

Source: Gilbert and Sullivan Archive, math.boisestate.edu/gas/pirates/web_op/pirates13.html. Accessed on October 8, 2005.

Gilbert had written a libretto based on a satiric mock trial that he had sketched for an 1868 issue of *Fun*. During a visit to Richard D'Oyly Carte, he found that that impresario was looking for a curtain raiser for Jacques Offenbach's *La Périchole*. Carte suggested that Gilbert write something that Arthur Sullivan could set to music, and the result, *Trial by Jury*, became not the curtain raiser but the main attraction. It opened March 25, 1875, and enjoyed a run of almost nine months. It was the first success for Gilbert and Sullivan, and their first teaming under the auspices of Carte. The success of this short operetta was a sign of things to come.

Though both men continued for a time to seek their separate fortunes, the team became famous in 1878 with the production of *H.M.S. Pinafore: Or, The Lass That Loved a Sailor*. Thus began a trying period of success for both. Together they completely reformed comic opera, moving operetta from the status of one-act light entertainment to full three-act main event, yet separately each man wished for a different kind of success. Gilbert longed to be taken seriously as a playwright, only giving up his dream in 1888, after the failure of *Brantinghame Hall*. Sullivan continued to think of himself as a serious composer, and he often chafed at what he believed was the disproportionate amount of attention the public paid to his operettas. The team became fabulously wealthy and famous as a result of their innovative efforts in operetta, yet both men felt stifled by that success, deprived of what each thought to be true destiny.

Despite their resentment of the operettas, the partners experienced one success after another. *The Pirates of Penzance*, their second full-blown operetta, led to American tours of both that operetta and *H.M.S. Pinafore*, and in 1881 the team debuted *Patience: Or, Bunthorne's Bride*, a spoof of the Aesthetic movement, which opened in April and moved in October into Carte's new theater, the Savoy, which was designed and built expressly for operetta. *Iolanthe* followed in 1882, *Princess Ida: Or, Castle Adamant* in 1884, *The Mikado: Or, The Town of Titipu* in 1885, *Ruddigore: Or, The Witch's Curse* in 1887, *The Yeoman of the Guard: Or, The Merryman and His Maid* in 1888, and *The Gondoliers: Or, The King of Barataria* in 1889.

The collaboration had been fruitful indeed, but the two men were not without their problems. Always combative, Gilbert was jealous of Sullivan's fame; he tended to bully the quieter Sullivan, who nevertheless believed that he, Sullivan, was the superior artist. The two fought often, several times breaking off their partnership, even during the periods of their greatest success. During the years from 1884 until 1890, Carte acted as referee, keeping the team together and smoothing over the affronts and slights, real and imagined. In 1890, however, Gilbert began a dispute that has become known as the carpet quarrel, an argument that ended in the dissolution of the partnership and in Gilbert's successful lawsuit against Carte.

The split lasted for three years, at which time Carte managed to bring Gilbert and Sullivan back together for *Utopia, Limited: Or, The Flowers of Progress* (1893) and *The Grand Duke: Or, The Statutory Duel* (1896), their last operetta. In 1900, Sullivan, always physically weak and troubled, from the 1870's onward, by serious recurrent kidney problems, contracted a cold that progressed into bronchitis. He refused to rest, and on November 21, his heart gave way. He died the next day. Gilbert also died of heart failure. On May 29, 1911, he rushed to the rescue of a woman who was drowning in a pond on his estate, Grim's Dyke, and the exertion proved to be too much for Gilbert's seventy-five-year-old heart.

SIGNIFICANCE

During their long and tempestuous relationship, Gilbert and Sullivan accomplished much, both together and separately. Sullivan's musical accomplishments, though overshadowed by the operettas, resulted in a resurgence in serious British music, for his fame and fortune made music a more respectable profession. Sullivan and Burnand resurrected comic opera, establishing it as a financially successful theatrical form. Sullivan brought the art of writing musical scores to a new height, providing all of his collaborators with music that enhanced but never detracted from their words. His scores complemented the librettos, a relationship that led to both the establishment of the musical theater and the increasing use of music as theatrical accompaniment. Today's theater orchestras and film scores owe much to Sullivan's pioneering work in the Victorian theater.

Gilbert, too, made his individual contribution. His nonsense verse, *The Bab Ballads*, made a major contribution to the genre. His muse was more acerbic than that of Edward Lear or Lewis Carroll, and he reestablished satire as a major subject for popular poetry. This vein he pursued avidly in his librettos, in which he lampooned his own abortive careers of law, the military, and even poetry. He rolled back the restrictions that Victorian society had long placed on the theater, determinedly and often gleefully violating conventional propriety with such exuberance and with such a deft comic touch that audiences and censors alike laughed, and acceded. Gilbert may not have achieved his dearest goal, that of becoming a serious poet and playwright, but his verse, in the form of librettos, forced open the narrow parameters

of the English stage, preparing the way for the giants of early twentieth century British drama.

Together, Gilbert and Sullivan almost single-handedly reinvented musical theater. Before them, operetta was lightly regarded. It had arisen in response to the Licensing Acts that, from 1739 through 1843, restricted plays with spoken dialogue to a limited number of theaters: In London, only Covent Garden and Drury Lane could produce actual drama. Operetta, in which the lines were sung, not spoken, combined with pantomime and tableau to form a program entertainment in houses such as German Reed's. It was Gilbert and Sullivan, however, who raised operetta to the stature of main attraction, ultimately propelling it to the point at which a full-length operetta was the only item on the evening's bill of entertainment. Their financial success brought actors, artists, money, and, more important, attention and respectability to the British stage, and their expansion of operetta from one-act play to full-length production laid the foundation for modern musical theater, most especially the modern musical.

—William Condon

FURTHER READING

Ainger, Michael. *Gilbert and Sullivan: A Dual Biography.* New York: Oxford University Press, 2002. A biography, comparing the backgrounds, personalities, and artistic aspirations of Gilbert and Sullivan. Ainger argues the pair's success was a result of their clashing personalities, with each man forcing the other to create his best work. Includes previously unpublished draft librettos and personal letters.

Bradley, Ian, ed. *The Complete Annotated Gilbert and Sullivan.* New York: Oxford University Press, 1996. Contains the complete works of Gilbert and Sullivan with extensive annotations and commentary on the text and stage directions. An informative book that describes the basis for each opera, identifies the real people mentioned therein, and more.

Goldberg, Isaac. *The Story of Gilbert and Sullivan: Or, The "Compleat" Savoyard.* New York: AMS Press, 1928. Reprint. 1970. A gossipy but detailed and fairly reliable account of the lives and careers of Gilbert and Sullivan, together and apart.

Helyar, James, ed. *Gilbert and Sullivan.* Lawrence: University Press of Kansas, 1972. A collection of essays covering much territory; includes essays by scholars who led the movement to reevaluate Gilbert and Sullivan's work.

Jones, John Bush, ed. *W. S. Gilbert: A Centenary of Scholarship and Commentary.* New York: New York

University Press, 1970. Spanning the century from 1868 to 1968, Jones's judiciously chosen collection provides a solid introduction to Gilbert's reputation through the years. The essay by Jane Stedman, in particular, is vital to an understanding of Gilbert's impact on the theater and the literary world of his day.

Moore, Frank L., ed. *The Handbook of Gilbert and Sullivan.* New York: Thomas Y. Crowell, 1972. An encyclopedic fact book about the famous partnership and all the collaborative productions. The book does not go into depth, but it covers a wide range of material about the operettas and the D'Oyly Carte company.

Stedman, Jane W. *W. S. Gilbert: A Classic Victorian and His Theatre.* New York: Oxford University Press, 1996. Well-written and accurate biography of Gilbert based on original sources and interviews with surviving contemporaries of the writer.

Wren, Grayden. *A Most Ingenious Paradox: The Art of Gilbert and Sullivan.* New York: Oxford University Press, 2001. Includes a separate chapter about each opera, arranged in chronological order, providing analysis of the work. Also includes information on the men's careers before and after their collaboration. Wren analyzes the pair's legacy, crediting the lasting popularity of their operas to universal themes and the characters' humanity. Includes an appendix of plot summaries and a bibliography.

SEE ALSO: Lewis Carroll; Felix Mendelssohn; Jacques Offenbach; Gioacchino Rossini.

RELATED ARTICLES in *Great Events from History: The Nineteenth Century, 1801-1900:* 1850's-1880's: Rise of Burlesque and Vaudeville; 1878-1899: Irving Manages London's Lyceum Theatre; October 10, 1881: London's Savoy Theatre Opens.

VINCENZO GIOBERTI
Italian politician

One of the founders of modern Italy, Gioberti developed the first comprehensive political program for the Risorgimento—the Italian national unification movement. He represented the progressive Catholic political tradition in nineteenth century Italy and sought to redefine the Church's political role in the process of creating the new Italian nation.

BORN: April 5, 1801; Turin, kingdom of Sardinia (now in Italy)
DIED: October 26, 1852; Paris, France
AREAS OF ACHIEVEMENT: Philosophy, religion and theology, government and politics

EARLY LIFE

Vincenzo Gioberti (joh-BEHR-tee) lost his father, Giuseppe, at an early age, and his mother, Marianna Capra—a learned and deeply religious woman—died on December 24, 1819. Gioberti received his education from a school run by a Catholic religious order—the Fathers of the Oratory, in Turin. Despite his ill health as a child, he studied diligently and demonstrated a particular interest in the writings of the Italian poet Vittorio Alfieri and the French philosopher Jean-Jacques Rousseau. Gioberti entered the religious order but apparently without much enthusiasm. In his studies for the priesthood, he became convinced of the need for religious reform and for the reconciliation between the Christian faith and modern science. After earning a theology degree in 1823, Gioberti joined the faculty of the theological college at the University of Turin. He was ordained a priest in 1825. The following year, he received an appointment as chaplain to the royal court of King Charles Felix of Piedmont-Sardinia.

Gioberti's service to the Savoy monarch in Turin did not alter his personal aversion to political authoritarianism. As a young man, he harbored the democratic and nationalist sentiments of many educated Italians during the early nineteenth century. The Italy of Gioberti's youth existed only as a "geographical expression"—an odd assortment of kingdoms, duchies, and principalities running the length of the Italian peninsula.

Inspired by the political ideas and events of the French Revolution, Italians nurtured their aspirations for an independent, united Italy. The obstacles to unification were immense. Much of northern Italy was part of the Austrian Empire; Spanish royalty ruled southern Italy and Sicily; and the pope exercised sovereignty over a large part of the central region. Moreover, the European powers had agreed to maintain the status quo in Italy, even by military intervention if necessary.

Many Italian nationalists, in their hopes for unification, looked to the strongest independent Italian state—Piedmont-Sardinia—for leadership. The conservative Savoy monarchs, however, had no desire to encourage political upheaval, nor did they wish to offend the Papacy or the European powers. Without the leadership of the Savoy monarchy or any other political authority, the task of Italian unification fell to a loosely connected network of secret patriotic societies. Gioberti's political activity began with his involvement with these conspiratorial organizations.

LIFE'S WORK

Gioberti first established contact with a secret society in 1828, when he traveled through northern Italy. During these travels (under the constant surveillance of the Austrian police), he also met with Giacomo Leopardi and Alessandro Manzoni, two leading nationalist writers. Later, he became acquainted with Young Italy, the republican society founded by Giuseppe Mazzini in 1831. He openly sympathized with Young Italy until Mazzini sponsored an unsuccessful insurrection in Piedmont in 1834.

Because of his preaching on civic and political matters, and his radical religious opinions, Gioberti was dismissed from the royal court in May, 1833. Shortly thereafter, he was arrested and imprisoned on the charge of advocating a republican form of government and distributing copies of Mazzini's newspaper *Young Italy* among Piedmontese soldiers. Given the choice between a lengthy prison sentence or exile, he left for France in September, 1833.

After a year in Paris without finding means for study or suitable employment, Gioberti accepted a teaching position at the Gaggia College in Brussels. There he began an intense period of writing. He published studies of aesthetics and the supernatural, a critique of Jesuit doctrines, and an introduction to philosophy. His most important work, *Del primato morale e civile degli Italiani* (on the moral and civil primacy of the Italians), was published in two volumes in 1843.

In *Del primato morale e civile degli italiani*, Gioberti presented a far-ranging theological and historical justification for Italian independence and unity. He recounted Italy's past greatness as the center of the Roman Empire and Christian civilization. He reminded Italians of the moral and political legacy that they had bequeathed to the modern world, and he called on his country to resume its historic role as a leader among nations. In his program for a new Italy, he envisioned a federation of independent states, free from foreign rule, united under the aegis of a papal president, and protected by the strong military arm of the House of Savoy. Gioberti dismissed the idea of unification through a popular insurrection as dangerous and impractical. Instead, he looked to the rulers of each Italian state to demonstrate their patriotism and their political wisdom by enacting progressive reforms and joining the national federation on a voluntary basis. Gioberti's outline for Italian independence and unification included several practical suggestions: abolishing tariffs and duties; standardizing weights, measures, and currency; and other forms of economic cooperation.

With *Del primato morale e civile degli italiani*, Gioberti established his reputation as the leading theorist of Italian unification. The tedious, seven-hundred-page work was widely read and discussed, despite the ban on its circulation outside Piedmont. *Del primato morale e civile degli italiani* lifted the morale of Italian nationalists. Both King Charles Albert of Piedmont-Sardinia and Pope Pius IX came under its spell. Gioberti's program for unification inspired political moderates to action. Many nationalists in the upper classes feared the economic and social upheaval that might accompany unification. They were wary of any participation of the masses in the unification movement, and they found much assurance in Gioberti's idea of creating an Italian nation "from above."

Some Italian nationalists, even among the moderate element, were skeptical of Gioberti's proposals. He gave no indication of how to deal with Austria and its powerful army in northern Italy. His hopes for political cooperation among the rulers of the Italian states seemed hopelessly naïve. The most controversial point was the idea of a pope as president of a federation of Italian states. Gioberti's critics scoffed at the notion that the pope could have any positive role in Italian unification. Their criticism was well justified. The Papal States had a reputation unsurpassed in Europe for political oppression, corruption, and misrule. The Papacy stood as a defender of the old order and an obstacle to political progress. Many nationalists believed that unification would be completed only when the pope surrendered civil authority over his territory and allowed Rome to become the capital of the new Italian nation.

When Pius became the new pontiff in 1846, the political climate in the Papal States changed markedly. The youthful, energetic ruler immediately instituted a series of democratic reforms within the Papal States, disbanded his mercenary army, and granted amnesty to political prisoners. His popularity grew throughout Italy, and he won support even among anticlerics. The explosion of revolutionary sentiment in 1848 eventually overtook the pontiff's program of reform, and Pius retreated behind a wall of intransigent conservatism. For a time, however, Gioberti's idea of a liberal pope seemed to be vindicated.

Gioberti's writing won for him national renown. He was recognized as the leader of the *Veri italiani* (true Italians), a circle of distinguished political moderates living in exile, and began corresponding with Charles Albert. The king, in turn, recognized his achievement by granting him an annual pension, which Gioberti donated to the church charity in Turin. While residing in Paris in 1846, he was elected to the Subalpine (Piedmontese) Parliament. He returned to Turin after almost fifteen years in exile, a celebrated figure in Italian political life. When he traveled through northern Italy, crowds greeted him as a national hero. In July, 1848, he was elected president of the Chamber of Deputies. In December, the king invited him to form a government.

Gioberti's tenure as prime minister was short and undistinguished. He lacked the requisite political skills and the ability to compromise. Somewhat vain and aloof, he refused to consult with his cabinet and advisers. His ineptness became apparent during a crisis in foreign affairs. An insurrection in Rome had driven the pope from the city. Gioberti sought ways to restore him to power before the European governments intervened. His attempts failed. The French army occupied the Papal States and ended the short-lived Roman Republic. The popular uprisings of 1848—particularly the one in Rome—left Pius frightened, embittered, and vindictive. He disavowed all progressive ideas and reforms, placed Gioberti's *Del primato morale e civile degli italiani* on the Index (list of works banned by the Church), and restored authoritarian rule to the Papal States.

Gioberti resigned in February, 1849, over the crisis in Tuscany. A popular uprising there had opened the way for unification with Piedmont. He refused to send troops to secure the region, and Austrian forces eventually restored order. In the spring of 1849, he accepted the post of ambassador to France and remained in Paris until his death. His frustrating experience in Italian politics led him to write *Il rinnovamento civile d'Italia* (the civil renewal of Italy) in 1851. By this time, he had accepted the position of other political moderates that national unification was possible only under the auspices of the king of Piedmont-Sardinia. Gioberti died suddenly on October 26, 1852, leaving many of his writings unfinished.

SIGNIFICANCE

In calling for papal leadership in Italy, Vincenzo Gioberti revived Guelphist politics—a tradition that dated from the Middle Ages, when the popes vied with the Holy Roman Emperors for political power in Europe. As a neo-Guelphist, he sought to restore papal authority as the moral and political arbiter of Christian nations. His critics dismissed this as a medieval solution to a modern problem, but some of Gioberti's ideas were validated by subsequent events.

Gioberti's belief that Italy needed to build a strong navy and acquire a colonial empire reflected foreign policy goals followed by Italian governments until the end of World War II. The idea of making Italy "from above" was ultimately affirmed in the statesmanship of Count Cavour. For all of his assurances of the "moral and civil primacy of the Italians," Gioberti actually had little faith in the political maturity of his countrymen. He believed in paternalistic, Christian government—"everything for the people, nothing by the people." As he had envisioned, Italy was unified without the involvement of most Italians, but this lack of popular participation in the unification process ultimately proved a source of political weakness for the new Italian state.

—*Michael F. Hembree*

FURTHER READING

Beales, Derek, and Eugenio Biagini. *The Risorgimento and the Unification of Italy*. Rev. 2d ed. Harlow, England: Longman, 2002. This examination of the relationship between the Italian national movement and Italian unification includes chapter 12, "Gioberti's 'philosophy.'"

Berkeley, C. F. H. *Italy in the Making*. Vol. 1. Cambridge, England: Cambridge University Press, 1932. This survey of Italian unification is a helpful source. The author, sympathetic to the Roman Catholic Church and the moderate political elements in the unification movement, deals at length with Gioberti's intellectual and political contributions.

Coppa, Frank J., ed. *Dictionary of Modern Italian History*. Westport, Conn.: Greenwood Press, 1985. Contains a brief biography of Gioberti taken from Italian sources.

DiScala, Spencer. *Italy from Revolution to Republic: 1700 to the Present*. 3d ed. Boulder, Colo.: Westview Press, 2004. Part three provides information about the Risorgimento, mentioning Gioberti's role within the movement.

Gioberti, Vincenzo. *Essay on the Beautiful.* Translated by Edward Thomas. London: Simpkin, Marshall, 1860. An English translation of one of Gioberti's several published works.

Grew, Raymond. *A Sterner Plan for Italian Unity: The Italian National Society in the Risorgimento.* Princeton, N.J.: Princeton University Press, 1963. Places Gioberti in the broader context of the moderate political tradition in the unification movement.

Mack Smith, Denis. *The Making of Italy, 1796-1870.* New York: Harper & Row, 1968. A survey of the Italian unification movement, more balanced than Berkeley's history in its assessment of Gioberti and the political moderates.

SEE ALSO: Count Cavour; Giuseppe Garibaldi; Alessandro Manzoni; Giuseppe Mazzini; Pius IX.

RELATED ARTICLES in *Great Events from History: The Nineteenth Century, 1801-1900:* 1831: Mazzini Founds Young Italy; January 12, 1848-August 28, 1849: Italian Revolution of 1848.

WILLIAM EWART GLADSTONE
Prime minister of Great Britain (1868-1874, 1880-1885, 1886, 1892-1894)

The dominant figure in British politics in the Victorian age, Gladstone was a leader in Parliament for fifty years, during which time he held a number of key cabinet positions, including four stints as prime minister, and he helped lead his country on the path toward full democracy.

BORN: December 29, 1809; Liverpool, England
DIED: May 19, 1898; Hawarden, Flintshire, Wales
AREA OF ACHIEVEMENT: Government and politics

EARLY LIFE

The fourth son of businessperson John Gladstone, William Ewart Gladstone was born into a middle-class family that was on the rise socially and financially. The future prime minister's father had moved to the growing port city of Liverpool from his native Scotland, establishing his fortune in shipping, real estate, insurance, and commercial ventures that included trade in the slave-based industries in the West Indies. John Gladstone was elected to Parliament in 1827; he lived to see three of his sons seek similar office and to watch his most gifted son, William, rise meteorically in a variety of cabinet positions under the mentorship of Prime Minister Robert Peel.

Gladstone's upbringing was influenced decidedly by strong Christian principles, and though he moved gradually through a phase of rigorous commitment to the established Anglican Church to toleration for differences of form among worshipers, he was consistent in applying religious and moral touchstones to his personal and political life. Educated at Eton and then at Oxford, where he took a double first in classics and mathematics, the young Gladstone displayed his firm commitment to Tory principles while still an undergraduate.

Gladstone's speech at the Oxford Union so impressed a classmate, Lord Lincoln, that the latter persuaded his father, the duke of Newcastle, to support Gladstone for a seat in Parliament representing Newark, a borough that the duke controlled. Gladstone, who had difficulty deciding whether to seek a career in the Church or enter politics, agreed to stand for election and received Newark's nomination in 1832. As fate would have it, he entered Parliament in a session during which British history was changed: Under pressure from various groups throughout the country, the Parliament in that year passed the First Reform Bill, significantly enlarging the number of eligible voters and setting Great Britain on an inevitable course toward modern democracy.

At the same time that he was making a name for himself in politics, though, Gladstone was finding his social life a bit more perplexing. Though considered one of the handsomest young men in Parliament—tall with dark eyes and flowing brown locks—he suffered for half a decade the emotional paroxysms of youth in his pursuit of the opposite sex. After being rebuked by two women, each of whose hand he had ardently sought, he ultimately succeeded in winning the heart of Catherine Glynne, to whom he was married on July 25, 1839. Their union was to last a lifetime, and Mrs. Gladstone was to play a significant role in supporting her husband during his political career.

LIFE'S WORK

The man who is remembered as the leader of the Liberals in nineteenth century England entered politics as a Tory. Gladstone's remarkable ability as an orator and his capacity for work so impressed the Conservative leadership of the House of Commons that within two years he was offered a position in the cabinet, as Junior Lord of the Treasury (1834); within a year he had been elevated to undersecretary for the colonies. His busy schedule as a politician did not keep him from working at his first love, religious studies, and in 1838 he published *The State in Its Relations with the Church*, in which he supported the Church of England's privileged political status, a position he was later to repudiate.

In 1841, Gladstone accepted a position as vice president of the Board of Trade, not considered a choice position for a young politician on the rise, but one from which he was able to grow as a manager and financial expert. In 1843, he was elevated to president of the Board of Trade. During the 1840's, Gladstone began supporting measures that put distance between him and the leadership of the Tory Party, which now called itself the Conservative Party: tariff reform, state supervision of railroads, state subsidy for the Roman Catholic Church in Ireland, the rights of minorities to hold seats in Parliament.

When Peel's government fell over the question of handling the famine in Ireland in 1845, Gladstone joined Peel in a move that broke apart the Conservative Party. In the new administration that Peel headed, Gladstone became colonial secretary but lost his seat in Newark, because he no longer held favor with the conservative duke of Newcastle. In 1847, he was returned to Parliament for Oxford, a seat he held until 1865, when his ever-advancing liberalism made him unacceptable to that electorate.

Gladstone resigned his seat in Peel's government in 1846, over the issue of his support for the Catholic-controlled Maynooth College in Ireland. He remained a leading member of the Peelites, as the followers of Peel were called, distrustful of either the Liberals under Lord Palmerston or the Conservatives, whose leadership was passing to Benjamin Disraeli. In 1853, the Conservatives were turned out on a vote of no confidence following Disraeli's presentation of the 1852 budget.

When Lord Aberdeen formed a coalition government, Gladstone joined the cabinet as Chancellor of the Exchequer. His 1853 budget was hailed as one of the most imaginative and comprehensive of the century, and se-

William Ewart Gladstone. (Library of Congress)

cured his reputation as a financial wizard. He continued in this position until 1855 and returned to it for almost seven years, from 1859 to 1866. For a brief interlude when out of office, Gladstone served as Lord High Commissioner of the Ionian Islands in the Mediterranean, though his record there was not especially salutary.

As early as 1865, Gladstone was being touted as a candidate for prime minister. The call finally came to him in 1868, only months after he had succeeded Lord John Russell as head of the Liberal Party. In that year he formed the first, and by all assessments the most successful, of four administrations. He assumed the prime ministership with a primary goal of settling the political turmoil in Ireland, something that had haunted him for years.

Gladstone saw his ascendancy to the head of government as a mission, and treated his work with religious fervor. Among his objectives were the disestablishment of the Church of England, a reversal of his earlier position of support for the political primacy of that religious body, and the resolution of problems between Irish tenants and their landlords, many of whom were absentee owners. His foreign policy was based on high-minded principles of mutual cooperation among nations and a belief that individual nations could operate on good faith with other countries—a policy that sometimes made Great Britain look foolish or weak within the international community. During this first administration, sweeping changes occurred in education in England, largely as a result of the Education Act of 1870, although Gladstone had little interest in or influence on the outcome. He did, however, work to abolish religious tests at the universities.

After almost eight years, the Liberals were turned out of office in 1874. Gladstone, by then in his sixties, retired from the leadership of his party, though he retained his seat in Parliament. He turned his attention to classical studies, specifically to translations of Homer and extended commentary on the Greek writer, in which he sought to establish links between Homer and Christianity, a position scoffed at in his own day and discounted by later critics. He also wrote a series of tracts on religious issues.

Turkish atrocities in the Balkans in 1876 prompted Gladstone's return to an active role in politics. For the next four years, he argued vociferously in Parliament and throughout the country against Disraeli's conservative policies. In 1880, a barnstorming campaign on behalf of Liberal ideology swept his party back into office, and Gladstone once again became prime minister. This second administration lasted until 1885. These years were more tumultuous than those of the first administration, and Gladstone was forced to deal with the growing violence in Ireland and problems caused by British imperialism.

On the home front, Gladstone's growing association with Irish Nationalist Charles Stewart Parnell caused dissension within his own party and gave enemies a prominent target for political attacks. The murder of Gladstone's close friend and nephew-in-law Frederick Cavendish in Phoenix Park, Dublin, in May of 1882, escalated the difficulty, as he was forced to take sterner measures in dealing with the violence.

Abroad, British actions in the Middle East and North Africa caused additional difficulties for the prime minister. A major crisis in the Sudan in 1883 led to the massacre of a British garrison at Khartoum and the death of General Charles Gordon. Gladstone, who had hesitated to take strong action in the region for fear that it would lead Great Britain into yet another brush war, was blamed by the press and by the queen herself for Gordon's death. Ultimately, he was forced to deal with the problems in the area and to assume some responsibility

IRISH HISTORY

One of the major issues that William Ewart Gladstone faced during his terms as prime minister was the seemingly intractable problem of home rule for Ireland. This extract comes from an essay on Irish history that he contributed to a book on home rule.

Ireland for more than seven hundred years has been part of the British territory, and has been with slight exceptions held by English arms, or governed in the last resort from this side the water. Scotland was a foreign country until 1603, and possessed absolute independence until 1707. Yet, whether it was due to the standing barrier of the sea, or whatever may have been the cause, much less was known by Englishmen of Ireland than of Scotland. Witness the works of [William] Shakespeare, whose mind, unless as to book-knowledge, was encyclopædic, and yet who, while he seems at home in Scotland, may be said to tell us nothing of Ireland, unless it is that—

The uncivil kerns of Ireland are in arms. [*2 Henry VI*, act 3, scene 1]

During more recent times, the knowledge of Scotland on this side the border, which before was greatly in advance, has again increased in a far greater degree than the knowledge of Ireland.

It is to Mr. [William Edward Hartpole] Lecky that we owe the first serious effort, both in his *Leaders of Public Opinion* and in his *History of England in the Eighteenth Century*, to produce a better state of things. He carefully and completely dovetailed the affairs of Ireland into English History, and the debt is one to be gratefully acknowledged....

That history, until the eighteenth century begins, has a dismal simplicity about it. Murder, persecution, confiscation too truly describe its general strain; and policy is on the whole subordinated to violence as the standing instrument of government....

Source: William E. Gladstone, "Lessons of Irish History in the Eighteenth Century," *Handbook of Home Rule*, edited by James Bryce (2d ed. London: Kegan Paul, Trench, 1887).

for the deteriorating political system in Egypt, a country in which England had significant interest. The height of ignominy occurred for Gladstone in June, 1885, when his government, which had supported stronger home rule measures for Ireland, was defeated on the issue of the budget by a coalition of Conservatives and Irish Nationalists.

Gladstone returned almost immediately to the prime ministership, and his third, short-lived administration was committed almost exclusively to one issue: home rule for Ireland. Only months after he began his crusade to give Ireland its own parliament and greater control over its own destiny, Gladstone saw his efforts dashed in Parliament in the summer of 1886, when the Home Rule Bill was defeated. Gladstone immediately resigned.

For the next six years, Gladstone worked as the leader of the opposition while the Conservatives held office. He continued to press for Irish home rule, working to hold his Liberal Party together as the radical element within the organization gained strength. In 1892, he formed his fourth and last administration, once again championing Irish home rule. The pressures of leadership finally proved to be too much for a man in his eighties; Gladstone resigned in March, 1894. He spent the last four years of his life at Hawarden, the estate of his wife's family that he had helped preserve when the family was almost forced to sell it during the 1840's. He died May 19, 1898, and after an elaborate funeral ceremony was buried in Statesmen's Corner at Westminster Abbey.

SIGNIFICANCE

William Ewart Gladstone's political career can be seen as the movement of a high-minded and deeply religious individual from conservative principles and High Church convictions to an eventual championship of individual rights and religious tolerance. Some have viewed it as a four-decade struggle against the other dominant figure in nineteenth century British politics, Conservative statesman Benjamin Disraeli. From whatever angle his life is observed, there is no doubt that Gladstone, never the pragmatist, believed deeply in the rightness of any cause he championed, and often sacrificed himself, his reputation, and his political party to ideals.

Gladstone's liberalism troubled Queen Victoria, and his manner in promoting it often offended her. The monarch who loved Disraeli frequently chastised Gladstone for his decisions and his behavior, but he always acted respectfully toward his sovereign. In spite of this stormy relationship, he was able to lead his country on the path toward democracy. Under his direction, and often only because of his strong hand, the British nation struggled—with remarkable success, in retrospect—with important human issues such as greater enfranchisement, improved working and living conditions for the lower classes, and greater concern for individual rights.

The force of his personality on British politics was recognized in his own time; during the later years of his life both friend and enemy alike took to calling him the "Grand Old Man," or "G.O.M." In a century that produced more than its share of giants in statesmanship, Gladstone has emerged as the dominant figure in British politics in the Victorian age.

—*Laurence W. Mazzeno*

FURTHER READING

Biagini, Eugenio F. *Gladstone*. New York: St. Martin's Press, 2000. Biagini, a historian specializing in the nineteenth century, takes a thematic approach to assessing Gladstone's life and political career.

Feuchtwanger, E. J. *Gladstone*. New York: St. Martin's Press, 1975. A detailed political biography, with extensive analysis of British politics, Gladstone's career in Parliament, and the cabinet. Extensive treatment of Gladstone's years as prime minister. Contains a useful bibliography.

Hammond, John Lawrence. *Gladstone and the Irish Nation*. London: Longmans, Green, 1938. A careful scholarly study of Gladstone's attempts to deal with the Irish nation and the question of Irish home rule, an issue that dominated his later administrations. Provides a wide-ranging look at both England and Ireland in the latter half of the nineteenth century.

Knaplund, Paul. *Gladstone and Britain's Imperial Policy*. London: Allen & Unwin, 1927. Reprint. Hamden, Conn.: Archon Books, 1966. Focuses attention on Gladstone's policies regarding the various colonies of the British Empire, which was the largest of all European empires in the nineteenth century. Gladstone had extensive impact on decisions regarding the colonies throughout his career, especially during his service as secretary for the colonies in Peel's cabinet, then later as prime minister.

_____. *Gladstone's Foreign Policy*. New York: Harper & Brothers, 1935. Reprint. Hamden, Conn.: Archon Books, 1970. An assessment of Gladstone's views on foreign policy and a review of his actions in that area during his four terms as prime minister. Includes extensive analysis of his handling of crises in the Near East and Middle East.

Marlow, Joyce. *The Oak and the Ivy: An Intimate Biography of William and Catherine Gladstone*. Garden City, N.Y.: Doubleday, 1977. A dual biography of Gladstone and his wife, focusing on the personal qualities of the statesman, his personality, and his psychological makeup.

Matthew, H. C. *Gladstone, 1809-1898*. New York: Oxford University Press, 1997. A concise biography by a noted Gladstone scholar. Topics include Gladstone's education, political career, and his public and private lives.

Morley, John. *The Life of William Ewart Gladstone*. 3 vols. New York: Macmillan, 1903. Written by a younger contemporary; contains much detail and includes extensive quotations from Gladstone's letters and diaries. Still a primary source for those wishing to understand the complexity of Gladstone's character and the magnitude of his achievements in politics and other fields.

Partridge, Michael. *Gladstone*. London: Routledge, 2003. A reassessment of Gladstone's life and political career. Describes how Gladstone tried but failed to resolve his great obsession—the Irish question.

Shannon, Richard. *Gladstone*. 2 vols. Chapel Hill: University of North Carolina Press, 1984-1999. A comprehensive biography by an expert on Victorian history. Originally published as two separate volumes, volume one covers the years from 1809 until 1865, while volume two covers 1865 through 1898.

SEE ALSO: Lord Acton; F. H. Bradley; John Bright; Joseph Chamberlain; Benjamin Disraeli; William Edward Forster; Lord Palmerston; Charles Stewart Parnell; Sir Robert Peel; Baron John Russell; Third Marquis of Salisbury; Queen Victoria.

RELATED ARTICLES in *Great Events from History: The Nineteenth Century, 1801-1900:* August, 1867: British Parliament Passes the Reform Act of 1867; December 3, 1868-February 20, 1874: Gladstone Becomes Prime Minister of Britain; June 13-July 13, 1878: Congress of Berlin; September-November, 1880: Irish Tenant Farmers Stage First "Boycott"; December 6, 1884: British Parliament Passes the Franchise Act of 1884; June, 1886-September 9, 1893: Irish Home Rule Debate Dominates British Politics.

AUGUST VON GNEISENAU
German military leader

As a Prussian field marshal and member of King Frederick William III's Military Reorganization Commission, Gneisenau fashioned the Prussian strategy that finally defeated Napoleon I in the campaigns of 1813 and 1814 and played a key role in reforming the Prussian army into the most professional military force in nineteenth century Europe. Gneisenau's organizational and operational reforms survive today as accepted elements in most of the world's armies.

BORN: October 27, 1760; Schildau, Saxony (now in Germany)

DIED: August 23, 1831; Posen, Prussia (now Poznan, Poland)

ALSO KNOWN AS: August Wilhelm Anton Graf Neidhardt von Gneisenau (full name)

AREA OF ACHIEVEMENT: Military

EARLY LIFE

The scion of a noble but poor German military family, August von Gneisenau (g-NI-zeh-now) was born during the Seven Years' War. His father, an artillery lieutenant in the Austrian army, abandoned him to friends who reared him in near poverty. A moneyed maternal grandfather subsequently assumed responsibility for the young orphan and entrusted his education to Jesuits. With the death of his benefactor, young Gneisenau inherited enough money to attend Erfurt University from 1777 to 1779. With his inheritance depleted, Gneisenau prematurely left the university, joined a local Austrian regiment as a cavalry subaltern, and fought against Prussia during the 1778 War of Bavarian Succession.

Gneisenau subsequently joined the army of Bayreuth-Ansbach, a tiny principality that hired out its soldiers to the highest bidder. It was within this context that Gneisenau, now a lieutenant of chasseurs, traveled to North America in 1782 to fight as a British mercenary against the American colonists. He arrived too late to fight, but he came upon and embraced new concepts that would later define his role as a leading Prussian military reformer: the belief in a politically active citizenry and the use of open order tactics by civilian militias in warfare.

Gneisenau returned to Europe after one year and personally petitioned Frederick the Great to allow him to join the Prussian army. In 1786, he received a commission as a first lieutenant in the infantry. Although he did participate in the Polish campaign of 1793-1794, Gneisenau served for the next twenty years in different Silesian garrisons, where he immersed himself in military studies and further developed the unique blend of combat and staff skills for which he is rightfully famous.

Gneisenau was an undistinguished forty-six-year-old captain when war broke out between France and Prussia in 1806. On October 14, 1806, he commanded a company of infantry at the Battle of Jena and experienced at first hand Napoleon's annihilation of the once-invincible Frederican army. The defeat was a profound blow to Gneisenau, but even more devastating was the complete indifference shown by the Prussian middle class to the loss of the army. In fact, their perception of the army as a royal instrument promoting reactionary interests was in direct contrast to the nascent "people in arms" concept Gneisenau had seen in the colonies.

Gneisenau adopted the citizen-soldier concept in his 1807 defense of Kolberg, a Pomeranian coastal town situated on the Baltic Sea and besieged by the French. Gneisenau's defense of Kolberg was the only successful Prussian military operation at the time and was directly attributable to his deliberate attempt to transform the local civilians from detached bystanders into active defenders who fought with the same spirit as his regular troops. Gneisenau's success earned for him the highly prized Pour le Mérite award, a promotion to lieutenant colonel, and the notoriety that laid the foundation for his major accomplishments.

LIFE'S WORK

Subsequent to the Prussian debacle at Jena-Auerstadt, King Frederick William III established the Military Reorganization Commission on July 25, 1807. Its charter was to review the army's performance and propose necessary reforms. Major General Ger-

hard von Scharnhorst, after rejecting a position as the director of an English artillery school, became chairman of the commission. Gneisenau, who saw himself as Scharnhorst's "Saint Peter," also became a member, as did two other protégés, Majors Karl Grolman and Herman von Boyen. Carl von Clausewitz, although never a full member of the commission, worked indirectly with it as Scharnhorst's aide. With royal sanction, these five military reformers would resurrect a new Prussian army from the ashes of the one previously destroyed by Napoleon. Gneisenau's influence was second only to Scharnhorst's; with the latter's premature death in 1813, he became the most prominent military reformer.

Gneisenau and his peers quickly ascribed the Prussian defeat to an outdated military and a reactionary society. The Frederican army that faced Napoleon relied on rigid tactics, brutal and unenlightened discipline, and over-centralized control. Common people, in turn, felt no sense of responsibility toward the state and greeted Prussian military failures with apathy. Gneisenau and the

August von Gneisenau. (Library of Congress)

other reformers decided to reverse the situation, but they realized that to be competitive the Prussian army would have to revise its tactics, organization, and working relationship with civilians completely. A mere reorganization of the old-style army would not suffice.

Gneisenau also realized that the reformers needed to inspire a new loyalty to the state; they had to transform Prussian subjects into self-motivated citizens, inspired by patriotism and a belief in national honor. However, Gneisenau believed that a people's army was impossible if Prussia did not change from a feudal society, dominated by landed Junkers, into a liberal, constitutional monarchy. In Gneisenau's estimation, neither a serf in hereditary bondage nor a member of the middle class restricted from local government or the officer corps would develop a devotion to the state in the absence of basic social and political rights. The regeneration of the Prussian military would occur only through the reformation of the state.

Gneisenau and the other commission members quickly introduced a number of enduring military reforms. In contrast to the murderous discipline of the past, an edict issued on August 3, 1805, introduced a humane system of rewards and punishments that deliberately limited corporal punishment. Humane treatment, the reformers hoped, would inspire soldiers to become self-motivated and thus develop a more enduring commitment to both the army and the state. Grolman, with the active support of Gneisenau, sponsored an August 6, 1808, decree that transformed the officer corps into a meritocracy, where members of the middle class could enter and succeed based on their demonstrated performance rather than on their family background.

A third innovation was the introduction of professional military education. By 1810, the Prussian army had reorganized all of its schools and introduced the prototype for the *Kriegsakademie*, the first modern war college. Those who attended the college received a liberal education that included, for the first time, a systematic study of war. Thanks to Gneisenau and his fellow reformers, war was no longer for a brave dilettante but for cool professionals who subjected it to lifelong study.

Gneisenau also supported Baron Heinrich von Stein, the king's chief minister and a fellow reformer on the Military Reorganization Commission, who laid the foundation for a War Ministry responsible for directing, coordinating, and controlling the Prussian army. The nascent general staff, organized within the General War Department of the War Ministry, would begin to flourish

as the intellectual center of the German military under Helmuth von Moltke the Elder.

Gneisenau's most cherished reforms, however, were the most imperfectly realized. He and the Military Reorganization Commission called for universal conscription as early as 1808, but Frederick William, who feared the destruction of the monarchy in a civil war between economic classes, balked at the idea of a nation in arms. It was only in 1814, when the defeat of Napoleon seemed possible, that Frederick William accepted national conscription. The principle survived, but Gneisenau did not see a lasting union of regular soldiers and militia into a military force crusading for freedom in Europe. The militia (*Landwehr*) enjoyed a brief, independent life but ultimately was subsumed under regular army control beginning in 1819.

Gneisenau worked hard for the above reforms and functioned as chief of the fortifications and engineering corps until Napoleon forced a powerless Frederick William to dismiss Stein and other reformers. In disgust, Gneisenau resigned and quietly undertook missions to Great Britain, Russia, and Sweden in order to muster support against France. His passionate humanism now focused on liberating Europe from Napoleon. When Prussia discarded its role as an unwilling satellite to France, Gneisenau returned to active service as Scharnhorst's *Ia*, or first general staff officer. When Scharnhorst died in June, 1813, Gneisenau became chief of the general staff and served Marshal Gebhard von Blücher. In this capacity, Gneisenau planned the Prussian strategy for the major campaigns of 1813-1814, including the Battle of Leipzig.

During this phase of his career, Gneisenau introduced battlefield innovations that had a lasting influence. He was the first to make the chief of staff of a major command equal in responsibility with the commander. He believed that this arrangement would strengthen the general staff system and establish spiritual unity between staff officers and combatants. He also developed the practice of issuing clear and comprehensive objectives while leaving room for the combat commander to exercise individual initiative and freedom of action. Gneisenau directly influenced Clausewitz's subsequent theory of war by insisting that the goal of an army was not to engage in maneuver warfare but to destroy enemy forces directly. Finally, he was an early practitioner of the battle of encirclement, later used with great success by Helmuth Karl Bernhard von Moltke and Alfred von Schlieffen. For these innovations and other successes, Frederick William ennobled Gneisenau in 1814.

Upon Napoleon's return from Elba in March, 1815, Gneisenau once again became Blücher's chief of staff. Each was good for the other: Gneisenau's powerful intellect and organizing skills tempered Blücher's mercurial personality and bulldog tenacity. It was Gneisenau, with prodding from Grolman, who at the Battle of Ligny decided not to retreat toward Prussia but north to Wavre, Belgium. Thus, when the Battle of Waterloo hung in the balance, the Prussians tipped it in the duke of Wellington's favor by attacking the French flank. The murderous pursuit of the French troops that followed was yet another example of Gneisenau's vigorous style of war.

With the final defeat of Napoleon, Gneisenau fell into disfavor. The absence of a common foe enabled the reactionary Junkers to reverse the more extreme changes he and the other reformers had introduced. Gneisenau subsequently resigned in 1816. He became governor of Berlin in 1818 and a field marshal in 1825. In 1831, during the Polish Revolution, he commanded the army of occupation on Prussia's eastern border. While on border duty, both he and Clausewitz, now his chief of staff, died of cholera.

SIGNIFICANCE

As a reformer and combatant, August von Gneisenau had a lasting and widespread influence. He and the other Prussian reformers on the Military Reorganization Commission forever changed the character of modern armies. Following the Prussian example, rival powers introduced universal conscription and opened the officer corps to those with talent, regardless of their social background. They increasingly relied on nationalism rather than harsh discipline to motivate troops. They also formalized their military establishments by introducing war ministries, professional military education, and the general staff system. Gneisenau was instrumental in developing and popularizing these innovations.

Gneisenau was bitterly disappointed for two reasons. Prussia, rather than becoming a liberal constitutional monarchy, remained thoroughly autocratic. As a result, the army remained an isolated enclave of military technicians rather than a democratic institution manned by enlightened citizen soldiers who had a personal investment in supporting their government. Gneisenau overestimated the state's willingness to turn over a new leaf. Instead, the pattern for future Prussian jingoism was set.

As a combatant, Gneisenau believed that the army was the enemy's "center of gravity" and thus had to be destroyed. A vigorous pursuit was part of the process. Both concepts found expression in Clausewitz's *Vom*

Kriege (1832-1834; *On War*, 1873), which later had an impact on German strategy and tactics (beginning in the Wars of German Unification). Given the influence of these combat techniques and his earlier organizational reforms, Gneisenau's sustained influence on modern military establishments is undeniable.

—Peter R. Faber

FURTHER READING

Britt, Albert Sidney. "Field Marshal August Neidhart von Gneisenau." In *The Consortium on Revolutionary Europe, 1750-1850: Proceedings, 1983*, edited by Clarence Davis. Gainesville: University of Florida Press, 1985. A basic treatment of Gneisenau's accomplishments that tries to prove that he was an outstanding example of ability improved by study.

Craig, Gordon. *The Politics of the Prussian Army, 1640-1945*. New York: Oxford University Press, 1956. Craig's seminal work traces the role of the army in modern German history. Gneisenau and the reformers receive a sympathetic look for their attempts not only to resurrect an army but also to change a society.

Dupuy, Trevor Nevitt. *A Genius for War: The German Army and General Staff, 1807-1945*. Englewood Cliffs, N.J.: Prentice-Hall, 1977. Dupuy performed statistical analyses of World War II battles and discovered that German combat effectiveness per man was better than for the Allies. He concludes that the Germans developed the ability to institutionalize military excellence. Analyzes how the Germans did this, beginning with Gneisenau and the reformers in 1807. The specific details on Gneisenau are valuable but limited.

Gneisenau, August Wilhelm Anton, Graf Neidhardt von. *The Life and Campaigns of Field Marshal Prince Blücher of Whalstaff: From the Period of His Birth and First Appointment in the Prussian Service Down to His Second Entry into Paris in 1815*. Translated by General Count Gneisenau and J. E. Marston. London: Constable, 1996. A reprint of Gneisenau's biography of his military superior. Offers an idea of how Gneisenau viewed the Napoleonic Wars and the army in which he served.

Goerlitz, Walter. *History of the German General Staff, 1657-1945*. Translated by Brian Battershaw. New York: Praeger, 1953. This German historian traces the growing incompatibility between the German army and a society evolving toward a democratic-capitalistic system. Goerlitz identifies Gneisenau's zealotry as one reason that the reformers fell so quickly into disfavor. He also treats Gneisenau's impact as a combatant.

Müffling, Baron Carl von. *The Memoirs of Baron Von Müffling: A Prussian Officer in the Napoleonic Wars.* London: Greenhill Books, 1997. Müffling, the Prussian liaison to Wellington during the Waterloo campaign, provides his recollections of the wars, including his impressions of Gneisenau, Blücher, and others.

Ritter, Gerhard. *The Sword and the Scepter: The Problem of Militarism in Germany.* Translated by Heinz Norden. Coral Gables, Fla.: University of Miami Press, 1969. As the title implies, this three-volume study analyzes the growth of German militarism from 1740 to the present. Gneisenau receives a factual review for reform efforts that unwittingly created the possibility for subsequent military adventurism.

SEE ALSO: Gebhard Leberecht von Blücher; Carl von Clausewitz; Karl von Hardenberg; Napoleon I; Gerhard Johann David von Scharnhorst; Freiherr vom Stein; Duke of Wellington.

RELATED ARTICLES in *Great Events from History: The Nineteenth Century, 1801-1900:* October 16-19, 1813: Battle of Leipzig; June 18, 1815: Battle of Waterloo.

VINCENT VAN GOGH
Dutch painter

Van Gogh's artistic career was brief, but in giving expression to a passionate vision of nature and humanity, he has become one of the most revered and influential painters of his time. Following his death, his paintings came to be acknowledged by critics and the public as constituting one of the highest achievements of nineteenth century art.

BORN: March 30, 1853; Zundert, the Netherlands
DIED: July 29, 1890; Auvers-sur-Oise, France
ALSO KNOWN AS: Vincent Willem van Gogh (full name)
AREA OF ACHIEVEMENT: Art

EARLY LIFE

Vincent Willem van Gogh (van goh) was the son of the Reverend Theodorus van Gogh, who was thirty-one years old at the time of Vincent's birth. His mother, Anna Cornelius Carbentus, was three years older than her husband. Among van Gogh's three sisters and two brothers, Vincent was to be close only to his brother Theodorus (called Theo), who was an important influence in his life. Vincent's family had been established for generations in the Dutch province of North Brabant, near the southern border with Belgium. Among his ancestors could be found preachers, craftspeople, and government officials, and his living relatives included several uncles prominent in business and government. Vincent's father, a Protestant minister, was a handsome man but not a gifted preacher. Working quietly in several rural parishes until his death at the age of sixty-two, he was able to provide for his family in a respectable but modest fashion.

Vincent enjoyed a happy childhood and was especially attached to the natural world; drawings he made as early as age eleven show a keen observation of plant life. His skill at drawing, which seems to have been fostered by his mother, does not foreshadow his later artistic genius, but it testifies to his capacity for solitary concentration. The recollection of Vincent's sister Elizabeth was that Vincent could be unapproachable and that he enjoyed solitude. If he seems to have had a somewhat changeable personality as a boy, his education proceeded normally when he was sent at the age of twelve to a boarding school in the nearby village of Zevenbergen, from which he progressed to a state secondary school in the town of Tilburg. By age fifteen, he was well on the way to being a literate, if not yet sophisticated, young man.

After more than a year at home in Zundert, Vincent left in the summer of 1869 to work as a junior clerk in the branch of the French firm of Goupil and Sons in The Hague, a post for which his uncle Vincent, a partner in the firm, had recommended him. He enjoyed his work, found favor with his employers, and was transferred after four years to the London branch of the firm. Beginning with this period, there is a substantially continuous documentation both of Vincent's activities and of his emotional and intellectual experiences, for in August, 1872, he and Theo began a correspondence that was to last to the end of the artist's life.

In the summer of 1874, the first of several romantic

disappointments struck van Gogh, when he declared his love for his landlady's daughter, Eugénie. Finding that she was engaged and had been playing upon his innocent devotion, he was cast into a despair, which he was unable to dispel during a three-month assignment to Goupil's Paris gallery. Returning to his London job in January, 1875, he once again failed to win Eugénie's love, and his distress, now colored by religious concerns, was intensified. In May he was permanently transferred to Paris, where his spiritual preoccupations distracted him from his work and led to his dismissal from Goupil's in March, 1876.

Van Gogh returned to England the following month and took an unpaid position in Ramsgate as a teacher of French, German, and arithmetic. In July, he changed jobs again, teaching at a boys' school in Isleworth and preaching occasionally. The prospect of a religious vocation began to dominate his thoughts, but with his health failing he returned to his parents' home, which was now in Etten. Soon after, his uncle found him another job in a bookstore in the city of Dordrecht, but by May, 1877, van Gogh had determined to study for admission to the faculty of theology at the University in Amsterdam.

For a little more than a year, van Gogh studied Greek and Latin with a congenial young Jewish scholar, Mendes da Costa, but in July, 1878, declaring his inability to learn these languages, he enrolled in a preparatory course for evangelists in Brussels. Failing to qualify for a regular parish, van Gogh was given a trial appointment as a missionary in the Borinage, a coal-mining district of Belgium, but the church authorities soon dismissed him for his unconventionally zealous behavior. Continuing his work alone, van Gogh seems to have gone through a period of extreme spiritual crisis, during which he began to draw the very people to whom he had been preaching. In the autumn of 1880, believing that his destiny was to be an artist, van Gogh left the Borinage for Brussels, seeking advice there from painters and attempting to improve his drawings.

During the following spring and summer, van Gogh was again in Etten, where a second disappointment in love occurred. At his parents' home he met a recently widowed first cousin, Kee Vos Stricker, and fell in love with her, but she fled to her parents when van Gogh declared his affection. In this affair, van Gogh's capacity for creating strained relationships with those closest to him had reached a new peak, and as a result he left again for The Hague, where he established a small studio in January, 1882, and lived with a prostitute, Clasina Hoornik, known as "Sien."

LIFE'S WORK

Through his employment at the Goupil establishments, van Gogh had been exposed to much art that was merely fashionable, but he had also seen the paintings of notable French and English painters such as Jean-François Millet, Thomas Gainsborough, and John Constable. In his own early work, however, he was guided less by artistic precedents than by a profound urge to render the life of laboring peasants and miners and to evoke compassion for the suffering of his fellow man.

Van Gogh was, from the start, temperamentally incapable of following a commonplace path in his art, but he valued the advice of his fellow painters, including popular ones such as his cousin by marriage, Anton Mauve, from whom he received instruction in The Hague during the winter of 1881-1882. Perhaps for family considerations, van Gogh's uncle, Cornelius, also lent the struggling artist encouragement in 1882 by commissioning from him a series of drawings of city views, but it was Theo's regular allowance that kept van Gogh from abject poverty throughout his artistic career. Just as important, Theo gave moral support to his erratic and socially inept elder brother, becoming a spiritual as well as financial guardian. He was also the recipient of much of van Gogh's best work, as van Gogh did not sell a painting until the last year of his life.

Van Gogh's passionate devotion to his artistic self-education yielded solid results during his stay in The Hague; to the emotional conviction of his drawings he was able to add increasing fluency of form. His subjects, principally peasants and workers, are often shown in a wintry landscape that seems both accurately rendered and true to the artist's social vision. There is experimentation with materials, but it is always aimed at rendering a particular subject rather than at producing an attractive appearance.

In the summer of 1883, van Gogh began to work in earnest with oil paints and during the next two years, living again at home with his parents in the village of Nuenen, he produced dozens of canvases of the countryside and its people. The culmination of this work is a masterpiece, *The Potato Eaters*, completed in October of 1885. It is a canvas approximately three feet high and four feet wide, depicting a family of five peasants seated around a rough table, about to eat a meal of boiled potatoes. Each figure, including that of a girl whose face cannot be seen, is a distinct portrait of human dignity in the face of adversity. Darkly monochromatic and roughly textured, *The Potato Eaters* is an uncompromising study of the human condition and has none of the sentimental-

Vincent van Gogh, self-portrait. (Courtesy, The Art Institute of Chicago)

ity that van Gogh sometimes found appealing in other artists and writers.

The year 1885 brought important new influences to van Gogh. In October, he saw old master paintings in the Rijksmuseum in Amsterdam and found special inspiration in the work of Rembrandt and Frans Hals. In late November, while studying briefly in Antwerp, he first saw Japanese prints, which were just beginning to be widely appreciated in Europe. The clarity and brilliance of the Japanese woodblock print, together with the freshness of van Gogh's seventeenth century Dutch predecessors, helped change his conception of light and color, which had been dominated by earth colors and dark tones.

Early in 1886, this change was accelerated by van Gogh's move to Paris, where the Impressionist painters were gaining recognition for their innovative style of rendering effects of light and color by applying brilliant, unblended pigments to their canvases. Van Gogh was soon associating with the Impressionists and befriending such artists as Camille Pissarro and Henri de Toulouse-Lautrec. Theo, as a representative of the new owners of Goupil's, was an agent for Impressionist paintings and fueled van Gogh's appreciation and understanding of them.

During the summer of 1886, Theo and Vincent took an apartment together in the Paris suburb of Montmartre. Despite the deep affection of the brothers for each other, their relationship was often strained almost to the breaking point; perhaps the remarkable progress of van Gogh's painting was Theo's reward for tolerating his volatile and inconsiderate brother. For van Gogh, however, the Paris years of 1886 and 1887 were a time of relative stability. He became acquainted with many personalities with valuable experiences and opinions to share.

Among these people were artists such as Émile Bernard, who later wrote perceptively about van Gogh, and the celebrated Julien Tanguy, an art-supply dealer who offered a haven—and quiet financial help—to many painters who were subsequently recognized as leading artists of their day. Van Gogh's 1887 portrait of "Père" Tanguy shows the quiet gentleman seated against a wall on which Japanese prints—which he also sold—are hung. In this celebrated work, van Gogh unites his affection for Tanguy and his reverence for Japanese art with a post-Impressionist technique likely borrowed from Paul Signac.

After a remarkable two years in Paris, van Gogh may have believed that he had exhausted the city's possibilities; in any case, the stress underlying his relationship with Theo could not continue indefinitely, and in February, 1888, he left Paris abruptly for the town of Arles, near the Mediterranean coast, arriving on February 20. The south of France had then, as it has continued to have, rich associations for artists. In addition to the many reminders of classical Latin culture, the climate, light, and atmosphere could be powerful stimuli to creative work. In van Gogh's case, Arles and its environs was in some sense the cause of the astonishing outpouring of drawings and paintings that occurred between February, 1888, and May, 1890.

Ironically for an argumentative person such as van Gogh, he had been preoccupied by the idea of creating a brotherhood of artists, and his move to Arles was partly intended as a step in that direction. During the early months in Arles, he associated with several artist acquaintances, but more typically he formed friendships with local people such as the postman Joseph Roulin, whose portrait he painted many times. However, in mid-October, van Gogh welcomed to his rooms in the "Yellow House" the stockbroker-turned-artist Paul Gauguin, another strong, even rebellious, personality with whom conflict might have been foreseen.

Gauguin had traveled to Arles and was to be maintained there at Theo's expense in exchange for paintings.

For a time, van Gogh and Gauguin valued their artistic relationship, but the domestic situation abruptly deteriorated, culminating—by Gauguin's account—in van Gogh's attack upon him with a razor blade. Before Gauguin could effect a departure from Arles, van Gogh had cut off part of his own earlobe, delivering it to the door of a local prostitute before returning, delirious and bleeding profusely, to his room at the Yellow House.

Following his recovery in the local hospital, van Gogh returned to the Yellow House on January 7 and began painting on the following day. The next month, he suffered hallucinations and was interned in a hospital cell for ten days, then released. By early May, he had agreed with Theo that he ought to enter an asylum in Saint-Rémy, several miles northeast of Arles, where he remained under the humane but ineffectual care of the asylum staff for slightly more than one year. A diagnosis of epilepsy, easily doubted but less easily supplanted by modern speculation, was made by the director, Dr. Peyron.

Throughout van Gogh's year at Saint-Rémy, his condition varied enormously; sometimes he was not only calm and productive but also optimistic, and at other times he was uncommunicative and even suicidal. Remarkably, during his period of lucidity and physical well-being, he created many of his great masterpieces, including *The Starry Night* and a *Self-Portrait* of 1889. Like many of the works painted during his stay at Saint-Rémy, these canvases are characterized by vibrant color and the use of a sinuous line that make the surface of the painting seem to pulsate with energy. *The Starry Night* and another Saint-Rémy picture of irises were included in a fall exhibition in Paris, where they attracted attention.

In January, 1890, the first article on van Gogh, and the only one published in his lifetime, appeared in *Mercure de France*. Entitled "The Isolated Ones: Vincent van Gogh," the article was the work of a perceptive young critic named G.-Albert Aurier, who had seen many of van Gogh's works at Theo's home. Aurier's observations were overwhelmingly enthusiastic, yet van Gogh wrote to Theo asking him to dissuade Aurier from writing any more about him. Although there was an element of modesty in this, it was more Vincent's accelerating exhaustion of spirit that caused him to be wary of acclaim. Events that buoyed his spirit, such as Theo's marriage and the birth of a nephew—also named Vincent Willem—could also have created new strains in his fragile mind.

Van Gogh left the asylum at Saint-Rémy on May 16, 1890, and traveled alone to Paris without incident, where he stayed four days with Theo and his family before traveling to nearby Auvers-sur-Oise to live under the supervision of Paul Gachet, an art-loving doctor of sixty-two. For several weeks, van Gogh carried on with his painting and even printed an etching using Gachet's press, but on July 27 he walked several hundred yards to a farm near Auvers and shot himself in the stomach. He managed to return to his room, and in the last thirty-six hours of his life he dozed, smoked his pipe, and spoke at length with Theo, who had been summoned from Paris. He died during the early morning hours of July 29, 1890. Only weeks later, Theo suffered a breakdown that seemed clearly connected to his grief over his brother's death, and on January 25, 1891, he died in Utrecht, the Netherlands.

SIGNIFICANCE

Vincent van Gogh's tumultuous life is so well documented by his letters and the recollections of family, friends, and associates, that an unusual degree of study and speculation has been devoted to his personal circumstances and particularly to the tragedy of his illness. In this respect, van Gogh has become virtually an archetype of the modern artist—a man ill at ease with himself and society, and restless in the personal as well as the artistic sphere. Van Gogh himself was well aware of the implications of his personality and his social situation, accepting his dependence upon his brother as well as his status as an outsider in order to pursue his art without compromise.

As compelling as van Gogh's story has been for critics and public alike, it is his paintings, and to a lesser extent his drawings, that are the cornerstone of his lasting significance. From the early drawings made during his ministry in the Borinage to the final paintings made in the weeks preceding his death in Auvers-sur-Oise, van Gogh's works are characterized by passionate sincerity. As important as their psychological authenticity is their adventurous form. Starting during the early 1880's from a vigorous but rather insular style, he assimilated the heritage of Dutch painting, then went on to adapt the lessons of Impressionism to new and visionary purposes. Van Gogh's singular artistic triumph, differentiating him from his post-Impressionist colleagues such as Gauguin and Georges Seurat, was his ability to communicate both his visual experience of nature and his insight into humankind's social and spiritual condition.

Van Gogh, whose personal relationships were often catastrophic, saw his art as an act of love for humanity, and one avenue of psychological analysis views the fervor of his career as compensation for the emotional failures of his life. Although there is doubtless some truth to this view, if taken too literally it can reduce the immense complexity of his life to a formula. Van Gogh was both highly intelligent and acutely self-aware, and it seems likely that even as he descended toward a tragic suicide, he was aware of the great, though painfully forged, achievement of his life as a painter.

—C. S. McConnell

FURTHER READING

Barr, Alfred H., Jr., ed. *Vincent van Gogh: With an Introduction and Notes Selected from the Letters of the Artist*. New York: Arno Press, 1966. This reprint edition of the catalog to a 1935 exhibition of the artist's work at the Museum of Modern Art, New York, is joined to an annotated bibliography, originally published in 1942, of articles, books, and other materials on van Gogh.

Gogh, Vincent van. *Complete Letters, with Reproductions of All Drawings in the Correspondence*. 3 vols. Greenwich, Conn.: New York Graphic Society, 1958. Van Gogh's letters rank among the finest literary artifacts in the sphere of visual art. Books of selected letters are useful but almost inevitably omit even items of general interest.

_____. *Van Gogh: A Retrospective*. Edited by Susan Alyson Stein. New York: Macmillan, 1986. A magnificent collection of documentary material and excellent color plates, this large book also contains a lengthy chronology of the artist's life, which corrects a number of factual errors scattered throughout many earlier sources.

_____. *Vincent van Gogh*. Text by Meyer Schapiro. New York: Harry N. Abrams, 1950. This volume, in a uniform series of artist monographs, contains a fine essay coupled with large color plates annotated on the facing page. The text is excellent as an introduction to the artist, but the plates do not reach the quality of modern reproductions.

_____. *The Works of Vincent van Gogh: His Paintings and Drawings*. Text by J.-B. de la Faille. New York: William Morrow, 1970. A complete (so far as scholarship can ascertain) catalog of the artist's works, each one illustrated, follows an essay, "Van Gogh and the Words," by A. M. Hammacher, which provides a history of the appreciation of van Gogh's works by leading writers and critics.

Krauss, André. *Vincent van Gogh: Studies in the Social Aspects of His Work*. Göteborg: Acta Universitatis Gothoburgensis, 1983. This compact study is a doctoral dissertation investigating the issue of social messages in the painter's work. Though it is specialized, it is very readable.

The Portable Van Gogh. New York: Universe, 2002. Focuses on Van Gogh's paintings, providing a comprehensive overview of all genres and periods of his work. Includes an essay about Van Gogh by Robert Hughes, a prominent art critic.

Sund, Judy. *Van Gogh*. New York: Phaidon, 2002. Biography using Van Gogh's correspondence to trace his artistic development and personal vision.

Wallace, Robert. *The World of Van Gogh, 1853-1890*. New York: Time-Life Books, 1969. Aimed at a popular audience, the text of this well-illustrated book is reliable, though sketchy. A justifiable, and even valuable, limitation is that van Gogh is presented alongside his contemporaries Toulouse-Lautrec and Seurat.

SEE ALSO: John Constable; Paul Gauguin; Hiroshige; Camille Pissarro; Georges Seurat; Henri de Toulouse-Lautrec.

RELATED ARTICLES in *Great Events from History: The Nineteenth Century, 1801-1900:* April 15, 1874: First Impressionist Exhibition; Late 1870's: Post-Impressionist Movement Begins; 1892-1895: Toulouse-Lautrec Paints *At the Moulin Rouge*; 1893: Munch Paints *The Scream*.

NIKOLAI GOGOL
Russian writer

Gogol made an important contribution to the development of modern comic fiction in literature, particularly short fiction. By combining such disparate narrative elements as oral folklore and literary Romanticism, Gogol paved the way for such modernist writers as Franz Kafka.

BORN: March 31, 1809; Sorochintsy, Ukraine, Russian Empire (now in Ukraine)

DIED: March 4, 1852; Moscow, Russia

ALSO KNOWN AS: Nikolai Vasilyevich Gogol (full name)

AREA OF ACHIEVEMENT: Literature

EARLY LIFE

Nikolai Gogol (GOH-gahl) was born on his family's country estate in the Ukraine near the small town of Sorochintsy. A sickly child, he was so pampered and idolized by his mother when he was young that he developed an inflated opinion of himself. At the age of twelve, Gogol entered a boarding school in the city of Nezhin, where he stayed for seven years; however, probably because he was bored with the routine of the classroom, he was only an average student. He was, however, enthusiastic about literature and drama, actively taking part in school theatricals in every capacity, from stagehand to actor and director.

By all accounts, Gogol was a skinny, unattractive child with a bad complexion and a long nose; he was often called dwarfish by his schoolmates. Although there is no indication that he gave serious thought to a writing career while in school, Gogol did write one long poem during his adolescence entitled "Hans Küchelgarten" (1829), which he took to St. Petersburg with him after graduation in 1828 and published at his own expense. Yet, as most critics agree, the poem is highly imitative and immature; the derisive reception it received by the few reviewers who noticed it at all probably made Gogol decide to abandon poetry forever and focus instead on drama and prose, in which his talent for mixing traditional styles and genres could best be exhibited.

After his father's death, Gogol's mother was unable to manage the family estate profitably; as a result, Gogol found himself without funds and without prospects. Securing a position in the civil service to support himself, he began writing stories in his spare time about the Ukraine and submitting them to a St. Petersburg periodical. By gaining the attention of such influential Russian

writers as Baron Anton Delvig and Vasily Zhukovsky with these pieces, Gogol was introduced to the great Russian poet Alexander Pushkin, who admired Gogol's fiction. Gogol's early stories were published in two volumes in 1831 and 1832 as *Vechera na khutore bliz Dikanki* (*Evenings on a Farm Near Dikanka*, 1926), and they received an enthusiastic response from critics in Moscow and St. Petersburg; Gogol had thus arrived as an exciting new talent and was admitted to the highest literary circles.

LIFE'S WORK

The stories in *Evenings on a Farm Near Dikanka* introduce readers to Gogol's major stylistic innovation—the combining of the fanciful and earthy folklore of his native Ukraine with the literary and philosophic imagination of German Romanticism, about which he had learned in school. The hybrid generic form that resulted from the combination of fantastic events and realistic detail not only characterizes Gogol's short stories in particular but also typifies similar narrative experiments being conducted with the short prose form in the United States, Germany, and France; Gogol's experimentation with short prose fiction gives him a place in the creation of the short story equal in importance to Edgar Allan Poe, E. T. A. Hoffmann, and Prosper Mérimée.

In 1834, Gogol obtained a position as a history professor at the University of St. Petersburg and lectured there for a little more than a year; however, he was so bad at it that the administration gently compelled him to leave. Essays in art, history, and literature on which Gogol had been working while teaching appeared in 1835 under the title *Arabeski* (*Arabesques*, 1982). Although these essays were not distinguished in any way, the three new stories that appeared in the collection—"Portret" ("The Portrait"), "Nevsky Prospekti" ("Nevsky Prospect"), and "Zapiski sumasshedshego" ("Diary of a Madman")—are significant Gogol works. Along with "Nos" (1836; "The Nose") and "Shinel" (1839; "The Overcoat"), and often referred to as the Petersburg Cycle, these stories are his major contribution to the short story and the novella forms.

Of the three stories that appeared in *Arabesques*, "Diary of a Madman" is perhaps the best known. Drawing some of his ideas from the German Romantic writer Hoffmann, Gogol has his central character, a minor government official, tell his own story of his hopeless infatuation with the daughter of the chief of his department. The story is an effective combination of social criticism, psychological analysis, and grotesque comedy, for, by intertwining the "mad" perception of the narrator with the supposedly "sane" perception of the bureaucratic world that surrounds the narrator, Gogol manages to underline the relativity of madness itself.

Gogol's story "The Nose" is perhaps second only to his masterpiece "The Overcoat" in its influence on subsequent fiction. The fantastic plot of the story begins when a St. Petersburg barber finds the nose of the assessor Major Kovalev, whom he shaves regularly, in his breakfast roll one morning. On the same morning, Kovalev wakes up to find a smooth, shiny place on his face where his nose used to be. When he goes to the police to have the case of the missing nose investigated, he is astonished to see his nose on the street wearing a gold-braided uniform. After finally recovering the nose, Kovalev tries unsuccessfully to stick it back on his face; finally, he wakes up one morning to find it back where it belongs. Although, like "Diary of a Madman," the story is filled with ironic social criticism, what makes it so influential is the integration of this fantastic plot premise with the most straightforward style of narration. Like Franz Kafka's twentieth century masterpiece *Die Verwandlung* (1915; *The Metamorphosis*, 1936), Gogol's "The Nose" only asks that the reader accept the initial incredible premise; all the rest follows in a strictly realistic fashion.

This combination of different realms of reality reaches a powerful culmination when Gogol unites it with two different literary styles in what all critics agree is his most nearly perfect work, "The Overcoat." The story of the poverty-stricken copyist with the absurd name of Akakii Akakiievich Bashmachkin is so well known that it has been said that most modernist Russian fiction springs from under Gogol's "overcoat." Once again, Gogol combines what seems to be social realism of everyday St. Petersburg life with the fantastic style of folklore. Indeed, most of the commentary that has been written on the story focuses on either its realistic nature or its fantastic style. Irish short-story writer Frank O'Connor has said that what makes the story so magnificent is Gogol's focus on the copyist and his emphasis on Akakii's implicit call for human brotherhood. On the other hand, in what is perhaps the best-known discussion of the story, Russian formalist critic Boris Eichenbaum claims that the genius of the story depends on the role played by the author's personal tone and the story's use of the oral conventions of Russian folktales.

GOGOL'S MAJOR WORKS	
Fiction	
1831-1832	*Vechera na khutore bliz Dikanki* (*Evenings on a Farm Near Dikanka*, 1926)
1835	*Mirgorod* (English translation, 1928)
1835	*Arabeski* (*Arabesques*, 1982)
1842	*Taras Bulba* (revision of his 1835 short story; English translation, 1886)
1842, 1855	*Myortvye dushi* (*Dead Souls*, 1887)
Drama	

Years in left column are earliest dates of production or publication.

1836	*Revizor* (*The Inspector General*, 1890)
1836	*Utro delovogo cheloveka* (revision of *Vladimir tretey stepeni*; *An Official's Morning*, 1926)
1842	*Vladimir tretey stepeni*
1842	*Zhenit'ba* (*Marriage: A Quite Incredible Incident*, 1926)
1842	*Lakeyskaya* (revision of *Vladimir tretey stepeni*; *The Servants' Hall*, 1926)
1842	*Tyazhba* (revision of *Vladimir tretey stepeni*; *The Lawsuit*, 1926)
1842	*Otryvok* (revision of *Vladimir tretey stepeni*; *A Fragment*, 1926)
1842	*Igroki* (*The Gamblers*, 1926)
1926	*The Government Inspector, and Other Plays*

Although Gogol published more ambitious works, at least in terms of scope, than these three short fictions, none of his later work surpasses them in narrative and stylistic control. Among Gogol's longer works, only one drama—*Revizor* (1836; *The Inspector General*, 1890)—and one novel—*Myortvye dushi* (part 1, 1842, part 2, 1855; *Dead Souls*, 1887)—remain as influential indicators of Gogol's genius. *The Inspector General*, although comic like his short fictions "The Nose" and "The Overcoat," is not fantastic like them. In fact, it has been called his most conventionally realistic work. Because of its satirical thrusts at government bureaucracy, the play was attacked, when it was first produced, by conservative critics as a slander on Russian government. Today it is remembered as one of Gogol's most emphatic social satires.

Many critics, more impressed with the broader scope of the novel than the more limited perfection of the short story, consider Gogol's novel *Dead Souls* to be his undisputed masterpiece. Indeed, it is an ambitious work, taking Gogol six years to complete. Building on an idea given him by Pushkin—that dead souls, or serfs, are taken as live ones—Gogol creates the character Tchitchikov, who buys dead souls to bolster his own wealth. Boasting an unforgettable assembly of grotesque comic characterizations, *Dead Souls* is often called one of the great comic masterpieces of European literature.

During the last ten years of his life, after the publication of part 1 of *Dead Souls*, Gogol worked on part 2. All that remains, however, are the first four chapters and part of a final chapter. In 1845, he burned all the other manuscript pages of the novel he had been working on for four years. Before his death in March, 1852, he once again put a match to the work he had subsequently done on part 2. He died a little more than a week later.

SIGNIFICANCE

Although Nikolai Gogol died when he was only forty-two, thus leaving a body of work that is relatively small—certainly nothing to rival the monumental output of such nineteenth century greats as Leo Tolstoy and Fyodor Dostoevski—his influence has loomed much larger than his output would suggest. Although he is generally remembered as a writer of biting social satire on Russian government bureaucracy and as a creator of comic types that rival those of Charles Dickens, it is his short fiction in particular that has had the most significant impact. Gogol is indeed a writer's writer, for short-story writers themselves are the ones who most recognize his greatness. From his countryman Ivan Turgenev to Irish short-story writer Frank O'Connor to American philosopher and fiction writer William H. Gass, Gogol has been recognized as a powerful nineteenth century innovator in the creation of that strange blend of fantasy and reality—the comic grotesque—that has come to be recognized as an essential element of modernism and postmodernism.

—*Charles E. May*

FURTHER READING

Bloom, Harold, ed. *Nikolai Gogol*. Philadelphia: Chelsea House, 2004. One of a series of books aimed at introducing students to major authors. Features a short biography, critical essays about Gogol's writing, a chronology, and an introductory essay by Bloom.

Driessen, F. C. *Gogol as a Short-Story Writer: A Study of His Technique of Composition*. Translated by Ian F. Finlay. The Hague, Netherlands: Mouton, 1965. A formalist study of Gogol's technique as a short-story writer. Focuses on anxiety as a major Gogol theme before analyzing selected stories, including "The Overcoat," which Driessen says represents an isolated attempt of Gogol to overcome his anxiety.

Erlich, Victor. *Gogol*. New Haven, Conn.: Yale University Press, 1969. A study of Gogol by an expert on Russian formalist criticism. Focuses on Gogol's technique and his most typical themes and images. More theoretical than practical in its approach to Gogol, the study contains numerous provocative ideas and concepts for understanding his genius.

Fanger, Donald L. *The Creation of Nikolai Gogol*. Cambridge, Mass.: Harvard University Press, 1979. An attempt to compensate for what the author calls the overabundance of eccentric views of Gogol in American criticism. Fanger outlines the Russian cultural context of Gogol's work and then examines his works to elucidate the progressive development of its basic underlying pattern.

Lindstrom, Thaïs S. *Nikolay Gogol*. Boston: Twayne, 1974. A general introduction to Gogol's life and his art, presented in chronological order. The focus is on Gogol's essential modernity and his creation of the comic grotesque. Includes a chronology of his life as well as a brief annotated bibliography of criticism.

Maguire, Robert A. *Exploring Gogol*. Stanford, Calif.: Stanford University Press, 1994. Fresh look at Gogol that presents his life and work as a whole through examination of the major texts set in a broad, intellectual context.

_____, ed. *Gogol from the Twentieth Century: Eleven Essays*. Princeton, N.J.: Princeton University Press, 1974. Contains eleven essays on Gogol from the perspective of various twentieth century Russian critical approaches, including formalist, psychological, religious, sociological, and historical criticism. Includes a famous essay by Boris Eichenbaum, "How Gogol's 'Overcoat' Is Made."

Peace, Richard. *The Enigma of Gogol*. Cambridge, England: Cambridge University Press, 1981. A study of Gogol's works from the point of view of their place in the Russian literary tradition, particularly focusing on the enigma of the scope of Gogol's influence on a realistic tradition in spite of his own grotesque rhetorical style.

Setchkarev, Vsevolod. *Gogol: His Life and Works*. Translated by Robert Kramer. New York: New York University Press, 1965. A readable introduction to Gogol's life and art. This straightforward study does not pretend to break any new critical ground but rather summarizes previous criticism and analyzes Gogol's works both thematically and formally.

SEE ALSO: Charles Dickens; Fyodor Dostoevski; Modest Mussorgsky; Nicholas I; Edgar Allan Poe; Alexander Pushkin; Nikolay Rimsky-Korsakov; Leo Tolstoy; Ivan Turgenev.

RELATED ARTICLE in *Great Events from History: The Nineteenth Century, 1801-1900:* December, 1849: Dostoevski Is Exiled to Siberia.

SIR GEORGE GOLDIE
British colonial administrator

One of the major figures of late nineteenth century British imperialism, Goldie employed his commercial skills and great administrative abilities to form the Royal Niger Company, which made possible the extension of British influence in Nigeria, which became one of Britain's most valuable African possessions.

BORN: May 20, 1846; Douglas, Isle of Man
DIED: August 20, 1925; London, England
ALSO KNOWN AS: George Dashwood Goldie Taubman (birth name)
AREA OF ACHIEVEMENT: Government and politics

EARLY LIFE
Born George Dashwood Goldie Taubman, Sir George Goldie changed his name to George Taubman Goldie in 1887, when he received his knighthood. His father was a wealthy Manx merchant and landowner who was married twice. George Goldie, like his two brothers from his father's second marriage, entered the army and attended the Royal Military Academy at Woolwich for two years. Following graduation, the death of a wealthy relative left him financially independent, and Goldie journeyed to Egypt. While in Egypt and the Sudan, Goldie acquired a mistress, learned Arabic, and, most important, developed a deep interest in the Sudan area of West Africa. He studied intently Heinrich Barth's five-volume *Travels and Discoveries in North and Central Africa* (1857-1858).

After returning to England, Goldie failed to conform to the accepted norms of middle-class Victorian Britain. In 1870, he fell in love with the family governess, Mathilda Catherine Elliot, with whom he departed abruptly for France. There they were trapped by the siege of Paris during the latter phases of the Franco-Prussian War. Goldie returned to England in 1871 and married Mathilda the same year. They had one son and one daughter.

At the mature age of thirty, Goldie still had no settled career, having already resigned his commission in the army. A thin, intense man with a large mustache and piercing eyes, Goldie impressed his contemporaries with his determination, pride, and quick temper. These personality traits, his atheism, and his scandalous background and marriage made it difficult for him to be accepted into polite Victorian society. Goldie was simply too unconventional and unpredictable to gain or to hold a position in government service or in politics. Like many of Great Britain's great empire builders, Goldie was to find fulfillment in the freer environment of the colonies.

Goldie's career opportunity came in 1875 through a member of his family. A sister-in-law's father, Captain Joseph Grove-Ross, was attempting, largely unsuccessfully, to conduct commerce on West Africa's Niger River. Anxious to rid itself of an embarrassment, the Taubman family suggested Goldie as a man who could restore the company's prosperity. Still fascinated with Africa, Goldie took up the challenge and left for the Niger in 1876. Between his arrival in West Africa in 1876 and the revocation of the charter of his later Royal Niger Company in 1900, Goldie spent much of his time overseas. During these turbulent years, Goldie would remake the commercial structure of the Niger region and ultimately contribute to Britain's annexation of what was later known as Nigeria.

LIFE'S WORK
On arriving on the Niger, Goldie quickly discerned the problems facing the English merchants seeking to trade in palm oil, a valuable lubricant for machinery and an important ingredient in fine soap. Powerful coastal African states, such as that of the Brassmen, were determined to protect their role as middlemen in this commerce and to prevent the European merchants from using the Niger River to trade directly with the palm-oil-producing regions farther to the north.

Travel by steamer remained dangerous on the river during the 1870's because of the absence of effective British protection. Furthermore, Goldie discovered that the intense rivalry among the large number of merchant companies conducting business on the Niger gave the African producers the opportunity to demand higher prices. Unless competition were restricted, Goldie feared, European profits would remain low and smaller companies such as his own would fail.

By 1879, Goldie had consolidated most of the European companies into the United African Company. Through his natural leadership abilities, he convinced his rivals of the benefits of establishing a monopoly that would restrict competition and lower the prices paid to the Africans for their palm oil. Goldie's problems were not, however, over. It was difficult to prevent new companies from being formed to challenge his United African Company. Also, by the early 1880's both the French and the Germans were beginning to show interest in the Niger, an area not yet claimed by any European government.

To counter these new threats, in 1882 Goldie formed the National African Company, and he attempted to obtain a royal charter from the British government giving him administrative control over the Niger region. The British government, still reluctant to extend its political responsibilities in West Africa, refused Goldie's request. The French annexation of Dahomey in 1883, however, and the German annexation of the Cameroons the following year strengthened Goldie's position.

In 1884, Goldie was given permission to make treaties with African chiefs. He also attended the Berlin Conference of 1884-1885, called by Germany to establish guidelines for African annexations, and he worked successfully to preserve British influence in the region and to ensure his control of navigation on the Niger River. Finally, in 1886, after almost two years of negotiation, he received a royal charter for his new Royal Niger Company. This charter gave Goldie administrative control of the lower Niger, over which Great Britain had belatedly established a protectorate in 1885. For his work in strengthening Great Britain's position in West Africa, Goldie received a knighthood in 1887.

Goldie's charter gave him the power to "protect" African states that had treaties with his company, to acquire new territory with the approval of the British government, and to levy taxes to pay for administrative costs. Goldie remained concerned, however, over the growing French influence in the Niger region. In 1894, he dispatched Captain Frederick Lugard to the Dahomey border to secure treaties with several African chiefs. These treaties forestalled French expansion from the west, but the two nations continued a rivalry in the north. It was not until 1898, after a major diplomatic crisis, that the British

and French governments established by treaty the western and northern boundaries of what is now Nigeria. Goldie's territorial position was finally secure.

Goldie's last years in Nigeria also saw intense conflict with the powerful Muslim city-states in the north. In 1897, he waged war on the emir of Nupe, who had engaged in slave trading in the territory of the Royal Niger Company. With only eight hundred men, Goldie defeated Nupe's army of fifteen thousand men, entered the Nupe capital, Bida, and deposed the emir. The state of Ilorin was also subdued by force.

By 1899, Goldie's African work was largely over. Nigeria had been brought under British control at little expense to the British taxpayer, but the 1898 crisis with France illustrated the crucial importance of official British possession of Nigeria. Goldie's private company simply could not compete with a hostile foreign government. As a result, in 1899 the British Parliament revoked the charter of the Royal Niger Company and deprived it of its administrative powers. On January 1, 1900, Frederick Lugard became the new British high commissioner for Northern Nigeria.

The revocation of the Royal Niger Company's charter ended Goldie's direct contact with Africa, although he remained interested in the empire and active in imperial affairs. He traveled widely and served as a member of a Royal Commission on the South African (Boer) War. In 1904, he visited Rhodesia (now Zimbabwe) to report on the status of the British South Africa Company. In his later life, he became involved in London politics and chaired the finance committee of the London County Council. Upon his death, on August 20, 1925, Goldie and his African work had largely faded from the public's consciousness.

SIGNIFICANCE

In many ways, Sir George Goldie caught the spirit of imperial Great Britain during the late nineteenth century. His romantic view of Africa, which led him early in life to contemplate an east-west crossing of the Sudan, drew him to the so-called Dark Continent. Once in Africa, Goldie personified the private imperialist, using his business skills not only to make money but also to ensure British control of the most commercially valuable portion of West Africa. During much of his early career in Nigeria, a reluctant British government opposed an extension of its imperial responsibilities in such a remote area.

Without Goldie's perseverance, Great Britain could easily have been squeezed out of the region by Germany and France. By maintaining a British commercial and administrative presence on the Niger during the 1870's and 1880's, Goldie retained for Great Britain the opportunity during the 1890's to consolidate its rule over the region. By 1900, after his company had lost its charter, Goldie was acknowledged "the Founder of Nigeria."

Goldie not only gave Nigeria its modern boundaries, but he also was instrumental in the development of British techniques of colonial administration. Largely because of financial necessity, he instituted a system of government whereby a few district officers ruled largely through the native chiefs, retaining much of the traditional African culture and law. Because of his desire to shun publicity and his decision to destroy his private papers, however, Goldie received little credit for this system of administration, which Lord Lugard later made famous as "indirect rule." It would be more than one hundred years after his death before Goldie would be rightfully recognized as one of the great British imperialists of the late nineteenth century.

—Brian L. Blakeley

FURTHER READING

Ajaiji, J. F. A., and Michael Crowder, eds. *History of West Africa*. Vol. 2. New York: Columbia University Press, 1973. Excellent study of West Africa from the early nineteenth century to 1960. Puts Goldie's work in perspective and highlights the role of the Royal Niger Company in the partition of West Africa.

Baker, Geoffrey L. *Trade Winds on the Niger: The Saga of the Royal Niger Company, 1830-1971*. New York: St. Martin's Press, 1996. Chronicles the company's history, explaining its creation and subsequent growth and development.

Falola, Toyin. *The History of Nigeria*. Westport, Conn.: Greenwood Press, 1999. Concise overview of Nigerian history. Chapters 3 and 4 include information on Goldie, the Royal Niger Company, and British colonial rule.

Flint, J. E. *Sir George Goldie and the Making of Nigeria*. London: Oxford University Press, 1960. The first and only complete study of Goldie's life and work. An excellent analysis of the methods by which he consolidated British influence in Nigeria. Weak on Goldie's private and personal life because of the destruction of his papers.

Geary, Sir William N. M. *Nigeria Under British Rule*. New York: Barnes & Noble Books, 1927. Written by a former British colonial official. An early laudatory account of British administration in Nigeria that more than most accounts from this period praises the efforts of Goldie.

Hargreaves, John D. *West Africa Partitioned*. 2 vols. London: Macmillan, 1974, 1985. Excellent study of the role of the Royal Niger Company in the diplomacy leading to the partition of Africa.

Perham, Margery. *Lugard: The Years of Adventure, 1858-1898*. Hamden, Conn.: Archon Books, 1956. The last section is an excellent discussion of Goldie's policies in Nigeria and his early relations with his friend and successor, Sir Frederick Lugard.

Wellesley, Dorothy. *Sir George Goldie: Founder of Nigeria*. Introduction by Stephen Gwynn. London: Macmillan, 1934. The first lengthy study of Goldie. Written by a friend, it contains valuable information on Goldie's character and personality. An early, uncritical attempt to resurrect Goldie's central role in the creation of modern Nigeria.

SEE ALSO: Muḥammad Bello; Samuel Ajayi Crowther; Louis Faidherbe; Cecil Rhodes.

RELATED ARTICLES in *Great Events from History: The Nineteenth Century, 1801-1900:* May 4, 1805-1830: Exploration of West Africa; November 15, 1884-February 26, 1885: Berlin Conference Lays Groundwork for the Partition of Africa; July 10-November 3, 1898: Fashoda Incident Pits France vs. Britain.

SAMUEL GOMPERS
English-born American labor leader

Gompers helped create the first successful national organization of trade unions in the United States, the American Federation of Labor, and led it almost continuously through four decades.

BORN: January 27, 1850; London, England
DIED: December 13, 1924; San Antonio, Texas
AREA OF ACHIEVEMENT: Social reform

EARLY LIFE

Samuel Gompers was the son of Dutch parents who had emigrated to London in 1844. His father was a cigar-maker whose family lived in poverty. Gompers's total formal education consisted of attendance, from the ages of six to ten, at a free school provided by the Jewish community, plus some free evening classes. Samuel left school because of the family's poor financial condition, and, after a brief try at shoemaking, his father arranged for an apprenticeship as a cigar-maker. Gompers worked in this trade until he became a full-time union leader.

In 1863, the Gompers family followed relatives to the United States and settled in New York City. Gompers married Sophia Julian in 1867. Although they had many children, only five lived to reach adulthood. Sophia died in 1920, and Gompers remarried the next year. His second wife, Gertrude Neuschler, was thirty years younger than he, and the marriage was an unhappy one.

Gompers was Jewish by birth; however, he neither practiced his religion nor exhibited any strong identification with other Jews. He had an attraction to fraternal orders, including the Foresters, the Odd Fellows, and the Masons. Gompers's father had been a union member in London, and father and son joined the Cigar-makers' Union in 1864. Gompers, however, was more involved with fraternal than with union activities until the early 1870's.

Hard times for skilled cigar-makers ultimately impelled Gompers into active involvement with the union. The introduction of a new tool, the mold, into the trade in 1869 simplified cigar-making and threatened the position of the skilled workers. The long depression of 1873-1877 made the situation worse. By 1872, Gompers had joined Adolph Strasser and Ferdinand Laurrell in trying to remake the faltering Cigar-makers' Union. In 1875, Gompers became president of a reorganized cigar-makers' local union in New York City. Gompers then helped elect Strasser as president of the national union in 1877. Together, they reconstructed the Cigar-makers'

Union on the model of British trade unions. This meant high dues; financial benefits, such as a death allowance, sick pay, and out-of-work payments; and centralized control of strikes. From 1880 onward, Gompers held office in his local union, and, after 1886 and for the remainder of his life, in the national union.

In these early years, Gompers demonstrated the personal qualities that were to mark his later activities. He was pragmatic, indefatigable, honest, and totally devoted to the union cause, passing up many more lucrative job opportunities. Although short in stature and initially hampered by a stammer, Gompers became an accomplished speaker. Despite his meager formal education, he wrote extensively, including many articles as editor of the journal of the American Federation of Labor (AFL). He gave his life to the labor movement, and he expected others to accept his leadership. Gompers rarely admitted a mistake or forgave an enemy.

LIFE'S WORK

As early as the 1870's, Gompers believed in the importance of a national organization to represent the trade unions of the country. Earlier efforts during the 1860's to create such an organization had failed. Gompers helped to form a weak federation of trade unions in 1881, and he was the leader, in 1886, in establishing a more powerful body, the AFL. He became its first president, and with the exception of 1894, he was reelected annually until his death. As president, Gompers developed his mature views on how the American labor movement should function, and he worked tirelessly to put them into practice.

Gompers believed that the labor movement must win acceptance by employers and the public as the representative of the workers' legitimate interests within the existing capitalist system. Any resort to violence or support of radicalism would lead to repression by the state. Thus, the labor movement must work within the law for goals understandable to most Americans: an improved standard of living, better opportunities for one's children, and security in one's old age.

Gompers was familiar with socialist doctrine from his exposure to the movement during the 1870's. Although he retained certain elements of Marxism, particularly an intense belief in class as the determinant of political behavior, by 1880, he opposed the socialists as being dangerous to the labor movement. He believed that the so-

Samuel Gompers. (Library of Congress)

The trade union was the only institution in society fully under the control of the working class and responsive to its interests. This doctrine of voluntarism brought him into frequent conflict with social reformers, who pointed out that most workers were not members of trade unions. Strong opposition to Gompers's views also came from important elements within the labor movement—principally the weaker unions that saw little prospect of substantial immediate gains through their own efforts and who were therefore attracted to an alliance with middle-class reformers to secure labor legislation. This trend was most apparent during the two decades prior to World War I, known as the Progressive period.

On occasion, Gompers believed that political action might be necessary for limited objectives that were unachievable by trade union action alone, or to protect the labor movement against assault. An example of the latter was the campaign by the AFL, from 1906 to 1914, to win relief from the use of the Sherman Antitrust Act against the labor movement. In such a case, however, labor had to follow a policy of rewarding friends and punishing enemies, without reference to party. Gompers argued that this practice would counteract the allegiance of workers to the two major parties and avoid the permanent commitment to any political party that Gompers wanted to avoid.

Despite his foreign birth, Gompers led the AFL in its demand for a restriction of immigration. He undoubtedly expressed the views of most trade unionists, who feared that the newcomers would accept lower wages and that the arrival of vast numbers of both skilled and unskilled workers would create an additional pool of labor that employers could use to crush strikes or to operate new machinery. The AFL consistently supported immigration restriction, beginning in 1897.

Gompers initially favored the organization of all workers. He opposed the tendency in some trade unions to bar immigrants, black people, women, or the less skilled, because by doing so a nonunion work force that could weaken the labor movement would be created. However, Gompers eventually yielded on this point and left the issue to individual unions.

Gompers also increasingly favored the organization of workers by craft, rather than through unions representing all the workers in an industry. Gompers believed that the creation of industrial unions would produce conflict with the existing craft unions, thus weakening the labor movement. Moreover, he argued that the craft unions could effectively organize the less skilled workers. In the event, however, this did not occur—and as a conse-

cialists did not represent the views of most Americans on matters such as private property. Moreover, their demand for radical change threatened to stimulate repression. Because many workers were supporters of the two major political parties, the attempts of the socialists to create an alliance between the trade unions and a radical third party were divisive. Gompers's struggles with the socialists increased in intensity after 1890, and they were the major opposition to his leadership within the AFL.

For Gompers, legislation was not a major means for workers to win gains. Ultimately, this position flowed from his belief that politics was controlled by class interests. For Gompers, because the demands of workers would eventually conflict with the interests of other classes and because workers did not control the government and were unlikely to do so, political action would be dangerous for the labor movement. Gompers carried this idea to the point of opposing most labor legislation, because once the government intervened in the lives of workers, it would be more likely to do harm than good.

Rather than risk the danger of governmental intervention in labor matters, Gompers called upon workers to organize trade unions and to win their gains by this means.

quence, the scope of the American labor movement was severely limited. It took a split in the AFL during the 1930's and the subsequent formation of the Congress of Industrial Organizations (CIO) to make industrial unionism a significant force in the United States.

Gompers consistently supported the peaceful settlement of international disputes until 1916, when he embraced the concept of preparedness. Gompers strongly supported the war effort once the United States entered World War I in 1917. This shift in attitude reflects several of his basic beliefs. First, he contended that the nation overwhelmingly supported preparedness and then the war, and it weakened the labor movement to oppose popular opinion. Second, Gompers viewed the issue with his usual pragmatism: He correctly believed that the administration of Woodrow Wilson would cooperate with the AFL to maximize production during the war. However, the gains for the labor movement could not be sustained after the war, in the face of the severe Red scare of 1919 and the political and economic conservatism of the 1920's. By the time of Gompers's death in 1924, the AFL was only slightly larger than it had been prior to the war.

SIGNIFICANCE

Samuel Gompers's views strongly influenced the character of the American labor movement until the appearance of the CIO during the 1930's. Gompers's leadership was a combination of experience, tenacity, hard work, and the web of personal contacts that he had built in the labor movement. He could only persuade and implore; he could not command. Because Gompers was elected annually by the votes of the larger craft unions in the AFL, he had to represent their interests. However, Gompers was too strong a personality to stay with a labor movement that he could not support. The AFL was not exactly what Gompers might have wanted, but it did reflect many of his basic views. Thus, he was able to develop, defend, and lead the organization for more than four decades.

—*Irwin Yellowitz*

FURTHER READING

Buhle, Paul. *Taking Care of Business: Samuel Gompers, George Meany, Lane Kirkland, and the Tragedy of American Labor*. New York: Monthly Review Press, 1999. A radical attack on Gompers and other American labor leaders. Buhle charges that labor leaders allied with corporate executives and government officials instead of representing the best interests of workers.

Dick, William M. *Labor and Socialism in America: The Gompers Era*. Port Washington, N.Y.: Kennikat Press, 1972. Traces Gompers's relations with the Socialists over the course of his career.

Gompers, Samuel. *The Samuel Gompers Papers*. Vol. 1, *The Making of a Union Leader: 1850-86*. Edited by Stuart B. Kaufman, et al. 9 vols. Urbana: University of Illinois Press, 1986-2003. Excellent documentary history that covers Gompers's early life and career up to the AFL's activities from 1913-1917. Other volumes to follow.

_____. *Seventy Years of Life and Labor: An Autobiography*. 2 vols. New York: E. P. Dutton, 1925. Gompers's version of his life and times. Contains valuable information, but it must be used with care. Includes photographs.

Greene, Julie. *Pure and Simple Politics: The American Federation of Labor and Political Activism, 1881-1917*. New York: Cambridge University Press, 1998. A study of the AFL under Gompers's leadership, examining the organization's political participation during the Progressive Era.

Grob, Gerald. *Workers and Utopia: A Study of Ideological Conflict in the American Labor Movement, 1865-1900*. Chicago: Quadrangle Books, 1960. Examines Gompers's efforts to establish the AFL in competition with the Knights of Labor.

Livesay, Harold. *Samuel Gompers and Organized Labor in America*. Boston: Little, Brown, 1978. Brief, interpretive, and readable study of Gompers.

Mandel, Bernard. *Samuel Gompers: A Biography*. Yellow Springs, Ohio: Antioch Press, 1963. Full-length biography that is rich in detail. Includes photographs.

Reed, Louis. *The Labor Philosophy of Samuel Gompers*. New York: Columbia University Press, 1930. Descriptive and analytical presentation of Gompers's views. The author sees a need for the AFL's type of unionism in the nineteenth century, but he believes that it became outdated in the twentieth century.

Taft, Philip. *The A.F. of L. in the Time of Gompers*. New York: Harper & Row, 1957. Detailed account of the AFL; necessarily stresses Gompers's role. Generally supports the policies of the AFL and its leader.

SEE ALSO: Felix Adler; Henry George.
RELATED ARTICLES in *Great Events from History: The Nineteenth Century, 1801-1900:* December 8, 1886: American Federation of Labor Is Founded; May 11-July 11, 1894: Pullman Strike.

CHARLES GOODYEAR
American inventor

Goodyear is remembered for inventing the first practical process for vulcanizing rubber, which made possible an immense range of products that have become central to everyday life—from pneumatic tires to modern condoms.

BORN: December 29, 1800; New Haven, Connecticut
DIED: July 1, 1860; New York, New York
AREA OF ACHIEVEMENT: Science and technology

EARLY LIFE

Charles Goodyear was the first child born to Amasa Goodyear and Cynthia Bateman Goodyear, whose family later grew to include six children. Stephen Goodyear, an ancestor from London, had been one of a group of merchants who founded a colony in New Haven in 1638. Amasa Goodyear was also a merchant, selling hardware supplies to farmers, as well as an inventor. One of his patented farm tools was a hay pitchfork made from steel; it was a great improvement over the heavy cast-iron pitchforks that were used during the early nineteenth century.

Charles attended public schools in New Haven and Naugatuck, Connecticut, his father having moved the family in 1807 to a farm near Naugatuck to take advantage of a water-powered factory he had bought there. Charles helped his father, to whom he was a close companion, at both the factory and the farm. Contemporaries remembered him as a serious youth with a studious nature. An excellent Bible student, he considered being a minister, but when he finished public school at the age of seventeen, he agreed with his father that he should enter the hardware business and was apprenticed, as a clerk, to a large Philadelphia hardware store run by the Rogers family.

Charles's tenure at the store was brief. He felt overworked, and his small, frail body soon wore out; ill health forced him to return to his father's house. Amasa Goodyear worked with his son as a business partner starting in 1826; together they sought to improve the farm tools of their era. During this time, in August of 1824, Charles married Clarissa Beecher, whose father was an innkeeper in Naugatuck.

Amasa Goodyear soon felt that his hardware sales were sufficiently good for him to open a branch store in Philadelphia. He sent his son to manage the new store; there the Goodyears sold only American-made goods, becoming the first United States hardware firm to eliminate British imports. However, the young Goodyear's business sense was not acute. He often sold goods on credit, as did his father in Connecticut, and reached a point where his creditors became too numerous and he was deep in debt. Rather than declare bankruptcy (as the law allowed), he decided to pay off his debts gradually. When young Goodyear's creditors pressed for their money, he was put in debtor's prison for the first time. This was in 1830 in Philadelphia. Charles Goodyear would spend time in and out of debtor's prison for the next ten years.

During one of the times Goodyear was out of prison, in 1834, he traveled to New York to try to secure bank loans to pay his debts. He was caught in a harsh rainstorm on the streets of Manhattan and entered the Roxbury India Rubber Company to get dry. Inside the store, he noticed a life preserver made with a faulty valve. He purchased it, hoping to redesign the valve and impress the firm's owners. Perhaps they would pay him for his invention. Goodyear spent the next few weeks on this project, but when he returned to the Roxbury Company with a perfected valve, he was surprised to learn of the great difficulties the firm was having with rubber goods.

Rubber goods had been produced and marketed in the United States since 1830. The demand for these products was high, especially in New England, where residents wore rubber boots and raincoats. The gum rubber that was used to make these items, however, was a sticky substance that melted in the summer and froze in the winter. When Goodyear first contacted the Roxbury Company, it was closing down. Goodyear came away from this encounter with the idea of curing rubber so it could be used more readily for clothing, life preservers, and other goods.

LIFE'S WORK

When Charles Goodyear returned to his Philadelphia home in the summer of 1834, he began what would be a five-year period of experimenting to cure rubber. Because he was not trained in chemistry, his experiments were conducted on a trial-and-error basis. He worked in the kitchen of his small cottage, or in prison when he was confined there. He was fortunate in that gum rubber was inexpensive and plentiful. Goodyear had no tools, so he worked the rubber with his hands. He first mixed it with a variety of substances (one at a time) to see if he could eliminate its stickiness. The good properties of rubber that he wished to retain were its elasticity and flexibility, along with its strength. Among the items Goodyear mixed with rubber were sand, ink, castor oil, witch hazel, and even salt, pepper, and sugar.

When Goodyear tried a mixture of rubber, magnesia, and quicklime, he thought he had a successful type of rubber. It appeared smooth and flexible and was no longer sticky. He jubilantly announced his news of a discovery to the press. He even produced some small items from the mixture to display at two institute fairs in New York in 1835, the New York American Institute and the New York Mechanics' Institute. Although both fairs awarded Goodyear prize medals for his discovery, it soon proved to be a failure. This treated or "tanned" rubber, as he called it, was destroyed when any acid (even a very weak acid) came in contact with it.

Goodyear was not discouraged by this failure; rather, he continued to mix other substances with gum rubber to find a useful compound. So intent was he to promote his products that he would dress all in rubber.

The hardships Goodyear and his family endured while he worked to perfect rubber were many. They often had no shelter, at one point living in an abandoned rubber factory on Staten Island, or no food—neighbors reported seeing the Goodyear children digging in their gardens for half-ripe potatoes. They never had money;

Charles Goodyear. (Library of Congress)

Goodyear sold furnishings and even his children's school books to purchase supplies.

The only way the family survived was by Goodyear's finding a series of financial backers for his experiments. Among the men who funded him were Ralph Steele of New Haven and later William de Forest, who had been a tutor to young Charles and later would become his brother-in-law. De Forest's total investment in Goodyear's work rose to almost fifty thousand dollars. Another pair of backers, William and Emery Ryder of New York, had to withdraw all their funds when the economic panic of 1837 ruined them financially.

On June 17, 1837, Goodyear had obtained a patent for a procedure to treat rubber that he called the "acid-gas process." The bankruptcy of the Ryder brothers shortly thereafter, however, gave Goodyear another setback— only a temporary one, however, for he soon met John Haskins in New York, who next helped him. Haskins was the former owner of the Roxbury India Rubber Company; he still owned an empty factory in Roxbury, Massachusetts, and Goodyear and his family moved to nearby Woburn. Goodyear manufactured various rubber items using the acid-gas process; among the thin products he sold in 1838 were tablecloths and piano covers.

Goodyear had another meeting while he resided in Woburn. He became acquainted with Nathaniel Hayward, who had himself worked out a method of treating rubber. Hayward mixed gum rubber with sulphur and set the substance to dry in the sun; he called his process "solarization." Sharing their knowledge, Goodyear and Hayward began manufacturing what they believed to be permanent rubber products, no longer sticky and not likely to melt or freeze. As their reputation grew, the two men were awarded a U.S. government contract to produce 150 mailbags. After they had completed their order, they were disheartened to see that all the bags melted in the summer heat.

Ironically, although totally defeated (financially and publicly) by the mailbag disaster, Goodyear was close to a successful curing of rubber. In the winter of early 1839, he accidentally dropped a piece of a ruined mailbag on the stove in his Woburn kitchen. He noticed that the sulphur-treated rubber did not melt, but charred as leather would when burned. Goodyear had worked long enough with rubber to realize he now had made a major breakthrough. The piece of charred rubber, when hung in the winter air overnight, also did not freeze.

The inventor still had a problem—no one, except his family, believed his new method was a success. Because of his past failures, the American press and any financial backers considered Goodyear a disturbed man who would never make a genuine discovery. It would be five more years before Charles Goodyear could slowly perfect his new treatment of rubber and have it patented on June 15, 1844. By that time, samples of Goodyear's new rubber had reached England, where one inventor, Thomas Hancock, had copied Goodyear's process. Hancock successfully obtained a British patent on this method of treating rubber, which he called "vulcanization," after the Roman god of fire, Vulcan.

Goodyear, however, did hold the American patent on vulcanization. When his countrymen began to realize that Goodyear finally had a truly usable product, he began to earn money. Royalties were paid to Goodyear by each company using his process to manufacture rubber goods in the United States.

Even after his great success with vulcanization, Charles Goodyear continued to spend large sums of money experimenting with rubber. After 1844, he concentrated on devising new rubber products. He also spent large sums of money promoting his products, especially in Europe. In 1855, Goodyear had built two elaborate exhibits abroad. In England, at the Crystal Palace Exhibition, he built a three-room Vulcanite Court completely furnished in rubber, at a cost of thirty thousand dollars. In France, at the Exposition Universelle in Paris, he constructed a similar exhibit for fifty thousand dollars. These expenditures, along with other debts, explain why Goodyear never became wealthy from his discovery of vulcanization.

Goodyear's wife Clarissa died in England in 1853, worn out by their lives of hardship and poverty; only six of their twelve children had survived to adulthood. Goodyear himself had always been a frail man, but in his final years he looked very old (although only in his fifties), and he had such severe gout and neuralgia that he could walk only with crutches for his last six years. He collapsed and died in New York City on July 1, 1860, on the way to see his gravely ill daughter in New Haven.

SIGNIFICANCE

It is ironic that Charles Goodyear's experiments with rubber aided Americans and all humankind so greatly and his family hardly at all. He was able to renew his patent on vulcanized rubber during his lifetime, but his heirs were refused renewals. The Goodyear Rubber Company, organized decades after his death, merely used his name to promote their rubber tires; the company was founded by strangers.

The rubber tire, so vital to modern transportation, is considered one of the most important outcomes of Goodyear's invention, as well as many other products essential to a life of good quality: in medicine, telecommunications, electronics—indeed, virtually every modern industry. It is difficult to imagine what daily life would be like without the availability of vulcanized rubber.

—*Patricia E. Sweeney*

FURTHER READING

Beals, Carleton. *Our Yankee Heritage: New England's Contribution to American Civilization.* New York: David McKay, 1955. Beals titles his chapter on Goodyear "Black Magic." In it, he emphasizes the inventor's personal life as well as his experimentation. This essay contains many details on Goodyear's family life not found in other sources. Beals also provides an analysis of Goodyear's character traits.

Chamberlain, John. *The Enterprising Americans: A Business History of the United States.* New York: Harper & Row, 1963. Originally a series in *Fortune* magazine on famous American businesspeople. In his lively and engaging account of Goodyear, the author places emphasis on the inventor's Yankee ingenuity. Includes a bibliography.

Gies, Joseph, and Frances Gies. *The Ingenious Yankees.* New York: Thomas Y. Crowell, 1976. The authors focus on how Yankee inventors helped transform a farming country into a powerful technological nation. A biographical sketch of Goodyear is included, as well as an extensive bibliography.

Korman, Richard. *The Goodyear Story: An Inventor's Obsession and the Struggle for a Rubber Monopoly.* San Francisco: Encounter Books, 2002. Biography recounting Goodyear's invention, patent battles, and other business struggles. The book features nontechnical explanations of vulcanization and descriptions of conditions in a nineteenth century rubber factory.

Patterson, John C. *America's Greatest Inventors.* New York: Thomas Y. Crowell, 1943. The author covers fully the lives and careers of eighteen inventors, including Goodyear. He includes interesting facts concerning Goodyear's work and personal difficulties, motivations, and thoughts.

Slack, Charles. *Noble Obsession: Charles Goodyear, Thomas Hancock, and the Race to Unlock the Greatest Industrial Secret of the Nineteenth Century.* New York: Hyperion, 2002. Describes the rivalry between Goodyear and Hancock over vulcanization—a process that engendered business speculation similar to the Internet boom of the 1990's. Although Slack discusses both men, he focuses on Goodyear, crediting him with greater persistence and business acumen than Hancock.

Wilson, Mitchell. *American Science and Invention: A Pictorial History*. New York: Simon & Schuster, 1954. A large volume that relies on period illustrations and photographs to describe the course of American invention. Concise and accurate on Goodyear's

life as well as his discovery, with descriptions of how his experiments progressed. Also interesting on Goodyear's personal character.

SEE ALSO: Thomas Alva Edison; Leopold II.
RELATED ARTICLES in *Great Events from History: The Nineteenth Century, 1801-1900:* June 15, 1844: Goodyear Patents Vulcanized Rubber; December 7, 1888: Dunlop Patents the Pneumatic Tire.

CHARLES GEORGE GORDON
English military leader

Gordon is remembered primarily for his dramatic death in the British defense of Khartoum. All the associations one might make with a man of the British Empire during the Victorian age—soldier, statesman, and adventurer—were forcefully expressed in his life.

BORN: January 28, 1833; Woolwich Common, England
DIED: January 26, 1885; Khartoum, Sudan
ALSO KNOWN AS: Gordon Pasha; Chinese Gordon
AREA OF ACHIEVEMENT: Military

EARLY LIFE

Charles George Gordon was the fourth son of eleven children born to Henry William Gordon and Elizabeth Enderby. His mother, for whom he had a special affection, came from a rather prosperous merchant family, and his father was an officer in the Royal Artillery. His grandfather and great-grandfather had served in the military—the latter having fought with General James Wolfe at Quebec. It was hardly surprising, therefore, when young Gordon decided to follow in the steps of his paternal ancestors and chose to pursue his own career in the military.

At the age of fifteen, Gordon entered Woolwich Academy, where he soon became better known for his volatile temper and impetuous pranks than for his scholarly achievements. When he was graduated in 1852 as a sublieutenant in the Royal Engineers, he was posted first to Chatham and then to Pembroke. His first combat experience came in early 1855 in the Crimea, where he quickly established a reputation for bravery and almost reckless courage. He was cited for special distinction by his own government, received the French Legion of Honor, and won the friendship and admiration of future field marshal Garnet Wolseley.

LIFE'S WORK

After the war, Gordon spent almost two years in Bessarabia and Armenia surveying and mapping the new boundaries created by the 1856 Treaty of Paris. Following his return to England, he was promoted to captain and made adjutant at the headquarters of the Royal Engineers at Chatham. At the age of twenty-five, Gordon was described by those who knew him best as a man who was absolutely fearless, who possessed boundless energy, and who had a great capacity to adapt and survive under the most trying circumstances. His courage, energy, and durability were attributes that would serve him well in the future. He was of average height—approximately five feet, nine inches—with brown curly hair, a small mustache, and a thin beard that served to accentuate a noticeably square jaw. Undoubtedly, Gordon's most striking physical feature was his vivid blue eyes, which, according to Wolseley, "seemed to court something while at the same time they searched the inner soul." Whatever the eyes may have disclosed about Gordon, they revealed to him a world cast in infinite shades of gray, for he was color-blind.

Gordon left his post at Chatham in July, 1860, when he was ordered to China, where the third in a series of trade wars between the British and the Chinese had been raging for almost two years. He arrived in Hong Kong in September, only two months before the conflict came to an end, and was subsequently assigned to the Tianjin (Tientsin) area. In early 1863, he received permission from the British government to enter the service of the Chinese emperor, whose forces were attempting to crush the Taiping rebels. Assuming command of a rather modest force known pretentiously as the Ever Victorious Army, Gordon won a series of brilliant victories over the rebels and gave substance to what had earlier been an empty title. His campaigns in China made him at once a hero and a legend. The small rattan cane that he always carried into battle became known as the "Wand of Victory," and he would forever more be known as "Chinese Gordon."

When he returned to England in early 1865, Gordon received a grand reception from the British public but found himself almost ignored by the War Office. In fact, for the next ten years, he received assignments that hardly matched his demonstrated military abilities. He spent almost six years as Royal Engineer in command at Gravesend and later served for three years as governor of Equatoria, where he waged a partially successful campaign to end the slave trade there.

Gordon had little more success with the slavers in the Sudan, where he served as governor-general from January, 1877, to January, 1880. During those three years, however, Gordon grew to love the Sudanese people and they to revere him. Appropriately enough, it would be in defense of the Sudan and its people that he would wage his last campaign in 1884-1885. In the years that intervened, the government once again seemed unable to find a place for him. He served briefly as secretary to Lord

Charles George Gordon. (Library of Congress)

Ripon, viceroy of India, returned to China in the summer of 1881, and in the spring of 1882, having been promoted to the rank of major general, went to South Africa to help bring the war with the Basuto to an end.

Gordon returned to England in the fall of 1882 for a brief visit, and in January, 1883, he traveled to Palestine, where he remained in virtual seclusion for almost a year. He both relished and needed this time, for though he was a public figure, Gordon remained throughout his life a private individual. He once confided while in Cairo, following his appointment as governor-general of the Sudan, that

> the idea of dinner in Cairo makes me quail. I do not exaggerate when I say that ten minutes per diem is sufficient for all my meals and there is no greater happiness to me than when they are finished.

Gordon was also a deeply religious man, though he never joined the Church or belonged to any particular sect. In his mind, "Catholic and Protestant are but soldiers in different regiments of Christ's army. . . ." He believed that the Bible was directly inspired by the Holy Spirit, and much of his time in Palestine was spent attempting to locate the exact site of the Crucifixion, the tomb of Christ, and the Garden of Eden. This proved to be a time for self-examination as well, and Gordon determined that he would make his life more "Christ-like."

Gordon decided while in Palestine that he would resign his commission and enter the service of Leopold II of Belgium for duty in the Congo. These plans changed, however, when he learned that Mohammed Ahmed—the self-proclaimed Mahdi or "Expected One"—had called for a Holy War in the Sudan and was marching on the capital of Khartoum. Though opinion in London was by no means unanimous, circumstances seemed to dictate that Gordon was the most logical choice to send to Khartoum. According to Lord Elton, a Gordon biographer, the harried government of William Ewart Gladstone found quite attractive the idea of sending "out the solitary, heroic figure, cane in hand, into the maelstrom of the Sudan."

Gordon left for Khartoum in January, 1884, under rather vague orders that required him to evacuate the city and report on the situation in the country. After reaching Khartoum, however, he attempted to hold the city, hoping thereby to compel the government to send sufficient forces to crush the Mahdi. Sir Evelyn Baring, British Minister Resident in Cairo, had earlier expressed some reservations about sending Gordon into the Sudan when he advised the Gladstone government that "a man who

EPITAPH TO GENERAL GORDON

Charles George Gordon's heroic death at Khartoum was a great emotional blow to the British people. Poet Alfred, Lord Tennyson, summed up the nation's feelings in this epitaph that appears on Gordon's tomb in London's Westminster Abbey:

> Warrior of God, man's friend, not here below,
> but somewhere dead far in the waste Soudan
> Thou livest in all hearts, for all men know
> This earth hath borne no simpler, nobler man.

habitually consults the prophet Isaiah when he is in difficulties is not apt to obey the orders of any one." Whatever his reasons, Gordon did not evacuate the city, and Gladstone, though ultimately pressured into sending a relief force to Khartoum, did so too late. The city fell on January 26, 1885, and among those who perished defending it was General Charles Gordon.

SIGNIFICANCE

It is difficult to imagine how Charles George Gordon might have been remembered had it not been for his heroic, if tragic, defense of Khartoum. History affords numerous examples, and this may be one, where an untimely death has intervened to save a deserving reputation and career from the ignominy of passing into history as an obscure and soon-forgotten footnote. Gordon will never endure that fate, though it is equally unlikely that he will enjoy the status of greatness accorded to one such as the first duke of Marlborough or the duke of Wellington. He would appear to be more of the ilk of T. E. Lawrence or Orde Wingate—both of whom combined eccentricity with a certain genius much like that of Gordon himself.

Save for the Crimean War, imperial interests dominated British foreign policy during the latter half of the nineteenth century, and it was from the vast stage provided by the empire itself that Gordon won wide acclaim from an appreciative British public. His exploits inspired little such enthusiasm among members of Great Britain's political leadership, who, despite Gordon's demonstrated gifts as an officer of exceptional ability, a natural leader, and a progressive administrator, never felt comfortable with him.

Gordon was the embodiment of many of the values that dominated the Victorian age and may have considered himself to be, as he has been described, the epitome of the Christian warrior. Whether, at Khartoum, he died

in defense of his empire or his faith is a question only he could have answered. To those who mourned him, it made little difference.

—*Kirk Ford, Jr.*

FURTHER READING

Blunt, Wilfrid Scawen. *Gordon at Khartoum*. New York: Alfred A. Knopf, 1923. A contemporary of Gordon, Blunt was initially critical of the general. He later developed a more favorable appreciation of Gordon and his work, as reflected in this book.

Buchan, John A. *Gordon at Khartoum*. Edinburgh: Peter B. Davies, 1934. A sympathetic treatment of Gordon that focuses on his last days at Khartoum. Buchan assesses the tragedy of Khartoum in terms of general British policy and gives some insight into the personalities who shaped that policy.

Chenevix, Charles Trench. *The Road to Khartoum*. New York: W. W. Norton, 1979. The passage of time provides the historian with perspective and usually new sources of information. Chenevix uses both to good advantage in this well-researched and balanced treatment of Gordon and the empire he served.

Elton, Godfrey. *Gordon of Khartoum*. New York: Alfred A. Knopf, 1955. A well-written biography that scarcely conceals the author's great admiration for his subject. Elton does not overlook Gordon's many shortcomings, but neither does he dwell on them.

Gordon, Charles George. *The Journals of Major-General Charles George Gordon, C.B., at Khartoum*. Edited by Egmont A. Hake. Boston: Houghton Mifflin, 1885. Although these journals cover only the period between September 10 and December 14, 1884, they provide the best insight into Gordon's mind during his last days at Khartoum.

Moore-Harrell, Alice. *Gordon and the Sudan: Prologue to the Mahdiyya, 1877-1880*. Portland, Oreg.: Frank Cass, 2001. Examines the years preceding the Mahdist revolution in Sudan by focusing on Gordon's administration as governor general. Provides details about the political, economic, and social developments under Gordon's leadership.

Nicoll, Fergus. *Sword of the Prophet: The Mahdi of Sudan and the Death of General Gordon*. Stroud, England: Sutton, 2004. Focuses on Mahdi's role as the charismatic leader of the Sudanese independence movement, recounting Gordon's death from Mahdi's perspective.

Strachey, Lytton. "The End of General Gordon." In *Eminent Victorians*. Garden City, N.Y.: Garden City, 1918. A controversial and critical treatment of Gordon that has been excoriated by the general's more ardent defenders—particularly Lord Elton.

Thompson, Brian. *Imperial Vanities: The Adventures of the Baker Brothers and Gordon of Khartoum.* London: HarperCollins, 2001. A nontraditional view of Gordon, depicting him as an eccentric anarchist.

SEE ALSO: William Ewart Gladstone; Leopold II; Menelik II; Henry Morton Stanley; Duke of Wellington.

RELATED ARTICLE in *Great Events from History: The Nineteenth Century, 1801-1900:* July 10-November 3, 1898: Fashoda Incident Pits France vs. Britain.

CHARLES GOUNOD
French composer

Because of his great popularity and stylistic influence on the next generation of composers, Gounod is often considered to be the central figure in French music in the third quarter of the nineteenth century.

BORN: June 17, 1818; Paris, France
DIED: October 18, 1893; St. Cloud, France
ALSO KNOWN AS: Charles-François Gounod (full name)
AREA OF ACHIEVEMENT: Music

EARLY LIFE

The father of Charles-François Gounod (gew-noh), Nicolas-François Gounod, was a gifted painter and winner of a Second Prix de Rome in 1783. His mother, Victoire Lemachois, a pianist, gave her son his early musical instruction. After completing his academic studies at the Lycée Saint-Louis, Charles Gounod received private musical training from composer-theorist Antoine Reicha; in 1836, when Gounod entered the Paris Conservatoire, he studied with such professors as Jacques Halévy (counterpoint), Jean-François Le Sueur (composition), and Pierre Zimmermann (piano). The extent of his musical education before entering the Paris Conservatoire, coupled with his exceptional talent, led him to win a Second Prix de Rome in 1837 and the Grand Prix de Rome two years later.

On December 5, 1839, Gounod left Paris for Rome; it was during his years in Rome that he met several women who played a significant role in his musical development. Felix Mendelssohn's married sister, Fanny Hensel, an accomplished pianist, introduced Gounod to the music of her brother, the music of Johann Sebastian Bach and Ludwig van Beethoven, as well as to the works of Johann Wolfgang von Goethe. Pauline Garcia was the sister of Maria Felicia Garcia Malibran, a singer who had been much admired by the young French artistic world before her death in 1836 at the age of twenty-eight. Pauline, besides being an excellent singer with a unique

mezzo-soprano voice, was also married to Louis Viardot, director of the Théâtre-Italien and a valuable ally for a young composer.

Another important influence in Gounod's life was the Dominican Friar Père Lacordaire. Lacordaire's sermons, which caused a great stir in Rome between the years 1838 and 1841, also impressed the young Gounod, whose sensibilities were constantly engaged in a battle between the sacred and the profane.

In the fall of 1842, Gounod left Rome for Vienna, where he received commissions for two masses, which were performed at the Karlskirche on November 2 (a requiem) and on March 25, 1843. During his stay in Vienna, Gounod had an opportunity to hear the Gewandhaus orchestra, probably the best orchestra in Europe at the time. Fortunate among French musicians of his generation, Gounod became acquainted with music, past and present, that was neither operatic nor within the French tradition.

After his return to Paris, Gounod became organist of the Missions Étrangères. However, he soon found himself in conflict with congregations who viewed the music of Bach and Giovanni Palestrina, music that Gounod greatly admired, as strange and unattractive. At this time in his life, Gounod's inclinations as well as his work led him to frequent ecclesiastical circles. Undoubtedly, this fact, combined with the influence of Lacordaire's sermons, inspired his decision to study for the priesthood. Although he took courses at St. Sulpice between 1846 and 1848, Gounod later referred to this interest in the priesthood as but a passing fancy.

LIFE'S WORK

The music that Gounod wrote immediately after his ecclesiastical studies was still intended for the Church. When he discontinued his studies at St. Sulpice, however, he soon turned to the field cultivated by most French composers of his day, the opera. In fact, it was Pauline Viardot who persuaded him to write his first opera, *Sapho* (1851), by promising to sing the title role. Although Hector Berlioz praised the music, and another critic detected in it the influence of Christoph Gluck, the work was generally considered a failure.

Since her performance as Fides in *Le Prophète* in 1849, Pauline Viardot had been one of the favorite artists of Giacomo Meyerbeer, whose reputation in Paris was at its zenith. It is therefore not surprising that Gounod's next opera, *La Nonne sanglante* (1854), based on Matthew Lewis's *The Monk*, should have been crafted in the Meyerbeer tradition. However, this opera also proved to be a failure. In the meantime, however, Gounod had written music for the choruses of François Ponsard's drama *Ulysse*, performed at the Comédie Française in 1852, and these earned for him an appointment as conductor of the largest male choir in Paris, L'Orphéon de la Ville de Paris. At this time he married Anna, the daughter of Pierre Zimmermann, who from 1820 to 1848 had been chief professor of the piano at the Paris Conservatoire.

During the decade 1855-1865, Gounod was at the height of his musical powers. In the area of church music, in which he had already succeeded, the *Messe solennelle de Sainte Cécile*, first performed on November 22, 1855,

Charles Gounod. (Library of Congress)

was a masterpiece in an ornate style that had come to replace the austere style in which he composed his early masses.

In 1858, Gounod began his association with the Théâtre-Lyrique, a theater founded in 1851 and dedicated to the performance of musico-dramatic works. Of the seven stage works that Gounod wrote between 1855 and 1865, five were first performed at the Théâtre-Lyrique; it is these five operas for which he is remembered more than a century later.

Two of the five Gounod operas are small-scale, light-hearted works in which his refined craftsmanship and unpretentious lyrical abilities were joined to well-known stories: Molière's play adapted by Jules Barbier and Michel Carré in *Le Médecin malgré lui* (1858) and the same adapters' version of the classical myth in *Philémon et Baucis* (1860). In these, Gounod finally discarded his Meyerbeerian pretensions and cultivated his own unique brand of wit and lyricism. The same librettists wrote for him not only the comic opera *La Colombe* (1860) but also the far more important *Faust* (1859), the work by which Gounod first became famous with the general public.

The success of *Faust* had already opened the doors of the opera to Gounod. However, it was only when he returned to the Théâtre-Lyrique and to the singer Marie Miolhan-Carvalho, who had sung the role of Marguerite in *Faust*, that Gounod scored two more major successes. The first was *Mireille* (1864), based on Frédéric Mistral's Provençal poem *Mirèio*, which had appeared in 1859. The second was the opera *Roméo et Juliette* (1867).

A disruption in Gounod's career as well as his private life came during the Franco-Prussian War of 1870-1871. On September 13, 1870, he and his family took refuge with English friends outside London. Although he was offered the directorship of the Conservatoire in June, 1871, it was not until June, 1874, that he returned to Paris.

Although Gounod never stopped writing occasional motets and cantatas for church use, he had written no mass since 1855; his major energies had been devoted to the opera. Even now it was an opera in which he eventually decided to incorporate for the first time his new musical ideals, which included writing music of tranquillity and feeling, music that transported the listener outside the realm of everyday life. While completing his opera *Polyeucte* (1878) in England, Gounod recognized the popularity of choral music in that country and was anxious to exploit both his own status as the composer of *Faust* and his experience as a choral conductor.

When the Royal Albert Hall Choral Society was formed in 1871, Gounod became its first conductor. During this period in his life, Gounod was high in the royal favor (*Faust* was Queen Victoria's favorite opera) and was glad to indulge the demand for sentimental ballads popular in mid-Victorian England. He had already written the notorious *Bethléem* and *Jésus de Nazareth* during the mid-1850's; the *Méditation sur le prélude de S. Bach* (1852), from which come the endless arrangements of *Ave Maria*, was composed in 1852.

Gounod gave up all the advantages of his position in England, however, when, in February, 1871, he met Georgina Weldon, an amateur singer separated from her husband and well connected socially. Weldon sang the solo part in Gounod's patriotic cantata *Gallia* (1871) at the reopening of the Conservatoire and again at the Opéra-Comique that summer. When she returned to London in 1871, she took Gounod with her. He was installed in Tavistock House, Bloomsbury, which Weldon had taken for her projected National Training School of Music. Gounod was quite seriously ill at the time and responded with growing hysteria to the hectic life in which he found himself at the school.

In spite of these conditions, Gounod managed to write most of *Polyeucte*, the incidental music to Jules Barbier's *Jeanne d'Arc* (1873), a requiem, ten psalms and anthems, twelve choruses, and three songs and short pieces. However, his social position was rapidly deteriorating. He was soon to enrage not only his own son, Jean, but also the English court as well when Weldon attempted to blackmail Queen Victoria into giving Gounod royal support for the Tavistock Academy and reinstatement in the Royal Albert Hall Choral Society after his falling out with the director.

For many reasons, then, Gounod's years in England seem to mark the end of his fruitfulness as a composer. As his ideals became loftier and his ideas more profound, his art became increasingly repetitive and platitudinous. The simplicity at which Gounod aimed in *Polyeucte* and *La Rédemption* (1882) disintegrated more and more into banality. Between 1882 and 1885, *La Rédemption* was performed all over Europe, including Vienna and Rome. However, while it was immensely popular, it was sharply attacked by the critics. *Polyeucte* fared little better.

It was not until June, 1874, that Gounod finally returned to France after a frightening cerebral attack during which he lay unconscious for long periods of time. With failing eyes but much determination, he struggled to complete his last piece of music, a requiem for his grandson Maurice, who had died prematurely. While reading through the manuscript, Gounod lapsed into a coma and died two days later, on October 18, 1893.

SIGNIFICANCE

In England, Charles Gounod had a strong and long-lasting influence on choral music, especially in the ecclesiastical and oratorio spheres, where *La Rédemption* occupied a prominent position during the 1880's. Like Giacomo Puccini and Richard Strauss a generation later, both Gounod and Mendelssohn expressed with skill and dignity the hopes and dreams of the contemporary bourgeoisie. The combination in *Faust* of tender sentiment and power of musical characterization with clean and imaginative craftsmanship made a deep impression on Peter Ilich Tchaikovsky, who owed almost as much to Gounod as to Georges Bizet and Léo Delibes.

Only a generation after Gounod's death, François Poulenc and Georges Auric were proclaiming as characteristically French the virtues of *Le Médecin malgré lui*, *La Colombe*, and *Philémon et Baucis* in their reaction against the music of Richard Wagner. All three works were revived by Sergei Diagilev in January, 1924. At the same time, a number of Gounod's songs were also revived; they have remained in the French repertory ever since. It was Gounod's belief that France was the country of "precision, neatness, and taste," and it is as a master of these qualities that he is best remembered.

—*Genevieve Slomski*

FURTHER READING

Abraham, Gerald, ed. *Romanticism, 1830-1890*. Vol. 9 in *The New Oxford History of Music*. New York: Oxford University Press, 1990. This standard music reference includes an essay on Gounod's life and work.

Cooper, Martin. *French Music: From the Death of Berlioz to the Death of Fauré*. New York: Oxford University Press, 1951. Provides a historical perspective on French music and includes a brief section on Gounod. Offers a succinct overview of the composer's life. Contains a bibliography and a table of events listing the major composers and other artists (and their principal works) during the years 1870-1925.

Gounod, Charles-François. *Memoirs of an Artist*. Translated by Annette E. Crocker. New York: Rand McNally, 1895. Gounod's intriguing but sentimental autobiography, spanning the years from his childhood to the writing of *Faust*.

Harding, James. *Gounod*. New York: Stein & Day, 1973. This informative biography discusses Gounod as a man of contradictions and extremes, demonstrating how the elements at war within his personality were reflected in his music. Assesses the impact of Gounod's music on later composers. Bibliography and appendix.

Hervey, Arthur. *Masters of French Music*. New York: Charles Scribner's Sons, 1894. This work contains a lengthy chapter devoted to Gounod. The author also focuses his discussion on Gounod's *Faust*, especially on the themes of love and religion in the work.

Johnson, Graham, and Richard Stokes, eds. *A French Song Companion*. New York: Oxford University Press, 2000. Includes an essay on Gounod as well as English translations of the lyrics of more than 700 French songs composed by Gounod and others, dating from the fifteenth through the twentieth centuries.

Tiersot, Julien. "Charles Gounod: A Centennial Tribute." *Musical Quarterly* 6 (July, 1918): 409-439. Tiersot examines the work and career of Gounod, as well as the man. Attempts to assess more objectively Gounod's contribution to French music.

SEE ALSO: Ludwig van Beethoven; Hector Berlioz; Georges Bizet; Léo Delibes; Felix Mendelssohn; Peter Ilich Tchaikovsky; Queen Victoria; Richard Wagner.

RELATED ARTICLE in *Great Events from History: The Nineteenth Century, 1801-1900:* October 22, 1883: Metropolitan Opera House Opens in New York.

WILLIAM GILBERT GRACE
English cricket player

Grace's brilliance as a cricket player, coupled with his immense personal popularity, consolidated cricket's position as England's national game. He became a symbol of the manly competitiveness that Victorians regarded as an essential element in the British character.

BORN: July 18, 1848; Downend, Gloucestershire, England
DIED: October 23, 1915; Mottingham, England
ALSO KNOWN AS: W. G. Grace
AREA OF ACHIEVEMENT: Sports

EARLY LIFE

William Gilbert Grace was born in a village a few miles from Bristol, England. He came from a cricketing family: His father, Henry M. Grace, a doctor, was captain of a local team, and his mother, Martha Pocock, was also devoted to the game. Both parents coached Grace and his brothers (two of whom also became famous players), and there was constant practicing in the orchard next to their house, with the family's dogs helping with the fielding.

Grace received a few years of education at private schools in nearby villages, but cricket always meant more to him than his studies. He was good enough to play in adult matches at the age of ten, and at the age of fourteen, he made more than fifty runs against the Somerset County XI, also distinguishing himself as a bowler in the same match. He played against the All-England XI (a powerful team of itinerant professionals) in that same year. By 1864, he was well enough known to be selected

for major matches outside the Bristol area, and he made his first big score, 170 runs, at the Oval ground in London. Two years later, he had an even bigger innings—224 not out for the Rest of England against Surrey—that confirmed his reputation as the finest English batsman of his day.

A large man—six feet, two inches tall and powerfully built—Grace was a superb all-round athlete. He excelled in all aspects of cricket. Besides being the greatest of English batsmen, he was also a fine bowler—fast in his youth, later turning to deceptive slow spin bowling—and a brilliant fielder with a magnificent throwing arm and huge hands that made breathtaking catches at point-blank range. As a young man, he regularly competed at athletics meetings, once being given temporary leave from an important cricket match at Lord's ground to run in a 440-yard hurdles race, which he duly won, at the Crystal Palace track. As a teenager, he was clean-shaven, but in his twenties he grew the massive black beard that made him instantly recognizable wherever he went.

LIFE'S WORK

Grace did more than anyone else to transform cricket from the relatively primitive stage that it had reached when he burst on the scene into something close to its modern form. Until the 1860's, cricket had been dominated for many years by two professional touring clubs—the All England XI and the United England XI—which played exhibition games against local teams. By the mid-1860's, however, county clubs containing a

William Gilbert Grace. (Library of Congress)

mixture of amateurs ("Gentlemen") and professionals ("Players") were growing in both strength and popularity. In 1873, the County Championship, a league of nine teams (by the end of Grace's career the number had grown to sixteen), was formed to meet the public appetite for more competitive cricket. Increased opportunities for leisure activities for both the middle and working classes, improved communications following the development of the railway, and widespread newspaper publicity combined to make cricket an extremely popular spectator sport.

Grace dominated the County Championship in its early years as no player since his time has ever done. His brilliant batting and astute leadership enabled his county, Gloucestershire, to win the championship four times in the first eight seasons. Year after year, he headed the national batting averages, sometimes with an average more than double that of his nearest rival, making light of the rough and physically dangerous conditions of many of the grounds on which he played. Before this time, an individual score of more than one hundred was almost unheard-of; Grace made it commonplace, occasionally going on to score a double or even a triple century.

Crowds flocked to see him, the county clubs prospered financially, and no benefit game for a needy professional was complete without him.

Although Grace's career flowered before the beginning of regular international cricket, he played a major role in promoting the game's popularity in other countries. He was one of a team that toured the United States and Canada in 1872, he took part in two tours of Australia, and, when the regular series between England and Australia began during the 1880's, he was an automatic first choice for the England team. By then, he was devoting a bit less time to the game. In 1873, he married Agnes Nicholls Day, and during the next few years, he qualified as a doctor at Bristol Medical School and two London hospitals, St. Bartholemew's and Westminster.

Grace still captained England in five series against Australia, winning four of them, and continued to represent his country until he was past fifty. Many of his greatest triumphs occurred in the annual exhibition matches between the Gentlemen and the Players (the amateurs against the professionals). Before 1864, the Players had won twenty-two of the previous twenty-five games; from 1867, the Gentlemen were victorious in seventeen of the next twenty-five, several of which Grace won almost single-handedly.

Grace's dominance was founded on two things: technical mastery and power of personality. His contribution to batting technique was thus described by the great Indian batsman, K. S. Ranjitsinghi:

> He revolutionized batting. He turned it from an accomplishment into a science. . . . What W. G. did was to unite in his mighty self all the good points of all the good players, and to make utility the criterion of style. He founded the modern theory of batting.

Great physical strength, superb coordination, high technical skill, immense powers of concentration, and a certain ruthlessness: That was the formula that made "W. G." (as he was known to legions of admirers) and led one despairing opponent to declare that he ought to be made to play with a smaller bat.

Assessments of Grace's personality are more ambiguous. The crowds adored him, and those who knew him well thought him a genial, straightforward person, with a genuinely kind heart. However, from some of the stories told about him it may seem surprising that he was a folk hero to followers of a game in which fair play and good sportsmanship were (and are) prized above all else. His high-pitched voice (another curious feature of so huge a man) was often raised in arguments with umpires, and he was said to "talk out" opposing batsmen by methods that certainly bordered on the unfair. He never actually went outside the laws, but an old professional once observed that it was wonderful what he could do inside them.

For someone who was ostensibly not paid for playing, Grace also made much money from cricket. There was always a clear distinction between the working-class amateur who played for money and the upper-class amateur who played for the love of the game, but the middle-class Grace seems to have been exempt from this. He always received lavish expenses, and after he began to practice medicine in Bristol in 1879 (with a substitute on call when Grace was away playing cricket), he was the recipient of several generously subscribed testimonial funds, the biggest of them after his spectacularly successful 1895 season. A malicious cartoon by Sir Max Beerbohm depicts the great "amateur" receiving a handsome check, with the funeral of one of his patients in the background. However, the patients do not seem to have complained; when available, Grace was devoted to their welfare, and they could bask in the reflected glory of being treated, at least occasionally, by England's most famous sportsman.

The year 1895 was Grace's "golden summer," in which, at the age of forty-seven, he completely recovered his old form and broke yet more batting records. That season was a brief interruption, however, in a slow and inevitable decline. In 1899, he lost his place on the England team (he had put on so much weight that he could no longer field effectively), and during the same year he broke with Gloucestershire to run his own team, London County, which played a few seasons of exhibition matches. He still appeared in the Gentlemen-Players matches until 1904, played his last first-class match at the age of fifty-eight, and turned out in local club games at Eltham, where he was then living, until 1914. Before the end of his first-class career, he had taken up golf and bowls, achieving some prominence in the latter sport: He was president of the English Bowling Association in 1903 and captained the national team for two seasons.

Grace's later years were darkened first by the deaths of his daughter in 1898 and his eldest son in 1905, and then by the outbreak of World War I. A patriotic Englishman, Grace wrote to *The Sportsman* newspaper in August, 1914, urging younger cricketers to volunteer, but soon he was mourning the slaughter of many of them in the carnage of Flanders. He seems to have lost the vitality and zest for life that had been so marked a feature of his character, and after a stroke, he died at Eltham on October 23, 1915.

SIGNIFICANCE

William Gilbert Grace was one of the most famous Englishmen of the Victorian Age. His great black-bearded figure, with cricket cap perched over his forehead, was known to millions, more familiar from cartoons in *Punch* and the sporting press than even the most celebrated statesman or military hero. He captured the public imagination and epitomized the spirit of vigorous, good-natured competition that, its adherents liked to think, was at the heart of the Victorian value system. Cricket was becoming a major ingredient in the cult of "muscular Christianity" instilled into generations of English schoolboys; Grace provided the hero figure necessary for that cult's success.

Grace was also a powerful symbol of national unity. Cricket already differed from other sports in that working-class professionals played alongside aristocratic amateurs, although the latter naturally controlled the organization of the game. Grace was undeniably middle class, but he became immensely popular among people of all classes: Admiration for his heroic deeds was something in which everyone could share. He thus contributed to a sense of English identity transcending class divisions, and indirectly promoted the growing spirit of patriotic nationalism on which mass support for British imperialism was built. Grace created modern cricket, but he also stood high in the ranks of Victorian heroes.

—*David Underdown*

FURTHER READING

Altham, Harry Suntees, and E. W. Swanton. *A History of Cricket*. 2 vols. London: Allen & Unwin, 1926, rev. ed., 1962. Volume 1 is a revision of Altham's older history, published in 1926; volume 2 (by Swanton) covers the period from 1914. A fine, detailed account of cricket history. Altham's volume is in three parts, the middle one being appropriately entitled "The Age of Grace."

Arlott, John, ed. *The Oxford Companion to World Sports and Games*. London: Oxford University Press, 1975. Contains a good, short description of cricket and its history, with illustrations and also a brief entry on Grace.

Darwin, Bernard. *W. G. Grace*. London: Duckworth, 1934, rev. ed. 1978. Darwin was primarily an expert on golf but also wrote extensively on cricket. This is a short but elegantly written biography, lively and interesting, maintaining a clear narrative line, with lavish illustrations. The best written of the numerous Grace biographies.

Grace, W. G. *Cricket*. Bristol, England: J. W. Arrowsmith, 1891. Partly autobiographical, partly a history of cricket, with comments on the players Grace knew and the issues confronting the game around 1890. Contains statistics of Grace's career until that year as well as many interesting anecdotes.

Howat, Gerald M. D. "William Gilbert Grace." In *Oxford Dictionary of National Biography*, edited by H. C. G. Matthew and Brian Harrison. New York: Oxford University Press, 2004. The entry on Grace sets out the essential facts of his life and athletic career.

Thomson, Arthur Alexander. *The Great Cricketer*. London: Hale, 1957. 2d ed. London: Hutchinson, 1968. A competent and thorough narrative of Grace's career, followed by chapters summarizing his achievements as cricketer, doctor, and "eminent Victorian." Useful for personal details as well as for the explanation of cricket; Thomson makes some effort to place Grace in historical context.

Trelford, Donald. *W. G. Grace*. Stroud, England: Sutton, 1998. Concise 128-page biography, recounting Grace's life and athletic achievements. Includes a bibliography.

SEE ALSO: Annie Oakley.

RELATED ARTICLES in *Great Events from History: The Nineteenth Century, 1801-1900:* c. 1845: Modern Baseball Begins; 1869: Baseball's First Professional Club Forms.

ULYSSES S. GRANT
President of the United States (1869-1877)

Grant was the preeminent military commander of the American Civil War, demonstrating the persistence and strategic genius that brought about the victory of the North. Afterward, a grateful nation twice elected him president, but his administration must be counted a failure.

BORN: April 27, 1822; Point Pleasant, Ohio
DIED: July 23, 1885; Mount McGregor, New York
ALSO KNOWN AS: Ulysses Simpson Grant; Ulysses Hiram Grant; Hiram Ulysses Grant (birth name); Unconditional Surrender Grant
AREAS OF ACHIEVEMENT: Military, government and politics

EARLY LIFE

Born Hiram Ulysses Grant, Ulysses S. Grant was the eldest child of Jesse Root Grant and Hannah Simpson Grant. His father had known poverty in his youth, but at the time of his first son's birth, he had established a prosperous tannery business. In 1823, Jesse moved his business to Georgetown, Ohio, where Grant spent his boyhood. He received his preliminary education at Georgetown, at Maysville Seminary in Maysville, Kentucky, and at the Presbyterian Academy, Ripley, Ohio. He did not show special promise as a student and lived a rather ordinary boyhood. His most outstanding gift turned out to be a special talent with horses, enabling him to manage the most fractious horse. He also developed a strong dislike for work at the tannery and a lifelong fondness for farming.

Jesse Grant secured an appointment for his son to the United States Military Academy at West Point in 1839. His son did not want to go but bowed to parental authority. Concerned about the initials on his trunk, "H.U.G.," he decided to change his name to Ulysses Hiram Grant. Arriving at West Point, Grant had his first skirmish with military bureaucracy. His congressman, evidently confusing Grant with his brother Simpson, had appointed him as Ulysses S. Grant. The army insisted that Ulysses S. Grant, not Ulysses H. or Hiram Ulysses, had been appointed, and eventually Grant surrendered. Grant wrote to a congressman in 1864: "In answer to your letter of a few days ago asking what 'S' stands for in my name I can only state *nothing*."

Grant was graduated in the middle of his class in 1843. While at West Point, he developed a fondness for novels and showed a special talent for mathematics. Appointed a brevet second lieutenant in the Fourth United States Infantry, Grant served with distinction in the Mexican War (1846-1848). He fought in the battles of Palo Alto, Resaca de la Palma, and Monterrey under the command of Zachary Taylor, "Old Rough and Ready." Taylor impressed Grant with his informal attire and lack of military pretension, a style that Grant later adopted. He participated in all major battles leading to the capture of Mexico City and won brevet promotion to first lieutenant for bravery at Molino Del Rey and to captain for his behavior at Chapultepec. Although he fought with distinction, Grant believed that the Mexican War was unjust and later said that he should have resigned his commission rather than participate.

Grant married Julia Dent, the daughter of a St. Louis slaveholding family, on August 22, 1848. He had been introduced to his future wife in 1843 by her brother, a West Point classmate, while stationed at Jefferson Barracks, Missouri. The Mexican War, however, interrupted their romance. The Grants had four children, Frederick Dent, Ulysses S., Jr., Ellen Wrenshall, and Jesse Root, Jr. A devoted husband and father, Grant centered his life on his family. Indeed, the many surviving letters to his wife during absences caused by a military career provide the most poignant insights into the man.

Ordered to the Pacific coast in 1852 with his regiment, Grant could not afford to take his wife and children. He grew despondent without his family, decided to resign his commission in 1854, and returned to live on his wife's family land near St. Louis to take up farming. For the remainder of Grant's life, rumors that he had been forced to resign on account of heavy drinking followed him. The next seven years were difficult for Grant. His attempt at farming did not work out, and he tried other occupations without real success. Finally, in 1860, he moved his family to Galena, Illinois, to work as a clerk in a leather-goods store owned by his father and operated by his two younger brothers.

Grant had never been a strident, political man. His father had been an antislavery advocate, yet Grant married into a slaveholding family. At one time, he owned a slave but gave him his freedom in 1858 at a time when Grant sorely needed money. His wife retained ownership of slaves throughout the Civil War. When news of the firing on Fort Sumter reached Galena, Grant believed that he had an obligation to support the Union. Because of his military experience, he assisted in organizing and escorting a volunteer company to Springfield, Illinois, where he stayed on to assist Governor Richard Yates in mustering in and organizing volunteer troops. Eventually, Yates appointed Grant colonel of the Twenty-first Illinois Volunteers, a disorganized and undisciplined unit. Grant quickly worked the regiment into shape, marched it to Missouri, and learned much about commanding volunteer soldiers.

LIFE'S WORK

On August 7, 1861, President Abraham Lincoln appointed Grant brigadier general, and Grant established headquarters at Cairo, Illinois, an important staging area

for Union movement farther south. On September 6, he occupied Paducah, Kentucky, near the strategic confluence of the Tennessee, Cumberland, and Ohio Rivers. Grant's first battle followed shortly. He attacked Confederate forces at Belmont, Missouri, with mixed results. He lost control of his troops after initial success and had to retreat when Confederate reinforcements arrived.

Grant gained national prominence in February, 1862, when authorized to operate against Fort Donelson and Fort Henry, guarding the Cumberland and Tennessee Rivers, obvious highways into the Confederate heartland. He moved his small army in conjunction with naval forces and captured Fort Henry on February 6 and immediately moved overland against Fort Donelson, twelve miles away. The Confederates attempted to escape encirclement on February 15 in a brief, but bloody, battle. On February 16, the Confederate commander asked Grant

Ulysses S. Grant. (Library of Congress)

for surrender terms. His response brought him fame: "No terms except an unconditional and immediate surrender can be accepted." The Confederates surrendered on Grant's terms, and Lincoln rewarded him for the first significant Union victory with promotion to major general.

Grant's next major engagement, the Battle of Shiloh, April 6-7, left him under a cloud. Surprised by Rebel forces, Grant suffered heavy losses but managed to rally his army on the first day. The second day, General Grant counterattacked and drove the Confederates from the field. This bloody engagement cast a long shadow, and Grant faced newspaper criticism, with rumors of his heavy drinking appearing in the press. Major General Henry W. Halleck arrived on the scene to take command of Grant's forces, placing him in a subordinate position with little to do. Grant considered leaving the army. He retained his humor, however, writing to his wife, "We are all well and me as sober as a deacon no matter what is said to the contrary." Halleck, however, was called to Washington to act as general in chief, and Grant resumed command. Although many had criticized Grant, Lincoln refused to relieve a fighting general, thus setting the stage for Grant's finest campaign.

Confederate control of the Mississippi River rested on extensive fortifications at Vicksburg, Mississippi, effectively barring midwestern commerce. In the fall and spring of 1862-1863, Grant made a number of attempts against this bastion. The overland campaign through northern Mississippi came to grief when Confederate forces destroyed his supply base at Holly Springs, Mississippi, on December 20, 1862. Grant then decided to move down the Mississippi to attack the city. Ultimately, Grant bypassed the city, marching his army down the west bank of the river. At night, he sent steamboats past the batteries to assist in crossing the river from Louisiana into Mississippi. The general then launched a lightning campaign into the interior of the state to destroy Confederate communications before turning back against Vicksburg. Thoroughly confusing his opposition, he won five separate battles and besieged the city on May 19. On July 4, 1863, Grant accepted the surrender of his second Confederate army.

After a brief respite, Grant was given command of all Union forces in the West on October 18 and charged with rescuing Union forces besieged in Chattanooga, Tennessee. In a three-day battle (November 23-25), Grant smashed the Confederate forces and drove them back into Georgia.

In March, 1864, Lincoln promoted Grant to lieutenant general and gave him command of all Union armies.

Grant left Halleck at Washington as chief of staff to tend to routine matters and established the beginning of a modern military command system. He stayed in the field with the Army of the Potomac, commanded by Major General George G. Meade. Grant made Union armies work in tandem for the first time. Using the telegraph, he managed troop movements across the country, keeping pressure on the Confederacy at all points. The two major efforts consisted of Major General William Tecumseh Sherman, moving against Atlanta, and Meade attacking Confederate forces in Virginia, commanded by the South's finest general, Robert E. Lee.

The final campaign opened in May, 1864, with the Battle of the Wilderness (May 5-6). After a series of bloody engagements, Grant maneuvered Lee into Petersburg, Virginia, where siege operations commenced on June 16. While Grant held Lee at Petersburg, Sherman proceeded to gut the South, capturing Atlanta in September, then marching across Georgia and capturing Savannah in December. Grant then planned for Sherman to march his army up through the Carolinas into Virginia. On March 29, 1865, Grant launched his final campaign. He smashed Confederate lines at Petersburg, then tenaciously pressured the retreating Confederates, and accepted Lee's surrender at Appomattox Courthouse on April 9. Grant's magnanimous surrender terms attest to his humanity and sensitivity. Seventeen days later, the last major Confederate force surrendered to Sherman and the Civil War ended.

Lincoln's assassination on April 14 deeply affected Grant, but he believed that President Andrew Johnson would be able to reestablish the Union on an equitable basis. Grant busied himself with the reorganization of the army, threatening French forces operating in Mexico, marshaling forces to fight Indians, and seeking to avoid political questions. However, he could not avoid the growing antagonism between Johnson and the radical Republicans. Increasing doubts about Johnson's Reconstruction policy brought the two men into conflict. In the face of growing southern persecution of black people, Grant came to believe that black people had to be protected by the federal government. In 1868, the breach between Johnson and Grant became public, and Grant believed that it was his duty to accept the Republican nomination for president.

A reluctant candidate, Grant easily defeated his Democratic opponent. His military background, however, had left him with a distaste for the hurly-burly of politics, and his two-term presidency (March 4, 1869, to March 4, 1877) had many problems. Already convinced of the

CIVIL WAR MEMOIRS

"Man proposes and God disposes." There are but few important events in the affairs of men brought about by their own choice.

Although frequently urged by friends to write my memoirs I had determined never to do so, nor to write anything for publication. At the age of nearly sixty-two I received an injury from a fall, which confined me closely to the house while it did not apparently affect my general health. This made study a pleasant pastime. Shortly after, the rascality of a business partner developed itself by the announcement of a failure. This was followed soon after by universal depression of all securities, which seemed to threaten the extinction of a good part of the income still retained, and for which I am indebted to the kindly act of friends. At this juncture the editor of the Century Magazine asked me to write a few articles for him. I consented for the money it gave me; for at that moment I was living upon borrowed money. The work I found congenial, and I determined to continue it. The event is an important one for me, for good or evil; I hope for the former.

In preparing these volumes for the public, I have entered upon the task with the sincere desire to avoid doing injustice to any one, whether on the National or Confederate side, other than the unavoidable injustice of not making mention often where special mention is due. There must be many errors of omission in this work, because the subject is too large to be treated of in two volumes in such way as to do justice to all the officers and men engaged. There were thousands of instances, during the rebellion, of individual, company, regimental and brigade deeds of heroism which deserve special mention and are not here alluded to. The troops engaged in them will have to look to the detailed reports of their individual commanders for the full history of those deeds.

The first volume, as well as a portion of the second, was written before I had reason to suppose I was in a critical condition of health. Later I was reduced almost to the point of death, and it became impossible for me to attend to anything for weeks. I have, however, somewhat regained my strength, and am able, often, to devote as many hours a day as a person should devote to such work. I would have more hope of satisfying the expectation of the public if I could have allowed myself more time. I have used my best efforts, with the aid of my eldest son, F. D. Grant, assisted by his brothers, to verify from the records every statement of fact given. The comments are my own, and show how I saw the matters treated of whether others saw them in the same light or not.

With these remarks I present these volumes to the public, asking no favor but hoping they will meet the approval of the reader.

—*U. S. Grant.*
Mount Macgregor, New York, July 1, 1885.

Source: *Personal Memoirs of U. S. Grant* (New York: Charles L. Webster, 1886), vol. 1.

need to protect black people. Grant sought in vain to advance civil rights for them. With the Force Acts (1870-1871), he succeeded in breaking up the first Ku Klux Klan, but by 1876, conservative southerners had regained control and reasserted their dominance.

In foreign policy, Grant did much to normalize relations with Great Britain with the Treaty of Washington in May, 1871, which settled the *Alabama* claims arising out of the Civil War. His stubbornness and persistence, which had served him so well in war, however, proved to be an embarrassment in his unsuccessful attempts to annex Santo Domingo.

Grant made a number of unfortunate appointments to federal office, and official corruption even reached into the White House with the Whiskey Ring Scandal. Although Grant was not personally involved, these scandals tainted his second term. Plagued by corruption and

politics, Grant resisted attempts to draft him for a third term in 1876.

After completing his presidential terms, Grant made a two-year journey around the world, indulging a passion for travel that he had developed early in his life. This triumphant tour brought him worldwide renown. Restless after returning to the United States, he unsuccessfully sought a third term in 1880. He then moved to New York City to pursue business interests in connection with his son, Ulysses S. Grant, Jr., and became a silent partner in Grant and Ward. Ferdinand Ward turned out to be a swindler, and in 1884, Grant found himself penniless. To support his family, Grant started writing his Civil War memoirs for a magazine. When his friend Mark Twain learned how poorly he was being paid for his articles, he was outraged. Twain was starting his own publishing firm at that time and offered Grant a generous book contract.

Around that same time, Grant—who had long been a heavy smoker—learned that he had contracted cancer of the throat. He completed his memoirs only days before his death, on July 23, 1885. The two-volume work that was made from his writings has become a literary classic and is recognized as one of the best military memoirs ever written. It also enriched his widow, to whom Mark Twain made the largest royalty payments in history, up to that time.

SIGNIFICANCE

Grant's boyhood had been ordinary, showing nothing of the extraordinary man he would become. He had not sought a military career and did not like things military. He detested military parades, disliked military dress, and rarely carried a weapon. He left the army in 1854 and suffered through seven years of disappointment. The outbreak of Civil War, for all its national trauma, rescued Grant from a life of obscurity.

This seemingly common man turned out to have a genius for war unmatched by his contemporaries. Grant perhaps had an advantage in that he had time to learn gradually the art of war. Grant made mistakes, learned from them, and never repeated them. He grew into the responsibilities of higher command. He also understood volunteer soldiers and their motivations for fighting.

Grant's military writings are extraordinary. His instructions are clear, brief, and to the point. Subordinates made mistakes, but not because of ambiguity of instruction. Grant became the finest general that the Civil War produced, indeed, the greatest American military figure of the nineteenth century.

The Grant presidency had many shortcomings. Not a politician, Grant never really understood presidential power and its uses. In this sense, he was a nineteenth century man: He believed that Congress decided policy and the president executed it. Had Grant viewed the presidency in the same manner that he perceived military command, his two terms might have been far different.

Grant returned to wartime form in the fight to complete his memoirs. This literary classic is really a gift to the ages as he again demonstrated that he was truly an extraordinary American.

—*David L. Wilson*

FURTHER READING

Bunting, Josiah, III. *Ulysses S. Grant*. New York: Times Books, 2004. One in a series of books analyzing presidential administrations. While acknowledging Grant's flaws, Bunting generally admires Grant, granting him high marks for "nobility of character" and for his achievements in attaining civil rights for African Americans.

Catton, Bruce. *Grant Moves South*. New York: Little, Brown, 1960. This biography of Grant, covering his early Civil War career, is thoroughly researched and superbly written.

_____. *Grant Takes Command*. Boston: Little, Brown, 1969. Catton continues his brilliant work, taking Grant from Chattanooga to Appomattox.

Garland, Hamlin. *Ulysses S. Grant: His Life and Character*. New York: Doubleday & McClure, 1898. This nineteenth century biography of Grant is among the best written. It is especially valuable because the author interviewed a number of Grant contemporaries.

Grant, Ulysses S. *The Papers of Ulysses S. Grant*. Edited by John Y. Simon. Carbondale: Southern Illinois University Press, 1967-   . Twenty-six volumes of this comprehensive series have been published, following Grant through 1875. This work makes it possible to evaluate Grant's career using documentary sources and demonstrates that Grant's literary flair in his memoirs was not a fluke.

_____. *Personal Memoirs of U. S. Grant*. 2 vols. New York: Charles L. Webster, 1885-1886. These volumes are magnificent from both a literary and a historical perspective. Grant's assessment of his life through the Civil War is powerful, compelling, and accurate.

Korda, Michael. *Ulysses S. Grant: The Unlikely Hero*. New York: Atlas Books/HarperCollins, 2004. Brief biography providing an overview of Grant's early life, military career, and presidency. Accessible and accurate.

McFeely, William S. *Grant: A Biography*. New York: W. W. Norton, 1981. A well-written biography that uses modern standards to judge Grant harshly, emphasizing what Grant should have done to protect black civil rights during Reconstruction.

Neillands, Robin. *Grant: The Man Who Won the Civil War*. Cold Spring Harbor, N.Y.: Cold Spring Press, 2004. Neillands, a military historian, focuses on Grant's military career, describing his military training and providing details of the Civil War battles in which he participated. The book ends in 1865, with Lee's surrender at Appomattox.

Porter, Horace. *Campaigning with Grant*. New York: Century, 1897. Written by a Grant staff officer, this account is excellent for a personal view of Grant during the last eighteen months of the war.

Young, John Russell. *Around the World with General Grant.* 2 vols. New York: American News, 1879. Although there is considerable padding in these volumes, they have real significance because of the author's numerous interviews with Grant.

SEE ALSO: Caleb Cushing; Rutherford B. Hayes; Andrew Johnson; Robert E. Lee; Abraham Lincoln; Thomas Nast; Zachary Taylor; Mark Twain.

RELATED ARTICLES in *Great Events from History: The Nineteenth Century, 1801-1900:* July 1, 1863- November 25, 1863: Battles of Gettysburg, Vicksburg, and Chattanooga; December 8, 1863-April 24, 1877: Reconstruction of the South; November 15, 1864-April 18, 1865: Sherman Marches Through Georgia and the Carolinas; April 9 and 14, 1865: Surrender at Appomattox and Assassination of Lincoln; February 24-May 26, 1868: Impeachment of Andrew Johnson; September 24, 1869-1877: Scandals Rock the Grant Administration; March 3, 1871: Grant Signs Indian Appropriation Act; May 8, 1871: Treaty of Washington Settles U.S. Claims vs. Britain.

ASA GRAY
American botanist

The leading botanical taxonomist in nineteenth century United States and the founder of the discipline of plant geography, Gray was the first advocate of Darwinian evolution in the United States.

BORN: November 18, 1810; Sauquoit, New York
DIED: January 30, 1888; Cambridge, Massachusetts
AREA OF ACHIEVEMENT: Biology

EARLY LIFE

The son of Moses Gray, a tanner, and Roxana Howard Gray (New Englanders who had migrated to upstate New York after the Revolutionary War), Asa Gray was born in upstate New York and educated at local schools and academies. He entered the College of Physicians and Surgeons of the Western District of New York in 1826. Alternating attendance at the lectures at the medical school with apprenticeship with practicing physicians, Gray received his medical degree in January, 1831.

Slight, short, and clean-shaven until his middle age, Gray was physically agile and appeared ever-youthful. This physical agility was matched by his mental quickness. Complementing these traits was a self-assuredness that led him to abandon medical practice in 1832 to follow his dream of becoming a botanist.

LIFE'S WORK

Gray's interest in botany had been sparked by James Hadley, one of the faculty at the College of Physicians and Surgeons, but his real mentor was John Torrey, one of the outstanding American botanists. After a tryout in 1832, Torrey hired Gray the following year to collect specimens for him. Ultimately, Gray moved into the Torrey home and became Torrey's collaborator on his *Flora of North America* (1838-1843).

Finding employment as a scientist during the 1830's was not easy. For the first few years after he rejected a medical career, Gray supported himself through part-time teaching and library jobs. In 1836, he was selected as botanist on the United States Exploring Expedition but resigned the position in 1838, before the expedition ever sailed, disgusted by the delays that had plagued the venture. Instead, he became professor of botany (the first such professorship in the United States) at the University of Michigan, spending the next year in Europe purchasing books and equipment for the university. The university's financial problems resulted, however, in the suspension of his salary in 1840, before he had ever taught a class.

Not until April, 1842, with his appointment as Fisher Professor of Natural History at Harvard University, with responsibility for teaching botany and maintaining the botanical gardens, did Gray obtain a stable and permanent institutional home. He remained at Harvard (which also indirectly supplied him with his wife, Jane Lathrop Loring, the daughter of a leading Boston lawyer who was a member of the Harvard Corporation) for the rest of his life.

Manifest Destiny helped shape the contours of Gray's scientific career: Overseas exploration and domestic reconnaissance and surveying during the two decades before the Civil War had resulted in a huge flow eastward of botanical specimens gathered by army engineers, naval explorers, and collectors accompanying the expeditions. Gray spent most of his professional life worrying about the nomenclature and taxonomy of these plants. Through either his own research or the coordination of the activities of other botanists, he was responsible for the description of flora gathered from Japan to Mexico.

By the 1850's, Gray was clearly the leading botanist in the United States. He was the cement that held together a huge network of amateur collectors. His publications included the *Manual of the Botany of the Northern United States* (1848) and extremely popular textbooks for college, high school, and elementary school students. A frequent visitor to Europe, he was well known in international scientific circles.

The opportunity for Gray's greatest contribution to science came about because of his international reputation, but his connection with this flow of specimens enabled him to exploit fully the opportunity. Charles Darwin had written him in April, 1855, inquiring about the geographical distribution of Alpine plants in the United States. In response, Gray produced a statistical analysis of the flora of the northern United States, drawing on his wide knowledge of the botany of the Northern Hemisphere. This in turn encouraged Darwin in 1857 to let Gray in on his great secret—the theory of evolution.

Asa Gray. (Library of Congress)

At this point, Gray had in hand an extensive collection from Japan, gathered by Charles Wright during the North Pacific Exploring Expedition, as well as smaller collections from Matthew C. Perry's expedition, which opened up Japan. Gray discerned that the flora of Japan was much more similar to that of eastern North America than western North America or Europe. He rejected the possibility of separate creation and, applying Darwin's ideas, proposed instead that the similarities reflect the evolution of the flora from common ancestry under similar conditions. A single flora, Gray theorized, had stretched round the earth before the Ice Age; changing geological conditions resulted in the differences in Northern Hemispheric flora.

This public endorsement of Darwin in early 1859, the first in the United States, was followed by many others. Gray quickly became the leading American spokesperson for Darwin's theory, and he negotiated the American publishing contract for *On the Origin of Species by Means of Natural Selection* (1859). Moreover, the review of this work in the *American Journal of Science*, the leading American scientific journal of the day, was written by Gray. Time and again he debated the leading anti-evolutionist in the American scientific community, the Swiss-born Louis Agassiz, director of Harvard's Museum of Comparative Zoology. In 1860, in a series of articles in the *Atlantic Monthly*, Gray defended Darwin from critics who charged that the theory of evolution was hostile to religion, taking a position on the compatibility of Darwinian evolution with theism that the author of the theory himself was unable ultimately to accept.

After his retirement from teaching in 1873, Gray continued his research and field trips. He spent six triumphant months in Europe in 1887, returning to the United States in October. A month later, he was taken ill and died in his home in Cambridge on January 30, 1888. He left behind the Harvard Botanic Garden, the Gray Herbarium, and a generation of botanists and collectors for whom he had provided training, guidance, and assistance.

SIGNIFICANCE

Asa Gray was fortunate to be a botanist in the United States at a time when the expansionist drive of the nation resulted in its soldiers and sailors crisscrossing the North American continent and the Pacific Ocean. Describing the botanical fruits of these exploring and surveying expeditions was Gray's lifelong work. His skill helped set American botany on a par with its European counter-

DARWIN VS. AGASSIZ

In an article that he originally published in the American Journal of Science and Arts *in 1860, Asa Gray analyzed the differences between the evolutionary theory of Charles Darwin and that of the American scientist Louis Agassiz. After laying out his broad observations, he offered this conservative judgment.*

Who shall decide between such extreme views so ably maintained on either hand, and say how much of truth there may be in each? The present reviewer has not the presumption to undertake such a task. Having no prepossession in favor of naturalistic theories, but struck with the eminent ability of Mr. Darwin's work, and charmed with its fairness, our humbler duty will be performed if, laying aside prejudice as much as we can, we shall succeed in giving a fair account of its method and argument, offering by the way a few suggestions, such as might occur to any naturalist of an inquiring mind. An editorial character for this article must in justice be disclaimed. The plural pronoun is employed not to give editorial weight, but to avoid even the appearance of egotism, and also the circumlocution which attends a rigorous adherence to the impersonal style.

We have contrasted these two extremely divergent theories, in their broad statements. It must not be inferred that they have no points nor ultimate results in common.

In the first place, they practically agree in upsetting, each in its own way, the generally-received definition of species, and in sweeping away the ground of their objective existence in Nature. The orthodox conception of species is that of lineal descent: all the descendants of a common parent, and no other, constitute a species; they have a certain identity because of their descent, by which they are supposed to be recognizable. . . .

Source: Asa Gray, "The Origin of Species by Means of Natural Selection," in *Darwiniana: Essays and Reviews Pertaining to Darwinism* (New York: D. Appleton, 1876).

cept such an interpretation, however, and Gray's vision died with him. If Darwin had made another choice, the intellectual, cultural, and philosophical history of the West might have taken a course much different from that which it subsequently followed.

—*Marc Rothenberg*

FURTHER READING

Dupree, A. Hunter. *Asa Gray: 1810-1888.* Cambridge, Mass.: Belknap Press of Harvard University Press, 1968. The standard biography, well documented, interpretive, and accurate. Views Gray within the context of the social and intellectual history of the United States.

Evans, Howard Ensign. *Pioneer Naturalists: The Discovery and Naming of North American Plants and Animals.* Drawings by Michael G. Kippenhan. New York: Holt, 1993. Provides information about more than 100 people who lent their names to North American plants and animals. Includes information about Gray and other prominent naturalists.

Eyde, Richard H. "Expedition Botany: The Making of a New Profession." In *Magnificent Voyagers: The U.S. Exploring Expedition, 1838-1842*, edited by Herman J. Viola and Carolyn Margolis. Washington, D.C.: Smithsonian Institution Press, 1985. Discusses the problems surrounding the botanical activities of the expedition.

Fry, C. George, and Jon Paul Fry. *Congregationalists and Evolution: Asa Gray and Louis Agassiz.* Lanham, Md.: University Press of America, 1989. Compares the lives and philosophies of Gray and his Harvard colleague, zoologist Louis Agassiz, focusing on their dispute over Darwin's theory of evolution and their membership in the Congregationalist Church.

Goetzmann, William H. *Exploration and Empire: The Explorer and the Scientist in the Winning of the American West.* New York: Alfred A. Knopf, 1966. A well-researched history of American exploration in the nineteenth century and the scientific discoveries that were its by-product. Although Gray is mentioned only briefly, this book describes the context of much of his scientific efforts.

parts. Prodded by Charles Darwin, he asked some important questions about plant distribution that led to the development of a new scientific field and further evidence for the evolutionary thought of Darwin.

Gray's greatest impact on American society, however, was as the defender of Darwin's theory of evolution. Gray, a member of the First Congregation Church of Cambridge, understood that if evolution was to be accepted by the deeply religious American scientific community of the mid-nineteenth century, it would have to be reconciled with a belief in the existence of God. Gray believed that Darwin's theory, whatever its scientific merits, had to be defended from accusations of atheism. His solution was to suggest that the Creator intervened by limiting or directing variations. Darwin could not ac-

Gray, Asa. *Darwiniana*. Edited by A. Hunter Dupree. Cambridge, Mass.: Belknap Press of Harvard University Press, 1963. A collection of Gray's essays on evolution, first published in 1876. Essential for understanding Gray's attempt to reconcile evolution and religion.

_____. *The Letters of Asa Gray*. Edited by Jane Loring Gray. 2 vols. Boston: Houghton Mifflin, 1893. This collection, edited by Gray's widow, includes Gray's autobiography.

Keeney, Elizabeth. *The Botanizers: Amateur Scientists in Nineteenth-Century America*. Chapel Hill: University of North Carolina Press, 1992. In the nineteenth century, tens of thousands of amateur botanists (or "botanizers") collected plant samples, exchanged specimens, and corresponded with expert botanists. Using popular magazines, textbooks, letters, diaries, and other contemporary sources, Keeney traces the rise and fall of botany as a popular recreational science. Includes information about Gray's participation in the movement.

Lurie, Edward. *Louis Agassiz: A Life in Science*. Chicago: University of Chicago Press, 1960. The essential biography of Darwin's chief American scientific opponent.

Rodgers, Andrew Denny, III. *American Botany, 1873-1892: Decades of Transition*. Princeton, N.J.: Princeton University Press, 1944. Discusses the evolution of American botany from a descriptive to an experimental science and Gray's role in that transition.

_____. *John Torrey: A Story of North American Botany*. Princeton, N.J.: Princeton University Press, 1942. A scholarly, although somewhat dated biography of Gray's mentor. Provides an excellent account of Torrey's scientific accomplishments and his role in developing American botany.

Sᴇᴇ ᴀʟsᴏ: Louis Agassiz; Ferdinand Julius Cohn; Charles Darwin; Charles William Eliot; John Muir; Matthew C. Perry.

Rᴇʟᴀᴛᴇᴅ ᴀʀᴛɪᴄʟᴇs in *Great Events from History: The Nineteenth Century, 1801-1900:* 1809: Lamarck Publishes *Zoological Philosophy*; 1854-1862: Wallace's Expeditions Give Rise to Biogeography; November 24, 1859: Darwin Publishes *On the Origin of Species*; 1871: Darwin Publishes *The Descent of Man*.

Hᴏʀᴀᴄᴇ Gʀᴇᴇʟᴇʏ
American journalist

A daring journalist and lecturer, Greeley engaged himself personally with a wide range of social issues—labor rights, abolitionism, territorial expansion, women's rights, and political reform—and his paper, the New York Tribune, *became a medium for the best thought of his time. He also dabbled in politics and was the Democratic candidate for president of the United States shortly before he died.*

Bᴏʀɴ: February 3, 1811; Amherst, New Hampshire
Dɪᴇᴅ: November 29, 1872; New York, New York
Aʀᴇᴀs ᴏꜰ ᴀᴄʜɪᴇᴠᴇᴍᴇɴᴛ: Journalism, social reform, government and politics

Eᴀʀʟʏ Lɪꜰᴇ
Among the founding families of New England, the first of Horace Greeley's ancestors arrived in North America in 1640. Greeley himself was the third of seven children of Zaccheus and Mary (Woodburn) Greeley. As a boy, he was frail and uncoordinated and had a large head on a small frame. His mother was very protective of him, keeping him close as he was physically weak. She held great influence on him, and she urged him to read and study rather than risk injury in the rough-and-tumble world of children. Greeley could read at an early age, and with his delicate manners he became a favorite of teachers in Bedford, whose trustees were also impressed with the boy's brilliance. Some influential citizens even offered to underwrite Greeley at Phillips Academy in nearby Exeter. His parents declined the offer, as hard times seemed continually to press them to move from farm to farm, from Connecticut to Massachusetts and on to Westhaven, Vermont, all before Horace was ten years old.

Greeley continued with his self-education, aided and watched over by his mother. His ungainly appearance and odd wardrobe of baggy short trousers and a coat topped by equally odd slouching hats and caps did little to mitigate the impression made by the high-pitched, whining voice that came from his large, moonlike head. Youngsters called him "the ghost," and he became a subject for their merriment. Throughout his life he lacked social polish and a sense of dress.

At the age of fifteen, Greeley was apprenticed to a small newspaper, the *Northern Spectator* of East Poultney, Vermont; there, he learned the rudiments of what was to become his life's work. He joined the local debating society, and, with his intense and serious attention to public affairs, he became a respected member of the community. The paper folded, however, and Greeley joined his family, who had moved to the Pennsylvania-New York border village of Erie, where his father had again taken up farming. There he helped with the farm and gained printing jobs in Erie, Jamestown, and Lodi, all towns in New York State. The struggle for existence, let alone success, in the dismal marginal area depressed him, and in 1831, with ten dollars, he set out on foot for New York City.

LIFE'S WORK

Finding employment in New York was difficult, but Greeley was willing to take on a technically difficult job that no other printer would do: set up print for an edition of the New Testament with Greek references and supplementary notes on each book. This job, which strained Greeley's already weak eyesight, brought him to the attention of other printers. He began work on William Leggett's *Evening Post*, from which he was fired because he did not fit the model of "decent-looking men in the office."

Greeley had been able to save some money and formed a partnership with Francis Vinton Story, and later, Jonas Winchester. They did job-printing as well as printing *Bank Note Reporter* (1832) and the *Constitutionalist* (1832), which dealt with popular lottery printing. They attempted a penny paper called the *Morning Post* using patronage investment by H. D. Shepard and supply credit from George Bruce, but a general lack of business acumen caused the venture to fail. With the failure of the penny daily, Greeley turned to putting out a successful weekly, the *New-Yorker*, which, coupled with his other publications, made the partnership now called Greeley and Company a success in journalism although not in the cash box. The habit of newspapers to extend credit rather than work on a cash basis was not to be changed until James Gordon Bennett's *Herald* demanded it during the 1840's. Greeley's weekly was nonpartisan in politics, stimulating, well written, and well edited. Greeley also made extra money by selling his writing to other papers, such as the *Daily Whig*.

In 1836, Greeley married Mary Youngs Cheney, formerly of Cornwall, Connecticut, then a teacher in North Carolina. They had first met while virtual inmates of

Horace Greeley. (Library of Congress)

Sylvester Graham's boardinghouse; Cheney was a devoted follower of the Grahamite cause, while Greeley was simply a teetotaling vegetarian satisfying his curiosity about Graham's unique regimen for healthy living. They were an odd match. She was plain, dogmatic, humorless, supercilious, and uncommunicative; he was compassionate, outgoing, and egalitarian. From the first day of their marriage, on July 5, 1836, they did not get along.

As a matter of personal conscience, Greeley was never inclined to pyramid debt, and this contributed to the failure of his weekly. In addition, nonpartisanship was never Greeley's strong suit. Opinionated, he found advocacy journalism more to his liking; therefore, he was more than willing to accommodate the proposition of Whig boss Thurlow Weed of Albany, New York, to put out a New York paper favoring the party. The result was the *Jeffersonian*, which brought Greeley a guaranteed salary of one thousand dollars per year and proved a success.

More important, Greeley was mixing in state and national political circles. In 1840, the Whigs encouraged

Greeley to publish another weekly, called the *Log Cabin*; because it had a guaranteed subscription list among the party faithful, the journal was an immediate success. Greeley edited the *Log Cabin* as well as his struggling *New-Yorker* until, on April 10, 1841, he combined the two publications using three thousand dollars, of which one-third was his cash, one-third was in supplies, and one-third was borrowed from James Coggeshall. The result was his *New York Tribune*. He had built a personal following through the political papers, and he now sought to capitalize on his name recognition.

As a conservative Whig daily, the *New York Tribune* was carefully structured, with sober news stories, minimal sensationalism, and a strong editorial section. Greeley turned over the business affairs to another partner, Thomas McElrath, while he concentrated on the journalism. Unlike Bennett, who was both a newsman and a businessperson, Greeley was a man to whom opinions came first. His work was like an ongoing feature article. His Puritan background encouraged him to seek redress for the social wrongs that he saw everywhere.

Greeley's belief in the rectitude of his moral cause made him impregnable to criticism. The common denominator linking many of his positions was his advocacy of the downtrodden and the oppressed. He strongly opposed the death penalty, which he saw as a violation of life and also a violence done by society against the weakest elements, who did not have the wherewithal to defend themselves; he led the fight for the rights of women and laboring classes, took up the cause of temperance as early as 1824, and championed the farming classes and frontier development. The fact that he would join the cause against slavery was almost inevitable.

Greeley regarded both wage slavery and chattel slavery as outrages against humanity and admonished the press to be as "sensitive to oppression and degradation in the next street as if they were practiced in Brazil or Japan." However, Greeley was an economic nationalist where foreign trade was concerned, pushing for protective tariffs.

In the matter of women's rights, Greeley was not in favor of suffrage, but he championed virtually every other plea by the burgeoning women's movement of the mid-nineteenth century. These causes, which promoted confidence in the people, brought enormous success to the *New York Tribune*, both critical and financial. Despite his success, Greeley was always financially hard-pressed. He never held controlling interest in the paper and was indifferent to that fact until his last years. By then it was too late, as the brilliant talents that he had re-

cruited and cultivated had acquired dominant interest. His intuitive sense of talent brought the iconoclastic Margaret Fuller to the paper and even to live in his home for a time.

Charles A. Dana joined Greeley in 1847 and was followed by Bayard Taylor in the following year. George Ripley, in 1849, was given a free hand to develop the literary department. In a continual struggle with the *Herald* for circulation and dominance, the *New York Tribune* vigorously pursued talent to make the paper a complete publication. During the 1850's came James S. Pike as Washington correspondent and editorial writer, F. J. Ottarson as city editor, W. H. Fry as music editor, Solon Robinson as agricultural editor, and then Fry and Richard Hildreth as byline reporters. The quality and intensity of the paper's political reporting, though uneven, was unequaled in the Civil War years. The newspaper's circulation under Greeley grew enormously, reaching well over a quarter million per week. This number is incredible in that the paper attracted subscribers only in areas outside the South.

Greeley's paper took strong positions on virtually every topic. Though this might have doomed other newspapers, the compelling intelligence of Greeley and his staff kept the *New York Tribune* in the forefront. At first reserved in judgment, Greeley gained confidence as his paper matured. He opposed the Mexican War, supported the Wilmot Proviso limiting slavery, and reluctantly supported Zachary Taylor. Greeley was an avid abolitionist and, in 1850, during the course of the debate on the Compromise of 1850, he stated that rather than have slavery on free soil he would "let the Union be a thousand times shivered." The Kansas-Nebraska Act infuriated him. He inveighed against its supporters and called upon anti-slavery forces to arm themselves and ensure that Kansas be without slavery.

Greeley considered himself an astute politician, but when he fell out with his influential friends William H. Seward and Thurlow Weed, he destroyed his chances for political success. He broke from Seward as a result of a dispute over the status of slavery in Kansas and from Weed because of the latter's refusal to support him for governor of New York. Greeley had been a member of the House of Representatives for a brief three months in 1848-1849, and he enjoyed the excitement of political action. He failed reelection in 1850, however, and even failed in his attempt to gain the lieutenant governorship of New York in 1854. Greeley wanted Seward's Senate seat in 1861 and attempted to gain nomination to the Senate again in 1863, but he was thwarted by Weed's forces.

He also failed to gain candidacy for the House in both 1868 and 1870 as well as the office of state comptroller in 1869. The Weed-controlled state machine was determined to force Greeley out of political life forever in retaliation for his attack on Seward's presidential candidacy in 1860 in favor of Abraham Lincoln.

At the onset of the Civil War, Greeley was inconsistent. At first he was vehement in opposition to slavery, secession, and concessions on the expansion of slavery, but, shortly after, he suggested that secession might be allowed if a majority of Southerners wished it. In a return to his earlier position, Greeley's paper took up the cry of "Forward to Richmond" in an article by Charles Dana that was often attributed to Greeley and that committed him to join the crusade. He allied himself with the Radical Republicans Thaddeus Stevens, Charles Sumner, and Salmon P. Chase and opposed all attempts by Lincoln to conciliate the South. His paper supported the John C. Frémont emancipation in Missouri and followed with an article, "The Prayer of Twenty Millions," on August 20, 1862, which attacked the administration on Confiscation Act manipulation, which favored Southern slaveholders.

Although Greeley rejoiced at the passage of the Emancipation Proclamation, he worked to undercut Lincoln in 1864 by suggesting a new candidate. However, by September of that year his paper endorsed Lincoln's reelection. He had, in the interim, suggested that to save the nation from ruin a one-year armistice be declared during which the blockade would be lifted and each side would hold on to what it had gained. As a result of that suggestion, his judgment was questioned; his influence waned even more with his pronouncements on Reconstruction.

Greeley advocated full equality of the freedmen while at the same time calling for a general amnesty for Southerners. At a time when most politicians were "waving the bloody shirt," he signed the bail bond of Jefferson Davis in Richmond on May 13, 1867, and pushed for his freedom. Greeley's reputation and his paper's circulation both suffered. He supported the nomination of General Ulysses S. Grant but after two years turned against him. He committed himself to defeating Grant in 1872, determined to use both himself and his paper to develop an independent party. He feared the destruction of his paper, which by then was held by as many as twenty interests.

When the desperate Democrats made an alliance with liberal Republicans, Greeley was itching to become a presidential candidate. With enemies in all camps, he took up the crusade, which exhausted him physically and emotionally. He was pilloried by cartoonists, who mocked his odd build, his floppy hats and strange white duster fluttering in the wind as he waddled, and the chin whiskers circling his face. By October, it was clear that there was little prospect for victory or even a good showing. In the election, he carried only six border and southern states, suffering the worst defeat of any presidential candidate to that time.

Greeley's wife, who had been ailing for years, died on October 30, 1872, five days before the disastrous election. His love for this irascible woman was enduring, and he felt totally alone. They had seen the death of five of their seven children, and now there were only the daughters Ida and Gabrielle to stand with him. He attempted to return to the *New York Tribune*, but it, too, rejected him and humiliated him. His mind snapped, and he was institutionalized in the home of Dr. George S. Choate of Pleasantville, New York, where he died on November 29. The death of this great public man was noted throughout the nation. After a monumental funeral, he was buried in Greenwood Cemetery. He was remembered by his printer union friends with a bust over his grave and other statues.

SIGNIFICANCE

Horace Greeley was forever a child prodigy, a passionate friend of humankind, one who understood the uses of money but who held no commitment to either gaining it or keeping it, and one who was possessed of and by ideas and by any and all who harbored them. Politically, he was a vain naïf caught in a cynical world. He was a man who wanted greatness for his nation and for its people. He had a compelling need to communicate his ideas, and he attracted to his paper people who themselves had something to say. He loved to explain things to a nation that was moving too quickly to do its own thinking.

Whether the issue was corruption in politics, the plight of women, love and marriage, crime, the burdens of the laboring classes, or the complexities of socialism, Greeley had something to say about it in a way that common people could understand. The people were his true family, and his *New York Tribune*, his lectures, his books, and his essays were the instruments by which he instructed this family.

—*Jack J. Cardoso*

FURTHER READING

Baehr, Harry, Jr. *The New York Tribune Since the Civil War*. New York: Dodd, Mead, 1936. A useful book, especially the first section, which has some good illustrations of personalities associated with Greeley.

Cross, Coy F., III. *Go West Young Man! Horace Greeley's Vision for America.* Albuquerque: University of New Mexico Press, 1995. Describes Greeley's ideas about westward expansion and his promotion of an agrarian utopia. Cross examines Greeley's efforts in support of land grant colleges, land reform, restricting slavery in western territories, and transcontinental railroads. Also discusses Greeley's role in creating the utopian Union Colony that later became Greeley, Colorado.

Greeley, Horace. *The American Conflict: A History of the Great Rebellion in the United States of America, 1860-'65.* 2 vols. Hartford, Conn.: O. D. Case, 1864-1866. This is an involved personal overview of the events leading to the Civil War, and the war itself, by a less than disinterested observer who nevertheless maintained a reasonable objectivity.

_____. *An Overland Journey from New York to San Francisco in the Summer of 1859.* New York: C. M. Saxton Barker, 1860. This, along with Greeley's other works, gives a sense of the charm and intelligence of the man.

_____. *Recollections of a Busy Life.* New York: J. B. Ford, 1869. This book should be read by anyone who wants to know Greeley. He was such a public man that even academics presume to know him without reading what is an unsung but truly remarkable autobiography.

Hale, William Harlan. *Horace Greeley: Voice of the People.* New York: Harper & Brothers, 1950. Shows Greeley's intuitive understanding of the issues of his time.

Horner, Harlan Hoyt. *Lincoln and Greeley.* Urbana: University of Illinois Press, 1953. An examination of the curious relationship between Lincoln and the often presumptuous Greeley on issues of war and peace.

Isely, Jeter Allen. *Horace Greeley and the Republican Party, 1853-61: A Study of the "New York Tribune."* Princeton, N.J.: Princeton University Press, 1947. This work is necessary to an understanding of the making of the Republican Party and the exploitation of the Greeley paper toward that end.

Maihafer, Harry J. *The General and the Journalists: Ulysses S. Grant, Horace Greeley, and Charles Dana.* Washington, D.C.: Brassey's, 1998. Describes how Greeley and other journalists influenced the conduct of the Civil War and public opinion of Presidents Lincoln, Andrew Johnson, and Grant.

Seitz, Don C. *Horace Greeley: Founder of the "New York Tribune."* Indianapolis: Bobbs-Merrill, 1926. Seitz provides a journalistic biography of Greeley with some useful information on the editor's family life.

Van Deusen, Glyndon G. *Horace Greeley: Nineteenth Century Crusader.* Philadelphia: University of Pennsylvania Press, 1953. This is the standard biography. Balanced, readable, well documented; includes a general bibliography, "bibliography by chapter," and illustrations (a number of which are cartoonists' caricatures of Greeley).

SEE ALSO: James Gordon Bennett; Salmon P. Chase; Jefferson Davis; John C. Frémont; Margaret Fuller; Ulysses S. Grant; Andrew Johnson; Abraham Lincoln; William H. Seward; Thaddeus Stevens; Charles Sumner; Zachary Taylor.

RELATED ARTICLES in *Great Events from History: The Nineteenth Century, 1801-1900:* July 6, 1854: Birth of the Republican Party; May 20, 1862: Lincoln Signs the Homestead Act; January 1, 1863: Lincoln Issues the Emancipation Proclamation; September 24, 1869-1877: Scandals Rock the Grant Administration.

THOMAS HILL GREEN
English philosopher

Both a theorist and a reformer, Green established the Idealist school of philosophy at Oxford, contributed political ideas that facilitated the movement away from liberalism, and was a powerful advocate of educational reform.

BORN: April 7, 1836; Birkin, Yorkshire, England
DIED: March 26, 1882; Oxford, Oxfordshire, England
ALSO KNOWN AS: T. H. Green
AREAS OF ACHIEVEMENT: Philosophy, education

EARLY LIFE

The youngest of four children, Thomas Hill Green was born into a family with extensive clerical affiliations. His mother died when he was one year old, and his father, the Reverend Valentine Green, assumed full responsibility for his youngest child, educating him until he was fourteen. The personality traits Green displayed during early childhood did not augur well for the future—he was shy, awkward, and indolent—and, indeed, these characteristics occasionally asserted themselves during his later life.

At the age of fourteen, Green was sent to Rugby, a public school that enjoyed some fame as a result of its recent leadership by Thomas Arnold, the father of poet and critic Matthew Arnold. Green appears to have been a willful student, choosing to do well only when his interest was aroused by the subject matter. While compounding his indolence with rebelliousness, Green did assert himself in translating a passage from John Milton's *Areopagitica* (1644) and won a prize. On graduation, Green entered Balliol College at Oxford and began an association that lasted the rest of his life. That association did not begin auspiciously, because Green retained the same independence in pursuing his own interests and the same indolence that characterized his earlier life. Typical of his Oxford days was his fulfillment of the requirement that an essay be turned in every Friday. One of his friends remarked that Green's essay was usually submitted on Saturday, but it was also the best essay submitted.

Green chose to stand apart from most of his fellow undergraduates. His strong sense of personal purpose and commitment to social equality made him interested in the working class and the poor. His reputation as a political and religious radical kept him out of the mainstream of undergraduate life; most of Oxford was not ready to accept a serious undergraduate whose politics were directed toward practical rather than romantic ends, and his

view that law and morality are the sole result of humankind's reason rather than natural law or innate rights undercut the foundation of popular liberalism as it existed in Oxford during his student days. Green's appearance may have led his peers to make assumptions about his personality. Green had thick black hair, a pale complexion, and brown eyes that were deep-set and thus gave the impression of seriousness.

Green was undecided about a career: The Church attracted him, but his unorthodox ideas led him to conclude that ordination in the Unitarian Church was the only honest possibility available to him; he also considered journalism a possibility. The problem was solved for him by the offer of a one-year appointment teaching ancient and modern history at Balliol, and by the end of the year he was elected to be a Fellow of Balliol College. During the subsequent eighteen years, Green assumed ever-greater responsibilities for running Balliol. He also accepted a broad range of responsibilities dealing with social and political reform outside the university.

LIFE'S WORK

The work of historian Thomas Carlyle and two summer visits to Germany in 1862 and 1863 made Green reject the philosophy of John Stuart Mill, which was popular at that time. Instead, Green's philosophical thinking was shaped by Aristotle and the Germans Georg Wilhelm Friedrich Hegel and Immanuel Kant. Like Kant, Green objected to the proposition of David Hume that knowledge was gathered by the impressions of the senses (that is, that knowledge was empirical) and to the notion that one should make choices based on the ability of the choice to give one happiness or to help one avoid pain, thus making morality and ethics a matter of calculating the alternatives.

Green argued that information gathered by the senses was connected in the mind by a "consciousness" or a "spiritual principle" that actively participated in creating knowledge. "Consciousness" also allowed one to establish and obey moral rules higher than the pursuit of happiness or the avoidance of pain. The mere pursuit of happiness does not explain humanity's pursuit of excellence, observance of duty, concept of a higher and lower self, or willingness to sacrifice oneself in so many varied ways. There was a spiritual principle ultimately underlying everything that could be realized through the practical activities of humankind.

For Green, it was imperative for a person to make decisions based on whether the action would further his own development or that of others. Self-development and social development were the fundamental goals in Green's system of thought. That emphasis marks the distinction between social reformers who believe that social problems can be solved by reforming the system and those who, like Green, consider the solution to social problems to lie in correcting the defects of individuals.

Green's metaphysics complemented his long-standing interest in social problems, and since his arrival at Oxford as an undergraduate, he had been active in various enterprises designed to help the working class. In December, 1864, he received an appointment to the Royal Commission on Middle Class Schools, headed by Lord Taunton. Many objections to popular education had prevented its introduction. Some opposed it as too expensive and a burden to taxpayers. Others opposed it on religious grounds as not offering instruction in their religion; there was serious disagreement between members of the Church of England and Dissenters as to the religion that should be taught.

As a member of the Royal Commission and afterward, Green put forward arguments that advocated popular education as both expedient and morally desirable. Green proposed expanding and improving the secondary schools, reforming the existing universities, and creating new universities throughout the country. The benefits from his scheme were numerous. Social barriers would be broken down. Members of different social classes would be at ease with one another because they would become familiar with one another. Although Green normally favored improvements through the voluntary association of interested parties, education was an exception.

The task was so large that it was beyond the capacity of voluntary associations; only the state could create and run a successful system of education. Furthermore, the voluntary principle would not be effective because some could not afford to pay for education; others were too mired in ignorance to want education for their children. Thus, while Green preferred voluntarism whenever possible, education was central to the self-development that would make social equality and justice possible, and state action was necessary.

The result of the Taunton Commission's work was the Elementary Education Act of 1870. From Green's point of view, this was a sorry compromise that commissioned the Education Department of the government to determine whether a district ought to have state schools. School boards were to be created in districts where they did not exist, but these authorities would have no jurisdiction over existing voluntary schools, which could not be given state aid.

Green proposed a scheme of interlocking schools that would permit intelligence to be recognized and forwarded through the highest level appropriate to the child's ability. All children were to be educated to the age of thirteen; those destined for business might stay until fifteen or sixteen, and others would remain in school until eighteen, when they would go to a university. That was, indeed, a radical proposal. According to Green, universities would be occupied by real scholars instead of those who were merely economically advantaged. Green believed that his system of education would produce civil servants who represented the best minds in society and who were committed to the pursuit of the betterment of all. The very basis of the state would be changed by educational reform.

Green remained active as a champion of educational reform throughout the remainder of his short life. He became active in the National Education League, formed to promote reforms that would make school attendance compulsory and to support schools in places that lacked adequate financial support. Green also was active at the community level. In 1874, he was elected to the school board in Oxford (the following year, he was elected to the Oxford town council), led a movement to establish a grammar school in Oxford, established a scholarship for boys from Oxford, and served on the governing board of King Edward's School in Birmingham. At the university, Green extended efforts to make Oxford more accessible to poorer students; he also supported the extension movement, which offered Oxford's services to working men, and worked to create new universities. He died in Oxford on March 26, 1882.

SIGNIFICANCE

Thomas Hill Green's diverse achievements have caused him to be considered by subsequent generations for his individual achievements. He is considered an important figure in the introduction of German Idealist philosophy into Great Britain. His political theory, which redefined freedom, not as the legal possibilities open to a person, but as access to the possibilities for self-development that are available to the person, in fact, was, for a time, considered a necessary assumption for state intervention, and Green is considered by some to be one of the forebears of the welfare state.

In the long run, the position that Green delineated regarding the place of education in society is his most significant legacy. Green proposed that education be provided to all children and that it be based on the abilities of the student rather than membership in a social class. Each individual would get the access necessary to allow him to realize his all-important self-development. Society would be reshaped by a government composed of the subsequent meritocracy, becoming more egalitarian. Omitting the Idealist emphasis on the importance of self-development, these practical issues have been at the heart of English educational social policy since Green first addressed them during the 1860's. Considered together, Green's separate achievements mark him as one of the most important intellectuals who helped shape the transition from the nineteenth to the twentieth century.

—Glenn O. Nichols

FURTHER READING

Barker, Ernest. *Political Thought in England from Herbert Spencer to the Present Day*. London: Williams & Norgate, 1915. This is a classic study in the Home University Library series. Barker's chapter "The Idealist School—T. H. Green" is an excellent brief interpretation of Green's thought, although it should be read in conjunction with Clark (see below).

Brink, David O. *Perfectionism and the Common Good: Themes in the Philosophy of T. H. Green*. New York: Oxford University Press, 2003. After a brief chapter discussing Green's life and work, the remaining chapters analyze various aspects of his philosophy, including metaphysics, idealism, self-realization, and the common good. Other chapters determine Green's impact, legacy, and relationship to other philosophers.

Clark, Peter. *Liberals and Social Democrats*. Cambridge, England: Cambridge University Press, 1981. Clark has written an excellent survey of political thought that questions the notion that Green was one of the forefathers of the welfare state.

Dimova-Cookson, Maria. *T. H. Green's Moral and Political Philosophy: A Phenomenological Perspective*. New York: Palgrave, 2001. Analyzes Green's theories of human practice, the moral idea, the common good, and freedom and human rights. Discusses how Green's idealism has the potential to address contemporary debates about human rights, moral agency, and positive and negative freedom.

Green, Thomas Hill. *The Works of Thomas Hill Green*. Edited by R. I. Nettleship. 3 vols. London: Longmans, Green, 1885-1888. This collection contains almost all of Green's works, except for his *Prolegomena to Ethics*, edited by A. C. Bradley and first published in 1883. The first two volumes are devoted to Green's philosophical works. Volume 3 contains a memoir that Nettleship assembled from Green's speeches and personal papers. The same volume includes Green's writings on education and religious essays.

Leighton, Denys. *The Greenian Moment: T. H. Green, Religion, and Political Argument in Victorian Britain*. Charlottesville, Va.: Imprint Academic, 2004. Analyzes Green's philosophy through his public life and political commitments, describing how some of his ideas were informed by evangelical theology, popular Protestantism, and nineteenth century British liberalism.

Milne, A. J. M. *The Social Philosophy of English Idealism*. London: Allen & Unwin, 1962. Milne examines the influence of Kant and Hegel on Green's thought.

Richter, Melvin. *The Politics of Conscience: T. H. Green and His Times*. Cambridge, Mass.: Harvard University Press, 1964. Richter's study is unusually good as a biographical sketch, a survey of Green's intellectual context, and an analysis of the content and meaning of Green's thought. It is unquestionably the best single volume about Green.

Rodman, John R., ed. "Introduction." In *The Political Theory of T. H. Green: Selected Writings*. New York: Appleton-Century-Crofts, 1964. Rodman gives an accessible, insightful, and convenient introduction to Green's political thought, as well as reprinting Green's essays "Liberal Legislation and Freedom of Contract," "The Senses of Freedom," and "The Principles of Political Obligation."

Ward, Mrs. Humphry. *Robert Elsmere*. London: Macmillan, 1888. Reprint. Lincoln: University of Nebraska Press, 1967. Mrs. Ward, a friend of Green, wrote a novel that includes a character (Mr. Grey) who is modeled on Green. Indeed, Mrs. Ward dedicated this novel to Green and put portions of his work into the mouth of her character.

SEE ALSO: Matthew Arnold; Thomas Arnold; F. H. Bradley; Thomas Carlyle; Georg Wilhelm Friedrich Hegel; John Stuart Mill; Herbert Spencer.

RELATED ARTICLE in *Great Events from History: The Nineteenth Century, 1801-1900*: July 14, 1833: Oxford Movement Begins.

FRANCIS GREENWAY
Australian architect

Although surrounded by controversy, Greenway attempted to legitimate and regulate building practices in Australia during the period when it was regarded primarily as a British penal colony. More important, however, he gave to the early buildings aesthetically unique designs combining both beauty and practicality.

BORN: November 20, 1777; Mangotsfield, England
DIED: September 26, 1837; East Maitland, New South Wales, Australia
ALSO KNOWN AS: Francis Howard Greenway (full name)
AREA OF ACHIEVEMENT: Architecture

EARLY LIFE

Not much is known of Francis Howard Greenway's early life beyond the fact that he was the fourth son of Francis Greenway and Ann Webb. His birthright links him with a two-hundred-year tradition of Greenways who were involved in stonemasonry, architecture, and construction in the Bristol area. Thus, his choice of occupation comes as no surprise. There is an indication that Greenway was educated in England and afterward was employed by and became the protégé of the famous architect John Nash, with whom he began to build both a minor reputation and career. In 1800, Greenway exhibited two architectural drawings at the Royal Academy, and he later designed the "market house," the Chapel Library, the Clifton Club, and the restoration of the Thornbury Castle.

In 1804, he married a woman whose identity is established by her first name only, Mary, by whom he probably had three or four children. A self-portrait pictures Greenway as a "fair and ruddy" man of approximately five feet, six inches, with auburn hair, hazel eyes, and a prominent nose. Accounts of Greenway's personality vary. His friends and admirers saw him as an extremely moral and practical man with a genius and passion for art and beauty. His enemies viewed him as a haughty and volatile man with grandiose ideas about his talents and abilities. His later actions seem to bear out both viewpoints.

Shortly after his marriage, Greenway went into business with his two brothers, Olive Greenway and John Tripp Greenway, offering the following services advertised in the *Bristol Gazette* in 1805: "All orders for marble monuments, Chimney Pieces, and every kind of orna-

mental stone work shall be carefully attended to, and executed in the most artist-like manner." It appears that for the next four years, the business ran smoothly until April, 1809, when legal questions were raised regarding both the family business and some of its present and past contracts. One month later, the word "bankruptcy" appeared in the paper, and Greenway's career became jeopardized. As a result, the Greenways' possessions were put up for auction in order to satisfy their creditors. The precise reasons for the legal actions and subsequent bankruptcy have been lost in local legend and unclear newspaper reports regarding a long-standing issue of water rights in and around Bath (where construction of buildings for the use of visitors who wanted to take advantage of the healing waters was common). Greenway tried to show how he had been fooled by speculators and false promises, but his attempt proved fruitless.

Despite this setback, Greenway was still working as an architect in 1810, but another tragedy was in the making. Problems arose regarding a contract that Greenway had made with Colonel Richard Doolan, for whom he was doing some work. Greenway swore that the colonel had authorized an additional £250 for some extra work Greenway had provided. However, the contract was lost and the colonel denied the charge. Greenway eventually produced the lost contract. In the court proceedings that followed, it was proved that Greenway had forged the contract, and Greenway was held at Newgate prison for sentencing. Three months later, in March of 1812, Greenway found himself in the dock at the Bristol Assizes. He pleaded guilty to the charges and was sentenced to death by hanging. However, he still had some influential friends, and they managed to get his sentence reduced first to lifelong exile in Australia (which was then a penal colony) and later to transportation to this colony for a term of fourteen years.

LIFE'S WORK

On February 7, 1814, Greenway arrived in Sydney, Australia, a colony made up largely of convicts with a population numbering about twelve thousand. There he found an architect's dream: a large, sprawling city with scattered houses and buildings showing little sign of any plan, direction, or beauty. Even more amazing to Greenway was the fact that there was little to distinguish private buildings from public or government buildings. The opportunities were immediately apparent to Greenway, and although in his mind he began construction on the future buildings of Sydney, it took him five months to reach Governor Luchlan Macquarie, who had his own visions of a new city.

Greenway assumed not only that the governor would put him to work but also that, as an architect, he would have complete freedom to do as he pleased. The governor, however, even in his desperate need for an architect, had plans of his own and asked Greenway to produce copies of a new courthouse and town hall from a book of previously constructed buildings. Greenway took immediate offense and instead sent to the governor a portfolio of his architectural drawings and a letter dated July, 1814, letting Macquarie know that for an artist merely to copy another's work is a "rather painful" undertaking. There is no record of the governor's reaction, but a few days later Greenway sent a letter of apology and a drawing of the buildings just as Macquarie had requested. The governor accepted the architect's apology, gave permission for Greenway's wife and family to join him, and unwittingly became Greenway's benefactor.

Francis Greenway. (Courtesy, Museum of Australian Currency Notes)

It would be quite some time before Greenway would become the "sole designer" of the colony, for the governor was cautious. For the next year or more, rather than fulfilling his role as an architect (despite the fact that he opened a private practice in December, 1814), Greenway acted as a surveyor of the public buildings already in progress. In these reports, Greenway not only cited the aesthetic and structural flaws he found but also made outraged statements against fraudulent contracts, the waste of materials and labor, and the inhumane treatment of the workers. The governor, whose entire building budget had already been used with little to show for it, must have been grateful for Greenway's reports, for in March, 1816, Greenway found himself appointed acting government architect and assistant engineer for Australia. Along with this position went a house, rations for him and his family, a convict servant, a horse, and a salary of three shillings per day plus the promise of traveling expenses.

It seemed as if Greenway, a convicted exile, had indeed come a long way. Yet, he was not satisfied. He believed that his destiny to bring to the world, in this case Australia, the physical and spiritual merits of art and architecture was being hampered. He wanted to offer humankind the combination of "beauty, strength and convenience," and he wanted to do this through his idealistic and grand architectural visions. Greenway found that such far-reaching and idealistic ambitions did not fit in with the concerns of the building contractors and suppliers with whom he had to deal. Thus, he continued to keep a close watch on what he saw as unethical building practices and continued to expose fraud, low-quality work, poor structural designs, substandard building materials, and ill-trained workers. In the process he made himself a number of enemies.

Macquarie, however, remained his friend, and between the two of them plans began to emerge for a new Australia. One of the first buildings attributed solely to Greenway was more a monument to the governor's and Greenway's artistic visions than a needed public facility. This building was the Macquarie Tower and Light House, for which the foundation stone was laid on July 11, 1816. This first building not only marked the beginning of a continuous building program for the cities of Sydney, Liverpool, Windsor, and Parramatta but also initiated a series of arguments, legal battles, and personal and professional setbacks that were to plague Greenway for the rest of his life.

Between the years 1816 and 1819, however, Greenway managed to break ground on a number of different projects—buildings that were considered superior to anything previously constructed in Australia. Among some of Greenway's most successful, although controversial, buildings were structures such as Fort Macquarie, the Military Barracks at Sydney, the Female Orphan School at Parramatta, the Liverpool Hospital, and the Government House.

While no one could question Greenway's artistic talents, and despite the fact that he fought to upgrade the quality of both the structures and the skills of the contractors, many of Greenway's own buildings became the subject of disputes, delays, structural flaws, or overcosts. Nevertheless, thanks to his friendship with Macquarie, he went ahead with his plans in the midst of controversies and arguments with private contractors. In fact, the governor saw fit to grant Greenway a conditional pardon in 1817, which was then made official in 1819, seven years before the end of his original sentence. He was, in effect, free to move into the higher social classes of Australia, a position to which he felt entitled.

However, freedom, social status, and professional and economic success would not be enough to guard Greenway against his own propensity to make enemies. Also, many in England were becoming concerned that the original plan to keep Australia a penal colony was being diverted (a result, in large part, of Greenway's architectural plans). Thus, in 1822, with the removal of Governor Macquarie, Greenway's rocky rise to success received a troubling blow. In June, a letter from John Thomas Bigge, who had been sent in 1819 to Australia to survey and report on the troublesome progress being made in this so-called penal colony, recommended that the "Colonial Architect" (referring to Greenway) introduce a more "uniform and simple style of architecture" into the public and government buildings. Furthermore, Bigge recommended that a corps of engineers be appointed to oversee all future work in the colony.

It appears, however, that Greenway was unaware of Bigge's recommendations, for, as usual, he was embroiled in arguments and controversies. The most damaging of these ongoing controversies came to a head in 1822, when Greenway faced a libel suit, again over matters of lost contracts and promised payments. When he was denied the right of inquiry and appeal regarding the matter, he refused to continue his official work of "inspecting the progress of public works."

This refusal, along with Bigge's earlier letter, produced the following results: "By direction of the Governor I am to acquaint you that from the present date your services to the Government will be dispensed with."

Greenway received this letter on November 15, 1822, and for the second time in his life he was financially and professionally ruined.

Greenway, refusing to admit defeat, continued to live in the house Macquarie had appointed to him in 1814. Meanwhile, he tried in vain to appeal to the government for reimbursements of traveling expenses, compensation for work done by him at the "request" of his old friend and benefactor, and the usual "percentages" of revenues from buildings completed, as well as plans for future buildings. The amount he believed was due him came to £11,232. His petitions were continually denied, and for a third time in his life Greenway came under suspicion of document forgery, although he was never tried or convicted in this last matter. There also arose questions regarding Greenway's claim to eight hundred acres of land at Tarro in the Newcastle district.

Again, documents proved faulty, causing Greenway additional anger and embarrassment, and he spent his last years writing letters and haranguing public officials. His efforts were in vain, however, for he died of unknown causes on September 26, 1837, impoverished and disgraced. A century later, a memorial tablet was erected on the North Porch of St. James's Church that reads: "In Memory of Francis Greenway Architect of This Church and of the Artisans and Labourers Who Erected It."

SIGNIFICANCE

It is difficult to assess accurately Greenway's life and career. The legal controversies in which he was embroiled, coupled with the personal and professional conflicts that followed Greenway his entire life, cast shadows that cannot be easily dispelled. However, Greenway's buildings speak for themselves; they are monuments to "beauty, strength and convenience" just as he had intended. He not only raised the standard of architectural design, but he also raised the standards of building construction and workmanship. Although clearly trained in the classical tradition of strict control of form and obviously influenced by the Georgian designs of Bristol during the early nineteenth century, Greenway managed to impose his own vision and imprint upon his designs, marking them as clearly the work of one talent, one man.

For all of his faults and failures, Greenway held firm to his passion for artistic beauty and its benefit to humankind. Australia, especially Sydney, owes much to Greenway's vision.

—Deborah Charlie

FURTHER READING

Ellis, M. H. *Francis Greenway: His Life and Times*. Sydney: Shepherd Press, 1949. Ellis has put together an exhaustive study of Greenway's life and times, as the title indicates. It is the only study of its kind and for this it is extremely valuable. It contains numerous references to and quotations from letters, documents, and papers, some of which were left behind by Greenway, others of which are official public documents and letters. Although the chronology is sometimes difficult to follow, the material proves both interesting and enlightening.

Freeland, J. M. *Architecture in Australia: A History*. Melbourne, Vic.: F. W. Cheshire, 1968. This is a fascinating account of Australia's history, from the late eighteenth century to the late 1960's. The pages dealing with Greenway, although not as specific as they could be, provide a good overview of the importance of his work in Australia's architectural growth. Freeland manages to highlight both the successes and failures of Greenway's career without being sidetracked by the turmoil that surrounded much of his life.

_____. *The Making of a Profession*. Sydney: Angus and Robertson, 1971. Although Freeland's comments about Greenway barely cover three pages of this study, the information provided is interesting, for it places Greenway at the beginning of a new and rising tradition of architects in Australia.

Herman, Morton. *The Early Australian Architects and Their Work*. Sydney: Angus and Robertson, 1954. Herman's book is a straightforward account of the beginnings of Australia's early architecture and architects. The material pertaining to Greenway provides a general overview of his career, referring only briefly to his personal life. It focuses primarily on Greenway's work and how it fits into the pattern of a new profession in a new land.

SEE ALSO: Charles Bulfinch; Daniel Hudson Burnham; John Nash.

RELATED ARTICLE in *Great Events from History: The Nineteenth Century, 1801-1900:* 1884: New Guilds Promote the Arts and Crafts Movement.

CHARLES GREY
Prime minister of Great Britain (1830-1834)

Grey was prime minister of Great Britain for a relatively brief period, but he oversaw one of the most important political transformations in British history. Recognizing that parliamentary reform was necessary in order to maintain the ascendancy of the aristocracy in a rapidly changing English society, he led the government that passed the Reform Bill of 1832.

BORN: March 13, 1764; Fallodon, Northumberland, England
DIED: July 17, 1845; Howick, Northumberland, England
ALSO KNOWN AS: Baron Grey; Viscount Howick; Second Earl Grey
AREA OF ACHIEVEMENT: Government and politics

EARLY LIFE

Charles Grey was born in his family's country house only a few miles from the sea in England's county Northumberland. His uncle was a baronet, whose nearby estate, Howick, Grey was later to occupy and then inherit. His father, Sir Charles Grey, had distinguished himself in military service, rose to the rank of general, and was made a peer in 1801. As the eldest surviving son (an older brother died no more than a few weeks after his birth), Charles Grey would succeed to his father's title and a seat in the House of Lords.

At the age of six, Grey was sent to a boarding school in Marylebone (London), where he spent three unhappy years until he arrived at Eton at the age of nine. During his eight years at Eton, Grey excelled in the largely classical curriculum, and in 1781, at the age of seventeen, he made the short journey to Trinity College, Cambridge. As was the case with many sons of the aristocracy and greater gentry, Grey did not take a degree. In 1784, he embarked on the Grand Tour, considered an essential part of the education of a young English aristocrat in the eighteenth century. He visited the south of France, Switzerland, and Italy. In 1786, during his last months on the Continent, Grey was elected a member of Parliament for the county of Northumberland. He was to remain a county member until 1807, after which he represented the pocket boroughs of Appleby and Tavistock.

In 1794, Grey married Mary Elizabeth Ponsonby, with whom he had fifteen children. Although he developed a reputation in public life for being stiff and aloof, Grey's marriage was happy, his family life warm and affectionate. The contentment he found with his family would later account, at least in part, for his occasional tardiness in arriving for the parliamentary session, his absences for a session or more, or, once parliamentary business was completed, his prompt return to Howick, a four-day journey from London by coach during the late eighteenth and early nineteenth centuries.

Like many military families, Grey's family had moderate Tory connections. However, Grey affiliated himself with the Foxite Whigs. This association may well have been the result of personal friendships rather than political principle. During the 1780's, it would have been difficult to distinguish the Foxites from other aristocratic factions that claimed the Whig name and, thereby, connected themselves with the legacy of the Glorious Revolution, with which the Whigs had become identified. During the 1790's, however, the Foxites reinforced the association of Whiggery with liberty in general and with a number of specific liberal causes. Grey was instrumental in this development.

LIFE'S WORK

Grey earned a reputation as an excellent orator in an age when oratory was highly valued. After participating in the proceedings to impeach Warren Hastings, he gained special attention, even notoriety, for his role in founding the Society of the Friends of the People in April, 1792. The society was an organization of young men, most of them aristocrats like Grey, that supported the reform of Parliament. Decades later, Grey was embarrassed about his youthful ardor which, in these early years of the French Revolution, inspired him to organize the society.

From the outset, Grey and most of the Friends distinguished themselves from radicals. The very name, Friends of the People, signified an attitude of paternalism and benevolent condescension toward the lower orders. The Foxite Whigs with whom Grey associated remained an aristocratic party, and Grey considered aristocracy as the intermediary between the Crown, which might be inclined toward arbitrary power, and the people, whose liberties aristocrats were to defend. Grey was never a democrat, a designation he associated with varieties of radicalism, and always cherished his aristocratic connection. Nevertheless, among other aristocratic factions, proposals for parliamentary reform appeared as assaults

on both aristocracy and monarchy, especially as the French Revolution entered its more radical phase.

Grey's motions for inquiries into the state of the representation during the 1790's and his proposal in 1797 for a reform of Parliament with triennial parliaments, a uniform property qualification for the suffrage, and abolition of rotten boroughs—parliamentary constituencies that had little or no population and were controlled by the owners of specific properties—were immediately rejected. The Friends of the People, however, succeeded in widening an already existing rift in the Whig opposition, enlisting the acquiescence if not the enthusiasm of Fox, and driving the more conservative Whigs to support William Pitt's government. During the 1790's, Grey also endorsed Fox's opposition to legislation considered to infringe on liberty—the suspension of habeas corpus (1794-1801), the Seditious Meetings Act (1795), and the Alien Bill (1799). After 1797, Grey joined the general Foxite withdrawal from parliamentary attendance for several sessions.

In 1806, Grey joined the cabinet as First Lord of the Admiralty in the Fox-Grenville coalition government. (He was then styled Lord Howick, a courtesy title resulting from his father's elevation to an earldom, but he remained in the House of Commons.) When Charles James Fox died in September, 1806, Grey succeeded him as secretary of state for foreign affairs and was generally acknowledged as leader of the Foxite Whigs. The ministry was dismissed by George III, technically on a matter concerning the appointment of Catholics as staff officers in the army, something that Grey thought an important gesture to conciliate Catholic Ireland. From their dismissal in 1807, the Whigs supported the right of Catholics to sit in Parliament.

In November, 1807, after Grey's father died, Grey became the second Earl Grey. Twenty-three years were to elapse before he returned to government. During those years, he was generally considered to be the leader of the Whig Party, which in 1817 separated from the Grenvillites with whom they had cooperated in opposition since the dismissal of the Fox-Grenville government. Grey was so often removed from London and from Parliament, however, that he was little more than a titular leader, dispensing advice from afar. He frequently had to be coaxed by such friends as Lord Holland to take a more active part in politics.

No longer enthusiastic about parliamentary reform, Grey often considered retirement. He was occasionally active, as in 1819, when he vigorously protested the Tory government's repressive Six Acts, and the following year, when he opposed George IV's divorce proceedings against Queen Caroline, thereby earning the king's enmity and ensuring that he would never be called to cabinet office during the new reign. Other Whigs were drawn to join or to support George Canning's government in 1827 (Grey despised Canning), and when Wellington's government was compelled to pass a bill for Catholic Emancipation, the Whigs were deprived of the one issue that had unified them in opposition. Some Whigs, moreover, began to look for a new leader.

Several developments dramatically transformed the prospects of both the Whigs and Grey. George IV's death, his succession by William IV, and the elections of 1830 encouraged the Whigs in their organized opposition to Wellington's government. Wellington's subsequent intransigence on parliamentary reform resulted in his government's defeat (though, technically, it was defeated on another matter). Grey, at the age of sixty-six, was chosen by the king as his prime minister in November, 1830. It was understood that the government would be pledged to parliamentary reform.

Grey's government was a coalition, ministers being drawn from Whigs of Grey's generation, younger members of the party, Canningites, and Ultra-Tories. Of the thirteen men who formed the original Grey cabinet, nine were in the House of Lords and one was an Irish peer in the Commons. Three others were in the Commons, of whom one, the leader of the House, Lord Althorp, was heir to an earldom. Indeed, Grey's government was the most aristocratic of the century. A commitment to the ascendancy of the aristocracy and the preservation of existing institutions bound the cabinet together, along with the conviction that if an effective measure of parliamentary reform were not passed, the country would face the alternative of revolution. Although the government was a coalition, its moving spirits were Whigs, and the committee of four ministers that Grey appointed to draft a reform bill—Lord Durham, Lord Duncannon, Lord John Russell, and Sir James Graham—had impeccable Whig credentials.

While the Reform Bill underwent numerous changes from its introduction in March, 1831, until its final passage in July, 1832, its central features remained the abolition of rotten boroughs, the addition of representation to hitherto neglected populous towns, and the extension of the franchise in the boroughs to all householders who either owned a house worth, or paid rent of, more than ten pounds yearly. When the government was defeated on an amendment in the House of Commons, the subsequent election of April, 1831, ensured a lower house favorable

to reform. When the House of Lords defeated the bill on its second reading in October, 1831, however, Grey and the cabinet were confronted with the problem of overcoming the resistance of the Lords while retaining the confidence of the king.

Grey was a masterful politician during those years. His occasional threats to resign proved to be remarkably effective in stemming cabinet dissension. Moreover, the king's confidence was reposed in Grey personally rather than in the cabinet collectively. Retaining that confidence was crucial, all the more so because it became increasingly apparent that the only way to persuade the House of Lords to pass the bill was by resorting to a creation of peers by the king. Only with great reluctance did Grey eventually acquiesce in this alternative. It was his personal influence with King William that ultimately persuaded the monarch to consent to a creation, but only after the duke of Wellington failed to form a coalition government in May, 1832. The Lords finally consented to the bill rather than witness a mass creation of peers.

The English Reform Bill of 1832 is one of the most significant acts of Parliament in British history. It was followed by bills for Ireland and Scotland. Grey's ministry also was responsible for other significant legislation, some of which it initiated, some of which it merely supervised. The Irish Church Reform Act of 1833 reduced the number of bishops in the Church of Ireland and eliminated the church cess, a tax paid by occupiers of land, mostly Catholic, to support the Protestant church. The Factory Act of 1833 was the first effective regulation of the conditions of factory labor. The abolition of slavery in the empire in 1833 complemented the abolition of the slave trade in 1807 by the Fox-Grenville ministry. Though it was passed after his resignation, the Poor Law Amendment Act was initiated when Grey was prime minister. Complementing its liberal record in domestic affairs, in foreign affairs Grey's government became associated with the defense of constitutionalism, especially in Belgium and Spain, against the reactionary policies of the eastern powers.

Grey's government came to an end in July, 1834. When Lord Althorp resigned as a result of an imbroglio involving secret dealings by other ministers with Daniel O'Connell concerning a renewal of an Irish Coercion Bill, Grey followed him into retirement. Grey declined the king's proposal that he form a new government after the defeat of Peel's ministry in April, 1835. He spent his remaining years in tranquillity at Howick, where he died on July 17, 1845.

SIGNIFICANCE

The second Earl Grey cherished his aristocratic connections and once observed that he had a predilection for old institutions. Both in his youthful days with the Friends of the People and during his premiership, he thought that parliamentary reform was necessary to preserve those institutions and the ascendancy of the aristocracy. He argued that reform was conservative. It was a concession to popular opinion that was necessary to maintain stability. He sincerely believed as prime minister that failure to implement a substantial reform of Parliament would result in a revolution that would destroy monarchy as well as aristocracy. One of his achievements, which few of his contemporaries could have managed, was to persuade the king that the alternative to reform was revolution; for without the king's support, however grudging, the Reform Bill could not have passed.

Grey never doubted the propriety of the aristocracy's ascendancy. However, he recognized that to govern effectively, it had to retain the confidence of the people. He sometimes thought of reform legislation as a boon to be bestowed from above by an enlightened aristocracy, whose benevolence was to be properly acknowledged by a grateful populace. The deference of the people was a reflection of their proper subordination to their governors. Although Grey recognized that the emerging middle classes had developed a new form of property that deserved representation in Parliament, he retained the idea that substantial landed property owners should direct the affairs of society for the benefit of all. Throughout his career, Grey scorned radicals and opposed any Whig connection with them, which, he thought, could only undermine the social order he sought to preserve. Committed to maintaining that order, he supported reform in order to preserve it.

—Abraham D. Kriegel

FURTHER READING

Brock, Michael. *The Great Reform Act*. London: Hutchinson, 1973. This study considers the recent scholarship on the Reform Bill but accepts the established interpretation that it was a concession designed to maintain stability.

Davis, H. W. C. *The Age of Grey and Peel*. London: Oxford University Press, 1929. An old but still valuable study of the Whigs and their values, especially good on the Whig suspicion of radicals. More critical of Grey than is G. M. Trevelyan (see below).

Derry, John W. *Charles, Earl Grey: Aristocratic Reformer*. Cambridge, Mass.: B. Blackwell, 1992. Derry is more critical of Grey than other writers, stressing his aristocratic values and the traditionalism of his outlook. Derry describes the events and influences that affected Grey's political career, discusses Grey's relationships with other politicians, and places the Reform Bill of 1832 into a historical and political context.

Kriegel, Abraham D. "The Irish Policy of Lord Grey's Government." *English Historical Review* 86 (January, 1971): 22-45. Discusses the association of concession with coercion in the government's Irish policy and relates it to the Whigs' policy on parliamentary reform.

_____. "Liberty and Whiggery in Early Nineteenth-Century England." *Journal of Modern History* 52 (June, 1980): 253-278. Considers the Whig idea of liberty and its relationship to Whig legislation such as the Reform Bill.

Mitchell, Austin. *The Whigs in Opposition, 1815-1830*. London: Oxford University Press, 1967. An excellent study of the Whig Party from the end of the Napoleonic Wars until the eve of Grey's government. Grey is portrayed as a reluctant leader during this period.

Roberts, Michael. *The Whig Party, 1807-1812*. London: Macmillan, 1939. Follows the intricate politics of the Whigs in opposition from the dismissal of the Fox-Grenville ministry until the establishment of George IV's regency in 1812.

Smith, E. A. *Lord Grey, 1764-1845*. New York: Oxford University Press, 1990. The late E. A. Smith was a historian who wrote several books about early nineteenth century British politics. His biography of Grey is a comprehensive account of the man and politician.

Trevelyan, G. M. *Lord Grey of the Reform Bill*. London: Longmans, Green, 1920. Not among Trevelyan's better studies, this old and dated biography is insufficiently critical but remains the only modern biography.

SEE ALSO: George Canning; First Earl of Durham; George IV; Daniel O'Connell; Sir Robert Peel; Baron John Russell; Duke of Wellington; William IV.

RELATED ARTICLES in *Great Events from History: The Nineteenth Century, 1801-1900:* June 4, 1832: British Parliament Passes the Reform Act of 1832; August 28, 1833: Slavery Is Abolished Throughout the British Empire.

SIR GEORGE GREY
British imperialist

One of the great proconsuls of the British Empire, Grey fused the arrogant, autocratic, decisive man of action with eclectic, radical, and democratic beliefs. He had a particularly profound influence on settlement, political developments, native policy, and ethnography, on three colonial frontiers: South Africa, South Australia, and New Zealand.

BORN: April 14, 1812; Lisbon, Portugal
DIED: September 19, 1898; London, England
ALSO KNOWN AS: George Edward Grey
AREA OF ACHIEVEMENT: Government and politics

EARLY LIFE

George Edward Grey was the son of George Grey, a British army lieutenant colonel who was killed at the storming of Badajoz a few days before Grey was born. Colonel Grey was a member of a family associated with the earls of Stamford, and his wife, Elizabeth Vignoles, was an Anglo-Irish woman from County Westmeath whose evangelical religious fervor had a powerful influence on her young son. Grey was educated at Guildford Boarding School but ran away and was then tutored by the Reverend Richard Whately, late archbishop of Dublin. He entered the Royal Military College, Sandhurst, in 1826 and as an ensign and lieutenant served in Ireland with the Eighty-third Regiment between 1830 and 1836.

Grey was sickened by his experiences in Ireland, where he was employed in collecting tithe payments from the destitute and miserable peasantry in the interests of Anglo-Irish landlords and the Church of England. Until the end of his life, he advocated the emigration of the industrious poor from Great Britain to the new colonies of white settlement, Jeffersonian democracy on the American model, and radical measures designed to prevent the aggregation of land by a few large proprietors. Although he obtained an excellent report following a postgraduate course at Sandhurst in 1836 and was promoted to captain, he sold his commission and left the army.

In 1838, under the auspices of the Royal Geographical Society, Grey made two journeys of exploration, one to Shark Bay on the central coast and the other to Hanover Bay on the northwest fringe of Western Australia. Both expeditions found little land of economic importance and resulted in great hardships. Grey displayed exceptional bravery and endurance and was the first to find unique Aboriginal rock carvings, but his bushcraft was

poor and he suffered a deep Aboriginal spear wound in the thigh, which gave him severe pain until his death. After recovering his health, Grey was made resident magistrate at King George Sound, and on November 2, 1839, he was married to Elizabeth Lucy, daughter of Sir Richard Spencer. The marriage was a most unhappy one. Their only son died in 1841, and, after domestic agonies, the couple was formally separated in 1860, although they were partly reconciled in 1896. Grey's solitary withdrawal and aloofness were reinforced by his tragic private life.

Grey's star, however, was in the ascendant as his report on how to civilize native peoples attracted the favorable opinion of the Colonial Office. At only twenty-eight years of age, Grey was appointed governor of the struggling colony of South Australia in 1840.

LIFE'S WORK

Grey immediately stabilized the economy of South Australia by financial retrenchments that offended private interests dependent on the state. He brought order and uniformity to the public service, facilitated the profitable occupation of pastoral land rather than urban speculation, and was lucky in presiding over the discovery of copper and the successful development of wheat growing for export. He ruled alone and successfully by misrepresenting Adelaide opinion to London authority, and London instructions to Adelaide gentry, and he was politically dexterous and astute in dividing and governing South Australia. He was a skillful writer of reports and memoranda and was "as amiable in private life as he was cold and unscrupulous in public affairs." Grey's achievement in setting the infant Australian colony on the road to prosperity was nevertheless considerable, and he gained a deserved reputation as an imperial troubleshooter who could be relied upon to rescue infant British colonies from a wide range of teething problems.

In 1845, Grey was appointed governor of New Zealand, a colony beset by Maori-European confrontation, land disputes, and financial shortfalls. Here he gained his greatest triumph—a knighthood in 1848. Seizing military command, he ended the Bay of Islands rebellion of Kawiti and Hone Heke by capturing their *pah*, or fort, Ruapekapeka ("the bat's nest"), on a Sunday morning when the Maori defenders were at their devotions. By a variety of means he pacified the Maoris of the south, and he captured the savage chief Te Rauparaha, whom he detained without trial. He displayed his brilliant flair for being on the spot when successful military operations were being conducted, and, like a modern general, managed news, dispatches, and personnel with confidence and a talent for public relations. He was indifferent to money but, as William Pember Reeves suggests, greedy for credit. At this time he was a blue-eyed, quick, energetic young officer with a square jaw, a Roman nose, a firm yet mobile mouth, and a queer trick of half closing one eye when he looked at the person whom he was addressing.

Grey learned the Maori language and customs, and through flattery, force, and *mana* (prestige and "face") secured the adherence of Maoris on the fringes of the European frontier. While he built hospitals and schools and encouraged Maori agriculture and their absorption into the European economy, land sales proceeded apace. The lasting merit of his racial policies is still the subject of much dispute. Before he left New Zealand in 1853, he introduced a scheme of representative government, based on elected Provincial Assemblies and a national House of Representatives. This quasi-federal system later proved unworkable, although Grey, when he entered New Zealand politics as an elected member of Parliament, continued to uphold it.

Grey's first New Zealand governorship, like his South Australian tenure, was viewed as a great success. The mess created by his predecessors was dramatically rectified. His assessment of his own achievements was generally accepted in London, and he was transferred in 1854 to another trouble spot in the British Empire. He was made governor of Cape Colony and high commissioner for South Africa and remained in that post until 1861. His task was to protect and pacify the eastern Cape frontier against unrest among the Southern Nguni people (known as "Kaffirs") and to regulate the struggling white settlements. His formula, which he had developed as a result of his Australian Aboriginal and New Zealand Maori experiences, was applied on the frontier with the creation of a new buffer province of British Kaffraria.

Grey believed that while native customs were intrinsically interesting, they should be condemned as incompatible with European reason. As Christianity was a superior religion, all native peoples would eventually receive the Gospel, abandon superstition, and adopt more European modes of life. Through European-sponsored magistrates, schools, hospitals, and farms, backed by a powerful army of white frontiersmen, the native peoples would become absorbed into the processes of colonization and development. Multiracial harmony, based on settler superiority and eventual amalgamation, would

then inevitably follow. Grey's policies in South Africa, however, were disastrous for black Africans.

Grey miscalculated the amount of agricultural land available, and charismatic prophets persuaded the Xhosa people to kill all of their cattle and cease planting corn. Devastation (1856-1857) resulted. The Kaffraria and Transkei populations were reduced by two-thirds. The chiefs were arrested and ruined, thirty thousand refugees were deported, and white farmers filled the vacuum. For the first time, Grey ran foul of the Colonial Office by his overspending and disobedience of orders not to attempt to federate Cape Colony, Natal, and Kaffraria with the Afrikaner Orange Free State. He was recalled by Sir Edward Bulwer-Lytton in 1859 but reinstated by the duke of Newcastle with a warning to obey orders. Grey seldom did. He had the man-on-the-spot mentality and always took authoritarian command, believing that success in the end justified all devious means used to attain it.

In 1861, Grey was sent to New Zealand again at his own request to prevent further fighting between Maoris and white settlers over land. This time his regime was a mixed one of success, military gain, confusion, betrayal, and failure. For the first time he had to deal with an elected Parliament and a responsible ministry. Grey played a lone, autocratic hand. He created policy and left his ministers to take the responsibility when things went wrong. He quarreled with the British general, Cameron, and pursued complicated and deceitful policies that, although militarily successful, resulted in major wars in the Waikato, West Coast, and Bay of Islands areas, the confiscation of hundreds of thousands of acres of Maori land, and the ruin of much of their society.

Grey was sacked by the Colonial Office in 1868 for disobeying instructions. He had retained British troops rather than sending them home, had increased expenditures, and was believed to have intensified the conflict by his forward military policy and huge land confiscations from the Maoris. His health broke, nervous problems appeared, his marriage disintegrated, and his self-control sometimes snapped. Increasingly isolated from his ministers and the Colonial Office, Grey was regarded as a dangerous, unscrupulous, and idiosyncratic autocrat. He retired to his retreat on Kawau Island in the Hauraki Gulf, where he devoted himself to literary, acclimatization, ethnographic, and scientific pursuits.

In 1874, Grey returned to politics, this time as the elected superintendent of Auckland Province. Two years later he became a member of the New Zealand House of Representatives and, between 1877 and 1879, led a radical ministry. His program of electoral reforms, the dismantling of big estates, labor regulation, and popular education was premature, but it was later carried out by Richard John Seddon. Grey proved a secretive, unstable, and autocratic leader who could not hold his disorderly group of followers together.

Grey consistently advocated British annexation and New Zealand control of Pacific islands. New Caledonia, the New Hebrides, Tonga, Samoa, and Fiji were all part of his grand vision to make Auckland the great mercantile capital of the Southwest Pacific and New Zealand the country "ordained by Nature to be the future Queen of the Pacific." Grey opposed New Zealand's entering the Australian Federation on the grounds that only colored labor could properly develop that continent. A prophet to the last, he looked forward to a grand confederation of all the English-speaking peoples of the British Empire and the United States.

Grey again retreated to Kawau but, in 1894, precipitately left New Zealand for London, where the queen made him a privy councillor. He died of senile decay in London on September 19, 1898, and, a rare honor for an Empire man, was buried in St. Paul's Cathedral.

SIGNIFICANCE

Sir George Grey was a complex, enigmatic colonial administrator whose life spanned almost the entire reign of Queen Victoria. Grey decisively influenced events in three major British colonies—New Zealand, South Australia, and Cape Colony. He was a peculiar mixture of autocrat and democrat, a visionary and political manipulator. He is still capable of arousing controversy among historians, repeating in death the passions, hatreds, and adulation that he engendered in life. Grey was a man with a tremendous variety of talents—an able soldier, an intrepid explorer, a man of letters, a mature scientist, and a talented administrator—but he never attained the great reputation that his initial brilliance and creative powers might have been expected to produce.

Grey's published collection of Maori legends, *Polynesian Mythology and Ancient Traditional History of the New Zealanders, as Furnished by Their Priests and Chiefs* (1855), is a classic, and his other writings on African, Aboriginal, and Maori languages are still of use to scholars. His generous donations of two magnificent libraries to the cities of Auckland and Cape Town are still remembered. Grey never accepted defeat. As his biographer James Rutherford comments, "He combined romantic idealism with a fierce determination to carry his ideas into immediate practice . . . he never altered what he once said."

Grey was a man of immense physical and moral courage, but his talents were flawed by his arrogance, disregard for orders, unscrupulous manipulation of evidence and events, and impetuosity. Above all, as his critics claimed, he never had the supreme courage—the courage to recognize at critical times that he was wrong. His virtues carried him through his halcyon days in Adelaide and Auckland, but as matters grew more complex, and he became more opportunistic and corrupted by office and his desire for a major place in imperial and democratic history, his judgment faltered. Contemporaries such as Seddon and Reeves saw much to admire in "good Governor Grey." He retained the affection of many of the Maori chiefs, although his native policies have come increasingly under critical scrutiny. His marriage was a disaster but he took great delight in children. He wanted to play all the major roles on several colonial stages, but, in the end, his audiences had departed and the applause had ceased.

—*Duncan Waterson*

FURTHER READING

Bohan, Edmund. *To Be a Hero: Sir George Grey, 1812-1898*. Auckland, New Zealand: HarperCollins, 1998. Balanced and comprehensive biography. Bohan, a New Zealand historian, has used some new material to provide fresh insights into his subject's political career and private life.

Dalton, Brian John. *War and Politics in New Zealand, 1855-1870*. Sydney: Sydney University Press, 1967. Like Ian Wards's book (see below), Dalton's study criticizes Grey's often insolent behavior as a statesman.

Frame, Alex. *Grey and Iwikau: A Journey into Custom*. Wellington, New Zealand: Victoria University Press, 2002. In 1849-1850, Grey, the governor of New Zealand, and Iwakau Te Heu Heu, paramount chief of Towharetoa, made an overland journey from Auckland to Taupo. Frame traces the journey, focusing on the interaction between the British and Maori cultures before war erupted between the government and the tribes.

McLintock, Alexander H. *Crown Colony Government in New Zealand*. Wellington, New Zealand: Government Printer, 1958. The best work on the constitutional issues in the period before New Zealand was granted representative government in 1854. Grey's role is clearly delineated.

Pike, Douglas Henry. *Paradise of Dissent: South Australia, 1829-1857*. London: Longmans, Green, 1957. An account of Grey's successful governorship when the infant colony of South Australia was transformed from a group of disheartened settlers and parasitic land sharks into a progressive agricultural settlement.

Rees, William Lee, and Lily Rees. *The Life and Times of Sir George Grey, K.C.B.* 2 vols. London: Hutchinson, 1892. Rambling, highly flavored, and entertaining memoirs based on interviews and the selected and selective personal thoughts of Sir George Grey before he retired to die in England.

Reeves, William Pember. *The Long White Cloud: Ao Tea Roa.* 3d ed. London: Allen & Unwin, 1950. Chapter 12, "Good Governor Grey," is a brilliant portrait by a younger New Zealand radical that frankly illustrates the enigma and contradiction that was Grey.

Rutherford, James. *Sir George Grey: A Study in Colonial Government.* London: Cassell, 1961. Excellent biography, based on a thorough mastery of a host of sources. Although he has not solved some of the challenging puzzles of Grey's personal life and controversial public actions, Rutherford, an Empire historian, is essential reading.

Sinclair, Sir Keith. *The Origins of the Maori Wars.* Wellington: New Zealand University Press, 1957. The classic analysis of the New Zealand race wars, detailing Grey's ambiguous motives and authoritative role in both major episodes.

Wards, Ian. *The Shadow of the Land: A Study of British Policy and Racial Conflict in New Zealand, 1832-1852.* Wellington, New Zealand: Government Printer, 1968. Wards's book is a powerful indictment of Grey's character and, particularly, his policy toward native people.

Wilson, Trevor G. *The Grey Government.* Auckland, New Zealand: Auckland University College, 1954. Critical, scholarly, and incisive, Professor Wilson takes a forensic look at a premature—and disastrous—radical New Zealand administration. Grey's shortcomings as a practical representative politician are clearly exposed.

SEE ALSO: Meri Te Tai Mangakahia; Richard John Seddon; Queen Victoria; Sir Julius Vogel; Edward Gibbon Wakefield.

RELATED ARTICLE in *Great Events from History: The Nineteenth Century, 1801-1900:* 1830's-1840's: Scientists Study Remains of Giant Moas.

EDVARD GRIEG
Norwegian composer

Drawing on Norwegian folk culture for inspiration, Grieg created an original, distinctive music of Romantic nationalism that made him the foremost composer in Norway and the first Scandinavian composer to achieve world renown.

BORN: June 15, 1843; Bergen, Norway
DIED: September 4, 1907; Bergen, Norway
ALSO KNOWN AS: Edvard Hagerup Grieg (full name)
AREA OF ACHIEVEMENT: Music

EARLY LIFE

Edvard Grieg (greeg) was the fourth of five children born to Gesine Hagerup Grieg and Alexander Grieg. His mother was musically gifted and, having been reared in a prominent and prosperous family, had received the best musical training available in Bergen and Hamburg. She was in great demand as a pianist and throughout her life played an important role in the musical life of Bergen. She gave Edvard his first piano lessons when he was six. His father, Alexander, the son of a prosperous merchant, also took an active interest in music, playing piano duets with his wife and invariably attending concerts on his many business trips abroad. Even when his own financial position deteriorated, he selflessly supported Edvard's lengthy and expensive musical education.

Grieg was undoubtedly fortunate to be born into a home in which music was a part of everyday life, and to have cultivated, sympathetic, and even indulgent parents. In an autobiographical reminiscence, "My First Success" (1903), Grieg states that his early childhood years were deeply formative and that his later creativity would have been stifled if constraints had been placed too early upon his sensitive and imaginative nature. Not surprisingly, his temperament resulted in an increasing dislike of school:

> School life was to me deeply unsympathetic; its materialism, harshness, and coldness were so contrary to my nature that I would think out the most incredible things to be quit of it even if only for a little while.

Although Grieg was fond of composing and improvising at the piano, he never thought of becoming an artist; he was certain that he would follow the path of numerous ancestors and become a minister. Yet, in the summer of 1858, the famous Norwegian violinist Ole Bull visited the Griegs and after hearing Edvard play persuaded Grieg's parents to send Edvard to the Leipzig Conservatory. Thus began for Grieg at the age of fifteen an experience that he always remembered with distaste.

After overcoming his initial homesickness, Grieg found the pedantic methods at the conservatory dry and uninspiring, even occasionally absurd, as when he was required to write a string quartet although he had received no instruction in the form and knew nothing of the technique of string instruments. He applied himself diligently to what he considered sterile exercises, but he was at best a mediocre student and left the conservatory nearly as ignorant as when he had entered it (an account of himself as a student that is curiously contradicted by the records that survive).

At the bottom of Grieg's always-bitter reflections on his student days in Leipzig (1858-1862) was the conflict between his inherently lyrical-romantic nature and the German classicism that the conservatory required. He acknowledged that the quantity of music he was able to hear performed in Leipzig was important to his development, particularly the works of the Romantics Robert Schumann, Felix Mendelssohn, and Frédéric Chopin—compensation, he said, "for the instruction in the technique of composition which I did *not* get at the Conservatory."

In 1862, Grieg received his certificate and returned to Bergen, where he gave his first concert. In 1863, he took up residence in Copenhagen—then the cultural center of Denmark and Norway—where he met a number of musicians and artists: Hans Christian Andersen, some of whose poems he had already set to music; author Benjamin Feddersen; singer Julius Stenberg; and Niels Gade, the leader of the Scandinavian Romantic school of music. He also met his cousin Nina Hagerup, a gifted singer who would, a few years later, become his wife. He had, however, not yet discovered his own distinctive musical personality.

LIFE'S WORK
In 1864, Grieg met the charismatic young composer and fiery champion of Norwegian nationalism Rikard Nordraak. While still a student in Berlin, Nordraak abandoned German music and literature and turned for inspiration to Norwegian sagas, folk tales, ballads, folk music,

Edvard Grieg. (The Granger Collection, New York)

anecdotes, and history. He saw clearly what Grieg had only dimly felt: not only the sterility of German classicism but also the impossibility of using German Romanticism to create a new, distinctly Norwegian music.

Prior to meeting Nordraak, Grieg had known little of Norway's folk culture. He had heard Ole Bull praise Norwegian folk music and had heard him play a few folk tunes, but Norwegian music had not been played in Grieg's home. In Copenhagen, he had met Gade, supposedly the leader of a new school of northern music, but whose compositions were actually heavily derivative of German Romanticism. Grieg's discovery of a rich native heritage was liberating and transforming. He at last felt able to link the best that was within him (his lyric-romantic nature) with the best that was in his native land—the untainted peasant culture with its long memory of an ancient past, its uninhibited expressions of both joy and sorrow, and its intense awareness of Norway's spectacular mountains, waterfalls, and fjords.

In 1865, Grieg, Nordraak, and Danish musicians C. F. E. Horneman and Gottfred Matthison-Hansen founded Euterpe, an organization to promote contemporary Scandinavian music. Although Euterpe flourished for only a brief time, it was one indication of Grieg's ori-

entation toward northern music. The early death of
Nordraak from pulmonary tuberculosis in 1866 only
strengthened Grieg's resolve to champion and create a
truly national music, and Nordraak's death became the
occasion for one of Grieg's most original and powerful
compositions, *Sörgemarsch over Rikard Nordraak* (1866;
funeral march in memory of Rikard Nordraak). In 1866,
Grieg gave an overwhelmingly successful concert of
Norwegian music in Christiania (modern Oslo), which
established him as one of his country's foremost young
musicians.

Grieg became a popular teacher and collaborated with
critic Otto Winter-Hjelm to establish a Norwegian Academy of Music. In 1867, Grieg and Nina Hagerup were
married, the same year Grieg's first book of *Lyriske
smaastykker*, Op. 12 (lyric pieces) for piano appeared,
some of whose titles reflect a growing nationalism:
Norsk (Norwegian), *Folkevise* (folktune), and *Faedre-
landssang* (national song). In 1868, Grieg composed his
famous Piano Concerto in A Minor, the same year his
only child, Alexandra, was born; she died thirteen
months later. His discovery in 1869 of Ludvig Linde-
man's collection of folk music was a further important
impetus in his evolution toward a distinctively Norwegian style; it became a rich source of inspiration for the
numerous tone poems he composed.

Partly because of the enthusiastic support Grieg received from the famed Franz Liszt, he obtained a government grant to further his musical education by travel and
study abroad. In 1870, he went to Rome, where he was
gratified by Liszt's appreciation of his work, particularly
of the recently completed Piano Concerto in A Minor.
Grieg's prestige was further enhanced by his close association during the 1870's with Norway's most prominent dramatist-poets, Henrik Ibsen and Bjørnstjerne
Bjørnson.

Grieg set many of Bjørnson's poems to music and collaborated with him to produce an opera, *Olav Trygvason*
(a project that was never completed and that occasioned
a long period of estrangement between the two artists).
In 1874, Ibsen invited Grieg to compose music for a
stage production of *Peer Gynt* (1867; English translation, 1892), which resulted in some of Grieg's best-
known and most-loved compositions. Additionally, some
of Ibsens's poems provided the inspiration for Grieg's
highest achievements in song, his *Sex digte*, Op. 25 (six
songs).

A government pension given to Grieg in 1874 freed
him from his teaching responsibilities and allowed him
to devote himself to composition. Nevertheless, Grieg

continued to the end of his life to give substantial
amounts of time and energy to conducting and to concert
tours (both at home and abroad), possibly as an escape
from periods of nonproductivity as a composer but additionally to renew himself by contact with the centers of
creative life abroad. Grieg's best remedy for artistic sterility, however, was to seek regeneration through contact
with nature, particularly through Norway's spectacular
scenery.

In 1877, Grieg moved to Lofthus in the Hardanger
district, where he composed *Den bergtekne*, Op. 32 (the
mountain thrall); the String Quartet in G Minor, Op. 27;
Albumblade, Op. 28 (album leaves); and *Improvisata
over to norske folkeviser*, Op. 29 (improvisations on two
Norwegian folk songs). His love of "the great, melancholy Westland nature" caused him eventually to build a
villa at Troldhaugen, overlooking the fjord a short distance from Bergen, even though the damp climate was
not the best for the health problems that increasingly beset him in later life.

When the Griegs moved to Troldhaugen in 1885, they
were moving into their first settled home, such had been
the roving nature of their lives. Nevertheless, the final
two decades of Grieg's life reveal the same restless lifestyle. As an internationally known composer-conductor-
pianist, Grieg undertook numerous concert tours to England, Paris, Brussels, Germany, Sweden, Vienna, the
Netherlands, and Warsaw. He met other famous musicians such as Johannes Brahms, Max Reger, Frederick
Delius, and Peter Ilich Tchaikovsky. The German ruler
Kaiser William II invited Grieg aboard his yacht
(moored in Bergen Harbor) to hear a program of Grieg's
works performed by his private orchestra.

Despite increasing complaints about his failing powers and health, Grieg continued to be productive in
composition, revising earlier compositions and creating
new ones, including the important works for the piano,
Norske folkeviser, Op. 66 (1896; nineteen Norwegian
folk tunes), and seven books of *Lyrische Stücke* (1901;
lyric pieces). He also composed the last of his Norwegian
songs and one of his most original works, *Haugtussa*,
Op. 67 (1895). *Slåtter*, Op. 72 (1902-1903), published as
a work for piano, was inspired by Hardanger violin tunes.
His final composition was a choral work, Four Psalms,
Op. 74.

Many years earlier, while a student at Leipzig, Grieg
had suffered an attack of pleurisy so severe that it had interrupted his studies and left him with a permanent health
liability—a collapsed lung. Although his active life
seemed to belie it (frequent walking trips through the

mountains, exhausting concert tours, and great bursts of creativity), Grieg's health was always frail. During his last years, it deteriorated significantly. Nevertheless, in the last year of his life, he made a tour to Copenhagen, Munich, Berlin, and Kiel, sustaining himself largely through nervous energy and sheer will. Characteristically, Grieg was preparing to leave Norway for a concert tour of England when his doctor, realizing the gravity of Grieg's condition, insisted that he go instead to the hospital in Bergen. He died there the next day. His funeral in Bergen, on September 9, 1907, was an important national and international event, a final tribute to the eminence that Grieg attained as conductor, performer, and composer.

SIGNIFICANCE

In assessing Edvard Grieg's contribution to music, typically two questions have been raised: How original an artist was he? and How major? Much that is attractive and uniquely expressive of the northern spirit in Grieg's mature style derives from Norwegian folk songs and dances: a bold use of dissonance reminiscent of the Hardanger fiddle; frequent use of second, seventh, and perfect as well as augmented fourth and fifth intervals; irregularities of rhythm and accent. However, his music is far from being a transcription or adaptation of sources. Comparisons of Grieg's works with the sources of his inspiration reveal how thoroughly he assimilated their color and spirit and how he transformed them by his own romantic imagination. The result is a fresh, original music that is uniquely expressive of his country's spirit but that invariably bears the deep impress of Grieg's own musical gifts: his ability to express a wide range of emotions and ideas, and particularly his genius for idiosyncratic and impressionistic use of harmony.

The second question about Grieg's ranking among composers is more problematic. Although he attained a popularity such as few artists experience during their lifetimes and achieved numerous distinctions (among them membership in the French Legion of Honor and honorary doctorates from Cambridge and Oxford), Grieg himself was ambivalent about his popularity and unimpressed by his many honors and awards. He was aware that his very popularity caused critics to view him with suspicion, lamenting that his "standing as an artist suffers thereby.... More fortunate are those artists who do not win so-called popularity while they are still living."

Undoubtedly influenced by the prevailing critical standards that confounded greatness with bigness, Grieg was also dismayed by his inability to handle the so-called larger forms, such as oratorios, operas, and symphonies. However, Wolfgang Amadeus Mozart, a great master of the larger forms, observed: "Our taste in Germany is for long things; BUT SHORT AND GOOD IS BETTER." Qualified critics today tend to view Grieg's songs and piano compositions as his most substantial and distinctive achievements.

—Karen A. Kildahl

FURTHER READING

Abraham, Gerald, ed. *Grieg: A Symposium*. London: Lindsay Drummond, 1948. A collection of specialized critical essays that examines every aspect of Grieg's music. A bibliography (focused on the music rather than the man) contains few entries in English. Includes a chronological list of compositions and forty pages of musical examples.

Benestad, Finn, and Dag Schjelderup-Ebbe. *Edvard Grieg: The Man and the Artist*. Translated by William H. Halverson and Leland B. Sateren. Lincoln: University of Nebraska Press, 1988. This English translation of a book first published in Norway in 1980 has been called the definitive biography of Grieg. The two authors spent decades conducting research, and their book presents a lively and objective discussion of the composer's life and music. The English translators added material after a cache of Grieg's manuscripts and letters was uncovered during the 1980's.

Finck, Henry T. *Grieg and His Music*. New York: John Lane, 1929. Includes the author's visit with Grieg a few years before his death. An ardent supporter of Grieg, Finck offers an uncritical appraisal of Grieg's music and a warmly sympathetic account of his life. Contains numerous photographs, a bibliography, and a catalog of Grieg's compositions.

Grieg, Edvard. *Diaries, Articles Speeches*. Edited and translated by Finn Benestad and William H. Halverson. Columbus, Ohio: Peer Gynt Press, 2001.

_____. *Letters to Colleagues and Friends*. Edited by Finn Benestad, translated by William H. Halverson. Columbus, Ohio: Peer Gynt Press, 2001. These two collections, including material unearthed during the 1980's, provide insights into Grieg's personality, life, and compositions. The volume of letters contains more than five hundred of Grieg's letters, arranged alphabetically by the name of the person with whom he corresponded. The collection of manuscripts is arranged chronologically by document type and contains annotations and footnotes.

Horton, John. *Grieg*. London: J. M. Dent & Sons, 1974. A succinct overview of Grieg's life and works. The survey of Grieg's life is concise and authoritative; the discussion of Grieg's music is scholarly but eminently readable. Contains an illuminating calendar of Grieg's life (correlated with the birth/death dates of contemporary musicians), an index identifying names important in any study of Grieg, a complete catalog of works, and an extensive bibliography.

Layton, Robert. *Grieg*. London: Omnibus Press, 1998. A concise overview of Grieg's life and music. Part of the Illustrated Lives of Great Composers series.

Monrad-Johansen, David. *Edvard Grieg*. Translated by Madge Robertson. Princeton, N.J.: Princeton University Press, 1938. A full-length biography of Grieg by a well-known Norwegian composer who had access to documents and letters unavailable to other writers. A balanced and objective but enthusiastic appreciation of Grieg's work and life, especially of his significance for Norway. Contains a few photographs.

SEE ALSO: Hans Christian Andersen; Johannes Brahms; Frédéric Chopin; Henrik Ibsen; Franz Liszt; Countess of Lovelace; Felix Mendelssohn; Robert Schumann; Peter Ilich Tchaikovsky.

RELATED ARTICLES in *Great Events from History: The Nineteenth Century, 1801-1900:* April 7, 1805: Beethoven's *Eroica* Symphony Introduces the Romantic Age; December 22, 1894: Debussy's *Prelude to the Afternoon of a Faun* Premieres.

SARAH AND ANGELINA GRIMKÉ
American abolitionists and women's rights activists

After renouncing their family's social class, southern traditions, and proslavery views, the Grimké sisters became the first prominent white female abolitionists in the United States. They were criticized for speaking against slavery to groups mixing men and women, and this criticism helped make them leading advocates for women's rights.

SARAH GRIMKÉ

BORN: November 26, 1792; Charleston, South Carolina
DIED: December 23, 1873; Hyde Park, Massachusetts
ALSO KNOWN AS: Sarah Moore Grimké (full name)

ANGELINA GRIMKÉ

BORN: February 20, 1805; Charleston, South Carolina
DIED: October 26, 1879; Hyde Park, Massachusetts
ALSO KNOWN AS: Angelina Emily Grimké (birth name); Angelina Grimké Weld
AREAS OF ACHIEVEMENT: Social reform, women's rights

EARLY LIVES
The sixth of fourteen children, Sarah Moore Grimké (grihm-KAY) was the daughter of John Faucheraud Grimké, a respected South Carolina lawyer, accomplished politician, and wealthy plantation owner. Sarah's mother, Mary "Polly" Smith Grimké, was a leading socialite from a prominent Charleston family. As members of Charleston's elite, the Grimkés were both devout members of the Episcopal Church and staunch supporters of slavery.

Educated at home, Sarah was bright, inquisitive, and studious. She admired her father and spent many hours in the family library reading his law books. John Grimké encouraged his daughter's intellectual development but drew the line when she expressed a desire to become a lawyer herself. Societal norms dictated that a young woman accept the traditional role of wife and mother. Sarah not only chafed under such expectations, but she also rebelled against the idea that slaves should not be educated. When she was eleven, her father punished her for teaching a young slave girl to read, an illegal act in the antebellum South. Sarah also rejected the prevailing view of the religious establishment that Christian Scripture sanctioned slavery and refused to become a member of the Episcopal Church.

Sarah's sister Angelina, who was thirteen years her junior, came to share her unconventional views on slavery. Angelina looked upon her older sister as a substitute mother in place of her real mother, who was distant and difficult. The two girls grew inseparable, and Angelina adopted many of the same attitudes toward religion and slavery that her sister had. Her views were cemented when she was a student at the elite Charleston Seminary. When a recently flogged slave boy entered her classroom to open the windows, his bloody wounds so sickened

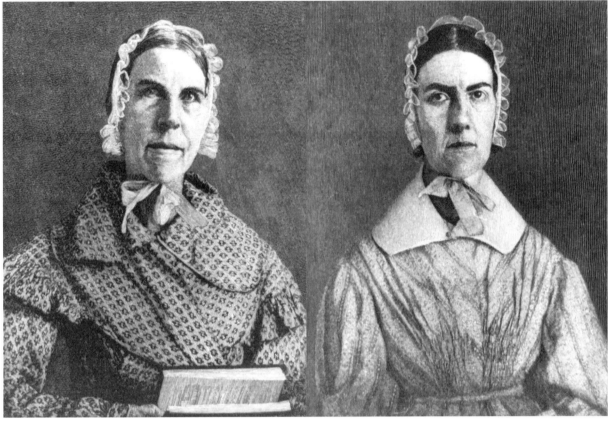

Sarah (left) and Angelina Grimké. (Library of Congress)

Angelina that she fainted. The image of the boy's lashed body haunted her through the rest of her life.

LIVES' WORK

In 1819, when Sarah was about twenty-seven, she traveled to Philadelphia with her ailing father to consult with medical specialists about his condition. While she was there, she became acquainted with the Quakers, whose abolitionist stance appealed to her. After her father's death in New Jersey, Sarah briefly returned to Charleston, but the rift between her and the rest of her family had become too great for her to stay with them. In 1822, she returned to Philadelphia permanently and became involved in the Fourth and Arch Street meeting of Quakers. Angelina adopted her sister's Quaker faith and abolitionist views, but remained in Charleston. Her outspoken activism and rebellious nature also damaged her relationship with other members of her family, especially her mother, and in 1829, she moved north to Philadelphia to live with Sarah.

The Grimké sisters began to be recognized as leaders in the national abolitionist movement after joining the

Philadelphia Anti-Slavery Society in 1835. As they gained a reputation as ardent and articulate opponents of slavery, New York abolitionists invited them to give "parlor talks" to small groups of women. These gatherings were so popular that the sisters soon moved into larger venues, where they addressed hundreds of women at a time. New England activists took note of the sisters' growing influence and invited them to speak in Boston in 1837. The meetings were geared toward women, but men began to attend as well. The sisters were criticized for speaking to mixed groups, most notably by Catharine Beecher, who, in "An Essay on Slavery and Abolitionism with Reference to the Duty of American Females," took the sisters to task for overstepping accepted social boundaries that restricted women to the domestic sphere. In response, Angelina wrote "Letters to Catherine Beecher," in which she equated the silencing of women with the subjugation of slaves.

One of the most notable events during the Grimké sisters' stay in Massachusetts took place in February, 1837, when Angelina became the first woman to address the state legislature. The public attention that the sisters received continued to draw the ire of critics, both inside and outside the abolitionist movement. In a pastoral letter issued by the Council of Congregationalist Ministers of Massachusetts, the Grimkés were censured for violating New Testament strictures and societal norms regarding proper womanly behavior. Sarah fired back with the first feminist manifesto published in the United States. Appearing in both the *Boston Spectator* and William Lloyd Garrison's abolitionist newspaper *The Liberator*, Sarah's "Letters on the Equality of the Sexes and the Condition of Women" deplored "the servitude of women," rejected biblical patriarchy, condemned marriage as an oppressive institution, argued for equal pay for equal work, and supported equal education for women. This essay profoundly influenced women's rights advocates of the time, including Elizabeth Cady Stanton and Lucretia Mott.

Although Angelina also supported the struggle for women's rights, she considered slavery the more urgent issue. In October, 1836, she wrote "An Appeal to the Christian Women of the Southern States." This thirty-six-page document is unique in the history of the antislavery movement because it was written by a southern woman for other southern women from slaveholding families like her own. Using a religious approach, Angelina's appeal branded slavery a sin and assured women that if they were to rise up against "the peculiar institution," their voices would be heard above those of men—a shocking idea at a time when women had no political power. Although Angelina's appeal did not produce the response from southern women for which she had hoped, it did mobilize many northern women to work against slavery by convincing them that they had the power to change society.

After Angelina married fellow abolitionist Theodore Dwight Weld in 1838, the sisters retired from the lecture circuit but not from activism. They helped Weld gather information for his influential volume *American Slavery as It Is*, which was published in 1839. Among the book's readers was Harriet Beecher Stowe—a sister of Catharine Beecher—who drew on the book for her famous antislavery novel *Uncle Tom's Cabin: Or, Life Among the Lowly* (1852).

In 1868, the sisters' concern for the plight of former slaves took a personal turn when they discovered that their brother Henry had fathered three sons with his slave Nancy Weston. Sarah and Angelina welcomed their mixed-race nephews into the family, providing them with love and financial support. After moving to Boston during the 1860's, the sisters continued to agitate for women's rights. On March 7, 1870, when Sarah was seventy-eight and Angelina was sixty-five, they held a demonstration promoting woman suffrage at a polling place in Hyde Park, a suburb of Boston. Sarah died three years later at the age of eighty-one. After suffering several strokes, Angelina died in 1879 at the age of seventy-four.

SIGNIFICANCE

As crusaders and political reformers, Sarah and Angelina Grimké set the stage for both the Civil Rights movement and feminist revolution of the twentieth cen-

APPEAL TO THE CHRISTIAN WOMEN OF THE SOUTH

Angelina Grimké's publication of this appeal to women of slave-owning families to turn against the institution of slavery was an unprecedented act for a woman of her background. This brief extract is a representative example of her unrestrained call for abolition.

The *women of the South can overthrow* this horrible system of oppression and cruelty, licentiousness and wrong. Such appeals to your legislatures would be irresistible, for there is something in the heart of man which *will bend under moral suasion*. There is a swift witness for truth in his bosom, *which will respond to truth* when it is uttered with calmness and dignity. If you could obtain but six signatures to such a petition in only one state, I would say, send up that petition, and be not in the least discouraged by the scoffs and jeers of the heartless, or the resolution of the house to lay it on the table. It will be a great thing if the subject can be introduced into your legislatures in any way, even by *women*, and *they* will be the most likely to introduce it there in the best possible manner, as a matter of *morals* and *religion*, not of expediency or politics. You may petition, too, the different ecclesiastical bodies of the slave states. Slavery must be attacked with the whole power of truth and the sword of the spirit. You must take it up on *Christian* ground, and fight against it with Christian weapons, whilst your feet are shod with the preparation of the gospel of peace. And *you are now* loudly called upon by the cries of the widow and the orphan, to arise and gird yourselves for this great moral conflict, with the whole armour of righteousness upon the right hand and on the left.

Source: Angelina Emily Grimké, *Appeal to the Christian Women of the South* (New York: Anti-Slavery Society, 1836).

tury by pioneering approaches to activism that have become commonplace in modern culture. For example, because their views on abolition were rooted in their Christian religion, they understood that people of faith could be a powerful force for political and social change. Angelina's "Appeals" reflected this view. Similarly, the mobilization of churchgoers and clergy during the 1960's was crucial to the success of the modern Civil Rights movement. In addition, the sisters understood that to gain adherents to a cause one must appeal to the heart as well as to the mind. They pioneered the tools of grassroots activism, including manifestos, pamphlets, petitions, direct fund-raising, rallies, and public speaking—approaches that are commonplace today among contemporary social and political activists.

The Grimké sisters were also among the first American activists to perceive that, given the chance, women could become a potent political force in their own right. When they spoke in front of mixed audiences, their appearances on podiums gave women a public voice for the first time and set the tone for the next eighty years as women fought to gain the vote. Their radical vision of social change defined the struggle for equal rights for women and foreshadowed the modern women's movement.

—Pegge Bochynski

FURTHER READING

Browne, Stephen Howard. *Angelina Grimké: Rhetoric, Identity, and the Radical Imagination.* East Lansing: Michigan State University Press, 2000. In this first full-length study of Angelina's letters and speeches, Browne argues that she used rhetoric not only to perfect her message but also to forge her identity as a moral force.

Ceplair, Larry, ed. *The Public Years of Sarah and Angelina Grimké: Selected Writings, 1835-1839.* New York: Columbia University Press, 1989. Accompanied by an informative critical introduction by Ceplair, this collection of letters, diaries, and speeches produced by the Grimké sisters includes writings that document their activism in women's rights.

Durso, Pamela. *The Power of Woman: The Life and Writings of Sarah Moore Grimké.* Macon: Mercer University Press, 2004. The first book-length treatment showing how religion and faith influenced Sarah Grimké's life and work.

Lerner, Gerda. *The Grimké Sisters from South Carolina: Pioneers for Women's Rights and Abolition.* Chapel Hill: University of North Carolina Press, 2004. A traditional biography illuminating the contributions of the Grimké sisters to the abolitionist and feminist movements during the nineteenth century. Includes selected speeches and essays.

Perry, Mark. *Lift Up Thy Voice.* New York: Viking Press, 2001. A well-researched biography focusing on the activism of the Grimké sisters, as well as the accomplishments of their three nephews who were born to their brother Henry Grimké and his slave mistress.

SEE ALSO: Catharine Beecher; Frederick Douglass; Charlotte Forten; Abby Kelley Foster; William Lloyd Garrison; Lucretia Mott; Elizabeth Cady Stanton; Harriet Beecher Stowe.

RELATED ARTICLES in *Great Events from History: The Nineteenth Century, 1801-1900:* July 19-20, 1848: Seneca Falls Convention; May 28-29, 1851: Akron Woman's Rights Convention; May, 1869: Woman Suffrage Associations Begin Forming; June 27, 1874-June 2, 1875: Red River War; February 17-18, 1890: Women's Rights Associations Unite.

JACOB AND WILHELM GRIMM
German fabulists

Remembered as the authors of what may be the best-known book of fairy tales in the Western world, the Grimm brothers were two of the most noted philologists of the nineteenth century. In addition to the fairy tales they recorded, they made significant contributions to linguistic theory, folklore, and the study of the German language and its literature.

JACOB GRIMM

BORN: January 4, 1785; Hanau, near Kassel, Hesse-Kassel (now in Germany)
DIED: September 30, 1863; Berlin, Prussia (now in Germany)
ALSO KNOWN AS: Jacob Ludwig Carl Grimm (full name)

WILHELM GRIMM

BORN: February 24, 1786; Hanau, near Kassel, Hesse-Kassel (now in Germany)
DIED: December 16, 1859; Berlin, Prussia (now in Germany)
ALSO KNOWN AS: Wilhelm Carl Grimm (full name)
AREAS OF ACHIEVEMENT: Literature, linguistics

EARLY LIVES

Jacob and Wilhelm Grimm were born into a comparatively prosperous family in a small village in what is now central Germany. Their father was a lawyer, judge, and public servant; however, he died suddenly at the age of forty-four, leaving his widow and his eleven-year-old son Jacob to take care of the other five children. Though times were financially difficult, Jacob and Wilhelm advanced academically, and by 1803 they were both studying law at the University of Marburg. Under the influence of a professor of legal history, the Grimm brothers became interested in the origins of the law and its growth and development in a cultural context. They also took up the study of philology (the investigations of ancient languages and texts) and began a serious inquiry into German folklore and linguistics. In 1825 Wilhelm married Dortchen Wild (who, along with other members of her family, provided the brothers with many of the folktales they would later use in their collections); Jacob never married.

In 1813, after the defeat of Napoleon Bonaparte, Jacob became a member of the local parliament. However, the local German princes regained their power, ending German reunification and democratization. The Grimm brothers took jobs as librarians and, from around 1815 to 1830, produced several books on German legends, legal history, and grammar. However, both brothers lost their librarianships and university teaching opportunities after failing to take loyalty oaths to the local monarchs. By 1840, however, their fortunes had changed, and both were appointed professors at the University of Berlin, where they continued the work they had already begun on their massive *Deutsches Wörterbuch* (1854; German dictionary). Both became involved in politics again during the German revolution of 1848 and were elected to the local legislature, only to resign when the revolutionary movement collapsed.

LIVES' WORK

The work of the Grimm brothers cannot adequately be appreciated without some understanding of the intellectual and political climate of early nineteenth century Europe. By this time, most of the people and places of the world had been "discovered" by Westerners, though to be sure, much of the details still needed to be filled in. What European scholars at the time faced was a world of almost infinite variety in terms of cultural customs, races, languages, and religious beliefs. The task, then, was to try to put order into this apparent chaos: Why was the world so diverse? Why did people look so different? Why were there so many different languages? Previous answers, often based on biblical stories (such as the Tower of Babel to account for linguistic heterogeneity), were proving inadequate in light of new data coming in from ethnology, geology, and biology.

The American and French Revolutions had also called into question the notion of the monarch state, the role of the governor and the governed, and the nature of the political unit. Who should govern whom? What constitutes a "country"? Does every different group of language speakers deserve to be a separate nation? The work of the Grimm brothers was informed by all these questions.

In 1786 (the year of Wilhelm's birth), the British legal scholar and Asian specialist William Jones shocked the world by claiming that Sanskrit (the ancient holy language of India) was related to Greek and Latin, having "sprung from a common source which, perhaps, no longer exists." It had already been well known that many

European languages shared a common ancestor in the past (for example, modern Romance languages such as French, Spanish, and Italian were derived from classical Roman Latin). What was startling about Jones's hypothesis was that he claimed that most of the languages of Europe were also connected to many other languages hitherto thought to be quite dissimilar. This supposed common parent language was termed "Proto Indo-European," and much of linguistic scholarship in the nineteenth century centered on trying to prove or disprove the Indo-European hypothesis. The Grimm brothers, particularly Jacob, made some important discoveries in this field and helped to establish the now commonly accepted view that the languages of today in the Indo-European family are actually all descendants from a common source.

The Indo-European hypothesis was one of the most critical issues of the nineteenth century. At stake were some of the deepest and strongest convictions held by Europeans: If linguistic affinity between Europe and India could be shown, notions of culture, race, and national identity would have to be reevaluated. Also, European scholars began to wonder just who these Indo-Europeans were, where they might have come from, and what some of their customs and beliefs might have been. It was an attempt to address some of these issues that prompted the

Grimm brothers to begin their collection of fairy tales around 1806. They argued that the folktales they were finding had ancient Indo-European origins, and that the *Märchen* (magic fables or fairy tales) they were finding were survivals from old classical mythology. The characters in the folktales they gathered, then, were the modern remnants of old Teutonic gods and goddesses.

Also, the German *Volk* (people) in their folklore studies were always the primary focus for the Grimm brothers. In their time, the German-speaking people in northern and central Europe had not yet come together to form a nation-state. Thus, as one translator put it, "from the beginning [the Grimm brothers'] principal concern was to uncover the etymological and linguistic truths that bound the German people together and were expressed in their laws and customs." In other words, people with a common tongue, a common mythology, and a common set of customs constituted a distinct culture or race deserving their own sovereignty; therefore, the Grimms sought to demonstrate the unity and origins of the Germans through their linguistic and folklore studies.

The Grimm brothers spent about forty years gathering their stories, though the first volume of their *Kinder- und Hausmärchen* (*German Popular Stories*, 1823-1826; best known as *Grimm's Fairy Tales*) was published in 1812 when the brothers were still in their mid-twenties. A second volume appeared in 1815. These first two books contained scholarly annotations and 156 stories, fables, legends and the like. These initial collections were not primarily intended as mere children's entertainment, but were to be read by educated lay adults and specialists who were interested in German folklore and culture.

As time wore on, it became clear that children were as interested in these fairy tales as scholars were. In 1819, the second (one-volume) edition appeared with 170 stories, and the annotations were purged and published separately. By the time of the final 1857 seventh edition, the collection contained 211 tales, now highly refined and revised. This is the version upon which most English translations are based, and it contains some of the best-known stories in Western literature, including "Snow White," "Little Red Riding Hood," "Cinderella," "Sleeping Beauty," "The Frog Prince," "Hansel and Gretel," "Rapunzel," and "Rumpelstiltskin."

Contrary to popular belief, the Grimm brothers did not actually gather their stories from peasants in the field. Many informants were actually bourgeois friends or acquaintances who told stories to the Grimms at their leisure in their homes. Also, a number of stories were taken

Jacob and Wilhelm Grimm. (Library of Congress)

"THE STRAW, THE COAL, AND THE BEAN"

Although one of the briefest of the Grimm brothers' fairy tales, this story nevertheless makes a moralistic point.

In a village dwelt a poor old woman, who had gathered together a dish of beans and wanted to cook them. So she made a fire on her hearth, and that it might burn the quicker, she lighted it with a handful of straw. When she was emptying the beans into the pan, one dropped without her observing it, and lay on the ground beside a straw, and soon afterwards a burning coal from the fire leapt down to the two. Then the straw began and said: "Dear friends, from whence do you come here?" The coal replied: "I fortunately sprang out of the fire, and if I had not escaped by sheer force, my death would have been certain,—I should have been burnt to ashes." The bean said: "I too have escaped with a whole skin, but if the old woman had got me into the pan, I should have been made into broth without any mercy, like my comrades." "And would a better fate have fallen to my lot?" said the straw. "The old woman has destroyed all my brethren in fire and smoke; she seized sixty of them at once, and took their lives. I luckily slipped through her fingers."

"But what are we to do now?" said the coal.

"I think," answered the bean, "that as we have so fortunately escaped death, we should keep together like good companions, and lest a new mischance should overtake us here, we should go away together, and repair to a foreign country."

The proposition pleased the two others, and they set out on their way together. Soon, however, they came to a little brook, and as there was no bridge or foot-plank, they did not know how they were to get over it. The straw hit on a good idea, and said: "I will lay myself straight across, and then you can walk over on me as on a bridge." The straw therefore stretched itself from one bank to the other, and the coal, who was of an impetuous disposition, tripped quite boldly on to the newly-built bridge. But when she had reached the middle, and heard the water rushing beneath her, she was after all, afraid, and stood still, and ventured no farther. The straw, however, began to burn, broke in two pieces, and fell into the stream. The coal slipped after her, hissed when she got into the water, and breathed her last. The bean, who had prudently stayed behind on the shore, could not but laugh at the event, was unable to stop, and laughed so heartily that she burst. It would have been all over with her, likewise, if, by good fortune, a tailor who was travelling in search of work, had not sat down to rest by the brook. As he had a compassionate heart he pulled out his needle and thread, and sewed her together. The bean thanked him most prettily, but as the tailor used black thread, all beans since then have a black seam.

Source: Brothers Grimm, *Fairy Tales*, translated by Edgar Taylor and Marian Edwardes (London, 1897).

---

and details that might detract from a story's flow were eliminated.

The Grimm brothers were interested in the literary quality of the tales as much as anything else. Also, as time went on and it became apparent that children were reading the stories as often as adults, pains were taken by the brothers to make them more palatable for young middle-class Christian German sensibilities. Sexual innuendo and coarse language were eliminated, and the Grimm brothers spent an increasing amount of effort emphasizing morals in their tales.

SIGNIFICANCE

Jacob Grimm retired from his university post in 1848, as did Wilhelm in 1852. Throughout their lives, the brothers worked in consort and lived near or with each other. Jacob wrote twenty-one books during his lifetime, while Wilhelm wrote fourteen. They also produced eight books together. Jacob was noted for his linguistics work, while Wilhelm spent much of his energy as the primary editor and author of the fairy tales. When Wilhelm died in 1859, Jacob took the loss hard but continued to carry on their work until his own death in 1863.

Each generation seems to have to reassess the Grimm brothers in the context of their own times. By the 1870's, in Prussia and much of the rest of the German principalities, the Grimm tales had been incorporated into the school curriculum. Their popularity during the late twentieth and early twenty-first century English-speaking world has been attested by the number of film adaptations that have been based on Grimm tales.

There have been few academic disciplines that have not had something to say about these fairy tales. Psychologists have searched them for universal archetypes and symbols of the human psyche and have sometimes seen commentaries being made on human development. Edu-

directly from earlier written sources, including a few Latin poems of the fourteenth century. In all cases, however, the Grimm brothers greatly expanded and edited the tales for dramatic and stylistic effect. Indirect speech was put into direct quotation, colorful language was embedded, and motivations of the characters were sometimes expanded upon or created. Chronologies were improved,

cators and philosophers draw attention to how the human morality play becomes manifested in these seemingly simple fables. Marxists point out how the Protestant work ethic and bourgeois values underlay most of the lessons found in the Grimm stories. Feminists argue that patriarchal notions of sex roles are reinforced by the Grimm brothers and sometimes even try to retell these fairy tales using their own vocabulary. Literary critics of all persuasions have analyzed them for tropes, stylistic features, and motifs of all kinds.

The Grimm brothers reinvented—or at least highly refined—a special genre: the literary folk tale. Although the Grimms no doubt believed that their collection revealed the genius and essence of the German-speaking people, they also believed that their stories contained certain universal (or at least Western) truths that spoke to everyone from a culture or cultures long past. Nevertheless, they felt that the messages and wisdom they conveyed were still very much contemporary. In this sense, Grimm's fairy tales join some of the world's other great story collections—such as *The Arabian Nights' Entertainments* from the Middle East, *The Pañcatantra* from India, and *Aesop's Fables* from Greece—as exemplars and depositories of literary drama, human wisdom, and creativity, and as reflections of the human spirit. It is probably for these reasons that the stories are still read today and will likely be read for quite some time.

—James Stanlaw

FURTHER READING

Grimm, Jacob, and Wilhelm Grimm. *The Complete Fairy Tales of the Brothers Grimm*. Edited and translated by Jack Zipes. New York: Bantam Books, 1992. This is perhaps the best of the many translations in English. The introduction is informative and provides data on the informants the Grimm brothers used in their research. Also included are thirty-two tales that the Grimms dropped from earlier editions, as well as eight variants showing how the Grimms edited and recreated tales as they were compiling their collection.

_____. *The Complete Grimm's Fairy Tales*. Edited and translated by Padraic Colum. New York: Pantheon Books, 1972. This edition is famous for a fine thirty-page commentary by renowned mythologist Joseph Campbell.

_____. *Grimms' Tales for Young and Old: The Complete Stories*. Edited and translated by Ralph Man-heim. New York: Anchor/Doubleday, 1977. Another standard translation.

Kamenetsky, Christa. *The Brothers Grimm and Their Critics: Folktales and the Quest for Meaning*. Athens: Ohio University Press, 1994. Kamenetsky provides a good literary and social analysis.

McGlathery, James. *Grimm's Fairy Tales: A History of Criticism of a Popular Classic*. Columbia, S.C.: Camden House, 1993. McGlathery traces the place of the Grimm tales in popular German and Western literature.

Murphy, G. Ronald. *"The Owl," "The Raven," and "The Dove": The Religious Meaning of the Grimms' Magic Fairy Tales*. New York: Oxford University Press, 2000. Murphy maintains the Grimm brothers intended their tales to be Christian fables. He analyzes five stories, "Hansel and Gretel," "Little Red Riding Hood," "Snow White," "Cinderella," and "Sleeping Beauty," to interpret their religious meanings.

Paradiž, Valerie. *Clever Maids: The Secret History of the Grimm Fairy Tales*. New York: Basic Books, 2005. Paradiž describes how the Grimms got their stories from educated young women in Kassel, and provides information about the lives of these women, including the Grimms' sister, Lotte, and the woman who later married Wilhelm.

Peppard, Murry. *Paths Through the Forest: A Biography of the Brothers Grimm*. New York: Holt, Rinehart and Winston, 1971. An approachable general biography.

Tatar, Maria. *The Hard Facts of the Grimms' Fairy Tales*. 2d ed. expanded. Princeton, N.J.: Princeton University Press, 2003. Traces the evolution of the tales through manuscript form and various editions. Tater contends that the brothers eventually gave up their scholarly efforts to reproduce folk poetry, continually sanitizing and revising each new edition to make the tales more acceptable to parents and children.

Zipes, Jack. *The Brothers Grimm: From the Enchanted Forest to the Modern World*. New York: Routledge, 1988. A good biography and criticism by one of the foremost Grimm translators.

SEE ALSO: Hans Christian Andersen; L. Frank Baum; Heinrich Heine; Engelbert Humperdinck.

RELATED ARTICLES in *Great Events from History: The Nineteenth Century, 1801-1900:* 1812-1815: Brothers Grimm Publish Fairy Tales; May 8, 1835: Andersen Publishes His First Fairy Tales.

SIR WILLIAM ROBERT GROVE
English physicist

Although trained as a lawyer, Grove invented the electric cell that bears his name. He also discovered and popularized the conservation of energy principle and helped to reform the Royal Society of London.

BORN: July 11, 1811; Swansea, Glamorganshire, Wales
DIED: August 1, 1896; London, England
AREAS OF ACHIEVEMENT: Physics, science and technology

EARLY LIFE

William Robert Grove was the only son of Anne Bevan and John Grove; his father was a magistrate and deputy lieutenant for Glamorganshire. After receiving instruction from private tutors, Grove attended Brasenose College, Oxford, graduating with a bachelor's degree in 1832 and a master's degree in 1835. It appeared that he was fated to follow his father in the legal profession. He was admitted as a law student at Lincoln's Inn on November 11, 1831, and was called to the bar on November 23, 1835. On May 27, 1837, he married Emma Maria Powles, daughter of John Diston Powles of Summit House, Middlesex. They had two sons and four daughters.

Despite his preparation for a legal career, Grove had always been interested in science. In 1835, he appeared to suffer from bad health and turned from law to science, becoming a member of the Royal Institution in that same year. His scientific curiosity was drawn to the electric cell, invented by Alessandro Volta in 1800. As it evolved before 1835, the typical cell consisted of two pieces of different metals, called electrodes, placed in either one or two chemical solutions, called electrolytes. These cells were weak and provided current for only the shortest periods of time as a consequence of a phenomenon called polarization.

One of the first practical solutions to the problems of polarization was that of John Frederic Daniell, professor of chemistry at King's College, London. Unlike Grove, Daniell was a member of the Royal Society of London, which had awarded Daniell its prestigious Rumford Medal in 1832 for an improved pyrometer, an instrument for measuring very high temperatures. The Daniell cell, as it came to be called, brought its inventor another distinguished honor from the Royal Society, the Copley Medal, in 1837.

Starting in 1835, Grove experimented with different electrodes and electrolytes. In 1839, he hit upon the com-

bination that became the standard form of his cell: a zinc electrode in dilute sulfuric acid and a platinum electrode in strong nitric acid. A porous membrane separated the two acids and eliminated polarization, the same means used in the Daniell cell. Grove's electrodes and electrolytes were different, however, and provided about twice the voltage of the Daniell cell and a current of up to ten amperes.

From a technical point of view, Grove had invented a superior cell. However, it was not practical. Platinum was expensive. Worse, as the cell operated, the platinum and concentrated nitric acid reacted to create poisonous gas. The German chemist Robert Bunsen, inventor of the laboratory burner of the same name, substituted an inexpensive carbon electrode for the platinum in 1841. This variation somewhat decreased the cell's voltage, but it doubled the current produced. The higher cost of nitric versus sulfuric acid made the Grove-Bunsen cell costlier per unit than the Daniell cell. In terms of voltage and amperage, however, the Grove-Bunsen cell provided significant savings over the Daniell cell and became the workhorse battery for applications requiring large currents, especially early forms of electrical lighting, long-distance telegraph lines, and the growing electroplating industry.

The invention of his cell immediately helped Grove's scientific career and brought him honor. On November 26, 1840, he was elected a Fellow of the Royal Society of London. The next year, he was appointed professor of experimental philosophy (physics) at the Royal Institution, a position he held until 1847. The only cloud on the horizon was Daniell, who accused Grove of having stolen his idea. Grove denied the charges in a series of letters published in the *Philosophical Magazine* in 1842 and early 1843. The subject of the dispute was the use of the porous membrane, which the French scientist Antoine César Becquerel had used as early as 1829. Despite the sharp language of their letters, the two men did not become bitter enemies.

LIFE'S WORK

Grove's scientific work did not end with the electric cell, which he continually improved. The focus of his later work was the same as that which had brought him to study the cell in the first place: an understanding of the relationship between electrical and chemical phenomena. Throughout 1839 and 1840, he published the results of his experiments in British, French, and German scientific journals.

In 1841, Grove published an article on a method for etching daguerreotype plates. The daguerreotype was the first photographic process and involved chemically fixing an image on a metallic plate. At that time, there was no process for reproducing a number of prints from a negative. Grove devised an electrochemical process that converted the daguerreotype plate into a reverse etching from which positive copies could be printed.

Grove was especially interested in the possibility of using gases rather than liquids as electrolytes in electric batteries. Into sealed test tubes of hydrogen and oxygen, he inserted platinum strips so that one end was in the gas and the other end rested in a dilute solution of sulfuric acid. Grove discovered that a current flowed from one platinum strip to the other. He published his findings in 1842 and called this device his "gaseous voltaic battery." Later, he used hydrogen and chlorine gas and increased the current produced.

Grove used his gas battery to decompose water into hydrogen and oxygen gas. He noted the electrical current created as a result of the chemical activity of the cell and the ability of that current to separate water chemically into hydrogen and oxygen. In short, it was a process of chemical and electrical energy conversions. As Grove wrote in 1842 in the *Philosophical Magazine*:

> This battery establishes that gases in combining and acquiring a liquid form evolve sufficient force to decompose a similar liquid and cause it to acquire a gaseous form. This is to my mind the most interesting effect of the battery; it exhibits such a beautiful instance of the correlation of natural forces.

The "correlation of natural forces" was the subject of his Royal Institution lecture given on January 19, 1842, on advances in the physical sciences since the institution's founding. He further developed the subject during his lectures that year. For Grove, the "correlation of natural forces" meant that the forces of nature, such as electricity, magnetism, heat, light, and chemical energy, could be converted into one another, could neither be created nor destroyed, and were manifestations of a single force. It was a new idea that captured the excitement and built upon the discoveries of such contemporary scientists as Jöns Jakob Berzelius of Sweden, who attempted to explain all chemical reactions in terms of electricity; Hans Christian Oersted, the Dane who demonstrated the conversion of electricity into magnetism; and the English-

man Michael Faraday, who showed the production of magnetism from electricity.

The principle that Grove lectured about is fundamental to the modern understanding of the physical universe. Grove's single force that revealed itself as various physical forces such as electricity and light is now called energy. The "correlation of natural forces" is known as the conservation of energy, which was discovered simultaneously by a number of scientists. In addition to Grove, Faraday in England, Hermann von Helmholtz (a physicist), and Justus von Liebig (a chemist) in Germany, to name a few, published articles and other works during the 1840's, setting forth the principle of energy conservation. The large number of laboratory experiments that illustrated transformations of one force into another, especially electrical and chemical ones, led Grove to give his lectures on the convertibility of physical forces. He also made reference to Samuel Taylor Coleridge, the English writer and proponent of German *Naturphilosophie*, a philosophical movement that had lead many in Germany to discover the conservation principle as well.

Grove's importance for the discovery of the conservation of energy was also his role as a science popularizer. Whereas others published their findings in the major scientific journals of the day, Grove first developed his ideas in the popular lectures he gave as professor of experimental philosophy at the Royal Institution in 1842. Over the next year, he refined these lectures, and the Royal Institution published the kernel of Grove's ideas in 1846 as the fifty-two-page booklet *On the Correlation of Physical Forces: Being the Substance of a Course of Lectures Delivered in the London Institution, in the Year 1843*.

From this rather modest start, *On the Correlation of Physical Forces* grew in size from edition to edition and spread Grove's ideas throughout England as well as overseas. The second edition appeared in 1850 and was more than one hundred pages. The 1855 third edition was more than two hundred pages and was translated into French in 1856 and German in 1863. The fourth edition (1862) was nearly three hundred pages long and was republished in 1865 as the first American edition. The fifth edition (1867) was more than three hundred pages, and the sixth edition (1874) almost five hundred pages.

In addition to popularizing scientific knowledge, Grove was highly interested in scientific institutions. He was an original member of the London Chemical Society and president of the British Association for the Advancement of Science in 1866. Elected a Fellow of the Royal Society of London in 1840, he was voted a member of the

Council in 1845, a year when prominent members who wished to raise the society's standards were considering asking the government for a new charter. Grove joined the Charter Committee and played a significant role in realizing a number of reforms, such as the limitation of membership numbers, which were approved by the Council in 1847. Grove was also a member of the 1849 committee charged with reforming the process for awarding the society's important Royal Medal.

As a consequence of his reform efforts, Grove was proposed as a candidate to fill a vacant society secretary post in 1848, but lost because of fighting between representatives of the physical and life sciences. As late as 1870, he was considered as a candidate for president of the Royal Society and continued to play an active role in the society's life into the 1880's.

Although maintaining an interest in the reform of the Royal Society and revising his book on the conservation of energy, Grove ceased to conduct experiments, perhaps because of his growing family (six children). He pursued a more financially rewarding career in law starting in 1853. In this, too, he excelled. In November, 1853, he became a member of the Queen's Court. Between 1862 and 1864, he combined his knowledge of science and law as a member of the Royal Commission on patent law.

Grove then distinguished himself as a judge in various courts. He became a judge in common pleas court on November 30, 1871; a justice of the high court, November 1, 1875; and member of the queen's bench division, December 16, 1880. He was knighted at Osborne, February 21, 1872. Grove retired from the bench in September, 1887, and wrote a number of odd philosophical works on the equilibrium of forces in nature before his death in 1896.

The high point of Grove's legal career was his defense of William Palmer, the Rugeley poisoner. Palmer had been dismissed from his apprenticeship with a Liverpool wholesale druggist for embezzlement. Apprenticed to a surgeon, he ran away after some misconduct. He eventually learned some medicine, became a member of the Royal College of Surgeons, and started a general practice. He then gave this up, was married, and devoted himself to horse racing as an owner and breeder. Palmer was also a gambler and ran up enormous debts.

On September 29, 1854, Palmer's wife died of "bilious cholera" and Palmer collected thirteen thousand pounds in life insurance. His brother Walter died suddenly and suspiciously the next year. Palmer did not receive any of the thirteen thousand pounds of insurance

policies that he had on his brother. On December 15, 1855, Palmer was arrested and charged with poisoning his friend John Parsons Cook, a betting man. The multiple poisonings troubled the area's residents, who attributed a number of mysterious local deaths to the Rugeley poisoner, as Palmer came to be called. The case was therefore tried elsewhere, at the Old Bailey, on May 14, 1856. News of the trial and Palmer's poisoning of his wife, brother, and friend spread throughout England and Europe. Grove was Palmer's defense attorney. Palmer was found guilty and hanged at Stafford on June 14, 1856.

SIGNIFICANCE

Although dynamos driven by steam and water turbines provide homes and industries with an enormous amount of electric power, the predecessor of these large-scale generating systems was the electric battery. The multitude of nineteenth century electrical applications that preceded the dynamo, such as electroplating, telegraphy, telephony, railroad signals, doorbells, electric clocks, even electric motors and lights, depended upon the availability of a steady, inexpensive source of current. The batteries of the early decades of the nineteenth century were incapable of operating over extended periods because of polarization. The Daniell cell solved that problem inexpensively and set the stage for industrial use of the battery. Grove's cell provided an even higher voltage and amperage, both necessary for the increasingly larger-scale uses of the battery during the 1850's and 1860's. By 1870, the use of the Grove-Bunsen cell had grown to such an enormous extent, with many telegraph stations and electroplating plants each employing hundreds of them, that an alternative was sought: the dynamo.

As significant as the Grove-Bunsen cell was in the early development of electrical technology, Sir William Robert Grove's discovery of the conservation of energy has had more enduring impact. Energy conservation—the idea that energy is neither created nor destroyed—is fundamental to an understanding of the physical universe. Although he was not its sole discoverer, Grove was an important popularizer of the concept at a time when amateurs could and did make major contributions to scientific knowledge. This, undoubtedly, more than any of his other work, was the basis for Grove's scientific reputation during his lifetime.

Far less known, however, are Grove's efforts to reform the Royal Society of London. The consequence of those reforms increasingly turned the society into an organization of professional scientists. Since then, the growing professionalization of science and scientists has also left its mark on education, funding, and a range of other activities. Today, science often entails team research, specialized training, and multibillion-dollar equipment. The gifted, curiosity-driven amateur, such as Grove, is the exception. Ironically, Grove's reforms have contributed to the creation of a world that would have excluded him.

—Andrew J. Butrica

FURTHER READING

Dunsheath, Percy. *A History of Electrical Power Engineering*. Cambridge, Mass.: MIT Press, 1962. Dunsheath places the invention of Grove's cell within the history of batteries as well as electrical engineering in general.

"The Future of Fuel Cells." *Scientific American* 281, no. 1 (July, 1999): 72. An overview of fuel cell technology, including an explanation of Grove's 1839 research.

Grove, William Robert. *Address to the British Association for the Advancement of Science*. London: Longmans, Green, 1867. President of the British Association for the Advancement of Science in 1866, Grove delivered this speech on August 22, 1866, at the society's meeting in Nottingham. Its subject was Grove's favorite: the conservation of energy.

_____. *On the Correlation of Physical Forces: Being the Substance of a Course of Lectures Delivered in the London Institution, in the Year 1843*. 6th ed. London: Longmans, Green, 1874. This volume provides Grove's arguments in favor of the conservation of energy. The first edition reproduces the original series of lectures at the Royal Institution. Later editions include revisions and new material. The sixth edition also contains reprints of many of Grove's early scientific papers.

Hall, Marie Boas. *All Scientists Now: The Royal Society in the Nineteenth Century*. Cambridge, England: Cambridge University Press, 1984. Hall discusses Grove's role as a reformer of the Royal Society of London, though this book is mainly concerned with the evolution of the society from an amateur to a professional organization of scientists in the nineteenth century.

Hoogers, Gregor, ed. *Fuel Cell Technology Handbook*. Boca Raton, Fla.: CRC Press, 2002. Describes the principles of fuel cell technology and their applications. Includes a brief history of fuel cell development, including information on Grove's discovery of the basic technology in 1839.

Kuhn, Thomas S. "Energy Conservation as an Example of Simultaneous Discovery." In *Critical Problems in the History of Science*, edited by Marshall Clagett. Madison: University of Wisconsin Press, 1959. Reprinted in Thomas S. Kuhn, *The Essential Tension*. Chicago: University of Chicago Press, 1977. An important work for understanding the discovery of energy conservation by Grove and others. It underlines the role of laboratory experiments and German *Naturphilosophie*.

Moore, Keith. "First Cell." *Professional Engineering* 17, no. 13 (July 28, 2004): 50. Describes Grove's fuel cell experiments and the technology he developed.

Webb, K. R. "Sir William Robert Grove (1811-1896) and the Origins of the Fuel Cell." *Journal of the Royal Institute of Chemistry* 85 (1961): 291-293. A short article on what Grove called his "gaseous voltaic battery," which led him to his understanding of the conservation of energy.

SEE ALSO: The Becquerel Family; Samuel Taylor Coleridge; Michael Faraday; Justus von Liebig.

RELATED ARTICLES in *Great Events from History: The Nineteenth Century, 1801-1900:* October 21, 1879: Edison Demonstrates the Incandescent Lamp; December 15, 1900: General Electric Opens Research Laboratory.

SIR ROBERT ABBOTT HADFIELD
English metallurgist

Hadfield's discovery of manganese steel ushered in the age of alloy steels, which have proven to be essential to the development of modern industrial technology and weapons.

BORN: November 28, 1858; Attercliffe, near Sheffield, England

DIED: September 30, 1940; Kingston Hill, Surrey, England

AREA OF ACHIEVEMENT: Science and technology

EARLY LIFE

Robert Abbott Hadfield was the only son of Robert Hadfield and Marianne Abbott. His father was the owner of Hadfield's Steel Foundry and one of England's pioneers in the manufacture of steel castings, an important step in the development of the English arms industry.

After studying at the Collegiate School in Sheffield, Hadfield chose to forgo further formal education at either Oxford or Cambridge, probably an early indication of his belief that learning by doing was superior to acquiring knowledge solely from books. Instead, in 1875 he briefly apprenticed with the local steel firm of Jonas and Colver. He also received private tuition in chemistry and established a personal laboratory in the basement of the family home. After only a few months at Jonas and Colver, Hadfield entered the family business, while at the same time initiating his systematic research into alloys. Combining a tremendous capacity for work with a practical interest in the efficient organization of labor, Hadfield managed to be highly productive both as a businessperson and as an experimental metallurgist.

LIFE'S WORK

It was during a visit to the Paris Exhibition in 1878 that Hadfield learned of the researches of the Terre Noire Company regarding the introduction of manganese into steel. They had discovered that adding up to 3 percent manganese hardened steel, but increasing the amount beyond that level left the steel extremely brittle. Hadfield decided to expand upon the French experiments by combining both manganese and silicon with steel in varying amounts.

Except for a break in the summer of 1882 to visit American steel-making facilities, especially those in Pittsburgh, Chicago, and Philadelphia, Hadfield worked on the first phase of his experiments on steel alloys for approximately four years. He increased the percentage of manganese considerably, ultimately discovering in late 1882 that 12 to 14 manganese produced a steel alloy of novel properties, relatively soft, yet resistant to crushing and abrasion. He patented his discoveries in 1883-1884, while spending five additional years confirming his results. Not until 1887 did he publicly display his new product.

At the age of twenty-four, Hadfield had taken responsibility for the family firm because of his father's failing health. Upon the death of his father in 1888, he became chairman and managing director of Hadfield's Steel Foundry. Having discovered manganese steel was only the first step for a practical businessperson. Hadfield still had to find commercial uses for it. He turned to the United States, which had impressed him greatly during his visit, as a potential market. (He would later turn to the United States for his bride, marrying Frances Belt Wickersham of Philadelphia in 1894.)

The first attempted commercial application of manganese steel was railway car wheels, but the alloy proved unsatisfactory. Hadfield quickly learned, however, that it was superior to other metals for railway rails and switches. Other uses for the alloy were in ore-crushing machinery, paper-pulp beaters, and burglar-proof safes. The mining industry was revolutionized: Manganese steel dredge buckets could be twice as large and operate at much greater depths than their predecessors. The alloy also proved to be ideal for tank treads, steel helmets for soldiers, and other forms of modern military technology.

Another Hadfield discovery during the 1880's was a low-carbon silicon steel alloy. Although patented in 1883, silicon steel attracted little interest until the first decade of the twentieth century. Again, the United States provided the market. Silicon steel proved to be the solution to energy losses in alternating-current transformers, increasing the efficiency of the transformers from 68 to 99 percent.

Hadfield's metallurgical research generally followed a standard pattern. Having decided to investigate the influence of a given element on steel, he would create a large number of alloys, steadily increasing the proportion of the added element. Each alloy would be tested for its mechanical, electrical, and magnetic properties, with an eye for possible industrial applications. Later in his career, Hadfield would collaborate with physicists in his investigations, providing them with alloys for experiments, for example, on the effect of very low temperatures on metals. He also became extremely interested in the history of metals and encouraged archaeological research into the antiquity of iron.

Success as a metallurgist was complemented by success in business. During his lifetime, combining great energy, technical expertise, and enlightened labor policies, Hadfield turned the family firm into one of the world's largest steel foundries. In 1891, he introduced the eight-hour day into his firm, one of the earliest examples of this reform. Not surprisingly, such policies were rewarded by a loyal workforce.

Photographs of the mature Hadfield show a high forehead, hooded eyes, and a full mustache. The impression is more of a scientist than a captain of industry. The elderly Hadfield looked much the same, except that the mustache had turned gray.

Hadfield won numerous honors. The Iron and Steel Institute awarded him its Bessemer Gold Medal in 1904. Knighted in 1908, he was made a baronet in 1917. He was elected a Fellow of the Royal Society of London in 1909, in recognition of his contributions to the field of metallurgy, and served as president of the Faraday Society from 1913 through 1920. In 1939, he was awarded

Sir Robert Abbott Hadfield. (Library of Congress)

the freedom of the city of Sheffield. In 1940, Hadfield died at home, on September 30.

SIGNIFICANCE

Sir Robert Abbott Hadfield was an important figure in the maturation of the British steel industry. When he entered the family firm, the Sheffield foundries were very traditional in their methods and their products. Trial and error was the system that governed the firms that had made Sheffield the world's leading steel-making center during the first half of the nineteenth century. There had been little or no interaction with the scientific community. Hadfield helped change that. Combining a systematic experimental approach, seemingly boundless energy, and an eye for the ever-increasing American market, he initiated the age of alloy steels.

Hadfield's genius did not lie in his methodology, which was essentially to interrogate nature slowly but surely, but in his rejection of his contemporaries' tendency to accept unproven assumptions about steel alloys rather than conduct tests and in his enthusiastic recognition of the potential of his discovery when others were indifferent. He saw the revolutionary possibilities when most steel makers did not. Once he proved the economic value of his experiments, however, others followed his example. The most significant of the later breakthroughs was the discovery of stainless steel by a fellow resident of Sheffield, Harry Brearley, in 1912.

Alloy steels have proven vital to the development of modern technology. In the United States in particular, the expansion of the railway system during the late nineteenth century and the progress of electrification during the early twentieth century were both dependent on Hadfield's discoveries. Indeed, so was the British military, which utilized the alloys for defensive purposes, such as steel helmets, and offensive purposes, such as armor-piercing shells. Hadfield's work, of clear benefit in many ways, helpful in the scientist's unraveling of the mysteries of metals, could also be applied in destructive ways. In that property it was not unique.

—*Marc Rothenberg*

FURTHER READING

Carr, James C., and Walter Taplin. *A History of the British Steel Industry*. Cambridge, Mass.: Harvard University Press, 1952. A standard history for the period after the mid-nineteenth century that puts Hadfield's work in perspective.

Desch, C. H. "Sir Robert Abbott Hadfield." Revised by Geoffrey Tweedale. In *Oxford Dictionary of National Biography*, edited by H. C. G. Matthew and Brian

Harrison. New York: Oxford University Press, 2004. This brief biography summarizes Hadfield's life and achievements.

"From Hammers to Gammas." *Professional Engineering* 11, no. 15 (August 5, 1998): 15. Discusses the family-owned Hadfield East Hecla steel works at Tinsley, Sheffield, England, including information on the equipment, machinery, and technology used there. Includes background information on Hadfield's career and management of his family's company.

Hadfield, Robert A. *Metallurgy and Its Influence on Modern Progress.* London: Chapman and Hall, 1925. Presents Hadfield's own views on his work and its impact.

Smith, Cyril S. *A History of Metallography: The Development of Ideas on the Structure of Metals Before 1890.* Chicago: University of Chicago Press, 1960. Provides an extensive discussion of metallurgical theory and the state of knowledge prior to Hadfield's experiments.

Tweedale, Geoffrey. "Metallurgy and Technological Change: A Case Study of Sheffield Specialty Steel and America, 1830-1930." *Technology and Culture* 27 (April, 1986): 189-222. Tweedale looks at the changing state of the Sheffield steel industry and the importance of the American market for the firms.

_____. "Sir Robert Abbott Hadfield, F.R.S. (1858-1940), and the Discovery of Manganese Steel." *Notes and Records of the Royal Society* 40 (November, 1985): 63-73. An account of Hadfield's early experimental work based on an analysis of his diaries, notebooks, and letters.

_____. *Steel City: Entrepreneurship, Strategy, and Technology in Sheffield, 1743-1993.* New York: Oxford University Press, 1995. Charts the rise and fall of Sheffield's steel industry, including information on Hadfield and his family's steel works.

SEE ALSO: Sir Henry Bessemer; Andrew Carnegie; James Buchanan Eads.

RELATED ARTICLE in *Great Events from History: The Nineteenth Century, 1801-1900:* 1855: Bessemer Patents Improved Steel-Processing Method.

ERNST HAECKEL
German biologist

Haeckel classified many marine organisms, especially the radiolaria and the medusae. He is most noted for his refinement of Charles Darwin's theory of evolution, its extension to humankind and the origin of life, the refinement of the biogenetic law, and the development of monism as a religion.

BORN: February 16, 1834; Potsdam, Prussia (now in Germany)
DIED: August 9, 1919; Jena, Germany
ALSO KNOWN AS: Ernst Heinrich Philipp August Haeckel (full name)
AREA OF ACHIEVEMENT: Biology

EARLY LIFE
Ernst Heinrich Philipp August Haeckel (HEHK-ehl) was the son of Karl and Charlotte Sethe Haeckel. Both his Haeckel and Sethe relatives contributed prominently to German history and intermarried on several occasions. In both families there were several prominent lawyers. Karl Haeckel was a state councillor. Shortly after Ernst was born, his family moved to Meresburg. There, he attended school until he was eighteen. As a boy he had a great love of nature, which was fostered by his mother. He collected and classified many plants as a youth; his father occasionally gave him words of encouragement. He had a strong sense of independence and individuality, and even as a youth he was a compulsive worker.

In 1852, Ernst entered the University of Jena to work with Matthias Schleiden, a codeveloper of the cell theory. Schleiden taught him how to combine his interests in botany and philosophy. Not long after entering Jena, however, he became ill and had to return to Berlin to stay with his parents. He entered the University of Würzburg in the fall of 1852 to work with the botanist Alexander Braun. His father's persistence, however, made him turn his attention to medicine. While at Würzburg, he studied under Albert Kölliker, Franz Leydig, and Rudolf Virchow. At Würzburg, he developed an interest in embryology.

The philosophy at Würzburg, where learning through research was emphasized, was well suited for the young Haeckel. Natural phenomena were explained and studied through cause-and-effect relationships and allowed little opportunity for the intrusion of mysticism and the supernatural. These philosophies laid the foundation for Haeckel's future work.

LIFE'S WORK

During the summer of 1854, Haeckel had the opportunity to study comparative anatomy under Johannes Müller. Müller gave Haeckel permission to work in the museum. During that summer, Müller took the young Haeckel to sea, where he taught him how to study living marine organisms. Haeckel stayed the winter at Berlin and wrote his first essay under the great Müller. In the spring of 1885, Haeckel returned to Würzburg, where, under Kölliker's influence, he earned a medical degree in 1857 with a zoological/anatomical emphasis rather than a strictly medical one. Although Haeckel earned a medical degree, he seldom practiced medicine. This resulted from the fact that he spent most of his time studying marine animals and saw patients only from 5:00 to 6:00 A.M. During his first year of practice, he saw only three patients.

In the winter of 1859-1860, Haeckel studied the radiolaria collected off Messina. This project laid the foundation for his interest and future work in zoology. By the spring of 1860, he had discovered 144 new species of radiolaria. His work at Messina culminated in the publication of *Die Radiolarien* (*Report on the Radiolaria*, 1887) in 1862. This work was one of his finest and most influential, and it established his position as a zoologist. After a fifteen-year hiatus, he again pursued the study of radiolaria and published the second, third, and fourth parts of *Report on the Radiolaria* from 1887 to 1888. He eventually classified more than thirty-five hundred species of radiolaria.

In March, 1861, he was appointed private teacher at the University of Jena, and in 1862 he was appointed extraordinary professor of zoology at the Zoological Museum. In 1865, he became a professor at Jena. In August, 1862, he married his cousin, Anna Sethe. Anna died two

---

MONISM

In an extemporaneous lecture that Ernst Haeckel delivered at Altenburg, Germany, in October, 1892, he outlined his views on monism.

At the outset, I am entirely at one with [Professor Schlesinger] as to that unifying conception of nature as a whole which we designate in a single word as Monism. By this we unambiguously express our conviction that there lives "one spirit in all things," and that the whole cognisable world is constituted, and has been developed, in accordance with one common fundamental law. We emphasise by it, in particular, the essential unity of inorganic and organic nature, the latter having been evolved from the former only at a relatively late period. We cannot draw a sharp line of distinction between these two great divisions of nature, any more than we can recognise an absolute distinction between the animal and the vegetable kingdom, or between the lower animals and man. Similarly, we regard the whole of human knowledge as a structural unity; in this sphere we refuse to accept the distinction usually drawn between the natural and the spiritual. The latter is only a part of the former (or *vice versa*); both are one. Our monistic view of the world belongs, therefore, to that group of philosophical systems which from other points of view have been designated also as mechanical or as pantheistic. However differently expressed in the philosophical systems of an Empedocles or a Lucretius, a Spinoza or a Giordano Bruno, a Lamarck or a David Strauss, the fundamental thought common to them all is ever that of the oneness of the cosmos, of the indissoluble connection between energy and matter, between mind and embodiment—or, as we may also say, between God and the world—to which [Johann Wolfgang von] Goethe, Germany's greatest poet and thinker, has given poetical expression in his *Faust* and in the wonderful series of poems entitled *Gott und Welt*.

That we may rightly appreciate what this Monism is, let us now, from a philosophico-historical point of view cast a comprehensive glance over the development in time of man's knowledge of nature. A long series of varied conceptions and stages of human culture here passes before our mental vision....

Source: Ernst Haeckel, *Monism as Connecting Religion and Science: The Confession of Faith of a Man of Science*, translated by J. Gilchrist (London, 1895).

---

years later at the age of twenty-nine. Stricken with grief over the loss of his beloved wife, he became a hermit and a compulsive worker, often surviving on only three to four hours of sleep each day. In 1867, he married Agnes Huschke.

In May, 1860, Haeckel read Charles Darwin's *On the Origin of Species by Means of Natural Selection* (1859). The book profoundly influenced Haeckel's intellectual development, and he became Germany's most devout supporter and popularizer of Darwinism. It has often been said that without Haeckel there would have been Darwin, but there would not have been Darwinism. Haeckel came to view evolution as the basis for the explanation of all nature.

Haeckel, whose faith was enfeebled by the study of comparative anatomy and physiology, was also profoundly influenced by his friend Johann Wolfgang von Goethe and became a believer in Goethe's God of Nature. Haeckel no longer believed in a Creator, because Darwin's theory permitted him to explain nature without divine influence. This enabled Haeckel to accept Darwinism better than Darwin. For Haeckel, it became possible to develop a philosophy of nature without having to interject God or a vital force. Haeckel's support of Darwinism made him the target of attack by his German colleagues, many of whom were doubters of Darwinian ideas. Haeckel first revealed his belief in Darwinism in *Report on the Radiolaria*. He acknowledges that in the radiolaria there are several transitional forms that connect the various groups and that they form "a fairly continuous chain of related forms," and he expresses his "belief in the mutability of species and the real genealogical relation of all organisms."

In an address to the Scientific Congress of 1863, eight years before Darwin published *The Descent of Man and Selection in Relation to Sex* (1871), Haeckel said that humans must recognize their immediate ancestors in apelike mammals. He realized, however, that Darwin's theory may not be perfect and may need refinement. He especially realized that it explained neither the origin of the first living organism nor how humans were connected to the genealogical tree. Haeckel thought that the first living organism was a single cell, a cell even more primitive than the eukaryotic cell. Not long afterward, the prokaryotic cell, a primitive cell without a nucleus, was described. After studying the brains and skulls of the primates, Haeckel produced a genealogical tree that showed the relationship of humans to the other primates and to lower animals.

During the mid-1860's, Haeckel began to study the medusae, a study that culminated in the publication of *Das System der Medusen* (*Report on the Deep-Sea Medusae*, 1882) in 1879. The treatise was a detailed description of the medusae. During the later 1860's, he studied the social aspects of the medusae.

Haeckel's greatest achievement was his *Generelle Morphologie der Organismen*, published in 1866. The monograph is considered a landmark and one of the most important scientific works of the latter half of the nineteenth century. In *Generelle Morphologie der Organismen*, Haeckel clearly presented his reductionist philosophy. He reduced the cell to the laws of chemistry and physics, and through the influence of Darwin, raised the study of zoology to that of the physical sciences.

He strengthened the laws of evolution, refined the biogenetic law, and presented a philosophy of life and a new story of its creation. In it, too, he described his early education as defective, perverse, and filled with errors. He lambasted the educational system that emphasized memory of dead material that interferes with normal intellectual development.

In *Generelle Morphologie der Organismen*, Haeckel presented two ideas, monism and the biogenetic law, which would occupy the rest of his life. The biogenetic law, which was originally proposed by Darwin, was refined and expanded by Haeckel. According to the biogenetic law, ontogeny recapitulates phylogeny, which means that during embryological development animals pass through developmental stages that represent adult stages from which the developing animal evolved. Haeckel viewed embryonic development of an individual animal as a brief and condensed recapitulation of its evolutionary history. Haeckel used the biogenetic law to strengthen his case for evolution. Although the law was eventually proved to be in error, it was accepted by many scientists and stimulated much discussion and research. In *Generelle Morphologie der Organismen*, he presented a genealogical tree with bacteria and single-celled organisms on the bottom. From the bacteria and single-celled organisms arose two branches: the animals and the plants.

In his search for a religion that did not rely on a vital force or a personal god, Haeckel developed monism, a scientific and philosophical doctrine that advocated nature as a substitute for religion. The basic principles of monism can be summarized as follows: Knowledge of the world is based on scientific knowledge acquired through human reason; the world is one great whole ruled by fixed laws; there is no vital force that controls the laws of nature; living organisms have developed by evolution through descent; nothing in the universe was created by a Creator; living organisms originated from nonliving matter; humans and the apes are closely related and evolved from a common ancestor; God as a supreme being does not exist; and God is nature.

These outspoken and heretical ideas about God made Haeckel the target of attacks not only from the Church but also from his colleagues. Indeed, many of his colleagues called for his resignation as a professor, yet he stayed at Jena and raised it to the level of an intellectual metropolis. His reputation as a great scientist and thinker attracted many young, bright scientists to Jena.

Not being one to walk away from the battlefield and collapse under fire, Haeckel published *Natürliche Schöp-*

fungsgeschichte (*The History of Creation*, 1876) in 1868. This book was a condensation and a popularization on the ideas originally presented in *Generelle Morphologie der Organismen* and was written primarily for the layperson. In the book, Haeckel approached the problems of life through Darwinism. The book was attacked by theologians and by many scientists, but it became a best seller in its time.

The History of Creation was followed by *Anthropogenie* (1874; *The Evolution of Man*, 1879), a survey of all that was learned in the nineteenth century about the history of humankind, and *Die Weltratsel* (1899; *The Riddle of the Universe at the Close of the Nineteenth Century*, 1900), an intentionally provocative and popular study of monism that was translated into more than a dozen languages.

In his many popular writings, Haeckel unleashed a relentless attack on the Church and the clergy, which he thought preyed on the gullibility of the ignorant masses in order to further their selfish aims. He was criticized for being outspoken against established, organized religion while ignoring what his critics regarded as more serious ills of his country. He answered these charges in *Die Lebenswunder* (*The Wonders of Life*, 1904).

Haeckel founded the phyletic museum at the University of Jena and the Ernst Haeckel Haus to house his collections, books, and letters. He retired from active teaching and research in 1909 at the age of seventy-five and died at Jena in 1919.

SIGNIFICANCE

Ernst Haeckel was one of the greatest natural historians, zoologists, and philosophers of the nineteenth century. His descriptions of many marine organisms, especially of the radiolaria and the medusae, were monumental and unparalleled in the zoological sciences. He classified several thousand new species of plants and animals.

Moreover, Haeckel's knowledge of zoology provided him with a platform from which he launched an advocacy and popularization of the ideas of Darwin. He described evolution as "the most important advance that has been made in pure and applied science." He was quick to extend and develop Darwin's theory. He refined the biogenetic law and was one of the first to extend Darwin's ideas to the origin of life and humankind.

Haeckel's staunch support of Darwinism and his monistic philosophy alienated him from the clergy and from older scientists but attracted many younger scientists as disciples. Although he had many critics, more than five hundred university professors (many his critics) around

the world contributed to the making of a marble bust of Haeckel, which was unveiled at the University of Jena in 1894. Haeckel's ideas influenced a generation.

—*Charles L. Vigue*

FURTHER READING

Bölsche, Wilhelm. *Haeckel: His Life and Work*. Translated by Joseph McCabe. London: T. F. Unwin, 1902. This is the most extensive biography of Haeckel, and the only one to have been translated into English. It is an excellent account of Haeckel's work as a scientist and philosopher. Bölsche was one of Haeckel's students.

De Grood, David H. *Haeckel's Theory of the Unity of Nature: A Monograph in the History of Philosophy*. Boston: Christopher, 1965. Originally written as a master's thesis, it was reprinted in 1982 by Gruner of Amsterdam. Summarizes Haeckel's monistic philosophy.

Gasman, Daniel. *Haeckel's Monism and the Birth of Fascist Philosophy*. New York: P. Lang, 1998. Examines monist philosophy and its role in encouraging the birth of fascist ideology in Italy and France.

_____. *The Scientific Origins of National Socialism*. New Brunswick, N.J.: Transaction, 2004. Traces the connections between Darwinism, Haeckel's theory of monism, and other scientific ideas to Nazi racial doctrines.

Gould, Stephen Jay. "Abscheulich! (Atrocious!)" *Natural History* 109, no. 2 (March, 2000): 42. Describes the lives of Haeckel and two other scientists—Louis Agassiz and Karl Ernst von Baer—who became involved in the debate over Darwin's theory of evolution. Explains the trio's contributions to the debate.

Haeckel, Ernst. *The Evolution of Man*. Translated by Joseph McCabe. New York: G. P. Putnam's Sons, 1905. The first edition to be translated into English.

_____. *The Riddle of the Universe*. Translated by Joseph McCabe. New York: Harper & Row, 1902. This book offers a popularization of Haeckel's monistic philosophy "for thoughtful readers . . . who are united in an honest search for the truth."

Hanken, James. "Beauty Beyond Belief." *Natural History* 107, no. 10 (December, 1998/January, 1999): 56. Details Haeckel's contributions and influence on evolutionary biology, including a discussion of his more controversial ideas.

Weikart, Richard. *From Darwin to Hitler: Evolutionary Ethics, Eugenics, and Racism in Germany*. New York: Palgrave Macmillan, 2004. Examines Darwin's influence on German ethics and morality. Weikert explains how Haeckel and other German thinkers believed Darwin had overturned Judeo-Christian ethics. He describes how Haeckel exalted evolutionary fitness as the highest form of morality; this concept would become a central element in Nazi racial dogma.

SEE ALSO: Louis Agassiz; Karl Ernst von Baer; Charles Darwin; Ellen Swallow Richards; Rudolf Virchow; August Weismann.
RELATED ARTICLES in *Great Events from History: The Nineteenth Century, 1801-1900:* November 24, 1859: Darwin Publishes *On the Origin of Species*; 1871: Darwin Publishes *The Descent of Man*.

H. RIDER HAGGARD
English writer

Haggard is remembered primarily as a writer of adventure stories set in exotic African locales. His most famous stories, King Solomon's Mines *and* She, *explore human nature and Victorian taboos while transporting readers into realms far removed from Western civilization.*

BORN: June 22, 1856; Wood Farm, West Bradenham, Norfolk, England
DIED: May 14, 1925; London, England
ALSO KNOWN AS: Henry Rider Haggard (full name); Sir H. Rider Haggard
AREA OF ACHIEVEMENT: Literature

EARLY LIFE

The son of a Norfolk landowner, Sir Henry Rider Haggard was born on the family's estate and spent most of his early years in Norfolk and London. As a child, he was a dreamy, imaginative boy who did not do well in school, perhaps taking after his mother, Ella Doveton Haggard, a quiet woman who wrote poetry. His hot-tempered father, William Haggard, had a low opinion of him and instead of sending him to university, as he had done his older sons, arranged for him to go to South Africa as an assistant to Sir Henry Bulwer, the lieutenant governor of Great Britain's Natal colony.

During the 1870's, South Africa was the site of conflicts among the native Zulu people, British colonists, and Afrikaner settlers—who were known to the British as Boers (Dutch for farmers). Haggard was only nineteen years old when he arrived in South Africa in August, 1875, and found himself caught up in the conflicts. In May, 1877, he personally helped raise the British flag in the Transvaal, an Afrikaner republic after it was annexed by the British. Later that same year, he became an official of the high court of the Transvaal Colony, in which capacity he accompanied the high court judge around the territory. The two men slept in a wagon, and Haggard's duties included shooting and cooking game for their meals.

After returning to England in 1879, Haggard met and married Louisa Margitson, a friend of one of his sisters, with whom he had four children, but with whom he never felt truly close. The woman he was actually in love with had rejected him and married someone else while he was in Africa. In 1880, Haggard and his new bride returned to South Africa, where Haggard intended to take up ostrich farming near the border between Natal and the Transvaal. However, continuing strife between Afrikaners of the occupied Afrikaner republics and the British made the area unsafe. The following year, Haggard decided to go back to England once more, this time to pursue a career as a lawyer.

LIFE'S WORK

Bored by the law, Haggard devoted his spare time while studying for the bar to writing. He had already written some articles while in Africa, including "A Zulu War Dance," which appeared in *Gentleman's Magazine* in July, 1877. He next wrote a book-length account of the political situation in South Africa, *Cetywayo and His White Neighbours* (1882). This book earned some respectful reviews, but it did not sell well, and Haggard decided to turn his hand to fiction. The result was *Dawn* (1884), a complicated novel about romantic intrigue and property disputes, which he followed up with *The Witch's Head* (1885), a semiautobiographical novel about a love triangle.

Neither of Haggard's first novels was successful with the public, although reviewers did praise the African sections of *The Witch's Head*. Haggard was contemplating giving up on his writing career and concentrating on the law when *Treasure Island* (1883), the recently published adventure story by Robert Louis Stevenson, came to his attention. The success of Stevenson's novel inspired Hag-

H. Rider Haggard. (Library of Congress)

gard to write an adventure story himself, and in 1885 he published *King Solomon's Mines*, a tale of three Englishmen seeking a fabled treasure in an uncharted region of Southern Africa.

Advertised as the most amazing book ever written, *King Solomon's Mines* was a huge success with both the public and reviewers, who praised its imagination and excitement. Haggard followed this success with *Allan Quatermain* (1887), a sequel to *King Solomon's Mines,* and *She* (1887), a story of a two-thousand-year-old white goddess ruling over an African tribe. *She* was even more successful than *King Solomon's Mines* with the general public, but some reviewers criticized its prose style and even accused Haggard of plagiarism. Haggard did not endear himself with reviewers when he published an article on fiction in 1887 in which he condemned most of the novels being published and said that only his style of adventure writing had merit.

Haggard wrote more adventure stories over the succeeding decades, including *Cleopatra* (1889), a tale of Egypt's famous queen; *Eric Brighteyes* (1891), a saga set in Iceland; and *Nada the Lily* (1892), a tale set among South Arica's Zulu people. In his later years, the quality of his stories declined, his readership decreased, and reviewers began to dismiss him as third-rate.

In these later years, Haggard turned his attention to political matters. He ran unsuccessfully as a Conservative Party candidate for Parliament in 1895. He also became an advocate for agricultural reform and several books on the topic, including *Rural England* (1902). He also became involved in several government commissions, including one established in 1906 to investigate coastal erosion and forests and another established in 1912 on the status of the British dominions, which included Canada, Australia, and South Africa.

In 1905, Haggard visited the United States to investigate the Salvation Army's labor communities and wrote a book, *The Poor and the Land*, during that same year recommending resettlement of the urban poor on farm land in the colonies. After World War I, he became involved in the anti-Bolshevik Liberty League. He was knighted in 1912.

On May 14, 1925, Haggard died in a London nursing home of complications following an operation, after he had been ill for several months. He had written his autobiography, *The Days of My Life*, in 1911, but it was not published until the year after his death.

SIGNIFICANCE

Haggard achieved his greatest success as the writer of adventure stories, a genre sometimes considered less serious than novels of social realism or character studies. However, he was greatly admired both by later serious authors, such as D. H. Lawrence and Graham Greene, and by social scientists such as the two founders of psychoanalysis, Sigmund Freud and Carl Jung.

Freud and Jung were both fascinated by Haggard's novel *She*, which they saw as presenting a picture of the eternal feminine archetype. For Jung, Haggard's work also revealed the deeper workings of the human psyche, the dark and savage powers lurking beneath the veneer of civilization. Haggard himself had his famous character, Allan Quatermain, say that Europeans were nineteen parts savage and only one part civilized. Interestingly, Haggard does not seem to condemn the savage parts of human beings; his books seem rather to celebrate the savagery, to show Europeans being liberated by escaping from the restraints of civilization, something that may have appealed to his readers in civilized England and that may appeal still to those who feel constrained by the modern world.

Haggard also was able to explore issues usually taboo in the Victorian period, from the varieties of sexual at-

HAGGARD'S BOOKS

NOVELS
1884　*Dawn*
1885　*The Witch's Head*
1885　*King Solomon's Mines*
1887　*She*
1887　*Allan Quatermain*
1887　*Jess*
1888　*Colonel Quarich, V. C.*
1889　*Cleopatra*
1890　*The World's Desire* (with Andre Lang)
1890　*Beatrice*
1891　*Eric Brighteyes*
1892　*Nada the Lily*
1893　*Montezuma's Daughter*
1894　*Hear of the World*
1905　*Ayesha*

NONFICTION
1882　*Cetywayo and His White Neighbours*
1902　*Rural England*
1905　*The Poor and the Land*
1926　*The Days of My Life*

traction through the hostility that lurks beneath politeness to the fate of the soul after death. He also created several memorable characters, most notably the central character of *She*, the beautiful but diabolical Ayesha, also known as "She Who Must Be Obeyed." Others included Gagool, the terrifying witch in *King Solomon's Mines*, and Allan Quatermain, the rough and grizzled hunter who narrates *King Solomon's Mines* and appears in seventeen other stories and novels by Haggard.

Haggard's work also influenced later writers of adventure and fantasy stories. Edgar Rice Burroughs, the creator of Tarzan, cited Haggard's work as one of his inspirations, and commentators have seen Haggard's influence in such works as J. R. R. Tolkien's *Lord of the Rings* (1955) and in the film *King Kong* (1933). *King Solomon's Mines* itself has also been filmed a number of times.

—Sheldon Goldfarb

FURTHER READING

Chrisman, Laura. *Rereading the Imperial Romance: British Imperialism and South African Resistance in Haggard, Schreiner, and Plaatje*. Oxford, England: Clarendon Press, 2000. This study sees Haggard as carrying out an imperial ideological project and focuses on the economic significance of *King Solomon's Mines*. The text may be difficult to understand for those not familiar with postmodernist vocabulary.

Cohen, Morton. *Rider Haggard: His Life and Works*. London: Hutchinson, 1960. Solid biographical study marred by a negative attitude toward Haggard's writings.

Ellis, Peter Berresford. *H. Rider Haggard: A Voice from the Infinite*. London: Routledge & Kegan Paul, 1978. Competent retelling of the biographical story. Includes illustrations and a detailed bibliography.

Etherington, Norman. *Rider Haggard*. Boston: Twayne, 1984. Provides insightful analysis of Haggard's writings. Also provides a useful biographical sketch, a chronology, and an annotated bibliography.

Fraser, Robert. *Victorian Quest Romance: Stevenson, Haggard, Kipling, and Conan Doyle*. Plymouth, England: Northcote House, 1998. Analyzes *King Solomon's Mines* and *She*. Warns against easy condemnations of Haggard as racist or imperialist.

Higgins, D. S. *Rider Haggard: The Great Storyteller*. London: Cassell, 1981. Detailed biographical study adding new information, though not always explaining where the new information is from. Includes illustrations, a bibliography, and a useful list of Haggard's writings.

Katz, Wendy R. *Rider Haggard and the Fiction of Empire: A Critical Study of British Imperial Fiction*. Cambridge, England: Cambridge University Press, 1987. Offers interesting insights into Haggard's works, but they are overshadowed by an extended attempt to prove that Haggard was an imperialist and a racist.

Low, Gail Ching-Liang. *White Skins/Black Masks: Representation and Colonialism*. New York: Routledge, 1996. Postmodernist analysis of Haggard's works, focusing on the exclusivity of the European male bonding that he portrays.

SEE ALSO: Cetshwayo; Sir Arthur Conan Doyle; Olive Schreiner; Shaka; Robert Louis Stevenson; Mark Twain.

RELATED ARTICLE in *Great Events from History: The Nineteenth Century, 1801-1900:* July, 1881-1883: Stevenson Publishes *Treasure Island*.

SAMUEL HAHNEMANN
German homeopath

Hahnemann founded the science of homeopathy, a healing method that follows the principle of treating like with like. That is, diseases are treated with substances that, used on a healthy person, create the very symptoms of the disease, but that, used in minute amounts, are believed to cure the symptoms in a sick person.

BORN: April 10, 1755; Meissen, Saxony (now in Germany)
DIED: July 2, 1843; Paris, France
ALSO KNOWN AS: Christian Friedrich Samuel Hahnemann (full name)
AREA OF ACHIEVEMENT: Medicine

EARLY LIFE

Christian Friedrich Samuel Hahnemann (HAH-nehmahn) was the son of Gottfried Hahnemann, a painter of fine china for a well-known pottery factory in Meissen. Hahnemann began studying in the local Latin School. Before he could finish, however, economic disaster struck the community when the factory was raided by a neighboring prince. The factory suffered a great loss, and the Hahnemann family was thrown into financial hardship. Thinking that his son needed to prepare for a trade so that he could more quickly make his own living, Hahnemann's father withdrew him from school and apprenticed him to a grocer. Hahnemann was, however, unwilling to leave his studies, so he ran away and returned home, where his schoolmaster arranged for him to continue his studies tuition-free in exchange for assisting in the teaching.

Hahnemann was a passionate scholar who often studied late into the night, even against the wishes of his parents. The fact that his schoolmaster recognized his brilliance is clear, both from the arrangements he was willing to make to return Hahnemann to school and from the fact that he put the young boy in charge of a class of students of Greek. Early on, Hahnemann's interests began to be focused in the sciences, his favorite school subjects being botany, mathematics, and geometry.

LIFE'S WORK

In 1775, Hahnemann completed his local schooling and went on to Leipzig University; he later moved to Vienna, and he received his medical degree from the University of Erlangen in 1779. His early adult years were spent restlessly, moving from one town to another. In the city of Dessau, he attached himself to a pharmacist named Herr Haseler, with whom he carried out experiments in chemistry. While there, he became acquainted with Haseler's stepdaughter, Henriette Kuchler, whom he soon married.

The couple and their five children continued to move several times, Hahnemann always growing more and more disillusioned with current medical methods. Eventually, he gave up traditional medical practice altogether, leaving the translation of scientific writings as his only income. It was in the town of Stotteritz in 1790 that he translated a book discussing an herb known as cinchona bark, which had been found to cure malaria. Intrigued with this substance, he began to take it himself experimentally. He took rather large doses over a period of several days, finding himself becoming feverish and sick as a result. When he stopped taking the substance, he quickly got well.

Hahnemann's experiment formed the basis both for his later theories of homeopathy and for the method he used for identifying homeopathic cures, that is, experimenting on his own body and those of other volunteers. The principle he identified from this experiment was the idea that substances that in large doses harm the body, causing certain symptoms, can in small doses cure those very same symptoms. This principle he called *Similia Similibus,* or the law of treating like with like.

In 1796, Hahnemann wrote a paper in which he explained why traditional cures did not work. These treatment methods he called "allopathic," meaning that cures were attempted by introducing the opposites of the disease symptoms. For example, laxatives given for constipation are allopathic treatments, as is opium for insomnia and pain. Each tries to affect the body by opposing the symptoms. Sometimes, Hahnemann admitted, these methods work, at least temporarily, allowing the body to heal itself. However, another allopathic method popular at the time—the practice of bloodletting—was not so benign, and Hahnemann argued against it. Many diseases were thought to be caused by an excess of blood, so an allopathic method was to cause the patient to bleed. Needless to say, many patients died of this treatment, even though it was considered a useful and important technique.

During this time, Hahnemann was collecting records of a variety of medicines accidentally taken in too large doses, and their effects on the patients. In addition, he continued to experiment on his own body and on those of a group of volunteers. He called this process "proving." At first, the practice of homeopathy was not known much beyond Leipzig, but a scarlet fever epidemic in 1799 further publicized the method.

At that time, Hahnemann was treating a family of several children. One daughter was particularly fragile; however, she did not get scarlet fever. On investigating, Hahnemann noted that she had been taking belladonna, a usually poisonous substance sometimes taken as medicine, for another medical problem. Surmising that it was the belladonna that kept the girl from getting scarlet fever, he also gave it in small doses to the other children in the family, and none of them became sick. He then noted that healthy people who accidentally take belladonna, which comes from the red berries of the common plant deadly nightshade, suffered symptoms similar to those of scarlet fever. This case further popularized his method, and by 1838, the use of belladonna to

prevent scarlet fever had become common practice in Saxony.

In 1810, Hahnemann published *Organon of Rational Healing*, which he later retitled *Organon of the Healing Art*. In this book, he outlined the principles of homeopathy and the homeopathic remedies he had discovered. The work remains a classic of homeopathic medicine. In 1812, his methods again found some popular support, as Napoleon's armies straggled home from Russia, bringing with them the deadly disease typhus. Hahnemann's homeopathic cures proved far superior to allopathic methods, and his fame continued to spread.

Hahnemann, though, was never without detractors. Some of his most vocal critics were the apothecaries, or pharmacists, of Leipzig. The doses he was prescribing were so small as to be unprofitable to the apothecaries, who were further cut out of the business when Hahnemann began making his own remedies and giving them to patients. In 1820, the Apothecary Guild of Leipzig brought Hahnemann to court for making his own remedies, under a law that restricted the compounding of medicine to apothecaries. He was convicted and barred from making his own remedies, although the government eventually allowed him to continue, under certain restrictions. In addition, a few apothecaries who were willing to be trained by Hahnemann learned to prepare medicines according to his requirements.

During this period, a publisher, in an effort to discredit Hahnemann's work, commissioned a young man named Constantine Hering to write a book denouncing homeopathy. As part of his research, Hering carefully studied Hahnemann's work and even worked with him, helping him prove his remedies. In the end, Hering was converted; he later went to America and in 1848 founded Hahnemann Medical College in Philadelphia.

Life in Leipzig became increasingly difficult, however, and in 1821 Hahnemann was invited by Duke Ferdinand of Anhalt-Coethen to live and practice in Coethen. There he lived for eleven years, watching the

---

GUIDELINES FOR A MODEL MEDICAL CASETAKING

1. Freedom from bias.
2. Fidelity in recording the image of the disease as recounted by the patient.
3. Recording the case "with the very same expressions used by the patient and his relations."
4. "The physician keeps silent, allowing them to say all they have to say without interruption, unless they stray off to side issues."
5. The physician then "makes a closer determination of each single statement, without ever asking a question that would put words into the patient's mouth or that would be answerable with a simple yes or no."
6. "Only after the patient has finished freely relating the pertinent information upon simply being invited to do so, and upon being prompted [with general questions] . . . is it allowable and indeed necessary for the physician to ask more precise and specific questions if he feels he has not yet been fully informed."
7. "When the patient's symptoms are altered by the use of medications . . . symptoms and ailments suffered before the use of the medicine or several days after discontinuing its use give the genuine, fundamental concept of the original gestalt of the disease. . . ."
8. "In cases of chronic disease, the investigation . . . must be conducted as carefully and minutely as possible, and one must go into the smallest details."
9. "Once the totality of the symptoms . . . has been exactly recorded, the most difficult work is done."
10. "During the treatment (especially of a chronic disease), the medical-art practitioner then has the total disease image always before him. . . ."

Source: Adapted from Samuel Hahnemann, *Organon of the Medical Art*, edited by Wenda Brewster O'Reilly (6th ed. Redmond, Wash.: Birdcage Books, 1996).

fame of his cures spread. Homeopathy was gaining in popularity, and in 1829 his friends organized a jubilee celebration to honor his fifty years in the medical profession. Visitors and greetings arrived from all over the world. His time in Coethen, an otherwise peaceful period for Hahnemann, was saddened by the death in 1831 of his wife Henriette at the age of seventy-five.

Hahnemann's work was not finished, however, for another epidemic again found him in controversy and providing homeopathic cures that were superior to traditional methods. During the 1830's, the Asian disease of cholera was spreading through Europe, and there were no allopathic remedies that could be counted on to cure it. Hahnemann was asked to find a cure; without seeing a single case, relying only upon a description of the symptoms, he discovered that camphor produced similar symptoms if taken in large doses. Publication and use of this remedy saved many lives.

Hahnemann's life was soon to take a new path. In October, 1834, a young Frenchman arrived at his house for treatment and was given hospitality for the night. In the morning, it was discovered that the young man was in fact a young woman, who had heard of Hahnemann and his practice and wanted to learn from him. Three months later, the woman, Marie Mélanie d'Hervilly, became Hahnemann's wife. Soon after, the couple moved to Paris, to the chagrin of Hahnemann's two daughters, who had devoted their lives to assisting their father in his work. Hahnemann began a homeopathic practice in Paris, and there he died in 1843.

SIGNIFICANCE

Although the principles of homeopathy were first stated by Hippocrates in the fourth century and also were a basis of traditional Chinese medicine, Hahnemann was the first to name and popularize the practice of homeopathic cure. Having learned medicine during a time when dangerous practices such as the letting of blood were commonly used, Hahnemann provided a valuable alternative that saved many lives.

Nevertheless, homeopathy has always been controversial. Traditional modern medicine, while open to more varieties of treatments and constantly seeking more reliable cures, is primarily allopathic in philosophy. Homeopathic remedies are discounted as quackery, partly because they treat the symptoms of the disease rather than search for its cause, and partly because the use of infinitesimally small doses in homeopathic remedies seems counterintuitive and, to critics, absurd. During the late twentieth century, however, the increased popularity

of alternative therapies prompted renewed interest in homeopathy and in Hahnemann's legacy.

—*Eleanor B. Amico*

FURTHER READING

Cook, Trevor M. *Samuel Hahnemann: The Founder of Homeopathic Medicine*. Wellingborough, Northamptonshire, England: Thorson, 1981. A very readable biography, clearly written and including photos and maps. Divided into sections that detail the various stages of Hahnemann's life.

Gumpert, Martin. *Hahnemann: The Adventurous Career of a Medical Rebel*. New York: L. B. Fischer, 1945. Focuses on Hahnemann's rebellion against traditional medical practices and the difficulties and conflicts he encountered. Also gives a complete biography, beginning with Hahnemann's life as a young physician and the events that led to his unorthodox discoveries.

Handley, Rima. *A Homeopathic Love Story: The Story of Samuel and Mélanie Hahnemann*. Berkeley, Calif.: North Atlantic Books, Homeopathic Educational Services, 1990. Dual biography of Hahnemann and his wife, Mélanie, a Parisian artist and poet. Describes Mélanie's role in the development of homeopathy.

_____. *In Search of the Later Hahnemann*. Beaconsfield, England: Beaconsfield, 1997. Examines Hahnemann's medical practice in the final years of his life, when he moved from Germany to Paris. Using Hahnemann's casebooks and other sources, Handley describes his experiments and medical discoveries during this period.

Hobhouse, Rosa Waugh. *Christian Samuel Hahnemann: A Short Biography*. Ashingdon, Rochford, Essex, England: C. W. Daniel, 1961. This brief book is meant as both an update and summary of Hobhouse's earlier biography. Although its flowery language makes the book seem quaint, it does provide a good and succinct overview of Hahnemann's life.

_____. *Life of Christian Samuel Hahnemann*. London: C. W. Daniel, 1933. Hobhouse's original biography of Hahnemann, which goes into much greater detail than her later short biography. Includes photos of places and objects in Hahnemann's life and portraits of him and the people around him. Written in somewhat flowery prose, the book nevertheless is well organized and gives a good portrayal of the subject.

Mitchell, George Ruthven. *Homeopathy: The First Authoritative Study of Its Place in Medicine Today*. London: W. H. Allen, 1975. Begins with a good biography of Hahnemann and goes on to describe the history of homeopathy as a science. Included are discussions of Hahnemann's followers and disciples and an explanation of homeopathy and its history.

SEE ALSO: Mary Baker Eddy.
RELATED ARTICLES in *Great Events from History: The Nineteenth Century, 1801-1900:* October 5, 1823: Wakley Introduces *The Lancet*; October 30, 1875: Eddy Establishes the Christian Science Movement.

SARAH JOSEPHA HALE
American writer and journalist

The author of poetry, novels, plays, and cookbooks, as well as an important history of women, Hale is best known as the editor of Godey's Lady's Book, *the most popular magazine in the United States before the Civil War. She encouraged and supported women writers and advocated improved opportunities for women's education and work.*

BORN: October 24, 1788; Newport, New Hampshire
DIED: April 30, 1879; Philadelphia, Pennsylvania
ALSO KNOWN AS: Sarah Josepha Buell (birth name)
AREAS OF ACHIEVEMENT: Literature, journalism

EARLY LIFE
Born Sarah Josepha Buell on a New Hampshire farm, Sarah Josepha Hale was one of four children of Gordon and Martha Whittlesey Buell. Though opportunities for formal schooling for girls were limited at she was growing up, she received a good education at home and later credited her mother with inspiring her love of literature. Despite limited access to books, Buell read widely during her youth. By the time she was fifteen, for example, she had read all of William Shakespeare's works. Other favorites included the Bible, John Bunyan's *Pilgrim's Progress* (1678, 1684), and Ann Radcliffe's *The Mysteries of Udolpho* (1794). Buell also benefited from tutoring by her brother Horatio, who attended Dartmouth College. During Horatio's summer vacations at home, the two studied Latin, Greek, philosophy, English grammar, rhetoric, geography, and literature. Hale drew on her strong education when, at the age of eighteen, she opened a private school for children. She continued to teach until 1813, when she married David Hale, a lawyer in Newport.

During her marriage, Sarah Josepha Buell Hale continued her education. As she later recalled, she and her husband spent two hours each evening reading current literature and studying topics ranging from composition and French to science. During this period, Hale also worked on her own writing, publishing a few poems in local magazines.

Hale's life changed considerably when, in 1822, shortly before the birth of their fifth child, her husband died suddenly. Concerned with providing for her family, Hale turned first to the millinery business, but she soon focused on becoming an author. Her first volume of poetry, *The Oblivion of Genius and Other Original Poems*, appeared in 1823. After winning several literary prizes and becoming a regular contributor to magazines and gift annuals, Hale published her first novel, *Northwood: A Tale of New England*, in 1827. Though highlighting New England character traits, as the subtitle suggests, the novel focused on the contrasts between the North and South, including issues of race relations and slavery.

LIFE'S WORK
Soon after the publication of *Northwood*, Sarah Josepha Hale, at the age of thirty-nine, launched what to a great extent would become her life's work as a magazine editor. When a new periodical, the *Ladies' Magazine*, first appeared in January of 1828, Hale edited it from her home in Newport, but within a few months she moved to Boston, where the magazine was published. Though the *Ladies' Magazine* was not the first periodical intended for American women or edited by an American woman, it did differ considerably from earlier efforts, which often focused on fashion. Hale's *Ladies' Magazine* included fashion plates during part of its nine-year existence, but it was much more intellectual than previous women's magazines had been. Sketches of famous women were common features, and Hale's editorial columns often addressed issues of social reform, such as property rights for married women and the importance of women's education.

Publishing both poetry and fiction, the magazine also had a significant literary component, and Hale's support of American authors is particularly noteworthy. Whereas other magazine editors relied on anonymous material and reprinted British literature (generally without permission), Hale's magazine featured American authors, and she repeatedly encouraged her readers to recognize authorship as a legitimate profession. Therefore, she favored original submissions rather than reprints, encouraged attribution of authors, and supported the idea that authors should be paid for their work.

Throughout her editorship of the *Ladies' Magazine*, Hale continued her efforts as an author. Her own writings appeared frequently in the magazine, and some of them were published separately in book form. Her *Sketches of American Character* (1829) and *Traits of American Life* (1835) first appeared in the *Ladies' Magazine*. During this time, Hale also published two poetry collections, including *Poems for Our Children* (1830), which contained the poem "Mary's Lamb" (now famous as "Mary Had a Little Lamb").

Hale's career took an important turn in 1837, when after nine years of managing the *Ladies' Magazine*, Hale accepted a new position as editor of Louis Godey's *Lady's Book*, which Godey had founded in 1830 in Philadelphia. For the first several years, Hale edited the magazine from her home in Boston, but in 1841 she moved to Philadelphia. Even before the move, however, Hale carefully reformed the magazine, which initially lacked the intellectual and literary focus Hale had developed in the

Sarah Josepha Hale. (Library of Congress)

Ladies' Magazine. With Hale as editor, however, the *Lady's Book* (now often referred to by its later name, *Godey's Lady's Book*) became an important literary magazine for women. Though the magazine continued to publish the so-called "embellishments" for which Louis Godey had become famous (engravings, fashion plates, and so forth), Hale continued her earlier positions supporting American writers and improved opportunities for women's work and education. This combination of Godey's "embellishments" and Hale's literary and educational essays proved popular. By 1860, the magazine boasted 150,000 subscribers, making it the most popular U.S. magazine of its day.

With such a large audience, Hale was able to exert considerable influence on a number of social issues. Some of these, such as her efforts to preserve the Bunker Hill Monument and Mount Vernon, demonstrate her strong patriotic impulses. Many more of Hale's editorial campaigns were related to her belief in the power of what she and many of her contemporaries called "woman's sphere." Believing that women were innately more moral than men, Hale voiced strong support of women's charitable organizations, such as the Seaman's Aid Society, which tried to improve the lives of Boston's seamen and their families by founding schools, a library, a boardinghouse, and a clothing shop.

Although Hale believed that the domestic space was part of women's sphere, she did not wish to confine women within the home. Quite the contrary, Hale encouraged women to extend their influence as widely as possible. Thus, for example, Hale voiced strong support for the founding of Vassar College (the first U.S. college for women), campaigned for women's medical colleges, and repeatedly called for women to take professional positions as teachers and with the post office.

Hale also took a particular interest in issues of women's health, arguing, for example, for women's physical education and denouncing tight corsets as unhealthy (a charge that was later fully substantiated). Though the *Lady's Book* sometimes prided itself on avoiding political topics, many of Hale's editorial campaigns had significant political implications. Her long-standing efforts to establish Thanksgiving as a national holiday, for example, were based on her belief during the antebellum period that if a nation shared a meal together once a year, it would be less likely to engage in civil war. Though Hale's ultimate goal of preventing civil war was, of course, unsuccessful, she did manage to persuade President Abraham Lincoln to declare Thanksgiving a national holiday.

Throughout her editorship of the *Lady's Book*, Hale continued to publish her own work. In addition to contributing material to the *Lady's Book*, she published a number of poetry volumes and several short novels, and following the success of Harriet Beecher Stowe's *Uncle Tom's Cabin* in 1852, she issued a revised edition of *Northwood*. Hale also wrote a number of popular cookbooks. Hale's efforts as a writer were well regarded by her peers, and she was featured in many of the gift annuals and literary anthologies published before the Civil War. One of Hale's most ambitious projects as a writer was her 1853 *Woman's Record: Or, Sketches of All Distinguished Women from "The Beginning" till A.D. 1850*. This nine-hundred-page work presents biographical essays on more than two hundred women, with brief mentions of more than two thousand others.

After five decades as a magazine editor, Hale published her last column with the *Lady's Book* in December, 1877. She died on April 30, 1879, at the age of ninety and was buried in Philadelphia.

SIGNIFICANCE

Though she was not the first woman magazine editor, Sarah Josepha Hale enjoyed a longer and more influential career than had any American woman before her. During her fifty-year editorial career, Hale made significant contributions to American literature and to women's issues. She published or reviewed the work of such writers as Edgar Allan Poe, James Fenimore Cooper, and Herman Melville. As editor of a popular women's magazine, Hale was able to support women writers, many of whom, such as Harriet Beecher Stowe and Lydia Sigourney, published their work in her magazines.

Through her editorial columns, Hale was also able to support other issues related to women. Although she did not advocate women's voting rights, she was a strong spokeswoman for property rights for married women, improved women's education, and increased opportunities for women's wage-earning work. Ultimately, one of Hale's most lasting contributions may have been in encouraging other women to pursue careers in publishing and periodicals. By proving that a women's literary magazine could be the nation's most popular periodical and by demonstrating that a woman could manage such a magazine, Hale undoubtedly helped to pave the way for later women editors, authors, and journalists.

—*Patricia Okker*

FURTHER READING

Bardes, Barbara A., and Susanne Gossett. "Sarah J. Hale, Selective Promoter of Her Sex." In *A Living of Words:*

American Women in Print Culture, edited by Susan Albertine. Knoxville: University of Tennessee Press, 1995. A literary analysis of Hale's treatment of women in her book *Woman's Record*.

Entrikin, Isabelle Webb. *Sarah Josepha Hale and "Godey's Lady's Book."* Lancaster, Pa.: Lancaster Press, 1946. A published dissertation, this work provides a good overview of Hale's editorial career and includes a bibliography of Hale's published works.

Finley, Ruth E. *The Lady of Godey's: Sarah Josepha Hale*. Philadelphia: J. B. Lippincott, 1931. The first full-length biography of Hale, this work provides a good overview of Hale's life, including her work as an author and editor and her support of issues such as national union and women's education.

Hoffman, Nicole Tonkovich. "*Legacy* Profile: Sarah Josepha Hale." *Legacy: A Journal of Nineteenth-Century American Women Writers* 7, no. 2 (Fall, 1990): 47-55. This short sketch of Hale's life and career includes a selected bibliography as well as an excerpt from one of Hale's editorials.

Mott, Frank Luther. *A History of American Magazines, 1741-1850*. Vol. 1. New York: D. Appleton, 1930. Though subsequent studies show less bias against sentimental literature than evident here, this pivotal work includes a detailed sketch of *Godey's Lady's Book* and valuable information about the periodical industry.

Okker, Patricia. *Our Sister Editors: Sarah J. Hale and the Tradition of Nineteenth-Century American Women Editors*. Athens: University of Georgia Press, 1995. In addition to identifying more than six hundred women who edited periodicals in the nineteenth century, this work provides a thorough analysis of Hale's editorial career, focusing specifically on her literary significance.

Rogers, Sherbrooke. *Sarah Josepha Hale: A New England Pioneer, 1788-1879*. Grantham, N.H.: Tompson & Rutter, 1985. Though it presents little new information, this biography is particularly suited to older adolescents.

Tonkovich, Nicole. *Domesticity with a Difference: The Nonfiction of Catharine Beecher, Sarah J. Hale, Fanny Fern, and Margaret Fuller*. Jackson: University Press of Mississippi, 1997. Examination of four nineteenth century women writers and how they altered women's traditional roles in the home, school, and community. Tonkovich describes how the writers paradoxically prescribed domesticity for other women while they pursued careers outside the home.

SEE ALSO: Catharine Beecher; James Fenimore Cooper; Margaret Fuller; Abraham Lincoln; Herman Melville; Edgar Allan Poe; Harriet Beecher Stowe.

RELATED ARTICLE in *Great Events from History: The Nineteenth Century, 1801-1900:* 1859: Smiles Publishes *Self-Help.*

SIR WILLIAM ROWAN HAMILTON
Irish mathematician

While questioning a commonly accepted three-dimensional concept of space on a plane, Hamilton discovered quaternions and, in doing so, drastically altered the study of algebra, forcing the abandonment of the commutative law of multiplication that was dominant in his day and leading the way to new methods of vector analysis.

BORN: August 3/4, 1805; Dublin, Ireland
DIED: September 2, 1865; near Dublin, Ireland
AREA OF ACHIEVEMENT: Mathematics

EARLY LIFE

William Rowan Hamilton was born exactly at midnight, a moment poised equally between August 3 and 4, 1805. His father, Archibald Hamilton, was away in the north at the time of his son's birth, carrying out his duties as agent to Archibald Rowan, a post he had held since 1800. Archibald Rowan, who was William Rowan Hamilton's godfather, had been in exile for eleven years. His agent, William's father, worked tirelessly to make possible Rowan's return to his estate at Killyleagh, an effort that resulted in Rowan's repatriation in 1806.

To help Rowan meet his expenses, Archibald Hamilton borrowed heavily at high interest rates. When these loans were called, Rowan failed to back Hamilton, who, in a year or two, had no alternative but to declare bankruptcy. By 1808, the family was sufficiently impoverished not to be able to provide for William, then three years old, and his sisters, Grace and Eliza, who had to be sent away to be cared for by relatives. The two girls presumably were sent to live with their father's sister, Sydney, and young William became the ward of his uncle, James Hamilton, a Church of England clergyman who ran the diocesan school at Trim, some forty miles to the northwest of Dublin in County Meath. William was to remain there until 1823, when he returned to Dublin as a student at Trinity College.

In retrospect, it appears to have been a stroke of good fortune that young William was forced by circumstance to live with his uncle, a man of considerable intellect. Be-

fore the boy was four years old, he was able to read English and showed a remarkable understanding of arithmetic. By the time he was five, William was able to translate from Latin, Greek, and Hebrew. He knew Greek and Latin authors well enough to recite from their works, and he was also able to recite passages from works by John Milton and John Dryden. He is said to have mastered fourteen languages by the time he was thirteen. Before he turned twelve, he had compiled a Syriac grammar, and two years later he was sufficiently fluent in Persian to compose a speech of welcome that was delivered to the Persian ambassador when he was a guest in Dublin.

Always advanced in mathematics, Hamilton was enormously exhilarated when he met the American mathematician Zerah Colburn in 1820. Colburn was able to perform complex mathematical computations quickly in his head, a skill that enticed the fifteen-year-old Hamilton. The youth had already read Sir Isaac Newton's *Philosophiae Naturalis Principia Mathematica* (1687) and Alexis-Claude Clairaut's *Elémens d'algèbre* (1746) by the time he met Colburn. The excitement generated by his meeting with Colburn led Hamilton in the following year to study the completed volumes of Pierre-Simon Laplace's five-volume *Traité de mécanique céleste* (1798-1825; *A Treatise of Celestial Mechanics*, 1829-1839).

Hamilton's detection of a flaw in Laplace's reasoning brought him to the attention of John Brinkley, a distinguished professor of astronomy at Trinity College who was then also president of the Royal Irish Academy. The following year, when he was seventeen, Hamilton sent a paper he had written on optics to Brinkley, who, upon reading the paper, declared to the Royal Academy that Hamilton was already the most important mathematician of his time.

Hamilton entered Trinity College in 1823. By 1825, he had completed his paper "On Caustics" and submitted it to the Royal Academy, only to be rebuffed because the members of the Academy could not follow his often convoluted reasoning. Hamilton was awarded the *optime* in both classics and mathematics, the first Trinity College student to achieve this dual honor. While still an undergraduate, in 1827, he submitted his paper "Theory of Systems of Rays" to the Royal Academy, establishing with that paper a uniform method of solving all problems in the field of geometrical optics. The paper was of sufficient significance that before he had finished his undergraduate studies at Trinity College, the school's faculty elected William Rowan Hamilton to the Andrews professorship in astronomy, a post that established him as royal astronomer of Ireland and an examiner of graduate students in mathematics at Trinity College. He assumed that post immediately upon graduation.

LIFE'S WORK

The post to which the Trinity College faculty elected Hamilton carried with it a residence at the Dunsink Observatory, some five miles from Trinity College. In October, 1827, Hamilton moved into that residence and remained there for the rest of his life. Although he did not have a distinguished career as an astronomer, Hamilton had a large following of people who attended his lectures on astronomy because the range of his literary as well as his mathematical knowledge was sufficient to enliven his presentations.

Hamilton read encyclopedically and regularly wrote poetry, although his friend, the poet William Wordsworth, advised him that his lasting contributions would lie in mathematics rather than in poetry. In 1832, Hamilton published an important supplement to his paper on the theory of rays. This supplement was purely speculative, postulating a new theory about the refraction of light by biaxial crystals. Augustin Fresnel had already developed the theory of double refraction, but Hamilton took the theory an important step beyond where Fresnel had left it. He contended that in certain circumstances, one ray of incident light could be refracted into an infinite number of rays in a biaxial crystal and would be formed in such a way that a cone would then result. Humphrey Lloyd, following Hamilton's speculative lead, proved this theory of conical refraction within two months.

In 1833, after six years of living alone in his official residence, Hamilton—a man of average height and ruddy complexion—married Maria Bayley, whose father had been an Anglican rector in County Tipperary. Maria bore three children, two sons and a daughter. Not renowned for her domestic abilities, Maria presided over a somewhat chaotic household. Hamilton considered liquor a more reliable source of nourishment than anything Maria's cook could provide, and, through the years, he became a heavy drinker.

Hamilton's "On a General Method in Dynamics," published in 1835, brought together his work in optics and dynamics. He proposed a theory that showed the duality that exists between the components of momentum in a dynamic system and the coordinates that determine its position. In many ways, this work was some of Hamilton's most significant, although it took nearly a century for the development of research in quantum mechanics to demonstrate the brilliance and importance of Hamilton's theory.

Hamilton served as the major local organizer of the British Association for the Advancement of Science meeting in Dublin in 1835, an activity that led to his being knighted in the closing ceremonies of that event. In 1837, he ascended to the presidency of the Royal Irish Academy. In 1843, the Crown awarded him an annual life pension of two hundred pounds. During his final illness, Hamilton received word that he had been ranked first on the list of foreign associates of the National Academy of the United States.

The contribution for which Hamilton is best remembered is his discovery of quaternions. This discovery has fundamentally changed the way in which mathematicians deal with three-dimensional space. Hamilton had begun his extensive investigation into ordered paired numbers more than ten years before he made his monumental discovery of quaternions on October 16, 1843, when, during a walk along Dublin's Royal Canal, the answer to a question that had been haunting him for nearly a decade flashed almost supernaturally into his mind. So excited was he by this flash of insight that he carved the formula for his discovery, $i^2 = j^2 = k^2 = ijk = -1$, into the Brougham Bridge.

Hamilton suddenly realized that in three-dimensional space, geometrical operations require not triplets, expressed as i, j, and k and representing space, as had been previously supposed, but rather that, because in three-dimensional space the orientation of the plane is variable, another element, a real term that represents time, must also be considered, resulting in quadruplets rather than triplets. One of the major consequences of this insight was its negation of the previously accepted commutative law of multiplication, which postulates $(a \times b) = (b \times a)$.

Hamilton's work with quaternions, to which he devoted the last two decades of his life, was essential to the development of vector analysis. More recently, further important applications of his theory of quaternions have been instrumental in the description of elementary particles. Hamilton published his *Lectures on Quaternions* in

1853, and his influential *The Elements of Quaternions* appeared posthumously in 1866. William Rowan Hamilton died of gout on September 2, 1865, after a lingering illness.

SIGNIFICANCE

Sir William Rowan Hamilton's name lives in both the history of mathematics and the histories of physics and optics. His pioneering work in vector analysis forced specialists in that field to abandon the theory of double refraction and to replace it with Hamilton's expanded theory of conical refraction. The work that led to these changes began while Hamilton was still an undergraduate at Trinity College and reached its culmination in the supplement to his "Theory of Systems of Rays" in 1832.

Hamilton's next significant achievement posited a duality between the components of momentum in a dynamic system and the coordinates that determine its position, a theory that reduces the field of dynamics to a problem in the calculus of variations. This theory came to have considerable significance as the field of quantum mechanics developed.

Hamilton's most memorable contribution by far, however, was his discovery of quaternions, which forced mathematicians to break with the commutative law of multiplication. In its simplified form, termed vector analysis and adapted by J. Willard Gibbs from Hamilton's theory, Hamilton's theory of quaternions has been of great significance to modern mathematical physicists.

—*R. Baird Shuman*

FURTHER READING

Bell, Eric Temple. *Development of Mathematics*. New York: McGraw-Hill, 1940. Bell relates Hamilton to some of the salient mathematical developments of his time. The coverage is sketchy and has been superseded by Thomas L. Hankins's biography (see below).

_____. *Men of Mathematics*. New York: Simon & Schuster, 1965. Bell puts Hamilton in historical perspective. The chapter "An Irish Tragedy" focuses on Hamilton, but, although interesting, it is not factually dependable in all respects.

Crilly, A. J. *Arthur Cayley: Mathematician Laureate of the Victorian Age*. Baltimore: Johns Hopkins University Press, 2005. Cayley (1821-1895) was a contemporary of Hamilton; the two men devised a matrix algebra theory that bears their names. Although focusing on Cayley, this biography also describes Ham-

ilton and others who were part of a nineteenth century British mathematical vanguard.

Graves, R. P. *Life of Sir William Rowan Hamilton*. 3 vols. London: Longmans, Green, 1882. The three enormous volumes of this set include extensive selections from Hamilton's correspondence, poetry, and miscellaneous writings, as well as extensive commentary. The work, remarkable in its time for its thoroughness, is badly dated and suffers from lack of selectivity.

Hamilton, William Rowan. *The Mathematical Papers of Sir William Rowan Hamilton*. 4 vols. Cambridge, England: Cambridge University Press, 1931-2000. Volume 1, *Geometrical Optics* (1931), and volume 2, *Dynamics* (1940), are edited by A. W. Conway and J. L. Synge; volume 3, *Algebra* (1967), is edited by H. Halberstam and R. E. Ingram. Volume 4 (2000) is edited by Brendan Scaife and includes Hamilton's *Systems of Rays*, two lengthy letters regarding definite integrals and anharmonic coordinates, and reprints of numerous papers about geometry, astronomy, and other topics. Volumes 1 and 3 contain useful introductions. Despite some omissions, these volumes are superbly produced, and the highest standards of scholarship have been observed in their editing.

Hankins, Thomas L. *Sir William Rowan Hamilton*. Baltimore: Johns Hopkins University Press, 1980. Hankins's critical biography of Hamilton is the definitive work in the field. Meticulously documented, the book is written in such a lively style that it at times reads like a novel rather than like the eminently scholarly work that it is. The best book to date on Hamilton.

James, Ioan. *Remarkable Mathematicians: From Euler to von Neumann*. New York: Cambridge University Press, 2002. This collection of brief biographies of prominent mathematicians includes a seven-page biography of Hamilton.

Synge, J. L. *Geometrical Optics: An Introduction to Hamilton's Method*. Cambridge, England: Cambridge University Press, 1937. Highly technical in nature, this book contains a brief but valuable preface. This book is for the specialist rather than the beginner.

SEE ALSO: Hermann von Helmholtz; Pierre-Simon Laplace; William Wordsworth.

RELATED ARTICLE in *Great Events from History: The Nineteenth Century, 1801-1900:* 1899: Hilbert Publishes *The Foundations of Geometry*.

MARCUS A. HANNA
American politician

Hanna was the close political friend of William McKinley, whom he helped to secure the presidency in 1896, and he served as an influential United States senator until his death.

BORN: September 24, 1837; New Lisbon, Ohio
DIED: February 15, 1904; Washington, D.C.
ALSO KNOWN AS: Mark Hanna; Marcus Alonzo Hanna (full name)
AREA OF ACHIEVEMENT: Government and politics

EARLY LIFE

Marcus Alonzo Hanna was the son of Leonard Hanna, who had come from Scotch-Irish Quaker stock and was in the grocery business when he married Samantha Converse, a Vermont schoolteacher from Irish, English, and Huguenot stock. The younger Hanna attended public schools in New Lisbon and, after 1852, in Cleveland, where his family had moved. He enrolled in Western Reserve College but was suspended in 1857 for faking programs to a school function. Going to work for his father's firm of Hanna, Garretson and Co., he took over his father's position by the early years of the Civil War. He served briefly as a volunteer in that conflict in 1864 and later married Charlotte Augusta Rhodes, on September 27, 1864. She was the daughter of a Cleveland dealer in iron and coal.

By 1867, Hanna's business ventures had failed, and he became a partner in his father-in-law's firm of Rhodes and Company. From then on, Hanna was a success. In 1885, the coal and iron business was reorganized as M. A. Hanna and Company. He also had an interest in many aspects of the Cleveland economy. He owned an opera house, a local newspaper, several street railways, and a share of several banks. Hanna was a popular employer. "A man who won't meet his men half-way is a God-damn fool," he said in 1894, and he believed in high wages, the unity of capital and labor, and unions over strikes. By the time he was forty, Hanna was a capitalist of consequence in the Midwest, but it was his love for Republican politics in Ohio that made him a national figure.

LIFE'S WORK

Hanna began as a backstage fund-raiser for Republican candidates at the end of the 1870's; he played a large role in the campaign to elect James A. Garfield president in 1880. He first identified himself with the national ambitions of Senator John Sherman during the ensuing decade

and worked closely with Governor Joseph B. Foraker on Sherman's behalf. At the Republican National Convention in 1888, a dispute with Foraker over the Sherman candidacy ended the difficult alliance with the temperamental governor and started a feud that endured until 1904. Hanna then turned to the rising political fortunes of an Ohio congressman, William McKinley.

McKinley's friendship with Hanna was the dominant force in the latter's life for the next decade and a half. Cartoonists and critics after 1896 would depict a bloated, plutocratic Hanna as the manipulator of a pliable McKinley and thus create a popular image wholly divergent from the truth. In their political relationship, McKinley was the preeminent figure and Hanna was always the subordinate. The two men had met first during the 1870's but did not establish a working partnership until the years 1888 to 1892. McKinley relied on the fund-raising ability and the organization skills that Hanna supplied in his races for governor of Ohio in 1891 and 1893. For his part, Hanna accorded McKinley an admiration that, in its early stages, verged on hero-worship.

McKinley's political fortunes prospered during the 1890's, a difficult time for the Democratic Party. After Benjamin Harrison failed to win reelection in 1892, the Ohio governor became a leading choice for the Republican nomination in 1896. Hanna helped McKinley through the embarrassing financial crisis in the Panic of 1893, when the governor became responsible for a friend's bad debts. By early 1895, the industrialist gave up his formal connection with his business interests to push McKinley's candidacy. Hanna set up a winter home in Georgia and began wooing southern Republicans who would be convention delegates in 1896.

The campaign to nominate McKinley went smoothly in the first half of 1896, and a first-ballot victory came when the Republicans assembled in St. Louis in mid-June. Hanna's organizational abilities had helped McKinley gather the requisite delegate votes, but the candidate's popularity and advocacy of the protective tariff during the depression made the task of his campaign manager an easy one. The two men also agreed on the currency plank of the Republican platform, which endorsed the gold standard in the face of the Democratic swing to the inflationary panacea of free silver.

Hanna and McKinley expected a relatively easy race until the Democrats selected the young and charismatic William Jennings Bryan, the champion of free silver, at their convention in July. As chairman of the Republican National Committee, Hanna supervised the raising of the party's financial war chest during the late summer. The eastern business community, frightened of Bryan, contributed between three and four million dollars to the party's coffers. Hanna then used these resources in what he called a "campaign of education."

After setting up the major distribution point for campaign materials in Chicago, Hanna supervised the process that sent out more than 100 million documents espousing the virtues of the tariff and sound money; an equal number of posters depicted McKinley as "the advance agent of prosperity" and promised to workers "a full dinner pail" if McKinley were elected. By October, the diversified Republican appeal and the strength of McKinley's campaign had overwhelmed the Democrats. Bryan's whistle-stop campaign had not made his inflationary message popular. He was, said Hanna, "talking Silver all the time and that's where we've got him." Hanna's strategy brought a resounding Republican victory in November, 1896.

As the new president formed his cabinet, he gave Hanna the opportunity to become postmaster general. Hanna's real ambition, however, was to be senator from Ohio. When John Sherman resigned his seat to accept the State Department portfolio, the governor of Ohio appointed Hanna to fill out the remainder of his senatorial term. There was much talk at the time that a nearly senile Sherman had been kicked upstairs to make way for Hanna. In fact, Sherman wanted the place in the cabinet and accepted it voluntarily. Hanna was elected to a full term by the Ohio legislature early in 1898, after a close and bitter contest in which charges of bribery and other corrupt tactics were made against the Republican candidate. None of these allegations was proved, and Hanna took his seat in the Senate in January, 1897.

Hanna liked being in the Senate and the influence he enjoyed with his friend in the White House. He had a large voice in patronage decisions, especially in the South, and he was again important in the Republican campaign during the 1898 congressional elections. He advocated business consolidation into trusts, subsidies for the American merchant marine, and a canal across Central America. McKinley did not consult him as much on the large issues of foreign policy that grew out of the Spanish-American War. Initially, Hanna did not favor war with Spain over Cuba, but he accepted intervention when it came in April, 1898.

By 1900, the president and the senator had drifted apart. McKinley did not like the stories that Hanna dominated him, and some time passed before Hanna was named to head the Republican reelection drive in 1900. The vice presidential nomination in that year went to the New York governor and war hero, Theodore Roosevelt. Hanna did not trust the flamboyant Roosevelt. He asked those who were pushing him: "Don't you understand that there is just one life between this crazy man and the presidency if you force me to take Roosevelt?" When McKinley refused to oppose the New Yorker, Hanna had no choice but to accept Roosevelt's selection.

In the campaign, the Republican organization functioned even more smoothly than it had in 1896 against Bryan, who was once again the Democratic standard-bearer. With McKinley sitting out the canvass as an incumbent, Hanna went out on the stump and proved second only to Roosevelt as a speaking attraction. Senator Richard F. Pettigrew of South Dakota, a silver Republican, had become a bitter enemy of Hanna, and they had clashed on the Senate floor. The Ohioan campaigned against Pettigrew in his home state and helped to deny him reelection. As McKinley's second term began, there was some talk of a Hanna candidacy for president in 1904.

Marcus A. Hanna. (Library of Congress)

McKinley's assassination in September, 1901, and Roosevelt's accession to the presidency shifted the political balance against Hanna. Much of his power over Republican patronage vanished when McKinley died. As the embodiment of corporate power in politics who was often depicted as a plutocrat in cartoons, Hanna would not have been a credible challenger to the young, popular, and forceful Roosevelt. Hanna knew this, and he never seriously entertained the prospect of disputing Roosevelt's hold on the Republican nomination in 1904. At the same time, he was reluctant to acknowledge the new president's preeminence too quickly. The resulting ambivalence placed Hanna in an awkward position during the last two years of his life. Friends in the conservative, probusiness wing of the Republican Party wanted him to be a candidate: That idea he resisted. However, he could not bring himself to endorse Roosevelt wholeheartedly. The Hanna-Roosevelt relationship became tense.

Hanna and Roosevelt did cooperate fruitfully in the settlement of the anthracite coal strike of 1902. A believer in the essential harmony of capital and labor, Hanna became active in and eventually chaired the National Civic Federation, which sought the elusive goal of industrial peace through arbitration and conciliation. When the coal miners struck in 1902, for higher wages and shorter hours, Hanna tried to persuade the coal operators to negotiate with their men. He assisted Roosevelt's mediation efforts that finally brought a resolution of the dispute in October, 1902.

Within the Republican Party, Hanna remained the most plausible alternative to Roosevelt. His recommendation that the party should "stand pat" in the congressional elections of 1902 and make few concessions to reform contributed a phrase to the language of American politics and further endeared him to conservatives. Most of the talk about Hanna's hopes was illusory, as an episode in the spring of 1903 revealed. Hanna's old enemy, his senatorial colleague Foraker, asked that the Ohio Republican state convention endorse Roosevelt for the presidency. When Hanna hesitated to agree, the president sent him a public message that "those who favor my administration and nomination" would support Foraker's idea "and those who do not will oppose them." Hanna performed a "back-action-double-spring feat" and gave in.

Hanna was reelected to the Senate in 1903, after a difficult contest against the Democratic mayor of Cleveland, Tom L. Johnson. Hanna's success revived talk of the White House, and Roosevelt prepared for a test of strength in the winter of 1904. Before it could come,

however, Hanna fell ill with typhoid fever; he died in Washington, D.C., on February 15, 1904. Hanna had three children: Mabel Hanna had a mental disability and caused her parents much anguish, Ruth Hanna McCormick was active in Republican politics, and her brother Dan Hanna pursued a business career.

SIGNIFICANCE

Despite two sympathetic biographies, Hanna's reputation has never escaped the stereotypes that political opponents created during his lifetime. In fact, he was not the creator or mastermind of William McKinley but only a good friend and an efficient instrument who served the purposes of the twenty-fifth president. The Republicans won the presidential election of 1896 not because Hanna and his campaign organization bought votes or coerced industrial workers: With an appealing candidate, a divided opposition, and a popular program, Hanna used the money at his disposal to educate the electorate, not to manipulate it.

Hanna came to represent the power of big business in American politics. Part of that impression was deserved. He believed that size brought efficiency and a better standard of living. He also endorsed the protective tariff. At the same time, he thought that industrial workers should receive fair wages and a voice in the state of their working conditions. This view did not make him a New Dealer in the Gilded Age. It did reveal that his Republicanism had within it elements that explain why the GOP was the majority party of the nation between 1894 and 1929. As Theodore Roosevelt wrote of Hanna when he died: "No man had larger traits than Hanna. He was a big man in every way and as forceful a personality as we have seen in public life in our generation." That was a fitting epitaph for one of the most important politicians in the age of McKinley and Roosevelt.

—Lewis L. Gould

FURTHER READING

Beer, Thomas. *Hanna*. New York: Alfred A. Knopf, 1929. Beer's father was a political associate of Hanna, and this biography is written from an admiring point of view. It contains many shrewd insights and is a pleasure to read.

Blum, John Morton. *The Republican Roosevelt*. Cambridge, Mass.: Harvard University Press, 1954. Blum's short study of Roosevelt has a chapter on the rivalry with Hanna from 1901 to 1904 that is important to understanding the senator's career.

Croly, Herbert. *Marcus Alonzo Hanna: His Life and Work*. New York: Macmillan, 1912. Croly had access to the Hanna papers and interviews with the senator's associates, and these documents are now at the Library of Congress in the Hanna-McCormick Family Papers. This is the best full biography of Hanna and is positive about his political achievements.

Crossen, Cynthia. "The Man Who Made Political Campaigns All About the Money." *Wall Street Journal* (Eastern edition), March 24, 2004, p. B1. Describes how Hanna introduced new methods of fund-raising in American campaigns. Focuses on Hanna's fund-raising and promotional efforts on behalf of William McKinley during the presidential campaign of 1896.

Gould, Lewis L. *The Presidency of William McKinley.* Lawrence: Regents Press of Kansas, 1980. Places Hanna's role in McKinley's career in the context of the presidency between 1897 and 1901. There are discussions of Hanna's appointment to the Senate, his part in the election of 1900, and his relation to the president.

Jones, Stanley L. *The Presidential Election of 1896.* Madison: University of Wisconsin Press, 1964. Jones provides the fullest treatment of Hanna's participation in the McKinley campaign. The book is richly documented and provides direction for further research into Hanna's political career.

Leech, Margaret. *In the Days of McKinley.* New York: Harper & Brothers, 1959. Leech's is the most detailed study of McKinley as president, and there is much useful information about Hanna's dealings with the White House and the administration.

Morgan, H. Wayne. *William McKinley and His America.* Syracuse, N.Y.: Syracuse University Press, 1963. This is the best biography of McKinley, and Morgan offers a persuasive analysis of the Hanna-McKinley friendship as it affected his subject's life and political career.

Phillips, Kevin. *William McKinley.* New York: Times Books/Henry Holt, 2003. This examination of McKinley's presidency includes information about his rise to political prominence and the presidential campaign of 1896. One in a series of books about American presidents.

Williams, R. Hal. *Years of Decision: American Politics in the 1890's.* New York: John Wiley & Sons, 1978. Williams provides a penetrating look at the decade in which Hanna achieved national prominence. The book is essential for understanding why Hanna, McKinley, and the Republicans triumphed in this period.

SEE ALSO: James A. Garfield; Benjamin Harrison; William McKinley.

RELATED ARTICLE in *Great Events from History: The Nineteenth Century, 1801-1900:* November 3, 1896: McKinley Is Elected President.

KARL VON HARDENBERG
German politician and diplomat

A leader in the Prussian reform movement, Hardenberg also directed the foreign policy of his country during the eventful years 1810-1822 and played a pivotal role in forming the coalition of powers that defeated Napoleon. He was the spokesperson for Prussia at the Congress of Vienna in 1815, which determined the political fate of Europe for the next fifty years.

BORN: May 31, 1750; Essenrode, Hanover (now in Germany)

DIED: November 26, 1822; Genoa, Kingdom of Sardinia (now in Italy)

ALSO KNOWN AS: Karl August von Hardenberg (full name); Karl August, Fürst von Hardenberg; Karl August, Freiherr von Hardenberg; Karl August, prince of Hardenburg; Karl August, baron of Hardenburg

AREAS OF ACHIEVEMENT: Government and politics, diplomacy

EARLY LIFE

Karl August von Hardenberg (HAHR-dehn-behrk) was the son of Christian and Charlotte von Hardenberg. His father, the scion of an old Hanoverian family, had a distinguished military career. Hardenberg's parents determined that he should pursue a career in government service, and they sent him to Göttingen University in 1766, to study law and political science. He also studied briefly at the University of Leipzig in 1768. He completed his studies in 1770, having returned to Göttingen. Upon graduation he entered the Hanoverian bureaucracy in the department of justice.

In 1775, Hardenberg made an unfortunate marriage to the Countess Juliana von Reventlow, after which Hardenberg was appointed as the Hanoverian minister to England. His wife became involved in a sordid affair with the Prince of Wales, which, when it became a public scandal in 1781, forced Hardenberg's recall from England and ultimately his resignation from service. Hardenberg managed to find a new post in the Brunswick bureaucracy in 1782, serving for more than a decade. His service in Brunswick was also terminated by a scandal when, after securing a divorce from Juliana, he married a divorcée. Leaving Brunswick in 1792, Hardenberg obtained a position in the Prussian bureaucracy as minister for several newly acquired provinces.

LIFE'S WORK

Hardenberg quickly displayed to his new monarch unusual ability both in internal administration and in foreign affairs. In domestic affairs, he was entrusted with the reorganization of the Prussian administrations of finance, justice, education, and transportation. In foreign affairs, Frederick William II made him plenipotentiary to conclude a territorial settlement with the revolutionary government of France in 1795. Through his adroit handling of the negotiations resulting in the Peace of Basel, Prussia actually emerged stronger than before, despite having fared poorly in the War of the First Coalition. Hardenberg continued to grow in favor, and in 1804 Frederick William III appointed him foreign minister of Prussia.

As minister for foreign affairs, Hardenberg openly advocated a policy of territorial aggrandizement, contending that the Prussian government should seize every opportunity to acquire new territory. He pursued a policy of peace with Napoleon and territorial expansion through negotiation. In 1806, however, Hardenberg's counsel was disregarded and Prussia allied with Russia in a new war against Napoleon.

The war ended disastrously for Prussia. The Prussian army was overwhelmingly defeated at the Battles of Jena and Auerstedt in 1806, and the Prussian monarch was forced to sign the Treaty of Tilsit in 1807. The treaty not only diminished Prussia territorially but also limited its autonomy. Part of the settlement at Tilsit was that Hardenberg, whom Napoleon distrusted, should retire from government service. Before leaving office, however, Hardenberg began the restructuring of the old administrative system, the first step in what has come to be known as the Prussian reform movement.

In 1807-1808, the reform movement was expanded by Freiherr vom Stein, who oversaw the emancipation of Prussian serfs and the extension of self-government to the municipalities of Prussia before being forced from office by Napoleon. Hardenberg remained in contact with Stein; during his forced retirement he produced his famous Riga Memorandum in 1808, which became the blueprint for the further reforms of Prussian institutions. The central thesis of the memorandum was that if the monarchical form of government was to survive in Prussia, the government must adopt many of the liberal institutions produced in France by the Revolution of 1789. Hardenberg's memorandum showed that he, like Stein, recognized that the forces of nationalism and democracy unleashed by the revolution in France would ultimately destroy the old order of Europe if they were not

Karl von Hardenberg. (Library of Congress)

brought under control. He proposed that the Prussian government should introduce liberal reform from above to prevent revolution.

In 1810, Napoleon allowed Frederick William to recall Hardenberg to the Prussian government, this time as prime minister. His initial reforms aimed at making the tax structure of the kingdom more equitable and at simplifying tax collection. Hardenberg imposed a property tax on all citizens (the nobility had formerly been exempted), an excise tax on all areas, and a profit tax. Concurrently, most restrictions on trade and commerce were removed, and civic equality for Jews was established.

Hardenberg then took a hesitant step toward establishing a representative assembly to permit popular participation in the making of governmental policy. By convening an assembly of notables he hoped to create widespread enthusiasm for the further changes he intended to make. However, the *junkers* (aristocratic landowners) opposed the idea of representative government and used their influence with Frederick William to thwart the hope of a national parliament. Nevertheless, Hardenberg was able to open admission of the officer corps and of the bureaucracy (formerly the exclusive preserves of the *junkers*) to all citizens.

From 1812 until his death, most of Hardenberg's attention was focused on foreign policy. In 1812, Napoleon forced Prussia to sign a military alliance in preparation for his planned invasion of Russia. When Napoleon's Russian campaign ended in a French debacle, Hardenberg saw the possibility of escaping the domination Napoleon had exercised over Prussia since 1806. Moving cautiously, Hardenberg engineered a military alliance in 1813 between Prussia and Russia, the Treaty of Kalisz. Ironically, Stein, in his new capacity as political adviser to Alexander I, was the Russian representative at Kalisz.

During the ensuing War of Liberation, a wave of patriotic enthusiasm swept through Prussia. After Napoleon's defeat at Leipzig in 1813 led to his withdrawal from the German states, Hardenberg went to Vienna to represent Prussia at the international congress whose purpose was to restructure Europe.

At Vienna, Hardenberg immediately came into conflict with Metternich, the Austrian representative. Metternich, an archconservative intent on reestablishing the old aristocratic order in Europe, opposed German unification in particular (Hardenberg's aim) and nationalism in general, which he saw as destructive to the interests of the multiracial Austrian Empire. The clash between Austria and Prussia over this and other matters at Vienna al-

most led to war and was instrumental in Napoleon's decision to return from his first exile and reclaim the throne of France.

After Waterloo, Hardenberg and Frederick William seemed to become more and more dominated by Metternich. They acquiesced to the creation of the Germanic confederation, a weakly unified government of largely independent small states. Hardenberg gave up his plan to introduce a constitution and a parliament in Prussia and signed the Holy Alliance, which obligated Prussia along with the other signatories to intervene militarily whenever a legitimate monarch anywhere in Europe was threatened by revolution. Nevertheless, domestic reform continued and considerable passion for unification and parliamentary government flourished, especially in Prussian universities.

After the assassination of a conservative newspaper editor by a young nationalist in 1819, Metternich persuaded Hardenberg and Frederick William to adopt the Karlsbad Decrees, which ushered in a period of total reaction in the German states. The Prussian reform movement was ended. Hardenberg, completely under the spell of Metternich, continued to direct Prussian foreign policy until his death, in Genoa on November 26, 1822.

SIGNIFICANCE

Karl von Hardenberg enjoyed considerable successes in domestic reform and diplomacy. Under his leadership, the principle of civic equality became firmly established in Prussia. Prussian Jews began to play leading roles in government, in the arts, and in education after 1812, as a result of Hardenberg's leadership in social reform. The bureaucracy and the army became more efficient because careers in those organizations were opened to all men of talent and promotions became based on merit rather than family. Hardenberg laid the foundation for the Prussian educational system to become the model and the envy of the rest of the world. Hardenberg was responsible for the establishment of a more equitable system of taxation and for the removal of many archaic restrictions on trade and commerce in Prussia.

Through his diplomacy, Hardenberg was instrumental in the defeat of Napoleon. His leadership in foreign affairs allowed the Prussian kingdom not only to survive the dangerous times of the Napoleonic Wars but also to emerge from the era larger and more powerful than it had been in 1780. For these accomplishments, Hardenberg is often recognized as being second in importance only to Otto von Bismarck among Prussian prime ministers. Despite these impressive accomplishments, Hardenberg is sometimes criticized for missing opportunities to accomplish much more.

Hardenberg's goals in foreign and domestic policy were to preserve the old order insofar as possible. He could not have led a movement that would have dismantled that order when the possibility existed of preserving most of it under the Metternichian system. In the final analysis, Hardenberg was an effective diplomat and an able administrator whose tenure as prime minister of Prussia was a decisive step toward the transformation of his country into a modern nation-state.

—Paul Madden

FURTHER READING

Blackbourn, David. *History of Germany, 1780-1918: The Long Nineteenth Century*. 2d ed. Malden, Mass.: Blackwell, 2003. The chapter entitled "Reform from Above" includes information about Hardenberg's attempts to institute reforms after the French Revolution.

Chapman, Tim. *The Congress of Vienna: Origins, Processes, and Results*. London: Routledge, 1998. Recounts the negotiations conducted at the Congress, describing the historical background for these sessions, the agreements reached, and the long-term consequences of these agreements.

Holborn, Hajo. *1648-1840*. Vol. 2 in *A History of Modern Germany*. New York: Alfred A. Knopf, 1964. Contains several chapters on the reform movement and provides sketches of its most important leaders, including Hardenberg. Places the Prussian reform movement and the reformers in their proper perspective in German history.

Meinecke, Friedrich. *The Age of German Liberation, 1795-1815*. Translated by Peter Paret and Helmut Fischer. Berkeley: University of California Press, 1977. One of the best accounts of the period, Meinecke's book provides a good account of Hardenberg's life and work.

Schenk, H. G. *The Aftermath of the Napoleonic Wars: The Concert of Europe, an Experiment*. New York: Oxford University Press, 1947. Perhaps the best account of the congress system implemented by Metternich after 1815. Hardenberg's role in diplomatic affairs during this era is amply and sympathetically treated.

Simon, Walter M. *The Failure of the Prussian Reform Movement, 1807-1819*. New York: Simon & Schuster, 1955. Simon is critical of both the reforms and the reformers in Prussia, particularly Hardenberg. Simon argues that the failure of the reforms to establish a unified, parliamentary German state led directly to the development of the authoritarianism of the German Empire after 1871 and ultimately to the Third Reich.

Webster, C. K. *The Congress of Vienna*. New York: Oxford University Press, 1919. This older study of the Congress of Vienna is still the standard work on the subject.

SEE ALSO: Alexander I; Otto von Bismarck; Metternich; Barthold Georg Niebuhr; Gerhard Johann David von Scharnhorst; Freiherr vom Stein.

RELATED ARTICLES in *Great Events from History: The Nineteenth Century, 1801-1900:* September 15, 1814-June 11, 1815: Congress of Vienna; November 20, 1815: Second Peace of Paris.

KEIR HARDIE
Scottish labor leader and politician

Through agitation and enthusiasm, Hardie, more than any other British politician, helped inspire and organize both the Independent Labour Party and then the more broadly based Labour Party, which became one of Great Britain's two major parties after World War I.

BORN: August 15, 1856; Legbrannock, Lanarkshire, Scotland
DIED: September 26, 1915; Glasgow, Scotland
ALSO KNOWN AS: James Keir Hardie (full name); J. Keir Hardie
AREAS OF ACHIEVEMENT: Government and politics, social reform

EARLY LIFE

James Keir Hardie was born in a small Scottish mining village; he was the illegitimate child of a farm servant, Mary Keir. Keir later married David Hardie, an erratically employed ship's carpenter. They had a large family, and two of Hardie's half brothers later became Labour members of Parliament (M.P.'s). Constant moves and an unsteady income meant that the family circumstances were more like that of unskilled workers than of artisans.

Young Hardie was never apprenticed but began working odd jobs at the age of seven while in Glasgow. When the family moved back to the Lanarkshire coalfields, ten-year-old Hardie started working in the pits and continued working there until his early twenties. Already, Hardie's boldness, energy, and romanticism were apparent. Having been taught to read at home, he received his only formal education at a night school, improving his writing and learning shorthand. An avid reader, Hardie was enraptured with Robert Burns, both for his Scottish style and for his egalitarian ideas. Reared an agnostic, in his early twenties Hardie was converted to Christianity and joined the Evangelical Union Church, a less doctrinaire and a more evangelical and democratic denomination than the official Calvinist Presbyterian Church. Partially in reaction to his drunken stepfather, Hardie became a strong advocate of temperance. He thus reflected the late-Victorian pattern of self-help and self-control as a way to improve oneself.

In 1879, Hardie married Lillie Wilson, a simple patient woman with whom he had three children. She later kept their home in Cumnock (in Ayrshire, Scotland) when he resided in London. An active and passionate man, Hardie had brief affairs with several women. Hardie was stocky and of average height, but his unconventional dress and heavy beard would soon be the caricaturists' delight. His black beard turned gray by his late thirties, which reinforced his position as an "elder" pioneer in labor politics and his aura as a working-class folk hero.

LIFE'S WORK

Locally known as a public speaker on temperance, Hardie became involved in trade union activity in 1878, as a result of which he lost his job and never worked as a miner again. He soon became a local miners' union agent and then secretary of the struggling union in Ayrshire. His militant approach led to two humiliating strike defeats. He attempted but failed to create an effective Scottish Miner's National Federation.

Young, flamboyant, and well known through his speaking, writing, and trade union activities, Hardie became active in Liberal politics. The Liberal Party was in flux: Its leader, William Ewart Gladstone, was becoming a champion of the masses, his ministry was making both county and national government more democratic, most of its aristocratic element was leaving the party, and a radical wing was developing. Moreover, a few workingmen were elected as Liberal M.P.'s (dubbed "Lib-Labs").

At that time, Hardie was already evolving a political position of socialism or radical collectivism, advocating increased governmental involvement in society. Thus, it was unlikely that he would be selected as a Lib-Lab candidate when he formally sought the Liberal Party nomination in the 1888 Mid-Lanark parliamentary by-election. Rebuffed, he ran and lost badly as an independent, an experience that made him more distrustful of the Liberals.

At the age of thirty, by which time he was a Socialist, Hardie attended his first Trades Union Congress (TUC) and made incessant attacks on its cautious leaders. Although his views gained wider acceptance by the early 1890's as the more militant "new unionism" grew, he was still considered by the TUC establishment as a troublemaker. When in 1894 he was neither an active worker at his trade nor a full-time union official, he was barred under new standing orders from being a delegate to the TUC. By then, however, Hardie had persuaded the TUC to advocate the eight-hour day (1891) and nationalization of production, distribution, and exchange (1894).

Keir Hardie. (Library of Congress)

In 1888, Hardie organized and served as secretary of the short-lived Scottish Labour Party, a loose coalition of various Scottish protest or labor organizations. In 1892, Hardie was elected to Parliament for West Ham South in London's East End; he succeeded as an independent because of Liberal division there. Although he failed to nurture that constituency and was defeated in 1895, he cut a colorful figure in Parliament for those three intervening years.

Disdaining the staid conventional dress of most members, Hardie entered Parliament in yellow tweed trousers, a serge jacket, and a Sherlock Holmes-style deerstalker cap, all of which reflected his bohemian love of flashy clothes. While in the Commons, Hardie vehemently protested Parliament's recognition of a royal birth while it ignored a major Welsh mining disaster. Most significant, Hardie was the first to focus political attention on unemployment, which suddenly expanded during the early 1890's.

In 1893, while still in Parliament, Hardie was instrumental in founding the Independent Labour Party (ILP).

Wanting it to become a broad-based party with significant electoral support, Hardie steered it carefully away from becoming branded merely a doctrinaire organization ("Independent" not "Socialist" was used in its title) and based it on existing local working-class or socialist institutions. Serving as its first chairman (from 1894 to 1900, and later from 1913 to 1915), he then helped it become more centralized. Realizing that the ILP, however, was still only a small party based primarily in the north of England, Hardie championed the creation of the Labour Representation Committee (LRC, which became the Labour Party in 1906). It, too, was a coalition of organizations, socialist ones (such as the ILP) as well as many nonsocialist trade unions. Hardie harnessed the financial and electoral support of trade unions to an effective and unified political party separate from the existing main parties.

The general election in 1900 caught the new LRC unprepared, but Hardie was returned to Parliament from the Welsh mining constituency of Merthyr Burghs and served until 1915. He benefited from friendly Liberal support, and in 1903 he agreed with the secret Liberal-Labour arrangement that in certain constituencies the two parties would not compete. That agreement helped Labour win twenty-nine seats in the 1906 election. By a one-vote margin, Hardie was elected Labour Party leader in the Commons (1906-1907). Although not considered a good leader, he did help achieve a reversal of the Taff Vale decision and a guarantee of civil immunity for unions on strike.

Hardie did not have the temperament to serve as spokesperson for a consensus position within the party; he was the bold advocate of minority causes, be they socialist or radical. He opposed the South African (Boer) War (1899-1902), supported the native populations in India and South Africa, and championed the suffragettes. The latter cause hurt him within the Labour movement, for Hardie supported Emmeline Pankhurst's Women's Social and Political Union and its extraparliamentary tactics and symbolic violence, as well as its emphasis on enfranchising primarily middle-class women.

Hardie was also an internationalist. He loved to travel, making trips to the United States, Canada, Europe, and elsewhere. With his appearance at the inaugural conference of the Second International (1889 in Paris), he became a fixture of international socialism. As with the ILP and the Labour Party, Hardie opposed doctrinaire attempts to exclude unorthodox socialist organizations and to forbid cooperation of socialist parties with nonsocialist ones. An advocate of class solidarity (though not of class war), Hardie opposed the European drift toward World War I and tried in vain to persuade the Second International to declare a general strike should a world war start. When all the major socialist parties of Europe, as well as the British Labour Party, supported their governments' decisions for war, Hardie was crushed. After suffering from ill health, exhausted by his demanding schedule, Hardie died on September 26, 1915.

SIGNIFICANCE

Keir Hardie is the preeminent, first-generation Labour political figure. Agitator, propagandist, crusader, maverick—Hardie inspired two generations of Labour supporters. With little formal education, Hardie guided the creation of a Labour Party linking socialist organizations (which contained some middle-class intellectuals) with the trade unions (mostly of nonsocialist skilled workers). A Scotsman residing in London representing a Welsh constituency for fifteen years, Hardie supported workers everywhere. At a time before radio and television, Hardie carried his message by rousing public speeches and by his newspaper columns throughout Great Britain, and his portrait became a fixture in many working-class homes.

Always vain and egotistical, Hardie did not work well with colleagues. Lax in financial matters and disliking details and procedures, he was never an effective administrator. He spoke and wrote passionately on issues, but he never tried to develop coherent programs for implementing socialism. He disdained theoretical analysis, and his socialism was emotional, rather than intellectual. Hardie's reputation as the erratic, sometimes irresponsible, flamboyant, pioneering Labour agitator, however, belies his other significant attributes.

Hardie was practical and flexible. To him, socialism was not only a future system but also a practical system to improve the lot of working people in his own day. He realized that the workers needed political representation, not as a minor adjunct of the Liberal Party but through their own party. He also realized that an effective party could not be created from the top; it must be based on existing local organizations.

Hardie's range became increasingly wider and more effective: He had limited success with the ILP (1893) but achieved a significant victory with the LRC-Labour Party (1900), which finally included trade unions themselves. A romanticist (as well as an evangelical Christian who became also a spiritualist), Hardie never systematized his political views: He advocated a radical stress on personal liberties, governmental actions to improve

conditions and eliminate unemployment, and future nationalizations. This broad political spectrum encouraged both socialists and pragmatic trade unionists to participate in the Labour Party. His uncertainty as to whether this early party was a pressure group or a party seeking power furthered its broad-based appeal.

Within ten years of Hardie's death, Labour replaced the Liberals as one of Great Britain's two most important parties, even forming a government briefly in 1924. In the 1930's, the party became more precise in its programs and more determined to gain office to implement them, and it was successful following World War II. Although the pioneering Hardie would seem out of place in the mid-twentieth century party, it was his persistence and organizational foresight that helped make that Labour Party possible.

—Jerry H. Brookshire

FURTHER READING

Bealey, Frank, and Henry Pelling. *Labour and Politics, 1900-1906: A History of the Labour Representation Committee*. London: Macmillan, 1958. A sequel to Henry Pelling's *The Origins of the Labour Party*, this standard work well demonstrates Hardie's role in moving the LRC toward becoming an effective party by 1906. While stressing Labour's independence, Hardie worked carefully with the Liberal Party on both the national and local levels.

Benn, Caroline. *Keir Hardie*. London: Hutchinson, 1993. A critical biography written by the late Caroline Benn, a political activist whose husband, Tony Benn, is a former Labour M.P. and cabinet minister.

Howell, David. *British Workers and the Independent Labour Party, 1888-1906*. Manchester, England: Manchester University Press, 1983. This is a masterful but complex treatment designed for specialists in the field. Howell brilliantly synthesizes his and many other researchers' work as he deftly examines local trade union and ILP branches as well as the national ILP center. This major work is a must for any sustained investigation of early labor politics.

Hughes, Emrys. *Keir Hardie*. London: Allen & Unwin, 1956. This is a laudatory biography written by Hardie's son-in-law and latter-day political disciple. Although uncritical and subjective, Hughes helps recreate the passions and the feuds of Hardie's life.

Jeffreys, Kevin, ed. *Leading Labour: From Keir Hardie to Tony Blair*. London: I. B. Tauris, 1999. Contains biographies of every Labour leader during the past one hundred years, including Hardie.

Laity, Paul. *The British Peace Movement, 1870-1914.* New York: Oxford University Press, 2001. A history of the peace movement, based on previously unused materials in the Peace Society Archive. Includes information about Hardie's participation in the movement.

McLean, Iain. *Keir Hardie.* New York: St. Martin's Press, 1975. This excellent brief biography is favorable toward, but not uncritical of, its subject. It is the best introduction to Hardie, and it also explains background issues well for nonspecialist readers.

Morgan, Kenneth O. *Keir Hardie: Radical and Socialist.* London: Weidenfeld & Nicolson, 1975. This is the best comprehensive Hardie biography. Its generally favorable coverage fails to capture Hardie's flamboyance. It concludes with an excellent chapter relating Hardie's legacy on the party throughout the twentieth century.

Pelling, Henry. *The Origins of the Labour Party, 1880-1900.* London: Macmillan, 1954. This standard, judicious appraisal focuses primarily on the function of socialist organizations (and deliberately de-emphasizes trade unions) in establishing the Labour Party. Hardie's successes are recognized clearly in this treatment.

Reid, Fred. *Keir Hardie: The Making of a Socialist.* London: Croom Helm, 1978. Treating Hardie's early life through 1895, Reid focuses on his childhood, the fluid 1880's, and Hardie's establishing the ILP. Exhaustingly researched, it provides a deeper and more subtle understanding of Hardie's personality and his evolving political concepts.

SEE ALSO: William Ewart Gladstone.

RELATED ARTICLES in *Great Events from History: The Nineteenth Century, 1801-1900:* January, 1884: Fabian Society Is Founded; August 3, 1892: Hardie Becomes Parliament's First Labour Member; February 27, 1900: British Labour Party Is Formed.

THOMAS HARDY
English novelist and poet

One of the great English novelists and poets of the late nineteenth century, Hardy is representative of the Victorian trauma of the loss of God and the search for a new order, and his works are still widely read.

BORN: June 2, 1840; Higher Bockhampton, Dorset, England
DIED: January 11, 1928; Dorchester, Dorset, England
AREA OF ACHIEVEMENT: Literature

EARLY LIFE

Thomas Hardy was the son of a master mason. His father was content with his low social status and his rural surroundings, but his mother, whom Hardy later called "a born bookworm," encouraged his education and urged him to raise his social standing. John Hicks, a Dorchester architect, took the boy on as a pupil at the age of sixteen. While in Hicks's office, Hardy met the well-known poet William Barnes, who became an important influence on his career. Another early influence was the classical scholar Horace Moule, an essayist and reviewer. Moule encouraged Hardy to read John Stuart Mill and the iconoclastic *Essays and Reviews* (1860) by Frederick Temple and others, both of which contributed to the undermining of Hardy's simple religious faith.

At the age of twenty-two, Hardy went to London to pursue his architectural training; by this time, however, he had also begun to write poetry and to entertain hopes of a literary career. In 1866, after reading Algernon Charles Swinburne's *Poems and Ballads: First Series* (1866), he began an intensive two-year period of writing poetry. He submitted many poems for publication during this time, but none was published, although many of these were published later, when he began writing poetry only.

After returning to Bockhampton in 1867, Hardy decided to try his hand at writing fiction. His first effort in this genre, "The Poor Man and the Lady," based on his perception of the difference between city and country life, received some favorable attention from publishers. After a discussion with novelist George Meredith, however, Hardy decided not to publish the work but, on Meredith's advice, to strike out in a new direction. In imitation of the detective fiction of Wilkie Collins, he thus wrote *Desperate Remedies* (1871). In spite of his success Hardy did not stay with the melodramatic novel but instead took the advice of a reader who liked the rural scenes in his first work and wrote a pastoral idyll entitled *Under the Greenwood Tree* (1872). Although the book was well received by critics, its sales were poor.

Hardy had found his true subject—the rural English life of an imaginary area he called Wessex—and he was on his way to becoming a full-time writer. He began writing serials for periodicals, abandoned architecture, and launched himself on a career that was to last well into the twentieth century.

LIFE'S WORK

In 1874, Hardy married Emma Lavinia Gifford, a socially ambitious young woman who shared his interest in books. At about the same time, his first great novel, *Far from the Madding Crowd* (1874), appeared and received many favorable reviews. As a result, editors began asking for the works of Thomas Hardy. While living with his wife at Sturminister Newton in a small cottage, Hardy composed his next great novel, *The Return of the Native* (1878), and enjoyed what he later called the happiest years of his life. After a brief social life in London, Hardy returned to Dorset, had his home "Max Gate" built, and published the third of his five masterpieces, *The Mayor of Casterbridge* (1886). For the next several years, Hardy continued his writing, traveled with his wife, and read German philosophy.

By this time, Hardy himself was being seen as a philosophical novelist. What has been called his "philosophy," however, can be summed up in an early (1865) entry in his notebooks: "The world does not despise us; it only neglects us." The difference between Hardy and many nineteenth century artists who experienced a similar loss of faith is that while others such as William Wordsworth and Thomas Carlyle were able to achieve some measure of religious affirmation, Hardy never embraced a transcendent belief. He did not try to escape the isolation that his loss of faith created, although in all of his major novels and in most of his poetry, he continued to try to find some value in a world of accident, chance, and indifference. Indeed, all of Hardy's serious artistic work can be seen as variations on his one barren theme of the loss of God and the quest for a new value system.

Late in his life, Hardy said that he never really wanted to write novels and did so only out of economic necessity. Indeed, many of his minor works are imitations of popular forms of the time. Although he did imitate the detective novel or social comedy, however, when he wished to write a novel that more clearly reflected his own vision of humanity's situation in the world, he could find no adequate fictional model among the popular forms of the time. Thus, he returned to classical models such as the pastoral for *Far from the Madding Crowd* and *The Woodlanders* (1887), Greek tragedy for *The Mayor*

Thomas Hardy.

of Casterbridge and *The Return of the Native*, and the epic for *Tess of the D'Urbervilles* (1891) and *Jude the Obscure* (1896).

Because these early genres were based on some sense of there being a God-ordered world, Hardy could not imitate them exactly but rather had to transform them into his own grotesque versions of pastoral, tragedy, and epic. As a result, in his pastorals nature is neither benevolent nor divinely ordered; in his tragedies, his heroes are not heroic because they defy the gods but precisely because there is no God; and in his epic works, his epic figures— Tess and Jude—are not heroes who represent the order of their society but rather are outcasts because neither their society nor indeed their universe has inherent value.

Thus, if Hardy is a philosophical novelist, as is often claimed, his philosophy is a simple and straightforward one—the world is an indifferent place and the heavens are empty of meaning and value. Although Hardy did not have a unified philosophical system, he was more committed to metaphysical issues than he was to the various social issues that preoccupied many novelists of the late nineteenth century. This is true in spite of the fact that the surface plot of *Tess of the D'Urbervilles* deals with the so-called marriage question in England and *Jude the Obscure* ostensibly deals with the problem of equal education.

Hardy's initial enthusiasm for his fourth important novel, *Tess of the D'Urbervilles*, was dampened when it was turned down by two editors before being accepted for serial publication by a third. The publication of this work brought hostile reaction and notoriety to Hardy—a notoriety that increased after the publication of his last great novel, *Jude the Obscure*. Hardy was both puzzled and cynical about these reactions to his last two novels for their iconoclastic views of sexuality, marriage, and class distinctions, but he was by then financially secure and decided to return to his first love, poetry.

In poetry, Hardy believed that his views could be presented in a less obvious and more distanced way. For the rest of his career, he wrote little else. His poems, of which he published well over a thousand, were well received, and his experimental drama, *The Dynasts: A Drama of the Napoleonic Wars* (1903-1908), brought him even more respect, fame, and honor. The final years of Hardy's life were spoiled only by the death of his wife in 1912. Within four years, he married his secretary, Florence Dugdale, who cared for him in his old age. Hardy continued to write poetry regularly for the rest of his life; his final volume, *Winter Words* (1928), was being prepared for publication when he died on January 11, 1928. His death was mourned by all of England, and his ashes were placed in Westminster Abbey.

SIGNIFICANCE

Thomas Hardy is second only to Charles Dickens as the most read and most discussed writer of the Victorian era. New books and articles appear on his life and work each year with no signs of abating. In terms of volume and diversity of work, Hardy is a towering literary figure with two highly respected careers—one as a novelist and one as a poet.

Interest in Hardy's work has followed two basic patterns. The first is philosophical, with many critics creating elaborate metaphysical structures that supposedly underlay his fiction. During the late twentieth century, however, interest shifted to that aspect of Hardy's work that was most scorned before—his technical expertise and his experiments with many different genres. Only recently has what once was termed his fictional clumsiness been reevaluated as sophisticated poetic technique. Fur-

thermore, Hardy's career as a poet, which has always been under the shadow of his fiction, has been seen in a more positive light recently and has even been called by some critics the most significant and important part of his life's work.

Hardy was a curious blend of the old-fashioned and the modern. With a career that began in the Victorian era and did not conclude until after World War I, Hardy was contemporary with both the representative Victorian writer Matthew Arnold and the most frequently cited representative of the modern, T. S. Eliot. Many critics suggest that Hardy, more than any other writer, bridges the gulf between the Victorian sensibility and the modern era.

Although not a systematic philosophical thinker, Hardy was a great existential humanist. His hope for humanity was that humans would realize that creeds and conventions that presupposed a God-oriented center of value were baseless. He hoped that humans would loosen themselves from religious dogma and become aware of their freedom to create their own value system. If only human beings would realize that all people were equally alone and without divine help, Hardy believed, they would realize also that it was the height of absurdity for such lost and isolated creatures to fight among themselves. The breakout of World War I was thus a crushing blow to whatever optimism Hardy held for modern humanity.

In his relentless vision of a world stripped of transcendence, Hardy is a distinctly modern novelist. As one critic has said of him, he not only directs one's attention back to the trauma of the loss of faith in the nineteenth century, he also leads one into the quest for renewed value that characterizes the modern era.

—*Charles E. May*

FURTHER READING

Beach, Joseph Warren. *The Technique of Thomas Hardy*. Chicago: University of Chicago Press, 1922. A classic, pioneering study that focused on Hardy's fictional technique rather than his philosophy.

Brady, Kristin. *The Short Stories of Thomas Hardy*. New York: St. Martin's Press, 1982. A helpful study of an often-neglected part of Hardy's work, showing how his stories are a link between the old-fashioned tale and the modern short story.

Brooks, Jean R. *Thomas Hardy: The Poetic Structure*. Ithaca, N.Y.: Cornell University Press, 1971. An excellent study that focuses on readings of the major works from the standpoint of linguistic patterns and poetic structure.

Carpenter, Richard. *Thomas Hardy*. New York: Twayne, 1964. More than an introductory overview, this study reveals the mythic structures that underlie much of Hardy's fiction.

Dean, Susan. *Hardy's Poetic Vision in "The Dynasts."* Princeton, N.J.: Princeton University Press, 1977. An interesting study of Hardy's experimental epic drama that proposes that the work is an objectification of the human mind.

Guerard, Albert J., Jr. *Thomas Hardy: The Novels and Stories*. Cambridge, Mass.: Harvard University Press, 1949. One of the most important studies to stimulate the modern reevaluation of Hardy's work, this book did much to call attention to Hardy's antirealism and thus his similarity to such writers as Joseph Conrad and André Gide.

Hynes, Samuel. *The Pattern of Hardy's Poetry*. Chapel Hill: University of North Carolina Press, 1961. An important reevaluation of Hardy's poetry that did much to create a new interest in this neglected body of Hardy's work.

Kramer, Dale, ed. *The Cambridge Companion to Thomas Hardy*. New York: Cambridge University Press, 1999. Collection of essays examining, among other subjects, Hardy's life, his handling of matters of gender, and the influence of religion, science, and philosophy upon his work. Other essays analyze his novels and poetry.

Millgate, Michael. *Thomas Hardy, a Biography Revisited*. New York: Oxford University Press, 2004. Millgate, a leading Hardy scholar, has significantly revised and expanded his Hardy biography that was first published in 1982. The revised edition provides new information about Hardy's family background, self-education as a poet, secret collaborations with aspiring women writers, and other aspects of his life that round out this comprehensive biography.

Turner, Paul. *The Life of Thomas Hardy: A Critical Biography*. Malden, Mass.: Blackwell, 1998. Describes how Hardy used his life experience and his influences from classical literature, Shakespeare, and other authors to create novels and other writings.

Weber, Carl J. *Hardy of Wessex: His Life and Literary Career*. New York: Columbia University Press, 1940. A highly detailed biographical treatment of Hardy that is more valuable for the hard information it supplies about Hardy's life than it is for the somewhat old-fashioned and unenlightening criticism.

SEE ALSO: Matthew Arnold; Thomas Carlyle; Charles Dickens; John Stuart Mill; William Wordsworth; Émile Zola.

RELATED ARTICLES in *Great Events from History: The Nineteenth Century, 1801-1900:* 19th century: Development of Working-Class Libraries; March, 1852-September, 1853: Dickens Publishes *Bleak House*.

WILLIAM RAINEY HARPER
American educator

As the president of the University of Chicago during its formative years, Harper was a major figure in the reshaping of American higher education.

BORN: July 26, 1856; New Concord, Ohio
DIED: January 10, 1906; Chicago, Illinois
AREA OF ACHIEVEMENT: Education

EARLY LIFE
William Rainey Harper was the son of Samuel and Ellen Elizabeth (née Rainey) Harper. His forebears on both sides were Scotch-Irish immigrants; his father was a small-town dry goods merchant. Intellectually precocious, Harper entered the preparatory school of the local Muskingum College at the age of eight, was graduated to the college itself at ten, and received his bachelor of arts degree in 1870. By that time, he had acquired sufficient fluency in Hebrew—the study of which became his lifelong passion—to deliver the salutatory oration at graduation in that language. For several years, he worked in his father's store while keeping up his study of languages.

In 1872-1873, Harper taught Hebrew at Muskingum College. In September, 1873, he began graduate work at Yale. He received his doctoral degree in philology in 1875; his dissertation was titled "A Comparative Study of the Prepositions in Latin, Greek, Sanskrit, and Gothic." He served as principal of the Masonic College (in fact, a glorified high school) at Macon, Tennessee, from 1875 to 1876, and taught Greek and Latin in the preparatory department of Denison University in Granville, Ohio, from 1876 to 1878. Although his family background had been Presbyterian, he became a Baptist while at Denison.

In 1879, Harper moved to the Baptist Union Theological Seminary located in Morgan Park (a Chicago suburb) to teach Hebrew. In addition to earning a bachelor of divinity degree, Harper developed while at Morgan Park a set of correspondence courses in Hebrew, a series of Hebrew textbooks, and a summer course in Semitic languages and biblical studies that became the model for similar courses across the country.

Harper was founder and editor of two journals: the *Hebrew Student* (renamed first the *Old and New Testament Studies* and then the *Biblical Scholar*) and *Hebraica* (which later became the *American Journal of Semitic Languages and Literatures*). In 1886, he went back to Yale as professor of Semitic languages in the Divinity School. Teaching at Yale, he gained a national reputation as a scholar, organizer, and editor. A major factor in his growing prominence was his association, dating from the summer of 1885, with the Chautauqua Institute; Harper's connection with the institute included the principalship of its college of liberal arts.

In 1890, Harper was offered the presidency of the newly planned University of Chicago, to be established under Baptist auspices with major funding provided by the multimillionaire John D. Rockefeller. Before accepting, Harper laid down what he thought should be the guidelines for the institution. After the trustees accepted his proposal in December, 1890, Harper entered upon one of the most remarkably successful episodes in university building in history. By the time the University of Chicago opened in the fall of 1892, he had recruited the nucleus of a topflight faculty; he would go on to make the university into one of the world's great academic centers.

LIFE'S WORK

Harper's first love was teaching; throughout his years as president of the University of Chicago, he continued his classroom work. Unlike most of his fellow academic empire builders, he was a distinguished scholar in his own right. He was a major figure in the revival of Hebrew scholarship. In 1902, he published a detailed and exhaustive study, *The Priestly Element in the Old Testament*; three years later there appeared the companion *The Prophetic Element in the Old Testament* (1905), along with his monumental *Critical and Exegetical Commentary on Amos and Hosea* (1905). Although a professing, even devout, Christian, Harper was an adherent of the so-called higher criticism—that is, the application to the scriptural text of evidentiary tests drawn from philology and history.

While affirming that the authors of the Bible were divinely inspired, Harper believed that their language reflected the linguistic, cultural, and religious context of their time. He accordingly insisted that critical scholarship would not undermine belief but rather would assist modern readers in understanding the real meaning of the Word of God as revealed through the Bible.

After becoming president of the University of Chicago, Harper continued for a time his association with Chautauqua and his journal editorships. He served on the Chicago Board of Education from 1896 to 1898, but the bulk of his energies was devoted to building his university. Along with a detailed conception of the University of Chicago, Harper had the advantage of starting from scratch and thus having neither hallowed traditions nor vested interests to overcome. He had the further advantage of finding in John D. Rockefeller a benefactor who kept his hands off university matters; Rockefeller rarely proffered advice even when asked.

Harper could thus proceed with the plans he had outlined when accepting the presidency: the division of the year into four quarters with the summer quarter an integral part of the academic year, division of the undergrad-

William Rainey Harper. (Library of Congress)

uate program whereby the first two years (the junior college) would be devoted to general education and the second two (the senior college) to more specialized study, faculty control of athletics, establishment of a university press, and structural organization of the institution along departmental lines. He was determined from the start that Chicago should not be simply an undergraduate college, but a center for graduate training and advanced research.

Probably the most distinctively innovative aspect of Harper's plans for the University of Chicago was its extension program. The inspiration came from Harper's messianic zeal to spread his own enthusiasm for learning; the model largely came from his association with Chautauqua, which had in turn based its program upon the example of the English university extension movement.

Chicago's Division of University Extension had three major alternative programs of study. "Lecture-Study" involved traveling instructors giving a locally based series of lectures, one per week for six or twelve weeks; discussions with the instructor at the time of the lecture; and weekly written exercises based upon a printed syllabus. "Correspondence-Teaching" allowed students to pursue course work entirely via mail. Off-campus evening classes in the Chicago area provided classroom work for those who could not attend regular courses because of their jobs. Extension students could earn undergraduate and even graduate credit, but the larger aim was to bring culture to the uncultured. "If culture is not contagious," the *University Record* declared in 1903,

it should be . . . more or less infectious, and every person who is reaping some of the rewards of the earnest labors of scholarly men should see that something is done to bring others into touch with the same spirit.

Harper had his difficulties. One was the pressure to make the university into a Baptist institution in fact and not simply in name. The president and two-thirds of the trustees were required to be Baptists; the initial plans had envisaged compulsory chapel attendance for undergraduates. A man without much interest in theological debates, Harper parried questions from fundamentalist-minded Baptists about where he stood on the authority of the Bible with the equivocal answer that while the Bible was "in a very unique sense 'inspired,'" there was simultaneously present a "human element."

Harper followed a similar balancing act regarding university policy. He exhorted the students to attend the

voluntary religious services; he instituted strict moral supervision over undergraduate housing, activities, and publications; he even—to his eventual regret—acceded to sex segregation in the classroom for the first two undergraduate years. He successfully resisted, however, any screening of the faculty on the basis of religious belief. From the start, the faculty included a number of Jews; Jewish donors played an important part in supplementing the Rockefeller gifts.

Another difficulty faced by all university chief executives of the time was the pressure for conformity on political, social, and economic issues. The failure to renew in 1895 the contract of economist Edward W. Bemis, an outspoken critic of monopolies, led to widespread charges that the University of Chicago was under the thumb of Standard Oil. However, the Bemis case was the exception—and his firing appears to have been attributable primarily to his personal shortcomings. Under Harper, Chicago gained the reputation of a bastion of academic freedom. "In the University of Chicago," he affirmed in his decennial report,

neither the Trustees nor the President . . . has at any time called an instructor to account for public utterances. . . . In no single case has a donor to the University called the attention of the Trustees to the teaching of any officer of the University as being distasteful or objectionable. Still further it is my opinion that no donor of money to a university . . . has any right . . . to interfere with the teaching. Neither an individual, nor the state, nor the church has the right to interfere with the search for truth, or with its promulgation when found.

Establishing a new university was an arduous task. The most serious problem was money. Harper's ambitions were constantly threatening to outrun the institution's financial resources, and the result was continuing friction between him and a dollar-conscious board of trustees. Harper successfully induced Rockefeller, however, to come up with additional funds at critical junctures. At a time when the average faculty salary ranged from fourteen hundred to fifteen hundred dollars annually, Chicago was paying as much as seven thousand dollars to department chairmen. Having such resources to work with gave Harper the leverage to build a distinguished faculty—often by raiding less generously endowed schools.

The faculty during the first year included men who had achieved or were on their way to achieving leadership in their disciplines: Hermann E. von Holst in history, J. Laurence Laughlin in economics, Jacques Loeb in biology, Carl D. Buck in philology, and George Ellery Hale in astronomy. Later Harper brought in such future giants as historian J. Franklin Jameson, philosophers John Dewey and George Herbert Mead, economist Wesley C. Mitchell, Egyptologist James H. Breasted, and physicist Robert A. Millikan. Some would later depart Chicago—because, like Dewey, they became disappointed at failing to receive the financial support that they had been led to expect or because, like Loeb, they received offers too generous to refuse. Most, however, imbued with Harper's vision for the university, would remain there for their full academic careers.

A man with a keen advertising sense, Harper engaged from the start in an active publicity campaign to attract students. A larger student population was seen as evidence of the university's prestige—and more tuition money added to its financial resources. Simultaneously, he pushed forward with an aggressive program of physical and institutional expansion.

The Ogden Graduate School of Science was established in 1892 and within a few years was enrolling more than five hundred students doing graduate work. The Kent Chemical Laboratory was added in 1894, the Ryerson Physical Laboratory the same year, and the Hull Biological Quadrangle three years later. The Haskell Oriental Museum was completed in 1896. The Yerkes Astronomical Observatory, featuring one of the world's most advanced telescopes, was opened at Lake Geneva, in Wisconsin, in 1897. The College of Commerce and Politics (later renamed the School of Commerce and Administration) was organized in 1898, the School of Education in 1901, the Law School in 1902, and the School of Religious and Social Service in 1903-1904.

The Decennial Celebration of 1901 was marked by the laying of the cornerstones of five new buildings along with the publication of a twenty-six-volume set of papers and monographs by faculty members. ("No series of scientific publications," Harper boasted, "so comprehensive in its scope and of so great a magnitude has ever been issued at any one time by any learned society or institution.") The broad range of programs offered by the University of Chicago led to its becoming popularly known as "Harper's Bazaar."

Harper exercised strong centralized control over the institution. Deans were his appointees; he retained final say on faculty appointments and promotions. He was deeply immersed in the details of even the physical plant—and the university's imposing and architecturally unified campus owes much to his fascination with sys-

tematic planning. However, he largely eschewed the role of autocrat.

Harper was willing to listen to others and profit from their advice; he even had a sense of humor. He was sufficiently flexible to abandon his own ideas when their implementation proved impracticable—for example, he abandoned the Greek requirement for the A.B. and agreed to make Hebrew optional in the divinity school. As John D. Rockefeller observed, "He knows how to yield when it is necessary in such a way that no sting or bitterness is left behind, and very few men in the world know how to do that." Although there was a short-lived faculty revolt in 1902, Harper ruled more by the force of his personality than by administrative fiat. After talking with Harper, an admirer recounted, one emerged "slightly dazed but tingling with the excitement of a new project, uplifted by a vision of ultimate possibilities, vibrant with a sense of power, for a brief moment feeling indomitable."

Harper had married Ella Paul, the daughter of the president of Muskingum College, on November 18, 1875. The couple had a daughter and three sons—one of whom, Samuel N. Harper, would become a member of the University of Chicago faculty in Russian history. A man of prodigious energy, Harper had the reputation of "a dynamo in trousers." For years, he went to bed at midnight and rose at dawn. Eventually overwork began to take its toll on even his robust constitution. "To the unthinking mind," he confessed in an address to students,

> the man who occupies a high position . . . is an object of . . . envy. If the real facts were known, in almost every case it would be found that such a man is being crushed—literally crushed—by the weight of the burdens which he is compelled to carry.

He admitted that "with each recurring year it has required greater effort on my part to undertake this kind of service." In 1904, he was found while undergoing an operation for appendicitis to have a cancerous infection that proved inoperable. X-ray treatment similarly proved ineffective. He died January 10, 1906, at only forty-nine years of age.

SIGNIFICANCE

Harper's monument was the University of Chicago. He had succeeded in building within the brief span of a decade and a half one of the world's great institutions of learning. As of 1910, the university boasted the third largest total student enrollment in the country—behind

Harvard and Columbia. Columbia was its only rival in the areas of graduate training and faculty research. At the same time, Harper had maintained a balance that kept in mind the separate needs of undergraduates. There were gaps in the record: Library facilities remained inadequate, the support available for research was uneven, and Harper himself was too prone to follow the model of the older, established universities on the East Coast.

The most striking example of the latter was in regard to the law school, when he opted for the Harvard case-method approach rather than the more innovative ideas of political scientist Ernst Freund. Harper set the pattern for what became a long-term weakness in the university faculty appointment policy—too much emphasis upon bringing in established "stars" from outside while neglecting nascent talent within. His successors lacked his genius for combining organizational skills of the highest order with a larger educational vision. Nevertheless, the University of Chicago was firmly established as a major university. The first dean of the university's law school penned his fitting epitaph: "He had the mind and manners of a captain of industry, but he had the heart and soul of a scholar and a sage."

—John Braeman

FURTHER READING

Goodspeed, Thomas Wakefield. *A History of the University of Chicago: The First Quarter-Century.* Chicago: University of Chicago Press, 1916. A detailed "bricks and mortar" account drawing upon the author's personal knowledge as a fund-raiser and secretary of the board of trustees.

_____. *William Rainey Harper: First President of the University of Chicago.* Chicago: University of Chicago Press, 1928. A hagiography by one of Harper's close associates. Although Goodspeed did utilize archival materials, the work's major strength lies in the author's firsthand knowledge of the man and situation.

Gould, Joseph E. *The Chautauqua Movement: An Episode in the Continuing American Revolution.* New York: State University of New York Press, 1961. Deals extensively with Harper's association with Chautauqua and its relation to the University of Chicago extension program.

Lester, Robin. *Stagg's University: The Rise, Decline, and Fall of Big-Time Football at Chicago.* Urbana: University of Illinois Press, 1995. Harper's innovations extended outside the classroom and onto the football field. Amos Alonzo Stagg was the university's first football coach, and the first tenured coach at a university. Stagg and Harper built a team of national repute that changed the public's perception of college football. This history of Chicago's football team describes the relationship between the two men and university life in the school's initial years.

Nevins, Allan. *Study in Power: John D. Rockefeller, Industrialist and Philanthropist.* 2 vols. New York: Charles Scribner's Sons, 1953. An excellent biography that relates the early history of the University of Chicago to Rockefeller's larger philanthropic activities.

Storr, Richard J. *Harper's University: The Beginnings.* Chicago: University of Chicago Press, 1966. The first volume (and only one published so far) of a planned multivolume history of the University of Chicago, this work is the most thoroughly researched and fullest account of the institution's founding and formative years.

Veysey, Laurence R. *The Emergency of the American University.* Chicago: University of Chicago Press, 1965. An excellent and perceptive analysis of the transformation of American higher education during the late nineteenth and early twentieth centuries. Harper emerges as probably the most attractive of the empire builders of his time.

SEE ALSO: Felix Adler; Charles William Eliot; Alice Freeman Palmer; John D. Rockefeller.

RELATED ARTICLE in *Great Events from History: The Nineteenth Century, 1801-1900:* July 2, 1862: Lincoln Signs the Morrill Land Grant Act.

JOEL CHANDLER HARRIS
American writer

Harris was famous in his day for his retellings of folktales by Uncle Remus in black dialect. In the mid-twentieth century, his reputation suffered when his tales became regarded as negative stereotypes; however, later studies of folklore established Harris's importance as a folklorist who collected authentic black folktales.

BORN: December 9, 1848; Eatonton, Georgia
DIED: July 3, 1908; Atlanta, Georgia
AREA OF ACHIEVEMENT: Literature

EARLY LIFE

Joel Chandler Harris was the illegitimate son of an Irish laborer who deserted his family shortly after Harris was born; however, Harris spent a rather ordinary boyhood in rural Georgia. He was not very interested in school and seems to have preferred playing pranks to studying. At the age of fourteen, Harris was given a job as a printer's devil by Addison Turner, an eccentric planter who published a rural weekly newspaper, *The Countryman*, on his nearby plantation. It is impossible to overestimate Turner's influence on young Harris, for in addition to allowing him to contribute pieces to the paper, Turner also encouraged him to read extensively in his private library and to roam around his thousand-acre plantation. It was here that Harris first heard the black folk narratives that were later to become the heart of the Uncle Remus stories. After working for Turner for four years, Harris held brief jobs at several newspapers around the South. In 1873 he married Esther LaRose and soon settled in Atlanta, where he lived until his death in 1908.

In 1876, Harris was hired to do editorial paragraphing for the Atlanta *Constitution*. Soon after his arrival, he was asked to take over a black-dialect column from a retiring writer, and, on October 26, 1876, his first sketch appeared, featuring the witty observations of an older black man. A month later the older black man was officially called "Uncle Remus," and a major new voice in American humor was born. Uncle Remus began as a rather thin, almost vaudevillian caricature of a black man who supposedly dropped by the Atlanta *Constitution* office to offer practical comments, and some of Harris's own opinions, on corrupt politicians and lazy African Americans. The character grew, however, when Harris transferred the locale of the sketches to a plantation and incorporated tales he had heard in the slave quarters during his early days with Turner. In late 1880, Harris col-

lected twenty-one "urban" and thirty-four "plantation" Uncle Remus sketches along with black songs, maxims, and proverbs in *Uncle Remus: His Songs and His Sayings*. The collection was an immediate success, and, much to Harris's astonishment and embarrassment, he was famous.

LIFE'S WORK

Uncle Remus: His Songs and His Sayings proved so popular that Harris went on to publish a half-dozen more Uncle Remus volumes in his lifetime. In 1881, Harris, who now had a steady and comfortable income, moved his family to a large farmhouse in Atlanta's West End, where he did most of his writing at night after returning home from work. His second collection, *Nights with Uncle Remus* (1883), is the most important and the one that most fully shows the fruits of his labor. In it, Uncle Remus is rounded out much more to become a complete character in his own right, and other characters on the plantation are introduced as storytellers, principally Daddy Jack, a character who speaks in a Sea Island dialect called "Gullah," and who Harris used to tell stories he perceived to be of a different cultural origin than the stories that Uncle Remus tells.

As popular as these Uncle Remus collections were, Harris never considered that their merit was inherently literary. He always insisted that in them he was the "compiler" of a folklore and dialect that were fast disappearing in the South at the end of the nineteenth century. He was careful to include only the Uncle Remus tales that could be verified as authentic black oral narratives, and, with his usual diffidence, he minimized his own role in elevating them to artistic short fiction.

In *Mingo and Other Sketches in Black and White* (1884), Harris surprised his readers by temporarily moving away from the Uncle Remus formula. The collection was favorably reviewed, and Harris showed that his literary talents could be stretched to include what he considered to be more serious forms. The title story, "Mingo: A Sketch of Life in Middle Georgia," is an admirable local-color portrayal of class conflicts. The central conflict is between two white families, the aristocratic Wornums and the poor-white Bivinses. Before the Civil War, the Wornums' daughter, Cordelia, had married the Bivinses' son, Henry Clay, much to the displeasure of the Wornum family, who promptly disinherited her. Henry Clay was killed in the war, and Cordelia died shortly thereafter, leaving a daughter in the care of Mrs. Feratia Bivins, Henry's mother. Mrs. Wornum is overcome with grief after the death of the children and realizes that she has made a mistake in snubbing the Bivinses, but fiercely proud Feratia cannot forgive her.

In a comic yet pathos-filled scene, Mrs. Wornum asks Feratia Bivins to let her see her granddaughter, whom she has never seen. Feratia coolly replies, "if I had as much politeness, ma'am, as I had cheers, I'd ast you to set down," and adamantly refuses to let Mrs. Wornum see the baby. The final wise commentary, however, comes from Mingo, a former Wornum slave who is loyal to his old master and acts as the surrogate father for the surviving child. It is the black man's strength of character and endurance that promises reconciliation and social progress. Harris, a poor white by birth himself, is clearly antiaristocratic and sides with the underdog in times of changing social values, yet by applauding the virtues of loyalty and duty in the black, he comes close to advocat-

ing a servile and passive acceptance, as some of his critics have charged.

Harris's *Free Joe and Other Georgian Sketches* (1887) and the frequently anthologized title story, "Free Joe and the Rest of the World," further illustrate his ambivalence on the "Negro question." In 1840, a slave-speculator named Major Frampton lost all his property except one slave, his body-servant Joe, to Judge Alfred Wellington in a famous card game. Frampton adjourned the game, went to the courthouse and gave Joe his freedom, and then blew his brains out. Joe, although freed, remains in town because his wife Lucinda is now the property of the judge.

All goes well for Joe until the judge dies and his estate is transferred to the stern Spite Calderwood. Calderwood refuses to let Joe visit Lucinda. Joe's easy life comes to an end: The other slaves will have nothing to do with him, and he is an outcast from the white community, sleeping outside under a poplar tree. When Calderwood learns that in spite of his orders Lucinda has been sneaking out to meet Joe, he takes her to Macon and sells her; he even has his hounds kill Joe's dog. Joe, however, even when told the truth about Lucinda, seems incapable of understanding. Night after night he waits for his wife and his dog to return together in the moonlight, until one night he dies alone under the poplar tree, a smile on his face and humble to the last.

In "Free Joe and the Rest of the World," Harris achieves a balance between sentimentality and realistic portrayal in dramatizing the plight of the freeman in the antebellum South. Even though Joe is the humble, unassuming victim of white cruelty, his freedom also represents the vague, Gothic threat of social dissolution to the white community, which comes to view him as "forever lurking on the outskirts of slavery, ready to sound a shrill and ghostly signal" of insurrection. Unlike Brer Rabbit, Joe is no ingenious trickster, and Harris obliquely hints that, all things considered, Joe may have been better off a slave because his freedom leaves him "shiftless" and incapable of fending for himself.

Of the six stories collected in *Balaam and His Master and Other Sketches and Stories* (1891), three are portraits of loyal black people and three treat the fate of a white man in a crumbling society. In this collection Harris again illustrates his favorite themes: the changing social values between black and white people, and the need for reconciliation through patience and understanding. "Balaam and His Master" is the story of the fiercely loyal manservant of young Berrien Cozart—the sensual, cruel, impetuous, and implacable son of a respected plantation

Joel Chandler Harris. (Library of Congress)

family. As in many of Harris's aristocratic families, the older Cozart practices a benign paternalism toward his slaves, but his young son Berrien is nothing but a spoiled and dissolute gambler who abuses the privileges of his race.

Despite his master's excesses, Balaam remains a constant and loyal valet, even to the point of participating in a scam to sell himself to a new master and then returning to Berrien. Berrien is finally arrested for murder, and Balaam breaks into the jail to be with him; but it is too late—Berrien is already dead. The story ends with Balaam loyally crouching over his dead master, who died with a smile as sweet as a "little child that nestles on his mother's breast." Even though Balaam is morally superior to his white master, the message of the story is that loyalty and service are superior to social revolution.

"THE WONDERFUL TAR BABY STORY"

Joel Chandler Harris's Uncle Remus stories are noted for their authentic dialect, but the heavy dialect of plantation slaves is not easily understood by modern readers. In this famous tale, readers will benefit by knowing that "sez" means "says" and "sezee" means "says he." "Brer" is a contraction for "brother."

"Didn't the fox never catch the rabbit, Uncle Remus?" asked the little boy the next evening.

"He come mighty nigh it, honey, sho's you born—Brer Fox did. One day atter Brer Rabbit fool 'im wid dat calamus root, Brer Fox went ter wuk en got 'im some tar, en mix it wid some turkentime, en fix up a contrapshun w'at he call a Tar-Baby, en he tuck dish yer Tar-Baby en he sot 'er in de big road, en den he lay off in de bushes fer to see what de news wuz gwine ter be. En he didn't hatter wait long, nudder, kaze bimeby here come Brer Rabbit pacin' down de road—lippity-clippity, clippity-lippity—dez ez sassy ez a jay-bird. Brer Fox, he lay low. Brer Rabbit come prancin' 'long twel he spy de Tar-Baby, en den he fotch up on his behime legs like he wuz 'stonished. De Tar Baby, she sot dar, she did, en Brer Fox, he lay low.

"'Mawnin'! sez Brer Rabbit, sezee—'nice wedder dis mawnin', sezee.

"Tar-Baby ain't sayin' nuthin', en Brer Fox he lay low.

"'How duz yo' sym'tums seem ter segashuate?' sez Brer Rabbit, sezee.

"Brer Fox, he wink his eye slow, en lay low, en de Tar-Baby, she ain't sayin' nuthin'.

"'How you come on, den? Is you deaf?' sez Brer Rabbit, sezee. 'Kaze if you is, I kin holler louder,' sezee.

"Tar-Baby stay still, en Brer Fox, he lay low.

"'You er stuck up, dat's w'at you is,' says Brer Rabbit, sezee, 'en I'm gwine ter kyore you, dat's w'at I'm a gwine ter do,' sezee.

"Brer Fox, he sorter chuckle in his stummick, he did, but Tar- Baby ain't sayin' nothin'.

"'I'm gwine ter larn you how ter talk ter 'spectubble folks ef hit's de las' ack,' sez Brer Rabbit, sezee. 'Ef you don't take off dat hat en tell me howdy, I'm gwine ter bus' you wide open,' sezee.

"Tar-Baby stay still, en Brer Fox, he lay low.

"Brer Rabbit keep on axin' 'im, en de Tar-Baby, she keep on sayin' nothin', twel present'y Brer Rabbit draw back wid his fis', he did, en blip he tuck 'er side er de head. Right dar's whar he broke his merlasses jug. His fis' stuck, en he can't pull loose. De tar hilt 'im. But Tar-Baby, she stay still, en Brer Fox, he lay low.

"'Ef you don't lemme loose, I'll knock you agin,' sez Brer Rabbit, sezee, en wid dat he fotch 'er a wipe wid de udder han', en dat stuck. Tar-Baby, she ain't sayin' nuthin', en Brer Fox, he lay low.

"'Tu'n me loose, fo' I kick de natchul stuffin' outen you,' sez Brer Rabbit, sezee, but de Tar-Baby, she ain't sayin' nuthin'. She des hilt on, en de Brer Rabbit lose de use er his feet in de same way. Brer Fox, he lay low. Den Brer Rabbit squall out dat ef de Tar-Baby don't tu'n 'im loose he butt 'er cranksided. En den he butted, en his head got stuck. Den Brer Fox, he sa'ntered fort', lookin' dez ez innercent ez wunner yo' mammy's mockin'- birds.

"'Howdy, Brer Rabbit,' sez Brer Fox, sezee. 'You look sorter stuck up dis mawnin',' sezee, en den he rolled on de groun', en laft en laft twel he couldn't laff no mo'. 'I speck you'll take dinner wid me dis time, Brer Rabbit. I done laid in some calamus root, en I ain't gwineter take no skuse,' sez Brer Fox, sezee.

Here Uncle Remus paused, and drew a two-pound yam out of the ashes.

"Did the fox eat the rabbit?" asked the little boy to whom the story had been told.

"Dat's all de fur de tale goes," replied the old man. "He mout, an den agin he moutent. Some say Judge B'ar come 'long en loosed 'im—some say he didn't. I hear Miss Sally callin'. You better run 'long."

Source: Joel Chandler Harris, *Uncle Remus: His Songs and His Sayings* (Rev. ed. New York: D. Appleton, 1895).

In "Where's Duncan?"—another story in *Balaam and His Master and Other Sketches and Stories*—Harris gives a more apocalyptic version of the changing social values between black and white people. The story is narrated by old Isaiah Winchell, who meets a dark stranger named Willis Featherstone as he is hauling his cotton to market. As they camp for the evening, old Isaiah learns that Willis Featherstone is the mulatto son of a plantation owner who had educated him, grown to hate him, and then sold him. The next evening the group camps near the old Featherstone plantation, and a vampirelike mulatto woman comes to invite them to dinner at the "big house." Willis Featherstone, who seems to know the woman, enigmatically asks her, "Where's Duncan?" and she hysterically replies that old Featherstone has "sold my onliest boy." Later that evening, the camp is awakened by a commotion at the big house. Old Isaiah rushes up to see the house on fire, and through the window he glimpses the mulatto woman stabbing Old Featherstone and screaming, "Where's Duncan?" Willis Featherstone, say some of the observers, was inside enjoying the spectacle.

The story ends with a Gothic scene of fiery retribution as the old plantation house burns and collapses, and old Isaiah still dreams of the smell of burning flesh. Violent confrontation is possible, Harris suggests, if white society continues to abuse the black.

In 1900, Harris quit his job at the newspaper so he could concentrate on writing full time at his farmhouse. During his lifetime, he gained much attention from his book. He was admired by Mark Twain, and the two embarked upon a joint lecture tour. Harris was also invited to the White House in 1902 by President Theodore Roosevelt, who declared that Harris's books had been instrumental in repairing the rifts caused by the Civil War. In 1905, he and his son Julian began publishing a southern literary magazine called *Uncle Remus's Magazine*, which achieved a circulation of 200,000 and became another huge success for the writer. Harris, however, was beginning to face recurrent illness in his old age, and the pressures of publishing a magazine did little to restore his health. He died at his home in 1908 after being diagnosed with cirrhosis of the liver.

SIGNIFICANCE

As an editorialist, essayist, and humorist, Joel Chandler Harris was instrumental in trying to reconcile the tensions between North and South, black and white, left by the Civil War. Although he shared some of the racial prejudices of his time—one detects a paternalism for the black in much of the short fiction—he was a progressive

conservative who, as one critic has said, "affirmed the integrity of all individuals, whether black or white; and he could not countenance unjust or inhumane actions by any member of the human race."

During the 1870's and 1880's, his editorials in the Atlanta *Constitution* consistently argue against sectionalism, both literary and political, and in favor of a united country. Any literature, wrote Harris in 1879, takes its materials and flavor from "localism," yet "in literature, art, and society, whatever is truly Southern is likewise truly American; and the same may be said of what is truly Northern."

—*Robert J. McNutt, revised by Thomas J. Cassidy*

FURTHER READING

Baer, Florence E. *Sources and Analogues of the Uncle Remus Tales*. Helsinki, Finland: Academia Scientiarum Fennica, 1980. Essential to anyone trying to study the Brer Rabbit stories. For each tale, Baer gives a summary, the tale type number from *The Types of the Folk-tale* (1928), motif numbers from Stith Thompson's *Motif-Index of Folk Literature* (1955-1958), and a discussion of possible sources. She also includes an excellent essay discussing Harris's legitimacy as a collector of folktales.

Bickley, R. Bruce, ed. *Critical Essays on Joel Chandler Harris*. Boston: G. K. Hall, 1981. Traces the critical heritage about Harris, including contemporary reviews. Of particular importance is an article by Bernard Wolfe, which was printed in *Commentary* in 1949.

_____, ed. *Joel Chandler Harris*. Boston: Twayne, 1978. A full-length study, including chapters on the major as well as the later Uncle Remus tales, and Harris's other short fiction. Includes a brief, useful annotated bibliography.

Brasch, Walter M. *Brer Rabbit, Uncle Remus and the "Cornfield Journalist": The Tale of Joel Chandler Harris*. Mercer, Ga.: Mercer University Press, 2000. Biography detailing Harris's newspaper and literary career and the debate over the racist character of his stories. Brasch argues that Harris's tales accurately depicted American Black English and Reconstruction Georgia.

Cousins, Paul. *Joel Chandler Harris: A Biography*. Baton Rouge: Louisiana State University Press, 1968. A biography that the author worked on intermittently for more than thirty years and that includes material from interviews with friends of Harris. Not a reliable source for critical evaluations of Harris's work.

Harris, Joel Chandler. *Dearest Chums and Partners: Joel Chandler Harris's Letters to His Children: A Domestic Biography*, edited by Hugh T. Keenan. Athens: University of Georgia Press, 1993. Reprints 280 letters that Harris wrote to his four sons and two daughters between 1890 and his death. The letters reveal Harris's interest in Roman Catholicism; some of the letters, written in Uncle Remus's dialect and containing patronizing remarks about "negroes," reveal Harris's attitudes about race.

Hemenway, Robert. Introduction to *Uncle Remus: His Songs and Sayings*, edited by Robert Hemenway. New York: Penguin Books, 1982. Hemenway's introduction is clear and informative, one of the better all-around essays on the Brer Rabbit stories. Contains a brief bibliography.

Keenan, Hugh T. "Twisted Tales: Propaganda in the Tar-Baby Stories." *The Southern Quarterly* 22 (Winter, 1984): 54-69. This essay updates some arguments that Bernard Wolfe put forth in his *Commentary* article (included in R. Bruce Bickley's entry). Better researched than Wolfe's article and more even in tone.

SEE ALSO: Hans Christian Andersen; Henry Clay; Jacob and Wilhelm Grimm; Mark Twain.

RELATED ARTICLE in *Great Events from History: The Nineteenth Century, 1801-1900:* May 8, 1835: Andersen Publishes His First Fairy Tales.

BENJAMIN HARRISON
President of the United States (1889-1893)

Harrison took a narrow view of the powers of the U.S. presidency and neither innovated nor experimented with the office during his single term as the twenty-third president; however, he gave the country an honest and straightforward administration devoted to Republican principles.

BORN: August 20, 1833; North Bend, Ohio
DIED: March 13, 1901; Indianapolis, Indiana
AREA OF ACHIEVEMENT: Government and politics

EARLY LIFE

Benjamin Harrison came from a line of notable Americans. One of his great-grandfathers was a signer of the Declaration of Independence; his paternal grandfather, William Henry Harrison, was ninth president of the United States; and his own father, John Scott Harrison, served in the U.S. House of Representatives.

The farm on which Harrison grew up, known as The Point, was near Cincinnati, and his family was a large one. Harrison himself was the second of eight children, and two other children had the Harrisons as their guardians. Financial difficulties were not unusual, and the children learned the value of hard work and thrift. Benjamin spent much time with his grandmother at her home at North Bend, where he read widely in the excellent library gathered by his grandfather.

In 1847, Harrison went to Farmer's College in Cincinnati; two years later, he transferred to Miami University, where he met Carrie Scott, daughter of the Reverend Dr. John Scott, a professor. In 1853, a year after Harrison was graduated, he married Carrie; her father performed the ceremony.

The Harrisons settled at The Point while Benjamin studied law. He was admitted to the bar in 1854, and the couple moved to Indianapolis, where Harrison set up his law office. Difficult times faced the young couple initially, but Harrison's meticulous research, his command of the facts, and his ability to present those facts clearly and plainly soon won for him cases and respect. By 1855, Harrison was doing well, and he was drawn into politics.

An opponent of slavery, he was naturally attracted to the new Republican Party and was an avid supporter of John Charles Frémont in the 1856 election; this support was expressed so fiercely that it drew a rebuke from his father, who urged him to temper his language.

An extremely loyal party man throughout his life, Harrison became secretary to the Republican state central committee; this was to be his real entry into politics. His successes would be owed primarily to his steadfast devotion to the party's cause and the alliances he formed in its struggles.

Elected as reporter to the state supreme court in 1860, Harrison was torn between serving in that position and volunteering for the Union army. In 1862, he enlisted, and was given command of a regiment. He was a strict disciplinarian but was popular with his troops because he took care to see that they were always well supplied.

Harrison was an able officer, cool and judicious in combat. During the Atlanta campaign, he fought well at the Battle of Resaca and at Peachtree Creek; against a surprise Confederate attack, he helped save the Union army by holding a weak point in the line. By the war's end, he was a brigadier general; in politics, the veteran's vote was almost always his.

At the end of the war, Harrison looked much as he would for the remainder of his life. He was about five feet, six inches tall and stout. He wore a long, full beard, which, like his hair, was light brown and which turned silver as he aged. His deeply blue eyes could be steely or warm, depending upon his mood. He had a fine voice, clear and penetrating; it was admirably suited to his manner of speaking, which was to stress the orderly arrangement of facts.

LIFE'S WORK

After the war, Harrison allied himself strongly with the section of the Republican Party that favored a radical reconstruction of the South, including voting rights for the free blacks and harsh treatment of the defeated rebels. For a time, however, Harrison stuck to his law practice. It was not until 1872 that he took an active part in the political wars, campaigning successfully for Republican candidates.

In 1876, the Republican candidate for governor of Indiana abruptly quit the race when his associations with the corrupt Grant administration were revealed. The party central committee hastily nominated Harrison, who was away on a fishing trip

---

HARRISON'S INAUGURAL ADDRESS

Fellow citizens: There is no constitutional or legal requirement that the President shall take the oath of office in the presence of the people, but there is so manifest an appropriateness in the public induction to office of the chief executive officer of the nation that from the beginning of the Government the people, to whose service the official oath consecrates the officer, have been called to witness the solemn ceremonial. The oath taken in the presence of the people becomes a mutual covenant. The officer covenants to serve the whole body of the people by a faithful execution of the laws, so that they may be the unfailing defense and security of those who respect and observe them, and that neither wealth, station, nor the power of combinations shall be able to evade their just penalties or to wrest them from a beneficent public purpose to serve the ends of cruelty or selfishness.

My promise is spoken; yours unspoken, but not the less real and solemn. The people of every State have here their representatives. Surely I do not misinterpret the spirit of the occasion when I assume that the whole body of the people covenant with me and with each other to-day to support and defend the Constitution and the Union of the States, to yield willing obedience to all the laws and each to every other citizen his equal civil and political rights. Entering thus solemnly into covenant with each other, we may reverently invoke and confidently expect the favor and help of Almighty God—that He will give to me wisdom, strength, and fidelity, and to our people a spirit of fraternity and a love of righteousness and peace.

This occasion derives peculiar interest from the fact that the Presidential term which begins this day is the twenty-sixth under our Constitution. The first inauguration of President Washington took place in New York, where Congress was then sitting, on the 30th day of April, 1789, having been deferred by reason of delays attending the organization of the Congress and the canvass of the electoral vote. Our people have already worthily observed the centennials of the Declaration of Independence, of the battle of Yorktown, and of the adoption of the Constitution, and will shortly celebrate in New York the institution of the second great department of our constitutional scheme of government. When the centennial of the institution of the judicial department, by the organization of the Supreme Court, shall have been suitably observed, as I trust it will be, our nation will have fully entered its second century. . . .

Source: Benjamin Harrison, Inaugural Address, March 4, 1889, in *A Compilation of the Messages and Papers of the Presidents*, edited by James D. Richardson (Washington, D.C.: Bureau of National Literature and Art, 1904), vol. 9.

---

and had to be persuaded to run when he returned. He then mounted a vigorous campaign, promising government reform, supporting sound money, and waving the "bloody shirt" by accusing the Democrats of wartime treason. He covered the state and received much support from veterans but lost by five thousand votes. Nevertheless, he had greatly impressed party regulars. He increased this respect and won many supporters when he went on a speaking tour for presidential candidate Ruth-

erford B. Hayes. Harrison spoke across the country, from New Jersey to Chicago, and established himself as a nationally recognized Republican leader.

In 1878, there occurred a tragic and bizarre incident. John Scott Harrison died in May. Leaving the cemetery, John Harrison, Benjamin's brother, noticed that the grave of a recently buried cousin had been disturbed. At that time, grave-robbing was commonly practiced by "resurrection men" who sold the bodies to medical schools.

Fearing that this had happened, John Harrison and a sheriff visited the Ohio Medical College in Cincinnati. There they discovered the body, not of the cousin, but of John Scott Harrison, suspended in a pit in the school's basement.

Great public anger was aroused by what was called the Harrison Horror. After the father's reinterment, the cousin's body was located in Ann Arbor, a finding that revealed a widespread and regular traffic between medical schools and grave-robbers. Following this incident, reforms were enacted regulating the procurement of cadavers for medical studies.

Harrison was elected to the U.S. Senate in 1880. He sponsored extremely generous pensions for veterans and was a strong protectionist, favoring high tariffs. At the same time that he was voting to have the federal government protect private industry, Harrison opposed flood control projects on the Mississippi, maintaining that the government had no constitutional right to assist individuals. In making such an argument, Harrison was following the essential Republican Party line, which strongly and unabashedly favored business, particularly big business. He never deviated from this line, disregarding the rise of labor and the growing emphasis on workers' rights.

In 1884, Harrison worked diligently for the Republican nominee, James G. Blaine, despite the charges of corruption that clung to the candidate. (Blaine sometimes closed his correspondence with the injunction, "Burn this letter.") In a close race, Blaine was defeated by Grover Cleveland after a Republican clergyman derided the Democrats as the party of "rum, Romanism and rebellion."

After the defeat, Harrison was in the vanguard of efforts to rebuild the Republican Party. In 1887, he was ousted from the Senate when the Democrats took control of the Indiana legislature (this was before the popular election of senators). During that same year, President Cleveland launched a vigorous attack on the tariff, denouncing a protective system that allied the federal government and big business at the expense of the worker. This was a direct assault on the key Republican position and set the battle lines for the next campaign.

The Republicans had an issue but lacked a candidate, since Blaine declined to run and there was no other figure of national prominence in the party. Harrison, the dedicated and hardworking party man, won the nomination in 1888.

In the election, Harrison faced Grover Cleveland. The Republicans were well financed by business and trade associations, which naturally favored a high tariff to protect their interests. A dispute among Democrats in New York State proved decisive: Although Cleveland polled a ninety thousand popular-vote majority, he lost the electoral count by 233 to 168.

Personally honest and highly moral (he had considered the ministry as an alternative to law), Harrison was generally independent in selecting his cabinet. The one exception was his appointment of Blaine as secretary of state. Actually, this appointment proved productive, because both were strong believers in closer ties with Central and South America. Their efforts led to a pan-American conference in 1889, during which representatives from most nations in the hemisphere toured the United States.

In line with his earlier efforts as a senator, Harrison pushed for increased veterans' pensions. He was also firmly in favor of protecting black voting rights in the South, moderate civil service reform, and limited use of silver in the currency—the last adopted to satisfy Republicans in the West, an area rich in the metal. The main struggle in Congress was over the tariff, which the Republicans wished to increase; they succeeded, raising customs duties an average of almost 50 percent. The tariff would once again prove to be a key issue in the presidential election.

The so-called Mafia incident in New Orleans arose in 1890. A police officer scheduled to testify on the activities of the alleged society was murdered; before he died, he named several Italians. After a long, tense trial, the accused men were acquitted. A mob stormed the jail and killed eleven Italian inmates who had not yet been released. Harrison denounced the event and offered his regrets to the Italian government but pointed out that the Constitution left considerable powers to the states; in this case, the federal government was unable to act. The incident was short-lived, but one major result was increased support for Harrison's call for a larger navy: During the brief war scare, observers noted that Italy had a much larger fleet of armored ships than did the United States.

In the election of 1892, Harrison faced, once again, the redoubtable Grover Cleveland. The election turned into a referendum on Republican policies, especially those regarding labor. The high tariff had protected the captains of industry but not the workers. Wages had been repeatedly cut, and many workers had been fired. Worse yet, a wave of antilabor violence swept the country. During a strike at the Homestead Plant of the Carnegie Steel Company, twenty men were killed in combat between locked-out workers and Pinkerton detectives. In July, a fight between striking miners and strikebreakers left thirty miners dead in Idaho; Harrison ordered in federal troops to restore order and keep the mines open. Another mine-related battle erupted in eastern Tennessee, where miners fought convicts who had been brought in to dig coal. The result of all this was a defection of thousands of voters from the Republicans to the Populist Party or to the Democrats.

Harrison did not campaign. His wife was gravely ill, and she died on October 25. Harrison was despondent and seemed relieved when he lost the election. Following his presidential term, Harrison returned to the law but accepted only a few cases. He refused a chair at the University of Chicago, although he did give a series of lectures at Stanford, which later became the book *Views of an Ex-President* (1901). He continued his extensive charitable contributions, especially for support of educating southern black people and for orphans.

In April, 1896, at the age of sixty-two, Harrison remarried; his bride was the widow Mary Lord Dimmick, daughter of his dead wife's sister. In February, 1897, they had a daughter; by his first wife Harrison had a son and a daughter.

With few exceptions, family life now occupied Harrison. In 1896, he firmly discouraged any talk of renomination, although he did campaign for the candidate William McKinley. In 1899, Harrison was retained by Venezuela in an arbitration case with Great Britain over disputed boundaries. In the course of a fifteen-month period, Harrison amassed three volumes of evidence, which he masterfully presented to the arbitration panel in Paris from June through October. Despite this, the panel decided in favor of Great Britain; it was later revealed that improper pressure from London had influenced the decision.

In March, 1901, Harrison caught a cold, which rapidly worsened and developed into pneumonia. On March 13, at his home in Indianapolis, he died.

SIGNIFICANCE

Soon after Harrison entered the White House, his private secretary had a talk with him. The secretary later recalled:

> I asked the President if he had ever seriously thought about being President. He said the thought had been with him many times when suggested by others, but he had never been possessed by it or had his life shaped by it.

This frank, disarming reply is characteristic of Harrison, and it reveals much about him and his administration. He was not driven by desire for office or inspired by a specific sense of mission. He seems to have regarded the the presidency as a duty to discharge faithfully and honestly but not a position through which to effect profound changes in American life. With few exceptions, he was probably quite satisfied with American life: The Union had been preserved by the Civil War, slavery had ended, business was good, and public officials were becoming increasingly, if perhaps slowly, more honest.

Harrison was neither an innovator nor an experimenter. He clung closely to a narrow interpretation of the Constitution, one that limited the powers of the federal government and left private enterprise strictly alone. Exceptions were those activities that protected business: the tariff, a firm hand in labor disputes, and a strong currency. In this, he was in accord with the prevailing policy of his party and, indeed, of many in the country.

As a man, Harrison was honest, principled, and forthright. Personally, he was kind and generous, a charming and affectionate family man, and a devoted friend. Even his political foes admired and respected him. As president, he conducted himself within the constitutional limits he revered, and his term in office was like the man himself, solid and dependable.

—Michael Witkoski

FURTHER READING

Armbruster, Maxim. *The Presidents of the United States and Their Administrations*. 7th ed. New York: Horizon Press, 1982. Introductory sketch of Harrison and his times; good on the fundamental tenets of the Republican Party of the period.

Calhoun, Charles W. *Benjamin Harrison*. New York: Times Books, 2005. In this reassessment of Harrison's presidency, Calhoun concludes that Harrison was an activist who accomplished a great deal until the Democrats took control of Congress and his wife became ill.

Graff, Henry, ed. *The Presidents: A Reference History*. New York: Charles Scribner's Sons, 1984. A collection of articles by various historians. The essay on Harrison is an excellent short study of the man and his office, especially regarding foreign affairs. It is helpful to read also the biographies of other presidents contemporary with Harrison.

Harrison, Benjamin. *Public Papers and Addresses*. Washington, D.C.: Government Printing Office, 1893. Reprint. New York: Kraus Reprints, 1969. Some of Harrison's official documents are of interest to the serious student of the period, especially those dealing with veterans' pensions and treatment of the South. His writing style is usually plain, simple, and direct.

_____. *Speeches*. Compiled by Charles Hedges. Port Washington, N.Y.: Kennikat Press, 1971. During his career, Harrison had a reputation, at least among Republicans, of being an excellent orator. These examples demonstrate his clarity and suggest his forcefulness.

Nevins, Allan. *Grover Cleveland: A Study in Courage*. New York: Dodd, Mead, 1958. This work was first published in 1932 and won Nevins a Pulitzer Prize for American biography. It is an outstanding study of Cleveland and his times and provides much information relative to Harrison. The contrast between the two is considerable: Both were admirable individuals, but Cleveland was by far the better president.

Perry, James M. *Touched with Fire: Five Presidents and the Civil War Battles That Made Them*. New York: Public Affairs, 2003. Harrison's military leadership during the Civil War is explored in this examination of five presidents' military careers.

Sievers, Harry J. *Benjamin Harrison: Hoosier Warrior, 1833-1865*. 2d ed. New York: University Publishers, 1960.

_____. *Benjamin Harrison: Hoosier Statesman: From the Civil War to the White House, 1865-1888*. New York: University Publishers, 1959.

_____. *Benjamin Harrison: Hoosier President: The White House and After, 1889-1901*. Indianapolis: Bobbs-Merrill, 1968. Together, these three volumes form the definitive modern biography of Harrison, one that is not likely to be improved upon or replaced soon. Sievers makes excellent use of the sources, including many of Harrison's papers and letters, and his biography is detailed but briskly paced.

Socolofsky, Homer Edward, and Allan B. Spetter. *The Presidency of Benjamin Harrison*. Lawrence: University Press of Kansas, 1987. A critical assessment of Harrison's presidency. The authors maintain Harrison was a confident, hardworking president who laid the groundwork for American acquisition of Hawaii and expansion in the Far East.

SEE ALSO: James G. Blaine; Grover Cleveland; William Henry Harrison; Rutherford B. Hayes; William McKinley.

RELATED ARTICLES in *Great Events from History: The Nineteenth Century, 1801-1900:* October 28, 1886: Statue of Liberty Is Dedicated; July 20, 1890: Harrison Signs the Sherman Antitrust Act; July 4-5, 1892: Birth of the People's Party.

FREDERIC HARRISON
English philosopher

In his varied career as a professor of law, literary critic, and lecturer, Harrison was one of the staunchest advocates of the philosophy of positivism in mid-Victorian England.

BORN: October 18, 1831; London, England
DIED: January 14, 1923; Bath, Somerset, England
AREA OF ACHIEVEMENT: Philosophy

EARLY LIFE
Frederic Harrison was the son of Frederick Harrison (whose first name was spelled differently), an architect turned stockbroker, and Jane (née Brice) Harrison. The couple's firstborn had died in infancy; Frederic would become the eldest of the five sons who survived. The family, of some means, would often spend time in the English countryside. Frederic's mother taught him to appreciate history and French and Latin, while his father imparted a passion for the fine arts. Frederic's family life was characterized by stability and the loving concern of his parents and bordered on the aristocratic.

Before he was six, in 1837, Frederic witnessed the coronation of Queen Victoria. The family moved to Oxford Square, Hyde Park, in 1840, where Frederic attended the day school of Joseph King for two years, followed by enrollment in the sixth form (or grade) at King's College School, where he would remain until 1849. Because of the success of his earlier schooling, Frederic found himself in classes with boys several years older; though he played most sports and excelled as a student, for a time the others treated him condescendingly and nicknamed him "Fan."

The nickname vanished when Harrison was befriended by one of the older students, Charles Cookson, a passionate devotee of literature and the High Church movement. Associated with Edward Pusey, advocates sought to move the Anglican Church closer to the Roman Catholic tradition. Harrison had been reared in the Anglican tradition of William Paley, with its emphasis on moral utilitarianism, but he would come to reject all forms of Christianity in favor of a new "Religion of Humanity." Harrison would teach that one's duty to humankind was paramount, not obeisance to a metaphysical deity. As part of his future positivist belief, Harrison's faith would rest in the essential goodness and progress of humanity. However, what of individuals themselves, Harrison would wonder: Where should one's sympathies lie?

Revolutionary fervor was abroad on the Continent. With the publication of Karl Marx's *Manifest der Kommunistischen Partei* (1848; *The Communist Manifesto*, 1850), there were uprisings in Paris, Berlin, Vienna, and Rome; in England, bad harvests that same year brought a renewal of the working-class Chartist movement that sought parliamentary and electoral reforms. Harrison found himself sympathizing with the fall of the old regimes and with the demands of the working class; yet throughout his life he would struggle with the question of whether specific political action would ever usher in the universal positivist utopia.

Harrison was eighteen when he entered Wadham College in Oxford in 1849. He had come to detest the intense competition inherent in formal schooling in England, as well as professors who only "taught for the test." An exception was Richard Congreve, his history professor and the founder of the British positivist movement. Though, in later years, Harrison would lament Congreve's turn toward his own fanatical brand of positivism, Harrison applauded Congreve's presentation of history as the surging progress of humanity and not a list of names and dates and innumerable "periods."

Harrison was graduated from Wadham in 1853 but remained two more years as Librarian of the Union and as a tutor. Though still considering himself a Christian, Harrison was brought under the sway of the French positivist philosopher Auguste Comte, by a group of Oxford friends who called themselves "Mumbo-Jumbo" and who had already renounced the creeds of the Church. Harrison himself declined to take orders for a career in the Church and in 1855 began a study of law at Lincoln's Inn in London. In that same year, he met in Paris with Comte.

Harrison was the portrait of the active Victorian. An ardent mountaineer most of his life, he was physically rugged, with a large head, black hair, and fierce whis-kers. Incurably optimistic (at least after his student days), he was at times pompous, quick-tempered, and irascible. He dressed to befit his class; punctuality was his hallmark. As one of his sons later observed, Harrison

liked time-tables, inventories, and everything that contributed towards the regular life, and he probably was the most consistently normal man who ever wrote books.

He was a skilled debater and a personal friend of many of England's nineteenth century luminaries, including William E. Gladstone, Thomas Carlyle, and John Stuart Mill.

LIFE'S WORK

Harrison counted his meeting with Comte as the most significant of his life; his growing adherence to Comtian philosophy provided unity to a life full of many undertakings. Comte had rejected absolutist metaphysics as unproductive: People had argued for thousands of years about God's existence and had come no closer to agreement. Instead, Comte proposed a philosophic system that was scientific, relative, and human-centered. As Harrison explained in two lectures given in 1920, three years before his death, the new system was scientific because it saw physical and social activity ordered by laws, but relative and human-centered because formulation of those laws depended on fallible human observation.

However, there was progress in humankind's understanding of the world. In ancient times, the world was explained in terms of myth; that gave way to the absolute generalizations of metaphysics, which led, in turn, to the scientific and relative positive philosophy of the nineteenth century. It was "positive" in the sense that it depended on substantive observations of the world (relative to humankind) and not on the manipulation of contentless abstractions. The sciences could be ordered by their complexity relative to humans (with sociology, a term coined by Comte in 1837, the most complex), with each science having its own methodology. Thus ordered, the scientific enterprise becomes a powerful tool for progress (as heralded by the Industrial Revolution). Humankind's faith, then, turns from the worship of ill-defined abstractions to that of humanity itself, with one's highest goal the altruistic service to humankind.

Comte's was a grand vision, in many ways suited to the Victorian tones of optimistic progress amid the waning belief in the old verities preached by the Church, and yet it offered a renewed sense of the centrality of the family and the importance of personal morality. Positivism's appeal to Harrison was manifest with, as defined by Comte, its so-called Calendar of 558 names, from Homer to Moses, representing an overview of civilization, its library of 270 works divided into four categories as an organized scheme of general literature, and its emotional appeal in the worship of humanity.

Harrison did not want to promulgate merely a new sect; he was uneasy about partisan political involvement but believed that the lot of the working man had to be improved. Called to the bar in 1858, Harrison concentrated on the plight of those nations struggling for independence from imperialist regimes. He reported from Italy for the *Daily News* and *Morning Post* and believed that he won his countrymen to the Italian cause. In 1866, Harrison joined the Jamaica Committee to pressure the governor to lift the martial law imposed there, and he was on the Royal Commission on Trades Unions from 1867 to 1869. His work helped lay the foundation for future trade-union legislation.

Harrison married his cousin Ethel Harrison in 1870. Secure in his traditional marriage, he seemed never to waver from his new positive religion, to which he had converted Ethel. A decade earlier, Harrison had clarified his religious views in his reply to *Essays and Reviews* (1860), a series of articles, originating with the Broad Church or Liberal movement, which called for the redrawing of the boundaries of traditional Christian doctrines in the light of modern science (including Higher Criticism). Harrison, critical of the book, called the result "Neo-Christianity," an attempt to separate all religious feelings from matters of scientific fact. What was needed, he said, was a synthesis of the religious impulse in humans with that of science, in the Religion of Humanity. (The future, for Harrison, belonged to positivism. Just as Christianity was no longer tenable, so any idea of culture transforming the world, as advanced by Matthew Arnold, was simply wind.)

In the decade of the 1870's, Harrison saw Prussian imperialism at first hand in France as a correspondent for *The Times* of London. He joined the Chapel St. Group in 1870 under Congreve's leadership and during the mid-1870's worked for the disestablishment of the Church of England (though he did not succeed). He was appointed Professor of Jurisprudence, International and Constitutional Law by the Council of Legal Education in 1877, and lectured at Middle Temple Hall for twelve years thereafter.

Harrison reluctantly agreed to preside over a new positivist group that first met at Newton Hall in 1879. A year earlier, Congreve had broken with Comte and his successor in France, Pierre Lafitte, to develop further the ceremonial aspects of the Religion of Humanity; thus Newton Hall was founded to carry on the French tradition.

Harrison's only attempt to enter Parliament failed in the general election of 1886, and political activism gave way to his writing. Works on positivism as well as literary studies seemed to pour from his pen. He aided in the founding of the *Positivist Review* in 1893 (which died with his passing), journeyed to the United States for a series of lectures in 1901 (the year of Queen Victoria's death), and, succumbing to what he called a senile weakness, wrote a historical novel, *Theophano: The Crusade of the Tenth Century, a Romantic Monograph* (1904). He published two volumes of memoirs in 1911.

The Harrisons had four sons and one daughter. Harrison died of heart failure on January 14, 1923, while he was correcting proofs for a book of essays containing what was to be his last defense of positivism.

SIGNIFICANCE

Frederic Harrison believed passionately in the family as the foundation for any scientifically ordered society of the future; education must begin in the home, and women were to find their liberation in the care of the household. In criticizing John Stuart Mill's *Subjection of Women* (1869), Harrison affirmed that "nothing can be made right in sociology whilst society is regarded as made up of individuals instead of families." It was not the first time that theorists have envisioned a "new order" that is little but their own lives writ large and made universal.

Before his marriage, Harrison was a seeker, an activist. In the last half of his long life, he seemed to step back from the political fray for a longer view. He would be the librarian of the new positivist society, worshiping dutifully at the shrine of Humanity with a clear conscience, anticipating the social progress that was yet to come. His would be the genteel, the aristocratic role, in this most orderly revolution in history.

However, positivism from the first was philosophically unsound. Despite his ardent defense of positivist faith, Harrison never saw that simply declaring metaphysical speculation off limits would never silence God; that Comte's absolute principles of historical progress were themselves metaphysical; and that the basic dualism between observation and humankind's conceptualizing of his findings made the positivist interpretation itself suspect.

Harrison's life and pursuits were quintessentially Victorian; he was the consummate amateur, always busy.

Harrison the optimist lived to see one of his sons die in World War I, and, with positivism passing from the scene, he was regaled not for his advocacy but as the man who was the friend of the great men and women of the Victorian era; he was no longer the prophet, but the storyteller.

—*Dan Barnett*

FURTHER READING

Amigoni, David. *Victorian Biography: Intellectuals and the Ordering of Discourse*. New York: Harvester Wheatsheaf, 1993. An analysis of the works of nineteenth century biographers. Amigoni maintains that Harrison and other late nineteenth century writers sought to create a biography style that differed from their predecessor, Thomas Carlyle.

Harrison, Austin. *Frederic Harrison: Thoughts and Memories*. New York: G. P. Putnam's Sons, 1927. A valuable anecdotal view of Harrison by one of his sons. An impressionistic (not chronological) overview of Harrison's faith, character, and temperament. No substitute for a biography.

Harrison, Frederic. *Autobiographic Memoirs*. 2 vols. London: Macmillan, 1911. Good source material on Harrison's early life, though less an autobiography (Harrison did not want to focus attention on himself) than a personal history of Victorian times. Volume 1 covers the years 1832-1870; volume 2, 1870-1910.

_____. *De Senectute: More Last Words*. London: T. F. Unwin, 1923. Published posthumously, the book contains "A Philosophic Synthesis," two lectures given by Harrison in 1920, and his last published defense of positivism.

_____. *George Washington and Other American Addresses*. New York: Macmillan, 1901. In some of these addresses, Harrison struggled with the idea of democracy. How could the best minds surface in the United States if society treated everyone equally? Note also "Personal Reminiscences," a lecture given to Bryn Mawr Women's College in Pennsylvania, detailing Harrison's friendship with Comte, Charles Darwin, the novelist George Eliot, and many others.

_____. *The Meaning of History and Other Historical Pieces*. New York: Macmillan, 1894. In "The Use of History," Harrison advises his readers that knowledge of history is in large part knowledge of its great men; another chapter annotates some of the great books of history, and a third, "The Sacredness of Ancient Buildings," focuses on Harrison's love of architecture and expresses his view that buildings are living relics.

_____. *Tennyson, Ruskin, Mill, and Other Literary Estimates*. New York: Macmillan, 1899. Includes what amounts to almost a panegyric on Matthew Arnold (though it does reprise delicately some of Harrison's earlier criticism of Arnold's idea of Culture). This volume also contains a useful critique of Harrison's friend John Stuart Mill.

Himmelfarb, Gertrude. *Victorian Minds*. New York: Alfred A. Knopf, 1968. A good introduction to the Victorian period through studies of some of its leading personalities: John Stuart Mill, Leslie Stephen, Walter Bagehot, and others. Harrison is scarcely mentioned, though he is characterized (in a list of Victorian paradoxes) as a religious libertarian with a Puritan morality.

Kent, Christopher. *Brains and Numbers: Elitism, Comtism, and Democracy in Mid-Victorian England*. Toronto: University of Toronto Press, 1978. A technical study of the politics of reform, especially as it is mirrored by Harrison's friend John Morley and by Harrison himself. Characterizes Harrison's political problem as that of reconciling government by an elite (which seemed logical to him) with the rising tide of democratic sentiment. Sets Comte into a middle-class context and clarifies his appeal. The book includes a large bibliography and makes reference to Harrison's personal papers.

Metraux, Guy S., and Francois Crouzet, eds. *The Nineteenth-Century World*. New York: Mentor Books, 1963. This work is especially interesting for Henri Gouhier's essay on "Auguste Comte's Philosophy of History," an essay generally sympathetic to Comte, crediting him with shrewdly understanding the impact of the Industrial Revolution.

Sullivan, Harry R. *Frederic Harrison*. Boston: Twayne, 1983. A valuable survey of Harrison's life and major concerns, with good bibliographic references. The chapters on positivism are clear enough; the two long chapters on Harrison's literary critiques seem valuable only to the antiquarian. A generally sympathetic nontechnical study.

SEE ALSO: Matthew Arnold; Thomas Carlyle; Auguste Comte; Charles Darwin; Karl Marx; John Stuart Mill; Charles Sanders Peirce; Queen Victoria.

RELATED ARTICLES in *Great Events from History: The Nineteenth Century, 1801-1900:* 1851-1854: Comte Advances His Theory of Positivism; c. 1865: Naturalist Movement Begins.

WILLIAM HENRY HARRISON
President of the United States (1841)

Harrison's victory over the Indian forces of Tecumseh and the Prophet at the Battle of Tippecanoe in 1811 made him a national military hero. As a soldier and later governor of the Old Northwest Territory, he became identified with the ideas and desires of the West, eventually riding his military reputation to his election as president of the United States; however, he served only one month in that office and left no legacy as the nation's chief executive.

BORN: February 9, 1773; near Charles City, Virginia
DIED: April 4, 1841; Washington, D.C.
ALSO KNOWN AS: Old Tippecanoe
AREAS OF ACHIEVEMENT: Government and politics, military

EARLY LIFE

The son of a signer of the Declaration of Independence, William Henry Harrison was born at his family's famous Berkeley Plantation in tidewater Virginia. He attended Hampden-Sydney College and briefly studied medicine under the famous physician Benjamin Rush. Harrison entered the army in 1791, serving in the campaigns against the Indians in the Northwest Territory and eventually becoming a lieutenant and aide-de-camp to Anthony Wayne. After serving as a frontier army officer for seven years, in 1798 Harrison resigned his commission to accept appointment as secretary of the Northwest Territory. The following year, he was elected the territory's first delegate to Congress.

In Congress, Harrison was a spokesperson for the West and was author of the Land Act of 1800, which provided for the disposition of public lands on more liberal terms than previously practiced. The same year, he was appointed governor of the newly created Indiana Territory, which included all of the original Northwest Territory except Ohio. His new job would require the talents of both the diplomat and the soldier, and with his tall and slender build, soldierly bearing, and amiable countenance, Harrison looked the part.

LIFE'S WORK

Harrison was given a nearly impossible charge. He was to win the friendship and trust of the Indians and protect them from the rapaciousness of white settlers, yet he was also urged to acquire for the government as much land as he could secure from the Western tribes. It appears that Harrison was genuinely concerned for the Indians: He

ordered a campaign of inoculation to protect them from the scourge of smallpox and banned the sale of liquor to them. Nevertheless, he actively pursued the acquisition of Indian lands, and in 1809 negotiated a treaty with Indian leaders that transferred some 2,900,000 acres in the vicinity of the White and Wabash Rivers to the United States. This cession brought the tension between red and white men in the Northwest to a boiling point and instigated the events upon which Harrison's fame and later career were founded.

In view of the uneasy relationship between the United States and Great Britain, many Americans assumed that the British had encouraged the "Indian troubles" of the interior. In reality, the growing hostility of the Western tribes was largely an indigenous reaction to the constant encroachments upon their lands by white settlers. Their frustrations finally reached a focus with the rise of two Shawnee half brothers, the chief Tecumseh and a one-eyed medicine man called the Prophet. The concept of a great Indian confederation was developed by Tecumseh, who argued that Indian lands were held in common by all the tribes and that the unanimous consent of those tribes was required if those lands were to be sold. The Prophet promoted a puritanical religious philosophy, and as his following grew, religion and politics gradually merged.

Harrison developed a healthy respect for the brothers' abilities and hoped to be able to find a way to placate them. Finally, however, in what must be considered an aggressive move, Harrison marched a force of about one thousand men north from his capital at Vincennes toward Indian lands in northwestern Indiana. Early on the morning of November 7, 1811, Harrison's encampment near an Indian settlement called Prophetstown in the vicinity of the confluence of the Tippecanoe and Wabash Rivers suffered a surprise attack. The Indians who attacked Harrison were led, or at least inspired, by the Prophet; Tecumseh was in the South, organizing the tribes of that area. Harrison's forces beat back the attackers and later burned the Indian settlement.

Almost immediately there was controversy concerning the particulars of the Battle of Tippecanoe and Harrison's performance. Questions were asked about whether his troops were prepared for the Indian attack, why they had camped in a vulnerable position, whether Harrison or companion officers had actually commanded the defenses, and whether Harrison's men were outnumbered. What, in fact, was the size of the attacking Indian force?

In any case, Harrison, who was not a paragon of modesty, and his supporters immediately began to tell the story of a "Washington of the West" who represented the bravery and ambitions of Western Americans.

During the War of 1812 with Great Britain, Harrison served militarily in several positions, becoming supreme commander of the Army of the Northwest. He broke the power of the British and the Indians in the Northwest and southern Canada, his ultimate victory occurring in early October, 1813, at the Battle of the Thames. Although his reputation among the general public was apparently enhanced, his military performance once again met with controversy. In May, 1814, he resigned from the army and took up residence on a farm at North Bend, Ohio, on the banks of the Ohio River near Cincinnati.

At North Bend, Harrison worked at farming and undertook several unsuccessful commercial ventures, and the foundation for another aspect of his public image was established. Harrison's home at North Bend, a commodious dwelling of sixteen rooms, was built around the nucleus of a log cabin. This humble kernel of his residence became one of the misrepresented symbols of "Old Tip's" 1840 presidential campaign. In 1816, Harrison resumed public life. He served successively as a congressman, senator, and United States minister to Colombia with competence but without distinction. In 1830, he returned to North Bend, where he seemed destined for a quiet life in retirement.

During the height of "Jacksonian Democracy" during the 1830's, there was a growing reaction against the alleged pretensions and aspirations of "King Andrew" Jackson. This contributed to the emergence of the Whig Party, made up of old National Republicans, former Anti-Masons, and various others who reacted strongly against Jackson or his policies. In 1836 the Whigs made their first run for the presidency against Jackson's chosen successor, Martin Van Buren. Harrison ran as the candidate of Western Whigs and showed some promise as a vote getter. As a result, he became a leading contender for the nomination in 1840.

By now widely known as "Old Tippecanoe," Harrison the military hero presented an obvious opportunity for the Whigs to borrow a page from the Democrats who had ridden "Old Hickory," Andrew Jackson, to great political success. The general's positions on key issues of the day were almost irrelevant, for he was to be nominated as a symbol of military glory and the development of the West. The Whigs wanted a candidate who would appeal to a broad range of voters and who was not too closely identified with the issues of the Jacksonian era. They did not offer a real platform, only a pledge to "correct the abuses" of the current administration. If the campaign were successful, the real decisions in a Harrison administration would be made by Whig leaders in Congress.

When, during the battle for the nomination, a Henry Clay partisan suggested that Harrison should be allowed to enjoy his log cabin and hard cider in peace, the tone and lasting fame of the campaign were established. A Baltimore newspaper said that if Harrison were given a barrel of hard cider and a pension, he would spend the remainder of his days in a log cabin studying moral philosophy. Whig strategists, recognizing a good thing when they heard it, created a winning campaign by portraying Harrison as a man of the people, a wise yet simple hero whose log cabin and hard cider were vastly preferable to the pretensions and trickery of "Old Kinderhook" Martin Van Buren. The Whigs waged the first modern presidential campaign, selling souvenirs, publishing and widely distributing campaign materials, flooding the country with speakers, and using songs, slogans, and verses, including the famous cry "Tippecanoe and Tyler too." Harrison made numerous speeches to large crowds and became the first presidential candidate to stump the country on his own behalf.

William Henry Harrison. (Library of Congress)

Inauguration day was chilly and rainy, and the new president caught a cold, which continued to nag him. Overburdened by the demands of his office, Harrison attempted to escape its pressures by concentrating on such minor details as the efficiency of operations in various government offices and even the purchase of supplies for the White House—leaving the weightier matters to Congress and his cabinet. The only major problem of his anticlimactic presidency, the Caroline Affair, was handled by his secretary of state.

On a cold March morning, the president went to purchase vegetables for the White House and suffered a chill that aggravated the cold he had contracted on inauguration day. The cold developed into pneumonia, and on April 4, 1841, Harrison died in the White House. He was carried back to North Bend for burial.

SIGNIFICANCE

The fame of William Henry Harrison was somewhat out of proportion to the actual accomplishments of his life and career. He first became a major public figure through his victory in the Battle of Tippecanoe, a frontier conflict that was blown up to epic proportions by Harrison and his idolaters. There is even some doubt concerning the quality of Harrison's leadership in the battle, but it did establish him as a national hero who was particularly identified with the ideas and desires of the West.

Many Americans believed that the battle was the product of British machinations among the Indians of the West, and the bad feelings generated became part of the package of Western grievances that helped trigger the War of 1812. Harrison later rode his military reputation and identification with the common man of the West into the presidency, but he served only about a month and had virtually no direct impact on the office. The method of his election and the circumstances of his death, however, were of lasting importance. The 1840 campaign established a new style of presidential campaigning, and Harrison's death forced the nation for the first time to experience the elevation of a vice president to the Oval Office.

—*James E. Fickle*

FURTHER READING

Cleaves, Freeman. *Old Tippecanoe: William Henry Harrison and His Times*. New York: Charles Scribner's Sons, 1939. This is a full and detailed biography that contains a colorful account of the Battle of Tippecanoe and two chapters devoted to the campaign of 1840 and Harrison's presidency.

Curtis, James C. *The Fox at Bay: Martin Van Buren and the Presidency, 1837-1841*. Lexington: University Press of Kentucky, 1970. This study of the Van Buren presidency views the election of 1840 from the Democratic perspective.

Dangerfield, George. *The Era of Good Feelings*. New York: Harcourt, Brace & World, 1952. This Pulitzer- and Bancroft Prize-winning study contains an excellent chapter on the Battle of Tippecanoe, placing it in the general context of the War of 1812.

Goebel, Dorothy B. *William Henry Harrison: A Political Biography*. Indianapolis: Indiana Historical Bureau, 1926. This is a major, although dated, biography. Goebel is highly critical of Harrison's Indian policies as well as his military preparations before the Battle of Tippecanoe.

Green, James A. *William Henry Harrison: His Life and Times*. Richmond, Va.: Garrett and Massie, 1941. A laudatory popular account that inflates the Battle of Tippecanoe into one of the epic battles in American military history.

Gunderson, Robert G. *The Log-Cabin Campaign*. Lexington: University Press of Kentucky, 1957. This is a good narrative account of the election of 1840.

Peterson, Norma Lois. *The Presidencies of William Henry Harrison and John Tyler*. Lawrence: University Press of Kansas, 1989. Although most of the book describes Tyler's presidency, the book discusses Harrison's presidential campaign, illness, and death.

Simon, Roger. "To the Log Cabin Not Born." *U.S. News & World Report* 133, no. 8 (August 26, 2002): 48. Focuses on Harrison's presidential campaign of 1840, in which he was deceptively portrayed as a backward populist. Describes how this campaign set a precedent for image advertising in American politics.

Tucker, Glenn. *Tecumseh: Vision of Glory*. Indianapolis: Bobbs-Merrill, 1956. This is a fast-moving, colorfully written, and sympathetic biography that is especially critical of Harrison's efforts to embellish his own reputation.

SEE ALSO: Henry Clay; Caleb Cushing; Benjamin Harrison; Andrew Jackson; Oliver Hazard Perry; Tecumseh; John Tyler; Martin Van Buren; Daniel Webster.

RELATED ARTICLES in *Great Events from History: The Nineteenth Century, 1801-1900:* April, 1808: Tenskwatawa Founds Prophetstown; November 7, 1811: Battle of Tippecanoe; October 5, 1813: Battle of the Thames; April 24, 1820: Congress Passes Land Act of 1820; April 14, 1834: Clay Begins American Whig Party; December 2, 1840: U.S. Election of 1840; August 1, 1846: Establishment of Independent U.S. Treasury.

NATHANIEL HAWTHORNE
American fiction writer

In writing short stories and novels that bring to life the moral and spiritual complexity of New England's Puritan past, Hawthorne achieved one of the most distinguished literary careers of nineteenth century America.

BORN: July 4, 1804; Salem, Massachusetts
DIED: May 19, 1864; Plymouth, New Hampshire
AREA OF ACHIEVEMENT: Literature

EARLY LIFE

Nathaniel Hawthorne was the great-great-grandson of John Hathorne, one of the three judges in the Salem witchcraft trials in 1692. When he was four years old, his father, Nathaniel Hathorne, a sea captain, died in Dutch Guinea (Hawthorne added the "w" to his surname when he was a young man). His mother, née Elizabeth Manning, came from a Massachusetts family prominent in business. Her brother, Robert Manning, was a well-known pomologist who assumed much of the responsibility for Hawthorne's care after the death of his father.

Hawthorne spent much of his adolescence in Raymond, Maine, where his Manning uncles owned property, and attended Bowdoin College in nearby Brunswick. He was a Bowdoin classmate of Henry Wadsworth Longfellow and Franklin Pierce (who would later become president of the United States). As a student, Hawthorne was adept in Latin and English, but was disciplined for gambling and faulty chapel attendance. He was a handsome young man of slender build, with dark hair and eyes. Although quiet, he had a reputation for conviviality and joining friends in clubs and outdoor sports.

Hawthorne took his degree in 1825—he stood eighteenth in a class of thirty-eight—and spent the next twelve years in Salem, where he read extensively and taught himself to write. The product of these twelve years was the indifferent novel *Fanshawe: A Tale* (1828) and more than forty stories and sketches, including such well-known pieces as "The Gentle Boy," "Roger Malvin's Burial," and "My Kinsman, Major Molineux." It was a rewarding apprenticeship in terms of his artistic accomplishment, and although it did not bring him much immediate fame or income, the publication of *Twice-Told Tales* in 1837 successfully launched his career.

In 1838, Hawthorne fell in love with Sophia Peabody of Boston, whom he married in 1842. During their courtship, he spent two years working at the Boston Custom House, and he joined the utopian community at Brook Farm for several months. Both of these experiences later proved fruitful for him as a writer. Hawthorne took his bride to live in the Old Manse in Concord, and there began a life as a happy and devoted husband and father of three children.

A second edition of *Twice-Told Tales* appeared in 1842, and in 1846, the year he left the Old Manse, Hawthorne published *Mosses from an Old Manse*. With these volumes, he began to receive high critical recognition. Edgar Allan Poe praised the second edition of *Twice-Told Tales* in a review that has become famous for its perceptive commentary on Hawthorne's "invention, creation, imagination, originality." When he left the Old Manse, Hawthorne was a mature artist, ready to write the novels for which he became famous.

LIFE'S WORK

With the help of influential friends, Hawthorne received in 1846 an appointment as surveyor of the Salem Custom House. He was dismissed from this position in 1849, a victim of the political spoils system, and then wrote his greatest work, *The Scarlet Letter* (1850). In the introduction to *The Scarlet Letter*, Hawthorne settled what he perceived as some old injustices at the customhouse and invented the fiction of having found his story in an old manuscript in the customhouse.

In *The Scarlet Letter*, Hawthorne develops his most powerful theme of the hardening of the heart in what he called the Unpardonable Sin. This theme, essentially an expansion of Saint Paul's admonition in I Corinthians 13 to practice charity, is dramatized in miniature in "Ethan Brand: A Chapter from an Abortive Romance" (1850). Ethan Brand has sought knowledge tirelessly, searching for the Unpardonable Sin, and when he learns that in his quest he has allowed his heart to atrophy, he realizes that he has found the answer in himself: The Unpardonable Sin is the cultivation of the intellect at the expense of one's humanity.

Thus, the Unpardonable Sin in *The Scarlet Letter* is not the very human adultery of Hester Prynne and the Reverend Arthur Dimmesdale, a sin that takes place before the novel opens and that results in Hester's scarlet letter "A" that she has to wear on her bosom, but the relentless, unforgiving persecution of Dimmesdale by Hester's cuckolded husband, Roger Chillingworth. Sadly, Chillingworth is a learned man to whom the implications of his uncharitable obsession with revenge are

Nathaniel Hawthorne. (Library of Congress)

absolutely clear. The inescapable conflict between nature and civilization stands out tragically in *The Scarlet Letter*: Hester and Chillingworth are united in marriage, a civil institution, but it is a marriage without true feeling for Hester, whereas the passion between Hester and Dimmesdale is deep and natural yet adulterous and unsanctioned. The outcome is tragic for all three of them.

In *The House of the Seven Gables* (1851), Hawthorne returns to the Puritan past and works out another fable of the effects of sin, this time in the form of a hereditary curse. The story of the Pyncheons is a fable of guilt and expiation, of the impossibility of escaping the past. Hawthorne thought it a greater novel than *The Scarlet Letter*.

During his residence at the Old Manse in Concord, Hawthorne had formed close friendships with his Transcendentalist neighbors, Ralph Waldo Emerson, Henry David Thoreau, William Ellery Channing, and Bronson Alcott. (The Old Manse had been built by Emerson's grandfather.) However, Hawthorne's sensibilities were too burdened by a sense of sin for him to accept the optimism and idealism expressed by these thinkers. Furthermore, his experience at Brook Farm had made him distrust the ideals expressed in the notion of intellectuals living together communally. In *The Blithedale Romance* (1852), he satirized many of the goals and values of uto-

pian thinkers. The novel is exceptionally acute in its perceptions of human psychology and is a measure of the distance between the student of Puritanism and the sin in the human heart and the Transcendentalists with their lofty vision of human possibilities.

Hawthorne also published in 1852 *The Life of Franklin Pierce*. This campaign biography of his Bowdoin classmate led to Hawthorne's appointment as United States consul in Liverpool, a post he held from 1853 to 1857. He left Liverpool to live in Italy for three years, an experience that culminated in *The Marble Faun* (1860). This novel made him one of the first American writers to treat the experiences of his countrymen in Europe, a theme developed by such later writers as Henry James, William Dean Howells, and Ernest Hemingway.

When he came home to the United States, Hawthorne bought a home in Concord, which he named The Wayside. After his death four years later while on a tour in Plymouth, New Hampshire, he was buried in Concord. By the time of his death he had earned a considerable reputation for his romances.

SIGNIFICANCE

After the success of *The Scarlet Letter*, Hawthorne had lived for three years in Lenox, Massachusetts, in the Berkshire Mountains, and had there established a close friendship with his literary neighbor, Herman Melville. Melville had been one of the first to recognize Hawthorne's unique powers as a writer, and in a famous review—written anonymously—he had praised Hawthorne's "great power of blackness." Hawthorne's influence certainly became one of the influences on Melville's own masterpiece, *Moby Dick: Or, The Whale* (1851).

Melville was responding to Hawthorne's skill in portraying imaginatively the mysteries of the human spirit. Hawthorne's preferred approach to his fictions was through symbolism and allegory, a technique that locates his plots on the ambiguous dividing line between the real and the imaginary. Some critics, such as Poe and Henry James, faulted him for the indirectness of his method in such cloudy parables as "The Minister's Black Veil" and "Rappaccini's Daughter," and Hawthorne himself admitted that "I am not quite sure that I entirely comprehend my own meaning in some of these blasted allegories."

Hawthorne's propensity for unfolding humankind's struggle with sin in these romances prompted Melville to comment on Hawthorne's "Calvinistic sense of Innate Depravity and Original Sin, from whose visitations, in some shape or other, no deeply thinking mind is always and wholly free." Another great writer, D. H. Lawrence, saw in Hawthorne a genius for perceiving the most "disagreeable" secrets in humankind's soul and presenting them in clever extended tropes and figures.

As an American writing in the nineteenth century, Hawthorne faced the problem of where to find his materials in a country short in a history of manners and morals. James Fenimore Cooper's solution was the frontier, Melville's the sea, and Poe's the psyche. For Hawthorne, the answer lay in the Puritan past and its theology rich in moral and spiritual complexity. When Young Goodman Brown goes into the dark forest and is hosted by the Devil to a Black Mass, he comes to know evil in his soul. When Robin searches for his kinsman, Major Molineux, in the nighttime town, he experiences his own introduction to the dark side of humankind's nature. In such stories of initiation and experience as these, Hawthorne shaped in fiction a superb body of moral philosophy that is unequaled in the dark stream of American literature.

—*Frank Day*

FURTHER READING

Bloom, Harold, ed. *Nathaniel Hawthorne*. Philadelphia: Chelsea House, 2003. This book, one in a series aimed at literature students, provides an introduction to Hawthorne's work. It includes an introduction by Bloom, a biography, an essay by Henry James analyzing Hawthorne's early writings, and a description of some of the elements of Hawthorne's fiction.

Crews, Frederick C. *The Sins of the Fathers: Hawthorne's Psychological Themes*. New York: Oxford University Press, 1966. A sensitive analysis of the psychological implications of Hawthorne's fiction. Especially perceptive in its explication of Hawthorne's sense of the past. Suggestive chapter entitled "Hawthorne, Freud, and Literary Value."

Hawthorne, Julian. *Hawthorne and His Circle*. New York: Harper & Brothers, 1903. Reprint. New York: Archon Books, 1968. A reprint of the 1903 book by Hawthorne's son. Rich source of intimate recollections.

Hawthorne, Nathaniel. *The American Notebooks*. Edited by Randall Stewart. New Haven, Conn.: Yale University Press, 1932. The notebooks Hawthorne kept intermittently from 1837 to 1853. Excellently edited with discussions of Hawthorne's character types, his adaptations of the notebooks in his fiction, and his recurrent themes. Indispensable for all students of Hawthorne.

_____. *The English Notebooks*. Edited by Randall Stewart. New York: Russell & Russell, 1962. The notebooks Hawthorne kept while United States consul in Liverpool between 1853 and 1857.

Mellow, James R. *Nathaniel Hawthorne in His Times*. Boston: Houghton Mifflin, 1980. A detailed biography that portrays Hawthorne in relation to his contemporaries.

Miller, Edward Haviland. *Salem Is My Dwelling Place: A Life of Nathaniel Hawthorne*. Iowa City: University of Iowa Press, 1991. A full-scale scholarly biography, including notes and bibliography. Miller's aim is to carefully analyze Hawthorne's many different poses in life and in art.

Moore, Margaret B. *The Salem World of Nathaniel Hawthorne*. Columbia: University of Missouri Press, 1998. Explores the relationship between Salem, Massachusetts, and its most famous resident, author Nathaniel Hawthorne.

Newman, Lea Bertani Vozar. *A Reader's Guide to the Short Stories of Nathaniel Hawthorne*. Boston: G. K. Hall, 1979. Extremely helpful guide to the short stories, spelling out for each story its publication history, circumstances of composition, sources, influences, and relationship to other works by Hawthorne. Includes summaries of interpretations and criticism.

Scharnhorst, Gary. *The Critical Response to Hawthorne's "The Scarlet Letter."* New York: Greenwood Press, 1992. Includes chapters on the novel's background and composition history, on the contemporary American reception, on the early British reception, on the growth of Hawthorne's reputation after his death, on modern criticism, and on *The Scarlet Letter* on stage and screen. Includes bibliography.

Stewart, Randall. *Nathaniel Hawthorne: A Biography*. New Haven, Conn.: Yale University Press, 1948. A skillful interpretation of Hawthorne by an excellent scholar. Well written.

Wineapple, Brenda. *Hawthorne: A Life*. New York: Alfred A. Knopf, 2003. An analysis of Hawthorne's often contradictory life that proposes that many of Hawthorne's stories are autobiographical.

SEE ALSO: Bronson Alcott; William Ellery Channing; James Fenimore Cooper; Ralph Waldo Emerson; Washington Irving; Henry James; Henry Wadsworth Longfellow; Herman Melville; Elizabeth Palmer Peabody; Franklin Pierce; Edgar Allan Poe; Henry David Thoreau.

RELATED ARTICLES in *Great Events from History: The Nineteenth Century, 1801-1900:* 1819-1820: Irving's *Sketch Book* Transforms American Literature; 1851: Melville Publishes *Moby Dick*.

JOHN HAY
American writer and government administrator

After a distinguished career as presidential assistant, poet, novelist, editor, and historian, Hay served as U.S. secretary of state and helped to implement the foreign policy initiatives that elevated the United States to world power.

BORN: October 8, 1838; Salem, Indiana
DIED: July 1, 1905; Newbury, New Hampshire
ALSO KNOWN AS: John Milton Hay (full name)
AREAS OF ACHIEVEMENT: Diplomacy, literature

EARLY LIFE

John Milton Hay was the fourth child of Dr. Charles and Helen Leonard Hay. Charles Hay, an Indiana country physician of Scottish and German lineage who was the grandson of Adam Hay, who emigrated from Germany to Virginia about 1750. Hay's mother, who had been born Helen Leonard, had deep New England roots.

Shortly after Hay's birth, his family moved to Warsaw, Illinois, where he began his education, studying first in the local public schools and then at a private academy in Pittsfield, Pike County. An excellent student and a voracious reader, he had completed six books of Vergil in Latin by the time he was twelve. In 1852, when he was fourteen, he enrolled at a Springfield college. Though barely more than a high school, the institution prepared him to enter Brown University as a sophomore three years later. Quickly establishing himself as a scholar, he was graduated near the top of his class in 1858. He also demonstrated a flair for rhyming that resulted in his election as class poet.

Although Hay was born and reared in the West, his education at Brown gave him an appreciation for polished, sophisticated eastern society. His trim, handsome features and neat mustache, combined with his courtly manners, social charm, conversational wit, and appreciation for feminine beauty, marked him as a true gentleman. Accompanying these traits, however, were periodic rounds of melancholy that remained throughout his life.

Hay returned to Warsaw after graduating from Brown, but remained only briefly before moving back to Springfield, the state capital. In 1859, he joined the law office of his uncle, Milton Hay, and began preparing for a legal career. He also had the opportunity to observe the inner workings of state politics and to meet such figures as Stephen A. Douglas, Senator Lyman Trumbull, and Abraham Lincoln, whose law office was next door to Milton Hay's. After Lincoln's election as president of the United States in 1860, his secretary, John G. Nicolay, persuaded the president-elect that young John Hay would be valuable as an assistant secretary.

Hay remained with Lincoln until near the end of the Civil War, receiving callers, writing letters, smoothing the ruffled feathers of politicians and generals, and listening to the jokes, stories, and innermost concerns of the wartime president. In early 1864, Hay received an appointment as assistant adjutant general, with the rank of major, and was assigned to the White House as a military aide. Although not a military expert, Hay had a sensitivity for the political implications of military affairs that made him an invaluable asset in Lincoln's efforts to bring the war to a swift conclusion. Hay's association with Lincoln had a profound impact upon his career.

LIFE'S WORK

Hay's apprenticeship in diplomacy began in March, 1865, just before the end of the Civil War, when Secretary of State William H. Seward appointed him secretary to the American legation at Paris. There he enjoyed the social delights of diplomatic life at the court of Napoleon III and composed verse that expressed his youthful democratic political ideas. He had little influence, however, in diplomatic matters. In mid-1867, after a brief furlough in the United States, he accepted an appointment as American chargé d'affaires in Vienna, Austria. With few serious diplomatic duties to perform, he traveled extensively, making tours of Poland and Turkey before his resignation in August, 1868. Ten months later, he became secretary of the American legation in Madrid, Spain, where he served until the summer of 1870.

After his initial round of diplomatic assignments, Hay embarked upon a remarkable literary career. In 1871, he published *Pike County Ballads and Other Pieces*, a collection of poems that celebrated life in Warsaw and the other Mississippi River towns of his youth. In *Castilian Days*, which appeared the same year, he reflected upon his travels in Spain. These books mirrored his early democratic optimism, established his reputation as a major literary figure, and led to friendships with authors such as Mark Twain, William Dean Howells, and Bret Harte. He also exercised his considerable talents as an editor for Whitelaw Reid's powerful *New York Tribune*.

Hay's writings acquired an increasingly conservative tone after his marriage in January, 1874, to Clara L. Stone, a daughter of Amassa Stone, a wealthy Cleveland industrialist and railroad builder. Already a gentleman by predisposition and education, Hay became an aristocrat by marriage. The extent of his change in attitude became fully apparent in 1884 with the publication of *The Bread-Winners*, a stinging attack against both labor unions and social mobility, and a defense of European-style class stratification. In the meantime, Hay had commenced an even more significant literary venture. In 1875, he and John Nicolay initiated their massive *Abraham Lincoln: A History*. By its completion in 1890, the project numbered ten volumes. Although it overly idealizes Lincoln, Nicolay and Hay's work remains a landmark study of the life of the sixteenth president.

Although Hay devoted most of his energies between 1870 and 1897 to literary and historical pursuits, he never completely divorced himself from foreign policy concerns. From 1879 to 1881, he served as assistant secretary of state, learning much about the intricacies of foreign policy formulation. During the next fifteen years, he traveled extensively in Europe, acquiring a wealth of information and contacts that would be beneficial in future diplomatic endeavors.

Hay also maintained close ties with leading Republican politicians. When his friend William McKinley won the presidency in 1896, Hay received the appointment as

John Hay. (Library of Congress)

ambassador to Great Britain. Convinced of the necessity of forging strong relations with the British, he used his considerable charm and tact to smooth friction created by the recent Venezuelan boundary dispute and the ongoing pelagic sealing controversy. When the Spanish-American War erupted in 1898, Hay's efforts ensured a stance of sympathetic neutrality on the part of England toward American intervention in Cuba.

In August, 1898, McKinley appointed Hay secretary of state. Although not an aggressive imperialist, Hay believed firmly that the United States should play a larger role in world affairs, and he worked vigorously throughout his tenure to accomplish that goal. During McKinley's administration, Hay focused much attention on affairs in Asia and the Pacific Ocean. In treaty negotiations to end the Spanish-American War, he supported the president's decision to acquire the Philippine Islands and then encouraged strong action to crush the insurrection led by Emilio Aguinaldo. Hay's most significant assertion of American influence in Asia was the famous Open Door notes, which sought assurances from the major powers that equal trading rights would be guaranteed within their spheres of interest. The following year, when the Boxer Rebellion triggered discussion of a partition of China by the European powers, Hay issued a second Open Door circular designed to preserve China's territorial integrity.

Hay also negotiated several treaties that paved the way for construction of the Panama Canal. In 1901, after the U.S. Senate rejected an earlier version, he concluded the Hay-Pauncefote Treaty with England, which abrogated the Clayton-Bulwer Treaty of 1850 and allowed the United States to construct and fortify an Isthmian canal. Two years later he negotiated the Hay-Herrán Treaty with Colombia, by which that nation was to allow the United States to build a canal across Panama. When Colombia refused to ratify the document, a convenient revolt erupted in Panama, and President Theodore Roosevelt promptly recognized its new government; Hay followed up by working out a treaty with Philippe Bunau-Varilla in which Panama gave the United States rights to a Canal Zone through which a canal would be constructed.

One of the most persistent Anglo-American problems as the twentieth century dawned was a controversy over the location of the Canada-Alaska boundary. In January, 1903, after months of effort, Hay and British ambassador Michael Herbert signed a treaty that called for the establishment of a tribunal made up of six impartial judges, three representing each side, to resolve the matter. President Roosevelt generated new controversy when he appointed Senators Henry Cabot Lodge and George Turner

"JIM BLUDSO, OF THE *PRAIRIE BELLE*"

Wall, no! I can't tell whar he lives,
Becase he don't live, you see;
Leastways, he's got out of the habit
Of livin' like you and me.
Whar have you been for the last three year
That you haven't heard folks tell
How Jimmy Bludso passed in his checks
The night of the *Prairie Belle*?

He weren't no saint,—them engineers
Is all pretty much alike, —
One wife in Natchez-under-the-Hill,
And another one here, in Pike;
A keerless man in his talk was Jim,
And an awkward hand in a row,
But he never flunked, and he never lied, —
I reckon he never knowed how.

And this was all the religion he had, —
To treat his engine well;
Never be passed on the river;
To mind the pilot's bell;
And if ever the *Prairie Belle* took fire, —
A thousand times he swore,
He'd hold her nozzle agin the bank
Till the last soul got ashore.

All boats has their day on the Mississip,
And her day come at last, —
The *Movastar* was a better boat,
But the *Belle* she WOULDN'T be passed.

And so she come tearin' along that night —
The oldest craft on the line —
With a nigger squat on her safety-valve,
And her furnace crammed, rosin and pine.

The fire bust out as she clared the bar,
And burnt a hole in the night,
And quick as a flash she turned, and made
For that willer-bank on the right.
There was runnin' and cursin', but Jim yelled out,
Over all the infernal roar,
"I'll hold her nozzle agin the bank
Till the last galoot's ashore."

Through the hot, black breath of the burnin' boat
Jim Bludso's voice was heard,
And they all had trust in his cussedness,
And knowed he would keep his word.
And, sure's you're born, they all got off
Afore the smokestacks fell, —
And Bludso's ghost went up alone
In the smoke of the *Prairie Belle*.

He weren't no saint,—but at jedgment
I'd run my chance with Jim,
'Longside of some pious gentlemen
That wouldn't shook hands with him.
He seen his duty, a dead-sure thing, —
And went for it thar and then;
And Christ ain't a-going to be too hard
On a man that died for men.

Source: John Hay, *Pike County Ballads* (Boston: J. R. Osgood, 1871).

---

to the tribunal, but the American position prevailed when the British jurist, in an effort to preserve Anglo-American harmony, rejected the views of his two Canadian colleagues and voted with the American representatives. Settlement of the Alaska boundary dispute was one of Hay's last major accomplishments. On July 1, 1905, after an extended illness, he died in Newbury, New Hampshire.

SIGNIFICANCE

John Hay was a major literary and diplomatic figure whose life and works symbolize the momentous transformation of American society and the significant expansion of the nation's role in world affairs during the late nineteenth and early twentieth centuries. The dra-

matic shift in Hay's ideological perspective between the publication of *Pike County Ballads* and the appearance of *The Bread-Winners* suggests the growing uneasiness within the American upper class over labor unrest, immigration, political radicalism, and other perceived threats to the status quo.

Hay's high literary reputation and his ability to inspire trust and make friends also made it possible for him to gain the respect and friendship of those with whom he strenuously disagreed. Thus he retained the friendship of anti-imperialists such as Mark Twain and William Dean Howells, even when they opposed his conduct of American policy in the Philippines. When his reputation led to his election in 1904 as a charter member of the American

Academy of Arts and Letters over such great writers as Henry Adams and Henry James, he rectified the error by arranging for their election on a later ballot.

Hay's accomplishments as secretary of state had lasting foreign policy implications. The Open Door notes undergirded American policy in Asia through World War II and beyond. The Panama Canal treaties and construction of the canal vastly expanded the nation's political and economic stake in Central America and the Caribbean region. The Hay-Herbert Treaty and the settlement of the Alaska boundary dispute contributed to a new era of Anglo-American friendship, which became a foundation stone of twentieth century foreign policy. Finally, Hay's skill, dignity, and restraint as a negotiator helped to placate some of the ill will created by Theodore Roosevelt's bellicosity in foreign policy matters. By the time of his death, Hay had participated fully in the emergence of the United States as a world power.

—Carl E. Kramer

FURTHER READING

Beale, Howard K. *Theodore Roosevelt and the Rise of America to World Power*. Baltimore: Johns Hopkins University Press, 1956. John Hay is a central figure in this detailed, well-researched account of American expansion under Theodore Roosevelt. This volume is essential to understanding the values as well as the political and economic forces behind American imperialism.

Campbell, Charles S. *The Transformation of American Foreign Relations, 1865-1900*. New York: Harper & Row, 1976. A well-written synthesis of scholarship on American foreign relations during the last thirty-five years of the nineteenth century. Excellent source of historical context for understanding foreign policy issues during the McKinley and Roosevelt administrations. Deals with Hay primarily in relation to the Open Door policy and Anglo-American relations.

Clymer, Kenton J. *John Hay: The Gentleman as Diplomat*. Ann Arbor: University of Michigan Press, 1975. A full-length treatment of Hay, this volume is especially useful for its explanation of his intellectual background and literary career. Although sympathetic to Hay, it is less satisfactory, on balance, in its discussion of his diplomatic service. Organized thematically, the volume is generally quite readable; the lack of a continuing chronology, however, sometimes makes it difficult to keep events in perspective.

Dennett, Tyler. *John Hay: From Poetry to Politics*. New York: Dodd, Mead, 1933. The best single biography of John Hay. Based upon extensive research into un-published manuscripts, published works, and official documents. Although sympathetic to Hay and his accomplishments, it also admits his defects and failures.

Dulles, Rhea Foster. "John Hay." In *An Uncertain Tradition: American Secretaries of State in the Twentieth Century*, edited by Norman A. Graebner. New York: McGraw-Hill, 1961. Summarizes Hay's major accomplishments as secretary of state. Pictures Hay as an implementor rather than as an initiator of policy whose ability to compromise and to accommodate were his major assets.

Hay, John. *At Lincoln's Side: John Hay's Civil War Correspondence and Selected Writings*. Edited by Michael Burlingame. Carbondale: Southern Illinois University Press, 2000. Compilation of 220 letters and telegrams that Hay drafted when he worked for President Lincoln. The documents, including some Hay composed for Lincoln's signature, provide a picture of Lincoln's presidency and Hay's position within it.

McCullough, David. *The Path Between the Seas: The Creation of the Panama Canal, 1870-1914*. New York: Simon & Schuster, 1977. A colorful, prizewinning study of the social, economic, political, and technological events surrounding construction of the Panama Canal. Based upon archival and manuscript sources from both sides of the Atlantic as well as interviews with surviving participants. Sympathetic to Hay in respect to his relationship with Roosevelt.

Thayer, William Roscoe. *Life and Letters of John Hay*. 2 vols. Boston: Houghton Mifflin, 1915. A detailed account drawn heavily from Hay's personal letters, many of which are quoted at length or reprinted in their entirety. Although severely dated in interpretation, it remains a useful background source, especially on Hay's early life.

Zimmerman, Warren. *First Great Triumph: How Five Americans Made Their Country a World Power*. New York: Farrar, Straus and Giroux, 2002. John Hay's activities as secretary of state to Presidents McKinley and Theodore Roosevelt are examined in this study of five people who helped make American an international power at the start of the twentieth century.

SEE ALSO: Henry Adams; Stephen A. Douglas; Abraham Lincoln; William McKinley; Napoleon III; William H. Seward; Mark Twain.

RELATED ARTICLE in *Great Events from History: The Nineteenth Century, 1801-1900:* September 6, 1899-July 3, 1900: Hay Articulates "Open Door" Policy Toward China.

FERDINAND VANDEVEER HAYDEN
American explorer

During the 1860's and 1870's, Hayden organized and led scientific explorations of the Rocky Mountains that generated publicity that helped to make Yellowstone the first national park in the United States.

BORN: September 7, 1829; Westfield, Massachusetts
DIED: December 22, 1887; Philadelphia, Pennsylvania
ALSO KNOWN AS: Ferdinand Vandiveer Hayden
AREA OF ACHIEVEMENT: Exploration

EARLY LIFE

Ferdinand Vandeveer Hayden (HAY-dehn) was born in southwest Massachusetts in 1829. After his father's death, his mother sent him at the age of ten to live with an uncle on a farm near Rochester, New York. An ambitious young man, Hayden left the farm at the age of sixteen. He taught school for two years before walking to Oberlin College in Ohio; he gained entrance despite a lack of financial assistance and worked his way through to graduation. Hayden studied geology at the school and graduated in 1850. He then entered Albany Medical School, completed his doctor of medicine degree in 1853, and continued his study of geology and paleontology.

Instead of practicing medicine, Hayden traveled to the South Dakota Badlands with one of his professors to study geology. The trip promised adventure and began Hayden's lifelong obsession with the American West and its natural history. During the 1850's, he explored the area from the Missouri River to the Rockies, often alone, making geologic and scientific observations of the vast, uncharted regions. By 1860, having gained invaluable training and experience in exploration and science, he was ready to explore the legendary region of Yellowstone. However, the Civil War forced him to postpone these plans.

Hayden returned to medical practice during the war as a volunteer surgeon; he ended the war with the rank of lieutenant colonel. By 1865, he had become well known for his early explorations, and he gained additional experience and respect during the Civil War. After the war's end, he accepted an appointment as a professor of mineralogy and geology at the University of Pennsylvania. In 1866, he again returned west to the Dakota Badlands for further exploration and study. During the next several years, he performed respected and well-received geological and topological surveys in Nebraska, Wyoming, and Colorado. In 1869, Hayden was asked to lead a series of surveys of the Rocky Mountains, which became one of the four great post-Civil War scientific explorations of the American West. His work was known as the United States Geological Survey of Territories.

LIFE'S WORK

Hayden assembled a group of experienced scientific professionals to accompany him on his surveys. Along with geologists, botanists, engineers, and topographers, he brought artists and photographers to sketch, paint, and photograph the wonders of the Rocky Mountains. These artists introduced the scenery of the Rocky Mountains to Americans and made the area a popular destination for farmers, settlers, and miners, who went to seek their fortunes. Such visual work helped to dramatize the beauty and wonders of the West for the American people. Hayden's surveys, which were published as books with photographs, sold well.

Hayden began his reconnaissance of the Rocky Mountains with about one dozen men. Later his party would grow to include between twenty and thirty people, all professional scientists and hardy outdoorsmen. His *Third Annual Report* of 1869 detailed their explorations in New Mexico and Colorado and told of the great mineral wealth and possibilities for settlement in these areas. This report was highly successful, and the popularity of his explorations gained him support in Congress for continued surveys, this time in the northern Rocky Mountains. In the summer of 1870, Hayden and his party left for Wyoming. After yet another successful year and another popular annual report, he finally set out to explore the legendary Yellowstone and the magnificent Teton Mountains.

In 1871, Hayden led the first official government expedition into Yellowstone, one of the last truly unknown areas in the United States. Fur trappers and Native Americans had virtually avoided the area, finding easier game outside the rugged area. Rumors of the great geysers, hot springs, and spectacular waterfalls had persisted for decades. Such rumors, combined with Congress's desire to map the area and discover its possible fur and mineral wealth, helped spur Hayden's discoveries.

When Hayden and his men entered Yellowstone Valley, they found hundreds of bubbling hot springs that fed the streams that became tributaries of the Yellowstone River. Green pines and aspens covered the mountains, and the serene surface of Yellowstone Lake reflected the crystal blue sky. The meadows were covered with dark green grass and acres of multihued wildflowers. Mud pots and geysers dotted the valley. Mammoth Hot Springs, officially discovered by Hayden's survey, had dozens of springs with water ranging in color from pure white to bright yellow. In the morning, steam rose from the numerous vents in the earth and obscured the valley in a volcanic mist. Wildlife was abundant, and moose, beaver, deer, and grizzly bears could be seen everywhere. The party also stumbled across the Grand Canyon of the Yellowstone River and its two waterfalls. There seemed to be something unfinished and unearthly about the region. It was a wonder to behold, and the area fascinated Hayden. He wrote in awe of its stunning beauty. The survey left Yellowstone in late August, 1871, and returned east later that year.

Hayden's report on Yellowstone immediately grabbed the interest of the American people and Congress. A map of the region was published, the photos were reproduced, and Hayden wrote a number of articles for popular magazines such as *Scribners* to urge the nation to turn the rare wonders of Yellowstone into a protected park for all Americans. Congress unanimously passed such a bill, and on March 1, 1972, President Ulysses S. Grant signed the Yellowstone Park Bill, creating the first national park in the United States.

In 1872, Hayden returned to the northern Rockies, this time to the Grand Teton Mountains. Like Yellowstone, the Tetons were an area of natural grandeur with dense spruce forests, deep canyons, and cascading streams. Above it all towered the famed jagged mountain peaks, their glory reflected off pristine mountain lakes. The survey climbed many of the peaks, named streams and other natural landmarks, and collected information on the natural history of the Tetons. The party departed in early fall, before the first snows. From 1873 to 1876, the Hayden survey explored Colorado.

The four years that Hayden and his men spent in Colorado were just as exciting and rewarding as the previous years in the northern Rockies. They mapped the mountains, rivers, and drainage basins of the state; studied its geology and natural history; and gave names to many of the peaks. Hayden's men braved electrical storms, forest fires, blizzards, blistering heat, and wild animals. In 1873, the expedition discovered the legendary Mountain of the Holy Cross. This peak appeared to have a one-thousand-foot-tall cross of white snow blazed into its side. Photographs of this mountain were spectacularly popular and helped to further American interest in the recreational and developmental potential of Colorado.

The next year, in 1874, a group of his men stumbled across ancient American Indian ruins in the southwest portion of the state. These cliff dwellings were a wonderful archaeological and historical find that helped gain further fame and public support for both Hayden and his wildly successful surveys.

The last two years of the survey were spent in Wyoming, Montana, and Idaho, where Hayden and his men continued their job of mapping the land and studying its geology and natural history. By 1878, Hayden's United States Geological Survey of the Territories had completed the task assigned to it. Hayden's work in the field continued until 1882, when locomotor ataxia forced him to begin to abandon the writing and exploration that he loved so greatly. Hayden died on December 22, 1887, in Philadelphia, Pennsylvania.

SIGNIFICANCE

Ferdinand Hayden will be remembered for his twelve years of painstaking geological fieldwork in the American West. For eleven years, from 1867 to 1878, Hayden and his men explored, mapped, and studied areas in five states. His leadership of the United States Geological Survey of the Territories was superb, and his devotion to his task was unequaled. His survey not only discovered or publicized such natural wonders as Yellowstone and the Grand Tetons but also found such legendary places as the Mountain of the Holy Cross and the ancient cliff dwellings of the American Southwest. His explorations and the subsequent publicity that accompanied them were crucial to securing the support of the American public for conservation of natural areas.

Hayden's Geological Survey of the Territories laid the foundation for much of American knowledge of the geology, zoology, and topography of the Rocky Mountains. Farmers, miners, and railroad companies used his maps and reports to help settle and conquer the American wilderness. His eleven years of fieldwork also proved to be a magnificent training ground for late nineteenth century American scientists, who became the leaders for the next generation. Hayden and his men demonstrated to a suspicious and uncertain American public that science was practical and important. With each new dramatic discovery, science became more accepted. Millions of Americans learned from his popular reports, viewed the pictures from his surveys, and visited museums that built upon information uncovered by his expeditions.

Hayden's most important accomplishment, however, was the establishment of Yellowstone National Park in

1872. It is quite possible that Yellowstone's incredible natural wonders would have been devastated by commercial development during the late nineteenth century. Hayden's efforts on behalf of the region's preservation, combined with photographs of the area's scenery reproduced for the public, forced Congress and President Grant to set aside Yellowstone for future generations. Today, more than fifty national parks preserve the greatest natural treasures in the United States.

—*Jeff R. Bremer*

FURTHER READING

Bartlett, Richard A. *Great Surveys of the American West.* Norman: University of Oklahoma Press, 1962. This is the best work on Hayden's actual surveys and contains four excellent, exciting chapters on his explorations. Bartlett's fine book places the surveys in their historical and political context and has an excellent bibliography.

Bruce, Robert. *The Launching of Modern American Science, 1846-1876.* New York: Alfred A. Knopf, 1987. Bruce's work puts Hayden's surveys in the context of post-Civil War expansionism and explains the beginnings of the American scientific community and the American quest for knowledge about the natural world.

Cassidy, James G. *Ferdinand V. Hayden: Entrepreneur of Science.* Lincoln: University of Nebraska Press, 2000. Focuses on Hayden's ability to gain government funding for his expeditions, creating a government niche for science that eventually resulted in the establishment of the United States Geological Survey. Cassidy argues that Hayden's experience exemplifies how government patronage and science worked to benefit business during the Gilded Age.

Foster, Mike. *Strange Genius: The Life of Ferdinand Vandeveer Hayden.* New York: R. Rhinehart, 1995. This is the only modern full-length biography of Hayden. It covers Hayden's entire life in detail, with emphasis on his scientific explorations in the American West.

Goetzmann, William H. *Exploration and Empire: The Explorer and the Scientist in the Winning of the American West.* Austin: Texas State Historical Association, 1993. This Pulitzer Prize-winning book covers a century of exploration and conquest in the American West. It contains a fine, succinct chapter on Hayden's Survey.

_____. *New Lands, New Men: The Second Great Age of Discovery.* London: Oxford University Press, 1987. This book details the scientific explorations of the nineteenth and twentieth centuries and shows the historical importance of Hayden, as well as the four other great surveys.

Merrill, Marlene Deahl, ed. *Yellowstone and the Great West: Journals, Letters, and Images from the 1871 Hayden Expedition.* Lincoln: University of Nebraska Press, 1999. This collection of edited and annotated writings by three lesser-known members of the expedition provides an understanding of how expedition members conducted their daily activities and viewed the West.

SEE ALSO: John C. Frémont; Ulysses S. Grant; Meriwether Lewis and William Clark; Zebulon Pike.

RELATED ARTICLES in *Great Events from History: The Nineteenth Century, 1801-1900:* January, 1839: Invention of Daguerreotype Photography Is Announced; March 1, 1872: Yellowstone Becomes the First U.S. National Park.

RUTHERFORD B. HAYES
President of the United States (1877-1881)

Though an ardent Radical Republican early in the Reconstruction era, Hayes moderated his views and as president ended that era by withdrawing military support for Republican state governments in the South. He also opposed inflation, defended the presidency from congressional attacks, and fought for civil service reform.

BORN: October 4, 1822; Delaware, Ohio
DIED: January 17, 1893; Fremont, Ohio
ALSO KNOWN AS: Rutherford Birchard Hayes (full name)
AREA OF ACHIEVEMENT: Government and politics

EARLY LIFE

The posthumous son of Rutherford Hayes, Rutherford Birchard Hayes was so weak at his birth that his mother, Sophia Birchard Hayes, did not expect him to survive. His parents were of old New England stock and had migrated to Ohio from Vermont in 1817. On his death, his father left his mother a farm that she rented, some additional land, and a house in town, where she kept two lodgers. Her sorrow was deepened in January, 1825, when Hayes's older brother, a sturdy nine-year-old, drowned while ice skating, leaving only Hayes, a feeble two-year-old, and his four-year-old sister, Fanny. She was his constant companion, whom he adored and whose dolls he played with until he grew older and replaced them with toy soldiers. His understandably protective mother allowed him neither to do household chores nor to play games with boys until he was nine. A friendly, cheerful child, Hayes admired his mother's carefree, younger bachelor brother, Sardis Birchard, who left their household when Hayes was four but returned often for visits and paid for Hayes's education.

After Hayes's mother had taught him to read, spell, and write, he attended a private grade school and later was tutored by a local lawyer. When nearly fourteen, Hayes left home to attend Norwalk (Ohio) Academy, and the next year he attended Isaac Webb's Preparatory School in Middletown, Connecticut. In 1838, at the age of sixteen, Hayes entered Kenyon College in Gambier, Ohio, and in 1842, he was graduated at the head of his class. After studying law for a year with a lawyer in Columbus, Ohio, Hayes entered Harvard Law School; he received his bachelor of law degree in 1845.

LIFE'S WORK

From 1845 to 1849, Hayes practiced law in his Uncle Sardis's town of Upper Sandusky, Ohio, and was largely responsible for changing its name to Fremont. Eager to be on his own in a challenging city, Hayes in January, 1850, opened an office in Cincinnati, Ohio, achieved prominence, and on December 30, 1852, married Lucy Ware Webb, a recent graduate of Wesleyan Female College. She was religious and a reformer with strong temperance and ardent abolitionist beliefs. In contrast, Hayes, a lifelong disciple of Ralph Waldo Emerson, never joined a church and before his marriage had shown little interest in organized reform.

In September, 1853, Hayes defended captured runaway slaves free of charge and soon helped found the Republican Party in Ohio. From 1858 to 1861, he held his first public office as Cincinnati's city solicitor. When the lower southern states seceded (1860-1861), he was inclined to "Let them go," but he was outraged when on April 12, 1861, their new Confederacy attacked Fort Sumter at Charleston, South Carolina. He organized half the Literary Club of Cincinnati into a drilling company of which he was captain, and on June 27, he was commissioned a major in the Twenty-third Ohio Volunteer Infantry. Hayes served throughout the war, was wounded four times, and emerged from the struggle a major general and a member-elect of Congress.

Serving from 1865 to 1867, Hayes consistently supported Radical Republican Reconstruction measures, but, as chairman of the Joint Committee on the Library, he worked hardest in developing the Library of Congress into a great institution. Unhappy in Congress, he resigned to run successfully for governor of Ohio and was reelected in 1869. His greatest achievements in his first two terms as governor (1868-1872) were Ohio's ratification of the Fifteenth Amendment and the establishment of Ohio State University. Returning to Cincinnati in early 1872, he loyally supported President Ulysses S. Grant for a second term and ran for Congress to help the ticket. Although Hayes lost, Grant won, and Hayes's services in a pivotal state placed him in line for a major appointment. When he was asked merely to be assistant treasurer at Cincinnati, he refused and retired from politics "definitely, absolutely, positively." With Lucy and their five children, he returned to Fremont to live with Uncle Sardis, who died in January, 1874, leaving Hayes the bulk of his estate.

The Panic of 1873 reversed the Republican Party's fortunes, while the "corruptionists around Grant" tarnished its reputation in the eyes of Hayes and other

Rutherford B. Hayes.

respectable Republicans. By 1875, Ohio Republicans, eager to save their state for their party, nominated a reluctant Hayes for a third term as governor. He won by a narrow margin and became a contender for the 1876 presidential nomination, which he also won because his rivals were either too corrupt, too ill, too radical, or too reformist. In contrast, Hayes was a fearless soldier, who was impeccably honest and from a crucial state, and, though both a Radical and a reformer, he was by nature moderate and conciliatory. To oppose him, the Democrats nominated Samuel J. Tilden, New York's reforming governor. They campaigned for white supremacy and the removal of the federal troops that upheld Republican regimes in the South and attacked the Grant administration as corrupt. Republican orators warned voters not to let the rebels capture the federal government through a Democratic victory and promised that Hayes would reform the civil service.

When the election was over, both Republicans and Democrats disputed its result. Tilden had at least 250,000 more popular votes than Hayes, but Republicans, after some election night computations, claimed to have carried Florida, Louisiana, and South Carolina (states that

Republicans, supported by federal troops, controlled, but which Tilden appeared to have won), giving Hayes 185 electoral votes and Tilden, 184.

Republican-dominated returning boards reviewed the vote in those states, legally eliminating the entire vote in districts where they believed black people were intimidated into not voting, and certified that Hayes had carried all three states. Charging the returning boards with fraud, Democrats certified that Tilden had carried those three states. To decide which electoral votes to count, the Democratic House of Representatives and the Republican Senate in January, 1877, agreed on the Electoral Count Act, creating the fifteen-member Electoral Commission, drawn from both houses of Congress and the Supreme Court and comprising seven Republicans, seven Democrats, and one independent. The independent, who was a Supreme Court justice, resigned to become a senator and was replaced on the commission by a Republican. By a strict eight-to-seven party vote, the Electoral Commission decided the disputed election in favor of the Republicans and Hayes.

The commission failed to end the crisis. The electoral votes had to be counted in a joint session of Congress, and its angry Democratic majority obstructed the count with repeated adjournments. Some southern Democrats, who had belonged to the pre-Civil War Whig party, while meeting with Republicans close to Hayes (who were also of Whig extraction), offered to cooperate in completing the count and suggested that they would desert their party to help Republicans organize the next House of Representatives (which the Democrats appeared to have won) and even join the Republican Party. In return, they wanted Hayes to withdraw the federal troops from Louisiana and South Carolina (the Florida Republican government had collapsed) and in effect complete the restoration of white supremacy governments in the South, and to appoint to his cabinet one of their political persuasion to augment their strength with federal patronage. A few of them pressed for a federal subsidy to construct the Texas and Pacific Railroad. There is no doubt that these negotiations took place, but how crucial they were in changing the Democratic votes that permitted completing the count is debated.

Hayes was inaugurated on schedule, becoming the nineteenth president of the United States. He appointed a southern Democrat with a Whig background to his cabinet and in April, 1877, ended the Reconstruction era by removing the federal troops from South Carolina and Louisiana, after receiving assurances from their incoming Democrat regimes that they would observe the Fourteenth and Fifteenth Amendments, granting civil and voting rights to black men. The amendments were not faithfully observed, southern Democrats neither helped Republicans organize the House nor joined their party, and Hayes ignored the Texas and Pacific Railroad.

Having disposed of the southern question, Hayes moved on two fronts to reform the civil service. Because it suffered because political parties depended on government workers to finance and organize the nomination and election of candidates, Hayes ordered that civil servants not be assessed a portion of their salaries for political purposes and that they not manage "political organizations, caucuses, conventions, or election campaigns." He also determined to make the New York Customhouse, the largest federal office in the land, where more than half the nation's revenue was collected, a showcase to prove that civil service reform was practical. That effort led to a spectacular but successful struggle with New York Senator Roscoe Conkling, who regarded the Customhouse as part of his political machine. Hayes's victory struck twin blows to promote reform and to restore executive power over appointments.

Despite enormous pressure to inflate the currency, Hayes was a consistent hard-money advocate. In February, 1878, he would not approve the mildly inflationary Bland-Allison Act (requiring the government monthly to purchase and coin two to four million dollars worth of silver), but Congress overrode his veto. In January, 1879, he was pleased when the Treasury Department began to pay gold for greenbacks (paper money issued during the Civil War without gold backing).

The Democrats challenged Hayes during the second half of his administration, when they controlled both houses of Congress. To necessary appropriation bills, they repeatedly attached riders that would repeal the federal election laws ("force bills") enforcing the Fourteenth and Fifteenth Amendments, but Hayes consistently vetoed those bills. He argued that the federal government was justified in preventing intimidation and fraud in the election of its Congress and also that Congress, by attaching these riders, was trying to destroy the executive's constitutional right to veto legislation. Hayes won the battle of the riders; his vetoes rallied his party and the people outside the South to his side. Responding to political pressure, Congress passed the appropriations without the riders.

Returning prosperity and a united Republican Party bolstered Hayes's financial and political views and left him in a strong position, but he had vowed to serve only one term. He left office confident that his policies were instrumental in electing as his successor James A. Garfield, a fellow Ohio Republican.

In retirement, Hayes served effectively as a trustee of the Peabody Education Fund and as president of the Slater Fund, both dedicated to further the education of black southerners. He died in Fremont, Ohio, on January 17, 1893.

SIGNIFICANCE

Hayes was a man of integrity, courage, and decision, but he was also a man of reason and moderation. He was an uncompromising defender of the Union and an opponent of inflation, but on other issues he was willing to compromise as he worked to achieve his goals. Although he was a reformer, he sought to convince people rather than coerce

---

HAYES'S FIRST STATE OF THE UNION ADDRESS

It is generally acknowledged that Reconstruction ended with the election of Rutherford B. Hayes in 1876. After the withdrawal of Union troops from the southern states, former slaves were left to the mercy of white politicians who returned to power in their state governments. In his first state of the union address, Hayes issued a mild appeal to all citizens to respect the rights of African Americans.

It may not be improper here to say that it should be our fixed and unalterable determination to protect by all available and proper means under the Constitution and the laws the lately emancipated race in the enjoyment of their rights and privileges; and I urge upon those to whom heretofore the colored people have sustained the relation of bondmen the wisdom and justice of humane and liberal local legislation with respect to their education and general welfare. A firm adherence to the laws, both national and State, as to the civil and political rights of the colored people, now advanced to full and equal citizenship; the immediate repression and sure punishment by the national and local authorities, within their respective jurisdictions, of every instance of lawlessness and violence toward them, is required for the security alike of both races, and is justly demanded by the public opinion of the country and the age. In this way the restoration of harmony and good will and the complete protection of every citizen in the full enjoyment of every constitutional right will surely be attained. Whatever authority rests with me to this end I shall not hesitate to put forth. . . .

Source: Rutherford B. Hayes, "State of the Union Address," December 3, 1877.

them. He had, for example, lectured in favor of temperance, but only after becoming president did he totally abstain from alcoholic beverages, and he opposed prohibition legislation and one-issue political parties founded on temperance. His moderate, pragmatic, piecemeal approach often angered those who were impatient to right wrongs. Out of the entire government service, his administration instituted reform in only the Department of the Interior under Secretary Carl Schurz and the New York Customhouse and Post Office, but, in these showcases, reform succeeded and proved its practicality. Had it been universally applied, hostile administrators would have discredited civil service reform.

Hayes, who was in a no-win position, has been criticized for his southern policy. With neither political support nor congressional appropriations, he could not reverse the policy of the preceding Grant administration and reclaim southern states by military force. From an impossible situation, he extracted promises from southern Democrats to uphold Reconstruction amendments if he would remove the troops supporting powerless Republican governments. At the start, he naïvely believed that southern Democrats would keep their word and thought that his policy would attract to his party respectable southern whites who would not interfere with black civil rights. Even though his policy failed, given the bleak prospects for southern blacks and Republicans in April, 1877, Hayes took the only feasible course by which their rights might have been protected.

—Ari Hoogenboom

FURTHER READING

Barnard, Harry. *Rutherford B. Hayes and His America.* Indianapolis: Bobbs-Merrill, 1954. An excellent psychological study that stresses Hayes's close relationship with his sister. In doing justice to Hayes's personal life, however, this biography underemphasizes his public life; less than half of the book is devoted to his election and presidency.

Hayes, Rutherford B. *Diary and Letters of Rutherford Birchard Hayes: Nineteenth President of the United States.* Edited by Charles Richard Williams. 5 vols. Columbus: Ohio State Archaeological and Historical Society, 1922-1925. Hayes kept a diary most of his life (one of the few presidents to do so) but did go for weeks at times without an entry. To form a readable narrative, the editor has corrected spelling and grammatical lapses, included letters, and supplied introductions and transitions.

_____. *The Diary of a President, 1875-1881: Covering the Disputed Election, the End of Reconstruction, and the Beginning of Civil Service.* Edited by Harry T. Williams. New York: David McKay, 1964. Virtually a facsimile edition of the diary, with the minor errors, gaps, deletions, and corrections made obvious.

Hoogenboom, Ari. *Outlawing the Spoils: A History of the Civil Service Reform Movement, 1865-1883.* Urbana: University of Illinois Press, 1961. The standard work on a major issue confronting the Hayes administration, this study reflects the exasperation of the reformers with Hayes's moderate course.

_____. *Rutherford B. Hayes: Warrior and President.* Lawrence: University Press of Kansas, 1995. A revisionist history. Hoogenboom refutes other historians who depict Hayes as a southern sympathizer or an example of Gilded Age greed; instead, Hoogenboom maintains, Hayes was a devout, pragmatic supporter of civil rights.

Morris, Roy, Jr. *Fraud of the Century: Rutherford B. Hayes, Samuel Tilden, and the Stolen Election of 1876.* New York: Simon & Schuster, 2003. The presidential election dispute of 2000 spurred new interest in Hayes's contested election. The publication of Morris's book was one result of this interest; his account of the 1876 election wrangling provides information on the lives and characters of both candidates as well as the nature of the political process. U.S. Supreme Court chief justice William H. Rehnquist has also written a book about the dispute: *Centennial Crisis: The Disputed Election of 1876*, published by Random House in 2004.

Polakoff, Keith Ian. *The Politics of Inertia: The Election of 1876 and the End of Reconstruction.* Baton Rouge: Louisiana State University Press, 1973. This superb study of the disputed election argues that the negotiations between southern Democrats and Hayes's friends had no effect on the settlement, that both parties were faction-ridden, that Hayes held the Republicans together better than Tilden held the Democrats together, and that in actuality Congress drifted into a settlement.

Trefousse, Hans L. *Rutherford B. Hayes.* New York: Times Books, 2002. Concise, informative account of Hayes's life and career, focusing on his Ohio governorship and his presidency. One in a series of books about American presidents.

Unger, Irwin. *The Greenback Era: A Social and Political History of American Finance, 1865-1879.* Princeton, N.J.: Princeton University Press, 1964. In following the greenback issue in American politics to the resumption of specie payments under Hayes, Unger not only analyzes the complex forces favoring inflation but also explores the equally complex attitudes of people such as Hayes, for whom hard money was not an economic issue but an undebatable article of faith.

Williams, Charles Richard. *The Life of Rutherford Birchard Hayes: Nineteenth President of the United States.* 2 vols. Boston: Houghton Mifflin, 1914. Reprint. Columbus: Ohio State Archaeological and Historical Society, 1928. First published in 1914, this old-fashioned biography is uncritical of Hayes but is full of information on Hayes's public career that the Barnard study ignores. The book is also valuable for its quotation of letters and speeches that otherwise are unavailable in print.

Williams, T. Harry. *Hayes of the Twenty-Third: The Civil War Volunteer Officer.* New York: Alfred A. Knopf, 1965. An outstanding military historian follows Hayes throughout the Civil War as he rose from major to major general.

Woodward, C. Vann. *Reunion and Reaction: The Compromise of 1877 and the End of Reconstruction.* 2d ed. Garden City, N.Y.: Doubleday, 1956. This classic study of the disputed election, first published in 1951, argues that a crucial element in the compromise was a land grant for the Texas and Pacific Railroad, which southern Democrats desired and Hayes's friends agreed to support but failed to deliver.

SEE ALSO: Chester A. Arthur; James G. Blaine; Ralph Waldo Emerson; James A. Garfield; Ulysses S. Grant; Benjamin Harrison; William McKinley; Thomas Nast; Carl Schurz.

RELATED ARTICLES in *Great Events from History: The Nineteenth Century, 1801-1900:* September 25, 1804: Twelfth Amendment Is Ratified; December 8, 1863-April 24, 1877: Reconstruction of the South; July 28, 1868: Burlingame Treaty; March 5, 1877: Hayes Becomes President; May 9, 1882: Arthur Signs the Chinese Exclusion Act; October 15, 1883: Civil Rights Cases.

GEORG WILHELM FRIEDRICH HEGEL
German philosopher

Hegel developed many theories of great philosophical importance that influenced the twentieth century social sciences, anthropology, sociology, psychology, history, and political theory. He believed that the mind is the ultimate reality and that philosophy can restore humanity to a state of harmony.

BORN: August 27, 1770; Stuttgart, Württemberg (now in Germany)
DIED: November 14, 1831; Berlin, Prussia (now in Germany)
AREA OF ACHIEVEMENT: Philosophy

EARLY LIFE

Born into a Protestant middle-class German family in Stuttgart, Georg Wilhelm Friedrich Hegel (HAY-gehl) was the eldest of three children. His father was a minor civil servant in the duchy of Württemberg, and his family had roots in Austria. To escape persecution by the Austrian Catholics in the sixteenth century, his ancestors settled among the Lutheran Protestants of the German territories, which consisted of more than three hundred free cities, duchies, and states loosely united under the rule

of Francis I of Austria. Little is known about Hegel's mother, but all accounts describe her as having been highly intelligent and unusually educated for a woman of that time.

Hegel had the conventional schooling for his social class, entering German primary school in 1773, Latin school in 1775, and the Stuttgart gymnasium illustre in 1780. Upon graduating from the gymnasium (equivalent to high school) in 1788, he entered the famous seminary at the University of Tübingen to study philosophy and theology in preparation for the Protestant ministry. As a student, Hegel became friends with Friedrich Hölderlin, a Romantic poet, and Friedrich Schelling. He shared the top floor of the dormitory with Schelling, who became famous before Hegel as an Idealist philosopher. In 1790, Hegel received a master's degree in philosophy.

After passing his theological examinations at Tübingen in 1793, Hegel began many years of struggle to earn his living and establish himself as a philosopher. Instead of entering the ministry, he began working as a house tutor for a wealthy family in Bern, Switzerland. In 1797, he became a tutor in Frankfurt, continuing throughout this time to read, think, and write about philosophical questions, usually along radical lines. For example, he considered Jesus inferior to Socrates as a teacher of ethics, and he considered orthodox religion, because of its reliance on external authority, an obstacle in restoring humankind to a life of harmony. Although Hegel always retained some of his skepticism toward orthodox religion, he later in life considered himself a Lutheran Christian. In 1798, he began to write on the philosophy of history and on the spirit of Christianity, major themes in his philosophical system. Upon his father's death in 1799, Hegel received a modest inheritance and was able to stop tutoring and join his friend Schelling at the University of Jena, in the state of Weimar.

LIFE'S WORK

Hegel's life's work as a teacher and philosopher began at Jena. From 1801 to 1807, Hegel taught as an unsalaried lecturer at the University of Jena, his first university position as a philosopher, for which he was paid by the students who attended class. While in Jena, Hegel cooperated with Schelling in editing the *Kritisches Journal der Philosophie*. He also published the *Differenz des Fichte'schen und Schelling'schen Systems der Philosophie* (1801; *The Difference Between Fichte's and Schelling's Philosophy*, 1977). During this time, Hegel began to lecture on metaphysics, logic, and natural law. In 1805, he was promoted to Ausserordentlicher Professor (Distinguished Professor) on the recommendation of the German Romantic poet Johann Wolfgang von Goethe. Hegel was prolific, yet beginning in 1802 he announced each year a significant forthcoming book to his publisher without producing it.

These were momentous times. In 1789, just before Hegel's nineteenth birthday, the fall of the Bastille announced the French Revolution across Europe; in 1806, after putting an end to the thousand-year Austrian Empire, Napoleon I crushed the Prussian armies at the Battle of Jena. On October 13, 1806, Napoleon victoriously entered the walled city of Jena, an event that Hegel described to a friend as follows:

> I saw the Emperor—that world-soul—riding out to reconnoiter the city; it is truly a wonderful sensation to see such an individual, concentrated here on a single point, astride a single horse, yet reaching across the world and ruling it.

October 13, 1806, was also the day that Hegel finished his book, long promised to his publisher, and sent the manuscript amid the confusion of war. The book was

his early masterpiece, *Die Phänomenologie des Geistes* (1807; *The Phenomenology of Spirit*, 1868, also known as *The Phenomenology of Mind*). On October 20, the French army plundered Hegel's house, and his teaching position at the University of Jena came to an end. Hegel left for Bamberg in Bavaria, where he spent a year working as a newspaper editor. He then became headmaster and philosophy teacher at the gymnasium in Nuremberg, where he worked successfully from 1808 until 1816.

The Phenomenology of Spirit, which exemplifies the young Hegel, was strongly influenced by German Romanticism. This movement provided a new and more complete way of perceiving the world and was developed by German philosophers and artists, such as Schelling and Hölderlin. German Romanticism stood in opposition to French rationalism and British empiricism, the two major philosophies of the seventeenth and eighteenth centuries dominated by reason and immediate sensory experience, respectively. German Romanticism had been influenced by the German philosopher Immanuel Kant, whose theory of knowledge synthesized rational and empirical elements. Kant argued that the laws of science, rather than being the source of rationality, were dependent on the human mind and its pure concepts, or categories, such as cause and effect. Kant believed that it is the mind that gives its laws to nature, and not the reverse.

Georg Wilhelm Friedrich Hegel. (Library of Congress)

Hegel's philosophical system expands upon this philosophy, which has reality depend on the rational mind for its perception. Hegel's absolute Idealism unites the totality of all concepts in the absolute mind or spirit, which he also referred to as the ultimate reality, or God. Hegel's metaphysics thus takes from German Romanticism the "inward path" to truth; the notion of nature as spirit, or the immanence of God within the universe; the quest for the totality of experience, both empirical and rational; and the desire for infinity.

Hegel argued that reality belongs to an absolute mind or a totality of conceptual truth, and that it consists of a rational structure characterized by a unity-amid-diversity. The purpose of metaphysics is to reveal the truth of this unified diversity. To this end, Hegel developed his highly influential theory of dialectic, a process involving three concepts: the thesis, the antithesis, and the synthesis. This dialectical process provides a way of transcending oppositions to a higher level of truth. Hegel argued that the dialectical triad, as the rhythm of reality, underlies all human knowledge and experience. Moreover, he defined the absolute mind as being the totality of concepts in a dialectical process.

Hegel believed that contradictions are never entirely overcome. Rather, the dialectic is both the essence of reality and the method for comprehending reality, which is always a unity-amid-diversity. Hegel's notion of conceptual truth, being immanent within the world, is time-bound rather than transcendental, despite his ambiguous reference to the absolute mind as God. Hegel's dialectic thus differs from that of Plato, which gives rise to timeless forms.

On the basis of his dialectic, Hegel begins *The Phenomenology of Spirit* by introducing his theory that the history of philosophy is a biography of the human spirit in its development over the course of centuries. The relationship between successive philosophies is one not of conflict but of organic growth and development. Hegel describes philosophy as a living and growing organism like the world itself. Each philosophy corresponds to the stage of a plant: the bud, the blossom, and the fruit. In addition to organicism, Hegel developed the metaphor of historicism, which holds that the understanding of any aspect of life is derived through its history, its evolution, and not through its static condition in the present. Hegel ends *The Phenomenology of Spirit* by arguing that the Age of Reason and philosophy must supersede the age of religious consciousness. He also argued that history evolves toward a specific goal, a state of freedom, and that the purpose of history is the unfolding of the truth of

reason. Hegel's arguments on this topic are collected in his *Sämtliche Werke* (1927; translated in *Lectures on the Philosophy of History*, 1956).

During the time Hegel taught in Nuremberg, he published *Wissenschaft der Logik* (1812-1816; *Science of Logic*, 1929) and *Encyklopädie der philosophischen im Wissenschaften Grundrisse* (1817; *Encyclopedia of Philosophy*, 1959). Hegel regarded the latter as having a dialectical structure, with the opposites of thought and nature united in mind and society, and ultimately in the self-referential act of philosophical self-consciousness. In 1811, Hegel married Maria von Tucher of Nuremberg, and in 1816 his nine-year-old illegitimate son, Ludwig, joined the household. Also in 1816, Hegel became a professor at the University of Heidelberg, and in 1817 for the first time he taught aesthetics. By this time, his reputation was so well established that the Prussian minister of education invited him to accept the prestigious chair of philosophy at the University of Berlin, where Hegel taught from 1818 until his death during a cholera epidemic in 1831.

During this final period, the climax of his career, Hegel lectured for the first time on the philosophy of religion and the philosophy of history. He published one of the great works of genius of Western culture, *Grundlinien der Philosophie des Rechts* (1821; *Philosophy of Right*, 1855), which exemplifies the mature or late Hegel in contrast to the early Hegel seen in *The Phenomenology of Spirit*. Hegel argued in his moral philosophy that ethics, like the individual, has its source, course, and ultimate fulfillment in the nation-state, particularly the state of Germany. The nation-state is a manifestation of God, which Hegel defines not as a personal God but rather as the Absolute. This totality of truth manifests itself in stages to each of the key nations of history, culminating in Germany.

During the 1820's, Hegel toured Belgium and the Netherlands and also traveled to Vienna and Prague. In 1824, he interceded with the Prussian government to free his friend Victor Cousin, a French liberal philosopher. Hegel was not an eloquent lecturer, but after his death, a group of his students collated their lecture notes and published an edition of his works in eighteen volumes (1832-1840). Hegel's writing is notoriously difficult, both stylistically and conceptually.

SIGNIFICANCE

Georg Wilhelm Friedrich Hegel's Idealist philosophy has been criticized for elevating the reality of concepts over the material aspects of reality, such as economics, environment, technology, and natural resources. Moreover, there seems to be a contradiction in Hegel's notion of the Absolute, in his definition of God as being externalized or existing in human consciousness. Finally, Hegel's philosophy of history has been criticized for masking a hidden defense for German nationalism, an aversion to democracy and individualism, and a fear of revolutionary change.

Nevertheless, Hegel has contributed many profound concepts to Western philosophy: the dialectical nature of thought, organicism and historicism, the concept of culture, the theory of ethics, and the theory of humanity's need for wholeness, in terms of both consciousness and social unification. Hegel believed that there are three important dialectical stages in ethical life responsible for social unity: the family, its antithesis in civil society, and their synthesis in the developed national state. As the French philosopher Maurice Merleau-Ponty says,

> All the great philosophical ideas of the past century, the philosophies of Marx, Nietzsche, existentialism and psycho-analysis had their beginning in Hegel.

Although he supported Christianity, Hegel placed philosophy above religion. He believed that religion and art are different ways of understanding the absolute idea, but that philosophy is a better way because it allows one to comprehend the absolute conceptually, not in religious symbols, and thereby subsumes both religion and art. For Hegel, ethical ideals, such as the ideals of freedom, originate in the spiritual life of a society.

—*William S. Haney II*

FURTHER READING

Althaus, Horst. *Hegel: An Intellectual Biography.* Translated by Michael Tarsh. Malden, Mass.: Blackwell, 2000. An English translation of a German biography published in 1992. The book recounts the major incidents in Hegel's life, providing a chronological account of how he developed his philosophical ideas. The book also discusses Hegel's role in the cultural and political life of his time.

Butler, Clark. *G. W. F. Hegel.* Boston: Twayne, 1977. A comprehensive study of Hegel that aims not to be merely about Hegel but to communicate the essence of Hegelian philosophy to a wider public. Presenting Hegelianism in an abstract philosophical context, Butler strives to be accessible but not oversimplistic. Approaches Hegel from the cultural standpoint of the

present. Contains a selected annotated bibliography and a chronology of Hegel's life.

Christensen, Darrel E., ed. *Hegel and the Philosophy of Religion: The Wofford Symposium.* The Hague, Netherlands: Martinus Nijhoff, 1970. Collection from the proceedings of the first conference of the Hegel Society of America. These excellent essays analyze many aspects of Hegel's philosophy of religion in relation to his historical context, his philosophical system, and the philosophies of Immanuel Kant, Friedrich Wilhelm Nietzsche, and Karl Marx. More appropriate for the advanced student.

Findlay, J. N. *Hegel: A Re-examination.* New York: Humanities Press, 1958. Findlay is the one most responsible for reviving Hegel scholarship in the English-speaking world. Provides a close exposition of Hegel's system, paragraph by paragraph, and is especially good in its treatment of his logic and philosophy of nature.

Fox, Michael Allen. *The Accessible Hegel.* Amherst, N.Y.: Humanity Books, 2005. As the title suggests, this is a concise, comprehensible overview of Hegel's philosophy that introduces readers to his ideas.

Hegel, Georg Wilhelm Friedrich. *Hegel: The Essential Writings.* Edited by F. G. Weiss. New York: Harper & Row, 1974. Contains an excellent introduction to Hegel's philosophy and also concise introductions to the different selections, which include *Encyclopedia of the Philosophical Sciences in Outline*, *The Phenomenology of Spirit*, and *Philosophy of Right*. Weiss also provides a useful annotated bibliography of primary and secondary texts. A popular text for introductory college philosophy.

Houlgate, Stephen. *An Introduction to Hegel: Freedom, Truth, and History.* 2d ed. Malden, Mass.: Blackwell, 2005. An expanded version of the book first published in 1991. Includes chapters on various aspects of Hegel's thought, including his philosophy of logic, religion, aesthetics, phenomenology, nature, and the subjective spirit. Relates Hegel to other thinkers and discusses his relevance to current philosophical debates.

Kojève, Alexandre. *Introduction to the Reading of Hegel: Lectures on the Phenomenology.* Translated by J. H. Nichols, edited by A. Bloom. New York: Basic Books, 1969. Although he describes Hegel's thought as historicist and atheistic, Kojève has been instrumental in reviving Hegel's philosophy. Appropriate for beginning students; makes lucid Hegel's influential theories in *The Phenomenology of Spirit*.

Lavine, T. Z. *From Socrates to Sartre: The Philosophic Quest*. New York: Bantam Books, 1984. A survey of six major Western philosophers, Hegel being the fourth and receiving a sixty-page condensed review. Lavine lucidly presents for the general public Hegel's life and work in relation to his intellectual and historical context, highlighting Hegel's influence on the theories of Marx. The book was aired as a Public Broadcasting Service television series.

Singer, Peter. *Hegel*. New York: Oxford University Press, 1983. A clearly written, ninety-page book in the Past Masters series intended for readers with no background in philosophy. Singer provides a broad overview of Hegel's ideas and a summary of his major works. He also discusses Hegel's influence on Marx and the Young Hegelians. Contains a useful index.

SEE ALSO: Mikhail Bakunin; Heinrich Heine; Aleksandr Herzen; Søren Kierkegaard; Ferdinand Lassalle; Karl Marx; Napoleon I; Friedrich Nietzsche; Albrecht Ritschl; Friedrich Wilhelm Joseph von Schelling; Arthur Schopenhauer.

RELATED ARTICLES in *Great Events from History: The Nineteenth Century, 1801-1900:* April, 1807: Hegel Publishes *The Phenomenology of Spirit*; 1824: Ranke Develops Systematic History.

HEINRICH HEINE
German writer

Through his literary and journalistic works, Heine exposed the hypocrisy and oppressiveness of feudal society as it existed in many parts of Europe during the first half of the nineteenth century.

BORN: December 13, 1797; Düsseldorf, Prussia (now in Germany)
DIED: February 17, 1856; Paris, France
ALSO KNOWN AS: Christian Johann Heinrich Heine; Chaim Harry Heine (birth name)
AREA OF ACHIEVEMENT: Literature

EARLY LIFE

Heinrich Heine (HI-neh) was born Chaim Harry Heine. He was a member of a respected Jewish family in Düsseldorf, the economic and cultural capital of the German Rhineland. His father, Samson Heine, was a moderately successful textile merchant who had little influence on Heinrich's upbringing. Indeed, the boy was reared almost exclusively by his well-educated, rationalist mother, Betty, who instilled in him—as well as in his siblings Charlotte, Gustav, and Maximilian—a deep sense of justice and morality, on one hand, and an aversion for anything deemed impractical (such as art, literature, and theater), on the other.

Despite his mother's efforts, Heine was eventually introduced to the arts and humanities—and also to Christian ideology—when he, at the age of ten, enrolled in the Jesuit school near his home. There, encouraged by his teachers, he began to develop his innate talent for writing, a talent upon which he hoped to build one day a successful literary career. His parents envisioned an entirely different future for him, however, and sent him to Hamburg in 1817 to begin an apprenticeship in business with his uncle Salomon Heine, a wealthy and influential banker, who was to become his longtime benefactor. Salomon attempted to transform his rather reluctant nephew into a true entrepreneur and even established a textile trading firm in the boy's name, but Salomon finally succumbed to the youth's wish to study law at the University of Bonn.

Once in Bonn, Heine did not pursue jurisprudence as he had originally planned, but instead took his course work in literature and history. Most noteworthy among his courses was a metrics seminar taught by the famed German Romanticist August Wilhelm von Schlegel, from whom he received valuable advice concerning the style and form of his early poetic attempts. After a year in Bonn, Heine transferred to the University of Göttingen to begin his legal studies in earnest, but involvement in a duel—strictly prohibited by university code—soon forced him to transfer again.

In 1821, he settled in Berlin, where he continued his education by electing courses in law and by visiting a series of lectures held by the renowned philosopher Georg Wilhelm Friedrich Hegel, a major proponent of the historical dialectic, of the history of ideas, and of personal and intellectual freedom. While in Berlin, Heine was befriended by Karl and Rahel Varnhagen von Ense, a liberal aristocrat and his outspoken Jewish wife, who were the focal points of a literary salon frequented by Hegel and other intellectual luminaries of the day. At the age of twenty-seven, Heine returned to Gøttingen to complete his legal studies, earning his doctorate in 1825, a year significant in that it also marks his conversion to Christianity and thus to a way of life that could, in his estimation, promote him from a Jewish outsider to an active participant in European culture.

LIFE'S WORK

Heine's career as a writer—inspired by the events of his youth, which culminated in a series of travels to Poland, England, northern Germany, and the Harz Mountains during the 1820's—formally began in 1827, when he published his immensely popular *Buch der Lieder* (*Book of Songs*, 1856), which pairs such traditionally Romantic elements as idealism, melancholy, and sentimentality with a unique brand of satire and irony. This collection, containing poems written as early as 1819, has love or, more specifically, unrequited love as its central theme. It no doubt was influenced by Heine's unsuccessful attempt at wooing his cousin Amalie during his apprenticeship in Hamburg.

The year 1827 proved to be an eventful one for Heine. In addition to his *Book of Songs*, he published two volumes of *Reisebilder* (*Pictures of Travel*, 1855), describing his aforementioned trips and containing detailed commentaries on social and political ills, especially the oppression of Jews, black people, and other minorities in many parts of Europe. *Pictures of Travel* brought Heine instant fame and notoriety—so much so, in fact, that Johann Friedrich von Cotta, the liberal-minded publisher of the great German masters Johann Wolfgang von Goethe and Friedrich Schiller, invited him to Munich early in 1827 to become coeditor of a new journal, *Politische Annalen* (political annals).

Not particularly overjoyed by this offer because he had set his sights on a university appointment, Heine allowed himself a considerable amount of time to complete the journey to Munich from the north German city of Lüneburg, his home since 1825. Indeed, he made lengthy stops while en route, visiting the famous folklorists the Brothers Grimm in Kassel and Ludwig Børne, one of Germany's most controversial political writers, in Frankfurt. When he finally did arrive in Munich, he was only willing to commit himself to the *Politische Annalen* for a scant six months.

In the latter half of 1828, Heine left Bavaria and, following Goethe's example, traveled to northern Italy. His sojourn in this romantic area was cut short, however, by

Heinrich Heine. (Library of Congress)

news of his father's death, upon which followed a rather abrupt return to Germany. Heine now settled with his grieving mother at the home of his Uncle Salomon in Hamburg. There, he put forth two additional volumes of *Pictures of Travel* (1830-1831), in which he primarily recounted his Italian travels. He also used these volumes to comment on the political situation in France, a nation that had, in July, 1830, experienced a revolution, in the course of which the Bourbon Charles X was replaced by the more liberal "citizen-king," Louis-Philippe. So enthralled was Heine by this development that he proclaimed France the new "Promised Land" of the liberal cause and, in so doing, contrasted it with conservative Germany, still ruled by the oppressive proponents of the old feudal order.

In May, 1831, Heine, still subsidized by his Uncle Salomon, journeyed to Paris to experience the new wave of liberalism at first hand. There, he joined the ranks of the ultraliberal Saint-Simonians and, as a foreign correspondent for the *Allgemeine Zeitung* (city of Augsburg newspaper), attempted to acquaint Germans with the major tenets of French progressivism. Heine also attempted, in book form, to acquaint Germans with contemporary trends in French literature through the various volumes of his *Der Salon* (1834-1840; *The Salon*, 1893), which combine commentaries written in a distinctly conversational tone with a variety of original literary pieces, including the fragmentary novel *Der Rabbi von Bacherach* (1887; *The Rabbi of Bacherach*, 1891).

Heine was extremely popular in France. His extensive circle of admirers included such luminaries as Honoré de Balzac, Victor Hugo, George Sand, Hector Berlioz, and Frédéric Chopin. In his native Germany, however, where the archconservative Metternich government banned his works in 1835 because they allegedly represented an affront against "altar and throne," his circle of supporters was comparatively small. In fact, it was not until 1840, the year the ban was lifted, that it again became safe to appreciate Heine in Germany.

The year 1840 is significant in that it also marks the beginning of a productive period in Heine's life, during which he resumed his reports for the *Allgemeine Zeitung* and began work on a wide variety of literary projects. These included the well-known mock epics *Atta Troll* (1847; English translation, 1876) and *Deutschland: Ein Wintermärchen* (1844; *Germany: A Winter's Tale*, 1892), both of which were directed against the hypocrisy and self-righteousness of the German bourgeoisie. In 1843, Heine interrupted his heavy work schedule for several months to travel to Hamburg, where he met with his mother as well as with his publishers at the firm of Hoffmann and Campe. Accompanying him on this journey was Mathilde (née Eugénie Mirat), his Belgian-born wife of nearly two years. Shortly after he returned to Paris in 1844, his Uncle Salomon died, leaving Heine's economic future uncertain. His health also began to fail drastically, and in 1848, the year of the German revolution, his health deteriorated completely, leaving him disabled and permanently confined to his bed.

Almost miraculously, Heine managed to remain lucid throughout the entire ordeal and, on his better days, even continued his writing. Using secretaries, he was able to produce a final great collection of poems in 1851, *Romanzero* (English translation, 1859).

After eight years of intense suffering, Heine—having readied many of his writings for publication in a collected works—died in February, 1856, at the age of fifty-eight. According to his wishes, he was buried in Paris's Montmartre Cemetery under a headstone bearing the simple yet significant inscription: "Here lies a German poet."

SIGNIFICANCE

Heinrich Heine's fame is rooted primarily in his lyric poetry, which not only gave rise to some of the most beloved folk songs ever written in the German language but also appeared in countless foreign translations. On the basis of his early poetry, Heine is often classified as a major proponent of the Romantic tradition. In truth, however, he often criticized the Romantic movement for its idealism and its lack of social and political commitment. During the turbulent period preceding the revolutions of 1848, he called for a new German literature focusing on such pressing issues of the day as human rights, women's emancipation, and equal representation of the masses in national government. Indeed, Heine is still known as one of Germany's most outspoken champions of the liberal cause. His name is frequently associated with the progressive Saint-Simonians in France as well as with Young Germany, a prerevolutionary movement among liberal authors, of which Heine was generally regarded the spiritual leader.

Heine has often (and by no means incorrectly) been described as an anomaly, a literary outsider of sorts, who combines Judaism and Christianity, Romanticism and realism, rationality and imagination, and beautiful verses and the most biting forms of satire and irony in a single person. However, it is Heine's uniqueness that has prompted such a lively interest in his life and works, an interest that has led to the formation of both a Heine Institute and a Heine Society in Düsseldorf and that has spawned countless scholarly publications throughout the world.

—*Dwight A. Klett*

FURTHER READING

Atkins, H. G. *Heine.* New York: E. P. Dutton, 1929. A standard biography providing detailed information on Heine's life and work. Characterizes Heine as an unusually gifted poet but, at the same time, questions the validity of his political writings. Includes an excellent bibliography of secondary sources.

Brod, Max. *Heinrich Heine: The Artist in Revolt.* Translated by Joseph Witriol. New York: New York University Press, 1957. A standard biography that frequently utilizes excerpts from Heine's works to illuminate important facts and events. Deals at length with Jewish-Gentile relationships and their bearing on Heine's life and career. Short but useful bibliography.

Browne, Lewis. *That Man Heine.* New York: Macmillan, 1927. This well-written, highly entertaining

Heinrich THE NINETEENTH CENTURY

biography focuses on Heine's outsider status in terms of both literature and society. It characterizes his existence as a constant exile from the German feudal order. Bibliography centers on biographical references.

Butler, E. M. *Heinrich Heine: A Biography*. London: Hogarth Press, 1956. This colorful account focuses on the Saint-Simonian influences on Heine, on his discovery of the Dionysian experience for German literature, and on his final years of great physical and emotional suffering spent in his "mattress grave."

Cook, Roger F., ed. *A Companion to the Works of Heinrich Heine*. Rochester, N.Y.: Camden House, 2002. A collection of scholarly essays about various aspects of Heine's writings, including his synthesis of German and Jewish cultures, nationalism, Romanticism, and irony. Aimed at graduate students and scholars.

Fejtö, François. *Heine: A Biography*. Translated by Mervyn Savill. London: Allan Wingate, 1946. A detailed account of Heine's life, aimed at identifying "the very essence of the man." Attempts to explain the personality capable of producing such a timeless and widely acclaimed works of art as the *Book of Songs*. Bibliography includes many sources on Heine's relationship to France.

Peters, George F. *The Poet as Provocateur: Heinrich Heine and His Critics*. Rochester, N.Y.: Camden House, 2000. Analyzes how Heine's work has been received in Germany, beginning with the critical reception during his lifetime through the revival of interest in his work after the fall of the Berlin Wall. Describes how opinion of Heine's literature has mirrored political events in Germany.

Rose, William. *The Early Love Poetry of Heinrich Heine: An Inquiry into Poetic Inspiration*. Oxford, England: Clarendon Press, 1962. In this excellent book, the author investigates—and seriously questions—the extent to which Heine's early love poetry can be viewed as an autobiographical confession.

Sammons, Jeffrey L. *Heinrich Heine: A Modern Biography*. Princeton, N.J.: Princeton University Press, 1979. One of the most critical studies ever written on Heine's life and work. Heine emerges as a problematic individual, perpetually at odds with his surroundings. This biography is fully documented and avoids the subjectivity that pervades many early treatments of Heine's life. Contains an excellent discussion of Heine's reception in Germany as well as a useful bibliography.

Spencer, Hanna. *Heinrich Heine*. Boston: Twayne, 1982. This Twayne series book provides a brief introduction to Heine's life and works, aimed at the beginning student of German literature. It includes a chronology of Heine's life, interpretations of his major works, and a select, annotated bibliography containing a large number of primary and secondary sources in English.

SEE ALSO: Honoré de Balzac; Hector Berlioz; Frédéric Chopin; Georg Wilhelm Friedrich Hegel; Victor Hugo; Emma Lazarus; Maximilian; Metternich; George Sand.

RELATED ARTICLE in *Great Events from History: The Nineteenth Century, 1801-1900:* January 2, 1843: Wagner's *Flying Dutchman* Debuts.

HERMANN VON HELMHOLTZ
German physiologist

Helmholtz contributed to the fields of energetics, physiological acoustics and optics, mathematics, hydrodynamics, and electrodynamics. His most important work was in establishing the principle of conservation of energy and in his experimental and theoretical studies of hearing and vision.

BORN: August 31, 1821; Potsdam, Prussia (now in Germany)
DIED: September 8, 1894; Charlottenburg, Berlin, Germany
ALSO KNOWN AS: Hermann Ludwig Ferdinand von Helmholtz (full name)
AREAS OF ACHIEVEMENT: Physics, science and technology

EARLY LIFE

Hermann Ludwig Ferdinand von Helmholtz (HEHLM-hohltz) was the eldest of four children of Ferdinand and Caroline Penne Helmholtz. His mother was a descendant of William Penn. His father studied philology and philosophy at the University of Berlin and was a teacher at the Potsdam gymnasium. He was a typical product of German Romanticism and Idealistic philosophy, with strong interests in music and art. These interests were passed on to his son, especially music, and became important aspects of his life and later work in physiological acoustics and optics.

Helmholtz was a sickly child, not entering the gymnasium until the age of nine, but he advanced rapidly and was encouraged by his father to memorize the works of Johann Wolfgang von Goethe, Friedrich Schiller, and the Greek poet Homer. His interest soon turned to physics. In 1837, he received a scholarship to study medicine at the Friedrich Wilhelm Institute in Berlin, with the provision that he would serve for eight years as an army surgeon after completing his degree.

While in Berlin, Helmholtz supplemented his medical studies with many science courses at the University of Berlin and studied mathematics on his own. In 1841, he began research under the great physiologist Johannes Peter Müller, who followed the German tradition of vitalism in explaining the unique characteristics of living organisms. Helmholtz joined the circle of Müller's students, including Emil Du Bois-Reymond, Ernst Wilhelm von Brücke, and Carl Friedrich Wilhelm Ludwig, and they later became known as the Helmholtz school of physiology for their rejection of the nonphysical vital forces in favor of purely physical and chemical explanations of life processes.

Helmholtz completed his medical degree in 1842, with a dissertation showing that nerve fibers are connected to ganglion cells. After some further research on fermentation that seemed to support vitalism, he was appointed as army surgeon to the regiment at Potsdam. From that time on, he wrote at least one major paper every year except 1849, publishing more than two hundred articles and books before he died. In 1849, he was granted an early release from his military duty to accept an appointment as associate professor of physiology at Königsberg. Just before leaving Potsdam, he married Olga von Velten, the daughter of a physician, by whom he had two children.

LIFE'S WORK

Helmholtz began to make major contributions to science even during his five-year tour of duty in the army, when he had little free time or access to laboratory facilities. Pursuing the ideas of the chemist Justus von Liebig, he made a quantitative study with homemade apparatus of the effects produced by muscle contraction and showed that it is accompanied by chemical changes and heat production. With this experimental evidence for transformation of energy (or force, as he called it), he undertook to establish the general principle that energy remains constant in all processes, whether animate or inanimate.

Arguing from the impossibility of perpetual motion with surprising mathematical sophistication, he demonstrated the principle of conservation of energy in its most general form and used it to refute vitalism. In 1847, "Über die Erhaltung der Kraft" ("On the Conservation of Force," 1853) was presented to the Physical Society in Berlin. The importance of this discovery led to fierce controversy over scientific priorities, but Helmholtz willingly shared the credit. Julius Robert von Mayer's prior announcement of this principle in 1842 was unknown to Helmholtz, whose work was much more detailed and comprehensive. James Prescott Joule is also given credit for this discovery for providing the first experimental verification.

After moving to his first academic post at Königsberg in 1849, Helmholtz began to try to measure the speed of nerve impulses, which Müller had considered too fast to be measured. This work led to the invention of the myograph for measuring short intervals from marks on a revolving drum. In 1851, he succeeded in measuring the speed along a frog's nerve by stimulating it at increasing distances from the muscle and found it to be surprisingly slow at about 30 meters per second. About the same time, he invented the ophthalmoscope, which brought him world fame in the field of medicine. This invention made it possible for the first time to view the inside of the living human eye, opening up the field of ophthalmology.

In 1855, Helmholtz became a professor of anatomy and physiology at Bonn. Continuing his work on sensory physiology, he published the first of three volumes of his massive *Handbuch der physiologischen Optik* (1856; *Treatise on Physiological Optics*, 1924). He also wrote several papers on acoustics. His interest in acoustics led to his first paper on theoretical physics in 1858, creating the mathematical foundations of hydrodynamics by finding vortex solutions. At this time he accepted a position as professor of physiology at Heidelberg.

After moving to Heidelberg in 1858, Helmholtz established the new Physiological Institute. At Bonn, his wife's health had started to deteriorate, and she died in 1859. During this stressful period, he achieved his greatest success in acoustical research, formulating his resonance theory of hearing, which explains the detection of differing pitches through variations of progressively smaller resonators in the spiral cochlea of the inner ear. He also published analyses of vibrations in open-ended pipes and of the motion of violin strings. In 1861, he wed Anna von Mohl, by whom he had three more children. In 1862, he completed the first edition of his highly influential treatise *Die Lehre von den Tonempfindungen als physiologische Grundlage für die Theorie der Musik* (1863; *On the Sensations of Tone as a Physiological Basis for the Theory of Music*, 1875).

During this time, Helmholtz also continued his optical research, amending Thomas Young's theory of color vision to distinguish between spectral primaries and physiological primaries of greater saturation. The resulting Young-Helmholtz theory could then explain all color perception by proper mixtures of three physiological primaries and could be used to explain red color blindness as well. He incorporated these results in the second volume of *Treatise on Physiological Optics* and began work on the third volume, in which binocular vision and depth judgments were treated. This included a defense of empiricism against the nativist view that some aspects of perception are innate, leading to original work in non-Euclidean geometry. After the third volume was published in 1867, he believed that the field of physiology

had grown beyond the scope of any one person, and he turned his attention almost exclusively to physics.

In 1871, Helmholtz accepted the prestigious chair of physics at Berlin after Gustav Robert Kirchhoff had turned it down. A new Physical Institute was established and he became the director, with his living quarters in the institute. He began his research in Berlin with a series of papers on electrodynamics, which brought James Clerk Maxwell's electromagnetic field theory to the attention of continental physicists. In Germany, the interaction between electric charges was explained by Wilhelm Eduard Weber's law of instantaneous action at a distance rather than action mediated by a field in an intervening ether. Helmholtz developed a more general action-at-a-distance theory but included Maxwell's field theory as a limiting case, allowing for wave propagation at the speed of light. This work inspired his former student Heinrich Rudolph Hertz to do experiments leading to the discovery of radio waves in 1887.

Returning to his early interest in energetics, Helmholtz began to investigate energy processes in galvanic cells and in electrochemical reactions. This led him to the idea that electricity consists of discrete charges, or atoms of electricity, and that chemical forces are electrical in nature. Research in thermochemistry resulted in the concept of free energy that determines the direction of chemical reactions. An analysis of solar energy led to an estimate of 25 million years as the amount of time since the formation of the planets; this estimate was far too conservative, however, because of the ignorance of nuclear processes. During the late 1880's, he formulated a theory for cloud formation and storm mechanics. One of his last great efforts was an unsuccessful attempt to derive all of mechanics, thermodynamics, and electrodynamics from Sir William Rowan Hamilton's principle of least action.

Helmholtz was elected Reactor of the University of Berlin for one year in 1877. He was granted hereditary nobility by Emperor William I in 1882. Helmholtz became the first president of the new Physical-Technical Institute in 1888, freeing him from teaching so he could spend more time in research. For several years, he had suffered from migraines and fits of depression, which only long vacations seemed to cure. In 1893, he traveled to the United States as a delegate of the German government to the Electrical Congress at Chicago. On his return voyage, he fell down the ship's stairs and injured his head. A year later, he suffered a cerebral hemorrhage, and, after two months of semiconsciousness, he died.

SIGNIFICANCE

Hermann von Helmholtz was one of the leaders among German scientists who rebelled against the scientific romanticism of the first half of the nineteenth century. He successfully replaced vitalism with a rigorous physicochemical empiricism, but he also shared the goal of his predecessors in his desire to find unifying principles in nature. He succeeded in this goal with his elaboration of the principle of the conservation of energy. He demonstrated the interconnections among physiology, chemistry, medicine, and physics; he fell short, however, in his efforts to extend the principle of least action. Especially important were his three-color theory of vision, his resonance theory of hearing, and his invention of the ophthalmoscope.

Helmholtz also contributed to the transition of German universities from teaching academies to research institutions. The great laboratories he established at Heidelberg in physiology and at Berlin in physics placed Germany in the forefront of scientific research. Some of the most famous scientists at the end of the century had been his students, including Hertz, who discovered radio waves and the photoelectric effect; Max Planck, who introduced quantum theory; and the Americans Henry Augustus Rowland and Albert Abraham Michelson.

As a master and leader in biology, physics, and mathematics, he surpassed all others in the imposing theoretical and experimental treatises he produced, especially in sensory physiology. As perhaps the greatest scientist of the nineteenth century, he was the last scholar whose work embraced virtually all the sciences together with philosophy, mathematics, and the fine arts.

—*Joseph L. Spradley*

FURTHER READING

Boring, Edwin B. *Sensation and Perception in the History of Experimental Psychology*. East Norwalk, Conn.: Appleton-Century-Crofts, 1942. This volume, dedicated to Helmholtz, is a comprehensive history of sensory physiology and psychology. Describes the work of Helmholtz in physiological optics and acoustics, its historical background, and later developments from his ideas.

Cahan, David, ed. *Hermann von Helmholtz and the Foundations of Nineteenth-Century Science*. Berkeley: University of California Press, 1993. This 666-page book is a compilation of essays analyzing Helmholtz's published and unpublished writings and describing his numerous contributions to science and philosophy. The essays are organized into three broad categories, discussing his work as a physiologist, a physicist, and a philosopher.

Elkana, Yehuda. *The Discovery of the Conservation of Energy*. Cambridge, Mass.: Harvard University Press, 1974. A history of the energy concept, including the physiological background and a chapter on the famous 1847 paper by Helmholtz on conservation of energy. Contains a bibliography and an appendix.

Helmholtz, Hermann von. *On the Sensations of Tone as a Physiological Basis for the Theory of Music*. Translated by Alexander Ellis. Mineola, N.Y.: Dover, 1954. An English translation of the fourth (and last) German edition (1877) of the great treatise on physiological acoustics. Includes a six-page introduction on the life of Helmholtz by Henry Margenau and a five-page bibliography of his major works with titles given in English translation.

_____. *Science and Culture: Popular and Philosophical Essays*. Edited by David Cahan. Chicago: University of Chicago Press, 1995. A collection of fifteen lectures that Helmholtz delivered between the 1850's and the 1890's. The topics of the lectures include the physiological causes of harmony in music, the conservation of force, the origins of the planetary system, and the theory of vision. Cahan's introduction places the lectures in historical and scientific context.

Jungnickel, Christa, and Russell McCormmach. *The Torch of Mathematics, 1800-1870*. Vol. 1 in *Intellectual Mastery of Nature: Theoretical Physics from Ohm to Einstein*. Chicago: University of Chicago Press, 1986. The first volume of this two-volume work on German science describes some of Helmholtz's physiological research. The second volume, *The Now Mighty Theoretical Physics, 1870-1925*, discusses his work in physics, especially in electrodynamics and energetics.

Königsberger, Leo. *Hermann von Helmholtz*. Translated by Frances Welby. Mineola, N.Y.: Dover, 1965. An abridged translation of the complete biography of Helmholtz in German published in 1906. The best source of information concerning his life and work, including discussions of his major publications.

Warren, Richard, and Roslyn Warren. *Helmholtz on Perception: Its Physiology and Development*. New York: John Wiley & Sons, 1968. Contains the English translations of six selections from lectures and articles by Helmholtz on sensory physiology. Includes a thirteen-page sketch of his life and work, a six-page evaluation of his work on sensory perceptions, and a five-page bibliography.

SEE ALSO: Gustav Theodor Fechner; Josiah Willard Gibbs; Justus von Liebig; James Clerk Maxwell.
RELATED ARTICLES in *Great Events from History: The Nineteenth Century, 1801-1900:* 1850-1865: Clausius Formulates the Second Law of Thermodynam-

ics; June 25, 1876: Bell Demonstrates the Telephone; July, 1897-July, 1904: Bjerknes Founds Scientific Weather Forecasting; 1899: Hilbert Publishes *The Foundations of Geometry.*

FELICIA DOROTHEA HEMANS
English poet

Hemans was one of the most popular poets of the English-speaking world during the nineteenth century and is credited with making contributions to Romantic poetry whose influence was felt throughout the following century.

BORN: September 25, 1793; Liverpool, England
DIED: May 16, 1835; Dublin, Ireland
ALSO KNOWN AS: Felicia Dorothea Browne (birth name)
AREA OF ACHIEVEMENT: Literature

EARLY LIFE

Felicia Hemans (HEHM-ahnz) was born Felicia Dorothea Browne, the daughter of George Browne, a banker and merchant from County Cork, Ireland, and Felicity Wagner of Lancashire. Before Felicia was six, financial problems forced the family to move to Gwrych, near Abergele in Wales, where they lived for nine years in a mansion that looked out over both sea and mountains. When she was thirteen, her father moved to Canada but continued to support his family in Wales. He died when she was nineteen.

Felicia was reading by the age of six and was beginning to write poetry at the age of eight. She had a photographic memory and could recite long passages from what she read. She was educated at home in literature, languages, art, and music. Her home had an extensive library, and she was provided with private tutoring. Thanks to her father's continental connections and the Italian and Austrian heritage of her mother, she became fluent in French, Italian, and German and then in Spanish, Portuguese, Welsh, and Latin.

LIFE'S WORK

Felicia began the career that would make her the century's best-selling English poet at the age of fourteen with her collection *Poems* (1808), which she dedicated to the Prince of Wales. That book's publication initiated a

correspondence between her and Percy Bysshe Shelley—of whom her mother disapproved. Some of Felicia's poems reflect military themes. Two of her brothers were in the British army's Twenty-third Royal Welsh Fusiliers, with whom they served in the Peninsular War against France. Felicia's patriotic enthusiasm can be heard in the martial tones of *England and Spain: Or, Valour and Patriotism* (1808). Her sister, Harriet Hughes, wrote that for Felicia, the "days of chivalry seemed to be restored."

In 1809, Felicia's family moved to Bronwylfa at St. Asaph, Flintshire. Three years later, she published *The Domestic Affections.* During that same year, 1812, she married Captain Alfred Hemans and then moved to Daventry, where her husband served with the Northamptonshire militia. Following his discharge from military service in 1814, he, Felicia, and their infant son, Arthur Wynne, moved into the home of Felicia's mother at Bronwylfa. In 1818, the couple separated for reasons that are now unknown. Captain Hemans moved to Rome, leaving a pregnant Felicia a single mother with five sons: Arthur, George Willoughby, Claude Lewis, Henry William, and Charles Isidore.

During Felicia's years at Bronwylfa, she became celebrated for her poetry. She published widely to critical acclaim and was admired by such literary luminaries as Sir Walter Scott and George Gordon, Lord Byron. During that period, she published *The Restoration of Works of Art to Italy* (1816), *Modern Greece* (1817), and *Tales and Heroic Scenes* (1819). Her fluency in foreign languages led to her publishing *Translations from Camões and Other Poets* (1818), which contained her translations from Portuguese, Spanish, Italian, and German poems. She also published *Welsh Melodies* (1822), which demonstrated her talent for writing songs, many of which would be sung in Victorian parlors throughout the nineteenth century.

Encouraged by friends and colleagues, Hemans had her verse drama *The Vespers of Palermo* produced at Covent Garden in 1823. It played unsuccessfully, possibly because of the incompetence of its lead performer.

By contrast, the same play was acclaimed when Harriet Siddons performed in an Edinburgh production, to which Sir Walter Scott and Joanna Baillie lent their support.

Praised in *The Quarterly Review* by John Taylor Coleridge and celebrated in *The Monthly Review* as a writer of "high chivalric poetry," Hemans continued to publish in that vein, with *The Siege of Valencia* and *The Last Constantine* (1823) and shorter lyrics, including "Songs of the Cid." These books were followed by *The Forest Sanctuary* (1824) and *The Lays of Many Lands* (1826). The former book praised American religious freedoms and won her a large transatlantic audience.

With her sons, mother, and sister, Hemans moved to Rhyllon, about one mile from Bronwylfa, in the spring of 1825. Her reputation continued to grow, and her works were collected and published in both American and British editions. However, a series of personal tragedies soon began: the deaths of her mother and one of her brothers and the beginning of chest pains, palpitations, and general inflammation that would plague her for the rest of her life.

In 1827, Hemans was offered the editorship of an American periodical but declined it. During that same year, her *Hymns on the Works of Nature for the Use of Children* was published in Boston. To Joanna Baillie, who had acclaimed the *The Vespers of Palermo*, she dedicated *Records of Women* in 1828.

In 1828, Hemans's sister married, and her brother George moved to Ireland, dispersing the family circle that had been closely knit and of great importance in Hemans's life. Hemans and her sons moved to Wavertree in the Liverpool area, where she had friends and where she hoped that her new surroundings would prove culturally stimulating and provide educational opportunities for her three youngest sons. Her two eldest sons had gone to live with their father in Rome. However, these hopes went unfulfilled, and she looked back on her peaceful and secure years at Bronwylfa and Rhyllon with nostalgia. Meanwhile, she continued to be sought after as a famous woman (*femme celèbre*) and was often asked to produce literary works, ranging "from the divinity treatise to the fairy tale," as her friend and biographer Henry Fothergill Chorley later noted.

Despite Hemans's disappointments at Wavertree, the locale proved convenient for travel to England's Lake District and the Lowlands. She made the acquaintance of Dorothy and William Wordsworth, visited Sir Walter Scott at Abbotsford, and met Sir Francis Jeffrey, the editor of the *Edinburgh Review*, who afterward provided glowing notices of her works. When she and her sons needed a quiet place to recuperate from whooping cough, she discovered a sanctuary across the Mersey River at Seacombe.

Rooted in themes initiated as early as 1812, *Songs of the Affections* (1830) earned Hemans a reputation as the poetess of the affections, of hearth and home. At that time, Hemans considered moving to Edinburgh but was warned off by her physicians, who thought the colder climate there might prove deadly. She instead decided to move to Dublin, where she would be near her brother George. In August, 1831, she made the move to Ireland, where she spent the last four years of her life among family and friends. Hemans's many friends were concerned that the move to Ireland had proved too taxing for her because it was followed by attacks of "oppression" of the chest and shortness of breath. However, Hemans was determined that her sons should grow up near their uncle, who had become chief commissioner of police in Ireland.

During her last years, Hemans's reading tastes became more religious, and she enjoyed seventeenth century poetry by writers such as George Herbert. Although her health continued to deteriorate, with episodes of arrhythmias, she continued to write—usually in a reclining position—predominantly on religious themes. During 1834 alone, she published *Scenes and Hymns of Life, with Other Religious Poems*; *Hymns for Childhood*; and *National Lyrics and Songs for Music*. During that same year, she also began a new series of critical pieces on continental literature in *The New Monthly*, but only the first part ever appeared.

Hemans and her sons moved to Redesdale, seven miles outside Dublin, but she soon returned to her Dublin residence to be near her doctors. Completely incapacitated, she died there on May 16, 1835. She was buried in St. Anne's Church on Dawson Street in Dublin, where she is commemorated by a memorial window and a tablet inscribed with verses from *The Siege of Valencia*. Her brothers later erected a memorial to her in St. Asaph's Cathedral with an inscription stating that her "character is best portrayed in her writings." William Wordsworth elegized her in a poem as "that holy Spirit,/ Mild as the spring, as ocean deep."

SIGNIFICANCE

Felicia Dorothea Hemans contributed works of literature and criticism to many of the major periodicals of her time, including *The Edinburgh Annual Register*, *Blackwood's Edinburgh Magazine*, the *Edinburgh Review*, *The Literary Gazette*, and *The New Monthly*. She received several literary prizes, was celebrated in Great Britain and America, and was translated on the Continent. She drew her themes from historical episodes, embodied national and imperial pride, and enshrined the domestic affections.

Hemans's Romantic melancholy was a melancholy overcome by faith and hope. As one of the last Romantics, Hemans, along with Letitia Landon, wrote a vital poetry during the supposed literary "interregnum" between the deaths of Byron, Shelley, and John Keats and the emergence of Alfred, Lord Tennyson, as a major Victorian voice. Although her particular style of writing, which sought to "sound the depths" of the human heart, fell into disfavor with the advent of modernism, leaving her works thereafter unread and unpublished, literary historians have noted that works widely celebrated and in print for one hundred years merit reevaluation. Although her "Casabianca" (also known as "The boy stood on the burning deck") and "The Stately Homes of England" were favorite recitation pieces, and "The Landing of the Pilgrim Fathers in America" was sung with the fervor of a hymn, current critical reevaluation of her work opens new perspectives on nineteenth century mentality and sensibilities.

—*Donna Berliner*

FURTHER READING

Curran, Stuart. "Women Readers, Women Writers." In *The Cambridge Companion to British Romanticism*, edited by Stuart Curran. Cambridge, England: Cambridge University Press, 1993. An important introduction to women writers of Hemans's era.

Sweet, Nanora, and Julie Melnyk, eds. *Felicia Hemans: Reimagining Poetry in the Nineteenth Century*. New York: Palgrave, 2001. Collection of significant articles assessing Hemans's poetry from a variety of perspectives.

Wolfson, Susan J. "'Domestic Affections' and 'The Spear of Minerva': Felicia Hemans and the Dilemma of Gender." In *Re-visioning Romanticism: British Women Writers, 1776-1837*, edited by Carol Shiner Wilson and Joel Haefner. Philadelphia: University of Pennsylvania Press, 1994. Places Hemans in context and assesses the contradictory gender implications in her works.

_____, ed. *Felicia Hemans: Selected Poems, Letters, Reception Materials*. Princeton, N.J.: Princeton University Press, 2000. Selection of Hemans's writings that provides primary materials that are otherwise difficult to find.

SEE ALSO: Elizabeth Barrett Browning; Lord Byron; Lord Jeffrey; John Keats; Sir Walter Scott; Percy Bysshe Shelley; William Wordsworth.

RELATED ARTICLE in *Great Events from History: The Nineteenth Century, 1801-1900:* November 5, 1850: Tennyson Becomes England's Poet Laureate.

JOSEPH HENRY
American physicist

As the first secretary of the Smithsonian Institution, president of the National Academy of Sciences, and a leading experimental physicist, Henry was one of the most important molders of an American professional scientific community of the nineteenth century.

BORN: December 17, 1797; Albany, New York
DIED: May 13, 1878; Washington, D.C.
AREA OF ACHIEVEMENT: Science and technology

EARLY LIFE

Joseph Henry was descended from Scots who immigrated to North America at the time of the Revolutionary War. His father, William Henry, was a cartman—a hauler and mover—of modest financial circumstances, but his mother, née Ann Alexander, was from a more affluent family. Henry was brought up by an uncle in Galway, New York, and educated in the village school, learning arithmetic, reading, and writing (but little about spelling, as his future letters would demonstrate). At the age of ten, he was working in a general store. The death of his father in 1811 and of his uncle shortly thereafter led to his return to Albany, where he was apprenticed to a silversmith, but was attracted to the theater.

According to Henry's later recollection, the turning point in his life occurred in about 1815 when he read a popular introduction to the physical sciences, William Gregory's *Lectures on Experimental Philosophy, Astronomy and Chemistry* (1808), the first book he had ever read with attention. The questions that Gregory asked and answered about the way the natural world behaved piqued Henry's interest and led to his decision to devote his life to science.

The reality of his situation, however, was a lack of any training in science and the immediate need to earn a living. Henry worked as an actor, a schoolteacher, and a private tutor during the late teens and early twenties of the nineteenth century. Most important for his future, he attended the Albany Academy as an overage student between 1819 and 1822, his only formal education beyond the elementary level. His intelligence, capacity for hard work, ambition, and determination attracted the attention of the faculty of the academy and the scientific leaders of the community, leading to his election as a member of the Albany Lyceum of Natural History and its successor, the Albany Institute. He found work as a tutor and a surveyor until his appointment in September, 1826, as professor of mathematics and natural philosophy (physics) at the Albany Academy.

LIFE'S WORK

The Albany Academy was not the ideal place for an ambitious scientist. The teaching load was heavy and much of it was on the elementary level, providing little intellectual stimulation. Research facilities were limited. Nevertheless, Henry's years on its faculty were fruitful, marked by great creativity and insight. He initiated his lifelong research program of exploring the phenomena of and interrelationship of the so-called "imponderables"—electricity, magnetism, light, and heat—the major field of research in the physical sciences during the first half of the nineteenth century. During his Albany years, he developed his great electromagnet, created the telegraph, invented the first electric motor, and discovered (independently of Michael Faraday) electromagnetic self-induction and mutual electromagnetic induction.

The Henry of this phase, however, was a scientist who was not in control of his research program. Both of his major publications of this period were in response to European scientists announcing discoveries paralleling or anticipating Henry's research. In the case of the electromagnet, it was Gerrit Moll; in the case of induction, it was Faraday. He was always in danger of losing his claim of priority, of being ignored by the European community. He was not, however, ignored by his compatriots. His fame, especially for his great electromagnet, led to a professorship at the College of New Jersey (now Princeton University) in 1832, despite the lack of a college degree.

The Joseph Henry who arrived in Princeton in November, 1832, to teach natural philosophy was a mature family man. He had married Harriet Alexander, a first cousin, in 1830, and had a son by this time. Three daugh-

Joseph Henry. (Library of Congress)

ters would follow. Paintings and photographs of Henry show an oval visage and stocky build. He had brown hair, gray eyes, and a light complexion. As he aged he put on weight. At five feet, ten inches, he must have given the physical impression of solidity, which was also one of his significant mental traits.

Henry's chief characteristic, however, was his curiosity. No natural phenomenon was too trivial for observation or experimentation, whether it was snow melting on his porch, light changing color as it passed through a syrup, or water evaporating while being heated for shaving. This curiosity may explain why he often experimented in short, intense bursts with frequent shifts among topics. With all the unanswered questions to be examined, Henry had difficulty giving a single problem his undivided attention.

Henry's years at Princeton were his most productive quantitatively. During this period, he examined lightning paths, discovered the concept of the transformer and the oscillational nature of the discharge of a capacitor, became the first individual to measure empirically the temperature difference between sunspots and the solar surface, and studied ultraviolet light—simply to point out the highlights. These were also the years of his friendly interaction with Samuel F. B. Morse. Their first documented contact was in 1839, and subsequently Henry supplied Morse with technical advice and private and public support for his telegraph. By 1846, however, Henry was unhappy over what he perceived to be Morse's failure to give Henry proper credit for his contributions to the invention and development of a practical electromagnetic telegraph. Ultimately, the two men found themselves on opposite sides during the various court tests of Morse's telegraph patent during the 1850's.

By that time, Henry was in Washington, D.C. In December, 1846, he had accepted the position as secretary (director) of the newly established Smithsonian Institution. Although there had been tremendous confusion in Congress over the meaning of James Smithson's bequest to the United States to establish an institution for "the increase and diffusion of knowledge," there was no confusion in Henry's mind. The funds provided a unique opportunity to support research and scholarly publication, to encourage cooperation and international exchange. Henry defeated an effort to use the bequest to develop a national library and worked out an arrangement with Congress for the federal government to support the National Museum, which was under Smithsonian management, through appropriations. This left Henry relatively free to support research in a diversity of fields, including meteorology, botany, zoology, anthropology, and archaeology.

Administrative responsibilities did not leave much time, however, for personal scientific research. The acoustics of public buildings and investigations of fog-signals for the United States Light-House Board were the only major projects carried out by Henry during his years as secretary. There were also the responsibilities that came from being a senior leader of the scientific community. During 1849-1850, Henry served as president of the American Association for the Advancement of Science. One of the original members of the National Academy of Sciences, he was elected its president in 1868 and served in that office until his death, turning the academy into an impartial supporter of research and the voice of the American scientific community. He was president of the Philosophical Society of Washington from 1871 until his death and chairman of the Light-House Board during the same period.

After decades of excellent health, Henry was struck by temporary paralysis in December, 1877. A victim of Bright's disease, he died in the Smithsonian Institution building on May 13, 1878.

SIGNIFICANCE

When speaking of Henry, his contemporaries often compared him to Benjamin Franklin. The contributions to the understanding of electricity, the preeminence within the scientific community, and the international standing of the two men were all analogous. Like Franklin, too, Henry was to make contributions to his country that proved to be more far-reaching than his scientific discoveries; the reputation that he secured as an experimenter gave him the prestige and respect necessary for his success as a science administrator and leader.

On behalf of his vision of science, Henry was able to call upon the support of intellectuals, community leaders, and politicians. Intensely patriotic, Henry viewed the shortcomings of the American scientific community with dismay. As secretary of the Smithsonian and president of various scientific organizations, he nurtured the small community of research-minded American men and women, asserted the primacy of basic research over applied, and fought to raise American science to international standards and gain European recognition of American achievements. He served as an articulate spokesman for the power, value, and necessity of basic scientific research, as well as a symbol of what Americans could accomplish in science.

—*Marc Rothenberg*

FURTHER READING

Cochrane, Rexmond Canning. *The National Academy of Sciences: The First Hundred Years, 1863-1963.* Washington, D.C.: National Academy of Sciences, 1978. An official history of the academy based upon its archives. Discussion of Henry and his circle dominates the early chapters.

Coulson, Thomas. *Joseph Henry: His Life and Work.* Princeton, N.J.: Princeton University Press, 1950. The standard biography, now dated. Although marred by factual errors and a lack of understanding of Henry's milieu, it is still useful.

Hafertepe, Kenneth. *America's Castle: The Evolution of the Smithsonian Building and Its Institution, 1840-1878.* Washington, D.C.: Smithsonian Institution Press, 1984. An architectural historian discusses Henry's struggle to focus the resources of the Smithsonian on the support of original research and the role the Smithsonian Building played in thwarting his dreams. Especially valuable for its insights into the political struggles surrounding the Smithsonian.

Hinsley, Curtis M., Jr. *Savages and Scientists: The Smithsonian Institution and the Development of American Anthropology, 1846-1910*. Washington, D.C.: Smithsonian Institution Press, 1981. An excellent integrative history of the rise and professionalization of a discipline. Provides a case study of Henry's role as a supporter of research.

Mabee, Carleton. *The American Leonardo: A Life of Samuel F. B. Morse*. New York: Alfred A. Knopf, 1943. This work presents a nonpartisan, well-researched account of the telegraph controversy.

Moyer, Albert E. *Joseph Henry: The Rise of An American Scientist*. Washington, D.C.: Smithsonian Institution Press, 1997. Focuses on the early phases of Henry's career, concluding in 1846, just before Henry became secretary of the Smithsonian. Moyer describes how Michael Faraday's discoveries about electromagnetic induction were dependent upon the electromagnet designed by Henry.

Reingold, Nathan, and Marc Rothenberg. "The Exploring Expedition and the Smithsonian Institution." In *Magnificent Voyagers: The U.S. Exploring Expedition, 1838-1842*, edited by Herman J. Viola and Carolyn Margolis. Washington, D.C.: Smithsonian Institution Press, 1985. Considers the creation of the National Museum at the Smithsonian in the context of the need for the federal government to find a home for its scientific collections.

Reingold, Nathan, et al., eds. *The Papers of Joseph Henry*. 10 vols. Washington, D.C.: Smithsonian Institution Press, 1972-2004. When complete, this will be a fifteen-volume collection of approximately six thousand letters, diary entries, laboratory notebook entries, and other manuscripts. The current ten volumes cover the period from Henry's birth through December, 1865.

Washburn, Wilcomb E. "Joseph Henry's Conception of the Purpose of the Smithsonian Institution." In *A Cabinet of Curiosities: Five Episodes in the Evolution of American Museums*, edited by Walter Muir Whitehill. Charlottesville: University Press of Virginia, 1967. Although challenged by recent scholarship that considers the picture presented of Henry as too simplistic, this article offers what has become the standard interpretation of Henry's attitude toward the Smithsonian and especially the role of a museum in the Institution.

SEE ALSO: Michael Faraday; Josiah Willard Gibbs; Samuel F. B. Morse.

RELATED ARTICLES in *Great Events from History: The Nineteenth Century, 1801-1900:* May 24, 1844: Morse Sends First Telegraph Message; August 10, 1846: Smithsonian Institution Is Founded.

O. HENRY
American short-story writer

O. Henry so advanced the state of American short stories that he made his pen name synonymous with surprise endings. In a little more than a single decade, he published more than two hundred stories in magazines and books, some of which are still read a century later.

BORN: September 11, 1862; Greensboro, North Carolina
DIED: June 5, 1910; New York, New York
ALSO KNOWN AS: William Sydney Porter (birth name)
AREA OF ACHIEVEMENT: Literature

EARLY LIFE

The life of William Sydney Porter was much like the literature he wrote as O. Henry: a short story punctuated by unforeseen twists. He was born during the midst of the Civil War and grew up under the postwar occupation government. His father, Algernon Sidney Porter, had a well-known drinking problem and no medical degree, but he was known as the best doctor in the county. His mother, Mary Jane Virginia Swaim, died of tuberculosis when Porter was only three years old. Porter and his older brother Shirley ("Shell") were mostly raised in their grandmother's boardinghouse by their Aunt Lina, a schoolteacher who encouraged Porter's love of books. By age ten, he was reading Charles Dickens and Sir Walter Scott. At the age of fifteen he left school and became an apprentice pharmacist in his uncle's drugstore, just as his father had done. Four years later, he was a licensed pharmacist.

In March of 1882, Porter went to Texas with family friends, hoping that the Texas climate would help his persistent, racking cough. He spent two years on the Dull-Hall Ranch near Cotulla, where he lived as a sheltered guest in Dick Hall's home doing little real ranch work. He sent some stories and letters to Greensboro, some of which appeared in the local newspaper.

In 1884, the Halls deposited Porter in Austin, the state capital. He worked briefly in a pharmacy and then part time in a cigar store, but mostly he did little for two and one-half years but socialize, sing in a quartet and church choirs, and serenade women. Late in 1886, he was given a job as a real estate bookkeeper. He learned this job quickly but soon moved to a $100-per-month job as a draftsman in Hall's new Texas Land Office. Many of his later stories drew on the experiences of his four years there. In January, 1891, Hall had lost his gubernatorial bid, so his job as land commissioner and Porter's job as draftsman both ended. Within one month, however, Porter's friends got him a new job as a bank teller, also at $100 per month.

Meanwhile, Porter's serenading had been fruitful. A rather normal-looking but foppish man at a height of 5 feet, 7 inches, with broad shoulders, blue eyes, chestnut brown hair, and a fashionable mustache, he eloped with young Athol Estes on July 1, 1887, less than three weeks after her graduation from high school. Athol apparently stimulated Porter into more frequent writing, as he sold some humorous items to the *Detroit Free Press* in 1887. On May 6, 1888, they had a son who died only hours after birth. This seems to have begun the decline in Athol's health that finally resulted in her death nine years later. On September 30, 1889, she bore their only other child, Margaret.

LIFE'S WORK

In March, 1894, Porter and a partner bought a struggling scandal sheet and its press and used it to publish humorous commentary and stories, many of them poking fun at the large German community of central Texas. They soon changed its name to *The Rolling Stone*, stimulating Austin through the next twelve months.

A crucial change in Porter's life began in December, 1894, when bank examiner F. B. Gray uncovered shortages in the accounts and charged him with embezzlement of bank funds. Porter left the bank to spend more time with *The Rolling Stone*, but it folded in April. In July, a grand jury refused to indict Porter, but Gray persisted.

In October, 1895, Porter accepted a new job writing for the *Houston Post*. In February, 1896, Gray succeeded in getting four indictments against him. Porter wrote his last *Houston Post* column on June 22. On July 6, he boarded a train heading up to Austin for his trial; after fifty miles he apparently got off and, hours later, boarded an eastbound train to seek anonymity in New Orleans,

Louisiana. With his excellent command of Spanish, he decided that he could build a new life in Honduras, which had no extradition treaty with the United States, and that he could then send for his wife and daughter to join him there until the statute of limitations expired. Honduras was at that time a stereotypical banana republic but politically more stable than most of its neighbors. Once there, he mixed with the swindlers, bank presidents, confidence men, and other brigands who would later populate some of his stories. The pueblo of Trujillo, Honduras, later became Coralio, Anchuria, in his *Cabbages and Kings* (1904).

The flaw in Porter's Honduras plan was that Athol's tuberculosis was too serious to let her leave her mother's care. In January, 1897, he returned to Austin. He posted a new court bond and spent the next several months caring for his wife until, on July 25, she died. Porter stayed in Austin writing freelance articles and stories. He finally went to trial on February 15, 1898. The evidence seems to imply that Porter was innocent but unwilling to implicate others. However, the jury convicted him on three

O. Henry. (Courtesy, Austin History Center, Austin Public Library)

counts, and he was sentenced to the lightest possible term, five years in the Ohio State Penitentiary.

When Porter became prisoner 30664 on April 25, 1898, he showed the strains of the past two years, during which he had lost his young wife, his home, his job, and his good name. The good news, though, was that he was allowed to work in the night shift of the prison pharmacy, leaving him plenty of time to write stories. It was there that he was to really begin the writing career that brought his fame. The twist, however, was that the more famous he became, the more he feared that people would discover his imprisonment. He submitted his stories through friends in New Orleans and elsewhere.

A model prisoner, he was released from prison on July 24, 1901, and went to Pittsburgh, Pennsylvania, to stay with Athol's parents and his eleven-year-old daughter. He wrote some stories and newspaper features, but it was soon clear that he hated Pittsburgh. In April, 1902, he moved to New York City, which he was to call "Baghdad by the Subway." In New York, Porter's frequent drinking companion Bill Williams said he "drank as the Southern gentleman he was and carried his liquor as a gentleman does. I . . . never once saw him or heard of his being intoxicated."

Although Porter might not have gotten roaring drunk, he nonetheless drank whiskey steadily throughout his short life. In 1909 he began to fade from cirrhosis of the liver. He spent six months back in North Carolina in the hope that the healthier environment might help to cure his illness but eventually moved back to New York City.

Porter collapsed on June 2, 1910, and friends took him to the Polyclinic Hospital. As an attending nurse dimmed the light on the evening of June 4, Porter said, "Turn up the lights. I don't want to go home in the dark." Porter died the following day soon after sunrise.

It was apparently in the Travis County Jail as Porter awaited transportation to Ohio that his middle name migrated from the "Sidney" of his birth and of his father to the "Sydney" of his later years. An April, 1898, letter addressed him as "Mr. Sydney Porter," and prison records also used "Sydney." On the other hand, many theories purport to explain how he settled on his plebeian nom de plume. The first story published by "O. Henry" was also the first one he wrote in prison: "Whistling Dick's Christmas Stocking," which drew on his experiences in New Orleans and appeared in *McClure's Magazine* in December, 1899. In the December, 1901, *Ainslee's Magazine*, he used "Olivier Henry."

While Porter was awaiting trial after his wife's death, McClure's Syndicate bought "The Miracle of Lava Can-

yon" and published it months later under the name of W. S. Porter. A revision of that story later appeared as "An Afternoon Miracle." In all, Porter used twelve different names for his writing, and it was several years before he settled on using only O. Henry. Some say the name was abbreviated from the name of a French pharmacist, Etienne Ossian Henry. Porter told one writer that he picked "Henry" from a list of notables in the New Orleans society pages, then a friend suggested using a single initial, and he decided that "O is about the easiest written." An Ohio Board of Clemency chairman noted that the prison had employed a Captain Orrin Henry who had retired eleven years before Porter's incarceration but whose signature Porter could well have seen.

Porter's reason for using the pen name is clearer than its precise origin: He was embarrassed about his prison record and did his best to keep it a secret from friends and public alike.

SIGNIFICANCE

Even after his death, the ending of Porter's life story took a characteristically ironic twist. Somehow, the Little Church Around the Corner had scheduled a wedding for 11:00 A.M. on June 7—the same time as Porter's funeral. The bridegroom's brother, trying to hide this omen from the bride, told the wedding party that another wedding was under way, so they spent the next hour in a nearby hotel while William S. Porter and O. Henry were eulogized in the church.

In the decade after his death, Americans bought nearly five million copies of his books, second only to Rudyard Kipling. They were translated into French, Spanish, German, Swedish, Danish, Norwegian, Russian, and Japanese. Ironically, this man's stories of the Western and urban life of the United States became even more popular in the new Soviet Union than in his own country. While American writers were using the Russian Anton Chekhov as their model, Russian writers were putting out O. Henry twist endings. In 1962, a Soviet postage stamp commemorated the one hundredth anniversary of Porter's birth, although his own country had never so honored him. His Christmas story "The Gift of the Magi" eventually became universally known to American schoolchildren, and one of his characters, the Cisco Kid, became a mainstay first to many radio listeners and then to a new generation of television viewers.

—*J. Edmund Rush*

FURTHER READING
Blansfield, Karen Charmaine. *Cheap Rooms and Restless Hearts: A Study of Formula in the Urban Tales*

of William Sydney Porter. Bowling Green, Ohio: Bowling Green State University Popular Press, 1988. Analyzes the character types and plot patterns in O. Henry's short stories. Examines how his varied jobs and life experiences, and conditions in nineteenth century New York City, influenced his writing. Reevaluates his contributions to American literature.

Current-Garcia, Eugene. *O. Henry: A Study of the Short Fiction*. New York: Twayne, 1993. Interprets O. Henry's short stories and surveys how critical attitudes toward his stories have changed over the years. Includes an annotated bibliography and index.

_____. *O. Henry (William Sydney Porter)*. Boston: Twayne, 1965. Summarizes O. Henry's life in one chapter, then focuses on the literary influences of his southern upbringing, Texas development, prison experiences, and New York life. Includes chronological summary, endnotes, extensive bibliography, and index.

Langford, Gerald. *Alias O. Henry: A Biography of William Sidney Porter*. New York: Macmillan, 1957. Covers O. Henry's entire life, with emphasis on his two marriages, his time in Houston, and the evidence in his embezzlement trial. Includes photographs, endnotes, index, and an extensive appendix about *The Rolling Stone*.

O'Connor, Richard. *O. Henry: The Legendary Life of William S. Porter*. Garden City, N.Y.: Doubleday, 1970. Covers O. Henry's entire life. Includes photographs and index.

Porter, Jenny Lind, and Trueman E. O'Quinn. *Time to Write: How William Sidney Porter Became O. Henry*. Austin, Tex.: Eakin Press, 1986. Focuses on O. Henry's life in Texas. Includes index and twelve short stories written while he was in federal prison in Columbus, Ohio, each with notes.

Stuart, David. *O. Henry: A Biography of William Sydney Porter*. Chelsea, Mich.: Scarborough House, 1990. Biography focused on O. Henry's life; does not provide literary analysis. Stuart maintains O. Henry was wrongly convicted of embezzlement and describes how the author's shame about his imprisonment made him obsessively paranoid and desperate to maintain a secret identity.

Watson, Bruce. "If His Life Were a Short Story, Who'd Ever Believe It?" *Smithsonian* 27 (January, 1997): 92-102. Biography strewn with anecdotes and some literary criticism. Includes photographs.

Williams, William Washington. *The Quiet Lodger of Irving Place*. New York: Dutton, 1936. Firsthand account of Porter's life in New York written by a long-time friend and newspaper reporter with emphasis on the people and locations that inspired many of O. Henry's stories.

SEE ALSO: Ambrose Bierce; Anton Chekhov; Charles Dickens; Rudyard Kipling; Guy de Maupassant; Edgar Allan Poe; Sir Walter Scott.

RELATED ARTICLES in *Great Events from History: The Nineteenth Century, 1801-1900:* 1819-1820: Irving's *Sketch Book* Transforms American Literature; December, 1884-February, 1885: Twain Publishes *Adventures of Huckleberry Finn*; December, 1887: Conan Doyle Introduces Sherlock Holmes.

ALEKSANDR HERZEN
Russian writer and social reformer

As one of the "fathers" of the Russian intelligentsia, Herzen urged an increased pace of Westernization for Russia, yet harbored a Slavophile attraction for the village commune. From his offices in London, he edited an influential émigré newspaper and helped to shape the direction of Russian radical opinion.

BORN: April 6, 1812; Moscow, Russia
DIED: January 21, 1870; Paris, France
ALSO KNOWN AS: Aleksandr Ivanovich Herzen (full name)
AREAS OF ACHIEVEMENT: Social reform, journalism

EARLY LIFE

Aleksandr Herzen (HEHR-tsen) was the illegitimate son of Ivan Alekseyevich Yakovlev, of a distinguished aristocratic family, and of Louise Ivanovich Haag, a German daughter of a minor official from Württemberg. The name "Herzen" was given him by his father to indicate that he was the product of matters of the "heart," as was his elder and also illegitimate brother, Yegor Herzen.

In the family home on Arbat Street in Moscow, young Herzen was isolated from many children, but he developed a close friendship with Nikolay Ogaryov, with whom he developed a lifelong partnership. Attracted to the Romanticism of Friedrich Schiller, the two boys took an oath to avenge the five Decembrist rebels executed by Czar Nicholas I after the abortive uprising of 1825. Both entered the University of Moscow in 1829, and Herzen joined the department of natural sciences. At the university, he also acquired a deep interest in history, philosophy, and politics. His circle of friends included Ogaryov, Nikolai Satin, Vadim Passek, Nikolai Kh. Ketscher, and Anton Savich. These friends reflected a popular mystical bent for politics, and they avidly read the works of Friedrich Schelling and Saint-Simon, espousing the radical democracy of brotherly love, idealism, and even socialism. In 1834, following a critical remark about the czar that was reported to the police, Herzen was arrested, jailed for nearly a year, and exiled to Perm and Viatka.

LIFE'S WORK

In 1838, after three years in exile, he married Natalya Alexandrovna Zakharina in Vladimir, and the next year they had a son, Aleksandr, Herzen's only surviving male heir. The czar pardoned Herzen in 1839, and he entered state service in Novgorod, partly to qualify for noble status and partly to acquire the rights of inheritance. His

work caused him to travel often to St. Petersburg, where he quarreled with Vissarion Grigoryevich Belinsky over the ideas of Georg Wilhelm Friedrich Hegel. Ironically, Belinsky abandoned Hegelian thought shortly before Herzen's own conversion to that system. Herzen won the admiration of Belinsky, however, when he published two installments of his early memoirs, *Zapiski odnogo molodogo cheloveka* (1840-1841; notebooks of a certain young man).

In 1840, Herzen again ran afoul of the authorities and was arrested, only to be released owing to his wife's illness. It was about this time that he rejected his wife's religious inspiration for Hegel's more radical thought, blaming police harassment for his wife's new illness and the subsequent death of their second child. He abandoned the Idealism of Schelling for the realism of Hegel and a materialist worldview; hence, he was regarded as a Left-Hegelian. He wrote *Diletantizm v nauke* (1843; dilettantism and science), an essay reflecting his new radicalism. His newfound hostility toward religion and all officialdom caused difficulties with his wife.

From 1842 to 1846, Herzen formed a new circle of friends in Moscow, including Ketscher, Satin, Vasily Petrovich Botkin, E. F. Korsh, Timofei Granovski, Mikhail Shchepkin, and Konstantin Kavelin. Belinsky and his St. Petersburg friends were sometimes in attendance. Although an avowed admirer of Western socialist thought, Herzen was increasingly attracted to the Russian peasant and the commune, central to the thought of the Slavophile community. The Slavophile attraction to religion and disdain for the West kept Herzen from entering their circles. In 1845-1846, Herzen published *Pisma ob izuchenii prirody* (letters on the study of nature), which combined his interest in science and philosophy.

In 1846, Herzen inherited a substantial fortune from his father, including a Moscow house and 500,000 rubles. During that same year, he left Russia, never to return. His wife, his three children, his valet, and two of his friends escorted him to the West. The year of his departure, he published a novel, *Kto vinovat?* (1845-1846; *Who Is to Blame?*, 1978), in which he paid his homage to George Sand and the women's movement. In Europe, Herzen read deeply the socialist literature of Louis Blanc, Charles Fourier, and Pierre-Joseph Proudhon. There followed *Pisma iz Frantsii i Italii* (1854; letters from France and Italy), *Vom andern Ufer* (1850; *From the Other*

Shore, 1956), "Lettre à M. Jules Michelet" (1851), and "Lettre d'un Russe à Mazzini" (1849). These works reflected his pessimistic reactions to the revolutions in Europe two years earlier; he concluded that western institutions were fatally ill.

Herzen's commitments to socialism and atheism made life difficult for his wife, Natalya, whose own affair with the German poet Georg Herwegh led to a crisis in the marriage. Shortly after the couple's reconciliation in 1851, their deaf-mute son, Nicholas, and Herzen's own mother died in a boating accident in the Mediterranean Sea. On May 2, 1852, his wife died after giving birth to a stillborn child.

In 1852, Herzen left for England, where he lived for the next eleven years. There he worked on his *Byloe i Dumy* (1861-1867; *My Past and Thoughts: The Memoirs of Alexander Herzen*, 1924-1927). In London, Herzen also founded a journal, *Poliarnaia zvezda* (the polar star), which was founded in the year that Nicholas died and on the exact anniversary of the rebellion of the five Decembrists, whose pictures were in the first issue. He wrote a public letter to the new czar, Alexander II, giving him advice on the need for freedom for his people.

During these years, Herzen's home in London was a haven for Russian revolutionaries. There, Herzen carried on a vigorous dispute with his boyhood friend Mikhail Bakunin. With the visiting Ogaryov, he launched his newspaper *Kolokol* (the bell). It was Ogaryov who suggested the title, reminiscent of the assembly bell of the Novgorodian republic that Grand Prince Ivan III removed, an action symbolically destroying the freedom of that community in the fifteenth century. The paper was extremely popular for eight years in Russia, where it was distributed bimonthly, despite the interference of the security police. Throughout this period, Herzen campaigned for the emancipation of the serfs, relief from government censorship, elimination of corporal punishment, and establishment of legal due process.

Despite his disappointment with the terms of the emancipation edict in 1861, Herzen's revolutionary radicalism was muted, because he began to doubt the efficacy of violence. Younger radicals were drifting to the more uncompromising positions of Nikolay Chernyshevsky, depicted often as the leader of the "sons" among the intelligentsia. Fearing loss of influence among the young radicals, Herzen was persuaded by Bakunin to support the Polish rebels in 1863, thereby risking the loss of many moderate liberals in Russia. By then Herzen seemed to have resolved his ambivalence toward revolution and to have approved the new radical party, Land and Freedom. When the expected peasant uprisings failed to occur, Herzen was left without his former supporters.

Meanwhile, complications arose in his personal life. Ogaryov's wife, Natalya, arrived in London in 1856, and she and Herzen began an affair that resulted in a daughter, born in 1858, and in twin boys two years later. Strangely enough, he and Ogaryov remained close friends. Four years later, the twins died of diphtheria in Paris. In 1865, Herzen moved his paper and journal to Geneva, but publication ceased two years later. When the radicals of Sergey Gennadiyevich Nechayev attempted to enlist Herzen's support in new conspiracies, he was wise enough to resist. Ogaryov, however, used his portion of the fund from *Kolokol* to aid the new movement in 1869. During that same year, Herzen first began to mention to Ogaryov his desire to return home, and he wrote to Bakunin expressing new reservations about violent revolt. On January 21, 1870, however, after a short illness, Herzen died in Paris. His remains were later removed to Nice.

SIGNIFICANCE

Through *Kolokol* Aleksandr Herzen gave advice to czar and radical alike. Influenced by German philosophy and French socialism, he belonged to those educated Russians who looked upon their own nation as backward. As Herzen grew older, however, he strengthened his belief in the values of the Russian peasant and his unique village commune. He viewed the Russian peasant not as a backward and embarrassing example of Russian culture but as an exemplar of moral purity. Observing the seamier side of Western industrialism and capitalism, Herzen, like the Slavophiles, saw an opportunity to build socialism in Russia with the peasantry. By avoiding industrial capitalism, Russia could catch up with and even surpass Western Europe. The village commune offered a romantic alternative to, and an escape route from, the urban degradation that marked so many European cities of his day.

Unlike his younger colleagues, Herzen saw hope in political reform. He once addressed the czar as a true populist and a benevolent father. When the emancipation came for the serfs, he was disappointed by the terms of the edict but nevertheless recognized that the government had moved in a liberal direction and that further reforms were to be expected. He reproached those who refused to see anything positive in the state reform. To Herzen, they were more interested in revolution as an end in itself than they were in bettering society. To the younger radicals, however, Herzen was a haughty nobleman offering advice to his servants.

If Herzen typified the fathers, Chernyshevsky typified the sons. This split among the intelligentsia of the 1860's was best described by the writer Ivan Turgenev in his novel *Ottsy i deti* (1862; *Fathers and Sons*, 1867). How understandable that Leo Tolstoy, the famed pacifist novelist, deplored the decline of Herzen's influence because his influence was the last opportunity for radicalism to avoid terror and bloodshed. However, his ambivalent attitude toward revolution enabled liberal, radicals, and Marxists to claim his support. What was not ambivalent was his constant defense of the dignity and freedom of the individual.

—John D. Windhausen

FURTHER READING

Acton, Edward. *Alexander Herzen and the Role of the Intellectual Revolutionary*. Cambridge, England: Cambridge University Press, 1979. Stresses the era of 1847-1863, when Herzen struggled with the concept of revolution. The author's biographical approach shows the interaction between Herzen's personal life and his career.

Gershenzon, M. O. *A History of Young Russia*. Translated by James P. Scanlon. Irvine, Calif.: Charles Schlacks, Jr., 1986. Although not a single chapter is devoted to Herzen, this book remains a brilliant mine of ideas and information about him. The chapters on Ogaryov and others reveal different sides of Herzen.

Herzen, Aleksandr. *Letters from France and Italy, 1847-1851*. Edited and translated by Judith Zimmerman. Pittsburgh: University of Pittsburgh Press, 1995. Collection of Herzen's letters written during his exile from Russia, including descriptions of the 1848 revolution in Paris and revolutionary activities in the Italian peninsula.

_____. *My Past and Thoughts: The Memoirs of Alexander Herzen*. Translated by Constance Garnett. New York: Alfred A. Knopf, 1973. Still the best source not only for Herzen but also for all members of his circle. Beautifully translated and rendered enjoyable to read in a single volume.

Kelly, Aileen M. *Views from the Other Shore: Essays on Herzen, Chekhov, and Bakhtin*. New Haven, Conn.: Yale University Press, 1999. Analyzes the writings of three Russians, describing the shared humanism and the emphasis on the role of chance and contingency in the works of Herzen, Anton Chekhov, and M. M. Bakhtin. Describes how the three men helped develop European thought.

Malia, Martin. *Alexander Herzen and the Birth of Russian Socialism, 1812-1855*. Cambridge, Mass.: Harvard University Press, 1961. The principal study of Herzen, treating his career up to the death of Nicholas. Malia seeks to explain why the basis for Russian socialism was laid in an era without an industrial working class.

Pomper, Philip. *The Russian Revolutionary Intelligentsia*. New York: Thomas Y. Crowell, 1970. This short survey focuses on the principle that ideologies are as much traced to individual personalities as they are to ideas.

Ulam, Adam B. *In the Name of the People: Prophets and Conspirators in Prerevolutionary Russia*. New York: Viking Press, 1977. A fascinating account of nineteenth century radicals. Ulam sees the turning point in the conspiratorial caste of mind that was fashioned during the early 1860's.

Walicki, Andrzej. "Alexander Herzen's Russian Socialism." In *The Slavophile Controversy: History of the Conservative Utopia in Nineteenth Century Russian Thought*. Oxford, England: Clarendon Press, 1975. Walicki describes how Herzen merged the utopias of the Slavophiles and the Western liberals. He shows Herzen's faith in the future of Russia despite his frequent bouts with disillusionment.

Zimmerman, Judith E. *Midpassage: Alexander Herzen and European Revolution, 1847-1852*. Pittsburgh: University of Pittsburgh Press, 1989. Recounts Herzen's experiences during exile from Russia. Although he lost his family and his optimism, he became a tougher and more effective political figure during these years.

SEE ALSO: Alexander II; Mikhail Bakunin; Louis Blanc; Charles Fourier; Georg Wilhelm Friedrich Hegel; Mikhail Lermontov; Jules Michelet; Nicholas I; Pierre-Joseph Proudhon; George Sand; Leo Tolstoy; Ivan Turgenev.

RELATED ARTICLE in *Great Events from History: The Nineteenth Century, 1801-1900:* March 3, 1861: Emancipation of Russian Serfs.

THEODOR HERZL
Austrian Zionist

Often called the founder of modern Zionism, Herzl expounded on the need for a Jewish homeland and created an effective organizational framework for this political movement. His diplomatic missions to secure a Jewish state lent worldwide credibility to early Zionism and contributed to the future establishment of Israel.

BORN: May 2, 1860; Pest, Austro-Hungarian Empire (now Budapest, Hungary)
DIED: July 3, 1904; Edlach, Austria
AREAS OF ACHIEVEMENT: Diplomacy, social reform

EARLY LIFE

Theodor Herzl (HEHR-tsehl) was born into a Jewish family, which—like many other Jewish families of its time and place—had confused notions about its cultural heritage. Herzl's grandfather, Simon Loeb Herzl, adhered to traditional religious observance, while his two brothers converted to Christianity. A successful businessperson and banker, Theodor's father, Jacob, hewed a middle line: He remained a culturally assimilated Jew. As the young Herzl approached his thirteenth year, his parents announced a "confirmation" rather than a "bar mitzvah." Thus, Theodor made the passage into Jewish manhood.

The city of Pest (which merged with Buda in 1872 to become Budapest) similarly polarized its residents into either the Hungarian or the German cultural camp. Nationalism was only beginning to stir Europe. With a respect for what she deemed the more refined and cosmopolitan culture, Jeannette Herzl inculcated in her son a love of German language and literature.

Herzl began his formal education at the age of six, attending a bilingual (German and Hungarian) parochial school, the Israelitische Normalhauptschule. In 1869, he moved to a municipal technical institute, where he could pursue his alleged proclivities for the sciences. During the course of four years, however, Herzl found himself motivated only by the humanities. He even initiated and presided over a literary society, an activity that foretold both his journalistic interests and his leadership drive. The anti-Semitic remarks of a teacher finally hastened Herzl's departure from the institute.

After these early educational experiments, the young Herzl at last entered the Evangelical Gymnasium, a nondenominational academy with a largely Jewish student body, which emphasized German culture and classical learning. He proved to be committed to his writing and, while still in secondary school, published a political article in the Viennese weekly *Leben*, and book reviews for the *Pest Journal*. As Herzl neared graduation, his only sibling, an elder sister, Pauline, died of typhoid fever. The Herzls moved to Vienna one week later. Theodor returned to Budapest in June to complete his examinations, then entered the University of Vienna's law school.

Law school proved to be rather routine, except for one incident. Herzl joined Albia, a fraternity at the University of Vienna. When the organization endorsed a memorial rally—with strong anti-Semitic overtones—for the composer Richard Wagner, Herzl issued a vehement protest letter and offered his resignation. Albia responded by expelling him. Herzl received his law degree in 1884. He was admitted to the Vienna bar and subsequently worked for criminal and civil courts. A year after commencing his legal practice, he left law altogether, finally choosing a writer's life.

Perhaps Herzl most vigorously aspired to be a playwright. Though one of his works made it to the German-language stage in New York, critics generally judged his plays mediocre. He achieved far greater success writing *feuilletons*, observations of the various people, places, and characteristics defining late nineteenth century life. Summer travels, heavily subsidized by the elder Herzls, also yielded articles for the vaunted *Neue Freie Presse*. With his career advancing, Herzl married Julie Naschauer, an attractive young woman from a prosperous Jewish family. The union was to produce three children—and numerous difficulties. Thought to have had emotional problems, Julie probably also clashed with her domineering mother-in-law. Herzl's prolonged absences only exacerbated the situation.

LIFE'S WORK

Herzl, now married and in his thirties, received a professional assignment that, in its own way, was to change his life. October, 1891, brought a telegram from the *Neue Freie Presse*: The paper's editors wanted Herzl to serve as Paris correspondent. For the rest of his days, he remained affiliated with the journal. Herzl's locus, Paris, stood at the nucleus of late nineteenth century culture, and as a writer, he developed from a *feuilletonist* into a journalist. With the trial of Captain Alfred Dreyfus, however, he also added a new element to his restless personality.

Theodor Herzl. (Library of Congress)

Dreyfus, a Jew, had been accused by the French government of treason. Perhaps the most egregious aspect of the 1894 trial was the virulent, far-flung anti-Semitism that it invoked. True to journalistic ethics, Herzl did not debate Dreyfus's guilt or innocence; rather, he reported on the less-than-humane treatment meted out to the captain in this most civilized of Western European nations. As a result of the Dreyfus trial and a resurgence of anti-Semitism across the continent, Jewish issues emerged in Herzl's writings, thoughts, and, most important, actions. Mid-1895 marked the initiation of his Zionist career.

Preparing for visits with millionaire Jewish philanthropists Baron Moritz Hirsch and members of the Rothschild family, Herzl crystallized and committed to paper his developing ideas about a Jewish state. The meetings did not go well. As some scholars note, the philanthropists dwelled on charity; Herzl instead pondered nationhood as a self-help mechanism for the Jewish people. The notes that Herzl prepared for these visits, however, subsequently appeared in a revised, printed form. *Der Judenstaat* (1896; *A Jewish State*, 1896) became both the inspiration of and the primer for a fledgling Zionist movement.

Herzl's booklet identified Jews as a people, rather than merely as a religious group. Moreover, it indicated that the absence of a homeland denied Jews the status en-

joyed by other nations. Even those attracted to the more tolerant Western European countries, for example, could only assimilate and advance to a certain point before their increasing numbers and greater visibility would provoke anti-Semitism. Eastern European Jews lived in a constant state of racially based poverty and repression. Herzl concluded that statehood would "liberate the world by our freedom" and allow Jews—both individually and collectively—to realize higher goals.

These themes were not new, but Herzl added articulation and administrative structure to them. Small, loosely organized groups, *Hoveve Zion*, already had initiated isolated migrations to Palestine. Herzl argued, however, that without the existence of an autonomous state, a Jewish presence could easily kindle anti-Semitism. In order to advance nationhood, *A Jewish State* proposed a political/moral "Society of Jews" and a "Jewish Company," capable of conducting economic activities and land acquisition. Herzl suggested both Palestine and sparsely populated, fertile Argentina as possible sites for the homeland.

Reactions to *A Jewish State* varied. Comfortable Western European Jews believed that they had been granted adequate civil liberties and that Herzl's concept of nationhood might only raise anti-Semitic furor. Much to their discomfort, "Jewish unity" also linked them with their impoverished, ill-educated brethren in Russia and other countries. However, Herzl did find an audience. His backers included intellectuals, students, and many eastern European Jews for whom assimilation proved impossible and for whom misery was a way of life. With increasing fervor and occasional encouragement, he commenced publication of *Die Welt* (the world), the movement's premier communications vehicle. Supporters also urged their leader to organize a world conference in Basel, Switzerland. On August 29, 1897, the first Zionist Congress met, attracting 197 delegates. An organizational statement was adopted, membership goals and fees set, and a committee structure devised. A total of six Zionist conferences would convene during Herzl's lifetime. Each drew more delegates, media participation, and, sometimes, controversy.

In the interim, Herzl traveled through Europe, seeking diplomatic support for an automonous Jewish state. He financed his own trips, just as he underwrote the publication of *Die Welt*. The money came from his salary; by late 1895, the *Neue Freie Presse* had promoted him to literary editor. Journalistic renown may have opened diplomatic doors, but Herzl's demeanor won for him converts among heads of state. He was an impeccable dresser; his proud stance and trim profile added greatly to his five-foot, eight-inch frame. However, the perfect manners and piercing, dark good looks belied ill health. Maintaining a demanding job, filling every spare minute with political activity, and balancing family finances with those of his organization slowly weakened an already ailing heart.

If Herzl was to grow weary by the failure actually to procure a Jewish homeland, his persistence lent Zionism global credibility. He eventually obtained audiences with the German kaiser Wilhelm II; Russian ministers Count Sergei Yulievich Witte and Vyacheslav Pleve; Pope Pius X; British ministers Neville Chamberlain, David Lloyd George, and Arthur James Balfour; Sultan Abdul Hamid II; and Italian king Victor Emanuel III. His approach was pragmatic: Sometimes he presented the Jewish state as a neutral, autonomous buffer in a region that would change radically after the inevitable collapse of the Ottoman Turkish Empire; on other occasions, he suggested that Zionism might help European countries alleviate "Jewish problems," anti-Semitic hatred, and the internal discord it evoked. Diplomatic efforts, however, were directed mainly at Turkey and England. The former was a rapidly deteriorating power, with a huge territory to administer and an equally large foreign debt. Turkey also held Palestine.

The Jewish Colonial Trust had been established by the second Zionist Congress for the purpose of generating funds to purchase land. Now Herzl sought an acquisition. He told the sultan that a sale of Palestine would boost the sagging Turkish economy. Furthermore, the Jewish settlers would bring new commerce to the empire and remain faithful to the Ottomans in the face of adversaries. However appealing the financial aid, Turkey refused to grant the Zionists a fair measure of autonomy. Negotiations broke in 1902.

Great Britain, on the other hand, had internal problems. With a reputation for political tolerance, it attracted eastern European Jews fleeing repression. British leaders became concerned about limited jobs and other domestic issues; they sought to restrict Jewish immigration. While the debate proceeded, the British offered Herzl El Arish, in the Sinai peninsula, but irrigation and other problems barred the agreement. Then, in the wake of the Kishinev pogrom, which killed forty-five Jews and precipitated an outpouring of worldwide sympathy, the British suggested a Zionist charter for Uganda.

Herzl took the proposal to the sixth Zionist Congress in 1903. He explained that East Africa merely represented an interim step to Palestine. The congress voted,

narrowly, to send a delegation to Uganda, but the powerful Russian delegation—fresh from the Kishinev pogrom—refused to accept anything resembling a territorial substitute and stormed out of the session. The Russian group presented Herzl with a leadership ultimatum several months later. Tremendously hurt, he nevertheless proved somewhat successful in ending the dispute. Herzl also continued on his diplomatic missions until halted by a severe heart attack in May, 1904. Ordered to rest, he became more sedentary but constantly accepted work and visits from his supporters. Pneumonia set in, further aggravating his heart condition. Herzl died on July 3, 1904, at the resort of Edlach, Austria. His remains were moved to the new state of Israel in 1949.

SIGNIFICANCE

Theodor Herzl came to his mission relatively unaware of contemporary Zionist philosophy or Jewish issues in general. However, he left many astute prophecies. Following the first Zionist Congress, he wrote, "I founded the Jewish State. If I were to say this today, I would be met by universal laughter. In five years, perhaps, and certainly in fifty, everyone will see it."

Israel came into being fifty years and three months after Herzl committed these visions to his diary. The connection, however, is far more direct. While the Uganda episode almost divided the fledgling Zionist movement and hastened Herzl's own death, it enabled him to establish relations with Lloyd George and Balfour, two British leaders responsible for the 1917 Balfour Declaration mandating Jewish settlement in Palestine.

Herzl's novel *Altneuland* (1902; *Old-New Land*, 1941) introduces the reader to a utopian state, circa 1923. The book describes conditions that were to inspire Israel's settlers: a desolate land transformed through agricultural technology; modern, gleaming cities; and a progressive social system. Most telling, however, the title page bears an inscription: "If you will it, it is no dream."

—Lynn C. Kronzek

FURTHER READING

Bien, Alex. *Theodore Herzl*. Translated by Maurice Samuels. Philadelphia: Jewish Publication Society, 1945. This sympathetic general biography views Herzl as an exemplary, independent, and selfless leader whose Zionist organization strongly advanced democratic participation while abiding by an ordered structure.

Elon, Amos. *Herzl*. New York: Holt, Rinehart and Winston, 1975. Drawing heavily on archival material made accessible since the release of Bien's work, this book presents Herzl, the sensitive journalist, sometime playwright, and driven activist, who infused a sense of drama into statecraft.

Herzl, Theodor. *Theodor Herzl: A Portrait for This Age.* Edited by Ludwig Lewisohn. Cleveland: World, 1955. The book uses Herzl's writings to show the personal conflicts behind the Zionist leader. An interesting psychological study, employing historical analysis and assessment of the subject's literary career.

Kornberg, Jacques. *Theodor Herzl: From Assimilation to Zionism.* Bloomington: Indiana University Press, 1993. Intellectual biography examining Herzl's life from 1878 to 1896, focusing on how and why he became a Zionist.

Lacquer, Walter. *A History of Zionism.* New York: Schocken Books, 1972. Perhaps the most authoritative source on Zionism. Lacquer devotes fifty pages exclusively to Herzl. Excellent chronological overview of the subject's politics, diplomatic efforts, and organizational endeavors, with a fine summary of *A Jewish State*, his most influential work. The book includes a concise, useful bibliography, a glossary, and six maps.

Neumann, Emanuel. *Theodor Herzl: The Birth of Jewish Statesmanship.* New York: Herzl Press, 1960. Unfailingly sympathetic in its depiction of Herzl, this brief work proves most valuable when discussing the philosophical differences between the practical Zionists, seeking colonization or infiltration into Palestine, and the political Zionists, who focused their efforts on securing an independent, autonomous homeland. Contains a timetable.

Patai, Raphael, ed. *Herzl Year Book.* Vol. 3. New York: Herzl Press, 1960. Twenty-one scholars address little-known aspects of Herzl's life, gather reminiscences, argue the merits of his political and diplomatic involvements, and reflect upon his legacies. Part of a six-volume set, this collection is designed for those who want to research more specific Herzelian issues.

Robertson, Ritchie, and Edward Timms, eds. *Theodor Herzl and the Origins of Zionism.* Edinburgh: Edinburgh University Press, 1997. Essays examining numerous aspects of Herzl's career, including his relations with his Viennese contemporaries, his negotiations with Germany and Britain to acquire land for a Jewish homeland, and his attempts to reshape Jewish identity in his fictional writings.

Shimoni, Gideon, and Robert S. Wistrich, eds. *Theodor Herzl: Visionary of the Jewish State.* Jerusalem: Magnes Press, 1999. Esays examining Herzl's Zionist visions and ideas.

SEE ALSO: Jean-Henri Dunant; The Rothschild Family; Richard Wagner; Isaac Mayer Wise.

RELATED ARTICLES in *Great Events from History: The Nineteenth Century, 1801-1900:* 19th century: Arabic Literary Renaissance; February, 1896-August, 1897: Herzl Founds the Zionist Movement.

WILD BILL HICKOK
American frontier lawman

Hickok's prowess with a pistol made him one of the deadliest gunfighters in the American West and one of the most forceful and accomplished lawmen of the Kansas cattle towns. His exploits as a soldier, scout, gunfighter, and lawman made him one of the most recognized figures from the American frontier.

BORN: May 27, 1837; Troy Grove, Illinois
DIED: August 2, 1876; Deadwood, Dakota Territory (now South Dakota)
ALSO KNOWN AS: James Butler Hickok (birth name)
AREA OF ACHIEVEMENT: Law

EARLY LIFE
Wild Bill Hickok was born James Butler Hickok, the fourth of six children born to William Alonzo and Polly Hickok. In 1836, the family moved to Troy Grove, Illinois, where Hickok's father opened the community's first general store. Known as the Green Mountain House, the store doubled as a way station on the Underground Railroad. Slavery deeply troubled William, and his boys regularly assisted their father in helping runaway slaves escape. William's business failed during the financial panic of 1837, forcing him to turn to farming.

As a young boy, James Hickok kept to himself, and many considered him a loner. Early in his life, he demonstrated a penchant for weaponry, and he acquired his first gun around the age of twelve. At every opportunity, young Hickok retreated into the woods to practice his marksmanship. When William died in 1852, his boys took over the family farm. Because of his prowess with a gun, James was given the responsibility of supplementing his family's diet. He spent much of his time prowling through the woods and fields, hunting deer and small game. He also earned extra income by killing wolves and collecting bounties on their pelts. By his late teenage years, Hickok was known as one of the best shots in La Salle County. His skill and dexterity with firearms would later serve him well as a frontier lawman and soldier.

Throughout Hickok's life, he had a tendency to never back down from a threat, and he regularly stood up for those who could not defend themselves. His first recorded altercation with another man occurred at the age of eighteen while he was working for the Illinois and Michigan Canal. Charles Hudson, a local camp bully, did not like Hickok and, after exchanging some heated words, a fight broke out. As the pair exchanged blows and wrestled along the bank of the canal, the edge gave way, sending them into the water. Bystanders jumped into the water and pulled Hickok off Hudson, who lay motionless in the canal. Thinking that he had killed his adversary, the youthful Hickok fled the scene and retreated to the family farm. Shortly thereafter, Hickok, along with his brother Lorenzo, left home and headed west to Kansas.

Wild Bill Hickok.

LIFE'S WORK

Hickok arrived in Kansas in 1856 as a nineteen-year-old teenager and, except for brief trips east, spent his entire adult life in the American West. During his twenty years on the Great Plains, Hickok worked as a frontier scout, spy, soldier, teamster, showman, gunfighter, gambler, and lawman. He witnessed many of the important events associated with the development and settlement of the American West, and he personally participated in the Indian Wars, policed the cattle towns, and saw the decimation of the buffalo.

The man who would become one of the most recognized figures of the frontier era stood more than six feet tall. He had piercing gray-blue eyes that reportedly looked right through people. His long and curled auburn hair tumbled to his shoulders, and a drooping mustache hung over his lip. He sometimes dressed in the buckskin clothing of the plainsmen but later became more elegant, sporting a Prince Albert frock coat. Topping off Hickok's appearance were his ever-present guns, two Navy Colt revolvers tucked butts-forward into a red sash wrapped around his waist.

When the Hickok brothers arrived in Kansas in 1856, the territory was on the verge of civil war. Hickok briefly labored as a plowman in Johnson County, but when hostilities erupted over the issue of slavery along the Kansas-Missouri border, Hickok joined Jim Lane's Free-State Army of Kansas. Whether he saw battle is unknown, but legend claims that he became Lane's personal bodyguard.

After leaving Lane's Kansas militia in late 1857, Hickok took his first job in law enforcement as a constable for Monticello Township in Johnson County. He held this position for less than one year before he went to work for the transportation and freighting outfit of Russell, Majors, and Waddell. For two years he drove wagons and stagecoaches on the Santa Fe Trail. While on one of these trips to Santa Fe, Hickok reportedly met Kit Carson, his boyhood hero. Little did Hickok know that within a few years his own status as a Western hero would equal or surpass that of Carson.

In 1861 Hickok was working at Rock Creek Station in southeastern Nebraska. It was here, on July 12, 1861, that Hickok fought his first gun battle. The incident grew out of an ongoing feud between a local bully named Dave McCanles and the station's manager. When McCanles, his son, James Woods, and James Gordon appeared at the station and threatened the manager and his wife, Hickok stepped in and shot the elder McCanles, Woods, and Gordon. McCanles died almost instantly. Woods and

Gordon, both wounded by Hickok, attempted to escape but were hunted down and dispatched by station employees. Nebraska authorities arrested Hickok and two others, but a jury determined that they had acted in self-defense.

After his acquittal, Hickok drifted into Kansas, where he enlisted as a civilian scout in the Union Army. During the war he served as a wagon master, scout, sharpshooter, and spy. He fought at the battles of Wilson's Creek and Pea Ridge. Hickok also spent time behind enemy lines, scouting enemy positions and intercepting Confederate orders and documents. It was during the Civil War that Hickok first gained notoriety. While in Independence, Missouri, Hickok, with his pistols in his hands, dispersed a mob that was threatening to lynch a man. It was from this incident that Hickok earned the name "Wild Bill." After breaking up the mob, a lady from the crowd yelled out, "Good for you, Wild Bill." The name stuck and from then on James Butler Hickok went by the name Wild Bill.

Hickok's Civil War service as a scout and an 1865 gunfight in which he killed Dave Tutt in Springfield, Missouri, enhanced the name of Wild Bill around Missouri and Kansas. In 1867, an article about Wild Bill in *Harper's New Monthly Magazine* made Hickok a household name and a national hero. The story, written by George Ward Nichols, greatly exaggerated Hickok's Civil War exploits and claimed that he killed ten men at the Rock Creek gunfight. Nichols's portrayal of Hickok influenced later writers who further embellished Hickok's law enforcement career by claiming that he had killed one hundred men in the line of duty. Hickok did not like his image as a "man-killer," but this portrait of him as a deadly gunman earned him respect, which made policing the rowdy cattle towns easier.

Although Hickok's career in law enforcement lasted only a few years, he gained notoriety as one of the best Western lawmen. From 1867 to 1870 he served as a deputy U.S. marshal, chasing army deserters and stock thieves. In 1869 Ellis County, Kansas, elected Hickok sheriff. Hays City, the county seat, was an end-of-the-line railroad town full of gamblers, brawlers, soldiers, buffalo hunters, prostitutes, and gunmen. In three months of service, he killed two men in gunfights and was largely credited with establishing law and order. After losing his reelection bid to his deputy sheriff, Hickok drifted around from place to place. On July 17, 1870, while back in Hays City, Hickok became involved in a drunken altercation with five soldiers from Fort Hays. In the fracas that ensued, Hickok shot two soldiers, killing one and seriously wounding the other.

Because of Hickok's reputation as a lawman and gunfighter, the Kansas cattle town of Abilene hired him as city marshal in 1871. Hickok largely succeeded in quelling disturbances by prohibiting cowboys from carrying guns and keeping a close eye on the drinking and gambling establishments that they frequented. Hickok was involved in only one shooting during his stint in Abilene. On October 5, 1871, Hickok confronted Phil Coe and a number of Texans who had shot their revolvers at stray dogs. Sensing danger from the gun in Coe's hand, Hickok pulled out his revolvers. The two exchanged shots, but only Hickok's found their mark. In the heat of the conflict, Mike Williams, a friend of Hickok who was a special police officer for the Novelty Theater, came running to Hickok's assistance. Catching a glimpse of the fast-approaching Williams out of the corner of his eye and believing him to be a friend of the wounded Coe, Hickok fired two shots, killing Williams.

The death of Williams had a tremendous impact on Hickok. Shortly thereafter he retired from law enforcement and supposedly never again fired his pistols at anyone. After 1871 Hickok tried his hand at acting. He performed with several Wild West shows, including that of William Frederick "Buffalo Bill" Cody. Realizing that acting was not for him, Hickok returned to the Great Plains, where, in March, 1876, he married Agnes Lake Thatcher, a former circus performer. Legend holds that Hickok also had a relationship with Martha "Calamity Jane" Cannary, but there is no basis for such a claim. In July, 1876, Hickok joined the gold rush to the Black Hills in the Dakota Territory hoping to strike it rich and return to his new wife. Hickok, however, seems to have known that his days were numbered. He regularly told his friends that Deadwood in the Dakota Territory might be his last camp. On August 2, 1876, Hickok's premonitions came true when Jack McCall shot him in the back of the head while he played poker in a local saloon. The cards held by Hickok—aces and eights—have come to be known as the "dead man's hand."

SIGNIFICANCE

The historical life of James Butler Hickok is quite interesting but of little significance. He served his country bravely during the Civil War, scouted during the Plains Indian Wars, killed up to ten men in gunfights, and policed some of the rowdiest cattle towns in the West. Perhaps his role as a lawman made those wild and rollicking towns a safer place to live, but on a larger scale, his contributions to history and his impact on American society were minimal.

The legendary Wild Bill Hickok, however, is a much different story. He has had a tremendous impact on American culture. Hickok's life and his exploits—whether fact or fiction—have received attention in films, in dime novels, on television shows, and from serious historians. Places such as Deadwood, South Dakota; Abilene, Kansas; and Hays City, Kansas, consider Wild Bill as one of their own and continue to promote his name and his image as a colorful frontier figure. Hickok's life has captured the imagination of thousands of people, and he has gone down as one of the true heroes of the American frontier.

—Mark R. Ellis

FURTHER READING

Dykstra, Robert S. *The Cattle Towns*. New York: Antheum, 1970. Analyzes the origins and development of the Kansas cattle towns of Abilene, Ellsworth, Wichita, Dodge City, and Caldwell. Although Hickok is not a central figure, this work is important to understanding the social world in which he worked as a lawman.

Miller, Nyle H., and Joseph W. Snell. *Great Gunfighters of the Kansas Cowtowns, 1867-1886*. Lincoln: University of Nebraska Press, 1967. Formerly published under the title *Why the West Was Wild*, this book provides a documentary history of the violence associated with the Kansas cattle towns. Using excerpts from newspapers, diaries, letters, and public documents, this work examines the gun battles and exploits of twenty-one Western gunfighters, including Hickok.

Rosa, Joseph G. *They Called Him Wild Bill: The Life and Adventures of James Butler Hickok*. Norman: University of Oklahoma Press, 1964. The definitive Hickok biography. Probably the best work on any Western gunfighter and lawman.

_____. *The West of Wild Bill Hickok*. Norman: University of Oklahoma Press, 1982. A pictorial biography of Hickok and the people and places associated with his career. Almost every known photograph, drawing, and painting of him appears in this volume.

_____. *Wild Bill Hickok, Gunfighter: An Account of Hickok's Gunfights*. College Station, Tex.: Creative, 2001. Chronicles Hickok's gunfights, providing detailed descriptions of the guns he used, his legendary abilities as a marksman, and the "dead man's hand" Hickok held in the poker game when he was shot to death.

_____. *Wild Bill Hickok: The Man and His Myth*. Lawrence: University Press of Kansas, 1996. An examination of the many myths and legends surrounding Hickok's exploits in the American West. Addresses his reputation as a "man-killer" among other topics.

SEE ALSO: Calamity Jane; Kit Carson; Wyatt Earp.

RELATED ARTICLES in *Great Events from History: The Nineteenth Century, 1801-1900:* February 25, 1836: Colt Patents the Revolver; 1867: Chisholm Trail Opens.

MIGUEL HIDALGO Y COSTILLA
Mexican priest and nationalist leader

Although he personally failed and died for his attempt, Hidalgo initiated the process that led to Mexico's independence from Spain and left an example that inspired the leaders who achieved his goal.

BORN: May 8, 1753; Corralejo, Mexico
DIED: July 30, 1811; Chihuahua, Mexico
AREAS OF ACHIEVEMENT: Religion and theology, government and politics

EARLY LIFE

Miguel Hidalgo y Costilla (mee-GEHL ee-DAHL-goh ee kohs-TEE-yah) and his four siblings were raised on a ranch managed by his father in Guanajuato, northwest of Mexico City. Descended from a Spanish *criollo* family that had lived in Mexico for several generations, Hidalgo was encouraged to advance himself through education. He was sent to Valladolid (now known as Morelia), in Michoacán, southwest of Guanajuato, and his acute intellect developed in the best educational institutions of New Spain, as colonial Mexico was known. Educated first by Jesuits, he became exposed to Enlightenment thought. After the government's suppression of the Jesuits in 1767, Hidalgo studied at the Colegio de San Nicolás Obispo, a noted seminary. From Morelia he went to the Royal and Pontifical University of Mexico in Mexico City, where he received degrees in philosophy and theology. In 1778, he was ordained a Roman Catholic priest.

LIFE'S WORK

Hidalgo's initial career was not as a parish priest but as a teacher in San Nicolás Obispo. Keen-witted and sociable, he was admired by his students and appreciated by colleagues for his intellectual prowess and became the college's head in 1790. However, Hidalgo's clerical vocation had decidedly secular characteristics. He fathered three children with two women and acquired several ranches. After falling into debt, he took up gambling and mismanaged college funds. In 1792 he was removed as college head and assigned to parish duties.

Hidalgo spent the pastoral phase of his career at churches in several provinces, mostly within in an arc north and west of the capital city. The last of his parishes, from 1803 to 1810, was in the poor Indian village of Dolores, in Hidalgo, northeast of Mexico City. What distinguished Hidalgo's work in his parish assignments was not so much his zeal for the spiritual life of his parishioners but his concern for their intellectual development and material welfare. As an apostle of the Enlightenment, he evangelized for human betterment through development of practical skills and applied knowledge.

Hidalgo organized musical, theatrical, and social events. He favored free public education and built a personal library of works in numerous languages on literature, natural philosophy, economics, and government that he shared with others. Many of his Dolores parishioners saw their lives significantly improved. He organized manufacturing activities, setting up curing tanks to tan hides and firing kilns to form tiles and bricks. He managed agricultural activities with practical commercial benefits: cultivating grapes to make wine, silkworms to make fine fabrics, and bees to make honey.

Hidalgo confidently carried out these measures in an atmosphere of acceptance and admiration. However, he was challenging an established order that demanded deference from subordinate masses at a time when larger sociopolitical forces increasingly destabilized that order. Toward the end of the eighteenth century, the English-speaking colonies north of Mexico had formed a democratic republic. An armed revolution in France overthrew the monarchy, attracting significant clerical support. Revolutionary anarchy in France also led to the rise of Napoleon Bonaparte, who successfully overthrew established monarchies throughout Europe. In 1808, Napoleon forced the Spanish king Ferdinand VII to flee, laying the entire Spanish Empire open to turmoil.

Like many members of provincial Mexican elites during this period, Hidalgo grew increasingly critical of the fiscal deprivations, economic stagnation, and political repression of the Spanish government. The heaviest burden of these policies fell on the mass of the indigenous and mixed-blood mestizo populations. The overthrow of royal government in Madrid presented an ideal opportunity to remove its representatives in Mexico.

Through his friendship with a member of the local militia, Captain Ignacio Allende, Hidalgo began attending secret meetings in 1810 that discussed replacing the Spanish government with a local one. With the nascent manufacturing base he had established in Dolores, Hidalgo supervised the production of primitive armaments. On September 16, 1810, after the group's plot was denounced. Hidalgo and Allende decided to begin their uprising immediately, as further planning was no longer an option. During the religious service he conducted on that day, Hidalgo announced his historic "cry [*grito*] of Dolores," launching the process that eventually would separate Mexico from Spain.

Forging an alliance of militant local elites and an enraged mass of rural workers, Hidalgo led his followers behind a banner of Our Lady of Guadalupe and became their commanding general. He and Allende initially enjoyed a series of victories. From late September to the end of October, they captured the important urban centers of Guanajuato, Morelia, and Guadalajara, and advanced to the outskirts of Mexico City. However, with his troops poorly organized and short of munitions, Hidalgo decided to delay taking the capital. Local elites, moreover, were becoming increasingly fearful of supporting Hidalgo because of the ferocious tactics his peasant followers used.

Meanwhile, government forces began to reverse the advances of the rebellious forces. After losing Guanajuato, Hidalgo attempted to establish a formal government in Guadalajara, where he appointed ministers, proclaimed laws, managed propaganda, reorganized the militia, and authorized executions. Tens of thousands of volunteers joined him. Nevertheless, on January 17, 1811, Hidalgo and Allende suffered massive losses against government forces in a decisive battle at Calderón Bridge.

Hidalgo and his colleagues attempted to escape to the north, into the United States, but Hidalgo was captured, imprisoned in Chihuahua, and tried before both martial and ecclesiastical courts. Stripped of his status as a priest, he was put before a firing squad on July 30, 1811, and then beheaded at Chihuahua. His head and those of the other conspirators were then displayed on stakes in a public square.

SIGNIFICANCE

The call for independence that Hidalgo announced on the morning of September 16, 1810, became the iconic symbol of the birth of the Mexican nation. That image is as important in Mexican history as the midnight ride of Paul Revere is in American history. Sometimes called the Father of the Nation, Hidalgo nonetheless produced a stillborn revolution, and his military failures brought about his own death. Nevertheless, he lit the spark that would ignited the rebellion that resulted in Mexico's full independence in 1821. Following Hidalgo's example, a former seminary student of his, José María Morelos (1765-1815), led the next phase of the independence movement.

Hidalgo's uprising recalls that of Tupac Amaru II in 1780 against repressive colonial authority in Spanish Peru. Both men enjoyed initial successes. However, they lost important local support as the enraged peasants, who constituted the mass of the popular militia, increasingly frightened the powerful upper classes because of the brutal revenges they inflicted on their oppressors.

With independence, Mexican *criollo* elites supplanted the Spanish. However, they continued the subordination of the indigenous masses. This repression eventually set off the Mexican Revolution of the early twentieth century. Nonetheless, despite the considerable subsequent incorporation of indigenous culture into the definition of the independent Mexican nation, economic and sociopolitical divisions have continued to challenge the country's sovereignty.

—Edward A. Riedinger

FURTHER READING

Archer, Chirston I., ed. *The Birth of Modern Mexico, 1780-1824*. Wilmington, Del.: Scholarly Resources, 2003. Collection of articles by various scholars concentrating on conditions and strategies for Mexican independence, placing ideas and actions of Hidalgo in historical context.

Fariss, Nancy M. *Crown and Clergy in Colonial Mexico, 1759-1821: The Crisis of Ecclesiastical Privilege*. London: Athlone, 1968. Examines intellectual, political, social, and economic dilemmas and contradictions of Roman Catholic clergy in the decades preceding Mexico's independence and positions them in relation to it.

Hamil, Hugh M. *The Hidalgo Revolt: Prelude to Mexican Independence*. Westport, Conn.: Greenwood Press, 1981. Examines the complex of historical factors and settings that gave Hidalgo the role of a catalyst and initiator, but not the cause, of Mexican independence.

Hammett, Brian R. *Roots of Insurgency: Mexican Regions, 1750-1824*. New York: Cambridge University Press, 1986. Details over the course of the late eighteenth and early nineteenth centuries the changing socioeconomic circumstances and political responses in Guadalajara, Guanajuato, Michoacán, and Puebla, the central Mexican provinces from which the independence movement emerged.

Lynch, John. *Spanish American Revolutions, 1808-1826*. 2d ed. New York: W. W. Norton, 1986. Noted work by a renowned scholar on the wars of independence in Mexico and Central and South America, placing the uprising of Hidalgo in a wider historical context.

Miller, Hubert J. *Padre Miguel Hidalgo: Father of Mexican Independence*. Rev. ed. Edinburgh: University of Texas-Pan American University Press, 2004. Brief biography of Hidalgo that includes illustrations and maps; originally produced as part of Texas's sesquicentennial celebration.

Tutino, John. *From Insurrection to Revolution in Mexico: Social Bases of Agrarian Violence, 1750-1940*. Princeton, N.J.: Princeton University Press, 1986. Places Hidalgo's uprising within the context of two centuries of the straitened rural conditions and peasant rebellions that fomented Mexico's independence movement at the beginning of the nineteenth century and its revolution at the beginning of the twentieth century.

Viles, Donald M. *Battles, Cuautla and Bridge of Calderon*. Garibaldi, Oreg.: Donald M. Viles, 1985. Study, accompanied by maps, of areas in which Hidalgo led most his decisive military actions in his thwarted attempt for Mexican independence.

SEE ALSO: Fanny Calderón de la Barca; Benito Juárez; Maximilian; Antonio López de Santa Anna.

RELATED ARTICLES in *Great Events from History: The Nineteenth Century, 1801-1900:* March, 1805-September 1, 1807: Burr's Conspiracy; September 16, 1810: Hidalgo Issues El Grito de Dolores; September 16, 1810-September 28, 1821: Mexican War of Independence; October 2, 1835-April 21, 1836: Texas Revolution; October 31, 1861-June 19, 1867: France Occupies Mexico.

THOMAS WENTWORTH HIGGINSON
American writer and social reformer

Higginson wrote prolifically but is best known in the literary world as the discoverer of Emily Dickinson's poetry. He is also noted for commanding a regiment of black enlisted men during the Civil War and for laboring in social causes such as the abolition of slavery and women's rights.

BORN: December 22, 1823; Cambridge, Massachusetts
DIED: May 9, 1911; Cambridge, Massachusetts
ALSO KNOWN AS: Thomas Wentworth Storrow Higginson (full name)
AREAS OF ACHIEVEMENT: Literature, military, social reform

EARLY LIFE
Although the large family into which Thomas Wentworth Storrow Higginson (HIHG-ahn-sahn) was the youngest child was not as wealthy as it had once been, there was never any doubt that Higginson would be educated at Harvard. In 1823 Stephen Higginson, then serving as Harvard University steward, had retained a library of one thousand books from more prosperous days, and by the age of four Thomas was rummaging among them. The boy's grandfather and great-grandfather had been merchants and shipowners, and the former continued to live in style despite hard times. Thomas's mother, Louise, was descended from Appletons and Wentworths, both colonial New England families of note, but she had been orphaned early and had lodged with relatives.

Thus the young Thomas Higginson knew early that he came from a privileged family with concomitant civic and social responsibilities but one forced to come to terms with the limitations and impediments of relative poverty. These lessons would later help guide him in his multifaceted career. Because his bright sister Louisa numbered the brilliant Margaret Fuller among her friends, Higginson, the future champion of women's rights, also became aware that girls could not expect the Harvard education that young men of good families in his area could virtually take for granted. After five years in a "Dame School," the nine-year-old Higginson began to study the obligatory Latin grammar in a private school, where one of his friends was the future poet James Russell Lowell. The next year Higginson's father, who had been dismissed from his Harvard post several years earlier, died; in 1837, the thirteen-year-old boy entered Harvard as its youngest freshman.

Higginson's next decade began and ended there, with several short-lived jobs sandwiched between. As an undergraduate, Higginson absorbed Harvard's liberal intellectual atmosphere and took up one of its more extreme liberal positions: abolition. During the 1840's he began to write poetry and grew a beard, then a symbol of defiance of the established order. At length he settled on a career as a minister, earned an impressive record at the Divinity School, and graduated in 1847.

LIFE'S WORK
In 1847, after a long engagement, Higginson, buoyed by the prospect of a pastorate in Newburyport, Massachusetts, married Mary Channing. He also met and came to admire Lucy Stone, one of the pillars of the movement for women's rights, but his own advocacy of women and black Americans won him few friends among the prominent white males in his congregation, and after two years he was asked to leave.

Shaken by the rejection, Higginson did not seek another pastorate but for the next three years worked for various liberal causes. In 1852, however, he accepted an appointment as the first pastor of the newly organized Free Church in Worcester, Massachusetts, and found there a congregation receptive to his abolitionist views. Increasingly, he preferred action to sermonizing on behalf of his causes, and his activities turned disruptive and even violent. He accompanied Stone and Worcester reformer Abby Kelley Foster to the World's Temperance Convention in New York in 1853, and when the efforts of Higginson, Stone, and Susan B. Anthony to instill women's rights issues into the convention split the delegations, they formed their own "Half World's Convention."

The following year, Higginson spearheaded an abortive rescue of a captured fugitive slave, Anthony Burns, in the course of which a police officer was killed. Those arrested and indicted for promoting a riot included Higginson, although he was never brought to trial. In the fall of 1856, he left his congregation to an assistant pastor and joined a group of Free-Soil activists in Kansas. Although he does not seem to have participated directly in violence there, this adventure acquainted him with the militant activities of John Brown, whom Higginson championed thereafter. One of Higginson's more peaceful efforts of the 1850's was performing the marriage ceremony of Lucy Stone and Henry Blackwell, brother of Elizabeth Blackwell, the nation's first female physician.

Thomas Wentworth Higginson. (Library of Congress)

Higginson also wrote industriously during these years. His output included a considerable body of largely unsuccessful poetry and, more important, a series of essays on various topics in the *Atlantic Monthly*. The essay with the most far-reaching effects did not appear until early in 1862. Titled "A Letter to a Young Contributor," it inspired some of the most intriguing letters ever written by a literary person.

After reading Higginson's essay of advice to young writers, a totally unknown poet in Amherst, Massachusetts, responded in April of 1862 with an idiosyncratic letter enclosing four of her poems. A correspondence developed between Higginson and Emily Dickinson, and he befriended and encouraged this strikingly unconventional poet. Because Higginson has been accused of shortcomings as a critic of Dickinson's poetry, it is appropriate to note that he stands as the first professional man of letters to recognize her as (to use his phrase) "a wholly new and original poet."

Higginson's letters to Dickinson have not survived, but hers to him make clear his importance to her. When she died in 1886 with her poems, nearly 1,800 of them,

still in manuscript, Higginson coedited them with Mabel Todd, wife of an Amherst College professor. The volume that they produced in 1890, *The Poems of Emily Dickinson*, has suffered in comparison with the collection edited by Thomas H. Johnson more than a half century later, its most serious flaw being a tendency to "correct" not only her unusual punctuation but also, at times, her diction. It appears, however, that Todd, not Higginson, was mainly responsible for these editorial shortcomings.

The year that marked the beginning of the Higginson-Dickinson correspondence, 1862, also saw the beginning of Higginson's military career. In March of that year he decided to forgo regular duties as a clergyman and began recruiting a Massachusetts regiment of volunteers for the war that had erupted between the North and the South the previous year. Before the regiment could join the conflict, Higginson, whose abolitionist sentiments had long been well known, was asked to command the First South Carolina Volunteers, a regiment made up of black southern refugees. Higginson learned to admire the spirit and resourcefulness of the African American soldiers. Wounded in his regiment's unsuccessful attempt to cut the railroad between Charleston, South Carolina, and Savannah, Georgia, in the summer of 1863, Higginson, who had attained the rank of colonel, was in and out of hospitals for the duration of the war.

Thereafter Higginson wrote, lectured, and cared for his invalid wife. Along with Stone, Julia Ward Howe, and others, he organized the New England Woman Suffrage Association and contributed to its publication, *The Woman's Journal*. In 1870 he published *Army Life in a Black Regiment*. By this time his activities other than writing had slowed considerably. The abolition battle had been won, and though much remained to be done before anything like full civil rights would be extended to the freed slaves, the task would require the efforts of a new generation of reformers long after Higginson's death.

The same pattern can be seen in Higginson's struggle for women's rights. In 1850, shortly after Elizabeth Blackwell obtained her medical degree, the first medical school for women opened in Philadelphia, Pennsylvania, and the states gradually began admitting women to the bar. Property rights for married women and free universal secondary education for all girls were other goals that the women's movement attained as the nineteenth century wore on. After about 1870, Higginson offered mainly moral support. For various reasons the suffrage movement lost momentum, and it was not until 1920 that

THE FIRST BLACK REGIMENT

In the introduction to his book about his experience commanding the Union Army's first African American regiment, Thomas Wentworth Higginson commented on the extra burden placed on his men by the publicity they received.

I am under pretty heavy bonds to tell the truth, and only the truth; for those who look back to the newspaper correspondence of that period will see that this particular regiment lived for months in a glare of publicity, such as tests any regiment severely, and certainly prevents all subsequent romancing in its historian. As the scene of the only effort on the Atlantic coast to arm the negro, our camp attracted a continuous stream of visitors, military and civil. A battalion of black soldiers, a spectacle since so common, seemed then the most daring of innovations, and the whole demeanor of this particular regiment was watched with microscopic scrutiny by friends and foes. I felt sometimes as if we were a plant trying to take root, but constantly pulled up to see if we were growing. The slightest camp incidents sometimes came back to us, magnified and distorted, in letters of anxious inquiry from remote parts of the Union. It was no pleasant thing to live under such constant surveillance; but it guaranteed the honesty of any success, while fearfully multiplying the penalties had there been a failure. A single mutiny, such as has happened in the infancy of a hundred regiments, a single miniature Bull Run, a stampede of desertions, and it would have been all over with us; the party of distrust would have got the upper hand, and there might not have been, during the whole contest, another effort to arm the negro.

Source: Thomas Wentworth Higginson, *Army Life in a Black Regiment* (Boston: Fields, Osgood, 1870).

the passage of the Nineteenth Amendment to the Constitution guaranteed women the right to vote.

In 1877 Higginson's first wife died; two years later he married Mary Thacher. His only two children, both daughters, were born in 1880 and 1881. Only one survived to adulthood. Poetry, both its composition and criticism, now engaged Higginson more than social reform. Between 1877 and 1904 he wrote all the poetry reviews for *The Nation.* His health, generally robust until about the age of sixty, declined. The women whose work he did so much to foster began to die. He spoke at funeral services for Dickinson in 1886 and Stone in 1893. Higginson's later books—a good example is *Cheerful Yesterdays* (1896)—reflect the mellowing of this once-fire-breathing liberal activist. When he died in 1911, few remembered the social activist of the 1850's and 1860's; instead, he was mainly regarded as a "grand old man of literature." However, in an appropriate gesture, the pallbearers at his funeral, a half century after the war in which he had accepted a command unprecedented in U.S. military history, were young black soldiers.

SIGNIFICANCE

Because of their subject's versatility, the biographers of Thomas Wentworth Higginson do not agree about his most important achievement. To lovers of American literature, his relationship to Emily Dickinson, a great poet who once wrote him, "You have saved my life," stands out. Admirers of his activities on behalf of social justice cite his early championing of women's rights initiatives and his militant—and military—efforts to abolish forever the evil of slavery. He combined literary competence and bold activism to an unusual degree; he impresses both by his word and deeds in his attack on injustices in American society.

Both women and black Americans continued to suffer from the heavy weight of injustice. From the perspective of several generations later, it is obvious that their battles had scarcely begun and that Higginson was limited by his vision, which was the vision of a white American male born early in the nineteenth century into an old New England family. Nevertheless, he contributed mightily to a great wave of social reform in the third quarter of that century. It would require further bursts of reforming energy in the twentieth century to consolidate and extend the earlier advances that Thomas Wentworth Higginson helped bring about.

—*Robert P. Ellis*

FURTHER READING

Broaddus, Dorothy C. *Genteel Rhetoric: Writing High Culture in Nineteenth-Century Boston.* Columbia: University of South Carolina Press, 1999. Analyzes the work of Higginson, Ralph Waldo Emerson, and other nineteenth century writers who created a more refined rhetoric and aesthetics. Broaddus shows how this gentility was lost when the writers addressed slavery, abolition, and other serious topics related to the Civil War.

Edelstein, Tilden G. *Strange Enthusiasm: A Life of Thomas Wentworth Higginson.* New Haven, Conn.: Yale University Press, 1966. The best source of information concerning Higginson's literary activity, including not only a substantial discussion of his literary criticism but also the only sustained criticism of Higginson's little-known poetry.

Higginson, Thomas Wentworth. *Army Life in a Black Regiment*. New York: W. W. Norton, 1984. A modern edition of Higginson's account of his experiences as a commander of a controversial regiment of black soldiers in the Civil War. His assessments of his troops, though displaying the prejudices characteristic of even the most liberal thinkers of his time, stand out as beacons of enlightenment in that time.

_____. *The Complete Civil War Journal and Selected Letters of Thomas Wentworth Higginson*. Edited by Christopher Lobby. Chicago: University of Chicago Press, 2000. In his journal, Higginson recounts his experiences as commander of a Union regiment of black soldiers; his journal was the basis for his book *Army Life in a Black Regiment*. Also includes some of Higginson's letters exploring changing racial relations in the South during the Civil War.

_____. *The Magnificent Activist: The Writings of Thomas Wentworth Higginson (1823-1911)*. Edited by Howard N. Meyer. Cambridge, Mass.: Da Capo Press, 2000. Collection of Higginson's essays on various subjects, including his response to the Fugitive Slave Law, his advocacy of women's suffrage, and his analysis of Sappho's poetry.

Meyer, Howard N. *Colonel of the Black Regiment: The Life of Thomas Wentworth Higginson*. New York: W. W. Norton, 1967. Emphasizes Higginson's military distinction as the commander of a regiment of southern black fugitives, his interest in race relations, his early championing of Susan B. Anthony, and his later promotion of the woman suffrage movement.

Tuttleton, James W. *Thomas Wentworth Higginson*. Boston: Twayne, 1978. Stresses Higginson's unusual relationship with Emily Dickinson as his chief contribution to American literature but also portrays Higginson as an original writer who illuminated the place of the professional man of letters in nineteenth century America.

Wells, Anna Mary. *Dear Preceptor: The Life and Times of Thomas Wentworth Higginson*. Boston: Houghton Mifflin, 1963. The first of several biographies marking the resurgence of interest in Higginson during the 1960's. As the title suggests, the book highlights the Dickinson connection, but at the same time it is the most balanced and readable life of Higginson.

SEE ALSO: Susan B. Anthony; Elizabeth Blackwell; John Brown; Lydia Maria Child; Emily Dickinson; Ralph Waldo Emerson; Charlotte Forten; Abby Kelley Foster; Margaret Fuller; Julia Ward Howe; Helen Hunt Jackson; Lucy Stone.

RELATED ARTICLE in *Great Events from History: The Nineteenth Century, 1801-1900:* October 16-18, 1859: Brown's Raid on Harpers Ferry.

JAMES JEROME HILL
American industrialist

Hill used his tenacity and entrepreneurial skills to amass a personal fortune and create a railroad empire in the American Northwest. At the same time, he contributed substantially to both the region's and the nation's prosperity and growth.

BORN: September 16, 1838; Rockwood, Ontario, Canada
DIED: May 29, 1916; St. Paul, Minnesota
AREA OF ACHIEVEMENT: Business

EARLY LIFE
Born in a Quaker village in Ontario, James Hill added the middle name Jerome later in life. The name of the French emperor Napoleon's brother, "Jerome" was an appropri-

ate addition for the man who would become known as the "Empire Builder." The Hill family farmed for a living, though Hill's father pursued other occupations as well, and was frequently unemployed. Through his father, young James encountered many different personalities and learned the often harsh realities of the business world. After the death of his father in 1852, James's mother kept an inn, and the future transportation magnate worked as a grocer's assistant. The Reverend William Wetherald, a local schoolmaster, played an important role in preparing Hill for what lay ahead. Wetherald taught him algebra, geometry, literature, and grammar. The instructor also instilled a sense of purpose in his pupil and increased his awareness of the world beyond rural Ontario.

Both of Hill's parents were of Anglo-Celtic descent, and neither came from a distinguished or wealthy family. They had immigrated to Canada during the early 1820's. Ann Dunbar Hill, James's mother, adhered to the tenets of the Methodist Church, but his father had been reared a Baptist. As parents, they reared their children among Quakers. James had one sister and one brother; a second brother died in infancy. The two boys enjoyed numerous outdoor activities, one of which had an unfortunate and lasting impact on James: At the age of nine, an archery accident caused him to lose the sight in one eye. He later claimed that this loss prevented him from pursuing a career in medicine.

In April, 1856, James made one of the most important decisions of his life. Like other Canadian youths of his day, he decided to go to the United States. His migration coincided with the opening of the Old Northwest—roughly the states surrounding the western Great Lakes—and the onset of railroad building within the region. Hill flirted with the idea of making his way to the Orient, but he wisely chose not to undertake the journey. He visited New York City, Philadelphia, and other eastern cities before making his way to St. Paul, Minnesota. The young man arrived in the city on July 21, 1856. There he found a burgeoning community filling with migrants from the East and immigrants from abroad. Hill soon met the city's civic and commercial leaders. He began his business career as a shipping agent. An astute observer, Hill rapidly learned the workings of the transportation business, both steamboat and railroad.

In 1865, the James J. Hill Company opened for business. Its namesake and part owner developed a procedure to facilitate the smooth transfer of goods from water to land conveyances and vice versa. Two years later, he married Mary Theresa Mehegan, a Roman Catholic of Irish descent, and a family soon followed. Hill continued to expand his business interests. At the same time, the Red River Valley region of northern Minnesota and southern Canada enjoyed increased prosperity, and Hill played a significant part in its development. He involved himself in the area's fur trade, tried to help resolve the Riel Rebellion in Winnipeg, Canada, and worked to bring steamboats to the Red River. During the late 1860's and early 1870's, Hill became a leader in the St. Paul coal industry. The emerging entrepreneur demonstrated a marked talent for commercial endeavors and rapidly established himself as one of the region's shrewdest businesspeople.

Hill's personal wealth and local prestige grew considerably during the 1870's. In 1877 and 1878, he intensi-fied his study of the area's railroads, particularly the ailing St. Paul and Pacific railroads. In concert with a group generally known as the "Associates," Hill moved toward obtaining control of the financially troubled line. The consortium included Norman W. Kittson, an old friend and one of St. Paul's first citizens, as well as representatives of prominent eastern banking interests. Through acumen, tenacity, and perseverance, the Associates acquired the object of their quest. In 1878, the St. Paul, Minneapolis, and Manitoba Railroad began operation. Hill first served as general manager and had to address such problems as corporate organization, local political pressures, and powerful competitors. He also had to learn the logistics of running a transportation company. He vigorously accepted the challenge, and the Manitoba line quickly emerged as an important regional railroad.

LIFE'S WORK

The 1880's witnessed many changes in the life of James Hill as he took his place as one of the nation's preeminent railroad executives. He became a United States citizen during the decade's first year. In 1882, he assumed the presidency of the St. Paul, Minneapolis, and Manitoba Railroad. Hill continued to involve himself in the company's day-to-day operations. He dealt with Minnesota's long and frigid winters, confronted labor problems, acquired new rolling stock, oversaw the upgrading of right-of-way, and contemplated expansion.

From 1881 to 1883, Hill participated in the Canadian Pacific Railroad syndicate. He provided those trying to build a transcontinental railroad north of the border with expert counsel. His efforts helped them secure the most advantageous route to the west of Winnipeg. Hill, for a time, hoped that his road would serve as a partial link between the eastern and western sections of the Canadian line. When the Canadian Pacific Railroad showed a marked determination to lay track north of Lake Superior, it spurred the Manitoba's president to the realization that his railroad must have its own route to the Pacific coast. Without it, the regional north-south conveyor could simply not compete.

Hill's rise to prominence coincided with a time of significant social and economic change in the United States. Rail construction continued at a furious pace, often with little forethought and no comprehensive planning. The years also saw considerable human turbulence, much of it associated with the nation's spectacular industrial growth. Hill took these changes in stride. He weathered competition from old adversaries such as the Northern

Pacific Railroad and new ones such as the Soo Line Railroad. In addition, railroad operation became a major political issue. Legislators from across the country began to contemplate greater federal control of the industry. Hill disliked this trend because he believed that it would minimize individual initiative, but he realized its inevitability. By the end of the 1880's, despite a host of new problems and conditions, he was ready to extend the Manitoba line to the Pacific coast.

The railroad advanced to the West in two stages and underwent important changes. In 1887, it entered Montana. During that summer, crews laid 643 miles of track, from the then western terminus at Minot, North Dakota (named for Hill's somewhat brash young associate at the time, Henry D. Minot), to Helena, Montana. Hill tried to involve himself in every detail, as was his style, and stressed the need for utility. The track layers completed their task in mid-November, before the onset of the harsh Montana winter. They thereby escaped Hill's anticipated wrath had they failed to finish the line that season. Almost immediately, the Manitoba executive began to plan for continuation to the Pacific coast.

On December 11, 1889, one of his agents located the Marias Pass through the Rocky Mountains. Its low altitude allowed Hill to push straight west from Havre, Montana, instead of using the more difficult and costly route out of Helena. Crews drove the final spikes on a cold January day in 1893. During the years of westward progression, Hill undertook a major reorganization. In 1889, the Manitoba became the Great Northern Railroad. This line, which now extended from Superior, Wisconsin, to Seattle, Washington, would become Hill's most lasting legacy.

Though his business interests occupied much of his attention, Hill found time to spend with his family and delve into numerous other pursuits. The former had grown to include nine children by the 1880's. The clan provided many happy moments and more than a few minor panics as a result of childhood illnesses and accidents. The parents educated their progeny at home and brought them up as Catholics. Hill never joined the Church, though he provided it with substantial financial support. The family spent much time at one of Hill's favorite spots, his property at North Oaks, Minnesota. There, he engaged in a second occupation, gentleman farming. Every spring, Hill and his cronies assembled for the annual "salmon kill" on the River St. John in Quebec, Canada. Though he dutifully promised his wife they would soon spend more time together, business came first for Hill.

New commercial challenges engaged much of Hill's attention in the years after the completion of the Great Northern Railroad. The onset of a serious depression in 1893 severely tested the railroad industry's mettle. Several lines encountered dire financial difficulties, but the Hill line persevered, in no small part because of the efforts and prudence of its chief executive. During the 1890's, Hill contemplated some form of unification between the Great Northern and the Northern Pacific railroads. He secured a major interest in the latter and tried, with the help of financial giant J. P. Morgan, to consolidate the two concerns under the umbrella of the Northern Securities Company. The Supreme Court, in 1904, ruled that the company would restrict commerce and ordered it dissolved. Hill disapproved of such government interference, believing that railroad leaders were best able to direct their own affairs, but his efforts to convince others were of no avail.

Other activities brought Hill more success and less bitterness. He found himself constantly in demand on the lecture circuit, speaking on subjects ranging from agriculture to education. In 1915, he embarked on a final major task. Under the stewardship of J. P. Morgan, Hill helped arrange a huge loan for the Anglo-French alliance.

SIGNIFICANCE

The success of Hill, and other American captains of industry, made for an apparent anomaly. In a democratic society, theoretically based on human equality, the concentration of such extreme wealth and power in the hands of a few appeared to many to be a gross injustice. The myth of the self-made man notwithstanding, the nation could not hide the marked disparity between its rich, as exemplified by Hill, and its laboring class, characterized by his employees. Hence, the designation of "robber baron" attains some legitimacy when applied to Hill. There are other factors, however, which those who are quick to condemn should pause to consider. Hill and his peers played major roles in transforming the fledgling, preindustrial United States into a major world power. They created its vast industrial complex from the ground up. Almost every American, in at least some small manner, shared the benefits of the economy these men helped create. To James Hill, however, there was only one perspective. He believed that at least he among the moguls of industry had made a uniquely positive contribution to the development of America.

—Robert F. Zeidel

FURTHER READING

Blegen, Theodore C. *Minnesota: A History of a State.* Minneapolis: University of Minnesota Press, 1963. Minnesota was the location of Hill's early railroad career. Blegen traces the history of the region in great detail and places Hill's career in perspective.

Holbrook, Stewart H. *James J. Hill: A Great Life in Brief.* New York: Alfred A. Knopf, 1955. This short volume provides an overview for the reader who does not wish to read several hundred pages. A popular biography rather than a detailed historical analysis, it lacks footnotes but does contain a short bibliography.

McCraw, Thomas K. *Prophets of Regulation.* Cambridge, Mass.: Harvard University Press, 1984. This volume looks at railroad regulation and its advocates. It provides fresh insight into the industry in which Hill played a leading role.

Malone, Michael P. *James J. Hill: Empire Builder of the Northwest.* Norman: University of Oklahoma Press, 1996. Comprehensive, interpretive biography, describing Hill's business career and role in developing the economy of the northwestern United States.

Martin, Albro. *James J. Hill and the Opening of the Northwest.* New York: Oxford University Press, 1976. Martin thoroughly researched his subject in both the Hill Papers and the Great Northern Railroad Papers. His work is detailed and well footnoted. Though its treatment of corporate intricacies may be tedious for some readers, it is an excellent starting point for those who wish to do further research.

Pyle, Joseph G. *The Life of James J. Hill.* 2 vols. Garden City, N.Y.: Doubleday, Page, 1917. Pyle wrote the official or sanctioned biography, published shortly after Hill's death. The author also served as Hill's literary agent during the last years of his life. The work is biased, but it is still valuable.

Strom, Claire. *Profiting from the Plains: The Great Northern Railway and Corporate Development of the American West.* Seattle: University of Washington Press, 2003. Examines Hill's efforts to increase agricultural production along the route of the Great Northern Railway. Hill knew that increased crop yields would increase the amount of merchandise his railroad would haul, and increased haulage would increase the railroad's profits. Strom describes the obstacles and successes Hill encountered in his attempts to promote farming.

SEE ALSO: John Jacob Astor; J. P. Morgan; Napoleon I.
RELATED ARTICLES in *Great Events from History: The Nineteenth Century, 1801-1900:* September 8, 1810-May, 1812: Astorian Expeditions Explore the Pacific Northwest Coast; 1818-1854: Search for the Northwest Passage; January 7, 1830: Baltimore and Ohio Railroad Opens; May 10, 1869: First Transcontinental Railroad Is Completed.

OCTAVIA HILL
English social reformer

Hill sought to cope with the social consequences of slum housing by creating and managing a system of humane and personal contact between landlord and tenant. Concern with the urban environment also led her to preserve open spaces for public use, to fight against smoke pollution, and to assist in the establishment of the National Trust.

BORN: December 3, 1838; Wisbech, Cambridgeshire, England
DIED: August 13, 1912; London, England
AREA OF ACHIEVEMENT: Social reform

EARLY LIFE

Octavia Hill was the eighth of the ten daughters of James Hill and the third of five daughters of Caroline Southwood Smith, James Hill's third wife. She was born shortly before her father entered into a bankruptcy and despondency that necessitated the division of the family. The children of the first two marriages were shipped off to maternal grandfathers, but the third Mrs. Hill, with the help of her father, Dr. Thomas Southwood Smith, an important sanitary reformer, managed to keep her five daughters together.

Hill thus grew up without brothers, while her weak and bewildered father hovered ineffectually in the background. Hill's mother was left with responsibility for the large contingent of daughters and Hill herself, obviously the most competent of the brood, rapidly became their recognized leader, as their mother necessarily busied herself with earning the cash required to keep the family going. Hill, then, functioning from an early age in an essentially all-female household, became accustomed to exercising leadership. This youthful experience, foreign to most Victorian women, was the source of her strength. Physically, Hill was short, in later life even dumpy, but her broad shoulders and massive head reinforced the power of her personality.

The family's unsettled finances resulted in frequent uprooting during Hill's childhood, and Hill lived in a succession of villages implanted in the fields on the outer fringes of London. Hill received no formal schooling but, mastering reading and writing before she was five, was educated by her mother, by interaction with her sisters, and through her own voracious reading. In consequence of her mother's connection with Frederick Denison Maurice's Christian Socialist movement, Hill at the age of fourteen was put in charge of a workshop where Ragged School girls made toy furniture.

Hill used her burgeoning artistic talents to design the furniture; she was also responsible for the management of the girls, some of them older than she, and for the operation's finances. From her experience at the workshop, Hill learned for the first time about living conditions for the poor in London. During the same period, she made the acquaintance of John Ruskin, the art critic, who visited the workshop and supplied advice on color. The connection with Ruskin led to lessons in art with Hill copying paintings at the public museums under Ruskin's direction. By 1862, the sisters had established a girls' school in Nottingham Place, Marylebone, in north-central London, where Hill shared in the teaching tasks.

LIFE'S WORK

In time, Ruskin became convinced that Hill did not have real artistic talent. While that realization was taking hold, Hill's experience in Marylebone turned her mind to serious consideration of the social problems arising from wretched inner-city housing. Ruskin and Hill, in a fruitful meeting of minds, determined to establish Hill as a landlord, purchasing a few working-class houses with Ruskin's money and utilizing Hill's managerial talent. Three houses, virtually slums, the first of many, were acquired in Paradise Place, Marylebone, in 1864. The plan was to improve the working-

class tenants by improving their living environment. The houses were cleaned, repaired, and painted, and their surroundings were spruced up, all the work being done under Hill's close supervision and much of it at first by her personally. Tenants were assured that a certain percentage of their rent money would be spent on the buildings, on repairs if necessary, but on improvements if tenants cared for their own quarters in such a way as to obviate the need for repairs. It was hoped and expected that tenants in more pleasant houses would become themselves more civilized, more sober, and more productive members of society.

An important part of the scheme was to become acquainted with the tenants as individuals—to convert the weekly calls for the collection of rent into social occasions at which the rent collectors, first Hill in person, and later one of the many young ladies she mobilized to help in the work, would meet the tenant's family over tea, offer advice and friendship, and treat them as respected hu-

Octavia Hill. (The Granger Collection, New York)

man beings. Tenants' parties and country outings conducted by Hill supplemented the rent collection visits as part of the effort to establish friendly guidance for the tenants. Tenants who fell behind on the rent were, after suitable grace periods, evicted. Hill was convinced that there was good in most people, but not in all. She was willing to abandon those who did not live by her rules, which she assumed were the rules of respectable society.

An annual report, entitled "Letters to My Fellow Workers," which Hill first issued in 1871, supplied a means of communication for Hill to her ever-widening circle of assistants and trainees. The work was not totally philanthropic. The houses were expected to produce a small income, both in order to protect the tenants from any feeling that they were relying on charity, and to demonstrate to other landlords that money could be made from decently maintained dwellings. By the early 1880's, properties managed under the Hill system housed 378 families, or about two thousand individuals. These numbers increased substantially during the mid-1880's when she became the agent for the Ecclesiastical Commission's properties in south London. Even with the great expansion of her work, her interest always lay in the rehabilitation of small preexisting dwellings, not in the construction by charity or public money of vast new and, she thought, dehumanizing housing projects.

In 1877, by which time she was already well known for her work in housing, Hill was forced to face unambiguously the choice between career and marriage that in a less obvious manner confronted many other Victorian women. In that year, she became engaged to Edward Bond, a colleague in housing work. Nevertheless, it soon became clear that Bond's widowed mother did not want to give up her son. For Hill, it was not an attractive proposition to abandon public activity for a role as a dutiful and reclusive wife in a household dominated by a mother-in-law. Hill chose to continue her career. The engagement was canceled, but the strain of the decision led to a severe nervous breakdown. Hill withdrew from her work for two years to recuperate by traveling on the Continent with a new companion, Harriot Yorke, chosen by her friends to watch over her. Yorke stayed with Hill throughout the rest of Hill's life, being her chief of staff, best friend, and personal companion.

Hill's work with her tenants led directly to her second area of activity, her concern with issues of conservation and preservation encompassed at the time by the word "amenity." Swiss Cottage Fields, an undeveloped area where Hill had played as a child and where she often took her Marylebone tenants on outings, was in 1873 carved up into streets and house lots. In an unsuccessful fight against its urbanization, Hill was introduced to the Commons Preservation Society and became acquainted with its solicitor, Robert Hunter. Her connections with both were immensely important in her subsequent work.

Shortly after the failure at Swiss Cottage, one of Hill's sisters, Miranda, urged the establishment of a society to introduce beauty into the lives of the poor. Hill, seizing upon the idea, founded in 1875 the Kyrle Society, named for John Kyrle, who had, through his personal endeavors, as celebrated by Alexander Pope, beautified his own surroundings. Hill's new society sought to bring to the people of the London slums beauty in all of its forms: in small gardens and green spaces, in freshly cut wildflowers, in works of art liberated from intimidating museums, in bright paint splashed on dull gray walls, in great literature, in choral music. Hill sought in Kyrle, as in her housing activity, close personal involvement with the poor.

Of the greatest public importance was Kyrle's Open Spaces Division, which supplied the organizational structure enabling Hill to begin her efforts for the preservation of open spaces near London. Hill, working sometimes in coordination with the Commons Preservation Society, raised money to prevent building at Hilly Fields, Parliament Hill, Vauxhall Park, and other areas in the metropolis. In concert with the Metropolitan Public Gardens Association, Kyrle's Open Spaces Division acquired rights over disused burial grounds in central London, redesigning them as small open air sitting rooms for the neighborhood. Similar Kyrle Societies came into existence at Birmingham, Bristol, Nottingham, Leicester, and Liverpool.

In 1895, Hill and Hunter, reinforced by Canon Hardwicke Rawnsley, an acquaintance from early years in inner London social work, founded the best known of the Victorian environmental organizations, the National Trust. The trust was designed to protect buildings or areas of natural beauty or historic interest by buying or otherwise acquiring title to them. It focused originally on saving ancient monuments, medieval buildings, ocean cliffs, and pleasant south-of-England hilltops. Hill took no formal office in the National Trust but attended its committee meetings regularly, actively solicited and explored projected National Trust properties, and raised money through numerous contacts within her oft-exploited personal network.

Hill's interest in housing also led her to become closely involved with the movement for smoke abatement. She organized a Smoke Abatement Exhibition during the winter of 1881-1882, where 116,000 people examined devices designed to burn fuel more cleanly and efficiently so as to reduce smoke while, incidentally, saving money. The exhibition's manifest success led to the establishment of the National Smoke Abatement Institution, which in turn inspired the foundation in 1898 of the Coal Smoke Abatement Society.

Indicative of Hill's reputation as an expert on social issues was her inclusion among the members of the Royal Commission on the Aged Poor, in 1893 and 1894, and on the Royal Commission on the Poor Laws, of 1905 to 1909. As an active proponent of the doctrine of the Charity Organization Society, with which she had worked since the late 1860's, Hill on both commissions supported the role of private initiative and the free economy as against suggestions for active state involvement, clashing against Beatrice Webb's socialistic views on the latter of the two commissions. Hill died on August 13, 1912, at the home on Marylebone Road, London, which she and Yorke had shared during the last twenty-one years of her life.

SIGNIFICANCE

Octavia Hill was best known to her contemporaries for her work in housing, although her approach appears to later twentieth century observers as distastefully patronizing to the tenants. It has left no mark on housing policies of late twentieth century England. Hill's labor-intensive system could offer shelter to only a minute percentage of the vast and increasing London lower classes. Hill herself pointed out in 1875 that the twenty-six thousand people housed through various philanthropic schemes in the preceding thirty years represented about six months' increase in London's population. It has been argued that the public attention that became focused on Hill's endeavors actually delayed any effective overall attack on the problem of housing of the London poor.

More significant for the future was Hill's lesser-known work in conservation and preservation. Many London open spaces were protected from urban development by the fund-raising efforts of Hill and her Kyrle Society. Although Kyrle died with Hill, her well-publicized successes helped encourage other private groups and, eventually, the state, to pursue similar objectives. The National Trust survives and prospers as a major civilizing element in contemporary England. Concentrating on acquisition and preservation of many of the great English country houses and on protecting the remaining unspoiled segments of the English coastline, the National

Trust has become the third largest landowner in England and one of the country's most visible voluntary agencies.

Hill's work in smoke abatement encouraged establishment of the Coal Smoke Abatement Society in 1898. A lineal descendant of that society was active in passage of mid-twentieth century legislation that at long last effectively dealt with smoke pollution in Britain. When during the 1960's there came a great surge of interest in environmental protection, Hill's status as a significant and constructive environmental pioneer became recognized.

—John Ranlett

FURTHER READING

Bell, E. Moberly. *Octavia Hill*. London: Constable, 1942. The standard biography, although imprecise in documentation and generally uncritical.

Boyd, Nancy. *Three Victorian Women Who Changed Their World: Josephine Butler, Octavia Hill, Florence Nightingale*. New York: Oxford University Press, 1982. Section 2 sketches Hill's career as an introduction to an examination of its religious and moral motivation.

Hill, Octavia. *Octavia Hill and the Social Housing Debate: Essays and Letters by Octavia Hill*. Edited by Robert Whalen. London: IEA Health and Welfare Unit, 1998. Whalen has edited this collection of Hill's letters, lectures, and other writings about housing issues, including some documents that have never before been published.

Hill, William Thomson. *Octavia Hill: Pioneer of the National Trust and Housing Reformer*. London: Hutchinson, 1956. Readable and uncritical; goes beyond Bell primarily in reference to Hill's environmental work.

Liebman, George W. *Six Lost Leaders: Prophets of Civil Society*. Lanham, Md.: Lexington Books, 2001. Hill's efforts to improve housing are included in this examination of six people who believed their individual efforts could improve social conditions.

Maurice, C. Edmund. *Life of Octavia Hill as Told in Her Letters*. London: Macmillan, 1914. The authorized biography, by Hill's brother-in-law, based largely on her letters, many of which are quoted at length. Detailed, but reticent on personal matters.

Owen, David. *English Philanthropy, 1660-1960*. Cambridge, Mass.: Harvard University Press, 1964. Treats its massive topic with grace and penetrating insight. Owen describes Hill's work in housing and in open spaces preservation with understanding while fitting it into its wider contexts.

Ranlett, John. "'Checking Nature's Desecration': Late-Victorian Environmental Organization." *Victorian Studies* 26 (Winter, 1983): 197-222. An overview of the organization of the late-Victorian environmental movement, emphasizing the network of personal connections that linked the various volunteer societies and identifying Hill's position in that network.

Wohl, Anthony S. *The Eternal Slum: Housing and Social Policy in Victorian London*. Montreal: McGill-Queen's University Press, 1977. A comprehensive discussion of lower-class housing and of a variety of private and public efforts for its regulation and improvement. Wohl finds Hill's contribution important but not altogether admirable.

SEE ALSO: Josephine Butler; Frederick Denison Maurice; Florence Nightingale; John Ruskin.

RELATED ARTICLES in *Great Events from History: The Nineteenth Century, 1801-1900:* 1864: Hill Launches Housing Reform in London; September 18, 1889: Addams Opens Chicago's Hull-House.

HIROSHIGE
Japanese poet

Famed for his poetic landscapes, Hiroshige was one of the last masters of the ukiyo-e *woodblock prints in Japan and is permanently inextricably linked with an artist named Hokusai in historical reputation.*

BORN: 1797; Edo (now Tokyo), Japan
DIED: October 12, 1858; Edo (now Tokyo), Japan
ALSO KNOWN AS: Ichiyūsai Hiroshige; Andō Hiroshige (full name); Ryusai; Utagawa Hiroshige; Andō Tokutarō (birth name)
AREA OF ACHIEVEMENT: Art

EARLY LIFE

Andō Hiroshige (hihr-oh-shee-gay) was born Andō Tokutarō. His father, Andō Gen'emon, was an official of the fire department attached to Edo Castle. Hiroshige's talent for drawing surfaced early; even as a child, he showed an interest in art. First he studied with Okajima Rinsai, a painter and also a fireman, who had been trained in the traditional Kano school of classical Chinese academic painting. Hiroshige's mother died when he was twelve years old, and when his father resigned shortly thereafter, Hiroshige was obliged to assume the hereditary duties. Attempting to study with the popular Utagawa Toyokuni, he was turned down; persevering, he managed, however, when he was fourteen, to be accepted as a pupil of the less popular Utagawa Toyohiro.

The following year, Hiroshige was allowed to use the name "Utagawa Hiroshige," a sign of his promise as an artist. Despite this honor, Hiroshige did not publish until 1818, when book illustrations with the signature Ichiyūsai Hiroshige appeared. When Hiroshige was thirty-one, his master died, but Hiroshige did not take over his name or his studio, as would have been customary for the best pupil to do. About this time, he called himself "Ichiyūsai," then dropped the first character and signed himself simply "Ryusai."

Art historians sometimes divide Hiroshige's artistic career into three stages. In his student days, from 1811 to 1830, he spent his time learning from his predecessors, working on the figure prints of actors and warriors, and, in his mid-twenties, on figure prints of beautiful women. Lessons with Ōoka Umpō taught Hiroshige the Chinese-influenced Nanga style of painting, with its use of calligraphy in depicting landscape. From the Shijō style of painting, Hiroshige learned the art of using ink washes in paintings for a softer effect. His master, Toyohiro, passed on the Western technique of the single-point perspective, which he himself had learned from his teacher, Toyoharu. Hiroshige's early, limited success came from his representation of flowers and birds, sometimes with his own accompanying poem. Prints of these are rarer than his landscapes and are much treasured.

LIFE'S WORK

Hiroshige's early work featured sketches of warriors, courtesans, actors, and other subjects typical of *ukiyo-e*, the art form that resulted from the political and geographical shift of power from Kyoto, the old capital, to Edo. By the time Hiroshige was born, Edo, a relatively new capital established by the Tokugawa shogunate, had turned into a populous city with more than one million inhabitants. Because of the complexity of the caste system then prevailing, the change in the capital of the country led to a series of other complex artistic, social, and commercial changes that defined the art form Hiroshige was to master so successfully.

The main patrons of the arts in the old capital of Kyoto, the wealthy merchants called *machischū*, refused to be lured by the economic possibilities offered by the new capital, leaving the path open for merchants of a lower class (*chōnin*) to profit from Edo's position as the commercial capital of Japan. Though now successful economically, the lower-class merchants still had no social clout. In search of entertainment, they would seek out the pleasure districts that sprang up outside the city limits and allowed members of different classes to mingle. This "floating world" was composed of the world of the highly trained and respected courtesans in the pleasure districts, and the art form that evolved to record their activities was the *ukiyo-e* woodblock print.

Although the staple subject of the *ukiyo-e* print was the varying fashions in hair, dress, customs, and manners of the evanescent world of the pleasure districts, the

View of Edo with Cat, 1857. Woodblock print by Hiroshige. (The Granger Collection, New York)

landscapes of which Hiroshige became a skilled master had always been traditional in Japanese painting, if only as background for the figures in *ukiyo-e* prints.

In the second and most productive stage of his career, from about 1830 to 1844, Hiroshige left the competitive field of figure designs and concentrated on landscapes. His most famous and finest series seemed to be a result of a journey he took around 1832, directly connected to his family tenure. The shogun in Edo, the real seat of power, annually presented horses from his stables to the emperor, secluded in Kyoto. As a minor official of the shogunate, Hiroshige joined the expedition so as to Kyoto to paint the ceremony of the presentation for the shogun. During the journey, he made several sketches of the Tōkaidō, as the main highway between Edo and Kyoto was called.

These sketches were the basis of the first *Tōkaidō Gojūsantsugi* (fifty-three stations of the Tōkaidō), a collection of fifty-five scenes consisting of the fifty-three stations on the highway and one each in Kyoto and Nihonbashi, the beginning and ending of the road. Published separately at first, the complete series was issued as a set in 1834. It brought Hiroshige immediate and enduring fame and success. Over the course of the next twenty-five years, in response to popular demand, Hiroshige designed some twenty additional sets of these views of the Tōkaidō.

Hiroshige's prints were so popular that some of his designs had runs of ten thousand, and he was kept so busy producing a series of prints on Edo, the suburbs, Lake Biwa at Otsu, and Kyoto that he was seldom present to direct the reproduction of his designs. Greedy publishers were responsible for turning out inferior copies of his designs in their haste to cash in on their popularity, and Hiroshige himself was not consistently good.

The first Tōkaidō series is considered the most original of his landscape series. What distinguished Hiroshige's vision of the highway were his personal and direct reactions to what he saw. Though inspired by the landscape, Hiroshige adapted freely; he changed the seasons or the time of day or added nonexistent features if his sense of composition required it. Unlike the famous Hokusai, Hiroshige was interested in the human drama around him, not merely in the possibility of the design. Thus, his prints are praised for their humorous point of view, their warmth and compassion, and their close observation of the changing atmospheric conditions, their poetic sensitivity to the relationship between humans and nature. He is even referred to as master of rain, mist, snow, and wind.

In the third stage of his career, from around 1844 to his death in 1858, Hiroshige became more interested in depicting figures in his landscapes. He worked in collaboration with Utagawa Kunisada, a figure print designer, and Utagawa Kuniyoshi, a designer of historical prints, to produce another Tōkaidō series jointly. Kunisada added the figures to Hiroshige's landscapes; the two also produced several other series. *Meisho Edo Hyakkei* (1856-1858; one hundred views of Edo), which Hiroshige produced at the age of sixty, is particularly remarkable for the interesting points of view and the placement of the figures in the landscape.

By this time, Commodore Matthew Perry and the U.S. fleet had intruded upon the closed Japanese society. Japan's opening its market to world trade brought the end of the feudal Tokugawa era and the way of life reflected in the *ukiyo-e* prints. With the passing of Hiroshige, who probably died in the great cholera epidemic in 1858, went the world he had recorded with such wit and warmth.

Because popular artists were not deemed worthy of official records, relatively little is known of Hiroshige's personal life. Such skimpy details as are known suggest a life of personal sorrows. Not only was Hiroshige orphaned as a teenager, but his family also had to be rebuilt. He was married twice, once to Tatsu, the widow of a samurai, by whom he had one son, Nakajiro; his wife died in 1840, his son in 1845. Hiroshige's second wife, Yasu, was twenty years younger. His small government pension kept Hiroshige from starving, but he was hardly ever a wealthy man.

Despite these personal setbacks, Hiroshige was a fun-loving man who was enormously productive as an artist. It is estimated, for example, that Hiroshige designed eight thousand woodcuts and that more than forty publishers were involved in publishing his designs. He was also enormously popular in his day, once receiving a commission from thirty innkeepers who wanted prints of their winehouses to present as souvenirs to their guests.

SIGNIFICANCE

The last major figure in the development of *ukiyo-e*, Hiroshige is inextricably linked with Hokusai in historical reputation. Hiroshige was the more melancholy, romantic, and poetic artist, but like most of the great Edo masters of the woodblock print who came from middle-class artisan families, his work, intended for and appealing primarily to bourgeois circles, was not considered fine art until Western artists, particularly the Impressionists, discovered and glorified the woodblock print. The

prints of Hokusai and Hiroshige, the last of the masters, were at the time still readily obtainable. The roster of great Western artists influenced by them includes James Whistler, Paul Cézanne, Henri de Toulouse-Lautrec, Paul Gauguin, and Vincent van Gogh.

James Michener, while criticizing Hiroshige for his weak designs, his undistinguished drawing, and his lack of focus, accords him the rare talent of an "honest, clean eye." Though many of the Hiroshige prints available are the late copies that do not convey his subtlety, he is probably the most accessible of the *ukiyo-e* artists because, in Michener's words, Hiroshige's inspired eye "can teach an entire nation, or even a substantial segment of the world, to see."

—*Shakuntala Jayaswal*

FURTHER READING

Addiss, Stephen, ed. *Tōkaidō, Adventures on the Road in Old Japan*. Lawrence, Kans.: Spencer Museum of Art, 1980. A collection of essays about the Tōkaidō, including chapters on Hiroshige's humor and his Tōkaidō prints in the context of traditional Japanese painting.

Andō, Hiroshige. *The Fifty-three Stages of Tōkaidō*. Edited by Ichitaro Kondo. English adaptation by Charles S. Terry. Tokyo, Japan: Nippon Express, 1960. A brief introduction to Hiroshige's most popular series. Each print is accompanied by text in English and Japanese.

_____. *Hiroshige*. Edited by Walter Exner. London: Methuen, 1960. An oversized book, with large-print text and color plates throughout. Contains a general introduction to the life and work of Hiroshige, written by the son of the Viennese art dealer who collected Hiroshige's work.

_____. *The Sketchbooks of Hiroshige*. Introduction and commentaries on the plates by Sherman E. Lee. Foreword by Daniel J. Boorstin. 2d ed. New York: George Braziller, 2001. Features reproductions of Hiroshige's sketches that were drawn as he traveled in Japan around 1840.

Faulkner, Rupert. *Hiroshige Fan Prints*. London: V & A, 2001. Contains full-color reproductions of the 126 Hiroshige fan prints owned by London's Victoria and Albert Museum and comments about each print.

Jansen, Marije. *Hiroshige's Journey in the Sixty-Odd Provinces*. Amsterdam: Hotei, 2004. Contains color reproductions of this series of Hiroshige woodblock prints, with a detailed description of each print and notes on variations evident in the different paintings.

Lane, Richard. *Images from the Floating World: The Japanese Print*. New York: G. P. Putnam's Sons, 1978. Provides historical background, tracing the rise of *ukiyo-e* through the seventeenth and eighteenth centuries. Contains color photographs, a bibliography, an index, and an illustrated dictionary of *ukiyo-e*.

Michener, James A. *The Floating World*. New York: Random House, 1954. Traces the life and death of the art known as *ukiyo-e* through the individual artists who practiced it. Contains sixty-five prints, a chronological table, brief biographies, a bibliography, and an index.

Narazaki, Muneshige. *Studies in Nature: Hokusai-Hiroshige*. Translated by John Bester. Tokyo, Japan: Kodansha International, 1970. Focuses on the achievements of these two artists in the depiction of flowers and birds, with a brief introduction to the development of the genre.

Whitford, Frank. *Japanese Prints and Western Painters*. New York: Macmillan, 1977. Discusses the influence of Japanese woodblock prints on European painting in the nineteenth century. Contains a chronology, a glossary, a bibliography, an index, and color plates.

SEE ALSO: Paul Cézanne; Paul Gauguin; Vincent van Gogh; Henri de Toulouse-Lautrec.

RELATED ARTICLES in *Great Events from History: The Nineteenth Century, 1801-1900:* 1823-1831: Hokusai Produces *Thirty-Six Views of Mount Fuji*; 1831-1834: Hiroshige Completes *The Tokaido Fifty-Three Stations*.

HO XUAN HUONG

Vietnamese poet

Ho Xuan Huong's clever and technically brilliant erotic poems have assured her a place among Vietnam's finest poets, despite the fact that very little is known about her life.

BORN: c. 1776; near Hanoi, Vietnam
DIED: 1820?; probably Hanoi, Vietnam
AREA OF ACHIEVEMENT: Literature

EARLY LIFE

No public records survive to give birth information on Ho Xuan Huong (ho zoo-ahn hoo-ohng). Most scholars estimate that she was born around 1776 near the northern Vietnamese capital of Thanh Long in a place that is now part of Hanoi—the modern name for Thanh Long. There is also a general consensus among scholars that she was born into the aristocratic Ho family of Vietnam's northern Nghe An province. Many historians believe that her father was Ho Phi Dien, who died in 1786. However, because her father was a scholar, some historians suggest that the man was actually Ho Si Danh, who died in 1783. In either case, Xuan Huong's father was in his seventies when she was born. Ho's mother, known only by her given name, Ha, was a high-ranking second wife, or concubine, to Ho's father. Some historians also believe that Ho Xuan Huong was related to the Tay Son rebels of central Vietnam. In 1788, their leader, Nguyen Hue, proclaimed himself Emperor Quang Trung. It is possible that Xuan Huong was his cousin.

Ho Xuan Huong's father decided to give her a classical education, allowing her to learn to read and to write. Tragedy struck the family when Xuan Huong was between seven and ten years old and her father died. To support herself and her daughter, her mother became the concubine of another man. It is likely that she herself taught Xuan Huong, who proved extraordinarily intelligent and poetically gifted.

Based on one of her later poems, some historians have argued that Ho Xuan Huong had somewhat dark skin, perhaps with small scars similar to those of a jackfruit, to which she seems to compare herself in her poem "The Jackfruit." She appears to have been tall and energetic, and her poetic brilliance quickly distinguished her.

LIFE'S WORK

The Tay Son rebellion changed life in Thanh Long while Ho was growing up. In December, 1788, Chinese forces invaded and conquered the capital before being decisively defeated by Emperor Quang Trung during the Tet festival of 1789. Ho's poem "At the Chinese General's Tomb" derisively challenges the valor of the invaders and pointedly asks if she herself might not have done better had she been a man.

Before Emperor Quang Trung died in 1792, he instituted reforms that affected Ho's poetry. To assert Vietnam's independence, he decreed that all official correspondence should be written not in Chinese, but in

Nom, a Vietnamese writing system invented during the tenth century. Nom uses Chinese characters to express spoken Vietnamese phonetically as well as some Chinese words. It was used among the Vietnamese elite until the 1920's, when a new national script that employs the Roman alphabet became the standard for written Vietnamese.

Ho Xuan Huong's brilliance in writing poetry in Nom brought her immediate fame as a poet in the new society. As a young woman, she lived in western Thanh Long. According to some sources, she opened a tea shop near the Tran Quoc Pagoda overlooking West Lake that features in one of her poems. There she exchanged poetry and engaged in intellectual literary discourse with the male students and scholars who frequented her shop along the route they followed to take the imperial exams in the capital. Because Quang Trung had ordered that the third part of these exams must require compositions in verse and rhymed prose written in Nom, Ho's advice, poetry, and intellectual banter became much valued by the people who patronized her tea shop.

Ho Xuan Huong soon became part of a vibrant intellectual scene, and her poetry became famous for its technical brilliance and its daring use of erotic double entendre. In a society that officially frowned upon erotic expression and female literary creation and intellectual accomplishments, Ho boldly stood out and continued to assert herself. One reason why she could continue writing and disseminating her widely popular poetry came from its sheer literary force. Using the prestigious, centuries-long tradition of the Chinese *lu-shih* poetry, she invigorated the form with her use of genuine Vietnamese terms and images, most of which have double erotic meanings.

Some of Ho's most famous poems describe dramatic vistas of northern Vietnamese landscapes that she probably visited herself. Her poems "Three-Mountain Pass" and "Viewing Cac-Co Cavern" ostensibly describe a natural landscape of rocks, caverns, trees, and a little stream, but quickly turn into erotic images for human anatomy. Some of her other celebrated poems were highly personal. For example, she decried the patriarchal nature of her society that made women into concubines and generally suppressed women and their sexual desires. She also took issue with the hypocrisy of the Buddhist clergy in

---

"THE JACKFRUIT"

This poem is believed to reveal some clues about Ho Xuan Huong's physical appearance. The jackfruit grows on a tree native to wetlands in tropical Asia that is related to the better-known breadfruit tree. Individual fruits on the tree turn brown as they ripen and can weigh as much as forty pounds at maturity.

> I am like a jackfruit on the tree.
> To taste you must plug me quick, while fresh:
> The skin rough, the pulp thick, yes,
> But oh, I warn you against touching—
> The rich juice will gush and stain your hands.

Source: Translation by Nguyen Ngoc Bich. Electronic text from PoemHunter.com. Accessed on September 20, 2005.

---

poems such as "The Lustful Monk," about a Buddhist monk failing in his vows of celibacy, and a "Buddhist Nun," about a nun struggling to remain chaste. At the same time, many of Ho's poems joyfully embrace desire and mutual fulfillment, thinly camouflaging their content with natural images or popular metaphors.

Because Ho's family situation, she accepted that she herself would have to settle for being a man's second wife or concubine. According to some sources, she met her first husband at her tea shop. Impressed by his poetic skills, she married him. In her "Lament for the Prefect of Vinh-Tuong"—using her husband's official title—she expressed her sorrow that their happy life together lasted only twenty-seven months before he died.

Much of Ho's poetry asserts her longing for physical and spiritual love. After her first husband died, she became the concubine of another man. However, she mocked her second husband as a toad in her funeral lament for him. The poem begins traditionally but ends savagely, describing her dead husband as a man who was rich but stupid and had only a sexual interest in her. It is not certain who her second husband was. He may have been her last husband on record, Tran Phuc Hien, a governor who was executed for bribery in 1819. The proceedings against him stated that Ho Xuan Huong was his concubine. Those proceedings are the last historical record of Ho while she was alive.

As with her birth, details of Ho's death are not certain. Most historians argue that she died around 1820. A poem written in 1842 by a brother of the reigning emperor mentions a visit to her grave by a royal prince. However, nothing is known about the exact circumstances of the event, the date of her death, or even if she had any children.

SIGNIFICANCE

Even though Ho Xuan Huong's poems were widely popular, because their erotic content violated Confucian decorum they were not published during her lifetime. In 1909, a first woodblock publication appeared in Nom; it could be read by the cultural elite. In 1914, the Nom texts were printed in the collection *Quoc Âm Thi Tuyen* (selection with the competing national writing styles) along with transliterations into the romanized national script. Her work became widely known and often secretly admired in Vietnam.

Ho Xuan Huong's eroticism, her iconoclasm, and critique of patriarchy and religion gave unique force to her poetry, but official Vietnamese literary society remained ambiguous toward her achievements. A few of her poems that were not overtly erotic were taught in Vietnamese literature classes during the twentieth century. Her poem "The Floating Cake" was taught for its expression of nationalist sentiments, and its erotic allusions to the female body were ignored. In 1980, Ho was officially recognized in her home country when the Institute of Literature of Vietnam proudly included her in its official literary history. In the Western world, the French were the first to appreciate Ho Xuan Huong but sometimes claimed to be shocked by her. Marcel Durand published her work in French in 1968. In English, there were only occasional scholarly translations until the pioneering work of John Balaban in 2000.

By the early twenty-first century, it was generally recognized that Ho Xuan Huong's mastery of Nom made her poetry a key to Vietnamese and Vietnamese American attempts to save knowledge of that early writing form. The popularity of Ho's poetry gave fresh impetus to the efforts of a committed community of scholars to keep alive knowledge of the Nom script. Without a knowledge of Nom, several centuries of Vietnamese prose and poetry would be lost to posterity. To modern readers, Ho Xuan Huong's poetry remains fresh and engaging.

—R. C. Lutz

FURTHER READING

Balaban, John. *Spring Essence: The Poetry of Ho Xuan Huong*. Port Townsend, Wash.: Copper Canyon Press, 2000. Excellent introduction to the life and legend of Ho Xuan Huong. Her major poems are translated into English by Balaban, with the original Nom text as well as a modern Vietnamese text given for each poem.

Chapuis, Oscar. *A History of Vietnam*. Westport, Conn.: Greenwood Press, 1995. Chapter 6 of this book briefly discusses Ho Xuan Huong as the major woman Vietnamese poet to flourish during the Tay Son era. Discusses the Nom script of Vietnamese she used for her poetry; provides a historical framework for her life and times.

My-Van, Tran. "Come on Girls, Let's Go Bail Water: Eroticism in Ho Xuan Huong's Vietnamese Poetry." *Journal of Southeast Asian Studies* 33, no. 3 (October, 2002): 471-494. Thorough and appreciative discussion of Ho Xuan Huong's work, her life, her society, and her reputation among modern Vietnamese.

SEE ALSO: Gia Long; Tadano Makuzu; Tu Duc.
RELATED ARTICLE in *Great Events from History: The Nineteenth Century, 1801-1900:* August, 1858: France and Spain Invade Vietnam.

JOHN PHILIP HOLLAND
Irish-born American inventor

Holland was not the first person to build workable submarines, but he was the first to develop and manufacture submarines capable of traveling long distances under water, and his innovations fundamentally altered the future of naval warfare.

BORN: February 29, 1841; Liscannor, County Clare, Ireland
DIED: August 12, 1914; Newark, New Jersey
AREA OF ACHIEVEMENT: Engineering

EARLY LIFE

John Philip Holland was the second of four sons of John Holland and Mary Scanlon Holland. Although his father's living as a member of the British Coast Guard was secure, Holland witnessed the Irish famine years, an experience that left him with a lifelong anti-British resentment. Holland attended Saint MaCreehy's National School in Liscannor, where he learned English (the language of his home was Gaelic), and later went to the Christian Brothers secondary school at Ennistomy. After Holland's father died, the family moved to Limerick in 1853, where Holland entered the monastery school. On June 15, 1853, he took the initial vows, joining the Teaching Order of the Irish Christian Brothers. After a brief novitiate, he was sent to teach at the North Monastery in Cork, where he was significantly influenced by Brother James Dominick Burke, a talented science teacher credited with founding vocational education in Ireland.

In 1860, ill health interrupted Holland's teaching career for two years, during which time he first became interested in submarines and the mechanics of flight. He was subsequently assigned to a series of teaching positions at Maryborough (Portaloise), Enniscorty, Drogheda, and Dundalk. At Dundalk he experimented with a clockwork submarine model and prepared plans and sketches for a one-man iron submarine.

Holland's brother, who was deeply involved in recurrent nationalistic uprisings, was forced to leave Ireland with his mother in 1872. Shortly thereafter, on May 26, 1873, alone and in poor health, Holland withdrew from the Christian Brothers and followed his family to the United States.

LIFE'S WORK

Shortly after arriving in Boston, Massachusetts, in November, 1873, Holland slipped and fell on an icy street, suffering a broken leg and a slight concussion. While confined to his room during recovery, he completed another submarine design. For the next two years, however, Holland worked as a lay teacher in St. John's Parochial School in Paterson, New Jersey.

In February, 1875, perhaps urged by a pupil's father who was a friend of the secretary of the Navy, Holland sent his submarine plans to the Navy. Although his description of a fifteen-foot, treadle-driven, one-man boat was included in a lecture on submarines at the Naval Torpedo Station in Newport, Rhode Island, the Navy rejected his submarine as impractical. Undiscouraged, Holland continued brainstorming with an engineer named William Dunkerly.

In mid-1876, Holland's brother Michael introduced Holland to Jeremiah O'Donovan Rossa, a member of the Fenian Order, a secret society of Irish revolutionaries. Rossa then introduced Holland to Jerome Collins, founder of the Clan-na-Gael (the United Order), a Fenian "umbrella" group. Later in 1876, Holland met John Devoy, chairman of the Fenian Executive Committee, and John J. Breslin (alias James Collins). Convinced of the practicality of Holland's submarine as a weapon against the British Royal Navy, the Skirmishing Fund of the Clan-na-Gael allocated $5,000 to construct Holland's first full-scale submarine, the *Holland No. 1.*

The 2.25-ton boat was launched on May 22, 1878, and promptly sank. The boat was easily raised and underwent several days of tinkering. On June 6, Holland successfully dived and cruised a short distance. After several more dives, the longest lasting for one hour, the *Holland No. 1* was dismantled and sunk. In the process, Holland demonstrated the need for a constant reserve buoyancy and a low, fixed center of gravity to ensure lateral and longitudinal stability. He also proved the superiority of hydroplanes located at the stern and the practicality of an internal combustion engine for propulsion.

The trustees of the Skirmishing Fund then ordered a larger boat that was fully armed and capable of breaking an enemy blockade. With this order, Holland's teaching career ended, and he embarked on his life's work as an inventor, engineer, and promoter. Supported by the Fenians, Holland designed a three-man, 31-foot operational submarine. He engaged the Delamater Iron Works of New York to build the vessel, and work began on May 3, 1879. In spite of the continual argument and skepticism of the workers and staff of the iron works, the boat was

John Philip Holland. (Library of Congress)

launched on May 1, 1881, at an estimated cost of about $60,000. While the submarine was under construction, Swedish, Russian, Italian, German, and Turkish observers visited the yard; the Turks subsequently offered Holland a contract for a boat of their own.

The 31-foot *Fenian Ram* displaced 19 tons and was driven by a Brayton internal combustion engine rated at about 15 to 17 horsepower. The surface speed was 9 knots, and Holland believed the ship's submerged speed was probably about the same. (This was not an unlikely assumption because the ship was hydrodynamically clean, and similarly shaped nuclear submarines are faster submerged than on the surface.) In tests between May and November, 1883, the *Fenian Ram* submerged to 60 feet for one full hour. Holland also built a third submarine, the 16-foot *Fenian Model*, for testing modifications of the basic design. While Holland worked, the Fenians fell into dissension, and one faction "stole" both submarines. They sank the *Fenian Model* on their way to New Haven, Connecticut, and were incapable of operating the *Fenian Ram* after their arrival. Holland severed his association with them.

Holland later met William W. Kimball of the United States Navy, who introduced him to Edmund L. Zalinski, an artillery expert. Both of these men furthered Holland's plans. Kimball unsuccessfully sought a naval position for Holland, so the inventor went to work for Zalinski's Pneumatic Gun Company. Kimball and Zalinski then organized the Nautilus Submarine Boat Company to build Holland's fourth submarine. The 50-foot *Zalinski Boat*, constructed at Fort Lafayette during 1884, had a steel-framed wooden hull. Its centralized control station was a major innovation: The depth gauges, levers operating the flood valves, diving plane controls, steering lever, and throttle were all accessible to the operator's platform below the conning tower. An unsuccessful attempt to design a modified camera lucida for underwater visibility proved that underwater steering by direct vision was impracticable. The submarine was badly damaged during launch and made only a few trial runs. It was dismantled, and the Nautilus Submarine Boat Company was liquidated in 1886.

On January 15, 1887, Holland married Margaret Foley of Paterson, New Jersey. They had five children: John, Robert Charles, Joseph Francis, Julia, and Marguerite. Two additional children, John P. and Mary Josephine, died in infancy.

During the next three years, Holland and Charles A. Morris, an engineer who had been converted to Holland's projects during construction of the *Fenian Ram*, entered two Navy competitions for contracts to build a submarine. Both times, 1888 and 1889, their plans won, but problems with the contractor and political maneuvering prevented construction. As a consequence, Holland occupied himself with developing designs for a flying machine and, to support himself, took a job with the Morris and Cummings Dredging Company on May 1, 1890.

Finally, on March 3, 1893, Congress appropriated $200,000 to reopen the submarine competition. Holland and Morris, in association with Elihu B. Frost, a lawyer for the dredging company, organized the John P. Holland Torpedo Boat Company. Frost effectively dominated finances of the business as Holland's stockholdings were less than a controlling interest. All of Holland's patents, inventions, and devices became company property. The company submitted plans for the competition on June 4, 1893. After further political maneuvering, the John P. Holland Torpedo Boat Company finally received a $200,000 contract for construction of the *Plunger*.

In order to meet naval specifications, the 85-foot *Plunger* was powered with two triple-expansion steam engines generating 2,500 horsepower for surface operation and a 70-horsepower electric motor for submerged operation. Another steam engine drove a generator for the bank of storage batteries supplying current to the electric motor. Construction was plagued by the Navy's continual close supervision. Also, the steam power plant was too bulky and generated excessive heat within the hull. As a consequence, Holland promoted construction of a sixth submarine of his own design, with Morris as his superintending engineer.

Construction began in the winter of 1896-1897, and the *Holland VI* was launched May 17, 1897. The first surface run was made February 5, 1898, and the first dive on March 11, 1898. The first successful submerged cruise, however, occurred on March 17, when Holland demonstrated the boat and its dynamite gun before a representative of the Navy Board of Auxiliary Vessels. Although performance specifications set out for the *Plunger* were met, the board called for further modifications and testing. After two years, acceptance trials were completed, and on April 10, 1900, the Navy bought the *Holland VI*. On August 2, 1900, the Navy ordered six more submarines. In addition, England, Japan, and Russia ordered either Holland submarines or plans for them.

Meanwhile, the John P. Holland Torpedo Boat Company was merged with the Electric Boat Company, and Frost and his associates effectively eliminated Holland and Morris from further influence in the company. Naval architects in the Electric Boat Company began building submarines with flat decks that carried guns and other impedimenta contrary to Holland's advocacy of hydrodynamically streamlined hulls.

Holland resigned from the Holland Torpedo Boat Company on March 28, 1904, and on May 18, 1905, organized the Holland Submarine Boat Company to build submarines of his own design. The Electric Boat Company, however, successfully blocked Holland's access to his earlier patents, and his financial backers withdrew. This ended his career as a submarine designer and builder. Despite periodic spells of poor health, he survived to age seventy-three before dying of pneumonia.

SIGNIFICANCE

John Holland was not the first to build submarines: Cornelius van Drebbel attempted a submarine in 1620; during the American Revolution, David Bushnell's *Turtle* (1775) was the first submarine to attack an enemy ship; and during the Civil War, the Confederate *Hunley* (1864) was the first to sink an enemy ship. Holland's innovations, however, resulted in the first submarines capable of successfully attacking surface vessels and, equally important, escaping intact thereafter.

Other contemporaneous experimenters include the American J. H. L. Tuck and his *Peacemaker*; the Swedish manufacturer Thorsten Nordenfeldt, who described his first submarine in 1886 and subsequently built submarines for Greece and Turkey; the French, who built the *Gymnote*, the first submarine accepted by a major naval power in 1888; and other builders active in England, Italy, and Spain. Holland's *Holland VI*, later called the USS *Holland* (SS-1), however, was the first submarine capable of naval warfare. His John P. Holland Torpedo Boat Company, when it merged into the Electric Boat Company, became the principal U.S. submarine builder. Only sixteen years after the USS *Holland* was commissioned, submarines became a major naval weapon during World War I.

—Ralph L. Langenheim, Jr.

FURTHER READING

Cable, Frank T. *The Birth and Development of the American Submarine*. New York: Harper & Brothers, 1924. This book was written by one of Holland's close associates in the early development of the submarine.

Holbrook, S. H. *Lost Men of American History*. New York: Macmillan, 1947. This volume includes an easy-to-read account of Holland's career that will satisfy casual readers.

Hutchinson, Robert. *Jane's Submarines: War Beneath the Waves from 1776 to the Present Day*. London: Harper-Collins, 2001. This history of the submarine includes a ten-page chapter, "The Holland Boats," describing Holland's contributions to submarine development.

Morris, Richard Knowles. *John P. Holland, 1841-1914: Inventor of the Modern Submarine*. Columbia: University of South Carolina Press, 1998. A new edition, with a new title, of the book originally published in 1984. Morris's comprehensive biography covers all aspects of Holland's life. The definitive but uncritical account may be too detailed for the average reader.

Parrish, Thomas. *The Submarine: A History*. New York: Viking Press, 2004. Parrish, a military historian, includes information about Holland's contributions to the submarine's development.

Potter, E. B. *The Naval Illustrated History of the United States Navy*. New York: Galahad, 1971. Potter discusses the development and the tactical and strategic significance of submarines. As the title suggests, the book includes illustrations of the *Holland* and later U.S. Navy submarines.

Rush, C. W., et al. *The Complete Book of Submarines.* Cleveland: World, 1958. The authors provide an illustrated history of submarines from their beginning through the nuclear age. The volume shows Holland's place among his contemporaries and evaluates his significance.

SEE ALSO: Robert Fulton; Jules Verne.
RELATED ARTICLES in *Great Events from History: The Nineteenth Century, 1801-1900:* May 22-June 20, 1819: *Savannah* Is the First Steamship to Cross the Atlantic; January 31, 1858: Brunel Launches the SS *Great Eastern.*

OLIVER WENDELL HOLMES
American physician, poet, and essayist

Holmes was both a doctor and a teacher of medicine who helped pioneer many new medical techniques, including the use of microscopes and anesthesia, and a major poet and essayist whose writings were dominated by wit and inventiveness.

BORN: August 29, 1809; Cambridge, Massachusetts
DIED: October 7, 1894; Boston, Massachusetts
AREAS OF ACHIEVEMENT: Literature, medicine

EARLY LIFE

Oliver Wendell Holmes was born into a kind of New England aristocracy that he later called the Brahmin caste. His home atmosphere was a mixture of solid Puritanism dictated by his father, Abiel Holmes, a Congregationalist minister, and more liberal thought contributed by his mother, Sarah Wendell, the daughter of a successful Boston merchant with high social connections. Holmes received his early education fairly uneventfully in Cambridge, Massachusetts, where his scholasticism was termed average and where he was frequently punished for talking and whispering. This small fact foreshadowed his adult role as one of the premier lecturers, conversationalists, and wits of his day.

Also significant from his childhood years was his fear of being visited by doctors. Of small, frail stature both as a child and as an adult, Holmes also suffered from asthma. The misery brought on by these early doctors' visits may partially account for his lifelong discomfort with private medical practice, attributed to an oversensitivity to the patients' suffering.

Central to his beliefs as an adult were his early childhood revolts against the Puritan religious orthodoxy prevalent in his home and community. Holmes's father, while educated in the strictest Calvinist traditions, was a compassionate man and an occasional writer of poetry who apparently had some difficulty enforcing many of the unforgiving orthodox doctrines among his family. Holmes primarily rebelled against such inhumane religious beliefs as original sin—the idea that even an unbaptized baby who dies in infancy is guilty and unforgiven because of the Fall of Man in the Garden of Eden.

At the age of fifteen, Holmes boarded at Andover School for one year in preparation for his entrance into Harvard. Holmes entered Harvard in 1825 and graduated with the celebrated class of 1829. Upon his graduation, Holmes was not sure what profession to adopt and studied law for one year. Discovering that law was not his calling, he later encouraged his eldest son, who succeeded brilliantly as a U.S. Supreme Court justice, to enter the profession. Holmes then entered medical school, where one of his first-year professors identified Holmes's true spark as a medical man. While at first repelled by hospital wards and operating rooms, in which the use of anesthesia was rare, Holmes quickly became fascinated by anatomy. After two years of medical studies in Boston, Massachusetts, Holmes finished his studies in Paris, France. His choice of medicine as his permanent profession was cemented by these two years in France, where he attended lectures by the greatest and most progressive medical minds of his time.

LIFE'S WORK

During the ten years after Holmes graduated from medical school (1836-1846), he set up private practice in Boston, got married, and fathered three children. Holmes's wife, Amelia Jackson, has been described as his ideal mate. She was industrious and devoted and managed Holmes's affairs in an efficient manner that allowed him to apply himself to his profession and varied interests.

It was also during this period that Holmes wrote the medical essays on which his honorable reputation as a medical researcher is based. The most valuable and famous essay was "The Contagiousness of Puerperal Fever." Puerperal fever was an infection of the lining of the uterus that afflicted and killed many new mothers.

Holmes argued that the infection was actually carried from patient to patient unknowingly by the attending physicians. This idea was extremely unpopular among the medical community, and Holmes's paper was viciously attacked. However, Holmes's theory was indeed true, and the medical community eventually came to accept it. Although Holmes did not originate the contagiousness theory, it is believed that his essay was instrumental in getting doctors to accept and treat the real cause. The essay was meticulously prepared and argued, and one can argue that it was the calm and professional manner in which Holmes handled his critics that actually gave force to his position. Holmes researched and published other influential medical papers, which were collected in his *Medical Essays, 1842-1882* (1883).

In 1847 Holmes became a professor of anatomy and physiology at Harvard Medical School, a position he held for thirty-five years. This vocation released Holmes from the suffering of the actual sickroom while satisfying his thirst for knowledge in his area of fascination, anatomy. Holmes, ever the wit and entertainer, also enjoyed the opportunity to inform and amuse his audience at the same time.

Oliver Wendell Holmes. (Library of Congress)

The Harvard medical student's schedule at that time was grueling. Students were expected to sit for rigorous lectures from 9:00 A.M. to 2:00 P.M. daily, with no break for rest or refreshment. Holmes was specifically assigned the 1:00 P.M. lecture because of his outstanding ability to hold the exhausted students' attention. Although he was serious about presenting information clearly and simply, Holmes nevertheless interjected the occasional anecdote and pun. In addition to his fame as a medical essayist and professor, he lectured extensively outside the college venue and championed such advances in medicine as the use of stethoscopes, microscopes, and anesthesia.

Running parallel with Holmes's distinguished medical career were his accomplishments as a writer. Holmes often commented that he would rather be remembered as a poet than as any other thing. One of his most famous poems, "Old Ironsides," was penned in 1830 directly after his graduation from Harvard. Holmes had read in the newspaper that the Navy Department intended to destroy the *Constitution*, a historic warship nicknamed "Old Ironsides." Holmes quickly composed his poem and mailed it to a Boston newspaper, where the poem was printed. The popular reaction to the poem's plea not to "tear her tattered ensign down!" was so strong that the ship was preserved. The noble verses in "Old Ironsides" were no doubt partially the result of Holmes's love as a youth for Alexander Pope's poetical translations of Homer's heroic *Iliad* and *Odyssey*.

Holmes had dabbled in writing poems from his youth, but he was not proud of most of these early attempts. As a student at Harvard, he and his companions entertained themselves and others with light, humorous verses for assorted events. In 1836, after graduating from medical school, Holmes published his first collection of poetry called *Poems*. This volume contained "Old Ironsides" and "The Last Leaf," which rivals "Old Ironsides" in fame, largely because of his contemporary readers' reaction to it. Edgar Allan Poe wrote a copy of the poem in his own handwriting, and Abraham Lincoln quoted it from memory at a public event. Hundreds of readers less renowned have loved it.

Probably more significant than Holmes's serious poetical efforts were his poems that fell into the category of light verse. Such poems as "My Aunt" and "The Height of the Ridiculous" demonstrated the apt descriptions and humor that led many people to call upon Holmes to compose poems. For fifty years, he was invited to write poems for significant occasions around Boston by medical societies, universities, clubs, and other organizations.

HOLMES ON AUTHORS

I never saw an author in my life—saving, perhaps, one—that did not purr as audibly as a full-grown domestic cat . . . on having his fur smoothed in the right way by a skilful hand.

But let me give you a caution. Be very careful how you tell an author he is *droll*. Ten to one he will hate you; and if he does, be sure he can do you a mischief, and very probably will. Say you *cried* over his romance or his verses, and he will love you and send you a copy. You can laugh over that as much as you like—in private.

Wonder why authors and actors are ashamed of being funny?—Why, there are obvious reasons, and deep philosophical ones. The clown knows very well that the women are not in love with him, but with Hamlet, the fellow in the black cloak and plumed hat. Passion never laughs. The wit knows that his place is at the tail of a procession.

If you want the deep underlying reason, I must take more time to tell it. There is a perfect consciousness in every form of wit—using that term in its general sense—that its essence consists in a partial and incomplete view of whatever it touches. It throws a single ray, separated from the rest,—red, yellow, blue, or any intermediate shade,—upon an object; never white light; that is the province of wisdom. We get beautiful effects from wit,—all the prismatic colors,—but never the object as it is in fair daylight. A pun, which is a kind if wit, is a different and much shallower trick in mental optics throwing the SHADOWS of two objects so that one overlies the other. Poetry uses the rainbow tints for special effects, but always keeps its essential object in the purest white light of truth.—Will you allow me to pursue this subject a little further? . . .

Source: Oliver Wendell Holmes, *The Autocrat of the Breakfast-Table* (Boston: Phillips, Sampson, 1858), chapter 3.

Although light verse is often seen as casual and easy, it can be demanding. Holmes was accommodating and prolific, and the quality of his poems is affirmed by their contemporary popularity as well as their survival. Although literary critics largely agree that Holmes was not someone who possessed poetic genius, he is considered the master of a type of poetry that is clear, graceful, unsentimental, and often humorous.

In 1857, James Russell Lowell, a poet and social reformer, had been hired as the editor of a new literary magazine. Lowell insisted that Holmes be the magazine's first and regular contributor. Holmes originally declined the offer because he had written little creative nonfiction before, and, at the age of forty-seven, he considered himself too old to be truly creative. Lowell persisted, and Holmes agreed to contribute, beginning by naming the new magazine *The Atlantic*. The nonfiction essays that Holmes composed serially for the magazine were eventually collected in *The Autocrat of the*

Breakfast-Table (1858), which most critics agree established him as a genius.

The autocrat in Holmes's essays was an imaginary figure who lived in a boardinghouse and conversed with and about his imaginary fellow boarders around the breakfast table. Although this structure that surrounds the essays is fiction, the thoughts and ideas expressed in the essays genuinely belong to Holmes. The essays are reflective, thought provoking, sophisticated, and humorous. They comment insightfully on Holmes's contemporaries and nineteenth century New England, as well as on human nature in general. These "conversations" of literature continued to appear in *The Atlantic*, and additional volumes were eventually published: *The Professor of the Breakfast-Table* (1860), *The Poet of the Breakfast-Table* (1872), and *Over the Teacups* (1891). *The Atlantic*'s longevity has largely been attributed to the popularity of Holmes's essay series.

Holmes also wrote three novels, *Elsie Venner* (1861), *The Guardian Angel* (1867), and *A Mortal Antipathy* (1885), which are not well respected for their literary technique. However, the novels are considered entertaining and influential because they pioneered the importance of the characters' psychology and hereditary traits in determining their actions and moral choices.

SIGNIFICANCE

Oliver Wendell Holmes has come to be representative of the type of high-quality citizen that American society and culture can produce. Typically associated with the New England renaissance of his day, he exemplified the power and value of original thought tempered with a respectful conservatism and compassion. Possibly one of the most illustrative examples of Holmes's best characteristics was his famous attitude toward the controversial issue of allowing women into Harvard Medical School to be trained as doctors. Holmes was essentially a conservative product of his society who believed in the importance of good taste and structure. He originally voted against women's admission, arguing that women's basic natures made them the best nurses. Shortly thereafter, in a speech to a Harvard audience, he turned on his own argument and reasoned that if a woman wanted to work hard and help others as a doctor, she should be allowed to. This example was typical of Holmes's clear-headed logic coupled with the compassion for which he was well known.

—*Valerie Snyder*

FURTHER READING

Broaddus, Dorothy C. *Genteel Rhetoric: Writing High Culture in Nineteenth Century Boston*. Columbia: University of South Carolina Press, 1999. Analyzes the work of Holmes, Ralph Waldo Emerson, and other nineteenth century writers who created a more refined rhetoric and aesthetics. Broaddus shows how this gentility was lost when the writers addressed slavery, abolition, and other serious topics related to the Civil War.

Crothers, Samuel McChord. *Oliver Wendell Holmes: The Autocrat and His Fellow-Boarders, with Selected Poems*. Boston: Houghton Mifflin, 1909. Brief but useful summation of the generally accepted attitudes about Holmes's personality and works. Includes all of Holmes's most famous poems.

Gibian, Peter. *Oliver Wendell Holmes and the Culture of Conversation*. New York: Cambridge University Press, 2001. Analyzes the role Holmes played in America's "Age of Conversation" before the Civil War. Reexamines Holmes's writings and argues that Holmes was a true republican who encouraged democratic conversation.

Holmes, Oliver Wendell. *Oliver Wendell Holmes: Representative Selections*. Edited by S. I. Hayakawa and H. M. Jones. New York: American Book, 1939. The literary criticism of Holmes's work found in the introduction to this source is insightful and is often referred to by other critics and biographers.

Hoyt, Edwin P. *The Improper Bostonian, Dr. Oliver Wendell Holmes*. New York: William Morrow, 1979. This well-researched and accessible book contains valuable and entertaining anecdotes.

Morse, John T., Jr. *Life and Letters of Oliver Wendell Holmes, Volumes I and II*. Boston: Houghton Mifflin, 1896. Considered the definitive Holmes biography, particularly valuable because the author knew Holmes and many of his contemporaries. Morse's colorful writing style is not unlike Holmes's own.

Tilton, Eleanor M. *Amiable Autocrat: A Biography of Dr. Oliver Wendell Holmes*. New York: Henry Schuman, 1947. Extremely well documented, enjoyable biography with valuable critiques of Holmes's writing.

SEE ALSO: Ralph Waldo Emerson; Edgar Allan Poe; Ignaz Philipp Semmelweis.

RELATED ARTICLES in *Great Events from History: The Nineteenth Century, 1801-1900:* October 16, 1846: Safe Surgical Anesthesia Is Demonstrated; May, 1847: Semmelweis Develops Antiseptic Procedures.

FRIEDRICH VON HOLSTEIN
German diplomat

A controversial chief adviser on German foreign policy during the late nineteenth and early twentieth centuries, Holstein has sometimes been blamed for Germany's diplomatic isolation in the years leading up to World War I.

BORN: April 24, 1837; Schwedt an der Oder, Pomerania (now in Germany)
DIED: May 8, 1909; Berlin, Germany
AREA OF ACHIEVEMENT: Diplomacy

EARLY LIFE

An only child, Friedrich von Holstein passed a sickly and lonely boyhood while living on his family's estate and in the family's Berlin town house. His adolescence was spent with his parents and private tutors at European health resorts, where he became fluent in English, French, and Italian, before attending the University of Berlin. Physically unfit to follow the example of his father's army career, Holstein was briefly and unhappily in the Prussian government's legal division. Through the influence of a neighboring family friend, Otto von Bismarck, Holstein was admitted to the diplomatic service in 1860 and sent as attaché to the legation at St. Petersburg, where Bismarck was then Prussian minister.

In 1863, Holstein passed his foreign service examination and was assigned to Rio de Janeiro but was recalled to Berlin by his patron, Bismarck, who had become Prussian minister-president. In the Danish War of 1864, Holstein served as one of Bismarck's liaison officers to Prussian army headquarters and was later sent to London for the 1864-1865 Conference on the Danish Question.

An 1865-1867 sojourn in the United States began as a travel leave with the purpose of self-discovery, as his father's accidental death in 1863 had left Holstein without family but with some inherited wealth. Photographs of the young baron depict a slender man of medium height with conventionally bearded good looks but a somewhat wary expression. He combined adventures on the Western frontier with a vague assignment at the Washington legation. His friendship with the unconventional young wife of Senator Charles Sumner was later magnified by gossip into an improbable tale of scandalous romance. More prosaically, Holstein began, in the United States, an ultimately unprofitable business enterprise, which continued after his 1867 return to Germany, caused him to leave diplomatic service in 1868, and apparently consumed most or all of his inheritance.

When the Ems Telegram in July of 1870 foreshadowed the Franco-Prussian War, Holstein put himself at Bismarck's disposal and was sent to Italy as the chancellor's private agent to organize anti-French republican activists there in case King Victor Emmanuel II supported Napoleon III. During the 1871 Prussian siege of Paris, Holstein served as Bismarck's unofficial contact with Communard leaders in order to weaken the French government's position in the preliminary peace negotiations.

After the war, Holstein remained in France as chief secretary for Germany's Paris embassy, soon headed by the baron's new chief, Count Harry von Arnim, a political ambassador of great influence and aspirations. Arnim intrigued to overthrow the new French republic as a step toward himself replacing Bismarck as chancellor. His exposure led to sensational trials involving, among much else, purloined state documents. A courtroom charge that Holstein had taken the missing papers made headlines, and his subsequent vindication was not as widely remembered as the false but memorable accusation. Holstein entered the public mind as a man suspected.

LIFE'S WORK

In 1876, Holstein was promoted to the Berlin foreign office, where he spent the rest of his career. He became head of an information apparatus for whatever Bismarck needed to know as well as a conduit for some of what Bismarck decided to do. The baron gradually became a work-absorbed bureaucrat. Rustic in dress and slightly grotesque in the special glasses his eyes came to require, he avoided government social functions and lived simply in three small rooms in an unfashionably remote suburb, though sometimes hosting a few personal friends, generally at Borchardt's restaurant.

Occasionally rude to his superiors, jealous of his prerogatives though considerate of the clerical staff, and with no clear public role, Privy Councillor Baron Holstein seemed to be a consequential official, simply because he possessed important information. The possibilities for blackmail in the German society of the time were abundant, and speculation grew about the basis for Holstein's influence. The result was the Holstein legend, since discredited, of an intelligence chief with spies everywhere and a "poison cupboard" of secrets about those in high places—a dim-sighted but dangerous "mole." Bismarck, among many, fed the rumors, when he described "the man with the hyena eyes" as useful because "sometimes I must do evil things."

In the foreign policy field that was much, though not all, of his job, Holstein followed Bismarck's views almost entirely for about five years. By the mid-1880's, however, his own anti-Russian sentiments increasingly diverged from Bismarck's insistence on a "bridge to St. Petersburg." Like others in German politics, Holstein assumed that the 1888 accession of Kaiser William II would hasten the day of Bismarck's retirement. The baron's efforts to postpone the break while preserving his own position were at least made with the knowledge of both parties.

It is sometimes claimed that from Bismarck's dismissal by the kaiser in March of 1890 to Holstein's own resignation in April of 1906, Holstein was "the real master" of German foreign policy. This exaggerates Holstein's control and underrates the extent to which he was forced to yield to the judgment of his superiors, the impulses of the kaiser, and the pressures of the Navy League and the colonial enthusiasts. The chancellorship of Leo von Caprivi (1890-1894) was the administration most influenced by Holstein, especially in the 1890 decision to abandon the Russian reinsurance treaty in order to have a free hand for pursuing an alliance with England. However, the generous territorial exchanges of Caprivi's treaties with England were merely seen by the British government and press as "trying to buy our friendship." England showed no interest in joining the Triple Alliance of Germany, Austria, and Italy.

Meanwhile, Russia used its diplomatic "free hand" for the Franco-Russian Alliance of 1893-1894, a blow to German security on two fronts which caused wide criticism of the kaiser's new advisers, including Holstein. When Chlodwig von Hohenlohe succeeded Caprivi as chancellor, Holstein was often reduced to ineffective protests against the kaiser's insistence on the 1895 Triple Intervention, which alienated Japan, the needless Kruger Telegram of 1896, and the naval construction program begun by Alfred von Tirpitz in 1898.

Holstein's renewed attempts at an English alliance expired in fruitless negotiations between 1898 and 1901. The Anglo-French Entente Cordiale of 1904 was a heavy blow to Holstein's policy direction, but the Far Eastern War between Russia and Japan did give Germany some diplomatic opportunities. Holstein supported the kaiser's hope of attracting Russia and perhaps even France into an anti-British front. At the same time, Holstein pressed on Chancellor Bernhard von Bülow and the kaiser a policy of detaching England from the Entente Cordiale by challenging French claims in Morocco.

The kaiser's speech in Tangier escalated this move into a crisis, and a war between France and Germany seemed an imminent possibility. Holstein argued that Great Britain would not support a France whose Russian ally was temporarily helpless and that therefore France would back down. He urged going to the brink of war, but the responsibility for going over the brink was not one the kaiser wished to take. The Algeciras Conference of 1906 found Great Britain ready to support France, the United States unexpectedly pro-French, and Italy predictably neutral. That left the Austro-German alliance diplomatically isolated. Such a conspicuous failure of German diplomacy caused foreign office reverberations leading to Holstein's resignation on April 16, 1906.

SIGNIFICANCE

Friedrich von Holstein was a career foreign officer who became an important foreign policy adviser following Bismarck's dismissal. As such, he never possessed the real authority of policy decisions because he had no political power base. On the whole, his advice was better than the inconsistent policies of his superiors. Holstein worked in the unfavorable atmosphere of an autocratic regime on the way to the scrap heap of history. The kaiser, with his frequent delusions of grandeur, was surrounded by irresponsible flatterers who isolated him from reality. Too outspoken and abrasive for such an entourage, Holstein tried to promote sensible policies by influencing the monarch's key advisers. Inevitably his efforts were gossiped about as part of the court circle intrigues, and, after the defeat of 1918, memoirs of the fallen regime often made Holstein the scapegoat for the diplomatic blunders leading to the lost war.

Holstein's papers and modern research have vindicated his character from the charges of base motives. Of the men in the kaiser's government, he was certainly above average in ability, patriotic dedication, honesty, and courage, and less given to malice or feline remarks. That comparison does not elevate him to a place among leading statesmen. His long apprenticeship under Bismarck did not qualify Holstein as a diplomatic sorcerer.

On balance, Holstein's record shows an impressive command of European and world problems; he foresaw more clearly than most the danger to Europe of the growing power of Russia. However, he was unable to comprehend effectively "the other side of the hill." He lacked the penetration, vision, and intuitive human understanding of great statesmanship. If by that standard Holstein failed, so also did the Germany and Europe of his generation.

—*K. Fred Gillum*

FURTHER READING

Berghann, V. R. *Imperial Germany, 1871-1918: Economy, Society, Culture, and Politics.* Rev. and expanded ed. New York: Berghann Books, 2005. Comprehensive and accessible survey of Germany history, organized thematically. Includes a chapter on foreign policy before and after World War I.

Bülow, Bernhard von. *Memoirs of Prince von Bülow.* Translated by F. A. Voigt. 2 vols. Boston: Little, Brown, 1931-1932. References to Holstein are widely scattered but plentiful, negative, and frequently malicious. Bülow presents Holstein not as a masterful gray eminence but as incompetent, disagreeable, and emotionally unstable.

Feuchtwanger, Edgar. *Imperial Germany, 1850-1918.* London: Routledge, 2001. Chronicles the political development of Germany during this period, including the country's aggressive foreign policy before World War I. Contains information about Holstein.

Gooch, George Peabody. *Studies in Modern History.* Reprint. Freeport, N.Y.: Books for Libraries Press, 1968. This essay by a widely respected historian, revised from a 1923 article, had great influence in establishing the Holstein legend for a generation of students and presents a readable collection of anecdotes.

Haller, Johannes. *Philip Eulenburg: The Kaiser's Friend.* Translated by Ethel Colburn Mayne. 2 vols. New York: Alfred A. Knopf, 1930. Holstein's attempts to influence Wilhelm II through the kaiser's adviser are well presented. Haller's biography is a frame for Eulenburg's collection of expansive letters and recollections. An appendix gives Eulenburg's specific comments on Holstein.

Holstein, Friedrich von. *The Holstein Papers*. Edited by Norman Rich and M. H. Fisher. 4 vols. London: Cambridge University Press, 1955-1963. These four volumes collect the relevant data on which much of Rich's biography is based. Volume 1 includes a useful introduction as well as Holstein's autobiographical sketches. Volume 2 contains Holstein's diaries, and volumes 3 and 4 contain his correspondence.

Hull, Isabel V. *The Entourage of Kaiser Wilhelm II, 1888-1918*. New York: Cambridge University Press, 1982. The kaiser and Eulenburg are at the center of this comprehensive account, but Holstein's relation to the group is established in this study, which includes a useful examination of some of the Holstein-Eulenburg letters from a different perspective.

Rich, Norman. *Friedrich von Holstein*. 2 vols. New York: Cambridge University Press, 1965. A long-awaited work, this is the only full-length biography of Holstein. The narrative follows Holstein's viewpoint, but objective judgment is maintained. A historical context of considerable detail makes the book especially useful to scholars of German and diplomatic history.

Seligmann, Matthew S., and Roderick R. McLean. *Germany from Reich to Republic, 1871-1918: Politics, Hierarchy, and Elites*. New York: St. Martin's Press, 2000. Information about Holstein is included in this history of Germany during the era of of Kaiser Wilhelm II and Otto von Bismarck.

SEE ALSO: Otto von Bismarck; Napoleon III; Charles Sumner.

RELATED ARTICLES in *Great Events from History: The Nineteenth Century, 1801-1900:* July 19, 1870-January 28, 1871: Franco-Prussian War; September 1, 1870: Battle of Sedan; January 18, 1871: German States Unite Within German Empire; May 6-October 22, 1873: Three Emperors' League Is Formed; May 20, 1882: Triple Alliance Is Formed.

WINSLOW HOMER
American painter

One of the greatest self-taught artistic figures of his time, Homer was known for his luminous watercolors and powerful oils, especially those depicting the power, moods, beauty, and menace of the sea.

BORN: February 24, 1836; Boston, Massachusetts
DIED: September 29, 1910; Prouts Neck, Maine
AREA OF ACHIEVEMENT: Art

EARLY LIFE

Winslow Homer's first known work of art was a small drawing he made at the age of ten of a boy lying on the ground gazing into the distance, his head resting on his arm. Entitled *Adolescence* (1846), it displays no more than the proficiency that one would expect from a pre-teen who lacks training or apparent promise. The sketch would hardly be worth even a first glance were its creator unknown. However, the young artist no doubt received much encouragement from his mother, a decent watercolorist of flowers and birds. Henrietta Benson Homer was the mainstay of her family of three sons, keeping the home running even when her husband, Charles, sold his hardware business, invested in mining machinery, and traveled to California to prospect for gold, returning two years later, completely penniless.

Winslow was thirteen when his father left. At that time, the family was living in Cambridge, having moved there in 1842, when Winslow was ready for school. The Homer home was down the street from Harvard College, but Winslow was not to get much of a formal education; he probably did not even finish high school. He continued to draw, but when he was nineteen, his father had him apprenticed to the printmaking establishment of John Bufford, thereby launching his son's professional career.

In the days before photographs could be printed in newspapers, there was a great demand for capable commercial artists to draw scenes and portraits for newspapers and magazines. Homer's first artistic assignment was a portfolio of seventeen lithographs of pictures of Puritans for inclusion in a genealogical register. Other graphics followed: more drawings for books, mostly portraits or scenes from nature; title pages for sheet music, bearing such engaging titles as "The Ratcatcher's Daughter" and "The Wheelbarrow Polka"; and even a political cartoon.

Bufford also required his apprentices to do their share of drudgery—shopkeeping, cleaning lithographers' stones, and the like, tasks that increased Winslow's sense of frustration and resentment. Being a regular employee of a firm such as Bufford's held little attraction for Homer, and as soon as he turned twenty-one and his apprenticeship was officially over, he left, vowing to be his own master.

Homer rented a studio and began to work on commission; most of his early assignments were done for *Ballou's Pictorial Drawing-Room Companion* (known as *Ballou's Pictorial*), an all-purpose newsmagazine designed to appeal to those who did not like to think too much about what they were reading. *Ballou's Pictorial* had an impressive circulation of 100,000. Homer did various genre pictures, portraits, street scenes, and advertisements, which all appeared in the publication as woodcuts, a medium that limited the use of curves and made it difficult for artists to draw lines fine enough to produce variations of gray. Consequently, the wood engraving turned everything into black and white and gave its figures a static, or posed, quality. Homer did not do his own woodblocks, as that task was the job of special designers.

Homer's work for *Ballou's Pictorial* attracted the attention of the editors of the newly founded *Harper's Weekly* of New York City. His first drawing for them was followed by an eight-month hiatus; then commissions became more frequent, so much so that in 1859, Homer moved to New York to be closer to his major market. This move also brought him into a more stimulating artistic environment and prompted him, for the first and last time in his life, to take formal instruction in art. He enrolled in night classes at the National Academy of Design and also took some lessons from French painter Frédéric Rondel, who taught him the basics of oil painting, how to lay down color, use brushes, and set his palette. Even so, Homer remained mostly self-taught.

Working for the illustrated weeklies was Homer's chief source of income over the next two decades. He rapidly became one of the leading artists of *Harper's Weekly*, and, when the Civil War began, *Harper's Weekly* wanted to put him on staff as an artist-correspondent to draw pictures of the fighting. Homer, however, always insistent on his independence, remained freelance. He did go to the front though, following the Union armies in George B. McClellan's ill-fated Virginia Peninsular Campaign of 1862. Practically every week, *Harper's Weekly* ran at least one of his works.

Most of Homer's Civil War illustrations were not pictures of the fighting as such, but rather of the activities of soldiers in camp or on bivouac: in short, the military equivalent of the genre pictures that he was accustomed to doing. Even Homer's battle drawings rarely showed blood and gore, and the enemy was hardly ever seen. He

Winslow Homer.

soon became recognized as one of the best war artists, but as the conflict was reaching its climax, Homer increasingly avoided doing woodblock engravings in order to develop his talent in another and ultimately more satisfying and important direction.

LIFE'S WORK

Not until he was nearly thirty did Homer try his first painting in oils, using as a subject a sketch he had done the previous year, 1862, printed as an illustration in *Harper's Weekly*. *The Sharpshooter* shows a Union soldier sitting in a pine tree, sighting his gun at a target somewhere off the canvas. This work was followed by *Punishment for Intoxication* (1863) and *A Skirmish in the Wilderness* (1864), which were also taken from drawings he had made while he was with the army. The paintings were done in his New York studio and are surprising for being such good first attempts.

Homer's most famous painting of the war was *Prisoners from the Front*, also a studio piece, done in 1866, when the war was over. Only the uniforms and several muskets make the picture military; the composition is very basic: The six principal figures simply stand in a ragged line in the foreground in studio poses. The picture was so well received by the experts and the public that it ensured Homer's election to full membership in the National Academy.

During that same year, Homer made his first trip to Europe, staying in Paris, where two of his paintings, including *Prisoners from the Front*, were to be shown at the Exposition Universelle. The paintings he did while abroad were mostly portraits of women, including two engaging oils of farm girls with pitchforks. He returned home after ten months to begin a period of great artistic creativity. In the fourteen years between his return in 1867, and 1881, when he again left for Europe, he produced more than half of the works of his entire artistic career. His search for new subjects and scenes took him all over New England, through Pennsylvania and Virginia.

Homer liked painting in the mountains: the Catskills, the Adirondacks, the White Mountains of New Hampshire; he liked painting the beaches: New England, along the New Jersey shore. As he became more practiced in oils, he also began to develop his talent in watercolor, a medium he also taught himself to use. He exhibited with the American Watercolor Society for the first time in 1874. He also continued to produce drawings for woodcuts in *Harper's Weekly* and other magazines, to earn extra money, but abandoned this form altogether in 1875.

One of Homer's favorite subjects continued to be women, whom he showed partaking in all sorts of respectable middle-class activities: picking flowers, playing croquet, tossing hoops. Even if the task was gathering eggs or taking care of sick chickens, the subjects hardly seemed engaged in real physical labor. Homer also liked to depict the pleasures of youth: children playing games, wading, dreaming, sitting on fences, gathering clams. For these bucolically pretty pictures, he filled his palette with bright warm colors, exactly the sort of hues that would appeal to his bourgeois clients. However, he also did paintings that were not so commercially motivated, and these must be judged among the best of the period. These come from his stay in Virginia, where he had an opportunity to observe the rural poverty of African Americans. He revealed these people with a compassion

"Shipbuilding, Gloucester Harbor," by Winslow Homer. (Library of Congress)

and sensitivity rare for a time when African Americans were seen as objects of derision.

As Homer became more involved in his art, he seemed to relate less successfully to other people and became more attached to his solitude. In 1881, he again left the United States for Europe, but this time he did not go to a large urban center, but rather to Cullercoats, a drab fishing village on the eastern coast of England, near Tynemouth. There, surrounded by working-class people, he found the isolation he wanted, his loneliness reinforced by watching the dark, changing moods of the North Sea and studying its effect on those who relied on it for their livelihood. He painted storms and shipwrecks and fisherwomen watching the dark waters for the return of their men. It was in England that he did the visual research, the artistic counterpart of working in an archive, for canvases that he would complete when he returned home. His famous *The Herring Net* (1885) almost certainly had its origins in his experiences there.

Homer returned to New York in late 1882, but he could never readjust to the urban life he once knew. In England, he had discovered the kind of simplicity he was seeking in life and wanted to portray in his work. Therefore, in 1883, he decided to settle on the craggy coast of Maine, on a rough promontory jutting southward into Saco Bay, known as Prouts Neck, which had been purchased by his father. There Homer built a studio; there he would remain for the remainder of his life, leaving only occasionally on excursions to Canada, Florida, and Bermuda. He continued the course he had charted for himself while in England, painting his greatest masterpieces. In 1909, he painted his last picture, *Driftwood*, which is also one of his best. After he finished, he smeared his palette and hung it on the wall, never to take it down again. The following year, he died. He was seventy-four.

SIGNIFICANCE

Winslow Homer was one of the greatest self-taught artistic figures of the nineteenth century. His consuming passion for his craft, his intense struggle to succeed, perhaps an overcompensation for his lack of formal training, constantly nurtured his compulsion to improve, and the older he became, the better his technique became. He had many opportunities to see the works of famous predecessors, but he avoided doing so, reluctant to damage his own instincts and compromise his powers of observation and sense of style.

Homer visited museums in Paris and London, but more out of a sense of obligation than out of a search for inspiration. If he was impressed by the Elgin Marbles in the British Museum, it was because they offered him confirmation and reinforcement, not contrast. Homer also made little contact with other living artists, neither those who painted in the standard academic vein, nor those more revolutionary, such as the Impressionists and their successors. Homer's art remained grounded in his own narrow, artistic universe. He became wedded to a basic classical compositional framework established during his career as an illustrator.

Had Homer died at fifty, he would have left many pleasing canvases and watercolors—his Civil War woodcuts might be regarded as interesting period pieces, but not the stuff of greatness. A notable exception was the *The Carnival* (1877), one of his pictures of the black Virginians. Homer arranged his figures in his usual manner, marching them across the foreground in rough formation, but rarely had he used oil color more dramatically and skillfully. Also remarkable was his depiction of character. In showing the determination with which these people celebrated their holiday, he revealed their sense of hopelessness; in painting a scowl on the face of a barefoot girl, he projected their life of penury. To this he added a touch of irony: The two youngest children are carrying tiny American flags.

Homer's true greatness lay ahead, revealed in the last twenty years of his life, a time when he became a virtual recluse. If an artist's character is truly revealed in his art, then Homer presents something of a problem. There is a sense of pessimism and terror in many of his seascape oils, but his watercolors are full of joie de vivre and hope. These are boldly presented, not picky in color or detail, and convey a sprightly immediacy that is alien to many of his morose canvases.

Homer's reputation, however, will always be based on his great marine paintings. Compositionally, they are hardly revolutionary. There is a certain theatricality about the manner in which he arranges his subjects, as if he were a director constantly blocking his scenes in stage center or just back of the footlights. Although he liked to work outdoors, in many of these oils it almost seems as if the turbulent waters had come into his studio to pose. The waves crashing against the rocks often have the same sculptural quality as the rocks themselves. Homer depicts movement not so much by composition, for example in the frenetic way of a work by Eugène Delacroix, but in the fluidity of his brush strokes and in his use of color.

In the flesh tones of the bearded sailor in *The Look-out—All's Well* (1896), Homer builds up his colors in thin layers, juxtaposing warm with cool, until one can almost see underneath the man's saltwater-toughened skin. The sun-and-surf-punished decking of the small sailboat in *The Gulf Stream* (1899) and the water surrounding the hapless craft are painted with the skill of Claude Monet at his best. Homer also has a fine sense of drama and understanding of theme. For example, in *The Wreck* (1896), Homer concentrated on a rescue operation rather than the disaster itself. In the foreground, in full-length black rubber coat, stands a gaunt, spectral walrus-mustached veteran, his right hand raised as a signal for help or in warning to onlookers to keep away. The man has obviously been through such tragedies many times before.

In depicting such moments, Homer makes one forget the individual elements of his art, just as hearing a great symphony makes one forget the individual notes. However, only by mastering the fundamentals was Homer, like all great artists, able to transcend his medium and convey the true immensity of his talent.

—*Wm. Laird Kleine-Ahlbrandt*

FURTHER READING

Beam, Philip C. *Winslow Homer at Prout's Neck.* Boston: Little, Brown, 1966. Beam concentrates on the last and greatest period of the artist's life. He seeks to enhance understanding of Homer's work by evaluating the internal evidence in his pictures and by understanding his relation to other American and European art of his time.

Downes, William Howe. *Life and Works of Winslow Homer.* Boston: Houghton Mifflin, 1911. This biography, published a year after Homer's death, was the first attempt to create a chronology of the subject's life. The author was awed by his responsibility, for he seems to have included every scrap of information he could find. However, Homer himself was not too cooperative, once telling Downes that no part of his life was of much concern to the public: "Therefore I must decline to give you any particulars in regard to it."

Flexner, James Thomas. *The World of Winslow Homer, 1936-1910.* New York: Time, 1966. This study, from the Time-Life Library of Art series, gives a fine presentation of Homer in the context of the development of American art. Especially helpful are such special sections as Homer as a watercolorist and the description of two other contemporary giants, Thomas Eakins and Albert Ryder.

Goodrich, Lloyd. *Winslow Homer.* New York: Macmillan, 1944. An artistic biography rather than an account of Homer's personal life. The author treats his

subject with understanding and insight, the product of careful and meticulous research. Includes a twenty-page reminiscence by one of Homer's friends, John Beatty.

_____. *Winslow Homer.* New York: Macmillan, 1973. The catalog to accompany the Winslow Homer exhibition organized by the Whitney Museum of American Art. Most of the book features reproductions of the works on display; these are put in context by an intelligent essay on Homer's life and the important stages in his artistic development.

Griffin, Randall C. *Homer, Eakins, and Anshutz: The Search for American Identity in the Gilded Age.* University Park: Pennsylvania State University Press, 2004. Examines how artists and critics sought to create a new identity for the United States that would match the Gilded Age's taste for opulence. Focuses on Homer, Thomas Eakins, and Thomas Anshutz, describing how their work led to the development of modern American art.

Hannaway, Patti. *Winslow Homer in the Tropics.* Richmond, Va.: Westover, 1973. The restricted scope of this book is part of a recent development to concentrate on one aspect of the artist's life, in this case his output of watercolors done while he was in Florida and in the Bahamas. The book is a catalog of the principal products of those visits. The illustrations are particularly good and are accompanied by a short background piece and artistic commentary.

Hendricks, Gordon. *The Life and Work of Winslow Homer.* New York: Harry N. Abrams, 1979. This well-researched, sumptuously produced volume includes many excellent reproductions, supplemented by intelligent commentary and an exhaustive listing of the artist's works in public collections in the United States.

Hoopes, Donelson E. *Winslow Homer Watercolors.* New York: Watson-Guptill, 1969. Representative samples of Homer's work from 1878 to 1904. Intelligent analysis of Homer's color technique and sense of composition.

Johns, Elizabeth. *Winslow Homer: The Nature of Observation.* Berkeley: University of California Press, 2002. Analyzes Homer's work and artistic development from the perspective of development psychology, focusing on one hundred images that represent turning points in his life. Discusses Homer's illustrations, oil paintings, and watercolors.

Junker, Patricia A., et al. *Winslow Homer, Artist and Angler.* New York: Thames and Hudson, 2002. Catalog accompanying an exhibit of Homer's fishing paintings displayed in San Francisco and Fort Worth, Texas. The book's essays discuss Homer's love of fly-fishing, his fishing experiences, and the place of fish and fishing in his artwork. Includes 184 illustrations.

SEE ALSO: Albert Bierstadt; George Caleb Bingham; Mary Cassatt; Eugène Delacroix; Thomas Eakins; James McNeill Whistler.

RELATED ARTICLE in *Great Events from History: The Nineteenth Century, 1801-1900:* February 8, 1861: Establishment of the Confederate States of America.

HONG XIUQUAN
Chinese political reformer

Hong Xiuquan created and led the first revolutionary movement to shake the traditional Chinese political system. His movement, the Taiping Heavenly Kingdom, was a cataclysmic upheaval that greatly influenced both Sun Yat-sen and Mao Zedong.

BORN: January 1, 1814; Fuyuanshui, Guangdong Province, China
DIED: June 1, 1864; Nanjing, Jiangsu Province, China
ALSO KNOWN AS: Hung Hsiu-ch'üan (Wade-Giles); Hong Huoxiu (full name)
AREA OF ACHIEVEMENT: Government and politics

EARLY LIFE

Born in a small Chinese village thirty miles from Canton (Guangzhou), the great port of south China, Hong Xiuquan (hong chih-ew-kwahn) was the third son of a Hakka family, clannish, hardworking peasants who spoke a distinct dialect and were often discriminated against by the Han Chinese majority. He was later described as tall with a fair complexion and large, bright eyes.

For young Chinese men, there was one sure way to climb in the ancient society: to pass the civil service examinations used to assign positions in the bureaucracy. The examinations were based upon the Confucian classic texts and demanded proficiency in the Chinese language with its tens of thousands of characters. Students often had wealthy families who could support them, because study had to begin early and usually did not culminate before a man's late twenties or early thirties. Although poor, Hong had unusual intelligence; many of his relatives, therefore, sacrificed to enable him to study. At the age of sixteen, he had to quit studying and work on his father's farm. The villagers thought so much of his talents that they hired him to teach their children, giving him an opportunity for part-time study.

Despite Hong's intelligence and ambition, part-time study was not enough. He repeatedly failed the first level

of the examinations. In 1837, he collapsed in nervous exhaustion and was bedridden for some time. In this state, he had a series of religious visions combining traditional Chinese notions with themes derived from Western Christianity.

Earlier, China had been strong and self-reliant and had repelled the repeated attempts of Western diplomats, businesspeople, and missionaries to gain entrance. However, problems, above all overpopulation, mounted. China's last dynasty, the Qing (1644-1912), were Manchus, formerly a fierce warrior people. They had grown corrupt and incompetent and were unable to stem China's accelerating decline. By the time Hong was born, many Westerners were in China though their activities were closely regulated. Western businesspeople, primarily British, were selling increasing amounts of opium. Great Britain hoped both to defray the costs of controlling India, where the opium was grown, and to use opium profits to pay for British purchases of Chinese teas and silks. The numbers of Western missionaries also increased rapidly, and their access to Chinese society expanded.

The missionaries meant well and made a lasting contribution to Chinese society by improving education and social welfare; China, however, had never known a monotheistic religion, and the impact of Christian ideas upon the Chinese was unpredictable. Hong had cursorily examined some translations of missionary texts the year before his collapse. In his illness, Hong had visions that continued over some months. He believed that God was calling upon him to drive evil spirits and demons, represented by the Manchus, out of China.

LIFE'S WORK

Hong recovered and began to preach ideas that struck most listeners as strange. It was a time of great turmoil, however, and friends and relatives began to listen to Hong; soon he was making converts. In 1844, he damaged local temples and drew the attention of the authorities, who strictly prohibited teachings outside the three religions of Daoism, Buddhism, and Confucianism. Hong and one of his first converts, Feng Yunshan, left for the neighboring province, Guangxi (Kwangsi). Guangxi was poor, and many of its inhabitants were racial minorities such as the Yao, Miao, and Chuang peoples. The Chuang were the most numerous Chinese minority and had often served as mercenaries in Chinese armies in the past.

During the winter, Hong went back to Guangdong (Kwangtung), leaving Feng, who had relatives among the numerous Hakka in Guangxi, to stay and preach. In Guangdong, Hong continued to preach and write, studying briefly in Canton with a noted American missionary, Issachar J. Roberts. In 1847, Hong returned to Guangxi. Feng was a spellbinding speaker and had been successful in winning converts, particularly among the Chuang and the Hakka.

China was in increasing turmoil. The Manchus had fought and decisively lost a war with Great Britain in 1839-1842. The ostensible cause of the war was the Chinese attempt to control the opium trade, but the real issue was foreign demands for greater freedom of action in China. The Opium War, as it was called, caused immense dislocation in south China. Guangxi, already poor, suffered from recurrent drought; banditry became widespread. Many peasants joined secret societies, traditional organizations that frequently became violently antigovernment. The authorities created local militia, which easily became tools of local despots.

Hong's congregations, known as the Society of God Worshipers, became embroiled in local conflicts, and the authorities attempted to suppress them. However, the combination of Hong's messianic fervor and of Feng's mystical appeals was irresistible in troubled Guangxi. In 1850, the Society of God Worshipers won a battle at Jintian village, attracting new converts as well as the cooperation of the secret societies and pirate bands eager for plunder. In 1851, his forces swollen with tens of thousands of new followers, Hong declared the "Taiping Tienkuo" (the Taiping Heavenly Kingdom) as both a new Chinese dynasty and a new holy order on earth.

The group repelled government counterattacks and moved north, into the Chang Jiang (Yangtze) River valley, China's populous economic center. Disaffected peasants flocked to Hong's banner. From 1851 to 1853, victory followed victory, and the Taiping established their capital at Nanjing, a major city on the Chang Jiang River. However, the government in Beijing rallied, led by a new generation of Han Chinese more willing to adopt Western weapons and techniques than the traditional Manchu leadership had been.

A major question was the attitude of the Western powers, who had won many privileges following the Opium War. They now had access to many Chinese ports and were gaining control of import and customs duties, making trade much easier. They were dubious of Hong's religious ideas, which were based upon only a small portion of the Bible, particularly upon the mystical Book of Revelation. Some thought him insane. A decisive issue in the minds of many foreigners was that Hong absolutely prohibited the opium trade. After considerable debate, the Western powers decided to maintain a public posture of neutrality, but they encouraged private assistance to the Manchu regime and gave necessary financial support. Foreign adventurers, such as the American Frederick Townsend Ward and the Englishman Major Charles George "Chinese" Gordon, formed units of Filipino and Western mercenaries, who fought for the government and trained Chinese soldiers.

Fighting was widespread and savage. Armies of hundreds of thousands marched and countermarched across central China. Prolonged sieges of large cities resulted in mass starvation. Enormous fleets clashed on China's many lakes and rivers. The peasants often found it impossible to farm, and famines resulted. It has been estimated that from 20 million to 40 million Chinese died in these upheavals.

Feng died in battle in 1852, but Hong had many talented soldiers, some of whom were made "kings" in the Taiping Heavenly Kingdom. The Taiping could not, however, win over the Confucian bureaucracy, who were instrumental in governing local communities in China. The Confucians preferred the Manchus, who were a known quantity and themselves highly Confucian, to the alien ideas of the Taiping, who held land in common and preached social leveling and the equality of the sexes.

In August of 1856, the Taiping were split by a series of internal struggles in which several of the kings died. Other able generals arose, and the war seesawed; however, the Taiping failed to deal with their internal problems. Without the help of the local Confucian gentry, they could not produce the necessary revenues to fight an increasingly modern war. The foreigners openly supported the government. During the late years of the Taiping Heavenly Kingdom, Hong grew increasingly isolated and less and less realistic. He believed that God would ultimately protect the Taiping Heavenly Kingdom, but the capital at Nanjing fell on July 19, 1864. Hong died in June, reportedly by his own hand.

SIGNIFICANCE

Despite his ultimate failure, Hong Xiuquan had great impact for a Chinese peasant. The odds against him were great. In Chinese history, only one peasant had founded a new dynasty, and that had been more than five hundred years earlier. Hong's religious ideas inevitably were unconventional. He necessarily perceived Western Christianity through the veil of his own Chinese culture, which alienated contemporary Western observers. Some scholars have questioned his sanity.

As well as dreaming of a China divinely purified of the Manchus, Hong also dreamed of a China that would be a better place for common men and women, a strong China free of foreign influence, without opium, slavery, prostitution, and marked social inequality. His example influenced a later generation of revolutionaries, such as Sun Yat-sen, another Hakka peasant from Guangdong, who helped to overthrow the Manchus, becoming the first president of Republican China in 1913. Hong also influenced the communists led by Mao Zedong, who founded the People's Republic of China in 1949. The Chinese government and people revered Hong as the first Chinese revolutionary, a visionary who fought for a new and more equitable Chinese government.

—*Jeffrey G. Barlow*

FURTHER READING

Boardman, Eugene. *Christian Influence upon the Ideology of the Taiping Rebellion, 1851-1864*. Madison: University of Wisconsin Press, 1952. Many works on the Taiping Rebellion largely ignore Hong as an individual, but not Boardman's. This work brings together everything that is known about Hong and examines his beliefs in both the Chinese and Western Christian context of the period.

Hamberg, Theodore. *The Visions of Hung-Siu-tshuen, and Origin of the Kwangsi Insurrection*. San Francisco: Chinese Materials Center, 1975. This book was written during the Taiping Rebellion by a Western missionary who investigated Hong's background, particularly his exposure to Christian ideas, and his resulting religious beliefs.

Jen, Yu-wen. *The Taiping Revolutionary Movement*. New Haven, Conn.: Yale University Press, 1973. Most scholarly works on the Taiping Rebellion are primarily interested in the contemporary Chinese social scene or in the war or in Taiping institutions. This work treats in detail the issue of Christian influences upon Hong's values and beliefs.

Kuhn, Philip A. "The Taiping Rebellion." In *The Cambridge History of China Late Ch'ing, 1800-1911*, edited by John K. Fairbank. Vol. 10. Cambridge, England: Cambridge University Press, 1978. Kuhn is one of the foremost historians of the rebellion, and this is an excellent introductory essay to it and to China during that period. Several other essays in the volume also relate to the rebellion. Contains a bibliographic guide to sources in Asian and Western languages.

Michael, Franz, and Chung-li Chang. *The Taiping Rebellion: History and Documents*. 3 vols. Seattle: University of Washington Press, 1966-1971. The first volume of this massive work is a narrative history of the rebellion. The final two volumes are translations of important documents. The work is considered a standard history for research purposes.

Reilly, Thomas H. *The Taiping Heavenly Kingdom: Rebellion and the Blasphemy of Empire*. Seattle: University of Washington Press, 2004. Examines the religious underpinnings of the Taiping Rebellion, chronicling the development of Christianity in China and explaining how Hong and the rebels interpreted Christian religion as an indictment of the Chinese imperial order.

Spence, Jonathan D. *God's Chinese Son: The Taiping Heavenly Kingdom of Hong Xiuquan*. New York: W. W. Norton, 1996. Spence, a specialist in Chinese history, chronicles the rise and fall of the Taiping Heavenly Kingdom. Focuses on Hong's religious vision and how Hong's faith helped spur the rebellion.

_____. *The Taiping Vision of a Christian China, 1836-1864*. Waco, Tex.: Markham Press Fund, Baylor University Press, 1998. The text of a lecture about the social and political conditions that led to the Taiping Rebellion. Includes information about Hong's life, including an analysis of his intellectual development and the influence of Christian scripture upon Hong and the rebels.

Teng, Ssu-yü. *The Taiping Rebellion and the Western Powers*. London: Oxford University Press, 1971. Teng is a leading historian in the field. This is an excellent study of the diplomatic context of the rebellion, particularly of the relations between the foreign powers and the Chinese court.

SEE ALSO: Cixi; Kang Youwei; Lin Zexu; Zeng Guofan.
RELATED ARTICLES in *Great Events from History: The Nineteenth Century, 1801-1900:* September, 1839-August 29, 1842: First Opium War; January 11, 1851-late summer, 1864: China's Taiping Rebellion; October 23, 1856-November 6, 1860: Second Opium War; 1860's: China's Self-Strengthening Movement Arises.

SAM HOUSTON
American military leader and politician

Houston had one of the most diverse political careers in U.S. history. He served as governor of two different states, commanded the Texan army during Texas's revolt against Mexico, was elected president of the independent Republic of Texas, and served in the U.S. Senate.

BORN: March 2, 1793; Rockbridge County, Virginia
DIED: July 26, 1863; Huntsville, Texas
ALSO KNOWN AS: Samuel Houston, Jr. (full name)
AREAS OF ACHIEVEMENT: Government and politics, military

EARLY LIFE

Sam Houston—the name he always used, both formally and informally—was the son of Samuel Houston, Sr., a farmer and veteran of the American Revolution. His mother, née Elizabeth Paxton, came from pioneer stock. Young Sam was the fifth of six sons in a family that also included three daughters. He attended school intermittently until his father's death in 1807, when his formal education ended. The widow Houston moved her family to Marysville, Tennessee, where Sam spent the remainder of his youth. For a time, he worked in the village store, although this was not to his liking. In his teenage years, he sought escape and left home on several occasions to live with the Cherokee Indians. In total, he spent almost four years with them, mastering their language, customs, and culture. The Indians accepted him as one of their own, giving him the name "Raven." He eventually returned home to live with his family.

Houston joined the army during the War of 1812, serving with distinction at the Battle of Horseshoe Bend. His personal exploits attracted the attention of General Andrew Jackson, who promoted him to the rank of lieutenant. After leaving the military in 1818, Houston studied law and became a practicing attorney at Lebanon, Tennessee. A physically large man of greater than average height, he had a powerful build graced by curly dark hair and a pleasing countenance. Known for his gregarious personality and public speaking ability, he had a dramatic air about him that made him the center of attention and an individual of great personal popularity.

LIFE'S WORK

Houston's neighbors in Tennessee elected him a state militia officer in 1819. During 1823, he gave up the practice of law and entered politics, securing in that year election to the U.S. Congress as a representative. Houston quickly became a leader in the Tennessee Democratic Party. He also forged a lifelong personal friendship with Andrew Jackson. Houston became the governor of Tennessee in 1827 and looked forward to a promising career in that state. He married Eliza H. Allen, daughter of a prominent Tennessee family, on January 1, 1829. Within months, Houston's success turned to bitter failure because of problems with his bride. Although historians have never agreed on the specific causes, the marriage to Eliza lasted only a short time. She returned home to her parents (eventually securing a divorce) while Houston, with some despondency, resigned the governorship in the spring of 1829 and moved to Indian territory to start life anew. The Tennessee years became a closed chapter in his life.

Houston spent the following years among his boyhood friends, the Cherokee. He adopted Indian dress and customs, became a citizen of the Indian nation, and took a wife according to the dictates of Cherokee law. His Indian wife, Tiana, assisted him in operating a small trading post. In addition, he served as an advocate for the Cherokee in various matters before the U.S. government. By 1832, the wanderlust again struck Houston, and he began visiting Texas, although he maintained residence in the Indian nation for a time. He first arrived in the Anglo areas of Mexican Texas as an Indian agent and a representative of investors who sought land in the province. The exact date that he moved to Texas is lost in obscurity, but, by late 1833, he was taking an active part in Texas affairs as a resident. In the process, he left his life with the Cherokee, including Tiana, forever in the past.

Houston's removal to Texas came in the midst of growing revolutionary fervor on the part of Anglo residents unhappy with Mexican rule. Houston played an important role in events that resulted in the eventual break with Mexico. He served as presiding officer of the Convention of 1833, which wrote a proposed constitution for Texas, and attended the Consultation of 1835, which marked the start of the revolution. He signed the Texas Declaration of Independence from Mexico while serving as a delegate to the Convention of 1836. The revolutionary government of Texas appointed him commander in chief of the army with the rank of major general on March 4, 1836. Forever after, in spite of the other high offices he would hold in his career, Sam Houston preferred the title "general."

Taking command of the army at Gonzales shortly after the Alamo fell to Mexican troops commanded by Antonio López de Santa Anna, General Houston led his forces eastward across Texas in a retreat known as the "Runaway Scrape." Potential disaster for the Texans turned to stunning victory when Houston and his men met Santa Anna's army, which had pursued them, at the

Sam Houston. (Courtesy, University of Texas at Austin Portrait Gallery)

Battle of San Jacinto on April 21, 1836. Santa Anna was captured, his army soundly defeated, and General Houston became the hero of the day.

With independence secured, Houston won election as president of the Republic of Texas on September 5, 1836. His term saw Texas's failure to enter the Union because of opposition in the U.S. Congress, attempts to deal with the Comanche Indians, and growing political factionalism in the republic. While president of the republic, Houston married Margaret M. Lea on May 8, 1840. They eventually had eight children, including Andrew Jackson Houston, who served a short period as United States senator from Texas during the 1930's.

Because the republic's constitution forbade a president from succeeding himself, Houston left office after one term. Mirabeau B. Lamar, with whom Houston had political differences, replaced him. Houston, however, won election to the republic's congress, where pro-Houston and anti-Houston parties soon became the active political factions of the fledgling nation. Houston's opponents objected to several of his policies, including his attempts to keep Austin from becoming the capital city; others believed that he had failed to work hard enough for statehood. Other critics no doubt found the general's large ego and some of his personal habits objectionable, especially his frequent and heavy drinking of whiskey. Whatever the reasons for controversy, Houston would be at the center of politically motivated strife and criticism for the rest of his public career.

Houston's reelection to the presidency of the republic in 1841 came after a heated campaign with the Lamar faction. Houston attempted to undo some of the programs of his predecessor and was faced with additional problems, including a minor, abortive Mexican invasion of Texas in 1842. He was able to deal with all these efficiently, although not always with complete success. By the end of his second term, in 1844, the annexation of Texas by the United States had become a distinct possibility. Houston, however, wavered in the face of statehood for Texas, sometimes giving the impression that he favored continuing the republic. It fell to his successor, Anson Jones, to have the distinction of serving as the last president of the Republic of Texas.

Along with Thomas J. Rusk, Houston became one of the United States senators representing Texas once statehood had been secured in 1845. He would continue to serve in that body until the eve of the Civil War. Houston continued his pre-Texas affiliation with the Democratic Party during his days in the Senate. He played a role in the debates over the Compromise of 1850, siding with southern delegates while he lobbied for an acceptable settlement to the Texas boundary controversy. He had aspirations for the Democratic Party presidential nomination in 1848 and in 1852, but in both instances he failed to attract enough delegate votes to make a showing at the convention.

Houston's role as a leader in the southern bloc of the Senate came to an end with his vote on the Kansas-Nebraska Bill of 1854. A strong advocate of the Union, he voted with Free-Soilers and Whigs against the bill. This placed him at odds with his southern colleagues and many slaveholders in Texas, all of whom wanted the bill passed. By the mid-1850's, Houston became increasingly distanced from the Democratic Party when he embraced the Know-Nothing movement because of his strong commitment to the preservation of the Union. He attended Know-Nothing meetings and conventions. Texas Democrats denounced him for these activities. Houston ran for the governorship of Texas in 1857 but was defeated by Hardin Runnels. He remained in the Senate until the end of his term, in 1859, whereupon he returned to Texas. He ran once more against Runnels for governor in 1859, this time winning by a small margin.

Houston's term as governor, which began in December of 1859, proved to be a time of turmoil for Texas and a period of deep personal anguish for Houston. The election of Abraham Lincoln triggered the secession crisis and the formation of the Confederate States of America. Texas was a slave state, largely settled by persons of southern heritage, and most Texans favored secession although some preferred to remain with the Union. Houston fell into the latter camp. His commitment to the Constitution and the Union was stronger than his desire to secede.

As governor, Houston thus found himself out of step with most Texans and their political leaders. Houston refused to cooperate with the State Secession Convention that met in Austin. When the convention adopted a secession ordinance, the governor took the position that Texas had returned legally to her former status as an independent republic. He therefore refused as governor to take an oath of allegiance to the Confederacy. The Secession Convention therefore declared the office of governor vacant and named Edward Clark to the position. Houston, refusing an offer of federal troops from President Lincoln, decided to accede to the convention's decision and relinquished his office. He retired to Huntsville, Texas, where he died on July 26, 1863.

SIGNIFICANCE

Sam Houston played an important role in the westward movement of the United States during the nineteenth century. As a frontiersman, military figure, and political leader, he assisted in the development of two states (Tennessee and Texas) from frontier outposts into settled areas. His greatest contributions came in Texas, where he led an army to victory, helped to organize a republic, and participated in its transition into a part of the United States. As a senator during the 1850's, he was one of the few southern leaders to foresee the consequences of national political policies that would lead to the Civil War. Once the war came, he stood alone as the most prominent Texas Unionist willing to sacrifice his career for the preservation of the Union. It is fitting that the largest, most industrial city in Texas bears his name.

—*Light Townsend Cummins*

FURTHER READING

Bishop, Curtis Kent. *Lone Star: Sam Houston*. New York: Julian Messner, 1961. Written for young readers, the book provides a clear assessment of Houston's career and relates the major facts of his life in an easy-to-read narrative.

Campbell, Randolph B. *Sam Houston and the American Southwest*. Edited by Oscar Handlin. 2d ed. New York: Longman, 2002. Biography relating Houston's life and ideas to the development of Texas and other areas of the Southwest during the nineteenth century.

Friend, Llerena B. *Sam Houston: The Great Designer*. Austin: University of Texas Press, 1954. Excellent scholarly biography. Treats Houston's entire career with an emphasis on his impact on national events. It is based on extensive archival research and is a good starting place for a full-scale study of Houston and his time.

Gregory, Jack, and Rennard Strickland. *Sam Houston with the Cherokees, 1829-1833*. Austin: University of Texas Press, 1967. Develops in detail the story of Houston's Indian marriage to Tiana and his role as Cherokee advocate. It is based on solid research previously unconsidered by historians, thereby providing an exhaustive analysis of Houston's years among the Indians.

Haley, James L. *Sam Houston*. Norman: University of Oklahoma Press, 2002. A more personal view of Houston, in which the author seeks to discover what "made him tick" by examining topics of importance to Houston, such as Native American relations. Houston emerges as a deeply troubled man. Well-researched, accessible biography.

Houston, Samuel. *Autobiography of Sam Houston.* Edited by Donald Day and Harry Herbert Ullom. Norman: University of Oklahoma Press, 1954. Houston paints himself in the best possible light, but this edited version provides insight into the man and his era.

_____. *The Writings of Sam Houston, 1813-1863.* Edited by Amelia Williams and Eugene C. Barker. 8 vols. Austin: University of Texas Press, 1938-1943. A comprehensive collection of the most important letters and papers dealing with Houston's career. Contains most of the extant Houston letters.

James, Marquis. *The Raven: A Biography of Sam Houston.* Indianapolis: Bobbs-Merrill, 1929. Provides a readable narrative with a colorful style. Highlights Houston's role as friend and political associate of Andrew Jackson. Until the appearance of the above-noted study by Friend, this biography ranked as the most complete analysis of Houston.

Wisehart, Marion K. *Sam Houston: American Giant.* Washington, D.C.: R. B. Luce, 1962. A laudatory, popular biography, full of detail. Although not scholarly in nature, it is useful because it is based on the important biographies noted above. An excellent study for readers at the high school level.

SEE ALSO: Stephen Fuller Austin; Andrew Jackson; Matthew Fontaine Maury; Antonio López de Santa Anna.

RELATED ARTICLES in *Great Events from History: The Nineteenth Century, 1801-1900:* September 16, 1810-September 28, 1821: Mexican War of Independence; May, 1831-February, 1832: Tocqueville Visits America; October 2, 1835-April 21, 1836: Texas Revolution; February 8, 1861: Establishment of the Confederate States of America.

ELIAS HOWE
American inventor

In addition to being the first American inventor to build a workable sewing machine and have it successfully patented, Howe combined with other sewing machine manufacturers to minimize lawsuits and maximize profits by sharing patents for fees to avoid mutually destructive competition.

BORN: July 9, 1819; Spencer, Massachusetts
DIED: October 3, 1867; Brooklyn, New York
ALSO KNOWN AS: Elias Howe, Jr. (full name)
AREA OF ACHIEVEMENT: Science and technology

EARLY LIFE

Elias Howe, Jr., was one of eight children born to a poor farmer, Elias Howe, Sr., and his wife, Polly Bemis Howe. Among the Howe family, two of Howe's father's brothers were inventors. Elias, Sr., himself ran a gristmill and cut lumber, in addition to farming, to support his family. When Elias, Jr., was six, he worked along with his brothers and sisters sewing wires on cards by hand at home. This piecework, for a local cotton mill, brought in some extra money to help the family. His other work as a boy included repairs to his parents' farmhouse. He showed great patience and determination in his painstaking tasks, often repairing the farm machinery—work he enjoyed. The young boy's life, however, was not all work. Regarded as easygoing and companionable, he had several good friends. He attended school during the winter but spent the other seasons at work on the farm.

By the time Howe was twelve, his father realized that he could no longer feed and clothe him, so he was hired out to work on a neighbor's farm. This arrangement lasted for about one year but had to end when Howe's frailties interfered with his heavy chores. The youngster had been born small and frail, and he never had the endurance and strength necessary for hard labor, a fact with which he had to contend all of his life. He was also congenitally lame.

In 1835, Howe moved to Lowell, Massachusetts, where he found work repairing cotton-mill machinery. Although he was still a young man, he was admired for his advanced skill with machinery. However, the economic panic in 1837 forced the cotton mills in Lowell to close, and young Howe lost his job.

Howe next moved to Cambridge, Massachusetts, where he roomed with a cousin and worked as a foreman for a hemp-carding company; this job was boring and fatiguing, so Howe stayed for only part of a year. His next position was a fortunate one for him. He worked as a repairman for Ari Davis of Boston, a skilled watchmaker, who also made precision instruments for seamen and for the scientists at Harvard University. Davis's shop at-

Elias Howe. (Library of Congress)

tracted many inventors, and it was here that Howe got the idea to invent a sewing machine. One day in 1839, he heard the loud-voiced Davis tell a customer who was struggling to invent a knitting machine that the invention of a sewing machine would make a man rich.

On March 3, 1841, Howe married Elizabeth J. Ames of Boston. In a few years, the couple had three children to support. To help her husband, Mrs. Howe did hand-sewing for her neighbors. Many evenings, Howe watched her sew, pondering how a sewing machine would work. In part from his fascination with machinery and in part from his desire to escape poverty and support his family, Howe became obsessed with the idea of inventing a sewing machine.

LIFE'S WORK

Howe quit his job at Davis's shop and moved into the attic of Elias Howe, Sr.'s house—now in Cambridge. There in 1843, working diligently, Howe was beginning to put together his first version of a sewing machine when a fire destroyed the house. A friend, George Fisher, took an interest in Howe's invention and generously funded him five hundred dollars for the equip-

ment he needed; Fisher also boarded the Howes in his home.

From 1844 to 1845 (especially during the winter months), Howe worked at a feverish pace to complete a functioning sewing machine. He used no blueprints or sketches but worked from a mental design; he also used the trial-and-error method of putting his ideas into moving parts, often discarding pieces of the machine that had not worked to his satisfaction. One of his most serious challenges was the designing of the proper needle for his sewing machine; needles with holes at the head (as women use in hand sewing) did not work on the machine. Finally, Howe had a dream in which men were threatening to kill him with spears; he noticed that all the spears had holes near their points—this was his solution. Howe's machine sewed perfectly when he used such needles.

By April of 1845, Howe and his business partner Fisher had a machine that they could present to the public. A demonstration was held at the Quincy Hall Clothing Manufactory, where Howe, operating his machine, sewed at least five times faster than the best women hand-sewers. The stitching produced by Howe's machine was also neater and stronger than that done by hand.

Howe's sewing machine did not impress Boston's clothiers as a useful item for them to purchase. A few factors affected the marketing of Howe's invention to American industry. First, it was expensive—about three hundred dollars. Second, the hand-sewers would have to be retrained to work by machine, and their employers feared that they would refuse (the workers knew that the sewing machines would soon take most of their jobs). Finally, the clothiers already had cheap labor in their women workers, so they saw no need to buy machinery to do the sewing. Howe was also at a disadvantage in that the United States did not yet have a strong communication network. If news of his machine had reached major clothing firms in New York City, he may have found buyers for his invention.

When Howe realized that there were no eager buyers for his machine in the United States, he sent his brother Amasa Howe to London, England, to try to market it there. The British industries were more organized than the American ones at this time and were also more acquainted with manufacture by machine. In October of 1846, Amasa Howe sold his brother's sewing machine to William Thomas of London for 250 pounds in British money. Thomas was a maker of corsets, shoes, and umbrellas, and he was also a dishonest man. He obtained a British patent for the Howe machine in his own name, rather than in Howe's as he had promised. Thomas also made a verbal agreement with Amasa to pay Elias a royalty on each sewing machine Thomas sold—an agreement that he ignored.

Howe's profits from the first sale of his invention quickly went to pay his debts. He found himself in poverty again and so accepted an offer from Thomas (still seemingly a fair man) to move to London and build for him a stronger sewing machine (presumably to sew leather for shoes). Howe and his family moved to a poor section of London, and he worked for Thomas for fifteen dollars a week. At the end of eight months, Howe had created the desired machine, and Thomas, not too graciously, ordered Howe to work as a repairman in his factory. Howe felt insulted and left.

The year 1848 was an especially difficult one for Howe. First, he had to be separated from his family. Unable to support them, he sent them home to the United States, while he remained in England to build another sewing machine with the financial help of Charles Inglis, a relatively poor man himself. When this machine was finished, Howe sold it cheaply and also pawned his American patent papers on his first sewing machine (along with a working model), in order to buy passage back to the United States.

Howe landed in New York, where he found employment as a mechanic at a good wage, but he had held this job for only a few weeks when tragedy struck. His wife, having battled consumption for two years, was dying. Elias Howe, Sr., sent his son money to travel home to see Elizabeth before she died; his brother-in-law loaned him a suit to wear to her funeral. Howe also learned that the few household goods he owned had been lost in a shipwreck on their passage from England. His father and neighbors helped him through this crisis, taking care of his children.

Ironically, at about this time, Howe learned of several American copies of his sewing machine, produced with total disregard to his U.S. patent. However, Howe remained persistent, patenting his first sewing machine on September 10, 1846, even though he had to mortgage his father's farm for the money that he needed to travel to Washington, D.C., to receive that patent.

Howe's legal patent made a considerable difference in the outcome of his life's work. He now elicited the aid of George Bliss, who had bought the 50-percent business interest in Howe's invention from George Fisher. Bliss and Howe employed the lawyers necessary to wage long court suits against the makers of American sewing machines. Howe wished to win a royalty from these manu-

facturers for each sewing machine they had sold in the United States; as the patented inventor of the machine, he had this right.

One of Howe's opponents in court proved to be a determined man himself. Isaac M. Singer, wishing to retain the fortune he was making from selling Singer sewing machines, hired help to refute Howe's claim that he was the rightful inventor. Singer located Walter Hunt of New York State, who had built a model of a sewing machine earlier than had Howe. Singer lost his case, however, when it was shown in court that Hunt's rebuilt machine did not work and that Hunt had never patented it.

Howe, after battling in court from 1849 to 1854, was victorious and, instantly, a rich man. All of his American competitors who were manufacturing and selling machines had to pay royalties to him. Soon, his income was about four thousand dollars a week. However, Howe was a generous man, sharing his new wealth with the friends and relatives who had helped him in his years of struggle. His one deep regret was that his wife had died before he gained his fortune. The humorous and fun-loving aspects of Howe's personality had left him at her tragic death.

Howe was, however, left with his dedication, which he used to good advantage in his remaining years. In 1865, in Bridgeport, Connecticut, he built a large, modern plant for the manufacture of sewing machines (later managed by his brother Amasa). Howe became a prominent and respected citizen of Bridgeport. When he volunteered to serve as a private in the Union Army during the Civil War (despite his age and infirmities) many young Bridgeport men were moved by his example and volunteered as well. Howe generously outfitted the entire Connecticut Seventeenth Regiment Volunteers, which he helped to organize; he even provided horses for the officers and paid the men when their army wages were delayed. Howe served in a Union Army camp near Baltimore, Maryland, but was forced to leave when his chronic frailty made it impossible for him to continue his duties as the camp's postmaster.

While visiting at his daughter's home in Brooklyn, New York, in 1867, Howe contracted Bright's disease; he never recovered and died October 3, 1867. The large factory he had built in Bridgeport, Connecticut, passed on to his son, who managed it until a fire leveled it on July 26, 1883. In the following year, the city of Bridgeport, in gratitude, erected a statue of Elias Howe, Jr., in its Seaside Park. He stands, hat in one hand and cane in the other, overlooking Long Island Sound. His face is large and solid, with a prominent nose, soft eyes, and firmly set lips—the face of a determined Yankee inventor.

SIGNIFICANCE

With his invention of the sewing machine, Howe made a contribution to American industry that profoundly affected Americans' lives. The hand-sewn garments that women laboriously made for their families were replaced by mass-produced clothing that sold at affordable prices. Howe's invention also moved the making of many clothing items, including shoes, out of cottage industries and tailor shops and into manufacturing plants. The sewing machine became a reasonably priced, convenient piece of equipment that was also found in a large number of homes; there sewing became a creative task, rather than a painstaking necessity.

Howe also played an important role in another area of American industrial development. He, along with several successful sewing machine manufacturers, held a conference in Albany, New York, in 1856, with the purpose of avoiding further lawsuits. These manufacturers, known as the Combination, became the first American industrial group to form a patent pool; they shared one another's machine designs and improvements for a reasonable fee, rather than remaining rivals.

Howe's inventiveness, perseverance, and mechanical skill won for him many well-deserved honors in foreign nations, including a gold medal at the famed Paris Exhibition of 1867. His genius and Yankee know-how gained for this once poverty-stricken American the acclaim of a grateful nation and a grateful world.

—Patricia E. Sweeney

FURTHER READING

Burlingame, Roger. *March of the Iron Men: A Social History of Union Through Invention.* New York: Charles Scribner's Sons, 1938. A fascinating book, well researched and well organized. As an interpreter of social history, Burlingame has strong opinions, which he defends admirably. Outstanding bibliography, chronology chart, and illustrations. Good at showing inventors' motives, including Howe's.

Chamberlain, John. *The Enterprising Americans: A Business History of the United States.* New York: Harper & Row, 1963. Originally a series in *Fortune* magazine on famous American businesspeople. Includes an extensive and helpful bibliography. Emphasis is on the wit and ingenuity of some Yankee inventors, including Howe. A lively and engaging style throughout. A good book for the high school student.

Gies, Joseph, and Frances Gies. *The Ingenious Yankees.* New York: Thomas Y. Crowell, 1976. The authors focus on how Yankee inventors helped transform an agricultural country into a powerful technological nation. Offers clarity of exposition in an interesting narrative format. A biographical sketch of Howe is included, as well as an extensive bibliography.

Iles, George. *Leading American Inventors.* New York: Henry Holt, 1912. Iles offers a careful analysis of Howe's personality, focusing on the characteristics that caused Howe's success. Iles brings his subject to life for the reader. Some of the details of Howe's life covered here are not found elsewhere; a portrait of him is included.

Poole, Lynn, and Gray Poole. *Men Who Pioneered Inventions.* New York: Dodd, Mead, 1969. A book suitable for a young person, from the Makers of Our Modern World series. Less factual information in its chapter on Howe than in the other books listed here. The Pooles describe how the sewing machine affected American life.

Thompson, Holland. *The Age of Invention: A Chronicle of Mechanical Conquest.* New Haven, Conn.: Yale University Press, 1921. One volume in a series devoted to American life, history, and progress. It has an ample bibliography, as well as photographs and illustrations. Vivid descriptive passages of Howe at work (slightly fictionalized) are provided in a narrative account of his life and work. Also details the mechanics of Howe's sewing machine.

Wilson, Mitchell. *American Science and Invention: A Pictorial History.* New York: Simon & Schuster, 1954. A large volume that relies on period illustrations and photographs to describe the course of American invention. Concise and accurate on Howe's life as well as his inventing. Good descriptions of how his machine operated. Also interesting on Howe's character, including his mechanical skill.

SEE ALSO: Ottmar Mergenthaler; George Westinghouse.

RELATED ARTICLE in *Great Events from History: The Nineteenth Century, 1801-1900:* September 10, 1846: Howe Patents His Sewing Machine.

JULIA WARD HOWE
American composer and suffragist

Howe is best remembered for composing the lyrics to the patriotic song "The Battle Hymn of the Republic" and was an active crusader for women's right to vote.

BORN: May 27, 1819; New York, New York
DIED: October 17, 1910; Newport, Rhode Island
ALSO KNOWN AS: Julia Ward (birth name)
AREAS OF ACHIEVEMENT: Literature, women's rights

EARLY LIFE

Julia Ward Howe was born Julia Ward, the second daughter and the fourth of seven children of Samuel Ward and Julia Rush Cutler Ward. Another Julia had previously been born to the Wards, only to die at the age of three. All the surviving Ward children enjoyed good relations with one another for most of their lives, especially the girls. Samuel Ward's ancestors had migrated to the United States from Gloucester, England, and settled in Rhode Island, a state that two Wards served as early governors. Samuel Ward himself was a partner in the prestigious Wall Street banking firm Prime, Ward, and King. Julia Cutler Ward, young Julia's mother, had been born in Boston but had relatives living in South Carolina, where her own mother had been a southern belle. Among the Cutler ancestors was General Francis Marion, the celebrated "Swamp Fox" of the American Revolution.

Little Julia, or "Little Miss Ward," as her family called her, had an intelligent nature combined with a sometimes fiery temper. As an adolescent, she developed scholarly habits that would remain with her throughout her life. Her father saw to it that all of his daughters were well educated; their private tutor, Joseph Cogswell, had them follow the Harvard curriculum of the early nineteenth century. Julia was also tutored in the Romance languages and took lessons in voice and piano from an Italian master.

All these things Mr. Ward was able to provide because of his comfortable financial status. He had a roomy, well-decorated house built at the corner of Bond Street and Broadway; one section of this dwelling housed his private art gallery. Mr. Ward was also, however, a strict and deeply religious man; he did not like his daughters to attend the theater or to mix too freely in New York society. Indeed, he delayed their entrance into society formally for some time, much to Julia's disappointment.

Once Julia entered New York society, she was an instant favorite. She was a petite young woman, only five feet tall. She had bright blue eyes and red hair combined with a creamy white skin in a lovely, oval-shaped face. She began to attend New York parties with some regularity when her brother, Samuel Ward, Jr., married Emily Astor of the wealthy Astor family, in 1837.

Julia Ward faced two tragedies in her early life. Her mother died when she was five; she had been tubercular and died of a fever days after giving birth to her seventh child. Mr. Ward was devastated by the early death of his wife, who was only twenty-eight; he invited her intelligent, witty sister, Miss Eliza Cutler, to reside in his home and care for his children. Little Julia showed much of the wit for which her aunt was noted; she also liked to write poetry, as her mother had done.

Julia had recently turned twenty when her father died. At that time Edward Ward, an uncle, looked after the orphaned children and managed their finances. Julia was deeply upset by her father's death. Shortly after, in 1841, she journeyed to visit friends in Boston to try to end her depression. Among her Massachusetts acquaintances was Henry Wadsworth Longfellow, a longtime friend of her brother, Samuel. While in Boston, Julia accompanied Longfellow on a visit to the Perkins Institute for the Blind. There she met the school's director, a famous educator and reformer, Dr. Samuel Gridley Howe. Dr. Howe, also a physician, was a tall and handsome bachelor of forty. Julia, now twenty-two, was attracted to him. They first appeared publicly as a couple in 1842 at a farewell dinner given for Charles Dickens in Boston, and shortly thereafter, their engagement was announced. They were married on April 23, 1843, after what is recorded as a stormy courtship.

The transition from girlhood and a relatively happy life among the cultured society of New York to that of a wife, mother, and homemaker in the unfamiliar setting of Boston was not easy for Julia Ward Howe. In New York she had been a favorite child in the extended Ward family living on clannish Bond Street; she had a quick wit, a winning charm, and skill as a conversationalist—all of which endeared her to New York society on the whole. In Boston, however, the new Mrs. Howe was a stranger. Her husband's friends included such men as Horace Mann, an educator of the deaf, and Ralph Waldo Emerson, the Transcendentalist, and while she got along well with these men, Boston society as a group did not embrace her.

Some of Howe's own actions caused Bostonians to keep their distance from her during the early years of her marriage. She did not know how to entertain guests in her home, because she had had servants to do that in New York. She also became a controversial figure because of her gift for repartee, which she could at times direct sharply against people. Howe had always been high-spirited—meaning that she had a mind of her own and often spoke her opinions. These traits not only hurt her in Boston society, where women were demure and passive, but also caused trouble between her and Dr. Howe, especially during the 1850's.

Dr. Howe was attracted to his wife for her beauty and vitality, but he never reconciled himself to her independent spirit. One of the greatest sources of argument for the couple was her literary career. She had a volume of lyric poetry published anonymously in 1854 under the title *Passion Flowers*, and some of the pieces in it proved too passionate to meet with her husband's approval. Dr. Howe was infuriated when Julia Ward Howe (by rumor) became publicly known as the book's author. Dr. Howe did not approve of women working outside their homes,

and this was especially true for his own wife, who had their six children to rear.

LIFE'S WORK

In the tense, unstable years before the Civil War, Dr. Howe did turn to Julia for literary assistance. He was an active abolitionist and edited a newspaper, *The Commonwealth*, to aid the cause. Julia Ward Howe wrote literary columns for this paper and reviewed books, plays, and concerts, and was also its proofreader. Also, during the late 1850's, Howe and her husband helped shelter fugitive slaves, who were fleeing to Canada and freedom, in their South Boston home.

When the Civil War broke out, Howe was frightened that the North would not win. She had hoped to do volunteer work to aid the army, but she was not as adept at bandage-rolling and knitting as were her women friends. Instead, she joined the women's auxiliary unit of the United States Sanitary Commission, of which Dr. Howe was a prominent member. This group worked for sanitary conditions for soldiers in camps and in hospitals; the organization was a forerunner of the American Red Cross.

It was on work for the American Sanitary Commission that Dr. and Mrs. Howe traveled to Washington, D.C., in November of 1861. Howe, her minister, and his wife were taken by carriage one morning to review the Union troops just outside the city. A sudden Confederate raid, however, forced them all to march back into Washington. During the slow ride, Howe and her companions sang "John Brown's Body," a popular tune of the day. Her friends in the carriage suggested that she write more meaningful lyrics for the song. At dawn the next morning, Howe arose from her bed in the Willard Hotel to write the poetry that would make the song beloved and famous. Howe wrote "The Battle Hymn of the Republic" on the stationery of the American Sanitary Commission on the morning of November 18, 1861, and in February of 1862, it was published in the *Atlantic Monthly*.

The hymn quickly became a favorite, probably because of its inspirational quality. Howe had written her finest poem for this hymn; her language was evocative of the Bible and indicative of patriotism. The men of the Union Army sang the new tune as a spur to fight on for freedom for all men in the bloody months

Julia Ward Howe. (Library of Congress)

of the Civil War. Howe was always proud to have written "The Battle Hymn of the Republic," for she felt it was her own contribution to the cause of justice for which the Union Army was struggling.

Howe had a full and illustrious public career even after the war years. In 1868, she became a founding member of the New England Woman's Club, a group that advocated the improvement of woman's place in American society; she would serve as its president for forty years. A similar group on the national level was the Association for the Advancement of Women, which Howe helped begin during the mid-1870's; she would lead it as president from 1878 to 1888. Howe firmly espoused her beliefs that women had to be allowed the freedom of a complete education and admission into the professions; she also became an advocate of suffrage for women.

As an elderly man, Dr. Howe suffered increasingly from ill health. Howe nursed him in his final illness and was with him when he died of a stroke in January of 1876. In her widowhood, she became even more dedicated to the causes of woman suffrage and world peace. She traveled throughout the United States and Canada, inspiring women to form women's clubs and suffrage associations in their cities. She also helped found the Women's International Peace Association beginning in 1871 and attended conferences in Europe on its behalf. Howe, despite her long life, would not live to see either of these two major causes reach fruition. She firmly believed, however, that the glory in her life had been in waging a noble battle for justice and peace for all men and women. She remained an active lecturer and essayist up to the last day of her life. Howe died in Newport, Rhode Island, at her summer home on October 17, 1910; she was ninety-one years old.

SIGNIFICANCE

When Howe died, she was greatly mourned. She had been a popular lecturer and social reformer active in American life for several decades. Although not all Americans agreed with her ideas, almost all admired her courage in living by her convic-

---

"THE BATTLE HYMN OF THE REPUBLIC"

Mine eyes have seen the glory of the coming of the Lord;
He is trampling out the vintage where the grapes of wrath are stored;
He hath loosed the fateful lightning of His terrible swift sword;
His truth is marching on.
Glory! Glory! Hallelujah! Glory! Glory! Hallelujah!
Glory! Glory! Hallelujah! His truth is marching on.

I have seen Him in the watch fires of a hundred circling camps
They have builded Him an altar in the evening dews and damps;
I can read His righteous sentence by the dim and flaring lamps;
His day is marching on.
Glory! Glory! Hallelujah! Glory! Glory! Hallelujah!
Glory! Glory! Hallelujah! His day is marching on.

I have read a fiery Gospel writ in burnished rows of steel;
"As ye deal with My contemners, so with you My grace shall deal";
Let the Hero, born of woman, crush the serpent with His heel,
Since God is marching on.
Glory! Glory! Hallelujah! Glory! Glory! Hallelujah!
Glory! Glory! Hallelujah! Since God is marching on.

He has sounded forth the trumpet that shall never call retreat;
He is sifting out the hearts of men before His judgment seat;
Oh, be swift, my soul, to answer Him! be jubilant, my feet;
Our God is marching on.
Glory! Glory! Hallelujah! Glory! Glory! Hallelujah!
Glory! Glory! Hallelujah! Our God is marching on.

In the beauty of the lilies Christ was born across the sea,
With a glory in His bosom that transfigures you and me:
As He died to make men holy, let us live to make men free;
[*originally*: let us die to make men free]
While God is marching on.
Glory! Glory! Hallelujah! Glory! Glory! Hallelujah!
Glory! Glory! Hallelujah! While God is marching on.

He is coming like the glory of the morning on the wave,
He is wisdom to the mighty, He is honor to the brave;
So the world shall be His footstool, and the soul of wrong His slave,
Our God is marching on.
Glory! Glory! Hallelujah! Glory! Glory! Hallelujah!
Glory! Glory! Hallelujah! Our God is marching on.

tions. She was also much admired for her great vitality and sound intelligence, which she sustained for all of her ninety-one years.

Howe became a familiar figure at the Boston State House, where she testified for many years before the state legislature on bills advocating women's and children's rights, world peace, female suffrage, and improvement of sanitation systems. In her earliest days as a public speaker, Howe had specialized in lectures on philosophers (her favorites were Immanuel Kant and Baruch Spinoza) and religion. After reading her essays to her friends in her home during the mid-1860's, she was asked to speak at area churches as well. On her first such lecture in her own Unitarian church in January of 1864, she wore a sedate black dress and placed a white lace cap on her head; this garment was to become her standard dress on lecture platforms in the United States and Europe.

At the time of her death, Howe had written four volumes of poetry, two plays (one of which was produced), a memoir of Dr. Samuel G. Howe, a fine biography of Margaret Fuller, and several books of essays reflecting her travel experiences, social views, and religious beliefs. Howe accomplished all this in an era when women were strongly discouraged from having public careers.

—Patricia E. Sweeney

FURTHER READING

Clifford, Deborah P. *Mine Eyes Have Seen the Glory: A Biography of Julia Ward Howe, 1819-1910.* Boston: Little, Brown, 1979. A scholarly study with illustrations and a good bibliography. Clifford is the first modern author to write a life of Howe. She judges Howe's literary talents for the reader, demonstrating the brilliance of the lectures in comparison with the poetry. Interesting discussion of Howe's difficulties with her marriage.

Elliott, Maud H., and Laura E. Richards. *Julia Ward Howe: 1819-1910.* Boston: Houghton Mifflin, 1915. Howe's two daughters won a Pulitzer Prize for this excellent study of their mother. They relied on many of Howe's own letters to tell her fascinating story—her personal life as well as her public life is recounted in this lively narrative.

Grant, Mary H. *Private Woman, Public Person: An Account of the Life of Julia Ward Howe from 1819-1868.* Brooklyn, N.Y.: Carlson, 1994. A feminist biography, covering Howe's life from birth until her decision to become an activist on behalf of women. Describes her transformation from a frustrated housewife to the first president of the New England Women's Club.

Hall, Florence Marion Howe. *Memories Grave and Gay.* New York: Harper & Brothers, 1918. The eldest surviving daughter of Julia Ward Howe gives the reader an intimate portrait of her mother in her reminiscences. Hall includes chapters on the antislavery movement, the Civil War, and her mother's work on behalf of soldiers and women. She also pays tribute to her mother in closing this book.

_____. *The Story of "The Battle Hymn of the Republic."* New York: Harper & Brothers, 1916. Howe's eldest daughter re-creates the scene of the writing of the patriotic hymn. She also details how the song was used on subsequent occasions and how its fame affected her mother. Hall also carefully recalls the turmoil, bitterness, anguish, and tragedy of the Civil War era that affected the hymn's reception.

Howe, Julia Ward. *Reminiscences: 1819-1899.* Boston: Houghton Mifflin, 1899. Howe, from the perspective of age eighty, reminisces about many interesting and famous people she met in her life, including such luminaries as Charles Dickens, Thomas Carlyle, Henry Wadsworth Longfellow, and William Wordsworth. She also discusses her husband and their life together.

Howe, Maud. *The Eleventh Hour in the Life of Julia Ward Howe.* Boston: Little, Brown, 1911. Howe's daughter wrote this small volume immediately after her mother's death to read to family friends. It gives insight into the old age of a remarkably spry and solidly intelligent woman who faced her final years with unusual vigor and courage. Emphasizes Howe's keen wit and her need to give of herself for worthy causes.

Tharp, Louise H. *Three Saints and a Sinner: Julia Ward Howe, Louisa, Annie, and Sam Ward.* Boston: Little, Brown, 1956. A well-researched book with a good bibliography. The author keeps the reader eager for more of her engrossing and well-paced narrative. She is good at presenting the essential interactions among the Ward siblings, as she places them in the social background of nineteenth century New York, Boston, and Europe.

Williams, Gary. *Hungry Heart: The Literary Emergence of Julia Ward Howe.* Amherst: University of Massachusetts Press, 1999. Reexamines Howe's literary career and her emergence as a writer. Analyzes *Passion Flowers* and Howe's unpublished story about a hermaphrodite protagonist, relating these writings to Howe's life.

Ziegler, Valerie H. *Diva Julia: The Public Romance and Private Agony of Julia Ward Howe.* Harrisburg, Pa.: Trinity Press International, 2003. Balanced biography, depicting Howe as a "superwoman," juggling the demands of a troubled marriage, her children, and her desire to write and participate in the world.

SEE ALSO: John Brown; Charles Dickens; Ralph Waldo Emerson; Margaret Fuller; Samuel Gridley Howe; Henry Wadsworth Longfellow; Horace Mann; William Wordsworth.

RELATED ARTICLES in *Great Events from History: The Nineteenth Century, 1801-1900:* 1820's-1850's: Social Reform Movement; December 6, 1865: Thirteenth Amendment Is Ratified; May 10, 1866: Suffragists Protest the Fourteenth Amendment; May, 1869: Woman Suffrage Associations Begin Forming; February 17-18, 1890: Women's Rights Associations Unite.

SAMUEL GRIDLEY HOWE
American educator and social reformer

Howe was a universal reformer who made his greatest contributions to the education of the blind, the deaf-blind, and the mentally disabled. His monumental efforts significantly enhanced social concern for persons with disabilities in the United States.

BORN: November 10, 1801; Boston, Massachusetts
DIED: January 9, 1876; Boston, Massachusetts
AREAS OF ACHIEVEMENT: Education, philanthropy

EARLY LIFE

Samuel Gridley Howe was the son of Joseph Howe and Patty Gridley Howe, both of old New England stock. His father was a cordage manufacturer and steadfast Jeffersonian Republican. A man of principle, as his son was to be, he accepted government bonds in payment for purchases during the War of 1812 and suffered serious financial losses. Samuel attended Boston Latin School and was frequently harassed for his father's politics. The only one of three brothers to attend college, Samuel entered Brown, rather than Federalist-dominated Harvard, in 1817. Young Howe excelled at campus pranks, but his academic performance was mediocre. As a Unitarian among Baptists, Howe once again learned to appreciate the position of the underdog—a useful trait for a future philanthropist.

Being graduated in 1821, Howe enrolled at Harvard Medical School and began to apply himself, enjoying especially anatomy and dissection. After commencement, however, he decided against a traditional practice. Stirred by the Greek War of Independence, a popular cause of the time, Howe left for the Peloponnisos, arriving in early 1827. In Greece he played many roles with distinction. As a physician, he served Greek forces on land and sea. As the agent of American relief committees, he distributed emergency rations, briefly returning to the United States to raise additional funds. Once back

in Greece, he developed and ran sizable work relief programs. For his exertions, Howe was knighted by the Greek king as a Chevalier of the Order of the Holy Savior. With the war all but over, Chev, as his friends now called him, returned to Boston in April, 1831. Tall, dark, and handsome, not yet sporting the beard of later years, Howe was a knight-errant seeking a new cause to uplift humanity.

LIFE'S WORK

As luck would have it, the projected New England School for the Blind, incorporated in 1829, needed a director in order to become a reality; the trustees of the school offered Howe the job. Excited by the challenge, he accepted immediately and sailed for Europe to study current techniques for educating the blind. Howe soon became convinced that European efforts were either too intellectual or too mechanical. A more balanced curriculum, he believed, including physical education and greater encouragement of self-reliance, was required. After imprisonment in Prussia for assisting Polish refugees, Howe returned to Boston in July, 1832. During the following August, the first school for the blind in the nation opened its doors with seven students and three staff members.

As director, Howe tried to tailor the curriculum—reading, writing, mathematics, geography, music, physical education, and manual training—to the needs and abilities of the individual student. He fashioned letters of twine and glued them to cards for reading instruction; he invented an improved method of raised printing that significantly lowered costs of manufacture. (Braille was not yet in use.) Howe trooped his students before legislative committees and popular audiences to secure funds, went out into the country to recruit students, and traveled to other states to promote more schools for the blind. As a result of his strenuous activity, the school, renamed Perkins Institution, soon required larger quarters.

In 1837, Howe heard of Laura Bridgman, an eight-year-old who, at the age of two, had lost her sight and hearing through scarlet fever. Howe, who believed in phrenology and innate mental dispositions, was confident that the child could be taught, despite near-universal opinion that the deaf-blind were completely uneducable. He induced her parents to enroll Laura at Perkins.

For several tedious months, Howe tried to get Laura to match raised words with physical objects and make words of letters. Suddenly one day, Laura understood that here was a way to communicate her thoughts to other minds; her face "lighted up with a human expression." This was the greatest single moment in Howe's career. John Greenleaf Whittier proclaimed that Howe was "the Cadmus of the blind." Charles Dickens, who met Laura Bridgman in 1842, lionized Howe's accomplishment in *American Notes* (1842). Howe soon became a world-renowned figure.

Howe's international stature certainly aided his election as a Whig to the Massachusetts House of Representatives in November, 1842. Though only a freshman legislator, he chaired the committee on public charities. Working closely with Dorothea Lynde Dix, Howe personally wrote the bill reforming care of the mentally ill, which passed by overwhelming margins in March, 1843.

In April, 1843, Howe married Julia Ward, who was of a prominent New York family. Their marriage was frequently tempestuous; their personalities did not mesh well. Prideful, demanding, and eighteen years her senior, Howe never approved of Julia's literary aspirations. He normally placed his many reform interests ahead of his wife and his eventual family of six children.

After returning to work in September, 1844, after a European honeymoon, Howe immediately joined his friend Horace Mann, secretary of the state Board of Education, in a battle to reform the Boston grammar schools. In 1845, Howe turned to education of those with mental impairments, undertaking an extensive, two-year training program that he followed up with a comprehensive report to the legislature. Once again, the lawmakers followed his bidding and established in 1848 the Massachusetts School for the Idiotic and Feeble-Minded Youth, another first in American history. Howe served as superintendent of that institution as well as of Perkins until his death in 1876.

Although Howe disapproved of slavery, he remained aloof from agitation until the admission of Texas drew him into the fray. During the Mexican War, Howe became a Conscience Whig, running unsuccessfully for Congress in 1846; in 1851, he helped orchestrate the election of his close friend Charles Sumner to the U.S.

Samuel Gridley Howe. (Library of Congress)

Senate. In response to the Kansas-Nebraska Act, Howe moved toward radical abolitionism.

In 1854, Howe was an organizer of both the New England Emigrant Aid Company and the Massachusetts Kansas Aid Committee, the latter formed to obtain guns for antislavery settlers. In January, 1857, John Brown visited Howe and other Boston supporters (the "Secret Six"), obtaining money from the committee and several token guns from Howe personally. In March, 1858, the group gave Brown additional funding to liberate slaves, a plan that culminated in the Harpers Ferry raid of October, 1859. When authorities uncovered Brown's correspondence, Howe fled, panic-stricken, to Canada on the flimsy pretext that he was promoting education of the blind. Involvement of the nation's foremost humanitarian in Brown's scheme further unnerved the South and increased sectional tensions.

During the Civil War, Howe returned to less violent philanthropy. He helped to establish the United States Sanitary Commission in June, 1861, serving on its board for the duration. The commission made important recommendations for "preserving and restoring the health of the troops," which doubtless reduced fatalities. Howe was also a member of the three-man American Freedmen's Inquiry Commission set up in 1863 to investigate the condition of free blacks and make proposals for their future welfare. The commission laid the foundations for the later Freedmen's Bureau.

In 1863, Massachusetts governor John Andrew named Howe chairman of the new Massachusetts Board of State Charities, created to coordinate eleemosynary institutions and programs. After the war, Howe, who strongly disagreed with the sign language system used at the American Asylum in Hartford, sought a charter for a school for the deaf that would teach finger spelling and articulation. The legislature again complied, incorporating Clarke Institution at Northampton in 1867.

Although in declining health after the war, Howe embarked in 1871 on his last crusade. President Ulysses S. Grant, manipulated by speculators, favored annexing Santo Domingo. The Senate rejected the treaty, in part because of Charles Sumner's virulent opposition, but Grant named an investigative commission in hopes of recouping support. Despite his long friendship with Sumner, Howe agreed to serve and after a visit to the island became converted to annexation. Howe apparently had hopes of concluding his career as a territorial governor who in philosopher-king fashion would reform Santo Domingo into a tropical paradise. Such dreams were doomed by continuing Senate opposition.

After the disappointing conclusion of the Dominican affair, Howe's health steadily deteriorated. In constant pain and severely depressed, he collapsed on January 4, 1876, and died five days later. Several hours before the end, Laura Bridgman (symbolically on behalf of all those who had or would benefit from his tireless philanthropy) kissed the unconscious Howe farewell.

SIGNIFICANCE

Samuel Gridley Howe lived in an optimistic age, in a city and state seething with the ferment of reform; not only was he in harmony with the spirit of his times, he was a symbol of the age as well. In those heady days, true heroism was seen by many as victory over social evil and human suffering. As the foremost philanthropist in the nation, Howe was, in the words of John Greenleaf Whittier, "The Hero."

A Whig in politics and a Unitarian in religion, Howe was a Yankee elitist who accepted the essential goodness of God and humanity and the inevitability of progress. A nineteenth century romantic, Howe rejected John Locke's concept of knowledge drawn solely from the five senses for belief in innate mental dispositions. This thinking as well as Howe's emphasis on self-reliance was clearly in line with that of his friend Theodore Parker and other Transcendentalists. Like many other Americans of the era, Howe was also strongly influenced by phrenology. This pseudoscience (which posited a body-mind unity) maintained that a balanced education, both

intellectual and physical, could influence cerebral growth and skull dimensions. Howe's phrenological and vaguely Transcendentalist assumptions frequently guided his reform endeavors. His temporary obsession with the abolitionist movement during the 1850's was typical of most antebellum reformers.

Howe was involved in many causes, but his major impact on American society was in his efforts for the education of people with disabilities. He firmly believed that most people with physical and mental disabilities could become independent and productive citizens. His refusal to accept traditional prejudices concerning the capabilities of the blind, the deaf-blind, the deaf, and the mentally impaired led him to found institutions and develop instructional strategies still important today. Howe's most enduring legacy may be his creation of a continuing public consciousness that disabilities can be surmounted, that, in the words of his life motto, Obstacles Are Things to Be Overcome.

—*Parker Bradley Nutting*

FURTHER READING

Brooks, Van Wyck. *Flowering of New England, 1815-1865*. New York: E. P. Dutton, 1936. A scholarly, readable description of the intellectual environment within which Howe thrived. Howe is not discussed in detail, but many of his acquaintances, including Theodore Parker, are.

Clifford, Deborah P. *Mine Eyes Have Seen the Glory: A Biography of Julia Ward Howe*. Boston: Little, Brown, 1979. A well-researched biography quite favorable to Mrs. Howe. It illuminates Howe's stormy marriage and the more disagreeable aspects of his personality. For Howe, reform did not include the liberation of married women.

Dickens, Charles. *American Notes for General Circulation*. London: Chapman and Hall, 1842. Reprint. London: Oxford University Press, 1966. Though frequently critical of things American, Dickens was extremely impressed by Howe's work. He quotes extensively from Howe's annual *Reports* to the Perkins trustees concerning the education of Laura Bridgman, a source not readily available to the interested reader.

Freeberg, Ernest. *The Education of Laura Bridgman: First Deaf and Blind Person to Learn Language*. Cambridge, Mass.: Harvard University Press, 2001. One of two recent books about Howe's relationship with Bridgman. Although Gitter (see below) provides more biographical information, Freeberg focuses on Howe's specific methods for educating Bridgman, describing how he was influenced by Unitarianism and phrenology. Howe, Freeberg maintains, sought to make Bridgman's education a model of "moral discipline" so he could gain greater insight into human nature.

Gitter, Elisabeth. *The Imprisoned Guest: Samuel Howe and Laura Bridgman, the Original Deaf-Blind Girl.* New York: Farrar, Straus and Giroux, 2001. Describes how and why Howe educated Bridgman, explaining the social, intellectual and cultural context in which Howe and Bridgman transformed public perception of people with multiple disabilities.

Lamson, Mary Swift. *Life and Education of Laura Dewey Bridgman, the Deaf, Dumb, and Blind Girl.* Boston: New England Publishing, 1878. Lamson was one of Laura's teachers. She quotes extensively from her own journal, those of other teachers, and from Howe's *Reports.* A very personal account, it reveals the difficulties of working with Howe.

Richard, Laura E. *Laura Bridgman: The Story of an Opened Door.* New York: D. Appleton, 1928. A full-length biography, written by Howe's daughter, who was Laura Bridgman's namesake. Strong on the relationship between Howe and Bridgman. Includes source materials not readily available.

_____, ed. *Letters and Journals of Samuel Gridley Howe.* 2 vols. Boston: Dana Estes, 1906. Collection contains excerpts from Howe's letters, journals, and annual *Reports,* connected by a running commentary. The period to 1832 is accorded the same weight as the rest of Howe's life. Despite such unevenness, this is the closest thing to a printed collection of Howe's papers.

Sanborn, Franklin Benjamin. *Dr. S. G. Howe: The Philanthropist.* New York: Funk & Wagnalls, 1891. The first scholarly biography, still worth consulting. The author, one of the Secret Six, is laudatory, but the book contains extensive, frequently revealing quotations from original sources. Strong on the antislavery days.

Schwartz, Harold. *Samuel Gridley Howe: Social Reformer, 1801-1876.* Cambridge, Mass.: Harvard University Press, 1956. Based on extensive research in the Howe manuscripts in Houghton Library at Harvard. Places Howe solidly in his intellectual and social milieu. Notes influence of phrenology. A very balanced work.

SEE ALSO: John Brown; Charles Dickens; Ulysses S. Grant; Julia Ward Howe; Horace Mann; Theodore Parker; Charles Sumner; John Greenleaf Whittier.

RELATED ARTICLES in *Great Events from History: The Nineteenth Century, 1801-1900:* 1820's-1850's: Social Reform Movement; October 16-18, 1859: Brown's Raid on Harpers Ferry.

MARGARET LINDSAY HUGGINS
British astronomer

Huggins engaged in a lifelong collaboration with her husband, with whom she did pioneering work in the field of astronomical spectroscopy, which they employed to study planets, stars, and nebulae. Together, they established the gaseous nature of the Orion nebula and published an important atlas of stellar spectra.

BORN: August 14, 1848; Dublin, Ireland
DIED: May 24, 1915; Chelsea, England
ALSO KNOWN AS: Margaret Lindsay Murray (birth name); Margaret Lindsay Murray Huggins; Lady Margaret Lindsay Huggins
AREA OF ACHIEVEMENT: Astronomy

EARLY LIFE

Margaret Lindsay Murray was the second child of a solicitor, John Murray, and Helen Lindsay Murray, who were both of Scottish descent. Although her mother died

when she was only eight, Margaret was apparently well cared for and became accomplished in music, writing, painting, and knowledge of antique furniture. She spent considerable time with her grandfather, who kindled her interest in astronomy by teaching her about the constellations, and she attended private school in Brighton, England. Little opportunity for higher education was available for women at the time, so she developed many of her skills on her own.

From about the age of ten, Margaret began a systematic study of sunspots. While she was in her early teens, she constructed a small telescope and used it to map sunspots. After reading an article in the magazine *Good Word* on the new science of spectroscopy—which identified elements by the unique patterns of lines in their spectra—she made her own prism spectroscope. She used her spectroscope to observe the dark lines in the solar spectrum that had been discovered by Joseph von Fraunhofer in 1814 and that were used in 1859 by Gustav

Kirchhoff and Robert Bunsen to identify vaporized elements in the sun's atmosphere. Margaret also developed a considerable skill in photography. As a result of these interests, she was introduced to the English amateur astronomer William Huggins, whom she married on September 8, 1875, at the Monkstown Parish Church near her family home. He was fifty-one, some twenty-four years her senior.

LIFE'S WORK

After their marriage, Margaret and William Huggins became lifelong collaborators in the new field of spectroscopic astronomy. William already had an established reputation in astronomy, but Margaret brought new skills and energy to complement his efforts. William was from a wealthy family who lived at Tulse Hill in Lambeth, a suburb south of London. In about 1854, he sold the family business and built a private observatory in the garden of the family home.

Before he married Margaret, Huggins had been a lone observer, except for a brief collaboration with William Allen Miller during the early 1860's. He had begun visual observations with a spectroscope, and Miller had assisted him in making photographs using an inconvenient wet process that yielded few results. Huggins and Miller demonstrated that stars produce continuous spectra with dark (absorption) lines like those of the sun. Some nebulae had similar dark-line spectra, indicating that they might consist of clusters of stars, but other nebulae were found to have bright (emission) lines that suggested they were gaseous. In 1868, Huggins made the important discovery that the lines emitted by moving sources, such as double stars, shifted toward the blue end of the spectrum when their sources were moving toward the solar system, and they shifted toward the red end of the spectrum when they were moving away. He correctly interpreted this as a Doppler shift that made it possible to measure the speed of the stars in the line of sight.

As the wife of William, Margaret Huggins contributed her skills in the newly developed use of dry photographic plates in addition to her intense interest in astronomical spectroscopy. Together they began a systematic program of investigating the chemical and physical properties of celestial sources using the new techniques of spectroscopy and photography. The Royal Society had provided a fifteen-inch refracting telescope and an eighteen-inch reflecting telescope for use at the Tulse Hill observatory. In 1876, Margaret assisted her husband in fitting the telescopes with photographic

plates using the new dry-plate process, and they began their pioneering work in photographing astronomical spectra.

Although Margaret did not appear at first as coauthor of her husband's published papers, he acknowledged her help in them. She immediately began making the entries in their laboratory notebooks, which clearly reveal her active involvement in all aspects of their work. She took particular interest in experimental design and in obtaining photographs. During 1876, she experimented with a variety of photographic plates, using both dry and gelatin plates with differing light sensitivities. For several years, she and her husband worked on obtaining long-exposure photographs of the planets, and Margaret gained special skill in guiding the telescope. They then fitted the eighteen-inch reflecting telescope with two special prisms for photographing the ultraviolet spectra of the stars. Before 1880, they published "The Photographic Spectra of Uranus, Saturn and Mars," "Lines of Wolf-Rayet Stars in Cygnus," "The Photographic Spectra of Stars," and other papers in scientific journals.

During the 1880's, Margaret worked with her husband to determine the nature of nebulae. In 1882, they became the first astronomers to obtain a photograph of the spectrum from the dim light of a nebula, the gaseous nebula in Orion. Such gaseous nebulae were characterized by bright green emission lines. These lines were close to several spectrum lines of known elements, especially magnesium, leading the astronomer Norman Lockyer to suggest that nebulae result from swarms of colliding meteors rich in magnesium. However, the Hugginses compared the green line of the nebula with the much brighter lines of burning magnesium and demonstrated that it did not coincide with any magnesium lines. They thought that the nebula's green line might be produced by an unknown element, which they called nebulium; however, the line was later shown to be caused by the ionization of oxygen and nitrogen in conditions not attainable on earth. In 1889, this work was the subject of the first paper on which Margaret's name appeared as coauthor, "On the Spectrum, Visible and Photographic, of the Great Nebula in Orion" in the *Proceedings of the Royal Society*.

During the 1890's, Margaret continued to work with her husband on stellar spectra. Their work culminated in the publication of the *Atlas of Representative Stellar Spectra* in 1899. In 1906, she edited the addresses that her husband had given to the Royal Society during the five years he had been its president. In 1909, they published their collected *Scientific Papers*, which they edited jointly together. William, who was knighted in 1897, died on May 12, 1910. Margaret was working on his biography when she died five years later.

SIGNIFICANCE

Margaret Huggins was one of the few women who actually practiced astronomy before the twentieth century. Only by collaborating with husbands or other family members were these women able to gain access to the observatory. She made significant contributions as a pioneer in astronomical applications of both spectroscopy and photography, developing important techniques in both fields. Her most important achievement was in obtaining with her husband the first photograph of the spectrum from the dim light of a nebula and differentiating it from the spectral lines of any known element.

Margaret's work on stars and nebulae helped to identify the two main types of nebulae as either gaseous sources or clusters of stars. The latter discovery eventually led to the discovery of galaxies containing billions of stars. She and her husband demonstrated the possibilities of chemical and physical analysis of celestial objects and provided many examples of stellar spectra that could be further analyzed by others. These techniques and results led to the modern understanding of the evolution and structure of stars.

—*Joseph L. Spradley*

FURTHER READING

Becker, Barbara J. "Celestial Spectroscopy: Making Reality Fit the Myth." *Science* 301 (September 5, 2003): 1332-22. This article places the work of Margaret Huggins and her husband in its historical context.

Belkora, Leila. *Minding the Heavens: The Story of Our Discovery of the Milky Way.* Bristol, England: Institute of Physics, 2003. A chapter on William Huggins includes a good discussion of Margaret's role and contributions.

Pycior, Helena, Nancy Slack, and Pnina Abir-Am, eds. *Creative Couples in Science.* New Brunswick, N.J.: Rutgers University Press, 1996. This book on the contributions of women working with their husbands includes a chapter by Barbara J. Becker on Margaret Huggins documenting her important role as more than just an assistant to her husband.

Whiting, Sarah F. "Lady Huggins." *The Astrophysical Journal* 42 (July, 1915): 1-3. Obituary written by an American friend and fellow astronomer.

SEE ALSO: Williamina Paton Stevens Fleming; Samuel Pierpont Langley; Albert A. Michelson; Maria Mitchell; Simon Newcomb.

RELATED ARTICLES in *Great Events from History: The Nineteenth Century, 1801-1900:* January 1, 1801: First Asteroid Is Discovered; 1814: Fraunhofer Invents the Spectroscope.

VICTOR HUGO
French novelist

Hugo was one of the great authors of the nineteenth century, and by the force of his personality he also became one of its great public figures, using his enormous popularity in the service of many political and social causes. His literary career, spanning six of the most turbulent decades in modern European history, encompassed poetry, drama, the novel, and nonfiction writing.

BORN: February 26, 1802; Besançon, France
DIED: May 22, 1885; Paris, France
ALSO KNOWN AS: Victor-Marie Hugo (full name)
AREA OF ACHIEVEMENT: Literature

EARLY LIFE

Victor-Marie Hugo was the third son of Joseph Léopold Sigisbert Hugo and Sophie Trébuchet Hugo. At the time of their marriage in 1797, Joseph Hugo was a rising young Bonapartist soldier imbued with the ideals of the French Revolution; Sophie, the orphaned daughter of a Breton ship's captain, had been reared by an aunt of pronounced Royalist sympathies. Thus, in his earliest years, the two poles of contemporary French politics became factors in his life.

An early estrangement of Hugo's parents, the result of personal incompatibilities magnified by the dislocations of his father's military career, became permanent, and Victor and his brother Eugène went with their mother to live in Paris. Though Victor's childhood was touched by the color and the upheaval of the Napoleonic era, by the age of seven he was able to read and translate Latin, and by his tenth year his spotty education had been augmented by trips to Italy and Spain.

After 1814, Hugo's education proceeded along more

orthodox lines, but it left him time to write verse and plays; at the age of twenty, financial and critical recognition of his talent enabled him to wed his childhood playmate, Adèle Foucher, a shy, pious young woman to whom he had pledged his love in the spring of 1819. An early novel, *Han d'Islande* (1823; *Hans of Iceland*, 1845), is the feverishly emotional product of Hugo's courtship of Adèle, but more significant for Hugo's development at this time were his contributions to the short-lived periodical *Muse française*, which shows a modification of his Royalist sympathies and a recognition that a poet should play a role in society. Hugo's ideas of literary form were evolving from a conservative classicism, which had won for him early popularity, toward a forward-looking but less well-defined Romanticism. In 1826, a small book of poems, *Odes et ballades*, signaled Hugo's embrace of Romanticism by substituting the inspiration of "pictures, dreams, scenes, narratives, superstitious legends, popular traditions" for the authority of literary convention.

Though of somewhat short stature, Hugo was a strikingly attractive man in youth as well as old age. With a high forehead and penetrating eyes, he seemed both austere and engaging, and he had a reputation as an excellent conversationalist. Few nineteenth century personalities were portrayed as often as Hugo was; contemporary drawings and photographs show him as an extraordinarily intense and commanding personality.

As early as the 1820's, Hugo's home had become a magnet for other young authors and artists. Newly married to an attractive wife, he was often host to an informal group of Romantic personalities that included his friend Charles-Augustin Sainte-Beuve, the painter Eugène Delacroix, and the sculptor David d'Angers. Known as the *cénacle*, or brotherhood, Hugo's circle became not only a source of mutual support for its youthful members, but also a font of the new movement in art, Romanticism. Its ideals can be gauged by reference to Hugo's *La Préface de Cromwell* (1827; English translation, 1896), which was celebrated as a manifesto of Romanticism.

In this preface to his long play *Cromwell* (1827; English translation, 1896), Hugo contributes to the redefinition of the three unities of time, place, and action that lie at the heart of French classical literature. He calls for greater realism and freedom in dramatic production, stating that "all that is in nature belongs to art" and arguing for the union of the grotesque and the sublime in the work of literary art. *La Préface de Cromwell* has been called Hugo's masterpiece as a literary apprentice; it marks his liberation from the vestiges of eighteenth cen-

Victor Hugo. (Library of Congress)

tury ideas and heralds the beginning of a productive decade that brought his work into the mainstream of French culture.

LIFE'S WORK

The publication in 1829 of a book of poems, *Les Orientales* (*Les Orientales: Or, Eastern Lyrics*, 1879), placed Hugo at the head of the Romantic movement, a role that was confirmed with the appearance of his melodramatic five-act play *Hernani* (English translation, 1830) in February, 1830. *Hernani* was a popular sensation and brought much-needed income into the Hugo household, which was strained by nearly a decade of pregnancies and shaky finances. In fact, the artistic success Hugo enjoyed in these years had been invisibly pursued by Adèle's unhappiness and a growing, secretive love between her and Sainte-Beuve, who was as much a family friend as an artistic colleague. Hugo was deeply shaken by the failure of his imagined, ideal relationship with his wife and the treachery of his friend, but he responded to his misfortune by composing the poems issued in November, 1831, as *Les Feuilles d'automne*, a collection that far surpassed his earlier verses.

Hugo had signed a contract in 1828 to produce a novel, but the project was displaced by his many other projects and by the July Revolution of 1830, which Hugo and his liberal contemporaries embraced. In September, 1830, he set to work on this novel in earnest, and completed *Notre-Dame de Paris* (1831; *The Hunchback of Notre-Dame*, 1833) within six months. A descriptive tapestry of fifteenth century Paris, the novel embodies Hugo's extraordinary visual imagination and his affinity for art and architecture. Hugo had, by this time, shown a related capacity for drawing, and in the years to come his sketches often achieved a mastery of dramatic visual effect and characterization quite beyond his nominally amateur status as an artist.

The theater continued to attract Hugo's interest. In November, 1832, *Le Roi s'amuse* (1832; *The King Amuses Himself*, 1842) was banned by the government following its first performance; yet on November 8, 1838, he achieved another triumph with *Ruy Blas* (English translation, 1890), widely considered to be his best play. It was also his last success as a dramatist; after the failure of *Les Burgraves* (*The Burgraves*, 1896) in 1843, Hugo no longer wrote for the stage. By then, however, he had achieved one of his main objectives in courting public and critical acclaim in the theater: election to the Académie Française, an event that occurred on his fifth attempt, on January 7, 1841. Celebrated as a poet, dramatist, novelist, and critic, Hugo's role as a youthful, rebellious Romantic had been outgrown. Financially secure, perhaps emotionally battered but artistically more refined, he now pursued his career with determination but with no less passion than before.

Since 1833, Hugo had maintained a liaison with a beautiful female actor, Juliette Drouet, who for twelve years followed a cloistered existence relieved only by six-week summer holidays with her lover. Notwithstanding Hugo's devotion to Juliette and his increasingly frequent love affairs with other adoring women, he was a devoted father to two sons and daughters. In 1843, Léopoldine, Hugo's favorite, perished in a boating accident with her husband of six months. His sons, Charles and François-Victor, died prematurely in their middle years, after sharing in many of their father's trials and successes; his daughter Adèle died in 1915, after a life darkened by madness.

During the 1840's, Hugo was something of an establishment figure in French letters. In April, 1845, he was raised to the peerage, becoming Viscount Hugo—a circumstance that in July saved him from almost certain prosecution on the complaint of the husband of one of his mistresses. After this perilous event, Hugo remained prudently quiet for several years, but in 1848, with France again in political turmoil, he sought to renew his political influence. Initially supporting France's "bourgeois king," Prince Louis-Napoleon, through the newspaper that he had founded with his sons, Hugo soon came to oppose his rule. His sons were imprisoned, and Hugo himself skirted arrest until it seemed absolutely necessary to leave France. He departed for Brussels on December 11, 1851, probably with the unstated tolerance of the authorities.

Hugo's nineteen-year absence from France, at first a necessity, later became a matter of principle, which conferred upon him the distinction of an exile of conscience. In comfortable circumstances, first in Jersey and, from 1855, in Guernsey, Hugo wrote great quantities of verse and prose, much of it concerned with social and political problems. His popularity as a writer continued to grow. Among the notable volumes of poetry in these years are *Les Châtiments* (1853), which includes satiric poems aimed at Louis-Napoleon, *La Légende des siècles* (1859-1883; *The Legend of the Centuries*, 1894), and a collection of earlier work, *Les Contemplations*, which earned for him enough money within months of its publication in April, 1856, to buy Hauteville House, where he surrounded himself with his family and admirers. Drouet lived within sight of the house, and by 1867 her relationship with Hugo was acknowledged even by Hugo's wife. Madame Hugo was to die in her husband's arms in Brussels the following year, during a family holiday.

Hugo's prodigious and best-known novel, *Les Misérables* (English translation, 1862), was published in 1861. It weaves together many of the themes of earlier books and manuscripts as well as historical and autobiographical elements from Hugo's youth. It is a singular novel both in Hugo's career and in the whole of European literature—a sprawling, twelve-hundred-page narrative that overcomes its liabilities by sheer energy. Hugo seeks to show no less than

> the advance from evil to good, from injustice to justice, from falsity to truth, from darkness to daylight, from blind appetite to conscience, from decay to life, from bestiality to duty, from Hell to Heaven, from limbo to God . . .

Thus, the book is in some fashion a religious book. *Les Misérables* is centered upon an account of the pursuit of a convict, Jean Valjean, by the detective Javert. Valjean, released on parole after nineteen years of imprisonment for a trivial crime, experiences a transformation of character that is repeatedly challenged both by his conscience and by Javert's detection. Within a vast framework of historical events and human affairs, the two principal characters are shown locked in a social and existential combat that remains compelling even for modern readers who are not conversant with the novel's political context.

Hugo's attention never wandered far from the political scene, and in 1870, as a prosperous Germany threatened war with a weakened France, Hugo determined to return to his homeland to aid it in its crisis. He arrived on September 5 to a tumultuous welcome, but by then the military situation was desperate. Paris was soon under full siege and the population was approaching starvation—Hugo himself was said to have been sent bear, deer, and antelope meat from the zoo at the Jardin des Plantes. In late January, 1871, an armistice was concluded and elections called for a National Assembly to make peace with the Germans and to debate the terms of defeat. Hugo ran successfully for the assembly and traveled to Bordeaux to participate in it, but the rancorous events of the following months soon outpaced the capacities of a seventy-year-old man, and he returned first to Paris and then to Brussels, where, amid much public controversy, the Belgian government expelled him. After a few months in Luxembourg, he returned to Paris, where he was defeated in the elections of January, 1872.

From 1872 until his death in 1885, Hugo lived alternately in Guernsey and in Paris. His last years saw the completion of a major novel of the French Revolution, *Quatre-vingt-treize* (1874; *Ninety-Three*, 1874), and the revival of several of his major theatrical works. *L'Art d'être grand-père* (1877), a book about Hugo's experiences with his two grandchildren, became a sentimental classic with the French public. During the Third Republic—the more liberal political regime that followed the turmoil of 1869-1872—Hugo came to be regarded as a patriarch, and the nation gave him almost limitless affection.

The beginning of Hugo's eightieth year was celebrated as a national holiday on February 26, 1881, with 600,000 admirers filing past the windows of his apartment on the Avenue Eylau, which was soon renamed Avenue Victor-Hugo. In late summer, he made up his will, in which he stated:

> God. The Soul. Responsibility. This threefold idea is sufficient for mankind. It has been sufficient for me. It is the true religion. I have lived in it. Truth, light, justice,

conscience: it is God. . . . I leave forty thousand francs to the poor. And I wish to be taken to the cemetery in a pauper's hearse.

Hugo had suffered a slight stroke three years earlier, but otherwise his health was remarkably good for a man of seventy-nine. During the next two years, he supervised the publication of the little of his work that remained unpublished, but his creative activity was at an end. Juliette Drouet, who for fifty years had been his devoted friend, died in May, 1883. Hugo lived on until May 22, 1885, when an attack of pneumonia claimed him at the age of eighty-three. His last words were "I see black light."

SIGNIFICANCE

Victor Hugo had one of the broadest-ranging, most celebrated public careers of his time. He was a poet, dramatist, novelist, literary and social critic, journalist, politician, and social activist, and often pursued more than one of these roles at a time. Above all a man of feeling, Hugo turned from the ardent Royalism of his childhood and adolescence to an equally passionate Romanticism, in which his natural literary gifts reached their full potential. As a poet, he was a great musician of words, who brought increasingly refined ideas to his work. His legacy as a dramatist is not as great as in other literary forms, but he helped effect a transition from classicism to Romanticism, and he held contemporary audiences spellbound on more than one occasion.

The contributions made by Hugo to fiction were diverse and influential. Some novels, such as *The Hunchback of Notre-Dame*, are notable for their descriptive power; others, such as the early *Le Dernier jour d'un condamné* (1829; *The Last Day of a Condemned*, 1840), combine adventurous narrative devices with a profound concern for social justice. *Les Misérables*, despite its unwieldy length, combines much of what is best in Hugo's craft and his philosophy, and after a century is still read as a living masterpiece. Other books, suffering perhaps from the miscalculation that can attend unbounded productivity, embody his poetic craft more than his sense of narrative substance.

In his life as well as in his work, Hugo was a spokesman for the common person against the power of the state; his long association with the political Left, however, was more a matter of human compassion than of social theory. He had experienced a range of political regimes, which made him a shrewd political observer, but increasingly he applied his genius to projects that transcended the affairs of his own historical epoch, creating an imaginative world of mythic dimensions.

—C. S. McConnell

FURTHER READING

Brombert, Victor. *Victor Hugo and the Visionary Novel.* Cambridge, Mass.: Harvard University Press, 1984. The author of this sophisticated, scholarly study of Hugo's novels became a dedicated "Hugolian" in 1940 as a teenager, during the German Occupation. His method of analysis is to combine the resources of modernist formal criticism with an "intricate network of aesthetic, social, political, psychological, and ethical preoccupations." Twenty-seven remarkable drawings by Hugo are reproduced.

Grant, Elliott M. *The Career of Victor Hugo.* Cambridge, Mass.: Harvard University Press, 1945. This scholarly but very readable book is principally a survey of Hugo's literary production, although it deals of necessity with the circumstances of his life.

Grant, Richard B. *The Perilous Quest: Image, Myth, and Prophecy in the Narratives of Victor Hugo.* Durham, N.C.: Duke University Press, 1968. The author, who is the son of Hugo scholar Elliott Grant, defines the essential motif of Hugo's narrative works as the myth of the heroic quest toward an ideal. Isolating his discussion as much as possible from biographical detail, he argues the view that the novels, the main plays, and narrative poems can be viewed as self-contained artistic unities.

Ionesco, Eugène. *Hugoliad: Or, The Grotesque and Tragic Life of Victor Hugo.* New York: Grove Press, 1987. This uncompleted work of Ionesco's youth—written during the 1930's in Romanian—is a sort of polemical antibiography, intended to dethrone its subject. The reader must take responsibility for separating fact from fiction, to say nothing of judging the aptness of the playwright's cheerless embellishments of anecdotal material. Postscript by Gelu Ionescu.

Maurois, André. *Olympio: The Life of Victor Hugo.* Translated by Gerard Hopkins. New York: Harper & Row, 1956. Originally published in French in 1954. This is probably as close an approach as possible to an ideal one-volume biography dealing with both the life and the work of a monumental figure such as Hugo. Of the sparse illustrations, several are superb; the bibliography, principally of sources in French, provides a sense of Hugo's celebrity and influence, which persisted well into the twentieth century.

_____.*Victor Hugo and His World.* London: Thames and Hudson, 1966. The 1956 English translation of Maurois's text noted above was edited to conform to the format of a series of illustrated books. The result is interesting and intelligible, but rather schematic. In compensation for the vast cuts in text, a chronology and dozens of well-annotated illustrations have been added.

Porter, Laurence M. *Victor Hugo.* New York: Twayne, 1999. Overview of Hugo's life and writings, one of the volumes in Twayne's World Authors series. Porter refutes criticism that Hugo was a popularizer with a talent for self-promotion by pointing out the richness and subtlety of Hugo's writing.

Richardson, Joanna. *Victor Hugo.* London: Weidenfeld & Nicolson, 1976. Richardson's aim was to produce a comprehensive account of Hugo's life and work in the context of her specialty, the study of nineteenth century European culture. Her book is complementary to Maurois's account of Hugo and is somewhat more efficient as well as being agreeably less literary in style. There is an excellent biography and reproductions of several classic Hugo family photographs.

Robb, Graham. *Victor Hugo: A Biography.* New York: W. W. Norton, 1997. Comprehensive, intelligent and well-written biography, presenting Hugo with all of his contradictions and complexity. Robb traces Hugo's evolution from leading poet of the Romantic movement to spirited novelist of the downtrodden to political exile.

SEE ALSO: Hector Berlioz; Sarah Bernhardt; Eugène Delacroix; Gaetano Donizetti; Alexandre Dumas, *père*; Auguste Rodin.

RELATED ARTICLES in *Great Events from History: The Nineteenth Century, 1801-1900:* March 3, 1830: Hugo's *Hernani* Incites Rioting; October 1-December 15, 1856: Flaubert Publishes *Madame Bovary.*

ALEXANDER VON HUMBOLDT
German explorer and scientist

One of the founders of modern science and scientific methods, Humboldt undertook a famous four-year expedition to the Americas that led to the development of the new sciences of geography, plant geography, and meteorology. He took a holistic view of science, insisting on seeing each geographical site as a whole that encompassed climate, elevation, and distribution of plants, animals, and natural resources.

BORN: September 14, 1769; Berlin, Prussia (now in Germany)
DIED: May 6, 1859; Berlin, Prussia
ALSO KNOWN AS: Friedrich Wilhelm Heinrich Alexander von Humboldt (full name); Baron Alexander von Humboldt
AREAS OF ACHIEVEMENT: Geography, science and technology

EARLY LIFE

At the time of Alexander von Humboldt's birth, his family was not part of the ancient Prussian nobility. The title of baron that he would later inherit had only been in the family a few generations. Alexander's father, Major Alexander George von Humboldt, had fought in the Seven Years' War in the Prussian army and later became adjutant to the duke of Braunschweig. Because he was not of the ancient Prussian elite, Major Humboldt decided that his sons would not become military men, but scientists and politicians.

Alexander was the younger of two brothers, both destined to become famous scholars—albeit in different fields. His other brother, Wilhelm, was early perceived to be the one with scholastic aptitude, whereas Alexander did not seem interested in academic pursuits. He liked nature and spent much of his childhood in the parks surrounding his childhood home, Schloss Tegel, near Berlin. He also showed early talent for map drawing and reading, and for drawing nature.

The two brothers were, from the earliest years, inseparable and would remain so throughout their lives. They were only two years apart, and at least one biographer claims that the strong bonding between them compensated for some degree of parental neglect—especially of Alexander because of his perceived lack of talent.

Alexander read one of Georg Forster's works on the South Sea Islands while he was still quite young, and a desire to see the tropics was born in him. He fell in love with the dragon tree and dreamed of seeing one in real life. He collected plants, insects, birds' eggs, and rocks.

The two brothers were initially taught at home by tutors, but eventually Wilhelm went to university, and Alexander followed. The brothers studied at the University of Frankfurt an der Oder and later at the University of Göttingen. While Wilhelm studied philology and philosophy, Alexander focused his studies on mineralogy.

From his earliest years, Alexander had planned to undertake a major scientific journey. His studies and pursuits were all focused on this goal. In 1792, however, he was employed by the Prussian government as superintendent of mines. He worked in this capacity until 1797, gaining valuable experience. From 1797 to 1799, he prepared himself for his great journey.

LIFE'S WORK

While still a child, Humboldt met the towering spirit of his time, Johann Wolfgang von Goethe. Later, in 1797, he spent three full months in the company of the great poet and scientific theoretician. The exposure to Goethe and his ideas about nature and science became central to Humboldt. His life's work became the practical application of some of the key aspects of Goethe's theories: He saw the world as a *Naturganzes*, or natural whole. To the Romantic theory he added an emphasis on stringent empirical observation.

With his theoretical and scientific baggage securely packed in his fine mind, Humboldt embarked from La Coruña in Spain on June 5, 1799, on his expedition to the Americas. His companion on the trip was the French botanist Aimé Bonpland. The two scientists had strong mutual respect and divided the work between them, Bonpland being primarily responsible for collecting and studying plants.

The expedition was to last four years, from 1799 to 1803. The first part was focused on the Orinoco River in Venezuela, where Humboldt first tested his holistic theory, or his "idea of the physical nature of the world." He was interested in correlating facts and observations rather than in individual facts. He studied the biology, geology, geophysics, archaeology, and meteorology of the areas through which he passed. The two companions traveled the entire length of the seventeen-hundred-mile-long Orinoco River on foot and by canoe. Interestingly, the hardships of this travel restored Humboldt's health.

HUMBOLDT'S IMPULSE TO EXPLORE

From my earliest youth I felt an ardent desire to travel into distant regions, seldom visited by Europeans. This desire is characteristic of a period of our existence when appears an unlimited horizon, and when we find an irresistible attraction in the impetuous agitations of the mind, and the image of positive danger. Though educated in a country which has no direct communication with either the East or the West Indies, living amidst mountains remote from coasts, and celebrated for their numerous mines, I felt an increasing passion for the sea and distant expeditions. Objects with which we are acquainted only by the animated narratives of travellers have a peculiar charm; imagination wanders with delight over that which is vague and undefined; and the pleasures we are deprived of seem to possess a fascinating power, compared with which all we daily feel in the narrow circle of sedentary life appears insipid. The taste for herborisation, the study of geology, rapid excursions to Holland, England, and France, with the celebrated Mr. George Forster, who had the happiness to accompany captain Cook in his second expedition round the globe, contributed to give a determined direction to the plan of travels which I had formed at eighteen years of age. No longer deluded by the agitation of a wandering life, I was anxious to contemplate nature in all her variety of wild and stupendous scenery; and the hope of collecting some facts useful to the advancement of science, incessantly impelled my wishes towards the luxuriant regions of the torrid zone. As personal circumstances then prevented me from executing the projects by which I was so powerfully influenced, I had leisure to prepare myself during six years for the observations I proposed to make on the New Continent, as well as to visit different parts of Europe, and to explore the lofty chain of the Alps, the structure of which I might afterwards compare with that of the Andes of Quito and of Peru. . . .

Source: Alexander von Humboldt, *Personal Narrative of a Journey to the Equinoctial Regions of America*, translated and edited by Thomasina Ross (London: G. Bell & Sons, 1881), vol. 1, chapter 1.

For his entire youth, he had been frail and sickly, and he emerged from his trip along the Orinoco River the very image of good health. Contemporaries describe him as a short, healthy-looking, robust, and powerfully built man.

The work describing the trip and Humboldt's findings did not appear until many years later. It was published in French, because the bulk of Humboldt's life after the trip was spent in Paris. The work was published in thirty-three volumes under the title *Voyage aux régions équinoxiales du Nouveau Continent, fait en 1799, 1800, 1801, 1802, 1803, et 1804, par A. de Humboldt et A. Bonpland* (1805-1834; a historical description of the voyage to the tropical regions of the new continent made in 1799, 1800, 1801, 1802, 1803, and 1804, by Al. de Humboldt and A. Bonpland).

The eighteenth century was an age of grand voyages and explorations. Humboldt's expedition fits the pattern, but there was a difference: His voyage had infinitely more repercussions for the future of science than probably any other until Charles Darwin's famous voyage on the *Beagle* a half-century later. Humboldt had a program. He firmly believed that nature embodied an overarching idea and that studying nature as a whole and overlooking no aspect, however apparently insignificant, would bring him closer to an understanding of the idea.

Humboldt believed that there is a unity to the cosmos and to the world. He saw this not as a phylogenetic unity of evolution but as a Platonic, idealistic unity: He thought that for each type of animal or plant there was a prototype. Another aspect of this unity is the so-called compensation principle (also known as metamorphosis or transformation), which states that if an animal or plant is strongly developed in one aspect, it will be lacking in some other aspect. Thus, if the giraffe has a long neck, it must be less developed somewhere else. This type of thinking was typical for Goethe and his followers. Although the static, idealistic aspects of Humboldt's theorizing have since been abandoned in favor of evolutionary ones, the idea of studying environments as integrated wholes and the emphasis on empirical observation are central to modern geography and ecology. Exactly those aspects of his work have earned for him the reputation as a founder of modern geography.

Humboldt and Bonpland proceeded to Mexico, Peru, and Cuba to conduct further studies. They not only continued their meticulous studies of ecosystems wherever they went but also took the time to study indigenous cultures, dabble in archaeology, and take a fresh look at the Spanish-speaking societies of the New World. One witness who encountered them in Quito, Ecuador, recounts that Humboldt, after a long day's work of studying plants, minerals, and soil types, would spend most of the night gazing at the stars.

Many rivers, mountains, and counties in the New World bear Humboldt's name, and the entire expedition was a great success. He returned to Europe in 1804, sailing from Philadelphia to Bordeaux. Humboldt lived in Paris, working on his life's project. When the work was complete and his inheritance spent, he accepted a job as chamberlain of the Prussian court and lived the rest of his life in Berlin. However, he made one more substantial trip. At the request of the Russian czar, he visited the Urals, the Altai, and parts of China. The purpose of the trip was to give advice regarding the economic exploitation of the areas covered on the trip. The scientific outcome of Humboldt's last major trip was meager compared to his trip to the Americas, but it was a success in terms of its stated goals. Humboldt could indeed give lucrative advice and make predictions with regard to the mineralogical composition of the Urals. Humboldt lived to the age of eighty-nine and worked until the end. He died on May 6, 1859, in Berlin.

SIGNIFICANCE

Alexander von Humboldt represents the emergence of modern empirical science. He was a child of his times in that his theoretical ideas about the world were rooted in German Romanticism and in that he joined many of his contemporaries in exploring parts of the world that were comparatively new to Europeans. However, he also broke the mold by combining his Romantic idealism with a hard-nosed empiricism that helped usher in the new age of technology and science.

Humboldt was amazingly eclectic. He studied plants, rocks, volcanoes, fauna, archaeology, and comparative religions, and he studied everything in minute detail. The thirty-three volumes that constitute Humboldt's testimony to future scientists contain not only a catalog of his physiognomic-typological primary forms of plants but also the painstakingly accurate descriptions of ecological systems that have made his scientific heirs name him the founder of not only geography but also the specialized field of plant geography and modern, systematic, and scientific meteorology.

—Per Schelde

FURTHER READING

Bowler, Peter J. "Climb Chimborazo and See the World." *Science* 298, no. 5591 (October 4, 2002): 63. Provides an overview of Humboldt's personal life and work, including his influence on the development of natural evolution, his exploration in Latin America, and his contributions to science.

Gendron, Val. *The Dragon Tree: A Life of Alexander, Baron von Humboldt.* New York: Longmans, Green, 1961. More than anything else a psychological portrait of Humboldt. The approach is Freudian and verges, from time to time, on hero-worship. Written entertainingly, with bits of dialogue between the protagonist and his friends and colleagues. Especially good description of Humboldt's early life and relationships with his parents and brother.

Helferich, Gerard. *Humboldt's Cosmos: Alexander von Humboldt and the Latin American Journey That Changed the Way We See the World.* New York: Gotham Books, 2004. Re-creates Humboldt's expedition to Latin America, describing in meticulous detail the conditions of the voyage, the terrain and climate in each country Humboldt visited, and the voyage's significance.

Kellner, L. *Alexander von Humboldt.* New York: Oxford University Press, 1963. A solid, scholarly biography. Relates Humboldt's early life as it emerges from the record without Freudian or other interpretations. Excellent account of the two major expeditions and of their scientific import.

Klencke, W. *Alexander von Humboldt: A Biographical Monument.* London: Ingram, Cooke, 1852. Focuses on the role of the Humboldt brothers in the emergence of modern Germany. A political monument that contains a good description of Humboldt's early life and his education.

Meyer-Abich, Adolph. "Alexander von Humboldt and the Science of the Nineteenth Century." In *Biological Contributions: A Collection of Essays and Research Articles Dedicated to John Thomas Patterson on the Occasion of His Fiftieth Birthday.* Austin: University of Texas Press, 1959. A good exposition of eighteenth century scientific ideas and beliefs. Sets the intellectual stage for Humboldt's achievements, primarily by explaining Goethe's scientific views: the holism, the types, and the compensation principle. Explains Humboldt's law of plant geography, which states, among other things, that the same type of climate will foster the same types of flora and fauna. Gives a list of the nineteen plant types Humboldt established. Compares Humboldt's scientific theories to such later developments as mechanism and evolutionary theory.

_____. "Humboldt's Exploration in the American Tropics." *The Texas Quarterly* 1 (1958). Brief but full description of Humboldt's life and major expeditions. The focus is on exploring the nature of Humboldt's achievement. Outlines Humboldt's education and gives a good picture of the intellectual community to which he belonged.

ENGELBERT HUMPERDINCK
German composer

As the developer and chief exponent of "fairy-tale" operas, Humperdinck was briefly the most important German opera composer after Richard Wagner. Although he was soon eclipsed by other composers, his music survives in one enduringly popular work, Hänsel und Gretel.

BORN: September 1, 1854; Siegburg, near Bonn, Prussia (now in Germany)
DIED: September 27, 1921; Neustrelitz, Germany
AREA OF ACHIEVEMENT: Music

EARLY LIFE

Engelbert Humperdinck (HEWM-pahr-dihngk) was born in a small Rhineland town where his father was a teacher. Family pressures destined Humperdinck for a career in architecture, but he evidenced an early interest in music and began to study it around the age of seven. By his early teens, he was composing and was active in a number of musical organizations. After overcoming parental opposition to a musical career, he studied at the Cologne Conservatory for four years. In 1876 he won Frankfurt's Mozart Prize, which allowed him to study further in Munich. Some early compositions were performed during this period that demonstrated the influence of Richard Wagner. After winning Berlin's Mendelssohn Prize in 1879, he was able to travel to Italy, where he met his idol Wagner, who was then vacationing in Naples. Impressed by the twenty-five-year-old Humperdinck's honesty and geniality, Wagner soon drew the young man into his circle.

In Bayreuth, Humperdinck became Wagner's right-hand man during preparations for the premiere of the opera *Parsifal* in 1882. As chief copyist of the score, Humperdinck was called upon to add some music of his own; part of his contribution was eventually dropped, but it is likely that significant portions of what he wrote, especially in the area of the orchestration, remained in the final version of Wagner's last opera. Humperdinck fulfilled numerous other responsibilities while working with Wagner. However, after winning the Meyerbeer Prize of Berlin in 1881, Humperdinck broke free in the autumn of 1882 to take up residence in Paris, France. Wagner tried to get his young disciple to join him in Venice at the Marcello Conservatory, but this arrangement failed, although Humperdinck did assist Wagner in preparing for the latter's final performance. When Humperdinck returned to Paris, he was followed by the news of his idol's death on February 13, 1883.

In the following years, Humperdinck traveled widely around Europe and the Mediterranean. After an unhappy spell of teaching in Barcelona, Spain, he took an appointment at his alma mater, the Cologne Conservatory, in 1887. He also became adviser to the important music publishing firm of Schott and an active music critic. Still close to the Wagner family, he gave private music lessons to the late master's son, Siegfried. Like Humperdinck himself, Siegfried had been expected to train as an architect; perhaps recalling his own escape, Humperdinck was influential in steering the young man toward a career of his own as conductor and composer.

Humperdinck had not given up his interests in composing. An orchestral humoresque that he wrote met with some success, and he had composed a steady number of songs for voice and piano as well as choral pieces. However, his dreams of writing opera had gone unrealized: Wagner's lingering influence weighed heavily on him, and he had failed to find the right material. It was only when Humperdinck moved to new teaching and journalistic duties in Frankfurt that his breakthrough came.

LIFE'S WORK

In the spring of 1891, Humperdinck's sister, Adelheid Wette, a literary dabbler, invited him to join in one of her private theatricals using her children's miniature theater. She had adapted one of the Brothers Grimm's fairy tales as a *Singspiel* (a spoken play with songs and musical numbers), and she asked him to provide appropriate musical settings. The finished production was presented at a party for family and friends a few weeks later. One of the guests was Hugo Wolf, whose compositions Humperdinck had supported through his publishing connections.

Wolf thought this tiny theatrical piece should be made into a full-length opera. Wette set to work on an expanded libretto and, though the idea of performability by children persisted, the project grew into the opera *Hänsel und Gretel*.

Securing a performance for the new work proved to be difficult at first, but parallel productions—at Weimar on December 23, 1893, under Richard Strauss, and two weeks later at Munich under old Bayreuth colleague Hermann Levi—caused a sensation. Critics who had bemoaned the lapse in German opera after Wagner's death and who were alarmed at the inroads made by the new Italian verismo movement hailed Humperdinck's work as bringing new life to German lyric theater. The opera swept through Europe and traveled around the world, establishing a barely matched record of unbroken popularity.

In his fusion of complex Wagnerian style (sumptuous orchestral apparatus and modified use of leitmotif references) with a folksy simplicity of tone (the feeling of a folk song and the naïve subject matter of folktales), Humperdinck unintentionally created what he recognized as a new idiom, the *Märchenoper* or fairy-tale opera. He moved quickly to consolidate the new audience he had created for his music. Another collaboration with

his sister, *Die sieben Geisslein* (the seven little goats) was well received in 1895, but it failed to capture any lasting public interest. Meanwhile, after reluctantly being drawn into writing incidental music for a play by a friend's daughter, *Königskinder* (the king's children), Humperdinck turned it into a melodrama—a form of drama with lines spoken over closely keyed music. He went further, notating rhythms and pitches for the spoken words. It was an idea that anticipated the *Sprechgesang* (speech-song), which was soon to become part of the radical style of Arnold Schoenberg, but it proved too demanding for the performers in a doomed production that turned into a fiasco when it premiered in 1897.

After relocating to Berlin, Humperdinck returned to the fairy-tale idiom with *Dornröschen* (Thorn-Rosie), an adaptation of the Charles Perrault tale commonly known as "The Sleeping Beauty." This new confection of sumptuous Wagnerian orchestration and childish naïveté with spectacular stage effects was highly acclaimed at its Frankfurt premiere on November 12, 1902, but once again it could not win the same popularity as *Hänsel und Gretel* and slipped quickly into obscurity. A shift into comedy was attempted with *Die Heirat wider Willen* (the involuntary marriage), with a libretto by Humperdinck's wife, based upon Alexandre Dumas *père*'s drama *Les Demoiselles de Saint-Cyr* (1843; *The Ladies of Saint-Cyr*, 1870). Despite a lavish premiere in April, 1905, and praises accorded its music, a weak libretto (with copious spoken dialogue) doomed the work to neglect.

Still committed to theatrical composition, Humperdinck produced a Nativity-play opera for children, *Bübschens Weihnachtstraum* (1906; toddler's Christmas dream), and then turned to writing a series of highly praised incidental scores for productions (mostly by Max Reinhardt at the Deutsches Theater in Berlin) of plays by William Shakespeare, Aristophanes, and Maurice Maeterlinck. However, he felt bound to give the fairy-tale opera one more effort to prove that the success of *Hänsel und Gretel* had not been a one-time aberration.

Returning to the *Königskinder* play, which had been an abortive melodrama, Humperdinck decided to utilize his original idea and make it into a full-fledged opera by recasting the earlier text and overhauling his previous music. The premiere, arranged at the Metropolitan Opera House in New York, took place, after many delays, in December, 1910, in the same month as that of Giacomo Puccini's *La fanciulla del west* (the girl of the golden West). Puccini's opera, which went on to survive as a part of the working international repertoire, was coolly

Engelbert Humperdinck. (Library of Congress)

received at first, while Humperdinck's work (now long forgotten) was ecstatically acclaimed for its beautiful music and theatrical effects.

At a seeming pinnacle of success and fame, Humperdinck composed a pantomime opera called *Das Mirakel* (the miracle). However, at its London premiere in December, 1911, Humperdinck suffered a physical breakdown that initiated a deterioration of his health that plagued him for the remaining decade of his life. He continued to travel and compose, producing two more operas (in 1914 and 1919) that achieved no success at all and writing in other vocal and instrumental forms as well. Still receiving international honors, he retired from his Berlin posts in 1920, only to die on September 27 of the following year at the age of sixty-seven.

SIGNIFICANCE

Engelbert Humperdinck was not exclusively an operatic composer. Besides other vocal music, he produced one major orchestral work—the *Moorish Rhapsody* (1899)—three string quartets (1873, 1875, and 1920), and a quintet for piano and strings (1875). However, it was in the theater that he felt most at home and strove to make his mark.

It was already clear by the time of his death that Humperdinck's successes had mostly become ephemeral. His early champion, Richard Strauss, had stolen a march on him: After establishing his commanding position as a composer of German orchestral music, Strauss had then assumed true leadership in German opera with his scandalous and decadent *Salome* (1905) and the shocking and brutal *Elektra* (1909), followed by the mellow *Der Rosenkavalier* (1911). With his operatic initiative taken away, Humperdinck also found himself adrift in the larger musical world being shaken by Schoenberg, Igor Stravinsky, and Bela Bartók. The idiom of the fairy-tale opera, which satisfied German cultural appetites of the moment, was actually built upon the illusion that the traditions of Romanticism were still vehicles for continued growth. Wagner's "music of the future" had quickly become a stale reaction in its own turn, for the musical world was rapidly moving into radical experiments with alternatives that left Humperdinck's aesthetics far behind.

Some of Humperdinck's music is still heard, and, at least in German houses, *Königskinder* and even *Dornröschen* might occasionally be revived. However, Humperdinck has survived in the dubious status of a one-work composer. *Hänsel und Gretel*—whether in the original German or as translated into almost every Western language—has curiously escaped the eclipse of everything else Humperdinck created amid such optimism. Its appeal to children as well as adults has given it an almost unique role as an introductory opera, and it has become an unshakable staple of Christmas performances. It is also, quite simply, a score filled with gorgeous music—the first and only true *Märchenoper*, but one that justly deserves its enduring popularity.

—*John W. Barker*

FURTHER READING

Abell, Arthur M. *Talks with Great Composers*. Secaucus, N.J.: Carol, 1994. The most recent reprint of a book originally published in 1955. Contains interviews with Humperdinck and other composers conducted between 1890 and 1917; the composers discuss their musical works and the creative process.

Bettelheim, Bruno. *The Uses of Enchantment: The Meaning and Importance of Fairy Tales*. New York: Alfred A. Knopf, 1976. This book contains an analysis of the original fairy-tale form of the Hansel and Gretel story, which is still useful despite the decline in the author's reputation.

Denley, Ian. "Engelbert Humperdinck." In *The New Grove Dictionary of Music and Musicians*, edited by Stanley Sadie and John Terrell. 2d ed. London: Grove, 2001. This article discusses Humperdinck's life, works, musical style, and the critical reception of his music. Includes a list of his musical works and a bibliography that does not include any materials written in English.

Humperdinck, Wolfram. *Engelbert Humperdinck: Das Leben meines Vaters*. Frankfort-am-Main, Germany: Kramer, 1965. A German-language biography of Humperdinck.

Irmen, Hans Josef. *Die Odyssee des Engelbert Humperdinck, ein biographische Dokumentation*. Siegburg, Germany: Druck Schmitt, 1974. This represents the best access to the sources on Humperdinck's life. In German.

_____, ed. *Engelbert Humperdinck: Briefe und Tagebücher*. Cologne, Germany: Volk, 1976. Along with Irmen's other book, this is the best source of information on Humperdinck. In German.

Markow, R. "Humperdinck: Beyond *Hansel und Gretel*." *Opera News* 53, no. 7 (December 24, 1988): 24. Profile of Humperdinck, discussing his personal life, musical training, work for Wagner, the influence of Wagner upon his music, and his operatic works.

Pennino, John. "Metropolitan Opera Broadcasts." *Opera News* 66, no. 6 (December, 2001): 45. Recounts Humperdinck's arrival in New York in December, 1910, for the premiere of his opera *Königskinder* at the Metropolitan Opera House. Discusses the preparations for his stay, evaluates the performance of famed singer Geraldine Farrar, and compares *Königskinder* to *Hänsel und Gretel*.

SEE ALSO: Hans Christian Andersen; Nikolay Rimsky-Korsakov; Richard Wagner.

RELATED ARTICLES in *Great Events from History: The Nineteenth Century, 1801-1900:* 1812-1815: Brothers Grimm Publish Fairy Tales; May 8, 1835: Andersen Publishes His First Fairy Tales; August 13-17, 1876: First Performance of Wagner's Ring Cycle.

WILLIAM HOLMAN HUNT
English painter

Hunt's activities in the Pre-Raphaelite Brotherhood and his artistic success outside the Royal Academy allowed him to exert a broadening influence on British art, reforming ideas regarding lighting and color and bringing considerations of content back into primary importance in painting.

BORN: April 2, 1827; London, England
DIED: September 7, 1910; London, England
AREA OF ACHIEVEMENT: Art

EARLY LIFE

William Holman Hunt was the oldest child in a family of two sons and five daughters. He was named for his maternal grandfather. His own father, also named William Hunt, was a warehouseman in the Cheapside district. The father took care to introduce his son to art and literature but did not encourage the boy's interest in art. Until the age of thirteen, Hunt attended private schools, and then he became an assistant to Richard Cobden, a calico printer and minor politician. Dissatisfied with these pursuits, young Hunt gained permission to study art in the evenings, which he proceeded to do in the studio of portrait painter Henry Rogers.

By 1843, Hunt had given up his commercial employment for the full-time study of art, working as a student at the British Museum three days a week and making copies at the National Gallery for two more. After failing his first attempt to gain admission to the Royal Academy schools, he was admitted as a probationer in 1844 and was promoted to full studentship the next year. There Hunt became fast friends with John Everett Millais, a painter two years Hunt's junior, but one who had already gained recognition for his great promise as a painter. Hunt also formed his first acquaintance with Dante Gabriel Rossetti, with whom, along with Millais, he would form the Pre-Raphaelite Brotherhood (PRB) some years

later. Primarily, however, Hunt spent these years learning to paint, and he began exhibiting at the Academy in 1846, with a picture titled *Hark!*, which he followed the next year with *Dr. Rochecliffe Performing Divine Service in the Cottage of Joceline Jocliffe at Woodstock*, a scene from a novel by Sir Walter Scott.

In 1848, Hunt first won individual recognition with his *Flight of Madeline and Porphyro*, adapted from John Keats's poem *The Eve of St. Agnes* (1820). This painting attracted the attention of Rossetti, who thought it the year's best painting and who, as a result, pressed Hunt to allow him to work under Hunt in Hunt's studio in Fitzroy Square. Thus began both an artistic association and a close personal friendship that would last for nine years. Hunt introduced Rossetti to Millais, and in the fall of 1848 these three, flush with the enthusiasm of their early success, laid down the principles and formed the nucleus of the PRB.

LIFE'S WORK

Hunt was a tall man with striking blue eyes, a high forehead, brown hair, and a long, silky, red-golden beard. He made two major contributions to the history of the fine arts in England. First, Hunt's position as cofounder of the PRB established him as a leader in the reformation of painting as an art form. With Hunt, Rossetti, and Millais in the lead, the PRB led a revolt against fashionable painting of the time, which emphasized technical perfection at the expense of content. The Pre-Raphaelites vowed to express only important ideas; to paint directly from nature, disregarding the accepted rules of design and color, which had limited artists to a relatively narrow range of colors and lighting effects; and to paint events realistically, as they were likely to have happened, rather than in the idealized, highly refined manner of the day. These three tenets, together with the suspicion aroused by the presence of a secret brotherhood, led to a public outcry against the works of the PRB, but the group gained an able champion in 1851, when John Ruskin came to the defense of Hunt's *Valentine Rescuing Sylvia from Proteus*, inspired by William Shakespeare's *Two Gentlemen of Verona*.

Ruskin defended what the Pre-Raphaelites were trying to do, and he explained, in the process, that their works were a logical and a positive reaction against some bad influences in English painting. Thus, from 1851 onward, Hunt's works, as well as those of his fellow Pre-Raphaelites, gained in acceptance and value. More important, however, their principles gained wider and wider acceptance, even though Hunt was perhaps the only Pre-Raphaelite artist to follow them rigorously throughout his career. These early works of the PRB paved the way for later artists such as Edward Burne-Jones and William Morris, and for such widely divergent movements as aestheticism and purism, in which idea assumed the ascendancy over style and realism and faithfulness to nature overrode established ideas of composition and design.

In addition to this perhaps purely aesthetic success, Hunt's personal success in making a living from the proceeds of his art and in doing so outside the Academy blazed a trail for artists who came after him and who also violated the accepted practices of their day. Beginning during the 1850's, Hunt began to make a good living from his art, even though he showed fewer and fewer paintings at the Royal Academy and even though his work violated accepted standards of composition, color, and design.

By 1854, Hunt's *The Light of the World*, a work still widely reproduced, sold for about five hundred pounds, a significant sum of money at that time; *The Scapegoat* sold for a similar amount in 1856. The best, however, was yet to come. In 1860, when Hunt finished *The Finding of the Saviour in the Temple*, he sold the painting for fifty-five hundred pounds, and *The Shadow of Death* brought twice that sum in 1871. These were unheard-of prices for the time, and Hunt's ability to thrive outside the Royal Academy broke the stranglehold that that body had long exercised on the visual arts. Hunt had brought ideas back into art, and his paintings, most of which explored New Testament themes according to a typological scheme of symbolism, increased in value and popularity as their artist's methods were vindicated by the increasing public and critical acceptance his work gained.

Hunt's methods were intimately connected with the success of his painting. His attention to detail, one of the primary traits of Pre-Raphaelitism, resulted from his absolute dedication to accuracy. This principle made him something of a legend, for he insisted on painting on site whenever possible. Thus, his major religious works were painted in Palestine, and they display an immediateness that is missing from most painting of the era, which was done largely from the artist's often mistaken impression of what such a place must be like.

More than this trademark of authenticity, Hunt's attention to detail reinforced his typological method, allowing him to exploit a single moment in his subject's existence to encapsulate that subject's entire import. In *The Shadow of Death*, for example, Christ, a young man working in his father's carpentry shop, stops during the late afternoon to stretch. Behind him, his outstretched arms cast a shadow on the wall, and the shadow falls on a tool rack in such a way that it produces an image of the Crucifixion. In the lower left of the painting kneels the Virgin Mary, who has been looking at the contents of a trunk that is still open before her and in which can be seen the gifts the Magi brought to the child Jesus. However, Mary is no longer looking at the gifts; her attention has been drawn to the shadow behind her, and her position suggests alarm, as if she senses the significance of the shadow on the wall. This one moment, then, condenses a considerable expanse of biblical history, from David, a

William Holman Hunt. (Library of Congress)

type of Christ, to the Crucifixion itself, and, through the reference to the twenty-third Psalm, to the Resurrection.

The verse alluded to in the title does celebrate being led through the valley of the shadow of death. Hunt's method, then, brings not only a remarkable number of physical details into his work but also an impressive density of ideas, so that the painting must literally be explored by the viewer, who is responsible for dealing with all the complex resonances of the allusions in the work. By means of this typological method, Hunt brought ideas back into British art, and this is perhaps his greatest contribution to painting.

Hunt's personal life, in the meantime, was almost as stormy as his artistic career. Upon returning from his first trip to the Holy Land and soon after he had finished *The Finding of the Saviour in the Temple*, Hunt paid a visit, in the company of his friend and fellow Pre-Raphaelite Thomas Woolner, to the Waugh household, where Woolner had long been courting Fanny Waugh, the favorite daughter of her overprotective father. In the end, she refused Woolner, for she had already become attracted to Hunt, whose attachment to Fanny was tempered by his fear of a scandal involving some indiscreet love letters he had earlier written to Annie Miller, a model who had been much admired among the Brotherhood. The attraction weathered this possible scandal and the initial disapproval of Fanny's father, and on December 28, 1865, the two were married. A disastrous honeymoon, delayed by Hunt's insistence on finishing several pictures, followed.

When the couple set out for the Holy Land for a working honeymoon, Fanny was already seven months pregnant. At Marseilles, the ports were closed because of cholera, so the Hunts crossed into Italy via Switzerland, but to no avail, because the same conditions were in effect there. They settled in Florence, where the heat and the effort of sitting for her husband weakened Fanny so that she was unable, ultimately, to recover from the rigors of childbirth. On October 26, 1866, Cyril Benone Holman Hunt was born in Florence, and about two months later, on December 20, Fanny died.

Hunt returned to England, bringing Cyril, who had, in the meantime, been twice almost starved by fraudulent wet nurses. His return led to the discovery that Fanny's youngest sister, Edith, was and always had been in love with him, and whether she was so much like Fanny or he simply found her attractive in her own right, Hunt found himself in love with her. Their union was proscribed as incestuous by the Affinity Laws, she being Hunt's sister under the law, so the two decided, reluctantly, to resist their attraction, and Hunt left for another eastern journey,

on which he began *The Shadow of Death* and attempted to put Edith out of his mind. Upon his return, nothing had changed, and the two, after great struggle and vacillation, finally decided to marry, in spite of the laws forbidding their union.

Both families of the couple disowned and disinherited them, but in November of 1875 Edith Waugh married her brother-in-law in Neufchatel, Switzerland, nine years after Fanny's death. Their marriage would not be recognized in Great Britain until 1907, when the Deceased Wife's Sister's Marriage Act received royal approval. Hunt and Edith remained devoted to each other, a happy couple for the rest of his life. He died in 1910, and she survived him by twenty years.

SIGNIFICANCE

For the most part, William Holman Hunt's life is exemplified by his art. A stubborn perfectionist with an intense vision about what art should be and do, Hunt refused to compromise his ideas. His early works, largely misunderstood, did not sell, but rather than change his methods, in 1850 Hunt contemplated giving up art and becoming a farmer. Ruskin's intervention relieved Hunt's distress, and increasing acceptance led to greater influence on artists who surrounded or succeeded Hunt. Perhaps Hunt's greatest aesthetic contributions were in the areas of color, realism, and symbolism. Eschewing the limited color range and chiaroscuro effects of his day, Hunt painted in bright, natural colors, and the lighting in his paintings was as bright or as dark as the actual situation demanded.

In addition, Hunt concentrated on painting a scene the way it really appeared rather than imposing an unnatural conventional design onto the subject. This emphasis on verisimilitude was reinforced by his views on color and lighting, so that his work represents a return to realism, a desertion of the highly stylized artificiality that, Hunt believed, had increasingly marred European painting from the time of Raphael onward. Most important, Hunt brought serious ideas back into painting.

Reacting against the example of such painters as Edwin Landseer (1802-1873), technically accomplished but lacking in substance, Hunt brought content to the foreground of his art. Combining a heightened attention to detail with a pronounced typological symbolism, Hunt produced works that were meaningful in themselves and that made statements with relation to other texts as well, whether those other texts came from literature or the Bible. Thus, Hunt's greatest works are narrative in nature, informed by texts alluded to in the subject of the painting and, in turn, commented on in the painting itself. This dialogue between texts provides the vehicle for the painting's statement and for art's return to an active involvement in the larger context of its culture.

—*William Condon*

FURTHER READING

Bennett, Mary. *William Holman Hunt*. Liverpool: Walker Art Gallery, 1969. The catalog of the Hunt exhibition, this work is indispensable to the serious study of Hunt's art.

Bronkhurst, Judith. *William Holman Hunt: A Catalogue Raisonné*. New Haven, Conn.: Yale University Press, Paul Mellon Centre for Studies in British Art, 2004. An 800-page catalog of Hunt's work, with separate sections devoted to his oil paintings and his works on paper. Includes an introduction assessing his life, artistic techniques, aims, philosophy, and religious beliefs. The appendixes feature Hunt's illustrated letters, etchings, and other examples of his work.

Holman-Hunt, Diana. *My Grandfather, His Wives and Loves*. London: Hamish Hamilton, 1969. This rather luridly titled but quite readable account of Hunt's private life is also surprisingly well documented, as the author had access to family papers not generally available at the time.

Hunt, William Holman. *Pre-Raphaelitism and the Pre-Raphaelite Brotherhood*. 2 vols. London: Macmillan, 1905-1906. 2d rev. ed. London: Chapman and Hall, 1913. Hunt's account of his career and of the history of the PRB, this book is highly subjective and somewhat self-justifying, but an important primary source of information. The two editions are collated in Bennett's catalog of the 1969 Hunt exhibition.

Hutton, Timothy. *The Pre-Raphaelites*. 1970. Reprint. London: Thames and Hudson, 1983. Lavishly illustrated general introduction to Pre-Raphaelite painting and a particularly useful starting place to study Hunt.

Landow, George P. *William Holman Hunt and Typological Symbolism*. New Haven, Conn.: Yale University Press, 1979. The definitive interpretation of Hunt's accomplishments in painting. Landow explains Hunt's typological method and provides detailed and highly insightful explications of Hunt's paintings and those of other Pre-Raphaelites, most notably Rossetti.

Péteri, Éva. *Victorian Approaches to Religion as Reflected in the Art of the Pre-Raphaelites*. Budapest: Akadémiai Kiadó, 2003. Examines the religious beliefs of Hunt, Ruskin, Rossetti, and Millais, and how these beliefs are evidenced in their use of Biblical imagery, symbolism, and other artistic techniques.

Prettejohn, Elizabeth. *The Art of the Pre-Raphaelites*. Princeton, N.J.: Princeton University Press, 2000. An examination of the Pre-Raphaelite Brotherhood and an analysis of the group's artistic techniques. Discusses the distinctive characteristics of Pre-Raphaelite art and how the movement responded to and commented on its time and place.

Welland, D. S. R. *The Pre-Raphaelites in Literature and Art*. 1953. Reprint. Freeport, N.Y.: Books for Libraries Press, 1969. Besides a useful general introduction to Pre-Raphaelite art, the book contains selections from writings by and about Pre-Raphaelite artists, poets, and critics.

SEE ALSO: Aubrey Beardsley; Richard Cobden; John Keats; William Morris; Walter Pater; Christina Rossetti; John Ruskin; Sir Walter Scott.

RELATED ARTICLE in *Great Events from History: The Nineteenth Century, 1801-1900:* Fall, 1848: Pre-Raphaelite Brotherhood Begins.

THOMAS HENRY HUXLEY
English naturalist and philosopher

As the first and most influential defender of Darwin's theory of evolution, Huxley forcefully articulated its implications in the fields of religion, philosophy, and ethics.

BORN: May 4, 1825; Ealing, Middlesex, England
DIED: June 29, 1895; Eastbourne, East Sussex, England
ALSO KNOWN AS: T. H. Huxley
AREAS OF ACHIEVEMENT: Science and technology, religion and theology

EARLY LIFE

Thomas Henry Huxley was born in a Middlesex village not far from London. The seventh and youngest child of George and Rachel Huxley, he was reared in a family of limited means. Though his father had taught mathematics, Huxley had had only two years of formal education before the Ealing school closed and his father changed professions. At the age of ten, Huxley became responsible for his own education.

Ironically, the inquisitive and self-motivated boy probably learned more on his own, systematically working through his father's library, than he would have in the incompetent semipublic education system of early nineteenth century England. Demonstrating the drive that would characterize his later years, he taught himself both French and German in order to read such writers as René Descartes and Johann Wolfgang von Goethe in their native languages. He read widely both in the humanities and in the sciences, laying a foundation that would serve him in his later efforts to bridge the two disciplines.

In 1842, Huxley won a scholarship to study medicine at London University's Charing Cross Hospital. A swarthy, energetic young man, whose keen eyes betrayed a voracious intellectual appetite, he took full advantage of his first complete course of instruction, winning the university's Gold Medal in Anatomy and Physiology upon his graduation in 1845. A few months later, he discovered a cellular component of human hair that came to be known as "Huxley's layer."

During the following year, Huxley joined the navy and was appointed assistant surgeon on HMS *Rattlesnake*, a surveying ship that began a four-year cruise of the South Pacific. Though he was not officially the ship's naturalist, he undertook a rigorous study of marine plankton that earned for him the reputation of a serious and gifted young scientist upon its publication in Lon-

don. In 1851, a year following his return to London, he was elected a Fellow of the Royal Society of London for the Promotion of Natural Knowledge, England's most respected scientific institution.

In 1852, Huxley won the society's gold medal for his studies of invertebrate animals. In 1854, he resigned from the navy, hoping against the odds to secure a position that would allow him to do scientific research in London. During that same year, his gamble paid off and he received two such appointments, one as professor of natural history and paleontology in the Royal School of Mines, and the other as curator of fossils in the Museum of Practical Geography. Combining the two modest salaries, he earned enough to send for his fiancé, Henrietta Anne Heathorn of Sydney, Australia. In 1855, the two were married.

In the years that followed, Huxley built his reputation not only as a rigorous scientist but also as a gifted public speaker. He became known as a spokesperson for the sciences, never afraid to defend controversial findings from attacks by politicians and religious leaders. When Charles Darwin published his *On the Origin of Species by Means of Natural Selection* in 1859, these attributes brought Huxley to the forefront of the century's most heated debate.

LIFE'S WORK

Though Huxley eventually made much use of Darwin's study, demonstrating its implications in a wide number of fields, he had opposed all previous theories of evolution. His reviews of the versions of it put forward by Robert Chambers and Jean Baptiste Lamarck had been scathing. It was only upon reading Darwin's work, following the course of Darwin's logic and tallying his numerous observations, that Huxley could embrace the controversial idea. For his own part, Darwin had sought Huxley's approval before publishing the book. A shy, retiring man, Darwin lacked the stamina required to defend his work from the onslaught of vicious attacks it was sure to receive. In Huxley, Darwin found a respected and able supporter.

In a series of heated debates following the book's publication, Huxley championed Darwin's theory of evolution as the most successful framework yet proposed within which to organize the known biological facts. What is more important, he fought to defend the broader principle that such controversies are better set-

Thomas Henry Huxley.

tled by examining the observable evidence than by appealing to unsupported Scripture. In the most important of these debates, opposing the influential Bishop Samuel Wilberforce of Oxford, Huxley defiantly asserted his and his colleagues' intention to continue to test Darwin's theory, without regard to the clergy's attempts to discredit them.

From 1860 to 1863, Huxley began the first of a series of studies intended to carry out this intention, extensively comparing primate anatomies. In *On the Origin of Species*, Darwin had only hinted that the theory of evolution could be applied to humans. In Huxley's most important book, *Evidence as to Man's Place in Nature* (1863), the younger scientist demonstrated that humans bear a close enough resemblance to the great apes to be included in their taxonomical class. Though a number of scientists initially rejected his conclusions, Huxley, like Darwin, thoroughly documented his findings with an entire volume of observed phenomena. His observations were there to be checked, and eventually the majority in the scientific community was convinced. No longer considered separate from the animal kingdom, humans joined the class of primates.

Sensitive to the fears that such findings engendered, Huxley devoted a large part of his later years to is-

sues raised by the new science in the fields of religion, morality, and philosophy. In a line of his thought that culminated in the book *Evolution and Ethics* (1893), he attempted to ease concerns that a moral education could not be taught without religion, describing ethics as one of the human species' special survival mechanisms. He argued that when people in a group treat one another ethically, each member conscious of the well-being of the others, the survival of the group (and thus of each individual) is made more secure. For this reason, he firmly believed that in the public schools a good moral education should accompany both a rigorous scientific education and a firm grounding in the humanities. As one of the founding members of the school board of London, he had a chance to put these views into practice.

Huxley also took it upon himself to promote the education of adults who, like himself, had never had the benefit of a primary or secondary education. In his popular Workingman Lectures, he took the time to express complex scientific and philosophical concepts in language that people from all walks of life could understand. He emphasized that science itself is nothing more than observation and common sense, applied in a systematic fashion and stored in books.

When Huxley died on June 29, 1895, in Eastbourne, East Sussex, England, he had published a number of important books and countless influential articles, he had received honorary degrees from some of the finest universities both in Great Britain and in the United States, and he had been elected president of Great Britain's Royal Society. His life's work has been carried on impressively by his son Leonard Huxley, a biographer and man of letters, and by his grandsons Aldous Huxley, the novelist, Andrew Fielding Huxley, cowinner of the 1963 Nobel Prize in Medicine, and Julian Huxley, a leading biologist who served as the first director general of the United Nations Educational, Scientific and Cultural Organization (UNESCO).

SIGNIFICANCE

Though in the general public the controversy surrounding evolution has not ended, in the scientific community the theory has, with rare exceptions, been universally accepted since Thomas Henry Huxley's time. Had the theory been disproved, Darwin, Huxley, and the few other scientists who had fought initially for its acceptance would probably have been ridiculed out of their profession. Instead, evolution has survived to become the cornerstone of modern biology, and all who have

HUXLEY'S SCHOOLDAYS

My regular school training was of the briefest, perhaps fortunately, for though my way of life has made me acquainted with all sorts and conditions of men, from the highest to the lowest, I deliberately affirm that the society I fell into at school was the worst I have ever known. We boys were average lads, with much the same inherent capacity for good and evil as any others; but the people who were set over us cared about as much for our intellectual and moral welfare as if they were baby-farmers. We were left to the operation of the struggle for existence among ourselves, and bullying was the least of the ill practices current among us. Almost the only cheerful reminiscence in connection with the place which arises in my mind is that of a battle I had with one of my classmates, who had bullied me until I could stand it no longer. I was a very slight lad, but there was a wild-cat element in me which, when roused, made up for lack of weight, and I licked my adversary effectually. However, one of my first experiences of the extremely rough-and-ready nature of justice, as exhibited by the course of things in general, arose out of the fact that I—the victor—had a black eye, while he—the vanquished—had none, so that I got into disgrace and he did not. We made it up, and thereafter I was unmolested. One of the greatest shocks I ever received in my life was to be told a dozen years afterwards by the groom who brought me my horse in a stable-yard in Sydney that he was my quondam antagonist. He had a long story of family misfortune to account for his position, but at that time it was necessary to deal very cautiously with mysterious strangers in New South Wales, and on inquiry I found that the unfortunate young man had not only been "sent out," but had undergone more than one colonial conviction.

Source: Thomas Henry Huxley, *Autobiography and Selected Essays* (New York: D. Appleton, 1912).

Why trouble ourselves about matters of which, however important they may be, we do know nothing, and can know nothing? We live in a world which is full of misery and ignorance, and the plain duty of each of us is to try to make the little corner he can influence somewhat less miserable and somewhat less ignorant than it was before he entered it.

—*Keith Bowen*

FURTHER READING

Ashforth, Albert. *Thomas Henry Huxley*. New York: Twayne, 1969. An examination of Huxley's thought, focusing on the decade that followed Huxley's years defending Darwin. Ashforth discusses Huxley's reexamination of Western beliefs and values in the wake of nineteenth century scientific breakthroughs.

Bibby, Cyril. *T. H. Huxley: Scientist: Humanist, Educator*. New York: Horizon Press, 1960. Excellent modern biography. Provides a vivid picture of Huxley in his many activities. Well documented with original research.

Desmond, Adrian. *Huxley: From Devil's Disciple to Evolution's High Priest*, Reading, Mass.: Perseus Books, 1997. Exhaustive, well-reviewed biography, featuring extensive quotes from Huxley's writings.

Huxley, Leonard. *The Life and Letters of Thomas Henry Huxley*. 2 vols. London: Macmillan, 1900. The biography most often used as a source for other biographies, though not in itself complete. Notably lacking in details of Huxley's individual essays, lectures, and addresses.

Huxley, Thomas H. *Collected Essays*. 9 vols. London: Macmillan, 1893-1894. Huxley brought together this collection from among what he considered to be his most important miscellaneous essays and lectures. Focuses primarily upon the impact of science on other areas of human thought. Includes volumes titled *Science and Education*, *Science and the Hebrew Tradition*, and *Science and the Christian Tradition*, among others.

_____. *Evolution and Ethics*. London: Macmillan, 1893. One of Huxley's most important works, the cul-

benefited from the great strides in twentieth century medicine and disease control owe a debt to these courageous scientists.

In addition, Huxley in particular helped his contemporaries to see how helpful results could be obtained in any area of human thought through the application of scientific inductive reasoning—beginning with the observed facts and working up toward the answers to the larger questions. This aspect of Huxley's thought has been missed by many of his opponents. For example, his opposition in religious circles considered him an atheist, but Huxley did not actually believe that there was enough evidence either to prove or to disprove the existence of God. To describe his own position, he coined the term "agnostic," defining it as one who is not afraid to admit when there are not enough observable facts to have a reliable opinion on a given topic. As he stated in 1868 in his essay "On the Physical Basis of Life":

mination of much of his thought on this subject. In this book, Huxley explains why morality does not need to rest upon religion.

_____. *Man's Place in Nature*. Ann Arbor: University of Michigan Press, 1959. Huxley's most important scientific study. He demonstrates how, according to the established rules of taxonomical classification, humans belong in the primate group with the great apes, monkeys, and lower primates. Exhaustive in its documentation.

_____. *Scientific Memoirs*. Edited by E. Ray Lankester and Michael Forster. 5 vols. London: Macmillan, 1898-1903. Huxley's most important scientific essays, collected after his death.

Peterson, Houston. *Huxley: Prophet of Science*. London: Longmans, Green, 1932. A lengthy critical discussion of Huxley's life and accomplishments, focusing on the philosophical underpinnings of his work. Rich in biographical detail.

White, Paul. *Thomas Huxley: Making the "Man of Science."* New York: Cambridge University Press, 2003. Comprehensive biography situating Huxley's life and ideas within the context of nineteenth century science, religion, and literature.

SEE ALSO: Auguste Comte; Georges Cuvier; Charles Darwin; Asa Gray; Ernst Haeckel; Sir Edwin Ray Lankester.

RELATED ARTICLES in *Great Events from History: The Nineteenth Century, 1801-1900:* August, 1856: Neanderthal Skull Is Found in Germany; November 24, 1859: Darwin Publishes *On the Origin of Species*; 1861: *Archaeopteryx Lithographica* Is Discovered; 1871: Darwin Publishes *The Descent of Man*.

HENRIK IBSEN
Norwegian playwright

One of the leading world figures in modern drama, Ibsen moved beyond the melodramas of the nineteenth century to create a drama of psychological realism that helped to create modern realistic theater.

BORN: March 20, 1828; Skien, Norway
DIED: May 23, 1906; Christiania (now Oslo), Norway
ALSO KNOWN AS: Henrik Johan Ibsen (full name)
AREA OF ACHIEVEMENT: Theater

EARLY LIFE

Henrik Ibsen was the second child of Knud Ibsen, a well-to-do merchant, and his wife, Marchinen, née Altenburg. Ibsen's house, which faced the town square, was across from a church and a town hall that housed lunatics in its cellar. Early in life, Ibsen was faced with what he would later see as the symbol of spiritual freedom (the church spire) countered by the forces of confinement (the town hall). When his father went bankrupt and the family was forced to move to a small farm, Ibsen felt the pressures of being socially ostracized. Also, rumors that he was illegitimate haunted the young Ibsen.

Theater was one of Ibsen's outlets, and by the age of twelve he had seen six plays by Eugène Scribe and had read Friedrich Schiller. As a child, Ibsen amused himself by staging puppet shows, magic acts, and ventriloquist's routines. In 1843, Ibsen went as an apothecary's apprentice to Grimstead, where he fathered an illegitimate child by a servant girl. This event would account for the themes of guilt, fear, and burdensome responsibility attached to sexual relationships in his works. At Grimstead, Ibsen absorbed himself in the realism of Charles Dickens, the biting satire of Voltaire, the explosive dramas of William Shakespeare, and the Romantic tragedies of Schiller.

Ibsen also began to develop his skill as a social critic by writing lampoons and satires. In addition, he wrote poetry that ranged from introspective meditations to political propaganda, and he published *Catalina* (1850; *Catiline*, 1921), his first play. It focused on one of his favorite themes: the conflict between the lone individual and the forces of power. During that same year, Ibsen moved to Christiana to study medicine, but he paid more attention to his literary pursuits and never finished his degree. His play *Kjæmpehøien* (1850; *Burial Mound*, 1912) was produced by the Christiana Theater. Ibsen continued to sharpen his skill as a poet, ventured into political journalism, and wrote perceptive theatrical criticism. Active

in leftist political movements, he barely escaped being arrested. From then on, Ibsen distanced himself from political activism.

In 1851, Ibsen became stage manager and playwright-in-residence at Ole Bull's Norwegian Theater in Bergen. Having received a travel grant, he toured Denmark and Germany to learn the latest developments in theater. Overworked, underpaid, and unable to produce innovative works, Ibsen left Bergen to become the artistic director of the Norwegian Theater in Christiana. This job was no less frustrating, however, and Ibsen was eventually driven to bouts of depression and alcoholism. Given a small travel grant and aided by friends, Ibsen finally left Norway for Italy. He was to spend the better part of his career in exile from family and country.

During Ibsen's career in Norwegian theater, he wrote nationalistic sagas and satirical comedies. His experience as a director taught him how to structure his dramas and how to make effective use of visual and poetic imagery. Although the dramas of this early period are full of bombast and mechanical contrivances, Ibsen was starting to formulate a new kind of drama.

LIFE'S WORK

Ibsen's career as a major world dramatist began in Rome. Exiled from a Norway whose narrow provincialism had stifled him, and infuriated over his country's refusal to aid Denmark, Ibsen created *Brand* (1866; English translation, 1891), a monumental poetic drama delving into the spiritual crisis of a romantic idealist. Ibsen had now gone beyond the aestheticism of his earlier nationalistic sagas to write a profound drama that would rouse his countrymen from their complacency and force them to face the great issues of life. Widely discussed and hotly debated, *Brand* became a best seller and won for Ibsen a pension from his government. Ibsen countered *Brand* with another massive poetic drama, *Peer Gynt* (1867; English translation, 1892), the story of an opportunistic double-dealer who compromises his inner self to achieve material gains. These two dramas established Ibsen's reputation.

In 1868, Ibsen moved to Dresden. He was lionized by the king of Sweden and later represented Norway at the opening of the Suez Canal. By 1869, Ibsen started to move in the direction of modern realistic drama. *De unges forbund* (1869; *The League of Youth*, 1890) focused on a contemporary setting, employed colloquial speech patterns, and satirized political chicanery. In

IBSEN'S MAJOR PLAYS

Years in left column are earliest dates of production or publication.

1850	*Catalina* (verse drama; *Catiline*, 1921)
1850	*Kjæmpehøien* (dramatic poem; *The Burial Mound*, 1912)
1851	*Norma: Eller, En politikers kjærlighed* (verse satire)
1853	*Sancthansnatten* (*St. John's Night*, 1921)
1855	*Fru Inger til Østraat* (*Lady Inger of Østraat*, 1906)
1856	*Gildet paa Solhaug* (verse and prose drama; *The Feast at Solhaugh*, 1906)
1857	*Olaf Liljekrans* (verse and prose drama; English translation, 1911)
1858	*Hærmænde paa Helgeland* (*The Vikings at Helgeland*, 1890)
1862	*Kjærlighedens komedie* (verse comedy; *Love's Comedy*, 1900)
1863	*Kongsemnerne* (*The Pretenders*, 1890)
1866	*Brand* (dramatic poem; English translation, 1891)
1867	*Peer Gynt* (dramatic poem; English translation, 1892)
1869	*De unges forbund* (*The League of Youth*, 1890)
1873	*Kejser og Galilæer* (2 parts: *Cæsars frafald* and *Kejser Julian*; *Emperor and Galilean*, 1876, 2 parts: *Caesar's Apostasy* and *The Emperor Julian*)
1877	*Samfundets støtter* (*The Pillars of Society*, 1880)
1879	*Et dukkehjem* (*A Doll's House*, 1880; also known as *A Doll House*)
1881	*Gengangere* (*Ghosts*, 1885)
1882	*En folkefiende* (*An Enemy of the People*, 1890)
1884	*Vildanden* (*The Wild Duck*, 1891)
1886	*Rosmersholm* (English translation, 1889)
1888	*Fruen fra havet* (*The Lady from the Sea*, 1890)
1890	*Hedda Gabler* (English translation, 1891)
1892	*Bygmester Solness* (*The Master Builder*, 1893)
1894	*Lille Eyolf* (*Little Eyolf*, 1894)
1896	*John Gabriel Borkman* (English translation, 1897)
1899	*Naar vi døde vaagner* (*When We Dead Awaken*, 1900)

In *Et dukkehjem* (1879; *A Doll's House*, 1880) and *Gengangere* (1881; *Ghosts*, 1885), Ibsen helped to shape the path of modern drama. Both plays treat contemporary issues, center on a small ensemble of characters, and take place in confined settings. They are crafted around tightly constructed plots that are based on the careful unraveling of past events. Their terse, choppy dialogue is loaded with double meanings, their decor is reflective of the moods and shifts of the characters, and their conflicts are intensely psychological. Both plays deal with women who are asked to sacrifice their duty to themselves in order to meet social obligations. Nora in *A Doll's House* leaves her husband and children, whereas Mrs. Alving in *Ghosts* settles for a loveless marriage, wreaking destruction on her entire family.

In these two dramas, Ibsen exploded both the form and content of the contrived, sentimental, and moralistic melodramas of his time and considered such taboo subjects as venereal disease, incest, and mercy killing. Ibsen even attacked the cherished institution of marriage. On the legitimate stage, his plays were banned or rewritten, but in the new avant-garde theaters of Europe, Ibsen's works became staples of the new repertory. Ibsen created plays that attacked bourgeois values at the same time as he elevated domestic drama to the status of high tragedy.

Soon Ibsen would go beyond social drama to probe the recesses of the unconscious in such plays as *Rosmersholm* (1886; English translation, 1889). Ibsen now began to show that an individual's repressed drives can bring about his or her destruction. In *Hedda Gabler* (1890; English translation, 1891), Ibsen combined realistic techniques with psychological drama. He dropped the standard exposition, eliminated long monologues, and created broken dialogue infused with underlying meanings. Hedda is a middle-class woman with no purpose in life. She tries to release her pent-up drives by controlling the destinies of the men around her. Failing in this, she shoots herself in the head.

Kejeser og Galilæer (1873; *Emperor and Galilean*, 1876), Ibsen created an epic tragedy in prose. In this drama, Ibsen tried to reconcile the Christian call for self-sacrifice with the pagan command to enjoy the pleasures of life to the fullest, thereby exposing the underlying dilemma of the late nineteenth century.

Ibsen now began to dissociate himself from political reform movements in favor of a spiritual revolution based on a radical individualism bordering on anarchy. Influenced by the Danish critic George Brandes and the realist director George II, duke of Saxe-Meiningen, Ibsen shifted away from historical plays and poetic epics to concentrate on prose dramas set in contemporary Norway. Eventually, he also helped to give form and depth to the modern realistic problem play.

After wandering back and forth between Italy and Germany, Ibsen returned to Norway a national hero. He was given the Grand Cross in Denmark, honored by royalty, and celebrated in torchlight parades. Frightened and fascinated by the new generation, Ibsen passed through a series of platonic affairs with young girls such as Émile Bardach, Helene Raff, and Hildur Andersen. The theme of a young girl beckoning an aging architect to create a masterpiece appears in the first of his final plays, *Bygmester Solness* (1892; *The Master Builder*, 1893). In these plays, Ibsen experiments with a form of mystic and visionary drama. Ibsen now focuses on the artist and his relationship to art. These short, narrowly focused dramas have a somber, poetic quality laden with symbolic overtones. Their claustrophobic, intense, and anxious mood of finality foreshadows the techniques of the modernist dramas of the twentieth century.

In 1901, Ibsen suffered the first of a series of strokes, which would eventually lead to his death on May 23, 1906. His last words were "On the contrary!"—an appropriate exit line for a man who celebrated the individual's right to define himself contrary to both the wishes of the establishment and the pressures of the crowd.

SIGNIFICANCE

Henrik Ibsen was one of the first playwrights to create tragic dramas about ordinary people caught in the webs of fate and forced to choose between their self-fulfillment and their responsibility to others. Ibsen helped to create the modern psychological drama that probes the recesses of the unconscious. His scenic details, suggestive imagery, poetic symbols, and double-edged dialogue created a dramatic technique that would help to revolutionize the modern theater.

Ibsen's dramas depended on a subtle, truthful form of acting that inspired ensemble productions free from rhetoric, bombast, and posturing. Ibsen's plays challenged avant-garde directors such as André Antoiné, Otto Brahm, and Konstantin Stanislavsky. Ibsen also influenced a diverse group of dramatists. George Bernard Shaw saw him as the champion of the propaganda drama. Arthur Miller centered on Ibsen's social dramas, whereas Luigi Pirandello and Harold Pinter focused on Ibsen's existential pieces.

Ibsen defies classification. He sought to go beyond photographic realism, yet he shunned symbolism. He attacked the hypocrisy of social and political establishments but refused to attach himself to any liberal reform movements. He probed deeply into the problems of women but dissociated himself from feminist causes. Ibsen, the true existentialist, had his characters ask two questions that would become the focal questions of modern drama: Who am I? and How can I be true to myself?

—*Paul Rosefeldt*

FURTHER READING

Beyer, Edvard. *Ibsen: The Man and His Work*. Translated by Marie Wells. New York: Taplinger, 1978. A biographical, critical study of Ibsen that relates Ibsen's works to cultural and political events in Norway at the same time as it establishes his place in world literature. Profusely illustrated with drawings, editorial cartoons, and production photographs. Contains a substantial bibliography of critical works in English.

Bloom, Harold, ed. *Henrik Ibsen*. Philadelphia: Chelsea House, 1999. Provides an overview of Ibsen's life and work for literature students. Includes a brief biography, chronology of Ibsen's life, and essays analyzing his plays.

Chamberlain, John S. *Ibsen: The Open Vision*. London: Athlone Press, 1982. Analyzes *Peer Gynt*, *Ghosts*, *The Wild Duck*, and *The Master Builder*. Uses significant plays from the major periods in Ibsen's career to show how Ibsen creates dramatic tension by pitting a variety of intellectual positions against one another without settling on a single resolution. Offers detailed analysis of seminal works.

Clurman, Harold. *Ibsen*. New York: Macmillan, 1977. A very readable introduction to Ibsen's plays, covering his early works as well as his major plays. A theatrical director, Clurman pays careful attention to production values. Places Ibsen in perspective with other major dramatists. The appendix provides director's notes for several plays.

Ferguson, Robert. *Henrik Ibsen: A New Biography*. London: Richard Cohen Books, 1996. Comprehensive biography examining Ibsen's personal life and creative work, describing how a timid poet became a symbol of artistic courage and integrity.

Fjelde, Rolf, ed. *Ibsen: A Collection of Critical Essays*. Englewood Cliffs, N.J.: Prentice-Hall, 1965. A sampling of articles covering a wide variety of plays. Focuses on both Ibsen's major themes and his techniques. Contains a balanced sample of the works of important Ibsen scholars.

McFarlane, James, ed. *The Cambridge Companion to Ibsen*. New York: Cambridge University Press, 1994. Collection of essays analyzing Ibsen's historical dramas, comedies, feminism, working methods, and the theater during his lifetime. Also contains an essay by Arthur Miller about Ibsen's challenge to contemporary theater and film

Meyer, Michael. *Ibsen: A Biography*. Garden City, N.Y.: Doubleday, 1978. A lengthy and exhaustive biography detailing Ibsen's personal and professional life. It not only documents Ibsen's development as a dramatist, his working methods, and his philosophical shifts but also gives a detailed account of the production history of his plays in Germany, France, and England.

Northam, John. *Ibsen: A Critical Study*. Cambridge, England: Cambridge University Press, 1973. Covers Ibsen's major work, concentrating on the evolution of Ibsen's later prose plays from the themes of his earlier poetic works. Pays careful attention to Ibsen's imagery.

Thomas, David. *Henrik Ibsen*. New York: Grove Press, 1983. An excellent, concise introduction to Ibsen's work. Thomas offers a brief biographical sketch and discusses literary and theatrical influences. Analyzes selected plays using a thematic approach that highlights the role of women in Ibsen's plays as well as his use of symbolism. Also gives a brief production history of major dramas and a review of critical works in English.

SEE ALSO: Kate Chopin; Charles Dickens; Edvard Grieg.

RELATED ARTICLES in *Great Events from History: The Nineteenth Century, 1801-1900:* 1878-1899: Irving Manages London's Lyceum Theatre; 1879: *A Doll's House* Introduces Modern Realistic Drama; 1893: Munch Paints *The Scream*.

II NAOSUKE
Japanese politician

Ii was a conservative but pragmatic defender of the Tokugawa family's rule (bakufu) *in nineteenth century Japan. While he temporarily slowed the decline of the* bakufu, *his policies in the long run were ineffective in dealing with either the growing domestic hostility toward the shogunate or Western pressures to open Japan to full participation in world trade and politics.*

BORN: November 29, 1815; Hikone, Japan
DIED: March 24, 1860; Edo (now Tokyo), Japan
ALSO KNOWN AS: Ii Kamon-no-Kami
AREA OF ACHIEVEMENT: Government and politics

EARLY LIFE

Ii Naosuke (eh-eh nah-o-sew-keh) was born into the large family of the domain (*han*) lord (daimyo) of Hikone, in central Japan. As the fourteenth son, he had little prospect of a major political career, because hereditary succession determined domain leadership. Lacking favorable prospects within the domain's administration, he realistically could expect only that his father would secure his fortunes by arranging his adoption into a suitable family. A common practice in Japan, adoption was a principal means of solidifying a family's political and military ties to other important families. His limited expectations were further restricted by the death of his mother when he was only five years old. Her passing left him without an adult to argue that he might be uniquely suited to participate in domain administration. It was largely chance that ultimately saved Ii from sharing with many of his elder brothers this fate as an adoptee and provided him with the opportunity to play a leading role in the national politics and diplomacy of a Japan that faced grave crises.

There was little in Ii's upbringing that specifically prepared him to direct domain, much less national, policy in these tumultuous times. Reared with his younger brother in a small house by the castle moat, he trained until age seventeen in the traditional fashion of upper-class samurai. He studied poetry, religion (Zen Buddhism), the arts, and such traditional disciplines as tea ceremony. He also diligently practiced martial arts (fencing, archery, horsemanship, and gunnery) and studied strategy. As a young adult, the focus of his studies came to include discussion of current political and administrative matters. Among his acquaintances was Nagano Shuzen, who became a lifelong teacher, adviser, and friend.

Following custom, Ii's elder brother, Naoaki, became daimyo, succeeding their father in 1834. By this time, some of Ii's other brothers had died and the rest had been placed as adoptees in other prominent families. With the passage of time, it became clear that Naoaki would have no heirs, so Ii, in his early thirties, unexpectedly became the heir to the family headship. In 1850, when Naoaki died, Ii was installed as daimyo of Hikone.

LIFE'S WORK

With his rise to daimyo status, Ii was thrust onto the national political stage for the first time. In part, Ii would make his mark by dint of his forceful personality and his willingness to become the leader of the political faction that defended the Tokugawa shogunate. He was also virtually guaranteed a measure of prominence solely by virtue of the fact that his family was one of the few who could provide candidates for the powerful office of great councilor (*tairō*), a post he would assume in 1858.

When Ii took on the responsibilities for domain administration, he also joined the ranks of the highest class of warriors and political figures in Japan, the daimyo. During the mid-nineteenth century, these men came to exert uncharacteristic influence on national policies and actions. Because the daimyo as a group were not formally incorporated into the *bakufu*'s policy-making organization, there was no effective means for resolving disputes among the factions that arose among them. During the preceding two hundred years, when Japan had faced no major foreign threat or internal crisis, this absence mattered little. The arrival of Europeans, who pressed Japan to open its ports to trade, sparked a controversy that the *bakufu* could not control. In this setting, some daimyo sought to challenge *bakufu* authority, and Ii rose to defend that authority.

A key issue in disputes among daimyo factions was the question of how Japan should respond to Western entreaties to open its ports. Should Japan open its ports to trade with the West, and if so, under what conditions? Should Japan keep its traditional policy of trading only with the Dutch on a limited basis? As early as 1846, the emperor, encouraged by those who sought a means to intrude on the traditional authority of the *bakufu*, urged the shogun to keep these "barbarians" out of Japan. (That was the first of several important efforts by this faction to use the emperor's antiforeign opinions as a means to compromise shogunal authority.) Others, especially the students of the so-called Dutch Studies (actually, studies of Western nations), were aware of the growing technological and military power of the West. Some of these men argued that Japan could benefit from contact with the West. All suspected that Japan would have a difficult, if not impossible, time keeping Westerners at bay much longer.

Commodore Matthew C. Perry's arrival in Japanese waters in July of 1853 brought urgency to the debate. Accompanied by several large and powerful steamships, the Perry mission was intentionally designed to impress, even to intimidate, the Japanese. Yet, at the same time, Perry brought examples of Western technology designed to entice the Japanese to trade with the United States. Perry's visit was brief, but, before he left, he told the Japanese that he would return in a year to sign a treaty of friendship.

Perry's visit caused substantial consternation among the Japanese. The nation had not confronted a foreign crisis of this magnitude for two centuries. In order to develop a response to Perry that would enjoy the broadest possible support from domain lords, Abe Masahiro, the most important shogunal adviser, requested all the daimyo to submit their opinions on the matter. Abe's hopes of developing a consensus policy were dashed by the lack of agreement among the daimyo and the strident tone of many of those opposed to dealing further with Perry. Tokugawa Nariaki, who was to be the leading opponent of contact with the West, argued that Japan should refuse the American demands, strengthen the nation's defenses, and be prepared for war. Ii, who soon became the leading advocate for a more restrained and pragmatic approach, agreed that Japan should strengthen its defenses but went on to argue that minimum concessions should be granted to Perry in order to avoid war. His proposals included extending the trading privileges granted to the Dutch to other Westerners.

Despite the division of opinion among the domain lords, the shogunate did sign a treaty of friendship with Perry when he returned in 1854. This treaty was limited in scope, but it contained one provision that would keep the foreign policy dispute alive for several years—a provision to negotiate a full-scale commercial treaty with the United States. Townsend Harris was sent to Japan as ambassador, with the specific charge of completing the commercial treaty. From the time of his arrival in 1856, Harris was beset by Japanese attempts to limit the performance of his ambassadorial duties. Among the Japanese, his presence and his mission were always a source of contention, even an object of violent attack. Abe attempted to deal evenhandedly with each side in the debate. Ii was appointed to guard the emperor and to protect him from the Western barbarians. Ii's antiforeign nemesis, Tokugawa Nariaki, was placed in charge of coastal defenses. In the end, attempts to be fair only provoked heated reactions from each faction.

Between late 1855 and Ii's death in 1860, however, Ii was able to engineer the appointment of a number of his supporters to high positions. Beginning with the appointment of Hotta Masayoshi to the rank of senior councillor, the pragmatic defenders of the Tokugawa rule gained preeminence in that most powerful advisory body. This development would have put Ii's supporters in control under normal circumstances, but Nariaki was able to open another arena of competition that, if successful, would allow him to gain direct control of the shogunate itself.

The key issue was who would become the next shogun. Among the antiforeign faction, the preferred candidate was Nariaki's son, Keiki. If Keiki were to become the heir and eventually the shogun, Nariaki and his followers could dominate the councillors, reform the shogunate, make efforts to keep the West at bay, and generally guide national policy. Ii and his allies naturally opposed this effort.

In early 1858, the domestic and foreign policy disputes between these two factions came to a head. Hotta presented the emperor with a commercial treaty (the Harris Treaty with the United States) for his approval. Usually, the emperor's consent was automatic, but by this time the antiforeign faction and other supporters of Keiki had been able to convince the emperor that signing the treaty was not in Japan's best interests. They persuaded him to refuse to approve the treaty. Rebuffed and embarrassed, Hotta fell from power.

Now Ii was given a special opportunity: He was appointed to the position of great councillor in early June. This office was not a regular one in the Tokugawa administration. Someone was appointed to this position only in great crises, and the authority to act decisively accompanied the title. Ii's actions were forceful, even impolitic. By July, Ii determined to push ahead with the signing of the Harris Treaty. He also agreed to sign similar treaties with other Western nations. Determined to protect his political flank, he appointed his own candidate, the daimyo of Kii, heir to the shogunate. He also filled as many offices with his supporters as opportunity and his authority to force resignations allowed.

Finally, to remove further threats to his authority from Nariaki and others, he began a purge of his opponents. By 1860, he placed Nariaki under house arrest. About seventy people were arrested in all; seven were sentenced to death, and a number of others were either given short-term imprisonment or sentenced to exile. He dismissed other officials who disagreed with him. This aggressive assault on Ii's opponents created an atmosphere of retribution. Although Ii sought to close the rift between the court and the *bakufu*, his opponents moved quickly to secure their own position at the imperial court.

They created situations to embarrass Ii politically. Each of these efforts failed and frustration rose among Ii's enemies. His aggressive attempts to support his own position created new foes.

Finally, opposition to Ii peaked in the spring of 1860. As he approached the Sakurada Gate of Edo on March 24, his carriage was attacked by a band of dissatisfied warriors, allies of Nariaki. Ii was hauled from his carriage and beheaded on the spot.

SIGNIFICANCE

With Ii Naosuke's death, the last major attempt to preserve the traditional Tokugawa political order ended. In the arena of foreign affairs, he had tried to preserve Japan's independence by bending to Western demands enough to keep Westerners from invading Japan. Domestically, Ii sought to protect the traditional authority of the shogun, and he refused to grant additional authority to the emperor or the domains.

All Ii's efforts failed to stem the crescendo of anti-*bakufu* criticism. Had Ii defended the *bakufu*'s prerogatives less vigorously, the Tokugawa shogunate ultimately might have been able to compromise effectively with its critics, and Tokugawa rule might have continued for more than another decade. Contrary to his expectations, Ii's purges did not still the opposition but merely created more and deeper opposition to his policies. By 1868, four domains led a direct military assault on the *bakufu* and established a new, fully centralized government, which set Japan on the road to international preeminence.

—*Philip C. Brown*

FURTHER READING

Alcock, Rutherford. *The Capital of the Tycoon: A Narrative of a Three Years' Residence in Japan.* 2 vols. Reprint. Westport, Conn.: Greenwood Press, 1969. A widely available account of life and politics in late Tokugawa Japan by a British diplomat.
Beasley, W. G. *The Rise of Modern Japan.* 3d ed. New York: St. Martin's Press, 2000. Chapters 2 and 3 provide an overview of the Western challenge to Japan and the overthrow of the Tokugawa.
Hane, Mikiso. *Modern Japan: A Historical Survey.* 3d ed. Boulder, Colo.: Westview Press, 2001. Chapter 4, "The Fall of the Tokugawa Bakufa," includes information about Ii and Perry.
Lee, Edwin Borden. *The Political Career of Ii Naosuke.* New York: Columbia University Press, 1960. Lee argues that Ii was a patriot who temporarily fought off those who sought to compromise the authority of the

bakufu and who pragmatically dealt with the problems posed by Perry's arrival and the advent of the "unequal treaty" system.

McMaster, John. "Alcock and Harris: Foreign Diplomacy in *Bakumatsu* Japan." *Monumenta Nipponica* 22 (1967): 305-367. Diplomatic negotiations from the Western side, as seen by a British and an American ambassador. McMaster discusses the broader international context (economic and political) in which the negotiations took place and provides some sense of the military threat Japan faced.

Totman, Conrad. "From *Sakoku* to *Kaikoku*: The Transformation of Foreign-Policy Attitudes, 1853-1868." *Monumenta Nipponica* 35 (1980): 1-19. A general reassessment of Japanese attitudes toward intercourse with the West. Totman suggests that at first loyalists and defenders of the *bakufu* shared the same goal for Japanese foreign policy—keeping foreign contacts to a minimum—but that they disagreed over the means.

The ultimate victory of internationalization was the result of a change in fundamental Japanese perceptions of what was good for Japan, not the result of the ascendancy of a favorably disposed faction over isolationists.

Webb, Herschel. *The Japanese Imperial Institution in the Tokugawa Period.* New York: Columbia University Press, 1968. Chapter 4, "The Throne in Politics," analyzes the increased use of the emperor by the anti-Tokugawa forces. Ii's conflict with the imperial loyalists is discussed.

SEE ALSO: Itō Hirobumi; Matthew C. Perry; Saigō Takamori.

RELATED ARTICLES in *Great Events from History: The Nineteenth Century, 1801-1900:* March 31, 1854: Perry Opens Japan to Western Trade; January 3, 1868: Japan's Meiji Restoration.

JEAN-AUGUSTE-DOMINIQUE INGRES
French painter

Ingres championed sound draftsmanship and inspiration from Greek civilization. His idealized figures and flawless surfaces set an unequaled standard in the first half of the nineteenth century. In elevating aesthetic form and personal expression above orthodoxy, he inadvertently became one of the earliest examples of art for art's sake, a concept that became important for the later modern movements.

BORN: August 29, 1780; Montauban, near Toulouse, France
DIED: January 14, 1867; Paris, France
AREA OF ACHIEVEMENT: Art

EARLY LIFE

Jean-August-Dominique Ingres (ahn-gray) was born into a family of modest means in Montauban in southern France. His father, Joseph, originally from nearby Toulouse, practiced painting, sculpture, and architecture, but without much notice. He encouraged his young son to study the arts in general and gave him lessons in drawing, voice, and violin. By the age of eleven, Ingres was taking instruction in art at the Museum-du-Midi, Toulouse, under Jean Briant, a landscape painter. Not long after that, he entered the Académie de Toulouse to

study painting with Guillaume-Joseph Roques and sculpture from Jean-Pierre Vigan. During this period, Ingres did not neglect his music studies.

In 1797, when barely seventeen, Ingres left Toulouse with the son of his first instructor and traveled to Paris. Once there, Ingres was no doubt immediately recognizable as coming from the south of France, because he was short, round-faced, and had an olive complexion. Eventually, his stiff posture and deliberate walk suggested a slight arrogance. Ingres entered the studio of Jacques-Louis David, the greatest French talent of the time. This formal association lasted at least three years, wherein Ingres was thoroughly exposed to David's brand of neoclassicism in both topical works and commissioned portraits. Their approaches to eighteenth century classicism in art diverged when Ingres's studio apprenticeship ended. David subscribed to a type of painting activity whose content addressed contemporary issues and moral questions, as he hoped to influence political action. His figures and their settings, however, recalled the Greek republican era. Ingres, by contrast, was generally apolitical and content to explore and alter classical form as a satisfying concept in itself.

In 1800, he competed unsuccessfully for a Prix de Rome. The following year, he earned the coveted award, only to wait five more years in Paris as a result of unfavorable political events in Rome. Nevertheless, Ingres did not languish. Provided with studio space and a modest stipend, he delved into the art of past eras, especially antiquity. Surprisingly, Ingres's classical education to that point was poor, including a near-total deficiency in Greek and Latin. He began to correct his shortcomings by accumulating a modest library, including Greek and Latin poetry and books whose illustrations attracted him because of their special qualities of line.

Ingres traveled to Rome in 1806 to begin his postponed official stay of four years, but remained at the École de Rome for an additional ten years. The sixteen-year period was productive and was marked by several large commissions from Napoleon I for the Quirinale Palace, paintings sent from Rome as submissions to the annual Paris Salon, and stunning portraits of the French colony in Rome, which were characterized by stylization and purity.

Serious financial constraints, however, developed with the fall of the French Empire, the withdrawal of many in the French colony, and Ingres's first marriage.

Jean-Auguste-Dominique Ingres. (Library of Congress)

Collectively, these factors led to Ingres's initiation of graphite portraits as a speculative enterprise. This time, the resident English population in Rome provided Ingres with the majority of models, a number of whom were set in family compositions using a vitalistic line and almost no modeling. Already evident in these works is his preference for refined and delicate contour lines verging on the precious.

Ingres spent the years 1820 to 1824 in Florence, gathering data for a religious commission. While there, he came upon the works of Italian primitives that were either unknown or disdained in official circles at the time. These paintings, and the refinement he found in those of the centuries-earlier School of Fountainbleau, surfaced as influences in several quasi-historical genre paintings of that time, such as *Roger Freeing Angelica* (1819), *The Death of Leonardo da Vinci in the Arms of Francis I* (c. 1819), and *The Vow of Louis XIII* (1824).

LIFE'S WORK

Ingres returned to Paris at the end of 1824 and opened a studio that welcomed both commissions and students. He received both quickly. The return was a triumph, and official recognition, which he courted, came quickly too. By 1825, Ingres was awarded the Legion of Honor after experiencing salon success the previous year with *The Vow of Louis XIII*. The next year, he received a major commission for a ceiling painting in the new extension of the Louvre. It was known as *The Apotheosis of Homer;* its format conception was unusual, because it was destined for a ceiling but painted as an upright easel picture because Ingres sought to avoid traditional Baroque foreshortening devices.

Though this painting was received without enthusiasm in the 1827 Salon, it was quite important to Ingres as a defense of the classical tradition in art and, more acutely, as his participation in the neoclassical movement was threatened by the rise of the Romantic movement in painting. In *The Apotheosis of Homer*, Ingres assembled great men of the past and present, paying tribute to the ancient Greek poet Homer. In fact, it is a group portrait of fine arts luminaries most admired by Ingres, a catalog of his tastes, and, hence, his influences.

Ancient admirers of Homer occupy a raised forecourt in a handsome Ionic peripteral colonnaded temple. At the center of that assembly sits Homer, being crowned by a winged victory figure, enthroned atop a stone base. Seated respectfully below Homer are personifications of the *Iliad* and the *Odyssey*. More recent homage bearers occupy the steps and orchestra pit and include Dante, Raphael, Michelangelo, Nicolas Poussin, Jean Racine, William Shakespeare, Wolfgang Amadeus Mozart, and Joseph Haydn. The overall composition was derived from Raphael's *Parnassus* and confirms Ingres's clear debt to the High Renaissance master. Just as important, Ingres valued Raphael as the last of a line of Italian Renaissance primitives, including Fra Filippo Lippi, Sandro Botticelli, and Petro Perugino, in whose art he saw naïveté and mannered grace in contrast to artists after Raphael, in whom Ingres perceived decadence.

The artist's fear concerning the rise of Romanticism and the decline of classicism did not subside upon completion of *The Apotheosis of Homer*. Ingres immediately assessed the varied directions in his oeuvre and returned to ideas explored in his École de Rome period. One resulting desire was to reinstate academic studies of the nude to a position of official and critical acceptance, but the climate for that had passed. Ingres did the next best thing; he added figures and occasionally drama to early works and amplified projects once shelved. A brief examination of the artist's reworked themes easily establishes his intentions for the nude.

Prominent among the rethought paintings is *Oedipus Solving the Riddle of the Sphinx* (1808), an appealing study of a male nude in an acceptable antique pose with a respectably engaging myth as a foil for the artist's interest in human form. By 1827, it was enlarged and altered by the addition of a Theban in the background fleeing Oedipus's audacity in terror. The Theban's fright contrasts dramatically to the poise and concentration of Oedipus. The work was a salon success in 1827, but it typified a problem in European academic art of the time. Serious artists attached to the human form had to place their figures in historical, biblical, or mythological scenes lest the compositions be criticized as vulgar by salon juries. The attitude became entrenched, discouraging innovation while demanding technical excellence. Almost by default, it encouraged a glut of uninspired formula art. Ingres himself avoided academic mediocrity by building a career of fresh invention.

Even more of a testament to Ingres's faith in classicism was the ambitious work *Antiochus and Stratonice*, begun in 1807 and thoroughly transformed during the 1830's. The subject, originally told by Plutarch, was familiar to Ingres and his contemporaries in painting and theater during their student years in Paris and Rome. Ingres's second version illustrated the moment when a physician diagnosed the bedridden Antiochus's illness (by a racing pulse) as passion for his stepmother, Stratonice.

Ingres spent six years on the painting in Italy, where he had accepted the directorship of the École de Rome. He did so after being rejected by the Salon of 1834, vowing not to submit again. He researched the correct period setting, documented local color, constructed the convincing illusion of a three-dimensional interior with an air of gravity yet style, and tested forty-five times the gesture of Antiochus shielding himself from the near-fatal view of Stratonice. In 1840, the tenaciously constructed painting was shown privately in Paris at the Palais Royal, where it was a critical success, one that set the stage for Ingres's triumphant return to the capital city the next year.

Throughout his career, Ingres was obsessed with the potential of the female form for serene grace, especially the undraped female form. By the 1830's and 1840's, he was reworking single figures and groups devoted to sensuality. *The Bathing Woman*, a small half-torso study of 1807, and *The Valpincon Bather* of 1808 were the first of a long series of those expressions. In both pictures, the models are viewed discreetly, with turned heads and long, curved backs. A full-length, reclining nude also viewed from the back was used in 1814 for *The Grand Odalisque*, a statement of languid beauty and fantasized oriental exoticism, complete with feathers, silks, fur, jewelry, and incense.

In 1839, Ingres returned to the motif of the reposing nude in an oriental world. Entitled *Odalisque with the Slave*, the work benefited from a study of Persian miniatures and exotic bric-a-brac. Ingres's careerlong obsession with pliant female nudes culminated with *The Turkish Bath* of 1863, four years before the artist's death. The tondo-framed painting presents some two dozen nudes in a harem, bathing, lounging aimlessly, or admiring themselves.

There was at least one more vital aspect to Ingres's fascination with women, namely portraiture, especially of the rising middle class that dominated French society by the mid-1850's. As with the nudes, Ingres found helpful precedents in his own early work, for example, the 1805 portraits of Madame and Mademoiselle Rivière. Ingres's major portraits of the last phase of his career include the *Vicomtesse d'Haussonville* (1845), the *Baronne de Rothschild* (1848), two interpretations of Madame Moitessier in 1851 and 1856, and *Princess de Broglie* (1856). Collectively, the portraits project sensuality, a sense of power, the deceit of informality borrowed from David, and certainly the artist's love of flesh, hair, lush fabrics, patterns, and jewelry. These captivating women seem suitably dressed to receive visitors or to attend a ball.

When Ingres returned to Paris in 1841, he was immediately the honoree of a banquet with 426 guests presided over by the Marquis de Pastoret, plus a concert organized by the composer Hector Berlioz. More honors and commissions followed. One year before his death, Ingres bequeathed to the city of Montauban a collection of his own paintings and drawings, plus prints, books, Etruscan sarcophagi, Greek vases, and musical scores. In return, the city of his birth established the Musée Ingres in 1869 in his honor.

SIGNIFICANCE

Jean-Auguste-Dominique Ingres reached a position of prestige and professional success enjoyed by few other artists active from the Renaissance through the nineteenth century. However, his life and art were full of contradictions and paradoxes. For example, constantly acclaimed as the chief exponent of neoclassicism, he was actually one player in a larger heterogeneous artistic and literary community known as Romanticism. Furthermore, despite his adamant positions supporting classicism and academic techniques, his art could be just as arbitrary as that of his primary rival, Eugène Delacroix, leader of the Romantic movement in painting. Ingres, the neoclassicist, mastered historical genre painting, religious themes, and realistic portraiture. He managed to stay in official favor through the successive regimes of Napoleon I, the Bourbon Restoration, the civil wars of 1830 and 1848, and Napoleon III, though he detested change. Perhaps part of his genius is tied to his refusal to be locked into historical time. After all, he refused to change with the prevailing winds of art throughout his life.

Ingres professed to copy nature, stressing drawing as the first commandment of high art, using live models, and emphasizing the contours of forms. Yet, as if he were blinded by an obsession for human form, his figures frequently had suspect proportions, extra vertebrae, and rubbery necks. To Ingres, distortions and a mannered anatomy were justified in the service of his uppermost aims: first, the expression of humankind's feelings and situations, second, the attempt to place hybrid people in an idealized nature at once divine and within the measure of contemporary existence.

—*Tom Dewey II*

FURTHER READING

Condon, Patricia, et al. *Ingres, in Pursuit of Perfection: The Art of J.-A.-D. Ingres.* Louisville, Ky.: J. B. Speed Art Museum, 1983. A superbly crafted and highly didactic exhibition catalog. Draws together many versions and studies of works unlikely to have been seen in the United States until this exhibit and publication. Illustrations are of excellent quality and satisfying in number. The thoughtful appendix summarizing the artist's ancient and contemporary themes, plus the exhaustive separate indexes listing the artist's works by subject, location, medium, date provenance, and exhibition, are extraordinary.

Cummings, Frederick J., et al. *French Painting, 1774-1830: The Age of Revolution.* Detroit: Wayne State University Press, 1975. This 712-page book serves as a necessary aid in comprehending a blockbuster exhibition devoted to major and minor painters grouped under four historical periods: Louis XVI, Napoleon I, the Bourbon Restoration, and Napoleon III. Cummings and other authors weave events in art, politics, and intellectual thought and re-create the concept of period styles.

Ingres, Jean-Auguste-Dominique. *Ingres.* Text by Jon Whiteley. London: Oresko Books, 1977. A relatively brief but well-prepared and well-illustrated overview of the artist's major themes. Seventy carefully chosen works representing Ingres's lengthy career make up the plate portion. Eight appear in acceptable color. Most valuable are the well-researched and easily read notes adjacent to the illustrations.

_____. *Ingres.* Text by Georges Wildenstein. 2d ed. London: Phaidon Press, 1956. Part of Phaidon's French Art series, this work contains a concise examination of the artist's natural gifts and the goals he set for them as well as a discussion of his techniques. The chronology of Ingres's life is lengthy and detailed. The plate section of two hundred images, including good details, is highlighted by six key works in color.

Picon, Gaëton. *Ingres: A Biographical and Critical Study.* Translated by Stuart Gilbert. 2d ed. New York: Rizzoli, 1980. A large-format, handsomely produced monograph. Easily understood by professionals outside the field of art. The selected bibliography is extensive. The chronologically thorough listing of Ingres's exhibitions up to 1980 will assist serious students. Includes more than fifty images.

Ribeiro, Aileen. *Ingres in Fashion: Representations of Dress and Appearance in Ingres's Images of Women.* New Haven, Conn.: Yale University Press, 1999. Riberio, a dress historian, analyzes how clothing, accessories, and fabrics define and display the women in Ingres's portraits. Features more than 150 illustrations.

Rifkin, Adrian. *Ingres Then, and Now*. London: Routledge, 2000. Rifkin reinterprets Ingres's nineteenth century work within the context of twentieth century popular culture. Contains more than fifty images.

Vigne, Georges. *Ingres*. Translated from the French by John Goodman. New York: Abbeville, 1995. In this lavishly illustrated study, Vigne, the curator of the Musee Ingres in Montauban, France, examines Ingres's artistic life. The appendixes include reproductions of Ingres's notebooks in which he listed his paintings, a bibliography, and an exhibition list.

SEE ALSO: Hector Berlioz; Jacques-Louis David; Edgar Degas; Eugène Delacroix; Napoleon I; Napoleon III; Georges Seurat; Henri de Toulouse-Lautrec.

RELATED ARTICLE in *Great Events from History: The Nineteenth Century, 1801-1900:* May 15, 1863: Paris's Salon des Refusés Opens.

HENRY IRVING
English actor

Breaking with the conventions of acting and staging current in Victorian England during his time, Irving introduced a more natural acting style, greater reliance on authentic texts, and more realistic production values for the staging of William Shakespeare's plays.

BORN: February 6, 1838; Keinton Mandeville, Somerset, England
DIED: October 13, 1905; Bradford, Yorkshire, England
ALSO KNOWN AS: John Henry Brodribb (birth name); Sir Henry Irving
AREA OF ACHIEVEMENT: Theater

EARLY LIFE

The actor-manager who would become known to Victorian England as Henry Irving was born John Henry Brodribb, the only child of Samuel and Mary Behenna Brodribb. His father was a struggling shopkeeper, and he lived from the ages of four to eleven with his mother's sister Sarah and her husband, Isaac Penberthy, a mine manager, at Haseltown, Cornwall. In 1849, he joined his parents in London, where until 1851 he attended Dr. Pinches's City Commercial School. He entered the law firm of Patterson and Longman as a clerk, but in 1852, he became a clerk in a firm of East India merchants. Irving did not have his sights set on a business career. Ever since his school days, he had been attracted to the theater. Despite the opposition of his mother, a Methodist who objected to Irving's choice on religious grounds, his goal was a life on the stage.

There was no institution in Victorian England to provide young people with theatrical training, but Irving set out to prepare himself for a stage career. He took elocution lessons, studied acting privately with William Hoskins, and observed the performances of Samuel Phelps, London's leading Shakespearean actor. Irving turned down an offer to work with Phelps; in 1856, however, he joined the stock company of E. D. Davis, whom he had met through Hoskins, at the Lyceum Theatre in Sunderland. He gave his first public performance using the stage name Henry Irving in the role of the duke of Orleans in Edward Bulwer-Lytton's *Richelieu: Or, The Conspiracy* on September 18, 1856. During the next ten years, Irving learned his craft in provincial theaters throughout Great Britain. He worked with R. H. Wyndham for two and a half years in Edinburgh, with Charles Calvert in Manchester for nearly five years, and briefly in Dublin, Glasgow, and Liverpool. There were occasional London engagements during these years, but Irving was still mastering his craft and did not make strongly favorable impressions on audiences.

Irving struggled to overcome his Cornish accent and to control the lurching gait that gave him "the Crab" as a nickname. In time, he gained mastery over his tall, spare figure, and Ellen Terry, his most famous leading lady, thought his thin, pale face with its large nose and piercing eyes attractive. Those who saw him perform in his maturity commented on Irving's ability to convey a series of emotions using only facial expressions. His eyes were often called mesmeric. In 1866, Irving joined a company at the St. James's Theatre and had his first taste of London success that November as the villainous Rawdon Scudamore in Dion Boucicault's *Hunted Down* (pr. 1866). Work in the provinces and on tour, including an engagement in Paris, followed, however, and not until June, 1870, when he appeared as Digby Grant in James Albery's *Two Roses*, a new play at the Vaudeville that ran until March, 1871, did Irving have another solid success in London.

When Irving married Florence O'Callaghan on July 15, 1869, he used the name Brodribb when taking out the license. His sons Henry and Lawrence, born in 1870 and 1871, used that name until, as adults, they joined their father in the theater. Irving and his wife stopped living together in 1872, and in 1879 they effected a legal separation.

LIFE'S WORK

Irving's break with his wife was prompted, it is said, by a disparaging remark that Florence made after his opening-night performance of *The Bells*. Adapted by Leopold Lewis from Émile Erckmann and Alexandre Chatrian's *The Polish Jew* (1871), a vehicle for such famous French actors as Coquelin Aîné, *The Bells* was Irving's first solid success in London, running from November, 1871, to May, 1872, and it became a permanent fixture in the actor's repertoire. Indeed, Irving performed Mathias, the central character in *The Bells*, the evening before his death in 1905.

Irving achieved this success under the management of "Colonel" Hezekiah Bateman, an American who had taken over the Lyceum Theatre in 1871 and hired Irving to play opposite his daughter Isabel. Audiences and critics liked the comparative realism of Irving's performance in *The Bells*, and with Bateman, he embarked on a series of melodramas that were popular successes. Irving played the title characters in the premiers of William Gorman Wills's *Charles I* (1872) and *Eugene Aram* (1873), and in September, 1873, he took on the role of the cardinal in Bulwer-Lytton's *Richelieu*. His performance earned favorable comparisons with the acting of Phelps and William Macready, the critics finding impressive Irving's attention to authentic costuming, telling stage movements, and psychological motivation.

The same qualities marked Irving's performances in a series of plays by Shakespeare, the first a production of *Hamlet* (pr. c. 1600-1601) that ran two hundred nights following its opening on October 31, 1874. Irving went back to the original text of the play to construct an acting version that was tighter and more dramatic than the ones used by earlier performers. He invented new stage business, abandoning many of the conventions for staging the play, and presented a characterization of Hamlet decidedly more romantic than that of many of his Victorian contemporaries. Something of the sort happened every time Irving undertook a new production of a play by Shakespeare. By meticulous attention to detail, he gave audiences performances more unified in conception than other actors of his time. They were also productions that

Henry Irving. (Library of Congress)

were more beautifully staged and lighted than those to which his audiences had been accustomed.

While working with the Batemans, Irving staged *Macbeth* (pr. 1606) in 1875, *Othello* (pr. 1604) in 1876, and *Richard III* (pr. c. 1592-1593) in 1877. He came up with an entirely new text for the latter, rejecting the version by Colley Cibber that had prevailed since the eighteenth century. At the same time that he was working on these plays, Irving continued to add to his repertoire of non-Shakespearean kings. He appeared in 1876 as Philip II of Spain in Alfred, Lord Tennyson's *Queen Mary* (pb. 1875), and in 1878, he performed the title role in Boucicault's *Louis XI*.

After "Colonel" Bateman's death, Irving took over the management of the Lyceum from his widow in 1878, and he marked the occasion with a revival of *Hamlet* with Ellen Terry as Ophelia. The association of Irving and Terry continued until 1902, both at the Lyceum and on tour in England and the United States. Irving continued to provide audiences with new readings of the plays of Shakespeare, as he did with a sympathetic characterization of Shylock in *The Merchant of Venice* (pr. c. 1596-1597) in 1879, at the same time that he personally supervised every aspect of the staging of the plays in which Terry and he appeared.

In time, the company at the Lyceum comprised more than six hundred actors, technicians, and staff. Irving installed Henry Loveday and Bram Stoker as his lieutenants in management; he commissioned costume and set designs from artists as famous as Edward Burne-Jones and music from Sir Arthur Sullivan. The quality of the lighting and special effects at the Lyceum were noted by many critics, and Irving's ability to handle crowd scenes, as in the successful production of *Romeo and Juliet* (pr. c. 1595-1596) in 1882, was a striking feature of his direction. Although Ellen Terry was more successful as Juliet than Irving as Romeo, both were applauded in the roles of Beatrice and Benedick in the production of *Much Ado About Nothing* (pr. c. 1598-1599) later the same year. Irving staged a brief run of Shakespeare's *Othello* in 1882 as well, alternating in the roles of Othello and Iago with the American actor Edwin Booth.

For most of the rest of his professional career, Irving was the acknowledged head of the British theater. From October, 1883, to March, 1884, he took his company to the United States, the first of eight commercially successful tours. He continued to mount productions of new plays, such as Wills's version of *Faust* that ran from December, 1885, to April, 1887, in which Irving played the role of Mephistopheles, and productions of Shakespeare, such as the 1888 staging of *Macbeth*, for which Terry wore a green dress covered with iridescent beetles. Irving's conception of Macbeth as unheroic, even neurotic, did not please all audiences; it was an interpretation decades ahead of its time.

Meanwhile, Irving himself was increasingly a success with the upper and middle classes. He hosted lavish receptions on the stage of the Lyceum after important first nights or milestone performances of particular plays, receptions attended on occasion by the Prince of Wales. In April, 1889, Irving and Terry gave a command performance before Queen Victoria at Sandringham, enacting the entirety of *The Bells* and the trial scene from *The Merchant of Venice*. In 1893, there was a performance at Windsor Castle of Tennyson's *Becket*, itself a great commercial and critical success. Irving received a knighthood from the queen in 1895, the first actor to be so honored, and Her Majesty was pleased to bestow it.

The new productions of Shakespeare's plays that Irving mounted toward the end of his career, such as his *Henry VIII* (pr. 1613) and *King Lear* (pr. c. 1605-1606) in

---

ELLEN TERRY AND HENRY IRVING

In her autobiography, Ellen Terry recalled her last years working with Henry Irving, who had been both her fellow actor and manager.

I had exactly ten years more with Henry Irving after "Henry VIII." During that time we did "King Lear," "Becket," "King Arthur," "Cymbeline," "Madame Sans-Gene," "Peter the Great" and "The Medicine Man." I feel too near to these productions to write about them. . . .

In these days Henry was a changed man. He became more republican and less despotic as a producer. He left things to other people. As an actor he worked as faithfully as ever. Henley's stoical lines might have been written of him as he was in these last days:

> Out of the night that covers me,
> Black as the Pit from pole to pole,
> I thank whatever gods there be
> For my unconquerable soul.
> In the fell clutch of circumstance
> I have not winced nor cried aloud:
> Beneath the bludgeonings of chance
> My head is bloody but unbowed.

Henry Irving did not treat me badly. I hope I did not treat him badly. He revived "Faust" and produced "Dante." I would have liked to stay with him to the end of the chapter, but there was nothing for me to act in either of these plays. But we never quarreled. Our long partnership dissolved naturally. It was all very sad, but it could not be helped.

It has always been a reproach against Henry Irving in some mouths that he neglected the modern English playwright; and of course the reproach included me to a certain extent. I was glad, then, to show that I *could* act in the new plays when Mr. [James] Barrie wrote "Alice-sit-by-the-Fire" for me, and after some years' delay I was able to play in Mr. Bernard Shaw's "Captain Brassbound's Conversion." Of course I could not have played in "little" plays of this school at the Lyceum with Henry Irving, even if I had wanted to! They are essentially plays for small theaters. . . .

Source: Ellen Terry, *The Story of My Life* (New York: Doubleday, Page, 1908), chapter 14.

1892, were less successful than the run of Tennyson's *Becket* (pb. 1884) the following year. Having given *Henry VIII* so lavish a staging that it became more historical pageant than dramatic vehicle, Irving turned to a series of plays set in historical times. He played Corporal Gregory Brewster in Arthur Conan Doyle's *Waterloo* in 1894, Napoleon in 1897 in an adaptation of Victorien Sardou's *Madame Sans-Gêne* (pr. 1893) by Comyns Carr, and in 1898 the title role in his son Lawrence Irving's new play, *Peter the Great*.

Irving had always given attention to costuming and stage sets, but with these plays, he was in danger of staging nothing but costume drama. In 1898, a fire destroyed the warehouse in which the Lyceum stored the settings for Irving's plays, and the ensuing financial crisis caused Irving to turn over the theater to others. Under these circumstances, in 1899 he mounted a production of Lawrence Irving's translation of Sardou's new play *Robespierre* (1899), and in 1901 he did *Coriolanus* (pr. c. 1607-1608), his last new production of a Shakespeare play. Terry left the Irving company in 1902, and the new management of the Lyceum lost the lease on the building.

Nevertheless, Irving struggled to mount new productions. Tours in the British provinces and the United States offset the lack of financial success of his *Dante*, written by Victorien Sardou and produced in 1903 from a translation by his son Lawrence. In his final appearance in London, Irving revived Tennyson's *Becket*, and he was on tour with the play when he collapsed and died in Bradford on October 13, 1905.

Irving was buried in Westminster Abbey. It was the last in a series of public honors, including honorary degrees from universities in Dublin (1892), Cambridge (1898), and Glasgow (1899). The coffin was covered with a pall of laurel leaves. They turned gold in the light coming through the Abbey windows. Irving would have appreciated the theatricality of the effect.

SIGNIFICANCE

Henry Irving was the leading British actor-manager of the Victorian period. He wanted the middle and upper classes to accept theatrical work as genuine art, and he knew that would occur only if the public saw actors as respectable members of society. Irving worked consciously for social acceptance for himself and other members of his profession. He also worked hard to succeed as an actor. By supervising every element in the plays he staged at the Lyceum, Irving achieved greater stylistic and dramatic unity than had his Victorian predecessors.

Admittedly, many of the plays that Irving chose were sentimental and melodramatic. With the questionable exception of Tennyson, Irving worked with no first-rate contemporary dramatist. Both Henry Arthur Jones and Arthur Wing Pinero, successful as writers of an English drama more realistic than Irving usually selected, worked for a time in the Lyceum company, but Irving was comfortable with the romantic costume dramas of Sardou, Wills, and Carr. In his capacity as a drama critic, George Bernard Shaw argued that both Terry and Irving were wasted as actors in much of the material that they staged. He attempted, perhaps sincerely, to persuade both to appear in the sort of realistic play that he himself was starting to write.

Because so much of the quality of an actor's work lies in details of actual performances, it is hard to assess Irving's importance. Recordings of his voice exist, but contemporary reviews and memoirs are the chief evidence of the fact that Irving was a magnetic performer. The notes that he made for his productions of Shakespeare, however, do give a sense of Irving's originality. He sought, in every play in which he appeared, a unified characterization of the man he played. Like the Russian director Konstantin Stanislavsky, Irving saw each character as a unique human individual, and he looked constantly for the detail of phrasing, movement, or gesture that would convey that character's nature to an audience. Although later actor-managers such as Herbert Beerbohm Tree and John Martin Harvey followed Irving's lead in staging lavish productions of Shakespeare, they did not focus the details of a production toward the single, central effect characteristic of Irving. In a sense, Irving's heir as stage director was Terry's son, Edward Gordon Craig, and not Beerbohm Tree or Harvey.

Irving's real legacy to the English theater may lie less in his own acting than in his scholarly approach to the production of Shakespeare and his sensitivity to production values. His acting would perhaps not seem realistic to a twentieth century audience. Less mannered and stagey than the styles of his predecessors, Irving's acting was romantic in its emphasis on the individuality of the character and in its intuitive, rather than intellectual, approach to a role.

—Robert C. Petersen

FURTHER READING

Baker, Michael. *The Rise of the Victorian Actor*. Totowa, N.J.: Rowman & Littlefield, 1978. This study focuses on the development of acting as a profession in Victorian England.

Bingham, Madeleine. *Henry Irving: The Greatest Victorian Actor*. Foreword by John Gielgud. New York: Stein & Day, 1978. An excellent account of Irving's life, but the book fails to provide enough analysis of his work as actor and theatrical manager.

Darbyshire, Alfred. *The Art of the Victorian Stage: Notes and Recollections*. New York: Benjamin Blom, 1969. This chatty and anecdotal memoir, originally published in 1907, gives a theatrical associate's perspective on Irving.

Hughes, Alan. *Henry Irving, Shakespearean*. Cambridge, England: Cambridge University Press, 1981. Using prompt books and production notes, Hughes gives an invaluable scene-by-scene reconstruction of Irving's Shakespearean productions.

Joseph, Bertram. *The Tragic Actor*. London: Routledge & Kegan Paul, 1959. By placing Irving in the context of male tragic actors from the age of Elizabeth I to that of Victoria, Joseph makes it clear how Irving developed out of a long stage tradition.

King, W. D. *Henry Irving's Waterloo: Theatrical Engagements with Arthur Conan Doyle, George Barnard Shaw, Ellen Terry, Edward Gordon Craig: Late-Victorian Culture, Assorted Ghosts, Old Men, War, and History*. Berkeley: University of California Press, 1993. Recounts how late in the nineteenth century, critic George Barnard Shaw panned Irving's performance in *A Story of Waterloo*, a popular play by Arthur Conan Doyle. Shaw's attack was the first volley in a battle against the old guard of the Victorian stage.

Rowell, George. *The Victorian Theatre: A Survey*. Oxford, England: Oxford University Press, 1956. This book is especially useful in providing a sense of the technical and literary resources available to Irving at the start of his career as a stage manager.

Rozmovits, Linda. *Shakespeare and the Politics of Culture in Late Victorian England*. Baltimore: Johns Hopkins University Press, 1998. *The Merchant of Venice* was Shakespeare's most popular play in nineteenth century England, where the drama was part of the school curriculum, discussed in the press, and a big hit on the London stage. Rozmovits examines how and why this play was so meaningful to Victorian audiences. Includes information about Irving and his portrayal of Shylock.

Terry, Ellen, with additional chapters by Edith Craig and Christopher St. John. *Ellen Terry's Memoirs*. Westport, Conn.: Greenwood Press, 1970. The first half of the volume, written by Terry herself and published as *The Story of My Life* in 1908, contains a detailed account of her association with Irving at the Lyceum.

Wagenknecht, Edward. *Merely Playing*. Norman: University of Oklahoma Press, 1966. The chapter on Irving focuses on him as a performer, particularly in the romantic melodramas that sustained his career.

SEE ALSO: Edwin Booth; Sir Arthur Conan Doyle; W. S. Gilbert and Arthur Sullivan; Ellen Terry; Queen Victoria.

RELATED ARTICLE in *Great Events from History: The Nineteenth Century, 1801-1900:* 1878-1899: Irving Manages London's Lyceum Theatre.

WASHINGTON IRVING
American writer

Now considered the first "grand old man" of American letters, Irving was the first American writer to win international literary success and was responsible for making American letters respectable in the nineteenth century.

BORN: April 3, 1783; New York, New York
DIED: November 28, 1859; Tarrytown, New York
ALSO KNOWN AS: Jonathan Oldstyle (pseudonym); Geoffrey Crayon (pseudonym)
AREAS OF ACHIEVEMENT: Literature, diplomacy

EARLY LIFE

Washington Irving was born into the large family of William Irving and Sarah Sanders Irving. His father was a merchant of Scottish background and stern disposition. His mother, on the other hand, the granddaughter of an English curate, was gentle and kind. Although Irving's father, a church deacon, tried to restrict his children from simple pleasures, Washington, named after the first U.S. president, would slip away to wander throughout the then small town of New York City. The youngest of eleven children, Irving was frail as a child and had an undistinguished record as a student, being somewhat lazy as well as mischievous. He did read extensively the tales of adventure in his father's library, however, all of which influenced his writings later.

Irving began apprentice law studies in 1802 with Josiah Ogden Hoffmann. Also in that year, his brother Peter began publication of the *Morning Chronicle*, an Antifederalist newspaper that supported Aaron Burr, for which Irving began to contribute letter essays under the pseudonym "Jonathan Oldstyle, Gent." Although these early contributions were amateurish and imitative of essays in the British periodical *The Spectator*, they allowed Irving to experiment with various literary conventions and writing styles. Between 1804 and 1806, Irving traveled widely in England and throughout Europe, during which time he honed his powers of observation and strengthened his health. When he returned to the United States, he was admitted to law practice.

Irving's real interest and talent, however, lay in his writing. In 1807, along with his brother William and James Kirke Paulding, Irving helped establish another periodical, *Salmagundi*, a satiric and lively send-up of whatever the three young men thought needed parodying. Although Irving's father died in 1807, most biogra-

phers agree that the greatest tragedy during the early part of his life was the death of Matilda Hoffman, his first great love and the woman whom he intended to marry. In 1809, Irving published his first major work, *A History of New York*, a burlesquely comic narrative in which he created the persona Diedrich Knickerbocker, who appears later as the teller of Irving's most famous stories, "The Legend of Sleepy Hollow" and "Rip Van Winkle." The book brought Irving his first taste of literary success, and in 1812 he became the anonymous editor of *Analectic Magazine*.

In May, 1815, Irving traveled to Liverpool, England, on behalf of the hardware business of which he was a partner with his brothers Peter and William. It was here that he discovered what poor financial condition the business was in and here also that he faced with his brothers the bankruptcy courts. Thus, it was not a burning love of literature that made Irving begin his writing career in earnest, but rather his desperate need to make a living. Irving stayed in Europe for the next seventeen years, finally returning to the United States in 1832, but only after he had become the famous author of *The Sketch Book of Geoffrey Crayon, Gent.* (1819-1820).

LIFE'S WORK

A few months after the bankruptcy of his company, Irving began writing in earnest on the first installments of his series of tales and essays that were to become *The Sketch Book*. Sending them to his brother Ebenezer in the United States for publication, Irving wrote, characteristically, that his greatest desire was to make himself worthy of the goodwill of his countrymen. He did much toward achieving his goal by including in this first number perhaps the most memorable mythic figure in all of American literature, Rip Van Winkle. In the installments that followed, Irving almost single-handedly established the beginning of American literature. No American work of literature, and few works from any country, received the amount of praise heaped upon *The Sketch Book*. It was truly the first international literary sensation to come from the New World.

Irving's newfound success freed him and his brothers from their money worries and allowed Irving to indulge himself in his great love of travel. After several months in Paris, Irving returned to England to publish *Bracebridge Hall* (1822), which focused on the customs of England. Then he was off again, traveling through Europe until settling in Dresden for six months, after which he lived in Paris from August, 1823, until May, 1824. When he returned to London, he published the appropriately titled *Tales of a Traveller* (1824). This work was not well received by the critics, however, and caused Irving his first professional disappointment. His biographers call this an important transition period in Irving's literary development, a period during which he seems to have decided to cease writing the imaginative sketches that had brought him fame and to focus more on historical and biographical works.

After four months in southern France, Irving went to Spain with an American legation, thus beginning his career as an American diplomat and ambassador. The fruits of Irving's Spanish sojourn are *A History of the Life and Voyages of Christopher Columbus* (1828), *A Chronicle of the Conquest of Granada* (1829), *Voyages and Discoveries of the Companions of Columbus* (1831), and *The Alhambra* (1832), which included sketches and tales.

In 1829, Irving returned to London to become secretary of the American legation and thus began his diplomatic life in an even more formal way. In April, 1830, he was given a gold medal by the Royal Society of Literature for preeminent work in the field of literature, and in the following month he was presented an honorary doctor of letters degree from Oxford University. Thus, it was at the height of his professional career, some seventeen years after he left the United States, that he finally returned to his native country, having succeeded beyond his wildest dreams in earning the goodwill of his countrymen. He returned to great acclaim and public enthusiasm, much to his surprise, and had to refuse invitations from many cities for dinners and banquets in his honor. Still the wanderer, Irving began tours of the American West and South, keeping diaries of his travels from which he published *A Tour of the Prairies* in *The Crayon Miscellany* in 1835.

Also in 1835, Irving bought ten acres of land at Tarrytown, on which sat a Dutch stone house that he named Sunnyside and in which he took permanent residence. In the next six years, Irving published more historical and biographical works, including *Astoria* (1836), written at the request of John Jacob Astor; *The Adventures of Captain Bonneville, U.S.A.* (1837); and short biographies of Oliver Goldsmith and Margaret Davidson.

IRVING'S MAJOR WORKS

SHORT FICTION

1819-1820	*The Sketch Book of Geoffrey Crayon, Gent.*
1822	*Bracebridge Hall*
1824	*Tales of a Traveller*
1832	*The Alhambra*
1835	*Legends of the Conquest of Spain*

NONFICTION

1809	*A History of New York*
1813	*Biography of James Lawrence*
1828	*A History of the Life and Voyages of Christopher Columbus*
1829	*A Chronicle of the Conquest of Granada*
1831	*Voyages and Discoveries of the Companions of Columbus*
1835	*A Tour of the Prairies*
1836	*Astoria*
1837	*The Adventures of Captain Bonneville*
1849	*The Life of Oliver Goldsmith*
1855-1859	*The Life of George Washington* (5 volumes)

During this period he was offered, and refused, the position of secretary of the navy and the nomination for mayor of New York City. In short, as his biographers have noted, Irving took it easy in the ten years after returning to the United States. Although portraits of Irving as a young man present him as a keen-eyed, dark-haired Byronic dandy with curling dark locks of hair, the more popular image of him can be seen in a later sketch in which he looks the part of a genial middle-class landowner, reclining in a rural setting with his faithful dog Ginger beside him.

Irving did not, however, refuse the offer made to him by President John Tyler in 1842 to become minister to Spain, a position he held until the end of 1845, at which time he made his final return to the United States to spend the last years of his life in the idyllic setting of Tarrytown, expanding his biography of Oliver Goldsmith, arranging for the publication of his collected works, and writing his multivolume *The Life of George Washington* (1855-1859). Irving died at his home at Sunnyside on the evening of November 28, 1859.

SIGNIFICANCE

Washington Irving was the first "grand old man" of American letters, the nation's first internationally famous author, and the first American writer to make

American literature a tangible reality. *The Sketch Book*, although imitative of several genres such as the personal essay and the folktale that were popular in the nineteenth century, became a phenomenal success, unprecedented at the time. Irving had great influence not only on such British comic writers as Charles Dickens and William Makepeace Thackeray, but also on American writers such as Nathaniel Hawthorne, Herman Melville, and Edgar Allan Poe. Irving was successful in blending the eighteenth century essay style of the British writers Joseph Addison and Richard Steele with the Romantic folktale popular in Germany. In this way, Irving was instrumental in creating the short genre that Hawthorne and Poe would later deepen and develop and thus make the major American contribution to world literature.

Although Irving was a prolific writer and his works fill numerous volumes, and although he was widely read during his time, few people, other than students, read his work today, and they only read a small portion of his total output. However, two of his creations, Rip Van Winkle and Ichabod Crane, have become mythic figures in American folklore, comparable to Paul Bunyan and Johnny Appleseed. Everyone is familiar with these memorable icons of a more leisurely and peaceful time in American culture. In such tales as "Rip Van Winkle" and "The Legend of Sleepy Hollow," Irving used the persona of Diedrich Knickerbocker to give new life to old tales and thus allow his readers to identify with his comic characters. Regardless of age, many men have longed for a draught of the magic brew that allowed Rip Van Winkle to sleep through all of his adult responsibilities to emerge unscathed into a second childhood.

Washington Irving is responsible for making American literature a significant force in world culture at a time when the United States was felt to be England's cultural inferior. The secret of Irving's success, in addition to combining the essay and the tale form to sow the seeds for a new literary genre, was his own unique voice—a leisurely and genial point of view that expressed kindness, good humor, hospitality, and warmth, or, in short, the ideal of something uniquely American.

—*Charles E. May*

FURTHER READING

Aderman, Ralph M., ed. *Critical Essays on Washington Irving.* Boston: G. K. Hall, 1990. Collection of essays on Irving written during the nineteenth and twentieth centuries. Includes examinations of Irving's art and literary debts, the relationship of his stories to his culture, and his generic heritage.

Bowden, Mary Weatherspoon. *Washington Irving.* Boston: Twayne, 1981. An introductory critical study that focuses on the political forces that influenced Irving's work. Sketchy on biography but detailed on literary development.

Hedges, William L. *Washington Irving: An American Study, 1802-1832.* Baltimore: Johns Hopkins University Press, 1965. A sound and fully developed critical study that places Irving within his cultural milieu and examines the many literary genres that Irving mastered. Clarifies Irving's emphasis on dreams, fantasies, and symbolic fiction.

Hellman, George S. *Washington Irving, Esquire: Ambassador at Large from the New World to the Old.* New York: Alfred A. Knopf, 1925. An early informal biography that focuses on Irving's travels, his association with influential peers, and his role as a cultural ambassador for the United States.

Irving, Pierre M. *The Life and Letters of Washington Irving.* 4 vols. New York: G. P. Putnam's Sons, 1862-1864. Reprint. Detroit: Gale Research Co., 1967. Written by his nephew, this is the first biography of Irving. Although in its respectful treatment it is far from an objective account, it is valuable in its dependence on Irving's notebooks, letters, and journals.

Kime, Wayne R. *Pierre M. Irving and Washington Irving: A Collaboration in Life and Letters.* Waterloo, Ont.: Wilfrid Laurier University Press, 1977. A detailed account of the professional relationship between Irving and his nephew, the author of his first biography.

Myers, Andrew B., ed. *A Century of Commentary on the Works of Washington Irving.* Tarrytown, N.Y.: Sleepy Hollow Restorations, 1976. A collection of essays on Irving by artists and critics from Irving's own time up to the mid-twentieth century. Some of the most important criticism on Irving can be found here.

Roth, Martin. *Comedy and America: The Lost World of Washington Irving.* Port Washington, N.Y.: Kennikat Press, 1976. A helpful study of the literary genres of burlesque and satire that Irving borrowed from and developed, especially in his first important work, *The History of New York.*

Tuttleton, James W., ed. *Washington Irving: The Critical Reaction.* New York: AMS Press, 1993. Collection of essays analyzing Irving's literary works. Includes a chronology of his life.

Williams, Stanley T. *The Life of Washington Irving.* 2 vols. New York: Oxford University Press, 1935. The authoritative biography of Irving, based on extensive research in original manuscripts of Irving's journals, notebooks, travel notes, and letters. The most complete and dependable study of Irving's life and career.

SEE ALSO: Johnny Appleseed; Aaron Burr; Charles Dickens; Nathaniel Hawthorne; Herman Melville; Edgar Allan Poe; William Makepeace Thackeray; John Tyler.
RELATED ARTICLE in *Great Events from History: The Nineteenth Century, 1801-1900:* 1819-1820: Irving's *Sketch Book* Transforms American Literature.

ISABELLA II
Queen of Spain (r. 1833-1868)

Made queen of Spain at the age of three, Isabella II was the focus of considerable discord within the Spanish royal family because her uncle Don Carlos challenged the legitimacy of her reign. She eventually prevailed and held the throne for a total of thirty-five years but contributed little but discord to her realm.

BORN: October 10, 1830; Madrid, Spain
DIED: April 10, 1904; Paris, France
AREA OF ACHIEVEMENT: Government and politics

EARLY LIFE

Isabella II had the role of Spain's queen thrust upon her when she was only three years old, after her father, King Ferdinand VII, died on September 29, 1833. Though she could not have been aware of the fact, she immediately faced a crisis. Her father's brother Don Carlos was ambitious and expected to succeed his brother. A staunch conservative, he believed that under the Salic Law that had been enacted in 1713 by King Philip V, only male heirs could inherit the Spanish throne. King Ferdinand had failed to produce an heir with any of his first three wives. His fourth wife, Maria Cristina of Naples, whom he married on December 12, 1829, had given birth to Isabella in 1830. Upon Isabella's birth, Ferdinand, with the support and approval of the liberals, the legislature (Cortes), and the Progressists, rescinded the Salic Law, thereby intentionally clearing the way for Isabella to succeed him. Isabella's birth was followed by the birth of her younger sister, Luisa Fernanda. Thus, when Ferdinand died, Isabella, though only three weeks shy of her third birthday, appeared to be in direct line to assume the throne. However, Don Carlos was a resolute conservative and refused to recognize her accession, claiming that the throne was his by right of succession. Don Carlos had considerable support from the conservatives—called Carlists—who in late 1833 engaged in civil wars with the liberals who supported Isabella's succession.

Although Isabella's status remained uncertain, under the existing laws, she was queen, and for seven troubled years, during which the Carlists warred against the liberals, her mother, Maria Cristina, served as her regent. Finally, the Carlists were decisively defeated in 1839. In the following year, Baldomero Espartero, the most influential general in Spain and a strong supporter of Isabella's claim to the throne, pressured Maria Cristina to leave Spain. Isabella's mother had weakened her position in court by marrying a shopkeeper's son. She proved to be greedy and avaricious and was, to the great embarrassment of her liberal supporters, involved in the Cuban slave trade. Finally she left the country and had no recourse but to leave Isabella behind.

Espartero became Isabella's regent and served in that capacity until 1843, when, in a significant shift in power, the conservatives overthrew the liberals and banished Espartero. Joaquin Maria Lopez then presided over a cabinet that persuaded the Cortes to support Isabella. Thirteen years old and supported by the conservatives, Isabella was now officially proclaimed to be of legal age and, on November 8, she was formally installed as queen. She had officially held that title since her father's death, but it had been disputed for a decade.

Isabella had had no independence in asserting herself as queen during the first ten years of her reign, when her regents made all the decisions. During that tumultuous period, her education was spotty. She was essentially illiterate and ignorant in basic fields of study. Morever, Isabella, like her father, was not very intelligent. Nevertheless, despite her obvious limitations, she was said to be a charming person, although sometimes willful, and was physically attractive. During her thirty-five years as queen, she *reigned* rather than *ruled*, an important distinction. During most of her reign, Spain was run by a

Isabella II. (The Granger Collection, New York)

she turned her amorous attentions to the dashing General Francisco Serrano y Dominquez, twenty years her senior, who soon moved into her apartments.

Serrano had supported Isabella's claim to the throne and was directly behind the movement to banish Baldomero Espartero from his post as regent. His affair with Isabella caused a public scandal, but Serrano was merely the first of a procession of men who became romantically entangled with Isabella, whose sexual appetites became legendary. Meanwhile, Isabella was becoming unpopular because of her tendency to involve herself in politics in unprincipled ways. For example, she showed favoritism toward her conservative generals and toward the religious orders that held sway in her court. Never a good judge of character, Isabella became the unwitting pawn of many corrupt and dissolute courtiers.

Despite her sexual adventures, Isabella remained a devout Roman Catholic and was influenced by the nuns and monks prominent in her court. These religious people often verged on fanaticism and were extremely superstitious. Despite their influence and disapproval of her lascivious behavior, Isabella's wantonness continued unabated. Her sexual excesses brought her great popular disapproval in the Catholic nation over which she reigned, while her antiliberalism polarized the populace. These problems were intensified by an economic crisis that beset Spain in 1866 and led to a popular revolt in 1868.

While she was vacationing in San Sebastian in northern Spain's Basque region, Isabella and her current lover, Carlos Marfori, learned that she had lost the support of her generals, who were, ironically, led by her former lover Serrano y Dominquez. She realized that her only recourse was to escape into France, which she and Marfori did, accompanied by her rejected husband, Francisco de Asis, to whom she remained legally married.

Shortly after arriving in Paris, Isabella bought a house. Finally, two years later, realizing that she could not return to Spain, she formally abdicated in favor of her son, Alfonso XII, whose paternity was uncertain. In March of the same year, she legally separated from Francisco. When Alfonso, while still in his teens, went to Sandhurst in England to study military tactics, Prince Amadeo of Savoy took temporary control of the country.

bloc of conservative civilians who were beholden to Spain's powerful generals.

LIFE'S WORK

Isabella was by native intelligence and training ill-equipped to be a queen. On October 10, 1846, Isabella's sixteenth birthday, she and her sister, Luisa Fernanda, were forced into arranged marriages. Their mother, Maria Cristina—who was then living in France—and King Louis Philippe of France engineered both marriages. Isabella was betrothed to her cousin Prince Maria Fernando Francisco de Asis de Bourbon (1822-1902), and her sister was betrothed to the duke of Montpensier.

Isabella's marriage effectively ended on the same day that it began. On her wedding night, she expelled her homosexual husband from her bedroom. It is doubtful that he ever returned, or that the marriage was ever consummated. Isabella was an attractive, vigorous young woman who was fond of dancing and was sexually curious. After she rejected her shy and effeminate husband,

In 1873, Amadeo resigned and Spain fell into anarchy. The military restored order in 1874. The parliament was disbanded and Alfonso XII assumed the throne. Isabella meanwhile remained in France but did make some brief visits to Spain. She continued her amorous ways until the late 1890's, when she slipped into a depression. She succumbed to influenza at her home in Paris in April, 1904.

SIGNIFICANCE

Spain survived the chaotic regime of Isabella II by being run by generals and a coalition of responsible civilians. During Isabella's reign, Spain prevailed in a war with Morocco that resulted in the surrender of Moroccan territory that proved advantageous to Spain. Also during this period, advances were made in public works. Spain's railways were improved considerably, and before the economic crisis of 1866, there were minor gains in trade and in the economy. Isabella herself, however, contributed little to Spain in any positive way. When she attempted to involve herself in politics, the results were unfortunate. For example, during one of her trips to Madrid after her son Alfonso became king, Isabella tried to meddle in government matters, attempting to plot intrigues with some politicians. Alfonso summarily requested that his mother return to Paris and avoid any further intrigues. Thereafter, she remained out of the public eye until her death.

—*R. Baird Shuman*

FURTHER READING

Boetzkes, Ottilie G. *The Little Queen: Isabella II*. New York: Exposition Press, 1966. Boetzkes focuses largely on the early years of Isabella's life, detailing how she was manipulated by her regents and how her marriage failed from its first day.

Carr, Raymond. *Spain, 1808-1939*. Oxford, England: Clarendon Press, 1966. This is probably the best succinct source of information about the reigns of Ferdinand VII and his daughter Isabella.

_____, ed. *Spain: A History*. New York: Oxford University Press, 2000. Among the leading researchers of Spanish history, Carr has gathered a selection of essays that provide an excellent overview of the political climate in Spain before, during, and after Isabella's thirty-five year reign.

De Polnay, Peter. *A Queen of Spain: Isabella II*. London: Hollis & Carter, 1962. A detailed account of how Isabella became queen and of how she functioned in that capacity before her forced abdication, after serving for thirty-five years, in favor of her son, Alfonso XII.

SEE ALSO: Fanny Calderón de la Barca; Don Carlos.

RELATED ARTICLES in *Great Events from History: The Nineteenth Century, 1801-1900:* c. 1820-1860: *Costumbrismo* Movement; September 30, 1868: Spanish Revolution of 1868; 1876: Spanish Constitution of 1876.

ITŌ HIROBUMI
Prime minister of Japan (1885-1888, 1892-1896, 1898, 1900-1901)

Itō Hirobumi played a major role in the drafting of the Meiji constitution and modernizing the Japanese government. He served as president of the privy council and was Japan's first prime minister—an office to which he was elected a total of four times.

BORN: October 14, 1841; Tsukari Village, Chōshū Province (now Yamaguchi Prefecture), Japan
DIED: October 26, 1909; Harbin, Manchuria, China
AREA OF ACHIEVEMENT: Government and politics

EARLY LIFE

Itō Hirobumi (EE-toh heer-oh-BEW-mee) was not quite twelve years old when Japan's isolation from the outside world was ended by the arrival of U.S. Navy commodore Matthew C. Perry with four warships in 1853. Perry was the first representative of a Western government to arrive in Japan since the island nation had seal itself off from foreign religious and economic interference two centuries earlier.

By the time Itō began his career in the military, Japan was experiencing a political upheaval arising from the demise of the old ruling class. During the 1860's, he observed many tumultuous changes at first hand. Western ships were arriving in increasing numbers to supply markets in Yokohama, Nagasaki, and Kobe, and they controlled the bulk of Japan's export trade. Many leaders within Japan resented this new foreign intrusion and profiteering, and they rallied to the slogan "Revere the Emperor and Expel the Barbarians." Antiforeign nationalism was especially pronounced in Chōshû, an old castle town in which Itō was raised as the adopted son of a samurai warrior. He was in England studying in 1864 when he learned of plans to destroy foreign ships in Japan, so he rushed home to persuade Chōshū leaders from attacking the foreigners.

During the long Tokugawa period (1603-1867), Japan had a strong central government at Kyōto that was ruled by an imperial warlord known as the shogun. However, the rural areas and smaller towns were ruled by local chieftains known as daimyo and samurai who fought one another. The subsequent Meiji period (1868-1912) saw the restoration of the emperor, centralization of power, movement of the seat of government from Kyōto to Tokyo, and rapid modernization that included a fundamental reform of government. During the first few years of the Meiji period, small groups of political insiders, mainly from Chōshû and Satsuma, fought one another to gain influence in the new government. Itō was among the

Itō Hirobumi. (The Granger Collection, New York)

most influential of these new oligarchs and became both the first national prime minister and a major force for change. In 1873, he became a privy council member and led many government ministries.

During the rush to modernize and improve, Japan strived to learn from Western nations. Itō and other leaders knew that the era of isolation was over and that Japan must modernize and embrace the world or else become an inferior power. In 1882, Itō began traveling overseas with an influential group that included Prince Iwakura Tomomi, Ōkubo Toshimichi, and Kido Kōin to observe European models of government closely and to study their constitutions. The group first went to Berlin, the capital of Prussia, and Vienna, the capital of Austria.

Japanese government leaders believed that the Prussian constitution provided a better model for Japan than the constitutions of more democratically liberal England, France, and the United States. Prussia had a history that presented a number of similarities to Japan. For example, its government was a monarchy with a strong central government, its economy was late to industrialize, and its people were fearful of excessive political freedom. Itō conducted lengthy discussions with such German legal scholars as Albert Mosse, Hermann Roesler, Rudolph von Gneist, and Lorenz von Stein. He wanted to understand Western government and its sources of wealth and power at the same time he wanted to preserve the essentials of Japanese culture.

LIFE'S WORK

Itō Hirobumi was one of the principal framers of the Meiji imperial constitution, which he began drafting in 1887. That document established the structure of the Japanese government that was in force until the end of World War II in 1945. The constitution attempted to balance the voices favoring modernization, freedom, and democracy within the structure of an authoritarian monarch and small group of ruling elites. Itō oversaw the reestablishment of the young Emperor Meiji as the head of state and made sure that Emperor Meiji was invested with absolute powers and was regarded as a semi-divinity with an unbroken ancestral linkage to the ancient past and the Sun Goddess, the creator of Japan.

Itō personally oversaw every aspect of the drafting of Japan's constitution. He wanted it to be regarded as the "gift" of the emperor to his people. Principally written by Itō, the document was not reviewed for approval before being revealed to the citizens of Japan in 1889.

Although the emperor symbolically held a monopoly on power, the Meiji constitution also established a cabinet and a bicameral national legislature known as the Imperial Diet. The Diet's upper house was appointed, while its lower house was elected. The appointed house limited the powers of the elected house. The emperor could, if he so chose, initiate, dissolve, open, or close the Diet.

Itō also installed the emperor at the head of a state-sponsored Shinto religious system that cultivated a mystical reverence of his reign at the same time the bicameral Diet moved Japan toward democratic reform. The emperor's powers were limited by a complex system of checks and balances. Although the emperor's powers were absolute in theory, the reality was that political conservatives such as Itō could direct the emperor to act in certain ways to ensure their influence and undermine more liberal views from the lower house. Emperor Meiji could appoint or discharge government officials when he pleased, but his rulings needed the endorsement of the Diet to be acted on. A few oligarchs wanted the Diet to be advisory and empowered only to debate legislation with no real power, but Itō argued that constitutional government required the approval of the governed, especially in matters of the national budget. Thus, the Meiji constitution empowered the Diet to endorse important fiscal matters, to initiate new laws, and to accept or to overturn the emperor's edicts.

In international relations, Itō helped to form the policy that expansionist tendencies of China and Russia needed to be met with force. When China increased its involvement in Korean politics in 1894, Japan went to war and quickly defeated the Chinese with superior weaponry and tactics. Itō wrote the terms of the Treaty of Shimonoseki in 1895 that ended the war with China and freed Korea from Chinese meddling.

In 1900, Itō founded the Seiyukai Party, one of the two large political groups coming out of the Diet that disagreed over fundamental national issues. He was influential in moving the Japanese government toward open discussions of issues such as the balance of power, education, industry, transportation, foreign relations, and investment in business.

In 1904, Japan and Russia went to war over a territorial dispute. Both nations wanted their interests in Korea and Manchuria protected. Although Japan suffered casualties of over 100,000 citizens in mobilizing one-fifth of the able-bodied men to fight Russia, it emerged victorious in 1905 with sovereignty over Korea and Sakhalin Island. Many Asian nations regarded the swift Japanese victory as a miracle—a righteous revenge by the East over the West. Government leaders dispatched Itō to the Korean capital at Seoul, where he was installed as a resident general.

Itō planned to modernize Korea along the same lines followed by Japan and make Korea a Japanese protectorate. He believed that Koreans would welcome this assistance and sympathize with Japanese ideals, but he failed to consider Korean nationalist feelings. Because of his underestimation of Korean hostility toward the Japanese, he did not adequately protect himself and was assassinated by Korean nationalists at Harbin in Manchuria in 1909, shortly after he reached the age of sixty-eight.

SIGNIFICANCE

Itō's achievement in writing the Meiji constitution makes him a central figure in the history of Japan. As a statement of political philosophy, that document embraced contradictory notions of modern and ancient rule and was meant to ensure order and enshrine the emperor, while enabling Japan to move toward Western-style democratic government. Itō realized that the emperor should not rule directly but attributed to him mythic powers that allowed Japan to retain its traditional Confucian and Shinto values at the same time that it gradually allowed for political participation and reform. The new constitution gave Japan confidence to present itself to the outside world as equal in status to any European state.

—*Jonathan L. Thorndike*

FURTHER READING

Burma, Ian. *Inventing Japan*. New York: Modern Library, 2003. Focusing on the period 1853-1964, this book documents how Japan in just over one hundred years modernized through a process of cultural reinvention, borrowing and imagining a shared mythology. Itō and others attempted to adapt and limit the influence of Western ideas in Japan.

Duus, Peter. *Modern Japan*. 2d ed. Boston: Houghton Mifflin, 1998. Effective survey of the rise of Japan to world power status and postwar emergence as an economic superpower.

Jansen, Marius B., ed. *The Emergence of Meiji Japan*. New York: Cambridge University Press, 1995. Major chapters on the Tempō crisis, Tokugawa culture, the Meiji Restoration, opposing forces in Japanese society, and Japan's move toward imperialism and militarism.

_____, ed. *The Nineteenth Century*. Vol. 5 in *The Cambridge History of Japan*. Cambridge, England: Cambridge University Press, 1989. The authoritative six-volume *Cambridge History of Japan* is the standard in the field of Japanese history. The fifth volume expertly brings together the best scholars in nineteenth century history, while the other volumes cover Japan from its origins to the present.

Pyle, Kenneth B. *The Making of Modern Japan.* Lexington, Mass.: D. C. Heath, 1996. Analysis of the political and economic reform during the Meiji Era that allowed for Japan's transformation into a modern nation that rivaled or surpassed the traditional dominant nations of the West.

SEE ALSO: Ii Naosuke; Mutsuhito; Matthew C. Perry.

RELATED ARTICLES in *Great Events from History: The Nineteenth Century, 1801-1900:* March 31, 1854: Perry Opens Japan to Western Trade; January 3, 1868: Japan's Meiji Restoration; January-September 24, 1877: Former Samurai Rise in Satsuma Rebellion; August 1, 1894-April 17, 1895: Sino-Japanese War.

ANDREW JACKSON
President of the United States (1829-1837)

Possessing the characteristics of the roughly hewn Western frontiersman—in contrast to the aristocratic propensities of the eastern and Virginia "establishment"—Jackson came to symbolize the common person in the United States and the rise of democracy.

BORN: March 15, 1767; Waxhaw settlement, South Carolina
DIED: June 8, 1845; the Hermitage, near Nashville, Tennessee
ALSO KNOWN AS: Old Hickory
AREAS OF ACHIEVEMENT: Military, government and politics

EARLY LIFE

Andrew Jackson was born into a family that had come from County Antrim, Ireland. His father, also named Andrew, arrived in America in 1765 and died shortly before his son, the future president, was born. The younger Jackson's teenage years were "rough and tumble." Acquiring little formal education, Jackson made his way through early life by hand-to-mouth jobs, helping his two older brothers support their widowed mother.

During the Revolutionary War, the British invaded Waxhaw, an event that shaped much of Jackson's subsequent life and career. His two brothers were killed, and his mother died of cholera while caring for prisoners of war. Jackson, taken prisoner by the British, was orphaned at the age of fourteen, a situation that taught him independence, both in action and in thought.

In 1784, Jackson went to Salisbury, North Carolina, apprenticed to the law firm of Spruce McKay. Within three years, he was admitted to the bar, and in 1788, Jackson made the decision to go west, to Nashville, Tennessee, to seek his fortune.

While Jackson pursued a legal career as a practicing attorney, superior court solicitor, and judge, he also ventured into other activities. He became an avid horse breeder and racer, as well as a plantation owner. Jackson had no formal military training, but he quickly earned a reputation as an Indian fighter, and it was undoubtedly his experience in this area that led to his election in 1802 as major general of the western Tennessee militia. In 1791, Jackson married Rachel Donelson Robards, who had, she thought, been recently divorced from Lewis Robards. The divorce decree had not been issued in Virginia at the time Andrew and Rachel were wed in

Natchez, Mississippi. Three years later, when Jackson learned of the error, he and Rachel remarried, but this action did not stop enemies from slandering his wife in subsequent political campaigns.

Jackson was one of few serious duelists in American history (Aaron Burr was another), and his most famous confrontation was with Charles Dickinson, essentially over a problem that started with race horses. On the occasion, Jackson wore a borrowed coat that was too large for him. When Dickinson fired, he aimed for the heart, located, he thought, at the top of Jackson's coat pocket. Because the coat was too big, the top of the pocket was below Jackson's heart. Dickinson hit the target, but Jackson still stood. Dickinson exclaimed, "Great God, have I missed?" Jackson then fired at Dickinson, mortally wounding him. Dickinson lived for a time after being shot, and it was characteristic of Jackson not to allow anyone to tell Dickinson that he really had hit his opponent; he died thinking that he had missed. Jackson was seriously wounded in the duel, and he convalesced for several weeks.

Jackson was a tall, thin man, six feet one inch in height, usually weighing 150 pounds. His nose was straight and prominent, and his blue eyes blazed fiercely whenever he lost his temper, which was often. During the early years, his hair was reddish-brown; in old age, it was white. He had a firmly set chin and a high forehead. Paintings and daguerreotypes suggest a man accustomed to giving orders and having them obeyed.

LIFE'S WORK

Jackson became a nationally known figure during the War of 1812. Though he had been elected to his rank rather than earning it by training and experience, he soon proved to be a capable leader. He endeavored to neutralize the Creek Indians in Alabama, who periodically attacked white settlers. He accomplished this objective at the Battle of Horseshoe Bend. So tough and unremitting was he at this engagement that his soldiers began to call him Old Hickory. His greatest battle was against the British at New Orleans. Amazingly, there were some two thousand British casualties, and less than a dozen for the army of Westerners, black people, and pirates that Jackson had put together. Although the war was essentially over before the battle took place—news traveled slowly before the advent of modern communications—Jackson became a national military hero, and there was talk in some quarters of running him for president of the United States.

After the war, in 1818, President James Monroe ordered Jackson and his army to Florida, to deal with Indian problems. While there, Jackson torched Pensacola and hanged two Englishmen whom he thought were in collusion with the Indians as they attacked settlers across the border in Alabama. Jackson's deeds in Florida caused diplomatic rifts with Spain and England, and he clearly had exceeded his orders, but his actions appealed to a pragmatic American public, and the general's popularity soared.

When Jackson became a presidential candidate in 1824, some believed that it was the office to which all of his previous activities pointed. If ever there was a "natural" for the presidency, his supporters argued, it was Andrew Jackson. His opponents feared that if Jackson were elected, there would be too much popular government; Jackson, they argued, might turn the republic into a "Mobocracy." Worse yet, he had little experience with foreign policy, and his confrontational style might create one diplomatic crisis after another.

Jackson missed the presidency in 1824, although he received more electoral votes than anyone else. It was necessary to get a majority of electoral votes—more than all the other candidates combined. Because there was no majority in 1824, the election was decided by the House of Representatives, which selected John Quincy Adams; Jackson protested that Adams's victory was engineered by a "corrupt bargain" with Henry Clay, whom Adams appointed as secretary of state after Clay's supporters in the House ensured Adams's election. In 1828, however, there was no doubt that Jackson would defeat Adams. A political "revolution" had occurred in the four-year term. In 1824, four candidates amassed altogether less than a half million popular votes. In 1828, however, two candidates, Jackson and Adams, collected about 1,200,000, meaning that in four years 800,000 voters had been added to the polls—in large part the result of liberalized voting qualifications—and most of them voted for Jackson.

Jackson's great objective while in office was "executive supremacy." He reasoned: Who was the only government official universally elected to office? The answer was the president. Was it not reasonable, then, that the president was the chief symbol of the American people? Further, if he were the chief symbol, should not the executive branch be as powerful, or more so, than the Congress or the Supreme Court? This concept of executive supremacy displeased numerous congressional lead-

ers. Congress had dominated the federal government since the Revolution, out of a general distrust of administrative centralization. After all, Britain's King George III was a "typical" administrator.

Jackson pursued executive supremacy in a number of ways. One was the patronage system, by which he appointed friends to office. His enemies referred to this policy as the "spoils system"; Jackson called it "rotation in office." The number of those displaced, however (about 10 percent of the government workforce), was no greater than previous or future executive terms. Another procedure that strengthened Jackson's presidency, perhaps the most important, was the "county agent" system that Martin Van Buren created for the Democratic Party. The forerunners of what became known as "county chairmen," these agents enabled the Democrats to practice politics on a grassroots level, going door to door, as it were, to collect votes and support for the president.

An important part of Jackson's drive for executive supremacy was the presidential veto. He used this constitutional device twelve times, more than all of his predecessors put together. Moreover, he made good use of the "pocket veto." (If a bill comes to the president less than ten days before Congress adjourns, he can "put it in his pocket" and not have to tell Congress why he disapproves of it. A "pocket veto" enhances presidential power by preventing Congress from reconsidering the bill, an action that caused presidential critics to call Jackson "King Andrew I.") Though he was not the first president to use the pocket veto—James Madison was first—Jackson made more extensive use of it than any of his predecessors.

Perhaps the most significant presidential veto in American history was Jackson's rejection, in 1832, of the recharter bill, a bill that would have rechartered the Bank of the United States. Among other things, Jackson argued that the executive had the power to judge the constitutionality of a bill brought before him. According to Jacksonian scholar Robert Remini, Jackson's veto on this bill caused an ascendancy of presidential power that did not abate until Richard M. Nixon's resignation in 1974.

In foreign affairs, Jackson conducted a lively policy that gained new respect for the United States from major European powers. He nurtured good relations with England by a conciliatory attitude on the Maine-Canada boundary question and promising to exempt many English goods from the harsh tariff of 1828 (the Tariff of Abominations). He even held out the prospect of lowering the tariff against the British through a treaty. His pos-

JACKSON ON INDIAN REMOVAL

In his first state of the union speech, President Andrew Jackson addressed the subject of removing members of the Cherokee and other Indian tribes to the West of the United States. Despite the assurances Jackson provided in this speech, his administration was later responsible for the forced removal of the Cherokee in one of the most discreditable episodes in federal government relations with Indian tribes. This excerpt immediately follows Jackson's remarks on the impossibility of allowing Indian nations to assert their independence within the borders of U.S. states.

Actuated by this view of the subject, I informed the Indians inhabiting parts of Georgia and Alabama that their attempt to establish an independent government would not be countenanced by the Executive of the United States, and advised them to emigrate beyond the Mississippi or submit to the laws of those States.

Our conduct toward these people is deeply interesting to our national character. Their present condition, contrasted with what they once were, makes a most powerful appeal to our sympathies. Our ancestors found them the uncontrolled possessors of these vast regions. By persuasion and force they have been made to retire from river to river and from mountain to mountain, until some of the tribes have become extinct and others have left but remnants to preserve for a while their once terrible names. Surrounded by the whites with their arts of civilization, which by destroying the resources of the savage doom him to weakness and decay, the fate of the Mohegan, the Narragansett, and the Delaware is fast over-taking the Choctaw, the Cherokee, and the Creek. That this fate surely awaits them if they remain within the limits of the States does not admit of a doubt. Humanity and national honor demand that every effort should be made to avert so great a calamity. It is too late to inquire whether it was just in the United States to include them and their territory within the bounds of new States, whose limits they could control. That step can not be retraced. A State can not be dismembered by Congress or restricted in the exercise of her constitutional power. But the people of those States and of every State, actuated by feelings of justice and a regard for our national honor, submit to you the interesting question whether something can not be done, consistently with the rights of the States, to preserve this much-injured race. As a means of effecting this end I suggest for your consideration the propriety of setting apart an ample district west of the Mississippi, and without the limits of any State or Territory now formed, to be guaranteed to the Indian tribes as long as they shall occupy it, each tribe having a distinct control over the portion designated for its use. There they may be secured in the enjoyment of governments of their own choice, subject to no other control from the United States than such as may be necessary to preserve peace on the frontier and between the several tribes. There the benevolent may endeavor to teach them the arts of civilization, and, by promoting union and harmony among them, to raise up an interesting commonwealth, destined to perpetuate the race and to attest the humanity and justice of this Government.

This emigration should be voluntary, for it would be as cruel as unjust to compel the aborigines to abandon the graves of their fathers and seek a home in a distant land. But they should be distinctly informed that if they remain within the limits of the States they must be subject to their laws. In return for their obedience as individuals they will without doubt be protected in the enjoyment of those possessions which they have improved by their industry. But it seems to me visionary to suppose that in this state of things claims can be allowed on tracts of country on which they have neither dwelt nor made improvements, merely because they have seen them from the mountain or passed them in the chase. Submitting to the laws of the States, and receiving, like other citizens, protection in their persons and property, they will ere long become merged in the mass of our population.

Source: Andrew Jackson, "State of the Union Address," December 8, 1829.

itive stance on boundary lines and the tariff helped re-open full West Indies trade with the British. Although Jackson may have been an Anglophobe most of his life, it is nevertheless true that he gained concessions from the English that had been denied to his predecessor, the so-called Anglophile, Adams.

The United States almost went to war with its oldest and most loyal ally while Jackson was president. The United States presented France with a "spoliation" bill, going back to the depredations of American shipping during the Napoleonic Wars. When, for various reasons, the French government refused payments, Jackson's tone became strident. In a message to Congress, he said that a "collision" was possible between the two governments if the French remained obstinate. Ultimately, Britain intervened and urged the French to settle the "American matter," because of mutual problems developing with Russia.

Though Jackson personally believed that Texas would one day be a part of the American Union, he did not push its annexation while in office, for he feared that the slavery question that Texas would engender would embarrass his chosen presidential successor, Van Buren. After Van Buren was safely elected, Jackson publicly supported the annexation of Texas, which took place in 1845, the year Jackson died.

While Jackson was president, reforms occurred on state levels. Numerous state constitutions were revised or rewritten, all with liberal trends. Women found it easier to prosecute abusive husbands and, increasingly, they could purchase property and dispose of it as they chose, without getting permission from their nearest male kin. Prison reforms began in some states, and insane people were treated for their illnesses rather than being thought to be possessed by the devil. Public education systems started in several states, notably Massachusetts and New York. In all these reforms, suffrage ever widened, exemplifying the belief that political participation should be based on white manhood rather than property qualifications. Noted scholar Clinton Rossiter has shown that the Jacksonian presidency changed the base of American government from aristocracy to democracy without fundamentally altering its republican character.

After serving as president from 1829 to 1837, Jackson happily returned to the Hermitage. There, he continued as the father figure of his country, receiving dignitaries from around the world, and giving advice to those who followed him in the presidential office. He was especially pleased to see his protégé, James K. Polk, win the office in 1844 and become widely known as "Young Hickory." Jackson died at the Hermitage on June 8, 1845.

SIGNIFICANCE

It is fair to say that Andrew Jackson was first and foremost a beneficiary of rising democratic spirits in America. When he attained power, he put his stamp upon events and promulgated additional steps toward democracy. He suggested some reforms, many of which were ultimately enacted. He wanted senators to be popularly elected, as were members of the House of Representatives. He wanted additional judges to take the heavy burden off the judicial system. He believed that the United States Post Office should be reshaped into a semiprivate organization. He suggested some reforms that were not enacted but were widely discussed. He believed that a president should serve for six years and then be ineligible for further election. He thought that the electoral college should either be abandoned or drastically reformed, because, in his opinion, it did not always reflect the will of the electorate.

It is widely held that Jacksonian America heralded the "positive state," where government dominates the private sector. Jackson's presidency is frequently cited as starting the trend toward federal centralization. Jackson's legacy is most visible in his personification of the common American man, even though he, himself, was hardly a "common" man. His was an age of entrepreneurship in which it was believed that government should not grant privileges to one group that it withholds from another. This thought has motivated many reform philosophies in the twentieth century, not the least of which was the Civil Rights movement. In this and other significant ways, Andrew Jackson has spoken to Americans of subsequent generations.

—Carlton Jackson

FURTHER READING

Burstein, Andrew. *The Passions of Andrew Jackson.* New York: Alfred A. Knopf, 2003. Comprehensive biography painting a negative portrait of Jackson as a frontier bully, who was, in the author's words, "implacable," "humorless," "self-righteous," and a "rage-filled zealot."

Ellis, Richard E. *Andrew Jackson.* Washington, D.C.: CQ Press, 2003. Jackson's life, career, policies, and the impact of his presidency are examined in short chapters. Also includes pertinent documents and appendixes listing the major acts of Congress and U.S. Supreme Court decisions during his presidency. Part of *Congressional Quarterly*'s American Presidents Reference Series.

Gatell, Frank Otto, and John M. McFaul, eds. *Jacksonian America, 1815-1840: New Society, Changing Politics.* Englewood Cliffs, N.J.: Prentice-Hall, 1970. This collection of essays ranges from politics to societal judgments and lifestyles. The essays vary in quality, but the overall result is a lucid explanation of the Jacksonian era.

Pessen, Edward. *Jacksonian America: Society, Personality, and Politics.* Rev. ed. Urbana: University of Illinois Press, 1985. The best summary of the Jacksonian experience is to be found in this book. With an emphasis on social and economic affairs, the author clearly ties up all the various threads of the period.

Remini, Robert V. *Andrew Jackson.* 3 vols. Baltimore: Johns Hopkins University Press, 1998. This is the relatively new paperback edition of Remini's three-volume definitive biography. Volume one discusses Jackson's role in territorial expansion; volume two describes his first presidential campaign and his first term as president; and volume three explores his re-election and second presidential administration.

_____. *Andrew Jackson and the Bank War: A Study in the Growth of Presidential Power*. New York: W. W. Norton, 1967. In this book, Remini refers to the bank veto as the most significant presidential rejection in United States history, a culmination of Jackson's drive for executive supremacy. After the veto, presidential power grew considerably.

_____. *The Election of Andrew Jackson*. Philadelphia: J. B. Lippincott, 1963. Discusses the change in the number of eligible voters between 1824 and 1828, and how this change benefitted Andrew Jackson.

_____. *Martin Van Buren and the Making of the Democratic Party*. New York: Columbia University Press, 1959. Explains in detail how Martin Van Buren founded the Democratic Party. Van Buren was a politician par excellence, who always seemed to thrive while he held lower offices. His presidency (1837-1841), however, was not successful.

Rossiter, Clinton L. *The American Presidency*. New York: Harcourt, Brace & World, 1956. A work that explains the age-old practice of ranking the presidents, and of trying to determine what constitutes greatness in presidential terms. Jackson's presidency was a time of transition in American society, and the way he benefitted from it, and then helped to propel it, gave his tenure the label of "great."

SEE ALSO: John Quincy Adams; Thomas Hart Benton; Nicholas Biddle; Aaron Burr; John C. Calhoun; Henry Clay; David Crockett; James Gadsden; James Monroe; Osceola; James K. Polk; John Ross; John Tyler; Martin Van Buren.

RELATED ARTICLES in *Great Events from History: The Nineteenth Century, 1801-1900:* March, 1805-September 1, 1807: Burr's Conspiracy; July 27, 1813-August 9, 1814: Creek War; January 8, 1815: Battle of New Orleans; November 21, 1817-March 27, 1858: Seminole Wars; February 22, 1819: Adams-Onís Treaty Gives the United States Florida; December 1, 1824-February 9, 1825: U.S. Election of 1824; December 3, 1828: U.S. Election of 1828; 1830-1842: Trail of Tears; January 19-27, 1830: Webster and Hayne Debate Slavery and Westward Expansion; May 28, 1830: Congress Passes Indian Removal Act; March 18, 1831, and March 3, 1832: Cherokee Cases; May, 1831-February, 1832: Tocqueville Visits America; July 10, 1832: Jackson Vetoes Rechartering of the Bank of the United States; November 24, 1832-January 21, 1833: Nullification Controversy; April 14, 1834: Clay Begins American Whig Party; December 2, 1840: U.S. Election of 1840; September 4, 1841: Congress Passes Preemption Act of 1841; August 1, 1846: Establishment of Independent U.S. Treasury.

HELEN HUNT JACKSON
American writer and social reformer

Jackson received the first government commission on behalf of American Indians and fought vehemently for their civil rights and liberties. She was a major voice of the otherwise voiceless and was also an important poet in her own right.

BORN: October 15, 1830; Amherst, Massachusetts
DIED: August 12, 1885; San Francisco, California
ALSO KNOWN AS: Helen Maria Hunt; Helen Maria Fiske (birth name); H. H. (pseudonym)
AREAS OF ACHIEVEMENT: Literature, social reform

EARLY LIFE
Helen Maria Fiske was the daughter of Nathan Wiley Fiske and Deborah Vinal Fiske. Her father was a Congregational clergyman and a professor of philosophy and language at Amherst College who brought his children up under strict Calvinistic authority. Her mother Deborah was a quiet, demure woman whose influence on the young, vivacious Helen was minimal. Indeed, Helen's father's only real influence occurred when he either punished her physically or derided her in front of her friends. Although her home in Amherst provided her with stability and a strict code of ethics, little affection or warmth was conveyed to the young and impressionable Helen. For friendship and companionship, Helen would turn to her friend Emily Dickinson, who lived down the road from her house. Helen's friendship with the reclusive Emily proved to be a sustaining relationship throughout her life.

Illness was a common feature of New England life during the middle of the nineteenth century. Deborah contracted tuberculosis and died a few months after

Helen Hunt Jackson. (Library of Congress)

Helen's twelfth birthday—the year was 1844. Helen had been a devoted daughter and had received all of her education from her mother up to that point. By the summer of 1846, Nathan had also contracted tuberculosis, but he was set on traveling to the Holy Land. Since the death of Deborah, Helen had been separated from her younger sister Ann and had been attending various seminaries. A year after leaving Amherst, Nathan died, and he was buried on Mount Zion. Helen was nearly fifteen when she was faced with being separated from her only sister and living in seminaries with virtual strangers.

These early years of personal hardship and grief were formative in how Helen lived her life and clearly forged many of her later moral and political values. Despite such hardship, Helen maintained her somewhat carefree and unstructured lifestyle. From these early years as a young girl until she finally came to live in San

Francisco, Helen remained true to her own ideals rather than those of other people. Corresponding with Emily Dickinson was the one unaltered joy that sustained her through many personal and family hardships.

From this period in her life until her death in San Francisco, Helen was a traveler whose trunks and cases seemed to be permanently packed. These formative years gave the young, headstrong Helen a yearning to travel and to experience new and different places, becoming a part of society wherever she found herself.

LIFE'S WORK

Although Helen Hunt Jackson's novel *Ramona* (1884) made a lasting contribution to American literature, her literary and political endeavors had a rather inauspicious beginning. After the death of her first husband, Lieutenant Edward Bissel Hunt, in 1863 and the tragic death of her nine-year-old son two years later, Jackson turned to writing as a form of solace. (She became Helen Hunt Jackson when she later married William S. Jackson, a wealthy Quaker financier, in 1875.) Recognizing that she had an ability to write, she set out to become a well-known and respected writer. Helen undertook a life dedicated to writing. Articles, poems, sketches, and novels became her life-blood. Outwardly, at least, Helen Jackson remained vivacious and ebullient, seemingly undaunted by the tragic life that had been hers in only thirty-five years.

In the summer of 1865, Parke Godwin, the assistant publisher of the *New York Evening Post*, published Helen's poem "The Key to the Casket." This unexpected acceptance of her work inspired Helen to move to the writing community of Newport, Rhode Island. Thomas Wentworth Higginson, a respected writer and critic, soon became Helen's writing mentor, friend, and confidant. Newport allowed Helen the freedom to write even though woman writers were at that time far from being accepted. Because women writers were still an enigma, Jackson was forced to publish her works anonymously. Only when *Ramona* was published in 1884 did Jackson believe that her true identity was no longer an issue.

Because of the phenomenal success of *Ramona*, many

people have the impression that Jackson was really only the author of a solitary novel. This could not be further from the truth. From her early years at Newport and continuously throughout her life, Jackson wrote in many different subject areas.

JACKSON'S PRINCIPAL WORKS

LONG FICTION
1876	*Mercy Philbrick's Choice*
1877	*Hetty's Strange History* (as H. H.)
1878	*Nelly's Silver Mine: A Story of Colorado Life* (children's lit.)
1884	*Ramona* (as H. H.)

SHORT FICTION
1873-1878	*Saxe Holm's Stories* (2 volumes)
1879	*Letters from a Cat: Published by Her Mistress for the Benefit of all Cats and the Amusement of Little Children* (as H. H.)
1884	*The Hunter Cats of Connorloa* (as H. H.; better known as *Cat Stories*, 1886)
1887	*Between Whiles*

POETRY
1870	*Verses* (as H. H.)
1874	*The Story of Boon* (as H. H.)
1876	*Bits of Talk, in Verse and Prose, for Young Folks* (as H. H.)
1885	*Verses: New and Enlarged*
1886	*Sonnets and Lyrics* (as H. H.)
1888	*My Legacy* (as H. H.)
1891	*A Calendar of Sonnets*
1892	*Poems* (as H. H.)
1990	*A Selection of Poems* (with Emily Dickinson)

NONFICTION
1872	*Ah-wah-ne Days: A Visit to the Yosemite Valley in 1872*, by H. H. (serial), 1971 (book)
1872	*Bits of Talk About Home Matters* (as H. H.)
1872	*Bits of Travel* (as H. H.)
1878	*Bits of Travel at Home* (as H. H.)
1879-1885	*The Indian Reform Letters of Helen Hunt Jackson*
1881	*A Century of Dishonor: A Sketch of the United States Government's Dealings with Some of the Indian Tribes* (also as *A Century of Dishonor: The Early Crusade for Indian Reform*, 1965)
1883	*Father Junipero and His Work: A Sketch of the Foundation, Prosperity, and Ruin of the Franciscan Missions in California*
1886	*Glimpses of Three Coasts*
1897	*The Procession of Flowers in Colorado*
1902	*Glimpses of California and the Missions* (as H. H.; includes previously pb. essays)
1989	*Helen Hunt Jackson's Colorado* (includes previously pb. bits and essays)

Jackson's early writing, however, reveals little of the passion and conviction that the cause of the American Indians would eventually evoke in her. The seed for her later and most famous writing was planted during a trip to California in May of 1872. After crossing the Platte River, Helen was given her first close-up experience of what Indians looked like and how they lived. This singular encounter caused Helen a certain degree of heartache as she witnessed for herself the abject poverty in which those disenfranchised people lived.

Bits of Travel appeared in 1870, and *Bits of Travel at Home* was finally published in 1878. During the period between writing these complementary pieces, Jackson's successful "No Name" novels were hailed as drawing-room masterpieces. Jackson published *Mercy Philbrick's Choice* in 1876 and *Hetty's Strange History* in 1877. Up to this point in her writing career, Helen Hunt Jackson had published under the initials "H. H."

When *Century of Dishonor* appeared in 1881, Helen received all the criticism and vindictive press that was associated with writing about the plight of American Indians. Jackson's hope was that this laboriously researched work, which told the history of how badly the Indians had been treated, would spark some sympathy for them. In fact, the opposite proved to be the case. At her expense, she mailed a copy of *Century of Dishonor* to every congressman, again to little avail.

A woman who was no stranger to tragedy and who was relentless in pursuing what she believed to be right, Jackson continued to badger members of Congress. In particular, she focused on getting the attention of the secretary of the interior, Henry Teller, as well as appealing to Hiram Price, commissioner of Indian affairs. Both thought that Jackson was raising the controversial question of

Indian land rights as a means of gaining publicity, but eventually the constant letter writing and appeals paid off. Jackson's singular efforts gained for her the position of special commissioner of Indian affairs in Southern California. This was a major breakthrough, particularly because Jackson was the first woman to hold such a government position.

Abbot Kinney was her choice for coagent and interpreter—a traveler and visionary like herself. They met while she was on an assignment for *Century* magazine in California. Two years after *Century of Dishonor* had been published, Jackson and Kinney began their travels of the Southern California missions. What had originally begun as a crusade to gain land rights for the Ponca Indians in Nebraska turned into a full-scale investigation into how mission Indians were being treated under government laws.

By now, Jackson had become familiar with all of the missions in Southern California, and she undertook her commission with passion and zeal. Much of her traveling in Southern California in 1883 was done by carriage. With old stagecoach routes as their only means of traveling from one mission site to the next, Jackson and her troupe crisscrossed the sand plains and traversed the rugged mountains of the three most southerly counties of California.

Even though theirs was a fact-finding trip, Jackson's party continually came upon violations of Indian rights by white land settlers. Helen's passion for writing was now being used to record facts, figures, and names that she hoped would indict those early landowners.

To her dismay, Jackson's fifty-six-page report, which was appended to *Century of Dishonor*, created little stir. Perhaps the government hoped that the task would be more than one person could bear and that the society lady from New England would return to writing children's books and homilies. Realizing that the plight of the Indians was still in the balance, she took the advice of her close friend J. B. Gilder and began to write a novel.

When Gilder had first suggested that a novel might be the way to prick the conscience of a nation, Jackson balked at the immensity of such a project. Now, however, Jackson saw the need for such a book and was prepared to write her best. The many trips to California had steeped her in Indian culture and lifestyle. Despite the fact that *Ramona* forcefully portrays injustices toward the Indians, the novel quickly became a classic because it paints an exquisite, romantic portrait of mission life in old California.

SIGNIFICANCE

Helen Hunt Jackson was a woman who took up the cause of a people that had little or no voice in society. Like many other pioneering women of the nineteenth century, she contributed greatly to both literature and social reform. Her untimely death meant that she did not see the full effect of her efforts, but other people and groups took up where her work and unfailing devotion to the Indian people left off.

The Women's National Indian Association quickly recognized Jackson's contribution and hailed *Ramona* as a strong voice for Indian reform. Members of Congress, the commissioner of Indian affairs, members of various Christian organizations, and Indian reformers gathered at Lake Mohonk to discuss ways of dealing with Indian land rights. Many of the reforms that were later implemented by the government came directly as a result of these meetings. Jackson's message had little impact while she was alive, but soon after her death, groups and individuals were to carry that message throughout America.

Although Jackson's contribution to the American Indian cause has etched her name in American history, her personality and life also attest this same vision. Ralph Waldo Emerson considered Jackson one of the greatest American poets. Such an accolade only draws attention to Jackson as a woman who was forced to live in anonymity for much of her literary life. Helen Hunt Jackson provided the leadership and courage that would inspire many more American women to turn their dreams into reality.

—Richard G. Cormack

FURTHER READING

Banning, Evelyn. *Helen Hunt Jackson*. New York: Vanguard Press, 1973. Relying heavily on the work of Ruth Odell's 1939 biography, this work takes a painstaking look at Jackson's lesser writings. Indian rights are not a central theme, yet its scholarly approach makes this a useful reference.

Garner, Van H. *The Broken Ring: The Destruction of the California Indians*. Tucson, Ariz.: Westernlore Press, 1982. Thorough and well researched, this work covers the period from the 1840's to the 1980's. There are a number of useful entries concerning Jackson's specific dealings with various Indian tribes.

Jackson, Helen Hunt. *A Century of Dishonor*. Boston: Roberts Brothers, 1885. A thorough and meticulously researched document that became the backbone of Indian land reform. Much of the book resembles a legal brief, yet it manages to communicate the passion of Jackson's quest for reform.

_____. *The Indian Reform Letters of Helen Hunt Jackson, 1879-1885*. Edited by Valerie Sherer Mathes. Norman: University of Oklahoma Press, 1998. Contains more than two hundred of Jackson's letters to authors, editors, religious figures, and others expressing the concern about Native Americans that led her to write *A Century of Dishonor* and *Ramona*.

Mathes, Valerie Sherer. *Helen Hunt Jackson and Her Indian Reform Legacy*. Austin: University of Texas Press, 1990. The purpose of this work was to reestablish Jackson as a prominent author and reformer. With thoughtfulness and sound research, this work offers an excellent insight into American Indian history.

May, Antoinette. *Helen Hunt Jackson: A Lonely Voice of Conscience*. San Francisco: Chronicle Press, 1987. This is a complete bibliography of Helen Hunt Jackson's life from early childhood to her death. May's writing is based primarily on anecdotal sources, and she embellishes much of Jackson's life with an almost fictional style.

Phillips, Kate. *Helen Hunt Jackson: A Literary Life*. Berkeley: University of California Press, 2003. Comprehensive biography based in part on newly discovered material, including Jackson's unpublished private correspondence. Analyzes the full range of Jackson's writing, describes her beliefs and religion, and explores the significance of her chronic illnesses.

Senier, Siobhan. *Voices of American Indian Assimilation and Resistance: Helen Hunt Jackson, Sarah Winnemucca, and Victoria Howard*. Norman: University of Oklahoma Press, 2001. Describes how Jackson challenged the U.S. government's efforts to destroy Native American culture.

SEE ALSO: Emily Dickinson; Ralph Waldo Emerson; Thomas Wentworth Higginson.

RELATED ARTICLE in *Great Events from History: The Nineteenth Century, 1801-1900:* 1890: U.S. Census Bureau Announces Closing of the Frontier.

STONEWALL JACKSON
American military leader

The ablest and most renowned of Robert E. Lee's lieutenants, Jackson led daring marches and employed do-or-die battle tactics that resulted in key victories that helped to sustain the Confederacy through the first two years of the Civil War.

BORN: January 21, 1824; Clarksburg, Virginia (now in West Virginia)
DIED: May 10, 1863; Guiney's Station, Virginia
ALSO KNOWN AS: Thomas Jonathan Jackson (birth name)
AREA OF ACHIEVEMENT: Military

EARLY LIFE

Thomas Jonathan Jackson was born in a hilly, heavily forested region of what later became West Virginia that was sparsely populated by the Scotch-Irish settlers who were his forebears. Self-reliance was thrust upon the boy at an early age; the third of four children, he was orphaned by the age of seven. Taken in by an uncle, Cummins Jackson, he grew up in a farm environment in which he acquired numerous practical skills but little schooling. Even as a teenager, however, Jackson clearly demonstrated the traits of physical courage, uncompromising moral integrity, and high ambition serviced by an iron will. Resolved to improve his lot by education, Jackson obtained an appointment to the United States Military Academy at West Point. The shambling young man from the hills cut a poor figure among the generally more sophisticated and better educated cadets. Yet, impervious to taunts, he earned the respect of his classmates by perseverance and phenomenal concentration, finishing seventeenth in a class of fifty-nine.

Shortly after he was graduated in 1846, Jackson was ordered to Mexico as a second lieutenant of artillery. He took part in the siege of Veracruz and distinguished himself in several battles during the advance on Mexico City in the summer of 1847. Jackson's courage and effectiveness brought admiration from his superiors and a rapid succession of promotions; by the end of the war, at the age of twenty-two, he had attained the rank of brevet major. A photograph taken of him at that time shows a man with a trim figure (Jackson stood about five feet, ten inches, and weighed about 150 pounds) and a pleasant, earnest face characterized chiefly by the firm set of the mouth and clear, deep-set eyes that gaze out solemnly beneath a prominent brow. (The flowing beard that would give Jackson the appearance of an Old Testament prophet was to come later.)

Assigned to Fort Hamilton, New York, in 1848, Jackson entered the routine existence of a peacetime army garrison for the next two years. During this time, however, he became more and more deeply involved in religious pursuits. Jackson came to think of his rather frail health, with its persistent digestive disorders, as a visitation of Providence to lead him into more righteous ways. He was baptized, unsure whether he had been as a child, and from that time on, the course of his life was inseparable from his sense of consecration to the will of the Almighty.

LIFE'S WORK

In the spring of 1851, an instructor's position at the Virginia Military Institute, founded twelve years earlier on the model of West Point, became available. Jackson was nominated for it, and, bored with his work as a peacetime army officer, he resigned his commission and reported to Lexington in July, 1851, to take up the duties of a professor of natural philosophy (or, in modern terminology, general science) and artillery tactics for the next nine years.

Not by any account an inspiring teacher, Jackson nevertheless mastered topics in which he had no formal credentials, thereby earning at least the grudging respect of his students. Jackson also came to be regarded as something of an eccentric for his rigid ways and odd personal mannerisms—for example, his habit of frequently raising his left arm, ostensibly to improve circulation, and his silent grimace serving in place of a laugh—which would be remarked on by his troops during the Civil War and give color and distinction to the legend of "Old Jack."

Settled in his new life, Jackson turned his thoughts to marriage. Seeking a wife from the religious community of Lexington, in 1853 he married Eleanor Junkin, the daughter of the Reverend Dr. George Junkin. The union was tragically brief; Eleanor died the next year in childbirth. Two years later and after a summer tour of Europe that restored him from the lethargy of mourning, Jackson courted and married Mary Anna Morrison, the daughter of another clergyman, who would remain his devoted wife until his death and would eventually bear him a daughter.

Life for the Jacksons during the next three years was characterized by affection, tranquillity, and a mutual sense of religious purpose (Jackson was by now a deacon

Stonewall Jackson. (Library of Congress)

of the Presbyterian Church and maintained a Sunday school for black slaves). The impending events of the Civil War were to bring all that to an end. Although not a champion of either slavery or secession, Jackson felt loyalty deeply rooted to his native soil, and when Virginia seceded from the Union, his course was clear.

In April, 1861, Jackson was commissioned a colonel in the newly formed Confederate army and took command at Harpers Ferry. Within three weeks, he distinguished himself by establishing strict military order for the rather undisciplined garrison of raw, untrained soldiers and by capturing a large number of Northern locomotives and freight cars for use by the Confederate army.

Some three months later, Jackson earned the sobriquet of "Stonewall" at the Battle of First Manassas (or Bull Run). In this opening major conflict of the war, an army of some thirty-five thousand Federal troops under General Irvin McDowell marched south from Washington to crush the rebellion. On July 21, after some preliminary fighting, McDowell made his main attack near Manassas Junction. As the defending Confederates fell back toward Jackson's brigade, which was holding the ridge above Bull Run, General Barnard E. Bee rallied his troops with the cry "Look yonder! There is Jackson and his brigade standing like a stone wall!" Later in the day, it was Jackson's brigade that broke the Union line with a furious bayonet charge, thus halting General McDowell's offensive and forcing a rethinking of strategy in Washington.

With a huge increase in the Union army, the new strategy called for a seaborne assault upon Richmond via the Jamestown Peninsula, led by George McClellan (a classmate of Jackson at West Point) and supported by a secondary force coming down the Shenandoah Valley under the command of Nathaniel Banks. Jackson, now a major general, correctly surmised that a diversion up the Shenandoah Valley would not only neutralize Banks but also threaten Washington and thus divert troops from McClellan's peninsular offensive. Beginning in March, 1862, Jackson led his troops in a succession of battles renowned in military history as the Valley Campaign. Utilizing the tactics of deception, rapid forced marches, and hit-and-run assaults and retreats, Jackson blunted the Federal advance down the Shenandoah Valley, alarmed Washington, and consequently stalled McClellan's attack upon Richmond.

Jackson's victories continued to inspire the South and dismay the North during the year 1862. In August, Jackson played the pivotal role in defeating the new Union offensive led by General John Pope at the Second Battle of Manassas. In December, at the Battle of Fredericksburg, he and James Longstreet shared the responsibility for the Confederate victory over the forces of General Ambrose Burnside.

In the spring of 1863, the Union forces, under yet another commander, Joseph "Fighting Joe" Hooker, gathered for a massive offensive upon Richmond. Robert E. Lee, outnumbered two to one, decided to risk his defense on a hazardous division of his forces, with a corps led by Jackson, now a lieutenant general, tasked with flanking Hooker's army. On the evening of May 2, 1863, the unsuspecting Union Eleventh Corps was routed by Jackson's attack some four miles west of Chancellorsville. Darkness brought a lull to the fighting, during which Jackson and a small staff reconnoitered the battlefield to determine a route for a further Confederate advance. Returning to its own lines, however, Jackson's scouting party, in one of the great ironic moments of history, was mistaken for a Union cavalry patrol and fired upon. Hit by several musket balls, Jackson fell, his left arm shattered. Amputation failed to save his life, and on May 10,

1863, he succumbed to pneumonia. His last words uttered in a final, sublime moment of lucidity were, "Let us cross over the river and rest under the shade of the trees."

SIGNIFICANCE

Jackson's death was a mortal blow to the Confederacy. In subsequent battles in the eastern theater, the absence of his leadership was sorely missed; Lee was to remark later that if he had had Jackson at Gettysburg, he would have won that crucial battle. Beyond such speculation, however, there is no doubt that the loss of such an inspiring leader—by far the most popular commander on either side—seriously undermined Confederate morale.

Jackson's charismatic popularity was the product of both his brilliant generalship and his singular force of character. Merciless in driving his own troops and ruthless in pursuit of his enemy, he nevertheless was admired by both for his legendary courage, integrity, and lack of egoistical motive. Lee venerated his memory, referring to him as "the great and good Jackson."

Jackson's battles (in particular, the Valley Campaign) have been studied as models by successive generations of military students in the United States and Europe. Jackson understood and applied the principles of mass and maneuver as well as any commander in history, concentrating his forces at decisive points against numerically superior but more dispersed opponents. Beyond his significance as a tactical genius, however, "Stonewall" passed early into the realm of national epic, defining an ideal of valor for generations of American youths.

—*Charles Duncan*

FURTHER READING

Chambers, Lenoir. *Stonewall Jackson*. 2 vols. New York: William Morrow, 1959. Comprehensive, detailed biography. A lucid, graceful writer, Chambers brings admirable clarity and insight to his subject.

Churchill, Winston L. S. *The American Civil War*. New York: Fairfax Press, 1985. A reprint of the chapters on the American Civil War in Churchill's four-volume *A History of the English Speaking Peoples* (1956-1958). In any edition, Churchill's brief history of the Civil War is a masterpiece and focuses especially well on the significance of Jackson's role.

Clark, Champ. *Decoying the Yanks: Jackson's Valley Campaign*. Alexandria, Va.: Time-Life Books, 1984. As the title suggests, primarily a history of Jackson's Shenandoah Valley Campaign in the spring of 1862. Contains, however, a good short biography of Jackson in his early years as well. Lavishly illustrated with contemporary photographs, paintings, and drawings, the book gives a vivid account of the most spectacular achievement of Jackson's generalship.

Farwell, Byron. *Stonewall: A Biography of General Thomas J. Jackson*. New York: W. W. Norton, 1992. Thorough, balanced, and well-written account of Jackson's life.

Henderson, G. F. R. *Stonewall Jackson and the American Civil War*. 2 vols. New York: Longmans, Green, 1898. A classic biography of Jackson. Henderson's thoughtful, elegant study has gone through numerous editions and is still, after more than three-quarters of a century, a valuable resource cited in virtually every work on Jackson that has appeared since its publication.

Robertson, James I., Jr. *Stonewall Jackson: The Man, the Soldier, the Legend*. New York: Macmillan, 1997. Robertson, a Civil War historian, recounts the details of Jackson's life and military career, depicting his subject as a great military strategist and a man of strong religious faith.

Tate, Allen. *Stonewall Jackson, the Good Soldier*. New York: Minton, Balch, 1928. Reprint. Ann Arbor: University of Michigan Press, 1957. Short biography for the general reader by a leading southern man of letters. Tate's Confederate sympathies date the book but also provide an interesting partisan slant; he excoriates Jefferson Davis for not unleashing Jackson at decisive points that might have turned the tide for the Confederacy.

Vandiver, Frank. *Mighty Stonewall*. New York: McGraw-Hill, 1957. Comprehensive, well-balanced one-volume biography of Jackson by a respected Civil War historian. Vandiver's research is thorough, while his lively, anecdotal presentation brings to life the historical events for the reader.

Wheeler, Richard. *We Knew Stonewall Jackson*. New York: Thomas Y. Crowell, 1977. Extremely useful, well-conceived book of excerpts from contemporary accounts of Jackson linked by the author's commentary. In effect, an economical, accurate, short biography in which the author's sources speak for themselves.

SEE ALSO: John Brown; Jefferson Davis; John C. Frémont; Robert E. Lee.

RELATED ARTICLE in *Great Events from History: The Nineteenth Century, 1801-1900:* July 21, 1861: First Battle of Bull Run.

MARY PUTNAM JACOBI
American physician, educator, and writer

Through her personal example and work in improving medical education for women, Jacobi encouraged many women to become doctors at a time when they were not welcome in the medical profession.

BORN: August 31, 1842; London, England
DIED: June 10, 1906; New York, New York
ALSO KNOWN AS: Mary Corinna Putnam (birth name); Mary Corinna Putnam Jacobi
AREAS OF ACHIEVEMENT: Medicine, women's rights

EARLY LIFE

Mary Putnam Jacobi (Ja-KOH-bee) was born Mary Corinna Putnam, the oldest daughter of George Palmer Putnam, the founder of the book publishing firm of G. P. Putnam's Sons. Her parents were Americans, and she was born in London while her father was there managing the European branch of his business. When Mary was five, her family returned to the United States and settled in the New York City area.

Mary demonstrated her own literary talent by publishing a story in the June, 1860, issue of the prestigious *Atlantic Monthly* before her eighteenth birthday. Determined on a scientific career, she overcame the objections of her parents and attended the New York College of Pharmacy for two years. After graduating in 1863, she obtained the reluctant consent of her father—who considered medicine a repulsive career for a woman—to enter the Female Medical College of Philadelphia. She received a medical degree after attending only one semester of lectures, but her subsequent experience as a volunteer in army camps and in a Boston hospital during the Civil War convinced her that her medical training had been woefully inadequate. In 1866, she sailed to France for further study.

Persistence won Putnam permission to attend lectures and hospital clinics in Paris, but she was denied entry to the École de Médecine, which had never admitted a woman. Only direct intervention by the minister of education forced the faculty to accept her in 1868. Putnam remained in Paris through the Franco-Prussian War, the Siege of Paris, and the Commune. She described all these dramatic events and welcomed the birth of a new French republic in letters that she wrote home. In 1871, she passed all her examinations with high honors and graduated, while winning a bronze medal for her thesis.

LIFE'S WORK

After returning to New York City, Putnam was immediately hired to teach at the Women's Medical College of the New York Infirmary for Women and Children, which had been founded by Elizabeth and Emily Blackwell. She served as a professor of pharmacology and therapeutics until 1889, while setting high standards for her students. When her students complained about her demands, she in turn questioned the quality of the entering women, noting that many were inadequately prepared and had never previously faced rigorous intellectual challenges. To improve professional training of women, she organized the Association for the Advancement of the Medical Education of Women in 1872 and served as its president from 1874 to 1903.

Putnam was elected to many medical associations, beginning in November, 1871, with her election to the Medical Society of the County of New York, where her induction was presided over by Abraham Jacobi. During the following year, she married Jacobi, who had been born in 1830 of Jewish parents and had grown up in Germany, where he received his medical degree in 1851. During that same year he had been imprisoned for participating in the revolutions of 1848. Released after two years, he had fled Germany and opened a successful medical practice in New York City in 1853. He was a prolific author of books and articles on medical topics and served in leadership positions in many medical groups. He was one of the first physicians to focus on diseases of children and helped found the specialty of pediatrics in America.

Mary and her husband shared common interests in reform as well as medicine. Abraham was particularly active in civil service reform, along with Carl Schurz, his comrade in the 1848 German revolution. Mary helped establish the New York Consumers League as part of an effort to improve conditions for working women and vigorously supported the woman suffrage movement. She and her husband also assisted each other on medical publications. Mary published a popular book on infant diet in 1874, expanding upon her husband's lectures on that topic. A charming anecdote describes Mary and Abraham returning home on the horse cars after profes-

Mary Putnam Jacobi.

sional meetings, absorbedly discussing the evening's proceedings.

The marriage of two strong personalities was not without difficulties and quarrels. The greatest strain on the marriage, however, was the death from diphtheria of their only son in 1883, before his eighth birthday. Abraham, who had published a treatise on the disease three years earlier, blamed a nurse as a possible source of the child's infection. Mary, proud of her medical skills, reproached herself over her inability to prevent her son's death. The two grieved the rest of their lives and were never as close emotionally afterward as they had been before.

Mary lectured five times a week on therapeutics and pharmacology at the Women's Medical College, maintained a substantial private practice, and attended at several hospitals, including Mount Sinai, where she established an outpatient pediatric clinic. From 1882 to 1885, she lectured on diseases of children at the New York Postgraduate Medical School and thereby became the first woman to teach in a male medical school. In addition, she was a prolific writer. She published more than one hundred medical articles, chapters, and books, many of which were clinical reports of her observations of hospital patients, or descriptions of the action of specific drugs. She also contributed to popular magazines and social science journals on woman suffrage and educational reform.

Mary Jacobi was particularly proud of winning the prestigious 1876 Boylston Prize for Medical Writing awarded by the Harvard Medical School. The Harvard faculty set the question for that year's essay as: "Do women require bodily and mental rest during Menstruation, and to what extent?" The phrasing clearly solicited an answer that would support the assertion by a Harvard Medical School professor that the physical demands of the monthly cycle made the intellectual effort of higher education dangerous to the health of young women. Essays were submitted anonymously, and the judges were surprised to learn they had awarded the prize to a woman. Jacobi's winning entry, *The Question of Rest for Women During Menstruation*, used case studies and statistical analysis of survey data to argue that no special considerations were needed. She objected that only in reference to women were normal physiological functions labeled "pathological."

During the winter of 1895-1896, while vacationing in Greece with her daughter, Jacobi experienced the first symptoms of a brain tumor whose effects would turn her into a helpless invalid before her death. Her last medical paper described the slow progress of the disease, which adversely affected her speech and made it hard for her to manipulate a pen. The prolific writer of the past was reduced to laboriously inscribing a few succinct sentences to communicate her thoughts to her family and to prepare her final clinical report to her profession. She finally died in New York City on June 10, 1906, in her sixty-fourth year.

SIGNIFICANCE

Mary Jacobi was an active feminist, employing her pen in support of woman suffrage and striving to improve conditions of life for working women. She was particularly interested in increasing educational and vocational prospects for women, especially in medicine. However, she explicitly rejected the Victorian idea of a special sphere for women based on feminine virtues as too limiting. She agreed that women might be better at caring for sick people than men, but she thought that being a nurse was not good enough and that women should aspire to be doctors on an equal plane with men.

Jacobi set high standards for herself, for her students, and for women generally. She was proud of being the first woman admitted to the École de Médecine but regretted that she was unable to convince the faculty of the merits of her application and had had to depend on the intervention of a government minister to achieve her dream of earning a first-class medical degree. She was espe-

cially pleased that she had won recognition from the medical community of New York City, not merely as the foremost woman physician, but as a distinguished leader of the profession.

Mary Jacobi's greatest contribution to feminism, and to encouraging younger women to undertake scientific careers, was simply in being who she was—a physician better trained, more scientifically active, and more successful than the overwhelming majority of her male colleagues—a living refutation of the tenacious nineteenth century myth that females were biologically and intellectually incapable of learning science and practicing medicine.

—*Milton Berman*

FURTHER READING

Harvey, Joy. "Clanging Eagles: The Marriage and Collaboration Between Two Nineteenth-Century Physicians, Mary Putnam Jacobi and Abraham Jacobi." In *Creative Couples in the Sciences*, edited by Helena M. Pycior, Nancy G. Slack, and Pnina G. Abir-Am. New Brunswick, N.J.: Rutgers University Press, 1996. Analyzes the positive and negative aspects of Mary and Abraham Jacobi's marriage.

Morantz-Sanchez, Regina. *Sympathy and Science: Women Physicians in American Medicine*. 2d ed. Chapel Hill: University of North Carolina Press, 2000. Examines Jacobi as a woman doctor who personified a rational, scientific approach to medicine, in contrast to women physicians who stressed the value of feminine insight and empathy.

Putnam, Ruth, ed. *Life and Letters of Mary Putnam Jacobi*. New York: G. P. Putnam's Sons, 1925. Contains substantial selections from family letters that illustrate Jacobi's intellectual and writing skills.

Wells, Susan. *Out of the Dead House: Nineteenth-Century Women Physicians and the Writing of Medicine*. Madison: University of Wisconsin Press, 2001. Studies Jacobi's publications as an example of a woman physician who mastered the dispassionate tone in which male scientists wrote.

SEE ALSO: Elizabeth Blackwell; Marie Anne Victorine Boivin; Lydia Folger Fowler; Carl Schurz; Marie Elizabeth Zakrzewska.

RELATED ARTICLES in *Great Events from History: The Nineteenth Century, 1801-1900:* May 12, 1857: New York Infirmary for Indigent Women and Children Opens; July 19, 1870-January 28, 1871: Franco-Prussian War.

JAMĀL AL-DĪN AL-AFGHĀNĪ
Turkish politician and Islamacist

Afghānī was a pan-Islamist politician and teacher whose intense opposition to British colonial policies focused the energies of Middle Eastern, Central Asian, and Indian Muslim intellectuals on the plight of the masses. His untiring quest for Muslim solidarity influenced Egypt's nationalist movement and Iran's constitutional and Islamic revolutions during the twentieth century.

BORN: 1838; Asadābād, Persia (now in Iran)
DIED: March 9, 1897; Istanbul, Ottoman Empire (now in Turkey)
ALSO KNOWN AS: Jamāl al-Dīn al-Afghānī as-Sayyid Muḥammad Ibn-i Safdar al-Husain (full name)
AREAS OF ACHIEVEMENT: Government and politics, philosophy

EARLY LIFE

Jamāl al-Dīn al-Afghānī as-Sayyid Muḥammad Ibn-i Safdar al-Husain (jah-mahl ahl-deen ahl-ahf-GAH-nee) was born into a family of sayyids in the Persian village of Asadābād, near Hamadan. He claimed, however, that he was born in the village of Asʿadābād, near Kabul, Afghanistan. Only a sketchy account of Afghānī's childhood can be pieced together from the information provided by his biographer, Mīrzā Lutfullāh Asadābādī. Contrary to his own assertion that he grew up in Afghanistan, Afghānī was educated at home in Asadābād until age ten. He then attended school in Qazvīn and Tehran. During his teens, he studied theology and Islamic philosophy in Karbalā and An Najaf, centers of Shiʿite learning in Iraq.

In 1855, around the age of seventeen, Afghānī traveled to Büshehr, on the Persian Gulf, and from there to India. In India, he observed British imperialism at work. Indian Muslims were openly discriminated against in government appointments, religious institutions, and education. The Muslims' struggle against British tyranny left an indelible impression on the young Afghānī. He agreed with the Indians that the British intended to undermine and discredit Islam. From India, Afghānī journeyed to Mecca and then returned to the Shiʿite centers of learning in Iraq, where he had studied earlier. He remained in that area until 1865, when he traveled to Iran and, the following year, to Afghanistan.

Documented reports of Afghānī's early years date to 1866, when he was part of the entourage of Muḥammad A'zam Khān, the military ruler of Qandahār under Dōst Muḥammad Khān. When Dōst Muḥammad died in 1863,

his three sons fought among themselves for the rulership. Amīr Shīr ʿAlī Khān, Dōst Muḥammad's third son, assumed power in Kabul, pledging to modernize the nation. Shīr ʿAlī's brothers, however, rebelled in Quandahār and ousted him in 1866. A'zam became king, and Afghānī entered Afghan politics with him as his close confidant.

Afghānī reportedly drew up a national recovery plan that included provisions for a network of schools, a national newspaper, a centralized government, and a well-regulated communications system. In politics, he advised the king to ally himself with Russia against the British in neighboring India. A'zam's rule was short-lived. Shīr ʿAlī returned in 1868, deposing Muḥammad A'zam and expelling Afghānī—a foreigner who spoke Farsi with an Iranian accent. Afghānī's modernizing reforms, however, were retained.

LIFE'S WORK

Afghānī was a mullah with a strong constitution. He had a magnetic personality and a dogged determination, both of which he used competently to penetrate exclusive circles and promote his cause. He cherished secrecy at the expense of social norms. He wore a white turban, while calling himself a sayyid, and adamantly refused any association with women. He was quick-tempered, quick of action, and quick to envisage a British plot at every turn.

Afghanistan afforded Afghānī a worthy education by supplementing his understanding of the dynamics of struggle against imperialism with a possible response. He came to realize that the Shiʿi and Persian rational philosophy that had inspired him in India could rid the Muslim masses of ignorance and poverty, if it were enhanced with armed struggle and savage confrontation. If Afghans with bare hands could defeat Great Britain in the First Afghan War, he imagined what the impact of an Islamic army under a charismatic leader would be. Afghānī decided to inject himself into the growing confrontation between the Muslim East and the Christian West in Afghanistan.

The Muslim ruler charismatic enough to realize Afghānī's secret aspiration was Abdülaziz, an Ottoman sultan. In 1869, Afghānī traveled to Istanbul by way of Bombay and Cairo, expecting to be named confidant to the sultan. Turkish officials, busy with the *Tanzīmāt* reforms, appointed him instead to a lesser position on the Council of Education. While serving in this office,

Afghānī began a series of inspiring lectures on reform. These lectures, tinged with anti-imperialist allusions and modernist tendencies, and imbued with Shiʿite rational philosophy, raised the ire of the Sunnī ulema (holy men) in Istanbul, who found the lectures heretical. The powerful ulema waited for an opportunity to embarrass Afghānī publicly. This opportunity came when Afghānī compared the ulema with a human craft. The ulema brought their wrath down upon him, the sultan, and the *Tanzīmāt*. To save the *Tanzīmāt*, Abdülaziz was forced to expel Afghānī from Turkey.

With hopes dashed, Afghānī accepted Riyadh Pasha's invitation and, in 1871, went to Egypt. There he continued to teach and to pursue his dream of a pan-Islamic nation free from imperialist domination. In a series of provocative lectures, he grafted the example of Egypt's economic strangulation by European banks to medieval Islamic philosophy in order to foment revolt against Western exploitation. He also formed and led a Masonic lodge in Cairo, among whose members were counted such promising young leaders as Muḥammad ʿAbduh, a future leader of the pan-Islamic movement.

Afghānī's activities in Egypt brought him in direct confrontation with Khedive Ismāʿīl of Egypt and his suzerain, Sultan Abdülhamid II, as well as with European, particularly British, powers. Afghānī had placed Khedive Ismāʿīl in a difficult position by openly condemning his financial mismanagement as the cause of Egypt's capitulation to European bankers. To ward off Afghānī's allegations, Ismāʿīl blamed the foreign bankers, who, in turn, pressured the sultan to depose the khedive, which the sultan did in 1879. Muḥammad Tawfīq Pasha, Ismāʿīl's son, expelled Afghānī from Egypt that same year. From Egypt, Afghānī traveled to Hyderabad, south of India, where, for two years, he offered seminars, gave public lectures, and wrote. "The Refutation of the Materialists" (1881) was written at this time. This essay affords a glimpse of Afghānī's growing interest in social consciousness, modernism, and rational thinking.

Writing within the utopian tradition, Afghānī described his vision of the "Virtuous City" as a hierarchically structured society that functions on the principles of shame, trustworthiness, and truthfulness, and aspires to the ideals of intelligence, pride, and justice. Higher intelligence, Afghānī argued, leads to new capabilities and advanced civilizations; pride leads to competition and progress; and justice leads to global peace and harmony among nations. Naturalists (*neicherīs*), Afghānī argued, intended to destroy the solidarity of the Virtuous City through division and sectarianism.

From Hyderabad, Afghānī traveled to London and, shortly thereafter, to Paris, where he engaged the French philosopher Ernest Renan in a debate on the position of scientific discovery in Islam. Then, in 1844, Afghānī began his most consequential activity—his collaboration with Muḥammad ʿAbduh on editing a revolutionary journal in Arabic, *al-ʿUrwat al-Wuthqā* (the firmest bond). This publication established Afghānī as the champion of pan-Islamism, the movement rooted in the bitter memory of Abdülhamid's 1877 defeat in the Russo-Turkish War—whereby the *Tanzīmāt* reforms had been proved ineffective—and in the 1882 occupation of Egypt by Great Britain. *Al-ʿUrwat al-Wuthqā* published articles by Afghānī and ʿAbduh on diverse topics. The sultan was not impressed. Disappointed, Afghānī left for Russia. Waiting at Büshehr to collect his books, Afghānī received an invitation from Nāser od-Dīn Shāh, the sovereign in Tehran, who had read a translation of an essay from *al-ʿUrwat al-Wuthqā*. When this brief interview did not go well, Afghānī resumed his trip.

In Russia, Afghānī continued his anti-British activities. He argued that, with his mobilization of Indian and Central Asian Muslims, Russians would easily drive the British out of the subcontinent. The Russians humored him, delaying his departure to irk the British. Afghānī's two-year visit in Russia gained for him a second royal invitation to Tehran. Iran of the 1890's was much like Egypt of the 1870's. It was plagued with financial mismanagement and hounded by foreign investors, who sought concessions on every resource. The shah, however, unlike the khedive, ruled under the protection of divine right. He could sell Iran to whomever he pleased.

Afghānī arrived in Iran from St. Petersburg at a time when Iranians were growing increasingly alarmed by Nāser od-Dīn's doling out of their country's resources. Afghānī himself had distributed leaflets condemning these concessions. Afghānī was not received by his host, who also denied Afghānī's claim that he had been commissioned in Munich to go to St. Petersburg and make amends on Iran's behalf. Worse yet, Afghānī was clandestinely informed of orders for his arrest. To save himself from the shah's wrath, he took sanctuary (*bast*) in the shrine of Shāh Abdul ʿAzīm, south of Tehran. From there, using clandestine methods and superb oratorical techniques, Afghānī attracted Iranians in droves to his fiery attacks on the shah's past antireformist actions, especially the murder of Mīrzā Taqī Khān, Amīr Kabīr.

Afghānī predicted that Iran would capitulate to British might, as Egypt had in 1882. He demanded that Iranian revenues be spent on the construction of a railroad, on education and hospitals, and on an army to thwart imperialism, rather than on the shah's pleasure trips to Europe. Iranians, he said, must be given the right to express their opinions in publications independent of the government. Iran must have a constitution, a parliament, and a house of justice. Above all, he emphasized, Iranians deserved a just king.

Nāser od-Dīn was approaching his fiftieth year of rule. Because Afghānī had been instrumental in the shah's recent humiliation as the first shah to revoke his own writ—the tobacco concession—and because this action had precipitated Iran's first foreign debt, the shah ordered the unruly mullah to be expelled. Ignoring the rules of sanctuary, the shah's guards invaded the holy shrine in 1892, placed Afghānī, half naked and during the middle of winter, on the bare back of a mule, and deported him. Afghānī went to London, where he reestablished ties with his lodge members and then traveled to Turkey at the invitation of the sultan. Rather than becoming the sultan's confidant and pan-Islamist consultant as Afghānī had hoped, he became the sultan's prisoner.

From Turkey, Afghānī continued to foment revolt in Iran, using his devotees to carry out his behests. One such devotee was Mīrzā Rezā Kermānī, who, in 1896, was commissioned to murder Nāser od-Dīn. Mīrzā Rezā carried out his mission on the anniversary of the shah's fiftieth year of reign in the very sanctuary in which Afghānī had been humiliated a few years before. Afghānī died of cancer of the chin at the age of about sixty and was buried in a secret grave. In 1944, the government of Afghanistan claimed him as a citizen, and his supposed remains were transferred to and buried on the grounds of the University of Kabul under a respectful shrine.

SIGNIFICANCE

Jamāl al-Dīn al-Afghānī was an Iranian by birth. His activities and the corpus of his writings reflect that. When visiting Europe, he affiliated himself with Afghanistan; when in Afghanistan, he associated himself with Ottoman Turkey and called himself "Istanbūlī," to gain the confidence of Sunnī rulers and evade Iranian officials. There are several reasons that Afghānī failed in materializing his dream. First, he put too much trust in the goodwill of Muslim rulers and too little in the people of the Middle East.

In ignoring the grassroots support for his pan-Islamism, al-Afghānī violated the rules of his own Virtuous City, a violation that he regretfully acknowledged in a letter he wrote from prison before his death. Second, he used religion to achieve political aims, and, assuming that world rulers acted independently of one another, secretly groomed all for the same office—that of caliph. This policy backfired on him many times, finally costing him his life. Third, he annoyed rulers by lecturing them. Nāser od-Dīn dismissed him when Afghānī blatantly offered himself as a sword with which the shah could cripple the imperialists. The sultan was more gracious. Finally, Afghānī failed to distinguish between policy and personal disposition. He sought Queen Victoria's assistance against Nāser od-Dīn within a short time of the tobacco boycott against British interests in Iran, a boycott that he himself had helped bring to fruition.

—Iraj Bashiri

FURTHER READING

Ahmad, Aziz. "Sayyid Ahmad Khān, Jamāl al-Dīn al-Afghānī and Muslim India." *Studia Islamica* 13 (1960): 55-78. An important source of information on Afghānī's involvement in Indian Muslim affairs. Compares Afghānī's advocacy of *jihad* and *khilāfat* to Sayyid Ahmad Khān's policy of capitulation to British rule. Ahmad believes that Afghānī and Sayyid Ahmad Khān differed only in political matters.

Algar, Hamid. *Religion and State in Iran, 1785-1906*. Los Angeles: University of California Press, 1969. Provides the larger picture. Examines the life and works of Afghānī's colleagues and assesses Afghānī's contribution in the light of past philosophical and doctrinal efforts.

Hodgson, Marshall G. *Gunpowder Empires and Modern Times*. Vol. 3 in *The Venture of Islam*. Chicago: University of Chicago Press, 1974. Hodgson examines Afghānī's efforts in the context of an alliance among the Shi'i ulema, the *bazaaris*, and the intellectuals. Afghānī emerges as an opportunist in his calls for reform, emphasizing the political, religious, or social aspects depending on the weight each carried in a particular situation.

Karpat, Kemal H. *The Politicization of Islam: Reconstructing Identity, State, Faith, and Community in the Late Ottoman State*. New York: Oxford University Press, 2001. Examines the transformation of the Muslim world in the nineteenth and twentieth centuries, including the rise of pan-Islamism and the rule of Abdülhamid II. Includes information on Afghānī.

Keddie, Nikki R. *An Islamic Response to Imperialism: Political and Religious Writings of Sayyid Jamāl al-Dīn "al-Afghānī."* Berkeley: University of California Press, 1968. A comprehensive study of Afghānī's life.

Includes sample translations of his works as well as analytical notes on his worldview. Also contains a bibliography and a good index.

Kedourie, Elie. *Afghānī and ʿAbduh: An Essay on Religious Unbelief and Political Activism in Modern Islam*. London: Frank Cass, 1966. Kedourie discusses Afghānī's teachings from the point of view of his disciple, ʿAbduh, and of circumstances that influenced those teachings. Kedourie's discussion of Mahdīsm, as expounded by both Afghānī and Muḥammad Ahmad of Sudan, is noteworthy.

Kramer, Martin. *Islam Assembled: The Advent of the Muslim Congresses*. New York: Columbia University Press, 1985. The first two chapters deal with the genesis of the pan-Islamic ideal and its challenge to authority. The contributions of Afghānī are discussed in the context of a rising tide of discontent among Muslims from Indonesia, Sumatra, and Central Asia to Daghistan and the Crimea, as these are reflected at the court of the Ottoman sultans.

SEE ALSO: Muḥammad ʿAbduh; Sir Sayyid Ahmad Khan; Bahāʾullāh; Ernest Renan.

RELATED ARTICLE in *Great Events from History: The Nineteenth Century, 1801-1900:* 1811-1818: Egypt Fights the Wahhābīs.

HENRY JAMES
American writer

James is one of the preeminent and most influential writers of the modern American novel. Both his life and his work are closely related to the U.S. emergence in the twentieth century as a major world power.

BORN: April 15, 1843; New York, New York
DIED: February 28, 1916; London, England
AREA OF ACHIEVEMENT: Literature

EARLY LIFE

Henry James was born into a wealthy and distinguished American family tracing its roots to an immigrant ancestor, William James. This founder of the James family in the United States had come from Northern Ireland two generations before, just after the American Revolution, and had made a fortune in real estate in Albany, New York, then a small city greatly influenced by the Dutch. Henry James's father, Henry James, Sr., married Mary Robertson Walsh, originally from Northern Ireland, and together they produced five children: William, Henry, Garth (known as "Wilky"), Robertson, and Alice. Henry's brother William James, one year older than he, was to become one of the most famous American philosophers and psychologists.

Henry's first memory later in life was as an infant on his mother's knee, viewing the column in the center of the Place Vendôme in Paris, an extraordinarily fitting memory for someone whose attraction for Europe was to be one of the most pronounced aspects of his life. Indeed, the first two years of his life were spent with his family in England and France.

From 1845 to 1855, James lived in the United States and was educated by various tutors and schools. During this time, he knew Ralph Waldo Emerson, Washington Irving, and William Makepeace Thackeray, the first in a long line of renowned writers and artists with whom he associated throughout his life in the United States and Great Britain and on the Continent. As it turned out, this decade was also to be the longest continuous residence in the United States for James. As a boy, he was shy and a great reader.

Back in Europe in 1855 with his family, to improve his "sensuous" appreciation, he returned to the United States in 1858, only to leave again in 1859 for a year in Germany and Switzerland. His father, who in adult life became a devotee of the philosophy and theology of the Swedish thinker Emanuel Swedenborg, was dissatisfied with most of the schools available in both the United States and Europe; he continually sought other avenues of cultural enrichment for his children, particularly exposure to British and European society and heritage.

Having returned to Newport, Rhode Island, in 1860, James was prevented from joining the Union army in the American Civil War, which began in 1861, by a back injury, though his two younger brothers did so. Instead, he went to Harvard Law School in 1862 and began to write and publish stories; he dropped out of law school after one year to pursue his writing career full-time. In 1864, his family moved to Boston. His friend, William Dean Howells, soon to become an editor at the *Atlantic Monthly* magazine, was helpful to him, and James published several pieces in the prestigious magazine.

At the age of twenty-six, he traveled again to England and grew the beard and mustache that would mark his visage until the end of the century. He dined with the eminent art critic and social historian John Ruskin, visited cathedrals, and at last went to Italy, where he formed a permanent impression of how the past impinges on the present, a hallmark of his later writings.

After a brief return to the United States a year later, he spent the years 1872-1873 in Great Britain, Paris, and Rome (which he would revisit in 1874). His residence in Rome during these years gave impetus to the writing of *Roderick Hudson* (1876), published in the *Atlantic Monthly*, about an expatriate American sculptor whose life abroad works to destroy him; obviously, James wondered whether Europe's pull on him would do the same.

The fall of 1875 saw James in Paris, writing *The American* (1877), the story of an American businessperson who is treated badly in Parisian high society. James himself, though apparently welcomed at this time into exclusive literary and social circles in Paris, never felt fully accepted there. In 1877, at the age of thirty-four, James went to London, yearning to become fully integrated into English life, breaking down the barriers of being a mere observer and foreigner. He wrote *The Europeans* (1878), *Daisy Miller* (1878), and *The Portrait of a Lady* (1881) in quick succession, the second of which finally established his reputation.

LIFE'S WORK

James returned to the United States in 1881, though now resolved that his mission as a writer was to return to Europe; a notebook entry this same year reads, "My choice is the old world—my choice, my need, my life." An essay called "The Art of Fiction" (1884), written for *Longman's Magazine*, is a kind of literary manifesto inaugurating the "modern" novel, exemplified not only by the works of James but also by those of Marcel Proust, Virginia Woolf, and James Joyce. James's mother died in Boston in 1882 and his father soon thereafter. James went back to London, writing, "It is an anchorage in my life."

By the end of the 1880's, he had become a seasoned writer and a true expatriate, ready to enter his last, most mature phase as an artist, abandoning as his main subject the interrelationships of Europe and the United States and the impact of Europe upon Americans. Henceforward, his novels would have as their more major concern elucidating the inward states of mind in his characters. One already sees some of this new emphasis in *Portrait of a Lady*, whose main character, Isabel Archer, is married to Gilbert Osmond, an extreme narcissist with the

potential for bringing much evil into people's lives. It is the American expatriates in this novel, not the Europeans, who are the source of most of the deception and intrigue. The work contains portraits of various types of Americans abroad, all drawn with deft skill and subtlety; England, Florence, and Rome form the settings, all brought to life in the kind of convincing detail that only someone intimately familiar with life in these places could accomplish.

The novels of the later 1880's, *The Bostonians* (1886), *The Princess Casamassima* (1886), and *The Tragic Muse* (1889), were less successful in many ways. James himself believed that *The Bostonians* was diffuse and that he had also failed to bring to life people and places in the United States sufficiently well, because of his having lost touch with the American scene. *The Princess Casamassima* depicts the poverty of London in the most vivid terms; although it touches upon the most sensitive of political and social issues, this novel is also a good example of one of James's basic premises at work: that novels are meant to be "pictures," not "moral or immoral," not sermons or treatises. Not surprisingly, the work of Charles Dickens was a model here. *The Tragic Muse* has as its subject the total immersion of James as an artist into art with all the arduous sacrifice that entails; it undoubtedly reflected James's own state of mind at the time, because he, too, was poised on the edge of just such a total dedication of the rest of his life.

In 1896, James settled in England, finally moving into Lamb House at Rye, which would be his residence for his last and most intense productive period, the time when the legendary Henry James most familiar to contemporary readers came into full bloom. He found Sussex to be a suitable environment for this last prolonged stage of his life and work, steeped as it is in history still clearly visible, as had been the Europe of his experience. He grew attached to the coast and the sea and the ancient towns thereabouts. He could still travel to London with ease when moved to do so.

The middle period of his career culminated in the publication of *What Maisie Knew* (1897), the still-famous and widely read *The Turn of the Screw* (1898), and *The Awkward Age* (1899). Before proceeding into his final, most successful stage as a novelist, however, he made a highly unsuccessful bid for fame in the theater during the early 1890's. He had written a play based on the novel *Daisy Miller*, but it was never produced. He adapted another novel, *The American*, for the stage, but its London run was not long and the reviews were negative. After a number of other such attempts, he at last gave up, con-

---

JAMES'S MAJOR WORKS

LONG FICTION

1876	*Roderick Hudson*
1876-1877	*The American*
1878	*The Europeans*
1878	*Daisy Miller*
1878-1879	*An International Episode*
1879-1880	*Confidence*
1880	*Washington Square*
1880-1881	*The Portrait of a Lady*
1885-1886	*The Bostonians*
1885-1886	*The Princess Casamassima*
1888	*The Reverberator*
1889-1890	*The Tragic Muse*
1897	*The Spoils of Poynton*
1897	*What Maisie Knew*
1897-1899	*The Awkward Age*
1898	*In the Cage*
1898	*The Turn of the Screw*
1901	*The Sacred Fount*
1902	*The Wings of the Dove*
1903	*The Ambassadors*
1904	*The Golden Bowl*
1911	*The Outcry*
1917	*The Ivory Tower*
1917	*The Sense of the Past*

SHORT FICTION

1875	*A Passionate Pilgrim*
1879	*The Madonna of the Future*
1883	*The Siege of London*
1884	*Tales of Three Cities*
1885	*The Author of Beltraffio*
1888	*The Aspern Papers*
1892	*The Lesson of the Master*
1893	*The Private Life, Lord Beaupre, The Visits*
1893	*The Real Thing*
1895	*Terminations*
1896	*Embarrassments*

1898	*The Two Magics: The Turn of the Screw and Covering End*
1900	*The Soft Side*
1903	*The Better Sort*
1907-1909	*The Novels and Tales of Henry James* (24 volumes)
1910	*The Finer Grain*
1919	*A Landscape Painter*
1919	*Travelling Companions*
1920	*Master Eustace*

DRAMA

1883	*Daisy Miller*
1891	*The American*
1894	*Guy Domville*
1894	*The Reprobate*
1908	*The High Bid*
1909	*The Other House*
1909	*The Outcry*
1911	*The Saloon*

NONFICTION

1875	*Transatlantic Sketches*
1878	*French Poets and Novelists*
1879	*Hawthorne*
1883	*Portraits of Places*
1884	*A Little Tour in France*
1884	*The Art of Fiction*
1888	*Partial Portraits*
1893	*Essays in London*
1903	*William Wetmore Story and His Friends*
1905	*English Hours*
1907	*The American Scene*
1908	*Views and Reviews*
1909	*Italian Hours*
1913	*A Small Boy and Others*
1914	*Notes of a Son and Brother*
1914	*Notes on Novelists*
1917	*The Middle Years*

---

vinced that the theater was a vulgar medium, its audiences demanding the wrong things from writers.

In 1900, he shaved the familiar beard and mustache of his early career, perhaps as a symbol of his new inner resolve. His clean-shaven face and balding head would now take on the prominent well-known profile found in the John Singer Sargent portrait of him, painted much later in honor of his seventieth birthday, at the insistence of his friends; this famous painting now hangs in the National Portrait Gallery.

In 1904, after having lived twenty years abroad, James returned briefly to the United States and toured many regions and levels of society. He was in the end, however, quite dismayed with what he found and felt unable to identify with what the United States had become in his absence. Later, by the start of World War I, after his return to Rye, he was to conclude that the civilization of Europe that he had cherished so much was now dead. In truth, James's life, spent as it was between Great Britain and the United States for the most part, gave him a unique vantage point on the passing of an age. The more innocent and isolated United States of his youth was transformed, just as were the traditional rigidities of society in the Old World.

There are three novels that critics generally cite as representing the apex of James's career: *The Wings of the Dove* (1902), *The Ambassadors* (1903), and *The Golden Bowl* (1904). They are among the most difficult of his works to read but also probably the most rewarding. All three are concerned with the idea that improving one's perception of one's own personality and character, and thereby learning to understand better the personalities and characters of others, is the true road to freedom and maturity for human beings.

In *The Wings of the Dove*, the New York heiress Milly Theale is the leading character, the "dove" of the story. Upon her death, Merton Densher, who has pursued her for her money, finally cannot accept it; he has become a morally better person through his contact with Milly. Milly Theale is by no means naïve, but her simple grace and wisdom transcend the sordid materialism and artificial artfulness of those around her. The setting is London high society, perhaps best represented by the manipulative and grasping, polished and beautiful Kate Croy. This is perhaps the first modern novel to focus so intently and intricately upon subjective experience, the inner life; indeed, it is a forerunner in many ways of such major modernist fiction as that of Proust, D. H. Lawrence, Woolf, and Joyce.

The Ambassadors, actually written before *The Wings of the Dove* but published after it, was considered by James to be his best work; most critics and readers have come to agree. It is about the American Lambert Strether and his delayed liberation from the clutches of the deadening ethos of American Puritanism. Strether becomes an appreciator of European culture and enlightenment and an expert in understanding the importance of leading a sensitive and aesthetically fulfilling life; Paris is for him the new world that saves him, and this city is the ultimate symbol for James, too, of the best kind of life.

The Golden Bowl is in form and content a true culmination of James's progression as a novelist. The symbol of the golden bowl, taken from Ecclesiastes, represents life and sensibility; it must be broken near the end of the story, just as the protagonist Maggie Verver's life must be reconstituted on a higher plane, one more spiritual and refined. James obviously hoped that the American upper crust would similarly be transformed. Maggie remains essentially American but also an inheritor of the best of European culture, and she is triumphant in the end over

both European and American evils and distractions from the high road in life.

The "New York edition" of James's writings, *The Novels and Tales of Henry James*, was published in 1907-1909. He made revisions and wrote prefaces to these works, the prefaces being separately published in 1934 as *The Art of the Novel: Critical Prefaces*. In 1908, at the age of sixty-five, he once again suffered from what he called "black depression," a condition that he had last experienced fourteen years previously; this time it continued for a longer period. Harvard University granted him an honorary degree in 1911, which he accepted in memory of his famous brother William. In 1915, he became a naturalized British subject. In the same year, he suffered two strokes. James was given the Order of Merit by the king in early 1916, and shortly thereafter, he died, on February 28, 1916, and was cremated; his ashes were put in the family grave in Cambridge, Massachusetts. A memorial plaque was erected in his honor in Chelsea Old Church in London; it reads, "A resident of this parish who renounced a cherished citizenship to give his allegiance to England in the first year of the Great War."

Near the end of his life, James wrote, "One's supreme relation . . . is one's relation to one's country." Despite his attraction to England and Europe, Henry James was an American; his life and work are dominated by his "relation" to his homeland.

SIGNIFICANCE

The novels of Henry James are in marked contrast to most other literature written between the American Civil War and World War I, a whole epoch. His work is quite unlike the romanticism of O. Henry, the local color of Sarah Orne Jewett and Bret Harte, the realism of Howells and Mark Twain, or the naturalism of Stephen Crane, Frank Norris, and Jack London. James was intensely preoccupied with artistic technique, psychological verisimilitude, and the mores and manners of a highly sophisticated elite.

In both style and subject matter, James was the inaugurator of the modern novel. His belief in the power of consciousness as the ultimate shaper of people's lives and his denial of the fixed givens of life as determinants of destiny can be seen in retrospect as very American. Just as the United States itself was preparing to enter the world scene as a major power during his lifetime, James's life and work looks outward, despite its concern with interior states and developed sensibilities, to America's new adult relationship to England and Europe in the twentieth century. Although it took some time after his death for Henry James's reputation and influence to reach their height, he has finally come to be regarded as one of the great American authors; indeed, some would say the greatest.

—Thomas J. Elliott

FURTHER READING

Cargill, Oscar. *The Novels of Henry James.* New York: Macmillan, 1961. An informative commentary by a famous critic of James's novels. Cargill's criticism here is particularly useful because it summarizes and incorporates most of the outstanding scholarship on James (up to 1960).

Edel, Leon, ed. *Henry James: A Collection of Critical Essays.* Englewood Cliffs, N.J.: Prentice-Hall, 1963. Contains eighteen essays, published elsewhere previously, a selected bibliography, and a list of important dates in James's life.

_____. *Henry James: A Life.* New York: Harper & Row, 1985. Derived from Edel's monumental five-volume biography, published between 1953 and 1972, but updated and revised. This is the definitive work. Edel's additions to this one-volume version are particularly helpful on the subject of James's sexuality and its relationship to his writings. Based on unpublished correspondence, diaries, and other resources. This noted biography provides a comprehensive treatment of every aspect of James's life and career.

Graham, Kenneth. *Henry James, a Literary Life.* New York: St. Martin's Press, 1995. Critical overview of James's important writings and his literary career, charting his development as a writer.

Hadley, Tessa. *Henry James and the Imagination of Pleasure.* New York: Cambridge University Press, 2002. Describes how James's novels differed from other nineteenth century English-language novels that moralized about sexual passion. Hadley shows how James's novels dispensed with the belief that only bad women were sexual.

Haralson, Eric. *Henry James and Queer Modernity.* New York: Cambridge University Press, 2003. Examines gender politics and the emergence of modern male homosexuality in the writings of James and three writers who were influenced by him: Willa Cather, Gertrude Stein, and Ernest Hemingway.

Kaplan, Fred. *Henry James: The Imagination of Genius: A Biography.* New York: Morrow, 1992. Biography chronicling James's life and analyzing his writings. Among other subjects, Kaplan describes how James's repressed homosexuality influenced his fiction.

Matthiessen, F. O. *The James Family: Including Selections from the Writing of Henry James, Senior, William, Henry and Alice James.* New York: Alfred A. Knopf, 1948. An interesting view of Henry James's relationship with other members of his famous family, especially his brother William, the well-known philosopher and psychologist. This book is largely a collection of quotations. Contains short biographical introductions about the four James family members included. A postscript compares Henry and William.

Perry, Ralph Barton. *The Thought and Character of Henry James.* 2 vols. Boston: Little, Brown, 1935. Especially useful on the relationship of Henry James to his brother William. Deals with their education, upbringing, and correspondence. Contains many quotations from Henry James's letters and autobiographical writings. Attention is devoted to James's European experience and his impressions of the United States.

Putt, Samuel G. *Henry James: A Reader's Guide.* Ithaca, N.Y.: Cornell University Press, 1966. Introduction by Arthur Mizener. Contains fifteen chapters systematically commenting on most of James's major and minor works, attempting to make them more accessible to the general reader. Although the introduction claims that this book is aimed at beginning readers, it is really more helpful to the slightly advanced student of James's works. Covers all twenty-two novels and 112 tales.

Wagenknecht, Edward. *Eve and Henry James: Portraits of Women and Girls in His Fiction.* Norman: University of Oklahoma Press, 1978. A study of many, but not all, of James's female characters that discusses many sides of their personalities. Wagenknecht organizes his commentary by employing certain types, such as women as victors, women as losers, women as victims, women as femmes fatales, and certain qualities such as destiny, modernity, innocence, love, and honor.

SEE ALSO: Mary Elizabeth Braddon; Stephen Crane; Charles Dickens; Ralph Waldo Emerson; Nathaniel Hawthorne; O. Henry; Washington Irving; William James; Sarah Orne Jewett; John Ruskin; John Singer Sargent; William Makepeace Thackeray; Mark Twain.

RELATED ARTICLES in *Great Events from History: The Nineteenth Century, 1801-1900:* 1851: Melville Publishes *Moby Dick*; December, 1884-February, 1885: Twain Publishes *Adventures of Huckleberry Finn.*

JESSE AND FRANK JAMES
American outlaws

Although Jesse and Frank James won notoriety and lasting fame as criminals, they were regarded as heroes by many southerners who had suffered during the Civil War and harbored deep, bitter feelings toward the North.

JESSE JAMES

BORN: September 5, 1847; near Centerville (now Kearney), Missouri
DIED: April 3, 1882; St. Joseph, Missouri
ALSO KNOWN AS: Jesse Woodson James (full name); Dingus James; J. D. Howard; Thomas Howard; Tim Woodson

FRANK JAMES

BORN: January 10, 1843; Centerville (now Kearney), Missouri
DIED: February 18, 1915; near Kearney, Missouri
ALSO KNOWN AS: Alexander Franklin James (full name), Buck James; Ben Woodson; B. J. Woodson
AREA OF ACHIEVEMENT: Crime

EARLY LIVES

Frank and Jesse James were the sons of Robert and Zeralda James of Kearney, Missouri. The brothers had a difficult childhood. In 1850, while they were both still very young, their father left his family to prospect for gold in California, where he later died from food poisoning. Their mother's second husband, Benjamin Simms, died in a horse accident. In 1855, their mother married a third husband—Dr. Reuben Samuel, a general practitioner and farmer. The James brothers learned the farming trade.

When the Civil War broke out in 1861, it disrupted the peaceful farming life in Missouri. Frank and Jesse's parents owned slaves and supported the Confederate cause. On more than one occasion, reportedly, the family was treated harshly by Union soldiers who were occupying Missouri. Frank joined the Missouri State Guards, a force sympathetic to the Confederacy, on May 4, 1861. During the summer of 1862, he and his cousins, Cole and Jim Younger, joined a Confederate guerrilla band led by William Clarke Quantrill. Working as renegades, they robbed mail coaches, plundered towns that supported the Union, and murdered members of the Union Army and supporters of President Abraham Lincoln.

On August 21, 1863, Frank James participated in Quantrill's bloody attack on Lawrence, Kansas, in which nearly two hundred unarmed persons were murdered and 180 buildings burned. On September 20, 1864, Jesse James rode with a Quantrill group led by "Bloody" Bill Anderson into Centralia, Missouri, where the band robbed an incoming train and killed twenty-four unarmed Union soldiers. After a general amnesty for Confederate guerrillas was issued in 1865, Jesse and Frank rode to Lexington, Missouri, to surrender. On the way into town, federal soldiers opened fire on them, wounding Jesse in the chest. The James brothers were able to escape, but with increased feelings of embitterment toward the United States political establishment.

LIVES' WORK

In January, 1866, Jesse and Frank James formed a band of outlaws in partnership with their cousins, the Younger brothers. Under the direction of Frank James and Cole Younger, the gang robbed the Clay County Savings Association Bank in Liberty, Missouri, on February 13, 1866. They killed a teenage boy and got away with more than sixty thousand dollars. During this robbery, Jesse James was still at home recovering from his chest wounds.

During the gang's next exploit, Jesse led it in the robbery of the Hughes and Mason Bank in Richmond, Missouri, on May 22, 1867. This was followed by the robbery of the Southern Deposit Bank in Russellville, Kentucky, on March 20, 1868, that netted the gang fourteen thousand dollars. Through late 1868 and most of 1869, Jesse and Frank spent much of their time hiding out in the Nashville, Tennessee, area.

On December 7, 1869, the gang went back into action, robbing the Davies County Savings Bank in Gallatin, Missouri. While Jesse and Frank posed as customers, one of them shot the bank clerk, John Sheets. They made off with about seven hundred dollars. Now facing murder charges, Jesse and Frank James were placed on the most-wanted list of outlaws. Between 1866 and 1873, their gang held up numerous banks, and their fame and legend grew. Jesse and Frank James were considered heroes by many southerners and by the less fortunate, with whom they reportedly shared some of their stolen loot—a story reminiscent of the legendary Robin Hood.

As bank security improved and time-lock vaults replaced many of the older combination-lock vaults, it became increasingly risky to rob banks, so the James-

Jesse James. (Library of Congress)

Younger gang turned to robbing trains and stagecoaches. On July 21, 1873, they removed a section of railroad tracks near Adair, Iowa, and held up the Chicago, Rock Island, and Pacific Express. However, for this daring exploit, they collected only about three thousand dollars from the train's safe and passengers. On January 15, 1874, the gang robbed a stagecoach for the first time—the Concord Stage, near Malvern, Arkansas. Only sixteen days later, they held up the Little Rock Express train near Gadshill, Missouri, and rode away with twenty-two thousand dollars in cash and gold.

On April 23, 1874, Jesse James married his cousin Zee Mimms in Kansas City, Missouri. They had two children, whom Jesse adored. During the following June, Frank married Anna Ralston. With Pinkerton detectives in hot pursuit, the James brothers moved frequently and expanded their area of operation to encompass several states. They robbed the San Antonio Stage near San Antonio, Texas, on May 12, 1875; a bank in Huntington, Virginia, on September 6, 1875; and a Missouri-Pacific train near Otterville, Missouri, on July 7, 1876. The three robberies netted more than forty thousand dollars.

While attempting to rob the First National Bank in Northfield, Minnesota, on September 7, 1876, the James-Younger gang encountered stiff resistance from the town's citizens and law officers. Cole, Jim, and Bob Younger were wounded and captured, and three other gang members were killed. Jesse and Frank James were wounded but managed to escape to North Dakota and then return to Missouri. Over the next three years, Jesse and Frank laid low and kept moving about to avoid the law. They took on various aliases, lived on small farms in Tennessee and Kentucky, and prospected for gold in California and Colorado.

During the fall of 1879, Jesse James organized a new gang that included Charlie and Robert Ford. Between October of that year and September, 1881, this gang robbed five trains—the last on September 7, 1881, when they held up a train near Glendale, Missouri. In the meantime, Missouri governor Thomas T. Crittenden offered a ten-thousand-dollar reward for the capture of the James brothers.

On April 3, 1882, Jesse James was shot in the back of the head and killed by Robert Ford while he was adjusting a picture on a wall of his home. Ford apparently killed him for reward money and publicity. Although there were many claims that it was another man who had been killed, an examination of the body performed by a doctor on the night of the murder, as well as DNA testing on the exhumed remains in 1995, confirmed that the murdered man was indeed Jesse James.

After eluding the law for several more months, Frank James surrendered on October 5, 1882. He was released in 1885 and never returned to crime. To earn a living, he spent the last thirty years of his life doing a variety of jobs. He farmed, sold shoes, performed in a circus, and served as an usher, a doorman, and a bouncer in a saloon. He also turned the James family farm into a museum, at which he charged visitors thirty cents to view the grave of his brother Jesse.

SIGNIFICANCE

The James brothers gained notoriety as ruthless bandits who were at odds with the U.S. government. Because of their deep affection for the South and adverse feelings toward the North during the Civil War, they developed strong antigovernment attitudes that made them folk heroes in the eyes of many Confederate sympathizers. Their reputation was embellished by their legendary bank, stagecoach, and train robberies and stories that they shared their loot with the less fortunate. During their fifteen-year careers as outlaws, they robbed at least twelve banks, seven trains, four stagecoaches, and a county fair in Kansas City.

As the James brothers and their gang took out their wrath on an industrial society that was fast replacing the old agricultural lifestyle of America, many supporters saw them as the last remaining evidence of the South and the society that they once loved. Jesse James, in particular, became a symbol of the individuality that characterized the American West. The James brothers lives have been remembered in many books and movies, as well as a melodramatic ballad that was written about Jesse James one day after he was murdered.

—Alvin K. Benson

FURTHER READING

Block, Lawrence, ed. *Gangsters, Swindlers, Killers, and Thieves: The Lives and Crimes of Fifty American Villains.* New York: Oxford University Press, 2004. Insights into the lives and misdeeds of fifty notorious criminals, from John Wilkes Booth and Jesse James to Machine Gun Kelly.

Stiles, T. J. *Jesse James: Last Rebel of the Civil War.* New York: Alfred A. Knopf, 2002. Stiles explores the complicated life of Jesse James, addressing why he became a legend, and why he may be classified as the forerunner of a modern terrorist.

Tolzmann, Don. *Lives and Exploits of the Daring Frank and Jesse James.* Westminister, Md.: Heritage Books, 1992. Facts and myths are explored about the lives and outlaw careers of the notorious James brothers.

Yeatman, Ted P. *Frank and Jesse James: The Story Behind the Legend.* Nashville, Tenn.: Cumberland House, 2003. A detailed biography of the lives of Frank and Jesse James, from their births, to their days with William Quantrill's raiders, to their escapades as bank robbers, train robbers, and murderers.

SEE ALSO: Lizzie Borden; Abraham Lincoln; Abby Sage Richardson.

WILLIAM JAMES
American psychologist and philosopher

Seeking to reconcile a deep commitment to scientific thought with the emotional nature of human beings and longing for some kind of religious faith, James helped to create and popularize the modern science of psychology and the uniquely American approach to philosophy called pragmatism.

BORN: January 11, 1842; New York, New York
DIED: August 26, 1910; Chocorua, New Hampshire
AREAS OF ACHIEVEMENT: Psychology, philosophy

EARLY LIFE

The brother of novelist Henry James, William James was the eldest son of Henry and Mary (Walsh) James. His parents, who were of Scotch and Scotch-Irish ancestry, had four other children and provided one of the most remarkable home environments on record. There is little doubt that his childhood as part of this unusual family was instrumental in creating William James, the psychologist and philosopher, just as it helped mold his bother Henry to become a preeminent novelist.

Henry James, Sr., was a restless, perhaps even tortured intellectual with a religious bent, able to pursue his own private quest for truth because of a small inheritance. His family naturally became part of his search, and

conversation around the Jameses' dining table was more like a philosophical seminar than typical family chatter. The children were encouraged to think and to question and even defend their ideas under the watchful eyes of their parents. Education was considered too important to be left to chance.

Henry, Sr., moved his family from the United States to Europe and back again several times, enrolling his children in numerous schools in an attempt to find the perfect atmosphere for learning. This varied and unsettled experience gave both William and his brother Henry an excellent command of languages and the basics of a liberal education without providing deep knowledge in any particular area. The gypsylike introduction to the academic world and family debates did provide, however, a healthy respect for diversity and a tolerance for other opinions, including sometimes strange ones, that marked William James throughout his life.

As a youth, James was of slight to medium build with blue eyes and a less-than-robust constitution. Gradually, the determination to overcome his tendency toward physical and emotional illness became an important undercurrent in his celebrated attitude toward life. If by the force of will a sickly, neurotic youth could transform himself into a dynamic professor with an iron-gray beard, who seemed to his students perpetually engaged in productive thought, then others were also free to make such transformations. His mature outlook was open and optimistic, and his personality, dominated by humor and tolerance, made him almost impossible to dislike. His students treated him with near worship, and his many friends and acquaintances in the intellectual community of the world, even when they disagreed violently with his ideas, loved the man himself. However, the surface of this congenial thinker hid a storm raging beneath.

Life as part of the James family had been challenging, but it had not produced happiness. As a young man, William James continually struggled with bouts of emotional illness that at times necessitated an almost total retreat from the active world. At the center of the problem was the inability to reconcile his growing commitment to the rationalistic, scientific outlook of his age with the deep religious faith of his father. The elder James, who had rejected established religion as a young man, had been introduced to the ideas of Emanuel Swedenborg when William was two years old. Though Henry James, Sr., was never able to become a strict follower of the Swedish theologian, he constructed his own system of belief that became a necessary spiritual consolation. His son could never accept his father's simplistic faith, yet he always respected it and sometimes seemed to long for the certainty it provided. He later paid homage to his father's ideas when he published some of the elder James's letters in *The Literary Remains of Henry James* (1885).

The inability to please his father even haunted James's choice of vocation. When William was eighteen, the family had moved to Newport, Rhode Island, where he could study art with William M. Hunt. His father had not been happy with this choice, but he was even less happy when his eldest son abandoned art a year later and entered the Lawrence Scientific School at Harvard University. This decision, however, was a significant turning point.

Not only did it begin a lifelong connection between William James and Harvard but it also began the gradual development of his personality beyond the influence of his family. The process would be difficult and never complete, but it was well on its way when the young man gravitated almost naturally toward medical school at Harvard. His studies were interrupted for a year in order to accompany the famous anthropologist Louis Agassiz on an expedition to the Amazon, but James still received his medical degree in June, 1869.

RELIGION AND PSYCHOLOGY

William James's book The Varieties of Religious Experience *is a collection of lectures that he delivered at the University of Glasgow. In his first lecture, he issued a disclaimer on his own authority on the subject of religion.*

As regards the manner in which I shall have to administer this lectureship, I am neither a theologian, nor a scholar learned in the history of religions, nor an anthropologist. Psychology is the only branch of learning in which I am particularly versed. To the psychologist the religious propensities of man must be at least as interesting as any other of the facts pertaining to his mental constitution. It would seem, therefore, that, as a psychologist, the natural thing for me would be to invite you to a descriptive survey of those religious propensities.

If the inquiry be psychological, not religious institutions, but rather religious feelings and religious impulses must be its subject, and I must confine myself to those more developed subjective phenomena recorded in literature produced by articulate and fully self-conscious men, in works of piety and autobiography. Interesting as the origins and early stages of a subject always are, yet when one seeks earnestly for its full significance, one must always look to its more completely evolved and perfect forms. It follows from this that the documents that will most concern us will be those of the men who were most accomplished in the religious life and best able to give an intelligible account of their ideas and motives. These men, of course, are either comparatively modern writers, or else such earlier ones as have become religious classics. The documents humains which we shall find most instructive need not then be sought for in the haunts of special erudition— they lie along the beaten highway; and this circumstance, which flows so naturally from the character of our problem, suits admirably also your lecturer's lack of special theological learning. I may take my citations, my sentences and paragraphs of personal confession, from books that most of you at some time will have had already in your hands, and yet this will be no detriment to the value of my conclusions. It is true that some more adventurous reader and investigator, lecturing here in future, may unearth from the shelves of libraries documents that will make a more delectable and curious entertainment to listen to than mine. Yet I doubt whether he will necessarily, by his control of so much more out-of-the-way material, get much closer to the essence of the matter in hand.

Source: William James, *The Varieties of Religious Experience: A Study in Human Nature* (New York: Longman, Green, 1902), lecture 1.

Too unstable emotionally to begin a medical practice, he remained in a state of semi-invalidism until he was appointed instructor in physiology at Harvard, in 1872. Characteristically, James believed that the conquest of his emotional problem was made possible by a philosophical conversion. While in Europe during a phase of his medical education, he had been introduced to the ideas of the French philosopher Charles Renouvier, whose stress on free will helped James reject the paralyzing fear of determinism. James's struggle for personal independence would reach a climax of sorts with his marriage to Alice H. Gibbens of Cambridge, Massachusetts. By all accounts, the union was a happy one and eventually produced five children. More important, however, the establishment of his own family at the advanced age of thirty-six coincided with the beginning of his productive career.

LIFE'S WORK

In the same year as his marriage, James agreed to a contract with Henry Holt and Company for the publication of a textbook on psychology. The agreement was, in part, recognition of his growing influence in an area of study that was undergoing transformation from a kind of mental philosophy into a laboratory science. During his European travels James had been influenced by the experimental approach to psychology current in Germany, and he taught his first course in psychology in 1875. His approach was revolutionary. Rather than the vague, often theological, speculation that characterized psychology in American universities, James started with physiological psychology, stressing the relationship between body and mind, and insisted on a thoroughly empirical approach. He soon established one of the first laboratories dedicated to psychological research in the United States.

James's proposed textbook on psychology took almost as long to mature as James himself had. Scheduled for publication in 1880, the book did not appear until 1890, as *The Principles of Psychology*. It was hardly a textbook; instead, James had produced a monumental two-volume study covering the entire field as it stood in 1890 and proposing numerous theories that would influence psychology for years to come. However, the work was not the empirical tour de force that one might expect. In spite of his dedication to science, James never liked laboratory research, and his own contribution was more impressionistic and philosophical than scientific. Moreover, the enthusiastic reception of his work owed as much to literary eloquence as it did to sound research.

In fact, James had already tired of experimental psychology before *The Principles of Psychology* was ever published. Though he would continue to be influential in the field and engage in numerous scholarly debates, his primary interest had turned to philosophy. It was not as much a change of direction as it was a change of emphasis. Since youth, he had been interested in philosophical speculation, and he taught his first course in philosophy in 1879.

Much of James's psychological work had philosophical overtones, and he was appointed professor of philosophy at Harvard in 1885. He had also exhibited an unusual interest in psychic phenomena, infuriating many of his fellow psychologists with his tolerant attitude toward the claims of spiritualists, mediums, and such dubious ideas as telepathy. This tendency was not an indication that James actually accepted parapsychology without qualification. Instead, it was a continuation of his quest for a reconciliation between humanity's need for spiritual meaning and his commitment to rational inquiry. This problem became the core of his philosophical questioning for the last decade of the nineteenth century.

James had been thinking about the problem for most of his life and had published essays on the subject while writing *The Principles of Psychology*. He began to draw these ideas together with the publication of his collection of essays, *The Will to Believe, and Other Essays in Popular Philosophy* (1897). He carried his ideas further when invited to give the Gifford Lectures on natural religion at the University of Edinburgh. Ill health prevented him from appearing until 1901-1902. These lectures, published under the title *The Varieties of Religious Experience* in 1902, are his most definitive attempt at reconciling his empirical scientific approach with religion and the spiritual world. Although his conclusions would hardly please the most orthodox, they stand as a ringing defense of the "right" to believe beyond physical evidence and an important recognition of the limitations of science, which James believed had erected a new orthodoxy as limiting as the old.

The remainder of James's life would be dedicated to defining and explaining his approach to philosophy, which he generally called pragmatism. The term was borrowed from his friend and fellow student Charles Sanders Peirce. Although Peirce clearly meant something different from James with the concept, it was James who popularized the term and made it part of American philosophical tradition. Unfortunately or perhaps fortunately, depending on one's perspective, most of James's writing was directed toward a popular rather than a philosophical audience. As a result, many of the principles of pragmatism actually depend upon which pragmatist is responsible for the explanation. This vagueness, however, is probably inherent in the doctrine and is, at least partially, responsible for its widespread acceptance.

James's final philosophical position had been evolving throughout his life and rested on a concept of the human mind that he had explained in his famous *Principles of Psychology*. In this sense, James always remained a psychologist, but he carried his psychological perspective into the world of metaphysics.

Early in his intellectual development, James had committed himself to what he called "radical empiricism," which was firmly in the tradition of David Hume and John Stuart Mill and against the dominant rationalism implicit in the most influential philosophical school of his era, German idealism. Idealism, James believed, led to a concept of the "absolute" that resulted in a deterministic universe, something that he could not accept. However, materialism, the chief opponent of idealism, also leads to a deterministic universe. James sought the middle ground that, above all, would be useful to humankind.

Usefulness is perhaps the key to understanding James's version of pragmatism. The meaning of an idea can only be judged by the particular consequences that result from it. If an idea has no real consequences, then it is meaningless. When placed in the context of James's radical empiricism, which accepts reality as that which is experienced, this doctrine means that human motives play a key role in human beliefs. Such an approach would have its most radical impact on the philosophical conception of truth. To James, this hallowed term should not apply to some mysterious ontological reality. Instead, it should refer only to one's beliefs about the world. To be true, an idea must refer to some particular thing and have "cash value," that is, satisfy the human purpose for which it was intended. It is important to remember that for James and most pragmatists, this does not mean simply practicality or what might be called pure subjectivism. Rather, truth should be tied to rigid empirical criteria and motivations designed to maximize human values.

James spent the balance of his life defending his ideas in numerous essays and lectures, most of which have been published in various collections. In his last years, he became the best-known philosopher in the English-speaking world, and his ideas were seen as the American answer to the sterile speculations of continental rationalism. To answer those who criticized his tendency toward popularization, James hoped to bring his theories together in a complete metaphysical argument. However, the project was never completed. His less-than-robust health failed him, and he died at his country home in New Hampshire on August 26, 1910.

SIGNIFICANCE

Never the ivory-tower intellectual, James always tried to live his own philosophy. For him, philosophy could never be separated from the real needs of human beings, and the answers he sought, even in the rarefied atmosphere of metaphysics, must have use beyond the lecture halls of universities. This explains his own tendency to simplify his ideas that, while leading to philosophical sloppiness, made them available to men without the training or the inclination for abstract thinking. It also explains his commitment to contemporary causes, such as his opposition to imperialism during William McKinley's administration, his general opposition to war, and his defense of unpopular ideas such as faith healing. James was always concerned first and foremost with the real fate of human beings.

James's philosophy would become one of the most important intellectual influences in American life, particularly in the twentieth century. Like his famous personality that made him so popular with friends and students, his ideas were essentially optimistic and positive. To him, the universe was pluralistic and capable of being understood. Humankind was not a passive victim of the cosmos but an active agent, whose role was essentially creative. Although humans might not be able to change the dictates of nature, they could change the conditions of their own environment.

—David Warren Bowen

FURTHER READING

Allen, Gay Wilson. *William James*. New York: Viking Press, 1967. A full-length biographical study based on the James's family papers. The author argues that James's life should be understood as an attempt to overcome emotional problems based on his self-acknowledged neuroses. Provides an excellent account of James's early life.

Bjork, Daniel J. *The Compromised Scientist: William James and the Development of American Psychology*. New York: Columbia University Press, 1983. Concentrates on James as a founder of American psychology. The author is particularly interested in James's clashes with contemporary American psychologists and the development of the discipline as a field of professional inquiry.

Conkin, Paul K. *Puritans and Pragmatists: Eight Eminent American Thinkers*. New York: Dodd, Mead, 1968. One of the finest examples of American intellectual history. Places James within the context of the development of American thought from Jonathan Edwards to George Santayana.

Cooper, Wesley. *The Unity of William James's Thought.* Nashville, Tenn.: Vanderbilt University Press, 2002. Traces the systematic philosophy in James's writing, arguing that the doctrine of pure experience links his early psychological theories with his later ideas about epistemology, religion, and pragmatism.

Feinstein, Howard M. *Becoming William James.* Ithaca, N.Y.: Cornell University Press, 1984. A biographical treatment of James that concentrates on the first three decades of his life. The author focuses on the psychological influence of James's family and has a particularly interesting analysis of James as a frustrated artist.

Gale, Richard M. *The Philosophy of William James: An Introduction.* New York: Cambridge University Press, 2005. This book, a revised edition of *The Divided Self of William James*, published in 1999, is an accessible introduction to James's philosophy. Gale argues that James's philosophy is divided between his beliefs in active pragmatism and passive mysticism.

Perry, Ralph Barton. *The Thought and Character of William James.* 2 vols. Boston: Little, Brown, 1935. A collection of the letters and writings of William James, with biographical commentary.

Roth, J. K. *Freedom and the Moral Life.* Philadelphia: Westminster Press, 1969. Concentrates on the relationship of James's concept of pragmatism to ethics. The author is particularly interested in stressing the continued value of James's idea of moral behavior.

Talisse, Robert B., and D. Micah Hester. *On James.* Belmont, Calif.: Wadsworth/Thomson Learning, 2004. One in a series of books about philosophers, this volume offers a brief overview of James's philosophy.

Wild, John D. *The Radical Empiricism of William James.* Garden City, N.Y.: Doubleday, 1969. Places James within the continuing empiricist tradition. Contains excellent though technical discussion of the relationship of pragmatism and phenomenology.

Wilshire, Bruce. *William James and Phenomenology.* Bloomington: Indiana University Press, 1968. Concentrates on phenomenological aspects of James's ideas. Although the book is not for the philosophical novice, it provides an important insight into the relationship of philosophical theories in the twentieth century.

SEE ALSO: Louis Agassiz; F. H. Bradley; Henry James; William McKinley; John Stuart Mill; Charles Sanders Peirce.

RELATED ARTICLE in *Great Events from History: The Nineteenth Century, 1801-1900:* 1900: Freud Publishes *The Interpretation of Dreams.*

ANNA JAMESON
Canadian writer

Although her work was long neglected after she died, Jameson was one of the major writers of nonfiction prose during the nineteenth century. Her long and varied career encompassed both Europe and Canada, and her travel writing, art criticism, Shakespearean critiques, and social commentaries covered new subjects in sometimes controversial ways.

BORN: May 19, 1794; Dublin, Ireland
DIED: March 17, 1860; London, England
ALSO KNOWN AS: Anna Brownell Murphy (birth name); Anna Brownell Jameson; Mrs. Anna Jameson
AREA OF ACHIEVEMENT: Literature

EARLY LIFE

Anna Jameson was born Anna Brownell Murphy, the daughter of Richard Murphy, an Irish painter of miniature portraits. The Murphys were not well off, and when Anna was four they moved across the Irish Sea to England—first to Whitehaven in the English county of Cumbria. When Anna was eight, the family moved again, to Newcastle-on-Tyne, where they eked out a living on her father's paintings. However, after a few years. Murphy became more successful as a painter, and the family moved to London, where they began to mingle with prominent figures on the city's cultural scene.

In London, Anna became familiar with the literary world in which she was to spend the rest of her life. In 1820, she became engaged to Robert Jameson, a young lawyer on the fringes of that literary world, However, rather than marrying Jameson immediately, she chose to work as a governess for two families, the Rowles and the Hathertons. She got along well with the latter family, but her years as a governess were not happy ones. However, they provided her with insights into the plight of working-class women that she would later use in her books about social conditions.

Anna traveled with the Rowles to Italy—a trip that yielded literary fruit. In 1826, she published *Diary of an Ennuyée*. Now regarded as a classic account of a young Englishwoman's impressions of the Continent, her first book was badly reviewed at the time, both because of perceived infelicities of style and also because it seemed to embarrass the Rowles family. The fact that he book was actually a mixture of fact and fiction—a melding that would later intrigue literary historians—confused contemporary reviewers.

Also during 1825, Anna finally married Jameson. They lived together for four years, but when Jameson was sent to the Caribbean as a colonial official in 1829, Anna instead went to Europe with her father and a family friend. She found her travels in Germany particularly gratifying, as she made the acquaintance of Ottilie von Goethe, the daughter of the great German writer Johann Wolfgang von Goethe, who became a lifelong friend. She also gained an acquaintance with German culture rare for an English person of her generation.

It is unknown why Anna was separated from her husband for such a long time. However, when her husband was appointed a colonial magistrate in Canada, she decided to accompany him to Toronto.

LIFE'S WORK

In 1836, Canada was a country beginning to emerge into democracy and self-government. Robert Jameson's task was to serve as a constitutional official—speaker of the House of Assembly—without having the consent of the people, which inherently limited his position. Anna Jameson found Toronto drab and provincial, especially in comparison to the American cities that she had visited on her way to Canada. However, she enjoyed visiting the Georgian Bay area and walking around Lake Huron, where, at Sault St. Marie, she met the American ethnologist Henry Schoolcraft, who taught her about the customs of the Chippewa people who inhabited the area.

Jameson's book about her trip, *Winter Studies and Summer Rambles in Canada* (1838), is less about castigating Toronto as dull than it is about Jameson's ambivalent curiosity about the countryside and the native peoples that would capture the imagination of later generations. Written in diary form, *Winter Studies* is now seen, despite Jameson's frequent condescension toward Canada, as an early document of Canadian literature.

Some critics have theorized that the way that the imaginative energies of Jameson's book gravitate to-

ward the wild is also an allegory of the breakup of Jameson's marriage. In any event, she and her husband separated for good in 1837. She once again traveled around the Continent, returning to England only after her father died in 1842. From that moment, she lived in the midst of London's literary world, where she became acquainted with the younger poets Elizabeth Barrett and Robert Browning and developed a close friendship with Lord Byron's widow that eventually ended acrimoniously in 1854.

Jameson's work had three main focuses during the last twenty years of her life. As an art historian, she wrote, in *Sacred and Legendary Art* (1865) and *Legends of the Madonna* (1861), primarily about sacred art, especially the representation of the Virgin Mary and of women in general in Christian art of the medieval and Renaissance periods. She wrote about this material in strictly aesthetic terms, rather than promoting religious belief.

As a literary scholar, Jameson wrote, in *Shakespeare's Heroines* (1832), about the female characters in William Shakespeare's plays, in the very period when great women actors—instead of men—were beginning to play those roles in theatrical performances and in the Victorian cultural imagination. As a social commentator and reformer, Jameson wrote in *Characteristics of Women* (1832) and *Sisters of Charity* (1855) about the position of women in the social sphere, the ways they were mistreated in private situations, such as those of governesses, and the general waste that society made of women's talents. Although she did not write at length on the slavery question, she was active, with her friend Harriet Martineau, in the British abolitionist movement, which by that time was concerned only with slavery in the United States, as slavery had already been abolished throughout the British Empire.

Despite Jameson's status as a single woman, she remained a respectable figure in Victorian literary society. Her former husband never gave her the financial compensation that he had promised her, and her later years were marred by illness and quarrels with former friends. However, when she died in 1869, at the age of sixty-six, tributes were paid to her for her energy and longevity on the literary scene.

SIGNIFICANCE

After Anna Jameson died, she and her art books were soon forgotten. John Ruskin began to talk about Renaissance Art in a much more polemical, theoretical, and passionate manner. Jameson's travel books were also soon forgotten, and her social tracts were left behind as people moved on to new issues and concerns. However, Jameson's work serves as a bridge in literary history: between the European continent and the Canadian wilderness, between romanticism and Victorianism, and between the history of Western aesthetics and the development of a feminist sensibility.

Like many other nineteenth century women writers, Jameson had to be reclaimed in the late twentieth century from an obscurity that befell her after her death. In her case, she had two critical movements working to reclaim her: not only feminism but Canadian nationalism. Despite Jameson's brief stay and divided stance toward Canada, it is there that she is most highly regarded and seen as a part of a national literature.

—*Nicholas Birns*

FURTHER READING

Desmet, Christy. "'Intercepting the Dew-Drop': Female Readers and Readings in Anna Jameson's Shakespearean Criticism." In *Women's Re-Visions of Shakespeare: On the Responses of Dickinson, Woolf, Rich, H. D., George Eliot, and Others*, edited by Marianne Novy. Urbana: University of Illinois Press, 1990. Examines the key role of Jameson's Shakespeare criticism in calling attention to women's roles in the plays.

Henderson, Jennifer. *Settler Feminism and Race Making in Canada*. Toronto: University of Toronto Press, 2003. Occasionally dense but informative book examines Jameson's Canadian writing, *Winter Studies and Summer Rambles in Canada*, in the light of conceptions of gender roles and of the relationship of the white settlers to indigenous peoples.

Johnston, Judith. *Anna Jameson: Victorian, Feminist, Woman of Letters*. Brookfield, Vt.: Ashgate, 1997. The first comprehensive biography of Jameson to take the insights of feminist criticism into account. Johnston is especially insightful on Jameson's continental and artistic connections. This book is the foundation for the late twentieth century flurry of scholarly work on Jameson.

Lew, Laurie Kane. "Cultural Anxiety in Anna Jameson's Art Criticism." *SEL: Studies in English Literature, 1500-1900* 36, no. 4 (Autumn, 1996): 829-856. Provides a basic overview of Jameson's writings on art, centering on their pioneering exploration of women in artistic representation, while also discussing how Jameson admires the great European art of the past while nonetheless being perturbed by it.

Lootens, Tricia. "Fear of Cairina: Anna Jameson, Englishness and the 'Trite Placer' of Italy." *Forum for Modern Language Studies* 39, no. 2 (April, 2003): 178-189. Examines the influence on Jameson of her older contemporary, the French novelist Germaine de Stael, and how Jameson's portrait of Italy displays typically English anxieties about the delights and temptations of the European continent.

Monkman, Leslie. "Primitivism and a Parasol: Anna Jameson's Indians." *Essays on Canadian Writing* 29 (1984): 85-95. A noted Canadian scholar examines Jameson's representation of indigenous peoples in *Winter Studies and Summer Rambles in Canada*.

Thomas, Clara. *Love and Work Enough: The Life of Anna Jameson*. Toronto: University of Toronto Press, 1967. This first twentieth century biography of Jameson helped to put her work back on the literary map.

York, Lorraine M. "'Sublime Desolation': European Art and Jameson's Perceptions of Canada." *Mosaic* 19, no. 2 (Spring, 1986): 43-56. A beginning effort in an area that may become a major concern of Jameson studies: linking her insights into European art with her exploration of native American experience.

SEE ALSO: Lord Byron; Harriet Martineau; Susanna Moodie; John Ruskin; Thomas Talbot; Catharine Parr Traill.

RELATED ARTICLE in *Great Events from History: The Nineteenth Century, 1801-1900:* February 10, 1841: Upper and Lower Canada Unite.

JEAN JAURÈS
French politician

Through the use of his powerful oratorical skills and his philosophical studies, Jaurès became the founder of French socialism and a leading international advocate for peace in the years leading up to World War I, which began only days after he died.

BORN: September 3, 1859; Castres, France
DIED: July 31, 1914; Paris, France
ALSO KNOWN AS: Auguste-Marie-Joseph-Jean Jaurès (full name)
AREA OF ACHIEVEMENT: Government and politics

EARLY LIFE

Auguste-Marie-Joseph-Jean Jaurès (zho-rahz) was the first son of Jean-Henri Jules and his wife Marie-Adélaïde Barbaza, a family of traders and rural smallholders in Castres, France. Because of his family's lower-middle-class standing, Jaurès was not held to the strict rules of behavior set by the wealthier middle class. Instead, he was free to form his own opinions and could intermingle with the laboring classes of the region, which had been a largely agricultural area but was slowly developing some industry.

Jaurès first attended school at the pension Séjal, a small private establishment run by a priest. He enthusiastically participated in school and, in 1869, was admitted to the Collège de Castres with a scholarship. During his seven years at the school, Jaurès impressed many of his fellow students and teachers. In 1875, his impressive intellect was noticed by Inspector-General of Schools Nicolas-Félix Deltour, who was seeking to recruit young men to help boost the educational system in France. Through Deltour's assistance, Jaurès began his Parisian education at Sainte-Barbe in 1876 in preparation for his move in 1878 to the École Normale Supérieure, one of the most demanding and prestigious schools in the nation.

Jaurès's obvious love of learning allowed him to flourish at the École Normale Supérieure. He chose philosophy as his field of study, although he was attracted to both languages and history as well. In 1881, he participated in the aggregation, a series of oral and written examinations to determine who would receive the best teaching posts in France. He placed third and requested a post in philosophy at the Lycée d'Albi in order to be near his parents. When his father died in 1882 and his mother came to live with him, Jaurès decided to move to Toulouse, where he was offered a position in the Faculty of Letters at the University of Toulouse in 1883.

Because of his outstanding oratorical skill and his passion for republican politics, Jaurès was placed on the republican list for his region during the 1885 elections. He was the youngest deputy in the 1885-1889 parliament and soon became disillusioned with republicanism. His true political education began after his defeat in the elections of 1889 when he returned to the University of Toulouse and threw himself into studying various political ideas, particularly the socialist theories of Louis Blanc, Pierre-Joseph Proudhon, Ferdinand Lassalle, and Karl Marx. Gradually, he began to initiate closer contact with the urban working classes and to develop a fledgling socialist commitment.

LIFE'S WORK

For Jaurès, the Carmaux mining strike of 1892 was a critical turning point. He saw the struggle between the miners and their employers as an issue of human dignity, an attempt by the workers to free themselves. He championed their cause and was elected deputy for Carmaux in an 1892 by-election and then in the 1893 general election. Throughout the 1890's his oratorical skills and his socialist theories pushed him to the forefront of the socialist faction of parliament. He spoke on a variety of topics in the Chamber of Deputies, ranging from education to military affairs.

Although busy as a deputy and leader of the socialists, Jaurès continued to participate regularly in labor disputes and came to understand some of the strengths of working-class culture as well as the weakness of working-class collective organization. He firmly believed in the power of socialist politics rather than a dependency on the sudden strikes and calls to the barricades advocated by the syndicalist faction of the socialist movement. During the Fourth Congress of the Second International meeting in London in 1896, Jaurès attempted to unify the various factions by denying that anarchism constituted part of socialism (thus singling out an extremely divisive element of the Congress) and by supporting syndicalism as an important part of socialism. However, he continued to make it clear that working through standard government politics was the preferred and more effective path. Despite his eloquent speeches, he failed to make the distinction between anarchism and syndicalism apparent to all.

By 1897 Jaurès had become involved in the Dreyfus affair, in which a Jewish army officer was falsely accused of selling military secrets. Jaurès was consumed with a desire to see justice prevail. He believed that the future of the republic lay in how socialists reacted. For Jaurès, socialists had to defend the republic and fight for justice in this matter. Because the bourgeois parties were failing to uphold the banner of republican government, he concluded that the socialists must take it. Jaurès proceeded to rail against the government's actions in the Dreyfus case. His outspoken moves would serve to work against him in the coming year.

When Jaurès arrived back in his home region in the spring of 1898 to campaign for reelection, he found that his opponents had already begun campaigning against him. They denounced him as an enemy of religion and an agent of the Jews. The employers of Carmaux were determined to see Jaurès defeated at all costs. They broke up socialist meetings and prevented Jaurès from forming an audience for his speeches. When the May votes came in, Jaurès found himself defeated. Instead of turning away from the issues that had caused his defeat, he continued to involve himself in the Dreyfus affair. He also began editing the Paris daily *La Petite République* (the small republic) and writing the *Histoire socialiste de la révolution française* (1901-1907; socialist history of the French Revolution).

During his time away from the Chamber of Deputies, Jaurès devoted himself to supporting a reformist socialist approach to government. He backed the entry of Alexandre Millerand, a socialist lawyer, into the bourgeois government of René Waldeck-Rousseau in 1899 despite opposition from many leading socialists, such as Jules Guesde and Édouard Vaillant, who felt that he was compromising too many socialist ideas in the process. Despite this opposition, Jaurès continued to defend his position, believing that it was necessary for the socialists to defend and consolidate the republic. Breaking with Guesde and Vaillant in 1902, he formed the Parti Socialiste Français and joined with the radicals to form a leftist bloc that won a victory in the 1902 elections. Among the victorious electors, Jaurès was appointed one of the vice presidents of the Chamber of Deputies.

By 1904 Jaurès's leftist bloc had begun to disintegrate from attacks both within and without. Simultaneously, his Parti Socialiste Français was also dying. Realizing that his compromises with the bourgeois parties had diluted his message, Jaurès began calling for socialist unity. He repaired his relationships with Guesde and especially Vaillant. He abandoned his reformist notions in favor of a more traditional socialist line, embracing the class nature of the socialist struggle as well as its revolu-

tionary character. In April, 1905, under Jaurès's leadership, a pact of union was signed, and the Section Française de L'Internationale Ouvrière (SFIO), a new unified socialist party, was formed.

Jaurès emerged as the undisputed leader of the new party. He formulated policy on almost every subject but was particularly concerned with a desire for closer unity between the syndicalist socialists and the SFIO. He showed a great ability for political flexibility regarding the syndicalists and even developed a complex theory of the working class. Jaurès also made military reform a priority. In his work *L'Armée Nouvelle* (1911; *Democracy and Military Service*, 1972), he stated that socialists should not work to undermine the military. Instead, the military should be adjusted to the pattern of the French revolutionary armies of 1792-1795, which would bring back the national spirit of 1792 and promote social cohesion. This program ultimately proved unpopular.

Aside from his political and military reform interests, Jaurès was also concerned with the growing militarism of Europe in the years prior to World War I. He called for a political reconciliation between France and Germany and declared arbitration as the best method to resolve disputes. He made several trips to places such as Basel, Switzerland (1912), and Brussels, Belgium (1914), to make speeches in favor of peace. Many began to feel that he was the final barrier against the growing war fever of European governments. However, Jaurès's stance against war brought his downfall. On July 31, 1914, as Jaurès sat in a Paris café with a group of his colleagues with his back to a window, a right-wing fanatic named Raoul Villain, who thought Jaurès's pacifism would lead the nation astray, shot him twice. He died within minutes. His ashes were later moved to the Pantheon on November 23, 1924.

SIGNIFICANCE

Without the powerful leadership and oratorical grace of Jean Jaurès, it is doubtful that the socialist movement would have been able to unify itself in the turmoil of the early twentieth century. Too many divisive issues worked against this outcome. Jaurès was able to use his unique ability to compromise and speak to the hearts of the working classes to help bring about the necessary cohesion to achieve advances for the lower classes.

Jaurès's humble beginnings at Castres allowed Jaurès to identify with the working classes, and the educational opportunities he was given permitted him to bring the issues of the working classes to the government. By immersing himself in the works of great philosophers, he was able to conceive his own vision for how the Socialist Party should be constructed and run. His was a flexible policy. It was his strong personality that held the party to a middle course between the paths of reformists and revolutionaries. As Daniel Halévy stated in 1905, "What, then, was this party? I will define it in a word: it was Jaurès. It was his reflection. He created it. He kept it together."

—Michael R. Nichols

FURTHER READING

Goldberg, Harvey. *The Life of Jean Jaurès.* Madison: University of Wisconsin Press, 1962. The definitive biography of Jaurès. Traces the development of Jaurès's political ideas and his rise to the head of the French socialist movement. Includes a detailed bibliography and some photographs.

Jaurès, Jean. *Democracy and Military Service.* New York: Garland, 1972. An English translation of Jaurès's *L'Armée Nouvelle*, which details his ideas for the military and the importance of capturing a democratic spirit for the nation.

Pease, Margaret. *Jean Jaurès: Socialist and Humanitarian.* London: Headley Brothers, 1916. Written shortly after Jaurès's death, this book includes an excellent introduction by former British Prime Minister James Ramsay MacDonald. A fairly succinct biography of Jaurès but somewhat weakened by its lack of a bibliography.

Rebérioux, Madeleine. "Party Practice and the Jaurèsian Vision: The SFIO (1905-1914)." In *Socialism in France: From Jaurès to Mitterand,* edited by Stuart Williams. London: Frances Pinter, 1983. A short essay on the particulars of Jaurès's vision for the united Socialist Party. Also includes ideas for how to approach the study of Socialist Party politics at the beginning of the twentieth century.

Sowerwine, Charles. *France Since 1870: Culture, Politics, and Society.* New York: Palgrave, 2001. An overview of French history, politics, and culture during the Third Republic through the late twentieth century. Includes information about Jaurès.

Stuart, Robert C. *Marxism at Work: Ideology, Class, and French Socialism During the Third Republic.* New York: Cambridge University Press, 1992. Examination of French Marxism during the late nineteenth century focusing on the followers of Jules Guesde (Guesdists). Includes information about Jaurès.

Tuchman, Barbara W. "The Death of Jaurès." In *The Proud Tower: A Portrait of the World Before the War, 1890-1914.* New York: Macmillan, 1966. An essay in a collection devoted to the study of the period prior to World War I. Follows Jaurès's ideas leading up to World War I as well as the impact of his assassination on world events. Includes some photographs.

SEE ALSO: Louis Blanc; Ferdinand Lassalle; Karl Marx; Pierre-Joseph Proudhon.

RELATED ARTICLES in *Great Events from History: The Nineteenth Century, 1801-1900:* 1839: Blanc Publishes *The Organization of Labour*; September 28, 1864: First International Is Founded.

LORD JEFFREY
Scottish journalist

As founder and editor of the Edinburgh Review, *Jeffrey created a forceful instrument for critical analysis and the shaping of popular opinion, making him a unique force in early nineteenth century journalism. His review won readers through its courageous espousal of often unpopular causes, dissent from conventional wisdom, and sophisticated, readable style.*

BORN: October 23, 1773; Edinburgh, Scotland
DIED: January 26, 1850; Edinburgh, Scotland
ALSO KNOWN AS: Francis Jeffrey (birth name)
AREAS OF ACHIEVEMENT: Journalism, law

EARLY LIFE

Francis Jeffrey was the son of George Jeffrey. His mother, Henrietta Louden, was loving and gentle but died when Francis was thirteen. His father, a moody and pessimistic man, served as deputy clerk for the Court of Session. Jeffrey's education, shaped by his father's high Tory views, was conservative. He found his real education, however, among the bleakly beautiful hills of Scotland and the books of an uncle's library. In 1791, he spent a year at Queen's College, Oxford, but was miserable and returned to Edinburgh to study law.

At the age of twenty, Jeffrey was shy, slight of build, and romantic. He was barely five feet in height; his oval face was intensely expressive and his black eyes gleamed. It was a face, a friend noted, that reflected "honesty, intelligence and kindly fire." Like many sensitive young men maturing during the opening years of a revolutionary era, Jeffrey saw himself as a poet and dramatist. Nevertheless, economic reality dictated his career, and he was admitted to the Scottish bar in 1794.

Despite his father's Tory views and the strong patronage system of Scottish politics, Jeffrey had already made the great political transition. In 1793, in a youthful essay on politics, he adopted a lofty intellectual allegiance to the Whig Party, a loyalty that he never relinquished. He paid the price of conversion for nearly a decade. In Tory Scotland, legal fees and political opportunities were virtually nonexistent for young Whigs.

Jeffrey was married in 1801 and established his bride in a flat in Buccleuch Place. His wife, Catherine Wilson, was a cousin, and marriage gave the young Jeffrey a stable, happy home life. Around the young couple, a coterie of promising talent gathered. Edinburgh, long a center of learning, was filled with good conversation and conviviality. In 1802, a group of young men, including Sydney Smith and Henry Brougham, met at Buccleuch Place, and Smith proposed that they found a review. Jeffrey and the others had apparently discussed the idea for some time, but the expense of such a project was formidable. Nevertheless, their enthusiasm conquered their hesitation. Thus, almost casually, was born the *Edinburgh Review*, one of the foremost journals of the modern era.

LIFE'S WORK

The first issues of the *Edinburgh Review* were hastily put together in a dreary printing office off Craig's Close by a committee of friends, none of whom could have predicted its enormous popularity. Almost immediately, however, the sales startled the young contributors. In an era when a few hundred copies counted as a good circulation, the *Edinburgh Review* achieved a circulation of twenty-five hundred within six months. Clearly, financial success would have to breed greater efficiency. Although the witty Sydney Smith had acted as self-appointed editor of the earliest issues, he had little organizational ability. Moreover, although he remained a popular and eloquent essayist, Smith lacked intellectual depth. Within a year of its establishment, Jeffrey was appointed the official editor of the review.

One of his first and most important decisions was to pay contributors. Not yet thirty, Jeffrey had struggled with near-poverty for years. He recognized that a successful journal was often doomed after an original success when bright young authors had to choose between art and earning a livelihood. His own meager law practice made his income of fifty pounds an issue particularly precious. Others in the circle, he knew, would drift away to the dazzle of London. Generous payment for articles would hold young talent and attract proven authors. It was a wise decision and would be widely copied by later publications.

More important, Jeffrey set out to make the *Edinburgh Review* interesting, provocative, and authoritative. Although journalism traced its roots back to the formidable diatribes and satire of Joseph Addison and Sir Richard Steele, it remained, like acting, a somewhat suspect profession. Jeffrey constantly worried about the possible harm to his reputation or legal career from his editorship. The challenge and the work proved, however, irresistible. Under his direction, the *Edinburgh Review* continued to present the strongest essays on important issues as well as the most critical reviews of books and art in Great Britain. As a result, its circulation continued to expand, and by 1814 it was being read by a phenomenal thirteen thousand people.

Much of the *Edinburgh Review*'s popularity resulted from Jeffrey's ability to persuade others to work with him creatively. Although the original articles proudly proclaimed devotion to Whig, or liberal, principles, Jeffrey steered a moderate course politically. As a result, the early years of publication attracted writers of the stature and popularity of Sir Walter Scott. Scott, a staunch Tory, not only wrote several articles but also encouraged friends such as Robert Southey to consider the review. Nevertheless, the times were chaotic and dangerous and journalistic partisanship all too common. Increasingly, the *Edinburgh Review* reflected the Whig interpretations of events. Although kind and diffident with his family and friends, Jeffrey was a tiger when it came to his convictions.

In 1808, Jeffrey wrote, with minor assistance from Brougham, the famous Cevallos article. It was a scathing attack upon the Iberian campaign and British governmental policies in Spain. Scott was so incensed that he

Lord Jeffrey. (Library of Congress)

dropped his subscription and encouraged the founding of a rival publication, the *Quarterly Review*. Nevertheless, Jeffrey continued to express his opposition to the Napoleonic Wars and to the later war with the United States in 1812. Equally unpopular was his courageous support for Catholic emancipation.

The tone of the review after the Cevallos article became more openly liberal, and Jeffrey took pride in the quality of the discussion and the spread of liberal philosophy. In 1832, when the Reform Bill passed, he believed strongly that the *Edinburgh Review* for three decades had prepared the public for the great change in politics.

Ironically, it was not Jeffrey's politically controversial opinions that endangered his life, but rather his equally passionate views of poetry. Jeffrey, although an outstanding editor, was not always a good judge of poetic quality. A product of the Scottish Enlightenment in training, he disliked intensely the early outpourings of the "Lake Poets." In the fifteenth issue of the review, he attacked Thomas Moore's *Epistles, Odes, and Other Poems* (1806). Jeffrey considered them immoral and depraved. An indignant Moore challenged Jeffrey to a duel in 1806.

In the end, the meeting of editor and poet proved more ludicrous than dangerous. Moore had hastily borrowed pistols from a friend who in turn had reported the affair to the famous Bow Street Runners. As the two men tried to "do or die" on the field of honor, the police intervened and hauled both of them off to court. When the diminutive Jeffrey and the lanky Moore were questioned, it turned out that Jeffrey had intentionally not even loaded his pistol. He was willing to die for his views but not kill for them. Lord Byron later erroneously imputed the unloaded pistol to Moore.

As a result of their tumultuous introduction and their ignominious visit to the police, the two men wound up close friends. Moore later published articles in the *Edinburgh Review* and in 1825 visited Jeffrey in Scotland.

Although touched by the amusing and the occasionally absurd, Jeffrey's personal life had taken a tragic turn. Within a month in 1805, he lost his young wife and his favorite sister. His only child had died two years earlier. In late 1810, a French refugee family, related to the controversial parliamentarian John Wilkes, visited Jeffrey. On their voyage to the United States, they were accompanied by their niece Charlotte Wilkes. Jeffrey fell deeply in love but realized the depth of his feelings belatedly. By that time, Miss Wilkes had arrived in the United States. Despite the fact that he was thirty-seven years old and prone to seasickness, and despite the fact that the War of

1812 had begun, Jeffrey resolved, like a Scottish Lochinvar, to find Wilkes. Calling on friends to take over the review for the interim, Jeffrey set sail for New York. His daring won Wilkes's hand.

After his marriage in 1813, Jeffrey traveled in the United States and met with President James Madison and Secretary of State James Monroe. Even before the outbreak of the War of 1812, he had been highly critical of British foreign policy in North America, but he was conscientious in explaining British sentiments and official policies to Madison and Monroe. His genuine concern for the young nation expressed frequently in subsequent review articles did much to dissipate British ire following the war. In addition to his editorial work, Jeffrey carried on a growing legal practice. He developed a rapport with Edinburgh juries that, combined with a passion for detail, real charm, and kindness, won his clients' acquittal. By 1820, he was considered one of Scotland's finest criminal attorneys. In 1830, Whig victories enabled the party to recognize his years of service with an appointment as lord advocate.

Jeffrey's new position required him to enter Parliament in the rough-and-tumble elections of 1830-1832. Jeffrey was fifty-seven and in poor health. He soon found the seemingly endless committee meetings and innumerable details of the reform bills to be exhausting. In 1834, he retired from Parliament to accept a judgeship in the Court of Sessions, becoming, on June 7, 1834, Lord Jeffrey.

Gradually, his legal and political life diverted Jeffrey from the *Edinburgh Review*. In 1829, he resigned from the journal. MacVey Napier succeeded him as editor. Although he occasionally contributed articles to the review after his return from Parliament, his judicial work took up much of his time. In addition, his home near Edinburgh, Craigcrook, and its gardens became an absorbing interest. In his old age, he served as a mentor to younger authors such as Charles Dickens, whose novels he loved, and as a stylistic consultant to fellow Whigs such as Thomas Babington Macaulay, whose early volumes he proofread. He died on January 26, 1850, and was buried in the Dean cemetery near Edinburgh.

SIGNIFICANCE

Lord Jeffrey's contributions as editor to the *Edinburgh Review* made him a unique force in early nineteenth century journalism. The review soon captured a popular readership by the courage of its espousal of often unpopular causes, its dissent from conventional wisdom, and its sophisticated, readable style.

Everything that went into the early review was crafted and polished by Jeffrey, sometimes to the anger or dismay of the contributor. His legal logic, vivid style, and intellect made him a great and feared critic, yet he was quick to see both sides of an issue, generous to political foes, and swift to detect and encourage talent. Although the *Edinburgh Review* under Jeffrey soon faced competition from journals as renowned as the *Quarterly Review* and *Blackwood's*, its influence was unrivaled during the early decades of the century. Jeffrey's passionate devotion to liberal politics, combined with his love of literature, caused an unusual tension in analytical criticism. It created an entirely new tone in periodical literature, combining philosophical, political, and literary topics not only to entertain but also to educate a readership. Jeffrey had created in large measure a revolution in the scope and purpose of journalistic literature.

—*E. Deanne Malpass*

FURTHER READING

Carlyle, Thomas. *Reminiscences*. Edited by James Anthony Froude. 2 vols. London: Longmans, Green, 1881. Contains an excellent and penetrating sketch of Jeffrey, who admired Thomas and Jane Carlyle intensely. Carlyle gives a fine description of Jeffrey's appearance, character, and legal prowess in criminal cases.

Cockburn, Henry Thomas, Lord. *Life and Correspondence of Lord Jeffrey*. 2 vols. London: Longmans, Green, 1852. This voluminous work, written shortly after Jeffrey's death, is dated but still essential to any study of his career. The letters give a sense of Jeffrey's critical acumen.

Demata, Massimiliano, and Duncan Wu, eds. *British Romanticism and the "Edinburgh Review": Bicentenary Essays*. New York: Palgrave, 2002. A collection of essays reassessing the *Edinburgh Review*'s significance and influence during its first two hundred years of publication. The essays contain numerous references to Jeffrey.

Houghton, Walter Edwards, ed. *The Wellesley Index to Victorian Periodicals, 1824-1900*. Toronto: University of Toronto Press, 1966. An invaluable work on nineteenth century journals. It deals with the early years of the *Edinburgh Review* (1802-1823) in the context of the entire publication.

Jeffrey, Francis. *Contributions to the "Edinburgh Review."* 4 vols. London: Longman, Brown, Green, and Longmans, 1844. A selection of essays that indicates the quality and scope of Jeffrey's work. It includes his famous essay on beauty that appeared in the *Encyclopædia Britannica*.

Reid, Stuart J. *The Life and Times of Sydney Smith*. London: S. Low, Marston, 1884. Contains a discussion of the founding of the *Edinburgh Review* and the friendship between Smith and Jeffrey, as well as some useful correspondence.

SEE ALSO: Henry Brougham; Lord Byron; Thomas Carlyle; Charles Dickens; Thomas Babington Macaulay; James Mill; James Monroe; Sir Walter Scott.

RELATED ARTICLE in *Great Events from History: The Nineteenth Century, 1801-1900:* 1807: Bowdler Publishes *The Family Shakespeare*.

SARAH ORNE JEWETT
American novelist

The author of twenty books, Jewett was the most accomplished of the American writers associated with literary regionalism and was a major force in the creation and development of an American women's literary tradition.

BORN: September 3, 1849; South Berwick, Maine
DIED: June 24, 1909; South Berwick, Maine
ALSO KNOWN AS: Theodora Sarah Orne Jewett (full name)
AREA OF ACHIEVEMENT: Literature

EARLY LIFE

Theodora Sarah Orne Jewett was the second of three daughters of an established and wealthy Maine family. Her grandfather Captain Theodore Furber Jewett had prospered in the West Indies trade during the early part of the century, leaving the family financially independent. Although Sarah received her formal education at Miss Raynes's School and at Berwick Academy in South Berwick, much of her true education came from her father, a country doctor. She was her father's frequent companion on his house calls, especially when bouts of ill health kept her out of school. As they moved from house to house, he shared with her his close observations of the surrounding landscape as well as his thoughts on life and literature. Later, Sarah, by now an accomplished writer, would credit her father with pointing out to her that really great writers do not write *about* people and things, but describe them just as they are.

Young Sarah read widely in her parents' substantial library, and when, at the age of seventeen, she read Harriet Beecher Stowe's *The Pearl of Orr's Island* (1862), she found in Stowe's portrayal of scenes from Maine life a hint of the possibilities of the regionalist fiction in which Sarah herself would excel.

Jewett's first published story, "Jenny Garrow's Ghost," appeared in *The Flag of Our Union*, a Boston

weekly, on January 18, 1868. The nineteen-year-old author, unwilling at this point that others should know of her literary activities, used the pen name "Alice Eliot." In December of the following year, after two polite rejections, the prestigious *Atlantic Monthly* published her story "Mr. Bruce," confirming Jewett's conviction that she was at least an apprentice writer. She continued to write for the *Atlantic* and other publications. Finally, William Dean Howells, the novelist and editor, suggested to Jewett that she organize some of her sketches and short stories into a book. Jewett found this work painfully difficult, but the result, *Deephaven* (1877), marked her arrival at maturity as a writer.

LIFE'S WORK

The death of her father in 1878 was a difficult blow for Sarah Orne Jewett. Until his death, her relationship with him had been the most important of her life. Her closest adult emotional relationships were her friendships with women. The most important of these was with Annie Fields, whom Jewett met during the 1870's, when Annie was married to the publisher James T. Fields, Annie's senior by some seventeen years. After Fields's death in 1881, Jewett and Fields's friendship flowered into a "Boston marriage." The term denotes a virtually spousal—although not necessarily, or even usually, sexual—relationship between two women. Jewett and Fields lived together for part of each year, they traveled together, and, when physically separated, kept in touch by letter. To their friends, it became natural to think of them as a couple.

In the years following *Deephaven*, Jewett continued to develop as a writer. She enjoyed her greatest success in the sketches and short stories set in her native Maine. The fact that her life as an adult involved long periods of residence in Boston and of foreign travel seemed to strengthen her imaginative possession of the Maine setting. Her own experience justified the advice she later gave the younger novelist Willa Cather, that to know the parish one must first know the world.

Jewett was mastering a form that was very much her own: a short narrative devoid of plot in terms of dramatic event and linear structure. The form allows for patient observation of the gradual unfolding of human relationships and the interrelationship of the human and the natural in places Jewett had known since childhood. Many of her stories have a conversational quality: A speaker, usually a woman, moves, by what seems superficially like random association, toward a clarification of emotional, spiritual, or moral truth that is the heart of the story.

Jewett had less success with the more conventional sort of novel. Most readers find *The Country Doctor* (1884) her most interesting work in the novel form because of its content, the relationship of Nan Prince and Doctor Leslie, with its intriguing autobiographical resonance, and Nan's determination to enter the medical profession, which was regarded by her contemporaries as a male preserve. Nevertheless, the novel achieves only limited dramatic power.

Jewett continued to develop as a literary artist. Her progress was dramatically displayed in the collection *A White Heron, and Other Stories*, published in 1886. The title story of the collection, perhaps Jewett's most famous short story, exemplifies its author's respect for the reader's share in the literary experience. She credited her father for pointing out to her the importance in fiction of leaving readers some work to do, rather than bullying them into a passive acceptance of predigested motives and meanings.

In "A White Heron," indirection in presenting the moment of decision involves the reader centrally in the process of making meaning. This is an art based on process rather than product, on cooperation rather than conquest. Some readers have suggested that it is very much a woman's sort of art, although appreciation of this art is by no means denied to men. In this case, any attentive reader must admire the delicacy and force (the two easily coexist in Jewett's work) with which the author brings into play within the reader's active mind many of the themes central to her fiction. She includes meditations on innocence and experience, on continuity and change, on the city and the country, on nature and culture, on masculine and feminine, on the imagination's power to soar, and on the reaching of the mind toward an androgyny of the spirit that may obviate the need for the sexual union of man and woman. This is much to build on a moment in the life of a nine-year-old girl, but Jewett (who, in a letter written when she was forty-eight, stated that she always felt nine years old) makes it all work.

The collections of stories and sketches published in the decade following *A White Heron, and Other Stories* contain much of Jewett's best work in these forms. By now a fully mature artist, she published in 1896 *The Country of the Pointed Firs*, generally regarded as her masterpiece and the finest work of literary regionalism produced by any American writer. Like *Deephaven*, the new book consisted of a sequence of related short narratives unified by setting, characters, and, most powerfully, by the development of the narrator's involvement in the fictional community of Dunnet Landing. An important part of this development is the narrator's relationship with Almira Todd, a native of Dunnet Landing and one of Jewett's greatest triumphs of characterization. Structurally similar to *Deephaven*, *The Country of the Pointed Firs* is, because of its formal control and thematic depth, a much richer work. Writing in 1925, Willa Cather suggested that the work stands with Nathaniel Hawthorne's *The Scarlet Letter* (1850) and Mark Twain's *Adventures of Huckleberry Finn* (1884) as one of the three American literary works of its century likely to achieve immortality.

Jewett would publish only two more books in her lifetime, *The Queen's Twin and Other Stories* in 1899 and *The Tory Lover*, an attempt at a historical novel, in 1901. In 1901, she was awarded an honorary degree by Maine's Bowdoin College, an all-male institution. She was delighted, she said, to be the only sister of so many brothers. Then, in September, 1902, she suffered a severe spinal injury from which she would never fully recover. Writing fiction became increasingly difficult and, finally, impossible. On June 24, 1909, she died in the Jewett family home in South Berwick, Maine.

SIGNIFICANCE

Sarah Orne Jewett was inspired by Plato's maxim that the noblest service that can be done for the people of a state is to acquaint them with one another. The regionalist's literary vocation is precisely to acquaint the people of the larger society—ultimately, perhaps, of the world—with the life of a single region, often one remote from any cosmopolitan center. This vocation was realized by Jewett more fully than by any other American writer. The stature of *The Country of the Pointed Firs* has been recognized since its first publication. Although there is always the danger that this book will dominate Jewett's posthumous reputation to the extent of reducing her to the status of the "one-book author," the last quarter of the twentieth century has seen a resurgence of interest in the totality of her work. This resurgence has in part been fueled by feminist concerns. The fact that Jewett was a woman who wrote most powerfully about women and whose deepest emotional relationships were with women lends her an undeniable interest. However, audience has never been limited to women.

Jewett enjoyed considerable critical recognition in her lifetime. Among the writers who came to be associated with the regionalist movement, she was quickly and widely recognized as preeminent, as was the value of her sort of realism, even if it was a qualified sort. Although she tended to keep the grimmest of realities at the margins of her fiction, she did not expel them completely. For some of her characters, life in the country of the pointed firs follows a pattern of frustration and despair. Certainly, Jewett leaves her readers in little doubt that economic decline is the fundamental condition within which her characters live out their lives.

Jewett was an inspiration to such younger writers as Kate Chopin and Willa Cather, the latter of whom dedicated to Jewett the novel *O Pioneers!* (1913) and in 1925 edited and introduced a collection of Jewett's best fiction. Although Edith Wharton claimed to reject Jewett's influence, many critics who are familiar with both writers find that the truth of the matter is more complicated.

Jewett's stories continue to be published separately and in anthologies. Her work has been translated into German, Japanese, Spanish, and French. Critical interest in Jewett's work has never been higher. Narrow though her range may have been, her work within that range reveals clarity, compassion, and the courage of an artist who developed the forms that her imagination demanded. What Willa Cather said of *The Country of the Pointed Firs* may be said of its author: She confronts time and change securely.

— *W. P. Kenney*

FURTHER READING

Blanchard, Paula. *Sarah Orne Jewett: Her World and Her Work*. Reading, Mass.: Addison-Wesley, 1994. Examines Jewett's life and the circles of writers and friends in which she traveled. Blanchard explains why there has been a resurgence of interest in Jewett's work, and faults some male critics for overlooking and patronizing Jewett's fiction.

Cary, Richard, ed. *Appreciation of Sarah Orne Jewett: Twenty-nine Interpretive Essays*. Waterville, Maine: Colby College Press, 1973. This selection of criticism published prior to 1973 reflects the critical formalism dominant at the time of the book's publication. Supplemented by Nagel's collection.

_____. *Sarah Orne Jewett*. New York: Twayne, 1962. This book, the earliest full critical review of Jewett's work, analyzes her materials, methods, and forms, examining each work in relation to the long maturation of her genius. The organization is, for the most part, topical rather than chronological, and the case for Jewett as more than a one-book author is made convincingly.

Donovan, Josephine. *Sarah Orne Jewett*. New York: Frederick Ungar, 1980. The author explores the themes of city versus country and isolation versus community in Jewett's mature fiction and finds in *The Country of the Pointed Firs* the consummation of her thematic and formal concerns.

Mobley, Marilyn Sanders. *Folk Roots and Mythic Wings in Sarah Orne Jewett and Toni Morrison*. Baton Rouge: Louisiana State University Press, 1991. A critical study that asserts the importance of myth and folklore in the work of two women of different races and generations who draw on the cultural roots of their people.

Morgan, Jeff. *Sarah Orne Jewett's Pastoral Vision: "The Country of the Pointed Firs."* Lewiston, N.Y.: Edwin Mellen Press, 2002. A reassessment of Jewett's best-known novel. Morgan argues that the extra material included in many editions marred the novel's reputation; he maintains the book should be reconsidered as a feminist text and one of the finest novels in nineteenth century American literature.

Nagel, Gwen L. *Critical Essays on Sarah Orne Jewett*. Boston: G. K. Hall, 1984. A collection that supplements Cary's *Appreciation* and reflects later tendencies in Jewett criticism, including feminist perspectives.

Roman, Margaret. *Sarah Orne Jewett: Reconstructing Gender*. Tuscaloosa: University of Alabama Press, 1992. Argues that Jewett consciously collapses gender dichotomies, dissolving binary oppositions of gender.

Sherman, Sarah Way. *Sarah Orne Jewett: An American Persephone*. Hanover, N.H.: University Press of New England, 1989. Explores the growth of Jewett's art out of nineteenth century American culture and the terms in which that culture defined womanhood.

Silverthorne, Elizabeth. *Sarah Orne Jewett: A Writer's Life*. Woodstock, N.Y.: Overlook Press, 1993. This biography emphasizes the relationships between its subject's life and work and places her clearly within the literary and cultural life of her time.

SEE ALSO: Kate Chopin; Nathaniel Hawthorne; Henry James; Harriet Beecher Stowe; Mark Twain.
RELATED ARTICLES in *Great Events from History: The Nineteenth Century, 1801-1900:* 1819-1820: Irving's *Sketch Book* Transforms American Literature; December, 1884-February, 1885: Twain Publishes *Adventures of Huckleberry Finn.*

ANDREW JOHNSON
President of the United States (1865-1869)

A Tennessee politician who rose to the presidency of the United States at the conclusion of the Civil War, Johnson encountered powerful congressional opposition to his lenient Reconstruction policies in the defeated South and was the target of the first impeachment of a U.S. president.

BORN: December 29, 1808; Raleigh, North Carolina
DIED: July 31, 1875; near Carter Station, Tennessee
AREA OF ACHIEVEMENT: Government and politics

EARLY LIFE

Andrew Johnson was the son of Jacob and Mary (Mc-Donough) Johnson, illiterate tavern servants, and he grew up in poverty. In 1822, he was apprenticed to a tailor, under whom he learned a trade and the rudiments of reading. In 1826, he moved to Tennessee, opened a tailor's shop, and, shortly after his nineteenth birthday, married seventeen-year-old Eliza McCardle. Under Eliza's tutelage, Johnson learned writing and arithmetic and practiced his reading. Although never well educated, Johnson always strove for intellectual self-improvement.

Johnson was successful as a tailor but spent most of his spare time involved in debating societies and political discussions. In 1829, Johnson was elected alderman in Greeneville, Tennessee. Two years later, he was elected mayor of the town. He reached the state legislature in 1835, and the U.S. Congress in 1842.

LIFE'S WORK

By 1842, Johnson had permanently abandoned tailoring for the full-time pursuit of politics. He was extremely ambitious and anxious to rise to the top of the political heap.

From 1842 to 1852, Johnson served in Congress with a singularly undistinguished record. His congressional career, which would set a pattern for the remainder of his life, was marked by his inability to compromise, his unwillingness to work with anyone who opposed him, and his use of extremely vicious language against those who disagreed with him. Quick-tempered, ill-mannered, and notorious for his verbal assaults on his enemies, Johnson was popular with poor and nonslaveholding whites. Although not an imposing figure, the five-foot, eight-inch Johnson was physically strong and a vigorous campaigner, who scored points with the "plebeians," as he called them, by attacking the rich. He viewed each electoral success as something more than a personal triumph; for Johnson, a victory at the polls was a victory for the common person over those with education and wealth.

Throughout his political career, Johnson made the most of his humble origins and his status as a tradesman, portraying himself as "the little man," the representative of "the people," against the rich. His class hatred was profound. One contemporary asserted, with some truth, that "if Andy Johnson were a snake, he would hide in the grass and bite the heels of rich men's children." His opponents correctly called him a demagogue, but he was a successful one.

After the Whigs gerrymandered him out of his congressional district, Johnson successfully ran for governor in 1853 and again in 1855. Although his personality and style precluded an effective administration, Johnson was able to push through legislation creating the first public-school system in Tennessee. As governor, the man who grew up illiterate did not forget his roots, even though he had become well-to-do, having acquired a fine house, four slaves, and assets in land and bonds.

In 1852 and 1856, Johnson sought the Democratic nomination for vice president. In 1857, Johnson entered the U.S. Senate, where he accomplished little. He sought a Senate seat as part of his unquenchable thirst for success and political power. He saw the Senate as a way of thrusting him onto the national scene. In 1860, he was the favorite son of Tennessee at the Democratic National Convention, but he again failed to find a spot on the ticket and dutifully supported John C. Breckinridge.

During the secession winter of 1860-1861, Johnson worked for sectional compromise, even though he opposed compromises on principle. At this point, Johnson became a contradictory figure, and something of a heroic one. As a slaveholding Democrat, Johnson staunchly favored states' rights, disliked the Republicans, and was a vicious Negrophobe who especially hated free blacks. However, Johnson also believed, almost religiously, in the Constitution. He considered secession illegal, unconstitutional, and treasonous. Thus, in February, 1861, he successfully rallied Unionists in Tennessee to oppose secession. Johnson continued to oppose secession in the spring, often speaking while armed, in response to death threats. After the firing on Fort Sumter, sentiment shifted, and in June, Tennessee left the Union.

Unlike every other southerner in Congress, Andrew Johnson did not leave the Union. Johnson remained in the Senate, where he successfully sponsored a resolution asserting that the purpose of the war was to preserve the Union and not to end slavery. Consistent with his class analysis, Johnson saw secession as a plot by rich slaveowners to destroy the nation. He told one Union general that he cared nothing for the slaves but that he was "fighting those traitorous artistocrats, their masters."

As the only man from a Confederate state to remain in Congress, Johnson was something of a hero in the North. In 1862, Abraham Lincoln appointed Johnson military governor of Tennessee. This period was Johnson's finest hour. As military governor, he was resolute, firm, and brave, risking his life and property for the Union. He understood the nature of a civil war, and like Ulysses S. Grant and William Tecumseh Sherman, was willing to accept its costs. Thus, when rebel forces surrounded Nashville, Johnson declared that he would burn the city before surrendering it. In 1863, Johnson called a state constitutional convention for the purpose of reconstructing Tennessee's government. While military governor, Johnson reported directly to Lincoln. This experience made Johnson believe in the efficacy of direct presidential control of Reconstruction.

In 1864, Johnson was with Lincoln on a Union Party ticket. As a southern Unionist and a former Democrat, Johnson was seen as a man who could help bind the nation's wounds at the conclusion of the war. After the election, Johnson remained in Tennessee until February, 1865, when he was able to install a legally elected governor under a new Unionist state constitution.

When Johnson took the oath of office in March, he appeared to be drunk and gave a rambling and incoherent speech, glorifying his roots and declaring, "I'm a plebeian!" Although Johnson was not a drunkard and was, at the time of his inauguration, suffering from the aftereffects of typhoid fever, his performance was nevertheless shocking and disgraceful. Lincoln was mortified, Republican senators were humiliated, and few could argue when a Democratic newspaper called Johnson a "drunken clown." A group of senators, led by Charles Sumner, demanded his resignation. Although Lincoln was less harsh, he nevertheless did not meet with his vice president until the afternoon of April 14. Whether that meeting signaled an end to Johnson's isolation from the administration is unknown. By that night, the question was moot. At ten o'clock that evening, Johnson was awakened with the news that President Lincoln had been shot. The next day Johnson became president.

Johnson's presidency was a failure. His relationship with Congress was disastrous. Ultimately, Johnson was impeached by the House, tried by the Senate, and avoided conviction by only one vote. Because a conviction required a two-thirds guilty vote of the Senate, Johnson's acquittal could hardly be considered a vindication; a large majority in Congress believed that he should be removed from office. The impeachment trial was the culmination of conflicts with Congress that were rooted in two intractable problems: the nature of political Reconstruction and the role of African Americans in the post–Civil War South.

Although notorious for his harsh rule as a military governor, Johnson actually favored a mild Reconstruction policy. He was quick to offer pardons for most former Confederates. His amnesty proclamation of May 29, 1865, reinstated political rights for former rebels, except those with taxable property of more than twenty thousand dollars. Johnson believed that the war had been caused by the "aristocrats in the South" and that only they should be punished. However, his proclamation held out hope for the southern elite, because he also promised to grant individual pardons whenever the "peace and dignity" of the nation allowed it. In the next few months, Johnson presided over a steady stream of rich southerners asking for pardons. Johnson made the most of this opportunity to force the "aristocrats" to look up to a "plebeian," reveling in his power but also granting thousands of pardons. Instead of confiscating the property of former slaveowners and giving it to the former slaves, as radicals such as Thaddeus Stevens wished to do, Johnson was busy enfranchising the master class.

While giving much to the former enemies of the nation, Johnson offered little to southern Unionists, especially the former slaves. Johnson was a thoroughgoing racist, even by the benighted standards of the 1860's.

Andrew Johnson. (Library of Congress)

He supported emancipation, in part because it would undermine the power of the planter elite. However, he opposed black suffrage or any government aid to the freedmen. This attitude was made clear in his proclamation re-creating self-government in North Carolina. The proclamation, much to the disappointment of many Republicans, gave the state exclusive power to determine suffrage under the laws of North Carolina before secession: This meant that African Americans could not vote. Johnson's policies indicated that he saw the Civil War as having accomplished nothing more than ending slavery and permanently preserving the Union. Otherwise, Johnson wanted to re-create the Union as it had been before

the war, with a small federal government that could not interfere with states' rights, and no meaningful protections for former slaves.

Throughout 1865 and 1866, Johnson labored to have the southern states readmitted into the Union as quickly as possible and with no requirements that they grant equality to former slaves. When the southern states passed "black codes," severely restricting the movement and rights of free blacks, Johnson expressed only mild disapproval. Similarly, when southerners elected former Confederate officials and generals to Congress, Johnson indicated only slight displeasure and took no action.

Congress, however, did act. In December, meeting for the first time since Lincoln's death, Congress refused to seat representatives from the former Confederate states. Congressional hearings on conditions in the South revealed the continuing oppression of the freedmen by whites and the need for radical changes in the society. In February, 1866, Congress extended the life of the Freedmen's Bureau, a War Department agency, headed by war hero General Oliver Otis Howard, which had been established the previous spring to help black and white people in the wake of the war. The bill passed with the unanimous support of the Republicans in Congress. To the surprise of the Republican majority, Johnson vetoed the bill, arguing that Congress lacked the power or the right to spend money to feed, educate, or find land for freed slaves. In his veto message, Johnson argued that his role as president required him to protect the interests of the South, which was not represented in Congress. Despite feelings of betrayal, Republicans in Congress were not fully united, and the Senate narrowly sustained the veto.

The successful veto of the Freedmen's Bureau Bill led Johnson to believe that he controlled the Republican Party and that he could stop those who sought to enfranchise African Americans, create racial equality in the nation, or reconstruct the South in any meaningful manner. This illusion of power led Johnson to a major blunder. Three days after the Freedmen's Bureau veto, Johnson publicly blamed the war and the assassination of Lincoln on antislavery radicals. He specifically named Senator Charles Sumner, Congressman Thaddeus Stevens, and the abolitionist orator Wendell Phillips, asserting that these men, and other radicals, were traitors to the nation and the equivalent of southern secessionists. This speech undermined support for Johnson in Congress and throughout the nation, support that he would never regain.

Johnson, however, did not fully comprehend the damage done by the Freedmen's Bureau veto and his speech attacking radical Republicans and abolitionists. In another major miscalculation, he vetoed the Civil Rights Act of 1866, even though it was a moderate measure that made the freedmen citizens and guaranteed them "equal protection of the laws." Johnson believed that this law would interfere with states' rights and the ability of the states to regulate social policy. His veto also revealed Johnson's deep-seated racism. For the first time in American history, Congress overrode a presidential veto.

In May and July, whites killed or injured hundreds of African Americans in Memphis and New Orleans. In both cities, indecisive action by federal troops failed to stop the white mobs. Many of the victims of the mob in Memphis were black Union veterans who had been recently mustered out of service. These riots helped convince the North that southerners had not yet accepted African Americans as freedmen, much less equals, and that Johnson was more sympathetic to former rebels than he was to former slaves and Union veterans.

Johnson's support for southern recalcitrance was also clear in his reaction to the Fourteenth Amendment, which Congress sent to the states for ratification in June. Although the president has no right to veto an amendment, Johnson publicly opposed the amendment, which would guarantee African Americans citizenship and other rights and also fundamentally change the nature of the Union. Unlike the overwhelming majority of the Congress, Johnson seemed to be unaware that the Civil War had changed constitutional, racial, and political relations in the nation. By the end of the year, seven former Confederate states, taking their cues from Johnson, rejected the new amendment. Meanwhile, in July, Congress enacted a new Freedmen's Bureau Bill, over Johnson's veto.

In the fall of 1866, Johnson campaigned against Republican candidates for Congress. The result was an overwhelming rejection of Johnson. More than two-thirds of both houses were not only Republicans but also hostile to Johnson and leaning toward the progressive racial policies of Stevens, Sumner, and Senator Ben Wade of Ohio.

MOURNING ABRAHAM LINCOLN

In his first state of the union address, which he delivered only eight months after taking office, Andrew Johnson naturally opened his speech with a tribute to his assassinated predecessor, Abraham Lincoln. In the tradition of state of the union addresses, Johnson does not mention Lincoln by name.

To express gratitude to God in the name of the people for the preservation of the United States is my first duty in addressing you. Our thoughts next revert to the death of the late President by an act of parricidal treason. The grief of the nation is still fresh. It finds some solace in the consideration that he lived to enjoy the highest proof of its confidence by entering on the renewed term of the Chief Magistracy to which he had been elected; that he brought the civil war substantially to a close; that his loss was deplored in all parts of the Union, and that foreign nations have rendered justice to his memory. His removal cast upon me a heavier weight of cares than ever devolved upon any one of his predecessors. To fulfill my trust I need the support and confidence of all who are associated with me in the various departments of Government and the support and confidence of the people. There is but one way in which I can hope to gain their necessary aid. It is to state with frankness the principles which guide my conduct, and their application to the present state of affairs, well aware that the efficiency of my labors will in a great measure depend on your and their undivided approbation.

Source: Andrew Johnson, "State of the Union Address," December 4, 1865.

In January, 1867, Congress overrode Johnson's veto of a bill giving the vote to African Americans living in Washington, D.C. Veto overrides soon became almost commonplace. In the spring, Johnson vetoed the first Reconstruction Act, which gave the vote to black men in the South, excluded former Confederate leaders from office and voting, required new state constitutions in the South, and gave the military the power to enforce these laws. This was Congress's response to the Memphis and New Orleans riots, the black codes, and southern opposition to the Fourteenth Amendment. By an overwhelming vote, Congress overrode this veto. Johnson then vetoed Nebraska's statehood because, among other reasons, the state's constitution allowed black men to vote. Congress again overrode the veto. Congress also changed its meeting time from December to March, so that it could be in almost continuous session to watch over Johnson's activities.

In March, Congress specifically provided that all military orders from the president had to go through General Grant, and that Grant could not be assigned to a post outside Washington against his will. This law indicated that Congress placed more faith in the war hero Grant than in the president. This provision was part of a larger appropriations bill, which Johnson signed, despite his distaste for the provisions concerning Grant. Johnson then vetoed the Tenure of Office Act, but Congress overrode the veto. This law, which prevented Johnson from removing any cabinet officers without the permission of Congress, reflected congressional fear that Johnson would remove Secretary of War Edwin M. Stanton, who was sympathetic to congressional goals.

In March, 1867, Congress overrode Johnson's veto of the Second Reconstruction Act. Meanwhile, the House investigated whether Johnson ought to be impeached. On June 3, the House investigating committee adjourned, with four members in favor of impeachment and five against. In July, Congress overrode Johnson's veto of the Third Reconstruction Act.

In May, Johnson interpreted the Reconstruction Acts in a narrow fashion, to allow most former Confederates to vote and ordered all generals to act accordingly. Both Secretary of War Stanton and General Grant opposed this interpretation. When General Philip Sheridan, headquartered in New Orleans, asked Grant if he should obey Johnson's order, Grant replied that it was not a legal order, because it had not come from him, as specified in the legislation of March, 1867. When forced to choose, Grant chose to follow the laws of Congress and not the whims of President Johnson. The army followed Grant. It was not unlikely that in a confrontation, the people would follow the hero of Appomattox rather than an unelected president of doubtful abilities.

In July, 1867, Johnson attempted to remove Sheridan from his position as military commander of Texas and Louisiana and to remove Stanton from the cabinet. Sheridan had followed congressional intent in the Southwest by removing former Confederates from office, in opposition to Johnson's policies. Stanton was, by this time, openly in sympathy with Congress and thus openly hostile to Johnson. Johnson asked Grant to take Stanton's place. At first, Grant refused but then accepted an interim appointment, pending the return of Congress from its summer recess. Under the Tenure of Office Act, Stanton could not be removed until Congress returned to session and gave its approval.

Following the removal of Sheridan, Johnson also removed other generals who were sympathetic to Congress. In September, 1867, Johnson exacerbated the situation by issuing a pardon for all but a few hundred former Confederate politicians and generals. The pardons, and the removal of Sheridan and other generals, led to new calls for impeachment. In November, the House Judiciary Committee voted five to four in favor of impeach-

ment, but the entire Congress rejected this recommendation.

On January 13, 1868, the Senate, acting under the Tenure of Office Act, refused to concur in the removal of Stanton as secretary of war. General Grant immediately turned the keys to the office over to Stanton and then reported to Johnson that he was no longer secretary of war. In the days that followed, Johnson accused Grant of betraying him and of being a liar. Public opinion sided with the general, not with Johnson.

On February 21, Johnson, ignoring the recommendations of most of his confidential advisers, attempted to replace Stanton with Lorenzo Thomas, a lackluster general. Stanton, however, refused to give up his office or even, physically, to leave the War Department. The next day, the House of Representatives voted overwhelmingly to send a resolution for the impeachment of Johnson to the Committee on Reconstruction, chaired by the radical congressman Thaddeus Stevens.

On February 24, the House, by an overwhelming vote, approved a resolution of impeachment. The next day, Congressman Thaddeus Stevens, a radical, and John Bingham, a moderate, entered the Senate, where they informed that body that Johnson had been impeached and that specific articles of impeachment would be forthcoming. On March 2, the House adopted nine separate articles of impeachment. On March 12, the Congress passed, over Johnson's veto, the Fourth Reconstruction Act.

On March 13, the trial of Andrew Johnson began before the Senate, presided over by Chief Justice Salmon P. Chase. Postponements delayed the proceedings until March 30. Then, for more than a month, the Senate heard evidence and arguments on the constitutionality of the Tenure of Office Act and the legal requirements for impeachment. Finally, on May 19, the Senate voted thirty-five to nineteen in favor of conviction on one of the articles of impeachment. The same vote prevailed, on May 26, for the other articles. This was one vote short of the two-thirds majority needed to remove Johnson from office. A coalition of Democrats and conservative Republicans saved Johnson by the thinnest possible margin. Later that day, Stanton resigned his office.

Johnson served out the remainder of his term with a continuation of his lackluster style and predictable veto overrides. Despite his opposition, the Fourteenth Amendment was ratified while Johnson held office. The only thing on which Johnson and Congress seemed to agree was the appropriation of funds to purchase Alaska, which came in 1868, more than a year after the treaty with Russia had been approved.

Johnson sought the presidency in 1868, but neither party would have him. He retired to Tennessee, and in 1875, he was again elected to the Senate. Four months after taking office, he died of a stroke.

SIGNIFICANCE

Historians and scholars have long debated whether Johnson should have been removed from office. The question often turns on a point of law. If impeachment is strictly for an illegal act, then perhaps Johnson was innocent, because it is generally agreed that the law he violated—the Tenure of Office Act—was itself unconstitutional. On the other hand, no court had yet declared the law unconstitutional, and until the Supreme Court makes a final determination, Congress has the right to determine constitutionality on its own. If impeachment is essentially a political process, then the grounds for Johnson's removal are stronger. He was an accidental president, out of step with the nation and lacking the support of either political party. He had consistently thwarted the will of Congress and the American people. His racist response to black freedom mocked the consequences of the Civil War and certainly prevented African Americans from attaining equality and justice in its aftermath.

Whatever their opinion on how the impeachment trial should have ended, almost all observers agree that Johnson's presidency was a total failure. Few presidents were so ill-equipped to handle the job. Arrogant, mistrustful of anyone with an education, insecure, unwilling to compromise, pigheaded in his ideas, and a racist, Johnson left a legacy in the White House that took years to reverse; he left a legacy for black Americans that has still not been completely overcome.

—*Paul Finkelman*

FURTHER READING

Benedict, Michael Les. *The Impeachment and Trial of Andrew Johnson*. New York: W. W. Norton, 1973. An older and exceptionally good study of the impeachment. Concludes, with much supporting evidence, that the impeachment was justified and conviction would have been proper. Available in paperback.

Castell, Albert E. *The Presidency of Andrew Johnson*. Lawrence: Regents Press of Kansas, 1979. A balanced and judicious study of Johnson's presidency.

Franklin, John Hope. *Reconstruction: After the Civil War*. Chicago: University of Chicago Press, 1961. Short, easily read introduction to the era of Reconstruction by one of the nation's most important scholars. Available in paperback.

Hearn, Chester G. *The Impeachment of Andrew Johnson*. Jefferson, N.C.: McFarland, 2000. One of several books about Johnson's impeachment that were written after Congress initiated impeachment proceedings against President Bill Clinton. Hearn focuses on the political turmoil after the Civil War that led to Johnson's impeachment; he argues Johnson was impeached because "he attempted to prevent Congress from using executive authority and overriding the Constitution."

Litwack, Leon. *Been in the Storm So Long*. New York: Alfred A. Knopf, 1979. Pulitzer Prize-winning history of African Americans during the early part of Reconstruction, when Johnson was president. Although not about Johnson, this book demonstrates the tragedy of Johnson's policies toward the former slaves. Wonderfully written and superbly documented, this book shows what Reconstruction was like from the perspective of the freedmen.

McKitrick, Eric L., ed. *Andrew Johnson: A Profile*. New York: Hill & Wang, 1969. Contains ten essays by nine different historians, with each essay focusing on a different aspect of Johnson's career. Some of the essays are dated in their interpretation, but others, particularly those on his prepresidential career, hold up well. Includes a short biography of Johnson.

Sefton, James E. *Andrew Johnson and the Uses of Constitutional Power*. Boston: Little, Brown, 1980. An excellent short biography. Balanced, with modern interpretations. Probably the best comprehensive coverage of Johnson's life available.

Simpson, Brooks D. *The Reconstruction Presidents*. Lawrence: University Press of Kansas, 1998. Examines and compares the presidencies of Johnson, Abraham Lincoln, Ulysses S. Grant, and Rutherford B. Hayes. Simpson concludes that Johnson was an inflexible president, unable to overcome his racism and hatred.

Trefousse, Hans Louis. *Andrew Johnson: A Biography*. New York: W. W. Norton, 1989. An assessment of Johnson's career and presidency. Trefousse maintains that Johnson's upbringing made him unable to adapt to societal changes and new political realities after the Civil War.

_____. *Impeachment of a President: Andrew Johnson, the Blacks, and Reconstruction*. New York: Fordham University Press, 1999. Focuses on the reasons why the Congress was unable to convict Johnson, the consequences of this acquittal, and the relationship of impeachment to the failure of Reconstruction. Trefousse argues that Johnson knowingly risked impeachment so he could thwart Reconstruction and maintain white supremacy in the South.

SEE ALSO: Salmon P. Chase; Ulysses S. Grant; Rutherford B. Hayes; Abraham Lincoln; Wendell Phillips; William H. Seward; William Tecumseh Sherman; Edwin M. Stanton; Thaddeus Stevens; Charles Sumner.

RELATED ARTICLES in *Great Events from History: The Nineteenth Century, 1801-1900:* December 8, 1863-April 24, 1877: Reconstruction of the South; March 3,

1865: Congress Creates the Freedmen's Bureau; November 24, 1865: Mississippi Enacts First Post-Civil War Black Code; December 6, 1865: Thirteenth Amendment Is Ratified; April 9, 1866: Civil Rights Act of 1866; March 2, 1867: U.S. Department of Education Is Created; March 30, 1867: Russia Sells Alaska to the United States; February 24-May 26, 1868: Impeachment of Andrew Johnson; July 9, 1868: Fourteenth Amendment Is Ratified; December, 1869: Wyoming Gives Women the Vote.

SCOTT JOPLIN
American composer

Despite his humble origins and the burdens of racial prejudice and cultural barriers, Joplin became an admired piano player and composer of ragtime music that earned him the nickname of "King of Ragtime." His most famous composition, "Maple Leaf Rag," was the first song to sell one million copies of sheet music in the United States.

BORN: November 24, 1868; Bowie County, near Texarkana, Texas
DIED: April 1, 1917; New York, New York
AREA OF ACHIEVEMENT: Music

EARLY LIFE

Scott Joplin was one of six children of Giles and Florence Givens Joplin. Although they were a poor black family, music was an important part of their lives. Giles, a railroad worker and former slave, played the violin, and young Scott heard from him the waltzes, polkas, reels, and folk music that Giles had played for his former masters on the plantation. Scott's freeborn mother sang and played the banjo, while his brother Will played guitar and violin and another brother, Robert, sang baritone.

At the age of seven Joplin began showing an interest in the piano. Florence worked as a servant for several white families in Texarkana, and while she cleaned, Joplin played their pianos. Eventually, the family put together enough money to buy a used piano for him to play at home. By age eleven he was writing and playing his own music, and his talent was well known in the community. Several local residents took an interest in his musical talent and gave him free lessons. The most influential of these people was a German music teacher, fondly remembered, who taught Joplin technique, sight reading, and harmony and gave him the opportunity to learn classical and popular European music.

Joplin argued frequently with his father about finding a steady job or trade, and after the death of his mother, the teenager left Texarkana to make his living in music. He worked as an itinerant musician in brothels, saloons, gambling halls, and traveling shows in towns and cities from Texas to the Mississippi River. He heard a variety of music played by musicians and singers, including a syncopated "ragged" style of music later known as "ragtime." Arriving in St. Louis in 1885, he socialized with other piano players at John Turpin's Silver Dollar Saloon. Joplin found steady work as a piano player and entertainer in a variety of St. Louis establishments and in other surrounding towns and cities.

In 1893, like many other African American piano players, Joplin sought a job at the World's Columbian Exposition in Chicago but found most of his work in the red-light district of the city. It was here that many people from around the nation were first exposed to ragtime music. Joplin then met a young piano player, Otis Saunders, who became a close friend and would be an important adviser during his future career. When the exposition closed, Joplin and Saunders returned to St. Louis; in 1894 they moved to Sedalia, Missouri.

LIFE'S WORK

Sedalia greatly influenced Joplin's career, and it was here that he began to compose and sell his piano compositions. He joined the locally popular Queen City Concert Band and attended the Smith School of Music at the George R. Smith College for Negroes, where he learned fundamentals of harmony and composition. In 1895 he returned to St. Louis and began spending time at Turpin's ragtime headquarters, the Rosbud Cafe. Turpin, credited with the first published black American rag, "Harlem Rag" (1897), became an inspiration and friend to Joplin.

Upon his return to Sedalia, Joplin formed a vocalizing harmony group, the Texas Medley Quartette. His brothers Will and Robert were singers in the group, while Joplin sang and played the piano. They performed a variety of folk and popular songs as well as Joplin's new music. They became so popular in Sedalia and the surrounding area that they decided to join a vaudeville tour and traveled as far as Syracuse, New York, where Joplin found publishers for two of his Victorian parlor songs, "A Picture of Her Face" (1895) and "Please Say You Will" (1895). He also composed marches and waltzes, although none of these were in the ragtime style that would later make him famous.

A second tour ended in Joplin, Missouri, and the group disbanded. Joplin returned to Sedalia in 1897 to play in various bars, bordellos, and social clubs, especially the Maple Leaf Club, which as owned by Tony Williams. Acquaintances knew Joplin as a polite, quiet, and well-spoken man who wanted to be respected as a serious composer. He often received support and encouragement from the white community and businesspeople.

Joplin continued to compose music in Sedalia. He sold his first ragtime composition, "Original Rag" (1899), to publisher Carl Hoffman of Kansas City, Kansas, after a Sedalia publisher, A. W. Perry and Son, rejected it. After rejections by another publisher, Hoffman and Perry and Son, Joplin sold his second and most important ragtime composition, "Maple Leaf Rag" (1899), to John Stark and Son of Sedalia for fifty dollars and a one-cent royalty. The composition was an immediate success and quickly sold thousands of copies. Ragtime music was already popular, but the "Maple Leaf Rag" became the standard for the genre. With the royalties he earned, Joplin could now afford to stop playing the piano for a living and concentrate on composing and teaching. "Maple Leaf Rag" also made John Stark a leading publisher in ragtime music. He moved his music store to St. Louis and made music publishing his full-time business.

In 1900 Joplin and his new bride, Belle Hayden, also moved to St. Louis. Stark and Son published "Peacherine Rag" (1901), "The Easy Winner" (1901), "A Breeze From Alabama" (1902), and "The Entertainer" (1902). The Louisiana Purchase Exposition in St. Louis inspired Joplin to write a musical tribute to it called "The Cascades" (1904). During his career Joplin would use various other publishers for his many rags, waltzes, songs, and an instruction book, *School of Ragtime* (1908). He occasionally visited the old St. Louis clubs and saloons to stay in contact with fellow ragtime friends and composers such as Turpin, Louis Chauvin, and Sam Patterson. He also played the "Maple Leaf Rag" and other songs on request.

Two of Joplin's young Sedalia protégés were Arthur Marshall and Scott Hayden. Joplin's music influenced both of them, and they collaborated on several musical compositions. Joplin and Hayden produced "Sunflower Slow Drag" (1901), "Something Doing" (1911), "Felicity Rag" (1911), and "Kismet Rag" (1913). Joplin and Marshall collaborated on two compositions: "Swipsey Cake Walk" (1900) and "Lily Queen—A Ragtime Two-Step" (1907). Joplin continued to influence and help other composers of ragtime music, such as James Scott and Joseph Lamb, throughout his career.

In St. Louis, Joplin concentrated on his desire to compose serious classical music. He wrote *Ragtime Dance* (1902), a nine-page, twenty-minute folk ballet with dancers and singers, which Stark reluctantly published. Popular as a production in Sedalia, it was a failure as sheet music. Joplin then decided to compose a ragtime opera, *A Guest of Honor* (1903). It was performed once in a St. Louis rehearsal, but Joplin was unsuccessful in finding a backer or publisher for the opera, including Stark. Meanwhile, Joplin's personal life was not a success either. His wife was not interested in his musical career. After the death of their infant girl, Belle and Joplin separated; she died two years later.

Depressed and discouraged, Joplin moved to Chicago in 1906. He stayed a short time with his friend Marshall, but he wanted to move to New York City. Stark had already opened a new publishing store there in 1905 to compete with the Tin Pan Alley music firms. Joplin finally moved to New York in 1907, and from this base he traveled with vaudeville tours to supplement his income. In 1909 he married Lottie Stokes, a woman who was interested in and supportive of his career. They opened a boarding house, and Joplin continued composing and teaching violin and piano.

Despite his first failures to succeed as a more serious classical composer, Joplin began a three-act opera, *Treemonisha* (1911), that drew from his experiences growing up on the Texas-Arkansas state border during Reconstruction. Its theme dealt with African American society, superstitions, and the necessity of education to better their lives. Joplin became obsessed with this work, spending much of his time and income on it. Unable to find a publisher for *Treemonisha*, Joplin copyrighted and published it himself. He even financed a 1915 rehearsal in front of a select audience in Harlem's Lincoln Theater. Without scenery or costumes and with only Joplin playing the piano, the performance was a failure. *Treemonisha*'s rejection devastated him.

Although Joplin wrote many new compositions in New York, his health was deteriorating from the advanced stages of syphilis he had contracted earlier in life. He suffered from mood swings and an inability to concentrate. He even had difficulty playing the piano and speaking coherently. Finally, in the fall of 1916, Lottie admitted him to the Manhattan State Hospital on Ward's Island in the East River where he died on April 1, 1917, from dementia paralytica-cerebra. Lottie buried him in St. Michael's Cemetery on Long Island.

SIGNIFICANCE

Ragtime was the first distinctive American music. Although the height of its popularity lasted for only a short period, from 1896 to 1917, it was a forerunner and influence on other music, especially jazz. It came from the African music, plantation melodies, and folk songs played on banjos and fiddles. It offered exciting, bouncy, and infectious syncopations. Ragtime was not considered respectable by white and black middle- and upper-class society because musicians originally played it in the saloons, bordellos, and sporting clubs of the red-light districts. Despite its disreputable beginning, it eventually became popular and was played by bands and orchestras, in theaters, and on parlor pianos of respectable homes.

Scott Joplin is credited with shaping this new music and influencing other composers and imitators with his sophisticated and classical style. John Stark termed Joplin's music "classic rag" to sell it as the best type of ragtime music. It combined black folk music and rhythms with nineteenth century European classical music. Joplin raised ragtime from improvised entertainment to his own smooth style of published music. He was serious and less flashy than many of his contemporaries and encouraged his students and performers not to hurry the tempo of his compositions.

Joplin wrote sixty-six published compositions and two operas. Many other unpublished works were lost in the years following Lottie Joplin's death. When Scott Joplin died, Stark wrote a brief obituary that stated, "Scott Joplin is dead. A homeless itinerant, he left his mark on American music."

—*Vivian L. Richardson*

FURTHER READING

Berlin, Edward A. *King of Ragtime: Scott Joplin and His Era*. New York: Oxford University Press, 1994. A comprehensive biography with attention to Joplin's music. Examines new information from archives and newspapers. Contains photographs, illustrations, alphabetical and chronological listings of Joplin's works, extensive notes, and bibliography.

Blesh, Rudi, and Harriet Janis. *They All Played Ragtime*. New York: Oak, 1971. A history of ragtime music and a study of its composers and players. Uses extensive personal interviews and correspondence and includes illustrations, photographs, complete musical scores, and lists of ragtime compositions.

Curtis, Susan. *Dancing to a Black Man's Tune: A Life of Scott Joplin*. Columbia: University of Missouri Press, 1994. Scholarly biography with an interpretation of the communities and societies of Joplin's era. Contains extensive chapter notes and a bibliography.

Gammond, Peter. *Scott Joplin and the Ragtime Era*. New York: St. Martin's Press, 1975. A scholastic and historical look at ragtime and Joplin's works. Contains illustrations and photographs.

Jasen, David A., and Trebor Jay Tichenor. *Rags and Ragtime: A Musical History*. New York: Seabury Press, 1978. A history of ragtime and a description of the major ragtime composers and their pieces. Contains illustrations and photographs.

Waldo, Terry. *This Is Ragtime*. New York: Hawthorn Books, 1976. A history of ragtime music. Includes illustrations, photographs, bibliography, and a select discography.

SEE ALSO: Paul Laurence Dunbar.

RELATED ARTICLE in *Great Events from History: The Nineteenth Century, 1801-1900:* February 6, 1843: First Minstrel Shows.

CHIEF JOSEPH
Native American leader

The leader of his people in the Nez Perce War of 1877, Chief Joseph attempted to retain for his people the freedoms enjoyed prior to white American interest in their lands. Although he ultimately failed to preserve his people's independence, he became an enduring symbol of the fortitude and resilience of Native Americans.

BORN: c. 1840; Lapwai Preserve, Wallowa Valley, northeastern Oregon

DIED: September 21, 1904; Colville Indian Reservation, Washington

ALSO KNOWN AS: Joseph the Younger; Heinmot Tooyalakekt (birth name)

AREA OF ACHIEVEMENT: Government and politics

EARLY LIFE

Chief Joseph (Heinmot Tooyalakekt in his native tongue, which translates as Thunder-Rolling-in-the-Mountains) was born to Old Joseph (Tuekakas) and Asenoth. His exact birthdate is unknown, but he was baptized Ephraim on April 12, 1840, by the Reverend Mr. Henry H. Spalding, who maintained a Presbyterian mission at Lapwai in the heart of Nez Perce country. This area, which comprises parts of Idaho, Oregon, and Washington, contains some of the most desirable land in the United States. As such, white Americans desired the land upon which the Nez Perce and other bands of Indians lived.

In 1855, the U.S. government greatly reduced the holdings of all tribes and bands in the northwestern United States in a series of treaties at the Council of Walla Walla, called by the governor of the Washington Territory, Isaac Stevens. In those treaties, the Neemeepoo (meaning the people) or Nez Perce (pronounced nez purse) agreed to what amounted to a 50 percent reduction of their territory. The Nez Perce were able to keep this much of their land because the whites were not yet interested in the wild and remote country of west-central Idaho and northwestern Oregon. The Nez Perce had been exposed to Christianity as early as 1820. The existence of Christian names indicates that many practiced that religion. Chief Joseph was, or was generally believed to have been, baptized and named Ephraim. It would fall to him, a kind and gentle man, to deal with the problems—initially encroachment and then expropriation—which threatened the lands of his fathers.

The troubles of the Nez Perce began in 1861, when gold in quantity was discovered along the Orofino Creek,

a tributary of the Clearwater. Old Joseph attempted to keep the prospectors from the land but finally accepted the inevitable and sought to supervise rather than prohibit the activity. This plan failed. Once the area had been opened, many whites entered. In violation of the agreements, and of the treaties of 1855, which prohibited such white encroachments, some whites turned to farming.

The results were surprising. The government, rather than forcing the whites to leave, proposed an additional reduction of the Nez Perce lands. The federal government indicated that as much as 75 percent of the holdings should be made available for white settlement. Old Joseph refused; his refusal apparently split the Nez Perce peoples. Some of them agreed to the reduction. Aleiya, called Lawyer by the whites, signed the agreement that the Joseph faction of the Nez Perce would refer to as the thief treaty. Hereafter, the Nez Perce were divided into the treaty and nontreaty bands. Old Joseph refused to leave the Wallowa Valley, where his nontreaty Nez Perce bred and raised the Appaloosa horse.

Old Joseph died in 1871, and, at his parting, he reminded his eldest son, Heinmot Tooyalakekt, or Young Joseph,

> always remember that your father never sold his country. You must stop your ears whenever you are asked to sign a treaty selling your home. . . . This country holds your father's bones. Never sell the bones of your father and your mother.

Chief Joseph was as adamant in his refusal to sell or part with the land as had been his father, but he realized the power and inconstancy of the U.S. government. In 1873, President Ulysses S. Grant issued an executive order dividing the area that the whites were settling between the whites and the Nez Perce. In 1875, however, Grant opened the entire region to white settlement. In 1876, he sent a commission to see Chief Joseph. The decision had been made to offer Joseph's band of nontreaty Nez Perce land in the Oklahoma Indian Territory for all of their Idaho holdings.

What transpired as a result of this decision has been termed by Jacob P. Dunn, Jr., in *Massacres in the Mountains* (1886), "the meanest, most contemptible, least justifiable thing that the United States was ever guilty of. . . ." Chief Joseph refused the offer to move to Oklahoma. General Oliver Otis Howard arrived with orders to enforce the presidential decision. General Howard proposed a swift compliance with those orders. Joseph realized that his Nez Perce could not long stand against a government and an army determined to take their land and move them. Accordingly, a council of chiefs, including Joseph's younger brother Ollokot (a fine warrior), White Bird, Looking Glass, and the Wallowa prophet, Toohoolhoolzote, reached the decision to go to Canada rather than to Oklahoma. General Howard, however, declared that "the soldiers will be there to drive you onto the reservation. . . ."

LIFE'S WORK

The Nez Perce War of 1877 is misnamed. It would be more appropriate to label it a chase. It is the story of Chief Joseph's attempt to lead his people to the safety of Canada, where the geography and the climate were more similar to the traditional lands than were those of Oklahoma. The United States Army, under orders to deliver the Nez Perce to the Indian Territory, would pursue Chief Joseph's band during the 111-day war/chase that

Chief Joseph. (Library of Congress)

eventually found Joseph winding over fourteen hundred miles through the mountains. His attempt to elude the military would fail because of nineteenth century technology rather than his lack of ability.

Hostilities began when a member of White Bird's band of Nez Perce, Wahlitits, wanting to avenge the death of his father at the hands of white men, and two other youths, killed four white men. Apparently, some whites were of the opinion that only a war would guarantee the removal of the Nez Perce from the land, and some of them had been trying for some time to provoke that war. The men killed by Wahlitits had been the first white men killed by Nez Perce in a generation.

Joseph's reaction to the killings was one of regret and the realization that only flight would preserve his people. General Howard's reaction was to move immediately not only against White Bird's people but also against all the nontreaty Nez Perce. The initial engagement on June 17, 1877, was between two troops of the First Cavalry (about ninety men) under Captains David Perry and Joel Trimble. The cavalry was accompanied by eleven civilian volunteers. One of those civilian volunteers fired at the Nez Perce truce team. This action led to a short, unplanned, disorganized fight during which the Nez Perce, under Ollokot, killed thirty-four cavalry. (Important also was the capture of sixty-three rifles and many pistols.)

This initial defeat led Howard, fearing a general uprising of all Nez Perce—treaty and nontreaty alike—to call for reinforcements. Troops from all over the United States were quickly dispatched, including an infantry unit from Atlanta, Georgia, to the Washington Territory. Joseph's strategy was to seek protection from the Bitterroot Mountain range, where traditional cavalry tactics would be neutralized. Leading his approximately five hundred women and children and 250 warriors, he moved over the Lolo Trail, crossed the Bitterroots, and then, hoping to avoid detection, moved southward to the vicinity of the Yellowstone National Park, which he crossed in August, 1877. Joseph then swung northward into present-day Montana, hoping to reach Canada undetected. Seeking the security of the Bearpaw Mountains, Joseph moved his people as quickly as the women and young could travel. They were not quick enough: The Bearpaws would be the location of the final encounter with the military.

Joseph was not a military strategist; Ollokot was. Joseph urged that they try to reach Canada. Ollokot, Toohoolhoolzote, Looking Glass, and other chiefs preferred to fight. Battles had been joined several times

---

"I WILL FIGHT NO MORE FOREVER"

When Chief Joseph finally surrendered his people to the U.S. Army, he sent this message to the army commander, General Oliver Otis Howard:

Tell General Howard I know his heart. What he told me before I have in my heart. I am tired of fighting. Our chiefs are killed. Looking Glass is dead. Toohoolhoolzote is dead. The old men are all dead. It is the young men who say yes or no. He who led the young men [Ollokot] is dead. It is cold and we have no blankets. The little children are freezing to death. My people, some of them, have run away into the hills, and have no blankets, no food; no one knows where they are—perhaps freezing to death. I want time to look for my children and see how many I can find. Maybe I shall find them among the dead. Hear me, my chiefs. I am tired; my heart is sick and sad. From where the sun now stands I will fight no more forever.

---

along the route. At the Clearwater (July 11), at Big Hole (August 9-10), at Camas Meadows (August 16), at Canyon Creek (September 13), and at Cows Creek (September 23), sharp engagements were fought. Each resulted in Joseph's band eluding capture but with irreplaceable losses. The military, meanwhile, was receiving reinforcements in large numbers. Especially important was the arrival of Colonel Nelson Miles with nearly six hundred men, including elements of the Second and Seventh cavalries.

About thirty miles from the Canadian border, the Nez Perce halted, believing that they had succeeded in eluding the army and had the time to rest. Joseph was wrong: The telegraph and the railroad had outflanked him. Colonel Miles caught the Nez Perce unprepared on September 30, on the rolling plains of the Bearpaw Mountains. Joseph's band, hopelessly outnumbered, held out until October 4. After a hastily convened, makeshift council, Joseph decided to surrender. On October 5, he rode to the headquarters of Miles and General Howard, who had arrived in force the day before, and handed his rifle to Howard, who, in turn, passed it to Colonel Miles—still in command of the operation.

Joseph's surrender was apparently based upon an assumption that his people could return to the Lapwai. This was not to be. The Nez Perce were loaded onto boxcars and transported to the Oklahoma Indian Territory. In this new climate and country, many of the remaining Nez Perce died. Joseph repeatedly begged for permission to return to the northwestern hunting grounds. Partial success came in 1885, when Joseph was allowed to return with his people to the Colville Reservation in Washington. Thereafter, every attempt on Joseph's part to effect a re-

turn to the Lapwai was unsuccessful. Joseph died on September 21, 1904, on the Colville Indian Reservation.

SIGNIFICANCE

Chief Joseph of the Nez Perce was a dignified leader of his people. A man who loved the land of his ancestors, he attempted to retain it. His defiance of the U.S. government was a gallant, almost successful, effort. His failure marked the end of the wars of the Northwest and was the last important Indian resistance except for the Battle at Wounded Knee Creek. The removal of the Nez Perce to reservations marked the end of freedom as the American Indians had known it. As Joseph said, "you might as well expect the rivers to run backward as that any man who was born free should be content when penned up and denied liberty."

—Richard J. Amundson

FURTHER READING

Allard, William Albert. "Chief Joseph." *National Geographic* 151 (March, 1977): 408-434. A well-illustrated, concise, balanced, readily available source.

Andrist, Ralph K. *The Long Death: The Last Days of the Plains Indians.* New York: Macmillan, 1964. Includes a well-written, sympathetic chapter on the Nez Perce. Especially valuable for detailing the reasons for the decision to go to Canada.

Beal, Merrill D. *"I Will Fight No More Forever": Chief Joseph and the Nez Perce War.* Seattle: University of Washington Press, 1963. A carefully written, well-illustrated account that gives special attention to the hostilities.

Brown, Dee. *Bury My Heart at Wounded Knee: An Indian History of the American West.* New York: Holt, Rinehart and Winston, 1970. A classic study of white-Indian relationships that must be read by the serious student. It contains an excellent account of Chief Joseph and his attempted flight to Canada. White motivation in the contest is perhaps overstated.

Chalmers, Harvey, II. *The Last Stand of the Nez Perce: Destruction of a People.* New York: Twayne, 1962. Contains a valuable glossary of characters and a balanced account of the hostilities.

Dunn, Jacob P., Jr. *Massacres of the Mountains: A History of the Indian Wars of the Far West.* New York:

Harper & Brothers, 1886. A chapter devoted to what Dunn argues was an injustice committed by the U.S. government. Many later sources rely upon his analysis.

Josephy, Alvin M., Jr. *The Patriot Chiefs: A Chronicle of American Indian Leadership*. Harmondsworth, England: Penguin Books, 1958. One of the few sources that deals with Chief Joseph as an individual. The account of the war is excellent.

Miles, Nelson A. *Personal Recollections and Observances*. Chicago: Werner, 1896. The final days of the Nez Perce recounted by the officer in the field commanding the United States military. Unsympathetic toward Joseph's motivation.

Moeller, Bill, and Jan Moeller. *Chief Joseph and the Nez Perces: A Photographic History*. Missoula, Mont.: Mountain Press, 1995. Color photos and text depict the places in Idaho and Montana where the Nez Perce

Indians camped, followed trials, and sought refuge from government troops between June and October, 1877.

Moulton, Candy. *American Heroes: Chief Joseph, Guardian of the People*. New York: Forge Books, 2005. Well-documented biography, recounting Chief Joseph's attempt to lead his people to safety in Canada and his subsequent diplomatic initiatives to regain his people's homeland.

Park, Edwards. "Big Hole: Still a Gaping Wound to the Nez Perce." *Smithsonian* 9 (May, 1978): 92-99. Deals with a serious setback during the great chase of 1877.

SEE ALSO: Crazy Horse; Geronimo; Ulysses S. Grant; Sitting Bull.

RELATED ARTICLE in *Great Events from History: The Nineteenth Century, 1801-1900:* June 15-October 5, 1877: Nez Perce War.

JOSÉPHINE
First wife of French emperor Napoleon I

Joséphine's life exemplified the chaos and unpredictability of the French Revolution and subsequent warfare. She was popularly loved as "the good Joséphine," and her social talents assisted Napoleon Bonaparte in creating stability and reconciliation among the various factions dividing the citizens of France.

BORN: June 23, 1763; Trois-Îlets, Martinique
DIED: May 29, 1814; Malmaison, France
ALSO KNOWN AS: Joséphine Bonaparte; Viscountess de Beauharnais; Marie-Joséphe-Rose Tascher de la Pagerie (birth name); Joséphine de Beauharnais
AREA OF ACHIEVEMENT: Government and politics

EARLY LIFE

Joséphine was born Marie-Joséphe-Rose Tascher de la Pagerie on the French Caribbean island of Martinique. She descended from the middle ranks of the French nobility who had emigrated to the colonies to make their fortunes growing sugar and was therefore Creole (born overseas but of French ancestry). Everyone called her Marie-Rose until she met Napoleon Bonaparte, who preferred "Joséphine." She attended a local convent school for four years during a privileged childhood. When she was sixteen, her family arranged her marriage to a

wealthy and well-educated Frenchman named Viscount Alexandre de Beauharnais. In France she entered a sophisticated world where her lack of formal education disappointed her husband. The birth of their son Eugene (1781) and daughter Hortense (1783) did nothing to draw the couple together.

Soon the viscount demanded his freedom by falsely accusing Joséphine of infidelity and ordering her out of his house. She took refuge in a convent and complained to legal officials about his unreasonable behavior. The courts ordained a permanent separation and ordered Alexandre to pay modest alimony and child support. The separation left Marie-Rose in a precarious position in a society in which unattached women suffered serious disabilities: She had two preschool children, a small income, and no home. She had neither great beauty nor accomplishments; her one gift was charm, an aura of empathy and graciousness that won her loyal friends and sexual admirers. To support herself and her children, she became a woman of society, holding a salon where people of all political and social ranks fell under her spell and rendered her financial assistance.

LIFE'S WORK

The momentous events of the French Revolution engulfed and transformed Joséphine's life. Early in the

Revolution, her estranged husband rose to political prominence by advocating moderate reforms. When war broke out in 1792, Alexandre commanded French forces along the Rhine and suffered serious defeats. Austrians and Prussians dedicated to restoring the Bourbons invaded France. The republican revolutionists organized the nation for victory and wielded the Reign of Terror against domestic opponents. Some radicals charged that General Beauharnais's military failures suggested treason; they arrested and imprisoned him and his wife from April to August, 1794. Alexandre was guillotined on fabricated charges and Joséphine, fearing imminent death, became emotionally unstable. She survived because moderate revolutionaries, the Thermidorians, overthrew the Terrorists and established a new government comprising a five-man executive called the Directory. Joséphine became the mistress of Director Paul Barras and indulged in the atmosphere of dissolution that followed the Reign of Terror.

In 1795 the widowed Joséphine met the man who dominated the remainder of her life, a twenty-six-year-old revolutionary general named Napoleon Bonaparte. He fell passionately in love with Joséphine and proposed marriage. She hesitated to make this commitment but agreed after learning that Napoleon had received an important command in northern Italy that could bring fame and fortune. Napoleon's mother and adult brothers opposed the marriage, calling Joséphine an old woman (over thirty) with no money. Despite family bickering, they married in a simple civil ceremony in March, 1796. Within a week Napoleon departed to command the French army in northern Italy.

Napoleon brilliantly defeated the forces of monarchy clustered on France's southeastern borders. He sent home money and hundreds of artworks to enrich the Directory and practically dictated the terms of peace in 1797. Only Joséphine defied Napoleon's will; he implored her to come to Italy, but she resisted. She dallied in Paris, continued her relationship with Barras, probably took a new lover, and made money through war profiteering. When she finally traveled to Napoleon's headquarters near Milan, Italy, she had aroused his deepest suspicions and jealousy. In Italy Joséphine first assumed important public functions; she presided over lavish official ceremonies and was treated almost as royalty. Once the couple returned to Paris, their small home became a site of pilgrimage for French patriots.

Popular myths immediately developed about Joséphine, celebrating her as "Our Lady of Victories" and "the good Joséphine," a symbol of good fortune and prosperity. She indulged her joy in shopping and collecting items as diverse as clothing, art, jewelry, and rare plants. Her extravagance did possess positive aspects: She was generous to a fault, patronized charities, and loved giving gifts. She never ignored a plea for help, however humble, and she was gracious to all. Furthermore, she did not meddle in politics or attempt to influence her husband's policies. These characteristics rendered Joséphine "good" in the eyes of public opinion in marked contrast to the "bad" Queen Marie Antoinette.

While Napoleon remained in France, Joséphine appeared as his loyal spouse and helpmate. However, when he led the French expedition to Egypt and remained away for seventeen months (1798-1799), she reverted to some of her previous bad habits and companions. Joséphine did begin to reform her behavior, but negative reports had quickly reached Napoleon. His secret return in autumn of 1799 surprised Joséphine, and she attempted to intercept him before her critical in-laws did. Napoleon greeted her with silence behind a locked bedroom door,

Joséphine. (Library of Congress)

but within a short time her copious weeping melted his heart and brought reconciliation.

Napoleon had far more on his mind than his wife's behavior. The Directory had suffered military losses and regularly canceled any unfavorable election results. A wide spectrum of political and business leaders assured Napoleon that they would support him if he would overthrow the Directors. His brothers Joseph and Lucien were well positioned to assist him, and Napoleon decided to act. Thus occurred the coup of Brumaire VIII in November of 1799 and creation of the Consulate, a three-man executive with Napoleon as First Consul. A major aim of the Consulate was to bring reconciliation among the political, religious, and social factions dividing the French people. Joséphine was an asset to this policy because she always had friends in all political and social camps. The Consulate ended the unseemly social behavior of the Directory; the First Consul and his wife moved into the Tuileries palace and virtually reestablished a court.

Napoleon and Joséphine frequently escaped the formality of the Tuileries by visiting their country estate, Malmaison, where they relaxed with their extended families and Joséphine unleashed her domestic talents. She redecorated the chateau extravagantly and began monumental gardening projects. She aspired to collect an example of every plant in France and introduce many new ones. She patronized botanists who studied and classified thousands of species. Malmaison became Joséphine's true home and was closely associated with popular perceptions of her.

Napoleon's ability to solve France's problems made him a target for royalist assassination attempts and made the need for an orderly transition of power in case of his death obvious. Joséphine worried for his safety and also for her own position should someone else assume power. She also feared that Napoleon, who had always wanted children, might divorce her and remarry in hopes of having them. She temporarily protected herself by arranging for her daughter Hortense to marry Napoleon's brother Louis in 1802. This couple produced three grandsons for Joséphine, uniting Bonaparte and Beauharnais lines; Napoleon seriously considered adopting the oldest child before he died in 1808. The creation of the First Empire (May, 1804) intensified Joséphine's fears about succession and divorce. She invoked the sanction of the Roman Catholic Church against divorce by informing Pope Pius VII, who was visiting Paris for Napoleon's coronation ceremony, that her marriage had been civil only. At papal urging, Napoleon and Joséphine quickly had a brief religious wedding.

The spectacular coronation ceremony reached its high point as Napoleon crowned Joséphine and himself. Their relationship had grown into an affectionate partnership; they often dined privately at the end of long days in which she sustained the elaborate public rituals of the court, freeing him to work on pressing matters. When Napoleon was away, Joséphine calmly continued the court routine and assured France that all was well. She remained essentially apolitical and unhesitatingly supported Napoleon's policies. Joséphine's concerns about war and politics lay with loved ones serving the First Empire. Eugene was an active soldier and viceroy of the Kingdom of Italy; his politically dictated marriage to a Bavarian princess had turned out happily. Hortense became a queen as Louis Bonaparte was named king of Holland, but her marriage disintegrated.

A combination of personal and political pressures led Napoleon to divorce Joséphine in 1809. For years he doubted he could father a child; in 1806 and 1810, however, affairs produced two sons who were undoubtedly his, the latter by the Polish countess Maria Walewska. Simultaneously, political pressure mounted for Napoleon to divorce Joséphine and improve France's international position by marrying into the Russian or Austrian ruling house. Napoleon informed Joséphine of his decision and requested her understanding. This time her tears could not dissuade him. Joséphine retained Napoleon's affection, the title of empress, possession of Malmaison, and a handsome income. In 1810 Napoleon married the Austrian archduchess Marie-Louise and, in 1811, rejoiced at the birth of his son Napoleon-Francis, king of Rome.

Joséphine's life changed greatly after divorce, but Joséphine herself did not. At heart she understood Napoleon's decision, and she contrived to visit and play with his sons by Countess Walewska and Marie-Louise. She lived at Malmaison and again gathered about her interesting people of all political persuasions. Although she entertained many royalists, she remained loyal to Napoleon. She lamented the reverses Napoleon met in Russia and the subsequent campaigns. She was fiercely proud that Eugene remained faithful to the emperor as others betrayed him. In the spring of 1814, the victorious allies swarmed over Paris and restored the Bourbon monarchy. The new regime allowed Joséphine to keep Malmaison and receive important visitors, including the Russian czar. Her children and grandchildren found refuge with sympathetic rulers abroad. However, the downfall of the First Empire seemed to overwhelm her, and her health failed. Most likely it was a mere coincidence, but less than one month after Napoleon was exiled to Elba, on May 4, 1814, Joséphine died at Malmaison.

SIGNIFICANCE

Joséphine was as loved in death as in life. After she died, twenty thousand people paid their last respects, and a huge number of popular pamphlets praised her virtues. This outpouring was partly a measure of Napoleon's continued popularity and partly an expression of genuine regard. Massive changes swept France in her lifetime as the old feudal order collapsed and modern concepts of liberty, nationalism, and government arose. Joséphine transcended political divisions and softened the edges of Napoleon's authoritarian government as France entered a new age. Joséphine was beloved because she buffered the cruelties and harshness of her times and extended human sympathy in a society beset with turmoil.

—Sharon B. Watkins

FURTHER READING

Cole, Hubert. *Josephine*. New York: Viking Press, 1963. Reliable, basic account of Joséphine's life. Contains a useful bibliography.

DeLorme, Eleanor P. *Joséphine: Napoleon's Incomparable Empress*. Foreword by Bernard Chevallier. New York: H. N. Abrams, 2002. Focuses on the crucial role Joséphine played in Napoleon's political and military career and on her support of the arts.

Epton, Nina Consuelo. *Josephine: The Empress and Her Children*. New York: W. W. Norton, 1976. Adequately surveys Joséphine's entire life and suggests that what little happiness she found came mostly from her relationships with Hortense and Eugene.

Knapton, Ernest John. *Empress Josephine*. Cambridge, Mass.: Harvard University Press, 1963. A carefully researched scholarly biography that dispels some often-repeated inaccuracies and gives abundant historical details that carefully place Joséphine in relation to contemporary events and personalities. The bibliography is exceptionally informative.

Seward, Desmond. *Napoleon's Family*. New York: Viking Press, 1986. Joséphine's life after meeting Napoleon is woven throughout the complicated story of the Bonaparte and Beauharnais families; highlights family battles and hostility to Joséphine.

Stuart, Andrea. *The Rose of Martinique: A Life of Napoleon's Joséphine*. New York: Grove Press, 2003. Detailed, well-researched biography, based in part on Joséphine's diaries and letters.

Vance, Marguerite. *The Empress Josephine: From Martinique to Malmaison*. New York: E. P. Dutton, 1956. Romanticized view emphasizing themes from her childhood that persisted in later life. The author maintains, perhaps unfairly, that Joséphine was her own worst enemy because she always insisted upon having her own way.

Wilson, Robert McNair. *The Empress Josephine, the Portrait of a Woman*. London: Eyre & Spottiswoode, 1952. A reliable account that emphasizes the personal rather than public side of her life. Includes a bibliography.

SEE ALSO: Jean-Jacques-Régis de Cambacérès; Napoleon I.

RELATED ARTICLE in *Great Events from History: The Nineteenth Century, 1801-1900:* December 2, 1804: Bonaparte Is Crowned Napoleon I.

BENITO JUÁREZ
President of Mexico (1861-1872)

The dominant figure of mid-nineteenth century Mexican politics, Juárez embodied a liberal vision of a democratic republican form of government, economic development and modernization, virulent anticlericalism, and mandatory public education. Although he was prevented from fully implementing his ambitious agenda by years of warfare against foreign intervention and his policies were anathema to many entrenched conservative elements in Mexico, especially the Roman Catholic Church, Juárez's reform program laid the groundwork for a modern Mexican nation.

BORN: March 21, 1806; San Pablo Guelatao, Oaxaca, Mexico
DIED: July 19, 1872; Mexico City, Mexico
AREA OF ACHIEVEMENT: Government and politics

EARLY LIFE

Benito Juárez (wahr-ehs) was born in a small mountain hamlet in the southern Mexican state of Oaxaca. He was orphaned when his parents died before he reached the age of four. Reared by his uncle until the age of twelve in a remote Zapotec Indian community, Juárez had beginnings that could not have been more humble. In 1818, he walked forty-one miles to the state capital, Oaxaca City, and found work and shelter in the home of a Franciscan lay brother who was a part-time bookbinder. Juárez worked in the bindery and helped with chores, and in return was given school tuition.

Because he excelled in school, Juárez was encouraged to enter the seminary. He later changed his mind, however, and in 1829 chose a career in law, entering the Oaxaca Institute of Arts and Sciences. Two years later, he earned his lawyer's certificate, and that professional degree proved to be his passport to politics. The same year he was graduated from law school, he became an alderman in the city council and subsequently served as state legislator. His improved social and economic standing was reflected by his marriage in 1843 to Margarita Maza, the daughter of a prominent Oaxacan family.

Even as a successful young lawyer, Juárez always remembered his roots and did *pro bono publico* work for groups of impoverished peasant villagers. Convinced that major structural change was needed to make Mexico a more just society, Juárez decided to forgo his law practice and dedicate his career to public service.

When war erupted between Mexico and the United States in 1846, Juárez, who at the time was a deputy in the Mexican national congress, was recalled to his home in 1847 to serve an abbreviated term as interim governor. A year later, he was elected to a full term. Juárez proved to be a capable and honest governor, overseeing the construction of fifty rural schools, encouraging female attendance in the classroom, trimming the bloated state bureaucracy, facilitating economic development through the revitalization of an abandoned Pacific port, and making regular payments on the state debt. Moreover, the idealistic governor raised eyebrows around Mexico when he refused to offer his state as sanctuary to General Antonio López de Santa Anna, the powerful dictator (caudillo) who would serve as president on eleven separate occasions during the first thirty chaotic years of Mexican nationhood. Santa Anna never forgave Juárez for this slight, and, when he became president for the final time in 1853, he arrested Juárez, imprisoned him for several months, and then exiled him aboard a ship destined for New Orleans.

LIFE'S WORK

In New Orleans, Juárez made contact with a burgeoning expatriate community who represented the best and brightest of a new generation of young, idealistic Mexicans. These liberals, who called themselves *puros*, were committed to wholesale changes in the political system, to modernizing the nation's stagnant economy, and to creating a more equitable society for all Mexicans. These *puros* knew that Mexico had been racked by political instability, that Mexico had suffered a humiliating defeat at the hands of the United States, that corporate institutions such as the military and the Church had a viselike grip on Mexican society, and that a small, politically powerful, and economically wealthy elite dominated thousands of impoverished Indians and mestizos.

Influenced by nineteenth century European liberal thought and enamored of the North American republican experiment, the *puros* composed a statement of principles in exile and secured arms and ammunition for regional caudillos in Mexico who opposed Santa Anna. Juárez was smuggled into Mexico and served as an aide to Juan Alvarez, the caudillo who spearheaded the Ayutla Rebellion. In 1855, the rebels drove Santa Anna from power for the last time.

When the new government was formed, Juárez was named secretary of justice. Juárez's cohorts were determined to see Mexico erase the vestiges of the past and emerge from chaos and anarchy. The *puros* focused on the Roman Catholic Church as being the single most regressive institution in Mexican society and sought to curtail its pervasive influence. The secretary of justice was intimately involved with the first of a series of reform laws that attacked corporate interests.

There followed a series of reform laws—which gave the era its name, La Reforma—that systematically dismantled the power of the Catholic Church in Mexico. The *Ley Lerdo* prohibited corporate institutions from owning or administering property not used in their daily operations. The Church, local and state governments, and corporate Indian villages could retain their churches, monasteries, meeting halls, jails, and schools, but other property had to be put up for sale at public auction, with the proceeds destined for federal coffers. In the first six months following the implementation of the law, twenty-three million pesos worth of property was auctioned, twenty million of which had belonged to the Church.

The reform laws were incorporated in a new constitution (1857). This document gave Mexico its first bill of rights, abolished slavery and titles of nobility, and created a unicameral congress to diminish executive power. Conservatives, especially the Church, unleashed a torrent of invective against the liberal document. Priests who did not publicly disavow the constitution were suspended by the hierarchy. While bureaucrats who refused to take the oath of allegiance lost their jobs, soldiers who did take the oath were not treated in Catholic hospitals and were denied the last rites.

The War of the Reform broke out in 1858, when conservatives attacked and captured Mexico City, dissolved the congress, and arrested Juárez, who had recently been elected chief justice of the supreme court—a position that placed him next in line for the presidency. When President Ignacio Comonfort proved unequal to the task of reconciliation, he resigned. Juárez then managed to escape from conservative hands and was promptly named president by his liberal supporters. For three years, the war raged as Juárez made his temporary headquarters in the port city of Veracruz.

After a bitter and protracted struggle, the liberals persevered and in 1861 Juárez entered Mexico City triumphant. The president decided to treat his enemies leniently and tendered a generous amnesty. More pressing problems faced Juárez, because he inherited a depleted treasury and a destitute army that had not been paid. Moreover, Mexico owed a considerable amount of money to European creditors, who now demanded repayment. Juárez, in an act of fiscal desperation, ordered a

Benito Juárez. (The Institute of Texan Cultures, San Antonio, Texas)

two-year suspension of payments on the foreign debt. Spain, England, and France, in an effort to prod Mexican repayment, agreed jointly to seize ports along the Mexican coast to collect their claims.

Napoleon III viewed the joint occupation of the port of Veracruz as a vehicle to further his expansionistic aims. Hoping to re-create the empire of his great-uncle, Napoleon I, and to take advantage of a debilitated United States engaged in its own civil war, Napoleon III ordered his army to leave the port of Veracruz and march on Mexico City. (When the Spanish and English learned of Napoleon's true intentions, they withdrew their forces.) After a stiff fight, the French army reached Mexico City, only to find that Juárez had already evacuated the capital and had taken his government with him, constantly moving across the desert of northern Mexico to escape capture.

Napoleon III attempted to legitimate his imperialistic actions when he persuaded a Habsburg archduke, Ferdinand Maximilian, to leave Austria and become the emperor of Mexico (with the backing of the French army).

Conservatives and the Church, which had just been defeated in the War of Reform, were delighted and welcomed Maximilian. Maximilian, with his wife Carlota, arrived in Mexico in 1864 and quickly found that Juárez's liberals were still a force to contend with and that the French had not successfully pacified the country.

Portraying the conflict as a nationalistic struggle to oust the foreign usurper, the president inspired his forces to conduct a guerrilla campaign against the French. Juárez also asked and received war matériel from the United States, especially after the defeat of the Confederacy in 1865. Secretary of State William Seward sent threatening messages to the French king, protesting that the occupation was a violation of the Monroe Doctrine and demanding that the French withdraw from the Western Hemisphere. In addition, the French troops grew weary of the Mexican campaign, and Napoleon appeared to have lost interest as well. Concerned with Otto von Bismarck's aggressive foreign policy closer to home, Napoleon ordered his troops home in the spring of 1866. Soon thereafter, Maximilian's forces surrendered.

Maximilian was tried by court-martial, and the state asked for the death penalty. Despite intense pressure from the international community, Juárez stood by the sentence. After a devastating loss of territory to the United States and a nightmarish foreign interlude that cost more than fifty thousand Mexican lives, Juárez believed that Mexico had to make it clear that it would not countenance any more intervention. Maximilian was tried, convicted, and shot in 1867.

Most historians mark 1867 as the beginning of the modern Mexican nation. Juárez called for presidential elections and announced that he would run for an unprecedented third term. Because the first two terms were spent at war, most Mexicans believed that, under these extraordinary circumstances, the president was justified in seeking reelection. Moreover, given his back-to-back victories against the conservatives and Maximilian, Juárez's popularity was cresting.

Juárez's third term (1867-1871) was the first time the president had an opportunity to implement his liberal program in a peaceful atmosphere. The first order of business was to reconstruct Mexico's economy, which had been ravaged by nine years of war. To encourage foreigners to invest in Mexico, the president had to change the nation's image abroad. A rural police force was expanded to safeguard silver shipments and to protect highways from bandits. Mexico's first railroad from Mexico City to its chief port, Veracruz, was finally completed in 1872 by a British company with subsidies from Juárez's

administration. Juárez also revised Mexico's antiquated tax and tariff structures and sought to revitalize the mining sector to stimulate foreign investment further. Finally, Juárez appointed a commission to overhaul the national educational system. All of these policies collectively represented Juárez's vision for Mexico's future, and, although many were never fully implemented by his administration, they did put Mexico on the road to modernization.

One major problem that persisted throughout his third term was political unrest, especially at the regional and local level. Juárez spent much of his energies quieting one local uprising after another and found it necessary repeatedly to ask the congress to grant him extraordinary powers (martial law). Juárez's opponents believed that he had abused the constitutional principles he had fought so ardently to defend and that his rule was growing increasingly arbitrary and heavy-handed with time.

Despite the fact that his popularity had been falling for some time, Juárez decided to run for a fourth term in 1871. Two candidates, Sebastián Lerdo de Tejada (the brother of the author of the *Ley Lerdo*) and Porfirio Díaz, opposed him in the election. When no candidate received the requisite majority, according to the 1857 constitution, the congress would decide the outcome. The legislature, dominated by Juárez's supporters, elected him for a fourth term. Although Díaz revolted, federal forces quelled the rebellion. Soon after Díaz's defeat, however, Juárez suffered a coronary seizure and died on July 19, 1872.

SIGNIFICANCE

Benito Juárez defined Mexican politics from 1855 to 1872. The fact that a full-blooded Zapotec Indian could become president of the nation demonstrated that Mexico had broken with its aristocratic past. The leader of an ambitious group of idealistic liberals, Juárez knew that the power of the Catholic Church, the caudillos, and the army had to be diminished. Notwithstanding his more autocratic rule during his last years, especially his controversial decision to run for a fourth term, he remained true to his democratic principles.

Although Juárez is best known for his defeat of Maximilian and his anticlericalism, his greatest political legacy was his ambitious third term, which set the agenda for future presidential administrations. Juárez's successors, Lerdo de Tejada (1872-1876) and Díaz (1876-1911), faithfully followed his policies and programs. Although some economic policies proved successful, the breaking up of village lands led to the expansion of the great estates or haciendas, and the destruction of semi-autonomous Indian villages. Although Juárez's democratic principles were abused by Díaz during his long dictatorship, Díaz's policies and strategies for modernization bore the indelible stamp of Benito Juárez.

—Allen Wells

FURTHER READING

Bazant, Jan. *Alienation of Church Wealth in Mexico: Social and Economic Aspects of the Liberal Revolution, 1856-1857.* Cambridge, England: Cambridge University Press, 1971. A thorough analysis of the implications of the *Ley Lerdo* and its effects on church wealth in Mexico.

Berry, Charles R. *The Reform in Oaxaca, 1856-1876: A Microhistory of the Liberal Revolution.* Lincoln: University of Nebraska Press, 1981. A critical examination of how liberal policies were implemented in Juárez's home region, Oaxaca. Berry dispels certain myths about the land reform, arguing that it was not as thoroughgoing and disruptive as previously believed.

Hanna, Alfred J., and Kathryn A. Hanna. *Napoleon III and Mexico: American Triumph over Monarchy.* Chapel Hill: University of North Carolina Press, 1971. A fascinating account of the role of the United States in dislodging the French from Mexico. Utilizing Seward's diplomatic correspondence and other North American sources, the authors also investigate the moral and material help the American government gave Juárez against Maximilian and the French.

Krauze, Enrique. *Mexico: A Biography of Power: A History of Modern Mexico, 1810-1996.* Translated by Hank Heifetz. New York: HarperCollins, 1997. The book includes numerous references to Juárez, including descriptions of his presidency and his importance in Mexican history.

Meyer, Michael C., and William L. Sherman. *The Course of Mexican History.* 3d ed. New York: Oxford University Press, 1987. The best single-volume text on Mexican history. The material on Juárez is concise, thorough, and up-to-date.

Perry, Laurens B. *Juárez and Díaz: Machine Politics in Mexico.* De Kalb: Northern Illinois University Press, 1978. The only critical account of Juárez's arbitrary rule during his third term. Perry treats not only Juárez's administration but also the succeeding presidencies of Lerdo and Díaz.

Roeder, Ralph. *Juárez and His Mexico.* 2 vols. New York: Viking Press, 1947. A biography in English of Juárez, this massive, dated work details in narrative fashion his life and work.

Wasserman, Mark. *Everyday Life and Politics in Nineteenth Century Mexico: Men, Women, and War.* Albuquerque: University of New Mexico Press, 2000. Part 2, "The Age of Civil Wars," features a brief biography of Juárez and describes Mexican history, politics, economics, and everyday life from 1848 through 1876.

SEE ALSO: Otto von Bismarck; Porfirio Díaz; Maximilian; Napoleon III; Antonio López de Santa Anna.

RELATED ARTICLE in *Great Events from History: The Nineteenth Century, 1801-1900:* October 31, 1861-June 19, 1867: France Occupies Mexico.

KAMEHAMEHA I
King of the Hawaiian Islands (r. 1804-1819)

Through his prowess, astute leadership in battle, and adroit use of European advisers, ships, and weapons, Kamehameha overcame his rival and united the Hawaiian Islands for the first time in their history. In the process, he made himself their king and founded a dynasty that helped the islands preserve their independence from European and American rule through most of the nineteenth century.

BORN: c. 1758; Halawa, North Kohala, island of Hawaii, Hawaiian Islands

DIED: May 8, 1819; Kailua, Hawaii

ALSO KNOWN AS: Paiea (birth name); Kamehameha the Great

AREAS OF ACHIEVEMENT: Government and politics, military

EARLY LIFE

Because Kamehameha (kah-may-HAH-may-HAH)—whose Hawaiian name means the "lonely one" or the "silent one"—was born before the European arrival in the Hawaiian Islands, and therefore before there were any written records, scholars must rely on native tradition for information about his birth. Estimates of his birth year vary from 1736 to 1758, but the modern consensus favors 1758. Kamehameha's mother was Kekuiapoiwa, and his father was Keoua, although there is a story that his real father was Kahekili, king of Maui.

Kamehameha was described by European contemporaries as being well over six feet tall, athletically built, and savage in appearance. He was a member of the chiefly caste, the *alii*, who ruled despotically over the common people. The *alii* were considered to have descended directly from the gods and possessed varying degrees of divinity. The highest *alii* were those who were born to a high-ranking chief and his sister—a system reminiscent of ancient Egypt. Hawaiians worshiped a number of gods, including Kane, the god of creation; Ku, the war god; and Lono, the fertility god. Life was governed by many prohibitions and strict rules for behavior known as the *kapu* (taboo). A priestly caste had charge of worship in the *heiau*, or open stone temples.

Kamehameha's father, Keoua, died young, and from then on Kamehameha was reared at the court of his uncle, Kalaniopuu, the king of Hawaii. It was during this period that Captain James Cook happened upon the Hawaiian Islands, which he called the Sandwich Islands in honor of John Montagu, fourth earl of Sandwich. Cook came first to Kauai and Niihau in 1778, and in 1779 entered Kealakekua Bay near Kailua on the lee side of Hawaii. The Hawaiians at first considered Cook to be the god Lono, but an unfortunate series of events disillusioned them, and he was killed in a skirmish on the shore of Kealakekua Bay. Kamehameha accompanied Kalaniopuu during a visit to one of Cook's ships and even spent the night there, but he seems not to have been present when Cook died.

LIFE'S WORK

When Kalaniopuu died, he left the kingship to his son Kiwalao, who undertook a system of land distribution unfavorable to Kamehameha and the other chiefs of Kona. After a bloody battle at Mokuohai in 1782 in which Kiwalao was killed, and with the assistance of an eruption of the volcano Kilauea that wreaked havoc with other opposing forces and showed them that Pele (the goddess of volcanoes) was against them, Kamehameha gained control over all of Hawaii.

When King Kahekili died in 1794, he controlled all the islands of the Hawaiian chain except Hawaii, Kauai, and Niihau. With the assistance of foreign ships and weapons, Kamehameha soon conquered Maui, Molokai, Lanai, and Kahoolawe. In 1795 he proceeded to Oahu—which now had Kalanikupule, Kahekili's brother, as its king—and landed his forces at Waikiki and Waialae. They drove Kalanikupule's forces up the Nuuanu Valley and forced the bulk of them to fall to their deaths from cliffs. Kalanikupule escaped but was later captured and sacrificed to the war god Kukailimoku.

Kamehameha now ruled all the Hawaiian Islands except for Kauai. He soon started preparations for an invasion of Kauai, and in the spring of 1796, he headed toward the island with a large flotilla of canoes. However, rough seas forced him to turn back and postpone his invasion. Hearing that a rebellion was taking place in Hawaii, he returned there to squelch it. He spent the next six years in Hawaii, during which time he assembled a formidable fleet of double canoes and a number of small schooners constructed by European carpenters. With these ships and a large supply of European weapons, he sailed to Oahu in 1804. However, his invasion plans were frustrated again, this time by a terrible plague (probably cholera) that was brought by foreign ships. The population of Oahu was devastated, and large numbers of

Portrait of Kamehameha the Great. (Hawaii State Archives)

Kamehameha's army also succumbed. Kamehameha himself was stricken but managed to survive.

Kamehameha continued to plan his invasion of Kauai and even acquired a large ship, the *Lelia Byrd*, to lead the assault. He also entered into negotiations with the island's king, Kaumualii, to solve the problem without battle. An American captain, Nathan Winship, persuaded the two kings to meet on board his ship, the *O'Cain*, and Kaumualii submitted to Kamehameha's sovereignty on the condition that he could retain his position until death.

Now Kamehameha reigned over all the islands, apparently the first to do so. He was an absolute dictator but used his power wisely. He divided up the lands in such a way that no chief had enough power to be tempted to rebel and appointed governors to administer each island. He issued decrees that made life safer and often worked at menial tasks to set an example for his people to follow. He appointed a Hawaiian named Kalanimoku (known as Billy Pitt after the British prime minister William Pitt) as chief executive officer.

During Kamehameha's lifetime, foreign visitors to the Hawaiian Islands became increasingly numerous. The first ships to appear after Cook's unfortunate visit were those captained by George Vancouver, who had been a member of Cook's crew. Vancouver visited the islands in 1792, 1793, and 1794. He brought cattle and goats and other commodities to the islands but refused to provide any arms. He persuaded Kamehameha to cede the Hawaiian Islands to Britain, although Kamehameha apparently believed that he was entering into a defensive alliance in the hope that he would get help against his enemies. In any event, Britain made no effort to follow through, but a close connection between Britain and the "Sandwich Islands" continued. This is symbolized by the Hawaiian flag, which bears the Union Jack in the upper left corner.

Although most of the ships that visited Hawaii during this period were traders searching to replenish their ships, there were occasional visits of a different stripe. Anton Schäffer, a German surgeon in the employ of the Russian-American Company, was sent to Hawaii to recover or receive compensation for a Russian cargo lost from a ship wrecked off Kauai. Schäffer got grandiose ideas and attempted, with the help of Kaumualii, to establish Russian outposts in Kauai and Oahu. He was repulsed by the Hawaiians with the assistance of the Americans in Honolulu and was forced to make his escape by hiding on a ship to Canton.

When the Europeans first visited the Hawaiian Islands, they were able to obtain valuable goods from the native Hawaiians for baubles or for small pieces of iron, which were especially prized because they could be made into fishhooks or daggers. Fresh water, hogs, and other food items were needed. As time went by, the Hawaiians became aware of the value of their commodities, and prices went up accordingly. Kamehameha himself secured great amounts of goods in barter and even large amounts of hard money, which he retained in storehouses in Kailua, Lahaina, and Honolulu.

Kamehameha had a total of twenty-one wives, but his favorite was Kaahumanu, by whom he had no children. Kamehameha married Keopuolani for dynastic purposes when she was about thirteen years old. Keopuolani and Kamehameha had three children who survived, one of whom, Liholiho, was designated as the heir to the kingdom. Kamehameha spent most of his last years in Kailua, although he occasionally traveled to the other parts of his realm. In 1819, he contracted a malady that no one could cure, and on May 19, he died. His body was treated in the usual way for *alii*: His bones were stripped of their flesh and hidden somewhere in a cave by one of his faithful retainers.

SIGNIFICANCE

Only a few monarchs in world history have received the appellation "great." Kamehameha, by uniting all of the Hawaiian Islands under his sway and keeping his land independent of foreign dominance, probably deserves such a title. He was flexible enough to adapt to the changing times but still retained his way of life under the taboo system. If he was sometimes harsh and cruel by contemporary standards, he was also kind and generous. During his brief reign as Kamehameha II, his son Liholiho, upon the urging of Kaahumana (a *kuhina nui*, or prime minister), put a dramatic end to the taboo system by publicly eating with the women, which had been strictly forbidden. After Liholiho's death (by measles during a trip to England), Kaahumanu remained as regent until Liholiho's brother came of age, and she saw to it that the remnants of the taboo system were destroyed. In 1819, the same year that Kamehameha died, the missionaries came to Hawaii and transformed Hawaiian life forever.

—*Henry Kratz*

FURTHER READING

Daws, Gavan. *Shoal of Time: A History of the Hawaiian Islands*. New York: Macmillan, 1968. Reprint. Honolulu: University of Hawai'i Press, 1974. Daws's book, the best one-volume history of Hawaii, contains an excellent section on Kamehameha and his times, starting with Cook's discovery of the islands. It is very readable, with copious endnotes and an excellent bibliography.

Desha, Stephen. *Kamehameha and His Warrior Kekuhaupi'o*. Translated by Frances N. Frazier. Honolulu: Kamehameha Schools Press, 2000. Orginially published as a magazine serial in the Hawaiian language during the early 1920's, this book recounts the epic tale of King Kamehameha and a warrior named Kek-uhaupi'o. An engaging saga for younger readers that includes a great deal of information about Hawaiian history and culture. Glossary and detailed index.

Kuykendall, Ralph S. *The Hawaiian Kingdom 1778-1854: Foundation and Transformation*. Honolulu: University of Hawai'i Press, 1938. This first volume of Kuykendall's monumental history of Hawaii contains an extensive account of Kamehameha's life and the history of Hawaii since Cook's appearance there. The book also includes an appendix discussing Kamehameha's controversial birth year.

Malo, David. *Hawaiian Antiquities*. Translated by Nathaniel B. Emerson. 2d ed. Honolulu: Bishop Museum Press, 1951. This volume, written by a native Hawaiian in the Hawaiian language, was translated in 1898 by one of the great experts on Hawaiian culture. It contains a wealth of information about virtually every aspect of Hawaiian life before the European discovery, including old Hawaiian folktales and chants.

Mellen, Kathleen Dickenson. *The Lonely Warrior: The Life and Times of Kamehameha the Great of Hawaii*. New York: Hastings House, 1949. This is a well-researched and readable biography. Mellen used oral sources of Hawaiian traditions along with written sources and was aided in her work by Kawena Pukui, a distinguished scholar of Hawaiian culture and language employed by the Bishop Museum. The book contains several useful maps, including one denoting the battle on Oahu that ended at Nuuanu Pali.

Morrison, Susan. *Kamehameha: The Warrior King of Hawai'i*. Honolulu: University of Hawai'i Press, 2003. Brief biography written for younger readers.

Mrantz, Maxine. *Hawaiian Monarchy: The Romantic Years*. Honolulu: Aloha Graphics, 1973. This forty-seven-page booklet gives a quick summary of the monarchy by providing short biographies of all of the monarchs from Kamehameha I to Liliuokalani. It also contains portraits of all the monarchs, as well as other interesting photographs.

Tregaskis, Richard. *The Warrior King: Hawaii's Kamehameha the Great*. New York: Macmillan, 1973. Tregaskis relies heavily on unauthenticated sources and his own imagination to write what amounts to a fictionalized biography. Nevertheless, the main facts are there, and the book contains genealogical tables, a map of the Hawaiian Islands, sixteen pages of reproductions of contemporary paintings, and a useful bibliography.

SEE ALSO: Liliuokalani.

RELATED ARTICLE in *Great Events from History: The Nineteenth Century, 1801-1900:* January 24, 1895: Hawaii's Last Monarch Abdicates.

KANG YOUWEI
Chinese intellectual and nationalist leader

One of the leading Chinese political thinkers of his time, Kang wrote practical memorials concerning economic and political topics, as well as utopian essays. After he was forced to flee China as a dangerous radical in 1898, he became an influential agitator and organizer seeking Chinese political reform.

BORN: March 19, 1858; Guangdong Province, China
DIED: March 31, 1927; Qingdao, Shandong Province, China
ALSO KNOWN AS: K'ang Yu-wei (Wade-Giles)
AREAS OF ACHIEVEMENT: Government and politics, philosophy

EARLY LIFE

Kang Youwei (kahng yoo-way) was born into a relatively well-to-do family. His father, a government official, died when he was eleven years old, and his mother was challenged to manage with a much reduced income. Her coping skills and affectionate bullying left Kang with great admiration for her, and helps explain the favorable attitude toward women's rights that he developed later in his life.

Kang was tutored by his grandfather in the traditional literary and philosophical Chinese classics. These studies were aimed at helping him pass the government civil service examinations and qualify for an official position—then the most appealing route to wealth and power. However, he failed the examinations in 1876—perhaps because his rebellious and creative streak was beginning to surface.

From his early years, Kang displayed extraordinary self-confidence, reflecting his wide reading and unusual verbal skills. Aided by family financial support, he embarked on a career as a "public intellectual." His reading moved beyond the Chinese classics into the more mystical realms of Buddhism and Daoism and then into public affairs—government, history, geography, economics.

In 1876, Kang married Zhang Miaohua, a woman three years older than him, and they had two daughters together. Although Kang often affirmed Confucian endorsements of marriage, he was also involved successively with two concubines, in part because he was away from his wife for long periods of time. His writings repeatedly affirmed the value of pleasures and comforts, and his lifestyle reflected these convictions.

LIFE'S WORK

Like many contemporary Chinese thinkers, Kang was disturbed by the weakness of China's imperial government and the ease with which it was bullied by Japan and Western powers. He began writing about possible social and political reforms from several angles. The most noteworthy of these viewpoints involved reinterpretations of the writings of the ancient Chinese philosopher Confucius. In 1891, he produced a book the title of which translates as the "forged classics of the Wang Mang period." This work claimed that many of the revered Chinese classical texts were actually forgeries. His book generated so much public outrage that it was banned by the imperial court. In 1897, Kang published a book on Confucius that argued that the ancient sage had been a supporter of institutional change. Clearly Kang was using Confucius as a medium to advance his own agenda for political reform, sometimes at the sacrifice of truth and accuracy.

In 1891, Kang established an academy in Canton (Guangzhou). There, he provided instruction in the classics—according to his own interpretations—and also in modern subjects such as mathematics and the study of Western learning. His prize pupil was Liang Qichao, who became a remarkably prolific writer on Chinese public affairs and introduced into China many Western writers.

Kang finally passed the civil service examinations in 1893; two years later, he received an appointment in the government's board of works. China had just been defeated in a war with Japan and was in the process of accepting the Treaty of Shimonoseki, which gave Japan control of Korea. Kang petitioned Emperor Guangxu to reject the treaty, thus beginning his series of widely publicized memorials to the throne advocating reforms to strengthen China against imperialist pressures. In 1895-1896, he and Liang Qichao produced a reform-oriented newspaper, and Kang organized at least two associations dedicated to reform.

Emperor Guangxu, who sincerely desired modernizing reforms, invited Kang to an imperial audience in June, 1898. In response to the suggestions of Kang and other advisers, Guangxu issued a breath-taking series of decrees establishing a national university (later called Beijing University) and other modern schools, modernizing the civil service examinations, establishing a budget system, abolishing useless public offices, and reorganizing both the military and civil administrative systems.

These rapid moves were disturbing to the inner circle of palace officials, who feared for their own power and influence and claimed that reform measures were being used by foreign powers to weaken the monarchy and the state. Indeed, the Japanese were, in fact, trying to persuade the young emperor to give them a major role as advisers seeking China's modernization. An influential clique of palace insiders persuaded the dowager empress Cixi, the emperor's aunt, to take a more active role in warning Guangxu of the dangers they perceived in the reform program. They presented evidence that Kang and his associates were planning to assassinate some leading officials. Kang later claimed the emperor had been forcibly deposed and was being held prisoner, but Sterling Seagrave's 1992 book, *Dragon Lady*, refutes this claim.

In any event, the government moved vigorously to suppress the reform movement. Kang's brother was executed, and the same fate would have befallen Kang and Liang Qichao, had they not fled the country. After arriving in Hong Kong, Kang began a campaign to discredit the dowager empress and did in fact attempt to engage hired assassins to murder her. Kang then proceeded to Japan, Great Britain, and Canada, lobbying their governments to intervene to free the supposedly captive emperor and restore him to power. In July, 1899, when he was in Victoria, British Columbia, he organized the Society to Protect the Emperor, which developed branches among overseas Chinese in the United States and several other countries. During that same year that same emperor offered a reward of more than 100,000 dollars for Kang and Liang. During the Boxer Rebellion of 1900, Kang and other leaders of Chinese insurgent movements tried to organize the overthrow of the empress.

Kang spent most of 1900-1903 relaxing and writing in Penang in Malaya and in Darjeeling, India. He extended his discussions of Confucius as a reformer, attributing to him the idea that society was moving through three stages—an age of disorder, an age of "minor tranquility," and a final stage of "great peace." Kang then absorbed this sequence into a book—which is his most interesting to Western readers—*Datongshu*, the book of great harmony. Kang apparently began this work in 1885, and completed it in 1902, but published only a small portion of it during his lifetime. It was later translated into English. The book was a blueprint for a utopian socialist society, comparable to Edward Bellamy's *Looking Back-ward* (1888), which appeared in Chinese translation in 1891-1892.

Kang believed that much of the world's conflicts arose from the competitive striving after gain animated by the family system. In his ideal socialist system, marriages would be modified into short-term contracts and child-raising would be taken over by the state. Kang stressed the need to achieve equality and to eliminate barriers among races, classes, and the sexes. He envisioned the merging of national states into a democratic, federated world government.

Kang's composition itself displayed many conflicts. Many of his other writings had stressed the virtues of competition and free enterprise. He expressed contradictory views on the desirability of competition. In one place he wrote that competition was "the greatest evil to the public existing in the world." Elsewhere he wrote that "without competition there is laxness and decadence."

In 1903, Kang began shifting his political focus to press for China to adopt a constitution and become a limited monarchy similar to that of Great Britain. He traveled extensively, speaking to groups of overseas Chinese and raising money to support Chinese reform and—so his critics claimed—to enjoy a luxurious lifestyle.

Kang was not a supporter of the 1911 revolution. As it proceeded, he campaigned unsuccessfully against overthrowing the monarchy. He remained loyal to the fallen dynasty and urged that Confucianism be established as China's official religion. He returned to China in 1913. He was involved in 1917 in a plot to restore the deposed emperor and narrowly escaped arrest and possible execution. Disillusioned with public affairs, he turned his attention to cosmology, combining scientific knowledge and fantasy in his final writings.

SIGNIFICANCE

Kang symbolized the struggle of Chinese intellectuals to modernize their society, while at the same time preserving the esteemed values of Chinese culture celebrated in the Confucian classics. His conflicted inclinations are evident: He simultaneously wrote memorials supporting competition and market economy while designing a utopian socialist system.

Assessments of Kang's life and work vary widely. Most historians of Chinese intellectual development deal respectfully with his writings. In China he is praised as a hero of the reform movement of 1898. Sterling Seagrave gives a very different picture. He views Kang as a vain, pompous, and dishonest opportunist who greatly exaggerated his own originality and importance and whose main achievement was in helping to create a false negative image of the dowager empress Cixi. Kang's most praiseworthy effort was probably his consistent defense of constitutional monarchy during the years following 1903. Had the Chinese followed his path, they might have avoided the disastrous failures of the ill-fated republic that emerged from the 1911-1912 revolution.

—*Paul B. Trescott*

FURTHER READING

Hsiao, Kung-chuan. *A Modern China and a New World: Kang Yu-wei, Reformer and Utopian, 1858-1927*. Seattle: University of Washington Press, 1975. A comprehensive review of Kang's writings, effectively assessed on the context of what everyone else was saying and doing.

Karl, Rebecca, and Peter Zarrow, eds. *Rethinking the 1898 Reform Period*. Cambridge, Mass.: Harvard University Press, 2002. Places Kang's ideas and activities into the broader context of his times.

Lo, Jung-pang, ed. *K'ang Yu-wei: A Biography and a Symposium*. Tucson: University of Arizona Press, 1967. Lo was Kang's grandson and the tone of this volume is respectful rather than critical.

Seagrave, Sterling. *Dragon Lady: The Life and Legend of the Last Empress of China*. New York: Alfred A. Knopf, 1992. Written with a novelist's flair for drama. Stresses Kang's role in the 1898 political upheaval and in creating a false impression in the West about developments in China.

Thompson, Laurence G. *Ta T'ung Shu: The One-World Philosophy of K'ang Yu-wei*. London: G. Allen and Unwin, 1958. This is the English translation of Kang's utopian book.

SEE ALSO: Cixi; Hong Xiuquan; Zhang Zhidong.

RELATED ARTICLES in *Great Events from History: The Nineteenth Century, 1801-1900:* 1860's: China's Self-Strengthening Movement Arises; August 1, 1894-April 17, 1895: Sino-Japanese War.

EDMUND KEAN
English actor

Kean's capacity to identify deeply and sympathetically with the characters he portrayed and his ability to communicate passion to his audiences established him as the foremost tragic actor of his day and assured the dominance of Romantic over classical acting techniques on the nineteenth century British stage.

BORN: November 4, 1787; London, England
DIED: May 15, 1833; Richmond, England
AREA OF ACHIEVEMENT: Theater

EARLY LIFE

Considerable uncertainty surrounds Edmund Kean's date of birth. November 4, 1787, is the most frequently mentioned possibility, but March 17, 1789, has also been suggested, and both may be incorrect. Some doubt exists, too, about Kean's parentage, but the consensus is that his mother was Ann "Nance" Carey, an untalented actor and part-time street vendor, and that his father was Edmund Kean, at various times a surveyor's clerk, an architect, an amateur orator, a professional mime, a drunkard, and a madman. The great actor himself often speculated that he was the son of his sometime guardian, Charlotte Tidswell, and Charles Howard, the eleventh duke of Norfolk,

but this appears to be romantic fantasy. Contemporary testimony points with near unanimity to Nance Carey as Kean's mother, and the actor's physical and temperamental resemblance to the dark-eyed, dark-haired, alcoholic, unstable Edmund suggests, although it does not quite prove, the elder Edmund's paternity.

Because both the Carey and the Kean families had strong connections with the theater, it is hardly surprising that the younger Edmund Kean became a performer. In addition to Nance, her father, George Saville Carey, appeared on the stage both as an actor and an impersonator of figures from the entertainment world. George's father, Henry Carey, was a writer of ballad operas whose one claim to fame, other than being Edmund Kean's grandfather, is his composition of the song "Sally in Our Alley." Like George Carey, with whom he occasionally performed, Moses Kean, the actor's uncle and a man of considerable theatrical renown, was an impersonator of public figures.

Although the details of his childhood are almost as sketchy as the facts of his birth, it appears that Kean was primarily cared for not by his parents but by a Mrs. Price, his father's sister, and by Charlotte Tidswell, an actor who was Moses Kean's mistress for a time. Young Kean may also have been negligently attended by a professional nurse for a short while, resulting in health problems that required his temporarily wearing leg braces, but again the biographers contradict one another on this point.

What the biographers agree on, however, is that Kean began his stage career early and experienced a long and often frustrating apprenticeship in his craft. The earliest playbill that mentions him by name is dated June 8, 1796, and announces him as Robin in a Drury Lane production of *The Merry Wives of Windsor* (pr. 1597), but he is reputed to have played a goblin in a presentation of *Macbeth* (pr. 1606) as early as April 21, 1794, when the new Drury Lane first opened its doors, and his actual debut may have occurred still earlier. Separating fact from myth for this first stage of Kean's theatrical life is nearly impossible, but what emerges from the various accounts is the portrait of a gifted, undereducated, rebellious child performing sporadically in the major and minor theaters and entertainment halls of London and beyond while being shunted from guardian to exploitative mother to guardian. The young Kean is most likely to have been experienced in every form of theatrical entertainment, from singing to tumbling to Shakespearian recitation, by the time he was announced on May 18, 1802, at Covent Garden as "the celebrated Master Carey."

The above billing suggests that Kean was exhibited as a child prodigy, an assumption strengthened by the oft-repeated claim that he was capable, perhaps even before entering his teens, of reciting *The Merchant of Venice* (pr. c. 1596-1597) in its entirety from memory. Whatever the truth, Kean, despite his small stature, could hardly have passed for a prodigy beyond his mid-teens, and by 1804, he was working as a journeyman actor at a weekly wage of fifteen shillings for Samuel Jerrold, an organizer of a provincial touring troupe.

Kean played a wide variety of roles for several companies during the next decade, spent mainly in the provinces, and while mastering an impressive dramatic repertoire, he waited with growing impatience for the opportunity to prove himself before an audience at London's Drury Lane or Covent Garden. Compounding his troubles during this period of comparative obscurity were the attractions of alcohol and the financial responsibilities that accompanied his marriage to Mary Chambers on July 17, 1808, and the births of his sons Howard Anthony Kean, on September 13, 1809, and John Charles Kean, who eventually became a distinguished actor in his own right, on January 18, 1811.

Edmund Kean. (Library of Congress)

LIFE'S WORK

One of the terrible ironies of Kean's life is that his beloved Howard Anthony died during the complex contract negotiations that led to Kean's first London successes. The son died on November 22, 1813, and the father premiered at Drury Lane as Shylock on January 26, 1814. Reviewers for only two of the London papers, the *Morning Chronicle* and the *Morning Post*, were present for the historic performance, but both praised Kean's innovative, passionate, sardonic interpretation of Shakespeare's familiar Jew. The *Morning Chronicle*'s William Hazlitt, who was to become Kean's foremost champion and most insightful critic, was especially impressed with the variety of emotion Kean infused into the too-often predictable role.

After several performances of *The Merchant of Venice*, the patrons of Drury Lane, still uncertain of Kean's potential, looked forward with considerable anticipation to his appearance on February 12 as Richard III. This time, a full retinue of reviewers was present. The Richard to which London audiences were accustomed was the carefully cadenced, classically restrained Richard of John Philip Kemble. Kean's Richard, by contrast, was emotionally complex, unpredictable, electrifying; his gestures and vocal intonations were subtle at one moment and fiery at the next. This Richard was not simply a character played by a skillful actor with a mellifluous voice; this was the moody, richly varied human being as he might really have been.

For those who would accept nothing but Kemble's declamatory style, the evening was disconcerting, but for the rest, the performance was a revelation, and Kean's success was assured. Kean's subsequent performances of *Richard III* (pr. c. 1592-1593) filled Drury Lane to capacity and restored the financially ailing house to solvency. His appearance as Hamlet on March 12, although not quite the success that his Richard had been, was received well enough to confirm him as Kemble's primary rival for preeminence on the English stage and to raise the public's hope that Kean might become as great as the immortal David Garrick. His triumphs also ended the financial privations of his family. The provincial player who had so recently been earning a few shillings a week was now the most lionized actor in London, under contract to Drury Lane Theater for five years at the princely sum of eighty pounds a month.

The extraordinary season continued with Kean's portrayal on May 5 of Othello and, in the immediately following performance, of Iago. His Othello, eventually recognized as one of his greatest roles, at first received lukewarm reviews, but his Iago was immediately acknowledged as masterful. As generally happened when Kean performed, what the critics noted were the subtleties of gesture, the nuances of expression that set his version of the character apart from all others. Kean's voice lacked the grandiloquent music of that of Kemble, but he could communicate emotion with a glance, with some bit of body movement that no previous actor had thought to attempt, and he could shift the emphasis of a familiar dramatic line in such a way that it became startlingly new and the character astonishingly human.

Kean followed up his London successes with well-received performances in Dublin, Gloucester, and Birmingham. He returned to London in the fall of 1814, and in addition to repeating the roles that had made his reputation during his first London season, he played Macbeth, Romeo, Richard II, and various forgettable non-Shakespearian parts. Although his Richard II was widely admired and his Macbeth profitable, the season, which ran from October, 1814, through July, 1815, was not quite the dazzling triumph that the previous one had been. Nevertheless, Kean remained a vastly admired man, and he thoroughly immersed himself in the life that his recent fame and wealth had made possible. His friendship was cultivated by Lord Byron, and he began developing eccentricities that rivaled Byron's own. He

sometimes startled his guests by introducing them to his pet lion, often rode after dark at full gallop through the countryside on a black horse, and, most ominously, spent interminable hours drinking in the Coal Hole Tavern with his cronies of the Wolf Club, a notorious organization of his own founding.

By the season of 1815-1816, Kean was advising in the management of Drury Lane, with Byron and four others, and he continued to be the theater's major attraction. His performances were generally well attended, but when he added new roles to his previous successes, the public, having been disappointed by a number of his previous efforts to diversify, was slow to respond. Three new parts, however, were well received: Florez in Douglas Kinnaird's *The Merchant of Bruges: Or, Beggar's Bush* (1815), Sir Giles Overreach in Philip Massinger's *A New Way to Pay Old Debts* (1621-1622?), and Bertram in the play of that name by Charles Robert Maturin. Overreach, one of his finest portrayals, illustrates his genius for representing evil. During the final scene of the January 12, 1816, premiere, one of the supreme moments of his career, Kean rendered Overreach's culminating madness with such passionate conviction that his fellow actors were astounded, the pit enthralled, and the susceptible Lord Byron quite literally thrown into a convulsive fit. Needless to say, the play was profitably repeated for many nights thereafter.

Kean's drinking problem was increasing, and his first missed performance at Drury Lane, occurring on March 26, 1816, is probably attributable to drunkenness. He recovered well from this first misstep, however, and the season's end and the subsequent summer tour of the provinces were successful. All appeared prosperous as the 1816-1817 season began, but soon matters took a troublesome turn, with Drury Lane receipts falling disastrously and Kean's home life threatening to deteriorate. Furthermore, despite the retirement of Kemble at the end of the season, Kean's preeminence among English tragedians was still insecure because of the appearance of two new rivals, Junius Brutus Booth and William Charles Macready. Booth, the father of the great actor Edwin Booth and the infamous assassin John Wilkes Booth, was soon overcome, but Macready remained a thorn in Kean's side to the end.

The 1817-1818 and the 1818-1819 seasons were again mediocre, and Kean's health, which had already shown signs of decline, began growing worse under the various pressures of his intense acting and his equally intense carousing. He was also alienating many of his fellow actors through the ruthlessness with which he eliminated rivals to his theatrical fame. Booth was the most illustrious of Kean's victims, but there were others. In addition, Kean became entangled in disputes over which plays were to be performed at Drury Lane, and on more than one occasion, he helped to scuttle the hopes of an aspiring playwright by resisting the inclusion of a particular play in the season's schedule or by putting little effort into the performance of a role that did not provide him with any likelihood of further glory.

Because of various managerial difficulties, a number of them aggravated by Kean, control of Drury Lane was handed over at the beginning of the 1819-1820 season to an old theatrical enemy, Robert William Elliston, for whom Kean at first refused to work. The combination of a threatened lawsuit for breach of contract and various flattering promises soon changed his mind, and the season included Kean's London debut as King Lear, seen first on April 24, 1820, and repeated twenty-five times by May 27. The fact that Kean, despite his five-foot, seven-inch frame, could succeed as Lear, perhaps the most formidable of all dramatic roles, is a clear indication of his continuing power as an actor.

Kean spent the 1820-1821 season in the United States, dividing his time between New York, Philadelphia, Boston, and Baltimore. All went well until May 25, 1821, when he refused to perform before a Boston audience that he judged to be insultingly small. The ensuing national furor cut short his intended tour, and on June 6, he set sail for home. His return to Drury Lane was greeted enthusiastically, but his health failed him, as it would more and more frequently in the future, and he took several weeks off. The rest of the 1821-1822 season brought no new triumphs, and it was only through the shrewd introduction by Elliston of a rival tragedian, Kemble's heir apparent Charles Young, into the Drury Lane company that Kean was once more inspired to act to his full potential.

During the 1822-1823 season, both Young and Kean played to large houses, and when they played together, especially in *Othello, the Moor of Venice* (pr. 1604), the theater was packed. The 1823-1824 season saw Young at Covent Garden and Kean and Macready at Drury Lane, but nothing like the previous year's rivalry developed. Kean's performances were usually quite profitable, but provincial touring and sporadic bad health kept him frequently away from Drury Lane.

As the 1824-1825 season began, Kean's tempestuous personal life became even more the subject of scandalous rumor than it had formerly been. Town gossip alleged that a liaison had long existed between Kean and the wife of a close family friend and that the aggrieved husband, one Robert Cox, was about to seek damages for the insult to his marriage. When, on January 17, 1825, the suit actually materialized, resulting in a judgment of eight hundred pounds against Kean, the English and American newspapers gave the matter their full attention, and several of Kean's audiences reacted with predatory delight.

Kean's performance as Richard III on January 24 was shouted down, and disruptive behavior marred two or three of his subsequent appearances, but the Drury Lane patrons gradually shifted their sympathies back to Kean, and his London career survived the crisis. However, his long-abused marriage did not. Although there was no divorce, he and Mary were permanently estranged. Problems continued, too, during various performances away from Drury Lane. Partially because of public disapproval of his personal life and partially because of his own belligerence and more and more noticeable drunkenness on the stage, a tour of the provinces and a second North American tour, this time including Canada, were stormy. They were not without their triumphant moments, however; Kean's star was rapidly declining, but it had not quite set.

Kean's January 8, 1827, return to Drury Lane in *The Merchant of Venice* was a tumultuous success, but the Cox scandal still haunted him, and he escaped his sorrows through spectacular indulgences in liquor and women. The cumulative effect on his health, physical and mental, was disastrous, and he soon found it nearly impossible to memorize new roles. He failed miserably, for example, in the May 21, 1827, premiere of Thomas Colley Grattan's *Ben Nazir* (1827), only a few lines of which he was able to deliver correctly. He then quarreled with Stephen Price, the new manager of Drury Lane, deserted to Covent Garden for the 1827-1828 season, and found himself competing with his own inexperienced son, with whom he was also quarreling and whom the sly Price had signed straight from the amateur theatricals of Eton.

The final period of Kean's career is an odd mixture of the pathetic and the heroic, as Kean continued to act—sometimes badly, sometimes with a return of the old fire—despite continual announcements of his impending retirement. His final performance occurred on March 25, 1833, at Covent Garden, where he played Othello opposite the Iago of his son Charles, with whom he had since been reconciled. He collapsed into his son's arms halfway through the presentation and was taken to his home in Richmond, where he died on May 15.

SIGNIFICANCE

Edmund Kean was the quintessential Romantic actor, capable of stirring a depth and variety of emotion unmatched by the best of his contemporaries and perhaps unequaled in the history of the English theater. He was the perfect actor for his time, a period in which theaters were large and audiences attuned to the stormy emotive power of which Kean was the acknowledged master. Although the ephemeral nature of the performing arts, at least before the next century's audio and video recording, makes it impossible to know with certainty what a performance by Kean was like, contemporary accounts suggest that classical polish gave way entirely to passion and psychological exploration when Kean was on the stage.

Laurence Olivier's brooding Heathcliff and John Barrymore's eccentric Svengali, rather than John Gielgud's regal Hamlet, are the lineal descendants of the characters brought to vivid life by Kean. That dexterity of face and body that Kean developed during his long, obscure apprenticeship served him well in his years of triumph, and though his voice was not the sonorous, cadenced instrument of a John Philip Kemble, it was capable of both the subtlety and the projective power needed to stir the soul of the furthest spectator at Drury Lane.

As the comments of such writers as William Hazlitt and John Keats, another of Kean's admirers, make clear, Kean was capable of identifying so completely with his role that all distinction between actor and character disappeared. The intensity that was displayed by Kean both on the stage and in his tempestuous private life destroyed him, as it has destroyed other actors like him, but it created some of the most inspired moments in world theater and made the Romantic rather than the classical ideal the standard that English-speaking actors most frequently sought to emulate for decades following his untimely death.

—Robert H. O'Connor

FURTHER READING

Booth, Michael R., et al. *The Revels History of Drama in English.* Vol. 6. London: Methuen, 1975. A wide-ranging history invaluable for understanding the complex theatrical world in which Kean flourished. Volume 6 covers the years 1750 to 1880. The direct commentary on Kean's acting contrasts the passion of his technique with the classical restraint of John Philip Kemble. An evenhanded account of both Kean's strengths and weaknesses is presented through references to many of the roles with which Kean was most closely associated.

Crochunis, Thomas C. "Byronic Heroes and Acting: The Embodiment of Mental Theater." In *Contemporary Studies on Lord Byron,* edited by William D. Brewer. Lewiston, N.Y.: Edwin Mellen Press, 2001. Analyzes how actors portrayed the heroes in Byron's plays, focusing on Kean's performances of these roles.

FitzSimmons, Raymund. *Edmund Kean: Fire from Heaven.* New York: Dial Press, 1976. A popular biography that makes use of all preceding biographical material as well as some newly discovered documents. A vivid account of both the private and public lives of the great actor that leans a bit too strongly toward the credulous. Contains an extremely useful bibliography.

Hawkins, F. W. *The Life of Edmund Kean from Published and Original Sources.* 2 vols. London: Tinsley Bros., 1869. Reprint. New York: Benjamin Blom, 1969. One of the more influential and unreliable of the nineteenth century biographies. A repository of mingled fact and myth that has led many later researchers astray.

Hazlitt, William. *Hazlitt on Theater.* Edited by William Archer and Robert Lowe. New York: Hill & Wang, 1957. Reprint. Westport, Conn.: Hyperion Press, 1979. Fully one-third of the essays in this volume are reviews of particular performances by Kean directly witnessed by Hazlitt. An invaluable depiction by Kean's greatest champion and most astute critic of what Kean's acting was like. Hazlitt emphasizes the naturalness and the emotive power of Kean's stage presence.

Hillebrand, Harold Newcomb. *Edmund Kean.* New York: Columbia University Press, 1933. Reprint. New York: AMS Press, 1966. This is the definitive scholarly account of Kean's public life. A valuable resource, too, for some details of Kean's private life. Any serious research on Kean should begin with this volume.

Moody, Jane. "Romantic Shakespeare." In *The Cambridge Companion to Shakespeare on Stage,* edited by Stanley Wells and Sarah Stanton. New York: Cambridge University Press, 2002. Describes theatrical production during the Romantic period in the nineteenth century, focusing on the performances of Kean and John Philip Kemble.

Playfair, Giles. *Kean.* New York: E. P. Dutton, 1939. Rev. ed. *Kean: The Life and Paradox of the Great Actor.* London: Reinhardt and Evans, 1950. A revision of Playfair's widely respected 1939 study. Playfair has the advantage of familiarity with Hillebrand's work and improves on Hillebrand's treatment of the private life.

Proctor, B. W. *The Life of Edmund Kean*. 2 vols. London: Edward Moxon, 1835. Reprint. New York: Benjamin Blom, 1969. This earliest full-length biography of Kean has the advantage of direct access to those who knew him but is unreliable in many details. Less fanciful than Hawkins but should still be read with caution.

Thomson, Peter. *On Actors and Acting*. Exeter, England: University of Exeter Press, 2000. A collection of essays, including essays exploring the themes, episodes, and contemporary taste that established the reputations of Kean and other English actors of the eighteenth and nineteenth centuries.

SEE ALSO: Edwin Booth; Lord Byron; Edwin Forrest; John Keats; William Charles Macready; Ellen Terry.

RELATED ARTICLES in *Great Events from History: The Nineteenth Century, 1801-1900:* c. 1801-1850: Professional Theaters Spread Throughout America; 1878-1899: Irving Manages London's Lyceum Theatre.

JOHN KEATS
English poet

Through works exploring the significance of beauty, joy, and imagination in a world of suffering and death, Keats was one of the great poets of the Romantic era and is generally acknowledged to have been among the finest writers of personal correspondence in English.

BORN: October 31, 1795; Moorfields, London, England
DIED: February 23, 1821; Rome, Papal States (now in Italy)
AREA OF ACHIEVEMENT: Literature

EARLY LIFE

The eldest child of Thomas Keats and the former Frances Jennings, John Keats (keets) was born in the living quarters of the family's London business, the Swan and Hoop Stables. He had three brothers, George, Thomas, and Edward (who died in childhood), and a sister, Frances Mary. By all accounts, the family was lively and affectionate, and John's earliest years were probably happy. However, the Keats family fortunes received a disastrous shock with the death of John's father following a riding accident in April of 1804. John's mother, in desperate haste, married an unpropertied bank clerk, William Rawlings, on June 27, 1804, and left him soon thereafter, thus forfeiting everything she had inherited from her first husband.

The children had moved into the home of their grandparents, John and Alice Jennings, even before this second marriage, and it was there that their mother ultimately rejoined them. She lived on only until March of 1810, succumbing to what was almost certainly tuberculosis, the disease that would eventually kill both young Thomas and her favorite son, John. John is reported to have nursed her through some of the worst stages of her illness, thereby getting a foretaste of what he himself would experience a decade later.

Even before this, on March 8, 1805, the grandfather had died, leaving a will that provided fifty pounds annually for his daughter Frances and lump sums of 250 pounds plus interest for each of her children when they came of age, none of which was paid out during Keats's lifetime. Additional money, placed as a trusteeship in the hands of Richard Abbey by Alice Jennings several years before her death in December of 1814, was mishandled, perhaps criminally, and Keats spent much of his life on the brink of poverty, partially because his obsession with poetry brought him little income but also because Abbey, his legal guardian, gave him only a portion of the money that was rightfully his. Despite the various deaths and the family's financial problems, the Keats siblings remained close, maintaining their affectionate relationship through visits and regular correspondence after the breakup of the household.

During the summer before his father's death, Keats had entered the academy of schoolmaster John Clarke at Enfield, where the future poet was a student until his mid-teens. Although quick-tempered and often involved in fights, the result of boyish high spirits rather than malice, he formed friendships easily and was a favorite among his schoolmates. Despite his curly hair, rather delicate features, and diminutive stature—he stood less than five-foot-one at his full growth—Keats experienced little of the adolescent persecution that so plagued his contemporary, Percy Bysshe Shelley. Keats possessed the same sensitivity and generosity as Shelley, but he was more pugnacious and down-to-earth than the ethereal pacifist, and this gritty, bantam element made him more compatible with his peers. Indeed, throughout his short life, he had a talent for friendship exceeded only by his talent for poetry.

With the encouragement of John Clarke and his son Charles Cowden Clarke, Keats developed a passion for reading during his final years at Enfield, especially an interest in books of Greek mythology. After leaving the school in 1811 to become an apprentice apothecary-surgeon with Thomas Hammond of nearby Edmonton, Keats continued his reading, visiting the schoolmaster's son several times a month to discuss books and authors. On one memorable occasion, the young Clarke introduced Keats to Edmund Spenser's *The Faerie Queen* (1590, 1596).

The eventual result of Keats's enthusiasm for the Elizabethan poet was his first poem, "Imitation of Spenser," written in 1814, when he was approaching his nineteenth birthday—a comparatively advanced age for a poet who was to become one of the most important in the English (or any) language, especially when one considers how little time Keats had left to live. Although the conclusion of his apprenticeship with Hammond was still ahead, plus several months of study at Guy's Hospital in London, Keats's growing fascination with poetry would assure that he would never make significant use of the apothecary's license granted him in 1816.

LIFE'S WORK

Keats successfully completed his apothecary's examination on July 25, 1816, after which he vacationed in Margate with his ailing brother Tom. Following his return to London in September, he sought out Clarke, who had recently moved to London from Enfield, and the two read George Chapman's translation of Homer together. By the next morning, Keats had written the sonnet "On First Looking into Chapman's Homer," the first of his poems that bears the undeniable stamp of genius. Shortly thereafter, Clarke introduced Keats to Leigh Hunt, a fellow poet and the influential editor of the ultraliberal *Examiner*, where Keats's poem "To Solitude" had been published during the previous May. The two became immediate friends, and while visiting Hunt again later in the year, Keats wrote a large part of "Sleep and Poetry," a

work that explicitly announces his dedication to the poetic life.

Through Hunt, whose stylistic influence is evident in much of Keats's early work, not always happily, Keats became acquainted with the poets, artists, and intellectuals of London. At various times, Hunt's circle included such figures as the literary parodist Horace Smith, the political philosopher William Godwin, the painter Benjamin Robert Haydon, the critic William Hazlitt, the essayist Charles Lamb, and the poets John Hamilton Reynolds and Shelley. Haydon, with whom he discussed the grandeur of William Shakespeare and the beauty of the Elgin Marbles; Hazlitt, many of whose ideas on the poetic imagination he borrowed; and Reynolds, to whom he addressed several of his profoundest letters, were to be especially important to his future.

Hunt recommended Keats to his many friends as a gifted young writer and published an article in praise of Reynolds, Shelley, and Keats in the December 1, 1816, *Examiner*. The lure of poetry was now so great that Keats announced to the angry Abbey that he was giving up plans to earn his surgeon's license and turning his full attention to establishing himself as a poet. His first volume, a generally undistinguished collection that he dedicated to Hunt, was published by Charles and James Ollier on March 3, 1817. Within a few weeks, Keats had left London to work on a much more ambitious project, the sprawling poetic allegory of the questing imagination, *Endymion*. By late November, having moved restlessly from the Isle of Wight to Margate to Canterbury to Hastings back to London and finally to Oxford, he had the four-thousand-line poem ready for final revision. By April of 1818, *Endymion* had been published by the firm of Taylor and Hessey.

Keats spent several weeks of the period between completing the draft and seeing the final printed version of *Endymion* in London, where he met William Wordsworth, whose egotism offended him, and heard several lectures on poetry by Hazlitt, one of which gave him the inspiration for the grotesque verse romance drawn from Giovanni Boccaccio's "Isabella: Or, The Pot of Basil." He then visited his brother Tom in Teignmouth, Devonshire, and was troubled by Tom's obviously declining health. During the brothers' return to London, Tom, who had only a few months to live, experienced serious hemorrhaging. His brother George, meanwhile, had become engaged to marry Miss Georgiana Wylie and had committed himself to emigration to America.

George and Georgiana were married in late May and left England the following month, after which Keats and

"IMITATION OF SPENSER"

Now Morning from her orient chamber came,
And her first footsteps touch'd a verdant hill;
Crowning its lawny crest with amber flame,
Silv'ring the untainted gushes of its rill;
Which, pure from mossy beds, did down distill,
And after parting beds of simple flowers,
By many streams a little lake did fill,
Which round its marge reflected woven bowers,
And, in its middle space, a sky that never lowers.

There the king-fisher saw his plumage bright
Vieing with fish of brilliant dye below;
Whose silken fins, and golden scales' light
Cast upward, through the waves, a ruby glow:
There saw the swan his neck of arched snow,
And oar'd himself along with majesty;
Sparkled his jetty eyes; his feet did show
Beneath the waves like Afric's ebony,
And on his back a fay reclined voluptuously.

Ah! could I tell the wonders of an isle
That in that fairest lake had placed been,
I could e'en Dido of her grief beguile;
Or rob from aged Lear his bitter teen:
For sure so fair a place was never seen,
Of all that ever charm'd romantic eye:
It seem'd an emerald in the silver sheen
Of the bright waters; or as when on high,
Through clouds of fleecy white, laughs the coerulean sky.

And all around it dipp'd luxuriously
Slopings of verdure through the glossy tide,
Which, as it were in gentle amity,
Rippled delighted up the flowery side;
As if to glean the ruddy tears, it tried,
Which fell profusely from the rose-tree stem!
Haply it was the workings of its pride,
In strife to throw upon the shore a gem
Outvieing all the buds in Flora's diadem.

Woman! when I behold thee flippant, vain,
Inconstant, childish, proud, and full of fancies;

Without that modest softening that enhances
The downcast eye, repentant of the pain
That its mild light creates to heal again:
E'en then, elate, my spirit leaps, and prances,
E'en then my soul with exultation dances
For that to love, so long, I've dormant lain:
But when I see thee meek, and kind, and tender,
Heavens! how desperately do I adore
Thy winning graces;—to be thy defender
I hotly burn—to be a Calidore—
A very Red Cross Knight—a stout Leander—
Might I be loved by thee like these of yore.

Light feet, dark violet eyes, and parted hair;
Soft dimpled hands, white neck, and creamy breast,
Are things on which the dazzled senses rest
Till the fond, fixed eyes, forget they stare.
From such fine pictures, heavens! I cannot dare
To turn my admiration, though unpossess'd
They be of what is worthy,—though not drest
In lovely modesty, and virtues rare.
Yet these I leave as thoughtless as a lark;
These lures I straight forget,—e'en ere I dine,
Or thrice my palate moisten: but when I mark
Such charms with mild intelligences shine,
My ear is open like a greedy shark,
To catch the tunings of a voice divine.

Ah! who can e'er forget so fair a being?
Who can forget her half retiring sweets?
God! she is like a milk-white lamb that bleats
For man's protection. Surely the All-seeing,
Who joys to see us with his gifts agreeing,
Will never give him pinions, who intreats
Such innocence to ruin,—who vilely cheats
A dove-like bosom. In truth there is no freeing
One's thoughts from such a beauty; when I hear
A lay that once I saw her hand awake,
Her form seems floating palpable, and near;
Had I e'er seen her from an arbour take
A dewy flower, oft would that hand appear,
And o'er my eyes the trembling moisture shake.

Source: John Keats, *Poems* (London: C. & J. Ollier, 1817).

a new friend, Charles Brown, made a walking tour of the English Lake District and Scotland. Having written a bundle of poetic impressions of his journey, Keats returned in mid-August, feverish and susceptible to further infection, only to discover that Tom's tubercular symptoms had become much aggravated. To make matters worse, as Keats began the melancholy and dangerous task of nursing his brother through his last weeks of life, critical attacks on *Endymion* appeared in three conservative periodicals: *Blackwood's Edinburgh Magazine*, the *Quarterly Review*, and the *British Critic*. The particularly vicious and snobbish article in *Blackwood's Edinburgh Magazine*, probably written by John Gibson Lockhart, lumped Keats with Hunt and several others into the "Cockney School" of poetry, a condemnation by association echoed in John Wilson Croker's critique in the *Quarterly Review*. Although these attacks did not, as some have claimed, hasten Keats's death, they made an already unpleasant period of his life even less pleasant.

On December 1, 1818, nineteen-year-old Tom Keats died, leaving John with memories of suffering and death that would cast their shadow over much of his remaining poetry and add profundity to what had previously been beautiful, sometimes brilliant, but too often shallow and naïve. He had already begun the Miltonic fragment "Hyperion," a poem that he would later rework as *The Fall of Hyperion: A Dream* (1856), thereby making even more explicit his theme of the growth of the imagination that follows the human fall into full knowledge of the entwined joys and agonies of earthly life.

Deepening his sense of this inevitable entanglement of joy and sorrow was his love for the beautiful young Fanny Brawne, whom he had first met during Tom's final weeks of life and to whom many of his most passionate short lyrics were addressed. Often driven frantic by Fanny's flirtatiousness, Keats nevertheless won her pledge, late in 1819, to marry him, but their union was made impossible by his own impending death. On February 3, 1820, after months of uncertain health, he spat up a quantity of arterial blood that he immediately recognized as evidence of his doom.

What occurred between Tom's death and that terrible day on which he foresaw his own demise, however, was a flowering of poetic genius unmatched in English literary history. During his *annus mirabilis*, in addition to continuing "Hyperion" and working on *The Fall of Hyperion*, Keats wrote "The Eve of St. Agnes," "La Belle Dame Sans Merci," "Ode to a Nightingale," "Ode on a Grecian Urn," "Ode on Melancholy," "Lamia," and "To Autumn," as distinguished a manifestation of lyric power

as any poet has ever produced. Peripatetic as ever, Keats composed "The Eve of St. Agnes" during a visit to Chichester and Bedhampton early in 1819; "La Belle Dame Sans Merci," "Ode to a Nightingale," "Ode on a Grecian Urn," and probably "Ode on Melancholy" during a spring interlude at Wentworth Place in the Hampstead area of London; the first part of "Lamia" during a summer stay on the Isle of Wight; and the second part of "Lamia" as well as the whole of "To Autumn" in August and September at Winchester.

Tragically, when most of these poems, plus a handful of others, were published by Taylor and Hessey during June of 1820 in Keats's third volume of poetry, his poetic career had already ended. In a vain effort to recover his health, Keats had left England for Italy in September of 1820 with the painter Joseph Severn. He died in Rome on February 23, 1821, where he was buried, at his own request, under the inscription, "Here lies one whose name was writ in water."

SIGNIFICANCE

John Keats's personality and his poetry can best be understood through a careful reading of his letters, perhaps the most insightful written by any English poet. What emerges from his correspondence is the portrait of a charming, generous, surprisingly levelheaded young man who loves the world of the five senses with consummate intensity and who believes passionately in the power of poetry to create essential beauty from the unrefined ore of human experience.

During the earliest phase of Keats's career, this artistic intensity, this "gusto" as Hazlitt frequently referred to it, manifested itself as a power to suspend his own ego and to identify imaginatively and nonjudgmentally with objects and events beyond himself. Although he never lost this power of empathy, the intoxicated pastoralism that it frequently produced gradually gave way to a darker and, at the same time, more satisfying vision of human life, a vision in which our earthly existence is portrayed as an unresolvable mixture of bliss and pain whose mingled ecstasies and purgatorial trials fashion our souls. At its most mature, Keats's poetry never denies that the world is a place of suffering and death, but it courageously affirms that the sorrows of life must be embraced if life's beauty is to be realized. For Keats, the rejection of life is the worst of all possible errors.

—Robert H. O'Connor

FURTHER READING

Bate, Walter Jackson. *John Keats.* Cambridge, Mass.: Harvard University Press, 1963. For the advanced and the ambitious intermediate student of Keats, this Pulitzer Prize-winning critical biography is the place to begin. Bate analyzes the intellectual and artistic life of Keats with scrupulous scholarly care, weaving copious comments on the poetry and the more important letters into his account of the poet's everyday life.

Blades, John. *John Keats: The Poems*. New York: Palgrave Macmillan, 2002. Provides a detailed analysis of the themes and techniques in Keats's poetry. Places his poetry in context by examining his letters, nineteenth century Romanticism, and Keats's critical reception.

Finney, Claude Lee. *The Evolution of Keats's Poetry*. London: Russell & Russell, 1936. Reprint. New York: Russell & Russell, 1963. The reissue of Finney's impressive 1936 study of the development of Keats's poetry is recommended for the advanced and intermediate student rather than the beginner. Emphasis is on the impact of Keats's experiences and of the world in which he lived on his creative output. Still of great value.

Gittings, Robert. *John Keats*. Boston: Little, Brown, 1968. With access to certain British resources unavailable to American biographers, Gittings expands on the work of Finney, Bate, and Ward. A valuable supplement to the earlier studies.

Hebron, Stephen. *John Keats*. New York: Oxford University Press, 2002. Concise, fully illustrated biography, charting Keats's development as a poet. Good for students with little previous knowledge of Keats's life and work.

Hirst, Wolf Z. *John Keats*. Boston: Twayne, 1981. Like the other volumes in the Twayne series, this study is an excellent starting point for the beginner. Contains a convenient capsule biography, a helpful chapter on the letters, good critical assessments of the poems, and an extensive annotated bibliography.

Keats, John. *The Letters of John Keats, 1814-1821*. 2 vols. Edited by Hyder Edward Rollins. Cambridge, Mass.: Harvard University Press, 1958. This is the definitive collection of Keats's extensive correspondence. No thorough understanding of Keats as a poet or a man is possible without reading these extraordinary letters. Presented with meticulous editorial care.

_____. *The Poems of John Keats*. Edited by Jack Stillinger. Cambridge, Mass.: Harvard University Press, 1978. Stillinger's edition of the poetry supersedes all previous collections. The extensive textual notes are an invaluable source of information on the sometimes tortuous history of the individual poems.

Motion, Andrew. *Keats*. London: Faber & Faber, 1997. Scholarly biography, examining the social, familial, political, and financial forces that shaped Keats's life and poetry.

Stillinger, Jack. "John Keats." In *The English Romantic Poets: A Review of Research and Criticism*. Edited by Frank Jordan. New York: Modern Language Association of America, 1985. For the student of Keats who wishes to explore studies of the poet not mentioned in this bibliography, Stillinger's evaluation of available scholarship is definitive.

Ward, Aileen. *John Keats: The Making of a Poet*. New York: Viking Press, 1963. Ward's much-admired study attempts to analyze the complex psychological forces that produced Keats the poet. Usually, but not always, convincing.

SEE ALSO: Lord Byron; Percy Bysshe Shelley; William Wordsworth.

RELATED ARTICLE in *Great Events from History: The Nineteenth Century, 1801-1900:* December, 1816: Rise of the Cockney School.

BARON KELVIN
Irish physicist

Thomson contributed fundamentally to the mid-nineteenth century revolution in physics. By bringing together different approaches and different subjects in highly original conceptualizations, he deeply influenced the course of physical thought.

BORN: June 26, 1824; Belfast, Ireland (now in Northern Ireland)
DIED: December 17, 1907; Netherhall, near Largs, Scotland
ALSO KNOWN AS: William Thomson (birth name); Sir William Thomson
AREA OF ACHIEVEMENT: Physics

EARLY LIFE

William Thomson, the future Baron Kelvin, was the son of James Thomson, an Irishman who had been graduated from Glasgow University and who was teaching mathematics in Belfast at the time of William's birth. Thomson's mother, née Margaret Gardner, the daughter of a wealthy Glasgow merchant, died when William was six years old. In 1832, James Thomson took his motherless family of six children to Glasgow, where he had been appointed the professor of mathematics at Glasgow University. William's life was to be centered in Glasgow.

Thomson was a prodigy with a father who knew how to cultivate genius. James Thomson educated his children himself, and at the remarkably young age of ten, William became a student at Glasgow University. His older brother, James (1822-1892), later a professor of engineering at Glasgow University, entered the university at the same time. The Thomson brothers generally placed at the top of their classes, usually William first and James second. Along with ancient languages, mathematics, and moral philosophy, William studied chemistry and natural philosophy (that is, physics) at Glasgow. The broad natural philosophy course covered heat, electricity, magnetism, optics, and astronomy.

At the age of seventeen, Thomson published his first paper, a successful defense of work by a leading French mathematician against charges from the professor of mathematics at Edinburgh University. Thomson's father arranged for the publication of the paper, which appeared anonymously. The paper was published about the time that Thomson left Glasgow to enroll at Cambridge University, the leading British university for studies of mathematics and mathematical theories of astronomy and optics. Because Thomson was already an accomplished

mathematician, it is debatable how much mathematics he actually learned at Cambridge. Nevertheless, his stellar performance as an undergraduate there confirmed that he was a mathematician to be reckoned with. His abilities were also confirmed by the original papers in mathematical physics that he published as an undergraduate, while his fellow students were preparing for examinations.

Shortly after Thomson took his degree at Cambridge in 1845, the professorship of natural philosophy became vacant at Glasgow. With his father's guidance, Thomson successfully applied for the post, being appointed in 1846 at twenty-two years of age. The influential father and his talented son enjoyed membership in the same university faculty for only three years, for James died of cholera in 1849. William retained his position at Glasgow until he retired in 1899.

Thomson's early publications were mathematical studies of heat, electricity, and magnetism, which combined a Glasgow emphasis on those subjects with a Cambridge-like emphasis on high-level mathematics. Even early in his career, Thomson's exuberant brilliance readily drew others into his research program. He offered the most advanced physics instruction available in Great Britain during the late 1840's; he had established a laboratory where his students did experimental work in support of his own scientific and engineering research. He also worked closely at this time with the experimental physicists James Prescott Joule and Michael Faraday, collaborations that did much to transform the science of physics.

LIFE'S WORK

Thomson's easy-flowing genius spilled over into numerous areas of science and engineering. He wrote some 650 papers, coauthored a major physics textbook that helped establish the new science of thermodynamics, and took out some seventy patents. His research on heat during the 1840's and 1850's is embodied in what is now known as the Kelvin temperature scale and brought him into conflict with geologists over estimates of the age of the earth.

During the 1850's and 1860's, Thomson's inventions and his applications of mathematical physics to telegraphy problems were keys to the success in 1866 of the Atlantic cable, a submarine telegraph from Europe to North America. For his efforts, he was knighted in 1867, becoming Sir William Thomson. Later, his love of sailing led to patents for improved ships' compasses and methods of taking deep-sea soundings. Most momentous of all, however, was Thomson's lifetime of speculative thinking in physics: He brought together different approaches and different subjects in a highly original conceptualization that deeply influenced the course of physical thought.

In recognition of all of his accomplishments, Thomson was raised to the peerage in 1892. He chose the name Baron Kelvin of Largs, after both the River Kelvin that runs through Glasgow and the seaside town of Largs, where he had built a mansion financed from the proceeds of his patents.

To understand Thomson's contributions to physics, one must see the science as Thomson first saw it. The great success of early nineteenth century physics had been the establishment of the wave theory of light, according to which light consisted of waves in a rarefied form of matter called the luminiferous ether. New experimental results and sophisticated mathematical analysis of wave motion had combined to bring this theory to an advanced state. Heat, electricity, and magnetism, on the other hand, were not as well understood; experimental results in those areas had not yet been fit into a satisfactory mathematical theory comparable to the wave theory of light. Furthermore, the best mathematical physicists during the early nineteenth century were Frenchmen. In Great Britain, the most interesting work in physics tended to be done by experimentalists, such as Joule and Faraday, who knew little of high-level mathematics. Thoroughly familiar with French mathematical physics (as indicated by his first publication), Thomson was able to deal with Joule's and Faraday's results in heat, electricity, and magnetism in ways that they could not.

Joule claimed that his experiments proved that heat was not "conserved," that the total amount of heat in the world did not remain constant but could be created and destroyed in physical processes. Contemplating Joule's arguments, which he at first rejected, Thomson was led to publications at mid-century that were instrumental in founding the science known as thermodynamics. Now, it was energy, not heat, that was understood to be conserved. Different forms of energy (electrical, thermal, and magnetic) could be converted into one another (so that the total amount of heat, for example, could change), but in such conversions the total amount of energy remained the same. That was the first law of thermodynamics, the conservation of energy.

The second law, in Thomson's words, involved a "dissipation" of energy. In an example given by Thomson, the potential energy of a rock was converted into the

kinetic energy of motion as it fell. As it accelerated toward the ground, it lost potential energy but gained kinetic energy in such a way that their sum was constant. Upon impact with the ground, the rock's kinetic energy was converted not only into energy of sound but also into energy of heat, as the rock and the ground around it were slightly warmed. The energy, though constant, had "dissipated," for the sound and heat were not as usable as was the initial potential energy of the rock. Thermodynamics was a unifying science, because heat and other forms of energy were understood to be convertible into one another.

Faraday's experiments in 1845 had shown that the plane of polarization of polarized light was rotated by a magnetic field under certain circumstances. Experiments by Faraday and others had already demonstrated that there were mutual influences between magnetism and electricity, and in this context Faraday's findings of 1845 gave Thomson a case of what he later called his half century of "ether dipsomania."

Time and again over the decades, Thomson tried to figure out how—just as light consisted of waves within the ether—all physical phenomena could be reduced to activity of one kind or another in the ether. The overall strategy was to use analogies with ordinary matter to visualize properties of the ether and then to seek correlations between resultant theories of the ether with experimental results. For example, Faraday's experiment with polarized light suggested to Thomson that magnetism must involve microscopic rotational motions that could influence the direction of the ethereal vibrations of light.

Thomson's seminal results rendered highly influential his view of all physical phenomena unified in ethereal activity. The view eventually led Thomson's younger colleague, James Clerk Maxwell, a fellow Scot and Cambridge graduate, to his electromagnetic theory of light during the 1860's. Indeed, Maxwell's particular solution to the general problem prevailed over Thomson's and remains as a part of modern physics. Thomson himself never formulated a satisfactory theory of the ether, and pursuit of his own insights prevented him from accepting most of Maxwell's electromagnetic theory.

The drive toward unification, exemplified in Thomson's theories of ether and energy, reached its greatest extent in Thomson's vortex-atom theory, published in 1867. Thomson imagined material particles themselves to be microscopic whirlpools in a frictionless fluid, analogous to ordinary smoke rings. Experiments showed that smoke rings bounced off one another just as it seemed reasonable to suppose that atoms would.

Faraday's 1845 experiments had shown the importance of rotational motion in nature. In addition, Thomson argued that many of these fluid whirlpools packed together and repelling one another would possess the kind of elasticity that allowed the ether to transmit light waves. If successful, the vortex-atom theory would, therefore, have reduced both ordinary matter and the ether to the same underlying frictionless fluid. All physical phenomena would then be reduced to states of potential and kinetic energy within this cosmic fluid. Though Maxwell and others were highly impressed by the theory, the mathematics of such rotational motion were difficult to work out. Thomson himself finally decided that the theory was physically implausible, and during the early years of the twentieth century it gave way to quite a different conception of matter. Yet, during its late nineteenth century lifetime, Thomson's theory directed the research and imagination of many physicists and, indeed, represented the essence of the Victorian concept of physical nature.

SIGNIFICANCE

Rejecting Maxwell's electromagnetic theory, which guided so much of late nineteenth century research, Thomson was somewhat at odds with the physics community in the last decades of his life. So profound had his influence been, however, that a leading British physicist was correct when he declared in 1889 that he lived in a "Thomsonian era." Thermodynamics and Maxwell's Thomson-inspired electromagnetic theory of light survive as integral parts of physics.

Later physicists abandoned much of the "Thomsonian" worldview, especially that involving the ether, during the early twentieth century revolution in physics associated with relativity and quantum mechanics. This constant updating of theories inevitably occurs in the history of science, however, and it should not diminish appreciation of the power of Thomson's physical insight. In fact, at a fundamental level, there is considerable continuity between Thomson's views and those of modern physicists, for both sought a unified physical theory to be expressed mathematically and supported by precise experimental results.

—*David B. Wilson*

FURTHER READING

Burchfield, Joe D. *Lord Kelvin and the Age of the Earth.* New York: Science History, 1975. Burchfield discusses Thomson's various calculations of the age of the earth, their impact on geological thought, and their eventual downfall. Relying especially on thermodynamics, Thomson estimated the earth to be about one hundred million years old, far younger than uniformitarian geologists of the day thought. Thomson convinced them that he was right, but modern discoveries in radioactivity have undermined Thomson's calculations, extending the earth's age to a few billion years.

Cardwell, D. S. L. *From Watt to Clausius: The Rise of Thermodynamics in the Early Industrial Age.* Ithaca, N.Y.: Cornell University Press, 1971. Examines the growth of thermodynamics, especially as it related to technology. Thermodynamics successfully explained the operation of steam engines, so essential for the Industrial Revolution and the development of railway technology.

Dunsheath, Percy. *A History of Electrical Engineering.* London: Faber & Faber, 1962. Dunsheath gives an overview of the history of electrical engineering, placing Thomson's contributions in their technical context.

Harman, P. M. *Energy, Force, and Matter: The Conceptual Development of Nineteenth-Century Physics.* Cambridge, England: Cambridge University Press, 1982. Provides an introductory survey of nineteenth century physics with an excellent discussion of Thomson's various researches.

King, Elizabeth. *Lord Kelvin's Early Home.* London: Macmillan, 1909. Describes the domestic life of James Thomson's large family, written by Thomson's sister.

Lindley, David. *Degrees Kelvin: A Tale of Genius, Invention, and Tragedy.* Washington, D.C.: Joseph Henry Press, 2004. Biography examining Thomson's life and thought processes and the evolution of physics during the nineteenth century. Lindley describes how Thomson was initially an innovative scientist but eventually became an anachronism, refusing to accept new concepts.

Nye, Mary Jo. *Before Big Science: The Pursuit of Modern Chemistry and Physics, 1800-1940.* New York: Twayne, 1996. Includes information about Thomson's theories of ether and thermodynamics.

Purrington, Robert D. *Physics in the Nineteenth Century.* New Brunswick, N.J.: Rutgers University Press, 1997. This overview of nineteenth century physics includes information about Thomson's scientific contributions and relations to other physicists.

Thomson, Silvanus P. *The Life of William Thomson, Baron Kelvin of Largs.* 2 vols. London: Macmillan, 1910. Explores Thomson's entire life, often in year-by-year fashion, but also provides a good analysis of Thomson's search for a "great comprehensive theory."

Wilson, David B. *Kelvin and Stokes: A Comparative Study in Victorian Physics*. Bristol, England: Adam Hilger, 1987. Compares Thomson to another major physicist, concentrating on physics education, science and religion, ether theories, and Thomson's reasons for rejecting modern theories of atomic structure.

SEE ALSO: Charles Darwin; Michael Faraday; Josiah Willard Gibbs; Joseph Henry.
RELATED ARTICLES in *Great Events from History: The Nineteenth Century, 1801-1900:* 1850-1865: Clausius Formulates the Second Law of Thermodynamics; July, 1897-July, 1904: Bjerknes Founds Scientific Weather Forecasting.

FANNY KEMBLE
English actor

Kemble ranks as one of the finest actors on the British and American stage. Her Journal of a Residence on a Georgian Plantation in 1838-1839 *is one of the best firsthand accounts of slavery in the United States and is still considered one of the most important indictments of antebellum slavery.*

BORN: November 27, 1809; London, England
DIED: January 15, 1893; London, England
ALSO KNOWN AS: Frances Anne Kemble (full name); Frances Anne Butler
AREA OF ACHIEVEMENT: Theater

EARLY LIFE

Frances Anne Kemble was born into the most famous acting family in Great Britain. Her father, Charles Kemble, had succeeded his brother John as the manager of the Covent Garden theater in London, and two of her aunts were well-known actors. Her mother, Maria Therese De Camp, was an actor who appeared on the London stage with her husband. Known as Fanny, Frances was reared primarily by her aunt, Adelaide ("Dall") De Camp, but because of her excitable temperament she was sent to France for her elementary schooling. Her antics soon caused the school's neighbors to refer to her as "*cette diable* Kemble" (that devil Kemble). She returned to France for a finishing-school education in Paris. She became fluent in French, developed a lifelong interest in religion, and began to read Lord Byron and Sir Walter Scott. She was a natural bookworm despite her excitable nature. During her years in Paris, Fanny also discovered her histrionic ability when acting in a school production.

Aside from singing and piano lessons, Kemble spent the next three years in England pondering the question of a career, finding herself drawn to writing except for the uncertainness of the income. Perhaps a career on the stage would provide the income for her to pursue her literary aspirations. Her enthusiasm for the theater evaporated, however, when she pondered how much it had cost other members of the Kemble family.

LIFE'S WORK

Fanny Kemble's return to London in 1829 marked a dramatic change in her life's work. She found her family in dire financial circumstances because of the burden of managing Covent Garden, which was covered with bills of sale. Although Kemble disliked the theater and had never had any dramatic training, her mother enlisted her to learn the role of Juliet in William Shakespeare's *Romeo and Juliet* (pr. c. 1595-1596). On October 5, 1829, Kemble made her debut, was an overnight success, and soon became the darling of the British theater crowd.

Two other important events happened in this two-year period: Kemble's play *Francis I* was published, and Kemble met the woman who would be her lifelong friend and correspondent, Harriet St. Leger of Ireland. For two years, Kemble performed in London and the provinces and made enough money to keep the Covent Garden in business. The great economic and political crisis of the 1830's, however, finally caused Charles Kemble to abandon the Covent Garden and to take Fanny and her Aunt Dall to the United States in the hope of recouping the family fortunes.

Kemble determined to keep a journal of her sea voyage and the tour of America. She was a good writer and a keen observer of the American scene, which she recorded in what others would later see as blunt and unkind language that was unsuitable for a lady.

The tour of the United States was all that Kemble and her companions had hoped it would be. Kemble was as popular in the United States as she had been in Great Britain, and American dollars flowed into the family purse. Although Kemble found being an actor distasteful, she believed that it was her duty to help her parents,

Fanny Kemble. (Library of Congress)

ther the monies she expected to receive from the publication of her travel journal. Although Pierce Butler was well aware of Kemble's independent ways, he soon endeavored to make her over into the submissive wife that he wanted, a wife who would not embarrass him or his family by expressing her own ideas. His attempts resulted in failure and ultimately in the end of the marriage.

At the time of his marriage, Butler was heir, along with his brother, to a Georgia plantation that grew sea-island cotton tended by approximately seven hundred slaves. The Butler family had become one of the wealthiest Philadelphia families with the riches acquired from the absentee ownership of the lucrative slave property. At that time, Kemble knew nothing of the source of her husband's wealth—a circumstance that was not at all unusual. By the same token, Pierce Butler was unaware that his new wife had decidedly antislavery views that had been formed in the agitation that had only recently resulted in the abolition of slavery in England. To Fanny, to be anything but antislavery would have been a disowning of her English heritage.

Once Kemble was aware of the source of the Butler money, the overwhelming concern of her life was slavery and how she could persuade her husband to free his slaves. During these early days of her marriage, Kemble devoted herself to reading, writing, and elaborating her thoughts on slavery, which soon caused disagreements between husband and wife. The first battle was over the travel journal, which was published in 1835 as the *Journal*. Kemble proposed to include in this travel journal a treatise against Negro slavery. Although Butler was unsuccessful in convincing the publisher to suppress the *Journal*, he did succeed in keeping Kemble from including the tirade against slavery by throwing the offending manuscript into the flames.

Kemble's opinions about slavery were strengthened when she read William Ellery Channing's *Slavery* (1835) in 1836 and adopted his idea that the slave owner must be won to repentance. Kemble accepted that her duty was to become Pierce Butler's conscience and mentor. To accomplish this goal, she needed to go to the Butlers' Georgia plantation. After much resistance, Butler

and that was the only way that she could do so. As she had in Great Britain, Kemble met in the United States famous and about-to-be famous people, including John Quincy Adams, Dolley Madison, Andrew Jackson, Nathaniel Hawthorne, and Charles Sumner, to list but a few. She also came under the influence of William Ellery Channing, the spiritual leader of the Unitarians and abolitionists in New England.

During Kemble's two-year tour of the United States, two important changes in her life occurred: She met and was ardently pursued by Pierce Mease Butler of Philadelphia, and her beloved Aunt Dall died as a result of a coach accident. Some of Kemble's biographers opine that if her Aunt Dall had not died in April of 1834, Kemble might not have been so quick to marry Pierce Butler that June. Her marriage meant that Kemble was saying goodbye to both her father and her country. Her last act of filial duty was to arrange to turn over to her fa-

took her there in 1838 when he had to assume the running of the plantation. As she was accustomed to do, Kemble kept a journal of her experiences while living in Georgia for fifteen weeks.

The state of Georgia had one of the densest slave populations of any state. When Kemble arrived, the residences for both the Butler family and the slaves were in wretched condition. The slaves were in poor physical condition, especially the women, who were sent back to the fields immediately after giving birth. This resulted in high infant mortality as well as many gynecological problems that were not treated. Kemble soon sought to remedy some of these conditions. Despite the fact that the slave owner's wife traditionally served as a "doctor" to the slaves, Butler interpreted his wife's interest as female meddling. Anyone who complained to Kemble was promptly flogged. Although Butler sometimes showed compassion—for example, by buying a slave's children from another owner so that the family could remain together—he soon tired of Kemble's complaints. In retaliation, she began to teach slaves to read, which was a serious crime, and to pay them for doing tasks for her.

When the couple returned to Philadelphia, their marriage was already breaking apart, although it would be almost ten years before Pierce secured a divorce. In 1849, the marriage formally ended, and the two Butler children, Sarah and Fan (Fanny), were given into the custody of their father.

For some years, Kemble spent her time between the United States and Europe; eventually, she found herself back in England during the American Civil War. There was much interest in England in the war because of the question of the recognition of the Confederacy as an independent nation. The one thing that might prevent that recognition was slavery. She tried to give an accurate picture of slavery to British authorities she knew, such as Charles Grenville, the diarist, and Lord Clarendon, a liberal peer. Her lack of success led Kemble to publish her journal of the time spent in Georgia. *Journal of a Residence on a Georgian Plantation in 1838-1839* appeared in May of 1863, when recognition of the Confederacy was being debated in Parliament. There is no indication that it had any effect. It was brought out in the United States in July of 1863, shortly after the dual Union victories of Gettysburg and Vicksburg. The book did serve to fan the antislavery fire in what by then were war-weary Northerners.

During her years as a divorcée, Kemble earned her living by doing dramatic readings, which had become more popular than plays. She was successful at this and toured both the British Isles and the United States. Upon the death of her husband in 1867, Kemble was able to reestablish contact with her two daughters.

CHRISTIANITY AND SLAVERY

In the journal that Fanny Kemble kept during her residence in Georgia during the 1830's, she comments perceptively on the hypocrisies and contradictions in slave societies. In this extract she points out the dangers to slave owners of allowing their slaves to attend church.

I . . . was surprised to hear rising from one of the houses of the settlement a hymn sung apparently by a number of voices. The next morning I enquired the meaning of this, and was informed that those negroes on the plantation who were members of the Church, were holding a prayer-meeting. There is an immensely strong devotional feeling among these poor people. The worst of it is, that it is zeal without understanding, and profits them but little; yet light is light, even that poor portion that may stream through a key-hole, and I welcome this most ignorant profession of religion in Mr. ——'s dependents, as the herald of better and brighter things for them. Some of the planters are entirely inimical to any such proceedings, and neither allow their negroes to attend worship, or to congregate together for religious purposes, and truly I think they are wise in their own generation. On other plantations, again, the same rigid discipline is not observed; and some planters and overseers go even farther than toleration; and encourage these devotional exercises and professions of religion, having actually discovered that a man may become more faithful and trustworthy even as a slave, who acknowledges the higher influences of Christianity, no matter in how small a degree. Slave-holding clergymen, and certain piously inclined planters, undertake, accordingly, to enlighten these poor creatures upon these matters, with a safe understanding, however, of what truth is to be given to them, and what is not; how much they may learn to become better slaves, and how much they may not learn, lest they cease to be slaves at all. The process is a very ticklish one, and but for the northern public opinion, which is now pressing the slaveholders close, I dare say would not be attempted at all. As it is, they are putting their own throats and their own souls in jeopardy by this very endeavour to serve God and Mammon. . . .

Source: Frances Anne Kemble, *Journal of a Residence on a Georgian Plantation, 1838-1839* (London: Longman, Green, 1863).

As she entered old age, she wrote her autobiographies based on the letters that she had sent to St. Leger and that St. Leger now returned to her. She died at her daughter Sarah's home in England in 1893.

SIGNIFICANCE

Fanny Kemble's impact on her time rests on her acting and her writing. Despite the fact that she did not like acting, she is acknowledged to have been one of the finest female actors that England has produced. Her craft, whether acting or doing dramatic readings, brought the pleasures of Shakespeare and other writers to people throughout the British Isles and the United States. Her most significant written work, *Journal of a Residence on a Georgian Plantation in 1838-1839*, effectively gave the lie to the Southern claim that slavery had been a benign institution. Its publication ensured that Northerners would not lose heart in the struggle to end the Civil War and see that the slaves would be freed by the Thirteenth Amendment. Despite efforts to discredit the book in the post-Civil War period, it remains the best available firsthand account of slavery in the United States. Kemble had indeed accomplished her goal of being a writer.

—*Anne Kearney*

FURTHER READING

Blainey, Ann. *Fanny and Adelaide: The Lives of the Remarkable Kemble Sisters*. Chicago: I. R. Dee, 2001. Dual biography of Fanny and her younger sister Adelaide, an opera singer, based in part on the sisters' letters.

Clinton, Catherine. *Fanny Kemble's Civil Wars*. New York: Simon & Schuster, 2000. Detailed and comprehensive biography. Clinton is generally sympathetic to Kemble, whom she views as a woman trapped by her family and fame. Includes sixty-four black-and-white illustrations.

Driver, Leota Stultz. *Fanny Kemble*. New York: Negro Universities Press, 1969. Provides portraits, pictures from Butler's island, a bibliography, notes, and an index. Contains interesting facts not recorded in other biographies, but the reader must beware of the author's opinions and her use of emotional terms.

Furnas, J. C. *Fanny Kemble: Leading Lady of the Nineteenth-Century Stage*. New York: Dial Press, 1982. Well illustrated with copious notes and a good bibliography. Provides thorough coverage of Kemble's life up to the publication of *Journal of a Residence on a Georgian Plantation in 1838-1839*. At times, the author exhibits a male bias.

Kemble, Frances Anne. *Journal of a Residence on a Georgian Plantation in 1838-1839*. Edited by John A. Scott. Athens: University of Georgia Press, 1984. Scott's introduction provides a short biography of Kemble up to the publication of the journal in 1863. Evaluates the importance of the journal.

Marshall, Dorothy. *Fanny Kemble*. New York: St. Martin's Press, 1978. Written from an English viewpoint. Includes many illustrations of family and friends not found in other biographies. Accepts as fact that Kemble was mentally unbalanced.

Wise, Winifred E. *Fanny Kemble: Actress, Author, Abolitionist*. New York: G. P. Putnam's Sons, 1967. Places Kemble's life in historical context by identifying persons whom other biographers simply name. Provides little information about the second half of her life.

Wright, Constance. *Fanny Kemble and the Lovely Land*. New York: Dodd, Mead, 1972. The best of the Kemble biographies. Places Kemble in her historical setting by explaining the historical importance of the various people in Kemble's life. A good bibliography and many illustrations are included.

SEE ALSO: John Quincy Adams; William Ellery Channing; Nathaniel Hawthorne; Andrew Jackson; Dolley Madison; Charles Sumner; Ellen Terry.

RELATED ARTICLE in *Great Events from History: The Nineteenth Century, 1801-1900:* 1878-1899: Irving Manages London's Lyceum Theatre.

JAMES KENT
American legal scholar

Through his law lectures, written judicial opinions, and four-volume Commentaries on American Law, *Kent won renown as a legal scholar of profound intellect. His work set the standard by which future legal and constitutional scholarship in the United States was measured.*

BORN: July 31, 1763; Fredericksburg, New York
DIED: December 12, 1847; New York, New York
ALSO KNOWN AS: American Blackstone
AREA OF ACHIEVEMENT: Law

EARLY LIFE

The mother of James Kent, who had been born Hannah Fitch, was the daughter of a physician. Kent's father, Moss Kent, the son of a noted Connecticut Presbyterian minister, had been educated at Yale College and had become a successful lawyer. It was natural, as he was born into an educated and socially prominent family, that James would be sent to the best private schools and tutors available. Beginning at the age of five, he studied the traditional college preparatory curriculum for that era. He had a happy childhood, notwithstanding the loss of his mother at the age of seven and the troubles and loss of home during the early days of the American Revolution.

At the age of fourteen, James Kent entered Yale College, where he excelled as a student, being accepted into Phi Beta Kappa in his senior year. In 1779, he had to flee Yale when the British threatened to march through New Haven, Connecticut, and the college was closed down. During this brief interruption of his college studies, Kent discovered his father's four-volume set of William Blackstone's *Commentaries on the Laws of England* (1765-1769). He found the clear and eloquent prose of the *Commentaries* so profound that it turned his interest toward law.

By the time he was graduated from Yale at the age of eighteen in 1781, Kent had become a scholar and a gentleman. He was considered a handsome youth, slight of build and just under average height, with a high forehead and a friendly face. He was somewhat shy, but throughout his life he made friends easily. Kent was ambitious and understood that preferment often came to those who were respectful of their superiors. By 1781, Kent had acquired life-long beliefs in caution and conservativism, hard work and honesty, and a sense of duty to society in return for his position as a member of the country's elite upper class.

Because there were no law schools in the United States before 1784, the only way for Kent to become a lawyer was to "read for the law" while working for a practicing attorney or judge. He secured a clerk's position with New York's attorney general, Egbert Benson, in Poughkeepsie, New York. He soon reestablished his reputation for diligence, spending most of his own time reading and studying the classics in law by Hugo Grotius, Samuel von Pufendorf, John Locke, Blackstone, and Edward Coke, among others. By January of 1785, he easily passed the oral examination admitting him to the bar. While clerking for Benson, he lived with John Bailey and fell in love with his daughter Elizabeth. They were married on April 3, 1785, just after he had joined Gilbert Livingston, a prominent Poughkeepsie lawyer, as a partner. He was twenty-one and she was sixteen. It was to be a long and happy union with four children, three of whom survived to adulthood.

LIFE'S WORK

The events surrounding the adoption of the U.S. Constitution drew Kent into a short political career and brought him to the attention of prominent politicians. He was keenly interested in the proposed new federal constitution, attending as a spectator all sessions of New York's special convention to decide whether to adopt it. His interest was so piqued, he ran for and was elected to the New York Assembly in 1790 and reelected in 1792 as a delegate of Poughkeepsie. Although his voting record clearly aligned him with the more conservative Federalists, he gained the trust and admiration of all factions for his hard work and knowledge of law. In 1792, the governorship was also being contested. John Jay, the Federalist candidate, was defeated by George Clinton. Kent gained the recognition of Jay and the Federalist leadership of New York when he led the fight during that election to expose some questionable campaign practices by the Clinton forces. Jay and other leading Federalists persuaded Kent to run for the U.S. House of Representatives in 1793, a race he lost.

With a rare lapse of good grace, Kent moved his family to New York City and opened his own law office, saying Poughkeepsie was too provincial. In November of 1794, he also began teaching law at Columbia College. The lectures written for the course were well researched and systematically covered all areas of American law. They later were published and then expanded into his famous, four-volume *Commentaries on American Law* (1826-1830). The professorship lasted only four years. The course seemed to have been too demanding for undergraduate students to be popular.

In 1795, John Jay ran again for governor of New York and won, but he did so just as the news broke of the unpopular treaty with England he had just negotiated for President George Washington. Kent entered the public debate to defend Jay by writing and publishing several pamphlets and essays. Jay rewarded Kent in 1796 by appointing him one of the two masters in chancery for New York City. A year later, Jay also appointed Kent as recorder of the City of New York. These two appointments, held simultaneously, made keeping a private practice unnecessary, an outcome that Kent welcomed. Although he had proved himself to be a fine courtroom lawyer, Kent had learned that he did not like arguing against other attorneys.

In 1798, Jay promoted Kent to associate justice of the New York state supreme court, a position he held until 1804 when he became chief justice. The new position required him to move to the state capital, Albany, and did not pay particularly well. Neither proved a problem, however, because he and Elizabeth had come to dislike the squalor and noise of the city and Kent had made some wise real estate investments that had paid off handsomely. Wealth was never Kent's ambition, for he sought instead respect as a scholar and man of principle. Kent was an intellectual. In Albany he found time for the further study of law and literature, and his library increased considerably.

The majority of the five-man New York State Supreme Court were Democratic-Republicans (that is, Jeffersonians), a political orientation Kent wholeheartedly despised. He perceived in their philosophy a plot by the lower classes to plunder the wealth and property of the upper classes. This, he thought, was the worst threat to liberty facing the United States. The fact that Kent was successful in becoming the leading justice on the court was a testament to his congenial personality as well as his scholarship.

A major problem before the court, and all state and federal courts at this time, was whether English common law was still in force. Federalists such as Kent thought the answer was yes, while Democratic-Republicans favored developing an American common law spiced with French doctrines as needed. The contest in New York was decisively won by English common law and Kent was largely responsible. Drawing on his profound learning and using his extensive powers of logic and persua-

James Kent. (Library of Congress)

sion, Kent carried his colleagues. This situation did not go unnoticed in the press, which praised Kent for his clarity, impartiality, and precision. As chief justice after 1804, Kent arranged to have all of the Court's opinions written and published, an effort that spread his influence throughout the nation.

Kent did not embrace English common law wholly and without question. There were times when he found it either unsuited to a republican environment or contrary to his sense of justice. He was then willing to amend or alter English precedent. The result was that by the time he left the New York Supreme Court in 1814, a fair body of logically consistent judicial doctrine was in place as a heritage for New York's future. This included laying the foundations for free enterprise capitalism and the defense of rights such as the free press. In the latter case Kent argued, contrary to English common law, that truth with legitimate intent was an acceptable defense against libel.

In 1814, in recognition of his eminence as a jurist, Kent was appointed chancellor of New York, a judicial office that has since fallen into disuse in the United States. A chancery court was a court of equity that heard cases where the injustice claimed was not covered by statutory law. Such cases were decided on the basis of rules of equity developed by the equity courts over the years. The object of these rules was to render each man his due and make justice and right-dealing prevail in the regulation of people's affairs. Each case was an ethical rather than legal issue and required a wise and learned judge.

Kent approached his new position with characteristic vigor and scholarly acumen and was soon gaining renown in New York and throughout the nation for the quality of his decisions. As he had done before, Kent began the practice of written decisions that were then published in book form periodically. He became particularly famous for defending property and contract rights. Chancellor Kent did not, however, favor the wealthy, as some claimed. His decisions often provided relief for the poor, and he was known for being hard on those who violated the trusts of widows, orphans, and the feebleminded.

Chancellor Kent was reversed by the New York Court of Errors only on occasion and his reputation for honesty, fairness, high professionalism, and incorruptibility became legend. Many famous lawyers and politicians consulted him on difficult points of law. Chancellor Kent wanted to continue on as chancellor as long as he was physically and mentally able, but New York's constitution mandated retirement at the age of sixty, an age Chancellor Kent reached in 1823.

After retiring, Kent moved back to New York City to open a law office and became a successful lawyer's lawyer. Columbia College again asked him to accept a professorship of law. Kent reworked his old lectures, and in the process began his greatest work, the *Commentaries on American Law*, published between 1826 and 1830. Kent's retirement turned out to be the most important period of his life. Five editions of his *Commentaries* were published during his lifetime, and he had finished the sixth just before he died. In the years following his death, further editions under various editors were also published; the fourteenth, in 1896, was the last.

Kent's *Commentaries* were the first effort by anyone to study the American laws and the Constitution in a systematic and scholarly manner. Judges, lawyers, and law students throughout the nation bought and used these books. Every copy of every edition published during the chancellor's lifetime (indeed until nearly the last edition) was sold. Although the *Commentaries* reflect Kent's conservative bias, his careful scholarship and intellectual integrity made the books of great value to everyone regardless of their political philosophy. It is probable that, until about 1900, the number of American lawyers unfamiliar with Chancellor Kent's *Commentaries* were few.

Besides his professional work, Kent spent his declining years traveling and enjoying the company of his wife,

children, and grandchildren. He seemed especially to enjoy the many banquets held to honor him. He remained alert and vigorous until nearly the end of his life. Besides old age, a touch of arthritis was all that seemed to bother him. He died quietly at home in his sleep December 12, 1847, at the age of eighty-four.

SIGNIFICANCE

As a New York Supreme Court justice and then chancellor, Kent left a legacy of written opinions of exceptional merit and scholarly precision that had influence far beyond the state's borders. During Kent's tenure on these courts, only the U.S. Supreme Court was more highly respected or more frequently cited as precedent in the decisions of other courts. Kent set standards for the entire American legal profession and was studied even in Europe. Kent respected the power of justice to maintain a stable and free society, and through his writings helped teach this respect to American lawyers. He also helped significantly in creating the aura of impartiality, justice, and wisdom that typically surrounds American judges and inspires individual judges to live up to that standard.

Kent's *Commentaries* were often used as texts in colleges and law schools, teaching law to generations of American lawyers. More important, the four volumes also taught by example how to study the law. Some might disagree with some of Kent's conclusions and ideas, but few could fault the manner by which he arrived at them. The *Commentaries* stressed the significance of the unique American doctrine of judicial review. Kent believed that this doctrine, which allowed courts to declare actions by other branches of government unconstitutional, was the keystone of liberty and justice. Through the courts' exercise of judicial review, the power of the state could be confined to legitimate uses. This would both preserve the principles of the Constitution and build public faith and trust in government.

Kent, unlike many Jeffersonians, never questioned that the final arbiter of constitutional issues was the U.S. Supreme Court. He had lived through the years of the Articles of Confederation and understood that the United States could not long survive with a weak and powerless national government. Kent's *Commentaries* also contributed to the intellectual tradition favoring an indivisible union, based on the principles of the Constitution, with a national government strong enough to preserve those principles. When the crisis of secession came, it was this tradition that preserved the United States.

—Richard L. Hillard

FURTHER READING

Ferguson, Robert A. *Law and Letters in American Culture.* Cambridge, Mass.: Harvard University Press, 1984. Interesting and perceptive discussion of the impact of law and lawyers on American culture from the Revolution to the Civil War, an era during which lawyers were perhaps the most respected professionals. Mentions Kent only briefly.

Horton, John Theodore. *James Kent: A Study in Conservatism, 1763-1847.* New York: D. Appleton-Century, 1939. Reprint. New York: Da Capo Press, 1969. Not particularly profound, but the only published biography. What is lacking is insight into Kent's personality and any real appreciation of his impact on the American legal profession.

Horwitz, Morton J. *The Transformation of American Law, 1780-1860.* Cambridge, Mass.: Harvard University Press, 1977. Mentions Kent in a number of places. Probably the best legal history of the era to date. Emphasis is on the transformation of English law in the colonies into a modern national legal system, and how this transformation aided economic development.

Kent, James. *Commentaries on American Law.* Edited by Oliver Wendell Holmes, Jr. 12th ed. 4 vols. Boston: Little, Brown, 1864. The fifth and sixth editions are considered by many the best produced by Kent personally, although any of the fourteen will suffice. The twelfth, by Oliver Wendell Holmes, Jr., is considered the most definitive edition.

_____. *Memoirs and Letters of Chancellor James Kent.* Compiled by William Kent. Boston: Little, Brown, 1898. Reprint. Union, N.J.: Lawbook Exchange, 2001. Compiled by Kent's eldest son, William. For readers interested in more personal details of Kent's life and his correspondence with other famous people of his day. The selection is a bit biased in Kent's favor.

Langbein, John H. "Chancellor Kent and the History of Legal Literature." *Columbia Law Review* 93, no. 3 (April, 1993). Discusses Kent's influence on the development of law as a body of precedent based on published, written opinions.

Newmyer, R. Kent. *The Supreme Court Under Marshall and Taney.* New York: Thomas Y. Crowell, 1968. The best short discussion of the great legal and constitutional questions of Kent's era from the viewpoint of the Supreme Court. Although Kent is mentioned only briefly, this work is an excellent introduction to the important issues Kent had to face.

SEE ALSO: Salmon P. Chase; James Fenimore Cooper; John Marshall; Joseph Story; Roger Brooke Taney.

RELATED ARTICLES in *Great Events from History: The Nineteenth Century, 1801-1900:* March 2, 1824: *Gibbons v. Ogden*; November, 1828: Webster Publishes the First American Dictionary of English; May, 1831-February, 1832: Tocqueville Visits America.

FRANCIS SCOTT KEY

American composer

Key was a successful lawyer throughout his adult life and held several important government posts; however, he is most widely known as the author of "The Star-Spangled Banner," which became the national anthem of the United States in 1931.

BORN: August 1, 1779; Frederick County (now Carroll County), Maryland
DIED: January 11, 1843; Baltimore, Maryland
AREAS OF ACHIEVEMENT: Law, music

EARLY LIFE

Francis Scott Key was born on his family's Maryland estate. He was the son of John Ross Key, who owned a plantation, and Ann Phoebe Charlton. At the age of ten, Key was sent to Annapolis, Maryland, to live with his grandmother, Ann Ross Key. While in the state capital, Key attended St. John's College, where he received the modern equivalent of a high school and university education at the same institution. Following his graduation from college in 1796, Key decided to become a lawyer. In the days before law schools, students had to find an established attorney who owned a law library. Key found a patron in the form of Judge J. T. Chase and was allowed to read and study the law, as well as be tutored by Judge Chase, until he was prepared to take the bar examination. He succeeded in 1801 and immediately opened his own practice in the town of Frederick, Maryland.

On January 19, 1802, Key married Mary Tayloe Lloyd, the daughter of Colonel Edward Lloyd of Annapolis, Maryland. Shortly thereafter, the newlywed couple moved to Georgetown in the District of Columbia. The Keys remained residents of Georgetown for the next twenty-eight years. During that time they raised eleven children—-six boys and five girls. Key quickly established a successful law practice by specializing in federal court cases. He was also active at St. John's Episcopal Church in Georgetown and was known for his keen intellect and speaking ability.

LIFE'S WORK

The events that led to Key's writing of "The Star-Spangled Banner" began in 1814 during the War of 1812. The United States and Great Britain had been at war with each other for more than two years when Key was approached with an urgent request for his help. Dr. William Beanes, a popular doctor and town leader from Upper Marlboro, Maryland, had been arrested by the British. Beanes's friends went to Key to gain his help in securing the doctor's release.

Beanes's ordeal began with the British invasion of the Chesapeake Bay area in the summer of 1814. On August 23, the English troops under the command of Major General Robert Ross passed through Upper Marlboro, a town in Maryland located southeast of Washington, D.C. Beanes, one of the few residents who did not evacuate during the invasion, was forced to open his home to Ross and Rear Admiral George Cockburn for an overnight stay. The following day, the British entered Washington, D.C., and Ross ordered his troops to put the nation's capital to the torch. Beanes responded to the burning of Washington by helping to organize a vigilante group that jailed British soldiers who became separated from the rest of the invasion force. When news of Beanes's actions reached Ross, the British commander ordered his men to arrest the doctor.

The friends of Dr. Beanes succeeded in retaining Key to attempt to win the doctor's release. Although Key had no experience with negotiating the release of prisoners of war, he did have experience fighting the British. Key had been involved in the war effort as the aide-de-camp to General Walter Smith, commander of the militia protecting the District of Columbia. When Key agreed to help Beanes, he was granted permission by President James Madison to approach the British. Because Key had no experience in this area of diplomacy, the War Department sent John S. Skinner, an American prisoner-of-war exchange agent, to assist Key in the negotiations.

On September 6, Key and Skinner boarded the HMS *Royal Oak*. The Americans were told that Beanes, along

Francis Scott Key. (Library of Congress)

with Ross and Cockburn, were aboard the HMS *Tonnant*, a British warship that was anchored off the coast of Tangier Island near the mouth of Chesapeake Bay. On the following day, much to the surprise of everyone aboard the *Royal Oak*, the ship carrying Beanes was spotted heading right for them under full sail. Key and Skinner were transferred to the *Tonnant*, where they learned that Beanes was to be released. Not long after boarding the British man-of-war, the Americans were also told that the *Tonnant* was en route to Baltimore, where it would join the rest of the British fleet for a full-scale assault on the largest and most prosperous city in the state of Maryland. In order to keep the operation a secret, Key, Skinner, and Beanes would be held until the end of the invasion. They were transferred to the HMS *Surprise*, a larger warship, and the fleet headed north for Baltimore.

Clearly, the invasion of Baltimore did not remain a secret for long as the movement of so many enemy vessels in the Chesapeake Bay alarmed residents along the way. Word spread quickly among the people on shore. When the British assault began during the early morning hours of September 13, 1814, the people of Baltimore were prepared. Fort McHenry, the star-shaped fortification

THE STAR-SPANGLED BANNER

O say, can you see, by the dawn's early light,
What so proudly we hail'd at the twilight's last gleaming?
Whose broad stripes and bright stars, thro' the perilous fight,
O'er the ramparts we watch'd, were so gallantly streaming?
And the rockets' red glare, the bombs bursting in air,
Gave proof thro' the night that our flag was still there.
O say, does that star-spangled banner yet wave
O'er the land of the free and the home of the brave?

On the shore dimly seen thro' the mists of the deep,
Where the foe's haughty host in dread silence reposes,
What is that which the breeze, o'er the towering steep,
As it fitfully blows, half conceals, half discloses?
Now it catches the gleam of the morning's first beam,
In full glory reflected, now shines on the stream:
'Tis the star-spangled banner: O, long may it wave
O'er the land of the free and the home of the brave!

And where is that band who so vauntingly swore
That the havoc of war and the battle's confusion,
A home and a country should leave us no more?
Their blood has wash'd out their foul footsteps' pollution.
No refuge could save the hireling and slave
From the terror of flight or the gloom of the grave:
And the star-spangled banner in triumph doth wave
O'er the land of the free and the home of the brave.

O thus be it ever when free-men shall stand
Between their lov'd home and the war's desolation;
Blest with vict'ry and peace, may the heav'n-rescued land
Praise the Pow'r that hath made and preserv'd us a nation!
Then conquer we must, when our cause it is just,
And this be our motto: "In God is our trust!"
And the star-spangled banner in triumph shall wave
O'er the land of the free and the home of the brave!

guarding Baltimore's inner harbor, was stocked with fifty-seven cannons and nearly one thousand men.

The British attack on Baltimore began at 5:00 A.M. on September 13, and artillery fire from both U.S. and British guns continued for the next twenty-three hours. The primary target of the enemy's guns was Fort McHenry because the English warships could not proceed until the heavily fortified arsenal was captured and its guns silenced. Throughout the day, Key, Skinner, and Beanes observed the battle through a spyglass from the deck of the *Surprise*, which was anchored eight miles away from the fighting. Key and his colleagues knew that as long as

Fort McHenry withstood the invasion, Baltimore would not fall into enemy hands. Because they were so far away from the fighting, the only way they could be sure was to see the large red, white, and blue flag of the United States flying over the fort. As the fighting continued after nightfall, Key could see the flag still flying over Fort McHenry through the glare of bombs and rockets exploding in and around the arsenal.

At 4:00 A.M. the following day, the fighting finally ended. The American prisoners aboard the British warship wondered if the assault on Baltimore had succeeded. They anxiously waited until daybreak, only to discover that the heavy haze of smoke from the artillery fire obscured their view. When the smoke cleared, Key and his friends were relieved to see that the U.S. flag was still flying over Fort McHenry. The signal was given for the British fleet to withdraw, thereby ending the battle. Key was so moved by the sight of the flag that he scribbled a few phrases on an envelope that he carried in his pocket.

On the evening of September 16, the British deposited Key, Skinner, and Beanes at Hughes' Wharf in Baltimore. The men were taken immediately to the Indian Queen Hotel in order to rest and recuperate from their recent ordeal as prisoners of war. Key, however, found it impossible to sleep. The images of the recent battle—the blasts of cannon fire and the shrieking of shells cutting through the dark sky—still swirled in his head. He returned to the series of phrases that he had written on the envelope. Key completed the poem, then borrowed the melody from a popular British drinking song of the day titled "To Anacreon in Heaven" to complete his composition. The next day he showed the song to his family and friends.

Although it is not known exactly who was responsible for releasing the song to the public, someone passed the composition to the publisher of the *American and Commercial Daily Advertiser*, a small local newspaper produced in Baltimore. The song was printed on handbills under the title "Defence of Fort M'Henry," and the following week the song appeared in the *Baltimore Patriot and Evening Advertiser.* On September 27 it became a national sensation after being published in the *Daily National Intelligencer* of Washington, D.C. Several more weeks passed before the title of the song was changed to "The Star-Spangled Banner."

Following the War of 1812, Francis Scott Key resumed his law practice. In 1833, President Andrew Jackson appointed him to negotiate a treaty with the Creek Indians in Alabama. At the time, the Jackson administration was beginning preparations for removal of the remaining Native American tribes from the southeastern United States to areas west of the Mississippi River. In the same year, Key was selected to be the United States district attorney for the District of Columbia, a position he held for eight years. He died from a lung disease called pleurisy on January 11, 1843, at the home of his daughter in Baltimore.

SIGNIFICANCE

Key was a successful attorney throughout his life, but he will forever be known as the composer of "The Star-Spangled Banner." Although the song became popular almost immediately after it was written, it did not become the national anthem until Congress passed a resolution in 1931. The original flag that inspired Key to write his song hangs in the Smithsonian Institution in Washington, D.C.

—Jonathan M. Jones

FURTHER READING

Gelb, Norman. "Reluctant Patriot." *Smithsonian* 35, no. 6 (September, 2004): 66. A profile of Key, containing information on the War of 1812 and Key's experiences at Fort McHenry.

Hickey, Donald R. *The War of 1812: A Forgotten Conflict.* Urbana: University of Illinois Press, 1989. One of the best sources on the War of 1812. Contains only a few pages on Key, but provides a thorough study of the British operations in the Chesapeake Bay.

Kauffman, Bill. "O Say Can You Sing?" *American Enterprise* 14, no. 7 (October, 2003): 47. Describes how Key's poem *The Star-Spangled Banner* was selected and designated the U.S. national anthem.

Lord, Walter. *The Dawn's Early Light.* New York: W. W. Norton, 1972. Lord provides a lengthy and interesting explanation of how Key was inspired to write his song.

Molotsky, Irvin. *The Flag, the Poet, and the Song: The Story of the "Star-Spangled Banner."* New York: Dutton, 2001. Popular history of the American flag and the national anthem. Describes Key's background and how he wrote *The Star-Spangled Banner.*

Quaife, Milo M., Melvin J. Weig, and Roy E. Appleman. *The History of the United States Flag: From the Revolution to the Present.* New York: Harper & Row, 1961. Contains information on Key and instructions for the use and display of the U.S. flag.

Tucker, Glenn. *Poltroons and Patriots: A Popular Account of 1812.* Indianapolis: Bobbs-Merrill, 1954. Tucker's study provides information on Key as well as the British invasion of the Chesapeake Bay area.

SEE ALSO: Julia Ward Howe; Andrew Jackson; John Ross.

RELATED ARTICLE in *Great Events from History: The Nineteenth Century, 1801-1900:* April 22, 1864: "In God We Trust" Appears on U.S. Coins.

SØREN KIERKEGAARD
Danish philosopher

Kierkegaard's challenge to neat systems of philosophical thought, such as that propounded by Hegel, has highlighted his philosophical influence. His predominant assumption, that existence is too multiform to be systematized, created the fabric around which existentialism, and indeed much of Continental philosophy, has been woven.

BORN: May 5, 1813; Copenhagen, Denmark
DIED: November 11, 1855; Copenhagen, Denmark
ALSO KNOWN AS: Søren Aabye Kierkegaard (full name)
AREAS OF ACHIEVEMENT: Philosophy, religion and theology

EARLY LIFE

Søren Aabye Kierkegaard (SUHR-ehn KIHR-keh-gor) was the last of seven children of Michael Pedersen Kierkegaard and his second wife, Ane Sørensdatter (Lund). His mother had been the maid of Michael's first wife, who died childless after two years of marriage. His father, an affluent businessperson, had himself been born in poverty and virtual servitude, rising by dint of hard work and good fortune to the comfortable status the family enjoyed at Søren's birth.

Despite such prosperity, the Kierkegaard household was haunted by early death. Two of Søren's siblings died before he was nine; his mother and three more siblings died in a span of less than three years before his twenty-first birthday. Michael was never able to overcome the belief that these deaths were punishment for the unpardonable sin he committed when, as a boy of eleven, tending sheep and bitter at his lot, he cursed God.

The influence of the somber elder Kierkegaard upon his gifted son is certain, but the extent to which it permeated Kierkegaard's character and influenced his writings throughout his life is difficult to estimate. A key passage from Kierkegaard's journals suggests that his father's inadvertent revelation of some past misdeeds permanently altered their relationship:

> An affair between the father and son where the son finds everything out, and yet dare not admit it to himself. The father is a respectable man, God-fearing and strict; only once, when he is tipsy, he lets fall some words which arouse the most dreadful suspicions. Otherwise the son is never told of it and never dares to ask his father or anybody else.

Regarding this incident, Frederick Sontag says that it thrust Kierkegaard into a "period of dissipation and despair," causing him for a time to neglect completely his theological studies at the university.

In addition to his father's influence, Kierkegaard was indelibly marked by his engagement to Regina Olsen. He met her for the first time at a party, when she was fourteen. She was captivated by his intellectual sagacity; he later admitted that that had been his design. They both endured a difficult period of waiting until she was nearly eighteen before they became engaged. Yet, having endured such a lengthy period of waiting, within days after the engagement had been effected Kierkegaard was convinced that it was a mistake. Some years after he had broken the engagement, he wrote in his journal:

> I said to her that in every generation there were certain individuals who were destined to be sacrificed for the others. She hardly understood what I was talking about. . . . But just this spontaneous youthful happiness of hers, set alongside my terrible melancholy, and in such a relationship, must teach me to understand myself. For how melancholy I was I had never before surmised; I possessed no measure for conceiving how happy a human being can be.

In 1841, not long after breaking his engagement, Kierkegaard successfully defended his doctoral thesis and departed for Berlin, where he stayed for several months attending lectures. Within two years, he published his first books, the product of an intense period of creativity, and his career was fully launched.

LIFE'S WORK

Kierkegaard was a powerful and prolific writer. The bulk of his corpus was produced within a period of about seven years, spanning 1843-1850. Appreciative readers of Kierkegaard's writings can be thankful for the voluminous groundswell of production that came in his early thirties, for he died a young man of forty-two. During the course of his writing career, he pursued several recurring themes; it would be misleading, however, to treat his work as though he had systematically moved from one arena to another in a planned, orderly fashion.

Indeed, Kierkegaard's decided distrust of the systematizing of Georg Wilhelm Friedrich Hegel had pushed him in the direction of an existential methodology that would be expressive of his whole personality. Rather than creating a system for the whole of reality that was necessarily linked by chains of reasoning, Kierkegaard created in his writings psychological experiments centered on persons confronting life situations. By so doing, he avoided both the strict rationalism and the Idealism so characteristic of analytic philosophers, and pulled his readers into existential consideration of life's dilemmas.

Kierkegaard considered his life and cojointly his works as an effort to fulfill a divinely appointed task. This conviction had led to his breakup with Regina because of what he called his destiny "to be sacrificed for the others." It also led him to the realization that his vocation was to confront his contemporaries with the ideal Christian life. He saw that as his purpose in life and consequently chose to lay aside every weight that would hinder him from "willing that one thing."

Denmark had appropriated Hegelianism as the proper mode of informed thinking. Indeed, Kierkegaard's countrymen had even allowed Christianity to be absorbed into the Hegelian system. Hence, the Christian ideal of individuals choosing Christ was lost: Every person in Denmark was nominally a Christian. When applied to the Church, the totalizing attempt prefigured in Hegel made everyone a Christian by birth. It was within this context, and for the purpose of confronting this attitude, that Kierkegaard arose to do battle in print. He described himself as a "midwife," helping to bring forth authentic individuals. His goal was nothing short of arousing his age from its complacence. Whereas Hegelianism might encourage rigors of thought, it made things easy through its promise of certainty. Kierkegaard, on the other hand, made things difficult by thrusting the individual into the fray, thereby teaching him what it truly means "to become a Christian."

An important aspect of many of Kierkegaard's works had to do with his method. For his philosophical works, he used a variety of often-flamboyant pseudonyms, such as Victor Eremita, Constantine Constantius, Virgilius Haufniensis, Johannes Climacus, and Anti-Climacus. At the same time, under his own name, he produced a number of devotional works and religious meditations. Kierkegaard's indirect communication has caused not a little bewilderment.

Kierkegaard himself addressed what he referred to as his "polynymity" rather than "pseudonymity" in an appendix to *Afsluttende uvidenskabelig Efterskrift til de Philosophiske Smuler: Mimisk-pathetisk-dialektisk Sammenskrift, existentielt Indlæg* (1846; *Concluding Unscientific Postscript*, 1941, 1968). Given his consistent and unwavering emphasis upon "choice," it is reasonable to assume that Kierkegaard believed that this method of presentation enhanced his ability to confront the reader. As long as pseudonyms were used, his readers were not free to see what "Kierkegaard the authority" had to say about the issues. Readers would thus be thrown back upon themselves, having to choose an interpretive stance for themselves.

Because Kierkegaard was a difficult writer, ahead of his time, he received little income from his writings, depending largely on his substantial inheritance. Moreover, as a brilliant, acerbic, and uncompromising critic of his society, he was frequently embroiled in controversy; in his later years, he worked in great isolation. Near the end of his life, Kierkegaard wrote several books that dealt explicitly with Christianity. *Til Selvprøvelse* (1857; *For Self-Examination*, 1940) challenged his readers to view themselves in the light of New Testament descriptions of Christianity rather than simplistically accepting the terms that the established church was propounding. His final book, *Hvad Christus dømmer om officiel Chris-*

Søren Kierkegaard. (Library of Congress)

tendom (1855; *What Christ's Judgment Is About Official Christianity*, 1944), views the relationship between the state and Christianity. He shows that the official Christianity of which every Dane partook was far from New Testament Christianity.

On October 2, 1855, Kierkegaard collapsed while walking in the street. The nature of his final illness is not certain. He was hospitalized, accepting his fate with tranquillity. He died on November 11, 1855.

SIGNIFICANCE

At the time of his death, and for a long period thereafter, Søren Kierkegaard's works were little known outside Denmark. Both his striking originality and the fact that he wrote in Danish delayed recognition of his achievement. By the early twentieth century, however, a wide diversity of thinkers reflected his influence, which has continued to grow since that time; he is often hailed as the founder of existentialism.

Even Kierkegaard's most explicitly philosophical writings, it should be noted, bear an undeniable theological character. In *Philosophiske Smuler: Eller, En Smule Philosophi* (1844; *Philosophical Fragments: Or, A Fragment of Philosophy*, 1936, 1962), he plumbs the epistemological depths of how a historical consciousness can confront an eternal consciousness and come away with what one might call "knowledge." In other words, to what degree can eternal truth be learned within the categories of time or space? In *Concluding Unscientific Postscript*, he confronts the objective problem of the truth of Christianity. The issue involved here is often referred to as "Lessing's ditch." Gotthold Ephraim Lessing believed that there exists an intellectually impossible leap from the contingent truths of history to the necessary truths of divine revelation. Kierkegaard looked at this problem and concluded that "a leap of faith" was required for the individual bound by finiteness and historical necessity to encounter eternal truth. This assertion has caused most to claim that Kierkegaard equated truth with subjectivity.

—*Stephen M. Ashby*

FURTHER READING

Blackham, H. J. "Søren Kierkegaard." In *Six Existentialist Thinkers*. New York: Macmillan, 1952. A brief but incisive treatment of Kierkegaard's championing of individuality and inwardness as opposed to Hegel's notion of abstract system building. Emphasizes Kierkegaard's claim that any true philosophy confronts the intellectual, the aesthetic, and the ethical arenas in terms of the existing individual's life situations. Fur-

ther alludes that faith is a fourth category, not to be confused with any of the others.

Duncan, Elmer H. *Søren Kierkegaard*. Waco, Tex.: Word Books, 1976. Surveys Kierkegaard's thought for the stated purpose of "making him more accessible to all of us." Ties the theme of Kierkegaard's corpus to traditional problems of philosophy. Emphasizes Kierkegaard's lasting contribution of categories, such as "absolute paradox," "absurdity," and "angst," which have been used by the main voices of existentialism, as well as the key figures of contemporary theology.

Evans, C. Stephen. *Kierkegaard's "Fragments" and "Postscript": The Religious Philosophy of Johannes Climacus*. Atlantic Highlands, N.J.: Humanities Press, 1983. Provides a thorough and serious conceptual look at Kierkegaard's writings through the two books that he pseudonymously attributed to Johannes Climacus. Its intent is that of a "companion" to the two works. Provides as much elucidation as would a good commentary.

Gardiner, Patrick. *Kierkegaard: A Very Short Introduction*. Oxford, England: Oxford University Press, 2002. Concise overview of the full range of Kierkegaard's thought. Describes how he developed his ideas and how his philosophy has influenced modern ways of thinking.

Garff, Joakim. *Søren Kierkegaard: A Biography*. Translated by Bruce H. Kirmmse. Princeton, N.J.: Princeton University Press, 2005. Monumental, 872-page biography, recounting Kierkegaard's life in minute detail. Garff examines how Kierkegaard developed his philosophy from his life experiences.

Hannay, Alastair. *Kierkegaard: A Biography*. New York: Columbia University Press, 2001. Comprehensive biography examining Kierkegaard's life, philosophy, and faith. Hannay describes how Kierkegaard viewed his life as a series of collisions with a few significant people, such as his father and fiancé, and how these confrontations formed the basis of his philosophy.

Lowrie, Walter. *Kierkegaard*. 2 vols. Gloucester, Mass.: Peter Smith, 1970. This is a definitive biography of Kierkegaard, written by one of the most prominent translators of his writings. Follows Kierkegaard's life chronologically, providing a list of dates for major events and publications. Also includes a helpful fifteen-page synopsis of Kierkegaard's works.

Sontag, Frederick. *A Kierkegaard Handbook*. Atlanta: John Knox Press, 1979. Sontag provides for Kierkegaard's works what Kierkegaard himself conscientiously avoided: a systematic approach. Sontag intended this dialectical study of key concepts as a companion reader for the student of Kierkegaard's philosophy.

SEE ALSO: Georg Wilhelm Friedrich Hegel; Friedrich Wilhelm Joseph von Schelling.
RELATED ARTICLE in *Great Events from History: The Nineteenth Century, 1801-1900:* 1893: Munch Paints *The Scream.*

MARY KINGSLEY
British explorer

Kingsley was a rare woman explorer who made several hazardous trips to tropical Africa almost entirely on her own to collect specimens for the British Museum and observe African cultures and belief systems. She wrote several popular books about her travels and advanced the then controversial view that missionaries and colonial officials should develop greater knowledge of, and respect for, native cultures.

BORN: October 13, 1862; London, England
DIED: June 3, 1900; Simonstown, near Cape Town, Cape Colony (now in South Africa)
ALSO KNOWN AS: Mary Henrietta Kingsley (full name)
AREA OF ACHIEVEMENT: Exploration

EARLY LIFE

Mary Kingsley was born into an English literary family. Her father, George Kingsley, and his four brothers were all writers. The most famous brother was Charles Kingsley, a poet, novelist, and theologian. George Kingsley and his wife, Mary Bailey, were somewhat estranged from the rest of the family for several reasons. They questioned the Christian faith of other family members, Mary Bailey came from a lower social class, and their first child, Mary, was born suspiciously soon after their wedding. Mary's father was a private physician for a wealthy man who traveled frequently, so he was often away from his family. He traveled through most of the world—apart from Africa—and sent home exciting letters describing his adventures.

At home, Mary's mother was left alone to manage her, her younger brother, Charles, and a large household—often with insufficient money. Both mother and son were frail and unstable, so young Mary assumed most of the day-to-day responsibilities for running the home. In addition to chores traditionally regarded as female, she taught herself to repair pipes and do other

maintenance work by reading the magazine *English Mechanic.*

Mary had no companions and spent her free time working through her father's library of science textbooks, natural history, and geography. Aside from some tutoring in the German language, she had no formal education, as it was not considered appropriate for even the brightest and most curious girls; however, her brother, George, was sent to college. When George returned home, Mary helped him with research for his own scholarly projects. In 1888, sixteen-year-old Mary assumed the care of both her parents, who were too ill to live alone. She nursed them for four years, until both died within a period of several weeks in 1892. Through the rest of her own life, Mary looked after her brother, arranging her own career around his needs.

LIFE'S WORK

In August, 1893, twenty-nine-year-old Mary Kingsley set out on her first trip to West and equatorial Africa. In fact, it was her first long trip anywhere, and all she knew about surviving in a hostile environment she had learned from reading her father's travel books and listening to his stories. The primary purpose of her journey was scientific; she had persuaded the British Museum to allow her to collect fish specimens for its collection. Being a naturalist with an approved project made it possible for her to set out without the condemnation that Victorian society reserved for women traveling alone.

Kingsley traveled aboard a cargo steamer, on which she easily made friends with the rough traders who shared what they had learned about the African people and landscapes. With only a few porters to help carry her gear, and access granted by the various European trading companies scattered along the African coast, she trekked inland into the Congo. Always wearing a long skirt and a high collar as protection against insects and thorns and carrying a sharp knife, Kingsley mastered canoeing, climbing, fishing with nets, and hiking during a trip that lasted only a few months. Along the way, she survived a tornado and a crocodile attack.

Kingsley returned to Africa again in 1893 and then several more times, and continued to collect fish, lizards, snakes, and insects for the British Museum. Among her finds was at least one previously unknown fish, which was named after her. She also undertook a study of fetishes in African religions and tried to learn what she could about rumored cannibalism.

Her travels took her across several parts of equatorial Africa not previously explored by Europeans, and she became only the second European to climb a mountain

---

THE DECISION TO GO TO WEST AFRICA

Before Mary Kingsley went to tropical Africa, she had never even been out of England—a fact that makes her chosen travel destination extraordinary. At that time, much of tropical Africa was politically unsettled and health conditions for Europeans were considered highly dangerous: West Africa had been dubbed the "white man's grave." This extract from Kingsley's introduction to her book about her journey explains some of her reasons for going to Africa, while calling attention to the dangers that she faced. The "Mr. Bunyan" whom she mentions below is John Bunyan, the author of The Pilgrim's Progress *(1678, 1684), an allegory about a Christian's journey to the Heavenly City. Her allusion to Wallace refers to Alfred Russel Wallace's 1876 book,* The Geographical Distribution of Animals.

It was in 1893 that, for the first time in my life, I found myself in possession of five or six months which were not heavily forestalled, and feeling like a boy with a new half-crown, I lay about in my mind, as Mr. Bunyan would say, as to what to do with them. "Go and learn your tropics," said Science. Where on earth am I to go? I wondered, for tropics are tropics wherever found, so I got down an atlas and saw that either South America or West Africa must be my destination, for the Malayan region was too far off and too expensive. Then I got Wallace's *Geographical Distribution* and after reading that master's article on the Ethiopian region I hardened my heart and closed with West Africa. I did this the more readily because while I knew nothing of the practical condition of it, I knew a good deal both by tradition and report of South East America, and remembered that Yellow Jack was endemic, and that a certain naturalist, my superior physically and mentally, had come very near getting starved to death in the depressing society of an expedition slowly perishing of want and miscellaneous fevers up the Parana.

My ignorance regarding West Africa was soon removed. And although the vast cavity in my mind that it occupied is not even yet half filled up, there is a great deal of very curious information in its place. I use the word curious advisedly, for I think many seemed to translate my request for practical hints and advice into an advertisement that "Rubbish may be shot here." This same information is in a state of great confusion still, although I have made heroic efforts to codify it. I find, however, that it can almost all be got in under the following different headings, namely and to wit: -

The dangers of West Africa.
The disagreeables of West Africa.
The diseases of West Africa.
The things you must take to West Africa.
The things you find most handy in West Africa.
The worst possible things you can do in West Africa.

I inquired of all my friends as a beginning what they knew of West Africa. The majority knew nothing. A percentage said, "Oh, you can't possibly go there; that's where Sierra Leone is, the white mans grave, you know." If these were pressed further, one occasionally found that they had had relations who had gone out there after having been "sad trials," but, on consideration of their having left not only West Africa, but this world, were now forgiven and forgotten.

I next turned my attention to cross-examining the doctors. "Deadliest spot on earth," they said cheerfully, and showed me maps of the geographical distribution of disease. Now I do not say that a country looks inviting when it is coloured in Scheele's green or a bilious yellow, but these colours may arise from lack of artistic gift in the cartographer. There is no mistaking what he means by black, however, and black you'll find they colour West Africa from above Sierra Leone to below the Congo. "I wouldn't go there if I were you," said my medical friends, "you'll catch something; but if you must go, and you're as obstinate as a mule, just bring me—" and then followed a list of commissions from here to New York, any one of which—but I only found that out afterwards.

Source: Mary Kingsley, "Introduction," *Travels in West Africa* (London: Macmillan, 1897).

called Mungo Mah Lobeh. A shrewd trader, she packed tobacco and cloth to bargain with local communities for whatever she needed. Kingsley described her adventures and her discoveries in two highly successful books, *Travels in West Africa* (1897) and *West African Studies* (1899). She also worked over her father's notes and diaries from his years abroad and published them in 1900 as *Notes on Sport and Travel*.

While staying in England between her African journeys, Kingsley took care of her brother and embarked on a career as a public speaker and writer of political articles and essays. Her exploits were already well known to readers of newspapers, and she was a dramatic speaker, describing her travels with vivid detail and humor. In articles published in leading journals, she argued that traders, not government bureaucrats, should take the lead in administering the African lands being absorbed into the British Empire. She also argued that Christian missionaries did more harm than good in trying to eradicate traditional African cultures, and that Africans should be seen as sophisticated and intelligent, not as children who needed European assistance to become "civilized."

Kingsley resisted attempts to portray her as a feminist. She argued that women should not be granted the vote because they were not sufficiently intelligent or informed to vote wisely. She pointed out that everything that she herself had accomplished had been done with the guidance of men.

In March, 1900, Kingsley began her last journey to Africa—this time to South Africa, where Great Britain was engaged in the South African (Boer) War. She wanted to collect more fish specimens but instead volunteered as a nurse in a prisoner-of-war hospital in Simonstown near Cape Town. An outbreak of enteric fever was devastating both prisoners and nurses when she arrived there, and she contracted the fever herself. On June 3, 1900, she died of the fever in Simonstown. Following her own wishes, she was buried at sea.

SIGNIFICANCE

Kingsley is now remembered chiefly as a pioneering woman, a feminist heroine, a role at which she would have scoffed. In traveling on her own into tropical Africa—a place considered the most dangerous on Earth—in climbing mountains and canoeing through rapids—and doing it all in long wool skirts—she demonstrated that women could accomplish physical feats that seemed impossible in her day. However, she was not a feminist; she did not believe that women were the intellectual or physical equals of men, and she argued against woman suffrage.

Kingsley's significance may reside in her rejection of all labels and categories, which allowed her to connect with the African peoples she met on their own terms. In her modes of travel, in her dress and language and manners, in her writing style, in her politics, Kingsley steered a middle course. By refusing either to align herself with the expectations for women in the Victorian period or to fit into twenty-first century notions of early feminists, she expanded both groups. She thus remains as controversial in the twenty-first century as she was in the nineteenth century.

—*Cynthia A. Bily*

FURTHER READING

Blunt, Alison. *Travel, Gender, and Imperialism: Mary Kingsley and West Africa*. New York: Guilford, 1994. A poststructural analysis that uses the example of Mary Kingsley to examine the particular role in imperialism of white women traveling alone, rejecting an approach that focuses on "heroic" women travelers as feminist emblems.

Frank, Katherine. *A Voyager Out: The Life of Mary Kingsley*. Boston: Houghton Mifflin, 1986. An accessible and dramatic presentation, for the general reader, of Kingsley as a Victorian heroine, torn between her duties as a daughter and her wish for adventure. Includes photographs, maps, and liberal quotations from Kingsley's published and unpublished writings.

Gates, Barbara T. *Kindred Nature: Victorian and Edwardian Women Embrace the Living World*. Chicago: University of Chicago Press, 1998. Discusses Kingsley's life and works as one example among many of women whose writing contributed to the study and preservation of nature at the end of the nineteenth and the beginning of the twentieth centuries.

Harper, Lila Marz. *Solitary Travelers: Nineteenth-Century Women's Travel Narratives and the Scientific Vocation*. Madison: Fairleigh Dickinson University Press, 2001. In a chapter titled "Mary H. Kingsley: In Pursuit of Fish and Fetish," the author focuses on Kingsley's contributions to biology and anthropology and on Kingsley's struggles to interpret the conflicting roles of scientist and domestic in Victorian female society.

Kipling, Rudyard. *Mary Kingsley*. Garden City, N.Y.: Doubleday, Doran, 1932. Memoir by a Nobel Prize-winning writer and adventurer who, like Kingsley, accepted British imperialism as inevitable and glorious.

Kipling met Kingsley a few times, admired her courage, and wrote a memorial poem about her upon her death.

Stevenson, Catherine Barnes. *Victorian Women Travel Writers in Africa.* Boston: Twayne, 1982. A chapter of some seventy pages deals with Kingsley, focusing on her literary accomplishments in the form and style of travel writing. Self-taught as a writer and an ethnographer, Kingsley nevertheless crafted beautiful and accurate prose.

SEE ALSO: Sir Richard Francis Burton; H. Rider Haggard; David Livingstone; John Hanning Speke; Henry Morton Stanley.

RELATED ARTICLES in *Great Events from History: The Nineteenth Century, 1801-1900:* May 4, 1805-1830: Exploration of West Africa; November 17, 1853: Livingstone Sees the Victoria Falls; 1873-1880: Exploration of Africa's Congo Basin; November 15, 1884-February 26, 1885: Berlin Conference Lays Groundwork for the Partition of Africa.

RUDYARD KIPLING
English writer

The author of books of extraordinary insight about the world of childhood, as well as stirring popular poetry sympathetic to British soldiers, Kipling is best remembered for his depictions of life in India at the close of the nineteenth century, and he won the Nobel Prize in Literature.

BORN: December 30, 1865; Bombay, India
DIED: January 18, 1936; Hampstead, London, England
ALSO KNOWN AS: Joseph Rudyard Kipling (full name)
AREA OF ACHIEVEMENT: Literature

EARLY LIFE

Rudyard Kipling was born in India one year after his father had accepted a position as a teacher of architecture in Bombay (now Mumbai). His parents both came from prominent but not wealthy families, and the promise of a reliable source of income was sufficient inducement for the Kiplings to leave England. Rudyard Kipling always recalled his childhood in India as a time of exceptional happiness, a paradisiacal existence in an edenic setting where he was treated like a young god by a loving family and many friendly local servants.

Kipling's idyll came to an end in 1871, when his parents, in accordance with British cultural expectations about hygiene, social status, and racial purity, sent him to England to board with a retired sea captain in Southsea. For the next six years, Kipling lived in what he called "The House of Desolation," severely disciplined by the captain's widow. The only pleasure he had during this time was his holiday visits to the home of his uncle Edward Burne-Jones, the renowned Pre-Raphaelite painter, in whose "magical domain" Kipling learned the stories of the "Arabian Nights" from family group readings, and from whom he developed an appreciation for games of language and wit, for stories of invention and surprise, and for the eclectic decor of the Burne-Jones home.

In 1875, Kipling's father became curator of the museum in Lahore. The job represented a considerable advancement in status and financial remuneration. The promotion permitted Kipling to enter the United Services College, a new and minor public school with an unusual headmaster (Cormell Price) who shared the radical public views of William Morris and recognized Kipling's need for encouragement in his idiosyncracies of character.

Incompetent at and disdainful of the social-entry games of cricket and soccer, Kipling nevertheless became close friends with two other individualistic boys (the trio became the basis for the heroes of *Stalky & Co.*, 1899) who shared his early interest in writing, debating, and exotic gestures such as decorating their study with Japanese fans, old china, and glass from secondhand shops. Avidly pursuing a program of self-education, the boys read and discussed all the modern poets, including Walt Whitman, whom Kipling defended against attacks by the English master. Kipling was editor of the school magazine but otherwise an ordinary student, and he could not qualify for a scholarship at Oxford, a necessity because his parents could not afford to pay his tuition. With no other prospects immediately apparent, his parents used their social connections to make an arrangement for him to return to India as a reporter for *The Civil and Military Gazette* of Lahore. In 1882, Kipling accepted this position and returned to India, three months before his seventeenth birthday.

LIFE'S WORK

Kipling's return to the land of his birth gave him a renewed access to places and situations that fired his imagination and gave a direction to his tremendous latent creative energy. From his parents' place in Anglo-Indian society, he was able to get a clear picture of the workings of the British colonial administration. His journalistic assignments enabled him to learn about the daily life of the British soldiers "at the ready," and his desire to learn about Indian culture took him on excursions across much of the subcontinent.

In 1885, in collaboration with his parents and his sister, Kipling published *Quartette*, including his first major short story, "The Strange Ride of Morrowbie Jukes," a powerful evocation of the fears of the rulers who recognized the precariousness of their position in a country torn by mutiny only twenty years before. In 1886, the year of his majority, he published *Departmental Ditties*, poems primarily about life among the civil servants based in Simla, the summer home for the viceroy of India. Kipling's stories had become a regular feature of *The Civil and Military Gazette*, and the pace of his work drove him to the limits of his energy. Between November, 1886, and June, 1887, thirty-nine stories appeared. In 1888, the volume *Soldiers Three* was published. It contained many of the best stories of three "typical" British privates whose farcical adventures in a picaresque milieu gave Kipling a frame to probe the barracks' world of adultery, treachery, bullying, and even murder, and then to probe further into the brooding interior landscape of the soldier's life, a harsh existence relieved only by the deep, close friendship of the men.

In autumn, 1887, Kipling was transferred to the senior paper of the syndicate, *The Pioneer*, where his astute but opinionated political commentary led to the threat of a lawsuit, attempted assault, and the grievance of some high government officials. As Kipling was becoming increasingly famous in English literary circles, with his parents' encouragement he decided to test his skills as a freelance writer in London. In March, 1889, he left Calcutta, returning only once more to India to visit his parents in 1891. For the remainder of his life, the cultural and psychic landscape of India haunted his dreams; it had already become the foundation for his finest work.

Kipling established himself in London as a kind of tentative bohemian bachelor. Generally reserved and no self-promoter, his ambition was still quite clear. Above the door in his rooms, he declared, "To Publishers, A classic while you wait." Many others agreed, and his reception in London was encouraging, beginning with a London *Times* leading article in March, 1890. The style of his life is captured in the description by Kay Robinson, his editor at *The Pioneer*, who wrote in 1896 about a man

Rudyard Kipling. (Library of Congress)

in a white cotton vest and trousers who suggested a Dalmatian because of the mass of inkspots that covered him. Robinson saw him as mildly eccentric, with a "mushroom-shaped" hat and a fox terrier that looked like a "nice clean sucking pig."

In later years, Kipling tended to look more formal, a smallish man of soldierly bearing with glasses and a cartoonist's delight of a mustache, a high forehead, and, quite often, a hat when out in public. His first years in London saw the publication of the finest stories of his early period, *The Courting of Dinah Shadd and Other Stories* (1890), the two versions of *The Light That Failed* (1890, 1891), both in American editions, and *Barrack-Room Ballads and Other Verses* (1892), which included poems such as the well-known "Danny Deever." Kipling's visits to London music halls seem to have been instrumental in the development of the insistent jaunty rhythms that he fitted to poems of military life.

In spite of his success, Kipling was not entirely comfortable with the world of letters in London. Its innate conservatism in literary matters did not really suit his temperament or aesthetic principles. In addition, his usual regimen of constant, intensive writing and a continuing feeling of displacement or homelessness had brought him to the verge of a breakdown. Part of his course of recovery included a long sea voyage to Calcutta to visit his supportive family, and another part included his marriage to Caroline Balestier, the sister of his agent and a member of a prominent American family from Brattleboro, Vermont. By way of a kind of extended honeymoon, Kipling and his bride traveled extensively in the United States, where Kipling met Mark Twain, one of his favorite authors.

In 1893, Kipling and his wife settled in southern Vermont on five acres of land purchased from her family; they lived there until 1895. The distance from India may have given Kipling the perspective he needed to shape his experiences and impressions of India into literature, because it was in Vermont that he produced the Mowgli stories, publishing *The Jungle Book* in 1894 and *The Second Jungle Book* in 1895. He wrote the second half of *Barrack-Room Ballads and Other Verses* in Vermont and began work on *Kim* (1901), his great visionary epic of India. During this time he also made several trips to the whaling port of Gloucester, Massachusetts, to do research for *Captains Courageous* (1897). Several factors combined, however, to end his stay in the United States. His once-harmonious relationship with his wife's younger brother deteriorated into litigation, he feared that the Cleveland administration would draw the United States into war with Great Britain over a minor dispute in Venezuela, and he felt hounded by American reporters who pursued him for his celebrity without giving him the peace to continue the writing that produced it.

The Kiplings returned to England in time for the Jubilee of 1897, and Kipling contributed to the carnival atmosphere with his memorable poem "Recessional," which was published in the London *Times* after a family friend retrieved it from the wastebasket where Kipling had discarded it. Many people read their own political feelings into the poem, often missing its negative view of the imperial creed, but the poem contributed considerably to Kipling's reputation. Oxford granted him an honorary degree, compensating for the disappointment of his inability to matriculate there ten years earlier, and he was elected to the exclusive Athenaeum Club, a tribute considered "one of the greatest professional-class establishment honors of late Victorian England." The publication of "The White Man's Burden" (also in *The Times*) in 1898, with its explicitly racist title, was Kipling's statement of resistance to foreign tyranny and anarchy, two *bêtes noires* of his belief in the necessity of an ordered existence.

While visiting South Africa during the winter of 1898, Kipling met and was captivated by Cecil Rhodes, and he became a firm supporter of Rhodes's empire-building ideas, thus further developing an ideology particularly repugnant even to many people who much admired his other work. Perhaps more significantly, during his stay in South Africa he journeyed along the Limpopo River, a crucial part of his inspiration for the *Just So Stories* (1902), which he composed in a comfortable house made available on Rhodes's estate.

After returning from the United States, the Kipling family had lived in close proximity to various relatives in Rottingdean, in Sussex, from 1897 to 1902. Kipling completed *Kim* in this setting and pulled the Stalky stories together, as well as finishing the last of the *Just So Stories*, "The Elms." The death of his young daughter Josephine in New York City in 1899, however, spoiled the charm of the home in which she had been reared.

Kipling purchased a house in Burwash, in the country of East Sussex, in 1902, and there spent the remainder of the time he was in England. The failure of the British imperial venture in South Africa distressed him, and the ascendancy of the Liberal Party to power in 1906 made him feel like a member of the rejected Tory old guard. He believed that his cherished concept of "order," the foundation of his faith in existence, was now threatened by such new forces as "cosmopolitanism," "egalitarianism," and "individualism," unconventional ideas that, he thought, undermined England's "world-civilizing mission."

With his fabled India fading into the oblivion of memory, the deaths of both Kipling's parents in the winter of 1910-1911 cut him off from the possibility of recall in conversation, and he felt compelled to find a new locus for his faith. To some extent, he found it in the lush, unspoiled Sussex countryside that he established as a constant source of value in his cyclical stories of renewal set in medieval times, *Puck of Pook's Hill* (1906). Paradoxically, just as he was retreating from public life, he was named the first British laureate by the Nobel Committee (1907).

England's entry into World War I drew Kipling back into active public life, and the death of his son John in October, 1915, led him into two large-scale projects to combat his sorrow. As a kind of memorial for his son, he compiled *The Irish Guards in the Great War* (1923), interviewing many of his son's fellow officers, and he accepted an appointment to be Commissioner of War Graves, a post that took him to Gallipoli, Mesopotamia, Palestine, and other sites where British forces fell in battle.

Kipling's last two collections of stories deal primarily with the psychological effects of war on combatants and emphasize themes of compassion and healing. A striking exception to this, however, was his continuing hatred of everything German, which found expression in some virulent anti-kaiser poetry and in the famous story "Mary Postgate," in which a German airman dies in agony. Through the 1930's, Kipling continued to criticize the Germans, and with the rise of Nazism, acting with typical consistency in personal as well as political affairs, he removed the Indian "ganesh" sign from his publications because of its resemblance to the swastika.

Kipling's health had been declining for some time when, in 1922, he suffered a serious gastrointestinal attack (the result of an undiagnosed duodenal ulcer). This moved him further into what Angus Wilson called "an ever-growing introspective meditative frame of mind." During his later years, Kipling and his wife spent considerable time abroad, particularly in France, with Kipling writing occasional stories, verse, essays, and an interesting and revealing autobiography, *Something of Myself: For My Friends, Known and Unknown* (1937). He died in January, 1936, just as England was beginning to respond to the Nazi menace about which he had warned. Kipling was buried in Poets' Corner, Westminster Abbey, near the ashes of Charles Dickens, who had died the year before Kipling arrived in England.

SIGNIFICANCE

The passage of time has not been particularly kind to Rudyard Kipling. His strong political opinions earned for him the enmity of many people in Great Britain, the United States, Canada, and India during his lifetime, and while such eminent critics as Edmund Wilson and George Orwell paid him the compliment of taking him seriously, their attacks on his ideas and his art have contributed to a general attitude that Kipling is either a historical curiosity, a local colorist, a Tory bully, or, at best, the writer of cliché-ridden, jangling verse and a few charming children's books. Ezra Pound's caustic assessment, beginning "Rudyard the dudyard/ Rudyard the false measure . . . ," suggests how simple it is to dismiss Kipling in the style of his own poetry, how close he is to parody even at his best.

Pound, probably because he detested Kipling's politics, missed one of Kipling's greatest strengths, something that Pound himself (in *The ABC of Reading*, 1934) prescribes as an essential component of poetry: the sheer, unforgettable rhythmic musicality of Kipling's best work. There is a primal power of language in poems such as "Gunga Din" and "Mandalay" that has pressed them into the memory of at least three generations in the United States and the British Commonwealth, where they can be easily recalled and recited with evident sensual delight. Kipling instinctively sensed the energy of the popular song and knew how to seize and use it, though it is not only the sound of the best poems that is so compelling. Some of his most familiar lines—"East is East and West is West," "Somewheres East of Suez," "The female of the species is more deadly than the male," and "He travels fastest who travels alone"—have been incorporated into the collective subconscious as aphoristic folk wisdom.

Even if Pound were right about Kipling's politics— a bizarre anomaly in the light of Pound's own political theories—the chauvinistic, semiracist, cryptofascist declarations are distortions of some quite sensible and thoughtful political formulations. Kipling's idea of The Law is akin to Ernest Hemingway's famous "Code" in that it was not a rigid social contract but a method of maintaining personal integrity amid the forces of chaos, and a doctrine designed to ensure maximum individual freedom amid a cooperative social system. Because Kipling was so easily unsettled by personal demons, he tended to overcompensate by supporting what he hoped were organizational principles that would guarantee some stability in what he knew was a fragile world even for the strongest of men and women. A careful reading of Kipling's stories and poems will reveal a subtle mind.

Although his children's stories have been highly praised, they have also been appreciated *only* as children's stories. As Angus Wilson points out:

> the elusive magic which lies at the heart of most of his best work . . . came from the incorporation into adult stories and parables of two of the principal shapes which are to be found in the imaginative world of children. The first is the transformation of a small space into the whole world which comes from the intense absorption of a child. The second is the map-making of hazards and delights which converts a child's smallest journey into a wondrous exploration.

That aspect of the adult psyche that remains permanently tied to childhood has rarely been touched and projected as well as in Kipling's writing.

Finally, Kipling's sense of India, especially the Anglo-Indian world that he loved, gave him a subject and a sense of place from which a powerful literary vision could be drawn. Kim, the "Ariel of Kipling's magic kingdom," is one of the true originals of English literature. His delight in life, and his openness to people and things, make him a wonderful guide to Kipling's own India, and his story, as Wilson perceptively explains, is "an allegory of that seldom portrayed ideal, the world in the service of spiritual goodness." By contrast, the more ordinary but still complex mortals of his songs and stories are dreadfully human in their faults and limits, but the soldiers, civil servants, and their families that he wrote about are the subject of a kind of compassion and empathy surprising in a man regarded as an aloof defender of class and caste. If the worst of Kipling is caught in the crumbling of an obsolete empire, the best is preserved in the art of a man who understood how tenuous life is and how valiant the human struggle can be.

—Leon Lewis

FURTHER READING

Bodelson, C. A. *Aspects of Kipling's Art.* New York: Barnes & Noble Books, 1964. A superior interpretation of Kipling's writing, with attention to his symbols.

Cornell, Louis L. *Kipling in India.* New York: St. Martin's Press, 1966. Contains a considerable amount of important information about Kipling's early career, as well as an incisive interpretation of the crucial aspect of India as a visionary concept in Kipling's writing.

Dobrée, Bonamy. *Rudyard Kipling.* New York: Longmans, Green, 1951. An early examination of Kipling from the perspective of a professional soldier turned professor who provides a balanced view of Kipling's ideas.

Gilmour, David. *The Long Recessional: The Imperial Life of Rudyard Kipling.* New York: Farrar, Straus and Giroux, 2002. Gilmour argues that Kipling embodied his country's spirt in the nineteenth century the way Shakespeare did three hundred years earlier. Examines the way Kipling influenced Britons' view of their empire, transforming himself from apostle of success to predictor of national decline to match the empire's rise and eclipse.

Henn, T. R. *Kipling.* New York: Barnes & Noble Books, 1967. Brief but succinct discussion of Kipling and his writing, including a survey of criticism and a list of the short stories.

Kipling, Rudyard. *Something of Myself: For My Friends, Known and Unknown.* London: Macmillan, 1937. An underrated, candid, and revealing account of Kipling's life from the artist's own point of view. Important as a complement to any other study of Kipling.

Mallett, Phillip. *Rudyard Kipling: A Literary Life.* New York: Palgrave Macmillan, 2003. Focuses on Kipling's public life, examining his involvement in politics, his dealings with the literary community, and the rise and fall of his reputation.

Ricketts, Harry. *Rudyard Kipling: A Life.* New York: Carroll & Graf, 1999. Biography offering a sympathetic yet critical examination of Kipling's life and personality as well as a reinterpretation of his writings.

Rutherford, Andrew, ed. *Kipling's Mind and Art.* Stanford, Calif.: Stanford University Press, 1964. Includes the historical views of Lionel Trilling, George Orwell, and Edmund Wilson, as well as more recent essays of particular sensitivity that cover the full spectrum of modern criticism.

Stewart, J. I. M. *Rudyard Kipling.* New York: Dodd, Mead, 1966. A biographical and critical study of Kipling's writing and his personality.

Wilson, Angus. *The Strange Ride of Rudyard Kipling.* New York: Viking Press, 1977. A prominent novelist's quirky, passionate, and highly knowledgeable study of Kipling's life and writing, grounded in thorough scholarship and guided by a most sympathetic, individualistic series of insights. Indispensable for anyone interested in Kipling.

SEE ALSO: Charles Dickens; William Morris; A. B. Paterson; Cecil Rhodes; Mark Twain; Walt Whitman.

RELATED ARTICLES in *Great Events from History: The Nineteenth Century, 1801-1900:* 1839-1847: Layard Explores and Excavates Assyrian Ruins; 1885: Indian National Congress Is Founded.

HEINRICH VON KLEIST
German writer

Kleist was one of the most important literary figures in the development of the German Novellen *of poetic realism. Although he is better known in Germany than in English-speaking countries, he is usually acknowledged to have been ahead of his time, a forerunner of the modern literature of the grotesque, which became associated with Franz Kafka a century later.*

BORN: October 18, 1777; Frankfurt an der Oder, Prussia (now in Germany)
DIED: November 21, 1811; Wannsee bei Potsdam, Prussia (now in Germany)
ALSO KNOWN AS: Bernd Heinrich Wilhelm von Kleist (full name)
AREAS OF ACHIEVEMENT: Literature, theater

EARLY LIFE

Heinrich Wilhelm von Kleist (klist) was the first son of a Prussian army officer, Joachim Friedrich von Kleist, and his second wife, Juliane Ulrike Pannwitz. By the time he was fifteen, both of his parents had died and he, without much enthusiasm, had become a soldier. Although little is known about his childhood, what evidence there is available from letters and other sources indicates that he was bored and unhappy with his life as a soldier; although he was promoted to lieutenant, he resigned from the army in 1799 to enter the University of Frankfurt. While there for three semesters, Kleist threw himself wholeheartedly into his studies of mathematics, physics, and philosophy.

Also while at the university, Kleist met and became engaged to Wilhelmine von Zenge, the daughter of an army officer. His letters from this period suggest that he was an extremely serious young man, introspective and concerned with finding fulfillment in his life by means of intellectual pursuits. Even his love affair with Wilhelmine was characterized by his efforts to make her into a kind of idealized soul mate, an embodiment of intellectual and moral beauty. In letters to his sister and his fiancé, he talks of his "life plan," a rational pursuit that would prevent him from being merely a puppet at the mercy of fate.

Kleist's hopes for a purely rational plan of life were crushed in 1801 by what his biographers refer to as his "Kantian crisis." In a letter to Wilhelmine, he declared that as a result of reading Immanuel Kant all of his faith in rationality as a basis for leading a purposeful life had been destroyed, and his anguish at facing a life governed by chance, fate, and meaninglessness had become almost unbearable. In what some have called an attempt to escape his intellectual torment, Kleist left Frankfurt and began traveling, first to Paris and then to Switzerland, where he became fascinated with ideas learned from Jean-Jacques Rousseau about leading the "natural life." Because his fiancé refused to go along with his new enthusiasm to lead the simple life of a peasant, their engagement was broken the following year. It was while living in Switzerland that Kleist began writing and thus launched his short-lived career.

LIFE'S WORK

Some of his biographers suggest that Kleist's literary career began because he was attempting to compensate for his failure to achieve his intellectual goals by succeeding immediately as a writer. While living on a small island on the Lake of Thun in Switzerland, he completed his drama *Die Familie Schroffenstein* (1803; *The Schroffenstein Family*, 1916) and began work on *Der zerbrochene Krug* (1808; *The Broken Jug*, 1930) and *Robert Guiskard* (1808; English translation, 1962). Although he began two of his best-known short fictions at this time, "Die Verlobung in St. Domingo" (1811; "The Engagement in Santo Domingo," 1960) and "Das Erdbeben in Chili" (1807; "The Earthquake in Chile," 1946), he had been greatly encouraged to continue his work on *Robert Guiskard* by the high praise for an early fragment of the play received from Christopher Martin Wieland, one of the most respected literary figures in Germany at the time.

For reasons known only to the tormented mind of Kleist, when he returned to Paris he burned the fragment of *Robert Guiskard*, which Wieland had said was worthy of Sophocles and William Shakespeare. Stung by his own self-imposed sense of failure, he joined Napoleon I's forces, which were ready for an invasion of England, perhaps hoping, as some biographers suggest, that death in battle would redeem his failure in a glorious way. Shortly thereafter, however, he was sent back to Germany and hospitalized for a nervous breakdown.

After recovering, Kleist obtained a post with the government in the ministry of finance. During this time, he continued to write, finishing *The Broken Jug*, drafting both plays *Amphitryon* (1807; English translation, 1962) and *Penthesilea* (1808; English translation, 1959), and beginning his best-known fiction, *Die Marquise von O . . .* (1810; *The Marquise of O . . .*, 1960). He suffered, however, from both depression and physical ailments that made it necessary for him to take an indefinite leave from his government job.

While on a trip to Dresden with two friends in January, 1807, Kleist was arrested by French authorities in Berlin on suspicion of being a spy and sent to prison in France. For several months during his imprisonment, he continued to work on his plays, especially *Penthesilea*. After being cleared and released, Kleist returned to Dresden to enjoy literary success as the author of *Amphitryon*, which had been published during his incarceration.

Kleist's newly raised hopes for a successful literary career seemed dashed when *The Broken Jug* was poorly received by drama critics and when a literary journal he had begun to edit had to be sold for lack of sufficient subscribers. At first seemingly undeterred by these setbacks, Kleist continued his writing, reconstructing the destroyed *Robert Guiskard* fragment, finishing *The Marquise of O . . .*, and beginning another great novella, *Michael Kohlhaas* (1810; English translation, 1844).

Kleist traveled to Austria in 1809 and attempted to start a patriotic journal in support of Germany's efforts against Napoleon; however, that too failed, and during this time he once again suffered depression and physical illness. There were even rumors that he had died. Nevertheless, he returned to Dresden, in good health, although penniless, in 1810. His play *Das Käthchen von Heilbronn: Oder, Die Feuerprobe* (1810; *Cathy of Heilbronn: Or, The Trial by Fire*, 1927) was staged in Vienna to an approving audience, and he now was making plans to stage *Prinz Friedrich von Homburg* (1821; *The Prince of Homburg*, 1875), which he had completed during his travels to Austria. However, a planned performance of the play in the private theater at the palace of Prince Radziwill was canceled, the publisher of *Cathy of Heilbronn* refused to honor his promise to publish the work, and the director of the Prussian National Theater refused to allow the play to be staged. Again, Kleist's hopes for a literary career seemed dashed.

Kleist's next effort to support himself in the literary world was to become editor of the *Berliner Abendblätter*, the first daily newspaper to be published in Germany. Although the newspaper was popular with the public, it was somewhat too daring in its political editorials for the Prussian government censors. Although Kleist made strong pleas for freedom of the press, even to Prince Wilhelm, he was ignored. Despite the fact that the newspaper was forbidden from publishing what the government considered radical political ideas, it did publish Kleist's famous essay on the marionette theater, as well as some

of his short fictions. Also during 1810, a second volume of his short fiction was published. The newspaper, however, was doomed to failure; the last issue of the *Berliner Abendblätter* was published on March 31, 1811.

At this time, Kleist was alone and without means of support; a request for a position with the government was ignored; and his family, at a reunion at Frankfurt in October, was reluctant to support him. During this period, he met the young wife of a government official, Henrietta Vogel, who, biographers suggest, was suffering from an incurable illness. Together they made a suicide pact, and on November 21, 1811, near Berlin, Kleist shot Henrietta Vogel and then himself.

SIGNIFICANCE

Heinrich von Kleist remains a mysterious figure in the history of literature. Relatively little is known about his tragic life, and his art and ideas have not been discussed in the United States or Great Britain to the extent that they have in Germany. The major focus of the criticism of Kleist's work has been on its philosophical content, although some studies (mostly in German) have been made on his narrative technique. Despite the fact that critical attention on Kleist has shifted to structural and textual analyses of his *Novellen* and plays, the primary emphasis is still on the mysterious tension in his work between the nature of consciousness and the nature of external reality.

Kleist is an important German Romantic writer who represents the significant intellectual shift during the early nineteenth century from an earlier dependence on rational, intellectual assumptions and structures to a new approach to reality based on the individual's own perception. He is often referred to as a precursor to twentieth century existential thought in his emphasis on the tension between the individual's desire for meaning and unity and the cold and unresponsive external world.

—Charles E. May

FURTHER READING

Allan, Seán. *The Stories of Heinrich von Kleist: Fictions of Security*. Rochester, N.Y.: Camden House, 2001. Explores four central themes in Kleist's stories: justice and revenge, revolution and social change, education and the nature of evil, and art and religion.

Ellis, John M. *Heinrich von Kleist: Studies in the Character and Meaning of His Writings*. Chapel Hill: University of North Carolina Press, 1979. Contains detailed analyses of Kleist's most mature works. Based on these discussions, Ellis provides a summary chapter on the general nature of Kleist's fiction, primarily its typical themes.

Fischer, Bernd, ed. *A Companion to the Works of Heinrich von Kleist.* Columbia, S.C.: Camden House, 2003. Collection of essays interpreting Kleist's stories and dramas, including examinations of his narrative and theatrical techniques, aesthetic theory, and philosophical and political ideas.

Gearey, John. *Heinrich von Kleist: A Study of Tragedy and Anxiety.* Philadelphia: University of Pennsylvania Press, 1968. A helpful and readable general study of Kleist's major short fiction and plays. According to Gearey, the basic tension in Kleist's works is not simply between rationality and emotion or even self-consciousness and the external world. More basically, his works focus on the general nature of opposition itself.

Griffiths, Elystan. *Political Change and Human Emancipation in the Works of Heinrich von Kleist.* Rochester, N.Y.: Camden House, 2005. Places Kleist's writings within the context of the political and philosophical debates of his times and assesses the political implications of his works.

Heibling, Robert E. *The Major Works of Heinrich von Kleist.* New York: New Directions, 1975. A general introduction that surveys previous Kleist criticism, provides a brief biographical sketch, and then argues that Kleist's vision is tragic, not pathological. The predominant theme of Kleist's works is the conflict between the individual consciousness and the unresponsive external world.

Maass, Joachim. *Kleist: A Biography.* Translated by Ralph Manheim. New York: Farrar, Straus and Giroux, 1983. Maass's workmanlike biography, the first full-length account of Kleist's life available in English, was first published in German in 1957 and was reissued in a revised version in 1977, the basis for the English translation. Includes brief discussions of Kleist's major works. Illustrated, with indexes but no notes or bibliography.

McGlathery, James M. *Desire's Sway: The Plays and Stories of Heinrich von Kleist.* Detroit: Wayne State University Press, 1983. The primary focus of this relatively brief and highly documented critical study is the tension in Kleist's characters between their devotion to lofty ideas and their outbursts of passion—a tension that McGlathery says is typical of comedy.

March, Richard. *Heinrich von Kleist.* New Haven, Conn.: Yale University Press, 1954. Perhaps the best introduction to Kleist's life and art. Although this is only a brief (fifty pages) pamphlet, it provides a concise biographical sketch as well as an informed introduction to the basic themes in Kleist's work.

SEE ALSO: Napoleon I; Freiherr vom Stein.

RELATED ARTICLES in *Great Events from History: The Nineteenth Century, 1801-1900:* 1842: Tennyson Publishes "Morte d'Arthur"; January 2, 1843: Wagner's *Flying Dutchman* Debuts; November 5, 1850: Tennyson Becomes England's Poet Laureate.

ROBERT KOCH
German bacteriologist

A pioneer bacteriologist, Koch was the first to prove definitively that specific microorganisms cause specific diseases. His identification of the bacterium that causes cholera enabled the virtual elimination of that disease in the Western world. He also isolated the causative agent of tuberculosis, making possible the containment of that once-deadly scourge, and he discovered the reproductive cycle of anthrax, providing for the successful combating of that disease.

BORN: December 11, 1843; Clausthal, Hanover (now Clausthal-Zellerfeld, Germany)
DIED: May 27, 1910; Baden-Baden, Germany
ALSO KNOWN AS: Heinrich Hermann Robert Koch (full name)

AREAS OF ACHIEVEMENT: Medicine, science and technology

EARLY LIFE
Born in the mining country of central Germany's Harz Mountains, Robert Koch (kahk) was one of thirteen children of Hermann Koch and his wife, Mathilde Biewend. Hermann was a mining official and reasonably well-off, although provision for a large family taxed his resources. A timely promotion assisted him in educating Robert, a precocious child drawn to the study of nature, who was able to excel at the local gymnasium, or academic preparatory school. He went on to study at the nearby University of Göttingen. After a year of science and math, young Koch abandoned the idea of a teaching career and

in 1863 transferred to the medical school at Göttingen, hoping that that field would allow him to pursue his love of science and travel. Koch's greatest scientific mentor was Jacob Henle, an anatomy professor who had published on disease causation and who speculated that infection might be transmitted by living organisms. At that time, however, no medical school in the world offered courses in bacteriology.

In 1866, Koch received his medical degree, passed his medical examination, and went to Berlin, where for a few months he attended lectures by the famous Rudolf Virchow, author of the notion that disease is the result of disturbance of cell function in the body tissues. Koch, from the beginning of his career, was no mere medical practitioner concerned with diagnosis and treatment of disease but was a scientist interested in its causes.

After a brief internship at Hamburg General Hospital, where he learned about cholera at first hand, he returned home and in July, 1867, married Emmy Fraatz, a daughter of the mining superintendent of Clausthal. Koch and his wife then lived for about a year at Langenhagen, Hanover, where he served at a hospital for children with mental disabilities while he practiced medicine privately in the community. By the time the couple's only child, Gertrud, was born in September of the following year, they were living at Niemegk, near Berlin. The young doctor's practice did not flourish there, and Koch moved his family to Rakwitz, near Posen, where he became a successful country doctor.

During the Franco-Prussian War, Koch entered the Prussian Army Medical Corps and served in 1870 and 1871 in France, working both with the wounded and with soldiers afflicted with typhoid. He left the army and returned briefly to his patients at Rakwitz, but in 1872 he secured appointment as district physician for Wollstein, another small town in the province of Posen. It was from that area of lakes, woods, and fields that Koch moved into national and international acclaim. A ruralist would have called the setting idyllic; Koch's later friend and admirer Élie Metchnikoff, a city dweller, referred to Wollstein as "a God-forsaken hole in Posen." Nevertheless, it was the very rurality of Wollstein that provided Koch with his first great opportunity.

LIFE'S WORK

Koch had become a mature physician with a lengthy and varied record of civilian and military experience. A smallish man with a bristling beard and round spectacles, he was the stereotypical Germanic scientist, and he longed to do more actual research than he could perform

Robert Koch. (Courtesy, University of Virginia Health System)

by examining algae and lesions with a handheld magnifying glass. A good microscope would have enabled him to peer more deeply into diseased tissue, but he believed that he could not afford such an instrument. His wife, Emmy, however, saved coins in a beer mug and surprised Koch with the money: The right man and the right research tool had come together at last. Like all men of genius, however, Koch was a driven man and made a poor companion. Emmy was neglected while her husband devoted most of his spare time to his laboratory, where he began by investigating the cause of anthrax—a very rural disease, a malady of grazing animals, primarily, but sometimes an ailment that could infect humans.

During the 1860's, the French physician-researcher Casimir-Joseph Davaine had discovered that a bacterium was the cause of anthrax. He called the rodlike microorganism "bactéridie" (later known to science as *Bacillus anthracis*), but he was not able to ascertain how the disease was transmitted or how the bacteria, which did not seem to be very long-lived, managed to survive between hosts.

Koch first verified Davaine's work by using sterilized wood splinters to inject anthrax bacilli into the tails of mice that he kept in cages in his laboratory. When the first mouse died, a drop of its blood was injected into a second mouse, and so on, until after eight mice the conclusion had to be reached that the poison was a living, self-perpetuating entity. A chemical poison would eventually have become so attenuated as to lose its potency. To grow his anthrax bacilli without contamination from other bacteria, Koch invented the hanging-drop technique. He ground out a depression in a thick glass slide, put a drop of blood containing anthrax microbes on a thin glass coverslip, put sealant around the edges of both sterile slides, placed the thick one over the thin one, and quickly inverted the pair, causing the drop to hang suspended over the depression. As a culture medium for the bacilli, he used liquid from the interior of the eye.

Only about one hundred miles from Wollstein was the large university city of Breslau in Silesia, and there the renowned botanist Ferdinand Julius Cohn had been working with bacteria. He had predicted that anthrax bacilli might form small eggs or spores. Koch clearly observed the spores, as he had been keeping his slides at body temperature, thus allowing the bacteria to develop through their life cycle though outside a host. Koch noted that in the inert or spore stage, anthrax bacilli, normally quick to perish when not in a warm host, could survive for years and be destroyed only by burning. He found that the spores formed only when the host died but was still warm.

Koch wrote to Cohn at Breslau in 1876 and arranged to demonstrate his techniques and findings. Koch packed his equipment and animals and treated Cohn and other scientists to a history-making exhibition, during which the pathologist Julius Cohnheim was said to have rushed from the room in great excitement to summon his students to see the masterful work being demonstrated. Though self-taught, Koch handled his equipment like a master scientist, and his three-day re-creation of his experiments left no room for doubt that he had discovered the true etiology of anthrax. He was the first to prove that a microscopic one-celled organism caused a disease.

Cohn and Cohnheim became Koch's champions in the academic community. Cohn, in his biology journal, published Koch's paper on anthrax, and Koch's fame began to spread. While the Breslau scientists tried to find government support for Koch, he had to continue his researches in his tiny laboratory—a laboratory that Koch could hardly suspect would one day be turned into a museum. Koch, meanwhile, was making a definitive record of his observations by purchasing a special camera that he fitted to his microscope—a pioneer technique on which he wrote in 1877 in another article in Cohn's journal of biology. In the same article, he touted the use of the still fairly new aniline dyes for staining bacterial cultures on slides to make organisms contrast with the background. He had not been the first to employ the technique, but he was one of the earliest to advocate it.

By that time, the news of Koch's work had spread not only around Germany but also over all the world. Even the hidebound German bureaucracy began to pay attention. In 1879, Koch was given a post at Breslau, but it had an insufficient salary, so the Koch family returned to Wollstein. Finally, the following year, Cohnheim succeeded in having Koch named as government counselor to the Imperial Bureau of Health in Berlin. A country doctor no more, Koch was given a laboratory, two assistants, and financial support.

It was after moving into his new laboratory in the capital city that Koch innocently made a rather rural discovery: He saw bacterial colonies growing on a slice of leftover boiled potato. Several different kinds were on the slice, and it struck Koch that a solid medium would provide an excellent way to keep separate the bacteria he was culturing. After a while, he abandoned cooked potato slices and employed a mixture of gelatin and beef broth, which he allowed to set in petri dishes. Louis Pasteur, who always cultured microorganisms in a souplike mixture, had a difficult time separating the desired microbes.

In Berlin, Koch concentrated on finding the agent causing tuberculosis, a slow but usually fatal endemic disease that was at its height during the late nineteenth century. Tubercle bacilli are much smaller and harder to grow than those of anthrax, but Koch persisted and produced a special blood-serum jelly to culture tuberculosis outside the body. Although he did prove that the tubercle bacillus caused the disease, Koch's vaunted tuberculin, a serum designed to cure tuberculosis in nonterminal patients, proved ineffective. Nevertheless, tuberculin can be used to diagnose the disease and is thus quite valuable.

Koch's greatest success story was the discovery of the cause of cholera—a horrible and usually fatal disease whose deadly epidemics were the terror of nineteenth century Europe and America. In 1883, cholera spread into Egypt and threatened to cross into Europe. To prevent this, the governments of France and Germany sent their best scientists to Alexandria: a French team consisting of Pasteur's top men and a German squad led by Koch himself. They searched for a microbe guilty of causing the feared cholera, and Koch was rather sure that he had located it. Then the epidemic left Egypt as mysteriously as it had come, and Europe was temporarily safe, but no one knew why.

Back in Berlin, Koch asked the government to send him to Calcutta, in eastern India, to find the disease in its permanent home. There, Koch and his assistants in early 1884 positively identified the vibrio bacillus as the cause and found that it was transmitted by water and other substances polluted with fecal matter. When the German scientists arrived home in May, they were greeted as conquering heroes. With lavish ceremony, the German Emperor William I personally decorated Koch with the Order of the Crown, with Star, while the Reichstag voted the scientist a large monetary gift.

SIGNIFICANCE

Robert Koch shares with Pasteur the honor of founding modern medical bacteriology, but, in employment of solid culture media, discovery of improved sterilization by steam, use of staining techniques, and other innovations, he built the modern bacteriological laboratory. Koch's name is permanently associated with the conquest or taming of anthrax, cholera, and tuberculosis, but he did much other work. He always had a yearning to travel, frustrated in earlier years by family responsibilities. Leaving his perennial and only partially successful work on tuberculosis, Koch worked on malaria in Italy, rinderpest in South Africa, sleeping sickness and tick fever in German East Africa, and bubonic plague in northern India. He identified the rat and its flea as vectors of the plague, but it remained for Koch's Japanese disciple Kitasato Shibasaburo to isolate the actual microbe.

Koch scandalized Victorian mores in 1892 when, his marriage failing, he divorced his first wife and married a young actor, Hedwig Freiburg. Many of his biographers deliberately omitted any mention of the occurrence, as they themselves were scandalized—a comment on the strict middle-class morality of the late nineteenth century. Koch was awarded the Nobel Prize in Physiology or Medicine in 1905, primarily for his work on tuberculosis. It was an ultimate vindication for great efforts that bore fruit in many different ways that he was given such recognition for a disease that he had not managed to kill.

—*Allan D. Charles*

FURTHER READING

Brock, Thomas D. *Robert Koch: A Life in Medicine and Bacteriology.* Madison, Wis.: Science Tech, 1988. Reprint. Washington, D.C.: ASM Press, 1999. Biog-

raphy focusing on Koch's medical career, drawing upon his published work, correspondence, and nineteenth century bacteriological literature.

Daniel, Thomas M. *Pioneers of Medicine and Their Impact on Tuberculosis.* Rochester, N.Y.: University of Rochester Press, 2000. This history of tuberculosis and its treatment includes a chapter on Koch's pioneering work in bacteriology.

De Kruif, Paul. *Microbe Hunters.* New York: Harcourt, Brace & World, 1950. This readable yet detailed account has a lengthy chapter on "Koch: The Death Fighter." De Kruif's entertaining style makes the sometimes arcane world of microbiology accessible to the general reader.

Dormandy, Thomas. *The White Death: A History of Tuberculosis.* New York: New York University Press, 2000. This history of tuberculosis includes a portrait of Koch and his role in isolating the cause of the disease.

Dubos, René. *The Unseen World.* New York: Rockefeller Institute Press, 1962. This work has a large section on Koch's life and contributions, including several interesting photographs. The book is an excellent and easily understandable introduction to microbiology and gives great credit to Koch as a founder of the science.

Fox, Ruth. *Great Men of Medicine.* New York: Random House, 1947. This book has a lengthy, thorough, and entertaining chapter on Koch. Fox concentrates on the early and middle portions of the pathologist's career.

Metchnikoff, Élie. *The Founders of Modern Medicine.* New York: Walden, 1939. This outstanding volume by a man who was himself a famous medical scientist and who knew Koch personally provides a rare and valuable look at Koch's scientific and personal lives.

Riedman, Sarah R., and Elton T. Gustafson. *Portraits of Nobel Laureates in Medicine and Physiology.* New York: Abelard-Schuman, 1963. Contains an excellent chapter on Koch plus a considerable amount of discussion of him in other chapters relating to researchers who were indebted to or in contact with him.

Stevenson, Lloyd G. *Nobel Prize Winners in Medicine and Physiology, 1901-1950.* New York: Henry Schuman, 1953. This volume concentrates on and gives a good account of Koch's work on tuberculosis, as Koch's labor in this area was what won for him the Nobel Prize.

SEE ALSO: Emil von Behring; Ferdinand Julius Cohn; Louis Pasteur; Rudolf Virchow.

RELATED ARTICLES in *Great Events from History: The Nineteenth Century, 1801-1900:* May, 1847: Semmelweis Develops Antiseptic Procedures; March 24, 1882: Koch Announces His Discovery of the Tuberculosis Bacillus; December 11, 1890: Behring Discovers the Diphtheria Antitoxin; August 20, 1897: Ross Establishes Malaria's Transmission Vector; 1898: Beijerinck Discovers Viruses.

SOFYA KOVALEVSKAYA
Russian mathematician

Kovalevskaya was the first woman in the world to receive a doctorate in mathematics from a European university and was also the first woman to teach at a European university during the nineteenth century. Her achievements in mathematics provided evidence of the ability of women to conduct research at the highest level and were recognized throughout Europe.

BORN: January 15, 1850; Moscow, Russia
DIED: February 10, 1891; Stockholm, Sweden
ALSO KNOWN AS: Sofya Vasilyevna Korvin-Krukovskaya (birth name); Sonya Kovalevskaya; Sophia Kovalevskaya; Sofia Kovalevskaya
AREA OF ACHIEVEMENT: Mathematics

EARLY LIFE

Sofya Kovalevskaya (kah-vah-LYAYF-skah-yah) was born Sofya Korvin-Krukovskaya. Her family had an estate located near the borders of what are now Russia, Lithuania, and Belarus; was affluent; and had a tradition of education. Her mother had German roots; her mother's maiden name was Schubert, and her mother's grandfather had been a German mathematician and astronomer.

Sofya's mother had inherited her grandfather's concern for education, and Sofya herself enjoyed the attention of a sequence of governesses of various nationalities, none of them Russian. This was in accord with the attitude of the educated Russian class of the time, who saw the benefit in exposing children to cultures and languages other than their own. As a result, Sofya was able to read in English and French from an early age and made good use of her language skills.

Sofya also displayed an early interest in mathematics, supposedly linked to the fact that copies of lectures given by a distinguished Russian mathematician were used to paper the wall of a bedroom. One of her uncles stimulated her interest in the subject, and she taught herself trigonometry. Her interests also extended to other sciences, and she used a microscope she purchased herself to study biology. Within her home there was no limit to the extent to which she could pursue intellectual interests. However, in the wider world, it was a different story.

The University of St. Petersburg had opened its lecture halls to women in 1861, when Sofya was eleven, but subsequent agitation led to government crackdowns and the withdrawal of the privilege for women to attend. As a result, it was clear that Sofya would have to go abroad if she wanted to pursue the various studies to which she was attracted. The difficulty was that unmarried Russian women were not allowed to travel abroad on their own. The standard solution was for women who were interested in studying elsewhere to enter into marriages of convenience with men willing to support their endeavors without necessarily expecting anything more from their marriages.

The man who played the appropriate role in Sofya's life was Vladimir Kovalevskii, an individual with scientific interests as well as political ones. There was a definite political slant to the intellectual circles in which the two spent their time, usually characterized by the term "nihilist." That term, which came from the attitudes of a character in Ivan Turgenev's novel *Fathers and Sons* (1862), summarized the view of a generation of intellectuals who found unpersuasive the extensive rules governing life and political action in the old Russian Empire. Instead, they wanted to start over again without regard for rank and wealth. Not surprisingly, this attitude was not encouraged by the government, and ongoing battles between nihilists and government agents provided another reason for going abroad.

After Sofya married Kovalevskii in September, 1868, she went abroad to study mathematics. She and her husband were also eager to find an interesting political circle, so they went first to Vienna, Austria, and then to England. Neither place fully met their needs, so by the end of the summer of 1869 they had gone to Heidelberg, Germany. Kovalevskii studied paleontology there but decided to finish his degree at the University of Jena, another German institution. Sofya, meanwhile, had decided to go the fountainhead of mathematics to study at the University of Berlin under the eminent mathematician Karl Weierstrass. Sofya's separation from her husband was to be typical of much of the couple's marriage, which ended when Kovalevskii committed suicide in 1883.

LIFE'S WORK

The prestigious position that Weierstrass held in the world of German mathematics gave him opportunities to do things that lesser scholars would not have been permitted to do; however, even he could not manage to arrange for Kovalevskaya to get credit for the work that she did with him. It was difficult for him simply to get her permission to use the university library. While the general political atmosphere in Berlin might have been more liberal than it was in Russia, that did not mean that Berlin provided a comfortable environment for a woman to make academic progress. There existed a tendency to discount the mathematical achievements of women—especially women as physically attractive as Kovalevskaya—and to attribute any success they demonstrated to their borrowing the work of their male colleagues. One indication of the stature of both Weierstrass and Kovalevskaya is the fact that no whisper of such claims was ever made about Kovalevskaya's work.

The work for which Kovalevskaya was to become best known pertained to the study of partial differential equations, which govern the behavior of most physical processes and describe how certain quantities change with changes in other quantities, such as time and position. Solutions to such equations raised great difficulties, but Kovalevskaya was able to apply Weierstrass's ideas to build a theoretical foundation for the subject, while looking for solutions. Meanwhile, she earned a doctoral degree from the University of Göttingen; she received it *in absentia*, which was a means of avoiding the issue of her being a woman. Although women had previously earned reputations in Europe as mathematicians, Kovalevskaya was the first woman to get a doctorate, a degree whose importance in the research arena was of relatively recent creation.

When Kovalevskaya returned to Russia and her husband, she looked for a suitable job but found opportunities at the university level and academies of science limited—partly because of her unpopular political views. In 1878, she gave birth to the only child she had by her husband. Two years later, she returned to Berlin. From there she hoped to be able to find a position in mathematics in

some other country, but even Weierstrass's recommendation was not enough for some institutions. For example, the University of Helsinki did not offer her a position for which she was well qualified, but it is unclear whether being a Russian or being a woman was considered the greater disqualification in Finland.

In 1884, Kovalevskaya finally received a position in Stockholm, thanks to the efforts of the mathematician Gosta Mittag-Leffler, who had been so impressed by her work that he had traveled to St. Petersburg to hear her speak before she returned to Berlin. Mittag-Leffler arranged for Kovalevskaya to get a salaried five-year professorship after she had proven her mathematical skills during her first year in Stockholm. Her responsibilities in Stockholm included lecturing and tutoring, as well as carrying out research in collaboration with Mittag-Leffler.

Even at that stage in Kovalevskaya's career, she was not allowed to attend lectures in Berlin, a tribute to the continuing difficulties with which women mathematicians had to contend in Europe. It is also true that the distinguished Swedish playwright August Strindberg was openly negative about Kovalevskaya's presence on the faculty in Stockholm, although he was scarcely qualified to criticize her mathematical work.

Despite the efforts of Mittag-Leffler to make her feel at home, Kovalevskaya became bored with Stockholm. Her stock in the mathematical world rose considerably when she received the Borodin Prize of the French Academy of Sciences in 1888 for her solution of a problem about the motion of a rigid body rotating about a fixed point. The subject had been under investigation for some time, and Kovalevskaya was far from the only entrant in the competition for the prize. It was a measure of her success that the academy doubled its cash award to her in recognition of the elegance of her solution. On the strength of this award, Kovalevskaya hoped that she could find an academic post in Paris or Russia.

Kovalevskaya's quest for alternative employment proved unavailing, but the Russian mathematician Pafnuty Chebyshev succeeded in having her named the first woman corresponding member of Russia's Imperial Academy of Sciences. In 1891, she taught the first classes of the spring semester in Stockholm but died shortly afterward.

SIGNIFICANCE

At the time of her death, Sofya Kovalevskaya was best known to the general public in Russia for her writings, especially an autobiographical account of her childhood.

The mathematical community recognized her for her ability to carry on the research program of Weierstrass as applied to a variety of particular problems.

On one hand, Kovalevskaya was a mathematician whose work need not fear comparison with that of any of her contemporaries. She was educated in the best style of Weierstrassian analysis, and she made contributions to the study of partial differential equations in the form of textbooks and research articles. Those attacking more general problems involving rotations were able to build on her efforts.

On the other hand, there is no doubt that Kovalevskaya's life has received a great deal of attention because she was the first woman to do much of what she accomplished. She certainly did not enjoy having to overcome the difficulties placed in the way of women trying to do research in mathematics, and the intervals in her life when she stopped doing mathematics are representative of her own ambivalence. Nevertheless, the success that she achieved despite the handicaps enabled women following after to point to her distinguished precedent. During the late twentieth century a Kovalevskaya Fund was set up in her honor to help support the educational efforts of women in the sciences in underdeveloped countries. Her political and scientific testament could not have been better expressed.

—*Thomas Drucker*

FURTHER READING

Cooke, Roger. *The Mathematics of Sonya Kovalevskaya*. New York: Springer-Verlag, 1984. The most extensive analysis of Kovaleskaya's mathematics, tracing its historical roots from the work of Weierstrass and his predecessors.

James, Ioan. *Remarkable Mathematicians*. Cambridge, England: Cambridge University Press, 2002. The sketch of Kovalevskaya does not go into detail about her mathematics but spells out some of the mathematical connections that she built during her career.

Kennedy, Don H. *Little Sparrow: A Portrait of Sophia Kovalevsky*. Athens: Ohio University Press, 1983. A political and literary biography that steers away from mathematics.

Koblitz, Ann Hibner. *A Convergence of Lives*. 2d ed. New Brunswick, N.J.: Rutgers University Press, 1993. One of the books that started a revival of interest in Kovalevskaya's work in English, paying attention to her literary, political, and scientific careers.

Kovalevskaya, Sofya. *A Russian Childhood*. Translated and introduced by Beatrice Stillman. New York: Springer-Verlag, 1978. The autobiography that won Kovalevskaya the most recognition in her lifetime, translated into modern English. Contains an analysis of her mathematics by P. Y. Kochina.

Spicci, Joan. *Beyond the Limit: The Dream of Sofya Kovalevskaya*. New York: Forge Press, 2002. Although well researched, this biography borders on fiction and traces Kovalevskaya's career only up to the moment that she earned her doctorate in 1874.

SEE ALSO: Aleksandr Borodin; Sophie Germain; Nikolay Ivanovich Lobachevsky; Countess of Lovelace; Charlotte Angas Scott; Ivan Turgenev.

RELATED ARTICLES in *Great Events from History: The Nineteenth Century, 1801-1900:* 1899: Hilbert Publishes *The Foundations of Geometry*; 1900: Lebesgue Develops New Integration Theory.

PAUL KRUGER
President of the South African Republic (1883-1900)

The most important Afrikaner leader of the nineteenth century, Kruger rose from backcountry farmer to the presidency of the Transvaal region's South African Republic, which took on the British Empire in two wars. Although he was ultimately vanquished by the British, he helped raise Afrikaners to a position from which they would dominate modern South Africa through most of the twentieth century.

BORN: October 10, 1825; Colesberg, Cape Colony
 (now in South Africa)
DIED: July 14, 1904; Clarens, Switzerland
ALSO KNOWN AS: Stephanus Johannes Paulus Kruger
 (birth name); Oom Paul
AREA OF ACHIEVEMENT: Government and politics

EARLY LIFE

Paul Kruger (KREW-yer) was the son of Caspar Kruger, an Afrikaner (Boer) farmer of German ancestry who lived in the Cradock district of Cape Colony. Most of the British colony's Afrikaner families were scattered throughout the interior, where their living conditions were primitive, and most Afrikaners were poorly informed about the outside world. The Calvinist religion played a major role in Afrikaner homes, such as that of the Krugers. Paul's parents belonged to the Dopper branch of the Dutch Reformed Church, which was far more conservative than most branches of the Dutch church. Paul himself had little formal education, but he developed an ability to express himself clearly—in both spoken and written language.

Afrikaner resentment against British rule in the Cape Colony escalated after 1833, when Great Britain abolished slavery through its empire, with only little compensation for former slaveowners. Emancipation also flooded the colony with unemployed former slaves, whom Afrikaners regarded as potentially dangerous. Thousands of farmers organized what became known as the Great Trek—a mass exodus of Afrikaner families from the Cape Colony to the interior regions to the north and northeast. These pioneers, who became known as voortrekkers, gathered their belongings onto ox-wagons and formed wagon trains for the difficult trek inland. The Kruger family was among the slowest to leave but eventually caught up with a voortrekker group that had entered the region that soon afterward became Natal Colony. Twelve-year-old Paul bore much of the responsibility for protecting the family's livestock during the

journey. He was considered bright, capable, a good horseback rider, and an excellent shot—valuable traits in the face of the constant danger of attacks by both wild animals and human marauders.

In 1837, Kruger's family arrived in Natal at a moment when other voortrekkers were treacherously betrayed by the Zulu king Dingane, the half brother and assassin of King Shaka. When Piet Retief and other voortrekker leaders called on Dingane to deliver presents and sign a treaty giving the voortrekkers the right to settled on Zulu land, the Zulu king entertained them with a feast and signed their treaty. When the voortrekker men removed their weapons in order to share a toast to peace, Zulu warriors descended on them and slaughtered them. The Zulu then raided the settlers' farms and killed other Afrikaners. Paul's awareness of this example of African duplicity very likely reinforced whatever negative feelings he harbored toward black Africans; the experience almost certainly affected his adult attitudes toward Africans.

After leaving Natal, the Krugers settled in the fertile Rustenberg region of the western Transvaal in 1842. There, at the age of twenty-three, Paul was appointed an assistant field cornet, an important administrative post that gave him magisterial rights during peacetime and command over fighting men during wartime. A year later he became a field cornet, a post that he held for five years. When he was promoted to commandant, he set up his own home and married Marie du Plessis. The last events set the stage for his life's work in war and politics.

LIFE'S WORK

Kruger's life's work was the political consolidation and development of the Transvaal under Afrikaner rule. His work formally began in 1852, when he was a member of an Afrikaner delegation, under the leadership of Andries Pretorius, that signed the Sand River Convention with representatives of the British Empire. Under the terms of that convention, the British recognized the political independence of the Afrikaners living north of the Orange River. In 1855, Kruger was a member of the commission that wrote a constitution for the government of the Afrikaners in the Transvaal region, who named their new nation the South African Republic. Meanwhile, the Afrikaners living between the Orange and Vaal Rivers formed the Orange Free State.

Among the challenges that the new South African Republic faced was a serious fiscal problem. To obtain much-needed manufactured goods from other lands, Afrikaners needed to replace their local system of barter with a hard currency. Kruger was a member of the government's inexperienced executive council. Under the leadership of President Marthinus Pretorius (1857-1871), the council decided to manufacture currency by printing bank notes of nominal value. Unsupported by any tangible assets, the new currency proved almost worthless and contributed to civil unrest. Realizing that a major political change was needed to avert disaster, Pretorius resigned in 1871, and the citizens of the republic elected a new president—Dutch Reformed Church minister Thomas Burgers. Thirty-six-year-old Kruger was elected vice president.

Burgers procured European loans, built schools and roads, reorganized the government, and put his own personal fortune into the treasury. However, because he was not a member of the conservative Dopper sect, Kruger and other religious conservatives put obstacles in his way. Although the republic appeared again to be menaced by the Zulu of King Cetshwayo, its men did not respond enthusiastically to Burgers's calls to fight and to pay taxes. In response to the republic's international disorders, the British Empire stepped in and annexed the Transvaal in 1877.

In 1877 and 1878, Kruger led unsuccessful Afrikaner delegations to England to seek redress from Benjamin Disraeli's government. He then helped organize passive resistance campaigns against the British occupation of the Transvaal. Finally, in December, 1880, he agreed that it was time to fight the British. In the brief conflict that followed—which is sometimes called the First Boer War—the Transvaalers inflicted several defeats on the British. After a major Afrikaner victory in the Battle of Majuba Hill in February, 1881, the British agreed to negotiate their withdrawal from the Transvaal. In 1883, Kruger was elected president of the South African Republic. The last person to hold that position, he was reelected in 1888, 1893, and 1898.

Through his four terms as president, Kruger sought to preserve the traditional rural way of life of Afrikaners, whom he regarded as "God's People." However, the discovery of major gold deposits in the Transvaal's Witwatersrand region, near Pretoria, in 1886 started a gold rush that attracted perhaps sixty thousand foreigners—whom Afrikaners dubbed *uitlanders* (outlanders)—to the Transvaal. Although the national economy and many individual Afrikaners flourished, the outsiders—who were mostly Englishmen—posed threats to the cultural cohesiveness of Afrikaner society and Afrikaner control of their own republic. To protect his government, Kruger ruled that newcomers would not be eligible to vote until they had resided in the Transvaal for fourteen years. He also imposed a heavy tax on mines.

The predominantly British *uitlanders* naturally regarded Kruger's policies as unreasonably discriminatory and enlisted outside forces to bring pressure on the Afrikaner government. During the last few days of 1895, Cecil Rhodes's close associate Leander Starr Jameson led an armed body of men into the Transvaal from the British South Africa Company's territory north of the Limpopo River. Operating on the mistaken assumption that discontented *uitlanders* would spontaneously rise up against Kruger, Jameson and Rhodes believed that a strong show of arms would bring down Kruger's government. Instead, the members of the so-called Jameson Raid simply meekly surrendered to South African Republic police as they entered the Transvaal. The incident strengthened Kruger's resolve to resist British encroachments and also helped to bring down the government of Rhodes, who was then prime minister of the Cape Colony.

Afterward, Kruger attempted to divide *uitlanders* by playing English-speaking workers and investors' groups against one another. This tactic backfired, however, and prompted Britain to send an army to the Transvaal border in 1899. After months of armed confrontation—and an ultimatum to the British to withdraw—Kruger declared war on the British on October 11. The South African, or Boer, War then began. At first, Afrikaner forces made skillful use of guerrilla tactics to win victories. However, the vastly larger and better-equipped British forces eventually won the war, On June 5, 1900, they captured Pretoria, Kruger's capital. Kruger, who by then was nearly seventy-five years old, fled to Europe, where he unsuccessfully lobbied for help from continental governments. After the South African War finally ended, on May 31, 1902, the South African Republic and Orange Free State were transformed into British colonies, which became provinces when the Union of South Africa was formed in 1910. Meanwhile, Kruger quietly died in Switzerland, on July 14, 1904. He was buried in Pretoria five months later.

SIGNIFICANCE

Although Paul Kruger performed the impressive achievement of rising from a backcountry farmer with limited education to become the powerful leader of the South African Republic, his critics claim that he was doomed to failure by his narrow mind-set and prejudices against non-Afrikaners—both black and white. However, he was shaped by his environment. Had he been different, he—like Thomas Burgers—would have been unable to succeed politically. His greatest achievement was formulating policies that changed the Transvaal's Afrikaners from an almost inconsequential aggregation of farmers into a nation. Moreover, he held his republic's presidency for seventeen years, until he was brought down by foreign conquest.

Kruger helped knit the Transvaal's Afrikaners into a political entity that won the powerful British Empire's recognition of its independence. Then, after the South African Republic fell into such disorder that Britain annexed its territory, he sagaciously employed passive resistance, lobbying campaigns, and force of arms to persuade Britain to permit his country a second chance at independence. However, Kruger's narrow-minded pursuit of a nation governed solely by conservative rural Afrikaners—"God's People"—and his prejudice against black Africans were major shortcomings that eventually contributed to his fall.

—Sanford S. Singer

FURTHER READING

Farwell, Byron. *The Great Anglo-Boer War.* New York: W. W. Norton, 1990. A solid book on the South African War that describes battles and opposing policies, with consierable attention to Kruger's own role.

Fisher, James. *Paul Kruger: His Life and Times.* London: Martin Secker & Warburg, 1974. A general description of Kruger's life and Afrikaner society and culture. It weaves into a tapestry Kruger's presidency, wider South African developments, and the British-Afrikaner wars.

Hillegas, Howard Clemons. *Oom Paul's People: A Narrative of the British-Boer Troubles in South Africa, with a History of the Boers, the Country, and Its Institutions.* 1899. Reprint. New York: Negro Universities Press, 1969. This contemporary narrative describes Kruger, the Transvaal, and Afrikaners. It covers the Afrikaner religion, Afrikaner attitudes toward Africans and *Uitlanders*, and the British statesmen and generals involved in the wars with the South African Republic.

Holmes, Prescott. *Paul Kruger: The Life Story of the President of the Transvaal.* Philadelphia: Henry Altemus, 1900. This straightforward biography of Kruger contains useful pictures of aspects of the times. It is organized chronologically to deal with both his failures and accomplishments.

Kruger, Paul. *The Memoirs of Paul Kruger: Four Times President of the South African Republic—Told by Himself.* 1902. Reprint. New York: Negro Universities Press, 1969. This autobiography presents Kruger's own views on his life, career, and political and military battles.

Magubane, Bernard. *The Making of a Racist State: British Imperialism and the Union of South Africa, 1875-1910.* Trenton, N.J.: Africa World Press, 1996. This book, not primarily about Kruger, describes the times and considers his role in the wider framework of the events leading to the creation of the Union of South Africa.

SEE ALSO: Sir Robert Stephenson Smyth Baden-Powell; Cetshwayo; Joseph Chamberlain; Benjamin Disraeli; H. Rider Haggard; Lobengula; Cecil Rhodes; Olive Schreiner.

RELATED ARTICLES in *Great Events from History: The Nineteenth Century, 1801-1900:* June 21, 1884: Gold Is Discovered in the Transvaal; October 11, 1899-May 31, 1902: South African War.

ALFRED KRUPP
German industrialist

During the period of Germany's unification into one of the most powerful nations in Europe, Krupp expanded his family's steelmaking concern into one of the most powerful industrial enterprises of the nineteenth century.

BORN: April 26, 1812; Essen, Grand Duchy of Berg (now in Germany)
DIED: July 14, 1887; Essen, Germany
ALSO KNOWN AS: Alfred the Great; Cannon King
AREA OF ACHIEVEMENT: Business

EARLY LIFE

The son of Friedrich Krupp, the founder of the family steelmaking business, Alfred Krupp (kruhp) was born in a Ruhr River Valley town only five months after Friedrich had founded the firm in 1812. When Alfred was fourteen, his father died and Alfred, along with his widowed mother, Therese, was left in charge of the business. Alfred had already been removed from school, largely because of his father's inability to make enough money to pay for his eldest son's education. As Krupp was to say in later life, his education came at an anvil, not a school desk.

As befitting a boy who had the responsibility of both a family and a factory thrust upon him, Krupp became consumed with work. His family and friends at the time described him as tall, slim, and delicate looking, but at the same time stoic and resolute. When Krupp inherited the family concern, the factory was almost bankrupt. Only seven men remained on the payroll, and wages had not been paid for several weeks. Moreover, few orders for steel products—the firm specialized in cutlery—were placed during the next several years. As Krupp later acknowledged, his mother held the family together during those lean times by sheer industriousness, a trait in himself that Krupp attributed to his mother's influence. From 1826 until he reached full adulthood, Krupp devoted every waking hour to the firm—helping either on the foundry floor or in the bookkeeper's office. Instead of playing with the other boys his age, young Krupp became obsessed with making steel.

LIFE'S WORK

For the next twenty years, Krupp endured a perpetual grind of hard work and impending financial collapse. The chief problem lay in competing with foreign producers. As late as 1848, steel from England still dominated the Prussian market. What little profit Krupp made during this time he put back into the firm, constantly attempting to expand and improve the foundry works. He was not above telling potential customers outright lies to gain a contract, nor was he reluctant to steal useful ideas from competitors. Finally, in 1834 Krupp steel was united with a force that was to transform the company as well as the map of Europe. This force was the kingdom of Prussia.

Three years after the 1815 peace eliminated Napoleon I and restored the balance of power in Europe, the Prussian government abolished all hindrances to trade among its scattered provinces. On January 1, 1834, other German states joined Prussia in an economic union, the *Zollverein*, which extended to cover most of German-speaking Europe, with the exception of Austria and Hanover. Krupp was among the first businesspeople to exploit this new advantage. By the end of 1834, he had traveled to all parts of the customs union and increased his orders for steel threefold. A year later, he again doubled his production, was employing seventy workmen, and had purchased a steam engine to power his foundry tools.

In 1847, the Krupp firm cast its first steel cannon, a small three-pound field gun, which attracted interest but few orders. The foundry still specialized in the production of fine steel suitable for dies and machine tools. The big break came in 1851, however, at the London Exhibition. Krupp was determined to gain international renown for his firm by taking to London the best example of steel casting ever produced. The result, a flawless two-ton steel ingot, representing a giant step forward in metallurgy, caused a sensation and advertised Krupp's skill as no other demonstration could have. Following the London Exhibition, orders flowed in from around the world.

The next step in the Krupp concern's development centered on mass production. By the late 1850's, Krupp had fully converted to the new production system. With his adoption of two new methods for steel manufacturing, which both lowered costs and increased production—the Bessemer and Siemens-Martin processes—Krupp was able to achieve such innovations as the seamless railroad wheel. This wheel revolutionized the railroad industry and made a fortune for Krupp; three interlocking wheels were chosen as the company emblem.

In 1858, large-scale armaments orders from the Prussian government began to dominate the firm's business. Krupp steel cannons became world-renowned after they helped Prussia defeat both Austria and France between 1866 and 1871. As a result, Krupp became a close associate of both Kaiser William I, who dubbed Krupp the "Cannon King," and German chancellor Otto von Bismarck.

By 1871, Krupp employed sixteen thousand men in numerous foundries and workshops. Ever the paternalistic proprietor, Krupp furnished an elaborate social-welfare program for his workers, including low-cost housing, free medical care, pensions, and consumer cooperatives. Workers' unions, however, were vigorously opposed, and Krupp deemed any flirtation with unions a personal affront to him. Krupp became a leader of the other Ruhr industrialists in opposing workers' organizations, and he helped finance strident antiunion and antisocialist campaigns. Most of the Krupp employees remained loyal to the firm, however, and the majority enjoyed referring to themselves as "Kruppianer."

During the 1860's, Krupp pioneered the development of vertically integrated industry by his acquisition of coal

Alfred Krupp. (Library of Congress)

mines and railroads. By the 1870's, Krupp had amassed one of the largest fortunes in Europe. The associated Krupp steel and coal companies employed more than twenty thousand men. The German elite, including the royal family, were frequent guests at Krupp's colossal mansion in Essen, the Villa Huegel, a Renaissance-style house built entirely of stone and Krupp steel. On July 14, 1887, Krupp died at Villa Huegel, attended by his family and mourned by the kaiser. Krupp's eldest son, Friedrich Alfred, continued the Krupp family's sole control over its steel empire until his death, when the firm became a corporation.

SIGNIFICANCE

With the death of his father, the founder of the Krupp steelmaking dynasty, Alfred Krupp saved the firm from near collapse and built it into an industrial giant by making use of the newest metallurgical techniques, by instilling tough discipline, and by obsessive hard work. Krupp began by making machine tools, coin dies, and steel cutlery, but his fame emerged with his production of steel cannons for the Prussian army during the 1860's and 1870's. By 1887, the name Krupp was world famous for the manufacture of quality steel, especially steel cannons for the Prussian army, which became the standard for comparison throughout the world. As an industrial empire builder, Krupp pioneered vertical integration by acquiring a variety of mining, power, and transportation concerns. An avowed opponent of socialism and labor unions, Krupp nevertheless was one of the first modern industrialists to provide full welfare services, including health insurance, pension benefits, and low-cost housing for his workers. Krupp served as a model for the nineteenth century aggressive, innovative, and paternalistic industrialist.

—William G. Ratliff

FURTHER READING

Batty, Peter. *The House of Krupp.* Rev. ed. Lanham, Md.: Cooper Square Press, 2002. First published in 1967, Batty's survey of the Krupp dynasty from its founding to the post-World War II period is less ambitious than Manchester's, but it provides the most readable and concise study. Batty thoroughly investigates Krupp's youth, and the author is especially adroit at displaying the youthful factors that later played a role in Krupp's direction of the firm.

Henderson, William Otto. *The Rise of German Industrial Power, 1834-1914.* Berkeley: University of California Press, 1975. The author concentrates on the role of unification in the rise of Germany as an industrial power. Krupp and the development of the Krupp firm from near bankruptcy to world acclaim are placed in the context of Germany's overall economic growth in the nineteenth century.

Kitchen, Martin. *The Political Economy of Germany, 1815-1914*. London: Croom Helm, 1978. The book addresses the relationship between the growth of German industry and the creation of an industrialist class. Although the discussion centers largely on the political debate over tariffs and taxes, the Krupp dominance of German armaments is given partial credit for the direction of nineteenth century German foreign policy.

Manchester, William. *The Arms of Krupp, 1587-1968.* 1968. Boston: Back Bay Books, 2003. The standard popular biography of the Krupp dynasty. A major section of the work concerns Krupp and his career as proprietor of the firm. Of special interest is Manchester's investigation of Krupp's private life and eccentricities, including the construction of the Villa Huegel. The work is careless in some of the details of the Krupp family saga.

Showalter, Dennis E. *Railroads and Rifles: Soldiers, Technology, and the Unification of Germany*. Hamden, Conn.: Archon Books, 1975. This work provides a close study of Krupp's role in the unification of Germany. The author focuses on Krupp's early years of business and his successful association with the Prussian government through the acquisition of government contracts. Especially well covered are Krupp's armaments contracts during the critical period of German unification during the 1860's and 1870's.

SEE ALSO: Otto von Bismarck; Samuel Colt.

RELATED ARTICLES in *Great Events from History: The Nineteenth Century, 1801-1900:* March 11, 1811-1816: Luddites Destroy Industrial Machines; February 25, 1836: Colt Patents the Revolver.

JOSEPH LANCASTER
English educator

An advocate of mass education, Lancaster devised an intricate educational system that was economical and replicable, thus promoting its adoption by numerous countries.

BORN: November 25, 1778; London, England
DIED: October 24, 1838; New York, New York
AREA OF ACHIEVEMENT: Education

EARLY LIFE

The names of Joseph Lancaster's parents are unknown, but his father is known to have been a sieve maker and a soldier in the war against the American colonies. Both of Lancaster's parents were Nonconformists who intended their son for the ministry. Lancaster's own mystical bent appeared when he was very young. At the age of fourteen, he was compelled to walk to Bristol, intending to board a ship bound for Jamaica, where he hoped to "teach the poor blacks the word of God." In Bristol, Lancaster realized that he was without funds to embark on a voyage, so, with characteristic impulsiveness, he instead joined the Royal Navy. After one voyage, he was released from his obligation through the intervention of friends. He left the ship after delivering an impassioned sermon to the crew.

Lancaster returned to London, where he soon joined the Religious Society of Friends (Quakers), which shared his avid interest in the education of the poor. He then served as an assistant schoolmaster at two schools before securing his father's permission, in 1798, to bring home a few poor children to teach. As well as teaching reading, writing, and arithmetic, the young man often provided clothing and food for his students. Although his generosity was much appreciated by the children, it was not matched by prudence: Lancaster's financial irresponsibility would be a leading cause of his later downfall.

Lancaster's great enthusiasm and aptitude for teaching won for him many students, however, and in 1801, Lancaster rented a large room in Borough Road, a site that was to become internationally renowned as the home of the Lancasterian monitorial school system. Over the door he had inscribed:

All who will may send their children and have them educated freely, and those who do not wish to have education for nothing may pay for it if they please.

In an age in which the education of the poor was considered by the aristocracy to be dangerous, Joseph Lancaster not only championed the right to education for the masses but also devised an economical and coherent system that made such education possible.

LIFE'S WORK

The Borough Road school proved so popular that young Lancaster soon had three hundred pupils. Turning to some Quaker philanthropists for aid, he was able to provide for some of his pupils' material needs, but he still lacked funds to pay salaries for assistant teachers. He therefore adopted a strategy cited by several other previous and contemporary educators: the use of pupil-teachers, or monitors. Although Lancaster did not "invent" this system, he was responsible for popularizing it. His enthusiasm, his talent for fund-raising and public speaking, and his gift for meticulous systematizing (curious in an otherwise impulsive and extravagant person) quickly won for him many supporters.

Imbued with the nineteenth century's faith in the goodness of technology, Lancaster brought the virtues of standardization, uniformity, and technology to the classroom. By employing monitors—older boys who taught younger ones—Lancaster could divide his three hundred students into groups of ten of roughly the same ability in a subject area (reading, writing, or arithmetic). Lessons were conducted in the manner of a spelling bee, with each group gathered in a semicircle around their monitor and each pupil competing to better his standing. This afforded direct attention and immediate reinforcement from the monitor—not possible in the traditional system in which the entire class recited lessons *en masse* to one teacher.

In the Lancasterian system, each pupil's progress (or lack of it) was duly noted in meticulous logs kept by the monitors, who were also supposed to be learning according to the classical dictum "he who teaches learns." The regimented system lent itself favorably to comparisons with the military and with factories, because each placed emphasis on the system rather than the individual: Monitors, like officers or machine parts, were replaceable in a smoothly running system. Because the system was easily copied, many monitors went out to establish their own schools elsewhere.

Lancaster's fascination with efficient technology led him also to invent ingenious cost-cutting and time-saving devices and methods for his monitorial system of education. For example, he realized that the use of textbooks was inefficient, because only one page of the book could be used at one time, and by only one student. Therefore, he made large lesson cards on which to display each lesson. These could be read simultaneously by all ten boys in the group, and, because they were not handled except by the monitors, the cards would last indefinitely. Lancaster also invented time-saving routines for taking roll, checking on truants, and almost every other activity occurring in the school day.

In an age when students were often beaten for not learning their lessons, Lancaster's psychology offered some improvement. Although whippings were still considered an option, he advised adherents of his system that even the most unruly child responds better to encouragement than to punishment. Thus, he devised an intricate system of rewards, wherein prizes could be won by the most accomplished students. (It should be noted that Lancaster also invented cages in which boys could be hung from the ceiling and advocated some other strategies that relied on humiliation for effectiveness. Although it may be argued that such tactics might be less cruel than corporal punishment, these ideas are also indicative of Lancaster's increasing mental instability.)

One of the most important features of the Lancasterian system was its nondenominational religious training. Lancaster promoted "scriptural education," which consisted solely of readings from the Scriptures without providing any doctrinal interpretations, thus encouraging individual interpretations, a practice advocated by Nonconformists and Quakers. At first, even the powerful Church of England supported this program, but this was to change as Lancaster's monitorial schools met with increasing success.

By 1805, the twenty-six-year-old teacher was famous, having won the approval of George III and attracted international attention to his Borough Road School. Despite his increasing personal problems—he was deemed by some to be "thriftless, impulsive, extravagant, and sadly deficient in ordinary self-control"—Lancaster inspired many followers to begin Lancasterian schools elsewhere.

At this point, conservatives grew alarmed at Lancaster's success. The Church of England and various conservative leaders attacked the Lancasterian system as an attempt to undermine the High Church by educating the masses with a neutral point of view about religion. Andrew Bell, who had established his own (earlier) form of monitorial school in India, was persuaded to come out

of retirement to lead this opposition. The ensuing Bell-Lancaster controversy, which raged over the next twenty years, was centered on this difference in religious perspective. The fact that the debate really had its basis in politics is evident in the conservatives' objections to an educated underclass. Bell wrote, "It is not proposed that the children of the poor be educated in an expensive manner, or even taught to write and to cypher." Lancaster's advocates denounced this as elitism, and Lancaster himself declared that he was precluded from offering an even more extensive curriculum by expense only.

Lancaster's largess, devoid of prudence, quickly became a major problem. In 1807, a small group of benefactors had to step in to rescue him from his large debt. Recognizing signs of his increasing mental instability, they agreed in confidence that "the prudent management of J. L. was the first and great object" of their organization. In 1811, this group became the Royal Lancasterian Society, which solicited public funds and defended the movement from attack by the conservative Bellites, as well as promoting the movement abroad.

Although the Lancasterians dreamed of a national system of education, it was never to be in their homeland. The monitorial schools met with varying degrees of success in many foreign countries, however, including Ireland, France, Denmark, Sweden, Spain, Russia, Greece, the West Indies, and various nations in Latin America.

By 1814, Joseph Lancaster's shortcomings had overshadowed the strengths he had to offer his own educational movement. Burdened by a mentally ill wife and his own serious psychological problems—he was paranoid, deluded that he was being persecuted, even by those who most wanted to help him—Lancaster finally alienated even his most loyal supporters. He was "read out" (expelled) from the Society of Friends for his financial irresponsibility, and the British and Foreign School Society (previously the Royal Lancasterian Society) pressured him into resigning, following an incident in which he had apparently beaten some of his monitors for pleasure. As philanthropist Samuel Whitbread told Lancaster grimly, "If we have to choose between the man and the system, we shall save the system and reject the man." Ironically, Lancaster's success in creating an educational system in which individuals were replaceable had made him obsolete.

At only thirty-five years of age, Lancaster had passed the apex of his career and was destined for misfortune the rest of his life. Although he always commanded audiences wherever he went, his delusions of martyrdom precluded his being able to hold a position at monitorial schools in Philadelphia, Baltimore, Caracas, Trenton, or Montreal. Always inspired by visions of the great things he would do next, Lancaster was incapable of working responsibly in the present. His autobiographical sketch entitled *Epitome of Some of the Chief Events and Transactions in the Life of Joseph Lancaster* (1833) reveals the extent of his mental aberration. Still convinced of his persecution, he died in 1838 in New York City, having been trampled by a runaway horse.

SIGNIFICANCE

Joseph Lancaster himself was not a major figure in education, but he is notable for his good fortune in capturing the spirit of the age—the enthusiasm for the Industrial Revolution—in a manner that benefited the advocates of education for the masses. Whereas the opposers of public education cited exorbitant cost and unfeasibility as obstacles, Lancaster provided a systematized plan for the monitorial schools that was not only cheap but also relatively efficient. His genius lay in his ability to detail every aspect of the pedagogy so minutely that any follower could implement the system.

Although later generations derided the monitorial schools as being "factories," the fact that they were efficient is evidenced in the presence of many Lancasterian elements in schools today, such as emphasis on discipline, routine, and pride in the school community.

The reliance on a chain of command, wherein authority lay in an office rather than a person, had both advantages and disadvantages. Advantages included the clarity of organization and the regularity of discipline, the individualized attention, and the psychological motivation provided by competition and prizes; the disadvantages included the damage done by any incompetent monitors and the rigidity of the teaching. These weaknesses were quickly identified and were in part responsible for the movement toward the professionalization of teaching in subsequent decades. Although Lancaster enjoyed personal acclaim only from 1804 to 1814, his monitorial school system continued to influence the rise of mass education internationally, until its decline during the 1840's.

—*Leslie Todd Pitre*

FURTHER READING

Cohen, Sol, ed. "Joseph Lancaster's Monitorial System (1805)." In *Education in the United States: A Documentary History*. Vol. 2, edited by Fred L. Israel and William P. Hansen. New York: Random House, 1974. Contains excerpts from Lancaster's *Improvements in Education, as It Respects the Industrious Classes of the Community* (1803), affording a firsthand look at the educator's philosophy, as well as his methods of teaching and discipline.

Fouts, Gordon E. "Music Instruction in Early Nineteenth-Century American Monitorial Schools." *Journal of Research in Music Education* 22 (Summer, 1974): 112-119. Discusses the contributions of Bell and Lancaster to music education by describing Ezra Barratt's fifty-six-page *Sabbath School Psalmody*, prepared expressly for use in monitorial schools.

Jones, Rufus M. *The Later Periods of Quakerism*. Vol. 2. London: Macmillan, 1921. Chapter 17, "Friends in Education," provides brief biographies of Lancaster and other Quakers influential in the rise of public education.

Kaestle, Carl F., ed. *Joseph Lancaster and the Monitorial School Movement: A Documentary History*. New York: Teachers College Press, 1973. An informative collection of documents, including excerpts from the writings of Joseph Lancaster, his advocates, and his detractors. Kaestle provides a lengthy and highly informative overview of the monitorial movement, the Bell-Lancaster controversy, and the international spread of the Lancasterian system in his introduction.

Rayman, Ronald. "Joseph Lancaster's Monitorial System of Instruction and American Indian Education, 1815-1838." *History of Education Quarterly* (Winter, 1981): 395-409. Gives background on how Lancaster's plan was seized as the most efficient way to achieve the white settlers' goals of Indian education and cultural assimilation. The federally funded Brainerd School and the Choctaw Academy, supposedly model Lancasterian schools, soon abandoned any educational ideals in favor of manual labor. An extensive bibliography is included.

Read, Julie. "Working Class Hall of Fame Reopens." *Times Educational Supplement*, no. 4288 (September 4, 1998). Discusses an exhibition in Hitchin, Hertfordshire, England, depicting and describing Lancaster's educational system in detail.

SEE ALSO: Mary Putnam Jacobi; Emma Willard.

RELATED ARTICLE in *Great Events from History: The Nineteenth Century, 1801-1900:* 1820's-1830's: Free Public School Movement.

HELENE LANGE
German feminist

Lange was a teacher and writer who became one of the central activists for the women's movement in Germany at the end of the nineteenth century. Her speeches, polemic essays, and articles testify to her fight for improved women's education and for women's rights. She became the central spokesperson for the General German Women's Association and represented a moderate feminist position advocating gender difference.

BORN: April 9, 1848; Oldenburg (now in Germany)
DIED: May 13, 1930; Berlin, Germany
ALSO KNOWN AS: Helene Henriette Elisabeth Lange (full name)
AREA OF ACHIEVEMENT: Women's rights

EARLY LIFE

Helene Lange (lahng-eh) was the second of three children and only daughter of a German merchant named Carl Theodor Lange and his wife, Johanne Sophie Amalie. At the age of seven, Helene lost her mother; her father died when she was sixteen. As was customary for girls of her social status, she first attended elementary school before attending a local private school for bourgeois girls. After passing her exam in 1864—the same year in which her father died—she spent one year in the household of a southern German pastor who had known her father. It was in this situation that Helene first realized women's disadvantaged position, as she was not allowed to participate in the men's political and philosophical discussions. In her later memoirs, she described that period as the birth of her feminist awareness.

In what Lange called the "time of waiting" for young women—after finishing school and before getting married—she experienced boredom and further developed her growing awareness of the inequality of women and men. She would never marry and soon started to teach children in her home. Eventually, she obtained a position in a girls' boarding school in Alsace. She was forced to give up this position, however, because of a severe eye condition and migraine headaches that would afflict her throughout the rest of her life. In 1871, after she came of age, she moved to Berlin, where she passed the teachers' examination that her guardian had previously refused to allow her to take.

LIFE'S WORK

In addition to giving lessons at private girls' schools in Berlin, Lange learned both Latin and Greek and read history and philosophy, together with other women. In 1876, when she was twenty-eight years old, she founded a women teachers' training college, in which she worked until 1891. She was convinced that girls should be educated primarily by women, and that the teachers themselves should receive better training. At that time, the education of bourgeois girls—in contrast with that of boys—was not designed to prepare them for professions or entrance to universities but to prepare them for their roles as wives, mothers, and teachers of their own children. Lange accepted these prescribed roles for women but regarded the educational system as incapable of training women to meet even those limited objectives.

In 1889, Lange opened the *Realkurse* (which she later extended into *Gymnasialkurse*)—courses that were designed to offer an extended educational program for young women. These courses prepared graduates of the higher girls' schools for useful employment and also for the examination that led to Swiss universities, which, unlike German universities, were already open to women at that time. With those preparatory courses and her educational politics, Lange also paved the way for women's access to university education in Germany—a milestone in women's emancipation.

Lange drew attention to her ideas by raising her voice courageously. Her rhetorical brilliance and her polemical directness later made her a famous and well-respected spokesperson for the moderate wing of the women's movement. Most late nineteenth century feminists were members of the middle class and demanded improved rights for women that were based on essential differences between the sexes, rather than on sexual equality. According to the conservative and moderate representatives of the women's movement, a woman's proper sphere was the home; hence, they petitioned for more autonomy for women in a separate sphere. However, Lange's work also resulted in better educational and career opportunities that contributed significantly to the improvement of women's situation in German society. Lange did not live quite long enough to witness the Nazi attempt to force German women back to their hearths during the 1930's.

The bourgeois German women's movement of the 1870's and 1880's, represented by the General German Women's Association founded in 1865, concentrated on two issues: improving women's education and admitting women to the medical profession. Petitions to the government were an important tool in feminist politics. Lange played a prominent role in the 1888 petition as the author of the so-called "Yellow Brochure" (*Gelbe Broschüre*), a tract demanding a more important role for women teachers in the upper grades of girls' schools, as well as the training of the women who were necessary for such teaching. Despite its moderate demands, the tract aroused hostile reactions, and the petition was rejected at the time.

Lange became famous as the leader of the General German Women's Association from 1902 to 1923. She not only worked in practical ways to advance the situation of women but also published theoretical works commenting on the women's movement in Europe and in America and reflecting on the aims of the German movement. With Gertrud Bäumer, she edited the multi-volume *Handbook of the Women's Movement*. In 1893, she founded the monthly journal *Die Frau* (woman), which discussed the political, social, and economic situation of women in Germany. *Times of Struggle* (1928) was a collection of her essays and speeches spanning four decades; it best illustrates the broad range of topics that Lange addressed as a prolific writer and publisher.

Lange's private life was closely intertwined with her political work. The feminist teacher, activist, and writer Gertrud Bäumer was her life partner and close colleague from 1899 until her death. Lange's close friendship with the twenty-five-year-younger Bäumer was often described as a mother-daughter relationship. After Lange's death in May, 1930, following a long illness, Bäumer continued her political work through the remaining twenty years of her own life.

During the 1920's, Lange received many public honors, including honorary citizenship of Oldenburg and an honorary doctorate from the University of Tübingen. These honors testify to her great importance for the women's movement and at the same time to her acceptance within society despite the predominantly conservative political circumstances.

SIGNIFICANCE

Through the first years of the twenty-first century, none of Helene Lange's work had been translated into English. Moreover, Germany's late nineteenth century feminist movement had gained only limited attention outside Germany. This lack of interest in Lange is probably due to the conservative position on gender differ-

ence, which distinguishes the German movement from the movements in England and the United States. However, to understand fully the impact of Lange's arguments, her work must be read within the context of imperial Germany. In this conservative context, her argumentation becomes more effective because it helped to reform politics, albeit slowly, in a positive way for women. Hence, her political contribution to German feminism is uncontested today and most of her works are—at least in German—reprinted and easily accessible.

Scholarly attention has focused also on Lange's private life and especially her close friendship with Gertrud Bäumer. Instead of being subordinated to a husband who legally possessed many rights to his wife's person, Lange and Bäumer each found in each other a life partner who understood and supported her professional activities. Living a life of shared intellectual work and forging a relationship between equals formed the crucial prerequisites for Helene Lange's feminist writing and activism.

—*Miriam Wallraven*

FURTHER READING

Albisetti, James C. "Could Separate Be Equal? Helene Lange and Women's Education in Imperial Germany." *History of Education Quarterly* 22, no. 3 (1982): 301-317. Analyzes traditions and developments in German education and traces Helene Lange's crucial role in improving women's educational opportunities.

Evans, Richard J. *The Feminist Movement in Germany, 1894-1933*. London: Sage Publications, 1976. Although in some respects superseded by newer research, this book remains the only study in English that provides the political background and an overview of the development of the German women's movement. It presents activists such as Lange against the backdrop of German liberalism from the fall of Otto von Bismarck to the advent of Adolf Hitler.

Göttert, Margit. *Macht und Eros: Frauenbeziehungen und weibliche Kultur um 1900: Eine neue Perspektive auf Helene Lange und Gertrud Bäumer*. Königstein, Germany: Ulrike Helmer Verlag, 2000. Focuses on the political and private relationship between Lange and Bäumer and situates their lives within the women's movement and a culture of women's friendship and intellectual community.

Hopf, Caroline, and Eva Matthes, eds. *Helene Lange und Gertrud Bäumer: Kommentierte Texte*. 2 vols. Bad Heilbrunn, Germany: Julius Klinkhardt, 2001, 2003.

These collections provide easy and comprehensive access to the most important essays on feminist politics and education by Lange and Bäumer. They offer excellent comments on the main political topics and texts.

Schaser, Angelika. *Helene Lange und Gertrud Bäumer: Eine politische Lebensgemeinschaft.* Cologne, Germany: Böhlau, 2000. Analyzes the relationship between Lange and Bäumer and provides detailed research on their works and positions as well as biographies. Contains a comprehensive bibliography.

SEE ALSO: Luise Aston; Hubertine Auclert; Dame Millicent Garrett Fawcett; Marie Elizabeth Zakrzewska.

RELATED ARTICLES in *Great Events from History: The Nineteenth Century, 1801-1900:* May, 1869: Woman Suffrage Associations Begin Forming; July 4, 1876: Declaration of the Rights of Women.

SAMUEL PIERPONT LANGLEY
American astronomer, physicist, and aeronautical engineer

Through pioneering research, Langley discovered new portions of the infrared spectrum, and his invention of the bolometer aided in spectral measurements of solar and lunar radiation. He also established the principles of flight and demonstrated the practicability of mechanical flight with self-propelled, heavier-than-air machines.

BORN: August 22, 1834; Roxbury, Massachusetts
DIED: February 27, 1906; Aiken, South Carolina
AREAS OF ACHIEVEMENT: Astronomy, science and technology

EARLY LIFE

Samuel Pierpont Langley was the son of Samuel Langley, a Boston merchant of English descent, and Mary Sumner Williams. The family background included intellectuals as well as skilled mechanics and artisans. As a boy, Langley played with his father's telescope and, with his brother John, built a new telescope and made astronomical observations. In addition to astronomy, the flight of birds fascinated the young boy. Langley read extensively throughout his life and studied science, literature, and history. He was well read in the classics in several languages, including English, French, and German. Langley attended the Boston Latin School and Boston High School. He had a gift for drawing and an interest in mathematics, so, upon graduation in 1851, he turned his attention to civil engineering and architecture.

Rather than attending a university, Langley went to work for an architectural firm in Boston. In 1857 he moved west and worked as an architect and civil engineer for several years in both Chicago, Illinois, and St. Louis, Missouri. In 1864 he returned to New England, where he built a larger telescope with his brother from the ground up. He and his brother also went to Europe for one year and visited observatories, museums, and art galleries.

With this varied background and without university training, Langley began a career as a self-taught astronomer. Upon his return to the United States in 1865, the director of the Harvard College Observatory asked Langley to become an assistant. In 1866 Langley became an assistant professor of mathematics at the Naval Academy in Annapolis, Maryland, although his primary responsibility was as director of the observatory. In 1867 he became a professor of astronomy and physics at Western University in Pittsburgh, Pennsylvania, where for twenty years he taught and was the director of the Allegheny Observatory.

LIFE'S WORK

Langley did most of his original scientific investigations during his years in Pittsburgh. To get funding for the Allegheny Observatory, he tried to make astronomy practical and profitable. He convinced the Pennsylvania Railroad Company that he could produce an accurate time-keeping system for its train personnel. At that time, these personnel had to change time every forty or fifty miles along the railroad lines. The observatory sent out a signal two times per day based on astronomical observations that gave the accurate time to all Pennsylvania Railroad stations. This arrangement provided complete funding for the Allegheny Observatory for many years and established a practice of standard time that later became universal.

During his tenure at Allegheny Observatory, Langley determined that current measuring instruments were not precise enough for his astronomical work. From 1879 to

1881 he developed and invented the bolometer, an instrument that accurately measures heat in small increments and enables astronomers to study the infrared region of the solar spectrum. The bolometer is basically an electrical thermometer. The sensitive element is a thin, blackened metallic tape adapted to absorb radiation in very narrow bands of the spectrum and with precision to one ten-millionth of a degree centigrade.

Langley undertook many survey expeditions and investigated eclipses, sunspots, and other astronomical phenomena. He also studied the solar spectrum. One of his most important expeditions was to Mount Whitney in California, the highest point in the United States at that time (1881). His team measured the energy of solar radiation with the bolometer and discovered infrared areas of the solar spectrum that were far beyond the spectral limit that was recognized at that time.

Langley's research at the Allegheny Observatory also encompassed many fields: the distribution of radiation over the sun's surface and in sunspots, the solar energy spectrum and its extension into the infrared, the lunar energy spectrum, spectra of terrestrial sources and determination of unmeasured wavelengths, absorption of the ra-

Samuel Pierpont Langley. (Library of Congress)

diation of the sun by the earth's atmosphere, and the determination of the solar constant of radiation. This research contributed to what was originally known as the "new astronomy" and is now called astrophysics. Rather than investigating the existence and position of astronomical bodies, Langley studied their physical characteristics—heat, light, and radiant energy.

In 1887 Langley also began research into aerodynamics. He formulated Langley's law, which states that the faster a body travels through the air, the less energy is required to keep it aloft. Langley's experiments showed that the work of the wind aids soaring flight, just as buoyancy aids swimming. He discovered principles of lift and resistance for rapidly moving surfaces in air.

In January, 1887, Langley joined the staff of the Smithsonian Institution as assistant secretary in charge of exchanges, publications, and the library. This position interested Langley because he had been somewhat isolated in western Pennsylvania. His move to the Smithsonian brought him to the center of the scientific community in the United States. By November, 1887, Langley had become the third secretary of the Smithsonian, a position he held until his death in 1906. Under his leadership, the Smithsonian expanded its areas of research with the National Zoological Park in 1890 and the National Gallery of Art in 1904. The museum also added a "children's room" for science education. Langley's key contribution to the Smithsonian as an institution was the founding of the Smithsonian Astrophysical Observatory in 1890, where he continued his work on solar radiation during the 1890's.

Aerodynamics also continued to fascinate Langley. He built what he called an "aerodrome"—an unmanned flying machine with wide-spreading wings to sustain its flight while it was driven along by a gasoline-fueled, steam-powered engine. It had a wingspan of about 14 feet patterned after a four-winged dragonfly. On May 6, 1896, Langley sent up aerodrome model number 5, which landed safely after flying over one-half mile (3,000 feet) for about 90 seconds. On November 28 of the same year, a larger model traveled about three-quarters of a mile (4,000 feet). The two flights proved the practicability of mechanical flight and were the first sustained free flights of power-propelled, heavier-than-air machines.

Although Langley showed the scientific feasibility of mechanical flight, he wished to leave further development to commercial applications. However, under pressure from the U.S. government, he pursued experimentation on a model large enough to carry a human. In 1898 the U.S. War Department, with the Spanish-American

War looming, allotted $50,000 to Langley to develop, construct, and test a large aerodrome. The Smithsonian added another $20,000 to the project. Langley intended simply to build a larger version of the models already flown and add a different engine. He eventually used an engine based on a design by Stephen Balzer and modified by Charles Manly, who had been working with Langley over the previous few years. Manly tested the manned machine himself.

On August 8, 1903, a 14-foot model flew without a pilot for about 1,000 feet. However, two tests of the full-sized, manned machine failed on October 7 and December 8 of 1903. In both cases, failure occurred during the launch rather than during flight. In scaling up the models, Langley had not accounted for the fact that the drag would increase exponentially. Langley's last trial preceded the successful flight of the Wright brothers by only nine days. Langley's tests were well publicized in newspapers, unlike those of the Wright brothers, and the reporters called the machines "Langley's Folly." Less than two years after the failed tests, in November, 1905, Langley had a stroke. For rest and convalescence, he traveled to South Carolina in early February, 1906. He suffered a second stroke there and died on February 27, 1906.

SIGNIFICANCE

Samuel Pierpont Langley's work in aerodynamics followed a different technical path from that of the Wright brothers, but his work was key to aviation development. The notion of heavier-than-air flight by humans had been ridiculed, but Langley's research provided a scientific basis for experimentation in mechanical flight. Coming from a prominent member of the scientific community, Langley's beliefs carried weight. In addition, Manly's improvements to Langley's engine turned it into the world's first radial engine designed for flight, and it was the same basic engine used in aircraft through World War II.

Langley's primary contributions were in the field of astrophysics, where he developed new apparatus and techniques for the measurement of radiation. With his invention of the bolometer, it became possible not only to identify radiant energy but also to measure it. Langley used the instrument to discover and explore new portions of the solar spectrum and measure the heat of sunspots, various parts of the sun's disk, and the temperature of the moon. His experiments aided in determining the distribution of radiation in the solar spectrum, the transparency of the atmosphere to different solar rays, and the en-

hancement of their intensity at high altitudes. In 1947 his name was given to a new unit of measurement: The "langley" is defined as a unit of illumination used to measure temperature, equal to one gram calorie per square centimeter of irradiated surface.

Langley also contributed to the institutionalization and popularization of American science, particularly astronomy. His administration at the Smithsonian Institution also expanded the exchange and distribution programs for scientific research. Langley gave many public lectures and wrote essays on astronomical subjects in popular magazines of his day, including *Popular Science Monthly*, *Atlantic Monthly*, *Century Magazine*, and *McClure's*. He also wrote a book called *The New Astronomy* (1888). Langley not only advanced science but also diffused and distributed new scientific knowledge to both specialists and the public.

—Linda Eikmeier Endersby

FURTHER READING

Berliner, Don. *Aviation: Reaching for the Sky*. Minneapolis: Oliver Press, 1997. Contains a chapter on Langley and the aerodrome, while chapters on other aviation pioneers provide context for his aeronautical research. Includes illustrations, a glossary, and a chronology of aviation advances.

Crouch, Tom D. *A Dream of Wings: Americans and the Airplane, 1875-1905*. New York: W. W. Norton, 1981. Covers developments in American aviation, including several chapters on Langley. This work is the most complete research on Langley's aeronautical contributions and includes an extensive bibliography.

_____. *A History of Aviation from Kites to the Space Age*. Washington, D.C.: Smithsonian National Air and Space Museum, 2003. One of numerous aviation histories published during the celebration of the centennial of flight. Includes information about Langley's aerodrome and his other contributions to aeronautics.

Eddy, John A. "Founding the Astrophysical Observatory: The Langley Years." *Journal for the History of Astronomy* 21 (February, 1990): 111-120. Contains a short, general biography of Langley with major emphasis on his astronomical research and administrative duties at the Smithsonian.

Hallion, Richard P. *Taking Flight: Inventing the Aerial Age from Antiquity Through the First World War*. New York: Oxford University Press, 2003. This aviation history book contains information about Langley's research on and development of the aerodrome and other contributions to aeronautics.

Jones, Bessie Zuban. *The Golden Age of Science: Thirty Portraits of the Giants of Nineteenth-Century Science.* New York: Simon & Schuster, 1966. Contains a chapter on Langley and provides context for his research.

Meadows, A. J. *Early Solar Physics.* Elmsford, N.Y.: Pergamon Press, 1970. Contains an overview of the development of the new astronomy from 1850 to 1900, including Langley's accomplishments. Also includes the writings of contemporary astrophysicists and a reference list with technical and scientific details.

Oehser, Paul Henry. *Sons of Science: The Story of the Smithsonian Institution and Its Leaders.* New York: Schuman, 1949. Includes a chapter on Langley that contains information on all of his various activities and accomplishments. Includes a selected bibliography.

Vaeth, J. Gordon. *Langley: Man of Science and Flight.* New York: Ronald Press Company, 1966. Short but complete biography of Langley written for nonspecialists. Includes a short bibliographical essay on sources.

SEE ALSO: Alexander Graham Bell; George Cayley; Williamina Paton Stevens Fleming; Margaret Lindsay Huggins; Maria Mitchell; Simon Newcomb.

RELATED ARTICLE in *Great Events from History: The Nineteenth Century, 1801-1900:* April, 1898-1903: Stratosphere and Troposphere Are Discovered.

LILLIE LANGTRY
English actor

Widely recognized as a celebrity during the late nineteenth and early twentieth centuries, Langtry was famous as a mistress of the Prince of Wales and was also a successful actor who amassed a fortune through her stage career and product endorsements.

BORN: October 13, 1853; St. Saviour's Parish, Jersey, Channel Islands
DIED: February 12, 1929; Monte Carlo, Monaco
ALSO KNOWN AS: Emilie Charlotte Le Breton (birth name); Lady de Bathe; Lily Langtry; Jersey Lily
AREA OF ACHIEVEMENT: Theater

EARLY LIFE

Lillie Langtry was born Emilie Charlotte Le Breton. She was the only daughter of the dean of the island of Jersey, William Corbet Le Breton, and his wife, Emilie Davis Martin. Surrounded by six brothers, Lillie grew up in comfortable surroundings and was educated at home. Much of her adult personality was shaped by her father, who engaged in a string of marital infidelities that she observed throughout her life. His sexual exploits affected not only the lives of several of his neighbors but also Lillie's own life. When she fell in love with a young boy at the age of sixteen, her father forbade her to have a relationship with the boy. After Lillie refused to obey his order, he explained his reason: The boy was his own son by one of his illicit relationships.

At the age of fifteen, Lillie spent one social season in London that resulted in disaster. She returned home and resolved to learn how to fit into London society. She spent the next few years studying and appreciated the value of education. As she matured, she became both more beautiful and more socially ambitious.

On March 9, 1874, Lillie married Edward Langtry, the son of an Irish shipowner, and honeymooned with him on his boat, the *Gertrude.* Afterward, they settled into a Southampton home. By that time, Lillie realized that she had nothing in common with her new husband. However, she fell ill soon after their arrival in Southampton. Edward Langtry thought that Lillie was pregnant, but Lillie had contracted typhoid fever. After she recovered, the couple moved to London, under doctor's orders, so that Lillie could regain her strength.

LIFE'S WORK

After Lillie and her husband arrived in London in 1878, they enjoyed sightseeing tours through the local parks and met Lord Raneleigh, a family friend from Jersey, who invited them to a Sunday brunch at his home. Lillie was mourning the death of her brother Reggie, so she wore a simple black dress to the brunch party. The following week, the couple received an invitation to a party at the home of Lady Sebright, a London art patron. Wearing the same simple black gown with no jewels, Lillie retired to a chair in the corner of a room and suddenly became the center of attention. Attracted to her beauty and her simple dress, the men in the room scrambled to meet her. Some of the greatest artists of the time descended upon her and demanded that she pose for paintings and sculptures. In that one evening lay the seeds of Langtry's future as a famous face, mistress, and actor.

The painters and members of London society who discovered Langtry's beauty at that dinner party catapulted her into the public eye almost overnight. Realizing that Langtry was a paragon of beauty, the painters rushed to immortalize her image. Edward Poynter, a noted artist of the time, found in Langtry his ideal of beauty and painted her several times in as many years. Other painters who appreciated Langtry's beauty and painted her included John Everett Millais, Arthur Weigall, Sir Edward Burne-Jones, and George Frederick Watts.

Frank Miles, the struggling artist who had been Oscar Wilde's roommate, quickly sketched a pencil drawing of Langtry that was sold in shops days after their first meeting. This pencil rendition of Langtry elevated her to the status of a professional beauty. Comments were soon written about her perfect skin, her symmetrical features, and her voluptuous figure. Many observers agreed that she was the most beautiful woman in the world.

Langtry's beauty also provided the catalyst for her meeting and subsequent affair with the Prince of Wales, Albert Edward, who later became King Edward VII. The two met in 1877 and began their affair soon afterward. The prince and Langtry were very public with their relationship. The prince showered gifts on his official mistress, and every party to which he was invited had to include Langtry on its guest list, or he would not attend. Although their affair did not last for a long time, Langtry and the prince remained friends. Meanwhile, Langtry began another affair, with Prince Louis of Battenberg, who fathered her only daughter, Jeanne-Marie, in 1880.

After Langtry became pregnant, she found herself in dire financial straits. Facing bankruptcy, social ostracism, and the breakup of her marriage, she became the first upper-class woman in London society to pursue a

Lillie Langtry. (The Granger Collection, New York)

stage career. With the help of Oscar Wilde, she went on stage in 1881 as Kate Hardcastle in the Oliver Goldsmith play *She Stoops to Conquer* (1773). Her first London audience included the Prince and Princess of Wales. The reviews that she received were good enough to launch her acting career, and she continued to act in England and the United States for many years.

Most drama critics regarded Langtry as having only marginal acting talent at best; most of the people who attended her performances usually did so to view her costumes or her famous face. Langtry also endorsed a variety of products during her time as a stage actor. She became the first woman to endorse a commercial product when she was paid 132 pounds for endorsing a soap brand.

Langtry toured the United States several times and eventually purchased property in California's Lake County, in the hope of raising racehorses. She eventually sold that property, which she called Guenoc, at a loss; however, the property served the purpose of establishing Langtry's residence in the United States, and she gained American citizenship in 1887 in order to divorce Edward Langtry in 1897. Two years later, she married again. On July 27, 1899, she wed Hugo Gerald de Bathe on the island of Jersey. On the death of her father-in-law in 1907, her husband inherited his father's title and Langtry became Lady de Bathe.

Langtry continued to tour through and began working in vaudeville at the age of fifty-four. She gave her last performance in London during World War I, after which she retired to Monaco. She also found success off the stage. Her horses, Merman and Yentoi, won the Cesarewitch twice, in 1897 and 1908. She died in Monaco on February 12, 1929, and was buried in St. Saviour's Churchyard on Jersey.

SIGNIFICANCE

Lillie Langtry's personality and renowned beauty attracted both poets and princes, and she turned their friendships into professional alliances. When her financial resources fell into a precarious position and her social standing was threatened, she chose to market her image through acting and endorsements. Her close circle of friends, made up of painters, aesthetes, socialites, and poets, encouraged her to use her talent in a way that would celebrate her beauty. She also succeeded in making a name for herself on the stage when it was not entirely acceptable for "proper" women to embark on theatrical careers. Outstanding beauty, modest talent, and a deliciously scandalous personal life ensured Langtry fortune and fame in England and America. At the peak of her career, she was considered by many to be the most famous and most beautiful woman in the world. She raced horses, gambled large sums of money, and continued to act on the stage and in films.

—*Jennifer Hudson Allen*

FURTHER READING

Aronson, Theo. *The King in Love: King Edward VII's Mistresses—Lillie Langtry, Daisy Warwick, Alice Keppel, and Others.* New York: Harper & Row, 1988. Popular account of King Edward's relationships with his many mistresses, including Langtry.

Beatty, Laura. *Lillie Langtry: Manners, Masks, and Morals.* London: Chatto & Windus, 1999. This biography of Langtry provides an excellent discussion of her personal life and her love affairs with Artie Jones and the Prince of Wales.

Dudley, Ernest. *The Gilded Lily: The Life and Loves of the Fabulous Lillie Langtry.* London: Odhams Press, 1958. Biography of Langtry that chronicles her life in the context of her private affairs; it highlights her background in Jersey, her marriage, and her stage career.

Harper, Donna Lee. *The Diary of Lillie Langtry and Other Remembrances.* New York: Arrowhead Classics, 1994. Fictionalized account that emphasizes Langtry's relationships with other famous people.

Inglis, Alison. "Deathless Beauty: Poynter's *Helen*, Lillie Langtry, and High Victorian Ideals of Beauty." In *Love and Death: Art in the Age of Queen Victoria*, edited by Angus Trumble. Adelaide: Art Gallery of South Australia, 2000. This essay examines the impact of Langtry in Poynter's painting. Her image as Helen of Troy is compared to Dante Rossetti's painting of the same subject, with interesting parallels and conclusions.

Langtry, Lillie. *The Days I Knew.* New York: George H. Doran, 1925. Langtry published this highly selective autobiography a few years before her death. It chronicles her life with the discretion and decorum expected of her at the time.

Sichel, Pierre. *The Jersey Lily: The Story of the Fabulous Mrs. Langtry.* Englewood Cliffs, N.J.: Prentice-Hall, 1958. Sichel's basic biography of Langtry covers her childhood, marriage, stage career, and retirement to Monaco in terms that provide understanding for anyone interested in general facts about Langtry.

SEE ALSO: Sarah Bernhardt; W. S. Gilbert and Arthur Sullivan; Henry Irving; Fanny Kemble; Adah Isaacs Menken; Ellen Terry; Oscar Wilde.

RELATED ARTICLE in *Great Events from History: The Nineteenth Century, 1801-1900:* 1878-1899: Irving Manages London's Lyceum Theatre.

SIR EDWIN RAY LANKESTER
English naturalist

After studying invertebrates, Lankester systematized the field of embryology, and he researched major groups of living and fossil animals. He wrote more than one hundred scientific essays, mostly dealing with comparative anatomy and paleontology, and his series of books made scientific matters understandable and interesting to nonscientists.

BORN: May 15, 1847; London, England
DIED: August 15, 1929; London, England
AREA OF ACHIEVEMENT: Biology

EARLY LIFE

Sir Edwin Ray Lankester (LAHNG-kesh-tehr) was the son of Edwin Lankester, a medical doctor who served as a coroner and lectured and wrote articles about natural history, diseases, and foods. Lankester's mother, née Phebe Pope, was also interested in science; she both assisted her husband with his scientific articles and wrote her own on botany and on health.

When he was eleven years old, Lankester entered St. Paul's School, where he earned several classical prizes and won cups for sculling and the long jump. At the age of seventeen, he entered Downing College, Cambridge, on a scholarship, but he transferred to Christ Church, Oxford, in his second year and won a scholarship there for his junior year.

In 1868, Lankester was graduated from Oxford with first-class honors in natural science and was given a scholarship in geology. With this and the Radcliffe Traveling Fellowship granted him in 1870, he studied at Vienna, Leipzig, and Naples. He returned to Oxford to teach for two years and then became a professor of zoology and comparative anatomy at University College, London, until 1889.

Lankester was welcomed to London by Thomas Huxley, a British biologist and surgeon, and other scientists who had known him since childhood. Lankester's personal charm earned for him the respect and affection of these men as well as a wider circle of friends. He was sincere, unprejudiced, and tolerant of differences in method and opinion. Especially kind to young workers, he listened sympathetically to others and was gentle and affectionate. His wit and anecdotes made him a delightful companion as guest or host. He enjoyed golf, cards, country walks, and fireside chats.

Although he had many close friends, Lankester never married. Robust in appearance and able to handle stress, his health nevertheless was delicate, and he suffered several illnesses. As he grew older he experienced problems with indigestion, bronchitis, and depression.

As a professor he quickly became known by the success of his lectures and the results of investigations by his students and himself. His clear and skillful illustrations instilled in his students his own enthusiasm for science.

LIFE'S WORK

After his graduation from Oxford, Lankester assisted his father in editing the *Quarterly Journal of Microscopical Science.* Two years later, he became the editor and held that position until his death sixty years later. During that time he became one of England's most noted zoologists and received major honors in his field.

These honors recognized his varied activities, his energy in teaching, and his philosophical thinking. His work benefited because of his principle that speculation should be the servant, not the master, of the biologist. In 1875, Lankester was accepted as a member of the Royal Society, a scientific association that supports and promotes scientific research. He was Royal Medalist in 1885 and served as the society's vice president from 1882 to 1896. In 1884, Lankester founded the Marine Biological Association, serving as its president in 1892. The association's laboratory has aided in the training of British biologists.

Lankester was appointed Linacre Professor of Comparative Anatomy at Oxford in 1890. In addition to teaching, he reorganized the University Museum to make it useful in teaching and beneficial to the educational community. This experience proved invaluable when he became director of the British Museum (Natural History) in 1898, resigning from his Oxford post. Conflicts with the museum committees and opposition from the trustees frustrated his plans for the museum, however, and he resigned his post in 1907, the year he was knighted.

Despite his varied duties, Lankester was first a professional zoologist. His curiosity about nature, his observations of living creatures, his skill in dissection and microscopy, and his patience in acquiring facts combined to give him a wide interest in zoology and detailed knowledge of many of its branches. He wrote well, and the ability to coordinate and arrange facts made his scientific writings easy to understand. He loved to teach zoology to beginners and laypersons, and he could encourage researchers with criticism and praise in any area.

Lankester's brilliance and abilities in science were not matched by great success with officialdom. Often in defending a cause he would act impulsively and even violently, never bothering to apologize or rectify his mistakes. His character and intelligence made it almost certain that he was promoting the best course of action, but his impetuous behavior ruined his arguments and position; officials saw his conduct, not his wisdom. A misunderstanding with the University of Edinburgh, a lawsuit with Oxford University, and his poor relationships with the committees of the Natural History Museum all occurred because of disputes accentuated by his imprudence.

Some of Lankester's best work was in the area of morphology, the study of the form and structure of plants and animals, without regard to function. He saw beauty in the varieties of animal form, and he arranged them in categories, explaining them clearly. His essays on classification and natural history were illuminating, and he contributed to almost every branch of zoology.

Lankester wrote widely about zoology and more general problems of science. His books included *On Comparative Longevity in Man and the Lower Animals* (1870), *The Advancement of Science* (1890), *The Kingdom of Man* (1907), and *Great and Small Things* (1923). These and other writings were read widely by the general public as well as the scientific community.

In addition to his work in zoology, Lankester studied and promoted neo-Darwinism and followed Gregor Mendel's work in hybridizing cultivated plants. He had a keen interest in the application of bacteriology and protozoology to preventive medicine, and through his Royal Society work he encouraged the investigations into sleeping sickness and other tropical diseases. Close friends with Louis Pasteur and Elie Metchnikoff, the institute's director, he often visited the Pasteur Institute in Paris and was proud to have contributed to medical knowledge and theory.

Lankester was highly respected by the scientific community, and this respect was demonstrated by the honorary degrees given him by Leeds, Exeter, and Christ Church College. He was still writing and studying when he died in London on August 15, 1929, after a short illness.

SIGNIFICANCE

The scientific discoveries of the eighteenth and nineteenth centuries revolutionized life and awakened a hope

that humans might master nature. This hope fostered a faith in science and an enthusiasm for learning. Sir Edwin Ray Lankester's books, which conveyed his zeal and knowledge in the layperson's language, were popular in this atmosphere because they made scientific achievements and information accessible to the public. The *Quarterly Journal of Microscopical Science*, which he edited, held an international reputation, and his encyclopedia articles were widely read.

Because of his own enthusiasm for comparative anatomy, Lankester inspired numerous students and colleagues to continue their own study and research. His most distinguished pupil, Edwin Goodrich, continued Lankester's work in zoology and spread his teaching.

Lankester brought order to an entire branch of biology when he studied the structure and embryos of invertebrates, systematized the field of embryology, and invented new technical terms to describe his discoveries. Adding greatly to humanity's knowledge of comparative anatomy, he researched major groups of living and fossil animals, from protozoa to mammals. He then showed the basic similarities in structure and close relationships among spiders, scorpions, and horseshoe crabs.

Scientists in the nineteenth century were using science for the power it gave to human society through mechanical and electrical devices, military weapons, food preservation, and control over disease. They discovered that science could lead to profit as well as to knowledge. Lankester, on the other hand, still saw the value of science in its gathering of information, its observations of nature, and its satisfaction to humankind's inner being. Pure science was, for Lankester, a thing of beauty.

—*Elaine Mathiasen*

FURTHER READING

Bowler, Peter J. *Life's Splendid Drama: Evolutionary Biology and the Reconstruction of Life's Ancestry, 1860-1940*. Chicago: University of Chicago Press, 1996. A comprehensive and critical study of evolutionary thought, focusing on research about the evolution of particular groups of organisms. Includes information on Lankester's theories of evolution.

Darwin, Charles. *The Illustrated Origin of Species*. Abridged and introduced by Richard E. Leakey. New York: Hill & Wang, 1979. An abridgment of Darwin's *On the Origin of Species by Means of Natural Selection* (1859) that explains his theory of evolution, a theory that Lankester advocated, although he later supported the school of neo-Darwinism. In his introduction, Leakey discusses Darwin's work and its problems, as well as the work of other scientists in that era.

Dubos, Rene J. *Louis Pasteur: Free Lance of Science.* Boston: Little, Brown, 1950. This biography of Lankester's friend and contemporary illuminates the work of other scientists of that period, and it includes background on previous scientific philosophy.

Gould, Stephen Jay. "A Darwinian Gentleman at Marx's Funeral." *Natural History* 108, no. 7 (September, 1999): 32. Describes the friendship between Lankester and Karl Marx and Lankester's role in communication between Marx and Darwin.

Lankester, Sir Edwin Ray. *Diversions of a Naturalist.* New York: Macmillan, 1915. A collection of essays and illustrations about nature suitable for reading by the general public. Contains articles previously written for *The Daily Telegraph*.

_____. *Great and Small Things.* London: Methuen, 1923. A miscellaneous collection of short articles related to the study of living things. The articles cover such varied subjects as the gorilla, the liver fluke, and human eyes.

_____. *Science from an Easy Chair.* London: Methuen, 1910. A collection of brief essays on a variety of scientific subjects, written for the layperson in common language. Readers are encouraged to do further research on ideas that interest them. Includes illustrations.

_____. *Science from an Easy Chair: A Second Series.* London: Adlard, 1912. An assortment of essays, originally written for *The Daily Telegraph*, to interest the layperson in scientific matters. Includes subjects such as elephants, smells and perfumes, museums, and parasites.

Metchnikoff, Olga. *Life of Elie Metchnikoff: 1845-1916.* Boston: Houghton Mifflin, 1921. This biography, with a preface by Lankester, describes Metchnikoff's life, research, and studies in medicine, including his work at the Pasteur Institute. Lankester and Metchnikoff were close friends and interested in each other's research.

SEE ALSO: Louis Agassiz; Karl Ernst von Baer; Louis Pasteur.

RELATED ARTICLES in *Great Events from History: The Nineteenth Century, 1801-1900:* November 24, 1859: Darwin Publishes *On the Origin of Species*; 1871: Darwin Publishes *The Descent of Man*.

PIERRE-SIMON LAPLACE
French mathematician

Laplace made groundbreaking mathematical contributions to probability theory and statistical analysis. Using Isaac Newton's theory of gravitation, he also performed detailed mathematical analyses of the shape of the earth and the orbits of comets, planets, and their moons.

BORN: March 23, 1749; Beaumont-en-Auge, Normandy, France
DIED: March 5, 1827; Paris, France
ALSO KNOWN AS: Marquis de Laplace
AREAS OF ACHIEVEMENT: Astronomy, mathematics, physics

EARLY LIFE
Pierre-Simon Laplace (lah-plahs) was born into a well-established and prosperous family of farmers and merchants in southern Normandy. An ecclesiastical career in the Church was originally planned for Laplace by his father, and he attended the Benedictine secondary school in Beaumont-en-Auge between the ages of seven and sixteen. His interest in mathematics blossomed during two years at the University of Caen, beginning in 1766.

In 1768, Laplace went to Paris to pursue a career in mathematics; he remained a permanent resident of Paris or its immediate vicinity for the rest of his life. Soon after his arrival in Paris, he sought and won the patronage of Jean Le Rond d'Alembert, a mathematician, physicist, and philosopher with great influence among French intellectuals. D'Alembert found Laplace employment teaching mathematics to military cadets at the École Militaire, and it was in this position that Laplace wrote his first memoirs in mathematics and astronomy.

In 1773, Laplace was elected to the Academy of Sciences as a mathematician. This achievement, at the relatively young age of twenty-four, was based upon the merits of thirteen memoirs he had presented to academy committees for review. Some of Laplace's earliest mathematical interests involved the calculation of odds in games of chance. At a time when there was not yet a field of mathematics devoted to the systematic study of probability, Laplace played a major role in carrying the early development of this topic beyond the rules of thumb of gambling and the preliminary conclusions of earlier mathematicians. In addition, Laplace emphasized the relevance of probability to the analysis of statistics. He believed that, because all experimental data are imprecise to some extent, it is important to be able to calculate an appropriate average or mean value from a collection of observations. Furthermore, this mean value should be calculated in such a way as to minimize its difference from the actual value of the quantity being measured.

Statistical problems of this type inspired Laplace's initial interest in astronomy. He became intrigued by the process through which new astronomical data should be incorporated into calculations of probabilities for future observations. In particular, he concentrated on the application of Sir Isaac Newton's law of gravitation to the motions of the comets and planets. Laplace's interest in physics thus had a strong mathematical orientation. Throughout his career, he retained his early concentration on the solution of problems suggested by the mathematical implications of physical laws; he never devoted himself to extensive experimental investigation of new phenomena. Laplace's primary motivation was a deep conviction that, even if human limitations prevent an exact knowledge of natural laws and experimental conditions, it is still possible progressively to eliminate error through increasingly accurate approximations.

Very little is known about Laplace's personal life during these early years. He does not seem to have stimulated strong friendship or animosity. In 1788, he married Marie-Charlotte de Courty de Romanges, who was twenty years younger than himself, and they had two children. Laplace established and maintained comfortable but disciplined living habits, and he retained an undiminished mental clarity to the moment of his death.

LIFE'S WORK

Although a brief summary of Laplace's life's work requires some classification by topics and an emphasis on final results rather than chronology, the highly integrated and developmental nature of his research should not be forgotten. For example, mathematical techniques that he

Pierre-Simon Laplace. (Library of Congress)

invented for the solution of problems in probability theory often were immediately applied to similar problems in physics or astronomy. Because Laplace was particularly interested in approximate or probable solutions and the analysis of error, he repeatedly revised his mathematical techniques to accommodate new data.

Laplace's contributions to probability theory were both technical and philosophical. This twofold concern is expressed in the titles of the influential volumes in which he summarized his work, *Théorie analytique des probabilités* (1812; analytic theory of probability) and *Essai philosophique sur les probabilités* (1814; *A Philosophical Essay on Probabilities*, 1902).

The *Théorie analytique des probabilités* was the first comprehensive treatise devoted entirely to the subject of probability. Laplace provided a groundbreaking, although necessarily imperfect, characterization of the techniques, subject matter, and practical applications of the new field. He relied on the traditional problems generated by games of chance, such as lotteries, to motivate his mathematical innovations, but he pointed toward the future by generalizing these methods and applying them to many other topics. For example, because the calculation of odds in games of chance so often requires the summation of long series of fractions in which each term in the series differs from the others according to a regular pattern, Laplace began by reviewing some of the methods he had discovered to approximate the sums of such series, particularly when very large numbers are involved.

Laplace then proceeded to state what has since come to be called Bayes's theorem, after an early predecessor of Laplace. This theorem states how to use partial or incomplete information to calculate the conditional probability of an event in terms of its absolute or unconditional probability and the conditional probability of its cause. Laplace was one of the first to make extensive use of this theorem; it was particularly important to him because of its relevance to how calculations of probability should change in response to new knowledge.

The *Théorie analytique des probabilités* includes Laplace's applications of his mathematical techniques to problems generated by the analysis of data from such diverse topics as census figures, insurance rates, instrumentation error, astronomy, geodesy, election prognostication, and jury selection. In particular, he gave an important statement of what has since been called the least square law for the calculation of a mean value for a set of data in such a way that the resulting error from the true value is minimized.

A Philosophical Essay on Probabilities has been one of Laplace's most widely read works; it includes the conceptual basis upon which Laplace constructed his mathematical techniques. Most important, Laplace stated and relied upon a definition of probability that has been a source of considerable philosophical debate. Given a situation in which specific equally possible cases are the results of various processes (such as rolling dice) and correspond to favorable or unfavorable events, Laplace defined the probability of an event as the fraction formed by dividing the number of cases that correspond to or cause that event by the total number of possible cases. When the cases in question are not equally possible (as when dice are loaded), the calculation must be altered in an attempt to include this information. Laplace's definition thus calls attention to his treatment of probability as an application of mathematics made necessary only by human ignorance.

In one of the most famous passages in *A Philosophical Essay on Probabilities*, Laplace expresses this view by describing a supreme intelligence with a complete knowledge of the universe and its laws at any specific moment; for such an intelligence, Laplace believed that probability calculations would be unnecessary because the future and past could be calculated simply through an application of the laws of nature to the given perfectly stipulated set of conditions. Because knowledge of natural laws and the state of the world is always limited, probability is an essential feature of all human affairs. Nevertheless, Laplace's emphasis was not on the negative aspect of this conclusion but on the mathematical regularities to which even seemingly arbitrary sequences of events conform.

The domain in which Laplace saw the closest human approach to the knowledge of his hypothetical supreme intelligence was the application of Newton's theory of gravitation to the solar system. Since Newton's publication of his theory in 1686, mathematicians and physicists had reformulated his results using increasingly sophisticated mathematics. By Laplace's time, Newton's theory could be stated in a type of mathematics known as partial differential equations. Laplace made major contributions to the solution of equations of this type, including the famous technique of "Laplace transforms" and the use of a "potential" function to characterize a field of force.

Laplace made remarkably detailed applications of Newton's results to the orbits of the planets, moons, and comets. Some of his most famous calculations involve his demonstration of the very long-term periodic variations in the orbits of Jupiter and Saturn. Laplace thus contributed to an increasing knowledge of the stability and internal motions of the solar system. He also applied gravitation theory to the tides, the shape of Earth, and the rings of Saturn. His hypothesis that the solar system was formed through the condensation of a diffuse solar atmosphere became a starting point for more detailed subsequent theories.

Newtonian gravitation theory became Laplace's model for precision and clarity in all other branches of physics. He encouraged his colleagues to attempt similar analyses in optics, heat, electricity, and magnetism. His influence was particularly strong among French physicists between 1805 and 1815. By his death in 1827, however, this attempt to base all physics upon short-range forces had achieved only limited success; aside from the mathematical methods he developed, Laplace's conceptual contributions to physics were not as long-lasting as his more fundamental insights in probability theory.

SIGNIFICANCE

Pierre-Simon Laplace's cultural influence extended far beyond the relatively small circle of mathematicians who could appreciate the brilliant technical detail in his work. In several ways he has become a symbol of some important aspects of the rapid scientific progress that took place during his career as a result of his role in institutional changes in the scientific profession and the implications that have been drawn from his conclusions and methods.

Laplace was very active within the highly centralized French scientific community. As a member of the French Academy of Sciences, he served on numerous research or evaluative committees that were commissioned by the French government. For example, following the French Revolution in 1789, he was an influential designer and advocate of the metric system, which has become the most widely used international system of scientific units. The academy was disbanded during the radical phase of the Revolution in 1793, but in 1796 Laplace became the president of the scientific class of the new Institute of France.

Highly publicized institute prizes were regularly offered for essays in physics and mathematics, and Laplace exerted a powerful influence on French physics through the attention he devoted to choice of topic and support for his preferred candidates. He also played an important part in the early organization of the École Polytechnique, the prestigious school of engineering founded in 1795. Although Laplace lived through turbulent political changes, he remained in positions of high scientific status through the Napoleonic era and into the Bourbon Restoration, when he was raised to the nobility as a marquis. Laplace seems to have held few strong political views, and he thus is sometimes cited as an example of a powerful scientist indifferent to social or political conditions.

Aside from his work in probability and statistics, which has quite direct impact on modern societies, other aspects of Laplace's work have contributed to general perceptions of the goals, limitations, and methods of science. With Newton's theory of gravitation as his model, Laplace was convinced that, although human knowledge of nature is always limited, there are inevitable regularities that can be expressed approximately with ever-increasing accuracy. Laplace thus has become a symbol of nineteenth century scientific determinism, the view that the uncertainty of the future is only the result of human ignorance of the natural laws that determine it in every detail.

When Napoleon I asked Laplace why God did not play a role in Laplace's analysis of the stability of the solar system, Laplace replied that he had had no need for such a hypothesis. Laplace thus contributed to a growing association of the scientific tradition with atheism and

materialism. Finally, Laplace's style of mathematical physics has become a primary example of a reductionistic research strategy. Just as the gravitational effect of a large mass is determined by the sum of the forces exerted by all of its parts, Laplace expected all phenomena to reduce to collections of individual interactions. His success in implementing this method contributed to widespread perceptions that this is a necessary component of scientific investigation.

—James R. Hofmann

FURTHER READING

Arago, François. "Laplace." In *Biographies of Distinguished Scientific Men*. New York: Ticknor & Fields, 1859. Arago was a student and colleague of Laplace for many years. His essay discusses only Laplace's work in astronomy and concentrates on his study of the stability of the solar system.

Brush, Stephen G. *The Origin of the Solar System and the Core of the Earth from Laplace to Jeffreys: Nebulous Earth*. Vol. 1 in *A History of Modern Planetary Physics*. New York: Cambridge University Press, 1996. Traces the evolution of Laplace's nebular hypotheses, the most popular nineteenth century explanation for the origin of the solar system.

Fox, Robert. "The Rise and Fall of Laplacian Physics." *Historical Studies in the Physical Sciences* 4 (1974): 89-136. This is an excellent summary of Laplace's efforts to direct French physics according to a research program based upon short-range forces.

Gillespie, Charles Coulston, Robert Fox, and Ivor Grattan-Guiness. *Pierre-Simon Laplace, 1749-1827: A Life in Exact Science*. Princeton, N.J.: Princeton University Press, 1997. Focuses on Laplace's research program and his work with the Academy of Science. Includes biographical information from a scientific point of view, a description of Laplace's efforts to gather young physicists who would work with the Newtonian model in physics, and an overview of the Laplace transform.

_____. "Pierre-Simon Marquis de Laplace." In *Dictionary of Scientific Biography*. Vol. 15. New York: Charles Scribner's Sons, 1978. This chronological survey of Laplace's scientific career combines discussion of significant concepts with summaries of important mathematical derivations.

Hahn, Roger. *Laplace as a Newtonian Scientist*. Los Angeles: Williams Andrew Clark Memorial Library, 1967. This short essay describes the philosophical debate concerning the status of laws of nature that occurred during Laplace's formative period at the University of Caen and his early years in Paris. Laplace's convictions about the law-governed structure of the universe are traced to his reading of d'Alembert and Marquis de Condorcet.

_____. *Pierre Simon LaPlace, 1749-1827: A Determined Scientist.* Cambridge, Mass.: Harvard University Press, 2005. Full biography of Laplace by a scholar who has studied him for decades.

Todhunter, Isaac. *A History of the Mathematical Theory of Probability from the Time of Pascal to That of Laplace.* New York: Chelsea House, 1965. Chapter 10 provides a technical and chronological account of the chief results and some of the derivations found in Laplace's publications on probability theory.

SEE ALSO: Joseph Fourier; Sir William Rowan Hamilton; Napoleon I; Mary Somerville.

RELATED ARTICLE in *Great Events from History: The Nineteenth Century, 1801-1900:* 1850-1865: Clausius Formulates the Second Law of Thermodynamics.

FERDINAND LASSALLE
German labor leader

One of the founders of the German labor movement, Lassalle was the most important advocate of scientific socialism in Germany after the revolutions of 1848. His theory of evolutionary socialism eventually triumphed within the German Social Democratic Party.

BORN: April 11, 1825; Breslau, Prussia (now Wrocław, Poland)
DIED: August 31, 1864; Geneva, Switzerland
ALSO KNOWN AS: Ferdinand Johann Gottlieb Lassalle
AREA OF ACHIEVEMENT: Philosophy

EARLY LIFE

Ferdinand Lassalle (lah-sahl) was the only son of Heymann Lassal, or Loslauer, a well-to-do Jewish silk merchant. Although admitted to the synagogue at the age of thirteen, the young Lassalle never took his ancestral faith seriously. Lassalle lived at home until he was fifteen. Much of his time as a teenager was spent playing cards or billiards for spending money. Not a particularly bright student, Lassalle was expelled from the classical high school (gymnasium) for forging his parents' signatures to his grade reports, an offense he committed repeatedly.

In May, 1840, Lassalle's father enrolled him in the Commercial Institute in Leipzig. His father had hopes that his son would eventually take over the family business, but Ferdinand was not willing. He announced his intention to study history, "the greatest subject in the world. The subject bound up with the holiest interests of mankind. . . ." After having passed his examinations in 1843, he was enrolled at the University of Breslau.

At the university, Lassalle studied history, archaeology, philology, and philosophy. It was while an undergraduate at Breslau that he was introduced to the works of the German philosopher Georg Wilhelm Friedrich Hegel. Hegel's dialectic soon became the cornerstone of Lassalle's worldview. This dialectic was for him, as it was also for Karl Marx, the key to understanding and interpreting the flow of human history. Like Marx, Lassalle came to believe that the future new order in society would be an inevitable product of the historical dialectic. Unlike Marx, who held to the necessity of revolution to move the dialectic forward, Lassalle came to understand it as a peaceful, evolutionary process.

In 1844, Lassalle entered the University of Berlin, where he continued studying philosophy. Although his interests extended to other philosophers such as Ludwig Feuerbach and the French utopian thinkers, Hegel remained his primary influence. He would often rise at four in the morning to begin the day with readings from Hegel's works. He also began work on his doctoral thesis, a Hegelian interpretation of the Greek philosopher Heracleitus. From 1845 to 1847, Lassalle lived in Paris, where he met and was influenced by the French socialist and anarchist philosopher Pierre-Joseph Proudhon and the German poet Heinrich Heine. It was also during his stay in Paris that he changed the spelling of his last name from "Lassal" to "Lassalle."

In 1846, Lassalle met the Countess Sophie von Hatzfeldt, who was seeking a divorce from her husband, one of the wealthiest and most influential noblemen in northwestern Germany. Although not a lawyer, Lassalle took up her cause. Between 1846 and 1854, he conducted thirty-five lawsuits on behalf of the countess before eventually winning her case. The countess rewarded Lassalle with a lifelong pension that made him financially independent. It was also the beginning of a lifelong relationship that both positively and negatively affected his political career.

LIFE'S WORK

Lassalle's career as a labor organizer and political agitator began in earnest during the revolutions of 1848. He was living in Düsseldorf, an emerging industrial center in the Prussian-ruled Rhineland. In November, 1848, Lassalle was arrested for making an incendiary speech, calling upon the populace and the militia to rise up in armed revolt. The occasion for the speech was a meeting called by Friedrich Engels, Marx's chief collaborator. Lassalle's relationship with Marx was not a smooth one. When they first met during the revolutions of 1848, Lassalle had not yet read *Manifest der Kommunistischen* (*The Communist Manifesto*, 1850), first published in 1848. Many scholars believe that many of Lassalle's theoretical assumptions, which were later harshly criticized by Karl Marx, were in fact borrowed from Marx's early

Ferdinand Lassalle. (Library of Congress)

writings, and may be found in *The Communist Manifesto*.

When the revolutions of 1848 collapsed, most of the revolutionary leaders fled the Continent. Marx settled in London. After his release from prison in July, 1849, Lassalle chose to remain in Germany. It was a choice that no doubt helped him in his subsequent bid for leadership of the German labor movement.

During the 1850's, and until their final estrangement in 1862, Marx and Lassalle remained hospitable toward each other, at least publicly. Marx looked to Lassalle for help in getting his books and articles published in Germany. He also called upon Lassalle for financial support. However, as Marx's own thought matured over the years, he became increasingly critical of Lassalle's writings and obviously envious of Lassalle's emergence as the leader of the German working class.

The tension between Marx and Lassalle was the result in large part of the differing historical roles to which each was called. Marx was basically an intellectual, addressing a small international audience of highly educated intellectuals like himself. He was a theorist, constructing the guiding principles of a future society. Lassalle, on the other hand, was a man of action. He was addressing the uneducated, illiterate, and backward German working class. He was attempting to shake it out of its political lethargy and mold it into a major political force. For Lassalle, unlike Marx, the future new order in society was immediately obtainable.

Toward the end of 1861, Lassalle made two speeches in which he called upon the working class to form its own political party. He believed that once the workers became a formidable political force, it would have the effect of altering the power relationships in the state. Because he believed that the written constitution of necessity reflects the true power ratio in society, Lassalle called upon the workers to organize and agitate for universal direct suffrage in all the German states.

In December of 1862, Lassalle was approached by the executive committee of the Central Committee to Convoke a General Congress of German Workers. It asked him to draw up a program for the congress. Lassalle's affirmative response marked the beginning of the final and most important phase in his life's work. Lassalle's response took the form of a pamphlet entitled *Offnes Antwortschreiben an das Central-Comité zur Berufung eines Allgemeinen Deutschen Arbeitercongresses zu Leipzig* (*Lassalle's Open Letter to the National Labor Association of Germany*, 1879), published in March, 1863. It contained his advice on what policies should be adopted by the working-class movement. Marx criticized the pamphlet as a vulgarization of his own ideas, but Lassalle's clarion call to action was well received by the workers. It led directly to the founding of the General German Workers' Association (Allgemeiner Deutscher Arbeiterverein) in Leipzig on May 23, 1863. Its chief goal, as stated in its bylaws, was to achieve justice for the German working class "through establishment of universal, equal, and direct suffrage."

Although Lassalle was a socialist, he was also a Prussian nationalist. He also felt the intellectual's usual frustration with the sluggishness of the working class. His attitude toward the workers was aristocratic and paternalistic, and his administrative style was authoritarian. He saw to it that the presidency of the association, the office he held, possessed dictatorial powers. "Otherwise," he said, "nothing will get done."

Being a nationalist, Lassalle did not find it necessary for the state to wither, as Marx did. In a letter to the Prussian prime minister Otto von Bismarck, in which he enclosed a copy of the association's bylaws, Lassalle said that the working class was instinctively inclined toward a dictatorship. He believed that the workers would prefer a monarchy, if only the king would look after their interests. Lassalle's willingness to consider the idea of a monarchical welfare state provided a common ground for his discussions and correspondence with Bismarck during late 1863 and early 1864. At that time, the prime minister was searching for allies in his struggle with the liberals in the Prussian parliament. The Bismarck-Lassalle talks came to nothing, however, in part because of Lassalle's presumptuousness and in part because of Bismarck's growing preoccupation with the unification of Germany.

By late spring, 1864, Lassalle was disappointed with the association's failure to increase its membership as rapidly as he had expected. He was also physically exhausted. His exhaustion was in part the result of his having contracted syphilis in 1847, when he was twenty-two. By the early 1860's, the disease was in the secondary stage, and the bones in one of his legs were deteriorating. In July, 1864, he decided to go to Switzerland for a rest.

In Geneva, Lassalle acted out the final chapter in his life as a romantic revolutionary. He had always pursued the conquest of women with the same enthusiasm as politics. He met and began courting passionately Helene von Dönniges. When he proposed marriage, he encountered opposition from her father and from her former fiancé, Yanko von Racowitza. In response to a challenge from

Lassalle, a duel between Lassalle and Racowitza was fought on August 28, in a forest outside Geneva. Lassalle was mortally wounded and died three days later on August 31, 1864.

SIGNIFICANCE

After Ferdinand Lassalle's death, Karl Marx and Friedrich Engels praised his memory in public, while continuing to criticize him in their correspondence with each other. Engels admitted that Lassalle had been politically "the most important fellow in Germany." In a letter to the Countess Hatzfeldt, Marx noted Lassalle's abilities, then added, "I personally loved him." He went on to lament the fact that they had drifted apart.

The General German Workers' Association continued to grow. By the late 1860's, it had split into two factions: the orthodox Marxists, who in 1869 founded the Social Democratic Labor Party (Sozialdemokratische Arbeiterpartei), and the Lassalleans, who were viewed by the former as reformist heretics. The two factions united in 1875 to form the Socialist Labor Party of Germany (Sozialistische Arbeiterpartei Deutschlands). The new party's program was largely based on theories and slogans associated with Lassalle.

In 1891, the party changed its name to the Social Democratic Party of Germany (Sozialdemokratische Partei Deutschlands), or SPD. The SPD was Marxist in theory, rather than Lassallean, but in practice it was becoming a mass parliamentary and reformist party, which is what Lassalle had advocated. The SPD became the largest and most influential socialist party in Europe prior to World War I. It was not until 1959, however, that the SPD formally abandoned all its Marxist ideology.

Much of what Lassalle had called for was later enacted by the German state under Bismarck's leadership. Perhaps, as some believe, Bismarck was only trying to win the workers away from socialism. In any case, speaking before the Reichstag in 1878, Bismarck said of Lassalle:

> He was one of the most intelligent and likable men I had ever come across. He was very ambitious and by no means a republican. He was very much a nationalist and a monarchist. His ideal was the German Empire, and here was our point of contact.

In 1866, Bismarck granted universal suffrage in elections to the Reichstag. In 1881, he began enacting a comprehensive social security program that included accident, health, and old age insurance. Bismarck's brand of "state socialism" may have been influenced by his earlier conversations with Lassalle. In any event, the German welfare program, inspired by Lassalle and initiated by Bismarck, served as a model for all other Western nations.

—*Paul R. Waibel*

FURTHER READING

Barer, Shlomo. *The Doctors of Revolution: Nineteenth-Century Thinkers Who Changed the World*. New York: Thames and Hudson, 2000. Lassalle is one of the thinkers included in this study of radical thought in nineteenth century Europe.

Bernstein, Edward. *Ferdinand Lassalle as a Social Reformer*. New York: Charles Scribner's Sons, 1893. Reprint. New York: Greenwood Press, 1969. A sympathetic but critical study by the founder of revisionism in German social democracy. Bernstein was the most important figure in the SPD from Lassalle to the Nazi seizure of power in 1933. Bernstein also edited the party's official publication of Lassalle's collected works.

Footman, David. *Ferdinand Lassalle: Romantic Revolutionary*. New Haven, Conn.: Yale University Press, 1947. A well-written and highly readable biography. It is the best book on Lassalle in English, and the place to begin a more detailed study. Footman believes that Lassalle's romantic nature is important for understanding his role in the birth of the German labor movement.

Gay, Peter. *The Dilemma of Democratic Socialism: Edward Bernstein's Challenge to Marx*. New York: Collier Books, 1962. Chapters 1 and 4 discuss Lassalle's influence on Bernstein and thus establish his place in

the revision of Marxism that resulted in the modern SPD.

Meredith, George. *The Tragic Comedians: A Study in a Well-Known Study*. Rev. ed. New York: Charles Scribner's Sons, 1906. Lassalle's final days in Geneva, including his courtship of Dönniges, is the subject of this romantic novel. The story is based largely on Dönniges's own account. It is considered to be a creditable attempt at making history come alive.

Mukherjee, Subrata, and Sushila Ramaswamy. *A History of Socialist Thought: From the Precursors to the Present*. Thousand Oaks, Calif.: Sage Publications, 2000. Detailed account of various schools of socialist thought, including an explanation of Lassalle's social democratic theories.

Wilson, Edmund. *To the Finland Station: A Study in the Writing and Acting of History*. Garden City, N.Y.: Doubleday, 1940. A popular study of the revolutionary tradition in European history from the beginning of the nineteenth century to the triumph of the Communist Revolution in Russia. Chapter 13, "Historical Actors: Lassalle," provides a brief account of Lassalle's life and thought, and tries to define his contributions to the rise of socialism in Europe.

SEE ALSO: Otto von Bismarck; Friedrich Engels; Georg Wilhelm Friedrich Hegel; Heinrich Heine; Wilhelm Liebknecht; Karl Marx; Pierre-Joseph Proudhon.

RELATED ARTICLES in *Great Events from History: The Nineteenth Century, 1801-1900:* 1839: Blanc Publishes *The Organization of Labour*; February, 1848: Marx and Engels Publish *The Communist Manifesto*; September 28, 1864: First International Is Founded; 1867: Marx Publishes *Das Kapital*.

For Reference

Not to be taken from this room